SOCIAL
PSYCHOLOGY

EIGHTH EDITION

SOCIAL PSYCHOLOGY

JOHN D. DeLAMATER   DANIEL J. MYERS   JESSICA L. COLLETT

WESTVIEW
PRESS

A Member of the Perseus Books Group

Westview Press was founded in 1975 in Boulder, Colorado, by notable publisher and intellectual Fred Praeger. Westview Press continues to publish scholarly titles and high-quality undergraduate- and graduate-level textbooks in core social science disciplines. With books developed, written, and edited with the needs of serious nonfiction readers, professors, and students in mind, Westview Press honors its long history of publishing books that matter.

Find us on the World Wide Web at www.westviewpress.com.

Every effort has been made to secure required permissions for all text, images, maps, and other art reprinted in this volume.

Westview Press books are available at special discounts for bulk purchases in the United States by corporations, institutions, and other organizations. For more information, please contact the Special Markets Department at the Perseus Books Group, 2300 Chestnut Street, Suite 200, Philadelphia, PA 19103, or call (800) 810-4145, ext. 5000, or e-mail special.markets@perseusbooks.com.

Library of Congress Cataloging-in-Publication Data
DeLamater, John D.
Social psychology / John D. DeLamater, Daniel J. Myers,
Jessica L. Collett. — Eighth edition.
pages cm
Includes bibliographical references and index.
ISBN 978-0-8133-4950-3 (paperback) — ISBN 978-0-8133-4951-0 (e-book)
1. Social psychology. I. Myers, Daniel J. II. Collett, Jessica L. III. Title.
HM1033.D45   2014
302—dc23
2014011421

Editorial production by *Marra*thon Production Services. www.marrathon.net

Design by Jane Raese
Set in 10.5-point Warnock Pro

10 9 8 7 6 5 4 3 2 1

ABOUT THIS BOOK

When revising a textbook, the authors always seek to build on the strengths of the prior editions, introducing new material reflecting developments in the field and changes in our larger society, while maintaining thorough coverage of the subject covered by the book. As in past editions, we seek to cover the full range of phenomena of interest to social psychologists. Not only do we address intrapsychic processes in detail, but cover social interaction and group processes, as well as larger-scale phenomena, such as intergroup conflict and social movements. Our goal in writing this book is, as it has always been, to describe contemporary social psychology and to present the theoretical concepts and research findings that make up this broad and fascinating field. We have drawn on work by a wide array of social psychologists, including those with sociological and psychological perspectives, drawing on both classic works and more recent studies. Throughout the book we have used the results of empirical research—surveys, experiments, observational and qualitative studies, and meta-analyses—to illustrate this wide range of social psychological ideas.

ABOUT THE AUTHORS

John D. DeLamater, Conway-Bascom Professor of Sociology at the University of Wisconsin-Madison, received his education at the University of California, Santa Barbara, and the University of Michigan. He earned his Ph.D. in Social Psychology in 1969. He has been teaching the undergraduate course in social psychology since 1970, and graduate courses and seminars in the area since 1981. He leads a seminar on teaching for graduate students, and has won several teaching awards, including the Chancellor's Award for Distinguished Teaching. He is the co-editor of the *Handbook of Social Psychology, 2nd edition,* published by Springer. His research and writing are focused on the effects of life-course transitions on sexuality. He has published papers on the effects of having a child, of dual-career couples, of divorce, and influences on sexual desire and sexual behavior among men and women over 45. His current research is concerned with sexual behavior in later life, including the influence of hormones on sexual desire and sexual behavior.

Daniel J. Myers is Professor of Sociology and Vice President and Associate Provost for Faculty Affairs at the University of Notre Dame. He was educated at the Ohio State University and the University of Wisconsin-Madison, where he received his Ph.D. in Sociology in 1997. He has taught courses on social psychology, statistics and research methods, and protest, and he received the University of Notre Dame's highest honor for teaching, The Rev. Charles E. Sheedy Award, in 2007. He has also developed a teacher training practicum for graduate teaching assistants at the University of Notre Dame. His research focuses on race and protest, the diffusion of social phenomena, urban poverty, and negotiation strategies in small groups.

Jessica L. Collett is Associate Professor of Sociology at the University of Notre Dame. This very book, although a much earlier edition, inspired her own interest in social psychology during her time as an undergraduate at Winthrop University. After Winthrop, she went on to study social psychology at the University of Arizona, where she received her Ph.D. in Sociology in 2006. She is an award-winning instructor who regularly teaches social psychology at both the undergraduate and graduate levels, as well as courses on social inequality and socialization and the life course. Her research focuses on small group processes, self and identity, and the connection between the two.

NEW TO THIS EDITION

The last edition of the text, the seventh, was a radically consolidated and streamlined text that we hoped would better fit the introductory social psychology courses taught by the many users. However, in soliciting feedback for the most recent edition, we found that many users longed for the extended text and wanted us to move back to a format closer to that of earlier editions. In response to reviewer concerns, we moved the "Research Methods" appendix back to the core of the text (now Chapter 2), split the chapter on altruism and aggression into two chapters again (Chapters 10 and 11), and reintroduced a chapter on "Emotions" (Chapter 5).

The eighth edition also contains updated research, data, and examples throughout the book, new boxes providing research updates and "test yourself" opportunities, and an increased emphasis on diverse populations and their experiences. As in the past, we have made a special effort to incorporate research that reports differences among participants who vary on race, gender, and sexual orientation, but of course are limited by what is available, and point out these limitations.

CONTENT AND ORGANIZATION

Instructors who have used previous editions of the text will notice the most radical change in the first chapter of the book. Although the theories outlined in the previous edition were classics, they did not reflect the dominant perspectives in social psychology today. The revised introduction includes cognitive and evolutionary perspectives, as well as dual-process theories and evolutionary perspectives from psychology, as well as symbolic interaction, group processes, and social structure and personality from sociology. This introduction to the theoretical perspectives in social psychology and the subsequent chapter's overview of research methods provide the groundwork for all that follows.

The remainder of the book is divided into four substantive sections. Section 1 focuses on individual social behavior. It includes chapters on socialization, self and self-presentation, emotions, social perception and cognition, and attitudes. Section 2 is concerned with social interaction, the core of social psychology. Each of the chapters in this section discusses how persons interact with others and how they are affected by this interaction. These chapters cover such topics as communication, social influence and persuasion, altruism and prosocial behavior, aggression, and interpersonal attraction. Section 3 provides extensive coverage of groups. It includes chapters on group cohesion, conformity, and intergroup conflict, as well as an overview of the dominant research focuses in the social psychological student of groups today, including status characteristics and expectation states theory, decision-making in groups, social exchange, and distributive and procedural justice. Section 4 considers the relations between individuals and the wider society. These chapters examine the impact of social structure on the individual, especially on physical and mental health; deviant behavior; and collective behavior and social movements.

EASE OF USE

Although we have attempted to present the material in this book in a logical sequence that will appeal to many instructors, there are, of course, many different ways in which an instructor can organize an introductory course in social psychology. Therefore, we have written each chapter as a self-contained unit. Later chapters do not presume that the student has read earlier ones (although we insert appropriate cross-references to allow students to easily find related material in other chapters). This compartmentalization enables instructors to assign chapters in any sequence.

Chapters share a standard format. To make the material interesting and accessible to students, each chapter's introductory section poses four to six focal questions. These questions establish the issues discussed in the chapter. The remainder of the chapter consists of four to six major sections, each addressing one of these issues. A summary at the end of each chapter reviews the key points. Thus, each chapter poses several key questions about a topic and then considers these questions in a framework that enables students to easily learn the major ideas.

In addition, the text includes several learning aids. Tables emphasize the results of important studies. Figures illustrate important social psychological processes. Photographs dramatize essential ideas from the text. Boxes in each chapter highlight in-

teresting or controversial issues and studies and also discuss the applications of social psychological concepts in daily life. Some boxes are identified as "Research Update"; these boxes have been updated by including the latest research. Other boxes are identified as "Test Yourself"; these contain a questionnaire that the student can complete to find out his or her standing on the measure of interest. Key terms appear in bold and are listed alphabetically at the end of each chapter. A glossary of key terms appears at the end of the book.

A major new feature in the eighth edition is an emphasis on developing critical thinking skills. Critical thinking is an important goal of a quality education; it refers to the ability to use cognitive skills and strategies to increase the probability of a desirable outcome. Diane Halpern is an expert on critical thinking and developing these skills, and we drew heavily on her writings. Critical thinking is logical, rational, and free of self-deception. As the student learns about social psychology, they will learn that there are a number of important ways in which our everyday thinking is biased, and ways in which we engage in self-deception. Developing critical thinking skills and using them in daily life should lead the student to make better decisions and therefore lead a better life.

At the end of each chapter there is a section called Critical Thinking Skill. Each teaches a particular skill with an application to social psychology, and will have applications throughout the student's life. Let's get going!

ACKNOWLEDGMENTS

We extend our thanks to reviewers for the eighth edition, especially the 10 anonymous colleagues who gave us extensive feedback on the seventh edition. As we noted above, their careful evaluation led directly to several major changes in this edition.

Throughout the writing of the various editions of this book, many colleagues have reviewed chapters and provided useful comments and criticisms. We express sincere appreciation to these reviewers of the previous editions: Annelise Ayers, University of Wisconsin-Madison; Abdallah Badahdah, University of North Dakota; Robert F. Bales, Harvard University; Philip W. Blumstein, University of Washington; Lisa Boyd, University of Notre Dame; Marilyn B. Brewer, University of California at Los Angeles; Peter Burke, University of California at Riverside; Brad Bushman, Iowa State University; Peter L. Callero, Western Oregon State College; Bella DePaulo, University of Virginia; Donna Eder, Indiana University; Nancy Eisenberg, Arizona State University; Glen Elder, Jr., University of North Carolina at Chapel Hill; Gregory Elliott, Brown University; Rebecca Fahrlander, University of Nebraska at Omaha; Richard B. Felson, State University of New York-Albany; John H. Fleming, University of Minnesota; Jeremy Freese, Northwestern University; Irene Hanson Frieze, University of Pittsburgh; Jim Fultz, Northern Illinois University; Viktor Gecas, Washington State University; Russell G. Geen, University of Missouri; Christine Grella, University of California at Los Angeles; Allen Grimshaw, Indiana University; Elaine Hatfield, University of Hawaii-Manoa; John Hewitt, University of Massachusetts; George Homans, Harvard University; Judy Howard, University of Washington; Pamela M. Hunt, Kent State University; Michael Inbar, Hebrew University of Jerusalem; Julia Jacks, University of North Carolina; Dale Jaffe, University of Wisconsin-Milwaukee; Edward Jones, Princeton University; Lewis Killian, University of Massachusetts; Melvin Kohn, National Institute of Mental Health and Johns Hopkins University;

Robert Krauss, Columbia University; Marianne LaFrance, Boston College; Robert H. Lee, University of Wisconsin-Madison; Omar Lizardo, University of Notre Dame; David Lundgren, University of Cincinnati; Steven Lybrand, University of Wisconsin-Madison; Patricia MacCorquodale, University of Arizona; Scott Magnuson-Martinson, Normandale Community College; Armand Mauss, Washington State University; Douglas Maynard, University of Wisconsin-Madison; William McBroom, University of Montana; John McCarthy, Catholic University of America; Kathleen McKinney, Illinois State University; Clark McPhail, University of Illinois; David L. Miller, Western Illinois University; Norman Miller, University of Southern California; Howard Nixon II, University of Vermont; Pamela Oliver, University of Wisconsin-Madison; Edgar O'Neal, Tulane University; Terri L. Orbuch, Oakland University; James Orcutt, Florida State University; Daphna Oyserman, University of Michigan; Daniel Perlman, University of Manitoba; Jane Allyn Piliavin, University of Wisconsin-Madison; Bill Price, North Country Community College; Rebecca Reviere, Howard University; Michael Ross, University of Waterloo, Ontario; David A. Schroeder, University of Arkansas; Melvin Seeman, University of California at Los Angeles; Diane Shinberg, University of Memphis; Anson Shupe, Indiana University Purdue ; Roberta Simmons, University of Minnesota; Lynnell Simonson, University of North Dakota; Brent Simpson, University of South Carolina; Douglas Clayton Smith, Western Kentucky University; Lawrence Sneden, California State University-Northridge; Daphne Pedersen Stevens, University of North Dakota; Sheldon Stryker, Indiana University; Robert Suchner, Northern Illinois University; James Tedeschi, State University of New York-Albany; Richard Tessler, University of Massachusetts; Elizabeth Thomson,

University of Wisconsin–Madison; Henry Walker, University of Arizona; Nancy Wisely, Stephen F. Austin State University; Ron Wohlstein, Eastern Illinois University; Steve Wray, Averett College; Mark P. Zanna, University of Waterloo, Ontario; Morris Zelditch, Jr., Stanford University; and Louis Zurcher, University of Texas.

We also thank the many students who used the previous editions and who provided us with feedback about the book; we applied this feedback to improve the presentation, pace, and style of the new edition.

Finally, we express thanks to the professionals at Westview who contributed to the process of turning the manuscript into a book. Catherine Craddock, acquisitions editor, worked with us at every stage. Christine Marra oversaw the transformation of manuscript into printed pages. Our appreciation to them all. Although this book benefited greatly from feedback and criticisms, the authors accept responsibility for any errors that may remain.

CHAPTER 1

INTRODUCTION TO SOCIAL PSYCHOLOGY

INTRODUCTION

- Why are some people more effective leaders than others?

- What makes people fall in and out of love?

- Why can people cooperate so easily in some situations but not in others?

- What effects do major life events like graduating from college, getting married, or losing a job have on physical or mental health?

- Why do some people conform to norms and laws while others do not?

- What causes conflict between groups? Why do some conflicts subside and others progress until there is no chance of reconciliation?

- Why do people present different images of themselves in various social situations, both in person and online?

- What causes harmful or aggressive behavior? What motivates helpful or altruistic behavior?

- Why are some people more persuasive and influential than others?

- Why do stereotypes persist even in the face of contradictory evidence?

Perhaps questions such as these have puzzled you, just as they have perplexed others through the ages. You might wonder about these issues simply because you want to better understand the social world around you. Or you might want answers for practical reasons, such as increasing your effectiveness in day-to-day relations with others.

Answers to questions such as these come from various sources. One such source is personal experience—things we learn from everyday interaction. Answers obtained by this means are often insightful, but they are usually limited in scope and generality, and occasionally they are even misleading. Another source is informal knowledge or advice from others who describe their own experiences to us. Answers obtained by this means are sometimes reliable, sometimes not. A third source is the conclusions reached by philosophers, novelists, poets, and men and women of practical affairs who, over the centuries, have written about these issues. Often their answers have filtered down and become commonsense knowledge. We are told, for instance, that joint effort is an effective way to accomplish large jobs ("Many hands make light work") and that bonds among family tend to be stronger than those among friends ("Blood is thicker than water"). These principles reflect certain truths and may sometimes provide guidelines for action.

Although commonsense knowledge may have merit, it also has drawbacks, not the least of which is that it often contradicts itself. For example, we hear that people who are similar will like one another ("Birds of a feather flock together") but also that persons who are dissimilar will like each other ("Opposites attract"). We are told that groups are wiser and smarter than individuals ("Two heads are better than one") but also that group work inevitably produces poor results ("Too many cooks spoil the broth"). Each of these contradictory statements may hold true under particular conditions, but without a clear statement of when they apply and when they do not, aphorisms provide little insight into relations among people. They provide even less guidance in situations in which we must make decisions. For example, when facing a choice that entails risk, which guideline should we use—"Nothing ventured, nothing gained" or "Better safe than sorry"?

If sources such as personal experience and commonsense knowledge have only limited value, how are we to attain an understanding of social interactions and relations among people? One solution to this problem—the one pursued by social psychologists—is to obtain accurate knowledge about social behavior by applying the methods of science. That is, by making systematic observations of behavior and formulating theories that are subject to testing, we can attain a valid and comprehensive understanding of human social relations.

One goal of this book is to present some of social psychologists' major findings from systematic research. In this chapter, we lay the foundation for this effort by addressing the following questions:

1. What exactly is social psychology? What are the core concerns of the field of social psychology?

2. What are the broad theoretical perspectives that prevail in social psychology today? What are the strengths and weaknesses of each perspective? How do these perspectives relate to one another?

WHAT IS SOCIAL PSYCHOLOGY?

A Formal Definition

We define **social psychology** as the systematic study of the nature and causes of human social behavior. This definition has three main components. First, social psychology's primary concern is human social behavior. This includes many things—individuals' activities in the presence of others and in particular situations, the processes of social interaction between two or more persons, and the relationships among individuals and the groups to which they belong. Importantly, in this definition, behavior moves beyond action to also include affect (emotion) and cognition (thoughts). In other words, social psychologists are not only interested in what people do, but also what individuals feel and think (Fine, 1995).

Second, social psychologists are not satisfied to simply document the nature of social behavior; instead, they want to explore the causes of such behavior. This differentiates social psychology from a field like journalism. Journalists describe what people do. Social psychologists are not only interested in what people do but also want to understand why they do it. In social psychology, causal relations among variables are important building blocks of theory, and in turn, theory is crucial for the prediction and control of social behavior.

Third, social psychologists study social behavior in a systematic fashion. Social psychology is a social science that employs the scientific method and relies on formal research methodologies, including experimentation, structured observation, and sample surveys. These research methods are described in detail in Chapter 2.

Core Concerns of Social Psychology

Another way to answer the question "What is social psychology?" is to describe the topics that social psychologists actually study. Social psychologists investigate human behavior, of course, but their primary concern is human behavior in a social context. There are five core concerns, or major themes, within social psychology: (1) the impact that one individual has on another; (2) the impact that a group has on its individual members; (3) the impact that individual members have on the groups to which they belong; (4) the impact that one group has on another group; (5) the impact of social context and social structure on groups and individuals. The five core concerns are shown schematically in Figure 1.1.

BOX 1.1 Test Yourself: Is Social Psychology Simply Common Sense?

Because social psychologists are interested in a wide range of phenomena from our everyday lives, students sometimes claim that social psychology is common sense. Is it? Eight of the following common sense statements are true. The other eight are not. Can you tell the difference?

1. **T F** When faced with natural disasters such as floods and earthquakes, people panic and social organization disintegrates.

2. **T F** Physically attractive individuals are usually seen as less intelligent than physically unattractive individuals.

3. **T F** The reason people discriminate against minorities is prejudice; unprejudiced people don't discriminate.

4. **T F** Individuals who attended an Ivy League school end up earning more money than those who declined an offer of admission from an Ivy League school and chose to attend a less selective school.

5. **T F** Attractive people are more likely to have prestigious jobs and happier marriages than are less attractive people.

6. **T F** People tend to overestimate the extent to which other people share their opinions, attitudes, and behavior.

7. **T F** Rather than "opposites attract," people are generally attracted to those similar to themselves.

8. **T F** "Putting on a happy face" (that is, smiling when you are really not happy) will not make you feel any different on the inside.

9. **T F** People with few friends tend to live shorter, less healthy lives than do people with lots of friends.

10. **T F** We tend to view people in the groups and social categories that we belong to as more diverse and different from each other than we believe people in other groups are.

11. **T F** Parental disapproval for a relationship (for example, Romeo and Juliet) increases the chance that the partners will stay together.

12. **T F** If people tell a lie for a reward, they are more likely to come to believe the lie if they are given a small reward rather than a large reward.

13. **T F** Women with children are seen as the least desirable job candidates in most fields, while men with children are seen as the most desirable.

14. **T F** Most people would disobey an authority who orders them to hurt a stranger.

15. **T F** The more often we see something—even if we don't like it at first—the more we grow to like it.

16. **T F** The more certain a crime victim is about their account of events, the more accurate the report they provide to the police.

True: 5, 6, 7, 9, 10, 12, 13, & 15.

Impact of Individuals on Individuals. Individuals are affected by others in many ways. In everyday life, interactions with others may significantly influence a person's understanding of the social world. Much of this happens simply by observation. Through listening to others and watching them, an individual learns how she should act, what she should think, and how she should feel.

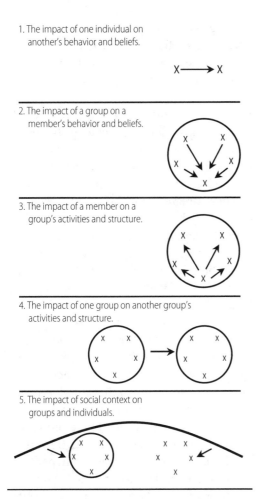

1. The impact of one individual on another's behavior and beliefs.

2. The impact of a group on a member's behavior and beliefs.

3. The impact of a member on a group's activities and structure.

4. The impact of one group on another group's activities and structure.

5. The impact of social context on groups and individuals.

FIGURE 1.1 The Core Concerns of Social Psychology

Sometimes this influence is more direct. A person might persuade another to change his beliefs about the world and his attitudes toward persons, groups, or other objects. Suppose, for example, that Mia tries to persuade Ashley that all nuclear power plants are dangerous and undesirable and, therefore, should be closed. If successful, Mia's persuasion attempt could change Ashley's beliefs and perhaps affect her future actions (picketing nuclear power plants, advocating non-nuclear sources of power, and the like).

Beyond influence and persuasion, the actions of others often affect the outcomes individuals obtain in everyday life. A per-

son caught in an emergency situation, for instance, may be helped by an altruistic bystander. In another situation, one person may be wounded by another's aggressive acts. Social psychologists have investigated the nature and origins of both altruism and aggression as well as other interpersonal activity such as cooperation and competition.

Also relevant here are various interpersonal sentiments. One individual may develop strong attitudes toward another (liking, disliking, loving, hating) based on who the other is and what he or she does. Social psychologists investigate these issues to discover why individuals develop positive attitudes toward some but negative attitudes toward others.

Impact of Groups on Individuals. Social psychology is also interested in the influence groups have on the behavior of their individual members. Because people belong to many different groups—families, work groups, seminars, and clubs—they spend many hours each week interacting with group members. Groups influence and regulate the behavior of their members, typically by establishing norms or rules. Group influence often results in conformity, as group members adjust their behavior to bring it into line with group norms. For example, college fraternities and sororities have norms—some formal and some informal—that stipulate how members should dress, what meetings they should attend, whom they can date and whom they should avoid, and how they should behave at parties. As a result of these norms, members behave quite similarly to one another.

Groups also exert substantial long-term influence on their members through socialization, a process through which individuals acquire the knowledge, values, and skills required of group members. Socialization processes are meant to ensure that group members will be adequately trained to play roles in the group and in the larger society. Although we are socialized to be members of discrete groups (sororities and fraternities, families, postal workers), we are also socialized to be members of social categories (woman, Latino, working class, American). Outcomes of socialization vary, from language skills to political and religious beliefs to our conception of self.

Impact of Individuals on Group. A third concern of social psychology is the impact of individuals on group processes and products. Just as any group influences the behavior of its members, these members, in turn, may influence the group itself. For instance, individuals contribute to group productivity and group decision making. Moreover, some members may provide leadership, performing functions such as planning, organizing, and controlling, necessary for successful group performance. Without effective leadership, coordination among members will falter and the group will drift or fail. Furthermore, individuals and minority coalitions often innovate change in group structure and procedures. Both leadership and innovation depend on individuals' initiative, insight, and risk-taking ability.

Impact of Groups on Groups. Social psychologists also explore how one group might affect the activities and structure of another group. Relations between two groups may be friendly or hostile, cooperative or competitive. These relationships, which are based in part on members' identities and may entail group stereotypes, can affect the structure and activities of each group. Of special interest is intergroup conflict, with its accompanying tension and hostility. Violence may flare up, for instance, between two street gangs disputing territorial rights or between racial groups competing for scarce jobs. Conflicts of this type affect the interpersonal relations be-

tween groups and within each group. Social psychologists have long studied the emergence, persistence, and resolution of intergroup conflict.

Impact of Social Context on Individuals and Groups. Social psychologists realize that individuals' behavior is profoundly shaped by the situations in which they find themselves. If you are listening to the radio in your car and your favorite song comes on, you might turn the volume up and sing along loudly. If you hear the same song at a dance club, you are less inclined to sing along but instead might head out to the dance floor. If your social psychology professor kicks off the first day of class by playing the song, chances are you won't sing or dance. In fact, you might give your fellow students a quizzical look. Your love for the song has not changed, but the social situation shapes your role in the situation (clubgoer, student) along with the expected behaviors based on that role. These contextual factors influence your reaction to the music.

These reactions are based, in part, on what you have learned through your interactions with others and through socialization in groups, the social influences discussed in the previous sections. However, as we grow and develop, the rules, belief systems, and categorical distinctions that have profound influence on our everyday lives seem to separate from these interactions. We forget that these things that appear natural were actually socially constructed (Berger & Luckmann, 1966).

Sociology, Psychology, or Both?

Social psychology bears a close relationship to several other fields, especially sociology and psychology.

Sociology is the scientific study of human society. It examines social institutions (family, religion, politics), stratification within society (class structure, race and ethnicity, gender roles), basic social processes (socialization, deviance, social control), and the structure of social units (groups, networks, formal organizations, bureaucracies).

In contrast, psychology is the scientific study of the individual and of individual behavior. Although this behavior may be social in character, it need not be. Psychology addresses such topics as human learning, perception, memory, intelligence, emotion, motivation, and personality.

Social psychology bridges sociology and psychology. In the mid-twentieth century, early in the history of social psychology, sociologists and psychologists worked closely together in departments and on research. In fact, top programs offered degrees in "Social Relations" or "Social Psychology" rather than Sociology or Psychology. However, over time, the interests of sociological social psychologists and psychological social psychologists have diverged somewhat. There is less collaboration today than there was early on, and most students get degrees in one of the two disciplines with a specialization or concentration in social psychology. That said, many still see the two areas as interdisciplinary.

Both sociologists and psychologists have contributed to social psychological knowledge. Sociological social psychologists use surveys, experiments, and observational techniques to gather data. These investigators are most interested in the relationship between individuals and the groups to which they belong. They emphasize such processes as socialization, conformity and deviance, social interaction, self-presentation, within-group processes, leadership, and cooperation and competition. Social psychologists working in the psychological tradition rely heavily on laboratory experimental methodology but increasingly use surveys and questionnaires. They are much less likely than sociological social psycholo-

gists to use observational methods outside the laboratory. Their primary concern is how social stimuli (often other persons) affects an individual's behavior and internal states. They emphasize such topics as the self, person perception and attribution, attitudes and attitude change, personality differences in social behavior, social learning and modeling, altruism and aggression, and interpersonal attraction.

Thus, sociologically oriented and psychologically oriented social psychologists differ in their outlook and emphasis. As we might expect, this leads them to formulate different theories and to conduct different programs of research. Yet these differences are best viewed as complementary rather than as conflicting. Social psychology as a field is richer for the differing contributions of both approaches.

THEORETICAL PERSPECTIVES IN SOCIAL PSYCHOLOGY

Yesterday at work, Warren reported to his boss that he would not be able to complete an important project on schedule. To Warren's surprise, the boss became enraged and told him to complete the task by the following Monday—or else! Warren was not entirely sure what to make of this behavior, but he decided to take the threat seriously.

That evening, talking with his girlfriend, Madison, Warren announced that he would have to work overtime at the office, so he could not go with her to a party on Friday evening as originally planned. Madison immediately got mad at Warren—she definitely wanted to go, she did not want to go alone, and he had promised several times to come along—and threw a paperweight at him. By now, Warren was distressed and a little perplexed.

Reflecting on these two events, Warren noticed they had some characteristics in common. To explain the behavior of his boss and his girlfriend, he formed a general proposition: "If you fail to deliver on promises made to another, he or she will get mad at you." He was happy with this simple formulation until the next day, when the car behind him at the stoplight started honking. He looked up and realized the light had turned green. As he moved forward, the car behind him passed him and the driver gave him an angry look. Warren thought about this event and concluded that his original theory needed some revision. Although he had not promised the driver behind him anything, the driver had become angry and aggressive because of Warren's actions. His new theory included a chain of propositions: "If someone's goals are blocked, he or she will become frustrated. If someone is frustrated, he or she will become aggressive. If someone is aggressive, he or she will lash out at either the source of the frustration or a convenient surrogate."

In his own way, Warren had started to do informally the same thing social psychologists do more elaborately and systematically. Starting from some observations regarding social behavior, Warren attempted to formulate a theory to explain the observed facts. As the term is used here, a **theory** is a set of interrelated propositions that organizes and explains a set of observed phenomena. Theories usually pertain not just to some particular event but rather to whole classes of events. Moreover, as Warren's example indicates, a theory goes beyond mere observable facts by postulating causal relations among variables. In other words, it describes not only what people do but also why they do it. If a theory is valid, it enables its user to explain the phenomena under consideration and to make predictions about events not yet observed.

In social psychology, no single theory explains all phenomena of interest; rather, the field includes many different theories. Many of these theories are discussed in this book. **Middle-range theories** identify the conditions that produce specific social behavior. One such theory is the frustration-aggression hypothesis, not unlike Warren's theory above, which describes the connection between blocked goals, frustration, and aggression. However, social psychology also includes **theoretical perspectives**. Broader in scope than middle-range theories, theoretical perspectives offer general explanations for a wide array of social behaviors in a variety of situations. These general explanations are rooted in explicit assumptions about human nature. Theoretical perspectives serve an important function for the field of social psychology. By making certain assumptions regarding human nature, a theoretical perspective establishes a vantage point from which we can examine a range of social behaviors. Because any perspective highlights certain features and downplays others, it enables us to "see" more clearly certain aspects or features of social behavior. The fundamental value of any theoretical perspective lies in its applicability across many situations; it provides a frame of reference for interpreting and comparing a wide range of social situations and behaviors.

Social psychology can be organized into a number of distinct theoretical perspectives. For sociologists who study social psychology, these theoretical perspectives are situated in three traditions—symbolic interactionism, group processes, and social structure and personality. James House (1977) referred to these as the three "faces" of social psychology, each with a unique perspective and emphasis. These faces as well as related theoretical perspectives are explained below. Also below is an introduction to theoretical perspectives that have dominated psychological social psychology over the last twenty years: cognitive theories (including both the dual-process model of information processing and social identity theory) and evolutionary theory.

Symbolic Interactionism

The theoretical perspective that guided much of the early work of sociological social psychologists—and that is still important today—is symbolic interactionism (Charon, 1995; Stryker, 1980, 1987). Although it is sometimes called **symbolic interaction theory**, symbolic interactionism is actually a perspective that guides the development of more specific theories. The basic premise of symbolic interactionism is that human nature and social order are products of symbolic communication among people. Society (from cultures to institutions to ourselves) is produced and reproduced through our interactions with others by means of language and our interpretation of that language. There are three main premises of symbolic interaction (Blumer, 1969):

According to symbolic interactionism, we derive the meaning of objects from how we (or others) plan to use those objects. The same bottle can be a vessel for liquid, waste, a vase, a weapon, or a game piece. Depending on how people intend to use the table the bottle is on, its meaning can also vary—from a table, to a desk, to a seat, to a place to lie down for a nap. © Tamas Panczel, Eross/ Shutterstock

1. We act toward things on the basis of their meanings.
2. Meanings are not inherent but are negotiated in interaction with others.
3. Meanings can be modified and changed through interaction.

People can communicate successfully with one another only to the extent that they ascribe similar meanings to objects. An object's meaning for a person depends not so much on the properties of the object itself but on what the person might do with the object. In other words, an object takes on meaning only in relation to a person's plans. Consider an empty glass bottle. Standing alone, a bottle has no meaning. The meaning of the bottle comes from how you plan to use it. If there is liquid in it, it becomes a vessel for a beverage. Placed in the recycling bin, it becomes waste. But if someone pulls it out of the recycling and puts flowers in it, it becomes a vase. Use it in a bar fight, it might be a weapon. Placed on its side at the center of a table filled with people, it becomes a game-piece for Spin the Bottle. We learn the meanings of things—whether bottles or smiles or pieces of linen and cotton printed with black and green ink—through interaction with others. These meanings can change and shift over time based on social interaction.

Negotiating Meanings. Symbolic interaction theory views humans as proactive and goal seeking. People formulate plans of action to achieve their goals. Many plans, of course, can be accomplished only through

This comic strip illustrates the negotiation of meaning between Calvin and his imaginary friend, Hobbes. They each have different labels for the same physiological reactions. Through interaction, Calvin learns that he had mistaken for cooties a feeling that Hobbes explains to him is actually love. CALVIN AND HOBBES © 1986 Watterson. Used by permission of Universal Uclick. All rights reserved.

cooperation with other people. To establish cooperation with others, the meanings of things must be shared and consensual. If the meaning of something is unclear or contested, an agreement must be developed through give-and-take before cooperative action is possible. For example, if a man and a woman have begun to meet after work for drinks and, one night, as they are leaving the bar, she invites him to her apartment, exactly what meaning does this proposal have? One way or another, they will have to achieve some agreement about the purpose of the visit before joint action is possible. In symbolic interaction terms, they would need to develop a consensual definition of the situation. The coworkers might achieve this through explicit nego-

tiation or through tacit, nonverbal communication. She might explain that she wants to show him her new guitar or to make him a cup of coffee before he drives home, or she might give him a wink and a smile along with the invitation. But without some agreement regarding the definition of the situation, the man may have difficulty deciding whether to accept the invitation; the woman, sensing the man's discomfort, may find herself behaving in an atypically awkward manner. Either way, cooperative action will be difficult.

Symbolic interactionism portrays social interaction as having a tentative, developing quality. Meanings can change over time or across situations. On the way home from his first day of kindergarten, a young boy was describing a little girl from his class—Maeve—to his mother. It was clear the boy was fond of Maeve as he spoke of her big brown eyes, long straight hair, pink lips, and chubby cheeks. But when he proceeded to tell his mother that Maeve looked like a dog, his mother was taken aback. To her, calling a woman a dog was an insult. The reverence in her son's voice suggested he would never insult Maeve, so the mother was confused. Thinking more about it, the mother realized that to her son, calling Maeve a dog was a compliment rather than an insult. There was nothing the young boy loved more than to cuddle up with the family dog. To him, a dog was something to love and cherish. He had not yet learned that dog was an insult. To fit their actions together and achieve consensus, people interacting with one another must continually negotiate new meanings or reaffirm old meanings. In the same way that the mother had to work to determine the boy's meaning to have interaction proceed smoothly, the coworkers will have to negotiate a working consensus to effectively communicate and interact. In this process, each person formulates plans for action, tries them out, and then adjusts them in light of others' responses. Thus, social interaction always has some degree of unpredictability and indeterminacy.

For an interaction among persons to proceed smoothly, there must be some consensus with respect to the **situated identity**—who one is in relation to the others in the situation—of each person. In other words, every person involved in the interaction must know who they are in the situation and who the other people are. In the example of the coworkers: are they friends, could she want more, or are they simply coworkers? Only by answering this question in some detail can each person understand the implications (meanings) that others have for his or her plan of action.

The Self in Relationship to Others. As we grow, we learn that the **self** is also a social object and its meaning is also developed and negotiated in interaction. As we interact with people, we try to imagine how they see us so we can come to understand how they see us and how we should see ourselves (Cooley, 1902). To do this, we engage in a process of **role taking**: we imagine ourselves in another person's role, including how we look from the other person's viewpoint. This serves two purposes. First, role taking can make cooperative action possible. Based on previous experience, we can imagine how another would react in any given situation. Consider a teenager whose mother has just asked him whether he completed his homework. Before answering, he will try to imagine the situation from his mother's perspective. If he tells her he played video games instead, she will be disappointed or even angry. If he lies and says it is all done, she will be satisfied—at least until she finds out the truth, and then she will be even angrier. By role taking, he can effectively guide subsequent interaction. However, there is a second important purpose of role taking. In imagining how he appears to his mother, the teenager is acquiring self-meanings. If he failed to do the homework, opting instead to play video games, he may see himself as lazy or unmotivated because that is how he imagines someone else (like his mother) would see him. If he lied about it, he might see himself as a liar. The self occupies a central place in symbolic interaction theory because social order is hypothesized to rest in part on self-control. Individuals strive to maintain self-respect in their own eyes, but because they are continually engaging in role taking, they see themselves from the viewpoint of the others with whom they interact. To maintain self-respect, they thus must meet the standards of others, at least to some degree.

Of course, an individual will care more about the opinions and standards of some persons than about those of others. The persons about whose opinions he or she cares most are called **significant others**. Typically, these are people who control important rewards or who occupy central positions in groups to which the individual belongs. Because their positive opinions are highly valued, significant others have relatively more influence over the individual's behavior.

Inherent in the above discussion is symbolic interactionism's assertion that a person can act not only toward others but also toward his or her self. That is, an individual can engage in self-perception, self-evaluation, and self-control just as he or she might perceive, evaluate, and control others. The ability to act toward oneself, taking the role of both subject an object, is a uniquely human trait. George Herbert Mead, a forefather of symbolic interactionism, referred to this ability as the **reflexive self** (1934).

In sum, the symbolic interactionist perspective has several strong points. It recognizes the importance of the self in social interaction. It stresses the central role of symbolic communication and language in personality and society. It addresses the processes involved in achieving consensus and cooperation in interaction. It illuminates why people try to maintain a positive image of self and avoid embarrassment. Many of these topics are discussed in detail in later chapters. The self, self-presentation, and impression management are discussed in Chapter 4, embarrassment and other social emotions in Chapter 5, symbolic communication and language are taken up in Chapter 8, and Chapter 16 addresses the importance of labeling on self and others.

Limitations of Symbolic Interaction Theory. Critics of symbolic interactionism have pointed to various shortcomings. One criticism concerns the balance between rationality and emotion. Some critics argue that this perspective overemphasizes rational, self-conscious thought and deemphasizes unconscious or emotional states. A second criticism concerns the model of the individual implicit in symbolic interaction theory. The individual is depicted as a specific personality type—an other-directed person who is concerned primarily with maintaining self-respect by meeting others' standards. A third criticism of symbolic interactionism is that it places too much emphasis on consensus and cooperation and, therefore, neglects or downplays the importance of conflict. The perspective does recognize, however, that interacting people may fail to reach consensus despite their efforts to achieve it. The symbolic interactionist perspective is at its best when analyzing fluid, developing encounters with significant others; it is less useful when analyzing self-interested behavior or principled action.

Group Processes

Social psychologists have long been interested in the ways individuals interact in groups. Throughout this text you will learn about ground-breaking social psychological experiments that explored the role of groups on individual behavior. Some of the most notable are the work of John Darley and Bibb Latané on helping in emergencies (Chapter 10) and Solomon Asch's research on majority influence in groups (Chapter 13). Like much of this early research, contemporary work on group processes tends to favor the experimental method over surveys or observational methods. Today's group processes researchers tend to work in sociological social psychology and draw on a number of theoretical perspectives and theories. These are described in detail in

BOX 1.2 Symbolic Interaction in Action: Roles and Identities

We do not infer who we are based solely on our actions—as the teenager might when he opts for video games instead of homework or lies to his mother; our definitions of self—as captured in roles and identities—also guide our actions. **Roles** consist of a set of rules (that is, expectations held by others) that function as plans or blueprints for behavior. **Identities** are categories—sometimes based on roles, other times based on group membership or personal characteristics—that specify the positions we hold in society and groups. Both of these concepts are tied to contemporary social psychological theories rooted in symbolic interactionism.

According to **role theory** (Biddle, 1979, 1986; Heiss, 1981; Turner, 1990):

1. People spend much of their lives participating as members of groups and organizations.
2. Within these groups, people occupy distinct positions (fullback, advertising executive, police sergeant, and the like).
3. Each of these positions entails a **role**, which is a set of functions performed by the person for the group. A person's role is defined by expectations (held by other group members) that specify how he or she should perform.
4. Groups often formalize these expectations as **norms**, which are rules specifying how a person should behave, what rewards will result for performance, and what punishments will result for nonperformance.
5. Individuals usually carry out their roles and perform in accordance with the prevailing norms. In other words, people are primarily conformists—they try to meet others' expectations.
6. Group members check each individual's performance to determine whether it conforms to the group's norms. If an individual meets others' role expectations, he or she will receive rewards in some form (acceptance, approval, money, and so on). If he or she fails to

perform as expected, however, group members may embarrass, punish, or even expel that individual from the group. The anticipation that others will apply sanctions ensures performance as expected.

Role theory implies that if we (as analysts) have information about the role expectations for a specified position, we can then predict a significant portion of the behavior (as well as the beliefs and attitudes) of the person occupying that position. If we want to change a person's behavior, role theory argues that it is first necessary to change or redefine his or her role (Allen & Van de Vliert, 1982).

Identity theory (Burke & Stets, 2009; Stryker, 1980; Stryker & Burke, 2000) also emphasizes the importance of self-meanings in guiding behavior. However, identity theorists extend beyond role identities to include three additional types of self-designations—person, social, and group identities. Olevia might be a student (role identity), but she is also a sister (another role identity), moral (person identity), a member of the Black Student Association (a group identity), and a woman (social identity). All five of these influence her behavior. Although our identities are often consistent, sometimes they come in conflict. Identity theory understands that because individuals occupy more than one identity at a time, their influence on our behavior is not as clear-cut as role theory might suggest. Therefore, much of the research in identity theory works to predict which identity we will enact in a given situation. Identity theory postulates that we are more likely to enact identities that we see as central to who we are; this centrality or salience is based in part on how much we have invested in the identity, the quality and quantity of social ties that we have through that identity, our need for identity support, and the situational opportunities (Stryker & Serpe, 1994).

Chapter 14, but two of the main orienting frameworks—social exchange and status—are introduced below.

Social Exchange. Like with symbolic interaction, there are many who refer to the exchange perspective as a theory. However, that is technically incorrect. Social exchange is a framework, within which a number of middle-range theories are situated (power-dependence theory, affect theory, reciprocity theory). The **social exchange** perspective (Cook, 1987; Homans, 1974; Kelley & Thibaut, 1978) has a unique set of concepts and assumptions that connect the various theories subsumed under the framework. In social exchange there are (1) *actors* who exchange (2) *resources* using an (3) *exchange process* while situated in an (4) *exchange structure* (Molm, 2006). These resources can be tangible goods or behaviors (an individual might give money, a smile, or a simple "thank you" in exchange for a cookie) and can be exchanged through different processes—a student might receive a cookie as a gift from a professor or she might purchase it in a negotiated transaction, by exchanging money for the cookie, at a bakery. These exchanges occur in relations that are structured by the size and shape of the exchange network and the types of relations between actors. According to this perspective, social relationships are primarily based on the exchanges of goods and services among persons.

The social exchange perspective assumes that individuals have freedom of choice and often face social situations in which they must choose among alternative actions. Any action provides some rewards and entails some costs. There are many kinds of socially mediated rewards—money, goods, services, prestige or status, approval by others, and the like. The theory posits that individuals are hedonistic—they try to maximize rewards and minimize costs. Consequently, they choose actions that produce good profits and avoid actions that produce poor profits. This view might seem overly rational and calculated, but social exchange theory suggest that these choices are actually often unconscious and are the result of **conditioning**—learning as the result of positive or negative responses to behavior (Mazur, 1998; Skinner, 1953).

People will be more likely to perform a specific behavior if it is followed directly by the occurrence of something pleasurable or by the removal of something aversive; likewise, people will more likely refrain from performing a particular behavior if it is followed by the occurrence of something aversive or by the removal of something pleasant. Individuals become embedded in ongoing exchange relationships because they experience these positive outcomes. They stop exchanging with particular others when the exchanges stop providing these positive reinforcements and there are alternative relations available that might provide comparable benefits.

Exchange theory also predicts the conditions under which people try to change or restructure their relationships. A central concept involved is **equity** (Adams, 1963). A state of equity exists in a relationship when participants feel that the rewards they receive are proportional to the costs they bear. For example, a chef may earn more money than a line cook and receive better benefits on the job. But the line cook may nevertheless feel the relationship is equitable because the chef bears more responsibility and has a higher level of education and training.

If, for some reason, a participant feels that the allocation of rewards and costs in a relationship is inequitable, the relationship is potentially unstable. People find inequity difficult to tolerate—they may feel cheated or exploited and become angry. Social exchange theory predicts that people will try to modify an inequitable relationship. Most likely, they will attempt to reallocate costs and rewards so that equity is established. However, they may also leave the relationship in search of one with a more equitable arrangement.

Status. Social psychologists are also interested in status differences. The chef has more than just a higher salary and better benefits compared to the line cook; she also has higher **status**—levels of esteem and perceived competence (Ridgeway, 2006). Sociological social psychology has explored how social differences in society—based on categories like gender, race, and education—become status differences. Why is it that men, across a range of domains, are held in greater esteem and thought to be more competent than women? Why is it that Whites are assumed, often unconsciously, to be more effective leaders and more skilled at any number of tasks than Blacks? Understanding the process through which status differences originate and are sustained in society and how they might decline (for example, how Irishness has lost its significance in the United States) offers important insight into inequality not only between groups but also within them (Ridgeway, 2011).

Early social psychological work on status focused on the emergence of status differences within groups. To illustrate, imagine you are assigned to work with a group of students from your social psychology class on a project. If you all were strangers but varied on status dimensions like gender, race, or year in school, how would that affect your behavior in groups? Over time, differences in contribution are likely to emerge. Some of the group members would talk more. Among those who contributed more, some have more influence. If they made sugges-

tions, these ideas would be more likely to be accepted by the group. Group members would also be less likely to interrupt these members while speaking. Based on status research, these integral members are more likely to possess attributes that are high status (white, male, juniors and seniors). They are afforded more influence in groups because we tend to hold higher performance expectations of high-status individuals. We assume they will perform better on any number of tasks unless we have explicit information that suggests otherwise or the task was explicitly seen as a domain of a lower-status group. For example, if we knew that Rich—the senior, white man in our group—was flunking social psychology, we would have lower expectations of his competence on the group task. Likewise, if the class was home economics rather than social psychology and the group task was related to sewing, the group would draw on the cultural belief that women would perform better on such tasks and defer to Monica.

In sum, the group processes tradition focuses on a number of interesting topics that are integral aspects of social life. Both social exchange and status, for example, are ubiquitous in our daily interactions, and the usefulness of theorizing on these processes is clear. The tradition recognizes the importance of the groups and relationships in shaping individuals' experiences. It explores processes both within and between groups. It also addresses inequality, a core sociological concern. Many topics of interest to this tradition are discussed in detail in later chapters. The role of groups in socialization processes is covered in Chapter 3, and the importance of social categories as shaping individual experiences are discussed in Chapter 6. Processes within and between groups, including group conflict and cohesion, are discussed in Chapters 13 and 14. Groups' potential to engage in collective efforts for social change is covered in Chapter 17.

Limitations of Group Processes. The main criticism of the group processes tradition and related theories is that they are based, in large part, on research that was conducted in laboratories, with North American college students as participants. There are concerns that any results from WEIRD—Western, Educated, and from Industrialized, Rich, Democratic countries—research participants are not generalizable to people from other social groups or cultures (Henrich, Heine, & Norenzayan, 2010) and that the way people behave in the artificial situations presented in the laboratory are not indicative of how individuals would respond in everyday situations. Although these concerns are certainly important to keep in mind, as you will see in this book, the theories tested and developed in the laboratory are often based on "real world" events. Furthermore, a growing number of social psychologists are incorporating non-laboratory-based methods to diversify their research participants and settings (Collett & Avelis, 2011; Correll, Benard, & Paik, 2007). Chapter 2 discusses the value of various research methods in social psychology.

Social Structure and Personality

The third tradition in social psychology argues that we are each situated in unique positions in the social structure. For example, Professor Collett is a white woman who is married with a teenage son. She grew up outside of Seattle, graduating high school in the early 1990s. Neither of her parents graduated college. They opened a small restaurant when Professor Collett was in elementary school, and she spent a lot of time hanging out—and later working—in the family business. Social psychologists who adopt a social structure and personality approach believe these attributes and experiences that situate Professor Collett in the social structure influence her personality—her attitudes, values, and goals, among other things. You might assume, for example, that Professor Collett cares about education, because she teaches college and has a school-aged son. You might think of Seattle as a liberal place or assume that someone from the Seattle area likes coffee, Microsoft computers, or the rain. As a product of the early '90s, you might imagine her to be more fond of Nirvana or Pearl Jam than Macklemore. You might assume that her parents' education level and exposure to a family business might have influenced her orientation toward college and work. Although social psychologists are interested in describing general trends rather than individuals' personalities, sociological social psychologists who work in this tradition are exploring similar topics. How does someone's position in the social structure influence their personality?

The seminal work in social structure and personality (SSP) was conducted by Melvin Kohn and Carmi Schooler (Kohn, 1969; Kohn & Schooler, 1973). Described in more detail in Chapters 3 and 15, this research found important social class differences in childrearing—with middle- and upper-class parents valuing self-direction and curiosity over conformity, for example—and argued that these differences were rooted in the parents' work conditions. Working-class parents were more likely to be employed in manufacturing jobs that rewarded conformity. Middle- and upper-class parents were more likely to be employed in sectors and positions that rewarded self-direction, creativity, and curiosity. The rewards at work reinforced these values in the parents, and through their child-rearing styles at home, the parents subsequently passed these values on to their children. These values likely influenced their children's work orientations as well, which would ultimately affect the types of work they would be drawn to and recreate the connection between class, work, values, and parenting (Kohn & Schooler, 1982).

Social class is only one of many aspects of social structure of interest to social psychologists. Others include occupation, gender, marital and parental status, and education. Additionally, personality—as conceived by those who work in this tradition—extends beyond values and beliefs to behavior and both physical and mental health. Many of these topics are covered in the chapters to follow. Chapter 3 discusses socialization as the process through which we come to acquire values. Chapters 6 and 7 describe how our positions in social structure can influence the way we perceive events and the attitudes we hold. The connection between social structure and both prosocial (altruism and helping) and antisocial (aggression) behavior is covered in Chapters 10 and 11. Finally, Chapter 15 takes the social structure and personality approach as its focus, introducing a wide array of research in the tradition.

Limitations of Social Structure and Personality. Although some assert that the social structure and personality tradition is the most sociological of the social psychological approaches because of its consideration of macrosociological structures (Kohn, 1989), SSP does have its critics. The main criticism launched is that much of the research only describes a relationship—attractive people are happier than unattractive people, married people live longer than single people, groups with members who are similar tend to be more cohesive—and falls short of pro-

viding a mechanism, an explanation of why one thing leads to another. As you will see as you progress through this book, however, this is a somewhat unfair criticism. There are a number of causal mechanisms suggested throughout social psychology. However, the SSP tradition's reliance on survey methods makes causal inferences difficult. The social structure and personality approach is also criticized because it fails to account for individuals who deviate from trends and averages. Not everyone from Seattle is liberal or appreciates musicians from the Pacific Northwest.

Cognitive Perspectives

Social psychologists who work in psychology tend to emphasize cognitive perspectives. The basic premise of **cognitive theory** is that the mental activities of the individual are important determinants of social behavior (Operario & Fiske, 1999). These mental activities, called **cognitive processes**, include perception, memory, judgment, problem solving, and decision making. Cognitive theory does not deny the importance of external stimuli, but it maintains that the link between stimulus and response is not direct; rather, the individual's cognitive processes intervene between external stimuli and behavioral responses. Individuals not only actively interpret the meaning of stimuli but also select the actions to be made in response.

Historically, the cognitive approach to social psychology has been influenced by the ideas of Koffka, Kohler, and other theorists in the Gestalt movement of psychology. Central to Gestalt psychology is the principle that people respond to configurations of stimuli rather than to a single, discrete stimulus. In other words, people understand the meaning of a stimulus only by viewing it in the context of an entire system of elements (the gestalt) in which it is embedded. A chess master, for example, would not assess the importance of a chess piece on the board without considering its location and strategic capabilities vis-à-vis all the other pieces currently on the board. To comprehend the meaning of any element, we must look at the whole of which it is a part.

Cognitive theorists depict humans as active in selecting and interpreting stimuli (Fiske & Taylor, 1991; Moskowitz, Skurnik, & Galinksy, 1999). According to this view, people do more than react to their environment; they actively structure their world cognitively. First, humans are cognitive misers. Because individuals cannot possibly attend to all the complex stimuli that surround them, they select only those stimuli that are important or useful to them and ignore the others. Second, they actively control which categories or concepts they use to interpret the stimuli in the environment. There are a wide range of cognitive tactics available for people to draw from, and they choose the approach they take (Operario & Fiske, 1999). Humans are "motivated tacticians" (Fiske & Taylor, 1991). This means, of course, that various individuals can form dramatically different impressions of the same complex stimulus in the environment.

Consider, for example, what happens when several people view a vacant house displaying a bright "for rent" sign. When a building contractor passes the house, she pays primary attention to the quality of the house's construction. She sees lumber, bricks, shingles, glass, and some repairs that need to be made. Another person, a potential renter, sees the house very differently. He notes that it is located close to his job and wonders whether the neighborhood is safe and whether the house is expensive to heat in winter. The real estate agent trying to rent the house construes it in still dif-ferent terms—cash flow, occupancy rate, depreciation, mortgage, and amortization. One of the young children living in the neighborhood has yet another view; observing that no person has lived in the house for several months, he is convinced the house is haunted.

Cognitive Structure and Schemas. Central to the cognitive perspective is the concept of **cognitive structure**, which refers broadly to any form of organization among cognitions (concepts and beliefs). Because a person's cognitions are interrelated, cognitive theory gives special emphasis to exactly how they are structured and organized in memory and how they affect a person's judgments.

Social psychologists have proposed that individuals use specific cognitive structures called *schemas* to make sense of complex information about other persons, groups, and situations. The term **schema** is derived from the Greek word for "form," and it refers to the form or basic sketch of what we know about people and things. For example, our schema for "law student" might be a set of traits thought to be characteristic of such persons: intelligent, analytic and logical, argumentative (perhaps even combative), and thorough with an eagle eye for details, strategically skillful in interpersonal relations, and (occasionally) committed to seeing justice done. This schema, no doubt, reflects our own experience with lawyers and law students as well as our conception of which traits are necessary for success in the legal profession. That we hold this schema does not mean we believe that everyone with this set of characteristics is a law student or that every law student will have all of these characteristics. We might be surprised, however, if we met someone who impressed us as unmethodical, illogical, withdrawn, inarticulate, inattentive, sloppy, and not very intelligent and then later discovered he was a law student.

Schemas are important in social relations because they help us interpret the environment efficiently. Whenever we encounter a person for the first time, we usually form an impression of what he or she is like. In doing this, we not only observe the person's behavior but also rely on our knowledge of similar persons we have met in the past; that is, we use our schema regarding this type of person. Schemas help us process information by enabling us to recognize which personal characteristics are important in the interaction and which are not. They structure and organize infor-

Many comedies make use of schemas. In order to find humor in Elle Woods pursuing a law degree at Harvard in the movie *Legally Blonde*, you must first understand that she does not fit the schema for a law student. Throughout the movie, Woods's interactions with those who do fit the law school student schema provide stark contrast and set the stage for humorous situations. © Bureau L.A. Collection/Sygma/Corbis

mation about the person, and they help us remember information better and process it more quickly. Sometimes they fill gaps in knowledge and enable us to make inferences and judgments about others.

To illustrate further, consider a law school admissions officer who faces the task of deciding which candidates to admit as students. To assist in processing applications, she uses a schema for "strong law student candidate" that is based on traits believed to predict success in law school and beyond. The admissions officer doubtless pays close attention to information regarding candidates that is relevant to her schema for law students, and she most likely ignores or downplays other information. LSAT scores do matter, whereas eye color does not; undergraduate GPA does matter, whereas ability to throw a football does not; and so on.

Schemas are rarely perfect as predictive devices, and the admissions officer probably will make mistakes, admitting some candidates who fail to complete law school and turning down some candidates who would have succeeded. Moreover, another admissions officer with a different schema might admit a different set of students to law school. Schemas also figure centrally in our stereotypes and discriminatory attitudes. If, for example, an admissions officer includes only the race "White" in her schema for successful law students, she will be less likely to admit African Americans. Despite their drawbacks, schemas are more efficient ways to process social information than having no systematic framework at all. Thus, they persist as important cognitive mechanisms even when less than perfect. Schemas will be discussed in more detail in Chapter 6.

Dual-Process Theory of Information Processing. Much of the recent work in psychological social psychology incorporates dual-process models. Like the sociological approaches outlined earlier, the dual-process theory is a theoretical perspective that subsumes a number of specific theories. Theories associated with this theoretical perspective are all based on the notion that we process information two ways—automatically and deliberately—and this influences perception, impression formation, and attributions (Chapter 6), attitudes (Chapter 7), persuasion (Chapter 9), attraction (Chapter 12), and stereotyping (Chapters 6 and 13), among other social psychological processes.

The automatic process of perception occurs so quickly that individuals fail to even notice it. This automaticity relies on the use of **heuristics**—cognitive shortcuts using readily accessible information based on experience—that aid in information processing. Schemas, as outlined above, are a good example. Individuals have learned, over time, the content of a variety of schemas. We have ideas about women and men, law students and sorority sisters, Blacks and Whites. When we encounter someone new, we use heuristics to classify them into a category using salient physical features, behaviors, or labels provided to us through means of an introduction or setting. Once classified, heuristics also help us determine what to expect from them and how to treat them—without giving any conscious thought to the categorization or these expectations. These processes are automatic and require little effort.

However, if we decide to keep processing, a more conscious and deliberate process occurs. This high-effort systematic processing as it relates to forming impressions of people we encounter is shown in Figure 1.2. This process takes place if the person is of even minimal relevance to us. If you are walking down the street late at night, for example, you want to know whether you can trust the person who is walking toward you. Are they a threat? Are they benevolent? Additional processing takes place because you are seeking out a more accurate judgment than what is provided through unconscious processing alone. It can also occur because the information presented to us is so inconsistent with our heuristics (Elle Woods does not fit our schema for a law student, the person walking toward us is a Black man whistling a concerto by Vivaldi [Steele, 2011]). Based on this dual-processing view, we are not doomed to be cognitive misers who act on autopilot throughout our lives. We are capable of more elaborate processing, but we must have reason to set that high-effort processing in motion (Moskowitz, Skurnik, & Galinksy, 1999).

Social Identity Theory. Social identity theory grew out of a concern that psychology had become too reductionist and was only concerned about the individual. This perspective argues that while we sometimes think, feel, and act as individuals, most of our behavior stems from the social groups that we belong to (Operario & Fiske, 1999). The most sociological of the psychological perspectives, social identity argues that individuals' identification with societal structures—groups, organizations, cultures—guides cognitive processes (Markus, Kitayama, & Heiman, 1996). Identification is central here. If someone does not identify with a group, it is not psychologically real (Hogg, 2006). This is why social identity theory is a cognitive theory. Self-categorization—a cognitive process—is instrumental in social identity processes (Turner 1987).

We categorize ourselves and others into groups using a type of schema called a prototype. We decide that we are a member of a group because we fit a schema of typical group members. This categorization affects our self-concept, of course, but it also influences our perceptions of others. We

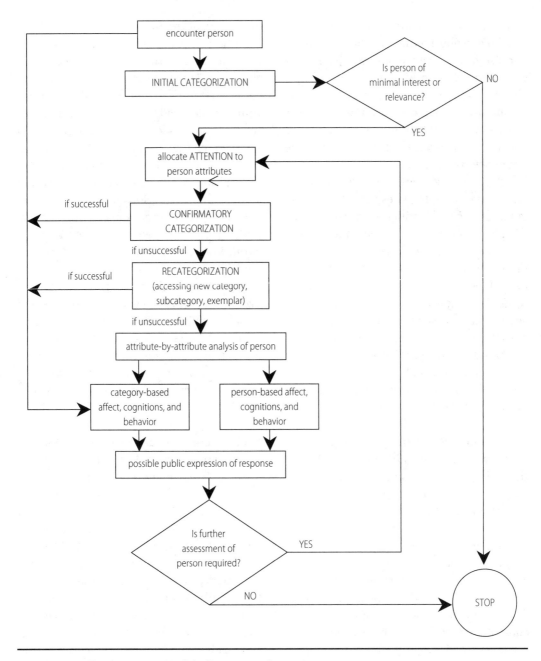

FIGURE 1.2 The Continuum Model of Impression Formation

This model illustrates the dual processes at work when we form impressions of people we encounter. The initial categorization is low effort and occurs immediately upon perception of the person. If the person we encounter is relevant to us, this sets in motion a high-effort process in which we allocate additional attention to the person to try to confirm our original categorization or to recategorize the person. These categorizations guide our responses (affect, cognition, and behavior) to the person. However, if we are unable to categorize (or recategorize) the person we encounter, we will conduct an attribute-by-attribute analysis of the person to determine how to respond to him or her and whether additional attention is needed. Adapted from Figure 11.1 in Fiske, Lin, and Neuberg (1999), *The Continuum Model: Ten Years Later.*

view ourselves and those who we classify as fellow group members more positively. Because of this, we feel a sense of camaraderie and cohesion with our social groups. However, the same processes lead us to feel distinct from those who are not in our social group, and the cognitive shortcuts we take in classification tend to exaggerate the differences between us and them.

Social identity processes appear throughout the text. Chapter 4 describes the importance of social identities in self-concepts. Chapter 6 covers prototypes and stereotypes. Chapter 13 discusses both inter- and intragroup dynamics like cohesion and conformity, ethnocentrism, and discrimination.

In sum, cognitive theory is an incredibly active area in psychological social psychology, and it continues to produce many insights and striking predictions regarding individual and social behavior. It is among the more popular and productive approaches in social psychology.

Limitations of Cognitive Perspectives. One drawback of cognitive theories is that they simplify—and sometimes oversimplify—the way in which people process information, an inherently complex phenomenon. Another drawback is that cognitive phenomena are not directly observable; they must be inferred from what people say and do. This means that compelling and definitive tests of theoretical predictions from cognitive theory are sometimes difficult to conduct. However, methodological advances—including the ability to subliminally prime subjects, to measure millisecond reaction times, and to use fMRI scans—are making such research increasingly possible (Operario & Fiske, 1999).

Evolutionary Theory

The last theoretical perspective of this chapter is evolutionary theory. Although it is not one of the main perspectives in contemporary social psychology, it is found throughout the topics in this book and, therefore, is still an important perspective to understand moving forward. When we think of Charles Darwin and evolution, we most often think of the development of physical characteristics. How, for example, did humans develop binocular vision or the ability to walk upright? How did some animals develop an acute sense of smell, whereas others depend for survival on their ability to see at low levels of light? Evolutionary psychologists—and sociobiologists—do not stop with strictly physical characteristics, however. They extend evolutionary ideas to explain a great deal of social behavior, including altruism, aggression, mate selection, sexual behavior, and even such seemingly arcane topics as why presidents of the United States are taller than the average man (Buss & Kenrick, 1998).

Evolutionary Foundations of Behavior. Evolutionary psychology locates the roots of social behavior in our genes and, therefore, intimately links the psychological and social to the biological (Buss, 1999; Symons, 1992; Wilson, 1975). In effect, social behavior, or the predisposition toward certain behaviors, is encoded in our genetic material and is passed on through reproduction. In physical evolution, those characteristics that enable the individual to survive and pass on its genetic code are ones that will eventually occur more frequently in the population. For instance, animals whose camouflage coloring allows them to escape predators will be more likely to survive and produce offspring—who will then receive the advantageous coloring from their parents. Animals of the same species whose camouflage coloring is less efficient will be more likely to be caught and killed before they can reproduce. Thus, over time, the share genetic material with their biological children but not with their stepchildren (Piliavin & LePore, 1995). These and many other topics will be examined using evolutionary ideas throughout the book, particularly in Chapters 3 (Socialization Through the Life Course), 6 (Social Perception and Cognition), 10 (Altruism and Prosocial Behavior), 11 (Aggression) and 12 (Interpersonal Attraction and Relationships).

Limitations of Evolutionary Theory. Although the perspective continues to guide some social psychological work, the evolutionary perspective never eclipsed other theoretical approaches to social psychology and has been subject to a fair amount of criticism (Caporeal, 2001; Rose & Rose, 2000). The most persistent critique accuses evolutionary psychologists of circular reasoning (Kenrick, 1995). Typically, the evolutionary psychologist observes some characteristic of the social world and then constructs an explanation for it based on its supposed contribution to genetic fitness. The logic of the argument then becomes: Why does this behavior occur? Because it improves the odds of passing on one's genes. But how do we know it improves those odds? Because it occurs. This logical trap is, in some sense, unavoidable because we cannot travel back in time to observe the actual evolution of social behavior.

The problem appears most clearly when we consider the possibility of alternative outcomes. For example, we may observe that men are more accepting of casual sex than women. The evolutionary explanation for this difference between men and women is that men can maximize the survival of their genetic material by spreading it as widely as possible. Women, however, need to know who the father of their children is and extract support from him to ensure the successful transmission of their own genes. Suppose, however, that women were actually more accepting of casual sex than men. This could also easily be explained by the evolutionary perspective. A man cannot be certain that a child is his, so a strong commitment to a monogamous relationship would help ensure that it is actually his genes that are being passed to a child. Women, however, are always 100 percent sure that their own genes are passed down to their children, so in terms of genetic fitness, it should not matter to them who is the father. Because these after-the-fact explanations are always easy to construct and difficult to prove, it can be very difficult to judge them against competing arguments. Therefore, although the evolutionary perspective has a number of supporters, it still has major obstacles to overcome before achieving widespread acceptance as a useful explanation for social behavior.

The five theoretical perspectives discussed here—symbolic interaction, group processes, social structure and personality, cognitive perspectives, and evolutionary theory—differ with respect to the issues they address, the concepts they draw on, and the behavior they attend to. The three sociological perspectives begin with society and consider how social forces influence the individual, favoring external—structural and interactional—processes. The two psychological perspectives, however, tend to privilege internal, cognitive processes because they start with the individual (Stryker, 2001). However, these perspectives should be seen as complementary rather than competing. For example, cognitive theories stress the importance of schemas and cognitive structure in determining judgments and behavior but connect with symbolic interaction in arguing that the content of these schemas and cognitive structures are learned in social interaction and with social structure and personality in that these schemas and cognitive structures are based on positions and roles individuals hold in social structures.

Because of the overlap, in the chapters that follow, insight from these perspectives is most often presented without explicit mention of the guiding theoretical perspective. Social psychology is a collective enterprise, with sociologists and psychologists routinely drawing on each other's work (Thoits, 1995). This textbook is unique in the way it bridges these two disciplines—giving voice to both sociological social psychology and the more psychological approaches—and presents social psychology to a new generation of students as a collective enterprise with much of interest to people regardless of their disciplinary orientation.

SUMMARY

This chapter considered the fundamental characteristics of social psychology and important theoretical perspectives in the field.

What Is Social Psychology? There are several ways to characterize social psychology. (1) By definition, social psychology is the systematic study of the nature and causes of human social behavior. When thinking about behavior, social psychologists are not only interested in what people do but also what they feel and think. (2) Social psychology has several core concerns, including the impact of one individual on another individual's behavior and beliefs, the impact of a group on a member's behavior and beliefs, the impact of a member on the group's activities and structure, the impact of one group on another group's activities

and structure, and the impact of social context on individuals and groups. (3) Social psychology has a close relationship with other social sciences, especially sociology and psychology. Although they emphasize different issues and often use different research methods, both psychologists and sociologists have contributed significantly to social psychology, and it can be an interdisciplinary enterprise.

Theoretical Perspectives in Social Psychology. A theoretical perspective is a broad theory based on particular assumptions about human nature that offers explanations for a wide range of social behaviors. This chapter discussed five theoretical perspectives: symbolic interaction, group processes, social structure and personality, a cognitive perspective, and evolutionary theory. (1) Symbolic interaction theory holds that human nature and social order are products of communication among people. It stresses the importance of the self, of role taking, and of consensus in social interaction. It is most useful in explaining fluid, contingent encounters among people. (2) The group processes perspective focuses its attention on interaction in social groups or networks. It mainly draws on experimental research to demonstrate how the structure of groups can influence individual behavior within groups. (3) Social structure and personality argues that individuals' positions in the social structure influence their thoughts, feelings, and behaviors. Some argue that it is the most sociological of the approaches because it considers how macrosociological structures influence individuals. (4) Cognitive theories hold that such processes as perception, memory, and judgment are significant determinants of social behavior. Differences in cognitions, including the use of low-effort or high-effort cognitive processing, help to illuminate why individuals may behave differently from one another in any given situation. (5) Evolutionary theory posits that social behavior is a product of long-term evolutionary adaptation. Behavioral tendencies exist in human beings because these behaviors aided our ancestors in their attempts to survive and reproduce.

List of Key Terms and Concepts

cognitive processes (p. 17)
cognitive structure (p. 18)
cognitive theory (p. 17)
conditioning (p. 14)
equity (p. 14)
evolutionary psychology (p. 22)
heuristics (p. 20)
identities (p. 13)
identity theory (p. 13)
middle-range theories (p. 8)
norms (p. 13)
reflexive self (p. 12)
role (p. 13)
role taking (p. 11)
role theory (p. 13)
schemas (p. 19)
self (p. 11)
significant others (p. 14)
situated identity (p. 11)
social exchange (p. 14)
social psychology (p. 3)
status (p. 15)
symbolic interaction theory (p. 9)
theoretical perspectives (p. 8)
theory (p. 8)

Critical Thinking Skill:
An Introduction to Critical Thinking

A variety of stakeholders, including employers and graduate and professional program faculty and administrators, are interested in college graduates with well-developed critical thinking skills. To help students develop these skills, this chapter and all that follow will include sections labeled Critical Thinking Skill. These exercises will not only improve your critical thinking skills as applied to Social Psychology but will also give you the tools to engage critical thinking in other classes and in other areas of your life.

According to Diane Halpern, an expert in critical thinking:

> Critical thinking is the use of those cognitive skills and strategies that increases the probability of a desirable outcome. It is purposeful, reasoned, and goal directed. It is the kind of thinking involved in solving problems, formulating inferences, calculating likelihoods, and making decisions. . . . Critical thinking also involves evaluating the thinking process—the reasoning that went into the conclusions we have arrived at or the kinds of factors considered in making a decision. (Halpern, 2002, p. 93)

Critical thinking is logical and fact based. Critical thinkers work to overcome bias and avoid self-deception. Most importantly, critical thinking is a skill set that we can acquire and can use throughout our lives. Once we acquire the ability, we can think critically in a range of situations to make better decisions and experience positive outcomes (Halpern, 1998).

Because of the benefits of critical thinking, colleges and universities are increasingly working to improve students' critical thinking skills to help graduates navigate a world with growing access to information. To help students be competitive in today's knowledge-based economy and to flourish in a world where individuals are inundated with information from a variety of sources, it is increasingly important that citizens are adept at evaluating information in a rational, deliberate manner.

Each Critical Thinking Skill exercise will engage a particular critical thinking skill as applied to social psychology. However, you will find that these skills will have applications throughout your life and that becoming a critical thinker will have benefits far beyond this course.

Understand Diverse Causal Forces. Most of us pay little attention to our everyday behaviors, feelings, and thoughts. Consider a trip to the movies. In American culture, we tend to sit quietly in a theater, laugh during comedies and cry during dramas, and think popcorn, candy, and soda are appropriate movie-viewing foods. We like to believe that we choose all of these actions freely, but do we?

As the theoretical perspectives covered in this chapter suggest, very little of what we do in our everyday life is based on individual actors making truly unique decisions. One of the best ways to see the social nature of our psychology—to learn social psychology—is to begin to question the motivation behind actions we often take for granted, "to recognize the social significance in mundane behaviors" (Fine, 1995, p. 6). Being attuned to the sources of our thoughts, feelings, and behavior is also important to critical thinking because understanding ourselves helps us understand our biases and reasoning.

Let's begin by thinking about a mundane behavior we all engage in: eating. I would bet that you gave little thought to what you ate for breakfast today (or if you decided to eat breakfast at all). However, the choice was actually socially significant. According to Gary Alan Fine, there are four dimensions at play in human action: body, mind, others, and culture.

I will use myself as an example. Today I had a cup of coffee and a bowl of cereal with milk for breakfast. I ate because my **body** signaled it was hungry, with a growling in my stomach. My **mind** interpreted this growling as a sign that I should eat. I learned to interpret sensations like the growling stomach in interaction with **others**. My mother always told me to eat breakfast, and she and others taught me, whether explicitly or implicitly, what an appropriate breakfast is and that the caffeine in coffee would wake me up. In this way, others influenced the way my mind processes information by teaching me to categorize foods as appropriate or inappropriate for breakfast. **Culture** also influences what we see as breakfast foods. Even though I know that soup would satiate my hunger, I was less likely to choose it or to crave it because of my cultural background. Whereas someone from an Asian culture might eat soup for breakfast, Americans traditionally do not. Cultural beliefs also shift over time. My grandparents would never have eaten cold cereal for breakfast. They would have eaten their cereal piping hot.

By stopping to think not only about why I ate breakfast (although that, too, is worth considering similarly) but also about why I chose what I did for breakfast, I can see how little physiological processes, innate cognition, or my own unique thoughts and desires had to do with my action. Instead, I recognize the social influences in shaping what I think, feel, and do. What did you eat for breakfast? How did these four dimensions or a subset of them influence that action? Similarly, what did you decide to wear today? Where are you reading this chapter? Are you doing anything else while studying? What other mundane behaviors can you see as socially significant by using this same framework?

When we stop to evaluate the sources of our mundane behaviors, we are not only recognizing the importance of social psychological processes and interaction; we are also training ourselves to evaluate all actions—whether mundane or not—to better interpret and understand them and those who engage in them.

CHAPTER 2

RESEARCH METHODS IN
SOCIAL PSYCHOLOGY

INTRODUCTION

The field of social psychology relies on empirical research, which is the systematic investigation of observable phenomena (behavior, events) in the world. Researchers try to collect information about behavior and events in an accurate and unbiased form. This information, which may be either quantitative or qualitative, enables social psychologists to describe reality in detail and to develop theories about social behavior.

When conducting empirical research, investigators usually employ a **methodology,** which is a set of systematic procedures that guide the collection and analysis of data. In a typical study, investigators begin with a question or hypothesis amenable to investigation. Next they develop a research design. Then, they go into a research setting and collect the data. Next, they code and analyze the data to test hypotheses and arrive at various conclusions about the behaviors or events under investigation. Throughout this process, investigators follow specific procedures to ensure the validity of the findings.

When investigators report their research to the wider community of social psychologists, they describe not only the results but also the methodology used to obtain the results. By reporting their methods, they make it possible for other investigators to independently verify their findings.

Independent verification of research findings is one of the hallmarks of any science. Suppose, for instance, that an investigator were to report some unanticipated empirical findings that ran contrary to established theory. Other investigators might wish to replicate the study to see whether they can obtain the same findings in other settings with different participants. Through this process, investigators with differing perspectives can identify and eliminate biases in the original study. If the results are replicable, they are more likely to be accepted by other social psychologists as reliable, general findings.

Questions about Research Methods

In this chapter, we will discuss the research methods used in contemporary social psychology. This discussion will provide a foundation for understanding and evaluating the empirical studies discussed throughout this book. We address the following questions:

1. What are the basic goals that underlie social psychological research? What form do research hypotheses assume? What steps can researchers take to ensure the validity of their findings?

2. What are the defining characteristics of research methods, such as surveys, naturalistic observation, archival research, and laboratory and field experiments? What are the strengths and weaknesses of each? What is a meta-analysis?

3. What issues are raised when we undertake research on diverse groups within a society or on members of other cultures?

4. What ethical issues are important in the conduct of social psychological research? Which safeguards are available to protect the rights of participants? Are there potential benefits to the participants?

CHARACTERISTICS OF EMPIRICAL RESEARCH

In this chapter, we discuss the major research methods used by social psychologists. These methods include surveys, field observation, archival studies, and experiments. Before looking at these in detail, however, we will review some issues common to all forms of empirical research. Specifically, we will consider the objectives that typically underlie empirical research, the nature of the hypotheses that guide research, and the factors that affect the validity of research findings.

Objectives of Research

Investigators conduct social psychological studies for a variety of reasons. Their objectives usually include one or more of the following: describing reality, identifying correlations between variables, testing causal hypotheses, and developing and testing theories.

In some studies, the central objective is simply to describe reality in accurate and precise terms. An investigator may wish to characterize some behavior or describe the features of a social process. Description is often the paramount goal when a researcher investigates a phenomenon about which little or nothing is known. Even when investigating more familiar phenomena, a researcher may wish to ascertain the frequency with which a particular attitude or behavior occurs in a specified group or population. For instance, during election years, researchers routinely conduct public opinion polls to learn how Americans feel about political candidates, issues, and parties. Their goal is to describe public sentiment with great accuracy and precision.

A second objective of research is to ascertain whether a correlation exists between two or more behaviors or attributes. Researchers might conduct a survey, for example, to find out whether growing older is associated with changes in a person's sexual behavior (Karraker & DeLamater, 2013) or whether how children spend their time is related to their scores on standard achievement tests (Hofferth & Sandberg, 2001). Although a

correlation between variables may reflect an underlying causal relation, two variables can be correlated without one causing the other; this will happen, for instance, if both are caused by a third variable. Correlation alone is not sufficient evidence for causation.

A third objective of research, then, is to discover the causes of some behavior or event. When pursuing this goal, the researcher first develops a causal hypothesis, which is a statement that differences or changes in one behavior or event produce a difference or change in another behavior or event. For instance, an investigator might hypothesize that studying for an exam in groups will produce higher grades than studying for the exam individually. After specifying the hypothesis, the investigator collects data to test the hypothesis. To support the hypothesis of causality, this test must show that differences or changes in one variable produce differences or changes in the other. Moreover, the design of the test must preclude or eliminate plausible alternative (noncausal) interpretations of the data. Frequently, the best way to test a causal hypothesis is by an experiment, a topic discussed in greater detail further on.

A fourth objective of social psychological research is to test existing theories and to develop new ones. A **theory** is a set of interrelated hypotheses that explains some observable behavior(s) or event(s). Frequently, a theory will serve as a basis for predicting future events. Tests of theories resemble tests of hypotheses, except that several interrelated hypotheses are assessed at once. In some cases, investigators juxtapose theories that make different predictions, and the results of the test may enable them to reject one theory in favor of another.

Research Hypotheses

In broad terms, a **hypothesis** is a conjectural statement of the relation between two or more variables. Many social psychological studies begin with one or more hypotheses. To test whether a hypothesis is correct, an investigator will first ask what observations would be expected if the hypothesis is true; then, he or she will take some observations or measures of reality and compare these with what is expected under the hypothesis. If a discrepancy is noted, it constitutes evidence against the hypothesis and may lead to its rejection.

There are various types of hypotheses. Some hypotheses are noncausal in nature; for example, "Variables X and Y are correlated, such that high levels of X occur with low levels of Y" (negative correlation). Noncausal hypotheses make statements about observed relations between variables.

Other hypotheses are explicitly causal in nature. For instance, a causal hypothesis relating two variables might take the form "X causes Y" or "Higher levels of X produce lower levels of Y" or "An increase in X will produce a decrease in Y." Sometimes, of course, causal hypotheses are more explicit and qualified in scope; for example, "If conditions A and B are present, then an increase of 1 unit in X will cause a decrease of 6 units in Y."

Causal hypotheses always include at least two variables—an independent variable and a dependent variable. An **independent variable** is any variable considered to cause or have an effect on some other variable(s). A **dependent variable** is any variable caused by some other variable. The dependent variable changes in response to changes in the independent variable. In the preceding example where X causes Y, X is the independent variable and Y is the dependent variable.

Another important type—the **extraneous variable**—is any variable that is not expressly included in the hypothesis but that nevertheless has a causal impact on the dependent variable. Extraneous variables are widespread in social psychology because most dependent variables of interest have more than one cause.

Validity of Findings

One cannot take for granted that the findings of any given study will have validity. Consider a situation where an investigator is studying deviant behavior. In particular, she is investigating the extent to which cheating by college students occurs on exams. Reasoning that it is more difficult for people monitoring an exam to keep students under surveillance in large classes than in smaller ones, she hypothesizes that a higher rate of cheating will occur on exams in large classes than in small. To test this hypothesis, she collects data on cheating in both large classes and small ones and then analyzes the data. Her results show that more cheating per student occurs in the larger classes. Thus, the data apparently support the investigator's research hypothesis.

A few days later, however, a colleague points out that all the large classes in her study used multiple-choice exams, whereas all the small classes used short answer and essay exams. The investigator immediately realizes that an extraneous variable (exam format) is confounded with the independent variable (class size) and may be operating as a cause in her data. The apparent support for her research hypothesis (more cheating in large classes) may be nothing more than an artifact. Perhaps the true effect is that more cheating occurs on multiple-choice exams than on essay exams, irrespective of class size.

We say that the findings of a study have **internal validity** if they are free from contamination by extraneous variables. Internal validity is a matter of degree; findings may have high or low internal validity. Obviously, the investigator's findings about the effect of class size on cheating have low internal validity due to the possibly confounding effect of exam format. Internal validity is very important. Without internal validity, a study cannot provide clear, interpretable results.

To achieve results with higher internal validity, the investigator might repeat the study with an improved design. For instance, our investigator might repeat her study with only one exam format (say, multiple choice) in both large and small classes. Then she could test whether class size affects the rate of cheating on multiple-choice exams. By holding constant the extraneous variable (exam format), her new design will have greater internal validity. Better still, she might use a more complex design that includes all four logical possibilities (that is, small class/multiple choice; small class/essay; large class/multiple choice; large class/essay). She could analyze the data from this design to estimate separately the relative impacts of class size and exam format on cheating. In effect, this design converts an extraneous variable (exam format) into a second independent variable. Although better, it is not a perfect design, because other extraneous variables could still be operating as causes of cheating—and they may be confounded with class size and exam format.

As important as internal validity is, it is not the only concern of the investigator. Another concern is external validity. **External validity** is the extent to which a causal relationship, once identified in a particular setting with a particular population, can be generalized to other populations, settings, or time periods. Even if an investigator's results have internal validity, they may lack external validity; that is, they may hold only for the specific group and setting studied and not generalize to others. For instance, if the investigator studying cheating and class size conducted her study in a 2-year col-

lege, there is no assurance that the findings (whatever they turn out to be) would also apply to students in other settings, such as high schools or 4-year colleges or universities. In general, external validity is important and desirable, because the results of a study often have general importance only if they generalize beyond the particular setting in which they appeared.

RESEARCH METHODS

Although there are many ways of collecting data about social behavior, most social psychological studies use one or another of four main methods. These methods are surveys, naturalistic observation, archival research based on content analysis, and experiments. We discuss each of these methods in turn.

Surveys

A survey is a procedure for collecting information by asking members of some population a set of questions and recording their responses. The survey technique is very useful for identifying the average or typical response to a question, as well as the distribution of responses within the population. It is also useful for identifying how groups of respondents differ from one another. For instance, Prince-Gibson and Schwartz (1998) used a survey to test a set of hypotheses about gender differences in values. They predicted that men would more strongly value power, achievement, hedonism, and stimulation, whereas women would value benevolence, conformity, tradition, and security. The hypotheses were tested using data from a probability sample of the Israeli Jewish population. Contrary to predictions, there were no significant differences in the mean ratings of the importance of these values given by men and women. Because some

Working from a schedule of questions, the survey interviewer carefully records the answers given by a respondent. © wdstock/iStock

research conducted in the 1970s and 1980s did report such differences, the authors concluded that their results suggest that men's and women's values are converging.

Purpose of a Survey. Investigators often conduct surveys to obtain self-reports from individuals about their own attributes—that is, their attitudes, behavior, and experiences. Information of this type enables investigators to discover the distribution of attributes in the population and to determine whether a relationship exists between two or more attributes of interest.

One form of survey—the public opinion poll—has become very common in the United States. Several organizations specialize in conducting surveys that measure the frequency and strength of favorable or unfavorable attitudes toward public issues, political figures and institutions, and candidates for office. These polls play

a significant role in American politics, for their findings increasingly influence public policy and the positions taken by political figures (Halberstam, 1979; Ratzan, 1989). Presidential candidates used the results of such polls to guide their decisions during the 2012 election campaign, and they will do so again in 2016.

Investigators also often use surveys to obtain data about various social problems. For instance, government agencies and individual researchers have conducted surveys on sexual activity and pregnancy risk among single women (Lindberg & Singh, 2008) and on alcohol and drug use by teenagers (Substance Abuse and Mental Health Services Administration, 2012). Information about the extent of such activities and the people involved in them is requisite to developing effective social policies.

Finally, investigators often conduct surveys with the primary objective of making basic theoretical contributions to social psychology. For instance, many studies of socialization processes and outcomes, psychological well-being, discrimination and prejudice, attitude-behavior relationships, and collective behavior have used survey methods.

Types of Surveys. There are two basic types of surveys—those based on interviews and those based on questionnaires. In an **interview survey**, a person serves as an interviewer and records the answers from the respondents. To ensure that each respondent in the study receives the same questions, the interviewer usually works from an interview schedule. This schedule indicates the exact order and wording of questions. In certain studies, however, the interviewer has flexibility in determining the exact order and wording of questions, but he or she is expected to make sure that certain topics are covered. One advantage of using an interview is that the interviewer can adjust the questioning to the respondent. That is, he or she can look for verbal or nonverbal signs that the respondent does not understand a question and repeat or clarify the question as needed (Moore, 2004).

In a **questionnaire survey**, the questions appear on paper or a computer screen, and the respondents read and answer them at their own pace. No interviewer is present. One advantage of questionnaires over interviews is that questionnaires cost less to administer. The cost of a national survey using trained personnel to conduct face-to-face interviews is rather large; it can run as much as $250 to $300 or more per completed interview, although this varies with the length of the interview and other factors. In contrast, the same survey using questionnaires mailed to respondents would cost considerably less—maybe as little as $15 per completed form. The same survey posted online may cost only two or three dollars per completed survey. The major disadvantage of questionnaires lies in the **response rate**—the percentage of people contacted who complete the survey. Whereas an interview study can obtain response rates of 75 to 80 percent or more, mailed questionnaires rarely attain more than a 50 percent response rate. Online surveys may have only a 20 percent response rate. Because a high response rate is very desirable, this is a significant disadvantage for mailed questionnaires and online surveys.

A compromise between interviews and questionnaires is the telephone interview. This is the standard method used by public opinion polling organizations, such as Gallup and Roper. Investigators are using it in basic research as well. The telephone interview uses a trained interviewer to ask the questions, but it sacrifices the visual feedback available in a face-to-face interview. It is cheaper (about $60 per completed interview, depending on length) than the face-to-face interview, although it typically involves a somewhat lower response rate (about 65 percent). Many surveys now use computer-assisted telephone interviewing (CATI). With CATI, the computer randomly selects and dials telephone numbers. Once a potential respondent is on the line, the interviewer takes over and conducts the interview. He or she reads some questions and enters the answers directly into the computer when the respondent gives them. In listing questions to ask, the computer may alter later questions in light of earlier answers by the respondent.

The latest innovation is the web survey, using the Internet to collect survey data. Researchers prepare a questionnaire using specially designed software and post it on the web. Potential participants are recruited either directly through targeted e-mail, or by banners on relevant webpages. The software may allow some tailoring of the later questions to the person's earlier answers, an advantage over the printed survey.

Potential advantages include the opportunity to recruit people with specific characteristics, or unique populations (Wright, 2005). Thus, a researcher in a racially homogenous community can recruit members of other racial/ethnic groups from around the United States (or indeed the world) for a study of prejudice. A researcher on a college campus can move beyond the study of students and recruit a more representative sample of adults of all ages. Further, one can recruit a large sample with a minimum of effort. For example, one web survey of gays, lesbians, and bisexuals yielded 2,800 completed surveys in just 2 months (Mustanski, 2001). Another advantage is that data are recorded in digital form, eliminating the need for coding handwritten material, facilitating a shortened analysis phase.

Disadvantages include sampling issues. Respondents to online surveys self-select and may not represent the spectrum of people in the group/population of interest. E-mail lists may include duplicates and inactive addresses, inflating the apparent size of the group. Also, there is no guarantee that the person completing the survey is the person who was invited.

As we will discuss below, the quality of data depends on the percentage of the sample members who complete the research. Completion rates for printed/mailed surveys are low, sometimes less than 30 percent. Researchers believe that participants are more likely to complete a web survey because it is readily accessible and uses a technology that is now widely used, especially by younger people. Web surveys of undergraduate students at one university may achieve a completion rate of 60 percent. At the same time, Internet users are not a random sample of the population, and so the sample may be biased by age, income, or education. In 2011, persons over 65, persons earning less than $50,000 per year, and Blacks and Hispanics were less likely to have Internet access (File, 2013).

Measurement Reliability and Validity. In any form of research, the quality of measurement is an important consideration. Of primary concern are the reliability and the validity of the instruments. **Reliability** is the extent to which an instrument produces the same results each time it is employed to measure a particular construct under given conditions. A reliable instrument produces consistent results across independent measurements of the same phenomenon. Reliability is a matter of degree; some instruments are highly reliable, whereas others are less so. Obviously, investigators prefer instruments with high reliability and try to avoid those with low reliability.

There are several ways to assess the reliability of an instrument. The first is to see if people's responses to an instrument are consistent across time. In this approach, called the *test-retest method*, an investigator applies the measuring instrument to the same respondents on two different occasions, and then he or she compares the first responses with the second responses. If the correlation between the first and second responses is high, the instrument has high reliability; if the correlation is low, the instrument has only low reliability.

A second way to assess the reliability of an instrument is to see if people's responses are consistent across items. This approach is called the *split-half method*. To illustrate, suppose we have a scale of 20 questions measuring psychological well-being. These questions ask the respondent about psychological states, such as how often he or she is sad, nervous, depressed, tense, or irritable, and how often he or she has trouble concentrating, working, or sleeping. Assume that we administer all the questions to 300 male respondents. To use the split-half method, we would randomly divide the 20 questions into two groups of 10, calculate a score for each respondent on each group of 10, and compute a correlation between the two scores. A high correlation (if it occurs) provides confirmation that the scale is reliable.

Just as findings must be valid, as discussed above, so must our measures. Does the instrument actually measure the theoretical concept we intend to measure? There are several types of validity, including face validity, criterion validity, and construct validity. First, an instrument has *face validity* if its content is manifestly similar to the behavior or process of interest. If a researcher wishes to measure the frequency of sexual intercourse, for example, the question "How often do you engage in sexual intercourse?" has face validity. The question "How often do you have sex?" has lower face validity, since "sex" includes behaviors other than intercourse.

Second, an instrument has *criterion validity* if we can use it to predict respondents' standing on some other variable of theoretical or practical interest. Suppose, for example, that an investigator is concerned with traffic safety on the roads and that she develops an instrument to distinguish good drivers from bad drivers. To establish the instrument's predictive validity, she first administers the instrument to young people getting their driver's license and then, several years later, checks their driving records for moving violations. If the drivers' scores on the instrument correlate highly with their level of subsequent violations, the instrument has criterion validity.

Third, an instrument has *construct validity* if it provides a good measure of the theoretical concept being investigated by the research. In general, an instrument will have construct validity if it measures what people understand the concept to mean and if it relates to other variables as predicted by the theory under consideration. Establish-ing the construct validity of an instrument can be difficult, especially if the underlying theoretical construct is highly abstract in nature. Suppose, for example, that an investigator's theory includes an abstraction like "intellectual development." The measurement of this concept is somewhat problematic, for there is no readily observable referent, no single behavior or occurrence that the investigator can point to as indicative of intellectual development. The usual method of establishing the construct validity of an instrument is to show that the pattern of correlations between respondents' scores on the instrument and their scores on other variables is what would be expected if the underlying theory holds true.

The Questions. The phrasing of questions used in surveys requires close attention by investigators. Subtle differences in the form, wording, and context of survey questions can produce differences in responses (Schwarz, Groves, & Schuman, 1998). Creating good survey questions is as much art as science, but there are certain guidelines that help. First, the more precise and focused a question, the greater will be its reliability and validity. If a question is expressed in vague, ambiguous, abstract, or global terms, respondents may interpret it in different ways, and this in turn will produce uncontrolled variation in responses. A second consideration in formulating survey questions is the exact choice of words used. It is best to avoid jargon or specialized terminology unless one is interviewing a sample of specialists. Likewise, it is important to adjust questions to the educational and reading level of the respondents. A third consideration is the length of questions. Several studies have shown that questions of moderate length elicit more complete answers than very short ones (Anderson & Silver, 1987; Sudman & Bradburn, 1974). A fourth consideration is whether the topic under investigation is potentially a threatening or embarrassing one (sex, alcohol, drugs, money, and so on). In general, threatening questions requiring quantified answers are better asked by presenting a range of alternative answers (say, 0, 1–5, 6–10) than by asking a question requiring an exact number (Rea & Parker, 1997).

Measuring Attitudes. Perhaps the most common purpose of surveys is to measure people's attitudes toward some event, person, or object. Because attitudes are mental states, they cannot be directly observed. Therefore, to find out someone's attitude, we usually ask them.

The most direct way of finding out someone's attitude is to ask a direct question and record the person's answer. This is the way most of us study the attitudes of the people with whom we interact. It is also the technique used by newspaper and television reporters. To make the process more systematic, social psychologists use several methods, including the single-item measure, Likert scales, and semantic differential techniques.

Single Items. The use of single questions to assess attitudes is very common. The single-item scale usually consists of a direct positive or negative statement, and the respondent indicates whether he or she agrees, disagrees, or is unsure. Such a measure is economical; it takes a minimum of time and space to present. It is also easy to score. The major drawback of the single item is that it is not very precise. Of necessity, it must be general and detects only gross differences in attitude. Using the single-item measure in Box 2.1, we could separate people into only two groups: those who favor premarital abstinence and everybody else.

Likert Scales. Often, we want to know not only how each person feels about the object of interest but also how each respondent's

attitude compares with the attitudes of others. The Likert scale, a technique based on summated ratings, provides such information (Likert, 1932).

Box 2.1 includes a two-item Likert scale. Each possible response is given a numerical score, indicated in parentheses. We would assess the respondent's attitude by adding his or her scores for both items. For example, suppose you strongly agree with item 1 (+2) and strongly disagree with item 2 (+2). Your score would be 4, indicating strong opposition to premarital intercourse. Your roommate might strongly disagree with the statement that people should wait until they marry (−2) and might also disagree that premarital sex strengthens a marriage (+1). The resulting score of −1 indicates a slightly positive view of premarital intercourse. Finally, someone who strongly disagrees with item 1 (−2) and agrees with item 2 (−1) would get a score of −3 and could be differentiated from a person who received a score of −4.

Typically, a Likert scale includes at least four items. The items should be counterbalanced—that is, some should be positive statements, and others should be negative ones. Our two-item scale in Box 2.1 has this property; one item is positive, and the other is negative. The Likert scale allows us to order respondents fairly precisely; items of this type are commonly used in public opinion polls. Such a scale takes more time to administer, however, and involves a scoring stage as well.

Semantic Differential Scales. Like most attitude scales, the single-item and Likert scales measure the denotative or dictionary meanings of the object to the respondent. However, objects also have a connotative meaning, a set of psychological meanings that vary from one respondent to another. For instance, one person may have had very positive experiences with sexual intercourse, whereas another person's experiences may have been very frustrating.

BOX 2.1 The Measurement of Attitudes

Suppose you want to assess attitudes toward premarital sexual behavior. Here are three techniques you could employ.

Single Item

The single item is probably the most common measure of attitudes. An example of this type is:

I think people should wait until they are married to have sex.

_____ Yes
_____ No
_____ Not sure

Likert Scale

The **Likert scale** consists of a series of statements about the object of interest. The statements may be positive or negative. The respondent indicates how much he or she agrees with each statement. For example:

1. I think people should wait until they are married to have sex.

_____ Strongly agree   (+2)
_____ Agree   (+1)
_____ Undecided   (0)
_____ Disagree (−1)
_____ Strongly disagree   (−2)

2. I think having sex before marriage strengthens the marriage.

_____ Strongly agree (−2)
_____ Agree (−1)
_____ Undecided (0)
_____ Disagree (+1)
_____ Strongly disagree (+2)

Semantic Differential Scale

The semantic differential scale consists of a number of dimensions on which the respondent rates the attitude object. For example:

Using the table below, rate how you feel about premarital sexual intercourse on each of the following dimensions.

Semantic Differential Scale

good	_____	_____	_____	_____	_____	_____	_____	bad
	(3)	(2)	(1)	(0)	(1)	(2)	(3)	
weak	_____	_____	_____	_____	_____	_____	_____	strong
	(3)	(2)	(1)	(0)	(1)	(2)	(3)	
fast	_____	_____	_____	_____	_____	_____	_____	slow
	(3)	(2)	(1)	(0)	(1)	(2)	(3)	
negative	_____	_____	_____	_____	_____	_____	_____	positive
	(3)	(2)	(1)	(0)	(1)	(2)	(3)	
light	_____	_____	_____	_____	_____	_____	_____	heavy
	(3)	(2)	(1)	(0)	(1)	(2)	(3)	
exciting	_____	_____	_____	_____	_____	_____	_____	boring
	(3)	(2)	(1)	(0)	(1)	(2)	(3)	

The semantic differential scale (Osgood, Suci, & Tannenbaum, 1957) is a technique for measuring connotative meaning. In using it, an investigator presents the respondents with a series of bipolar adjective scales. Each of these is a scale whose ends are two adjectives having opposite meanings. The respondent rates the attitude object on each scale. After the data are collected, the researcher can analyze them by various statistical techniques. Analyses of such ratings frequently identify three aspects of connotative meaning: evaluation, potency, and activity. Evaluation is measured by adjective pairs such as *good-bad* and *positive-negative;* potency, by *weak-strong* and *light-heavy;* and activity, by *fast-slow* and *exciting-boring.*

The example in Box 2.1 includes two bipolar scales measuring each of the three dimensions. Scores are assigned to each scale from +3 to −3; they are then summed across scales of each type to arrive at evaluation, potency, and activity scores. In the example shown, scores on each dimension could range from −6 (*bad, weak,* and *slow*) to +6 (*good, strong,* and *fast*).

One advantage of the semantic differential technique is that researchers can compare an individual's attitudes on three dimensions, allowing more complex differentiation among respondents. Another advantage is that because the meaning it measures is connotative, it can be used with any object, from a specific person to an entire nation. This technique is also used to assess the meaning of role identities (*mother, doctor*) and role behaviors (*hug, cure*) (Heiss, 1979; Smith-Lovin, 1990). Its disadvantages include the fact that it requires more time to administer and to score.

The Sample. Suppose a survey researcher wants to ascertain the extent of prejudice toward Blacks among White adults in the United States. These White adults consti-tute the **population** of interest—that is, the set of all people whose attitudes are of interest to the researcher. It would be virtually impossible—and enormously expensive—to interview all people in the population of White adults, so the researcher instead selects a sample, or representative subset, from that population to interview.

Sample selection is one of the most important aspects of any survey. In some cases, investigators may use a particular sample simply because it is readily available; samples of this type are known as *convenience samples.* A sample consisting of students taking a class, occasionally used in social science research, is a convenience sample. Convenience samples have a major drawback—they usually lack external validity and do not enable the investigator to generalize the findings to any larger population. For this reason, it is better research practice to select some other type of sample—one that is representative of the underlying population. Only when the sample is representative can the results obtained from it (for example, information regarding racial prejudice obtained from survey respondents) be generalized to the entire population. The nature of the sample, therefore, has a major impact on the external validity of the survey.

Two types of systematic samples are commonly used in social psychological surveys. One is the **simple random sample**, wherein the researcher selects units—usually individuals—from the population such that every unit has an equal probability of being included. To use this technique, the researcher needs a complete list of members of the population. At a university, for example, she might obtain a list of all students from the registrar. At the city or county level, she might use voter registration lists. A frequent problem, especially when the population being studied is large, is the absence of a complete list. Under these circumstances, researchers usually fall back on some substitute, such as a telephone directory. Of course, this will limit the population to which one can generalize, because people who are poor or who move frequently may not have telephones, others may choose not to list their numbers in the directory, and others only have cell phones. In 2012, only 66 percent of adults in the United States had a landline phone. Persons under 25 and Hispanics were least likely to have such phones (Blumberg & Luke, 2012).

Working from a complete list of the population, the researcher draws a random sample. A common way to do this is to number the people on the list consecutively and then use a table of random numbers to choose people for the sample. Once the researcher has drawn a random sample, she must take steps to ensure that all the members of the sample are interviewed; in other words, the researcher must strive for a high response rate. Without a high response rate, the results of the survey will not be generalizable to the whole population. Bias may result if the people who participate in the study differ in some significant way from those who refuse to participate.

If the population is very large, the investigator may not be able to list all its members and draw a random sample. Under these conditions, researchers frequently employ a **stratified sample**. That is, they divide the population into groups according to important characteristics, select a random sample of groups, and then draw a sample of individuals within each selected group. For example, public opinion polls designed to represent the entire adult population of the United States often use stratified samples. The population is first stratified on the basis of region (Northeast, Midwest, South, Southwest, and West). Next, the population within each region is stratified into urban versus rural areas. Within urban areas, there may be still further stratification by size of urban area. The result will be numerous sampling units—population subgroups of known regional and residential type. Some units are then selected for study in proportion to their frequency in the entire population. Thus, one would sample more urban units from the Northeast than from the South or Midwest; conversely, one would select more rural units in the latter regions. Finally, within each sampling unit, people are selected randomly to serve as respondents. Using this technique, one can represent the adult population of the United States with a sample of 1,500 people and obtain responses accurate within plus or minus 3 percent.

Causal Analysis of Survey Data. Social psychologists have long used computers to aid in the descriptive analysis of survey data. In recent years, however, some social psychologists have begun to use more sophisticated techniques to aid in the causal interpretation of survey data. Analysis techniques of this type (such as LISREL and path analysis) require the investigator to postulate a pattern of cause-and-effect relations among a set of variables (Bollen, 1989; Jöreskög & Sörbom, 1979). The computer then estimates coefficients of effect from the data. These coefficients indicate the strength of the relationships among the variables, and they provide a test of whether the causal linkages postulated by the theory are indeed present in the data. Using this approach, an analyst can test many alternative hypotheses. Typically, some hypotheses will turn out to be inconsistent with the data, and the analyst can reject these in favor of alternative hypotheses that survive the test. One difficulty with this approach is that for problems involving many variables (say, a dozen or more), there often exist numerous alternative hypotheses that are plausible. Although this process will eliminate many hypotheses, more than one may survive as tenable.

Panel Studies. One useful extension of the survey technique is the longitudinal survey or **panel study**, in which a given sample of respondents is surveyed at one point in time and then resurveyed at a later point. For instance, in a panel study, a sample of respondents would be surveyed by telephone interview or questionnaire (this is called the first wave of the panel). Then, at some future time (say, 1 year later), the same respondents would be surveyed again (the second wave); the questionnaire items in the second wave will be similar to—or an extension of—those used in the first wave. If desired, the same respondents could be surveyed again at a still later point in time (the third wave), and so on. In principle, there is no upper limit on the number of waves that might be included in a panel study, although there are practical constraints, such as the dollar cost of running the panel and the difficulties in tracking down members of the sample at various times. The waves in a panel study can be spaced either closely together or far apart in time, depending on the study's purpose.

The usual objective of a panel study is to determine whether various outcomes experienced by respondents at later points in time are related to or determined by their experiences, attitudes, and relationships at the earlier points in time. For instance, Orbuch, Veroff, Hassan, and Horrocks (2002) used a panel study with four waves to investigate the risk of divorce over a 14-year period. Initially, both members of 199 White couples and 174 Black couples who had recently married were interviewed. Couples were contacted and re-interviewed in years 3 and 7, and brief follow-up data were collected in year 14. The purpose of the research was to assess the role of social conditions (race, income) and interpersonal processes (positive interaction, frequency and type of conflicts). The results indicated that race and education were related to the risk of divorce. Blacks were twice as likely to be divorced in year 14, and couples in which the wife had more education (12 years or more) were less likely to be divorced. Reports of destructive conflict by husband and wife in earlier waves were related to subsequent risk of divorce. Thus, both social conditions, such as the disadvantaged conditions of some Blacks, and interactional style are related to divorce.

In general, data from a panel study lend themselves somewhat more readily to causal interpretation than data from a simple cross-sectional survey. The waves in the panel study provide a natural temporal ordering among the variables, which usually provides increased clarity when interpreting the results causally.

Strengths of Surveys. Surveys can provide, at moderate cost, an accurate and precise description of the characteristics of a specific population. When a social psychological researcher uses measures that are reliable and valid, employs a sampling design that guarantees representativeness, and takes steps to ensure a high response rate, the survey can produce a clear portrait of the attitudes and social characteristics of a population.

Surveys also provide an effective means to study the incidence of various social behaviors. A survey asking people to report their behavior is usually more efficient and cost-effective than observational studies of actual behavior. This is especially true for behavior that occurs only infrequently or in private settings.

Surveys are frequently used to test predictions based on symbolic interaction theory, such as predictions about influences on personal identity and self-esteem. These methods are also used to test hypotheses about attitude structure and function based on cognitive theory.

Weaknesses of Surveys. As with any methodology, there are certain drawbacks to the survey technique. Both questionnaires and interviews rely on self-reports by respondents. Under certain conditions, however, self-reports can be invalid sources of information. First, some people may not respond truthfully to questions about themselves. This is not usually a major problem, but it can become troublesome if the survey deals with activities that are highly personal, illegal, or otherwise embarrassing to reveal. Second, even when respondents want to report honestly, they may give wrong information due to imperfect recall or poor memory. This can be a nettlesome problem, especially in surveys investigating the past (for example, historical events or childhood). As an illustration, consider the question "When were you last vaccinated?" This may seem simple and straightforward, but it often produces incorrect responses because many people cannot remember the relevant dates. Third, some respondents answering self-report questions have a tendency to fall into a response set. That is, they answer all questions the same way (for example, always agree or disagree) or they give extreme answers too frequently. If many respondents adopt a response set, this will introduce bias into the survey's results.

Field Studies and Naturalistic Observation

Observational research—often termed a **field study**—involves making systematic observations about behavior as it occurs naturally in everyday settings. Typically, the data are collected by one or more researchers who directly observe the activity of people and record information about it. Field studies have been used to investigate many forms of social behavior in their nat-

ural settings. For instance, researchers have observed and recorded data about social interaction between judges and attorneys in the courtroom (Maynard, 1983), between teachers and students in the classroom (Galton, 1987), between couples in informal settings (Zimmerman & West, 1975), between working-class boys and girls in grade school (Thorne, 1993), and between street vendors and passersby in Greenwich Village (Duneier, 2001). Other studies have focused on socialization. Lois (2003) spent 3½ years observing a volunteer search and rescue group, studying the process by which individuals became willing to routinely risk their lives—often in dangerous situations such as blizzards—to save others.

Because field studies investigate social behavior in its natural setting, researchers usually make efforts to minimize or limit the extent to which they intrude on that behavior. In fact, field studies are usually less intrusive than surveys or experiments. Whereas a survey often intrudes on people by asking for self-reports and an experiment involves manipulation of the independent variable(s) and random assignment to treatment, a field study involves nothing more intrusive than recording an observation about the behavior of interest.

Field studies differ in how the observers collect and record information. In some studies, observers watch carefully while the phenomenon of interest is occurring and then make notes about their observations from memory at a later time. The advantage of recording afterward is that the observer is less likely to arouse curiosity, suspicion, or antagonism in the participants. In other studies, the observers may record field notes or make audiotapes at the same time that they observe the behavior. In still other field studies, researchers make audio or video recordings of interactions, and then analyze the tapes later (Whalen & Zimmerman, 1987). Tape recordings may seem a superior alternative to the use of human observers (who may have selective perception), but this is not always the case. The use of recordings maximizes the information obtained, but it can also inadvertently influence behavior if the participants discover that they are being taped.

Participant Observation. When the behavior of interest occurs in public settings, such as restaurants, courtrooms, or retail stores, researchers can simply go to the setting and observe the action directly. The researchers do not need to interact with the people being observed or reveal their identities. However, when the behavior of interest is private or restricted in nature (such as intimate sexual activity, use of illegal drugs, or recruiting new members for a cult), observation is usually more difficult. To investigate activities of this type, researchers occasionally use the technique of participant observation. In participant observation, members of the research team not only make systematic observations of others' behavior but also interact with them and play an active role in the ongoing events. Frequently, the fact of being an active participant enables the investigators to approach and observe behavior that otherwise would be inaccessible. In participant observation, researchers usually do not engage in overt coding or any other activity that would disrupt the normal flow of interaction. In some instances, they may even need to use an assumed identity, lest their true identity as investigators disrupt the interaction.

One study (Eder, 1995) used observational techniques combined with participation to investigate adolescent school culture in a Midwestern community. To observe interaction patterns and topics of conversation among junior high school students, the investigators participated over an extended period of time in students' lunchroom groups. They identified themselves (truth-

fully) as being from a nearby university, and they adopted the role of "quiet friend." They did not affiliate with teachers and avoided appearing to be authority figures of any kind. This approach enabled them to establish sufficient rapport and trust with the students that they could ask questions about the students' beliefs regarding gender differences and observe how students' behavior patterns fostered gender inequality.

Unobtrusive Measures. Field studies sometimes use unobtrusive measures, which are measurement techniques that do not intrude on the behavior under study and that avoid causing a reaction from the people whose behavior is being studied (Webb, Campbell, Schwartz, & Sechrest, 1981). For example, some unobtrusive measures rely on the physical evidence left behind by people after they have exited from a situation. One illustration is the analysis of inventory records and bar bills to unobtrusively measure the alcohol consumption patterns at various nightclubs and bars (Lex, 1986). Another investigator discovered that the rate at which vinyl floor tiles needed replacement in the Chicago Museum of Science and Industry was a good indicator of the popularity of exhibits.

Strengths and Weaknesses of Field Studies. Like any research method, field studies have both strengths and weaknesses. A major strength is that observational techniques allow researchers to study social activity in real-world settings. Careful observation can provide a wealth of information about behavior as it actually occurs in natural settings. These data can be used to investigate ideas about social interaction drawn from role theory or symbolic interaction theory. Moreover, because these techniques are relatively unintrusive, investigators can use them to investigate sensitive or private behaviors—such as drug use or sexual activity—that would be difficult to address through intrusive methods like surveys or experiments.

Many field studies involve only one period of observation, however long that period may be. Burawoy (2003) suggests that a focused revisit to a site can serve several purposes, one of which is to study social change. A revisit to a factory 32 years after the original observational research identified significant changes in the interaction between supervisors and workers. The researchers were able to relate the changes observed in this factory to national trends in labor relations over the 32-year period.

Weaknesses of field studies include their sensitivity to the specific recording methods used. Observations recorded after the fact are often less reliable and valid than those recorded on the spot or those based on audio or videotaping. Furthermore, the validity of the observations may depend in part on the identities that the investigators publicly project while making their observations; validity may be destroyed if the researchers have been operating covertly and the subjects suddenly discover that they are under observation. Then, too, the external validity of field observation studies can be problematic, because research of this type frequently focuses on only one group or organization, or on a sample of interactions selected for convenience.

In some cases, field investigators do not get informed consent from the people being observed prior to the collection of data. Permission for using the data is sought only after the behavior has been observed or the conversations tape-recorded. Some people construe this as a serious drawback and object to participant observation on ethical grounds. Of course, this concern has to be weighed against the fact that if permission were sought in advance, the behavior under investigation might never occur or might take a different form.

Archival Research and Content Analysis

Although social psychological researchers often prefer to collect original data, it is sometimes possible to test hypotheses and theories by using data that already exist. The term **archival research** denotes the acquisition and analysis (or re-analysis) of information collected previously by others. When archival data of suitable quality exist, a researcher may decide that analyzing them is preferable to collecting and analyzing new data. Archival research usually costs less than alternative methods.

Sources. There are many sources of archival data. In the United States, one important source is government agencies. The Census Bureau makes available much of the data it has collected over the years. Census data are a rich source of information about the U.S. population; they often include repeated measures taken at different points in time, which allow an investigator to assess historical trends. The Bureau of Labor Statistics, the Federal Bureau of Investigation, and other agencies also release data to investigators. A second important source of archival data in the United States is the data banks maintained at various large universities. These archives serve as locations where researchers can deposit data they have collected so others can use them. They include, among others, the Interuniversity Consortium for Political and Social Research and the Data Archive on Adolescent Pregnancy and Pregnancy Prevention. There are also several archives of public opinion data, enabling researchers to track attitude change across time. Foremost among these is the General Social Survey-NORC archive. A third source of archival data—less used by social psychologists but still important—is formal organizations such as insurance companies and banks. These typically entail over-time data with respect to various measures of financial and economic performance. A fourth source of archival information for research is news media. Newspaper and news magazine articles are a rich source of information about past events. For instance, an investigator wishing to study the reactions of those affected by a natural disaster, such as the impact of Hurricane Ike (September 2008), the third costliest in U.S. history, might use newspapers as a data source. Unfortunately, between January 2007 and July 2010, 166 newspapers in the United States stopped publishing, reducing the availability of this source for recent events. Other types of printed material (for example, corporate annual reports) can also provide archival data usable in research.

Content Analysis. In some cases, an investigator relying on newspaper articles, government documents, or annual reports as archival sources can use the information directly as it appears. All the investigator has to do is extract the information and analyze it, usually by computer. In other cases, however, the investigator faces the problem of how to interpret and code the information from the source. Under these circumstances, he or she may use content analysis, which involves undertaking a systematic scrutiny of documents or messages to identify specific characteristics and then making inferences based on their occurrence. For example, if newspapers serve as the source, one could use **content analysis** to code the reportage from newspaper articles into a form suitable for systematic statistical analysis.

Researchers have used content analysis to investigate a wide variety of topics. Some studies, for instance, have analyzed the content of personal advertisements on the Internet placed by gay men, lesbians, and heterosexual men and women (Lever et al., 2008). Other studies have addressed

such issues as whether the depiction of older people is distorted in American media (Dahmen & Cozma, 2009) and the relationship between the mortality rates associated with a disease, for example, AIDS, and newspaper coverage of that disease (Adelman & Verbrugge, 2000).

When a researcher conducts a content analysis, the first step is to identify the informational unit to be studied—is it the word, the sentence, the paragraph, or the article? The second step is to define the categories into which the units will be sorted. A third step is to code the units in each document into the categories, and the final step is to look for relations within the categorized data.

As an example of content analysis, consider a study of the relationship between rhetorical forms of speech and applause from the audience (Heritage & Greatbatch, 1986). The investigators hypothesized that political speakers will use certain rhetorical forms—for example, a three-element list—to signal the audience when to applaud. The raw data in this study were the texts of 476 speeches delivered by British political leaders at party meetings. The researchers carefully defined the rhetorical devices and identified their use in the speeches. Then they counted the number of times that the speakers used each device and noted whether the audience responded immediately to each use with applause. The results showed that applause was much more likely to occur immediately after the use of certain rhetorical devices (such as a three-element list) than at other points in the speech.

Strengths and Weaknesses of Archival Research. One significant advantage of archival research is its comparatively low cost. By reusing existing information, the investigator avoids the cost of collecting new data. A second advantage is that by using information already on hand, an investigator may complete a study more quickly than otherwise. A third advantage is that an investigator can test hypotheses about phenomena that occur over extended periods of time. In some cases, authorities have kept records (such as marriage licenses) for decades or even centuries, and these can serve as a basis for investigating various questions (such as who marries whom).

One major disadvantage of archival research is the lack of control over the type and quality of information. An investigator must work with whatever others have collected. This may or may not include data on all the variables the investigator wishes to study. Moreover, there may be doubts regarding the quality of the original research design or the procedures used for collecting data. A second disadvantage of archival research is that creating a reliable and valid content analysis scheme for use with records can be difficult, especially if the records are complex.

A third disadvantage is that some sets of records contain large amounts of inconsistent or missing information. Obviously, this will hinder the study and limit the validity of any findings.

Experiments

The **experiment** is the most highly controlled of the research methodologies available to social psychologists, and it is a powerful method for establishing causality between variables. For a study to be a true experiment, it must have two specific characteristics:

1. The researcher must manipulate one or more of the independent variables that are hypothesized to have a causal impact on the dependent variable(s) of concern.
2. The researcher must assign the participants randomly to the various

treatments—that is, to the different levels of each of the independent variables.

The term **random assignment** denotes the placement of participants in experimental treatments on the basis of chance, as by flipping a coin or using a table of random numbers. Random assignment is desirable because it mitigates the effects of extraneous variables. By using random assignment, the researcher creates groups of participants that are equivalent in all respects except their exposure to different levels of the independent variables. This removes the possibility that these groups will differ systematically on extraneous variables such as intelligence, personality, or motivation. Thus, random assignment enables the investigator to infer that any observed differences between groups on the dependent variable are due only to the effects of the independent variable(s) (or chance), not to extraneous variables (Haslam & McCarty, 2004).

Whereas researchers manipulate the independent variables in an experiment, they simply measure the dependent variable(s). Experimenters can measure dependent variables in many ways. For example, they can monitor participants' neural or physiological arousal, administer short questionnaires that assess participants' attitudes, record the interactions that occur between participants, or score the participants' performance on tasks. The exact type of measurement used in the experiment will depend on the nature of the dependent variable(s) of interest.

Laboratory and Field Experiments. It is useful to distinguish between laboratory experiments and field experiments. Laboratory experiments are those conducted in a laboratory setting, where the investigator can control much of the participants' physical surroundings. In the laboratory, the investigator can determine which stimuli, tasks, information, or situations the participants will face. This control enables the experimenter to manipulate the independent variables, to measure the dependent variables, to hold constant some known extraneous variables, and to implement the random assignment of participants to treatments. For instance, if an investigator is studying the impact of verbal communication on group productivity in a laboratory setting, he may wish to restrict the interaction among participants. To do this, he might limit communication to written notes or verbal messages sent by electronic equipment. This practice not only would eliminate the possibly contaminating influence of nonverbal communication, but also would permit the content of any messages to be analyzed later by the experimenter.

Field experiments, in contrast with laboratory experiments, are studies where investigators manipulate variables in natural, nonlaboratory settings. Usually, these settings are already familiar to the participants. Investigators have used field experiments to study topics ranging from pay inequity in large bureaucratic organizations to altruistic behavior on street corners and in subway cars. Compared with laboratory experiments, field experiments have the advantage of high external validity. When conducted in natural and uncontrived settings, they usually have greater mundane realism than laboratory experiments. Moreover, participants in field experiments may not be particularly conscious of their status as experimental participants—a fact that reduces participants' reactivity. The primary weakness of field experiments, of course, is that in natural settings, experimenters sometimes have difficulty manipulating independent variables exactly as they would wish and often have little control over extraneous variables. This means that

the internal validity of field experiments is often lower than in comparable laboratory experiments.

Conduct of Experiments. To illustrate how investigators conduct experiments, consider the following laboratory study, which sought to determine the impact of certain independent variables on whether one person will help another in an emergency (Darley & Latané, 1968). The investigators conducted the study at a university in New York City. Male and female students serving as participants came to the laboratory to participate in a discussion of problems they had encountered in adjusting to the university. The experimenters placed each participant in a separate room in the laboratory and instructed them to communicate with other participants via an intercom. The rationale given was that this procedure would permit them to remain anonymous while discussing personal problems.

The independent variable was the number of other persons who the participant believed were participating in the discussion (and who would, therefore, later witness an emergency). Depending on experimental treatment, participants were told there were one, two, or five other participants. Participants were randomly assigned to the various levels of this independent variable.

The discussion proceeded with each participant speaking in turn over the intercom for 2 minutes. Thus, depending on the experimental treatment, the participant heard the voices of one, two, or five others. In reality, the participant was hearing a tape recording of other people, not the voices of actual participants. (This was the real reason for putting participants in separate rooms and having them communicate via intercom.) One of these recorded voices admitted somewhat hesitantly that he was subject to nervous seizures. In his second turn, he started to speak normally, but

Experiments enable the investigator to manipulate independent variables and measure behavior in various ways. Many studies have replicated Darley and Latané's pioneering bystander intervention research, discussed in the text. Some have been field experiments, where an emergency is staged in a public area. As the photo suggests, most find that the more witnesses, the less likely anyone is to help.
© Shotshop GmbH/Alamy

suddenly his speech became disorganized. Soon, he lapsed into gibberish and choking sounds and then into silence. Evidently, an emergency was occurring. The participant realized that all participants could hear it, although the intercom prevented them from talking to one another.

The dependent variables were whether the participant would leave the room to offer help and how quickly he or she would do so. Participants who elected to help the victim typically came out of their room looking for the victim. The experimenter timed the speed of the participant's response from the beginning of the victim's speech. The results verified the research hypothesis that the greater the number of witnesses, the less likely a participant was to offer help to the victim.

This carefully controlled experiment allowed a straightforward test of the hypoth-

esis. The manipulated independent variable (number of witnesses) and the measured dependent variable (speed of helping response) were unambiguous. Confounds from extraneous variables could be ruled out due to the random assignment of participants to treatments. From these results, we can conclude that the number of witnesses has a causal effect on the speed of helping response.

Note, however, that although the experiment showed the causal effect to hold, it did so only under the conditions prevailing in the laboratory. The causal effect may or may not hold under other conditions. This can be problematic if the conditions that existed in the laboratory setting are uncommon in daily life. (When, for instance, was the last time you discussed personal issues over an intercom with five strangers in other rooms?) Thus, from this study alone, it is not clear whether we can generalize the cause-and-effect findings from the laboratory to everyday, face-to-face situations. The relationship between the number of others present and a person's reaction to an emergency might be different in other situations.

Although this experiment provides some answers regarding intervention in emergencies, it also raises further questions. Why, for instance, should the number of witnesses present affect a person's willingness to help in an emergency? The researchers conducting this study were aware of this question and, based on data from a brief questionnaire administered after the experiment, they proposed that participants in larger groups were slower to help because the responsibility for helping was more diffuse and less focused than in smaller groups. Although this diffusion of responsibility hypothesis is interesting, we must note that this experiment did not demonstrate it to be either true or false. The experiment showed only that under the conditions in the laboratory, the number of witnesses present affected the participants' helping behavior.

Strengths of Experiments. The strength of experimental studies lies in their high level of internal validity. This makes experiments especially well suited for testing causal hypotheses. Experiments excel over other methods (surveys, field observation, and so on) in this respect.

Experiments have high internal validity precisely because they control or offset all factors other than the independent variable that might affect the dependent variable. Techniques to accomplish this include (1) randomly assigning participants to treatments, (2) holding constant known extraneous variables, and (3) incorporating extraneous variables as factors in the research design—that is, manipulating them

as independent variables, so that they are not confounded with the main independent variables of interest. Another technique is (4) measuring extraneous variables and including them in the data analysis as covariates of the independent variables.

In principle, investigators can design both laboratory experiments and field experiments to have high internal validity. In practice, however, laboratory experiments often have higher internal validity than comparable field experiments. This happens because researchers have more control over extraneous variables in the laboratory than in the field. Field experiments, however, often surpass laboratory experiments with respect to external validity.

Experiments have been used to test many causal hypotheses drawn from social exchange theory and cognitive theory. Hundreds of experiments have been conducted in an effort to identify the causes of racial and ethnic prejudice.

Weaknesses of Experiments. There are many social phenomena investigators cannot study by this method. Oftentimes, they lack the capacity to manipulate the independent variables of interest or to implement random assignment. Numerous ethical, financial, and practical considerations in everyday life restrict what investigators can manipulate experimentally. For example, we cannot randomly assign children to various types of parental socialization.

Even when the independent variable(s) can be manipulated, experiments face several threats to internal validity. First, there is the possibility that the experimental manipulation may fail. This might occur, for example, if the participants interpret the manipulation as meaning something other than what the researcher intended. The usual remedy for this problem is to use manipulation checks—measures taken after the manipulation that show whether the

BOX 2.2 Using Research to Answer Questions

- What makes people fall in love? What makes them fall out of love?
- What causes harmful or aggressive behavior?

In Chapter 1, we suggested that social psychology answers these questions by applying the methods of science. So how might we answer these questions, using the research methods discussed in this chapter?

Consider the questions about love. First, we need to define *love*. Since love is something people experience, we could begin with a survey. We could ask open-ended questions, such as:

- Have you ever been in love?
- How did you know you were in love?
- What does it feel like to be in love?

We would want to ask these questions of an appropriate sample, so we might choose young adults (college students?). After gathering answers from many respondents, we would study the answers carefully, looking for common themes in the answers to each of the three questions. If we were able to identify certain themes, we could then construct a scale, such as the one in Box 12.3.

Now we can turn to the question of what makes people fall in love. Again, we want to study people's experience. So we might use the method of collecting personal narratives or stories, and conducting a content analysis of the stories. We could request that people "Write a description of the most recent love relationship that you experienced. Describe how you met, what happened in the early days and weeks of the relationship, how you fell in love, and where your relationship is now." Obviously, we would want these narratives from people who are or have recently been in love; we might recruit such people by newspaper ads or flyers on bulletin boards or posts on websites.

We would read a sample of the stories and try to develop a set of coding categories that capture the content of the stories. For example, categories for describing how people met could include school, work, party, bar, music concert, sports event, introduction by friends/relatives, and religious services. Then we would train at least two coders to use our categories and "score" each narrative. Suppose the results showed that one-half of the women and one-third of the men met through an introduction; what would that suggest about how people fall in love? What if 40 percent of the men and women met at a bar?

---

participants perceived the manipulation as intended. Use of manipulation checks is routine and widespread in social psychological experiments. Similar checks are used in surveys to ensure that participants understood directions or questions as intended.

Another threat to the internal validity of experiments is the existence of demand characteristics (also called *subject effects*). This refers to the possibility that participants may interpret certain subtle cues in the experimental setting as requiring particular responses (Aronson et al., 1998). A subject effect occurs, for instance, when participants bring a stereotyped role expec-

tation or mental set to the experiment and then something in the experimental situation activates that expectation, causing the participants to emit the role-defined behavior. To prevent this, some designs disguise the nature of the research and the research hypothesis by providing a cover story—a plausible, albeit false, description of its purpose.

Another threat to internal validity is experimenter effects. This refers to the possibility that an experimenter may expect participants to behave in a particular manner (aggressively, cooperatively, and so on) and may unwittingly telegraph these expectations to the participants (Rosenthal, 1966, 1980). The expectations communicated to participants will likely influence their behavior. This can be a serious problem, especially if the expectations conveyed by the experimenter change as a function of the experimental treatment. People designing an experiment can use several techniques to minimize or eliminate experimenter effects. First, they can restrict the experimenters' contact with the participants and standardize their behavior in the experimental setting. This will limit the opportunities to transmit expectations. Second, they can keep the research personnel "blind" regarding the hypotheses under study and the treatment to which each participant is assigned. Third, they can use a research design with two or more groups of experimenters, each holding a different hypothesis concerning the study. Analysis of the data from such a design will show whether experimenter effects are present or absent.

Beyond internal validity, experiments also face problems with external validity. Some experiments take place in settings that seem artificial to participants and have low apparent realism. This is often true of laboratory experiments, although less true of field experiments. One useful distinction is that between mundane realism and experimental realism (Aronson, Ellsworth, Carlsmith, & Gonzales, 1990). Mundane realism is the extent to which the experimental setting appears similar to natural, everyday situations. Experimental realism, in contrast, is the impact the experimental situation creates—that is, the degree to which the participants feel involved in the situation.

Low mundane realism need not imply low experimental realism. A laboratory study can have low mundane realism but high experimental realism. Participants were highly involved, for example, in the previously discussed study where the experimenters staged an emergency in the laboratory. Many participants were nervous and expressed concern when they came out of their room looking for the supposed victim. Most expressed surprise when they later learned that the seizure was simulated, not genuine.

There is no single solution to the problem of establishing high experimental realism. Some investigators use a combination of laboratory experiments and field experiments when investigating a phenomenon. This approach is often successful, for the field experiments provide the mundane realism that the laboratory experiments lack. Other investigators simply note that they are more concerned with experimental realism than with mundane realism. If the situation is real and involving to the participants, they maintain, then the behavior of the participants is real and worthy of study.

Comparison of Research Methods

We have discussed a variety of research methods—surveys, naturalistic observation, archival research, and laboratory and field experiments. Table 2.1 summarizes the strengths and weaknesses of each research method. As this table indicates, no one method of empirical investigation is best for all purposes. A method's appropriateness depends on the phenomenon under study and on the research characteristics most important to the investigator.

Surveys, which provide a useful way of obtaining an accurate description of the attributes of some population, usually have at least moderate internal and external validity, and they pose few ethical problems. Field studies relying on observational techniques will tend to have comparatively low internal validity and may confront a variety of ethical issues, but they may still be the best way to investigate previously unex-

TABLE 2.1 Strengths and Weaknesses of Research Methods

	METHOD				
	SURVEY	OBSERVATIONAL STUDY	ARCHIVAL RESEARCH	LABORATORY EXPERIMENT	FIELD EXPERIMENT
Internal Validity	Moderate	Low	Low	High	Moderate
External Validity	Moderate	Moderate	Moderate	Moderate	High
Investigator Control	Moderate	Moderate	Low	High	Moderate
Intrusiveness of Measures	Moderate	Moderate	Low	Moderate	Low
Difficulty of Conducting Study	Moderate	Moderate	Low	Moderate	High
Ethical Problems	Few	Many	Few	Some	Some

Note: Entries in the table indicate the strength of the research methods with respect to the various concerns (validity, control, intrusiveness, and the like).

plored social phenomena in their natural settings. Laboratory experiments, which can be especially useful in testing causal hypotheses, are generally high in internal validity, but they may pose some ethical problems (especially if deception is used).

Meta-Analysis

Social psychologists have been conducting empirical research for more than a century. There have been dozens and sometimes hundreds of studies of some phenomena. Unfortunately, the results of different studies on a specific question do not always agree. For instance, some studies show that contact with members of a group produces more positive attitudes (reduces prejudice) toward that group; other studies find that contact has no effect on attitudes. Meta-analysis is a technique that allows an investigator to bring order out of this apparent chaos.

Meta-analysis is a statistical technique that allows the researcher to combine the quantitative results from all previous studies on a question to determine what, collectively, they say. In conducting a meta-

analysis, the researcher performs three steps:

1. The researcher locates all previous studies on the question. Today, this is typically done using computerized searches of libraries and databases. It should also include a canvas of researchers known to have worked in the area to identify unpublished research.

2. For each study, the investigator computes a statistic that measures how big the difference was, say, between those who did and those who did not interact with members of the group, and what the direction of the difference was (whether those who had contact were more or less prejudiced). This statistic is called d. The formula for it is

$$d = \frac{M_c - M_{nc}}{s}$$

where M_c is the mean or average score for the participants who had contact and M_{nc} is the average score for those who did not; s is the standard deviation of the scores of all participants. The standard deviation is a measure of how much variability there is in the scores. The d statistic tells us—for this one study—how big the difference between the two groups of participants was relative to the variability in scores.

3. The researcher averages all the values of d over all the studies that were located. This average d value tells what the direction of the difference is in attitudes between those who do and do not have contact with the group and how large the difference is for all the studies combined. A general guide is that a d of .20 is a small difference, a d of .50 is a moderate difference, and a d of .80 is a large difference.

We include the results of a number of meta-analyses throughout the book.

RESEARCH IN DIVERSE POPULATIONS

For much of the twentieth century, the participants in research by social psychologists were often White, often middle-class, and often college students. In the past 30 years, there has been increasing interest in studying racial and ethnic minority groups in the United States, and members of other cultures around the world. It is important that research in such groups meet the standards of internal and external validity discussed earlier. This requires that we give careful consideration to the methods we use and be willing to adapt or change them.

Much research is based on theory. The theories and assumptions on which we base studies of diverse groups should take into account the cultural history and present social and economic circumstances of the group(s) being studied. For example, Orbuch and colleagues (2002), in developing the longitudinal study discussed earlier, assumed that the risk of divorce for Black couples is influenced by past and present social and economic conditions faced by Blacks. The measures must be linguistically equivalent—that is, be worded so that they are understood in the same way by all participants; if the participants speak a different primary language from that of the instrument, a careful process of translation and independent back translation should be employed to produce equivalent instruments. Measures should be standardized or interpreted using data from the population(s) being studied; for example, researchers should not use score distributions obtained from majority samples to interpret the scores of minority populations unless they have been shown to be equivalent. In this example (Orbuch et al., 2002), the measures of positive interaction and of conflict had been used in the earlier waves of the research, and their applicability to both Blacks and Whites had been demonstrated.

If the researcher's intent is to characterize groups or cultures, the samples studied must be representative. If they are not, it should be noted in any reports of the research, and the results should be interpreted accordingly. Whereas the samples in this study (Orbuch et al., 2002) were not representative of Blacks or Whites, they did appear to represent the population of couples marrying for the first time in both groups. Finally, the research team should include either researchers who are members of the group(s) or persons who are culturally competent based on supervised training and experience (CNPAAEMI, 2000).

Culture refers to an intersubjective (shared) set of schema, attitudes, and values that members use to perceive and understand the world. When we conduct research,

BOX 2.3 Crowdsourcing Social Psychological Research

Crowdsourcing refers to "the practice of obtaining needed services, ideas, or content by soliciting contributions from a large group of people, and especially from an online community" (http://en.wikipedia.org/wiki/Crowdsourcing). Employers needing services, and so forth, post requests for workers to provide what they need, with or without compensation. Online solicitation of contributions can provide access to a large number of people who may complete the task very quickly. One widely used online platform is Amazon's Mechanical Turk (AMT). Requesters can post various tasks using templates provided by the software, solicit workers to complete the tasks, and offer compensation to those who complete it. The task is referred to as a HIT (human intelligence task). Social psychologists have begun to employ AMT in conducting both online surveys and experiments.

A researcher can post a survey on AMT just as he or she would post it on a university server. The researcher creates a description of the HIT, which is posted on a list. Persons looking for work read the list and select the HITs they want to complete. The researcher can list prerequisites for completing the HIT, such as age, gender, and so on. AMT includes a payment mechanism. The researcher can deposit an amount of money in an online account, specify the compensation to be provided, and AMT will transfer the compensation to the worker's account upon completion of the task. If s/he wants to, the requester can specify that the worker's contribution be reviewed for quality/completeness before payment is transferred, giving the researcher some quality control.

It is also possible to conduct experiments on AMT. If the independent variable can be manipulated by exposing groups of participants to different information—different texts, images, decision-making problems—and measuring the DVs with questions or scales, it can be done online. In this case, each experimental condition is one HIT, and the researcher specifies how many "assignments" (participants) are allowed for each HIT. Again, the researcher can specify prerequisites, or even have potential workers complete a screening questionnaire or practice items. For example, one could conduct a bystander effect experiment on AMT by providing a story or video of a person suffering a seizure or being attacked; there could be four versions, varying the setting (university classroom, shopping mall) or gender of person needing help. The DV would be measured by a series of questions about whether the participant would intervene or help. Many laboratory experiments are now presented "live" to participants on laptop computers using digitized materials and recording the responses. It is easy to transfer such protocols to the AMT platform.

AMT has several advantages as a research site. It provides access to a very large participant pool (more than 100,000 people) and a streamlined recruitment procedure (Buhrmester et al., 2011). Research indicates that AMT participants are demographically diverse, certainly more diverse than an undergraduate subject pool. Also, the data obtained (personality scales) are as reliable as data obtained by traditional methods. Participation rates are affected by task length and compensation rate. A final advantage is fast cycles of developing theory, collecting data, revising theory, and collecting more data (Mason & Suri, 2012). Like other online data collection, the researcher has little control over the context in which the data is collected (classroom, bedroom, frat party), and must rely on the participant's report of "who" she or he is.

it is important that the results reflect the culture of the group(s) being studied. Some suggest that this requires that quantitative research be supplemented with methods focused on the cultural meanings that group members attribute to the quantitative measures. For example, a study of differences in gender role used scores on the Bem Sex-Role Inventory to compare a sample of European-American women with a sample of Women of Color (Landrine, Klonoff, & Brown-Collins, 1995). There were no significant differences between the groups in self-rating on traits such as "feminine," "assertive," and "independent." Following the self-rating items were questions designed to measure the meaning of these words to the respondent. Responses to these questions revealed differences in meaning between the groups. The most common meaning of "assertive" among European-American women was "standing up" for themselves, while among women of color it meant saying what was on their mind. Thus, understanding differences across groups requires research designs that will capture relevant aspects of the cultures of the groups.

ETHICAL ISSUES IN SOCIAL PSYCHOLOGICAL RESEARCH

As important as the methodological issues are the ethical issues involved in research on humans. There is a consensus among investigators and others affiliated with the scientific community that people who participate in research have certain rights that must be respected. In some cases, protecting those rights requires investigators to limit or modify their research practices.

In the following discussion of ethical issues, we focus first on potential sources of harm to participants. Then we discuss various safeguards, such as risk-benefit analysis and informed consent, to protect partici-

pants' rights. Finally, we consider potential benefits to participants in research.

Potential Sources of Harm

Harm to participants in research can take a variety of forms, including physical harm, psychological harm, and harm from breach of confidentiality. We will discuss each of these.

Physical Harm. Exposure to physical harm in social psychological research is uncommon. Investigations to measure the effects of stress do sometimes employ an exercise treadmill or tasks where participants immerse one hand in ice water. As a precaution, investigators usually screen prospective participants to exclude those with relevant medical conditions. At the onset of a study, investigators are expected to inform the participants about any risks so that they can decide whether they might be harmed by participating. In studies involving physical stress, investigators typically monitor participants for adverse effects throughout the research.

Psychological Harm. A more common risk in social psychological research is psychological harm to participants. This risk is present in studies where participants receive negative information about themselves. For example, a not uncommon experimental manipulation is to give participants false feedback about their physical attractiveness, about others' reactions to them, or about their performance on various tests or tasks. Investigators can use such feedback to raise or lower participants' self-esteem, to induce feelings of acceptance or rejection by others, or to create perceptions of success or failure on important tasks. These manipulations are effective precisely because they do influence the participants' self-perception.

Negative feedback may cause psychological stress or harm, at least temporarily. For this reason, some investigators believe that such techniques should not be employed in research. Others believe, however, that they are acceptable and may be used if alternative, less harmful manipulations are not available. When false feedback is used, an investigator can limit any long-term harmful effects by giving the participants a thorough debriefing after the study, providing the participants with a full description of the study, and emphasizing the falsity of the feedback. Debriefing should be done immediately after the study to minimize the time that participants labor under false impressions.

In 2003, a book was published by professor of psychology J. Michael Bailey with the provocative title *The Man Who Would Be Queen*. The book presents in lay language research and thinking about many aspects of sexual behavior. One of the topics discussed is transsexualism. Bailey presents the theory that some transsexuals are autogynephilic—that is, men who are erotically attracted to the image of themselves as a woman. The book included two "portraits" of transsexuals. The book generated a strong backlash (Dreger, 2008), leading to formal charges of misconduct by Bailey, including failure to inform transsexual people with whom he interacted that he was performing research. If true, this is a serious charge.

Breach of Confidentiality. Confidentiality is another important issue, especially in survey and observational research. Interviewers and observers are frequently able to identify participants, and they may recall details regarding the participants' behavior or responses to questions. Were confidentiality to be breached, the effects might be damaging to the participants. This concern arises especially in surveys inquiring about sexual behaviors, past physical or psychiatric illnesses, or other sensitive personal matters. It also arises in observational studies of deviant or criminal activities.

One important precaution against breach of confidentiality is to avoid including on the research team any people who are apt to have social contacts with respondents in other settings. Furthermore, many investigators refuse to attach any identifying information such as names and addresses to data after they have been collected. Another approach is to keep any identifying information separate from questionnaires or behavioral records to prevent breaches of confidentiality.

Observational research often deals with a specific group or organization. During their investigation, researchers may gather information about the organization itself and about various members. When these findings are published, the investigators typically refer to the organization by a pseudonym and to members by role only. This practice usually suffices to prevent outsiders from identifying the organization and its members, although it may not prevent members from identifying each other. There are obvious risks to members' positions, reputations, or jobs within the organization if compromising information becomes known to other members. Box 2.4 lists some of the major ethical questions that apply to many studies.

Institutional Safeguards

As noted earlier, researchers can take various steps to prevent harm to participants. Although many people feel that voluntary self-regulation by researchers suffices to protect the rights and interests of the participants, others feel that some agency other than the researcher should review proposed research designs. Accordingly, most institutions have developed and put into place

BOX 2.4 Ethical Considerations in Research Design

Before conducting a given study, investigators and members of review boards ask certain ethical questions about the proposed research design and its impact on participants. Among the most commonly asked ethical questions are the following:

1. Is it possible that participants in the study might be harmed physically, for example, by strenuous exercise?
2. Does the study give participants false information about themselves or use any other form of deception?
3. Does the study induce participants to engage in behavior that might threaten their self-respect?
4. If the investigators make audio or videotapes of the participants, will they obtain permission from the participants to use the tapes as a data source?
5. What steps will the investigators take to preserve the confidentiality of information obtained about the participants?
6. Will the investigators tell potential participants in advance about the foreseeable risks that their participation may entail?
7. Will participants have a chance to ask questions about the study before they consent to participate?
8. Will the investigators inform the participants that they have the right to terminate their participation at any time?
9. At the end of the study, will the investigators fully debrief the participants and tell them about the real nature of the study and its procedures?

safeguards against potentially harmful effects of research. The two most important safeguards are conducting a risk-benefit analysis and obtaining informed consent from all participants.

Risk-Benefit Analysis. The federal government is a major provider of funds for research in the social and biomedical sciences. Many federal departments and agencies have adopted common criteria for the review of research involving human participants (the Common Rule, 45 Code of Federal Regulations 46 A). Under these regulations, investigators and institutions are responsible for minimizing the risks, of whatever type, to participants in research. The rules encourage researchers to develop designs that expose participants to no more than "minimal risk"—meaning risk no greater than that ordinarily encountered in daily life or during the performance of routine physical or psychological examinations or tests (U.S. Department of Health and Human Services, 2010).

Furthermore, the regulations require each institution that receives funds from federal agencies to establish an institutional review board responsible for reviewing proposed research involving human participants. The IRB (sometimes called a human subjects committee or research ethics committee) assesses the extent to which participants in each proposed study will be placed at risk. As noted earlier, many social psychological studies involve no foreseeable risks to participants, but if the members of the board believe that participants might be harmed—physically, psychologically, or by breach of confidentiality—a detailed assessment must be made. That is, the review board conducts a **risk-benefit analysis**, which weighs potential risks to the participants against anticipated benefits to the participants and the importance of the knowledge that may result from the research. The review board will not approve research involving risk to participants unless it concludes that the risk is reasonable in relation to the benefits.

In the Bailey case, the IRB did not review his methods because his work did not fit the definition of research, "a systematic investigation designed to develop or contribute to generalizable knowledge" (U.S. Department of Health and Human Services, 2010, Sec. 42.102). His book from the outset was intended as a popularization, not a research report. Since it was not research, he was not required to obtain informed consent from those with whom he interacted. At the same time, the record suggests that he was quite candid about his intent to write a book from his first meetings with them. The case is a good example of the importance of lay people understanding the rules, and the researcher being clear about his/her purpose in interaction.

Informed Consent. The other major safeguard against risk is the requirement that investigators obtain **informed consent** from all individuals, groups, or organizations that participate in research studies. Informed consent exists when potential participants or respondents, on being informed by the investigators what their participation will involve, agree willingly to participate in the research. Specifically, six elements are essential to informed consent. (1) The researchers should give potential participants an explanation of the purposes of the research and a brief description of the procedures to be employed; however, they need not and usually do not tell the participants the hypothesis of the research. (2) The investigators should inform participants about any foreseeable risks of participation. (3) The researchers should provide a description of any benefits to the partici-

pant or others. (4) The investigators should provide information about which medical or psychological resources, if any, are available to participants who are adversely affected by participation. (5) The researchers should offer to answer questions about the study whenever possible. (6) The researchers should inform potential participants that they have the right to terminate their participation at any time.

In many survey and observational settings, investigators implement informed consent by giving this information to respondents orally. In experiments, especially those involving some risk to participants, investigators usually obtain written consent from each participant.

Potential Benefits

In the process of obtaining informed consent, participants are usually told that they will not benefit directly from the research. Although that is often true, there are exceptions. Field trials of new forms of treatment for physical or psychological problems may directly benefit participants if the new form of treatment proves to be effective. Similarly, participants in some studies may gain insight into themselves and others. For example, a longitudinal study of couples in premarital relationships included measures of how the men and women were affected. Many participants reported that they paid more attention to evaluating their relationship, and those who reported paying more attention reported more satisfaction with their relationship at the end of the yearlong study (Hughes & Surra, 2000).

Some people believe that being questioned about one's sexual behavior is upsetting, especially to youth. In one study, 15- to 25-year-olds completed such a questionnaire. Later, they rated how distressing and positive the experience had been. Few reported being distressed, and 89 percent said surveys like this should be carried out. Persons who were distressed were those who reported experiencing sexual coercion in the past (Kuyper et al., 2012).

SUMMARY

This chapter discussed the research methods used by social psychologists to investigate social behavior, activity, and events.

Characteristics of Research. (1) Objectives of research include describing reality, identifying correlations between variables, testing causal hypotheses, and testing theories. (2) Research is usually guided by a hypothesis, which may specify a causal relationship between two or more variables. (3) Ideally, the findings of empirical research should be high in both internal validity and external validity.

Research Methods. Social psychologists rely heavily on four methods—surveys, naturalistic observation, archival research based on content analysis, and experiments. (1) A survey involves systematically asking questions and recording the answers from respondents. Investigators use surveys to gather self-reported information about attitudes and activities. The quality of the data obtained in a survey depends on the reliability and validity of the measures used. (2) Naturalistic observation involves collecting data about naturally occurring events. In a field study, observers view an event or activity as it occurs and then record their observations. (3) Archival research involves the analysis of existing information collected by others. Sources of archival data include the Census Bureau and other federal agencies, data archives, and newspapers. Investigators use content analysis to study textual material such as speeches or reports. (4) An experiment involves the manipulation of one or more independent variables and the random assignment of participants to experimental conditions or treatments. Some experiments are conducted in a laboratory, where the investigator has a high degree of control, whereas others are conducted in natural settings.

Ethical Issues in Research. (1) There are several potential sources of harm to participants in research. These include physical harm, psychological harm, and breach of confidentiality. There are various steps that individual investigators can take to prevent or minimize such harm. (2) There are also institutional safeguards against harm. These safeguards require investigators to minimize risks to participants and to obtain informed consent from participants. Institutional review boards monitor research designs to ensure that these conditions are met by investigators. (3) In some cases, participants in research may benefit directly from their participation.

List of Key Terms and Concepts

archival research (p. 47)
content analysis (p. 48)
dependent variable (p. 34)
experiment (p. 49)
external validity (p. 35)
extraneous variable (p. 34)
field study (p. 45)
hypothesis (p. 33)
independent variable (p. 34)
informed consent (p. 61)
internal validity (p. 34)
interview survey (p. 37)
Likert scale (p. 41)
meta-analysis (p. 55)
methodology (p. 32)
panel study (p. 44)
population (p. 42)
questionnaire survey (p. 37)

random assignment (p. 49)
reliability (p. 38)
response rate (p. 37)
risk-benefit analysis (p. 60)
simple random sample (p. 42)
stratified sample (p. 43)
theory (p. 33)

Critical Thinking Skill:
Understanding the Importance of Sampling

Every type of research in social psychology involves a sample. Surveys involve asking questions of a sample of persons drawn from some population (students, adult voters, visitors to an Internet website, and so on). Experiments involve participants recruited/sampled from some population, often students at a college or university. Ethnographic and observational studies involve a sample of settings (such as bars) or persons (for example, workers at McDonald's). The character of the sample has a major impact on the conclusions one can make from the research.

A researcher was interested in studying the culture of alcohol consumption on the campus where he taught. In particular, he wanted to compare Black and White male students' attitudes and consumption patterns. He decided to approach several Black student groups and several White student groups to recruit men to be interviewed. He contacted two Black and two White fraternities, two Black and two White eating clubs, and two Black and two White professional groups (business students and engineering students). He distributed fliers to members of each group describing the research, and asked interested men to call him. He interviewed five men from each of the six groups, for a total of 30 men. He found that about two-thirds of the men drank four or more drinks on one or more nights each week, and that drinking didn't seem to vary by race/ethnicity.

What can we conclude from this study? Can we conclude that there is no difference in alcohol attitudes and behavior by race among college students generally? By race among students at this college? That business and engineering students are equally likely to drink? Think about these questions and then answer them. When you have finished, read on.

The sample in this study is a volunteer sample. The participants volunteered based on a flier that described the study as a study of drinking. It is likely that most of the volunteers were men who currently drank. A nondrinker would probably think the researcher wasn't interested in talking to him. The men are all from the same college; we certainly can't infer anything about men at other colleges and universities. And these men were all recruited from social groups on the campus, and so they probably aren't representative of Black and White male students on the campus. In fact, it takes money to belong to a fraternity or eating club. The researcher may have found that college students who have money drink a lot; not an especially newsworthy result!

So whenever you read a report of the results of research, find out the nature of the sample before you draw any conclusions. A sample that is representative of some group or population is usually a prerequisite for valid research.

CHAPTER 3

SOCIALIZATION THROUGH THE LIFE COURSE

INTRODUCTION

My daughter is the percussionist in her middle-school band. At the first session in September when the director asked for volunteers, six boys shouted "Me!" "I want to do it!" and so on. Then the director asked, "Who can play the piano?" Kimberly and two other girls raised their hands. The band director auditioned the three girls. He wanted a percussionist who could read music; a really good idea.

Kimberly got the position. She jumped right in, practicing on the bass drum, the snare drum, and the chimes after school; we had to pick her up when she finished because she missed the bus. She brought the drums home sometimes on weekends (I had to pick her up and transport the instruments on Friday, and return her and the instruments on Monday morning). I was amazed. I had no musical talent at all, and here she was improving every week.

I had gone to a small school. The administration wanted a big band. I knew I had no talent or even training. but *everybody* had to audition. The band director gave me a clarinet and said, "Just move your fingers in time to the music." I lasted about two concerts, after which he grudgingly conceded that I couldn't play at all and dismissed me from the band. Of course, the 95 percent of the students who were still in the band made my life hell for several weeks. So I was really pleased that Kimberly not only made the band, but was practicing and improving and getting good! I could hardly believe it. She wasn't like me at all. But I was really proud!

In late October, the band gave their first public concert. I was in the second row. It was great! They played the "Star Spangled Banner," then a couple of short pieces, a march by John Philip Souza, "The Tempest," and finished with "*The Pirates of the Caribbean* theme." It was awesome!! I was so proud of her. The audience, mostly parents of the band members, loved it. I waited outside the band room after the concert.

She was the last band member to come out. I saw her, smiled, and walked toward her with my arms out. I hugged her. She started crying. "Dad, I was awful." I was stunned. I stuttered and said, "No, you were great." She said, "I missed my cue once, and my timing was off in the Souza." I said, "I didn't notice, and I am sure no one else did."

She *is* like me—a perfectionist. It is wonderful that she has musical talent. She also got my perfectionism.

One of the striking features of social life is that there is great continuity from one generation to the next—continuity both in physical characteristics and in behavior. Genetic inheritance is one source of continuity. But a major contributor to intergenerational similarity is **socialization**, the ways in which individuals learn and re-create skills, knowledge, values, motives, and roles appropriate to their positions in a group or society.

How does an infant become "human"— that is, an effective participant in society? The answer is, through socialization. As we grew from infancy, we interacted continually with others. We learned to speak a language—a prerequisite for participation in society. We learned basic interaction rituals, such as greeting a stranger with a handshake and a loved one with a kiss. We also learned the socially accepted ways to achieve various goals, both material (food, clothing, shelter) and social (respect, love, help of others). As we learned these, we used them; as we used them, we re-created them—adapted them to our particular circumstances.

It is obvious that socialization makes us like most other members of society in important ways. It is not so obvious that socialization also produces our individuality. The sense of self and the capacity to engage in self-oriented acts (discussed in Chap. 4) are a result of socialization.

The first part of this chapter will examine childhood socialization. By childhood, we mean the period from birth to adolescence. Childhood is a social concept, shaped by historical, cultural, and political influences (Elkin & Handel, 1989). In contemporary American society, we define children as immature—in need of training at home and of a formal education. The second part examines socialization beyond childhood.

The discussion focuses on the following five questions:

1. What are the basic perspectives in the study of socialization?

2. What are the socializing agents in contemporary American society?

3. What are the processes through which socialization occurs?

4. What are the outcomes of socialization in childhood?

5. What is the nature of socialization in adolescence and adulthood?

PERSPECTIVES ON SOCIALIZATION

Which is the more important influence on behavior—nature or nurture, heredity or environment? This question has been especially important to those who study children. Although both influences are important, one view emphasizes biological development (heredity), whereas another emphasizes social learning (environment).

The Developmental Perspective

The human child obviously undergoes a process of maturation. He or she grows physically, develops motor skills in a relatively uniform sequence, and begins to en-

Responsiveness to another person develops early in life. By 16 weeks of age, a child smiles in response to a human face. By 28 weeks, a child can distinguish caregivers from strangers. © video1/ iStock

gage in various social behaviors at about the same age as most other children.

Some theorists view socialization as largely dependent on processes of physical and psychological maturation, which are biologically determined. Gesell and Ilg (1943) documented the sequence in which motor and social skills develop and the ages at which each new ability appears in the average child. They viewed the development of many social behaviors as primarily due to physical and neurological maturation, not social factors. For example, toilet training requires voluntary control over sphincter muscles and the ability to recognize cues of pressure on the bladder or lower intestine. According to developmental theory, when children around age 2½ develop these skills, they learn by themselves without environmental influences.

Table 3.1 lists the sequences of development of various abilities that have been identified by observational research. The ages shown are approximate; some children will exhibit the behavior at younger ages, whereas others will do so later.

As an example, consider the development of responsiveness to other persons. As early as 4 weeks, many infants respond to close physical contact by relaxing. At 16

TABLE 3.1 The Process of Development

	16 WEEKS	28 WEEKS	1 YEAR	2 YEARS	3 YEARS
Visual Activity	Follows objects with eyes; eyes adjust to objects at varying distances	Watches activity intently; hand-eye coordination	Enjoys watching moving objects (like TV picture)	Responds to stimuli in periphery of visual field; looks intently for long periods	
Interpersonal	Smiles at human face; responds to caregiver's voice; demands social attention	Responds to variation in tone of voice; differentiates people (fears strangers)	Engages in responsive play; shows emotions, anxiety; shows definite preferences for some persons	Prefers solitary play; rudimentary concept of ownership	Can play cooperatively with an older child; strong desire to please; gender differences in choice of toys, materials
Vocal Activity	Vocalizes pleasure (coos, gurgles, laughs); babbles (strings of syllable-like sounds)	Vocalizes vowels and consonants; tries to imitate sounds	Vocalizes syllables; practices two to eight known words	Vocalizes constantly; names actions; repeats words	Uses three-word sentences; likes novel words
Bodily Movement	Can hold head up; can roll over	Can sit up;	Can stand; can climb up and down stairs	Can run; likes large-scale motor activity— push, pull, roll	Motion fluid, smooth; good coordination
Manual Dexterity	Touches objects	Can grasp with one hand; manipulates objects	Manipulates objects serially	Good control of hand and arm	Good fine-motor control— uses fingers, thumb, wrist well

Source: Adapted from Caplan, 1973; and *The Infant and Child in the Culture of Today* (1943) by Arnold Gesell and Frances L. Ilg. Used with permission of the Gesell Institute of Human Development.

weeks, babies can discriminate the human face and usually smile in response. They also show signs of recognizing the voice of their usual caregiver. By 28 weeks, the infant clearly differentiates faces and responds to variations in facial expression. At 1 year, the child shows a variety of emotions in response to others' behavior. He or she will seek interaction with adults or with siblings by crawling or walking toward them and tugging on clothing. Thus, recognition of, responsiveness to, and orientation toward adults follow a uniform developmental pattern. The ability to interact with others depends in part on the development of visual and auditory discrimination.

Development continues throughout life. Important physical and hormonal changes occur during puberty, pregnancy, and menopause/later life and impact on motivation and behavior. Recognition of this lifelong process is one aspect of the life-course perspective, discussed later in this chapter.

The Social Learning Perspective

Whereas the developmental perspective focuses on the unfolding of the child's own abilities, the social learning perspective emphasizes the child's acquisition of cognitive and behavioral skills in interaction with the environment. Successful socialization requires that the child acquire considerable information about the world. The child must learn about many physical or natural realities, such as what animals are dangerous and which things are edible. Children also must learn about the social environment. They must learn the language used by people around them to communicate their needs to others. They also need to learn the meanings their caregivers associate with various actions. Children need to learn to identify the kinds of persons encountered in their immediate environment. They need to learn what behaviors they can expect of people, as well as others' expectations for their own behavior.

According to the social learning perspective, socialization is primarily a process of children learning the shared meanings of the groups in which they are reared (Shibutani, 1961). Such variation in meanings gives groups, subcultures, and societies their distinctiveness. Although the content—what is learned—varies from group to group, the processes by which social learning takes place are universal. This viewpoint emphasizes the adaptive nature of socialization. The infant learns the verbal and interpersonal skills necessary to interact successfully with others. The processes by which this occurs are the concern of reinforcement theory. Having acquired these skills, children can perpetuate the meanings that distinguish their social groups and even add to or modify these meanings by introducing innovations of their own.

Recent research on socialization has considered both the importance of developmental processes and the influence of social learning. The developmental age of the child obviously determines which acts the child can perform. Infants less than 6 months old cannot walk. All cultures have adapted to these developmental limitations by coordinating the performance expectations placed on children with the maturation of their abilities. However, developmental processes alone are not sufficient for the emergence of complex social behavior. In addition to developmental readiness, social interaction—learning—is necessary for the development of language. This is illustrated by the case of Isabelle, who lived alone with her deaf-mute mother until the age of 6½. When she was discovered, she was unable to make any sound other than a croak. Yet within 2 years after she entered a systematic educational program, her vocabulary numbered more than 1,500 words and she had the linguistic skills of a 6-year-old (Davis, 1947).

Thus, both nature and nurture influence behavior. Developmental processes produce a readiness to perform certain behaviors. The content of these behaviors is determined primarily by social learning—that is, by cultural influences.

The Interpretive Perspective

Socialization occurs primarily through social interaction. Whereas the social learning perspective emphasizes the process of learning—for example, the role of reinforcement in the acquisition of behavior—the interpretive perspective (Corsaro & Fingerson, 2003) focuses on the interaction itself. Drawing on symbolic interaction theory (see Chap. 1), this perspective views the child's task as the discovery of the meanings common to the social group (such as the family or a school band). This process of discovery requires communication with parents, other adults, and other children. Especially important is the child's participation in **cultural routines**, which are recurrent and predictable activities that are basic to day-to-day social life (Corsaro & Fingerson, 2003). Greeting rituals, common games, and mealtime patterns are examples of such cultural routines. These routines provide a sense of security and of belonging to a group. At the same time, their predictability enables children to use them to display their developing cultural knowledge and skills. A good example is Kimberly, who we met in the opening essay. There are cultural routines for playing a musical instrument, but Kimberly, like other young musicians, develops her own particular style in playing the snare drum.

According to this perspective, socialization is a process of interpretive reproduction. Children don't simply learn culture. In daily interaction, children use the language and interpretive skills that they are learning or discovering. As they become more proficient in communicating and more knowledgeable about the meanings shared in the family and school, children attain a deeper understanding of the culture. Children, through interaction, acquire and reproduce the culture.

When children communicate with one another (as in school or at play), they do not simply imitate the acquired culture. They use what they have learned to create their own somewhat unique peer culture. Children take a traditional game such as one group chasing another group and change the rules to fit their needs and the physical and social context in which they are enacting the game. In the 1950s the two groups were often cowboys and Indians; in the 2000s they might be cops and Blacks (Goffman, 2014). The changed rules become part of a new routine of chase. Thus, from an early age, children are not just imitating culture, but creating it.

The Impact of Social Structure

A fourth perspective emphasizes the influence of social structure. Socialization is not a random process. Teaching new members the rules of the game is too important to be left to chance. Socialization is organized according to the sequence of roles that newcomers to the society ordinarily pass through. In American society, these include familial roles, such as son or daughter, and roles in educational institutions, such as preschooler, elementary school student, and high school student. These are age-linked roles; we expect transitions from one role to another to occur at certain ages. Distinctive socialization outcomes are sought for those who occupy each role. Thus, we expect young children to learn language and basic norms governing such diverse activities as eating, dressing, and bowel and bladder control. Most preschool programs will not enroll a child who has not learned the latter.

Furthermore, social structure designates the persons or organizations responsible for producing desired outcomes. In a complex society such as ours, there is a sequence of roles and a corresponding sequence of socializing agents (see Box 3.1). From birth through adolescence, the family is primarily responsible for socializing the child. From ages 6 to 12, a child is an elementary school student; we expect elementary school teachers to teach the basics to their students. Next, the adolescent becomes a high school student, with yet another group of agents to further develop his or her knowledge and abilities. In adulthood, men and women become partners and coworkers, and need to learn these roles from persons in related roles.

This perspective is sociological; it considers socialization as a product of group life. It calls our attention to the changing content of and responsibility for socialization throughout the individual's life. This theme is fundamental to the life-course perspective, discussed later in this chapter.

AGENTS OF CHILDHOOD SOCIALIZATION

Socialization has four components. It always involves (1) an agent—someone who serves as a source for what is being learned; (2) a learning process; (3) a target—a person who is being socialized; and (4) an outcome—something that is being learned. This section will consider the four primary agents of childhood socialization—family, peers, school, and mass media. Later sections will focus on the processes and outcomes of childhood socialization.

Family

At birth, infants are primarily aware of their own bodies. Hunger, thirst, or pain creates unpleasant and perhaps overwhelming bodily tensions. The infant's primary concern is to remove these tensions and satisfy bodily needs. To meet the infant's needs, adult caregivers must learn to read the infant's signals accurately (Ainsworth, 1979). Also, infants begin to perceive their principal caregivers as the source of need satisfaction. These early experiences are truly interactive (Bell, 1979). The adult learns how to care effectively for the infant, and the infant forms a strong emotional attachment to the caregiver.

Is a Mother Necessary? Does it matter who responds to and establishes a caring relationship with the infant? Must there be a single principal caregiver in infancy and childhood for effective socialization to occur?

Psychoanalytic theory (as originally framed by Freud) asserts that an intimate emotional relationship between infant and caregiver (almost always the mother at the time Freud wrote) is essential to healthy personality development. This was one of the first hypotheses to be studied empirically. To examine the effects of the absence of a single, close caregiver on children, researchers have studied institutionalized infants. In the earliest reported work, Spitz (1945, 1946) studied an institution in which six nurses cared for 45 infants under 18 months old. The nurses met the infants' ba-

sic biological needs. However, they had limited contact with the babies, and there was little evidence of emotional ties between the nurses and the infants. Within 1 year, the infants' scores on developmental tests fell dramatically from an average of 124 to an average of 72. Within 2 years, one-third had died, 9 had left, and the 21 who remained in the institution were severely retarded. Recent research on children who lived in orphanages for an average of 16 months following birth found that at age 4½, they had significant difficulty matching facial expressions of emotion with stories, compared to children from control families (Fries & Pollak, 2004). These findings dramatically support the hypothesis that an emotionally responsive caregiver is essential.

Thus, infants need a secure **attachment**—a warm, close relationship with an adult that produces a sense of security and provides stimulation—to develop the interpersonal and cognitive skills needed for proper growth (Ainsworth, 1979). Moreover, being cared for in such a relationship provides the foundation of the infant's sense of self.

For many decades, gender role definitions in American society made mothers primarily responsible for raising children. Fathers' parental responsibility was to work outside the home and provide the income needed by the family. The division of labor in many families conformed to these definitions. As a result, some analysts concluded that a warm, intimate, continuous relationship between a child and its mother is essential to normal child development (Bowlby, 1965). Perhaps only in the mother-infant relation can the child experience the necessary sense of security and emotional warmth. According to this view, other potential caregivers have less emotional interest in the infant and may not be adequate substitutes.

Research on parent-child interaction indicates that if mothers are sensitive to the child's needs and responsive to his or her distress in the first year of life, the child is more likely to develop a secure attachment (Demo & Cox, 2001). This is true in both two-parent and mother-only families. Infants who are securely attached to their mothers in the first 2 years of life evidence less problem behavior and more cooperative behavior from ages 4 to 10. Thus, secure mother-infant attachment is associated with positive outcomes (see Box 3.1). Research also indicates that a father's sensitivity to the child at 13 months is associated with father-child attachment at 3 years of age (Brown, Manglesdorf, & Neff, 2012). Thus, parent-child attachment does not depend on the parent's gender.

A related question is whether children need or benefit from having both a male and a female parent—that is, does the gender of parents matter? Researchers (Biblarz & Stacy, 2010) compared studies of two-parent families with same or different gender co-parents with studies of single-parent families. The relationships between parenting practices and child outcomes reported in studies of heterosexual families were also found in lesbian families, and in the few studies of gay co-parents that have been published. In general, in single-parent families, children fared better with a single mother than a single father, but such families differ on important dimensions like circumstances of formation, gender of child, and income.

Since 1960, gender role definitions have been changing. Married women with children are increasingly working outside the home (see Figure 3.3). The effects of maternal employment on the child is a major continuing public concern.

Effects of Maternal Employment. What effect does maternal employment have on children? A meta-analysis of 69 studies found mostly nonsignificant effects on

children's achievement outcomes—IQ, test scores—and child behavior problems (Lucas-Thompson, Goldberg, & Prause, 2010). Early employment was most beneficial in single-parent families. Employment during the child's first year had a small negative effect.

The Fragile Families and Child Well-being researchers collected data from White, Black, and Hispanic families. Researchers analyzed the relationship between maternal employment during the child's first year and several outcomes at 3 years of age. Maternal employment was associated with lower vocabulary scores in White, but not Black or Hispanic families, and with higher levels of behavior problems in Hispanic families (Berger, Brooks-Gunn, Paxson, & Waldfogel, 2008). These outcomes were not related to maternal stress or parenting behaviors. A study of the effects of employment during the preceding year found that it was associated with fewer positive mother-child interactions, and less reading with parents at ages 2 and 4 (Nomaguchi, 2006).

There have been dozens of studies of the effects of maternal employment on achievement outcomes in children and adolescents. A meta-analysis of 68 studies looked at four outcomes: tests of achievement, tests of intellectual functioning, grades, and teacher ratings of cognitive competence (Goldberg, Prause, Lucas-Thompson, & Himsel, 2008). Comparing children of mothers who worked (including part- and full-time) with children of mothers who did not, there were no significant differences on the four outcomes. Part-time work was positively associated with all four outcomes; there were more positive effects for girls.

The effects of maternal employment on older children depend partly on work characteristics. Nonstandard work (for example, working nights or rotating shifts) can negatively affect parent-child closeness

BOX 3.1 Test Yourself: Attachment in Children and Adults

Which of the following best describes your feelings about relationships?

1. I find it relatively easy to get close to others and am comfortable depending on them and having them depend on me. I don't often worry about being abandoned or someone getting too close to me.
2. I am somewhat uncomfortable being close to others; I find it difficult to trust them completely, difficult to allow myself to depend on them. I am nervous when anyone gets too close, and often, love partners want me to be more intimate than I feel comfortable being.
3. I find that others are reluctant to get as close as I would like. I often worry that my partner doesn't really love me or won't want to stay with me. I want to merge completely with another person, and this desire sometimes scares people away. (Hazan & Shaver, 1987)

Each of these statements represents one attachment style, an individual's characteristic way of relating to significant others (Hazan & Shaver, 1987). The first describes a secure style, the second an avoidant style, and the third an anxious/ambivalent style.

The roots of the individual's style may be found in childhood. Ainsworth (1979) identified three styles of attachment in caregiver-child interactions. The attachment style of a young child is assessed by observing how the child relates to his or her caregiver when distressed (by, for example, a brief separation in a strange environment). The secure child readily approaches the caregiver and seeks comfort. The avoidant child does not approach the caregiver and appears detached. The anxious/ambivalent child approaches the caregiver and expresses anger or hostility toward him or her. Children as young as 2 years behave consistently in one of these ways when distressed.

We bring the style we developed as children into our intimate adult relationships. Surveys of adults (for example, Hazan & Shaver, 1987) have found that about 55 percent describe themselves as secure, 25 percent as avoidant, and 20 percent as anxious/ambivalent. Attachment style influences our responses to other people (Feeney, 1999). It leads us to pay attention to certain aspects of a person (for example, his or her trustworthiness), creates biases in memory (we remember events consistent with our style), and affects how we explain relationship events. A secure person will ignore an event (his partner talking to an attractive person) that would make an anxious person feel jealous. Attachment style also influences relationship quality. Men and women who describe themselves as secure report that their romantic relationships involve interdependence, trust, and commitment (Simpson, 1990). Adults who describe themselves as avoidant say that they do not trust others and are afraid of getting close (Feeney & Noller, 1990). Those who are anxious/ambivalent report intense emotions toward the partner and a desire for deep commitment in a relationship. Since attachment style develops on the basis of childhood experience, analysts assume that it precedes adult relationships. Longitudinal data point to stability in style over time (Feeney, 1999). However, particularly significant relationship experiences may lead to change in style. A secure person who spends a long time with someone who is chronically unfaithful understandably may become anxious.

and delay cognitive development (Crosnoe & Cavanagh, 2010). Mother's exposure to physical hazards at work also negatively affects cognitive development, and exposure to work-related stressors has a negative effect on behavior (Felfe & Hsin, 2012). Father's exposure to physical hazards and stressors may have similar effects.

What about the effects of child care? It depends on the type, quality, and amount of care. A large-scale research project conducted at 10 sites around the United States followed 1,000 children from birth. At age 4½, children who experienced higher-quality care and whose care was provided in a center had significantly better cognitive skills and language performance; quality was measured using observers who completed a standardized observational record. Children who received more hours of care between the ages of 3 months and 4½ years were given higher ratings on behavior problems (on the 113-item Child Behavior Checklist) by care providers. Twenty-four percent of the sample were children of color; it appears that the results do not vary by ethnicity (NICHD Early Child Care Research Network, 1997a, 1997b, 2002; Belsky, 2006).

Researchers have continued to follow these youth. At age 15, both quality and quantity of nonrelative child care at young ages were linked to adolescent outcomes. Higher quality care predicted higher cognitive and academic achievement, and youth reports of fewer school and emotional problems (Vandell et al., 2010).

Father's Involvement with Children. The broadening of maternal role definitions to include work outside the home has been accompanied by changes in expectations for fathers. This new ideology of fatherhood, promoted by television and film, encourages active involvement of fathers in child care and child rearing (Parke, 1996). Some men have adopted these expectations for themselves. Research finds that married fathers spent significantly more time with their child(ren) each day in 1998 than they did in 1965 (Sayer, Bianchi, & Robinson, 2004). The father's contribution is often through rough-and-tumble play; such play is thought to facilitate the child's development of motor skills. Fathers increasingly also engage in child care and developmental activities. These patterns are found in European-American, African-American, and Hispanic two-parent families (Parke, 1996).

Several variables influence the extent of fathers' involvement with their children. Maternal attitudes are one important factor; a father is more involved when the mother encourages and supports his participation. Maternal employment is another influence. Husbands of employed women are more involved in child care and in some cases provide full-time care for the child. Also, a study found that lower levels of stress on the job and greater support from coworkers for being an active father were associated with greater involvement (Volling & Belsky, 1991). Thus, research suggests that work stressors have negative effects on both fathers' and mothers' involvement in child rearing. Research on Mexican-American families finds that a positive relationship between mother and father was related to quality fathering (Formoso, Gonzales, Barrera, & Dumka, 2007). Finally, parental education is positively related to time spent with children by both fathers and mothers (Guryan, Hurst, & Kearney, 2008).

Child Rearing in a Diverse Society. There is diversity in the living arrangements of children in the United States today. Table 3.2 indicates the living arrangements of all children in 2000 (Lichter & Qian, 2004). Sixty-one percent of all children lived with married parents. Fifteen percent lived with a single mother; note that more than 2 mil-

TABLE 3.2 Children's Living Arrangements, 2000, 2007

ALL CHILDREN			BY RACE/ETHNICITY			
ARRANGEMENT	PERCENT	ARRANGEMENT	WHITE	BLACK	ASIAN	HISPANIC
Working father/ nonworking mother	21%	Two parents	78% 75	38% 34	87% 86	68% 63
Married, both working	41	Biological mother & father	68	31	82	61
Male-headed	2.3	Father	3.6	3.3	2	2
Female, previously married	10	Mother	16	50	9	26
Female, never married	5					
Cohabiting couple	4.1					
Grandparents	6	Grandparents	1.4	5.4	0.5	2
Unknown	10.6					

Source: All: Lichter and Qian. (2004). *Marriage and Family in a Multiracial Society.* New York Russell Sage Foundation, Table 6. By race/ethnicity: U.S. Bureau of the Census (2007). Survey of Income and Program Participation, 2004 Panel, Wave 2, Table 1.

lion children are living with a single father (U.S. Bureau of the Census, 2005). These arrangements vary by race/ethnicity, as seen in the right-hand panel of Table 3.2. In 2007, compared to White (18%) and Asian (9%), more African-American children lived with a single mother (50%). Asian children were most likely (82%) to live with married, biological parents, compared to White (68%), Hispanic (61%), and Black (31%) (Krieder & Ellis, 2011).

Studies of socialization have focused on child-rearing techniques or parenting styles and their impact on cognitive and social development. Research has consistently found that authoritative parenting—characterized by high levels of warmth combined with control—benefits children. Reliance by parents on this style is associated with greater achievement in school and positive relations with other adults and peers. Authoritarian styles, including physical punishment, and permissive styles are more likely to be associated with poor adjustment in childhood (Demo & Cox, 2001).

Spanking of children ages 1 to 3 is more likely when the child is fussy or has behavior problems, the mother is experiencing psychological distress, and the family is low SES (Hahlweg et al., 2008). In a large, ethnically diverse sample, spanking at ages 1 and 2 is associated with behavior problems at school entry (Slade & Wissow, 2004). In low-income White, African-American, and Mexican-American families, spanking at age 1 predicts aggressive behavior at age 2 and lower mental development scores at age 3 (Berlin et al., 2009).

The negative outcomes reported by research to be associated with physical punishment and authoritarian styles of parenting lead some observers to conclude that these are improper child-rearing techniques. Minority researchers challenge the validity of this conclusion for minority families (McLoyd, Cauce, Takeuchi, & Wilson, 2001). White and Black mothers living in poverty are more likely to use physical punishment, partly due to chronic financial stress (Demo & Cox, 2001). Research by

Deater-Deckard and Dodge (1997) has suggested that physical discipline is more common in African-American families and that they define it as positive parenting. Other research (Chao, 1994) has suggested that Asian-American parents rely on providing training and clear and concrete guidelines for behavior, and that this should not be seen as authoritarian.

With respect to values, White parents emphasize the development of autonomy (Alwin, 1990), which is consistent with the mainstream culture's emphasis on individualism and independence. Minority children are more likely to be socialized to value cooperation and interdependence (Demo & Cox, 2001). African-American parents tend to emphasize assertiveness, whereas Mexican-American families emphasize family unity and solidarity with the extended family. Asian-American parents teach children to value family authority. Thus, as we would expect, socialization in distinctive communities tends to emphasize the values of those communities.

Contemporary scholars stress that the meaning and the impact on the child of a parenting technique varies depending upon cultural background, family structure, and social context. This suggests that we should focus on specific techniques and not group differences in their use (Crosnoe & Cavanagh, 2010). Scholars also point to diversity within racial categories, rendering generalizations about a group, such as Blacks or Hispanics, questionable (Burton et al., 2010).

Effects of Divorce. Forty to fifty percent of all marriages end in divorce (Cherlin, 2010); the probability of marital disruption is much lower for a woman with a college education. About one-half of these divorces involve children under the age of 18 years. Divorce usually involves several major changes in the life of a child: a change in family structure, a change in residence, a change in the

family's financial resources, and perhaps a change of schools. Therefore, it is difficult to isolate the effects of divorce—the change in family structure—independently of these other changes. Research consistently finds that the number of transitions a child experiences is positively associated with undesirable outcomes (Cherlin, 2010). An additional confounding fact is that divorce is not a one-time crisis; it is a process that begins with marital discord while the couple is living together, continues through physical separation and legal proceedings, and ends, if ever, when those involved have completed the uncoupling process (Amato, 2001).

Research comparing children of divorced with children of married parents has consistently found that the children of divorced parents score lower on measures of academic success (such as grades), psychological adjustment, self-esteem, and long-term health, among other outcomes (Amato, 2001). Some research (for example, Hetherington, 1999) has reported that these deficits were present several years before the divorce, leading to the suggestion that children's problem behaviors cause the discord that leads to divorce. However, if we view the divorce as a process, problems prior to the divorce could be caused by the marital discord. A few studies report positive consequences for some children. Some offspring, especially daughters, develop very positive relationships with custodial mothers (Arditti, 1999).

The view of divorce as a one-time crisis implies that children will show improved function as the time since divorce increases. Some studies (for example, Jekielek, 1998) report that children's well-being does improve over time. On the other hand, longitudinal research finds that the gap in well-being between children of divorced parents and children of intact couples increases (Cherlin, Chase-Lansdale, & McRae, 1998) or remains the same (Sun & Li, 2002) over time. A unique study documents intergenerational effects of divorce. The researchers reported negative effects on subsequent academic achievement, later marital discord, and weak ties to mothers and fathers in both the second and third generations (that is, effects on children and grandchildren) (Amato & Cheadle, 2005).

Although most people acknowledge the undesirability of divorce, it is often justified with the argument that it is less harmful than growing up in a family with chronic marital, social, and perhaps economic problems. Is this true? A longitudinal study in Great Britain followed thousands of children from birth to age 33, enabling researchers to compare adults whose parents divorced when they were 7 to 16, 17 to 20, or 21 to 33 years of age (Furstenberg & Kiernan, 2001). The results show that men and women whose parents divorced when they were 7 to 16, compared to men and women whose parents divorced when they were older, completed less schooling and earned higher scores on an index of psychological symptoms; women were more likely to drink heavily as adults. The researchers also found higher rates of early and nonmarital pregnancy among those whose parents had divorced early. All of these results have been reported in studies of persons in the United States (Demo & Acock, 1988; Garfinkel & McLanahan, 1986). Reduced educational attainment and early parenthood and marriage result in a higher rate of poverty among adults raised in single-parent families (McLanahan & Booth, 1989).

A review of research on low-income families (often single-parent families) concludes that the need for the parent(s) to work long hours in order to earn enough money shifts the burden of family labor onto one or more children, usually girls. This labor includes caring for younger siblings, cooking, and cleaning; it prevents the person providing it from focusing on ed-

ucation and taking advantage of extracurricular and other opportunities, and may funnel her into early childbearing and marriage (Dodson & Dickert, 2004). Very few studies have been done of the effects of divorce in non-European-American families. We don't know whether we would find the effects described here in racial and ethnic minority groups.

Peers

As the child grows, his or her peers become increasingly important as socializing agents. The peer group differs from the family on several dimensions. These differences influence the type of interaction and thus the kinds of socialization that occur.

The family consists of persons who differ in status or power, whereas the peer group is composed of relative equals. From an early age, the child is taught to treat parents with respect and deference. Failure to do so will probably result in discipline, and the adult will use the incident as an opportunity to instruct the child about the importance of deference (Cahill, 1987; Denzin, 1977). Interaction with peers is more open and spontaneous; the child does not need to be deferential or tactful. Thus, children at the age of 4 years bluntly refuse to let children they dislike join their games. With peers, they may say things that adults consider insulting, such as "You're ugly," to another child. This interactional give-and-take is a basic aspect of the friendship process (Corsaro & Fingerson, 2003).

Membership in a particular family is ascribed, whereas peer interactions are voluntary (Gecas, 1990). Thus, peer groups offer children their first experience in exercising choice over whom they relate to. The opportunity to make such choices contributes to the child's sense of social competence and allows interaction with other children who complement the developing identity.

BOX 3.2 The Peer Group

American society is highly segregated by age. Most of us spend most of our time with people of about the same age. This is especially true in childhood and adolescence, because age segregation is the fundamental organizing principle of our schools. Research provides important sights into the nature of peer groups and their significance for socialization.

Among preschool-age children, a major concern is social participation. Kids in American society learn about the role of friends and the expectations associated with that role. Their understanding of this role provides a basis for evaluating their relationships with other children. As children begin to play in groups, maintaining access to the group becomes an issue. Children become concerned with issues of inclusion and exclusion—who is in the group and who is not. These issues remain important ones throughout childhood and into adolescence (Adler & Adler, 1995).

Peer groups reflect the desire of children to gain some control over the social environment and to use that control in concert with other children (Corsaro & Eder, 1995). Children become concerned with gaining control over adult authority, and they learn that a request or plea by several children is more likely to be granted. In elementary school, children develop a strong group identity, which is strengthened by minor rebellions against adult authority. Thorne (1993) observed that in one fourth-/fifth-grade classroom, most of the students had contraband—small objects such as toy cars and trucks, nail polish, and stuffed animals—which were prohibited by school rules. By keeping these items in desks and by displaying or exchanging them at key moments during class, the kids were displaying resistance, a form of nonconformity challenging the academic regime and rules in the classroom (McFarland, 2004). Both children and adolescents assert themselves by making fun of and mocking teachers and administrators. Peer groups play a major role in socializing young persons to gender role norms.

As children move through elementary school, they increasingly form groups that are homogeneous by gender. For instance, in one study, Thorne (1993) observed that there is a geography of gender in the school yard. Boys generally were

---

Unlike the child's family, peer groups in early and especially middle childhood (aged 6 to 10) are usually homogeneous in sex and age. A survey of 2,299 children in third through twelfth grade measured the extent to which they belonged to tightly knit peer groups, the size of such groups, and whether they were homogeneous by race and gender (Schrum & Creek, 1987). The proportion belonging to a group peaked in sixth grade and then declined. The size of peer groups declined steadily from third through twelfth grade. Boys' groups are generally larger than girls' groups (Rose & Rudolph, 2006). A study of third through eighth graders found, controlling for the number of boys and girls in each grade, substantial sex homogeneity in both boys' and girls' networks (Neal, 2010). Sex homophily was consistent from grades three through nine; significant homophiliy by race developed in seventh grade. Other research indicates that friendships of seventh- to twelfth-grade Black, Hispanic, and White students tend to be homogeneous by race (Quillian & Campbell, 2003).

Peer associations make a major contribution to the development of the child's identity. Children learn the role of friend in interactions with peers, contributing to greater differentiation of the self (Corsaro & Rizzo, 1988). Peer and other relationships found on the playing fields, whereas girls were concentrated in the areas closer to the building and in the jungle gyms. Children who violated these gender boundaries risked being teased or even ridiculed. Thorne identified several varieties of **borderwork,** which is "interaction across— yet interaction based on and even strengthening—gender boundaries" (1993, p. 64). One form of borderwork was the chase, which almost always involved a boy chasing a girl or vice versa. Another form was cooties, or treating an individual or group as contaminated, which also was often cross-gender; girls were often identified as the ultimate source of contamination, whereas boys typically were not. Finally, invasion occurred when a group of boys physically occupied the space that girls were using for some activity; Thorne never observed girls invading a boys' game. All of these activities involve the themes of gender and aggression—themes common to heterosexual relationships in American society. There is also the implicit message that boys and their activities are more important than girls and their activities.

In another study, Eder (1995) and her colleagues observed peer relationships in a middle school for 3 years. During the sixth, seventh, and eighth grades, young adolescents shift their focus from gender role norms to norms governing male-female relationships. Boys learn from other boys the "proper" view of girls; in some but not all groups, the prescribed view was that girls were objects of sexual conquest. Girls learn to view boys as potential participants in romantic relationships. Public teasing and ridicule of those who violate norms—common in elementary school—are replaced by gossip and exclusion from the group as sanctions for violations of group norms in middle school.

Eder (1995) also observed that the status hierarchy in the school generally reproduced the class structure of the wider community. Status was accorded to students based on popularity. One became popular by being visible. The most visible students were those on athletic teams and the cheerleader squad. Participating in these activities required money, as they were not funded by the school. Furthermore, the teams and cheerleaders relied on parents to transport them to games, giving an advantage to students who had one parent who did not work or parents whose jobs allowed them to take time off for such activities. Not surprisingly, the popular, visible students were those from middle-class families.

outside the family provide a basis for establishing independence; the child ceases to be exclusively involved in the roles of offspring, sibling, grandchild, and cousin. These alternate, nonfamilial identities may provide a basis for actively resisting parental socialization efforts (Stryker & Serpe, 1982). For example, a parent's attempt to enforce certain rules may be resisted by a child whose friends make fun of children who behave that way. As suggested in Box 3.2, children actively resist adult culture through peer interaction and talk (Kyratzis, 2004). Playing house may provide an occasion for mimicking a parent, using parentlike words and tone. It may also provide "mom" with the opportunity to be in charge, and decide which children are included and excluded from the game.

Although peer culture tends to be concerned with the present, it plays an important role in preparing children and adolescents for role transitions. An observational study of Italian preschoolers found that the transition to elementary school was a common topic of discussion and debate (Corsaro & Molinari, 2000).

School

Unlike the peer group, school is intentionally designed to socialize children. In the classroom, there is typically one adult and a group of children of similar age. There is a sharp status distinction between teacher and student. The teacher determines what skills he or she teaches and relies heavily on instrumental learning techniques, with such reinforcers as praise, blame, and privileges to shape student behavior (Gecas, 1990). School is the child's first experience with formal and public evaluation of performance. Every child's behavior and work is evaluated by the same standards, and the judgments are made public to others in the class as well as to parents.

We expect schools to teach reading, writing, and arithmetic, but they do much more than that. Teachers use the rewards at their disposal to reinforce certain personality traits, such as punctuality, perseverance, and tact. Schools teach children which selves are desirable and which are not. Thus, children learn a vocabulary that they are expected to use in evaluating themselves and others (Denzin, 1977). The traits chosen are those thought to facilitate social interaction throughout life in a particular culture or society. In this sense, schools civilize children.

A key feature of social life in the United States is making statements or "claims" about reality and supporting them with evidence. Each of us engages in such discourses many times each day. In legislative arenas and courtrooms, there are multiple perspectives, each with its claims and supporting arguments contending for adherents. Schools, especially public speaking and debate classes and clubs, are the settings in which youth learn and hone these skills (Fine, 2000).

Social comparison has an important influence on the behavior of schoolchildren. Because teachers make public evaluations of the children's work, each child can judge his or her performance relative to the performance of others. These comparisons are especially important to the child because of the homogeneity of the classroom group. Even if the teacher de-emphasizes a child's low score on a spelling test, the child interprets the performance as a poor one relative to those of classmates. A consistent performance will affect a child's image of self as a student.

An observational study of children in kindergarten, first, second, and fourth grades documented the development of social comparison in the classroom (Frey & Ruble, 1985). In kindergarten, comparisons were made to personal characteristics—for example, liking ice cream. Comparisons of performance increased sharply in first grade; at first, comparisons were blatant, but they became increasingly subtle in second and fourth grades.

Mass Media

In recent decades the mass media has become a very influential agent of socialization. Media portrayals—news articles, television programs, videos, films, internet sites—present information about every aspect of daily life and the world around us. These images shape our perception of people, places and events, and thus influence our attitudes toward these objects. The images also shape our *scripts*, our images of the people and behaviors that are appropriate in various types of relationships.

Media portrayals shape the child's image of self as male or female, as well as their expectations about and treatment of others based on gender (and of course, race and age). Older children and adolescents learn schemas and scripts for various types of relationships from watching familial, romantic, and work relationships unfold on the movie or television screen and on YouTube. For example, Ward and Friedman (2006) have shown that adolescents' attitudes and sexual behavior are associated with viewing sexual content on television. Prime-time television in particular portrays a heterosexual script that includes not only behavioral but cognitive and emotional guidelines for men and women in romantic relationships (Kim et al., 2007).

In the discussion of aggression we will summarize the correlational and experimental evidence linking exposure to portrayals of violence in the mass media with aggressive and violent behavior (see Chap. 11). There is also concern that viewing aggressive pornography contributes to violence against girls and women. Another concern is the link between frequent playing of violent video games and murder or mass murder. Anecdotal evidence suggests that some recent incidents in which many people died from gunfire were perpetrated by persons with extensive exposure to "shooter" video games.

Media have an especially powerful socializing effect because many children and adolescents are exposed to media content several hours per day. According to a survey of a nationally representative sample of children 6 and under, 75 percent watch TV, 32 percent watch videos, 16 percent use a computer, and 11 percent play video games (Rideout & Hamel, 2006). More than 40 percent of 2- to 6-year-olds spend two or more hours with screen media per day. The average number of hours per day spent in media activities by youth ages 8 to 18 are shown in Figure 3.1. Note that children 8 to 10 are exposed to media content almost 8 hours per day, while older children spend more than 11 with media.

PROCESSES OF SOCIALIZATION

How does socialization occur? We will examine three processes that are especially important: instrumental conditioning, observational learning, and internalization.

Instrumental Conditioning

When you got dressed this morning, chances are you put on a shirt or blouse, pants, a dress, or a skirt that had buttons, hooks, or zippers. When you were younger, learning how to master buttons, hooks, zippers, and shoelaces undoubtedly took considerable time, trial and error, and slow progress accompanied by praise from adults. You acquired these skills through **instrumental conditioning**, a process wherein a person learns what response to make in a situation in order to obtain a positive reinforcement or avoid a negative reinforcement. The person's behavior is instrumental in the sense that it determines whether he or she is rewarded or punished.

The most important process in the acquisition of many skills is a type of instrumental learning called *shaping* (Skinner, 1953, 1957). **Shaping** refers to learning in which an agent initially reinforces any behavior that remotely resembles the desired response and later requires increasing correspondence between the learner's behavior and the desired response before providing reinforcement. Shaping thus involves a series of successive approximations in which the learner's behavior comes closer and closer to resembling the specific response desired by the reinforcing agent.

In socialization, the degree of similarity between desired and observed responses required by the agent depends in part on the learner's past performance. In this sense, shaping is interactive in character. In teaching children to clean their rooms, parents initially reward them for picking up their toys. When children show they can do this consistently, parents may require that the toys be placed on certain shelves as the condition for a reward. Shaping is more likely to succeed if the level of performance required is consistent with the child's abilities. Thus, a 2-year-old may be praised

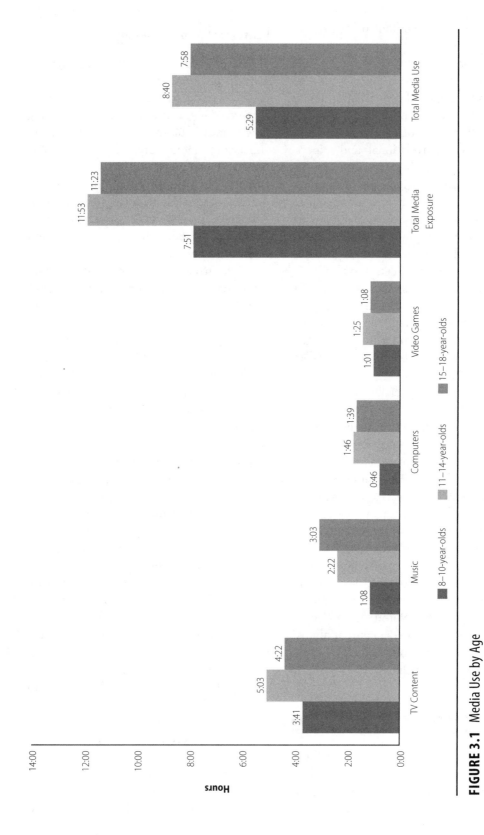

FIGURE 3.1 Media Use by Age

Source: Rideout, Foehr, & Roberts (2010). *Generation M2: Media in the Lives of 8- to 18-year-olds.* Menlo Park, CA: Kaiser Family Foundation (p. 9).

Shaping is a process through which many complex behaviors, such as playing the violin, are learned. Initially, the socializer (teacher or parent) rewards behavior that resembles the desired response. As learning progresses, greater correspondence between the behavior and the desired response is required to earn a reward, such as praise. © Bill Oxford/iStock

for drawing lines with crayons, whereas a 5-year-old may be expected to draw recognizable objects or figures.

Reinforcement Schedules. When shaping behavior, a socializing agent can use either positive reinforcement or negative reinforcement. Positive reinforcers are stimuli whose presentation strengthens the learner's response; positive reinforcers include food, candy, money, or high grades. Negative reinforcers are stimuli whose withdrawal strengthens the response, such as the removal of pain. (Shaw & Costanzo, 1982)

In everyday practice, it is rare for a learner to be reinforced each time the desired behavior is performed. Instead, reinforcement is given only some of the time. In fact, it is possible to structure when reinforcements are presented to the learner, using a reinforcement schedule.

There are several possible reinforcement schedules. The fixed-interval schedule in-

volves reinforcing the first correct response after a specified period has elapsed. This schedule produces the fewest correct responses per unit of time; if the learner is aware of the length of the interval, he or she will respond only at the beginning of the interval. It is interesting that many schools give examinations at fixed intervals, such as the middle and end of the semester; perhaps that is why many students study only just before an exam. The variable-interval schedule involves reinforcing the first correct response after a variable period. In this case, the individual cannot predict when reinforcement will occur, so he or she responds at a regular rate. Grading a course based on several surprise or "pop" quizzes uses this schedule.

The fixed-ratio schedule provides a reinforcement following a specified number of correct, nonreinforced responses. Paying a worker on a piece rate, such as 5 dollars for every three items produced, uses this pattern. If the reward is sufficient, the rate of behavior may be high. Finally, the variable-ratio schedule provides reinforcement after several non-rewarded responses, with the number of responses between reinforcements varying. This schedule typically produces the highest and most stable rates of response. An excellent illustration is the gambler, who will insert quarters in a slot machine for hours, receiving only occasional, random payoffs.

Punishment. By definition, **punishment** is the presentation of a painful or discomforting stimulus or the removal of a positive stimulus (by a socializing agent) that decreases the probability that the preceding behavior (by the learner) will occur. Punishment is one of the major child-rearing practices used by parents. The Gallup organization interviewed a nationally representative sample of parents in 1995 (Straus & Stewart, 1999; Straus & Field, 2003). The percentage of parents who reported using corporal punishment—pinching, slapping, spanking, or hitting—during the preceding year varied by the age of the child. The use of corporal punishment was reported by 94 percent of the parents of 3- and 4-year-olds; the prevalence declined steadily from age 5 to age 17. The use of psychological techniques—shouting, name-calling, threatening—was reported by more than 85 percent of parents of children of all ages. The results are displayed in Figure 3.2.

Punishment is obviously widely used in the United States, suggesting that our culture is tolerant of or encourages its use. As discussed earlier, corporal punishment was more commonly reported by African-American and low-income parents (Straus & Stewart, 1999), while the use of psychological techniques did not vary by race or other sociodemographic characteristics (Straus & Field, 2003).

So, does punishment work? Research indicates that it is effective in some circumstances but not in others. One aspect is timing. Punishment is most effective when it occurs in close proximity to the behavior. A verbal reprimand delivered as the child touched the toy was more effective than a prior warning or a reprimand following the action (Aronfreed & Reber, 1965). Also, the effectiveness may be limited to the situation in which it is given. Because punishment is usually administered by a particular person, it may be effective only when that person is present. This probably accounts for the fact that when their parents are absent, children may engage in activities that their parents earlier had punished (Parke, 1969, 1970).

Another factor in the effectiveness of punishments is whether they are accompanied by a reason (Parke, 1969). Providing a reason allows the child to generalize the prohibition to a class of acts and situations. Yelling "No!" as a child reaches out to touch the stove may suppress that behavior. Telling

FIGURE 3.2 Percentage of Parents Who Use Physical Punishment and Psychological Punishment

The Gallup Organization interviewed a representative sample of 991 parents in 1995. Each parent was asked whether and how often he or she used physical punishment (spanked the bottom; slapped hand, arm, or leg; pinched; shook; hit on the bottom with an object; or slapped head, face, or ears) and psychological punishment (shouted, yelled, or screamed; threatened to hit or spank; swore or cursed; threatened to kick out of the house; or called names, such as dumb or lazy). Most parents reported using both types. The use of physical punishment peaked with 4-year-old children and then declined steadily through age 17. By contrast, the use of psychological punishment was reported to be as common with 17-year-olds as with 1-year-olds (90 percent).

Source: Straus and Stewart, 1999; Straus and Field, 2003.

the child not to touch it because it is "hot" enables him or her to learn to avoid hot objects as a group. Finally, consistency between the reprimands given by parents and their own behavior makes punishment more effective than if parents do not practice what they preach (Mischel & Liebert, 1966).

What about the long-term consequences of punishment? Clearly, parents and caregivers need to control children's behavior. At the same time, they need to recognize that corporal punishment may be associated with subsequent antisocial behavior by children. Punishment should focus on the behavior and not the child, and should be balanced by praise and rewards.

Self-Reinforcement and Self-Efficacy. Children learn hundreds, if not thousands, of behaviors through instrumental learning. The performance of some of these behaviors will remain **extrinsically motivated**—that is, they are dependent on whether someone else will reward appropriate behaviors or punish inappropriate ones. However, the performance of other activities becomes **intrinsically motivated**—that is, performed in order to achieve an internal state that the individual finds rewarding (Deci, 1975). Research has demonstrated that external rewards do not always improve performance. Providing a reward for a behavior that is intrinsically motivated, such as drawing, may actually reduce the frequency or quality of the activity (Lepper, Greene, & Nisbett, 1973).

Closely related to the concept of intrinsic motivation is **self-reinforcement**. As children are socialized, they learn not only specific behaviors but also performance standards. Children learn not only to write but to write neatly. These standards become part of the self; having learned them, the child uses them to judge his or her own behavior and thus becomes capable of self-reinforcement (Bandura, 1982b). The child who has drawn a house and comes running up to her father with a big smile, saying, "Look what I drew," has already judged the drawing as a good one. If her father agrees, her standards and self-evaluation are confirmed.

Successful experiences with an activity over time create a sense of competence at the activity, or self-efficacy (Bandura, 1982b). This, in turn, makes the individual more likely to seek opportunities to engage in that behavior. The greater one's sense of self-efficacy, the more effort one will expend at a task and the greater one's persistence in the face of difficulty. For instance, a young girl who perceives herself as a good basketball player is more likely to try out for a team. Conversely, experiences of failure to perform a task properly, or of the failure of the performance to produce the expected results, create the perception that one is not efficacious. Perceived lack of efficacy is likely to lead to avoidance of the task. A boy who perceives himself as poor at spelling will probably not enter the school spelling bee.

Observational Learning

Children love to play dress-up. Girls put on skirts, step into high-heeled shoes, and totter around the room; boys put on sport coats and drape ties around their necks. Through observing adults, children have learned the patterns of appropriate dress in their society. Similarly, children often learn interactive rituals, such as shaking hands or waving goodbye, by watching others perform the behavior and then doing it on their own.

Observational learning, or modeling, refers to the acquisition of behavior based on the observation of another person's behavior and of its consequences for that person (Shaw & Costanzo, 1982). Many behaviors and skills are learned this way. By watching another person (the model) perform skilled actions, a child can increase his or her own skills. The major advantage of modeling is its greater efficiency compared with trial-and-error learning.

Does observational learning lead directly to the performance of the learned behavior? No; research has shown that there is a difference between learning a behavior and in more physical and relational aggression than girls (Lansford et al., 2012). By age 4, the games typically played by boys and girls differ; groups of girls play house, enacting familial roles, whereas groups of boys play space rangers. In middle childhood, gender-segregated play appears to be almost universal (Edwards, Knoche, & Kumru, 2001).

We noted early in this chapter the importance of "nature" in understanding children's development. Research involving almost 4,000 twin and non-twin sibling pairs (Iervolino, Hines, Golombok, Rust, & Plomin, 2005) identified both genetic and shared environmental (family) influences on sex-typed behavior (play activities) for both boys and girls. In related research, Hines and colleagues (2002) measured women's blood levels of testosterone during pregnancy, and gender-role behaviors when the children were 3½ years old. There was a positive relationship between testosterone and male-typed behavior among girls, but not among boys.

Parents are an important influence on the learning of **gender role**—the behavioral expectations associated with one's gender. Children learn gender-appropriate behaviors by observing their parents' interaction. Children also learn by interacting with parents, who reward behavior consistent with their expectations and punish behavior inconsistent with them. The child's earliest experiences relating to members of the other gender occur in interaction with the opposite-gender parent. A woman may be more likely to develop the ability to have warm, psychologically intimate relationships with men if her relationship with her father was of this type (Appleton, 1981).

Obviously, boys are not all alike in our society, and neither are girls. The specific behaviors and characteristics that the child is taught depend partly on the gender role expectations held by the parents. These in turn depend on the network of extended family—grandparents, aunts and uncles, and other relatives—and friends of the family. The expectations held by these people are influenced by the institutions to which they belong, such as churches and work organizations (Stryker & Serpe, 1982). With regard to religion, research suggests that the differences among denominations in socialization techniques and in outcomes such as gender role attitudes have declined in recent decades (Alwin, 1986). The data suggest that church attendance is more influential than the denomination to which one belongs.

Gender role definitions vary by culture. Some research suggests that Latino families teach more traditional expectations for behavior of boys and girls compared to other groups in U.S. society. These families also encourage a strong sense of family obligation, which has benefits but may tie offspring physically to the family, limiting educational and occupational mobility (Crosnoe & Cavanagh, 2010). Other research finds that as education and female labor-force participation increase, families have more egalitarian views of behavior and decision making (Ginorio, Gutierrez, Cauce, & Acosta, 1995). It is important to remember that "Latino" encompasses people from several different cultural backgrounds, including Mexican-American, Puerto Rican, and Cuban. Asian cultures are patriarchal, and parents may socialize female children to restrictive norms designed to serve the family rather than express their individuality (Root, 1995). Again, "Asian" includes persons of Chinese, Taiwanese, Japanese, Korean, and Vietnamese descent; these cultures may differ in the prevailing gender role definitions.

Schools also teach gender roles. Teachers may reward appropriate gender role behavior. A more subtle influence on socialization is the content of the stories that are

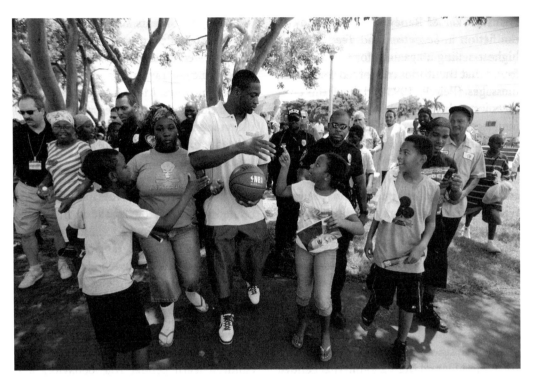

Children and adolescents learn gender-role expectations and behavior through interaction with adults. Meeting their hero, basketball player Dwyane Wade, may have a lifelong impact on these boys/girls/ youth. © AP Photo/J. Pat Carter

read and told in preschool and first-grade classes. Many of these stories portray men and women as different. In the past, men were depicted as rulers, adventurers, and explorers; women were wives (Weitzman, Eifler, Hokada, & Ross, 1972). A study of award-winning books for children published from 1995 to 1999 found men and women equally represented as main characters, but men played a greater variety of roles and were seldom shown engaging in child care, shopping, or housework (Gooden & Gooden, 2001). An analysis of 200 children's picture books found that males were title characters twice as often as females, and females were more often portrayed as nurturing, in indoor scenes, and appeared to have no paid employment (Hamilton et al., 2006). A study of illustrations in a sample of 56 contemporaneous coloring books found that males were more

active, and more likely to be portrayed as adults, and as superheroes (Fitzpatrick & McPherson, 2010).

A major influence on gender role socialization is the mass media. Media provide images of masculinity and femininity that can readily be imitated. Researchers analyzing the contents of television programs, television advertising, feature films, and other media report that portrayals of men and women and girls and boys reinforce traditional definitions of gender roles. A content analysis of 175 episodes of 41 animated TV series found that male characters were portrayed as independent, athletic, ambitious, and aggressive, whereas female characters were shown as dependent, emotional, domestic, and romantic (Thompson & Zerbinos, 1995). A content analysis of 160 hours of children's cartoons found that superheroes are defined in masculine

The next stage of language development is highlighted by the occurrence of private speech, in which children talk to themselves, often for extended periods. Private speech begins at about age 3, increases in frequency until age 5, and disappears by about age 7. Such private talk serves three functions. First, it contributes to the child's developing sense of self. Private speech is addressed to the self as object, and it often includes the application of meanings to the self, such as "I'm a girl." Second, private speech helps the child develop an awareness of the environment. It often consists of naming aspects of the physical and social environment. The repeated use of these names solidifies the child's understanding of the environment. Children also often engage in appropriate actions as they speak, reflecting their developing awareness of the social meanings of objects and persons. Thus, a child may label a doll a "baby" and dress it and feed it. Third, children engage in more private speech during novel or open-ended tasks than during tasks where the teacher or parent tells them what to do (Kyjonkova & Lacinova, 2010), or self-selected activity (Winsler, Carlton & Barry, 2000), suggesting that its use facilitates self-regulation of behavior by the child.

Gradually, the child begins to engage in dialogues, either with others or with the self. These conversations reflect the ability to adopt a second perspective. Thus, by age 6, when one child wants a toy that another child is using, the first child frequently offers to trade. She knows that the second child will be upset if she merely takes the toy. This movement away from a self-centered view also may reflect maturational changes. Dialogue requires that the child's own speech meshes with that of another.

Language is important in the socialization of gender. A meta-analysis of observational studies of parents' use of language in interaction with their children identified several differences between mothers and fathers in types of communication. For example, mothers were more supportive and less directive compared to fathers. Moreover, mothers and fathers differed in the way they talked to sons and to daughters (Leaper, Anderson, & Sanders, 1998). Thus children are socialized to gender differences in language use as they observe and interact with their parents/caregivers.

Language socialization involves much more than learning to talk. It also involves learning to think, how to behave, and how to feel and express feelings (Garrett & Baquedano-Lopez, 2002). As the interpretive perspective suggests, language learning occurs in the routine, everyday interaction of children and adults. It is responsive to and reflects local values, patterns of social organization, and (sub)cultural features.

Cognitive Competence. Children must develop the ability to represent in their own minds the features of the world around them. This capacity to represent reality mentally is closely related to the development of language.

The child's basic tasks are to learn the regularities of the physical and social environment and to store past experience in a form that can be used in current situations. In a complex society, there are so many physical objects, animals, and people that it is not possible for a child (or an adult) to remember each as a distinct entity. Things must be categorized into inclusive groupings, such as dogs, houses, or girls. A category of objects and the cognitions that the individual has about members of that category (for example, "dog") makes up a schema. Collectively, our schemas allow us to make sense of the world around us.

Young children must learn schemas (see Chap. 1). Learning language is an essential part of the process, because language provides the names around which schemas can develop. It is noteworthy that the first words that children produce are usually nouns that name objects in the child's environment. At first, the child uses a few very general schemas. Some children learn the word *dog* at 12 to 14 months and then apply it to all animals—to dogs, cats, birds, and cows. Only with maturation and experience does the child develop the abstract schema "animals" and learn to discriminate between dogs and cats.

Researchers can study the ability to use schemas by asking children to sort objects, pictures, or words into groups. Young children (aged 6 to 8) rely on visual features, such as color or word length, and sort objects into numerous categories. Older children (aged 10 to 12) increasingly use functional or superordinate categories, such as foods, and sort objects into fewer groups (Olver, 1961; Rigney, 1962). With age, children become increasingly adept at classifying diverse objects and treating them as equivalent.

These skills are very important in social interaction. Only by having the ability to group objects, persons, and situations can one determine how to behave toward them. Person schemas and their associated meanings are especially important to smooth interaction. Even very young children differentiate people by age (Lewis & Brooks-Gunn, 1979). By about 2 years of age, children correctly differentiate babies and adults when shown photographs. By about 5, children employ four categories: little children, big children, parents (aged 13 to 40), and grandparents (aged 40-plus).

As children learn to group objects into meaningful schemas, they learn not only the categories but also how others feel about such categories. Children learn not only that Catholics are people who believe in the Trinity of Father, Son, and Holy Spirit, but also whether their parents like or dislike Catholics. Thus, children acquire positive and negative attitudes toward the wide range of social objects they come to recognize. The particular schemas and evaluations that children learn are influenced by the social class, religious, ethnic, and other subcultural groupings to which those who socialize them belong.

Moral Development

In this section, we discuss moral development in children and adults. Specifically, we focus on the acquisition of knowledge of social rules and on the process through which children become capable of making moral judgments.

Knowledge of Social Rules. To interact effectively with others, people must learn the social rules that govern interaction and in general adhere to them. Beliefs about which behaviors are acceptable and which are unacceptable for specific persons in specific situations are termed **norms**. Without norms, coordinated activity would be very difficult, and we would find it hard or impossible to achieve our goals. Therefore, each group, organization, and society develops rules governing behavior.

Early in life, an American child learns to say "Please," a French child "S'il vous plait," and a Serbian child "Molim te." In every case, the child is learning the value of conforming to arbitrary norms governing requests. Learning language trains the child to conform to linguistic norms and serves as a model for the learning of other norms. Gradually, through instrumental and observational learning, the child learns the generality of the relationship between conformity to norms and the ability to interact smoothly with others and achieve one's own goals.

What influences which norms children will learn? The general culture is one influence. All American children learn to cover parts of the body with clothing in public. The position of the family within the society is another influence. Parental expectations reflect social class, religion, and ethnicity. Thus, the norms that children are taught vary from one family to another. Interestingly, parents often hold norms that they apply distinctively to their own children. Mothers and fathers expect certain behaviors of their own sons or daughters but may have different expectations for other people's children (Elkin & Handel, 1989). For instance, they may expect their own children to be more polite than other children in interaction with adults. Parental expectations are not constant over time; they change as the child grows older. Parents expect greater politeness from a 10-year-old than from a 5-year-old. Finally, parents adjust their expectations to the particular child. They consider the child's level of ability and experiences relative to other children; they expect better performance in school from a child who has done well in the past than from one who has had problems in school. In all of these ways, each child is being socialized to a somewhat different set of norms. The outcome is a young person who is both similar to most others from the same social background and unique in certain ways.

When children begin to engage in cooperative play at about 4 years of age, they begin to experience normative pressure from peers. The expectations of age-mates differ in two important ways from those of parents. First, children bring different norms from their separate families and, therefore, introduce new expectations. Thus, through their peers, children first become aware there are other ways of behaving. In some cases, peers' expectations conflict with those of parents. For example, many parents do not allow their children to play with toy guns, knives, or swords. Through

involvement with their peers, children may become aware that other children routinely play with such toys. As a result, some children will experience normative conflict and discover the need to develop strategies for resolving such conflicts.

A second way that peer norms differ from parental norms is that the former reflect a child's perspective (Elkin & Handel, 1989). Many parental expectations are oriented toward socializing the child for adult roles. Children react to each other as children and are not concerned with long-term outcomes. Thus, peers encourage impulsive, spontaneous behavior rather than behavior directed toward long-term goals. Peer norms emphasize participation in group activities, whereas parental norms may emphasize homework and other educational activities that may contribute to academic achievement.

When children enter school, they are exposed to a third major socializing agent—the teacher. In school, children are exposed to universalistic rules—norms that apply equally to all children. The teacher is much less likely than the parents to make allowances for the unique characteristics of the individual; children must learn to wait their

At school, children get their first exposure to universal norms—behavioral expectations that are the same for everyone. Although parents and friends treat the child as an individual, teachers are less likely to do so. © monkeybusinessimages/iStock

turn, to control impulsive and spontaneous behavior, and to work without a great deal of supervision and support. In this regard, the school is the first of many settings where the individual is treated primarily as a member of the group rather than as a unique individual. As noted in Box 3.2, children may engage in resistance in response to the authority structure in a school.

Thus, school is the setting in which children are first exposed to universalistic norms and the regular use of symbolic rewards, such as grades. Such settings become increasingly common in adolescence and adulthood, in contrast with the individualized character of familial settings.

Moral Judgment. We not only learn the norms of our social groups, we also develop the ability to evaluate behavior in specific situations by applying certain standards. The process through which children become capable of making moral judgments is termed **moral development**. It involves two components: (1) the reasons one adheres to social rules and (2) the bases used to evaluate actions by self or others as good or bad.

How do children evaluate acts as good or bad? One of the first people to study this question in detail was Piaget, the famous Swiss developmental psychologist. Piaget read a child stories in which the central character performed an act that violated social rules. In one story, for example, a young girl, contrary to rules, was playing with scissors and made a hole in her dress. Piaget asked the children to evaluate the behaviors of the characters (that is, to indicate which characters were naughtier) and then to explain their reasons for these judgments. Based on this work, Piaget concluded there were three bases for moral judgments: amount of harm/benefit, actor's intentions, and the application of agreed-upon rules or norms (Piaget, 1965).

Kohlberg (1969) extended Piaget's work by analyzing the reasoning by which people reach moral judgments. He uses stories involving conflict between human needs and social norms or laws. Here is an example:

In Europe, a woman was near death from cancer. One drug might save her, a form of radium that a druggist in the same town had recently discovered. The druggist was charging $2,000, ten times what the drug cost him to make. The sick woman's husband, Heinz, went to everyone he knew to borrow money, but he could only get together about half of what it cost. He told the druggist that his wife was dying and asked him to sell it cheaper or let him pay later. But the druggist said no. The husband got desperate and broke into the man's store to steal the drug for his wife (Kohlberg, 1969).

Respondents are then asked, "Should Heinz have done that? Was Heinz right or wrong? What obligations did Heinz and the druggist have? Should Heinz be punished?"

Kohlberg proposes a developmental model with three levels of moral reasoning, each level involving two stages. This model is summarized in Table 3.3. Kohlberg argues that the progression from stage 1 to stage 6 is a standard or universal one, and that all children begin at stage 1 and progress through the stages in order. Most adults reason at stages 3 or 4. Few people reach stages 5 or 6. Several studies have shown that such a progression does occur (Kuhn, Langer, Kohlberg, & Haan, 1977). If the progression is universal, children from different cultures should pass through the same stages in the same order. Again, data suggest that they do (White, Bushnell, & Regnemer, 1978). On the basis of such evidence, Kohlberg claims that this progression is the natural human pattern of moral development. He also believes that attaining higher levels is better or more desirable.

Kohlberg's model is an impressive attempt to specify a universal model of moral

Griffin, 1979) examined how maternal emphasis on self-direction affected the young person's grades in school, choice of curriculum, and participation in extracurricular activities. The researchers reasoned that parents who valued self-direction would encourage their children to take college-preparatory courses, because a college education is a prerequisite to jobs that provide high levels of autonomy. Similarly, they expected mothers who valued self-direction to encourage extracurricular activities, because such activities provide opportunities to develop interpersonal skills. The researchers did not expect differences in grades. The results confirmed all three predictions. Thus, parents who value particular traits in their children do encourage activities that they believe are likely to produce those traits. We met Kimberly in the opening essay; her mother started her in piano lessons in fourth grade because she valued music, and that gave her the skills required when the band director needed a percussionist.

By age 16, many adolescents have expectations about jobs they will hold as adults. A longitudinal study in the United Kingdom found that these expectations at 16 were influenced by both parents and teachers; these expectations, in conjunction with the level of education completed, were associated with adult occupational attainment at ages 23, 33, and 42 (Brown, Sessions, & Taylor, 2004). Thus, adolescents' expectations provide a basis for educational and career choices.

Occupational choices are associated with gender and sexual orientation in the United States, according to data from 9,000 men and women ages 18 to 56. Heterosexual males were significantly more likely to prefer such jobs as athlete, auto mechanic, electrician, high school coach, and police officer. Gay men's preferences were more likely to include actor, artist, beautician, nurse, and novelist. Heterosexual females were more likely to prefer accountant, beautician, and CEO (Ellis & Ratnasingam, 2006).

THE LIFE COURSE

Socialization continues throughout one's life. Maturation and social learning, parents, peers and media, and social structural positon continue to influence development as a social actor. In adulthood, prior experience and the cultural capital (education, wealth, and status) derived from it become important, as do historical events. A viewpoint that integrates all of these is the life-course perspective. First, an introduction.

"I still can't get over Liz," said Megan. "I sat next to her in almost every class for 3 years, and still, I hardly recognized her. Put on some weight since high school, and dyed her hair. But mostly it was the defeated look on her face. When she and Hank announced they were getting married, they were the happiest couple ever. But that lasted long enough for a baby. Then there were years of underpaid jobs. She works part-time in sporting goods at Sears now. Had to take that job when her real estate work collapsed in the recession."

Jim had stopped listening. How could he get excited about Megan's Lincoln High School reunion and people he'd never met? But Megan's mind kept racing. A lot had happened in 25 years.

John—Still larger than life. Football coach at the old school, and assistant principal too. Must be a fantastic model for the tough kids he works with. That scholarship to Indiana was the break he needed.

José—Hard to believe he's in a mental hospital! He started okay as an engineer.

Severely burned in a helicopter crash, and then hooked on painkillers. Just fell apart. And we voted him Most Likely to Succeed.

Precious—Thinking about a career in politics. She didn't start college until her last kid entered school. Now she's an urban planner in the mayor's office. Couldn't stop saying how she feels like a totally new person.

Tom—Head nurse at Westside Hospital's emergency ward. Quite a surprise. Last I heard, he was a car salesman. Started his nursing career at 28. Got the idea while lying in the hospital for three months after a car accident.

Maria—Right on that one, voting her Most Ambitious. Finished Yale Law, clerked for the New York Supreme Court, and just promoted to senior partner with Kennedy, Sanchez and Ortega. Raised two kids at the same time. Having a husband who writes novels at home made life easier. Says she was lucky things were opening up for women just when she came along.

Megan's reminiscences show how different lives can be—and how unpredictable. When we think about people like Liz or José or Tom, change seems to be the rule. There is change throughout life for all of us. But there is continuity too. Maria's string of accomplishments is based on her continuing ambition, hard work, and competence. John is back at Lincoln High—once a football hero, now the football coach. Even José had started on the predicted path to success before his tragic helicopter crash.

As adults, each of us will experience a life characterized both by continuity and by change. This section examines the **life course**—the individual's progression through a series of age-linked social roles embedded in social institutions (Elder & O'Rand, 1995), and the important influences that shape the life course that one experiences. Our examination of the life course is organized around three broad questions:

1. What are the major components of the life course?
2. What are the major influences on progression through the life course? That is, what causes people's careers to follow the paths they do?
3. In what ways do historical trends and events modify the typical life-course pattern?

Components of the Life Course

Lives are too complex to study in all their aspects. Consequently, we will focus on the three main components of the life course: (1) careers, (2) identity and self-esteem, and (3) stress and satisfaction. By examining these components, we can trace the continuities and changes that occur in what we do through the life course.

Careers. A **career** is a sequence of roles— each with its own set of activities—that a person enacts during his or her lifetime. Our most important careers are in three major social domains: family and friends, education, and work. The idea of a career comes from the work world, where it refers to the sequence of jobs held. Liz's work career, for example, consisted of a sequence of jobs as waitress, checkout clerk, clothing sales, real estate agent, and sporting-goods sales.

The careers of one person differ from those of another in three ways—in the roles that make up the careers, the order in which the roles are performed, and the timing and duration of role-related activities. For example, one woman's family career may consist of roles as infant, child, adolescent, spouse, parent, grandparent, and widow. Another woman's family career may include roles as stepsister and divorcée but exclude the parent role. A man's career might include the roles of infant, child, adolescent, partner, and uncle. The order of roles also may vary. "Parent" before "spouse" has very different consequences from "spouse" before "parent." Furthermore, the timing of career events is important. Having a first child at 36 has different life consequences than having a first child at 18. Research indicates that marrying before age 23 is strongly associated with returning to school as an adult (Hostetler, Sweet, & Moen, 2007). Finally, the duration of enacting a role may vary. For example, some couples end their marriages before the wedding champagne has gone flat, whereas others go on to celebrate their golden wedding anniversary.

Societies provide structured career paths that shape the options available to individuals. The cultural norms, social expectations, and laws that organize life in a society make various career options more or less attractive, accessible, and necessary. In the United States, for example, educational careers are socially structured so that virtually everyone attends kindergarten, elementary school, and at least a few years of high school. Thereafter, educational options are more diverse—night school, technical and vocational school, apprenticeship, community college, university, and so on. But individual choice among these options is also socially constrained. The norms and expectations of our families and peer groups strongly influence our educational careers; so do the economic resources available to us.

Events in the family affect the child's/adolescent's educational career, via linkages between adults and child(ren). Changes in family structure (exit or entry of mother/stepmother or father/stepfather) is a

Some parents are able to blend work roles and family roles by working at home. As further advances occur in telecommunications, more women and men may choose this option. However, some major companies have barred employees from working off-site. © Fertnig/iStock

stressor that affects the child's attachment to school and GPA (Heard, 2007). The timing of the event matters; changes occurring at age 6 or younger have greater impact than changes from age 7 to adolescence. Duration also matters; the number of years spent in a mother-stepfather or single-parent (mother or father) home is negatively related to GPA in grades 7 through 11.

A person's total life course consists of intertwined careers in the worlds of work, family, and education (Elder, 1975). The shape of the life course derives from the contents of these careers, from the way they mesh with one another, and from their interweaving with those of family members. Sally's classmates, Maria and Precious, enacted similar career roles: Both finished college, held full-time jobs, married, and raised children. Yet the courses of their lives were very different. Maria juggled these roles simultaneously, helped by a husband who was able to work at home. Precious waited until her children were attending school before continuing her education and then adding an occupational role. The different content, order, timing, and duration of intertwining careers make each person's life course unique.

Why and when do people move? A rarely studied phenomenon is the housing or residential career. A person may move upward—into a larger, more expensive, or single-family residence—or downward—into a smaller, lower-quality, or multi-family dwelling. This residential career is interwoven with educational, family, and occupational careers. In fact, a move is usually associated with events in these other realms. With regard to family careers, entering cohabitation or marriage often involves a move up for one or both partners; a separation or divorce often involves moves down. Comparing married and cohabiting couples, couples who divorced experienced a larger drop in housing quality (Feijten & van Ham, 2010).

Identities and Self-Esteem. As we engage in career roles, we observe our own performances and other people's reactions to us. Using these observations, we construct role identities—conceptions of the self in specific roles. The role identities available to us depend on the career paths we are following. When Liz's work in real estate collapsed, she got a job in sales at Sears; she was qualified to sell sporting goods because of her prior work experience.

As we will see in Chapter 4, identities are negotiated. To become a parent, one must negotiate with a partner, or with persons representing alternative paths (artificial insemination, surrogates, adoption) to parenthood. Many gay men see the identity

of prospective father as incompatible with the identity of gay man. However, some gay men are fathers. Interviews focused on how this identity change occurred; consideration by a man of parenthood was triggered by caring for a child, meeting a gay or lesbian parent, or contact with an adoption agency (Berkowitz & Marsiglio, 2007). Adoption of the identity was the product of negotiations with intimate partners, birth mothers, lawyers, and other agents of organizations associated with reproduction.

As we enact major roles, especially familial and occupational roles, we evaluate our performances and thereby gain or lose self-esteem—one's sense of how good and worthy one is. Self-esteem is influenced by one's achievements; Maria has high self-esteem as a consequence of being the first in her family to earn a law degree, and a senior partner in a prestigious law firm. Self-esteem is also influenced by the feedback one receives from others.

Identities and self-esteem are crucial guides to behavior, as discussed in Chapter 4. We therefore consider identities and self-esteem as the second component of the life course.

Stress and Satisfaction. Performing career activities often produces positive feelings, such as satisfaction, and negative feelings, including stress. These feelings reflect how we experience the quality of our lives. Thus, stress and satisfaction are the third component of the life course.

An important influence on the amount of stress or satisfaction experienced by a partner in a dual-earner relationship is the balance between marital and work roles. A study of dual-earner couples found that couples who shared in making decisions and in which both spent time doing household or housekeeping tasks experienced equity (see Chap. 14) (Bartley, Blanton, & Gilliard, 2005). Couples in which one person exerted should marry? Age is the primary criterion that every known society uses to assign people to such activities and roles (Riley, 1987). Throughout life, individuals move through a sequence of age-graded social roles. Each role consists of a set of expected behaviors, opportunities, and constraints. Movement through these roles shapes the course of life.

Each society prescribes a customary sequence of age-graded activities and roles. In American society, many people expect a young person to finish school before he or she enters a long-term relationship. Many people expect a person to marry before she or he has or adopts a child. There are also expectations about the ages at which these role transitions should occur. These expectations vary by race and ethnicity; Hispanic adolescent girls expect to marry and have a first child at younger ages (22, 23) than Whites (23, 24) or Blacks (24, 24) (East, 1998). These age norms serve as a basis for planning, as prods to action, and as brakes against moving too quickly (Neugarten & Datan, 1973).

Pressure to make the expected transitions between roles at the appropriate times means that the life course consists of a series of normative life stages. A **normative life stage** is a discrete period in the life course during which individuals are expected to perform the set of activities associated with a distinct age-related role. The order of the stages is prescribed, and people try to shape their own lives to fit socially approved career paths. Moreover, people perceive deviations from expected career paths as undesirable.

Not everyone experiences major transitions in the socially approved progression. Consider the transition to adulthood; the normative order of events is leaving school, performing military service, getting a job, and getting married. Analyzing data about the high school class of 1972 collected be-

Violating the age norms associated with a major transition, such as the transition to parenthood, may have lasting consequences. Having a baby at age 16 may force a young woman to leave school and limit her to a succession of poorly paid jobs. © Ian Hooton/Science Photo Library/Corbis

tween 1972 and 1980, researchers found that half of the men and women experienced a sequence that violated this "normal" path (Rindfuss, Swicegood, & Rosenfeld, 1987). Common violations included entering military service before one finished school and returning to school after a period of full-time employment.

In some cases, violating the age norms associated with a transition has lasting consequences. The transition to marriage is expected to occur between the ages of 19 and 25. Research consistently finds that making this transition earlier than usual has long-term effects on marital as well as occupational careers. A survey of 63,000 adults allowed researchers to compare men who married as adolescents with men of similar age who married as adults (Teti, Lamb, & Elster, 1987). Because the sample included people of all ages, the researchers could study the careers of men who married 20, 30, and 40 years earlier. Men who married as adolescents completed fewer years of education, held lower-status jobs, and earned less income. Furthermore, the marriages of those who married early were less stable. These effects were evident 40 years after marriage. Early marriage has similar effects on women. Women who marry before age 20 experience reduced educational and occupational attainment, and are more likely to get divorced (Teti & Lamb, 1989).

Movement from one life stage to another involves a **normative transition**—socially expected changes made by all or most members of a defined population (Cowan, 1991). Although most members undergo this institutional passage, each individual's experience of it may be different, reflecting his or her past experience. Normative transitions are often marked by a ceremony, such as a bar mitzvah, graduation, commitment ceremony, wedding, baby shower, or retirement party. But the actual transition is a process that may occur over a period of weeks or months. This process involves both a restructuring of the person's cognitive and emotional makeup and of his or her social relationships.

Transitions from one life stage to another influence a person in three ways. First, they change the roles available for building identities. The transition to adulthood brings major changes in roles. Those who marry or have their first child begin to view themselves as spouses and parents, responsible for others. Second, transitions modify the privileges and responsibilities of persons. Age largely determines whether we can legally drive a car, be employed full-time, serve in the military, or retire. Third, role transitions change the nature of socialization experiences. The content of socialization shifts from teaching basic values and motivations in childhood, to developing skills in adolescence, to transmitting role-related norms for behavior in adulthood (Lutfey & Mortimer, 2003). The power differences between socializee and socializing agents also diminish as we age and move into higher education and occupational organizations. As a result, adults are more able to resist socialization than children (Mortimer & Simmons, 1978).

Historical Trends and Events. Recall that Megan's classmate Maria attributed her rapid rise to senior law partner to lucky historical timing. Maria applied to Yale Law School shortly after the barriers to women had been broken, and she sought a job just when affirmative action came into vogue at the major law firms. Megan's's friend Liz attributed her setback as a real estate broker to an economic recession coupled with high interest rates that crippled the housing market. As the experiences of Maria and Liz illustrate, historical trends and events are another major influence on the life course. The lives of individuals are shaped by trends that extend across historical periods (such as increasing equality of the sexes and improved nutrition) and by events that occur at particular points in history (such as recessions, wars, earthquakes, and tsunamis).

Birth Cohorts. To aid in understanding how historical events and trends influence the life courses of individuals, social scientists have developed the concept of cohorts (Ryder, 1965). A **birth cohort** is a group of people who were born during the same period. The period could be 1 year or several years, depending on the issue under study. What is most important about a birth cohort is that its members are all approximately the same age when they encounter particular historical events. The birth cohort of 1970 graduated from college about 1992, the beginning of a decade of sustained economic growth. Most of the graduates got good jobs and experienced several years of growth in their average annual household income (www.demos.org/data-byte/changes-average-annual). Between 1990 and 2000, incomes grew between 10 and 28 percent. This growth facilitated establishing relationships and families and purchasing homes. In contrast, the cohort of 1980 graduated about 2002, the beginning of a decade of economic shocks—9/11, major corporate bankruptcies, and the recession of 2008. During that decade average annual household incomes declined between 5 and 15 percent.

A person's membership in a specific birth cohort locates that person historically in two ways. First, it points to the trends and events the person is likely to have encountered. Second, it indicates approximately where an individual is located in the sequence of normative life stages when historical events occur. Life stage location is crucial because historical events or trends have different impacts on individuals who are in different life stages.

To illustrate, consider the effects of the economic collapse of several large corporations in 2001 and 2002. Enron and Arthur Andersen virtually collapsed; several other firms went out of business; and K-Mart, Tyco, and others downsized. Tens of thousands of workers and managers ages 30 to 60 were laid off. Some people in their 50s found it impossible to get new jobs, perhaps due to age discrimination, and experienced prolonged unemployment. Some persons in their 30s and 40s returned to school and subsequently entered new fields. Workers who kept their jobs were left with insecurity and increased workloads. Persons just finishing college—the birth cohort of 1980—found fewer employment opportunities than those who graduated in 1995. Of course, not all members of a cohort experience historical events in the same way. Members of the class of 2002 who majored in liberal arts faced more limited opportunities than those earning professional degrees.

Placement in a birth cohort also affects access to opportunities. Members of large birth cohorts, for example, are likely to be disadvantaged throughout life. They begin their education in overpopulated classrooms. They then must compete for scarce openings in professional schools and crowded job markets. As they age, they face reduced retirement benefits because their numbers threaten to overwhelm the Social Security system. Table 3.4 presents examples of how the same historical events affect members of different cohorts in distinct ways. These historically different experiences mold the unique values, ideologies, personalities, and behavior patterns that characterize each cohort through the life course. Within each cohort, there are differences too. For example, the wars in Iraq and Afghanistan led to a father's or mother's absence for some children but not for others.

Cohorts and Social Change. Due to the differences in their experiences, each birth cohort ages in a unique way. Each cohort has its own set of collective experiences and opportunities. As a result, cohorts differ in their career patterns, attitudes, values, and self-concepts. As cohorts age, they succeed one another in filling the social positions in the family and in political, economic, and cultural institutions. Power is transferred from members of older cohorts with their historically based outlooks to members of younger cohorts with different outlooks. In this way, the succession of cohorts produces social change. It also causes intergenerational conflict about issues on which successive cohorts disagree (Elder, 1975).

Occasionally, a major event or trend occurs that is profoundly discontinuous with the past; examples include Operation Desert Storm in 1991, the attacks on the World Trade Center and the Pentagon on September 11, 2001, and the wars in Iraq and Afghanistan that began in 2003. Cohorts that are in late adolescence or early adulthood when such events occur may be profoundly affected by them and, in consequence, may develop a generational identity—a strong identification with their own generation and a sense of difference from older and younger cohorts (Stewart, 2002). This identity may shape their lives, influencing their

TABLE 3.4 History and Life Stage

TREND OR EVENT	COHORT OF 1970–1975		COHORT OF 1990–1995	
	LIFE STAGE WHEN EVENT OCCURRED	SOME LIFE COURSE IMPLICATIONS OF THE EVENT	LIFE STAGE WHEN EVENT OCCURRED	SOME LIFE COURSE IMPLICATIONS OF THE EVENT
Economic Expansion (1992–2000)	Young Adulthood	Good job opportunities, income. Affordable housing.	Childhood	Raised in dual-career family. Good schools.
Terrorist Attacks (9/11/01)	Adulthood	Increased awareness of family, reordered priorities. Anxiety about health, safety.	Youth	Shaken sense of security, uncertainty about the future. Increased stress.
War in Iraq, Afghanistan		Increased political awareness, Military service disrupts careers, families.	Adolescence	Crowded schools, school violence.
Recession of 2008–2010	Midlife	Economic uncertainty, possibly unemployment, loss of home.	Young Adulthood	High unemployment, poor job prospects. Difficulty launching.

choice of work, political views, and family relationships.

In this section, we have provided an overview of changes during the life course. Based on this discussion, it is useful to think of ourselves as living simultaneously in three types of time, each deriving from a different source of change. As we age biologically, we move through developmental time in our own biological life cycle. As we pass through the intertwined sequence of roles in our society, we move through social time. And as we respond to the historical events that impinge on our lives, we move together with our cohort through historical time.

We have emphasized the changes that occur as individuals progress through the life course. However, there is also stability. Normative transitions usually involve choices, and individuals usually make choices that are compatible with preexisting values, selves, and dispositions (Elder & O'Rand, 1995). More than 90 percent of all Americans experience the normative transition of marriage. Most persons choose when and whom they marry. Longitudinal research indicates that we choose a spouse who is compatible with our own personality, thus promoting stability over time (Caspi & Herbener, 1990).

Historical Variations

Unique historical events—wars, depressions, medical innovations—change life courses. And historical trends—fluctuating birth and divorce rates, rising education, varying patterns of women's work—also influence the life courses of individuals born in particular historical periods.

No one can predict with confidence the future changes that will result from historical trends and events. What we can do is to examine how major events and trends have influenced life courses in the past. Two examples will be presented: the historical trend toward greater involvement of

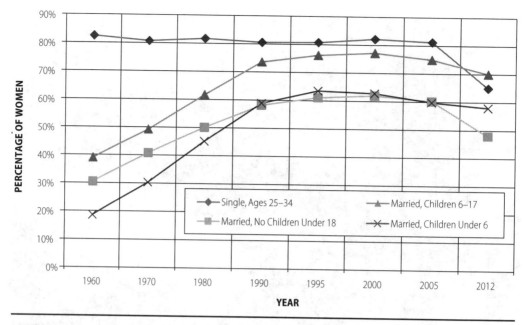

FIGURE 3.3 Women's Employment: 1960–2012

The percentage of married women who are employed rose steadily from 1960 to 1995. Young single women maintained virtually the same high level of employment throughout this period. Among married women, the level of employment rose slowly for those with no children and more rapidly among those with children under age 17. From 1995 to 2005, women's employment rates were stable, except for single women whose rate declined steadily from 2000 to 2012. Since 2005, employment rates have declined for all four groups, probably due in part to the recession of 2008–2009.

Source: U.S. Bureau of the Census and U.S. Bureau of Labor Statistics.

Other factors that may have promoted the increased employment of women include rising divorce rates, falling birth rates, rising education levels, and the invention of labor-saving devices for the home. None of these factors alone can explain the continuing rise in the employment of women over the whole century. However, at one time or another, each of these factors probably strengthened the historic trend, along with changes in gender role attitudes.

The specific changes in women's work behavior demonstrate that the timing of a person's birth in history greatly influences the course of his or her life. Whether you join the workforce depends in part on historical trends during your lifetime. So does the likelihood that you will get a college ed-

ucation, marry, have children, divorce, die young or old, and so on.

Impact of Events. Life course researchers are also interested in the impact of events on those who experience them. One dimension of impact is the magnitude of the event—that is, the number of people who are affected. The events of September 11, 2001, in the United States affected millions of people across the United States and in other parts of the world. The closing of a school affects hundreds of people in the community where the school is located.

How an event affects people depends on the life stage at which it is experienced. One model of this relationship is displayed in Table 3.5. In one sense, events have the great-

Processes of Socialization. Socialization is based on three different processes. (1) Instrumental conditioning—the association of rewards and punishments with particular actions—is a basis for learning both behaviors and performance standards. Studies of the effectiveness of various child-rearing techniques indicate that rewards do not always make a desirable behavior more likely to occur, and punishments do not always eliminate an undesirable behavior. The use of corporal punishment appears to increase the likelihood of later antisocial behavior. Through instrumental learning, children develop the ability to judge their own behaviors and to engage in self-reinforcement. (2) We learn many behaviors and skills by observation of models. We may not perform these behaviors, however, until we are in the appropriate situation. (3) Socialization also involves internalization—the acquisition of behavioral standards, making them part of the self. This process enables the child to engage in self-control.

Outcomes of Socialization. (1) The child gradually learns a gender role—the expectations associated with being male or female. Whether the child is independent or dependent, aggressive or passive, depends on the expectations communicated by parents, kin, and peers. (2) Language skill is another outcome of socialization; it involves learning words and the rules for combining them into meaningful sentences. Related to the learning of language is the development of thought and the ability to group objects and persons into meaningful categories. (3) The learning of social norms involves parents, peers, and teachers as socializing agents. Children learn that conformity to norms facilitates social interaction. Children also develop the ability to make moral judgments. (4) Children acquire motives—dispositions that produce sustained, goal-directed behavior. Orientations toward work are influenced primarily by parents; middle-class families emphasize self-direction, whereas working-class families emphasize conformity.

Components of the Life Course. To aid our understanding of adult lives, we focused on three components of the life course. (1) The life course consists of careers—sequences of roles and associated activities. The principal careers involve work, family, and friends. (2) As we engage in career roles, we develop role identities, and evaluations of our performance contribute to self-esteem. (3) The emotional reactions we have to career and life events include feelings of stress and of satisfaction.

Influences on Life Course Progression. There are three major influences on progression through the life course. (1) The biological growth and decline of body and brain set limits on what we can do. The effects of biological developments on the life course, however, depend on the social meanings we give them. (2) Each society has a customary, normative sequence of age-graded roles and activities. This normative sequence largely determines the bases for building identities, the responsibilities and privileges, and the socialization experiences available to individuals of different ages. (3) Historical trends and events modify an individual's life course. The impact of a historical event depends on the person's life stage when the event occurs.

Historical Variations. The historical timing of one's birth influences the life course through all stages. (1) Over the past 40 years, women's participation in the workforce has increased dramatically, and attitudes toward women's employment have become much more favorable. It is likely that the changes in attitudes reflect the changes in labor force participation, rather than the reverse. The likelihood that women will experience pressures and opportunities to work outside the home is now greater at every life stage. (2) Events also influence the life course of those affected by them. The impact of an event depends on its scope and on the life stage and social structural location of the persons influenced by it.

List of Key Terms and Concepts

attachment (p. 71)
birth cohort (p. 105)
borderwork (p. 79)
career (p. 99)
cultural routines (p. 69)
extrinsically motivated (p. 85)
gender role (p. 88)
instrumental conditioning (p. 81)
internalization (p. 87)
intrinsically motivated (p. 85)
life course (p. 99)
life events (p. 102)
moral development (p. 95)
normative life stage (p. 104)
normative transition (p. 105)
norms (p. 93)
observational learning (p. 85)
punishment (p. 83)
self-reinforcement (p. 85)
shaping (p. 81)
socialization (p. 66)
stress (p. 102)

Critical Thinking Skill: Understanding the Difference Between Truth and Validity

In this chapter we introduced several theories about how a person becomes an effective member of society: the developmental perspective, the social learning perspective, the interpretive perspective, and the life-course perspective. A common reaction by students is to ask "So which one is right?" or "Which one is the best?" These questions reflect the belief that a theory is correct or incorrect, right or wrong. Truth can be defined as consistent with facts or reality. The belief that some things are true and others are not is one that most of us rely on as we navigate the world, so we often try to sort out truth from falsity.

However, this belief will not serve us well if we apply it to evaluating theory. A theory is an abstraction, a simplification, an intentional focus on one or a few elements of a complex situation in order to make sense of that situation. Every observer of children notes that they develop the skills needed to interact successfully with adults. But the explanation the observer provides depends upon his or her theoretical lens. The developmental perspective says that this reflects the development of the brain so that it can process complex information, the development of motor control over posture, speech, and so on, and the maturation of vocal organs. The learning theorist would say that this reflects learning language via social learning and reinforcement, and interactional skills by observation of other children and adults interacting. The interpretive theorist would point out that she practiced many times per day interacting with other children, and developed her own unique brand of speech and gestures. Each theorist's interpretations are consistent with some of the reality they are observing in the child's behavior, so in this sense, each theory is "true." So asking "Which one is true?" doesn't help us evaluate the different theories.

Instead, we evaluate theories in terms of their validity. We look for *evidence*. We use the theory to generate testable questions or hypotheses, collect data or observations that are relevant to the hypotheses, and evaluate the consistency between the observations or data and the hypotheses. We described this process in detail in Chapter 2. To the extent that the evidence is consistent with the theory each time the theory is tested, we develop confidence that the theory is valid. Evidence that is not consistent, or evidence reported by one researcher/group that can- not be confirmed by subsequent research, gives us less confidence in the validity of the theory. In writing this book, we pay care- ful attention to the consistency of evidence, and often don't include theories or ideas because the evidence for them isn't consis- tent. So the next time you meet a new the- ory, what question will you ask?

SELF AND SELF-PRESENTATION

INTRODUCTION

He is a stranger to himself, a mystery to everyone else. Police call him Al, so at least he has a name, even if he knows it isn't his own.

Al's earliest memory takes him to the morning of September 10, when he woke up frightened and disoriented on the sidewalk in front of the World Trade Center in downtown Denver. Every memory before that moment is gone. "I want my past," Al says. "I want who I was. I don't care about anything else."

He learns something new about himself every day. He has discovered that he likes lasagna and "when it's warm outside." But he can't remember how to cook and isn't sure if he knows how to drive. When Al was examined, doctors found no drugs or alcohol in his system, or any sign of a head injury. Mental health experts who have interviewed Al believe he is suffering from retrograde amnesia.

He is expecting to go on national news shows in hopes someone will recognize him. Some clues come forward. Al was wearing a ring, a watch, yellow baseball cap, and glasses when he was found. He had a cigarette lighter and $8 in his pocket. Police have unsuccessfully tried to trace where his watch and ring were purchased. They ran his fingerprints through FBI databases, but no matches were found.

"I feel totally lost," Al said. "I feel totally alone, very depressed, very anxious about everything." Al now lives in a transitional housing facility where he spends much of his time contemplating what he doesn't have—family, friends, his past, his identity (Bernuth, *The Denver Post*, 10/22/2006).

"Who am I?" Few human beings in Western societies live out their lives without pondering this question. Some people pursue the search for self-knowledge and for a meaningful identity eagerly; others pursue it desperately. College students in particular are often preoccupied with discovering who they are. Few, however, have experienced existential uncertainty to the degree faced by Al.

Each of us has unique answers to this question, answers that reflect our **self-schema** or self-concept, the organized structure of cognitions or thoughts we have about ourselves. The self-schema comprises our perceptions of our social identities and personal qualities and our generalizations about the self based on experience.

One way to assess the contents of self-schema is by asking people to answer the question "Who am I?" This is the focus of Box 4.1. Before you read on, take a few moments and respond to this question yourself in the space provided in the box. For comparison, read the answers of a 9-year-old boy and a female college sophomore to the question "Who am I?" Their responses are listed at the bottom of the box.

The first half of this chapter addresses four major questions:

1. What is the self and how does it arise?

2. How do we acquire unique identities? How do we use them to locate ourselves in the world relative to others?

3. How do our identities guide our plans and behavior?

4. We are constantly experiencing self-evaluations. Where do they come from, and how do they affect our behavior? How do we protect our self-esteem against attack?

BOX 4.1 Test Yourself: Measuring Self-Concepts

In order to study self-concepts, we need ways to measure them. Several methods have been used. For example, one approach asks people to check those adjectives on a list (intelligent, aggressive, trusting, and so on) that describe themselves (Sarbin & Rosenberg, 1955). In another approach (Osgood, Suci, & Tannenbaum, 1957), people rate themselves on pairs of adjectives (strong-weak, good-bad, active-passive): Are they more like one of the adjectives in the pair or more like its opposite? Another technique, developed by Miyamoto and Dornbusch (1956), asks people whether they have more or less of a characteristic (self-confidence, likableness) than members of a particular group (such as fraternities, sororities, and so on). In yet another technique, people sort cards containing descriptive phrases (interested in sports, concerned with achievement) into piles according to how accurately they think the phrases describe them (Stephenson, 1953).

Each of these popular methods provides respondents with a single standard set of categories to use in describing themselves. Using the same categories for all respondents makes it easy to compare the self-concepts of different people. These methods have a weakness, however. They do not reveal the unique dimensions that individuals use in spontaneously thinking about themselves. For this purpose, techniques that ask people simply to describe themselves in their own words are especially effective (Kuhn & McPartland, 1954; McGuire & McGuire, 1982).

Instructions for the "Who am I?" technique for measuring self-concepts (Gordon, 1968) are provided below. You can try this test yourself.

In the 15 numbered blanks, write 15 different answers to the simple question "Who am I?" Answer as if you were giving the answers to yourself, not to somebody else. Write the answers in the order they occur to you. Don't worry about "logic" or "importance."

1. _____	9. _____
2. _____	10. _____
3. _____	11. _____
4. _____	12. _____
5. _____	13. _____
6. _____	14. _____
7. _____	15. _____
8. _____	

The following responses have been obtained from two persons, Josh and Arlene.

JOSH: A 9-YEAR-OLD MALE	ARLENE: A FEMALE COLLEGE SOPHOMORE
a boy	a person
do what my mother says, mostly	member of the human race
Louis's little brother	daughter and sister
Josh	a student
have big ears	people-lover
can beat up Andy	people-watcher
play soccer	creator of written, drawn, and spoken (things) creations
sometimes a good sport	
a skater	music enthusiast
make a lot of noise	enjoyer of nature
like to eat	partly the sum of my experiences
talk good	always changing
go to third grade	lonely
bad at drawing	all the characters in the books I read a small part of the universe, but I can change it I'm not sure? (Gordon, 1968)

THE NATURE AND GENESIS OF SELF

The Self as Source and Object of Action

We can behave in a wide variety of ways toward other persons. For example, if George is talking to Keisha, he can perceive her, evaluate her, communicate with her, motivate her to action, attempt to control her, and so on. Note, however, that George also can act in the same fashion toward himself—that is, he can engage in self-perception, self-evaluation, self-communication, self-motivation, and self-control. Behavior of this type, in which the individual who acts and the individual toward whom the action is directed are the same, is termed *reflexive behavior*.

For example, if George, a student, has an important term paper due Friday, he engages in the reflexive process of self-control when he pushes himself ("Got to work on that history paper now"). He engages in self-motivation when he makes a promise to himself ("You can go out for pizza and a movie Friday night"). Both processes are part of the self. To have a self is to have the capacity to engage in reflexive actions—to plan, observe, guide, and respond to our own behavior (Bandura, 1982c; Mead, 1934).

Our understanding of reflexive behavior and the self is drawn from symbolic interaction theory (see Chap. 1). By definition, the **self** is the individual viewed as both the source and the object of reflexive behavior. Clearly, the self is both active (the source that initiates reflexive behavior) and passive (the object toward whom reflexive behavior is directed). The active aspect of the self is labeled the *I*, and the object of self-action is labeled the *me* (James, 1890; Mead, 1934).

It is useful to think of the self as an ongoing process (Gecas & Burke, 1995). Action involving the self begins with the I—with an impulse to act. For example, George wants to see Keisha. In the next moment, that impulse becomes the object of self-reflection and, hence, part of the me ("If I don't work on that paper tonight, I won't get it done on time"). Next, George responds actively to this self-awareness, again an I phase ("But I want to see Keisha, so I won't write the paper"). This, in turn, becomes the object to be judged, again a me phase ("That would really hurt my grade"). So George exercises self-control and sits down to write. The I and me phases continue to alternate as every new action (I) becomes in the next moment the object of self-scrutiny (me). Through these alternating phases of self we plan, act, monitor our actions, and evaluate outcomes (Markus & Wurf, 1987).

Mead (1934) portrays action as guided by an internal dialogue. People engage in conversations in their minds as they regulate their behavior. They use words and images to symbolize their ideas about themselves, other persons, their own actions, and others' probable responses to them. This description of the internal dialogue suggests there are three capacities human beings must acquire in order to engage successfully in action: They must (1) develop an ability to differentiate themselves from other persons, (2) learn to see themselves and their own actions as if through others' eyes, and (3) learn to use a symbol system or language for inner thought. In this section, we examine how children come to differentiate themselves and how they learn to view themselves from others' perspectives. We also discuss how language learning is intertwined with acquiring these two capacities.

Self-Differentiation

To take the self as the object of action, we must—at a minimum—be able to recognize ourselves. That is, we must distinguish our own faces and bodies from those of others. This may seem elementary, but infants are not born with this ability. At first, they do not even discriminate the boundaries between their own bodies and the environment. Cognitive growth and continuing tactile exploration of their bodies contribute to infants' discovery of their physical uniqueness. So does experience with caregivers who treat them as distinct beings. Studies of when children can recognize themselves in a mirror suggest that most children are able to discriminate their own image from others' by about 18 months (Bertenthal & Fischer, 1978). Research indicates that children become capable of representing self-other contingencies (for example, "If I do X, she does Y") at 18 to 24 months old (Higgins, 1989).

Children must learn not only to discriminate their physical selves from others, but also to discriminate themselves as social objects. Mastery of language is critical in children's efforts to learn the latter (Denzin, 1977). Learning one's own name is one of the earliest and most important steps in acquiring a self. As Allport (1961) put it,

> By hearing his name repeatedly the child gradually sees himself as a distinct and recurrent point of reference. The name acquires significance for him in the second year of life. With it comes awareness of independent status in the social group. (p. 115)

A mature sense of self entails recognizing that our thoughts and feelings are our private possessions. Young children often confuse processes that go on in their own minds with external events (Piaget, 1954). They locate events in their own dreams, for example, in the world around them. The distinction between self and nonself sharpens as social experience and cognitive growth bring children to realize that their own private awareness of self is not directly accessible to others. By about age 4, children report that their thinking and

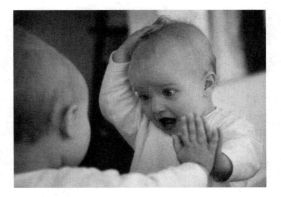

To take the self as the object of our action—observing and modifying our own behavior—we must be able to recognize ourselves. Although infants are not born with this ability, they acquire it quickly. © Plus/iStock

knowing goes on inside their heads. Asked further, "Can I see you thinking in there?" they generally answer, "No," demonstrating their awareness that self-processes are private (Flavell, Shipstead, & Croft, 1978).

Changes in the way children talk also reveal their dawning realization that the self has access to private information. At first, children's speech patterns are the same whether they are talking aloud to themselves or directing their words to others. Gradually, however, they begin to distinguish speech to self from speech to others (Vygotsky, 1962). Speech to self becomes abbreviated until it is virtually incomprehensible to the outside listener, whereas speech to others becomes more elaborated over time. "Cold" suffices for Shanice to tell herself she wants to take off her wet socks. But no one else would understand this without access to her private knowledge. When addressing others, Shanice would expand her speech to include whatever private information they would need to understand ("Gotta change my wet socks. They're making me cold").

Access to private information about the self leads to systematic differences in adults' self-descriptions compared to descriptions of others (McGuire & McGuire, 1986).

Descriptions of the self focus on what one does—on physical action and on cognitive and affective reactions to others. Descriptions of others focus on who the person is—as evidenced in his or her visible behavior and characteristics. Furthermore, people perceive themselves as more complex than other people (Sande, Goethals, & Radloff, 1988). Did your responses in Box 4.1 reflect these characteristics of self-descriptions?

Role Taking

Recognizing that one is physically and mentally differentiated from others is only one step in the genesis of self. Once we can differentiate ourselves from others, we also can recognize that the other person sees the world from a different perspective. The second crucial step in the genesis of self is **role taking**—the process of imaginatively occupying the position of another person and viewing the self and the situation from that person's perspective (Hewitt, 2000).

Role taking is crucial to the genesis of self because through it the child learns to respond reflexively. Imagining others' responses to the self, children acquire the capacity to look at themselves as if from the outside. Recognizing that others see them as objects, children can become objects (me) to themselves (Mead, 1934). They can then act toward themselves to praise ("That's a good girl"), to reprimand ("Stop that!"), and to control or regulate their own behavior ("Wait your turn").

Long ago, Cooley (1908) noted the close tie between role taking and language skills. One of the earliest signs of role-taking skills is the correct use of the pronouns *you* and *I*. To master the use of these pronouns requires taking the role of the self and of the other simultaneously. Most children firmly grasp the use of *I* and *you* by the middle of their third year (Clark, 1976). This suggests that children are well on their way to effec-

tive role taking at this age. Studies indicate that children develop the ability to infer the thoughts and expectations of others between ages 4 and 6 (Higgins, 1989).

The Social Origins of Self

Our self-schema is produced in our social relationships. Throughout life, as we meet new people and enter new groups, our view of self is modified by the feedback we receive from others. This feedback is not an objective reality that we can grasp directly. Rather, we must interpret others' responses in order to figure out how we appear to them. We then incorporate others' imagined views of us into our self-schema.

To dramatize the idea that the origins of self are social, Cooley (1902) coined the term **looking-glass self**. The most important looking glasses for children are their parents and immediate family and, later, their playmates. They are the child's **significant others**—the people whose reflected views have greatest influence on the child's self-concepts. As we grow older, the widening circle of friends and relatives, school teachers, clergy, and fellow workers provides our significant others. The changing images of self we acquire throughout our lives depend on the social relationships we develop. As children acquire digital devices, these provide another source of feedback about the self.

Play and the Game. Mead (1934) identified two sequential stages of social experience leading to the emergence of the self in children. He called these stages *play* and the *game*. Each stage is characterized by its own form of role taking.

In the **play** stage, young children imitate the activities of people around them. Through such play, children learn to organize different activities into meaningful roles (nurse, police officer, firefighter). For example, using their imaginations, children carry sacks of mail, drop letters into mailboxes, greet homeowners, and learn to label these activities as fitting the role of "mail carrier." At this stage, children take the roles of others one at a time. They do not recognize that each role is intertwined with others. Playing mail carrier, for example, the child does not realize that mail carriers also have coworkers and bosses to whom they must relate. Nor do children in this stage understand that the same person simultaneously holds several roles—that mail carriers are also parents, store customers, and golf partners.

The **game** stage comes later, when children enter organized activities such as complex games of house, school, and team

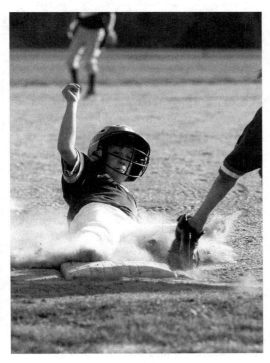

By playing complex games such as baseball, children learn to organize their actions into meaningful roles and to imagine the viewpoints of others at the same time. Role taking enables the third baseman to coordinate effectively with teammates, for example, to tag a runner out.
© jpbcpa/iStock

sports. These activities demand interpersonal coordination because the various roles are differentiated. Role taking at the game stage requires children to imagine the viewpoints of several others at the same time. For Michael to play center effectively, for example, he must adopt the perspectives of the guards and members of the defensive team as he dribbles the ball and decides whether to pass it or go for three. In the game, children also learn that different roles relate to one another in specified ways. Michael must understand the specialized functions of each position, the ways the players in different positions coordinate their actions, and the rules that regulate basketball.

The Generalized Other. Repeated involvement in organized activities lets children see that their own actions are part of a pattern of interdependent group activity. This experience teaches children that organized groups of people share common perspectives and attitudes. With this new knowledge, children construct a **generalized other**—a conception of the attitudes and expectations held in common by the members of the organized groups with whom they interact. When we imagine what the group expects of us, we are taking the role of the generalized other. We are also concerned with the generalized other when we wonder what people would say or what society's standards demand. As children grow older, they control their own behavior more and more from the perspective of the generalized other. This helps them to resist the influence of impulse or of specific others who just happen to be present at the moment.

Over time, children internalize the attitudes and expectations of the generalized other, incorporating them into their self-concepts. But building up self-concepts involves more than accepting the reflected views of others. We may misperceive or misinterpret the responses that others direct to us, for example, due to our less-than-perfect role-taking skills. Others' responses may themselves be contradictory or inconsistent. Also, we may resist the reflected views we perceive because they conflict with our prior self-concepts or with our direct experience. A boy may reject his peers' view that he is a "wuss," for example, because he previously thought of himself as brave and could still visualize his experience of beating up a bully.

Online Communication and the Self. Since 1995, there has been a rapid expansion in computer-mediated communication (CMC). People communicate using e-mail, instant messaging, participation in chat rooms and interest groups, and via personal webpages and social networking sites (for example, Facebook). We will discuss the relationship between CMC and other forms of communication, and the role of CMC in self-presentation and in relationships, in other sections. Here we focus on CMC as a potential influence on the development of self.

The self is heavily influenced by feedback from others. Our discussion so far has implicitly assumed feedback in face-to-face interaction. One difference between CMC and "real life" is that in CMC, the interaction partner is not physically present; thus, nonverbal cues (facial expressions, body language, and paralinguistic cues) are usually not available (Zhao, 2005). These are often the cues we use to assess the feedback we receive from others; without them, assessing the personal meaning of his or her statements is more difficult. Thus, we may be more skeptical of other's messages, and less likely to use them as a looking glass. On the other hand, teens are particularly heavy users of CMC (Ramirez & Broneck, 2009), and are in the life stage where feedback from others is especially influential.

The self constructed through online interaction may be termed the *digital self*. It has four characteristics (Zhao, 2005). First, it is *inwardly oriented*; people may use CMC to communicate about their inner world of thoughts and feelings. Second, like the self more generally, it is a *narrative* or a story—that is, a self-presentation that is expected by others to be coherent and consistent. Third, it is *retractable*; in real life, our various selves all inhabit the same body, and cannot easily be detached. In CMC, you can delete a self, and it is gone (or at least not ordinarily visible to others). Retracting a self will be more costly to the extent that it is salient, that the individual has invested time and resources in it, and receives valued rewards from it. Finally the digital self is *multiplied*; one can have several, diverse selves. According to one survey, more than one-half of teens who use CMC have more than one screen name or e-mail account (Lenhart, Rainie, & Lewis, 2001). The digital self is not constrained by geographic and institutional factors; this can be very important in allowing people with uncommon or stigmatized characteristics, such as survivors of breast cancer or persons struggling with issues of gender identity or sexual orientation, to contact similar others and form support networks.

Research suggests that online self-disclosure tends to be superficial. A study including students (ages 18 to 39) and non-students (ages 18 to 37) found that they were more likely to disclose information about their interests than their beliefs and intimate feelings (Attrill & Jalil, 2011). This constrains the feedback that one receives, and thus its influence on the self.

The impact of others whom we interact with online depends upon the nature of our relationship with them (Zhao, 2005). Some are strangers, people we don't know. Interaction with strangers usually does not impact the self. An exception would be members of an online support network. Others are people we know both online and off. If such persons are *significant others*, perceived feedback from them, both face-to-face and online, may be an important influence on self. The third category consists of people we know only online. These relationships may vary greatly in intimacy and longevity; intimate, long-term relationships may be very influential.

Self-Evaluation. The views of ourselves that we perceive from others usually imply positive or negative evaluations. These evaluations also become part of the self we construct. Actions that others judge favorably contribute to positive self-concepts. In contrast, when others disapprove or punish our actions, the self-concepts we derive may be negative.

We also form self-evaluations when reflecting on the adequacy of our role performances—on the extent to which we live up to the standards we aspire to. Our self-evaluations most commonly focus on our competence, self-determination, moral worth, or unity. Self-evaluations also influence the ways we express our role identities. A musician, for example, will pursue opportunities to perform in public more persistently if she sees herself as competent than if she thinks she is never quite good enough. Self-evaluations are so important that a later section of this chapter will be devoted to them.

IDENTITIES: THE SELF WE KNOW

In Box 4.1, Arlene described herself as a person, daughter, student, people-lover, and creator of things. This is the self she knows, a self that includes specific identities. **Identities** are the meanings attached to the self by one's self and others (Gecas & Burke, 1995). When we think of our identities, we are actually thinking of various plans of action that we expect to carry out. When Arlene identifies herself as a student, for example, she has in mind that she plans to attend classes, write papers, take exams, and so on. If Arlene does not engage in these behaviors, she will have to relinquish her student identity.

In this section, we consider four questions about the self we know: (1) How do our roles influence the identities we include in our self? (2) How do group memberships influence the self we know? (3) What evidence is there that the self we know is based on the reactions we perceive from others? (4) How do the aspects of self that people note vary from one situation to another?

Role Identities

Each of us occupies numerous positions in society—student, friend, son or daughter, customer. Each of us, therefore, enacts many different social roles. We construct identities by observing our own behavior and the responses of others to us as we enact these roles. For each role we enact, we develop a somewhat different view of who we are—an identity. Because these identities are concepts of self in specific roles, they are called **role identities**. The role identities we develop depend on the social positions available to us in society. As a result, the self we know is linked to society fundamentally through the roles we play. It reflects the structure of our society and our place in it (McCall & Simmons, 1978; Stryker, 1980). Role identities highlight the impact on self of social structure via reciprocal relationships with occupants of complementary roles.

Do societal role expectations strictly dictate the contents of our role identities? Apparently not. Consider, for example, the role expectations for a college instructor. Some instructors deliver lectures, whereas others lead discussions; some encourage questions, whereas others discourage them; some assign papers, and others do not. As this example indicates, role expectations usually leave individuals some room to improvise their own role performances. It is probably more accurate to think of people as "making" their roles—that is, shaping them—rather than as conforming rigidly to role expectations (Turner, 1978). Societal expectations do dictate the goals of role performance; instructors must instruct using means that are consensually agreed on (Burke, 2004).

Several influences affect the way we make the roles we enact. Conventional role expectations in society set a general framework. In the role of student, for example, you must submit assigned work. The person holding the complementary role also has expectations. As a student in Prof. Collett's class, you must write a 15-page lit review and research proposal. Within the boundaries set by these expectations, you can fashion your actual role performances to reflect your personal characteristics and competencies. You can select topics that interest you, highlight your strengths, and cover your weaknesses. You also mold your role performances to impress your audience (say, writing in the style that Prof. Collett prefers). Finally, you adjust your different performances to maintain some consistency among them (say, trying for a level of quality consistent with your other course work). Because each person makes roles in a unique, personal fashion, we each derive somewhat different role identities even if we occupy similar social positions. Consequently, our role identities as student, ball player, and so on differ from the role identities of others who also occupy these positions.

In describing themselves, people frequently mention the styles of interpersonal behavior (introverted, cool) that distinguish the way they fashion their unique role performances. People also mention the emotional or psychological styles (optimistic, moody) that characterize these performances. Individual preferences point to specific ways in which people express their role identities. For example, a person who sees herself as a musician expresses this role identity differently depending on whether she prefers Bach or rock. Body image—the aspect of the self we recognize earliest—remains important throughout life. Beyond this, our self extends to include our material possessions, such as our clothing, house, car, music collection, and so on (James, 1890).

Social Identities

A second source of identities is membership in social categories or groups based on criteria such as gender, nationality, race/ethnicity, sexual preferences, or political affiliation (Howard, 2000). A definition of the self in terms of the defining characteristics of a social group is a **social identity** (Hogg, Terry, & White, 1995; Tajfel & Turner, 1979). Each of us associates certain characteristics with members of specific groups. These characterizations—Chicago Bulls fans are loud, women are emotional—define the group. If you define yourself as a member of the group, these characteristics become standards for your thoughts, feelings, and actions. If your interactions with others, whether members or not, confirm the importance of these attributes, they become part of the self you know. Research indicates that cognitive representations of the self and of the groups to which the person belongs are closely linked (Smith & Henry, 1996). Social identities highlight the impact on self of social structure via consensually defined social groupings (Deaux & Martin, 2003). Note that one need not interact with other members to identify as a member of the group.

Social groups are often defined in part by reference to other groups. The meaning of being a Young Republican is related to the meaning of being a Young Socialist and a Young Democrat. The meaning of being a man in American society is closely related to the meaning of being a woman. Thus, when membership in a group becomes a salient basis for self-definition, perceptions of relevant out-groups are also made salient. Often there is an accentuation effect—an emphasis on perceived differences and unfavorable evaluations of the out-group and its members (Hogg, 2013). Thus, negative stereotypes directed at persons of a different gender, race, or religion are often closely related to the self-concept of the person who holds them. Research indicates that both in-group favoritism and out-group hostility are reinforced in conversations between group members (Harasty, 1997).

Research on Self-Concept Formation

Two of the key theoretical ideas discussed so far are that (1) the formation of the self-schema involves the adoption of role and social identities, and (2) a person's self-concept is shaped by the reactions that he or she receives from significant others during social interaction. Each of these ideas has been the focus of empirical research.

The Adoption of Role and Social Identities. Self-schemas are formed in part by adopting identities. The identities available to us depend on the culture. One difference between cultures is whether a culture is individualist or collectivist (Triandis, 1989). Individualist cultures emphasize individual achievement and its associated identities such as president, team captain, idealist, and outstanding player. Collectivist cultures emphasize values that promote the welfare of the group and its associated identities such as son (family), Catholic (religion), Italian (ethnicity), and American. According to research, the self-schemas of persons in individualist cultures (such as the United States) include more individual identities, whereas those of persons in collectivist cultures include more group-linked identities (Triandis, McCusker, & Hui, 1990).

The adoption of a role identity involves socialization into the group or organization of which the role is a part. A study of members of a volunteer search and rescue group, Peak, identified three stages of membership: new, peripheral, and core (Lois, 2003). New members were often attracted by the desire to meet people, develop and exercise their outdoor skills, or be a hero. To make the transition to (be accepted by others as) a peripheral member, they had to suppress self-oriented attitudes and behavior and acknowledge the importance of the team. They also had to learn survival skills and rescue techniques, demonstrating humility and persistence in the process. To make the transition to core member, they had to accept the roles offered by the team (sometimes very unglamorous ones) and demonstrate that they were skilled by leading training sessions. As members progressed through these stages, they increasingly shared in the sense of "we-ness," and their membership became an important social identity. They ultimately achieved the role of hero by becoming a committed member of the team, not by performing acts of individual heroism.

Adopting a social identity involves self-categorization—the defining of the self as a member of a social category such as Irish American, Black American, or feminist (Stets & Burke, 2000). Whereas enacting a role identity involves behavior conforming to a role, enacting a social identity involves adopting styles of dress, behavior, and thought associated with the social category. Successful adoption may require consensus by other members of the category that you can claim the identity (Wong, 2002). Whether one identifies with a social

Social identities are often displayed by wearing items of clothing displaying the group's name or logo.
© Tommy LaPorte/Icon SMI/Corbis

category in which one can claim membership depends on how easily one can be identified as a member of that group, for example, by name or skin color (Lau, 1989). It also depends on the general visibility and status of that group or category in society.

Reflected Appraisals. The idea that the person bases his or her self-schema on the reactions he or she perceives from others during social interaction is captured by the term *reflected appraisal*. Studies of this process (Marsh, Barnes, & Hocevar, 1985; Miyamoto & Dornbusch, 1956) typically compare people's self-ratings on various qualities (such as intelligence, self-confidence, physical attractiveness) with the views of themselves that they perceive from others. The studies also compare self-ratings with actual views of others. The results of these studies support the hypothesis that it

is the perceived reactions of others rather than their actual reactions that are crucial for self-concept formation (Felson, 1989). A study of 12- and 14-year-olds got self-descriptions from the youth and one of his or her parents, teachers, and a peer chosen by the youth. Agreement in self/parent, self/teacher, and self/peer descriptions increased with age, and was greater among girls than boys (van Aken, van Lieshout, & Haselager, 1996).

Research has focused on the differential effect of various significant others on one's appraisal of self in particular roles or domains. Felson (1985; Felson & Reed, 1986) has studied the relative influence of parents and peers on the self-perceptions of fourth- through eighth-graders about their academic ability, athletic ability, and physical attractiveness. The results indicate that parents affect self-appraisals in the areas of academic and athletic ability, whereas peers are an important influence on perceived attractiveness. One aspect of attractiveness is weight. Although there is an objective measure of weight (that is, pounds, or pounds in relation to height), it is the social judgment ("too fat," "too thin," or "just right") that is incorporated into the self-concept. A study of adolescent health obtained self-appraisals of weight from 6,500 adolescents, as well as appraisals from their parents and a physician (Levinson, Powell, & Steelman, 1986). These young people were generally unhappy with their weight, with boys judging themselves to be too thin and girls judging themselves to be overweight. For both, parental appraisal was significantly related to the young person's judgment, whereas the physician's rating was not. Research on a large sample of young adult athletes found that self-perceptions of athletic competence were strongly related to the athlete's perception of appraisals by coaches, teammates, and parents (Trouilloud & Amiel, 2011). However, athletes' perceptions of their future were negatively related to others' appraisals.

A study of married couples with one child examined the relative influence of self-appraisal and partner's appraisal on two types of behavior: caregiving (traditionally female) and breadwinning (traditionally male) (Maurer, Pleck, & Rane, 2001). The hypothesis was that self-appraisal would be more influential for gender-consistent behavior (male breadwinning, female caregiving), whereas partner's appraisal would be more influential for noncongruent behavior (male caregiving, female breadwinning). The results generally supported the hypothesis. Thus, the appraisals of those presumed to be more knowledgeable about the role were more important.

Typically, a person's self-ratings are related more closely to his or her perceived ratings by others than to the actual ratings by others. Why is this so? Three reasons are especially important. First, others rarely provide full, honest feedback about their reactions to us. Second, the feedback we do receive is often inconsistent and even contradictory. Third, the feedback is frequently ambiguous and difficult to interpret. It may be in the form of gestures (shrugs), facial expressions (smiles), or remarks that can be understood in many different ways ("That's nice"). For these reasons, we may know little about others' actual reactions to us. Instead, we must rely on our perceptions of others' reactions to construct our self-concepts (Schrauger & Schoeneman, 1979).

Evidence that self-concepts are related to the perceived reactions of others does not in itself demonstrate that self-concepts are actually formed in response to these perceived reactions. However, one study (Mannheim, 1966) does suggest such an impact of the perceived reactions of others on self-concepts. The investigators in this study asked college dormitory residents to describe themselves and to report how they thought others viewed them. Several months later, self-concepts were measured again. In the interim, students' self-concepts had moved closer to the views they had originally thought that others held. Change toward the perceived reactions of others had indeed occurred. Similarly, a longitudinal study of delinquent behavior found that parental appraisals of youth as delinquent were associated with subsequent self-appraisals as delinquent; self-appraisal as delinquent was in turn related to delinquent behavior (Matsueda, 1992).

Identity and Multiracial Heritage. In a racially diverse society, social identity based on racial heritage is a significant component of self-schema. According to the reflected appraisal model, it is perceived reactions of others that influence self-perception. Also, successful adoption of an identity requires acceptance by others of one's claims. Thus, an important influence on racial identity should be responses of others based on one's appearance. The racial identity of some persons seems obvious—that is, their skin color and physical features fit the social stereotype of what Asians, Blacks, or Whites look like. But the racial identity of others is not obvious. People with ambiguous appearance are frequently asked "What are you?" and may come to hate having to answer that question one more time (Navarro, 2005). To study multiracial identity, Khanna (2004) recruited adults who had one Asian parent and one White parent. She predicted that (apparent) phenotype or appearance (How would others categorize you, Asian or White?) would be the most important influence on racial identity. But what about persons whose phenotype is ambiguous? Khanna predicted that cultural exposure, language proficiency, eating foods, and celebrating holidays would influence identity—that is, identifying oneself as "Asian." Both hypotheses were confirmed. A study of hundreds of Asian and Latino students entering UCLA found that speaking the ethnic language at home and having high school friends of the same ethnicity were the main predictors of strong ethnic identity (Sears, Fu, Henry, & Bui, 2003).

The Situated Self

If we were to describe ourselves on several different occasions, the identities, personal qualities, and self-evaluations mentioned would not remain the same. This is not due to errors of reporting; rather, it demonstrates that the aspects of self that enter our awareness and matter most to us depend on the situation. The **situated self** is the subset of self-concepts chosen from our identities, qualities, and self-evaluations that constitutes the self we know in a particular situation (Hewitt, 1997). Markus and Wurf

(1987) refer to the current, active, accessible self-representations as the *working self-concept.*

The self-concepts most likely to enter the situated self are those distinctive to the setting and relevant to the ongoing activities. Consider a Black woman for whom being Black and being a woman are both important self-concepts. When she interacts with Black men, she is more likely to think of herself as a woman. When she interacts with White women, she is more likely to be aware that she is Black. Similarly, whether gender is part of your situated self depends in part on the gender composition of others present (Cota & Dion, 1986). Male and female college students placed in a group with two students of the opposite gender were more likely to list gender in their self-descriptions than members of all-male or all-female groups. Thus, self-concepts that are distinctive or peculiar to the social setting tend to enter into the situated self.

Our activities also determine the self-concepts that constitute the situated self. A job interview, for example, draws attention to your competence; a party makes your body image more salient. The self we experience in our imaginings and in our interactions is always situated, because setting characteristics and activity requirements prime or make distinctive and relevant particular self-concepts.

IDENTITIES: THE SELF WE ENACT

How does the self influence the planning and regulation of social behavior? The general answer to this question is that we are motivated to plan and to perform behaviors that will confirm and reinforce the identities we wish to claim for ourselves (Burke & Reitzes, 1981; Markus & Wurf, 1987). In elaborating on this answer, we will examine three more specific questions: (1) How are

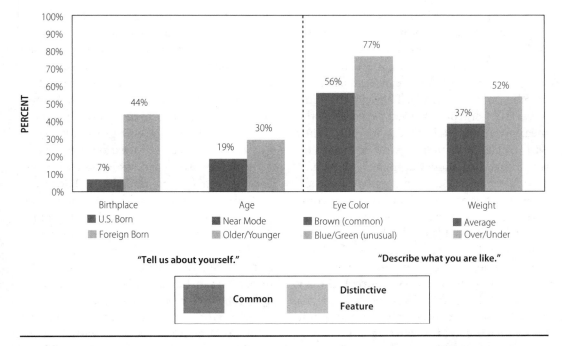

Figure 4.1 Students Spontaneously Mention a Distinctive Feature as Part of Their Self-Concept

A group of 252 sixth-graders from 10 classrooms were asked to describe themselves. Students mentioned a particular feature (for example, birthplace) more often if that feature distinguished them from their classmates. Because these are characteristics on which we stand out from our social groups, attracting more notice and social comment, we are more likely to build them into our self-concepts. Adapted from "Trait Silence in the Spontaneous Self-Concept" by W. J. McGuire and A. Padawer-Singer, *Journal of Personality and Social Psychology*, 33, 743–754. © 1976 by the American Psychological Association.

behaviors linked to particular identities? (2) Of the different identities available to us, what determines which ones we choose to enact in a situation? (3) How do our identities lend unity and consistency to our behavior?

Identities and Behavior

Each of us makes dozens of decisions every day; most of them influence our behavior. These decisions are influenced by explicit and implicit egotism—that is, giving undue prominence to the self. A study of major life decisions (where to live, choice of career) suggests that these decisions are influenced by our names (Pelham, Mirenberg, & Jones, 2002). We tend to choose places and occu-

pations with names that resemble our own. According to this study, it is not an accident that Susie sells seashells by the seashore.

Identities that are important to the person can motivate behavior that is consistent with or validates that identity. A longitudinal study of almost 800 seventh-, ninth-, and eleventh-graders measured how much each student identified with (from "not at all" to "very much like me") the characteristics "popular" and "troublemaker." The researchers expected that these identities at Time 1 would be related to sexual debut between Times 1 and 2. Among boys, identifying with both was associated with initiating sex. Among girls, identification with "troublemaker" was associated with sexual debut (Longmore, Manning, & Giordano, 2006).

The link between identities and behaviors is through their common meanings (Burke & Reitzes, 1981). If members of a group agree on the meanings of particular identities and behaviors, they can regulate their own behavior effectively. They can plan, initiate, and control behavior to generate the meanings that establish the identities they wish to claim. If members do not agree on these meanings, however, people have difficulty establishing their preferred identities. If Imani sees no connection between competitiveness and femininity, for example, she will have trouble establishing a feminine identity in the eyes of friends who think being feminine means being noncompetitive.

According to **identity control theory** (Burke, 1991), an actor uses the social meaning of his or her identity as a reference point for assessing what is occurring in the situation. The identities of the other actors and elements of the situation also have shared meanings. The behaviors of others and situational elements are evaluated by the actor according to whether they maintain his or her identity. Subsequent behaviors are selected and enacted in order to maintain one's identity in this situation. The (shared) meaning of an identity operates like a thermostat; if reflected appraisals or situational elements are inconsistent with identity, an actor will behave in ways designed to restore it (Smith-Lovin & Robinson, 2006).

Consider a woman whose identity is a "considerate professor." When students hand in assignments on time, her identity is reinforced. Occasionally, when an apparently hardworking student asks for an extension of a due date, it is consistent with her identity as "considerate" to grant the request. But if numerous students ask for extensions for reasons that seem trivial, she may "crack down" and refuse to give an extension to anyone, enacting the "professor" identity.

Since the meanings of role-identity elements, actions, and other identities are widely shared, Burke and other researchers use quantitative techniques to assess them. Adapting the techniques developed by Osgood (see Box 2.1), the meaning of an identity element or action is assessed on the dimensions of affect, evaluation, and potency. Researchers can compare these values across roles or groups or cultures to assess the impact of context on meanings.

Social identities are associated with category or group memberships. There are widely held meanings or stereotypes associated with many categories and groups. Thus, claiming a social identity creates a pressure to accept these stereotypes as self-descriptive. This can have a powerful impact on behavior. We may voluntarily adopt behavior or traits associated with positive stereotypes, such as adopting the food preferences associated with "veganism." On the other hand, we may avoid engaging in behaviors we associate with disliked out-groups. Researchers found that American-Indian, African-American, and Mexican-American college students and eighth-graders viewed healthy behaviors (for example, good diet, exercise) as white and middle-class, and were less likely to engage in them. Minority students were more likely to identify unhealthy behaviors as consistent with in-group identity (Oyserman, Fryberg, & Yoder, 2007).

We may be influenced by negative stereotypes as well; *stereotype threat* refers to a situation in which one is at risk of confirming as self-characteristic a negative stereotype about a group to which one belongs (see Chap. 6). For instance, Blacks may underperform in an academic testing situation because they believe that others stereotype them as "dumb," which creates anxiety that disrupts their performance.

On the other hand, some group members will obviously violate any stereotype of the group. We noted earlier that characteristics that distinguish us from others are more likely to be part of our self-concept. Indeed, research indicates that people are more likely to include in their self-schema areas in which their performance is counterstereotypic—that is, distinctive (von Hippel, Hawkins, & Schooler, 2001).

Choosing an Identity to Enact

Each of us has many different identities. Each identity suggests its own lines of action. These lines of action are not all compatible, however, nor can they be pursued simultaneously in a single situation. If you are at a family reunion in your parents' home, for example, you might wish to claim an identity as a helpful son or daughter, an aspiring rap artist, or a witty conversationalist. These identities suggest different, even conflicting ways of relating to the other guests. What influences the decision to enact one rather than another identity? Several factors affect such choices.

The Hierarchy of Identities. The many different role identities we enact do not have equal importance for us. Rather, we organize them into a hierarchy according to their **salience**—their relative importance to the self-schema. This hierarchy exerts a major influence on our decision to enact one or another identity (McCall & Simmons, 1978; Stryker, 1980). First, the more salient an identity is to us, the more frequently we choose to perform activities that express that identity (Stryker & Serpe, 1981). Second, the more salient an identity, the more likely we are to perceive that situations offer opportunities to enact that identity. Only a person aspiring to the identity of a rap artist, for example, will perceive a family reunion as a chance to demonstrate his or her skill. Third, we are more active in seeking opportunities to enact salient identities (say, searching for an open-mic session). Fourth, we conform more to the role

expectations attached to the identities that we consider the most important.

What determines whether a particular identity occupies a central or a peripheral position in the salience hierarchy? In general, the importance we attach to a role identity is affected by (1) the resources we have invested in constructing the identity (time, effort, and money expended, for example, in learning to be a sculptor); (2) the extrinsic rewards that enacting the identity has brought (for example, purchases by collectors, acclaim by critics); (3) the intrinsic gratifications derived from performing the identity (for example, the sense of competence and aesthetic pleasure obtained when sculpting a human figure); and (4) the amount of self-esteem staked on enacting the identity well (for example, the extent to which a positive self-evaluation has become tied to being a good sculptor). As we engage in interaction and experience greater or lesser success in performing our different identities, their salience shifts.

Social Networks. Each of us is part of networks of social relationships. These relationships may stand or fall depending on whether we continue to enact particular role identities. The more numerous and significant the relationships that depend on enacting an identity, the more committed we become to that identity (Callero, 1985). Consider, for example, your role as a student. Chances are that many of your relationships—with roommates, friends, instructors, and perhaps a lover—depend on your continued occupancy of the student role. If you left school, you could lose a major part of your life. Given this high level of commitment, it isn't surprising that for many students, being forced to leave school is traumatic.

The more commitment we have to a role identity, the more important that identity will be in our salience hierarchy. For instance, adults for whom participating in religious activities is crucial for maintaining everyday social relationships rank their religious identity as relatively important compared with their parent, spouse, and worker identities (Stryker & Serpe, 1981). Similarly, the importance rank that undergraduates give to various identities (student, friend, son or daughter, athlete, religious person, and dating partner) depends on the importance to them of the social relationships maintained by enacting each identity (Hoelter, 1983).

Online networks provide us with opportunities to enact identities. Some provide us with opportunities to enact and get feedback about our professional identities, for example, SPN (Social Psychology Network) or LinkedIn. Others such as eHarmony or Chemistry provide opportunities to enact identities related to meeting potential partners and intimate relationships. Obviously your posts on LinkedIn will be quite different from those on AVEN (Asexuality Visibility and Education Network)!

Need for Identity Support. We are likely to enact those of our identities that most need support because they have recently been challenged. For instance, suppose that someone has recently had difficulty "hooking up," or getting a date. That person may now choose actions calculated to elicit responses indicating he or she is an attractive dating partner. We also tend to enact identities likely to bring intrinsic gratifications (such as a sense of accomplishment) and extrinsic rewards (such as praise) that we especially need or miss at the moment. For example, if, after hours of solitary study, you feel a need for relaxed social contact, you might seek gratification by going to a student union or a bar to find someone to chat with.

Situational Opportunities. Social situations are restrictive; they let us enact only some identities profitably, not others. Thus,

in a particular situation, the identity we choose to enact depends partly on whether the situation offers opportunities for profitable enactment. Regardless of the salience of your identity as musician, if no one wants to listen to your music, there will be no opportunity to enact that identity.

In a series of studies, Kenrick, McCreath, Govern, King, and Bordin (1990) asked students to rate the extent to which various personal qualities could be displayed in each of six different settings. The traits were adjustment, dominance, intellectual ability, likableness, social control, and social inclination. The students agreed that one can display intellectual ability in academic settings but not in recreational ones. Behaviors expressive of dominance can be displayed in athletic and business settings but not in religious ones. Finally, there are opportunities to display adjustment and social inclination in recreational settings but not in church.

Opportunities to enact an identity depend in part on other persons offering access to the aspiring actor. Offers of access often depend on perceptions of actors or those who control access. In this situation, is it better to be perceived as a specialist or as someone who is versatile at a number of roles? In order to get invited to the party, is it better to have a reputation as the "life of the party" or as a bright, friendly, warm person? Research designed to answer this question looked at the careers of U.S. film actors, specifically at the odds they would get roles in subsequent films (Zuckerman, Kim, Ukanwa, & von Rittman, 2003). Specialization increased the odds that novices would get future roles, but decreased the odds for veterans; when you are relatively unknown, you are more likely to get opportunities if you are known to be good at a specialty. Once you are known, versatility will get you more opportunities than if you are a specialist.

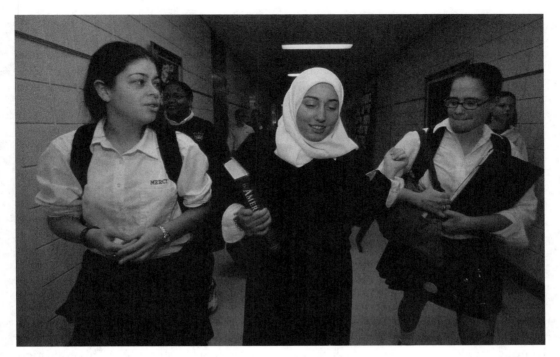

The more important an identity is to us, the more consistently we act to express it, regardless of others' reactions. Are any of your identities so important that you would express them by wearing such distinctive clothing as this high schooler? © Ed Kashi/VII/Corbis

Identities as Sources of Consistency

Although the self includes multiple identities, people usually experience themselves as a unified entity. One reason is the influence of the salience hierarchy. Another reason is that we use several strategies that verify our perceptions of self.

Salience Hierarchy. Our most salient identities provide consistent styles of behavior and priorities that lend continuity and unity to our behavior. In this way, the salience hierarchy helps us to construct a unified sense of self from our multiple identities.

The hierarchy of identities influences consistency in three ways. First, the hierarchy provides us with a basis for choosing which situations we should enter and which ones we should avoid. A study of the everyday activities of college students (Em-

mons, Diener, & Larsen, 1986) found clear patterns of choice and avoidance in each student's interactions; these patterns were consistent with the student's characteristics, such as sociability.

Second, the hierarchy influences the consistency of behavior across different situations. In another study, each person was asked to report the extent to which each of 10 affective states and 10 behavioral responses occurred in various situations over a 30-day period (Emmons & Diener, 1986). The results indicated a significant degree of consistency across situations.

Third, the hierarchy influences consistency in behavior across time. Serpe (1987) studied a sample of 310 first-year college students, collecting data at three points during their first semester in college. The survey measured the salience at each point of five identities: academic ability, athletic/

recreational involvement, extracurricular involvement, personal involvement (that is, friendships), and dating. There was a general pattern of stability in salience. Change in salience was more likely for those identities where there was greater opportunity for change, such as dating.

Although the self-concept exhibits consistency over time, it may change (Demo, 1992). Life transitions may change situations one encounters. This creates a need to exit from one or more roles, adopt new roles, and change the salience hierarchy. During times such as adolescence and retirement, we are likely to feel a weakened sense of unity and a confusion about how to behave. This has been called an *identity crisis* (Erikson, 1968). To overcome such confusion, we must reorganize our identity hierarchy, giving greater importance to identities based on our newly available or remaining social positions. A retiree may successfully reorganize the hierarchy, for example, by upgrading identities based on new hobbies (gardener) and on continuing social ties (witty conversationalist).

Self-Verification Strategies. We experience ourselves as consistent across time and situations because we employ several strategies that verify our self-perceptions (Banaji & Prentice, 1994).

One set of strategies consists of behaviors that lead to self-confirming feedback from others. First, we engage in selective interaction; we choose as friends, roommates, and intimates people who share our view of self. Second, we display identity cues that elicit identity-confirming behavior from others. In a hospital setting, most people treat a middle-aged person wearing a white coat as a physician. Third, we behave in ways that enhance our identity claims, especially when those claims are challenged. In one study, White students who viewed themselves as unprejudiced were led to believe they were prejudiced toward Blacks. When they were subsequently approached by a Black panhandler, they gave him more money than did students whose egalitarian identity had not been threatened (Dutton & Lake, 1973).

Another set of strategies involves the processing of feedback from others. As noted in the next section, we often do this in ways that make others' responses to us seem to support our self-concept.

There are limits to the extent to which we engage in self-verifying strategies. There are times when we want accurate feedback about our abilities or about another person's view of our relationship with him or her. When we want such feedback, and we have the necessary cognitive resources (attention, energy), we evaluate feedback from others by comparing it with our self-representations (Swann & Schroeder, 1995). This evaluation may lead to changes in behavior, such as moving toward a goal or a desired identity, or to a change in self-representation.

Self-Awareness and Self-Discrepancies

In this section, we discuss two ways in which the self affects our behavior. These include (1) ways in which focusing attention on the self influences the relationship between our identities and our behavior; and (2) the effect of self-discrepancies on emotional state and behavior.

Effects of Self-Awareness. While eating with friends, reading a book, or participating in conversation, your attention is usually directed toward the objects, people, and events that surround you. But what happens if, on looking up, you discover a photographer, lens focused on you, snapping away? Or what if you suddenly notice your image reflected in a large mirror? In such circumstances, most of us become self-conscious. We enter a state of **self-awareness**—that is, we take the self as the object of our attention and focus on our own appearance, actions, and thoughts. This corresponds to the "me" phase of action (Mead, 1934).

Numerous circumstances cause people to become self-aware. Mirrors, cameras, and recordings of our own voice cause self-awareness because they directly present the self to us as an object. Unfamiliar situations and blundering in public also cause self-awareness, because they disrupt the smooth flow of action and interaction. When this happens, we must attend to our own behavior more closely, monitoring its appropriateness and bringing it into line with the demands of the situation. In general, anything that reminds us that we are the objects of others' attention will increase our self-awareness.

How does self-awareness influence behavior? When people are highly self-aware, they are more likely to be honest and to more accurately report on their mood state, psychiatric problems, and hospitalizations (Gibbons et al., 1985). In general, people who are self-aware act in ways more consistent with personal and social standards (Wicklund, 1975; Wicklund & Frey, 1980). Their behavior is controlled more consciously by the self. In the absence of self-awareness, behavior is more automatic or habitual. Society gains control over its members through the self-control that individuals exercise when they are self-aware (Shibutani, 1961). This is because the standards to which people conform are largely learned from significant groups in society. Self-awareness is thus often a civilizing influence.

These findings suggest that groups enhance their social control over individual behavior when they expose individuals to conditions—like an attentive audience, unfamiliar circumstances, or socially awkward tasks—that increase awareness of the public self. Interestingly, these are precisely the conditions used by many groups—fraternities, sororities, military organizations—in initiation rituals.

Effects of Self-Discrepancies. Research has shown that the relationships between components of one's self-schema influence one's emotional state and behavior. There are three components of the self-schema: self as one is (actual), as one would like to be (ideal), and as one ought to be (ought). When we evaluate ourselves, we typically use the ideal self or the ought self as the reference point. When the actual self matches the ideal self, we feel satisfaction or pride. However, when there is a **self-discrepancy**—that is, a component of the actual self is the opposite of a component of the ideal self or the ought self—we experience discomfort (Higgins, 1989).

According to self-discrepancy theory, the two types of discrepancies produce two different emotional states. Someone who has an actual-ideal discrepancy will experience dejection, sadness, or depression. Someone who perceives an actual-ought discrepancy will experience fear, tension, or restlessness. The theory predicts that the larger the discrepancy, the greater the discomfort.

In a study designed to test these hypotheses (Higgins, Klein, & Strauman, 1985), students were asked to list up to 10 attributes each of the actual self, the ideal self, and the ought self. Discrepancy was measured by comparing two lists (say, the actual and the ideal); a self-state listed in both was a match, whereas a self-state listed on one list with its antonym (opposite) listed on the other was a mismatch. The self-discrepancy score was the number of mismatches minus the number of matches. Discomfort was measured by several questionnaires. The results showed that as the actual-ideal discrepancy increased, the frequency and intensity of reported dissatisfaction and depression increased. As the actual-ought discrepancy increased, the frequency and intensity of reported fear and irritability increased.

Self-discrepancy scores also are related to various behaviors. A study of satisfaction with one's body and of eating disorders found that a form of actual-ideal discrepancy was associated with bulimic behaviors, whereas an actual-ought discrepancy was associated with anorexic behaviors (Strauman, Vookles, Berenstein, Chaiken, & Higgins, 1991). A study of 100 women found that number of discrepancies was associated with both depressive symptoms and eating disorders. When experiencing symptoms was controlled, actual-potential discrepancies were associated with eating disorders (Sawdon, Cooper, & Seabrook, 2007). Research involving 112 female undergraduates found that exposure to ads portraying thin women increased body dissatisfaction and levels of depression, and lowered self-esteem. Women with high body-image self-discrepancy were more likely to experience these effects (Bessenoff, 2006).

SELF-ESTEEM

Do you have a positive attitude about yourself, or do you feel you do not have much to be proud of? Overall, how capable, successful, significant, and worthy are you? Answers to these questions reflect **self-esteem**, the evaluative component of self-concept (Gecas & Burke, 1995).

This section addresses four questions: (1) How is self-esteem assessed? (2) What are the major sources of self-esteem? (3) How is self-esteem related to behavior? (4) What techniques do we employ to protect our self-esteem?

Assessment of Self-Esteem

Our overall self-esteem depends on (1) which characteristics of self are contingen-cies of self-esteem, and (2) how we evaluate each of them. Some of our specific role and social identities and personal qualities are important to us; characteristics of self or categories of outcomes on which a person stakes self-esteem are **contingencies** of self-esteem (Crocker & Wolfe, 2001). Others are unimportant. For instance, you may consider yourself an excellent student and a worthy friend, an incompetent athlete and an unreliable employee, and not care about your social identity as Basque French. According to theory, our overall level of self-esteem is the product of these individual evaluations, with each identity weighted according to its salience (Rosenberg, 1965; Sherwood, 1965).

Ordinarily, we are unaware of precisely how we combine and weigh the evaluations of our specific contingencies. If we weigh our positively evaluated identities and traits as more important, we can maintain a high level of overall self-esteem while still admitting to certain weaknesses. If we weigh our negatively evaluated identities heavily, we will have low overall self-esteem even though we have many valuable qualities.

There are several approaches to measuring self-esteem. Probably the most widely used is the Rosenberg Self-Esteem Scale (see Box 4.2). It consists of 10 statements about feelings toward and evaluations of oneself, and assesses the extent of agreement or disagreement with each. A second approach is the attempt to measure implicit self-esteem—the unaware, automatic evaluation of the self—by assessing the person's evaluation of objects and qualities associated with the self (Greenwald & Farnham, 2000). A third technique involves using trained coders to assess autobiographical narratives; the coder reads the narrative and assigns two overall ratings, each on a 9-point scale. The coder rates the degree of self-liking and of self-confidence evident in the narrative (Anderson, 2006).

BOX 4.2 TEST YOURSELF: THE ROSENBERG SELF-ESTEEM SCALE

STATEMENT	STRONGLY AGREE	AGREE	DISAGREE	STRONGLY DISAGREE
1. I feel that I am a person of worth, at least on an equal plane with others.	_____	_____	_____	_____
2. I feel that I have a number of good qualities.	_____	_____	_____	_____
3. All in all, I am inclined to feel that I am a failure.	_____	_____	_____	_____
4. I am able to do things as well as most other people.	_____	_____	_____	_____
5. I feel I do not have much to be proud of.	_____	_____	_____	_____
6. I take a positive attitude toward myself.	_____	_____	_____	_____
7. On the whole, I am satisfied with myself.	_____	_____	_____	_____
8. I wish I could have more respect for myself.	_____	_____	_____	_____
9. I certainly feel useless at times.	_____	_____	_____	_____
10. At times I think I am no good at all.	_____	_____	_____	_____

Scores are calculated as follows:

For items 1, 2, 4, 6, and 7:

Strongly agree = 3
Agree = 2
Disagree = 1
Strongly disagree = 0

For items 3, 5, 8, 9, and 10 (which are reversed in valence):

Strongly agree = 0
Agree = 1
Disagree = 2
Strongly disagree = 3

Your score on the Rosenberg Scale:

The scale ranges from 0 to 30. Scores between 15 and 25 are within normal range; scores below 15 suggest low self-esteem.

Source: Morris Rosenberg, *Society and the Adolescent Self-Image,* 1989. Revised edition. Middletown, CT: Wesleyan University Press.

Sources of Self-Esteem

Why do some of us enjoy high self-esteem, whereas others suffer low self-esteem? To help answer this question, consider three major sources of self-esteem—family experience, performance feedback, and social comparisons.

Family Experience. As one might expect, parent-child relationships are important for the development of self-esteem. From an extensive study of the family experiences of fifth- and sixth-graders, Coopersmith (1967) concluded that four types of parental behavior promote higher self-esteem: (1) showing acceptance, affection, interest, and involvement in children's affairs; (2) firmly and consistently enforcing clear limits on children's behavior; (3) allowing children latitude within these limits and respecting initiative (such as older children setting their own bedtime and participating in making family plans); and (4) favoring non-coercive forms of discipline (such as denying privileges and discussing reasons, rather than punishing physically). Findings from a representative sample of 5,024 New York high school students corroborate these conclusions (Rosenberg, 1965). Note that these results are consistent with our discussion of socialization techniques in Chapter 3.

Family influences on self-esteem confirm the idea that the self-concepts we develop mirror the view of ourselves communicated by significant others. Children who see that their parents love, accept, care about, trust, and reason with them come to think of themselves as worthy of affection, care, trust, and respect. Conversely, children who see that their parents do not love and accept them may develop low self-esteem. A longitudinal study of adolescents found that excessive parental shaming and criticism were associated with low self-esteem and depression (Robertson & Simons, 1989).

Research also suggests that self-esteem is produced by the reciprocal influence of parents and their children on each other (Felson & Zielinski, 1989). Children with higher self-esteem exhibit more self-confidence, competence, and self-control. Such children are probably easier to love, accept, reason with, and trust. Consequently, they are likely to elicit responses from their parents that further promote their self-esteem.

As young people move into adolescence, their overall or global self-esteem becomes linked to the self-evaluations tied to specific role identities. A study of 416 sixth-graders found that evaluations of self as athlete, son or daughter, and student were positively related to global self-esteem (Hoelter, 1986). Also, the number of significant others expands to include friends and teachers in addition to parents. The relative importance of these others appears to vary by gender. A study of 1,367 high school seniors found that the perceived appraisals of friends had the biggest impact on girls' self-esteem, whereas the perceived appraisals of parents had the biggest impact on boys' self-esteem (Hoelter, 1984). For both boys and girls, teachers' appraisals were second in importance.

Both popular (Pipher, 1994) and academic (American Association of University Women, 1992) works have argued that a substantial difference between male and female self-esteem emerges in adolescence. Various causes have been suggested, such as the devaluing of female roles in U.S. society, the development of body consciousness and concern with appearance among girls, and the preferential treatment of boys by teachers. A meta-analysis of studies involving more than 146,000 participants of all ages finds a small difference in overall self-esteem favoring boys that is larger but not substantial in adolescence (Kling, Hyde, Showers, & Buswell, 1999). Furthermore, the difference declines from ninth grade to twelfth grade (Falci, 2011), and there is no gender difference at age 30 (Erol & Orth, 2011).

Performance Feedback. Everyday feedback about the quality of our performances—our successes and failures—influences our self-esteem. We derive self-esteem from experiencing ourselves as active causal agents who make things happen in the world, who attain goals and overcome obstacles (Franks & Marolla, 1976). In other words, self-esteem is based partly on our sense of efficacy—of competence and power to control events (Bandura, 1982c). People who hold low-power positions (such as clerks, unskilled workers) have fewer opportunities to develop efficacy-based self-esteem because such positions limit their freedom of action. Even so, people seek ways to convert almost any kind of activity into a task against which to test their efficacy and prove their competence (Gecas & Schwalbe, 1983). In this way, they obtain performance feedback useful for building self-esteem.

Social Comparison. To interpret whether performances represent success or failure, we must often compare them with our own goals and self-expectations or with the performances of others. Getting a B on a math exam, for example, would raise your sense of math competence if you had hoped for a C at best, but it would shake you if you were counting on an A. The impact of the B on your self-esteem also would vary depending on whether most of your friends got As or Cs.

Social comparison is crucial to self-esteem, because the feelings of competence or worth we derive from a performance depend in large part on with whom we are compared, both by ourselves and by others. Even our personal goals are largely derived from our aspirations to succeed in comparison with people whom we admire. We are

Few athletes win an Olympic gold medal. Those who do often experience great exhilaration. But for all of us, an inner sense of self-esteem depends on experiencing ourselves as causal agents who make things happen, overcome obstacles, and attain goals. © Tim Clayton/Corbis

most likely to receive evaluative feedback from others in our immediate social context—our family, peers, teachers, and work associates. We are also most likely to compare ourselves with these people and with others who are similar to us (Festinger, 1954; Rosenberg & Simmons, 1972). This reasoning suggests that the self-esteem of minority persons may benefit from being in a consonant environment, that is, one where most people are from the same group; a longitudinal study of a national sample of Blacks found that as the percentage of Blacks in the college attended increased, post-college self-esteem increased (St. C. Oates, 2004). A study of adult Chinese in Los Angeles County also found context effects on self-esteem; participation in Chinese culture, for example, speaking Chinese, eating ethnic foods, and celebrating ethnic festivals, was associated with higher self-esteem for persons living in predominantly Chinese neighborhoods, but not for Chinese living in predominantly White neighborhoods (Schnittker, 2002).

Losing one's job is generally interpreted as a serious failure in our society. A national survey of American employees reveals that job loss undermined self-esteem, but the size of the drop in self-esteem depended on social comparison (Cohn, 1978). In neighborhoods with little unemployment, persons who lost their jobs suffered a large drop in self-esteem. In neighborhoods where many others were unemployed too, the drop was less. This difference points to the importance of the immediate social context for defining success or failure.

Self-Esteem and Behavior

People with high self-esteem often behave quite differently from those with low self-esteem. At the same time, we should not overestimate the effects of self-esteem (Baumeister, 1998).

Compared with those having low self-esteem, children, teenagers, and adults with higher self-esteem are socially at ease and popular with their peers. They are more confident of their own opinions and judgments, and more certain of their perceptions of self (Campbell, 1990). They are more vigorous and assertive in their social relations, more ambitious, and more academically successful. During their school years, persons with higher self-esteem participate more in extracurricular activities, are elected more frequently to leadership roles, show greater interest in public affairs, and have higher occupational aspirations. Persons with high self-esteem achieve higher scores on measures of psychological well-being (Rosenberg, Schooler, Schoenbach, & Rosenberg, 1995). Adults with high self-esteem experience less stress following the death of a spouse and cope with the resulting problems more effectively (Johnson, Lund, & Dimond, 1986).

The picture of people with low self-esteem forms an unhappy contrast. People low in self-esteem tend to be socially anxious and ineffective. They view interpersonal relationships as threatening, feel less positively toward others, and are easily hurt by criticism. Lacking confidence in their own judgments and opinions, they yield more readily in the face of opposition. They expect others to reject them and their ideas, and they have little faith in their ability to achieve. In school, they set lower goals for themselves, are less successful academically, less active in the classroom and in extracurricular activities, and less popular. People with lower self-esteem appear more depressed and express more feelings of unhappiness and discouragement. They more frequently manifest symptoms of anxiety, poor adjustment, and psychosomatic illness.

Self-esteem influences our attributions regarding events in our close relationships. College students in dating relationships were recruited to participate in research. Their self-esteem was measured, and then they imagined two scenarios. In one, his or her partner was in a good mood; in the other, he or she was in a bad mood. When the partner's mood was negative and the cause ambiguous, those with low self-esteem felt more responsible, more rejected, and more hostile (Bellavia & Murray, 2003).

Most of these contrasts are drawn from comparisons between naturally occurring groups of people who report high or low self-esteem. It is, therefore, difficult to determine whether self-esteem causes these behavior differences or vice versa. For example, high self-esteem may enable people to assert their opinions more forcefully and, thus, to convince others. But the experience of influencing others, in turn, may increase self-esteem. Thus, reciprocal influence, rather than causality from self-esteem to behavior, is probably most common (Rosenberg, Schooler, & Schoenbach, 1989).

Protecting Self-Esteem

What grade would you like to get on your next exam in social psychology—an A or a C? Your answer depends in part on whether your self-esteem is high or low. We often think that everybody wants to get positive feedback from others, to have others like them, to be successful—that is, to experience self-enhancement. As noted in the previous section, people with high self-esteem expect to perform well and usually do. People with low self-esteem, on the other hand, expect to perform poorly and usually do. People are motivated to protect their self-esteem whether it is high or low—that is, to experience *self-verification* in the feedback they receive. Most people have high self-esteem and want self-enhancing feedback. Some people have low self-esteem; to verify their self-evaluation, they want self-derogating feedback.

Research with sixth- through eighth-graders assessed their perception of their strengths and their weaknesses, making them salient. They were then given the choice of self-enhancing or self-verifying feedback. These early adolescents preferred self-verification (Rosen, Principe, & Langlois, 2013). A meta-analysis of research on feedback found that context makes a difference; when the risk of rejection is high, people prefer self-enhancing feedback (Kwang & Swann, 2010).

People use several techniques to maintain their self-esteem. We will examine four of them (McCall & Simmons, 1978).

Manipulating Appraisals. We choose to associate with people who share our view of self and avoid people who do not. For example, a study of interaction in a college sorority revealed that women associated most frequently with those they believed saw them as they saw themselves (Backman & Secord, 1962). People with negative self-views seek people who think poorly of them (Swann & Predmore, 1985). Another way to maintain our self-esteem is by interpreting others' appraisals as more favorable or unfavorable than they actually are. For in-

stance, college students took an analogies test and subsequently were given positive, negative, or no feedback about their performance (Jussim, Coleman, & Nassau, 1987). Each student then completed a questionnaire. Students with high self-esteem perceived the feedback—whether positive or negative—as more positive than students with low self-esteem.

Selective Information Processing. Another way we protect our self-esteem is by attending more to those occurrences that are consistent with our self-evaluation. In one study, participants high or low in self-esteem performed a task; they were then told either that they succeeded or that they failed at the task. On a later self-rating, all the participants gave biased ratings. High-self-esteem participants who succeeded increased their ratings, whereas their low-self-esteem counterparts did not. Low-self-esteem participants who failed gave themselves lower ratings, whereas high-self-esteem participants who failed did not (Schlenker, Weigold, & Hallam, 1990).

Memory also acts to protect self-esteem. People with high self-esteem recall good, responsible, and successful activities more often, whereas those with low self-esteem are more likely to remember bad, irresponsible, and unsuccessful ones.

Selective Social Comparison. When we lack objective standards for evaluating ourselves, we engage in social comparison (Festinger, 1954). By carefully selecting others with whom to compare ourselves, we can further protect our self-esteem. We usually compare ourselves with persons who are similar in age, sex, occupation, economic status, abilities, and attitudes (Suls & Miller, 1977; Walsh & Taylor, 1982). We generally rate ourselves more favorably than we rate our friends (Suls, Lemos, & Stewart, 2002). We tend to avoid comparing ourselves with the class valedictorian, homecoming queen, or star athlete, thereby forestalling a negative self-evaluation.

Selective Commitment to Identities. Still another technique to protect self-esteem involves committing ourselves more to those self-concepts that provide feedback consistent with our self-evaluation, downgrading those that provide feedback that challenges it. This protects overall self-esteem because self-evaluation is based most heavily on those identities and personal qualities that are contingencies of self-esteem. This process may also lead us to change roles, exiting those that are associated with negative feedback.

People tend to enhance self-esteem by assigning more importance to those identities (religious, racial, occupational, family) they consider particularly admirable (Hoelter, 1983). They also increase or decrease identification with a social group when the group becomes a greater or lesser potential source of self-esteem (Tesser & Campbell, 1983). In one study, students were part of a group that either succeeded or failed at a task (Snyder, Lassegard, & Ford, 1986). On measures of identification with the group, students belonging to a successful group claimed closer association with the group (that is, basked in the reflected glory), whereas those in an unsuccessful group distanced themselves from the group. Similarly, students are more apt to wear clothing that displays their university affiliation following a football victory than after a defeat. They also identify more with their school when describing victories ("We won") than defeats ("They lost"), thereby enhancing or protecting self-esteem (Cialdini, Borden, Thorne, Walker, & Freeman, 1976).

People who want to verify their low self-esteem behave differently. Low-self-esteem participants who were members of a successful group downplayed their connection to the group and minimized their contribution to its success. Low-self-esteem participants were more likely to link themselves to the successful group when they were not members of it (Brown, Collins, & Schmidt, 1988).

All four techniques for protecting self-esteem described here portray human beings as active processors of social events. People do not accept social evaluations passively or allow self-esteem to be buffeted by the cruelties and kindnesses of the social environment. Nor do successes and failures directly affect self-esteem. The techniques described here testify to human ingenuity in selecting and modifying the meanings of events in the service of self-esteem.

SELF-PRESENTATION

Strolling down the aisle of the exhibition hall at the food fair, you notice the man in the next booth. He sees you at the same time and says, "Come on up. We're going to do it for you one more time." As you get closer, you see that he is surrounded by bowls of salsa and of coleslaw and piles of vegetables. On the table in front of him is a hard-plastic, hand-operated food processor—the Quick Chopper.

"Let me show you how to work these real quick, all right? You guys seen these on TV before? Cool. You didn't see me on TV, did you, *America's Most Wanted*, Saturday? Now the blades are the best part."

He makes it look effortless. He chops tomatoes, green peppers, and onions, all the while keeping up a steady banter. "Folks," he calls out, "come on up here. Help me get a crowd together. Sir, come on up here. You don't have to buy a thing, sir. Nobody else has." Other potential customers approach the booth.

He finishes the onions. "And then salt it to taste. This is my daddy's recipe, by

BOX 4.3 Minority Status and Self-Esteem

Members of racial, religious, and ethnic minorities might have special issues related to self-esteem. Because of prejudice, minority group members may see a negative image of themselves reflected in appraisals by members of majority groups. When they make social comparisons of their own educational, occupational, and economic success with that of the majority, they are likely to compare unfavorably. Therefore, we might assume that members of minority groups will interpret their performances and failures to achieve as evidence of a basic lack of worth and competence—that they will have low self-esteem.

Is this hypothesis true? Hundreds of studies have sought to determine whether minority status undermines self-esteem in America (Porter & Washington, 1993; Wylie, 1979). The vast majority of studies offer little support for the conclusion that minorities (racial, religious, or ethnic) have significantly lower self-esteem. Further research suggests that self-esteem among racial and ethnic minorities has two components. One is **group self-esteem**—how the person feels as a member of a racial or ethnic group. The other is personal self-esteem—how the person feels about the self (Porter & Washington, 1993).

A meta-analysis of data from more than 120 sources found that Blacks score significantly higher than Whites on global measures of personal self-esteem (Gray-Little & Hafdahl, 2000). Reflected appraisals from significant others affect minority group members just as they do majority group members. The self-esteem of Black schoolchildren is strongly related to their perception of what their parents, teachers, and friends think of them. These appraisals are not negative (Rosenberg, 1973, 1990). Living in segregated neighborhoods, minority group children usually see themselves through the unprejudiced eyes of their own group, not the prejudiced eyes of members of other groups. Similarly, the self-esteem of Black adults is related to the quality of their relationships with family and friends and their involvement in religion (Hughes & Demo, 1989).

What about other racial/ethnic groups? A meta-analysis of data from 354 samples of people of all ages, including Hispanics, Asians, and Native Americans (Twenge & Crocker, 2002), again found Blacks' mean scores on global measures to be somewhat higher than Whites'; the means of the other three groups were somewhat below the means of Whites.

Recent research has assessed self-esteem levels across the life course. Analyzing data from a longitudinal sample of 7,100 persons aged 14–30 (Add Health data), researchers found that self-esteem increases for everyone from adolescence into young adulthood. Hispanics had lower self-esteem in adolescence than Blacks or Whites, but subsequently experienced a larger increase. At age 30, Blacks and Hispanics had higher esteem than Whites (Erol & Orth, 2011). Data from 3,600 adults ages 25 to 75+ showed that Blacks and Whites had similar levels of esteem until age 65. Beyond 65, Blacks' self-esteem dropped more sharply than Whites' (Shaw, Liang, & Krause, 2010).

Group self-esteem, on the other hand, is not associated with reflected appraisals. Among Black Americans, group self-esteem includes Black consciousness, Black racial identity, and support for independent Black politics. High group self-esteem among Blacks is associated with higher education and more frequent contact with Whites, not with relationships with family and friends (Demo & Hughes, 1990). Research indicates that Puerto Ricans, Mexican Americans, and Asian Americans have high levels of group self-esteem (Porter & Washington, 1993). Other data suggest that when members of these groups receive negative feedback from members of other groups, they attribute it to racial prejudice (Crocker, Voelkl, Testa, & Major, 1991).

But what about the effects of social comparisons? Many minority group members are disadvantaged in terms of education, occupation, and income. Minority individuals do compare themselves with the majority, but they often do not blame themselves for their disadvantaged position. Minorities can protect their personal self-esteem by blaming the system of discrimination for their lesser accomplishments. Indeed, minority statuses such as race, religion, and ethnicity show virtually no association with self-esteem (Jacques & Chason, 1977; Rotheram-Borus, 1990). Social failure affects self-esteem only when people attribute it to poor individual achievement (Rosenberg & Pearlin, 1978).

the way. He's from Cuba. My mother's from Iceland. I'm an Ice Cube. What can I tell you? That's cool." A woman reaches into her purse. "Did you want to go ahead and get that now, ma'am? Cash, check, or charge? Folks, come on up here. Grab him by the hand. Hi there. I'll get your change, ma'am."

It looks easy. But it isn't. Bill Daniels and other product demonstrators who work food fairs spend weeks in training before they hit the stage. They are learning the art of "retailtainment"—how to run the demonstration, take the money, run the credit cards, keep talking the whole time, roll over the audience, and start another demonstration smoothly. Much harder than it looks, but very rewarding if you are good at it; you can earn $70,000 per year working long weekends. The successful ones have learned the art of tactical impression management and are making it pay (National Public Radio, 2002). (Watch the demonstration online: http://www.you tube.com/watch?v=a2HKYGn5oag.)

Although few of us make our living by creating such a finely tuned impression, we all present particular images of who we are. When we shout or whisper, dress up or dress down, smile or frown, we actively influence the impressions others form of us. In fact, presenting some image of ourselves to others is an inherent aspect of all social interaction. The term **self-presentation** refers to the processes by which individuals attempt to control the impressions that others form of them in social interaction (Leary, 1995; Leary & Kowalski, 1990; Schlenker & Weigold, 1992). The individuals involved may be aware of these processes or not.

For certain purposes, it is useful to distinguish between authentic self-presentation, ideal self-presentation, and tactical self-presentation (Baumeister, 1982; Kozielecki, 1984; Swann, 1987). In authen-

tic self-presentation, our goal is to create an image of ourselves in the eyes of others that is consistent with the way we view ourselves (our real self). In ideal self-presentation, our goal is to establish a public image of ourselves that is consistent with what we wish we were (our ideal self). In tactical self-presentation, our concern is to establish a public image of ourselves that is consistent with what others want or expect us to be. We may do this, for instance, by claiming to have some attributes they value, even if we really do not have them.

Persons engaging in tactical self-presentation usually have some ulterior motive(s) in mind. In some cases, they want others to view them positively because it will enable them to get some reward(s) that others control. Bill Daniels, for example, is earning money to support his lifestyle. In other cases, they are trying to pass as specific kinds of persons in hopes of gaining access to individuals and situations that are otherwise unavailable. If an undercover narcotics agent is trying to set up a sting, for example, he needs to infiltrate the drug operation, create the impression that he is an experienced drug runner, and gain the confidence of the bad guys. In tactical self-presentation, a person cares only about the impact of the image he or she is presenting to others, not about whether that image is consistent with his or her real self or ideal self. When a person uses self-presentation tactics calculated to manipulate the impressions formed of him or her by others, we say that he or she is engaging in **tactical impression management**.

Of course, there are hybrid situations in which a person uses several forms of self-presentation simultaneously. For instance, a woman might try to remain largely authentic in self-presentation (that is, giving others a correct impression of her) but also try to hide a few little flaws (so that others form a positive impression of her).

The second half of this chapter considers the ways in which people actively determine how others perceive them. It addresses the following questions:

1. What content is conveyed through self-presentation in everyday life? What factors—both personal and situational—affect self-disclosure between persons?
2. What impression-management tactics can we use when we want to claim a particular identity such as "overworked employee," "attractive date," or "competent student"? What factors influence our choice to use one impression-management tactic rather than another?
3. To what extent can people detect when others are using impression-management tactics against them? What cues reveal that an impression manager is trying to deceive them?
4. What are some of the consequences when people try but ultimately fail to project the social identities they desire?

SELF-PRESENTATION IN EVERYDAY LIFE

In this section, our primary concern is authentic self-presentation, although we must recognize that many processes in authentic self-presentation also are involved in tactical self-presentation. In everyday settings, people routinely project specific social identities, and they must take care that others understand and accept their identity claims. For example, when a temporarily out-of-work individual meets a potential employer during a job interview, she may naturally strive to create a positive first impression and claim the identity of "productive worker." However, she has to be careful to create an authentic impression and not to claim too much. If she is hired, it would be quite difficult to maintain a false image for very long when she has to perform on the job.

Successful self-presentation involves efforts (1) to establish a workable definition of the situation and (2) to disclose information about the self that is consistent with the claimed identity. We discuss each of these topics in turn.

Definition of the Situation

For interaction to be successful, participants in a situation must share some understandings about their social reality. Symbolic interaction theory (Blumer, 1962; Charon, 1995; Stryker, 1980) holds that for social interaction to proceed smoothly, people must somehow achieve a shared **definition of the situation**—an agreement about their situated identities, what their goals are, what actions are proper, and what their behaviors mean. In some interactions, they can establish a shared definition by actively negotiating the meaning of events (McCall & Simmons, 1978; Stryker & Gottlieb, 1981). In other interactions, people may invoke preexisting event schemas to provide a definition of the situation. Event schemas are particularly relevant when the event is of a common or recurring type, such as classes, job interviews, funerals, first dates, and the like.

To establish a definition of the situation, people must agree on the answers to two questions: (1) What type of social occasion is at hand? That is, what is the frame of the interaction? (2) What identities do the participants claim, and what identities will they grant one another? We consider these issues in turn.

Frames. The first requirement in defining the situation is for people to agree regarding the type of social occasion in which they are participating. Is it a commitment ceremony/wedding? A family reunion? A job interview? The type of social occasion that people recognize themselves to be in is called the *frame of the interaction* (Goffman, 1974;

Manning & Cullum-Swan, 1992). More strictly, a **frame** is a set of widely understood rules or conventions pertaining to a transient but repetitive social situation that indicates which roles should be enacted and which behaviors are proper. When people recognize a social occasion to be a commitment ceremony or wedding, for example, they immediately expect that two partners or a bride and groom, and someone authorized to perform the ceremony will be present. They also know that the other guests attending are mostly friends and relatives of the couple and that it is acceptable—indeed, appropriate—to congratulate both persons.

Participants usually know the frame of interaction in advance, or else they discover it quickly once interaction commences. Sometimes, however, there will be conflict and they must negotiate the frame of interaction. When parents send their wayward teenage daughter to a physician for a talk, for example, the discussion may begin with subtle negotiations about whether this is a psychiatric interview or merely a friendly chat. Once established, the frame limits the potential meanings that any particular action can have (Gonos, 1977). If the persons involved define the situation as a psychiatric interview, for example, any jokes the teenager tells may end up being interpreted as symptoms of illness, not as inconsequential banter.

Identities. Another issue in defining a situation is for people to agree on the identities they will grant one another and, relatedly, on the roles they will enact. That is, people must agree on the type of person they will treat each other as being (Baumeister, 1998). The frame places limits on the identities that any person might claim. For example, a teenager in a psychiatric interview cannot easily claim an identity as a "normal, well-adjusted kid." And employers would find it incongruous and bizarre if a young woman tried to claim the identity of "blushing bride" in a job interview.

Each person participating in an interaction has a **situated identity**—a conception of who he or she is in relation to the other people involved in the situation (Alexander & Rudd, 1984; Alexander & Wiley, 1981). Identities are "situated" in the sense that they pertain to the particular situation. For instance, the identity projected by a person while discussing a film ("insightful critic") differs from the identity projected by the same person when asking for a small loan ("reliable friend"). Situated identities usually facilitate smooth interaction. For this reason, people sometimes support situated identities claimed by others in public settings even though they may not accept them privately (Muedeking, 1992). To avoid unpleasant arguments, for example, you might relate to your friend as if she were an insightful or reliable person even though privately you believe she is not.

Much of the time, our identities are not self-evident to others because their perceptions of us filter through the person schemas and stereotypes they bring to a situation. These schemas bias the identities they perceive and grant to us. Thus, even if the identity claimed by us is authentic—in the sense of being consistent with our self-concept—we may need to highlight or dramatize it (Goffman, 1959b). For instance, consider some adolescents who are innocent of any wrongdoing. If they display their usual nonchalant, defiant image when stopped by police, they risk being detained or arrested. They are more likely to avoid arrest if they dramatize their innocence by presenting a polite, deferential demeanor (Piliavin & Briar, 1964).

Self-Disclosure

A primary means we use to make authentic identity claims is to reveal certain facts about ourselves. When we first meet someone, we usually discuss only safe or superficial topics and reveal rather little about

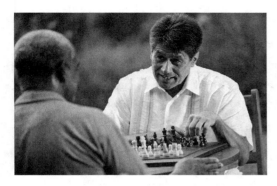

These chess players seem to be building trust and liking through reciprocal self-disclosure, an important process in authentic self-presentation. © Kali Nine LLC/iStock

ourselves. Eventually, however, as we get to know the other better, we disclose more revealing and intimate details about ourselves. This might include information about our needs, attitudes, experiences, aspirations, and fears (Archer, 1980). This process of revealing personal aspects of one's feelings and behavior to others is termed **self-disclosure** (Derlega, Metts, Petronio, & Margulis, 1993; Jourard, 1971).

Self-disclosure is usually reciprocal. There is a widely accepted social norm that one person should respond to another's disclosures with disclosures at a similar level of intimacy (Rotenberg & Mann, 1986; Taylor & Belgrave, 1986). This is termed the *norm of reciprocity in disclosure*. Most people follow it, although strict reciprocity in disclosure is more common in new relationships or developing friendships than in established ones where people already know a lot about one another (Davis, 1976; Won-Doornink, 1979). Furthermore, we are more likely to reveal more personal information to those we initially like and find attractive (Collins & Miller, 1994).

Self-disclosure usually leads to liking and social approval from others. People who reveal a lot of information about themselves tend to be liked more than people who disclose at lower levels (Collins & Miller, 1994). This holds especially true if the content of

the self-disclosure complements what their partner has revealed (Daher & Banikiotes, 1976; Davis & Perkowitz, 1979).

Although self-disclosure usually produces liking, there is such a thing as revealing too much about oneself. Self-disclosure that violates the audience's normative expectations may actually produce dislike. For instance, self-disclosure that is too intimate for the depth of the relationship (such as a new acquaintance describing the details of her latest bladder infection) will not strengthen the friendship and may just create the impression that the discloser is indiscreet or maladjusted (Cozby, 1972). Likewise, self-disclosure that reveals negatively valued attributes (such as a person discussing his prison record for felonious assault) or profound dissimilarities with the partner (such as a believer revealing his strong religious commitment to a nonbeliever) may produce disliking (Derlega & Grzelak, 1979). Constant updates of one's Facebook profile may result in disclosing more than your friends want to know.

Perhaps not surprisingly, the level of self-disclosure is related to loneliness. Young adults low in self-disclosure feel more lonely and isolated than those high in self-disclosure (Mahon, 1982). Lonely persons tend to have fewer skills in self-presentation and are less effective in making themselves known to others than are nonlonely persons (Solano, Batten, & Parish, 1982). The self-disclosure style of lonely persons may impair the normal development of social relations.

TACTICAL IMPRESSION MANAGEMENT

As we noted previously, self-presentation is inherent in social situations. Most people strive to create images of themselves that are authentic or true—that is, consistent with their own self-concept. These processes are automatic: The person is not

Physical appearance is important in impression management. If impression management is to be successful, one's appearance in the eyes of the audience must be consistent with the identity one claims. If he lacked the makeup and costume of a clown, this performer would have a hard time convincing even young children that he really is a clown. © REB Images/Blend Images/Corbis

conscious of them, they involve limited or no cognitive effort, and they are autonomous and involuntary (Schlenker, 2003).

Nevertheless, under certain conditions, individuals may try to present themselves in such a way as to create narrow, exaggerated, or misleading images in the eyes of others. The use of conscious, goal-directed activity to control information to influence impressions is called *tactical impression management.*

There are various reasons we might engage in tactical impression management (Jones & Pittman, 1982; Tetlock & Manstead, 1985). One is to make others like us more than they would otherwise (ingratiation). Other reasons for impression management are to make others fear us (intimidation), respect our abilities (self-promotion), respect our morals (exemplification), or feel sorry for us (supplication).

One aspect of the self that often requires management is the expression of emotion. The frame of a situation defines some emotions as appropriate and others as inappropriate. Service workers such as airline flight attendants and food servers are required to

be polite to customers and to conceal anger, even if the customer is being unreasonable or insulting (Hochschild, 1983). Professional hockey players, on the other hand, are required to act aggressively on the ice and even attack an opponent if provoked. An important part of the socialization into some professions involves learning to manage emotions; for instance, mortuary science students must learn to suppress negative reactions to dead bodies, bodily fluids, and disfigurement (Cahill, 1999). Some situations, such as the loss of a spouse, a job, or some other salient identity or resource, may elicit very strong emotions that the person has difficulty managing. One reaction to such loss is aggression directed at others (see Chap. 11). Alternatively, the person may seek professional help from a therapist, counselor, or support group. Support groups frequently provide a redefinition of the event (for instance, a divorce is an opportunity to start over—"turn your scar into a star") and an identity for the person that encourages emotions that are consistent with the group's ideology (Francis, 1997).

In this section, we examine some of the tactics used in impression management. In particular, we discuss managing appearances, ingratiation, aligning actions, and altercasting.

Managing Appearances

People often try to plan and control their appearance. As used here, the term *appearance* refers to everything about a person that others can observe. This includes clothes, grooming, overt habits such as smoking or chewing gum, choice and arrangement of personal possessions, verbal communication (accents, vocabulary), and nonverbal communication. Through the appearances we present, we show others the kind of persons we are and the lines of action we intend to pursue (DePaulo, 1992; Stone, 1962).

Physical Appearance and Props. Many everyday decisions regarding appearance—which clothes to wear, how to arrange our hair, whether and what to shave, and so on—stem from our desire to claim certain identities. In some situations, we arrange our clothing and accessories to achieve certain effects. This would be true, for example, if we were attending a party or going to a football game. It is also true when we go to a job interview, as illustrated in a study of female job applicants (von Baeyer, Sherk, & Zanna, 1981). Some applicants in this study were led to believe that their (male) interviewer felt that the ideal female employee should conform closely to the traditional female stereotype (passive, gentle, and so on); other applicants were led to believe that he felt the ideal female employee should be nontraditional (independent, assertive, and so on). The results showed that applicants managed their physical appearance to match their interviewer's stereotyped expectations. Those expecting to meet the traditionalist wore more makeup and used more accessories, such as earrings, than those planning to meet the nontraditional interviewer.

An important aspect of personal appearance is the location and visibility of hair on the body. U.S. social norms dictate groomed hair on the heads of both men and women unless one is bald; hair on parts of the body such as underarms and legs is expected on men but not on women. In fact, women who do not shave these areas are subject to harassment and ridicule (Hawkins, 2004). A woman may refuse to shave as a matter of principle, of not yielding to an arbitrary grooming norm, and may want this act of independence to be visible to others. But other women react with "How do you expect to get a boyfriend looking like that?"

and a man may pointedly ask "Are you a lesbian?" Thus, this nonconformity of appearance leads others to question the woman's sexual orientation.

Visible tattoos as a type of intentional personal adornment are becoming increasingly popular; one source estimates that 7 million people in the United States have tattoos, most of them between ages 18 and 40 (Knutson, 2002). Several studies have compared college students with and without tattoos on various measures; in these studies, 12 to 33 percent of the participants report having one or more tattoos. Those with tattoos do not differ in personality characteristics or reported childhood experiences from those without (Forbes, 2001). Men and women with tattoos do report significantly more risk-taking behavior and greater use of alcohol and drugs (Drews, Allison, & Probst, 2000; Dukes & Stein, 2011), and earlier experience with sexual intercourse (Gueguen, 2012). Studies of students' reactions to tattoos find that both men and women have significantly more negative reactions to a woman with a visible tattoo (Degelman & Price, 2002); also, participants with more conservative gender attitudes rank her more negatively (Hawkes, Senn, & Thom, 2004).

In a survey of 1,400 high school students, 9 percent of boys and 7 percent of girls reported tattoos, and 42 percent of girls reported piercings (not including ear lobes) (Dukes & Stein, 2011). Girls with piercings were less school oriented and reported more substance use. Apparently, unconventional body markers are associated with unconventional behavior.

The impression an individual makes on others depends not only on clothes, makeup, and grooming, but also on props in the environment. The impression Ashley makes on her friends and acquaintances, for instance, will depend in part on the props she uses—the titles in the pile of books she

We can see the embarrassment in former U.S. representative Anthony Weiner's face as he admits at a press conference that he had exchanged explicit messages and photos with several women. People experience embarrassment when an important social identity that they claim for themselves is discredited. © John Moore/Getty Images

places on her desk, the music she selects for her CD player, the wine she serves, and the like. A study of the impact of cleanliness of an apartment on perceptions of the resident found that persons (both male and female) with dirty apartments were given significantly lower ratings on agreeableness, conscientiousness, and intelligence, and higher ratings on openness and neuroticism. Ratings did not vary by the gender of the rater (Harris & Sachau, 2005). Thus, others make inferences about one's character and interests from the props that surround her.

Regions. Goffman (1959b) draws a parallel between a theater's front and back stages and the regions we use in managing appearances. He uses the term **front regions** to denote settings in which people carry out interaction performances and exert efforts to maintain appropriate appearances vis-à-vis others. One example of a front region is a restaurant's dining room, where waiters smile and courteously offer to help customers. **Back regions** are settings inaccessible to outsiders in which people knowingly violate the appearances they present in front regions. Behind the kitchen doors, the same

waiters shout, slop food on plates, and even mimic their customers. In general, persons use back regions to prepare, rehearse, and rehash the performances that occur in front regions.

Front and back regions are often separated by physical or locational barriers to perception, like the restaurant's kitchen door. These barriers facilitate impression management, because they block access of outsiders to the violations of images that occur in back regions. Any breakdown in these barriers will undermine the ability of persons to manage appearances. In recent years, for example, such breakdown has occurred regarding national political figures. Because the mass media are pervasive, they sometimes catch presidents, senators, and corporate officers off guard. National figures are shown expressing views and performing actions they would strongly prefer to keep hidden from the public. American presidents find it difficult to project a heroic identity when the media publicize one choking on a pretzel, another collapsing while jogging, and a third losing the TV remote. It was much easier to be a hero in the days of Jefferson or Lincoln, before the invention of electronic media that penetrate the barriers between front and back regions (Meyrowitz, 1985).

Ingratiation

Most people want to be liked by others. Not only do we find it inherently pleasant, but being liked may gain us a promotion or a better grade, and it may save us from being fired or flunked. How do we persuade others to like us? Whereas much of the time we are authentic and sincere in our relations with others, occasionally we may resort to **ingratiation**—attempts to increase a target person's liking for us (Wortman & Linsenmeier, 1977). The original theory (Jones, 1964) included the assumption that these attempts are conscious, but subsequent work has broadened the definition to include attempts that occur automatically due to social learning (Jones & Wortman, 1973).

Certain preconditions make ingratiation more likely. Individuals may try to ingratiate themselves when they depend on the target person for certain benefits and believe or assume that the target person is more likely to grant those benefits to someone he or she likes. Moreover, people are more likely to use ingratiation tactics when the target is not constrained by regulations and can therefore exercise his or her discretion in distributing rewards (Jones, Gergen, Gumpert, & Thibaut, 1965). In organizational settings, when roles are ambiguous, so that members are uncertain whether they are doing a good job, they may engage in ingratiation in an effort to ensure that they are perceived as competent and to receive rewards (Kacmar, Carlson, & Bratton, 2004).

There are a number of ingratiation tactics. Three of them are intended to increase the other's liking for an actor—that is, are other-focused. These are opinion conformity (that is, pretending to share the target person's views on important issues), other enhancement (that is, outright flattery or complimenting of the target person), and supplication (that is, convincing others you are deserving).

Opinion Conformity. Faced with a target person who has discretionary power, an ingratiator may try to curry favor by expressing insincere agreement on important issues. This tactic, termed *opinion conformity*, is often successful because people tend to like others who hold opinions similar to their own (Byrne, 1971). Of course, obvious or excessive opinion conformity on issue after issue would quickly arouse a target's suspicion, so a clever ingratiator will mix conformity on important issues with disagreement on unimportant issues.

Opinion conformity sometimes requires us to tailor the content of the opinions we express to match a target person's general values rather than any specific opinions he or she may hold. There is evidence that persons tend to show more ingratiation responses of all kinds toward their boss than toward a stranger or a friend (Bohra & Pandey, 1984). However, a meta-analysis of 69 studies (Gordon, 1996) indicates that ingratiation attempts directed upward (that is, toward persons of higher status) are less likely to be effective in promoting liking than are ingratiation attempts directed laterally (that is, toward persons of equal status) or downward (that is, toward persons of lower status). High-status targets, aware that others may have a motive to ingratiate, may be somewhat more vigilant than equal- or low-status targets.

Other Enhancement. A second ingratiation tactic is other enhancement—that is, using flattery on the target person. To be effective, flattery cannot be careless or indiscriminate. More than two centuries ago, Lord Chesterfield (1774) stated that people are best flattered in those areas where they wish to excel but are unsure of themselves. This hypothesis was tested in a study in which female participants were told that their supervisor valued either efficiency or sociability (Michener, Plazewski, & Vaske, 1979). The supervisor was a target for ingratiation because the participants' earnings depended on the evaluations they received from her. Before the supervisor made these evaluations, the participants had an opportunity to flatter her. The experimenter asked them to rate the supervisor's efficiency and sociability, and indicated that the supervisor would see the ratings. The results showed that the supervisor's assumed values channeled the form of flattery the participants used. Those who believed the supervisor valued efficiency publicly rated her higher on efficiency than on sociability, whereas those who believed she valued sociability publicly rated her higher on sociability than on efficiency. Thus, the participants were discriminating in their use of praise; moreover, they avoided extreme ratings that might suggest insincerity.

Ingratiation works. Research shows that targets of flattery are more likely to believe it—and to like the flatterer—than observers (Gordon, 1996). A set of experiments were conducted to identify which of several plausible reasons—vanity of the target, reduced ability to make accurate attributions, or the desire to like the other person—account for the target's reactions. The results suggest that it is the target's vanity; people like to be evaluated positively (Vonk, 2002). Other enhancement can also take forms other than flattery; one example, playing dumb, is discussed in Box 4.4.

Supplication. A third other-focused tactic is **supplication**—convincing a target person that you are needy and deserving (Baumeister, 1998). This is the tactic that roadside panhandlers use. By dressing in ragged clothes, they convey their need for money; by holding a sign that suggests a good use of the money ("Vet needs money to feed kids"), they attempt to convey that they are deserving. Students sometimes use this tactic in attempts to get an instructor to change a grade: "But I studied really hard and I knew a lot more than was on the exam." Whereas some people choose to use this tactic, others are forced to do so, for example, to get benefit payments from government or charitable agencies. In the latter case, the supplicant may feel embarrassed or angry, and will have to manage his or her emotional display.

Selective Self-Presentation. The fourth, self-focused ingratiation tactic is selective self-presentation, which involves the explicit presentation or description of one's own attributes to increase the likelihood of being judged attractive by the target. There are two distinct forms of selective self-presentation: self-promotion (Baumeister, 1998) and self-deprecation. When using self-promotion, a person advertises his or her strengths, virtues, and admirable qualities. If successful, this tactic creates a positive public identity and gains liking by others. A field study of job interviews in a campus placement office assessed the degree to which each applicant (61 men, 58 women, 91 percent White) used opinion conformity and self-promotion during the interview; the interviewer's perception of the applicant's fit to the job was assessed following the interview. The results indicated that opinion conformity enhanced perceived fit and influenced hiring recommendations, whereas self-promotion had little effect (Higgins & Judge, 2004).

In contrast, when using self-deprecation, a person makes only humble or modest claims. Self-deprecation can be an effective way to increase others' approval and liking, especially when it aligns the ingratiator with such important cultural values as honesty and objectivity in self-appraisal.

Although often effective, the tactic of selectively emphasizing our admirable qualities can be risky. This is especially true if the target knows enough about us to suspect we are boasting or if uncontrollable future events could prove our claims invalid. Wise ingratiators, therefore, use self-promoting descriptions only when these risks are minimal—that is, when the target person does not know them well and has no way to check their future performances (Frey, 1978; Schlenker, 1975).

Due to the risks inherent in self-enhancement, the opposite approach—self-deprecation or modest self-presentation—is often a safer tactic. To be effective, however, self-deprecation must be used in moderation. Excessively harsh and vigorous public self-criticism may gain expressions of

BOX 4.4 Research Update: Playing Dumb

"Playing dumb" is an ingratiation tactic used with some frequency in interaction. When playing dumb, impression managers pretend to be less intelligent or knowledgeable than they really are. By playing dumb, they present themselves as inferior, thereby giving the target person a sense of superiority. Thus, playing dumb is a form of other enhancement.

Although popular belief and early research suggested that women are more prone than men to playing dumb (Wallin, 1950), a national survey of American adults indicated just the opposite (Gove, Hughes, & Geerken, 1980). Significantly more men than women said that they had pretended at least once to be less intelligent or knowledgeable than they really were. Men reported playing dumb more often than women in most of the situations examined, including work.

A recent review of research on the use of impression management tactics in organizations found that both men and women use them, and use tactics consistent with gender-role expectations. In organizational settings, women reported "playing dumb" more than men (Guadagno & Cialdini, 2007).

What leads people to play dumb? The data indicate that people who use this technique tend to be young, highly educated men (Gove et al., 1980). In contemporary American society, these persons are likely to hold lower-status positions in competitive occupations where knowledge is valued (junior executives, law clerks, graduate students, and the like). Because of their youth,

many of these people are located at the bottom of an occupational ladder they aspire to climb.

These people interact with superiors in settings where intelligence and knowledge are prized. Under these circumstances, one's relatively low status may require deferring to superiors despite one's own knowledge and ability. People may stand to gain by hiding any intellectual superiority they feel—that is, by playing dumb.

Among college students, both men and women report playing dumb with dates, friends, and partners (Thornton et al., 2009). Measures of both hypercompetitiveness—desire to win—and competition avoidance were associated with more frequent use of the tactic.

Alternatively, playing dumb may be a defensive tactic, used to avoid action (Ashforth & Lee, 1990). The actor may attempt to avoid acting by pleading ignorance or lack of ability. Again, this may be more common in a highly structured, competitive organization, where midlevel personnel are motivated to avoid irritating others in order to enhance their long-term prospects. In the early years of the twenty-first century, playing dumb has become a common tactic for avoiding responsibility for corporate misconduct and fraud (Steffy, 2005). On trial for fraudulent financial practices, a CEO pleads ignorance, arguing that he didn't know what the CFO (chief financial officer) or the auditors were doing. In this case, the actor is playing dumb in an effort to avoid significant penalties rather than to enhance others' liking for him or her.

support from others, but these expressions run the risk that others may actually believe them and form a negative private evaluation of the person using them (Powers & Zuroff, 1988). A more effective form of self-deprecation is an assured, matter-of-fact modesty that understates or downplays one's substantial achievements. In one experiment, members of a group were asked to evaluate other members following the group's suc-

cess or failure at a task (Forsyth, Berger, & Mitchell, 1981). Group members reported greater liking for those who took blame for the group's failure or credited others for the group's success (self-deprecation) than for those who blamed others for failure and claimed credit themselves for the group's success (self-enhancement). These results suggest that when observers have evidence about someone's performance—whether favorable or unfavorable—self-deprecation can be an effective tactic of ingratiation.

Not only individuals but groups, organizations, and entire nations may experience stigma, or spoiled identity. The nation of Croatia has a "difficult past" as a result of the wars in the former Yugoslavia in the 1990s. The publicity about the wars, and the resulting deaths and destruction, had a big, negative impact on tourism, a major segment of the Croatian economy. After the conflict ended, the Croatian Tourist Bureau launched a public relations campaign based on selective self-presentation. Postwar brochures, advertisements, and feature articles on travel made no mention of the conflict, or of the region's Balkan roots; instead, they stressed Croatia's "European" character, proximity to Italy, and its lack of "Slavic roots" (Rivera, 2008).

Aligning Actions

During interaction, occasional failures of impression management are inevitable. Others may sometimes catch us performing actions that violate group norms (such as "dissing" other group members) or break laws (such as running a red light). Such actions potentially undermine the social identities we have been claiming and disrupt smooth interaction. When this occurs, people engage in **aligning actions**—attempts to define their apparently questionable conduct as actually in line with cultural norms. Aligning actions repair cherished social identities, restore meaning to the situation, and reestablish smooth interaction (Hunter, 1984; Spencer, 1987). In this section, we discuss two important types of aligning actions—disclaimers and accounts.

Disclaimers. When people anticipate that their planned actions will disrupt smooth social interaction, invite criticism, or threaten their established identity, they of-

ten employ disclaimers. A **disclaimer** is a verbal assertion intended to ward off any negative implications of impending actions by defining these actions as irrelevant to one's established identity (Bennett, 1990; Hewitt & Stokes, 1975). By using disclaimers, they suggest that although the impending acts ordinarily imply a negative identity, theirs is an extraordinary case. For example, before making a bigoted remark, a person may point to her extraordinary credentials (for example, "Some of my best friends are gay, but . . ."). Disclaimers are also used prior to acts that would otherwise undermine one's identity as moral (for example, ("I know this may sound weird, but . . .") or as mentally competent (for example, "Call me crazy, but . . ."). These disclaimers emphasize that although the speakers are aware the act could threaten their identity, they are appealing to a higher morality or to a superior competence.

Still other disclaimers plead for a suspension of judgment until the whole event is clear: "Please hear me out before you jump to conclusions." When individuals are not certain how others will react to new information or suggestions, they are more likely to preface their actions with hedging remarks (such as "I'm no expert, but . . ." or "I could be wrong, but . . ."). Such remarks proclaim in advance that possible mistakes or failures should not reflect on one's crucial identities.

Accounts. After individuals have engaged in disruptive behavior, they may try to repair the damage by using accounts. **Accounts** are the explanations people offer to mitigate responsibility after they have performed acts that threaten their social identities (Harvey, Weber, & Orbuch, 1990; Scott & Lyman, 1968; Semin & Manstead, 1983). There are two main types of accounts: excuses and justifications. Excuses reduce or deny one's responsibility for the unsuitable behavior by citing uncontrollable events (for example, "My car broke down"), coercive external pressures (for example, "My boss made me do it"), or compelling internal pressures (for example, "I suddenly felt dizzy and couldn't concentrate on the exam"). Presenting an excuse reduces the observer's tendency to hold the individual responsible or to make negative inferences about his or her character (Riordan, Marlin, & Kellogg, 1983; Weiner, Amirkhan, Folkes, & Verette, 1987). Excuses also preserve the individual's self-image and reduce the stress associated with failure (Snyder, Higgins, & Stucky, 1983). Justifications admit responsibility for the unsuitable behavior but also try to define the behavior as appropriate under the circumstances (for example, "Sure I hit him, but he hit me first") or as prompted by praiseworthy motives (for example, "It was for her own good"). Justifications are intended to reduce the perceived wrongness of the behavior.

Persons are more likely to accept accounts when the content appears truthful and conforms with the explanations commonly used for such behavior (Riordan et al., 1983). Accounts are honored more readily when the individual who gives them is trustworthy, penitent, and of superior status, and when the identity violation is not serious (Blumstein, 1974). Thus, we are more likely to accept a psychiatrist's quiet explanation that he struck an elderly mental patient because she kept shouting and would not talk with him than to accept a delinquent's defiant use of the same excuse to explain why he struck an elderly woman.

A staple of public life in many countries is the political scandal: allegations that a politician has engaged in some improper or illegal behavior. The politician typically either denies the allegation outright ("I did not have sex with that woman") or offers an excuse ("I did not know that my housekeeper was in the United States illegally") or a justification

("I did accept $200,000 from that group. I did so on the advice of my lawyer that it was legal"). How effective are these responses? Does their effectiveness vary depending on the transgression and the politician's gender? To answer these questions, researchers prepared four newspaper stories involving hiring an illegal alien, engaging in sex with a superior, accepting illegal gifts, and engaging in sex with a subordinate. Within each, gender was varied. Within each, the politician's response was denial, an excuse, or a justification. The results (mean ratings by undergraduates and adults from the community) show that denials and justifications were associated with more favorable ratings than were excuses. Contrary to predictions, respondents did not judge female politicians more harshly than men for the same offence. However, respondents did judge more harshly persons whose offense was consistent with gender stereotypes: men accepting illegal contributions and having sex with a subordinate, and women hiring an illegal alien and having sex with a superior (Smith, Powers, & Suarez, 2005). Thus, had Pres. Bill Clinton been a woman, he might have escaped impeachment!

Altercasting

The tactics discussed so far illustrate how people claim and protect identities. The actions of one person in an encounter will place limits on who the others can claim to be. Therefore, to gain an advantage in the interaction, we might try to impose identities on others that complement the identities we claim for ourselves. We might also pressure others to enact roles that mesh with the roles we want for ourselves. **Altercasting** is the use of tactics to impose roles and identities on others. Through altercasting, we place others in situated identities and roles that are to our advantage (Weinstein & Deutschberger, 1963).

In general, altercasting involves treating others as if they already have the identities and roles that we wish to impose on them. Teachers engage in altercasting when they tell a student, "I know you can do better than that." This remark pressures the student to live up to an imposed identity of competence. Altercasting can entail carefully planned duplicity. An employer may invite subordinates to dinner, for example, casting them as close friends in hopes of learning employee secrets.

People frequently use altercasting to put someone on the defensive. "Explain to the voters why you can't control the runaway national debt," says the challenger, altercasting the incumbent official as incompetent in dealing with the economy. Should the incumbent rise to her own defense, she admits that the charge merits discussion and that the negative identity may be correct. Should she remain silent, she implies acceptance of the altercast identity. Putting one's rivals on the defensive is an effective technique, because a negative identity is difficult to escape.

The news about self-presentation and impression management is not all good; these may have negative effects on health and relationships, as outlined in Box 4.5.

Impression Management Online

The widespread use of computer-mediated communication has multiplied the opportunities to engage in tactical self-presentation. As senders, CMC users can selectively present themselves; they have complete control over the content and timing of messages (Walther, 2007). The writer and the receiver are physically isolated from each other, so the receiver does not have access to nonverbal cues, which are often less controlled and therefore more revealing. Thus, messages and postings can be carefully crafted and manipulated (Lee, 2006).

A study of one user group included observation and analysis of messages for 2½ years (Lee, 2006). Members took a variety of steps to limit information about themselves. For example, 27 of the 66 members used a remailer to secure their privacy; only 5 included the URL of their personal webpage in their postings. Members based their "knowledge" of other members by inference from e-mail address and domain, name, signature, and message content. Members often tested identity inferences indirectly, by basing a communication on an inference about, for example, gender, and seeing how the recipient reacted. Occasionally, a member would pose a direct question about another member's identity (or identities). Over time, "regulars" revealed age, gender, careers, and hobbies. The researcher concludes that regulars carefully controlled interaction and employed a variety of protective practices.

Creating and posting a personal webpage or space is "conspicuous self-presentation that assumes external observation" (Schau & Gill, 2003). Researchers drew a sample of 326 sites and performed a content analysis on them; they also interviewed the creators of 35 of these sites. Creators carefully select and embed text, photos and drawings, icons, and hyperlinks. Hyperlinks may be used to tell one's story, such as links to schools attended and past/present employers. Some pages include references to or links to retailers, providing information about preferred clothing, makeup, or jewelry. The researchers observed variation in whether and how the site referenced the creator's physical body. One woman intentionally used the word *sexy* and professional photos of herself in lingerie on her site; other creators carefully avoided any reference to appearance or the body. People began to create a website in response to a life transition (graduation, career change), a desire for personal growth or experience, or to advocate for something. As they became more experienced through viewing other sites and getting feedback on their own,

BOX 4.5 Research Update: The Downside of Self-Presentation

Self-presentation facilitates smooth interaction, and impression management tactics may benefit the user. However, these practices also may have harmful effects.

Self-Presentation May Be Hazardous to Your Health. Leary and his colleagues (Leary, Tchividjian, & Kraxberger, 1994; Martin, Leary, & Rejeski, 2000) study the relationship between concern with how others perceive you and risky behavior. We usually want others to evaluate us favorably and support the identities we claim in interactions. We want to avoid failures in self-presentation because they are painful and because they tarnish others' images of us. These motives may lead to behaviors that jeopardize our physical health.

Teen pregnancy and sexually transmitted infections (STIs) are major public health problems and can be traumatic or life threatening to those affected by them. There are 750,000 pregnancies among teens and 4 million new cases of STIs among people under 25 in the United States each year. Most of these could be prevented by the correct and consistent use of condoms. Why don't sexually active young people, many of whom are aware of these risks, use condoms? Research indicates that self-presentational concerns are a major reason (Leary et al., 1994). Some men and women are afraid to buy condoms because others will infer they are sexually active. Some are afraid to produce a condom during sexual interaction for fear they will appear prepared (gasp!) for sexual activity. Some are afraid to suggest condom use because it might suggest that they are unfaithful or that they think their partner is unfaithful.

Consider skin cancer. The incidence of skin cancer increases every year in the United States. A major cause is excessive exposure to ultraviolet radiation. Many people intentionally expose themselves to this radiation by sunbathing. Why? To enhance others' impressions of their attractiveness. Research indicates that people who are concerned with others' impressions or high in body consciousness are more likely to sunbathe or use tanning facilities (Leary et al., 1994). More than 25 percent of teenage girls use tanning devices each year; the rate doubles from age 14 to 15, and again from age 15 to 17 (Balk, Fisher, & Geller, 2013).

Numerous other risky behaviors result in part from the desire to make a favorable impression on others, including excessive dieting and eating disorders; alcohol, tobacco, and drug use; and excessive use of steroids by athletes. Teens may engage in risky behavior in order to be accepted by their friends: Discussing why she started smoking, one woman said, "There are many times when I'll cross the line just so I won't lose friends" (Green, 2002, p. D1). Numerous teens die every year as a result of showing off, whether by driving recklessly or diving into shallow water.

Deception May Be Hazardous to Your Relationships. Many of us engage in selective self-presentation—that is, accentuating our positive features and withholding information or avoiding issues that might create negative impressions. Research indicates that we are most likely to engage in these practices in our romantic relationships. Obviously, we engage in these practices in an effort to preserve the relationship and to avoid costly interactions, such as conflict with or punishment by our partner. A study of 128 heterosexual couples found that many men and women reported using "misleading communication" with their partners for such purposes (Cole, 2001). However, they also reported using these practices when they perceived that their partner was using these tactics. And people who reported using deception or who perceived that their partner was dishonest reported lower levels of satisfaction with and commitment to their relationships.

One of the processes at work in this situation is the norm of reciprocity. Just as there is reciprocity in self-disclosure, there is reciprocity in withholding information and intentionally using misleading communication (that is, lying) in close relationships. These behaviors, motivated by a desire to preserve the relationship, can lead to a downward spiral and the eventual dissolution of the relationship.

they continuously upgraded or fine-tuned it, or created new sites, indicating the importance of intentionality in the construction of sites. The self presented on these sites was often an idealized or imagined self; the creators sometimes visually enhanced images of the body, for example, by careful attention to pose. So websites or spaces allow one to explore changing identities and monitor the feedback; obviously this could lead in some cases to a change in identity in the real world.

A study of social networking sites analyzed the content of sites posted by 51 men and 49 women (Magnusen & Dundes, 2008). Researchers were interested in the extent to which self-presentation was gendered. They found that men were less likely than women to mention their significant other in the space. They interpreted this as reflecting the norm of masculine individuality, in contrast to the expectation that women derive their identity in part from their relationships to others.

One group of researchers (Ellison, Hancock, & Toma, 2011) studied the sites posted by 37 online daters. These men and women are trying to construct a site that will appeal to potential partners for several months into the future. Thus, they were less concerned about the accuracy of the profile. Their criterion for what they posted was whether the self presented could be produced in the future. Thus, they perceived their presented self as a "promise" (losing 10 pounds, quitting smoking, reducing alcohol consumption, earning more money) that could be fulfilled if they met the right person. Promises, promises.

DETECTING DECEPTIVE IMPRESSION MANAGEMENT

Up to this point, we have discussed various techniques used by impression managers to project identities and control relationships. Now we will shift our focus to the person (target) toward whom impression management tactics are directed. Impression managers intentionally try to create a particular image. This image may or may not be challenged by the person targeted. In some cases, the target will accept a false image because he or she has little to gain by questioning the sincerity of the impression manager. For instance, funeral directors strive to convey an air of sympathy and concern although they usually did not know the deceased person. Mourning relatives realize that the sympathy is superficial, but they ask very few questions because they would only be more upset to discover the mortician's true feelings of boredom and indifference.

In other cases, however, the accurate detection of deception is crucial for protecting our own interests. In attempting to win a contract, for example, builders may claim to be reliable businesspeople and skilled artisans even when they are total frauds. For the homeowner about to make a down payment, it is literally worth thousands of dollars to determine whether the builder's hearty handshake belongs to a responsible contractor or to a fly-by-night operator.

How do people go about trying to unmask the impression manager? In general, they attend to two major types of information: (1) the ulterior motives the other person may have for an action, and (2) the nonverbal cues that accompany the action. In this section, we discuss both of these.

Ulterior Motives

The recognition that another person has a strong ulterior motive for his or her behavior usually colors an interaction. For example, when a used car salesman tells us that a battered vehicle with sagging springs was driven only on Sundays by his aged aunt, his ulterior motive is transparent, and we are certain to suspect deceit. In such a case, we will probably discount what the salesman says about any car on his lot or even refuse to do business with him.

Ironically, the very conditions that increase the temptation to use ingratiation tactics also make the target more vigilant. As noted earlier, ingratiators are especially prone to use such tactics as flattery or opinion conformity when the target person controls important rewards and can use discretion in distributing them. Unhappily for ingratiators, these same conditions alert the target to be vigilant and to expect deception. This state of affairs, termed the *ingratiator's dilemma*, means that ingratiators must be doubly careful to conceal their ulterior motives and avoid detection under conditions of high dependency. As documented by Gordon (1996) based on a meta-analysis, ingratiation attempts that are transparent tend to be relatively ineffective, sometimes to the point of backfiring. Ingratiators usually understand this, and indeed, there is some evidence that ingratiators avoid using tactics such as opinion conformity under conditions of blatant power inequality; they are more likely to use them under conditions that are less likely to alert the target (Kauffman & Steiner, 1968).

Nonverbal Cues of Deception

Research indicates that nonverbal cues do provide a basis for detecting deception at a rate somewhat better than chance (DePaulo, Zuckerman, & Rosenthal, 1980; Kraut, 1980).

Cues Indicating Deception. When people interact face-to-face, they send messages through both verbal and nonverbal channels. People transmit meanings not only by words (verbal expressions), but also by facial expressions, bodily gestures, and voice quality. The multichannel nature of com-

munication can pose problems for impression managers, because the meanings transmitted through some of these channels are more controllable than those transmitted through others. For instance, if an impression manager is trying to deceive a target, he or she may tell a lie verbally but then inadvertently reveal his or her true intentions or emotions through nonverbal channels. The term *nonverbal leakage* denotes the inadvertent communication of true intentions or emotions through nonverbal channels (Ekman & Friesen, 1969, 1974).

An impression manager will generally have a high level of control over his or her verbal expression (choice of words) and a fair amount of control over facial expressions (smiles, frowns, and so on). The deceiver may have less control, however, over body movements (arms, hands, legs, feet) and over voice quality and vocal inflections (the pitch and waver of his or her voice). The nonverbal channels that are least controllable—voice quality and body movements—are the ones that leak the most information (Blanck & Rosenthal, 1982; DePaulo & Rosenthal, 1979).

Several studies have demonstrated that the fundamental pitch of the voice is higher when someone is lying than when telling the truth (DePaulo, Stone, & Lassiter, 1985; Ekman, Friesen, & Scherer, 1976). The difference is fairly small—individuals cannot discriminate just by listening. Other vocal cues associated with deception include speech hesitation (liars hesitate more), speech errors (liars stutter and stammer more), and response length (liars give shorter answers; DePaulo et al., 1985; Zuckerman, DePaulo, & Rosenthal, 1981). Notice that interrogators on TV crime dramas use these cues.

Certain facial and body cues are also associated with deception. Tipoffs regarding deception include eye pupil dilation (liars show more dilation) and blinking (liars blink more); another tipoff is self-directed gestures (liars touch themselves more) (De-Paulo et al., 1985). The musculature of a smile is slightly different when people are lying than when they are telling the truth. Lying smiles contain a trace of muscular activity usually associated with expression of disgust, fear, or sadness (Ekman, Friesen, & O'Sullivan, 1988) (see Box 4.6).

Using a high-tech heat detection camera, researchers found that people who are lying get hot around the eyes (Pavlidis et al., 2002). In the popular mind and in the media, the lie detector is often associated with detecting deception, via the sensors that supposedly monitor pulse, breathing, and sweating. But the polygrapher rarely looks at the machine's output; he is busy listening for the verbal cues and watching for the behavioral changes listed here (Editorial, 2004).

Accuracy of Detection. Most of us rarely concern ourselves with the possibility of deception as we interact with others. But the events of September 11, 2001, led us to realize that in some situations, the costs of undetected deception are high indeed. As a result, there is much greater interest in the question "How good are observers at detecting acts of deception?" Although some people believe they can always detect deception when it is used by an impression manager, research suggests the contrary. The results of most experiments reveal that observers are not especially adept at correctly identifying when others are lying. Rates of detection are generally somewhat better than chance but not especially good in absolute terms (Ekman & O'Sullivan, 1991; Zuckerman et al., 1981). This occurs in part because observers often use the wrong cues or do not rely on the most useful kinds of information in judging whether someone is lying.

Difficulty in liar detection is illustrated by a study in which travelers at an airport in New York were asked to participate in a mock inspection procedure (Kraut & Poe, 1980). Some of these travelers were given "contraband" to smuggle past inspection, whereas others carried only their own legitimate luggage. All participants were instructed to present themselves as honest persons. As motivation, the researchers offered travelers prizes up to $100 for appearing honest. Later, professional customs inspectors and lay judges watched videotaped playbacks of each of the travelers and tried to decide which travelers ought to be searched. The results showed that both the customs inspectors and the inexperienced judges failed to identify a substantial proportion of the travelers who were smuggling contraband. The rate of detection, even by the customs inspectors, was no better than chance. Interestingly, however, the professional inspectors and the inexperienced judges agreed on which travelers should be searched. That is, the inspectors and the lay judges used the same (invalid) behavioral cues as indicative of deception. Travelers were more likely to be selected for search if they were young and lower-class, appeared nervous, hesitated before answering questions, gave short answers, avoided eye contact, and shifted their posture frequently. Unfortunately for the inspectors, these cues were imperfect indicators of deception. The results of this experiment remind us of the difficulties facing immigration and customs officials in airports and at border crossings.

Why aren't observers better at detecting deception? First, nonverbal behaviors that do reveal deception—such as high vocal pitch and short response length—are imperfect indicators. They do arise from deception, but they can also result from conditions unrelated to deception, such as excitement or anxiety. In such circumstances, the innocent will appear guilty, and observers will make mistakes in detection. Second, there are certain cues that

BOX 4.6 Test Yourself: Can You Detect the Deception?

Research indicates that most lay people are not very accurate in detecting deception. How about you? Can you tell the difference between Nicolas Cage's fake and genuine smiles?

On the surface, fake and genuine smiles may look quite similar, but there are distinct differ-ences between the two. To learn more and to test yourself on spotting fake smiles, go to http://www.bbc.co.uk/science/humanbody/mind/surveys/smiles/.

© EdStock/iStock

are commonly believed to reveal deception but that actually do not (DePaulo et al., 1985). These cues include speech rate (people think liars talk slower), smiling (people think liars smile less), gaze (people think liars engage in less eye contact), and postural shifts (people think liars shift more). If observers rely heavily on these cues, they will make mistakes in detection. Third, certain skilled impression managers are able to give near-flawless performances when deceiving. One study (Riggio & Friedman, 1983) finds evidence that certain people can give off what seem to be honest emotional cues (such as facial animation, some exhibition-ism, few nervous behaviors) even when they are deceiving. If an impression manager has this capability, he or she will appear inno-cent, again causing mistakes in detection by observers. Fourth, we note that face-to-face interaction is a two-way street; impression managers not only exhibit behavior, but they also observe the reactions of their au-diences. The feedback from audiences in face-to-face situations is fairly rich, and it often provides impression managers with a clear indication whether their attempts at deception are succeeding. If they are not succeeding, they may be able to adjust or fine-tune their deceptive communications to be more convincing.

The picture is not entirely bleak, however. First, members of some groups are accurate at catching liars. Law enforcement officers, judges, and professional psychologists were shown videotapes of the head and shoulders of 10 persons; each person was speaking about an issue he felt strongly about, and half of them were lying about their position. Federal officers (most from the CIA) attained an accuracy score of 73, while sheriffs, federal judges, and clinical psychologists interested in deception attained scores of 67 to 62. Law enforcement officers and academic psychologists attained the lowest scores (Ekman, O'Sullivan, & Frank, 1999). Second, observers' success in detecting deception can be increased by special discrimination training (Zuckerman, Koestner, & Alton, 1984). Moreover, success in detecting deception can be affected by the instructions given to observers. For instance, one study (DePaulo, Lassiter, & Stone, 1982) varied the instructions given to observers in face-to-face interaction. When given instructions to pay particular attention to auditory cues and to downplay visual cues, observers were more successful in discriminating truth from deception than when they were given instructions to pay attention to both visual and auditory cues. By emphasizing auditory and downplaying visual cues, observers more fully attended those cues that are least under an impression manager's control, such as voice quality. In general, lack of attention to verbal content and paralinguistic cues seriously impairs the ability to detect deception (Geller, 1977; Littlepage & Pineault, 1978). We can hope that the events of September 11, 2001, have led to changes in the training of officials who are supposed to detect deception—training based on the research results described here.

Notice that nonverbal cues play an important role in detecting false or inaccurate images. It is precisely these cues that are lacking in online communication, making it easier to engage in deceitful or fraudulent interactions online.

INEFFECTIVE SELF-PRESENTATION AND SPOILED IDENTITIES

Social interaction is a perilous undertaking, for it is easily disrupted by challenges to identity. Some of us may recover when a challenge occurs, but others will be permanently saddled with spoiled identities. In this section, we discuss what happens when impression management fails. First, we consider embarrassment—a spontaneous reaction to sudden or transitory challenges to our identities. Second, we examine cooling-out and identity degradation, which are deliberate actions aimed at destroying or debasing the identities of persons who fail repeatedly. Third, we analyze the fate of those afflicted with stigmas—physical, moral, or social handicaps that may spoil their identities permanently.

Embarrassment and Saving Face

Embarrassment is the feeling we experience when the public identity we claim in an encounter is discredited (Edelmann, 1987; Semin & Manstead, 1982, 1983). It is usually experienced in social interaction (Ho, Fu, & Ng, 2004). Many people describe it as an uncomfortable feeling of exposure, mortification, awkwardness, and chagrin (Miller, 1992; Parrott & Smith, 1991). It may entail such physiological symptoms as blushing, increased heart rate, and increased temperature (Edelmann & Iwawaki, 1987).

Whereas we experience embarrassment when our own identity is discredited, we also experience embarrassment when the identities of people with whom we are interacting are discredited (Miller, 1987). In this sense, embarrassment is contagious. It may be more acute when our own adequate performance serves as a frame of reference that highlights the inadequacy of others' performances (Bennett & Dewberry, 1989). We feel embarrassment at others' spoiled identities because we have been duped about the assumptions on which we built our interaction with them, including our unwarranted acceptance of their identity claims (Edelmann, 1985; Goffman, 1967). For example, someone who claims to be an outstanding ballplayer will experience embarrassment when he drops the first three routine fly balls to center field, but the manager who let him play in a crucial game also will feel embarrassment and chagrin for accepting the ballplayer's claim of competence.

Sources of Embarrassment. Investigators have analyzed hundreds of cases of embarrassment to ascertain the conditions that produce this feeling (Gross & Stone, 1970; Miller, 1992; Sharkey & Stafford, 1990). The results show that any of several conditions can precipitate embarrassment. To begin with, people feel embarrassed if it becomes publicly apparent that they lack the skills to perform in a manner consistent with the identity they claim. This is the plight, for example, of the math professor who suddenly discovers that he cannot solve the demonstration problem he has written on the chalkboard. Closely related to lack of skill is cognitive shortcoming, such as forgetfulness. A host's inability to remember others' names during introductions at a small party can cause embarrassment for all concerned.

Another condition that precipitates embarrassment is violation of privacy norms. If one person barges unaware into a place where he or she does not belong (such as a residential bathroom occupied by another), both persons are likely to experience embarrassment at the violation of privacy. The sudden and unexpected conversion of a back region into a front region is embarrassing for those whose identities are tarnished or discredited.

A further condition that often precipitates embarrassment is awkwardness or lack of poise. A person can lose poise if he or she trips, stumbles, spills coffee, or miscoordinates physically with others. Loss of control of equipment (a dentist dropping her drill), of clothing (a speaker splitting his pants), or of one's own body (trembling, burping, or worse) also will destroy poise. In general, poise vanishes and embarrassment increases whenever we lose control over those aspects of our self-presentation that we ordinarily manage routinely.

A study of Japanese undergraduates (Higuchi & Fukada, 2002) found that the causes of embarrassment include disruption of social interaction, fear of negative evaluation by others, inconsistency with self-image, and loss of self-esteem. The first two were rated as most important when the event occurred in the presence of others (criticism by an instructor during class, falling in public), and the last two as most important when the individual considered a prior event in private (failing to support a friend, failing an examination). In an experiment, male and female university students viewed slides of nudes and erotic couples either alone or with two strangers. Participants self-reported greater embarrassment when others were present, but careful analysis of videotapes showed fewer instances of nonverbal indicators of embarrassment, such as face touches and downward gazes, in the public condition (Costa, Dinsbach, & Manstead, 2001). It may be that we try to control nonverbal indicators in the presence of others.

Responses to Embarrassment. A continuing state of embarrassment is uncomfortable for everyone involved. For this reason, it is usually in everyone's interest to restore face—that is, to eliminate the conditions causing embarrassment. The major responsibility for restoring face lies with the person whose actions produced the embarrassment, but interaction partners frequently try to help the embarrassed person restore face (Levin & Arluke, 1982). For instance, if a party guest slips and falls while demonstrating his dancing prowess, his partner might help him save face by remarking that the floor tiles seem newly waxed and very slippery. Mutual commitment to supporting each other's social identities is a basic rule of social interaction (Goffman, 1967).

To restore face, the embarrassed person will often apologize, provide an account, or otherwise realign his or her actions with the normative order (Knapp, Stafford, & Daly, 1986; Metts & Cupach, 1989). When providing accounts, people will either make excuses that minimize their responsibility or offer justifications that define their behavior as acceptable under the circumstances. If the interaction partners accept these accounts—and partners have been known to accept the lamest excuses rather than endure continuing embarrassment—a proper identity is restored. If accounts are unavailable or insufficient, the embarrassed individual may offer an apology for the discrediting behavior and admit that his or her behavior was wrong. In this way, the person reaffirms threatened norms and reassures others that he or she will not violate those norms again. Research suggests that blushing is particularly important in restoring the normative order. Observers rated videotapes of a public gaffe; an actor who visibly blushed following the incident was judged less negatively, as less responsible, and as more trustworthy than an actor who did not blush (Jong, 1999). The results suggest that blushing communicates to others that the actor is attached to the social rules in question despite the violation.

When our behavior discredits a particular, narrow identity, we can sometimes restore face through an exaggerated reassertion of that identity. A man whose masculine identity is threatened by behavior suggesting he is infantile, for example, might try to reassert his courage and strength. In a test of this hypothesis (Holmes, 1971), some male participants were asked to suck on a rubber nipple, a pacifier, and a breast shield—all embarrassing experiences. Other participants were asked to touch surfaces such as sandpaper and cloth. The men were next asked how intense an electric shock they would be willing to endure later in the experiment. Men who had faced the embarrassing experiences indicated willingness to endure more intense shocks than men who had faced no threat to their masculine identity. By taking the intense shocks, the embarrassed men could present themselves as tough and courageous, thereby re-asserting their threatened masculinity.

Sometimes people embarrass others intentionally and make no effort to help them to save face. A study of self-reports of intentional embarrassment found that embarrassors reported that their goal was to negatively sanction the target, while targets reported that the embarrassor's goal was self-satisfaction (Sharkey, Kim, & Digs, 2001). In such circumstances, the embarrassed persons are likely to react aggressively. They may vigorously attack the judgment or character of those who embarrassed them. Some research indicates that an aggressive response to embarrassment is more likely between status unequals than between status equals (Sueda & Wiseman, 1992). Alternatively, the embarrassed persons may assert that the task on which they failed is worthless or absurd (Modigliani, 1971). Finally, they may retaliate against those who embarrassed them intentionally.

Retaliation not only reasserts an image of strength and achieves revenge, it also forestalls future embarrassment by showing resolve to punish those who discredit us. In these ways, embarrassment may lead to interpersonal aggression.

Cooling-Out and Identity Degradation

When people repeatedly or glaringly fail to meet performance standards or to present appropriate identities, others cease to help them save face. Instead, they may act deliberately to modify the offenders' identities or to remove them from their positions in interaction. Failing students are dropped from school, unreliable employees are let go, tiresome suitors are rebuffed, people with severe mental illness are institutionalized. Persons will modify an offender's identity either by cooling-out (Goffman, 1952) or by degradation (Garfinkel, 1956), depending on the social conditions surrounding the failure.

The term **cooling-out** refers to gently persuading a person whose performance is unsuitable to accept a less desirable, though still reasonable, alternative identity. A counselor at a community college may cool-out a weak student by advising him to switch from pre-med to an easier major, for example, or by recommending that he seek employment after completing community college rather than transfer to a university. Persons engaged in cooling-out seek to persuade offenders, not to force them. Cooling-out actions usually protect the privacy of offenders, console them, and try to reduce their distress. Thus, the counselor meets privately with the student, emphasizes the attractiveness of the alternative, listens sympathetically to the student's concerns, and leaves the final choice up to him.

The process of destroying the offender's identity and transforming him or her into a lower social type is termed **identity degradation**. Degradation establishes the offender as a nonperson—an individual who cannot be trusted to perform as a normal member of the social group because of reprehensible motives. This is the fate of a political dissident who is fired from her job, declared a threat to society, and relegated to isolation in a prison or work camp.

Identity degradation imposes a severe loss on the offender, so it usually is done forcibly. Identity degradation often involves a dramatic ceremony—such as a criminal trial, sanity hearing, or impeachment proceeding—in which a denouncer acts in the name of the larger society or the law (Scheff, 1966). In such ceremonies, persons who had previously been treated as free, competent citizens are brought before a group or individual legally empowered to determine their "true" identity. They are then denounced for serious offenses against the moral order. If the degradation succeeds, offenders are forced to give up their former identities and to take on new ones like "criminal," "insane," or "dishonorably discharged."

Two social conditions strongly influence the choice between cooling-out and degradation: (1) the offender's prior relationships with others, and (2) the availability of alternative identities (Ball, 1976). Cooling-out is more likely when the offender has had prior relations of empathy and solidarity with others and when alternative identity options are available. For example, during a breakup, lovers who have been close in the past can cool-out their partners by offering to remain friends. Identity degradation is more likely when prior relationships entailed little intimacy or when respectable alternative identities are not readily available. Thus, strangers found guilty of sexually molesting children are degraded and transformed into child molesters—immoral, subhuman creatures.

Observers have pointed out that in U.S. society, there are public degradation ceremonies for various types of offenders—trials and sentencing hearings, competency hearings, press conferences where one admits wrong-doing. However, there are no ceremonies when these persons return to society, and so they remain stigmatized. Redemption rituals could ease the reentry process. To be successful, they should be community based and public, and eliminate the person's "official" record (Fader, 2011).

Stigma

A **stigma** is a characteristic widely viewed as an insurmountable handicap that prevents competent or morally trustworthy behavior (Goffman, 1963b; Jones et al., 1984). There are several different types of stigmas. First, there are physical challenges and deformities—missing or paralyzed limbs, ugly scars, blindness, or deafness. Second, there are character defects—dishonesty, sexual attraction to inappropriate targets, psychological derangements, or treacherous beliefs. These may be inferred from a known record of crime, imprisonment, sexual abuse of children or partners, mental illness, or radical political activity, for example. Third, there are characteristics such as race, sex, and religion that—in particular segments of society—are believed to contaminate or morally debilitate all members of a group.

We discussed earlier the relationship between identity salience and self-esteem. Research involving 300 persons with various concealable stigmatized identities (for example, history of mental illness, rape, domestic violence, substance abuse) indicated that the amount of distress experienced was related to how much stigma the person expected, and the centrality (how important is it?) and salience (how often do you think about it?) of the identity (Quinn & Chandor, 2009).

Once recognized during interaction, stigmas spoil the identities of the persons having them. Stigmas operate via reflected appraisals; "normals" (nonstigmatized persons) convey expectations and negative evaluations of the stigmatized person (Kaufman & Johnson, 2004). No matter what their other attributes, stigmatized individuals are likely to find that others will not view them as fully competent or moral. As a result, social interaction between normal and stigmatized persons is shaky and uncomfortable.

Sources of Discomfort. Discomfort arises during interaction between normals and stigmatized individuals because both are uncertain what behavior is appropriate. Normals may fear, for example, that if they show direct sympathy or interest in the stigmatized person's condition, they will be intrusive (for example, "Is it difficult to write with your artificial hand?" "Can you dance with that artificial leg?"). Yet if they ignore the defect, they may make impossible demands (for example, "Would you help me move the refrigerator?"). To avoid being hurt, stigmatized individuals may vacillate between shamefaced withdrawal (avoiding social contact) and aggressive bravado ("I can do anything anyone else can!").

Another source of discomfort for normals is the threat, a sense of anxiety or even danger that they experience during interaction with stigmatized individuals (Blascovich, Mendes, Hunter, Lickel, & Kowai-Bell, 2001). Normals may fear that associating with a stigmatized person may discredit them (for example, "If I befriend a convicted criminal, people may wonder about my trustworthiness"). In recent times, this problem has arisen frequently with respect to AIDS, which is a heavily stigmatized condition due in part to its association with drug use and homosexuality as well as the lingering fear of transmission. Persons with AIDS experience the stigma, of course; but beyond that, the compassionate confidants who provide care and social support for persons with AIDS often encounter social difficulties as well. The stigma associated with AIDS results in some of these confidants being rejected by their friends and family (Jankowski, Videka-Sherman, & Laquidara-Dickinson, 1996).

Interestingly, stigmatized persons can use normals' discomfort in their presence to elicit a positive response to appeals. Confederates soliciting donations for charities were more successful when seated in a wheelchair than in a regular chair (Norton et al., 2012).

Effects on Behavior and Perceptions. Normals react toward stigmatized persons with an attitude of ambivalence (Katz, 1981; Katz, Wackenhut, & Glass, 1986). Toward a person with quadriplegia, for instance, normals have feelings of aversion and revulsion but also of sympathy and compassion. This ambivalence creates a tendency toward behavioral instability, in which extremely positive or extremely negative responses may occur toward the stigmatized person, depending on the specific situation.

When interacting with stigmatized individuals, normals alter their usual behavior. They gesture less than usual, refrain from expressing opinions that reflect their actual beliefs, maintain less eye contact, and terminate the encounters sooner (Edelmann, Evans, Pegg, & Tremain, 1983). Moreover, normals speak more rapidly in interactions with stigmatized persons than in interactions with other normals, ask fewer questions, agree less, make more directive remarks, and allow the stigmatized persons fewer opportunities to speak (Bord, 1976). By limiting the responses of the stigmatized person, normals reduce uncertainty and diminish their own discomfort. Negative messages are likely to be expressed nonverbally; normals often monitor their speech and try to restrain or suppress negative re-

marks, but nonverbal leakage may carry the day (Hebl & Dovidio, 2005).

For their part, stigmatized persons also have difficulty interacting with normals. Remarkably, the mere belief that we have a stigma—even when we do not—leads us to perceive others as relating to us negatively. In a dramatic demonstration of this principle (Kleck & Strenta, 1980), some female participants were led to believe that a woman with whom they would interact had learned that they had a mild allergy (a nonstigmatizing attribute). Other female participants believed that the woman would view them as disfigured due to an authentic-looking scar that had been applied to their faces with stage makeup (a stigmatizing attribute). In fact, the interaction partner had no knowledge of either attribute. In the allergy condition, the partner had received no medical information whatsoever. In the scar condition, there was actually no scar to be seen, because the experimenter had surreptitiously removed the scar just before the discussion. After a 6-minute discussion with the interaction partner, the participants described their partners' behavior and attitudes. Those participants who believed they had a facial scar remarked more frequently that their partners had stared at them. They also perceived their partners as more tense, more patronizing, and less attracted to them than the nonstigmatized participants did. Judges who viewed videotapes of the interaction perceived none of these differences. This is not surprising, as the partner knew nothing about either disability. However, these results show that people who believe they are stigmatized perceive others as relating negatively to them. This occurs even if the others are not, in fact, doing anything negative or irregular. These findings are illustrated in Figure 4.2.

When people believe they are stigmatized, they tend not only to perceive the

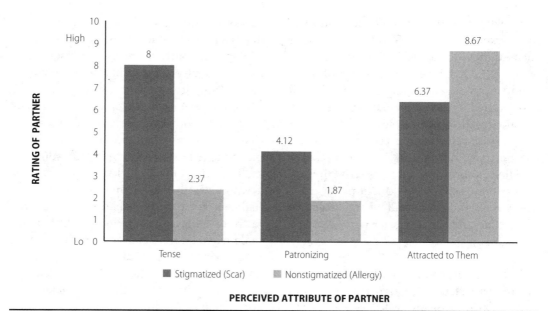

FIGURE 4.2 Perceptions of Interaction Partners by Stigmatized and Nonstigmatized Individuals

In this study, some female students were led to believe that a large facial scar stigmatized them in the eyes of their female interaction partner. Others were led to believe their partner knew they had a mild allergy—a nonstigmatized characteristic. In fact, interaction partners were unaware of either of these characteristics. Nonetheless, students who believed they were stigmatized perceived their partners as substantially more tense and patronizing and as less attracted to them. This suggests that the mere belief that we are stigmatized leads us to perceive others as behaving negatively toward us. Adapted from Kleck and Strenta, "Perceptions of the Impact of Negatively Valued Physical Characteristics on Social Interaction" by Kleck and Strenta, *Journal of Personality and Social Psychology,* 39 861–873. © 1980 by the American Psychological Association.

social world differently but also to behave differently. In one study, for instance, one group of mental patients believed that the person with whom they were interacting knew their psychiatric history, whereas another group thought their stigma was safely hidden (Farina, Gliha, Boudreau, Allen, & Sherman, 1971). Patients in the first group performed more poorly on a cooperative test and found the task more difficult. Moreover, outside observers of the interaction perceived these patients to be more anxious, more tense, and less well adjusted.

Coping Strategies. Stigmatized persons adopt various strategies to avoid awkwardness in their interactions with normals and to establish the most favorable identities

possible (Gramling & Forsyth, 1987). Persons who are handicapped or physically challenged often must choose between engaging in interaction (thereby disclosing their stigma) or withdrawing from interaction (concealing their stigma; Lennon, Link, Marbach, & Dohrenwend, 1989). A stutterer, for instance, may refrain from introducing himself to strangers; were he to introduce himself, he could do so only at the risk of stumbling over his own name and drawing attention to his stigma (Petrunik & Shearing, 1983). Men with spinal cord injury have a visible physical limitation. They also cannot engage in sexual intimacy using the traditional script. Some took control of the circumstances and enlisted their partners' active cooperation (helping them undress, positioning their bodies). Others rarely disclosed their difficulties and relied on their drugs and performance to maintain the semblance of the script. A third group simply stopped engaging in partnered sexual activity (Bender, 2012).

In interaction, stigmatized persons often try to induce normals to behave tactfully toward them and to build relationships around the aspects of their selves that are not discredited. Their strategies depend on whether their stigma can be defined as temporary—such as a broken leg on the mend or a passing bout of depression—or whether it must be accepted as permanent, such as blindness or stigmatized racial identity (Levitin, 1975). Persons who are temporarily stigmatized focus attention on their handicap, recounting how it befell them, detailing their favorable prognosis, and encouraging others to talk about their own past injuries. In contrast, people who are permanently stigmatized often try to focus attention on attributes unrelated to their stigma (Davis, 1961). They often use props to highlight aspects of the self that are unblemished, such as proclaiming their intellectual interests (say, by carrying a heavy book), their political involvements (say, by wearing campaign buttons), or their hobbies (say, by toting a knitting bag).

In cases where a stigma does not force excessive dependency, permanently stigmatized individuals often try to strike a deal with normals: They will behave in a nondemanding and nondisruptive manner in exchange for being treated as trustworthy human beings despite their stigma. Under this arrangement, they are expected to cultivate a cheerful manner, avoid bitterness and self-pity, and treat their stigma as a minor problem with which they are coping successfully (Hastorf, Wildfogel, & Cassman, 1979).

Everyone gains some benefit from handling stigmas in this way. Stigmatized persons avoid the constant embarrassment of indelicate questions, inconsiderateness, and awkward offers of help. They gain some acceptance and enjoy relatively satisfying interaction in most encounters. Normals gain because this resolution assuages the ambivalence they feel toward stigmatized persons and spares them the true pain the stigmatized person suffers.

Some persons are stigmatized because of some individual characteristic—birth defect, illness, disfigurement due to an accident, or history of deviant or criminal behavior. They often rely on these strategies. Others are stigmatized because they are members of certain groups—that is, because of a shared social identity: mental retardation, bipolar disorder, obesity, or racial/ethnic minority status (Crocker & Major, 1989). In these cases, stereotypes that are widely shared by both stigmatized and stigmatizers shape the attitudes and behavior of members of both groups, including the identities claimed in interaction (Renfrow, 2004). These persons have an additional coping strategy; they can attribute the stigma they experience to the prejudiced attitudes of others and base their self-perception on traits on which they rank well. They may also seek out relationships with others who share the stigma in an effort to experience positive reflected appraisals (Kaufman & Johnson, 2004).

The widespread advertising of medications for depression, bipolar disorder, and other forms of emotional disorders on television contributes to the stereotypes of the mentally ill (Smardon, 2007). On the one hand, the ads typically portray milder cases, and so in one sense they trivialize emotional disorders. On the other hand, persons taking a drug such as Prozac have a basis for forming a social network and supporting others who experience the condition or take the drug.

Another coping strategy is *passing*, distancing oneself from the stigmatized identity by hiding information (Renfrow, 2004). The person may hide the identity from normals while cultivating discreet associations with others who share the stigma; this will prevent negative appraisal by normals and provide the person with positive appraisals by the others. Millions of college students have used this strategy to gain access to bars and alcoholic beverages before they reach the legal drinking age. Or the person may distance themself from other stigmatized persons and associate with normals or withdraw from interaction (the closeted GLBT person); the latter strategy may result in great psychological distress. The central emotion in passing is fear: fear of the consequences of being identified by normals as stigmatized leads to passing, and fear of discovery dominates the passing experience.

Persons may attempt to cope with stigma by seeking therapy (Kaufman & Johnson, 2004). Physical and occupational therapy may reduce or remove the debilitating effects of accidents, loss of limbs, or loss of abilities. Psychological or behavioral therapy may change the beliefs and behavior that accompany mental retardation, mental illness, or unnatural passions. A final strategy is to join a social movement intended to change the perceptions and stereotypes of normals.

SUMMARY

The self is the individual viewed both as the source and the object of reflexive behavior.

The Nature and Genesis of Self. (1) The self is the source of action when we plan, observe, and control our own behavior. The self is the object of action when we think about who we are. (2) Newborn infants lack a sense of self. Later, they come to recognize that they are physically separate from others. As they acquire language, they learn that their own thoughts and feelings are also separate. (3) Through role taking, children come to see themselves through others' eyes. They can then observe, judge, and regulate their own behavior. (4) Children construct their identities based on how they imagine they appear to others. Both face-to-face and online interactions influence the development of self. They also develop self-evaluations based on the perceived judgments of others.

Identities: The Self We Know. The self we know includes multiple identities. (1) Some identities are linked to the social roles we enact. (2) Some identities are linked to our membership in social groups or categories. These identities may be associated with ingroup favoritism and out-group stereotyping. (3) We form self-concepts primarily through learning and adopting role and social identities. The self we know is primarily influenced by the perceived reactions of others. (4) The self we know varies with the situation. We attend most to those aspects of our selves that are distinctive and relevant to the ongoing activity.

Identities: The Self We Enact. The self we enact expresses our identities. (1) We choose behaviors to evoke responses from others that will confirm particular identities. To confirm identities successfully, we must share with others our understanding of what these behaviors and identities mean. Adopting these meanings may lead to poorer performance when we experience stereotype threat. (2) We choose which identity to express based on that identity's salience, need for support, and situational opportunities for enacting it. (3) We gain consistency in our behavior over time by striving to enact important identities. We also employ several strategies that lead to verification of our self-conceptions.

Self-Esteem. Self-esteem is the evaluative component of self. Most people try to maintain positive self-esteem. (1) Overall self-esteem depends on the evaluations of our specific role identities. (2) Self-esteem derives from three sources: family experiences of acceptance and discipline, direct feedback on the effectiveness of actions, and comparisons of our own successes and failures with those of others. (3) People with higher self-esteem tend to be more popular, assertive, ambitious, and academically successful, better adjusted, and happier. (4) We employ numerous techniques to protect self-esteem. Specifically, we seek reflected appraisals consistent with our self-view, process information selectively, carefully select those with whom we compare ourselves, and attribute greater importance to qualities that provide consistent feedback.

Self-Presentation in Everyday Life. *Self-presentation* refers to our attempts—both conscious and unconscious—to control the images we project of ourselves in social interaction. Some self-presentation is authentic, but some may be tactical. Successful presentation of self requires efforts to control how others define the interaction situation and accord identities to participants. (1) In defining the situation, people negotiate the type of social occasion considered to be at hand and the identities they will grant each other. (2) Self-disclosure is a process through which we not only make identity claims but also promote friendship and liking. Self-disclosure is usually two-sided and gradual, and it follows a norm of reciprocity.

Tactical Impression Management. People employ various tactics to manipulate the impressions that others form of them. (1) They manage appearances (bodily adornment, clothes, possessions, and so on) to dramatize the kind of person they claim to be. (2) They ingratiate themselves with others through such tactics as opinion conformity, other enhancement, and selective presentation of their admirable qualities. (3) When caught performing socially unacceptable actions, people try to repair their identities through aligning actions, which are attempts to align their questionable conduct with cultural norms. They explain their motives, disclaim the implications of their conduct, or offer accounts that excuse or justify their actions. (4) They altercast others, imposing roles and identities that mesh with the identities they claim for themselves. (5) Impression management is a major component of online communication. In e-mail, text messages, personal webpages, and online dating profiles, people intentionally select content to create a certain image in the mind of the receiver/ viewer.

The Downside of Self-Presentation. (1) Self-presentational motives such as the desire to be liked by or obtain rewards controlled by others may lead to behavior that is risky to your health, such as unprotected sexual intercourse or alcohol or drug abuse. (2) The desire to maintain romantic relationships may lead to withholding information from or lying to your partner; people who report deceiving their partner or who perceive their partner as deceptive report reduced commitment to their relationship.

Detecting Deceptive Impression Management. Observers attend to two major types of information in detecting deceitful impression management. (1) They assess others' possible ulterior motives. If a large difference in power is present, an impression manager's ulterior motives may become transparent to the target, making tactics like ingratiation difficult. (2) They scrutinize others' nonverbal behavior. Although detection of deceit is difficult, observers are more accurate when they concentrate on leaky cues, such as tone of voice, and discrepancies between messages transmitted through different channels. Some professionals are quite accurate in detecting deception.

Ineffective Self-Presentation and Spoiled Identities. Self-presentational failures lead to several consequences. (1) People experience embarrassment when their identity is discredited. Interaction partners usually help the embarrassed person to restore an acceptable identity. Otherwise, embarrassed persons tend to reassert their identity in an exaggerated manner or to attack those who discredited them. (2) Repeated or glaring failures in self-presentation lead others to modify the offender's identity through deliberate actions. They may try to cool-out offenders by persuading them to accept less desirable alternative identities, or they may degrade offenders' identities and transform them into lesser social types. (3) Many physical, moral, and social handicaps stigmatize individuals and permanently spoil their identities. Interaction between stigmatized and "normal" persons is marked by ambivalence and is frequently awkward and uncomfortable. In general, normals pressure stigmatized individuals to accept inferior identities, whereas stigmatized individuals seek to build relationships around the aspects of their selves that are not discredited. Some persons with stigma attempt to pass to avoid the negative reflected appraisals they would receive from normals.

List of Key Terms and Concepts

accounts (p. 156)
aligning actions (p. 156)
altercasting (p. 157)
back regions (p. 152)

contingencies (of self-esteem) (p. 138)
cooling-out (p. 167)
definition of the situation (p. 147)
disclaimer (p. 156)
embarrassment (p. 164)
frame (p. 148)
front regions (p. 152)
game (p. 123)
generalized other (p. 123)
group self-esteem (p. 145)
identities (p. 125)
identity control theory (p. 132)
identity degradation (p. 167)
ingratiation (p. 152)
looking-glass self (p. 122)
play (p. 122)
role identities (p. 125)
role taking (p. 122)
salience (p. 133)
self (p. 120)
self-awareness (p. 137)
self-disclosure (p. 149)
self-discrepancy (p. 137)
self-esteem (p. 138)
self-presentation (p. 146)
self-schema (p. 118)
significant others (p. 122)
situated identity (p. 148)
situated self (p. 130)
social identity (p. 126)
stigma (p. 168)
supplication (p. 154)
tactical impression management (p. 146)

Critical Thinking Skill: Defending Against Everyday Persuasive Techniques

The foundation of our efforts at self-presentation is our desire to have certain other people like and accept us, and treat us in particular ways. We want friends, we want a committed relationship, we want harmony with our roommates, and so we are motivated to conform to their expectations by presenting ourselves in certain ways. The means by which they communicate their expectations is often by using everyday persuasion techniques.

Imagine that you have not been in a relationship for several months. One day a close friend inquires about your "love life." You reply honestly, "I don't have one these days." The friend replies, "Well, maybe you're having trouble because of the way you look." "What do you mean?" "Well, you don't look healthy; you're not trim, and your skin is awfully white. I think you need to get some tan. Three times a week in a tanning bed will work wonders!"

This is an example of everyday persuasion. A well-meaning friend or coworker or roommate is trying to persuade you to solve a problem in the way she thinks will work. In this situation, many of us are tempted to follow the suggestion. She means well, you like her, you don't want to be critical or start an argument. You are inclined to accept in order to maintain a good relationship with her. But is it a good idea? She is suggesting tanning sessions to increase your attractiveness. Will it? Being tan is certainly considered attractive in your social group. But there is a good deal of evidence that tanning, especially in tanning beds, is related to increased risk of skin cancer in later life. And we reviewed evidence that persons who are concerned with others' impressions are more likely to use tanning facilities. So your inclination to accept the persuasive attempt probably reflects a heightened concern with self-presentation, not the merits of the suggestion.

As we suggest in a later Critical Thinking skill (Chapter 8), direct, honest communication is best in this situation. If you aren't sure your friend's suggestion is a good idea, you could say, "Thanks for that suggestion. I'll check it out." Then you can gather information about the effects of using tanning beds by going to recognized health care information sites like the one maintained by the Mayo Clinic (http://www.mayoclinic .org/news2012-rst/6777.html). If you conclude it isn't a good idea, you can ignore the advice. If your friend asks later, you can say that you learned there is a link between tanning bed use and skin cancer. That might lead to an interesting conversation!

EMOTIONS

INTRODUCTION

Robert Yu is a kindergarten teacher in a suburb of Columbus, Ohio, facing a Monday morning of teaching 25 energetic five-year-olds for three hours. Robert is a very dedicated teacher and always strives to give his best to his students. He is usually energized for class and follows well-developed lesson plans. His students love him and look forward to school every day.

Unfortunately, Robert is coming off a very difficult weekend. On Friday afternoon, he found out he was denied a loan for a new house he wanted to buy, and on Saturday he was in a serious car accident caused by a teenager who was texting rather than paying attention. No one was hurt, but Robert's car was damaged beyond repair and was towed to the junkyard. To top it all off, his favorite basketball team lost its final game of the season and, thus, was eliminated from the playoffs. On Monday morning, Robert got up in his shabby apartment, rode the bus to work, and proceeded to pay off a bet he had made on the basketball game with another teacher. Needless to say, he was not in a very good mood when he headed down the hall to his classroom.

But Robert still wanted to do a good job with the children in his class, so he decided to hide his feelings and put on a cheerful face. He bounced into the room acting as though absolutely nothing was wrong and, in fact, that he was just as happy as he could be. The students in the class thought Mr. Yu was in a great mood, as did the teacher's aide who helped in the class. They all reacted very positively toward him, and everyone had a great day in the classroom. As things progressed, Robert himself began feeling much better and, at the end of the day, thought this was one of the best days he'd ever had in the classroom.

In the space of a few days, Robert has experienced a wide range of emotions. He started off the weekend feeling fine, until he experienced a severe disappointment when he found out about his loan. When his car was hit, he first felt fear and then anger toward the other driver. Later, he started watching the basketball game with excited anticipation, rode a roller coaster of ups and downs as the game progressed, and came close to tears when the game was over. By Monday morning, he felt positively depressed but then managed to recover—very much by his own doing—during the course of teaching that morning.

How can we explain all of Robert's emotional experiences and the changes from one emotional state to another? During the basketball game, for example, Robert vacillates quickly between anger, sadness, disgust, joy, and satisfaction, all because of a few images on a television screen. On Monday morning, he is able to consciously choose behaviors that end up actually changing his mood. What is involved, both on an individual level and a social level, in producing all of these different emotional states and the changes from one to another? Given that Robert is not an inherently unstable individual, we need to understand the social context of his interactions to understand his emotional states.

To facilitate this social psychological interpretation of emotion, in this chapter we'll consider several key questions about emotions that can help us understand emotion stories like Robert's:

1. What exactly are emotions and psychological emotional states?

2. Where do emotions come from? What are the physiological, psychological, and social bases of emotions?

3. What kinds of emotions and expressions of them are universal human traits, and which are specific to social or cultural contexts?

4. How do social contexts produce emotions?

5. How do we psychologically and socially control the expression of emotions? Beyond limiting how we express them, how can we control our emotions, either by suppressing or producing them?

DEFINING EMOTIONS

To talk about emotions, we first need to know exactly what we mean by that term. This can be difficult because emotions are not particularly easy to define. To complicate things, there are other related terms that are partially synonymous with emotion, including sentiment, affect, mood, and, of course, feelings (Smith-Lovin, 1995). All of these terms are used in everyday conversation to refer to the experience of emotion, and social psychologists also use them in specific ways, so we first need to sort them out from one another.

Affect is usually considered the most general of the terms. It encompasses virtually any kind of subjective positive or negative evaluation of an object. This includes short-term reactions like the anger you might feel toward another after being the target of an insult as well as longer-term orientations such as the pleasant association many people have with the Christmas season. Affect can usually be described in terms of not just direction but also strength and the level of activity associated with it (Osgood, Suci, & Tannenbaum, 1957). In other words, it is not just whether one generally feels positive or negative toward something—perhaps a student, sports team, or riding the bus, in Robert Yu's case—but also how intense and dynamic that orientation is.

Emotions are often treated as a subset of affect. Usually, **emotions** are thought of as short-lived reactions to a stimulus out-

side of the individual. To distinguish emotions from other human stimulus-impulse reactions, sociologist Peggy Thoits (1989) delineates four components of emotions: (1) a situational stimulus, (2) physiological changes, (3) expressive gesturing of some kind, and, most importantly, (4) a label to identify a cluster of the first three. Being slapped by one's girlfriend plus elevated temperature and heart rate plus a furrowed brow and a clenched fist equals anger. Being slapped by one's girlfriend plus elevated heart rate plus laughter and smiling equals humorous teasing. Various culturally defined combinations produce what we typically think of and experience as an emotion.

Emotions tend to be related to goals. Whether we are frustrated by a blocked goal, joyful upon achieving one, anxious as we approach one, embarrassed that we failed at a goal, or motivated by an emotion to pursue a goal (such as fleeing from a fearful situation), emotions and goals are intimately entwined (Frijda & Mequita, 1994).

Sentiment is very close to emotion in meaning, but when social psychologists use the term sentiment, they emphasize the social aspect of emotion. Early social psychologists used sentiment to refer to the components of human responses that separate them from analogous responses that animals would have. For example, Cooley (1909) contrasts love and lust. Although lust is instinctive, we learn what love is through social interaction. In other words, sentiment relies not just on the responses of the individual to the stimulus but also on how other human beings understand that stimulus. In later years, as social psychologists have come to increasingly accept that social elements are a key piece of emotions, the idea of sentiment has become less distinguishable from that of emotion (Stets, 2003). In contemporary work, social psychologists often use the term **sentiment** to distinguish immediate emotional responses from longer-term emotional states such as love, grief, and jealously (S. Gordon, 1990). These sentiments can endure for days, weeks, and even years after the initial event that triggered them.

Moods are also more enduring than emotions. Whereas we might experience one emotion and move on to another in a matter of seconds or minutes (Ekman, 1992), a **mood** is a general psychological condition that characterizes our experience and emotional orientation for hours or even days. Moods are considerably less specific than emotions. When an emotion occurs, we have a very good sense of where it is directed and what stimulus caused it. Moods, however, are diffuse; they can be widely directed at anything that comes in our path—regardless of whether it has anything to do with the origin of the bad mood.

Returning to the experiences of the kindergarten teacher, Robert, almost all of the events described involve affect—some were stronger, such as when he was in the car accident, and some were weaker, such as when he paid his gambling debt. He also experienced many short-term emotional states with a great deal of social content (such as the disappointment of losing the loan) and others with much less social content (such as the initial fear and shock when hit by another car). These events accumulated, and by the time he got to work on Monday, he had probably been experiencing a morose mood for quite a number of hours.

CLASSICAL IDEAS ABOUT THE ORIGINS OF EMOTION

Where do emotions come from? Some of the earliest scientific work on emotions focuses largely on the nonsocial origins of emotions. Although these perspectives are now viewed as quite incomplete, they do provide some of the essential building blocks used in later understandings of emotions and, thus, require a brief review.

The beginnings of the study of emotion can be found in the work of Charles Darwin, especially in his important book, *The Expression of the Emotions in Man and Animals*. Darwin was motivated to write this book because he thought that if humans and other animals had common ancestors, there ought to be some similarities in emotional expression as well. At the time he wrote, Darwin was battling those who believed that humans had all kinds of unique characteristics not shared by other animals—and this included facial expressions. His book pointed out fascinating continuities in the emotional expressions made by humans and by other animals, such as monkeys and dogs, and also found some facial expressions and gestures that he thought were universal across cultures (Darwin, 1998).

The theory Darwin developed about emotional expression was based on these similarities across cultures and species. If some emotions and emotional expressions were universal, then they must be genetically encoded. And if they are genetically encoded, then they must have value that enhances genetic survival. Thus, emotional gestures, for example, were residual expressions related to threat or sexual attraction. The act of gritting and showing our teeth when angry could be a derivative of the act of biting in a battle for survival.

Although Darwin focused on the *expression* of emotions, other early thinkers were more concerned about the *internal sources* of emotions. Lange and James (1922) separately proposed a biological approach to emotions that focused heavily on the physiological responses to stimulus. In this model, the stimulus is followed by the biological reaction, and then the individual cognitively processes the physiological sensation and interprets it as an emotion. The physiological component of the emotional experience (for example, increased blood pressure) helps us to identify the emotion (anger) rather than anger causing the physiological change.

Sigmund Freud (1962) believed that repressed childhood sexual desires were the sources of emotions (principally anxiety and guilt). Although many of Freud's ideas have been discredited over time, he did contribute to the study of emotions in several ways. First, he drew attention to the ways emotions could develop unconsciously. Individuals can hide their feelings from themselves and yet still have these emotions affect the way they think and act. Second, he drew attention to the role an individual's past experience plays in helping to understand the meaning of emotions and the physical sensations that accompany them. Recognizing the past context of emotional reactions is an important step toward understanding the social forces that shape and define emotions.

UNIVERSAL EMOTIONS AND FACIAL EXPRESSIONS

The classic perspectives discussed above point to one of the more persistent questions in the study of emotions: Are some emotions genetically encoded in human biology? If so, are emotions universal human experiences that are similar across cultural and geographic boundaries as well as over historical epochs? When we feel anger, for example, are we feeling the same physiological and psychological sensations people experienced hundreds and thousands of years ago or experience in other parts of the world? Darwin's work suggests that at least some (but not all, he believed) emotions are universal—not just among humans but also across some different species.

As questions about the universality of emotions have developed over time, schol-ars have focused a great deal of attention on facial expression of emotion.

Facial Expressions of Emotions

Some of the facial expressions we make are largely involuntary—we perform them without thought or conscious effort. If we are trying to hide our emotions, we often try to look away or hide our face because we know we are involuntarily revealing our feelings (Goffman, 1959b). Other emotion displays are conscious. For example, we might express an emotion to emphasize a point, to appear friendly and welcoming, or to threaten others.

Social psychologists have used this distinction between involuntary and voluntary facial displays to study the issue of emotional universality. If involuntary facial expressions are (1) produced by the same emotional state across individuals and (2) identified by many observers as meaning the same thing, then we have reason to believe they are universal expressions of emotions (Ekman, Sorenson, & Friesen, 1969). Furthermore, if these emotional expressions are consistent across all world cultures, then Darwin's view of emotion is supported.

Paul Ekman has worked on this very problem for almost 50 years, finding support for the universality of particular emotional expressions. In his initial studies, Ekman showed photographs of varied facial expressions to thousands of people across a number of different cultures and asked them to identify the related emotions. He found six emotions that were widely agreed upon across groups, even in a preliterate culture in New Guinea (Ekman & Friesen, 1971, Ekman et al., 1969). These six fundamental emotions were happiness, sadness, surprise, fear, anger, and disgust (Ekman & Friesen, 1975). More recently, contempt has emerged as a seventh emotion that is

TABLE 5.1 Single-Emotion Judgment Task: Percentage of Participants Within Each Culture Who Chose the Predicted Emotion

NATION	HAPPINESS	SURPRISE	SADNESS	FEAR	DISGUST	ANGER
Estonia	90	94	86	91	71	67
Germany	93	87	83	86	61	71
Greece	93	91	80	74	77	77
Hong Kong	92	91	91	84	65	73
Italy	97	92	81	82	89	72
Japan	90	94	87	65	60	67
Scotland	98	88	86	86	79	84
Sumatra	69	78	91	70	70	70
Turkey	87	90	76	76	74	79
United States	95	92	92	84	86	81

Source: Adapted from P. Ekman and M. Friesen, "Single Judgment Emotion Task," *Journal of Personality and Social Psychology, 53,* 712–717. Copyright © 1987 by the American Psychological Association. Adapted with permission.

universally recognized (Ekman & Friesen, 1986).

Ekman also explored the universality of the expression of emotion. Most notably, he asked members of the Fore, the primitive, preliterate culture he studied in New Guinea, to act out their facial expression in different scenarios, such as, "Your child has died and you are sad," or "You are angry and about to fight." After returning to the United States, Ekman asked college students to look at the photographs and film clips he had taken of the Fore acting out these scenarios. Despite vast cultural differences across a number of dimensions, the American students were able to accurately identify the expressed emotion in the photos. Critics argued, though, that this study still captured the universality of emotion recognition and not of emotional expression. To combat these claims, Ekman did another study where he videotaped Japanese and American participants as they watched an emotional film (Ekman, 1972). He found that the expressions among the two groups throughout the viewing were not only similar but also the same expressions expected based on Ekman's previous

research on universal emotion displays. Later research on people who were born blind further supports Ekman's claim. Even though they never visually learned from other people how to express emotions, blind people still smile, laugh, and frown in much the same way as sighted people do (Eibl-Eibesfeldt, 1979).

In an effort to further this research, Ekman and his colleagues (Ekman & Friesen, 1978) developed the Facial Action Coding System (FACS), a methodology to classify visible facial behavior. Each of the fundamental emotions involves movement among a particular configuration of facial muscles. Ekman calls these **action units** (AU) and argues that any facial movement, even those unrelated to emotion, can be described using the action units that produced it. For example, happiness involves the "cheek raiser" (AU 6) and "lip corner puller" (AU 12). These configurations are not only crucial for the expression of each emotion but also what we use to determine the emotions of others. The importance of these action units is, in part, why younger people have difficulty interpreting emotion displays in the elderly (Hess, 2013). In

Upper Face Action Units					
AU 1	AU 2	AU 4	AU 5	AU 6	AU 7
Inner Brow Raiser	Outer Brow Raiser	Brow Lowerer	Upper Lid Raiser	Cheek Raiser	Lid Tightener
*AU 41	*AU 42	*AU 43	AU 44	AU 45	AU 46
Lid Droop	Slit	Eyes Closed	Squint	Blink	Wink
Lower Face Action Units					
AU 9	AU 10	AU 11	AU 12	AU 13	AU 14
Nose Wrinkler	Upper Lip Raiser	Nasolabial Deepener	Lip Corner Puller	Cheek Puffer	Dimpler
AU 15	AU 16	AU 17	AU 18	AU 20	AU 22
Lip Corner Depressor	Lower Lip Depressor	Chin Raiser	Lip Puckerer	Lip Stretcher	Lip Funneler
AU 23	AU 24	*AU 25	*AU 26	*AU 27	AU 28
Lip Tightener	Lip Pressor	Lips Part	Jaw Drop	Mouth Stretch	Lip Suck

Specific combinations of these action units (AU) have been categorized as emotional expressions that are fundamental across cultures (Ekman & Friesen, 1978). AU 6 ("cheek raiser") and AU 12 ("lip corner puller") combine for an expression of happiness, while AU 1 + AU 4 + AU 15 are a universal expression of sadness. © Paul Ekman Group, LLC

a recent research study, young people who were shown neutral faces—expressions with no emotion—were more likely to rate the faces as angry or sad not because of stereotypes they had about older people's emotional states but because wrinkles cause the mouth to drop or the forehead to crinkle (Garrido et al., 2013).

Recent technological developments have made real-time coding of facial expressions by computer software possible (Bartlett et al., 2006). Although this is useful across a variety of domains, including in emotions research, the technological advances are of particular interest to advertisers. When computers are able to recognize the emotions that users are feeling based on facial expressions, they can measure the efficacy of particular media—whether it be a commercial or movie trailer—or offer users advertising content based on those specific emotions (Bosker, 2013).

Criticisms and Limitations. Although most of the research about the facial expressions of emotions seems to support the notion that some emotions are universal across cultures, the research has its limitations as well. There are two main concerns about the methods. The first concerns the highly contrived circumstances of the experiments and contends that the results are in some ways elicited from the participants (Zajonc, 1998; Zajonc & McIntosh, 1992). The second argues that the research in the area that asks participants to identify the emotion expressed using a selection of possible emotion labels is more like a matching or multiple-choice test, which is likely to end up with much higher degrees of agreement than if the participants could give any emotional description they wish to the facial expression. Subsequent research has tried to address these concerns and in general has successfully supported Ekman's findings (see Haidt & Keltner, 1999).

There are two important limitations to Ekman's approach:

First, just because subjects who see a certain facial expression associate it with a particular emotion does not mean that the particular emotion is always expressed that way or even expressed on the face at all. For instance, we might recognize a smiling face as expressing happiness, but we do not smile every time we are happy. A study of sports fans who were watching their favored team win found that even during periods of intense happiness, these individuals often did not smile (Fernandez-Dols & Ruiz-Belda, 1995). Furthermore, some people are very good at faking their emotional displays and can smile very convincingly, even when they are angry or sad. Remember the story of Robert, who convinced his coworkers and students that he was in a very good mood. We will explore the selective display of emotion in more detail later in this chapter.

Second, Ekman's studies of emotional universality also examined a very limited set of emotions. Six emotions (happiness, sadness, anger, fear, disgust, and surprise) appear repeatedly in emotion studies and a seventh (contempt) is gaining in popularity (Ekman & Friesen, 1986). There is no reason to believe that these are the core emotions. Social psychologists using different methods have clustered "basic" emotions into five categories: love, joy, anger, sadness, and fear (Shaver, Schwartz, Kirson, & O'Connor, 1987). Whereas Ekman's approach focuses on those emotions that have uniquely identifiable facial expressions, Shaver uses a method by which subjects generate a list of emotions in a free-form way.

There may be other universal emotions missing from the list. For example, also using the emotional display approach, Keltner and colleagues have demonstrated that there is a unique way of expressing embarrassment that is widely recognized by others (Haidt & Keltner, 1999; Keltner, 1996). When we are embarrassed, we tend to avert our gaze, move our heads down, and touch our faces. Future research may find that additional emotions, beyond the seven currently identified, also have universal recognition.

CULTURAL DIFFERENCES IN BASIC EMOTIONS AND EMOTIONAL DISPLAY

Not all emotion is universal. Because of the importance of labels in emotion (Thoits, 1989), cultural expression and language influence the experience of emotion. For example, Shaver, Wu, and Schwartz (1992) discerned a unique category called "sad love" in Chinese culture that combined notions about unrequited love and nostalgia. The German culture has a word for vicarious embarrassment (being embarrassed for someone else): fremdschämen. Although Americans may understand these emotions and have similar feelings from time to time, they cannot label emotions as such because they lack the language or label to do so. Cultural forces can influence emotion in other ways. For example, emotions may not be distinct from each other in some cultures as they are in ours. In China, joy and love are not differentiable from each other as they are in the United States.

Even if some basic emotions are invariant across cultures, meaning that they lead us all to use certain combinations of facial muscles in a particular way, there are strong cultural influences that can suppress, exaggerate, or change the display of these emotions. As we interact in daily life, certain situations call for the display of a particular emotion or demand that we do not show others. In most situations, attending a funeral requires the expression of sadness and suppression of any levity or laughter. Typically, a reunion with a cherished brother or sister you haven't seen in 10 years requires the expression of excitement and joy. But if this reunion occurs at a funeral, it is usually required that the excitement and joy be suppressed. However, the requirement for solemn sadness at a funeral is not a cultural universal, and we must learn the norms of our culture in order to produce the proper emotional displays in each social situation.

Emotional Display

One set of cultural norms about emotional expression deals with how we must modify our facial expressions to make them fit social situations. These norms are called **display rules** (Ekman, 1972). Display rules are typically learned in childhood and sometimes become habits that automatically control facial muscles. Display rules may modify facial expressions of emotion

in one of several ways. They may require (1) greater intensity in the expression of an emotion, (2) less intensity in the expression of an emotion, (3) complete neutralization of the emotional expression, or (4) masking one emotion with a different one.

Cultures can vary more generally in their demands about emotional display in addition to providing guidance for displays in specific kinds of situations (Ekman & Freisen, 1969). For example, some cultures have a much more disapproving stance toward anger in general. In other cultures, anger and the expression of it is seen as a normal part of healthy social interaction. When anger is viewed more negatively, as in Eskimo culture (see Briggs, 1970), whatever natural expression of anger may exist can be moderated in such a way that people from other cultural groups, who are accustomed to a more open and obvious expression of anger, might not even recognize that there is a problem.

One of the most important cultural differences that affects the expression of emotions is how collectivist or individualistic the culture is (Matsumoto, 1990). **Individualistic cultures**, like in the United States, are usually more focused on the individual person as a key social unit. Individuals have their own goals, accomplishments, and behaviors that stand apart from group membership. **Collectivist cultures** are more focused on groups as the sources of identity. For example, individuals are seen in terms of their membership in their family and are much more affected by the interconnected behaviors, accomplishments, and failures of others in their groups. They are less independent and more interdependent in their social relationships and identities.

How does collectivism or individualism affect the expression of emotion? Most often, the studies compare American participants, who are usually highly individualistic, and Japanese participants, who are usually highly collectivist. It is important to note, however, that there are many cultural contexts that are more and less collectivist and individualistic than these two, and that individuals within each country vary a great deal in terms of their orientation toward collectivism and individualism.

To understand some of these differences, remember that collectivistic cultures are more concerned about disrupting social interaction. When social relations, as opposed to individual states, are at the center of identity and interaction, ensuring smooth, trouble-free exchange with others becomes more important. To avoid negative disruptions in social interaction, members of collectivist cultures such as Japan are more likely to suppress emotional expression and also to downplay the intensity of emotional reaction they observe in others' faces (Matsumoto, 1987; Matsumoto & Ekman, 1989). Thus, collectivistic cultures have not only more subdued display rules but also decoding norms that reduce the interpretation of emotional intensity.

This does not mean, however, that collectivist cultures are less sensitive to emotional expression. In fact, experimental research comparing Japanese and Americans showed that the Japanese were more sensitive to indirect emotional cues. In this study, the experimenters listened to words that were pleasant or unpleasant in meaning and were read in either a pleasant or unpleasant manner. Thus, the research subjects were presented with a curious mix of words with unpleasant meaning but were conveyed using positive vocal cues. Likewise, they were also presented with pleasant words conveyed using negative emotional cues. The results demonstrated that the Japanese participants were much more attentive to the vocal cues, whereas the Americans were more attentive to the

words themselves (Ishii, Reyes, & Kitayama, 2003). Thus, whereas collectivist cultures might work at reducing the expression and interpretation of negative emotions, they are actually more sensitive to them than those from individualistic cultures.

Collectivist and individualist cultures also differ in their approaches to happiness. What might those in individualist cultures be most likely to express happiness about? The answer, of course, is individual achievements and attributes. If the individual is good at something or has a characteristic that causes a positive reaction, then that individual has reason to be happy and to express it. Members of collectivist cultures express happiness in situations that emphasize their connectedness with others in their identity groups. When they feel close to and consonant with other people, this is the primary reason to experience and display happiness. This difference was demonstrated by Mequita and Karasawa (2002) in what is called a diary study. During the course of one week, American and Japanese students recorded information about their emotions every three hours. Japanese

Cultural norms strongly influence the expression of emotions. The expression of bereavement, for example, varies widely, ranging from solitary reflection to group wailing practices. Here, the tight-knit community of Hasidic Jews in Williamsburg, Brooklyn, come together in public to mourn the loss of a young couple killed in a car accident. © AP Photo/John Minchillo students, reflecting their collectivist orientation, reported pleasant feelings mainly when they experienced positive interdependent engagement with others. The American students reported positive feeling with respect to both interdependent events and independent events (such as having control or mastery).

Another important emotional experience that differentiates collectivist and individualist cultures is shame. We will discuss shame in more detail at the end of this chapter, but shame plays a substantially different role—in fact, a much more central role—in some cultures. Collectivist cultures emphasize the relationship of the individual to other people. Therefore, shame results from the negative evaluation that others have of the individual. The interpersonal sanctions that result are most important in the collectivist cultures. In contrast, individualistic cultures tend to focus more on guilt—failing to meet one's own standards, which is internally evaluated. Two studies suggest the relative importance of shame in different cultures. In one study, the researchers found that 95 percent of Chinese mothers reported that their children understood the concept of shame by the age of three (Shaver, Wu, & Schwartz, 1992). In another study, none of a group of Dutch seven-year-olds knew what shame was (Wellman, Phillips, & Rodriguez, 2000).

Anger is a very important emotion because it is so volatile. When people are angry, they can be extremely forceful, lose control, and even become highly destructive. When people express anger, they can make others angry—especially the targets of their anger. The expression of anger can lead to retribution and may set off a spiral of escalating anger and destruction. Therefore, anger is an emotion we must find ways to manage, control, and appropriately direct.

But how might collectivist and individualist cultures differently approach anger? Your first guess might be that collectivist cultures try to avoid the expression of anger. Given that it has such potential to upset and damage social interactions with others, we should expect that collectivists would work very hard to avoid experiencing and acting on anger. Briggs's (1970) study of an Eskimo culture provides dramatic support for this thesis. Briggs determined that she was studying a highly interdependent, collectivist culture. The group she studied depended heavily on the relationships among those in the group for survival. They were very isolated and often faced difficult conditions. Combined, these factors led them to emphasize group harmony very heavily, and anger was seen as a major threat to the stability and existence of the group. In Western, individualist cultures, however, anger is often encouraged because it is associated with assertiveness and individual rights (Averill, 1980; Braesicke et al., 2005). Anger is seen as a means to let others know how we feel, as a tool to rectify an unjust situation, and a way to blow off steam before the pressure builds to a catastrophic climax.

A final emotion to consider in the context of collectivist and independent cultural contexts is grief. As we look across cultures, we can witness an incredible range in the expression of grief and mourning. In almost all cultures, mourning a death involves sadness and tears. Given the wide variety of funeral and bereavement practices, it can be difficult to draw clear distinctions among the practices of collectivist and individualistic cultures. However, some of the most dramatic cultural mourning acts are associated with social groups in which there are strong interdependent relationships. These practices can range from elaborate wailing episodes to the suicide of a widow or widower. Individualist societies view these

BOX 5.1 Research Update: Social Status and Anger

For many years, social psychologists who studied emotions posited contradictory expectations about the relationship between social status (based on dimensions like class, education, or occupation) and the experience of anger. Some argued that status and anger were inversely related, with those of higher status less likely to experience or express anger than those of lower status. In other words, the higher one's status, the more positive one's emotion. Social psychologists believed this was the case for a number of reasons. Higher-status individuals were less likely to face obstacles than were lower-status individuals (Kemper, 1978), they were viewed more positively and were therefore more influential in interactions (Lucas & Lovaglia, 1998), and they were also more likely to have been socialized by their parents and others to suppress negative emotion (Hochschild, 1983). Others suggested that anger and status were positively related and that higher-status people experienced anger more and not less. Because anger is an emotion that signals mastery and dominance, it is seen as legitimate for higher-status people to employ it in interaction, and therefore, they likely use it more frequently than those of lower status. Higher-status people are also more inclined to blame others if they are unable to get their way, contributing to increases in both the experience and expression of anger.

These two accounts were considered in parallel by two researchers who combined them in the same analysis (Collett & Lizardo, 2010). The results show that these findings are not competing but rather are complementary. Individuals at both ends of the status hierarchy (those who are either very high or quite low on occupational status) are more likely to experience anger than are those who are in the middle. In fact, individuals at the top and bottom of the status ladder experience anger, on average, 36 more days a year than those in the middle. However, these two status groups differ on the type of anger they experience and the likely cause of it. Lower-status individuals are more likely to experience anger that is trans-situational. It endures across social situations and is due to chronic stressors in the day-to-day experience of those at the bottom of the status ladder. In other words, the anger is continuous and often directed at impersonal targets like objects or circumstances rather than other people. Without a tangible object toward which to direct their anger, this anger is difficult to discharge and tends to endure. High-status people, however, experience encounter-based anger. They get angry with specific others, most often people of lower status than themselves who fail to afford them the status they feel they deserve. They are more likely to get angry at relatively unfamiliar others in specific situations. Because they are able to focus and direct their anger in a specific situation, high-status people are more likely to have the anger dissipate more quickly than are lower-status individuals.

In sum, although rates of anger may be the same for those of high and low status, social psychological research suggests that the causes and the consequences of this emotion can be quite different.

Source: Collett & Lizardo, 2010.

kinds of practices as extremely strange and instead carry a belief that although mourning and grief after a death is normal, there are limits. Mourners who cannot get over a death are considered unstable and may end up being isolated until they can recover.

Looking across cultures and observing the different ways emotions are expressed, we see a complicated picture of basic emotions. For the most part, social psychologists agree that some emotions are universal and that they are physiologically connected to distinctive facial expressions, and yet the expression of even the most primary emotions is heavily influenced by cultural norms and can vary a great deal from place to place. If people are to communicate emotions effectively in everyday interaction, they must learn and use the display rules of their own culture. In addition, some emotions are far more conditioned on social processes than others, and sociologists who study emotion are much more focused on these kinds of social-emotional processes than on the biological links.

THE SOCIAL PSYCHOLOGY OF EMOTIONS

A social psychological approach to emotions moves beyond the notion that emotions are simply natural reactions to things that happen in the world around us. The above discussions demonstrate that although some aspects of emotion may be biologically hardwired, others are influenced by cultural norms and experiences. Social psychologists also argue that much of our emotional experience is a matter of interpretation. When we experience a physiological reaction that is part of an emotion, before we can decide which emotion is involved, we have to interpret the physical sensation in its social context.

Consider the feeling of being slightly nauseous and having sweaty palms. There are many potential interpretations of these physical symptoms. Perhaps you are a first-year medical student feeling disgusted upon seeing your first cadaver. Maybe you are grief stricken at the unexpected death of a cherished pet. Then again, perhaps you are excited about an upcoming date that you have been looking forward to. Or perhaps you are nervously heading into an exam you did not study enough for. When

we think more closely about emotions, we find that they are often just plausible explanations for our physiological reactions, and how we interpret them depends very much on what is happening in our social world. To the degree that we are actively experiencing, interpreting, and constructing our social world, we are also interpreting and constructing our emotions.

Cognitive Labeling Theory

One theory that tries to understand the social roots of emotions is **cognitive labeling theory** (Schachter, 1964). This theory proposes that emotional experience is the result of the following three-step sequence:

1. An event in the environment produces a physiological reaction.
2. We notice the physiological reaction and search for an appropriate explanation.
3. By examining situational cues ("What was happening when I reacted?"), we find an emotional label (disgust, grief, excitement, anxiety) for the reaction.

The theory further assumes that physical arousal is a general state. In other words, arousal does not substantially differ from one emotional state to another. Because one arousal state is not physiologically distinguishable from another, virtually any emotion can be attached to the arousal state. Which emotion becomes attributed to the arousal depends on the context.

Many social psychologists have demonstrated that individuals' understanding of physical arousal is indeed fairly easy to manipulate. For example, in an early study of cognitive labeling theory (Schachter & Singer, 1962), researchers gave students an injection of epinephrine, a drug that produces mild physiological arousal. The experimenters told one group of participants that this injection would probably cause them to experience a pounding heart, flushed face, and trembling. They told a second group nothing about the drug's effects. All students then waited with a confederate who, though appearing to be another participant, was actually employed by the researchers. Depending on the experimental treatment, the confederate behaved either euphorically (for example, shooting crumpled paper at a waste basket, flying paper airplanes, playing with a hula hoop) or angrily (for example, reacting with hostility to items on a questionnaire and finally tearing it up).

According to the theory, students in the informed group would not need to seek an explanation for their arousal because they knew their symptoms were drug induced. Students in the uninformed group, however, lacked an adequate explanation for their symptoms and thus would need to search the environment for cues to help them label their feelings. The results confirmed these predictions. Students in the uninformed group adopted the label for their arousal suggested by their environment. That is, those who waited with the euphoric confederate described themselves as happy, whereas those who waited with the angry confederate described themselves as angry. The self-descriptions of the informed group, however, were largely unaffected by the confederate's behavior.

Numerous later studies have expanded these findings to additional emotions (Kelley & Michela, 1980). They show that people who are unaware of the true cause of their physiological arousal can be induced to view themselves as anxious, guilty, amused, or sexually excited by placing them in environments that suggest these emotions (Dutton & Aron, 1974; Zillmann, 1978). As the theory predicts, environmental conditions strongly influence people's labeling of their physiological arousal.

Research suggests that the emotional label sometimes even precedes the awareness of arousal (H. Leventhal, 1984; Pennebaker, 1980). Our social context suggests that we should be experiencing a particular emotion, and only then do we search our bodily sensations for signs that will verify our belief. If environmental cues give us reason to believe we are angry, we attend to our flushed face and racing heart and verify our anger. If the cues suggest we are happy, we attend to our feelings of alertness and trembling and confirm our happiness. At any given time, our physiological state may afford evidence to support several emotional labels. Once the emotional label is applied, it can induce further physiological arousal that provides additional confirmation of the emotional label we have applied. Put another way, our expectations can help generate that affective response.

As the study of emotions has developed, researchers have come to better understand the centrality of the social situation in defining emotions. As cognitive labeling theory posits and the empirical research on the topic demonstrates, our immediate emotional reactions are products of internal physical processes that must also be recognized and interpreted in light of the present social context. This is true of not only immediate emotional reactions that are tied to arousal but also complex, enduring feelings like love and jealousy. These emotional states last even after physical arousal has passed (S. Gordon, 1990). Each is a pattern of sensations, emotions, actions, and cultural beliefs that are appropriate to a social relationship. Sentiments such as grief, loyalty, envy, and patriotism develop around our attachments to family, friends, fellow workers, and country.

Sentiments reflect the nature of our social relationships and the changes in them. Grief and nostalgia reflect social losses. Jealousy and envy reflect problems over control of possessions. Anger and resentment reflect betrayal of commitments. We label our feelings with the culturally appropriate sentiment to make sense of our diverse emotional responses. For example, a husband's joy in his wife's presence, his sorrow in her absence, his anger when she is criticized, and his fear when threatened with losing her make sense if he labels his feeling "love." Like simpler emotions, sentiments are produced by cognitive labeling. In choosing a sentiment label, however, we consider all the information we have about our enduring relationships, not just the immediate social context.

The Importance of Others in Emotional Experiences. At times, it is people in our social circles who define our emotions for us. Like us, they consider physiological reactions, social contexts, and our behavior to determine how we might be feeling and then communicate this to us. On the first day of kindergarten, a young child might describe to her father that she feels strange. When he asks her what she means by strange, she would try to describe her physical symptoms or emotions but may not have acquired the cognitive or linguistic skills to say "lightheaded" or "anxious" or even to interpret the physiological arousal as an indicator of an emotional state. If she describes the feeling as a bee buzzing through her body, from up in her head to down in her stomach, her father would likely explain to her that she is feeling excited or nervous and that such an emotion is completely normal in a new situation. From then onward, the young girl would understand that the buzzing response should be interpreted as a sign of nervousness or excitement and that those types of emotions are expected when she tries something new.

This emotional socialization occurs throughout our lives. In a study of a university-based evangelical Christian religious group, Amy Wilkins (2008) found that members of the group claimed to be happier than non-Christians. Rather than see this emotion as a positive mental health effect stemming from participation in the group, Wilkins saw it as originating in the culture of the group. She found that members of "Unity" (the pseudonym Wilkins gave the group) often talked about emotion, particularly happiness, and new members were taught to think of themselves as happy and learned how to actively produce that emotional response. Group members linked emotion to religiosity. They taught recruits that an important part of signaling a connection with God and differentiating themselves from nonmembers was experiencing elation. This prompted new members to both interpret their physiological responses as signs of happiness and to work to elicit positive feelings so they could feel a sense of belongingness and, thus, separate themselves from non-Christians.

Context in Interpreting the Emotions of Others. Just as individuals use context to determine their own emotional states, they use context to determine how others are feeling. In fact, context is routinely encoded in the perception of emotion (Barrett & Kensinger, 2010). Social psychologists conducted an experiment where they asked participants to determine either the specific emotion or the affective significance (positive, negative, or neutral) of a facial expression that was coupled with a context. Participants who were asked to label an emotional expression were much more likely to remember the context (a scene like a desert or a coffee shop) than those who were only asked to determine the affective significance of an expression. In other words, the facial expressions themselves provided all the information that the participants needed to determine general affect. However, to determine emotion, participants relied on context clues and, therefore, were more likely to remember them when prompted by experimenters.

Emotion Work

There are times when individuals want to either experience or express emotions that they might not currently be feeling, particularly if they want to elicit emotions that are more consistent with the social context. When a person enters into a social situation, he or she can make some decisions about what kind of emotions to display. Have you ever tried to psych yourself up for a performance, sporting event, or examination? Have you ever forced yourself to have a good time at a party even though you were tired? Maybe you have tried to feel grateful for a gift that you really didn't like or displayed a stiff upper lip despite severe disappointment. These are all instances of **emotion work**—attempts to change the intensity or quality of feelings to bring them into line with the requirements of the occasion (Hochschild, 1983).

We manage emotions in two ways: through evocation and suppression. In some situations, it is advantageous to evoke an emotion that is currently absent or at least beyond what one is really feeling. A mother who is tired after a long day in the office might put on her happy face when she picks her twins up from daycare. Although the mother might be glad to see her children, she will work to smile wider and express more excitement and cheer than she is actually feeling to appear involved and interested. This may be, in part, because she thinks that a good mother should be very happy to see her children and she wants to live up to that expectation for herself, her children, and the daycare workers. At other times, emotion work (also called emotion management) involves suppressing an emotion that is seen as inappropriate. A medical student who is examining a patient for the first time might suppress her disgust, embarrassment, or arousal so as to appear professional in front of the patient and her adviser (Smith & Kleinman, 1989).

Emotion work occurs because we are subject to **feeling rules**—rules that dictate what people with our role identities ought to feel in a given situation. If we are receiving a gift, the feeling rule is that we should feel grateful. If we are at a party, we should be having fun. Social psychologists have attempted to identify feeling rules by presenting scenarios to subjects and asking about appropriate or expected emotions. Many times, there was a high degree of agreement about which emotions should be present in certain social situations—evidence that there indeed are emotional expectation or feeling rules (Heise & Calhan, 1995). If our feelings are not in line with the current feeling rules and we were to unintentionally express our true feelings, we would be violating the norms of the situation. Therefore, we try to not only express the right feeling but also *feel* the right feelings. Efforts to change the experience of emotion stem, in part, from a desire to be consistent. It causes dissonance to feel sad while smiling on the outside.

To examine this phenomenon of actually working to alter the experience of emotion, Arlie Hochschild conducted a very interesting study of flight attendants (1983). Generally speaking, airline flight attendants are expected to feel calm and cheerful as they interact with passengers. But suppose a group of flight attendants has been working for ten hours, serving hundreds of people on three different flights. Fatigue and irritation may be the main feelings they are experiencing. If so, they must then work directly on their own emotions to evoke feelings of cheerfulness and to suppress feelings of irritation. In fact, Hochschild showed that this kind of emotion work was a fundamental requirement of the job and that flight attendants were trained to perform it (see Table 5.2).

TABLE 5.2 Emotion Work Tasks for Flight Attendants

EMOTION WORK CATEGORY	DETAILED DESCRIPTION
Relax and smile	Present a calm and cheerful demeanor. "It's incredible how much we have to smile, but there it is. We know that, but we're still doing it, and you would too."
Consider passengers as friends and family	Protect and comfort passengers as you would your own family.
Do not engage in ridicule	No matter how the passengers behave or what they demand, flight attendants may not ridicule them or their requests.
Never appear alarmed or frightened	No matter what the situation, flight attendants must suppress fear and panic. "Even though I am an honest person, I have learned not to allow my face to mirror my alarm or my fright."
Sincerity	Act from the heart. Manage others' emotions by remaining calm.
Do not blame passengers for anything	Even if it is their own fault.
Never display anger	Training programs emphasize strategies for reducing anger, including role-taking as passengers.

Source: Adapted from Hochschild (1983), *The Managed Heart.*

What is most interesting about emotion work is that when individuals act in accordance with feeling rules, they often begin to actually change their internal feelings to bring them in line with the way they are acting. A job requirement for flight attendants is to display upbeat, positive, energetic personas. Research has found that these portrayals of emotions can change the actual emotions the person is feeling under the surface of his or her performance. Flight attendants who appear to be cheerful even if they are actually fatigued and irritable tend to actually feel more cheerful as they continue the act. Recall our story about Rob the kindergarten teacher at the beginning of the chapter. Although he didn't feel like it at all, feeling rules demanded he act energetic and cheerful in front of his class. The longer he did this, the more cheerful he actually became. This may occur because of cognitive consistency effects (see Chapter 6), in which we are motivated to bring our attitudes in line with our behaviors. It can also occur because when we act cheerfully, people in turn interact with us in the way they would with a cheerful person. Their behavior reflects positively on us and can enhance our mood.

As individuals attempt to manage their emotions, they can engage in either surface acting or deep acting. Whereas surface acting only changes the expression of emotion (smiling and exchange pleasantries), deep acting transforms our emotional state (Larson & Yao, 2005). One method used to evoke suitable emotions and suppress unsuitable ones is simply to adopt an appropriate physical posture. Slumping over in a chair is unlikely to evoke feelings of cheerfulness, but standing up straight and walking briskly can. Other methods include breathing quickly or deeply or imagining a situation that produces the required feeling. To recapture some energy and become more upbeat, flight attendants may take a deep breath to relax and reduce irritation, imagining how good it will feel to be home tonight. Actively pursuing these strategies allows us to gain some control over our feelings and to project images necessary for a particular social situation.

Research suggests, however, that the demands for emotion work—and occupations that require emotional labor—are not evenly distributed. Those who have higher status in a social situation have more freedom in expressing their emotions. A boss or a parent can easily express anger or irritability in circumstances in which lower-level employees and children are expected to follow the feeling rules more closely. In effect, a person's status allows different feeling rules. Emotion work can also become a commodity, in that people who are proficient at it can be rewarded. For example, employers can demand emotion work from their employees as a part of their job requirements. When emotion work is done for pay and the emotion is one of the important goods a worker is producing, it is called **emotional labor**. Such is the case, in no uncertain terms, for flight attendants. Since Hochschild's seminal research on flight attendants and bill collectors, many other social psychologists have examined emotion management in workplaces such as Disneyworld and Disneyland (Reyers & Matusitz, 2012; Van Maanen, 1991), medical schools and offices (Larson & Yao, 2005; Smith & Kleinman, 1989), and police departments (Schaible & Gecas, 2010).

Emotion work is not always effective. When we are unable to effectively manage our emotions and instead project an emotion that is inappropriate (or too high or low an intensity of an emotion), this is referred to as **emotional deviance** (Thoits, 1990). In 2010, a flight attendant engaged in emotional deviance when he lost his patience when a passenger ignored his instructions and, in doing so, accidentally struck the flight attendant with a piece of luggage. Rather than make light of what happened—or smile and brush off the incident, as one might expect from a flight attendant—Steven Slater took to the plane's public address system and angrily cursed out the flier. Although some emotional deviance is expected in social life, persistent or pronounced emotional deviance can be seen as a sign of mental illness (Thoits, 1985). Sure enough, a subsequent mental health evaluation found that Slater was suffering from a clinical disorder and had a series of alcohol-abuse problems, perhaps contributing to this inability to regulate his emotional reaction that day.

Social Emotions

Although many emotions have both social and nonsocial components, there are certain emotions that simply cannot be understood or even defined without reference to the social world. These emotions are called **social emotions**, and they are defined as emotions that (1) involve an awareness of oneself in the social context, (2) emerge out of interaction with at least one other actor, and (3) are often experienced in reference to some kind of societal standard (Barrett, 1995; Stets, 2003). For many social emotions, it is necessary to place oneself in the role of others in order to experience the emotion (Shott, 1979).

To understand this rather complex definition, think about the notion of empathy. To experience emotional empathy, you first have to be aware that you have some kind of connection to a person who is experiencing an emotion. For example, when we feel empathy for someone who is feeling pain, we are at least partially recognizing that we are involved and perhaps even responsible for easing the person's pain. (The notion that helping can reduce empathic suffering is explored in greater detail in Chapter 10.) Second, there must be someone else in the social environment who is experiencing some kind of emotion in order for us to experience empathy. By definition, then, empathy is social. Third, when one experiences empathy, he or she is reminded of society's standards. If the object of our empathy is feeling pain, we may evaluate, based on societal standards, our own obligation to intervene to ease their pain. If their pain is minimal and the risk of harm to ourselves

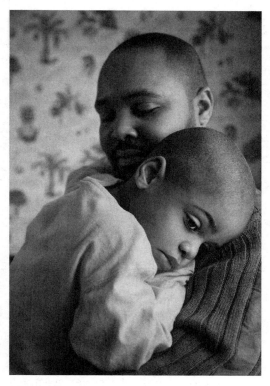

Parents experience strong empathic responses to the emotional states of their children. They find it easy both to recognize distress in their offspring and to put themselves in the place of their children. © iofoto/123rtf

is great, we are not obligated to intervene and, therefore, may experience minimal empathy.

In this section, we will examine the social bases of five emotions to illustrate how important social interaction is in experiencing and defining some of our most important social processes. There are many other social emotions, but here we focus on guilt, shame, jealousy, embarrassment, and love.

Guilt. We feel guilt when we judge that we have done something we should not have done. Guilt is, therefore, inherently evaluative. We are not necessarily a bad person if we have done something that causes us guilt, but we are certainly less good than we could be. Where do the standards come from that we use to judge ourselves? They come from others in our social groups or environment. Guilt, therefore, involves a self-reflexive judgment in which we see ourselves through other people's eyes. When we feel guilt, we are engaged in an appraisal of ourselves using standards that we may have accepted but were constructed by others. Guilt also implies action. Just like so many social psychological processes, guilt involves an uncomfortable feeling. Individuals who feel guilt need to do something to eliminate it so they can return to a more pleasant psychological state. They attempt to engage in some kind of reparative activity so they can be forgiven by someone who has the power to release them from guilt (Stets, 2003). Thus, not only is the negative emotion itself inherently social, so is the method of dealing with it.

Returning for a moment to our story about Rob, the kindergarten teacher, suppose in his frustration he had blown up at his teacher's aide for not getting the children settled for story time. After yelling at his aide, Rob may feel guilty for the unnecessary outburst, which made the aide feel underappreciated; the aide may feel guilty for not following classroom procedures properly; and if the children observed the outburst, they might also feel guilty for not getting into the story-time circle quickly enough. In each instance of guilt, there is a social standard of behavior (for Rob, for the aide, and for the children) that has been violated. Each guilty party can reduce or eliminate the guilt by, for example, apologizing to the offended party and receiving forgiveness.

Guilt has a number of social functions, the first of which is socialization (Hoffman, 2001). When a parent disapproves of a child's behavior, the result is a feeling of discomfort. If the parent can then induce the child to realize that the source of the discomfort is the child's own behavior, then the child will feel a sense of guilt. The child can then be taught to avoid the guilt by avoiding the behavior. Closely related, people can use guilt as a method to get what they want from others. If they can induce others to feel guilty about doing or not doing something, they may be able to change the target's behavior (Stets, 2003). Panhandlers use various methods of making their targets feel guilty for refusing to help them. By pointing out the disparities between the target and their own difficult circumstances, they can induce guilt and inspire giving (Basil, Ridgway, & Basil, 2008).

Finally, although we often think guilt has a negative impact on social relationships, social psychologists have found that it actually functions to support and strengthen relationships. It does this in two ways. First, it distributes the negative consequences of a bad social interaction. If I do something that hurts you, you are bearing all of the costs of the social exchange. But if I feel guilty about it, I also have to bear some costs—so guilt evens out the suffering to some degree (Baumeister, Stillwell, & Heatherton, 1994). Second, when we feel guilt and act to correct whatever problem caused the guilt, we are sending a powerful message to those who we harmed—we are telling them that we value the relationship and that we don't want our own poor behavior to damage it. If Rob apologizes to his classroom aide, his actions may actually endear him more to her than if he had never yelled at her in the first place.

Shame. A counterpart to the emotion of guilt is shame. Although both emotions share certain characteristics—a person feeling either of these emotions has committed some kind of offense against another—shame is a much deeper and longer-lasting state than guilt. When we feel guilty, it is typically tied to a single incident that is easy to identify and oftentimes has an eas-

ily identifiable response that will relieve the guilt. If, for example, you steal something and feel guilty, you can return what you stole or replace it. Shame, however, is not so much about an incident or transgression as it is about how you evaluate yourself as a person. When you feel shame, there is a deep sense of the self not as someone who has just done something wrong but as someone who is a bad person (Thoits, 2011). There is something wrong with your intrinsic character, and it is not something that can be easily rectified (Babcock & Sabini, 1990). As a result, the response to shame is not as simple as repairing the damage done to the social relationship. Most of the time the more likely response to shame is to flee. Shamed individuals want to run away from the situation, hide from everyone, or just disappear completely (Barrett, 1995; Tangney, 1995). Given that shame threatens the very core of an individual's self-regard, it is a very intense emotional experience—much more so than that of guilt.

Because shame is such an intense emotion, people are all the more motivated to try to escape it. One way of reducing shame is to escape the blame for the problems that caused it. Those who have been shamed sometimes try to accomplish this by blaming others. The result can be a volatile "shame-anger cycle" (Scheff & Retzinger, 1991) that escalates tension and shame. Imagine that one person, let's call her Karla, insults her husband, Leo, telling him that he is a worthless human being, as evidenced by his repeated failure to hold down a job. If Leo were to accept this appraisal, he would become ashamed. Escaping shame is a powerful motivator, so Leo responds by getting angry and insulting Karla with a retaliatory slur that implies she is the reason he has lost his job. He claims that he had to leave work early many times to deal with their son because she was an incompetent mother. Each partner now feels shame and sees the other person as the source of the problem. Shame leads to more anger through a retaliatory cycle. Oftentimes this is exactly the kind of interaction pattern that leads to spousal assault.

Jealousy. Jealousy is also an inherently social emotion. Jealousy is a negative emotional reaction we feel when something good happens to someone else (Ben Ze'ev, 2000). Because an individual cannot, by definition, experience jealousy without the participation of someone else, the emotional state is dependent on the social context. One situation that often produces jealousy is when a relationship moves from a dyad (group of two) to a triad (group of three), causing a person to lose a significant relationship with someone they were close to. The third person, who threatens an individual's relationship with the second person, is the object of the jealousy of the first person. A good example of this dynamic is the change that a couple experiences with the birth or adoption of a child. The mother may sense that the father loves the baby more than he loves her, and she may feel somehow displaced and, therefore, jealous of the baby. Later on, if the child grows close to the mother, the father may feel envious of the bond the two of them share and become jealous of the mother. Research on siblings shows that toddlers direct jealousy toward one another when a mother shifts her attention from playing with one child to the other (Draghi-Lorenz, Reddy, & Costall, 2001). This kind of dynamic can be observed in virtually any kind of paired relationship. Breakups of a romantically involved couple are another example. If the girlfriend, for example, leaves the relationship and starts dating a new partner, the boyfriend who is left behind may feel jealous of the new boyfriend.

If social emotions exist for a reason, what could be the functions of jealousy? We typically think of jealousy as being a destructive force—a green-eyed monster—that we must struggle to control. But if jealousy is really born of social forces and is not completely natural, it must have some useful purpose. One function may be to draw oneself back into a social interaction. When we express jealousy, we are signaling to others in the environment that we have been left out, that we want to be included, and that they are in some way responsible for helping to reintegrate us into the social relationship. A child who expresses jealousy when his mother is attending to some other child is sending the message that he wants to interact with her. If she responds, as parents often do, by increasing her interaction with him, picking him up, or drawing him into activities with the other child, then the expression of jealousy has been rewarded and, thereby, reinforced.

Jealousy can also signal to others in the environment that the jealous person has some kind of claim on the object in question (be it a person or a physical item). If, for example, a young girl expresses jealousy that her brother is getting to play with a favored toy, it would indicate that she is making a claim on the toy: She has a right to play with it, she deserves more time with the toy and he deserves less, and she wants to exercise that claim by playing with the toy. Thus, jealousy and envy help to establish turf boundaries around objects and around people.

Embarrassment. Another social emotion is embarrassment—an uncomfortable feeling of mortification or exposure. We become embarrassed when we fail to live up to an image or identity that we are trying to claim to an audience. For example, a math professor will likely experience embarrassment when he makes a simple calculation error on the board in front of his class. The embarrassment he feels is inherently social

BOX 5.2 Test Yourself: What's Your Emotional IQ?

Think you're smart? Think you're street smart? Maybe you are, but will those smarts help negotiate all social situations? Maybe not, say social psychologists who study **emotional intelligence**. A best-selling book called *Emotional Intelligence: Why It Can Matter More Than IQ* (Goleman, 1996, 2006), claims that an individual's ability to understand the emotional content in social interactions constitutes a unique dimension of intelligence that is substantially different from the different kinds of intelligences measured by IQ that had traditionally been the focus of the psychological literature on intelligence.

According to psychologists, emotional intelligence consists of four capacities:

1. Being able to accurately perceive emotions (one's own and others)
2. Being able to use emotional information in rational thinking
3. Being able to understand the meaning of emotions
4. Being able to manage emotions (both one's own and those of others)

These four capacities have been tied to success and failure in a number of social environments, including family and marital relationships, managing employees and coworkers, intergroup relations, and even personal health (Goleman, 2006).

A number of measures have been developed to assess emotional intelligence (see Brackett & Mayer, 2003; Lopes, Salovey, Cote, & Beers, 2005). One, developed by the Hay Group, is called the Emotional Competence Inventory (ECI). As with most other measures, the ECI is too long to be reproduced here, but some sample items give a preliminary sense of how emotional intelligence is typically measured.

1. *You are on an airplane that suddenly hits extremely bad turbulence and begins rocking from side to side. What do you do?*
   A. Continue to read your book or magazine or watch the movie, trying to pay little attention to the turbulence.
   B. Become vigilant for an emergency, carefully monitoring the stewardesses and reading the emergency instructions card.
   C. A little of both a and b.
   D. Not sure—never noticed.

2. *You are in a meeting when a colleague takes credit for work you have done. What do you do?*
   A. Immediately and publicly confront the colleague over the ownership of your work.
   B. After the meeting, take the colleague aside and tell her you would appreciate in the future that she credits you when speaking about your work.
   C. Nothing—it's not a good idea to embarrass colleagues in public.
   D. After the colleague speaks, publicly thank her for referencing your work and give the group more specific detail about what you were trying to accomplish.

3. *You are a customer service representative and have just gotten an extremely angry client on the phone. What do you do?*
   A. Hang up. It doesn't pay to take abuse from anyone.
   B. Listen to the client and rephrase what you gather he is feeling.
   C. Explain to the client that he is being unfair, that you are only trying to do your job, and you would appreciate it if he wouldn't get in the way of this.
   D. Tell the client you understand how frustrating this must be for him, and offer a specific thing you can do to help him get his problem resolved.

4. *You are a college student who had hoped to get an A in a course that was important for your future career aspirations. You just found out you got a C on the midterm. What do you do?*
   A. Sketch out a specific plan for ways to improve your grade and resolve to follow through.
   B. Decide you do not have what it takes to make it in that career.
   C. Tell yourself it really doesn't matter how much you do in the course; concentrate instead on other classes where your grades are higher.
   D. Go see the professor and try to talk her into giving you a better grade.

5. *You are a manager in an organization that is trying to encourage respect for racial and ethnic diversity. You overhear someone telling a racist joke. What do you do?*

A. Ignore it—the best way to deal with these things is not to react.

B. Call the person into your office and explain that their behavior is inappropriate and is grounds for disciplinary action if repeated.

C. Speak up on the spot, saying that such jokes are inappropriate and will not be tolerated in your organization.

D. Suggest to the person telling the joke that he go through a diversity training program.

6. *You are an insurance salesman calling on prospective clients. You have left the last 15 client meetings empty-handed. What do you do?*

A. Call it a day and go home early to miss rush-hour traffic.

B. Try something new in the next call, and keep plugging away.

C. List your strengths and weaknesses to identify what may be undermining your ability to sell.

D. Sharpen up your résumé.

7. *You are trying to calm down a colleague who has worked herself into a fury because the driver of another car has cut dangerously close in front of her. What do you do?*

A. Tell her to forget about it—she's okay now and it is no big deal.

B. Put on one of her favorite tapes and try to distract her.

C. Join her in criticizing the other driver.

D. Tell her about a time something like this happened to you and how angry you felt until you saw the other driver was on the way to the hospital.

8. *A discussion between you and your partner has escalated into a shouting match. You are both upset and, in the heat of the argument, start making personal attacks that neither of you really mean. What would be the best thing to do?*

A. Agree to take a 20-minute break before continuing the discussion.

B. Go silent, regardless of what your partner says.

C. Say you are sorry, and ask your partner to apologize too.

D. Stop for a moment, collect your thoughts, then restate your side of the case as precisely as possible.

9. *You have been given the task of managing a team that has been unable to come up with a creative solution to a work problem. What is the first thing you do?*

A. Draw up an agenda, call a meeting, and allot a specific period of time to discuss each item.

B. Organize an off-site meeting aimed specifically at encouraging the team to get to know each other better.

C. Begin by asking each person individually for ideas about how to solve the problem.

D. Start out with a brainstorming session, encouraging each person to say whatever comes to mind, no matter how wild.

10. *You have recently been assigned a young manager in your team and have noticed that he appears to be unable to make the simplest of decisions without seeking advice from you. What do you do?*

A. Accept that he "does not have what it take to succeed around here" and find others in your team to take on his tasks.

B. Get an HR manager to talk to him about where he sees his future in the organization.

C. Purposely give him lots of complex decisions to make so he will become more confident in his role.

D. Engineer an ongoing series of challenging but manageable experiences for him, and make yourself available to act as his mentor.

Scoring: Question 1. Either A, B, or C-10 points; 2. B-5, D-10; 3. B-5, D-10; 4. A-10, C-5; 5. B-5, C-10, D-5; 6. B-10, C-5; 7. C-5, D-10; 8. A-10; 9. B-10, D-5; 10. B-5, D-10. Higher scores suggest greater emotional intelligence.

Source: Hay Acquisition Company 1, Inc. Copyright © 1999–2005, used with permission.

because it stems from his imagination of how he appears to his students who realize his mistake. He worries that it threatens his students' impression of him (and his own identity) as a competent math professor. Lacking the skills necessary for an identity is only one source of embarrassment. As covered in Chapter 4, embarrassment can also come from a violation of privacy norms or awkwardness or lack of poise.

Embarrassment is also social because it is contagious; an additional source of embarrassment is the embarrassment of others. In a study of empathic embarrassment, groups of women observed another woman perform either a very embarrassing or an ambiguous task (Marcus, Wilson, & Miller, 1996). Most observers reported feeling embarrassed as they observed another perform the embarrassing task. Some observers of the innocuous task also reported feeling embarrassed, suggesting that people vary in their readiness to perceive emotion in others (empathy). Indeed, individuals vary a great deal in their ability to read, understand, and respond to the emotional cues and behavior of others. Those who are skilled in this process are said to have high emotional intelligence (see Box 5.2). High levels of empathy and emotional intelligence increase the likelihood that we will experience vicarious (or empathic) embarrassment.

Because of our ability to experience others' embarrassment, we work to help others save face in interaction. In a study of street-corner ciphers (impromptu rap sessions), Lee (2009) found that if a performer seemed at risk for messing up during a free-style performance, others would engage in collateral face-saving. If a rapper "fell off" and lost rhythm, someone else would "jump in" and begin rapping to keep the flow going in the cipher. Other onlookers would also use strategies to encourage the audience to turn their attention toward the person who jumped in. Both these tactics help minimize the embarrassment experienced by the rapper who fell off and the vicarious embarrassment of the onlookers.

Another indication of the social nature of embarrassment is the way it maps onto social organization (Goffman, 1956). For example, we are more likely to experience embarrassment in groups rather than when we are alone or with just one other person (Parrott & Smith, 1991; Tangney, Miller, Flicker, & Barlow, 1996). Embarrassment is also more common when we are among unfamiliar others, whose favorable impressions of us might seem more dependent on our performances in any one social situation. Family or close friends, however, would have more information to draw from and so are less likely to see any one instance of falling short of an identity claim as a threat to an identity. We are also more likely to experience embarrassment in front of a diverse audience than in a more homogenous one. For example, teenagers are much more likely to experience embarrassment among a mixed-gender group than if they are with their same gender peers (Lizardo & Collett, 2013).

Love. Despite our immediate sense that love is a happy, positive emotion, it is important to remember that it is not always so. As discussed earlier, in the section on culture and emotion, some Asian cultures actually identify a separate emotion that might be called "sad love," which usually involves some unrequited feelings of love. Nevertheless, most people experience love as a positive, mood-enhancing emotion.

Love is covered in greater detail in Chapter 12 (Interpersonal Attraction and Relationships), including different types of love that are experienced across a wide range of intensity. It is a complex emotion or, more appropriately, a set of related emotions. Love is, however, an inherently social emotion. It is plain that love involves at least two people—one who loves and one who is the object of the love. Growing up, we learn that to love someone implies a willingness to sacrifice something for the object of our affection (Nikolajeva, 2012).

The type of love involved and the experience of it depends very heavily on the relationship to the object of love and the reaction to any expression of love. Friends have different experiences of love than spouses, teenage boyfriends and girlfriends have different experiences of love than a couple who has been married for 30 years. Even within a single loving relationship, there can be significant asymmetry. A parent, for example, shares love with a child, but the adult's experience of love is considerably different from the child's. The differences in all of these experiences of love are not derived from some kind of natural reaction but rather from the different expectations associated with the role of parent, child, boyfriend, girlfriend, husband, wife, best friend, and so on. Parents have responsibilities for the growth, development, and well-being of their children that indicates a caretaking element in their concept of parental love, an element their children do not share. Other role demands produce very different conceptions of love, not only in different types of relationships but also across cultures.

SUMMARY

Defining Emotions. Affect is a general label that encompasses any kind of evaluation of an object. Affect varies in direction, intensity, and activity. Emotions are short-lived reactions to stimuli involving cognitive reactions, physiological reactions, and expressive gesturing and is also a label we associate with a cluster of the first three elements. Today's social psychologists use the term "sentiment" to refer to longer-term emotional states. Moods are general psychological conditions that can last for hours or even days.

Classical Ideas About the Origins and Expression of Emotion. Charles Darwin believed some emotions and their expression were universal not only among human beings but also across species. These ideas were developed to support his theories of evolution. James and Lange developed a physiological notion of emotion in which physical changes occurred first and then were cognitively processed and interpreted as demonstrated that facial expressions of happiness, sadness, surprise, fear, anger, and disgust are all readily recognized by almost all cultures, thereby suggesting they are universal, basic emotions. But there are also significant differences in the experience and expression of emotions across cultures. Some exaggerate or suppress basic emotions via complex display rules that may make emotions harder or easier to recognize. Collectivist cultures process and display emotion in ways that protect and reinforce social bonds. Individualist cultures display emotions in ways that broadcast individual states and draw attention to the individual as the key social unit.

The Social Psychology of Emotions. Social psychologists argue that much of our emotional experience is a matter of interpretation. Cognitive labeling theory describes the three-step sequence through which we experience a physiological reaction, search for an explanation for that reaction, and label our emotion based on that explanation. Others can also help us label our emotions, both teaching us how to interpret specific cues and helping us do so in interaction. We use context to interpret both our own emotions and the emotions of others. Social environments also define feeling rules, which dictate which emotions are appropriate for particular roles in that social context.

Individuals often engage in emotion work, in which they attempt to suppress or evoke particular emotions to bring their emotional expression and experience in line with situational expectations. Some occupations require workers, like flight attendants, to market their emotions as a commodity. If we fail to manage our emotions effectively and express or experience an emotion that is inappropriate in any given situation, we are engaged in emotional deviance.

Social Emotions. Many emotions, like empathy, cannot be defined or experienced without reference to the social context in which they exist. Guilt and shame require the judgments of others. Jealousy requires another person to compare oneself to. Embarrassment requires an audience, and love requires an object of affection.

List of Key Terms and Concepts

action units (p. 182)
affect (p. 179)
cognitive labeling theory (p. 189)
collectivist cultures (p. 185)
display rules (p. 185)
emotion work (p. 192)
emotional deviance (p. 194)
emotional intelligence (p. 198)
emotional labor (p. 194)
emotions (p. 179)
feeling rules (p. 192)
individualist cultures (p. 185)
mood (p. 180)
sentiment (p. 179)
social emotions (p. 194)

Critical Thinking Skill:
Effortful Consideration of Ideas

William Shakespeare famously said, "All the world's a stage, and all the men and women

merely players." By this point in the text, you have ample evidence that this is a perspective in social psychology as well. For example, the last chapter (Chapter 4) introduced you to the importance of self-presentation and impression management in everyday life, and the current chapter extended this by discussing the role of emotion management in social interactions. Although students seem to intuitively understand this material and enjoy these topics, it is important that they see beyond Shakespeare's stage. It is not simply that we are acting in social life; these performances have enduring effects. To consider this requires additional effort but provides great payoff.

As Thomas and Thomas (1928) wrote, if persons define situations as real, they are real in their consequences. If you put on a suit to present yourself as a respectable young man when meeting your girlfriend's parents for the first time, they are likely to accept that image and treat you as respectable. If you work to evoke tears at your godmother's funeral despite your excitement over your favorite team's win earlier that day, others around you will likely accept that performance as reality and empathize with you further. In other words, your expression of emotion might influence their own emotional experience.

To push this further, these performances can ultimately affect you as well. If your girlfriend's parents treat you as respectable, their treatment might influence your behavior and actually encourage you to live up to their expectations. If others at the funeral begin to express more sadness in response to your own, you may experience more "real" emotion.

Consider some of your recent performances. Given what you know about social psychology thus far—symbolic interaction, socialization, the self, deep acting—can you think of how they might have come to affect you and not just those around you?

A team of scientists (a doctor and a social psychologist) conducted research on medical students and their self-presentation and emotion management (Smith & Kleinman, 1989). They found that the tactics medical students use to make it possible for them to do their work came home with them, influencing them long after the performance was over. For example, medical students have to engage in intimate bodily contact with patients. To limit embarrassment or arousal, the medical students come to regard the patient's body as an intellectual puzzle or to see body parts as disconnected from any particular person. But neutralizing the body makes intimacy outside of work more difficult. One student reported that one night, while being intimate with his wife, he realized he was giving her a breast exam, searching for signs of cancer.

Although it might be easy to assume that the performative nature of social life discounts the importance of our socially constructed reality, the effortful consideration of the effects of these performances provides a more nuanced view of social psychological processes and social life.

CHAPTER 6

SOCIAL PERCEPTION AND COGNITION

INTRODUCTION

It is 10 p.m., and the admitting physician at the psychiatric hospital is interviewing a respectable-looking man who has asked for treatment. "You see," the patient says, "I keep hearing voices." After taking a full history, the physician diagnoses the man with schizophrenia and assigns him to an inpatient unit. The physician is well trained and makes the diagnosis with apparent ease. Yet to diagnose someone's mental condition correctly is a difficult problem in social perception. The differences between paranoia, schizophrenia, depression, and normality are not always easy to discern.

A classic study conducted by Rosenhan (1973) demonstrates this problem. Eight pseudo-patients who were actually research investigators gained entry into mental hospitals by claiming to hear voices. During the intake interviews, the pseudo-patients gave true accounts of their backgrounds, life experiences, and present (quite ordinary) psychological condition. They falsified only their names, occupations, and their complaint of hearing voices. Once in the psychiatric unit, the pseudo-patients immediately stopped simulating symptoms of schizophrenia. They reported that the voices had ceased and talked normally with other patients. The other patients began to suspect that the investigators were not really mentally ill, but the staff continued to believe they were. The nurses and orderlies made note of the pseudo-patients' "strange" behavior, including a tendency to line up very early for meals and to spend significant amounts of time writing in their notebooks. Although such behavior would not be seen as odd for healthy researchers with little else to do, the staff considered it evidence of mental illness. Because of these enduring beliefs, upon discharge, the pseudo-patients were still diagnosed with schizophrenia, although now it was "schizophrenia in remission."

A man voluntarily checking into a psychiatric hospital may pose a confusing problem for the hospital staff. Is he really "mentally ill" and in need of hospitalization, or is he "healthy"? Is he no longer able to function in the outside world? Or is he merely faking and trying to get a break from his work or his family?

To try to answer these questions, the admitting physician gathers information about the person and classifies it as indicating illness or health. Then the doctor combines these facts to form a general diagnosis (paranoia, schizophrenia, or depression) and determines what treatment the person needs. While performing these actions, the doctor is engaging in **social perception**. Broadly defined, social perception refers to constructing an understanding of the social world from the data we get through our senses. More narrowly defined, it refers to the processes by which we form impressions of other people's traits and personalities.

In making her diagnosis, the physician not only forms an impression about the traits and characteristics of the new patient, but she also tries to understand the causes of that person's behavior. She tries, for instance, to figure out whether the patient acts as he does because of some internal dispositions or because of external pressures from the environment. Social psychologists term this process attribution. In attribution, we observe others' behavior and then infer backward to causes—intentions, abilities, traits, motives, and situational pressures— that explain why people act as they do.

Social perception and attribution are not passive activities. We do not simply register the stimuli that impinge on our senses; rather, our expectations and cognitive structures influence what we notice and how we interpret it. This is closely tied to the dual-process model introduced in Chapter 1. The intake physician at the psychiatric hospital, for example, does not expect to encounter researchers pretending to be mentally ill; instead, she expects to meet people who are mentally ill. Thus, even before the interaction begins, the doctor has categorized the patient as mentally ill. With that categorization firmly in place, the doctor falls victim to **confirmation bias**, focusing on information relevant to that condition and ignoring or downplaying information that is inconsistent with a diagnosis of mental illness (Nickerson, 1998). In other words, her interpretation is influenced by her expectation that the patient is a real patient. Most of the time, the impressions we form of others are sufficiently accurate to permit smooth interaction. After all, few people who are admitted to psychiatric hospitals are researchers faking mental illness. Yet social perception and attribution can be unreliable. Even highly trained observers can misperceive, misjudge, and reach the wrong conclusions.

In February 1999, police officers in New York City were attempting to track down a serial rapist. Sketches of the rapist had been circulated to the police, and so they had some idea what the rapist looked like. Four White officers patrolling the Bronx encountered Amadou Diallo, a Black man, and thought he resembled the sketches of the rapist. As Diallo was entering his apartment building, the police officers ordered him to stop. Diallo stopped and began to reach for his wallet to produce his identification. The police officers interpreted this action quite differently, however. Believing he was reaching for a gun, the officers opened fire. They fired a total of 41 shots, and Diallo died immediately. Diallo was not the rapist and had no criminal record—the officers' snap judgments were wrong.

The image of a Black man in a bad neighborhood, reaching into his pocket as he was being stopped by the police, provided too many dangerous cues that caused the officers to act immediately. Many have wondered whether the police officers would have been slower to act if Diallo had been White. Did race help activate a dangerous image in the police officers' minds and encourage them to respond aggressively? Thirteen years later, the shooting of an unarmed Trayvon Martin prompted similar questions. George Zimmerman, a neighborhood watch coordinator, shot Martin, a 17-year-old African American, during a confrontation in Zimmerman's gated community. Just moments before the shooting, Zimmerman called the local police department because he was concerned about Martin's behavior: "There is a really suspicious guy....This guy looks like he's up to no good. Or he's on drugs or something. It's raining and he's just walking around, looking about" (CNN, March 20, 2012). The case received national attention and left many asking whether it was racially motivated. Did an African American teen in a hoodie elicit different reactions from what he would have if he been wearing something else? If Martin had been White, would Zimmerman have interpreted his actions—"walking through [the neighborhood], looking about"—as less threatening?

Studies conducted in laboratory settings confirm this type of dynamic. In one study, subjects were asked to act as police officers and decide whether to shoot at suspected criminals. The suspected criminals were either holding a gun (in which case the officer should shoot) or were holding a neutral object such as a cell phone (in which case the officer should not shoot). The results showed that the subjects were more likely to mistakenly shoot a suspect holding a cell phone if the suspect was Black. Similarly, they were also more likely to mistakenly hold back from shooting a suspect holding a gun if the suspect was White (Plant, Peruche, & Butz, 2005). Research replicated with actual police officers had similar results (Plant & Peruche, 2005).

This chapter focuses on these processes of social perception and attribution and addresses the following questions:

1. How do we make sense of the flood of information that surrounds us? How do we categorize that information and use it in social situations?

2. Why do we rely so much on notions about personality and group stereotypes? What problem does this practice solve, and what difficulties does it create?

3. How do we form impressions of others? That is, how do we integrate the information into a coherent, overall impression?

4. How do we ascertain the causes of other people's behavior and interpret the origins of actions we observe? For instance, when we judge someone's behavior, how do we know whether to attribute the behavior to that person's internal dispositions or to the external situation affecting that person?

5. What sorts of errors do we commonly make in judging the behavior of others, and why do we make such errors?

SCHEMAS

The human mind is a sophisticated system for processing information. One of our most basic mental processes is **categorization**—our tendency to perceive stimuli as members of groups or classes rather than as isolated, unique entities. For instance, at the theater, we see a well-groomed woman on stage wearing a short dress and dancing on her toes; rather than viewing her as a novel entity, we immediately categorize her as a "ballerina."

How do we go about assigning people or things to categories? For instance, how do

we know the woman should be categorized as a ballerina and not as an "actress" or a "cheerleader"? To categorize some person, we usually compare that person to our prototype of the category. A **prototype** is an abstraction that represents the "typical" or quintessential instance of a class or group— as least to us. It is the best example of the category. Perhaps your prototypical quarterback is Tom Brady. Others may have a different prototype for the same category, like Joe Montana or Peyton Manning. Although he was an outstanding quarterback, few might think of Donovan McNabb as a prototypical quarterback, in part because of his race. Although the number is growing, there have been very few Black quarterbacks in the history of the NFL. Usually, prototypes are specified in terms of a set of common attributes among members of a category. For example, the prototype of a "quarterback" may be someone who is tall, White, athletic, intelligent, and who has had a successful career, perhaps even winning a Super Bowl.

Categorizing people, objects, situations, events, and even the self becomes complicated because the categories we use are not isolated from one another; rather, they link together and form a structure. For instance, we may think of a person (Jonathan) not only as having various attributes (tall, wealthy) but also as bearing certain relations to other persons or entities (friend of Kareem, stronger than Bill, owner of a Lexus). These other persons or entities will themselves have attributes (Kareem: thin, athletic, Black; Bill: short, fat, balding; Lexus: silver, two-door, new). They also have relations with still other persons and entities (Kareem: co-worker of Bill, husband of Lisa; Bill: friend of Lisa, owner of a Prius). In this way, we build a cognitive structure consisting of persons, attributes, and relations.

Social psychologists use the term **schema** to denote a well-organized structure of cognitions about some social entity such as a person, group, role, or event. Schemas usually include information about an entity's attributes and about its relations with other entities. To illustrate, suppose Chandra, who is somewhat cynical about politics, has a schema about the role of "member of Congress." In Chandra's schema, the member of Congress will insist he or she serves the needs of his constituents but will actually vote for the special interests of those who contributed most to his campaign, will run TV advertisements containing half-truths at election time, will spend more time in Washington, DC, than in his home district, will put avoiding scandal above ethics, will vote for large pay raises and retirement benefits for himself, and, above all, will never do anything to lessen his own power.

Someone else, of course, may hold a less cynical view of politics than Chandra and have a different schema about the role of "member of Congress." But, like Chandra's, this schema will likely incorporate such elements as the congressional representative's typical activities, relations, motives, and tactics. Whatever their exact content, schemas enable us to organize and remember facts, to make inferences that go beyond the facts immediately available, and to assess new information (Fiske & Linville, 1980; Wilcox & Williams, 1990).

Types of Schemas

There are several distinct types of schemas, including person schemas, self-schemas, group schemas, role schemas, and event schemas (Eckes, 1995; Taylor & Crocker, 1981).

Person schemas are cognitive structures that describe the personalities of others. Person schemas can apply either to specific individuals (such as Barack Obama, Lady Gaga, your father) or to types of individuals (such as introvert, class clown, sociopath).

Person schemas organize our conceptions of others' personalities and enable us to develop expectations about others' behavior.

Self-schemas are structures that organize our conception of our own characteristics (Catrambone & Markus, 1987; Markus, 1977). For instance, if you conceive of yourself as independent (as opposed to dependent), you may see yourself as individualistic, unconventional, and assertive. To behave in a manner consistent with your self-schema, you may refuse to accept money from your parents, refuse to ask others for help with schoolwork, take a part-time job, or dye your hair an unusual color. Self-schemas are discussed in detail in Chapter 4.

Group schemas—also called stereotypes—are schemas regarding the members of a particular social group or social category (Hamilton, 1981). Stereotypes indicate the attributes and behaviors considered typical of members of that group or social category. These are rigid conceptions and widely shared by members of a culture or community. American culture uses a wide variety of stereotypes about different races (Blacks, Asians), religious groups (Protestants, Catholics, Jews), and ethnic groups (Arabs, Irish, Latinos, Italians).

Role schemas indicate which attributes and behaviors are typical of persons occupying a particular role in a group. Chandra's conception of the role of a congressional representative illustrates a role schema. Role schemas exist for most occupational roles—nurses, cab drivers, store managers, and the like—but they also exist for other kinds of roles in groups: group leader, captain of a sports team. Role schemas are often used to understand and predict the behaviors of people who occupy particular roles.

Event schemas (also called *scripts*) are schemas regarding important, recurring social events (Abelson, 1981; Hue & Erickson, 1991; Schank & Abelson, 1977). In our society, these events include weddings, funerals, graduation ceremonies, job interviews, cocktail parties, and hook-ups. An event schema specifies the activities that constitute the event, the predetermined order or sequence for these activities, and the persons (or role occupants) participating in the event. Scripts can be revealed by asking people to describe what typically happens during an event.

One type of script of interest to both social psychologists and college students alike is a hook-up script (Cohen & Wade, 2012). Hooking up—or engaging in a casual physical encounter—has replaced dating on many college campuses (Simon & Gagnon, 2003). As shown in Table 6.1, when asked to describe a "typical" hook-up, students tend to agree on a number of important characteristics (Paul & Hayes, 2002): Hook-ups tend to occur between strangers or acquaintances. Although someone may go out intending to hook-up, in most cases hooking up with a particular person is not planned. Men usually initiate the encounter, and the couples tend to meet one another at parties. Alcohol or drugs are often involved, and hook-up partners seldom talk about what is happening (or what has happened, after the hook-up ends). Although most hook-ups are one-time encounters, couples will occasionally engage in multiple hook-ups with the same person (Bogle, 2007). However, unlike a couple who is dating exclusively, a couple who is hooking-up—even repeatedly—has no obligations toward one another. The component of the hook-up script in which there is the least agreement among young people is what exactly "hooking up" implies (Glenn & Marquardt, 2001). Hooking up can range from kissing to intercourse. This ambiguity is one of the reasons the term "hooking up" appeals to young people, particularly women. Because it has a casual tone and could imply simply kissing or heavy petting, using the term can save women from potential damage to their reputations that may come from being seen as too promiscuous. Although people might sometimes ask for details, when a friend tells us that they attended a cousin's wedding or hooked up with a co-ed this past weekend, we usually fill in the gaps based on knowledge from our event schemas (and schemas for cousins and co-eds).

Schematic Processing

Why Do We Use Schemas? Although schemas may produce reasonably accurate judgments much of the time, they do not always work. Wouldn't it be better for us to rely less on schemas, perhaps to avoid the kind of tragic mistake the police made with Amadou Diallo or to not jump to conclusions about a friend's promiscuity (or chastity)? Perhaps, but we come to rely on schemas because they give us a way to efficiently organize, understand, and react to the complex world around us. It is simply impossible to process all the information present in each interaction. We have to find a way to focus on what is most important in defining the situation and the persons involved so we can respond appropriately. Schemas help us do this in several ways: (1) they influence our capacity to recall information by making certain kinds of facts more salient and easier to remember, (2) they help us process information faster, (3) they guide our inferences and judgments about people and objects, and (4) they allow us to reduce ambiguity by providing a way to interpret ambiguous elements in the situation. Once we have applied a schema to the situation, our decisions about how to interact in it become much more straightforward (Mayer, Rapp, & Williams, 1993).

Schematic Memory. Human memory is largely reconstructive. That is, we do not usually remember all the precise details of what transpired in a given situation—we

TABLE 6.1 Illustrative Descriptions of a Typical Hook-up (quotes from student questionnaires)

	FROM A 20-YEAR-OLD WOMAN	FROM A 21-YEAR-OLD MAN
Who is involved?	A guy and a girl who are somewhat attracted to each other but are strangers. It can also be a guy and a girl who are acquaintances and under the right conditions hook-up.	Any two people who find each other attractive or just there.
What leads to the hook-up? Is planning involved? Who instigates the hook-up?	The two may talk, flirt, dance together, drink together, make glances at each other. They are close to each other. Planning can be involved if one person scopes out the other or plans certain things to say. Usually the guy instigates the hook-up, but sometimes it is mutual instigation.	Sometimes investigation is done. One of the people may inquire about the other person in hopes of initiating the hook-up. Most often, however, the hook-up just kind of happens. The girl lets it be known (with eye contact or extremely friendly behavior) that she wants it, and generally the guy must then go and give it to her.
Where does it happen?	In rooms, at clubs, at parties. It can happen in a stairwell.	Anywhere possible. Most often on a couch or in adjacent chairs. Maybe in a bed if you're lucky.
Is alcohol or other drugs involved?	Sometimes, actually often. From my experiences, hook-ups always happen at parties.... Many situations involve alcohol and drugs because people lose inhibition and wear beer goggles, increasing the likelihood of hooking up.	Alcohol is almost always involved. This helps the guy with his confidence to initiate the hook-up.
What sexual behaviors take place? Are precautions taken to prevent transmission of sexually transmitted diseases (STDs)?	It depends. Some people just kiss. Others go further into oral sex and sexual intercourse. Usually in oral sex, precautions aren't taken to prevent the transmission of STDs. Sometimes in sex, condoms are used. In situations with alcohol and drugs, condoms are often forgotten.	Condoms are sometimes used if intercourse takes place. But a lot of hook-ups go to oral sex, in which case no preventative measures are used.
What communication takes place between the hook-up partners? Do they talk about what is happening?	Usually not a lot. They mainly just hook up or communicate with sexual noises.	Sometimes partners may say, "I can't believe I'm doing this. I don't even know you!" But this is generally only the females, and the males are just hoping this will not put a premature end to the hook-up.

These representative highlights demonstrate the consistency among students' event schemas for hook-ups and illustrate the tremendous agreement (and some differences) between men and women.

Source: Adapted from Paul & Hayes, 2002.

are not a camera capturing a video, instantly recording all the images and sounds. Instead, we typically remember some of what happened, enough to identify the appropriate schema and then rely on that schema to fill in other details. Schemas or-

ganize information in memory and, therefore, affect what we remember and what we forget (Hess & Slaughter, 1990; Sherman, Judd, & Park, 1989). When trying to recall something, people often remember better those facts that are consistent with their schemas. For instance, one study (Cohen, 1981) investigated the impact of an occupational role schema on recall. Participants viewed a video of a woman celebrating her birthday by having dinner with her husband at home. Half the participants were told the woman was a librarian; the other half were told she was a waitress in a local diner.

Some characteristics of the woman were consistent with the schema of a librarian: She wore glasses, had spent the day reading, liked classical music, and received a romantic novel as a gift. Other characteristics of the woman, however, were consistent with the schema of a waitress: She drank beer, had a bowling ball in the room, ate chocolate birthday cake, flirted with her husband, and received a nightgown as a gift. Later, when participants tried to recall details of the video, they recalled most accurately those facts consistent with the woman's occupational label. That is, participants who thought she was a librarian remembered facts consistent with the librarian schema, whereas those who thought she was a waitress remembered facts consistent with the diner-waitress schema.

What about memory for material inconsistent with schemas? Several studies have tested the recall of three types of information: material consistent with schemas, material contradictory to schemas, and material irrelevant to schemas. The results show that people recall both schema-consistent and schema-contradictory material better than schema-irrelevant material (Cano, Hopkins, & Islam, 1991; Higgins & Bargh, 1987). People recall schema-contradictory material better when the schema itself is concrete (for example, spends money wisely, often tells lies, brags about her accomplishments) rather than abstract (for example, practical, dishonest, egotistical).

Schematic Inference. Schemas affect the inferences we make about persons and other social entities (Fiske & Taylor, 1991). That is, they supply missing facts when gaps exist in our knowledge. If we know certain facts about a person but are ignorant about others, we fill in the gaps by inserting suppositions consistent with our schema for that person. For example, knowing your roommate is head of the campus PETA (People for the Ethical Treatment of Animals) chapter, you can infer he will not want to spend time with your new friend who enjoys hunting. Of course, the use of schemas can lead to erroneous inferences. If the schema is incomplete or does not correctly mirror reality, some mistakes are likely. For instance, the police officers who confronted Amadou Diallo applied a schema that was incorrect. Their schema for "a Black man who puts his hand in his pocket as he is being confronted by the police" includes the element that the suspect would be reaching for a gun in his pocket. From this, they inferred that he would try to shoot at them, and they reacted according to that erroneous inference.

Schemas—especially well-developed schemas—can also help us infer new facts. For instance, if a physician diagnoses a patient as having the flu, he can make inferences about how the patient contracted the disease, which symptoms might be present, what side effects or complications might arise, and what treatment will be effective. For another person who has no schema regarding this disease, these inferences would be virtually impossible.

Schematic Judgment. Schemas can influence our judgments or feelings about persons and other entities. The schemas themselves may be organized in terms of evaluative dimensions; this is especially true of person schemas. For example, Chandra's schemas for members of Congress had a negative valence, predisposing her to view any congressperson unfavorably. The complexity of a schema—or the variety of attributes included in a schema—also affects our evaluations of other persons. The complexity of schemas is directly tied to diversity of experience with the group (Crisp & Turner, 2011). The more members of a group we interact with, the less uniform we see group members (perhaps their personality, values, and so forth), and the more complex our schema of the group is. Conversely, less complex schemas lead to more extreme judgments and evaluations. This is called the **complexity-extremity effect**.

For instance, in one study (Linville & Jones, 1980), White college students evaluated a person applying for admission to law school. Depending on treatment, the applicant was either White or Black and had an academic record that was either strong or weak. The results showed an interaction effect between academic record and race. Participants rated a weak Black applicant more negatively than a weak White applicant, but they rated a strong Black applicant more positively than a strong White applicant. Judgments about Black applicants were more extreme—in both directions—than those about White applicants because the participants' schema for their own in-group (White) was more complex than their schema for the out-group (Black). Because these White students had more experience with a variety of Whites, it was difficult to infer competence based solely on this quality, and the schema was more complex. Further research (Linville, 1982) shows that the complexity-extremity effect also holds for other attributes, such as age. College students have less complex schemas for older persons than for persons their own age, so they are more extreme in judgments of older persons.

Drawbacks of Schematic Processing. Although schemas provide certain advantages, they also entail some corresponding disad-

vantages. First, people are overly accepting of information that fits consistently with a schema. In fact, some research suggests that perceivers show a confirmatory bias (also called a confirmation bias) when collecting new information relevant to schemas (Higgins & Bargh, 1987; Snyder & Swann, 1978). That is, when gathering information, perceivers tend to ask questions that will elicit information supportive of the schemas rather than questions that will elicit information contradictory to the schemas. Consider the intake process of Rosenhan's study at the mental hospital. The doctors asked particular questions of the researchers, assuming they were mentally ill, that biased responses toward confirmation of that belief. The nurses and orderlies interpreted information about pseudo-patients' behavior in ways that confirmed their schemas and ignored or downplayed information suggesting that the pseudo-patients were actually not ill, because it contradicted their existing schemas.

Second, when faced with missing information, people fill in gaps in knowledge by adding elements that are consistent with their schemas. Sometimes these added elements turn out to be erroneous or factually incorrect. When this happens, it will, of course, create inaccurate interpretations or inferences about people, groups, or events. As an example, research on eyewitness accounts of crimes finds that witnesses draw on event schemas of "typical crimes" when recalling specific incidents. This can distort memories in schema-consistent ways, leading to misinformation in reporting (Holst & Pezdek, 1992). Furthermore, as witnesses share their accounts of events, listeners who were not privy to the scene are likely to interpret events in ways that are influenced by their own existing beliefs (Allport & Postman, 1947). This introduces further distortion, like a children's game of telephone.

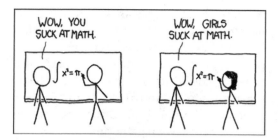

When schematic categories are not salient, we view persons as individuals and their behaviors as unique. However, when we view persons as category members, we tend to interpret their behavior as stereotypic and representative of the entire category or group. Comic courtesy of xkcd.com

Third, because people are often reluctant to discard or revise their schemas, they occasionally apply schemas to persons or events even when the schemas do not fit the facts very well. Forced misapplication of a schema may lead to incorrect characterization and inferences, and this in turn can produce inappropriate or inflexible responses toward other persons, groups, or events. A teacher who believes a child is lazy because she is not getting the class reading done may be less inclined to engage with the child in class or encourage the child's parents to have her tested for dyslexia or ADD (attention deficit disorder).

PERSON SCHEMAS AND GROUP STEREOTYPES

Person Schemas

As noted earlier, person schemas are cognitive structures that describe the personalities of other individuals. There are several distinct types of person schemas. Some person schemas are very specific and pertain to particular people. For example, Sarah is a 17-year-old high school student, and Joan is her mother. After years of interacting with Joan, Sarah has an elaborate schema of her mother. She can usually predict how Joan will react to new situations, information, or problems and plan accordingly. Similarly, we often have individual schemas for public figures (for instance, Oprah Winfrey, former talk show host, actor, advocate for women, Black, extremely wealthy) or for famous historical figures (for instance, Abraham Lincoln, political leader during the Civil War, honest, determined, opposed to slavery, committed to holding the Union together).

Other person schemas are very abstract and focus on the relations among personality traits. A schema of this type is an **implicit personality theory**—a set of unstated assumptions about which personality traits are correlated with one another (Anderson & Sedikides, 1991; Grant & Holmes, 1981; Sternberg, 1985). These theories tend to also include beliefs about the behaviors associated with various personality traits (Skowronski & Carlston, 1989). If you learn that a child is gifted, do you automatically assume the child has other attributes? Recent research explored the beliefs that teachers in Germany associate with giftedness (Baudson & Preckel, 2013). When a student was described as "gifted," teachers were more likely to also perceive the student as emotionally deficient. Although teachers believed gifted students would be more open to new experiences than students of average ability, they also saw them as more introverted, less emotionally stable, and less agreeable. These beliefs are considered implicit, or automatic, because we seldom subject our person schemas to close examination and are usually not explicitly aware of the schemas' contents. Therefore, the teachers were likely unaware of their biased judgments of gifted students and how these implicit assumptions were influencing their behavior toward the students in class.

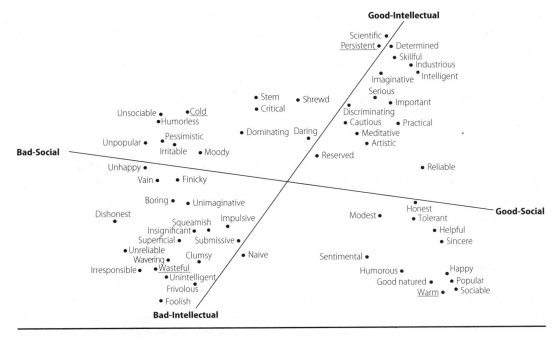

FIGURE 6.1 Relationships Among Attributes: A Mental Map

Each of us has an implicit theory of personality—a theory about which personality attributes tend to go together and which do not. We can represent our theories of personality in the form of a mental map. The closer attributes are located to each other on our mental map, the more we assume these attributes will appear together in the same person. The mental map shown above was created based on the mental maps of American college students. Adapted from Rosenberg, Nelson, & Vivekanandan, 1968

Implicit Personality Theories and Mental Maps. As do all schemas, implicit personality theories enable us to make inferences that go beyond the available information. Instead of withholding judgment, we use them to flesh out our impressions of a person about whom we have little information. For instance, if we learn someone has a warm personality, we might infer she is also likely to be sociable, popular, good-natured, and so on. If we hear that somebody else is pessimistic, we may infer he is humorless, irritable, and unpopular, even though we lack evidence that he actually has these traits.

We can depict an implicit personality theory as a mental map indicating the way traits are related to one another. Figure 6.1 displays such a mental map. This figure, based on judgments made by college stu-

dents, shows how various personality traits stand in relation to one another (Rosenberg, Nelson, & Vivekananthan, 1968). Traits thought to be similar are located close together within our mental map, meaning we expect people who have one trait to have the other. Traits thought to be dissimilar are located far apart, meaning we believe they rarely occur together in one person.

If your mental map resembles the one portrayed in Figure 6.1, you think that people who are wasteful are also likely to be unintelligent and irresponsible (see the lower left part of the map). Similarly, you think that people who are persistent are also likely to be determined and skillful (the upper right part of the map).

Early research, like that presented in Figure 6.1, believed that the two distinct evaluative dimensions traits fell upon were social and intellectual. For instance, the traits "warm" and "cold" differ mainly on the social dimension, whereas "frivolous" and "industrious" differ on the intellectual dimension (Rosenberg & Sedlak, 1972). Traits usually tend to be either good on both dimensions (like "important") or bad on both dimensions (like "unreliable," explaining a common bias in impression formation). We tend to judge persons who have several good traits as generally good and persons who have several bad traits as generally bad. Once we have a global impression of someone as, say, generally good, we assume that other positive traits (located nearby in the mental map) also apply. This tendency for our general or overall liking for a person to influence our subsequent assessment of more specific traits of that person is called the **halo effect** (Lachman & Bass, 1985; Thorndike, 1920). The halo effect produces bias in impression formation; it can lead to inaccuracy in our ratings of others' traits and performances (Cooper, 1981; Fisicaro, 1988).

In the decades since Rosenberg's mental map was published, social psychologists have worked to refine the dimensions and test impression formation across different cultures and groups. There is growing consensus that the two universal dimensions are better conceived of as warmth and competence (rather than social and intellectual). As early research (Asch, 1946, discussed later in this chapter) found, warmth is a highly influential trait in impression formation, and it appears to take precedence over competence, both in how rapidly it is judged and how much weight it carries in impressions (Fiske, Cuddy, & Glick 2007). Immediately upon encountering someone else, we must determine whether they are more likely to harm or help us. To do so, we gauge their level of warmth because it is the dimension that is tied to our perceptions of another's intent. The warmth dimension captures traits like friendliness, helpfulness, and sincerity. The competence dimension, however, is related to ability and includes traits like intelligence, creativity, and skill. Although everyone lends primacy to the warmth dimension in forming impressions, women and individuals from collectivist cultures appear particularly cued in to warmth (Abele, 2003).

Our impressions influence the emotions we feel toward others. We are likely to pity those who we consider high on warmth but low on competence and envy those who are high on competence and low on warmth. We admire those who we believe are high on both dimensions and hold contempt for those who are seen as low on both (Cuddy, Fiske, & Glick, 2007). Similar emotions are directed toward groups that we classify using the same two dimensions. We envy the rich (high-competence, low-warmth), admire the middle-class (high-competence, high-warmth), pity the elderly (low-competence, high-warmth), and have contempt for welfare recipients (low-competence, low-warmth).

Group Stereotypes

- "Politicians are liars and cheaters, with no compassion for ordinary people."
- "Asian women are 'tiger moms,' demanding perfection from their kids."
- "People on welfare are lazy, wasteful, and unemployed."
- "Arabs and Muslims are terrorists who hate America."
- "Jocks might be strong and athletic, but they're stupid and arrogant."

An unfortunate reality in our society is that we have all heard remarks like these—categorical, extreme, inaccurate characterizations. Each of these is an example of a group schema or stereotype. A **stereotype** is a set of characteristics attributed to all members of some specified group or social category (McCauley, Stitt, & Segal, 1980; Taylor, 1981). Just like other types of schemas, stereotypes simplify the complex social world. Rather than encouraging us to treat each member of a group individually, stereotypes encourage us to think about and treat all politicians, welfare recipients, or jocks the same way. By helping us quickly place people into categories, stereotypes enable us to form impressions of people and predict their behavior with only minimal information—the groups to which they belong.

Stereotypes, however, involve overgeneralization. They lead us to think that all members of a particular group or social category possess certain attributes. Although stereotypes might contain a kernel of truth—some members of the stereotyped group may have some of the imputed characteristics—it is almost never the case that all members have those characteristics. For this reason, stereotypes often lead to inaccurate inferences. Consider, for instance, all the feminists you know. Perhaps one of them is—as the stereotype suggests—a radical who would like to have the gender binary completely eradicated, and maybe

We can hardly avoid making a snap judgment about the personalities of these individuals, but are we right? We draw on stereotypes to form impressions about people merely by knowing the group to which they belong. © Renphoto/iStock

another is lesbian. It is certainly false, however, that all your feminist acquaintances are as politically active or eschew relationships—romantic or otherwise—with men. It is also false that all feminists are women.

Throughout our daily lives, we are constantly categorizing people who we encounter into existing groups to conserve mental attention. Walking down the street, we pass men and women, Blacks and Whites, young people and the elderly. Without much conscious thought, we sort these strangers into groups based on distinguishing characteristics and then draw on group schemas (stereotypes) to decide how to respond to these others without giving our actions much consideration (Fiske & Neuberg, 1990). We tend to not notice the work that our minds are doing until we encounter someone who does not neatly fit into one of our group schemas: an individual whose gender, race, or age is ambiguous. In these situations, because we need to gather additional information, processing takes longer and becomes more conscious. If it is difficult to determine a person's gender from a cursory glance, we may look for other nonverbal or vocal clues. If we are unable to classify someone—a running joke on *Saturday Night Live* with the infamous, gender-ambiguous character, Pat—we grow increasingly uncomfortable. Thinking back to moments when we sought such clarification and considering how seldom such moments occur demonstrates the ubiquity of categorization and stereotypes in our everyday lives.

Although stereotypes are overgeneralizations, we still constantly use them and are often unaware of their impact on our judgments of others (Hepburn & Locksley, 1983; Bornstein & Pittman, 1992). And although there is nothing inherent in stereotypes that requires them to be negative, many stereotypes do contain negative elements. Of course, some stereotypes are positive ("Asians excel at math"; "Blacks are gifted athletes"), but many others disparage or diminish the group stereotyped. Stereotypes can have many negative effects, especially when they are used to limit access to important social roles—for example, when an individual applies for a job or for admission to college.

To explore the effect of gender stereotypes on women's underrepresentation in science, a group of scientists recently asked science faculty at research-intensive universities to rate the materials of a student applying for a lab manager position (Moss-Racusin et al., 2012). The scientists used an experimental design and created fake applications that were randomly as-signed a masculine (John) or feminine (Jennifer) name. Other than the name, the application materials sent out were identical. Both men and women faculty who received John's application rated the applicant as significantly more competent and hireable than those who received Jennifer's (identical) application. Faculty also reported that they would offer a higher starting salary and more mentoring to John than to Jennifer. None of the faculty actively disliked women. In fact, faculty perceived Jennifer as a more likeable applicant than John. However, the pervasive gender stereotypes of women being less competent at science unintentionally influenced the raters' eval-

---

BOX 6.1   Research Update: Stereotype Threat

When people act on their stereotypes, this can produce many negative effects for those who are the subjects of these stereotypes. Members of racial groups may be denied jobs or promotions because of the stereotypes employers hold of their racial group (Pager, Western, & Bonikowski, 2009). As damaging as these direct uses of stereotypes can be, researchers have recently discovered a second, less direct negative effect of stereotypes called *stereotype threat* (Steele, 1997, 1999).

Stereotype threat occurs when a member of a group suspects that he or she will be judged based on a common stereotype that is held of that group. For example, one stereotype of women is that they are less proficient at mathematics than men are. If a woman enters a situation in which her mathematical ability is being judged and she believes the judgment will be negatively affected by the stereotype about women's mathematical ability, even without any conscious thought about the stereotype, her performance on the exam may suffer (Spencer, Steele, & Quinn, 1999). To test for this kind of effect, Steele and Aronson (1995) gave Stanford University students a very difficult test using questions from the Graduate Record Examination in literature. The difficulty of the test provided a stereotype threat for Black students because poor performance would confirm a stereotype that they were not as able as White students. Even though the White and Black students were matched on ability, the Black students scored much lower than the White students. However, when researchers told the students that the test was part of a study to understand how people solved problems and that it did not measure ability, the stereotype threat was removed and the Black and White students did equally well.

Why does performance deteriorate when stereotype threat is present? Isn't it possible that the desire to disprove the stereotype might cause students to try harder and thereby cause them to do even better than they normally would? In a follow-up study, students took the exam on a computer, so the researchers could time how long the students took with each question. The results showed that under conditions of stereotype threat, Black students were exerting extra effort and were overthinking the questions. They reread questions, changed their answers, and generally became less efficient at taking the test (Steele, 1999). This result also made sense of a finding that stereotype threat affected academuations. This is just one study of many suggesting that stereotypes can negatively affect work-related outcomes (see also Correll, Benard & Paik, 2007).

Stereotypes can also have less direct effects on members of stereotyped groups through a process called **stereotype threat** (Steele, 1997, 2010). When a member of a group believes there is a real threat of being judged based on group stereotypes, this can negatively affect their performance and actually cause an individual to perform more poorly than he or she would when not under stereotype threat. Box 6.1 explains how stereotype threat reduces the performance of some students on academic tasks and stan-

dardized tests and can also influence success among other groups in other domains.

Common Stereotypes. As the foregoing examples suggest, in American society, some widely known stereotypes pertain to ethnic, racial, and gender groups. Ethnic (national) stereotypes held by Americans might include, for example, the view that Mexicans are undocumented immigrants who struggle to speak English, the French are cultured and romantic, and Vietnamese people are hardworking and friendly. Investigators have studied ethnic, racial, and gender stereotypes for many years, and the results show that the content of stereotypes

---

ically strong students more than academically weak students—for those students who saw academics as an important part of their self-concept, the threat was much more meaningful than for those who cared less about academics (Steele, 2010).

The negative effects of stereotype threat are not limited to women or racial minorities, nor is it exclusively seen in academic spheres. In a novel application of stereotype threat, social psychologists tested racial stereotypes about athletic performance (Stone, Lynch, Sjomeling, & Darley, 1999). Black and White students were recruited to take an athletic test (simply ten rounds of miniature golf) in the laboratory. Black students who were told that this task was a diagnostic of "natural athletic ability" performed significantly better than those who were told that the task measured "sports intelligence." White participants, however, performed better in the "sports intelligence" condition than the "natural athletic ability" condition. Although stereotypes about Whites are generally more favorable than those about Blacks, students were aware of the stereotype that favors Blacks over Whites in athletic ability, and this caused differences in performance. Another study found that when primed with a stereotype of older people's propensity for memory problems, older adults performed worse on

a recall test than either younger people or older adults who had not had a threat induced by a prime (Hess, Auman, Colcombe, & Rahhal, 2003).

Outside the laboratory, it may be possible to reduce stereotype threat and to even the playing field. One way of doing this is to convince students who may be experiencing stereotype threat that the test being used is not biased. This is not easy to do given current deeply held beliefs about the unfairness of testing and the pervasiveness of racial stereotypes. However, Cohen, Steele, and Ross (1999) found that they could reduce stereotype threat by informing students that the evaluations of their performance would use very high standards and that they believed the students could perform up to those standards. Such an approach lets the student know that assessment is based on standards rather than stereotypes and that the student will not be viewed stereotypically. Another approach is to have individuals shift away from viewing themselves stereotypically by giving them the opportunity to construct a narrative of their selves that is about other positive attributes and values rather than the stereotyped characteristic. Simply asking individuals to write their primary values and why these are important to them before engaging in a threatening situation can improve performance (Steele, 2010).

changes over time (Diekman, Eagly, Mladinic, & Ferreira, 2005). For instance, few of us now believe—as many once did—that the typical Native American is a drunk, the typical African American is superstitious, or the typical Chinese American is conservative and inscrutable. Stereotypes may not have disappeared over time, but they have changed form (Dovidio & Gaertner, 1996).

Just as stereotypes about ethnic and racial groups are commonly held in our society, so also are stereotypes about gender groups. Usually, our first judgment when meeting people involves classifying them as men or women. This classification is likely to activate an elaborate stereotype. This stereotype depicts men as more independent, dominant, competent, rational, competitive, assertive, and stable in handling crises. It characterizes women as more emotional, sensitive, expressive, gentle, helpful, and patient (Ashmore, 1981; Martin, 1987; Minnigerode & Lee, 1978). Research on the nature of these gender stereotypes is discussed in Box 6.2. Within gender, stereotypes are linked to subtle cues like titles and surnames. For instance, research conducted in the 1980s found that women labeled "Ms." were seen as more achieving, more masculine, and less likable than women labeled "Mrs." (Dion & Schuller, 1991). These impressions were consistent with the high-competence, low-warmth stereotype of feminists in general (Fiske, Cuddy, Glick, & Xu, 2002), who were often associated with the term. However, today's college students are more likely to see "Ms." as related to marital status rather than concerns about sexism and, therefore, rate "Ms." as positively as "Mrs." or "Miss" (Lawton, Blakemore, & Vartanian, 2003).

Perhaps a more contemporary example related to the nuances of titles is the use of hyphenated surnames. Research finds that women who hyphenate their surnames after marriage are assumed to be well-educated

and more likely to have a career as well as more friendly, good-natured, industrious, and intellectually curious than married women who do not hyphenate. Men with hyphenated surnames are also perceived as good-natured, as well as more nurturing and more committed to their marriages than married men who do not hyphenate (Forbes, Adams-Curtis, White & Hamm, 2002).

Gender, ethnicity, and race are only a handful of the groups that are stereotyped in our culture. People also stereotype groups defined by occupation, age, political ideology, mental illness, hobbies, musical tastes, majors, school attended, and so on (Miller, 1982; Rahn, 1993; Rothbart 1996; Rentfrow & Gosling, 2007).

Origins of Stereotypes. How do various stereotypes originate? Some theorists suggest that stereotypes arise out of direct experience with some members of the stereotyped group (Campbell, 1967). We may once have known an Italian who was passionate, someone from Japan who was polite, or a southerner who was bigoted. We then build a stereotype by generalizing—that is, we infer that all members of a group share the attribute we know to be characteristic of some particular members.

Other theorists (Eagly & Steffen, 1984) suggest that stereotypes derive in part from a biased distribution of group members into social roles. Consider professional athletes. After professional sports integrated, Blacks quickly dominated a number of popular sports. In the late 1990s, 60% of professional football players and 85% of professional basketball players were African American (Sailes, 1998). The impressive athletic performances meant that Blacks also dominated the sports coverage in newspapers and on television (Davis & Harris, 1998). Roles have associated characteristics—professional sports players are athletically gifted—and eventually those characteristics are attached to the persons occupying the roles. The overwhelming athletic success and related images contributed to and helped maintain the stereotype that Blacks are athletically superior to other racial groups. If a social group is concentrated in roles with negative characteristics, an unflattering stereotype of that group may emerge that ascribes the negative characteristics of the role to members of the group.

Stereotyping may also be a natural outcome of social perception (McGarty, Yzerbyt & Spears, 2002). When people have to process and remember a lot of information about many others, they store this information in terms of group categories rather than in terms of individuals (Taylor, Fiske, Etcoff, & Ruderman, 1978). In trying to remember what went on in a classroom discussion, you may recall that several women spoke and a Black person expressed a strong opinion, although you cannot remember exactly which women spoke or who the Black person was. Because people remember behavior by group category rather than by individual, they attach the behavior to the groups (Rothbart, Fulero, Jensen, Howard, & Birrell, 1978). Remembering that women spoke and a Black person expressed a strong opinion, you might infer that in general, women are talkative and Blacks are opinionated. You would not form these stereotypes if you recalled these attributes as belonging to individuals rather than remembering them as attached to group membership.

Errors Caused by Stereotypes. Because stereotypes are overgeneralizations, they foster various errors in social perception and judgment. First, stereotypes lead us to assume that all members of a group are alike and possess certain traits. Yet individual members of a group obviously differ in many respects. One person wearing a hard

hat may shoulder you into the stairwell on a crowded bus; another may offer you his seat. Second, stereotypes lead us to assume that all the members of one group differ from all the members of another group. Stereotypes of football players and ballet dancers may suggest, for instance, that these groups have nothing in common. But both groups contain individuals who are athletic, hardworking, intelligent, and so on. If we see the two groups as nonoverlapping, we neglect to realize that there are ballet dancers who also play football.

Although stereotypes can produce inaccurate inferences and judgments in simple situations, they are especially likely to do so in complex situations when our minds are attending to a lot of stimuli. This is because we rely on stereotypes for efficiency (Sherman, Lee, Bessenoff & Frost, 1998). If an observer uses a stereotype as a central theme around which to organize information relevant to a decision, he or she may neglect information that is inconsistent with the stereotype (Bodenhausen & Lichtenstein, 1987). A process like this can contribute to bias in educational admissions or hiring decisions, like with the faculty ratings of lab assistant applications discussed earlier. With a large amount of material to be read and significant detail in each, our minds take shortcuts wherever they can. The stereotype that favors men with regard to scientific competence (and disfavors women) may overshadow specific evidence of competence from the applications.

Research also indicates that people of higher status have a tendency to use stereotypes more than people of lower status do. This seems to occur because people of higher status have more people competing for their attention and, thus, have more incentive to use shortcuts. They may also be able to afford to make more mistakes because of their power (Goodwin, Gubin, Fiske, & Yzerbyt, 2000). This dynamic

BOX 6.2 Test Yourself: Gender Schemas and Stereotypes

One of the most consistent findings on stereotypes is that many people believe men and women have different personality traits. What are the traits believed to be typical of each sex? Where do these sex stereotypes come from?

Studies of sex stereotyping have established a number of characteristics that people associate differently with men and women. In the chart opposite, 20 characteristics are listed that are consistently associated with men or women. To see how aware you are of these stereotypes, fill out the chart by indicating which of the traits listed are thought to be more typical of men and which are more typical of women. Also indicate if you consider each trait as a desirable or undesirable characteristic.

The Bem Sex Role Inventory (BSRI; Bem, 1974) is a widely used measure of sex-role stereotyping and self-perceptions. Although there has been some weakening of the distinctions between stereotypes of men and women over time, gender differences endure (Bergen & Williams, 1991; Holt & Ellis, 1998). The first five traits in the chart (*defends beliefs* to *individualistic*) are seen as more typical

of men, whereas the next five (*cheerful* to *childlike*) are considered more typical of women. Although there are subtle differences, the first seven traits are seen as desirable for both men and women. The next three (*gullible, shy,* and *childlike*), however, are rated as both feminine and generally undesirable (Colley, Mulhern, Maltby, & Wood, 2009). The next five (*affectionate* to *compassionate*) are seen as feminine and more desirable for women than for men, and the last five (*assertive* to *has leadership abilities*) are considered more desirable for men than for women. In general, research finds that traits associated with men are more desirable than those associated with women (Broverman et al., 1972). Did your evaluations of trait desirability favor the male stereotyped traits? If not, you may fit in with the trend among educated respondents toward valuing some traditionally feminine traits more positively and some more traditionally masculine traits more negatively (Der-Karabetian & Smith, 1977; Lottes & Kuriloff, 1994; Pleck, 1976). If this trend continues, even if sex stereotypes persist, women may be evaluated less negatively than before.

occurs even when subjects are randomly assigned to higher- and lower-status roles (Richeson & Ambady, 2003).

Although stereotypes involve overstatement and overgeneralization, they resist change even in the face of concrete evidence that contradicts them. This occurs because people tend to accept information that confirms their stereotypes and ignore or explain away information that disconfirms them (Lord, Lepper, & Mackie, 1984; Snyder, 1981; Weber & Crocker, 1983). Suppose, for example, that Omar stereotypes gay men as effeminate, nonathletic, and artistic. If he stumbles into a gay bar, he is especially likely to notice the men in the crowd who fit this description, thereby confirming his stereotype. But how does he

construe any rough-looking, athletic men who are there? It is possible that these individuals might challenge his stereotype, but reconstructing schemas is a lot of work, and Omar is more likely to find a way around this challenge. He might scrutinize those who don't fit his stereotype for hidden signs of effeminacy. He might underestimate their number or even assume they are straight. He may also engage in **subtyping**, a process through which perceivers create subcategories of stereotyped groups who serve as exceptions to the rule without threatening the overarching stereotype (e.g., these are "atypical gay men"). Through cognitive strategies like these, people explain away contradictory information and preserve their stereotypes.

TRAIT	MOST TYPICAL OF		DESIRABLE	
	MEN	WOMEN	YES	NO
Defends beliefs	_____	_____	_____	_____
Athletic	_____	_____	_____	_____
Strong personality	_____	_____	_____	_____
Makes decisions easily	_____	_____	_____	_____
Individualistic	_____	_____	_____	_____
Cheerful	_____	_____	_____	_____
Loyal	_____	_____	_____	_____
Gullible	_____	_____	_____	_____
Shy	_____	_____	_____	_____
Childlike	_____	_____	_____	_____
Affectionate	_____	_____	_____	_____
Flatterable	_____	_____	_____	_____
Tender	_____	_____	_____	_____
Eager to soothe hurt feelings	_____	_____	_____	_____
Compassionate	_____	_____	_____	_____
Assertive	_____	_____	_____	_____
Competitive	_____	_____	_____	_____
Independent	_____	_____	_____	_____
Dominant	_____	_____	_____	_____
Has leadership abilities	_____	_____	_____	_____

IMPRESSION FORMATION

Information about other people comes to us from various sources. We may read facts about someone. We may hear something from a third party. We may witness acts by the other. We may interact directly with the other and form an impression of that person based on his or her appearance, dress, speech style, or background. We even infer personality characteristics from people's facial features (Hassin & Trope, 2000; Zebrowitz et al., 1998). Regardless of how we get information about someone, we as perceivers must find a way to integrate these diverse facts into a coherent picture. This process of organizing diverse information into a unified impression of the other person is called **impression formation**. It is fundamental to person perception.

Trait Centrality

In a classic experiment, Asch (1946) used a straightforward procedure to show that some traits have more impact than others on the impressions we form. Undergraduates in one group received a list of seven traits describing a hypothetical person. These traits were *intelligent, skillful, industrious, warm, determined, practical,* and *cautious.* Undergraduates in a second group received the same list of traits but with one critical difference: The trait "warm" was replaced by "cold." All participants then wrote a brief paragraph indicating their impressions and completed a checklist to rate the stimulus person on such other characteristics as *generous, wise, happy, good-natured, humorous, sociable, popular, humane, altruistic,* and *imaginative.*

The findings led to several conclusions. First, the students had no difficulty performing the task. They were able to weave the trait information into a coherent whole and construct a composite sketch of the stimulus person. Second, substituting the trait "warm" for the trait "cold" produced a large difference in the overall impression the students formed. When the stimulus person was "warm," the students typically described him as happy, successful, popular, and humorous. But when he was "cold," they described him as self-centered, unsociable, and unhappy. Third, the terms "warm" and "cold" had a larger impact than other traits on the overall impression formed of the stimulus person. This was demonstrated, for instance, by a variation in which the investigator repeated the basic procedure but substituted the pair "polite" and "blunt" in place of "warm" and "cold." Whereas describing the stimulus person as warm rather than cold made a great difference in the impressions formed by the students, describing him as polite rather than blunt made little difference.

We say that a trait has a high level of **trait centrality** when it has a large impact on the overall impression we form of that person. In Asch's study, the warm/cold trait displayed more centrality than the polite/blunt trait because differences in warm/cold produced larger differences in participants' ratings.

A follow-up study (Kelley, 1950) replicated the warm/cold finding in a more realistic setting. Students in sections of a psychology course read trait descriptions of a guest lecturer before he spoke. These descriptions contained adjectives similar to those Asch used (that is, *industrious, critical, practical, determined*), but they differed

regarding the warm/cold variable. For half the students, the description contained the trait "warm"; for the other half, it contained "cold." The lecturer subsequently arrived at the classroom and led a discussion for about 20 minutes. Afterward, the students were asked to report their impressions of him. The results showed large differences between the impressions formed by those who read he was "warm" and those who read he was "cold." Those who had read he was "cold" rated him as less considerate, sociable, popular, good-natured, humorous, and humane than those who had read he was "warm." Because all students saw the same guest instructor in the classroom, the differences in their impressions could stem only from the use of "warm" or "cold" in the profile they had read.

How could a single trait embedded in a profile have such an impact on impressions of someone's behavior? Several theories have been advanced, but one plausible explanation holds that the students used a schema—a mental map—indicating what traits go with being warm and what traits go with being cold. Looking again at Figure 6.1, we note the locations of the attributes "warm" and "cold" on the map and the nature of the other attributes close by. If the mental maps used by the participants in the Asch (1946) and Kelley (1950) studies resembled Figure 6.1, it becomes immediately clear why they judged the warm person as more sociable, popular, good-natured, and humorous; these traits are close to "warm" and remote from "cold" on the mental map.

First Impressions

You have surely noticed the effort individuals make to create a good impression when interviewing for a new job, entering a new group, or meeting an attractive potential date. This effort reflects the widely held belief that first impressions are especially important and have an enduring impact.

In fact, this belief is supported by a body of systematic research. Observers forming an impression of a person give more weight to information received early in a sequence than to information received later. This is called the **primacy effect** (Luchins, 1957).

What accounts for the impact of first impressions? One explanation is that after forming an initial impression of a person, we interpret subsequent information in a way that makes it consistent with our initial impression. Having established that your new roommate is neat and considerate, you interpret the dirty socks on the floor as a sign of temporary forgetfulness rather than as evidence of sloppiness and lack of concern. Thus, the schema into which an observer assimilates new information influences the interpretation of that information (Zanna & Hamilton, 1977).

A second explanation for the primacy effect holds that we attend very carefully to the first bits of information we get about a person, but we pay less attention once we have enough information to make a judgment. It is not that we interpret later information differently; we simply use it less. This explanation assumes that whatever information we attend to most has the biggest effect on our impressions (Dreben, Fiske, & Hastie, 1979).

What happens if we make an effort to attend to all information equally? In such cases, recent information exerts the strongest influence on our impressions (Crano, 1977), an occurrence known as the **recency effect** (Jones & Goethals, 1971; Steiner & Rain, 1989). Jurors, for example, are asked to take the perspective that an individual on trial is innocent until proven guilty and instructed to weigh all the evidence presented at trial. Research shows the sequencing of the presentation of that evidence is important. Two groups witnessing identical courtroom arguments came to different verdicts based on whether it was the prosecution or defense who presented last (Furnham,

1986). When the defendant's case came second, perceptions of innocence increased significantly. A recency effect may also occur when so much time has passed that we have largely forgotten our first impression or when we are judging characteristics that change over time, like performance or moods. Perceivers' own moods also influence what information they attend to. Those in good moods seem to favor early information, while the primacy effect is eliminated for those who are experiencing a bad mood (Forgas, 2011).

In one study investigating the relative impact of primacy and recency effects on impression formation (Jones et al., 1968), participants observed the performance of a college student on an SAT-type aptitude test. In one condition, the student started successfully on the first few items but then her performance deteriorated steadily. In a second condition, the student started poorly and then gradually improved. In both conditions, the student answered 15 out of 30 test items correctly. After observing one or the other performance, participants rated the student's intelligence and tried to predict how well she would do on the next 30 items. Although the student's overall performance was the same in both conditions (15 of 30 correct), participants rated the student as more intelligent when she started well and then tailed off than when she started poorly and then improved. Observers also predicted higher scores for the student on the next series when the student started well than when she started poorly. Clearly, participants gave more weight to the student's performance on the first few items—a primacy effect.

Impressions as Self-Fulfilling Prophecies

Whether correct or not, the impressions we form of people influence our behavior toward them. Recall, for instance, the study in which students read that their guest instructor was "warm" or "cold" before meeting him (Kelley, 1950). Not only did the students form different impressions of the instructor, but they also behaved differently toward him. Those who believed the instructor was "warm" participated more in the class discussion than those who believed he was "cold." In a classic study, Rosenthal and Jacobson (1968) found that teachers act differently toward students who they expect to succeed—giving them more time, attention, and approval than other students—thereby creating more opportunity for those students to rise to the teachers' expectations and unintentionally disadvantaging the children for whom the teachers have lower expectations.

When our behavior toward people reflects our impressions of them, we cause them to react in ways that confirm our original impressions. When this happens, our impressions become **self-fulfilling prophecies** (Darley & Fazio, 1980). For example, if we ignore someone because we think she is dull, she will probably withdraw and add nothing interesting to the conversation, living up to our initial impressions. Because our own actions evoke appropriate reactions from others, our initial impressions—whether correct or incorrect—are often confirmed by the reactions of others.

The self-fulfilling prophecy can influence desirability in dating. In a recent study, researchers took the actual dating profiles of 100 men (both unattractive and attractive) from an online dating website and separated the photos from the text (Brand, Bonatsos, D'Orazio, & DeShong 2012). Fifty women then rated both the photos and the profile texts independently. Even without the photos attached, the women rated the attractive men's profile texts as more attractive than those of the unattractive men. The researchers argued that the confidence these men had established in their earlier dating history was the key factor. Having been treated as more attractive in previous inter-

actions, these men came to act in a way that was more appealing even long after those previous dating experiences had ended.

Heuristics

In most social situations, our impressions could be guided by a number of different schemas. How do we make decisions on how to characterize these situations? The answer comes in the form of another type of mental shortcut called a **heuristic** (Tversky & Kahneman, 1974). Heuristics provide a quick way of selecting schemas that—although far from infallible—often help us make an effective choice amid considerable uncertainty.

Availability. One factor that determines how likely we are to choose a particular schema is how long it has been since we have used that particular schema. If we have recently used a particular schema, it is easier for us to call up that schema for use in the current situation. There are other reasons why certain schemas are more available to us. If, for instance, certain examples of categorizations are easier to remember, schemas consistent with those examples are more likely to be called up and used. Suppose you were asked whether there are more words in the English language that begin with the letter *r* or if there are more words in which the third letter is an *r*. Most people find it much easier to think of examples of words that begin with *r*, and thus, the ease of producing examples makes it seem as if there are more words that begin with *r* (Tversky & Kahneman, 1974). These words are more easily available to us, and thus, they cause us to overestimate their frequency of occurrence (Manis, Shedler, Jonides, & Nelson, 1993).

Representativeness. A second heuristic we often use is called the representativeness heuristic (Tversky & Kahneman, 1974). In this case, we take the few characteristics we know about someone or something and determine whether that person or object is likely to be a member of a particular category (Dawes, 1998; Thomsen & Borgida, 1996). We use this type of heuristic when we judge the musical tastes of others (Lonsdale & North, 2012). The closer one is to a stereotypical country music fan—based on age (older), race (White), religion (Christian), and political beliefs (conservative)—the more likely we are to believe they listen to country music (Lonsdale, 2009). This heuristic holds even when less than half of the Whites (43%) in the United States consider themselves country music fans—and even with almost 10% of country fans people of color—because people tend to discount statistical information in the face of the representativeness heuristic (Kahneman & Tversky, 1973; National Endowment for the Arts, 2008).

Anchoring and Adjustment. When faced with making a judgment on something we know very little about, we grasp any cues we can find to help us make a decent guess. Oftentimes, we will use some particular standard as a starting point and then try to determine whether we should guess higher or lower than that starting point. Such a starting point is called an *anchor*, and our modification relative to the anchor is called *adjustment* (Mussweiler, Strack, & Pfeiffer, 2000; Tversky & Kahneman, 1974). Suppose you were asked on an exam to provide the population of Chicago. If you did not know that population but you did know the population of New York City, you might use the population of New York as an anchor and, thinking that Chicago must be somewhat smaller than New York, adjust the New York value downward to produce your guess.

When using this heuristic, however, we do not always have meaningful anchors. If a number is in our head for any reason, we are likely to use it as an anchor even if it has nothing whatsoever to do with the situation we are facing (Cadinu & Rothbart, 1996; Wilson, Houston, Etling, & Brekke, 1996). Suppose an employer is conducting an annual evaluation of employees and has the power to give employees a raise of anywhere from 0 to 40 percent depending on their performance. If the boss just attended a retirement party for someone who worked in the firm for 30 years, he or she may unconsciously use this value as an anchor and end up giving relatively high raises. If, however, the boss just attended the birthday party of a five-year-old niece, five may be used as the anchor, and although the boss may adjust up from five, the raises are likely to be considerably lower than if 30 were used as the anchor. These kinds of anchoring effects tend to occur even if we are explicitly warned not to allow arbitrary anchors to affect our decisions (Griffin, Gonzalez, & Varey, 2001).

Perhaps most often, we use ourselves as an anchor when judging social situations (Markus, Smith, & Moreland, 1985). We have a tendency to do this even when we know we are unusual. If you are a very generous person who always tips at least 25 percent at a restaurant and are asked whether your friend Emily is miserly or charitable, you would be likely to use your own rather unusual behavior as an anchor and report that she is tightfisted because you know she typically tips "only" 20 percent.

ATTRIBUTION THEORY

When we interact with other people, we observe only their actions and the visible effects those actions have. As perceivers, we often want to also know why others act as they do. To figure this out, we must usually make inferences beyond what we observe. For instance, if a coworker performs a favor for us, why is she doing it? Is she doing it because she is fundamentally a generous person? Or is she manipulative and pursuing some ulterior motive? Does her social role require her to do it? Have other people pressured her into doing it? To act effectively toward her and to predict her future behavior, we must first figure out why she behaves as she does.

The term **attribution** refers to the process an observer uses to infer the causes of another's behavior: "Why did that person act as he or she did?" In attribution, we observe another's behavior and infer backward to its causes—to the intentions, abilities, traits, motives, and situational pressures that explain why people act as they do. Theories of attribution focus on the methods we use to interpret another person's behavior and to infer its sources (Kelley & Michela, 1980; Lipe, 1991; Ross & Fletcher, 1985).

Dispositional versus Situational Attributions

Fritz Heider (1944, 1958), whose work was an early stimulus to the study of attribution, noted that people in everyday life use commonsense reasoning to understand the causes of others' behavior. They act as "naive scientists" and use something resembling the scientific method in attempting to discern causes of behavior. Heider maintained that regardless of whether their interpretations about the causes of behavior are scientifically valid, people act on their beliefs. For this reason, social psychologists must study people's commonsense explanations of behavior and events so we can understand their behavior.

The most crucial decision observers make is whether to attribute a behavior to the internal state(s) of the person who performed it—this is termed a **dispositional attribution**—or to factors in that person's environment—a **situational attribution**. For example, consider the attributions an observer might make when learning that her neighbor is unemployed. She might judge that he is out of work because he is lazy, irresponsible, or lacking in ability. These are dispositional attributions, because they attribute the causes of behavior to his internal states or characteristics. Alternatively, she might attribute his unemployment to the scarcity of jobs in his line of work, to employment discrimination, to the depressed condition of the economy, or to the evils of the capitalist system. These are situational attributions because they attribute his behavior to external causes.

What determines whether we attribute an act to a person's disposition or to the situation? One important consideration is the strength of situational pressures on the person. These pressures may include normative role demands as well as rewards or punishments applied to the person by others in the environment. For example, suppose we see a judge give the death penalty to a criminal. We might infer that the judge is tough (a dispositional attribution). However, suppose we learn that the law in that state requires the death penalty for the criminal's offense. Now we would see the judge not as tough but as responding to role pressures (a situational attribution).

This logic has been formalized as the **subtractive rule**, which states that when making attributions about personal dispositions, the observer subtracts the perceived impact of situational forces from the personal disposition implied by the behavior itself (Trope & Cohen, 1989; Trope, Cohen, & Moaz, 1988). Thus, considered by itself, the judge's behavior (imposing the death penalty) might imply that she is tough in disposition. The subtractive rule, however, states that the observer must subtract the effect of situational pressures (the state law) from the disposition implied by the behavior itself. When the observer does this, he or she may conclude the judge is not especially tough or overly inclined to impose the death penalty. In other words, using the subtractive rule in this situation served to weaken the dispositional attribution and strengthen the situational attribution.

There are other times, however, when applying the subtractive rule (by accounting for the situational influences) actually strengthens or augments the dispositional attribution—not unlike what happens when we subtract a negative number in arithmetic. This happens, for instance, when someone engages in an activity that his or her environment discourages or punishes. If we learn that the judge in the previous example gave the death penalty even though she was the first to give the death penalty for such a crime or that the jury suggested a lesser punishment or that she would face difficulty being reelected because of her decision, these situational factors would strengthen our dispositional attribution. She is more than tough; she is harsh.

Another factor that may influence our attributions is our attention to situational pressures and structural constraints. Social science students, whose coursework and training encourages them to think beyond the individual and to consider social structure, are more likely to blame the system for individuals' problems with unemployment and poverty than are either business or engineering students (Guimond, Begin, & Palmer, 1989; Guimond & Palmer, 1990). Some might argue that this is a selection effect; students who embrace system-blame are somehow drawn toward the social sciences. However, Figure 6.2 shows that students begin college with quite similar levels of system-blame, and it is over time that differences emerge. In a sense, as students are socialized into the norms of their disciplines, they acquire a particular view of the social world and reality—a type of cultural lens.

Culture plays an important role in the attribution process. One important cultural difference has to do with how individualist or collectivist a culture is (Norenzayan & Nisbett, 2000; Triandis, 1995). Individualist cultures emphasize the individual and value individual achievement; collectivist cultures emphasize the welfare of the family, ethnic group, and perhaps work group over the interests of individuals. This difference in emphasis turns out to have a substantial impact on the orientation toward dispositional versus situational attributions for behavior. Individualist cultures focus on the individual—thus, their members are predisposed to make individualist or dispositional attributions. In collectivist cultures, the focus on groups draws some attention to context—thus, members of these cultures are more likely to include situational elements in their attributions.

In one study, researchers compared attributions made by students from an individualist society (the United States) with those made by students from a collectivist society (Saudi Arabia). Participants in the study were 163 students recruited from U.S. universities and 162 students from a university in Saudi Arabia (Al-Zahrani & Kaplowitz, 1993). Each student was presented with vignettes describing eight situations—four involving achievement and four involving morality. Students were asked to assign responsibility for the outcome to each of several factors. Consistent with the hypothesis, the results showed that across the eight situations, U.S. students assigned greater responsibility to internal dispositional factors than did Saudi students.

Inferring Dispositions from Acts

Although Heider's analysis and the subtractive rule are useful in identifying some conditions under which observers make dispositional attributions, they do not explain which specific dispositions observers will ascribe to a person. Suppose, for

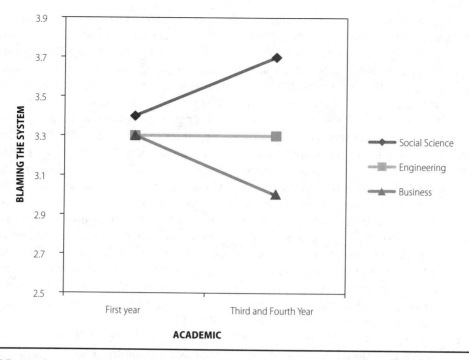

FIGURE 6.2 Situational Attributions for Poverty and Unemployment, by Field of Study and Academic Year

Students enter college with similar levels of "system-blame" for poverty and unemployment. College classes increase the likelihood of making situational attributions among social science students and decrease such attributions among business students. Because engineering classes are unlikely to engage discussions of poverty or unemployment, engineering students' views remain unaffected over the course of study. Adapted from Guimond & Palmer, 1990.

instance, that you are on a city street during the Christmas season and you see a young, well-dressed man walking with a woman. Suddenly, the man stops and tosses several coins into a Salvation Army pot. From this act, what can you infer about the man's dispositions? Is he generous and altruistic? Or is he trying to impress the woman? Or is he perhaps just trying to clear out some nuisance change from his coat pocket?

When we try to infer a person's dispositions, our perspective is much like that of a detective. We can observe only the act (a man gives coins to the Salvation Army) and the effects of that act (the Salvation Army receives more resources, the woman smiles at the man, the man's pocket is no longer cluttered with coins). From this observed

act and its effects, we must infer the man's dispositions.

According to one prominent theory (Jones, 1979; Jones & Davis, 1965), we perform two major steps when inferring personal dispositions. First, we try to deduce the specific intentions that underlie a person's actions. In other words, we try to figure out what the person originally intended to accomplish by performing the act. Second, from these intentions we try to infer what prior personal disposition would cause a person to have such intentions. If we think the man intended to benefit the Salvation Army, for example, we infer the disposition "helpful" or "generous." However, if we think the man had some other intention, such as impressing his girlfriend, we do not infer he has the disposition "helpful." Thus, we attribute a disposition that reflects the presumed intention.

Several factors influence observers' decisions regarding which effect(s) the person is really pursuing and, hence, what dispositional inference is appropriate. These factors include the commonality of effects, the social desirability of effects, and the normativeness of effects (Jones & Davis, 1965).

Commonality. If any given act produced one and only one effect, then inferences of dispositions from acts would always be clear-cut. Because many acts have multiple effects, however, observers attributing specific intentions and dispositions find it informative to observe the actor in situations that involve choices between alternative actions.

Suppose, for example, that a person can engage either in action 1 or in action 2. Action 1, if chosen, will produce effects a, b, and c. Action 2 will produce effects b, c, d, and e. As we can see, two of these effects (b and c) are common to actions 1 and 2. The remaining effects (a, d, and e) are unique to a particular alternative; these are noncommon effects. The unique (noncommon) effects of acts enable observers to make inferences regarding intentions and dispositions, but the common effects of two or more acts provide little or no basis for inferences (Jones & Davis, 1965).

Thus, observers who wish to discern the specific dispositions of a person try to identify effects that are unique to the action chosen. Research shows that the fewer noncommon effects associated with the chosen alternative, the greater the confidence of observers about their attributions (Ajzen & Holmes, 1976).

Social Desirability. In many situations, people engage in particular behaviors because those behaviors are socially desirable.

Yet people who perform a socially desirable act show us only that they are "normal" and reveal nothing about their distinctive dispositions. Suppose, for instance, that you observe a guest at a party thank the hostess when leaving. What does this tell you about the guest? Did she really enjoy the party? Or was she merely behaving in a polite, socially desirable fashion? You cannot be sure—either inference could be correct. Now suppose instead that when leaving, the guest complained loudly to the hostess that she had a miserable time at such a dull party. This would likely tell you more about her because observers interpret acts low in social desirability as indicators of underlying dispositions (Miller, 1976).

Normative Expectations. When inferring dispositions from acts, observers consider the normativeness of behavior. Normativeness is the extent to which we expect the average person to perform a behavior in a particular setting. This includes conformity to social norms and to role expectations in groups (Jones & McGillis, 1976). Actions that conform to norms are uninformative about personal dispositions, whereas actions that violate norms lead to dispositional attributions. An observer could be confident that a Michigan fan who cheered for his team while sitting in the middle of Notre Dame's student section is much more passionate about football (a dispositional attribution) than if the same fan was acting similarly in the heart of the Michigan student section.

Covariation Model of Attribution

Up to this point, we have examined how observers make attributions regarding a person's behavior in a single situation. Sometimes, however, we have multiple observations of a person's behavior. That is, we have information about a person's behavior in a variety of situations or in a given situation vis-à-vis different partners. Multiple observations enable us to make many comparisons, and these, in turn, facilitate causal attribution.

How do perceivers use multiple observations to arrive at a conclusion about the cause(s) of a behavior? Extending Heider's ideas, Kelley (1967, 1973) suggests that when we have multiple observations of behavior, we analyze the information essentially in the same way a scientist would. That is, we try to figure out whether the behavior occurs in the presence or absence of various factors (actors, objects, contexts) that are possible causes. Then to identify the cause(s) of the behavior, we apply the **principle of covariation**: We attribute the behavior to the factor that is both present when the behavior occurs and absent when the behavior fails to occur—the cause that covaries with the behavior.

To illustrate, suppose you are at work one afternoon when you hear your boss loudly criticizing another worker, Zach. To what would you attribute your boss's behavior? There are at least three potential causes: the actor (the boss), the object of the behavior (Zach), and the context or setting in which the behavior occurs. For example, you might attribute the loud criticism to your boss's confrontational personality (a characteristic of the actor), to Zach's slothful performance (a characteristic of the object), or to some particular feature of the context.

Kelley (1967) suggests that when using the principle of covariation to determine whether a behavior is caused by the actor, object, or context, we rely on three types of information: consensus, consistency, and distinctiveness.

Consensus refers to whether all actors perform the same behavior or only a few do. For example, do all the other employees at work criticize Zach (high consensus), or is

your boss the only person who does so (low consensus)?

Consistency refers to whether the actor behaves in the same way at different times and in different settings. If your boss criticizes Zach on many different occasions, her behavior is high in consistency. If she has never before criticized Zach, her behavior is low in consistency.

Distinctiveness refers to whether the actor behaves differently toward a particular object than toward other objects. If your boss criticizes only Zach and none of the other workers, her behavior is high in distinctiveness. If she criticizes all workers, her behavior toward Zach is low in distinctiveness.

The causal attribution that observers make for a behavior depends on the particular combination of consensus, consistency, and distinctiveness information that people associate with that behavior. To illustrate, Table 6.2 reviews the scenario in which your boss criticizes Zach. The table displays three combinations of information that might be present in this situation. These combinations of information are interesting because studies have shown they reliably produce different attributions regarding the cause of the behavior (Cheng & Novick, 1990).

As Table 6.2 indicates, observers usually attribute the cause of a behavior to the actor (the boss) when the behavior is low in consensus, low in distinctiveness, and high in consistency. In contrast, observers usually attribute a behavior to the object (Zach) when the behavior is high in consensus, high in distinctiveness, and high in consistency. Finally, observers usually attribute a behavior to the context when consistency is low.

Several studies show that, at least in general terms, people use consensus, consistency, and distinctiveness information in the way Kelley theorized (Hewstone & Jas-

TABLE 6.2 Why Did the Boss Criticize Zach?

Situation: At work today, you observe your boss criticizing and yelling at another employee, Zach.

Question: Why did the boss criticize Zach?

1. Kelley's (1973) model indicates that attributions are made to the actor (boss) when consensus is low, distinctiveness is low, and consistency is high.

   Example: Suppose no other persons criticize Zach (low consensus). The boss criticizes all the other employees (low distinctiveness). The boss criticized Zach last month, last week, and yesterday (high consistency).

   Attribution: The perceiver will likely attribute the behavior (criticism) to the boss. ("The boss is a very critical person.")

2. The model indicates that attributions are made to the stimulus object (Zach) when consensus is high, distinctiveness is high, and consistency is high.

   Example: Suppose everyone at work criticizes Zach (high consensus). The boss does not criticize anyone else at work, only Zach (high distinctiveness). The boss criticized Zach last month, last week, and yesterday (high consistency).

   Attribution: The perceiver will likely attribute the behavior (criticism) to Zach. ("Zach is a lazy, careless worker.")

3. The model indicates that attributions are made to the context or situation when consistency is low.

   Example: Suppose the boss has never criticized Zach before (low consistency).

   Attribution: The perceiver will likely attribute the behavior (criticism) to a particular set of contextual circumstances rather than to Zach or the boss per se. ("Zach made a remark this morning that the boss misinterpreted.")

pars, 1987; McArthur, 1972; Pruitt & Insko, 1980), although consensus seems to have a weaker effect on attributions than the other two aspects of covariation (Winschild & Wells, 1997). Of course, in any given situation, the combination of available information may differ from the three possibilities shown in Table 6.2. In such cases, attributions are more complicated, more ambiguous, and less certain. We usually assign less weight to a given cause if other plausible causes are also present (Kelley, 1972; Morris & Larrick, 1995).

BIAS AND ERROR IN ATTRIBUTION

According to the picture presented thus far, observers scrutinize their environment, gather information, form impressions, and interpret behavior in rational, if sometimes unconscious, ways. In actuality, however, observers often deviate from the logical methods described by attribution theory and fall prey to biases. These biases may lead observers to misinterpret events and to make erroneous judgments. This section considers several major biases and errors in attribution.

Overattribution to Dispositions

At the time of the Cuban Missile Crisis, the Cuban leader Fidel Castro was generally unpopular, even feared, in the United States. In an interesting study done shortly after the crisis, Jones and Harris (1967) asked participants to read an essay written by another student. Depending on the experimental condition, the essay either strongly supported the Cuban leader or strongly opposed him. Moreover, the participants received information about the conditions under which the student wrote the essay. They were told either that the essay was written by a student who was assigned by the instructor to take a pro-Castro or anti-Castro stand (no-choice condition) or that the essay was written by a student who was free to choose whichever position he or she wanted to present (choice condition). The participants' task was to infer the writer's true underlying attitude about Castro. In the conditions in which the writer had free choice, participants inferred that the content of the essay reflected the writer's true attitude about Castro. That is, they saw the pro-Castro essay as indicating pro-Castro attitudes and the anti-Castro essay as indicating anti-Castro attitudes. In the conditions in which the writer was assigned the topic and had no choice, participants still thought the content of the essay reflected the writer's true attitude about Castro, although they were less sure that this was so. Participants made these internal attributions even though it was possible the writer held an opinion directly opposite of that expressed in the essay. In effect, participants overestimated the importance of internal dispositions (attitudes about Castro) and underestimated the importance of situational forces (role obligations) in shaping the essay.

The tendency to overestimate the importance of personal (dispositional) factors and to underestimate situational influences is called the **fundamental attribution error** (Higgins & Bryant, 1982; Ross, 1977; Small & Peterson, 1981). This tendency was first identified by Heider (1944), who noted that most observers ignore or minimize the impact of role pressures and situational constraints on others and interpret behavior as caused by people's intentions, motives, or attitudes. This bias toward dispositional factors was labeled "fundamental" because it was documented in study after study over the years and assumed to be universal (for instance, Allison, Mackie, Muller, & Worth, 1993; Jones, 1979; Ross, 2001; Sabini, Siepmann, & Stein, 2001). However, more recent research suggests that the bias is less universal than it originally seemed. The tendency was mistakenly considered fundamental because early social psychological research relied almost exclusively on American and Western European participants in surveys and experiments. Members of these cultures have a more independent view of the self (Markus & Kitayama, 1991) than those in Eastern cultures, who were seldom studied. Contemporary social psychologists, now more attentive to cultural differences, find that members of collectivist cultures (e.g., China, India, Taiwan) tend to favor situational explanations over dispositional ones—the reverse of the fundamental attribution error (Smith & Bond, 1994). Although the term remains the same, through cross-cultural research social psychologists realize that the bias is not as fundamental as it once seemed.

Overemphasizing the importance of disposition is especially dangerous when it causes us to overlook the advantages of power built into social roles. For instance, we may incorrectly attribute the successes of the powerful to their superior personal capabilities, or we may incorrectly attribute the failures of persons without power to their personal weaknesses.

Focus-of-Attention Bias

A closely related error is the tendency to overestimate the causal impact of whomever or whatever we focus our attention on; this is called the **focus-of-attention bias**. A striking demonstration of this bias appears in a study by Taylor and Fiske (1978). The study involved six participants who observed a conversation between two persons (Speaker 1 and Speaker 2). Although all six participants heard the same dialogue, they differed in the focus of their visual attention. Two observers sat behind Speaker 1, facing Speaker 2; two sat behind Speaker 2, facing Speaker 1; and two sat on the sides,

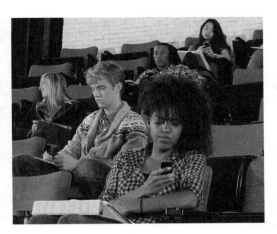

The students are visually focused on the professor, whereas the professor is visually focused on the students. These visual perspectives influence attributions. If a lecture is not going well, the professor may blame the class's inattention and apathy, but the students are more likely to blame the professor and his lack of teaching ability or enthusiasm. © Dirk Anschütz/Corbis

equally focused on the two speakers. Measures taken after the conversation showed that observers thought the speaker they faced not only had more influence on the tone and content of the conversation but also had a greater causal impact on the other speaker's behavior. Observers who sat on the sides and were able to focus equally on both speakers attributed equal influence to them.

We perceive the stimuli that are most salient in the environment—those that attract our attention—as most causally influential. Thus, we attribute most causal influence to people who are noisy, colorful, vivid, or in motion. We credit the person who talks the most with exercising the most influence; we blame the person who we see run past us when we hear a rock shatter a window. Although salient stimuli may be causally important in some cases, we overestimate their importance (Krull & Dill, 1996; McArthur & Post, 1977).

The focus-of-attention bias provides one explanation for the fundamental attribution error. The person behaving is the active entity in the environment. If we watch our math professor struggle with

a problem on the board, the professor is what captures our attention. In fact, many of the contextual influences on the actor (for example, things that happened earlier in the day or a pounding headache) may be completely invisible to us (Gilbert & Malone, 1995) or simply less salient (the distracting murmur from our classmates) as we focus on the professor. Because many of us are socialized to direct our attention more to people who act than to the context, we attribute more causal importance to people (the math professor is nervous or incapable) than to their situations.

Actor-Observer Difference

Actors and observers make different attributions for behavior. Observers tend to attribute actors' behavior to the actors' internal characteristics, whereas actors believe their own behavior is due more to characteristics of the external situation (Jones & Nisbett, 1972; Watson, 1982). This tendency is known as the **actor-observer difference**. Thus, although other customers in a market may attribute the mix of items in your grocery cart (beer, vegetables, candy bars) to your personal characteristics (hard-drinking, vegetarian, chocolate addict), you will probably attribute it to the requirements of your situation (preparing for a party) or the qualities of the items (nutritional value or special treat).

In one demonstration of the actor-observer difference (Nisbett, Caputo, Legant, & Maracek, 1973), male students wrote descriptions explaining why they liked their girlfriends and why they chose their majors. Then, as observers, they explained why their best friend liked his girlfriend and chose his major. When explaining their own actions, the students emphasized external characteristics like the attractive qualities of their girlfriends and the interesting aspects of their majors. However, when explaining their friends' behavior, they downplayed external characteristics and emphasized their friends' internal dispositions (preferences and personalities).

Two explanations for the actor-observer difference in attribution are that actors and observers have different visual perspectives and different access to information.

Visual Perspectives. The actor's natural visual perspective is to look at the situation, whereas the observer's natural perspective is to look at the actor. Thus, the actor-observer difference reflects a difference in the focus of attention. Both the actor and the observer attribute more causal influence to what they focus on. Consider the students and math professor from the focus-of-attention example above. The students in the example may think of their math professor as incapable because she is the students' visual focus. The professor, who cannot see herself and whose visual attention is turned toward the classroom, blames the disrespectful behavior of the students in her class.

Storms (1973) reasoned that if the actor-observer difference in attributions was due simply to a difference in perspective, it might be possible to reverse the actor-observer difference by making the actor see the behavior from the observer's viewpoint and the observer see the same behavior from the actor's viewpoint. To give each the other's point of view, Storms videotaped a conversation between two people, using two separate cameras. One camera recorded the interaction from the visual perspective of the actor, the other from the perspective of the observer. Storms then showed actors the videotape made from the observer's perspective, and he showed observers the videotape made from the actor's perspective. As predicted, reversing the visual perspectives reversed the actor-observer difference in attribution; finding ways to make individuals more self-aware can, therefore, reduce the actor-observer bias (Fejfar & Hoyle, 2000).

Information. A second explanation for the actor-observer difference is that actors have information about their own past behavior and the context relevant to their behavior that observers lack (Johnson & Boyd, 1995). Thus, for example, observers may assume that certain behaviors are typical of an actor when in fact they are not. This would cause observers to make incorrect dispositional attributions. An observer who sees a clerk return an overpayment to a customer may assume the clerk always behaves this way—resulting in a dispositional attribution of honesty. However, if the clerk knows he has often cheated customers in the past, he would probably not interpret his current behavior as evidence of his honest nature. Consistent with this, research shows that observers who have a low level of acquaintance with the actor tend to form more dispositional attributions and fewer situational attributions than those who have a high level of acquaintance with the actor (Prager & Cutler, 1990).

Even when observers have some information about an actor's past behavior, they often do not know how changes in context influence the actor's behavior. This is because observers usually see an actor only in limited contexts. Suppose that students observe a professor delivering witty, entertaining lectures in class week after week. The professor knows that in other social situations he is shy and withdrawn, but the students do not have an opportunity to see this. As a result, the observers (students) may infer dispositions from apparently consistent behavior that the actor (the professor) knows to be inconsistent across a wider range of contexts.

Motivational Biases

Up to this point, we have considered attribution biases based on cognitive factors. That is, we have traced biases to the types of information that observers have available, acquire, and process. Motivational factors—a person's needs, interests, and goals—are another source of bias in attributions.

When events affect a person's self-interests, biased attribution is likely. Specific motives that influence attribution include the desire to defend deep-seated beliefs, to enhance one's self-esteem, to increase one's sense of control over the environment, and to strengthen the favorable impression of oneself that others have.

The desire to defend cherished beliefs and stereotypes may lead observers to engage in biased attribution. Observers may interpret actions that correspond with their stereotypes as caused by the actor's personal dispositions. For instance, they may attribute a female executive's outburst of tears during a crisis to her emotional instability because that corresponds to their stereotype about women. At the same time, people attribute actions that contradict stereotypes to situational causes. If the female executive manages the crisis smoothly, the same people may credit this to the effectiveness of her male assistant. When observers selectively attribute behaviors that contradict stereotypes to situational influences, these behaviors reveal nothing new about the persons who perform them. As a result, the stereotypes persist (Hamilton, 1979). Social psychologists refer to our tendency to view our initial assumption as correct despite evidence to the contradictory as **belief perseverance** (Ross, Lepper & Hubbard, 1975).

Motivational biases may also influence attributions for success and failure. People tend to take credit for acts that yield positive outcomes, whereas they deflect blame for bad outcomes and attribute them to external causes (Bradley, 1978; Campbell & Sedikides, 1999; Ross & Fletcher, 1985). This phenomenon, referred to as the **self-serving bias**, is illustrated clearly by athletes' reporting of the results of competitions (Lau & Russell, 1980; Ross & Lumsden, 1982). Whereas members of winning teams take credit for winning ("We won"), members of losing teams are more likely to attribute the outcome to an external cause—their opponent ("They won," not "We lost"). Students are similar. In a study in which college students were asked to explain the grades they received on three examinations (Bernstein, Stephan, & Davis, 1979), students who received As and Bs attributed their grades much more to their own effort and ability than to good luck or easy tests. However, students who received Cs, Ds, and Fs attributed their grades largely to bad luck and the difficulty of the tests. Other studies show similar effects (Reifenberg, 1986).

Various motives may contribute to this self-serving bias in attributions of performance. For instance, attributing success to personal qualities and failure to external factors enables us to enhance or protect our self-esteem. Regardless of the outcome, we can continue to see ourselves as competent and worthy. Moreover, by avoiding the attribution of failure to personal qualities, we maximize our sense of control. This in turn supports the belief that we can master challenges successfully if we choose to apply ourselves because we possess the necessary ability.

Attributions for Success and Failure

Given motivational biases, how do observers (and actors) decide which of these is the "real" cause of success or failure? For students, football coaches, elected officials, and anyone else whose fate rides on evaluations of their performance, attributions for success and failure are vital. As observers realize, however, attributions of this type are problematic. Whenever someone succeeds at a task, a variety of explanations can be advanced for the outcome. For example, a student who passes a test could credit her own intrinsic ability ("I have a lot of intelligence"), her effort ("I really studied for that exam"), the easiness of the task ("The exam could have been much more difficult"), or even luck ("They just happened to test us on the few articles I read").

These four factors—ability, effort, task difficulty, and luck—are general and apply in many settings. When observers look at an event and try to figure out the cause of success or failure, they must consider two things. First, they must decide whether the outcome is due to causes within the actor (an internal or dispositional attribution) or due to causes in the environment (an external or situational attribution). Second, they must decide whether the outcome is a stable or an unstable occurrence. That is, they must determine whether the cause is a permanent feature of the actor or the environment or whether it is labile and changing. Only after observers make judgments regarding internality-externality and

TABLE 6.3 Perceived Causes of Success and Failure

DEGREE OF STABILITY	LOCUS OF CONTROL	
	INTERNAL	EXTERNAL
Stable	Ability	Task difficulty
Unstable	Effort	Luck

Source: Adapted from Weiner, Heckhausen, Meyer, and Cook, 1972.

stability-instability can they reach conclusions regarding the cause(s) of the success or failure.

As various theorists (Heider, 1958; Weiner, 1986; Weiner et al., 1971) have pointed out, the four factors aforementioned—ability, effort, task difficulty, and luck—can be grouped according to internality-externality and stability-instability. Ability, for instance, is usually considered internal and stable. That is, observers usually construe ability or aptitude as a property of the person (not the environment), and they consider it stable because it does not change from moment to moment. In contrast, effort is internal and unstable. Effort or temporary exertion is a property of the person that changes depending on how hard he or she tries. Task difficulty depends on objective task characteristics, so it is external and stable. Luck or chance is external and unstable. Table 6.3 displays these relations.

Determinants of Attributed Causes. Whether observers attribute a performance to internal or external causes depends on how the actor's performance compares with that of others. We usually attribute extreme or unusual performances to internal causes. For example, we would judge a tennis player who wins a major tournament as extraordinarily able or highly motivated. Similarly, we would view a player who has an unusually poor performance as weak in ability or unmotivated. In contrast, we usually attribute average or common performances to external causes. If defeat comes to a player halfway through the tournament, we are likely to attribute it to tough competition or perhaps bad luck.

Whether observers attribute a performance to stable or unstable causes depends on how consistent the actor's performance is over time (Frieze & Weiner, 1971). When performances are very consistent, we attribute the outcome to stable causes. Thus, if a tennis player wins tournaments consistently, we would attribute this success to her great talent (ability) or perhaps to the uniformly low level of her opponents (task difficulty). When performances are very inconsistent, however, we attribute the outcomes to unstable causes rather than stable ones. Suppose, for example, that our tennis player is unbeatable one day and a pushover the next. In this case, we would attribute the outcomes to fluctuations in motivation (effort) or to random external factors such as wind speed, court condition, and so on (luck).

Consequences of Attributions. Attributions for performance are important because they influence both our emotional reactions to success and failure and our future expectations and aspirations. For instance, if we attribute a poor exam performance to lack of ability, we may despair of future success and give up studying; this is especially likely if we view ability as given and not controllable by us. Alternatively, if we attribute the poor exam performance to lack of effort, we may feel shame or guilt, but we are likely to study harder and expect improvement. If we attribute the poor exam performance to bad luck, we may experience feelings of surprise or bewilderment, but we are not likely to change our study habits, because the situation will not seem controllable; despite this lack of change, we

might nevertheless expect improved grades in the future. Finally, if we attribute our poor performance to the difficulty of the exam, we may become angry, but we do not strive for improvement (McFarland & Ross, 1982; Valle & Frieze, 1976; Weiner, 1985, 1986).

SUMMARY

Social perception is the process of using information to construct understandings of the social world and form impressions of people.

Schemas. A schema is a well-organized structure of cognitions about some social entity. (1) There are several distinct types of schemas: person schemas, self-schemas, group schemas (stereotypes), role schemas, and event schemas (scripts). (2) Schemas organize information in memory and, therefore, affect what we remember and what we forget. Moreover, they guide our inferences and judgments about people and objects.

Person Schemas and Group Stereotypes. (1) One important type of person schema is an implicit personality theory—a set of assumptions about which personality traits go together with other traits. These schemas enable us to make inferences about other people's traits. We can depict an implicit personality theory as a mental map. (2) A stereotype is a fixed set of characteristics attributed to all members of a given group. American culture includes stereotypes for ethnic, racial, gender, and many other groups. Because stereotypes are overgeneralizations, they cause errors in inference; this is especially true in complex situations.

Impression Formation. (1) Research on trait centrality using the "warm/cold" variable illustrates how variations in a single trait can produce a large difference in the impression formed by observers of a stimulus person. (2) Information received early usually has a larger impact on impressions than information received later; this is called the primacy effect. (3) Impressions become self-fulfilling prophecies when we behave toward others according to our impressions and evoke corresponding reactions from them. (4) Impressions are informed by schemas that are selected through mental shortcuts called heuristics.

Attribution Theory. Through attribution, people infer an action's causes from its effects. (1) One important issue in attribution is locus of causality—dispositional (internal) versus situational (external) attributions. Observers follow the subtractive rule when making attributions to dispositions or situations. (2) To attribute specific dispositions to an actor, observers observe an act and its effects and then try to infer the actor's intention with respect to that act. Observers then attribute the disposition that corresponds best with the actor's inferred intention. (3) Observers who have information about an actor's behaviors in many situations make attributions to the actor, object, or context. The attribution made depends on which of these causes covaries with the behavior in question. Observers assess covariation by considering consensus, consistency, and distinctiveness information.

Bias and Error in Attribution. (1) Observers frequently overestimate personal dispositions as causes of behavior and underestimate situational pressures; this bias is called the fundamental attribution error. (2) Observers also overestimate the causal impact of whatever their attention is focused on. (3) Actors and observers have different attribution tendencies. Actors attri-

bute their own behavior to external forces in the situation, whereas observers attribute the same behavior to the actor's personal dispositions. (4) Motivations—needs, interests, and goals—lead people to make self-serving, biased attributions. People defend deep-seated beliefs by attributing behavior that contradicts their beliefs to situational influences. People defend their self-esteem and sense of control by attributing their failures to external causes and taking personal credit for their successes.

Attributions for Success and Failure. Observers attribute success or failure to four basic causes—ability, effort, task difficulty, and luck. They attribute consistent performances to stable rather than to unstable causes, and they attribute average performances to external rather than internal causes.

List of Key Terms and Concepts

Critical Thinking Skill:
Understanding Stereotyping

Although our culture makes it seem as though there are vast differences between men and women, the scientific data show a very different picture. Men and women are actually quite similar on most, though not all, psychological characteristics, including behaviors such as math performance and leadership (Hyde, 2005). If men and women are so similar, why do people like to believe they are so different?

The answers lie in stereotypes and motives for stereotyping. As noted in the chapter, a stereotype is a generalization about a group of people (e.g., men) that distinguishes those people from another group (e.g., women). Gender stereotypes abound. Women are talkative, and men have little to say. Women are submissive, whereas men are dominant. Women are best suited for the humanities and social sciences, whereas men excel at science and math. When we collect rigorous scientific data, it turns out that some stereotypes are fairly accurate and some are not. For example, it turns out that although men tend to dominate task-oriented groups and women acquiesce (Ridgeway, 2011), gender differences in talkativeness is tiny (Leaper & Smith, 2004) and girls and boys perform equally on standardized math tests (Hyde et al., 2008) (see also Box 15.1).

If so many stereotypes turn out not to be accurate, why do people continue to stereotype? Although this chapter introduced cognitive efficiency as a possible explanation, another motivation is self-enhancement.

We make ourselves feel better by denigrating people from another group. For example, if we say or think, "Teenagers are so irresponsible," by implication we, as adults, are much more responsible. Although when people stereotype for cognitive efficiency, the stereotypes can be positive or negative, when people stereotype for self-enhancement purposes, the stereotypes tend to be negative.

How does this illuminate potential reasons for gender stereotyping? Answer this question before you proceed to the next paragraph.

When people engage in gender stereotyping, sometimes it is for cognitive efficiency. Assuming that a man is interested in sports allows us to know what to ask him when we see him. Other times, people engage in gender stereotyping for self-enhancement purposes. A man might say, "You women are so emotional," which makes him feel emotionally in control and masculine. Or a woman might say, "Men are just clueless about how other people feel," making her feel good about her skills at reading others' emotions.

Good critical thinking involves understanding why people stereotype and acknowledging that stereotypes are often not accurate. The next time you hear someone (or yourself!) making a stereotyped comment (whether based on gender, race, age, or other differences), ask yourself two questions: (1) What is the person's/your goal in stereotyping? and (2) Is this an accurate stereotype that is supported by scientific data?

ATTITUDES

INTRODUCTION

- "The Yankees are awesome!"

- "My human sexuality class is really boring."

- "I like my job."

- "Something needs to be done about the nation's debt."

- "The drinking age should be lowered."

- "Guns don't kill people; people kill people."

What do these statements have in common? Each represents an **attitude**—a predisposition to respond to a particular object in a generally favorable or unfavorable way (Ajzen, 1982). A person's attitudes influence the way in which he or she perceives and responds to the world (Allport, 1935; Thomas & Znaniecki, 1918). For example, attitudes influence attention—the person who likes the Yankees is more likely to notice news stories about the team and its players. Attitudes also influence behavior—the person who thinks the drinking age should be lowered is more likely to drink before their 21st birthday.

Attitudes do not exist in isolation. The person who believes that the nation's debt is too high likely has a whole set of beliefs about the role of government in the economy. They are more likely to support austerity measures, to think that the government needs to cut items from its budget, and that entitlement programs like Medicare should be reformed. Because attitudes can influence behavior, holding these attitudes might influence who an individual votes for or whether they will write their congressperson before an important vote on the debt ceiling. If attitudes influence behavior, is it possible to change behavior by changing attitudes? Politicians, lobbyists, auto manufacturers, and restaurants

spend billions of dollars every year trying to create favorable attitudes. If they succeed, do these attitudes affect our behavior? What about when your parents or friends try to influence your attitudes? Are you less likely to smoke if your parents tell you it is a dirty and dangerous habit or to become vegetarian if your friends tell you about the documentary they watched on industrial animal farming?

In this chapter, we consider three main questions:

1. What is an attitude? Where do attitudes come from, and how are they formed?

2. How are attitudes linked to other attitudes? How does this organization affect attitude change?

3. What is the relationship between attitudes and behavior?

THE NATURE OF ATTITUDES

An attitude exists in a person's mind; it is a mental state. Every attitude is about something, the "object" of the attitude. This section introduces the components of an attitude, the sources of attitudes, and the functions of attitudes.

The Components of an Attitude

Consider the following statement: "My human sexuality class is really boring." This attitude has three components: (1) beliefs or cognitions, (2) an evaluation, and (3) a behavioral predisposition.

Cognition. An attitude is based on a set of **cognitions** or knowledge structures associated with the attitude object (Pratkanis & Greenwald, 1989). The person who doesn't like his or her human sexuality class perceives it as involving certain content, taught by a particular person. Often we cannot prove whether particular beliefs are true or false. For example, economists, politicians, and constituents disagree on whether the nation's debt is too high, with people on both sides equally convinced they are right.

Evaluation. An attitude also has an evaluative or affective component. "It's really boring" indicates that the course arouses a mildly unpleasant emotion in the speaker. An attitude is not just based on what people think but also how they feel about an object. Stronger negative emotions include dislike, hatred, or even loathing: "I can't stand punk rock." Of course, the evaluation may be positive: "Thai food is good" or "The Yankees are awesome!" The evaluative component has both a direction (positive or negative) and an intensity (ranging from very weak to very strong).

Behavioral Predisposition. An attitude also involves a predisposition to respond or a behavioral tendency toward the object. "It's boring" implies a tendency to avoid the class. "I like my job" suggests an intention to go to work. People who hold a specific attitude are inclined to behave in certain ways that are consistent with that attitude.

Relationships Among the Components. Cognitive, evaluative, and behavioral components all have the same object, so we would expect them to form a single, relatively consistent whole. However, these three components are distinct; if they were identical, we would not need to distinguish among them (Kothandapani, 1971).

Some attitudes are affect-based; they are primarily driven by the evaluative component of the attitude: "I am scared of snakes" (Edwards, 1990). Even if someone tried to influence the cognitive components of the attitude, such as assuring you that most snakes are not poisonous or that poisonous snakes are more scared of you than you are of them, if you have a phobia of snakes, you would jump at the sight of one. Your more affect-based attitudes are difficult to change with cognitive reasoning.

Other attitudes are cognition-based, with the cognitive components of that attitude taking priority: "The Toyota Prius is the best hybrid car." Less important for this attitude is whether you are aesthetically drawn to the car, which would be a more evaluative component, and more important is what you know—the cognitive component of your attitudes—about the car. It is reliable, gets good gas mileage, and has a lower carbon footprint than other models. It is not that how you feel about the car is unimportant; rather, it is simply that the affect-based evaluation is not central to the attitude.

Greater consistency between the cognitive and affective components is associated with greater attitude stability and resistance to persuasion (Chaiken & Yates, 1985). Greater consistency is also associated with a stronger relationship between attitude and behavior, a connection discussed later in this chapter.

Attitude Formation

Where do attitudes come from? How are they formed? The answer lies in the processes of socialization (discussed in Chapter 3). Attitudes may be formed through reinforcement (instrumental conditioning), through associations of stimuli and responses (classical conditioning), or by observing others (observational learning).

Attitudes toward our classes and jobs might be formed through instrumental conditioning—that is, learning based on direct experience with the object. If you experience rewards related to some object, your attitude will be favorable. Thus, if your work provides you with good pay, a sense of accomplishment, and compliments from your coworkers, your attitude toward it will be quite positive. Conversely, if you associate negative emotions or unpleasant outcomes with some object, you will dislike it. If you experience frequent embarrassment in your human sexuality class or have struggled to stay awake while doing the course reading and scored poorly on every test and assignment, you are likely to have a very negative attitude toward the course.

However, only a small portion of our attitudes are based on direct contact with objects. We can also acquire attitudes and prejudices toward objects through classical conditioning, in which a stimulus gradually elicits a response through repeated association with other stimuli. Children learn at an early age that "lazy," "dirty," "stupid," and many other characteristics are undesirable. Children themselves are often punished for being dirty or hear adults say, "Don't be stupid!" If they hear their parents (or others) refer to members of a particular group as lazy or stupid, children increasingly associate the group name with the negative reactions these terms initially elicited. Several experiments have shown that classical conditioning can produce negative attitudes toward groups (Lohr & Staats, 1973; Staats & Staats, 1958). Furthermore, these learned associations play an important role in the automatic (low-effort) processing and unconscious reactions to stimuli (Moskowitz, Skurnik, & Galinsky, 1999). In other words, these attitudes affect our behavior regardless of whether we realize we have them (see Box 7.1 and the photos on p. 248).

We also learn attitudes more directly by observing others and interacting with them. For example, we acquire many of our attitudes from our parents. Research shows that children's attitudes toward gender roles, divorce, and politics frequently are similar to those held by their parents (Glass, Bengston, & Dunham, 1986; Sinclair, Dunn, & Lowery, 2005; Thornton, 1984). This is in part because of observational learning, but the similarity between parents' and children's attitudes may also be a product of instrumental learning because parents typically reward their children—consciously or unconsciously—for adopting the same or similar attitudes. Friends are another important source of our attitudes. The attitude that the drinking age should be lowered, for example, may be learned through interaction with peers.

Many of us grow up in homogeneous settings, within families that are similar to us and among neighbors and friends who hold both similar attributes (race, social class) and attitudes. However, when we attend college, we often encounter people—both students and faculty—who are quite different from us. This is one of the reasons significant attitude shifts often occur during young adulthood. A classic study of Bennington College women by Newcomb (1943) demonstrated the impact of peers on the political attitudes of college students. Although the majority of these women grew up in wealthy, politically conservative families, most of the faculty—and a number of students—at Bennington had very liberal political attitudes. The study demonstrated that first-year students who maintained close ties with their families and did not become involved in campus activities remained conservative. However, women who became active in the college community and interacted more frequently with other students and with faculty gradually became more liberal.

Another source of attitudes is the media, especially television and films. The media provide interpretive packages or frames about objects that may influence viewers' and readers' attitudes. By portraying events and actors in certain ways, TV news, news

BOX 7.1 Research Update: The Implicit Associations Test

Social psychologists are increasingly aware that people are sometimes unwilling—and often unable—to report their attitudes on surveys. Although people's unwillingness often stems from concerns about political correctness, their inability to report attitudes has also been attributed to people's limited awareness of those attitudes. When it comes to attitudes—in the words of dual-process theories—some them are low-effort rather than high-effort.

Although these automatic or implicit attitudes are beyond our consciousness, they profoundly influence our perceptions and behavior. For social scientists to fully explore the impact of implicit attitudes on social life, they had to find a way to measure them. To do that, they developed the Implicit Associations Test (IAT).

The IAT is a computerized test that measures individuals' response latencies when they encounter attitude-consistent and attitude-inconsistent stimuli. For example, if someone holds the attitude that men are more inclined toward math and science and that women are more inclined to the humanities and liberal arts, they should be able to process information linking men and math (attitude-consistent) more quickly than they would women and science (attitude-inconsistent) and, therefore, have a shorter response latency.

To test this, the IAT has subjects complete a number of blocks. First, respondents are asked to use two keys (often E and I) to classify exemplars of two contrasted concepts (for example, men and women's names). The next block will, once again, ask respondents to use the keys to classify exemplars of contrasted concepts (for example, algebra and English). The third and fourth blocks are combined tasks, in which all four exemplars are shown in various combinations, and respondents are explicitly instructed on how to classify objects (to categorize men's names and science and math subjects using E and women's names and humanities and liberal arts classes using I). If they hold implicit attitudes that are consistent with these pairings, they should be able to complete this task more quickly (and with fewer errors) than they will the final block (in which the pairing will be reversed). In the last block, the same key will be used for women's names as for science and math and another key for both men's names and humanities and liberal arts.

If a respondent possesses an attitude—even an unconscious one—they have a mental association between the affective or cognitive component of the attitude (academic strengths) and the attitude object (gender). The implicit association is able to gauge that mental association by comparing individuals' response latencies in the third and fourth blocks and then considering the number of errors (Greenwald, Nosek, Banaji, 2003).

The IAT has been used to measure a variety of implicit attitudes—including racial stereotypes, ageism, and gender roles. It is particularly useful for socially sensitive topics, in which respondents' concerns about impression management might distort their self-report responses. Research finds that the IAT is often more predictive of behavior than self-reports.

You can try the IAT yourself by visiting http://implicit.harvard.edu.

Source: Adapted from Greenwald, Poehlmann, Uhlmann, & Banaji, 2009.

magazines, and newspapers can produce cognitive images that influence attitudes. For example, television coverage of racially charged riots depicting a racial group as being volatile, dangerous, or unreasonable fosters negative attitudes toward that group (Myers & Caniglia, 2004). Similarly, portrayals of families of various social classes—such as *The Real Housewives* or *Roseanne*—shape viewers' attitudes toward those groups, whether positive or negative (Kendall, 2011).

Left: Two residents wade through chest-deep water after finding bread and soda from a local grocery store after Hurricane Katrina came through the area on August 29, 2005, in New Orleans, Louisiana. Katrina was downgraded to a category 4 storm as it approached New Orleans. © AP Photo/Dave Martin

Above: A young man walks through chest-deep flood water after looting a grocery store in New Orleans on Tuesday, August 30, 2005. Flood waters continue to rise in New Orleans after Hurricane Katrina did extensive damage when it made landfall on Monday. © Chris Graythen/Getty Images

Implicit associations were likely at play when the same behavior (taking items from stores) was described in one news agency photo caption (left) as "finding" when attributed to Whites and in another caption (right) as "looting" when attributed to Blacks.

The Functions of Attitudes

We acquire attitudes through learning, but there would be no reason to retain them—and to draw on them so frequently—if they did not serve at least some important functions (Katz, 1960; Pratkanis & Greenwald, 1989).

The first is the heuristic function. Once they are developed, attitudes provide a simple and efficient means of evaluating objects (Fazio, 1995). Attitudes help us decide whether objects are something we want to approach or avoid (Ajzen & Sexton, 1999). Because the world is too complex for us to completely understand, we group people, objects, and events into categories or schemas and develop simplified (stereotyped) attitudes that allow us to treat individuals as members of a category. Our attitudes about that category (object) provide us with meaning—a basis for making inferences

about that category's members. The affective and cognitive components of our attitudes influence our behavior (Bodenhausen & Wyer, 1985; Fiske, Lin, & Neuberg, 1999). Reacting to every member of the group in the same way is more efficient, even if less accurate and satisfying, than trying to learn about each person as an individual.

Stereotypes of groups are often associated with intense emotions. A strong like or dislike for members of a specific group is called a **prejudice**. Prejudice and stereotyping (discussed in Chapter 6) go together, with people using their stereotyped beliefs to justify prejudice toward members of the group. The emotional component of prejudice can lead to intergroup conflict (see Chapter 13).

Second, attitudes define the self and maintain self-worth. Some attitudes express an individual's basic values and reinforce his or her self-image. Think about your musical tastes, your attitudes toward particular music. What does your dislike of rap or your love of country or your tolerance of "anything but heavy metal" say about you (Bryson, 1996)? We tend to adopt attitudes we see as consistent with our identities. For example, many political conservatives in our society have negative attitudes toward abortion, immigration, and government-sponsored entitlement programs that help the poor. Thus, a person whose self-concept includes conservatism might adopt these attitudes because they align with that self-image.

Even if an individual never gave a particular attitude much thought, he or she will see attitudes as symbolic of his or her identification with or membership in particular groups or subcultures. A first-year student at Notre Dame who never gave a thought to football might suddenly adopt the attitude that the Fighting Irish are the best football team ever simply because it is consistent with his self-image as a member of the Notre Dame community. The attitudes "Guns don't kill people; people kill people" and "The only way to stop a bad guy with a gun is a good guy with a gun" are widespread among members of the National Rifle Association (NRA). Holding these attitudes may be both a prerequisite to acceptance by other group members and a symbol of loyalty to the group.

Finally, some attitudes protect the person from recognizing certain thoughts or feelings that threaten his or her self-image. For instance, Sarah may have received a negative performance review at work. In order to maintain a positive self-image, she may adopt attitudes that shift the blame toward other entities (van Dellen, Campbell, Hoyle, & Bradfield, 2011). If she originally held a positive attitude toward her job or her manager, she might adopt a more negative one instead, thinking "that job is not fulfilling" or "my manager fails to appre-

ciate me." Research indicates that experiences that threaten a person's self-esteem are particularly likely to lead to a more negative evaluation of other groups (Crocker, Thompson, McGraw, & Ingerman, 1987). This is particularly true among people who have high self-esteem. If self-esteem is already low, there is no reason to shift attitudes to protect it.

ATTITUDE ORGANIZATION

Attitude Structure

Have you ever tried to change another person's attitude toward an object (global warming) or a behavior (recycling)? If you have, you probably discovered that the person had a counterargument for almost every argument you put forth. She or he probably had several reasons why her or his attitude was correct. This tendency flows from how attitudes are arranged in our minds. Attitudes are usually embedded in a cognitive structure, linked with a variety of other attitudes. Not only would changing one attitude require shifting a slew of other attitudes, but the other attitudes also work as a support structure to keep the original attitude intact.

We can often discover which other cognitive elements are related to a particular attitude by asking the person why he or she holds that attitude. Consider the following interview:

INTERVIEWER: Why do you think same-sex marriage should be legal?

JUSTIN: Because the Constitution's Bill of Rights says that all Americans should have equal rights and protections. To exclude same-sex couples from the rights and protections of marriage is unfair.

INTERVIEWER: Are there any other reasons?

JUSTIN: Well, I think children do best in homes with two parents, and marriage would encourage more people to stay together and raise their children.

INTERVIEWER: Any other reasons?

JUSTIN: Um ... yeah. I believe that who we are attracted to is not usually a choice. I have always been attracted to women. I was born that way. Why is someone who is attracted to the same sex any different? Shouldn't we all be able to marry who we love?

This exchange indicates Justin's reasons for his attitude. More than that, it illustrates the two basic dimensions of attitude organization: vertical and horizontal structure (Bem, 1970).

Vertical Structure. Justin's favorable attitude toward same-sex marriage is rooted in his belief that all citizens of the United States should have equal rights and protections. Justin's attitude toward same-sex marriage ultimately rests on his belief in equality, which stems from his acceptance of the Constitution. The unquestioning acceptance of the credibility of some authority, such as the Constitution, is termed a **primitive belief** (Bem, 1970).

Attitudes are organized hierarchically. Some attitudes (primitive beliefs) are more fundamental than others. The linkages between fundamental beliefs and minor beliefs in cognitive structure are considered *vertical*. Vertical linkages signify that a minor belief is derived from or dependent on a primitive belief. Such a structure is portrayed in the center of Figure 7.1.

A fundamental or primitive belief, such as a belief in the Constitution, is often the basis for a large number of specific or minor beliefs (Bem, 1970). For example, Justin probably supports the democratic political system in the United States, freedom of speech, and race and gender equality. Changing a primitive belief may result in widespread changes in the person's atti-

tudes. If Justin were to align himself with the Chinese Communist Party and declare the U.S. Constitution untenable and unreasonable, the change in his primitive beliefs will likely lead to changed attitudes toward many objects, including his views of democracy, freedom of speech, and equality.

Horizontal Structure. When the interviewer asked Justin why he supports same-sex marriage, Justin gave two other reasons. One was his belief that it is best for children to be raised in homes with two adults and that marriage encourages couple to stay together. The other reason was his belief that attraction is something we are born with, not a choice, and that we should be able to marry the people we love. These belief structures are portrayed in the right-hand and left-hand columns of Figure 7.1. When an attitude is linked to more than one set of underlying beliefs—that is, when there are two or more different justifications for it— the linkages are termed *horizontal*.

An attitude with two or more horizontal linkages, or justifications, is more difficult to change than one based on a single primitive belief. Even if you show Justin statistical evidence that couples are no more likely to stay together if married than if simply cohabiting, his belief in equality and the roots of romantic attraction make it unlikely his attitude toward same-sex marriage will change.

Studying links like these is one way to identify attitude structures. A different approach to study how close attitudes are to one another is to measure response latency—how long it takes a person to reply to an attitude question—like the IAT (Box 7.1) does. What is your attitude toward homosexuality? What is your attitude toward vegetarians? Chances are it took you longer to retrieve from memory your attitude toward vegetarians. Your attitudes about sexual behavior were primed or activated

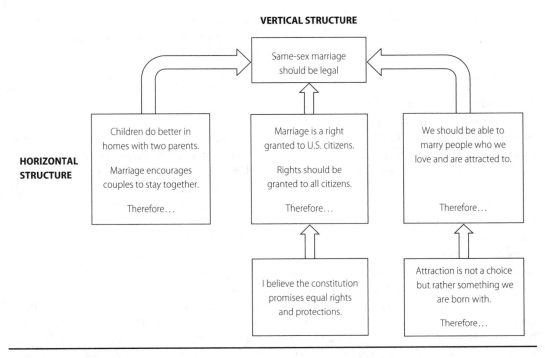

FIGURE 7.1 The Structure of Attitudes

by our discussion of same-sex marriage and should be associated with short latencies. The shorter the latency, the closer two attitudes are in a person's attitude structure (Judd, Drake, Downing, & Krosnick, 1991).

COGNITIVE CONSISTENCY

Alysia lives a "green" life. She composts and recycles. She has her own garden and thinks organic produce is better than nonorganic options. She identifies as an environmentalist and believes she is intentional about her consumption and waste patterns. These beliefs (we should be intentional consumers) and attitudes (organic is better than nonorganic) fit together. It is not surprising that Alysia perceives both as applying to her. Many of her attitudes and behaviors are also consistent with what she perceives as green or environmentalist. For example, she prefers to give handmade, wooden toys

to her nieces for gifts rather than mass-produced plastic toys, and she likes to purchase her clothes at thrift stores and second-hand shops.

Consistency among a person's cognitions—that is, their beliefs and attitudes—is widespread. If you have liberal political values, you probably favor housing assistance programs for people living in poverty. If you value public education, you are likely to support a property-tax increase to generate additional revenue for the local schools or choose to send your children to public schools rather than to a private school in the area. Cognitions are usually consistent because people are motivated to maintain that consistency. If an inconsistency develops between cognitive elements—for example, if you value public education yet oppose a tax increase or decide to enroll your children in private school—you will be motivated to restore harmony between those elements. Several theories of attitude organization are based on this principle of consistency.

Balance Theory

One important consistency theory is **balance theory**. This theory was originally formulated by Heider (1958) and later elaborated by Rosenberg and Abelson (1960) to explain how we seek consistency in three-element cognitive structures.

Balance theory is concerned with cognitive systems like this one: "I'm going to vote for Liz Brown. Like me, she is also in favor of reducing taxes." This system contains three elements—the speaker, another person (candidate Liz Brown), and an impersonal object (taxes). According to balance theory, two types of relationships may exist between elements—*unit relations* and *sentiment relations*. Unit relations describe the relationship between two elements (ownership, proximity) that are nonevaluative. Sentiment relations are evaluative and based on positive or negative evaluation. For example, a positive sentiment relation may result from a social relationship (such as friendship or marriage) between elements. A negative sentiment relation indicates not only dissociation, like that between ex-spouses or members of groups with opposing interests, but also a negative evaluation of that other element—"I don't like my ex-husband" or "I hate those greedy politicians."

Using these terms, let's analyze the above example. We can depict this system as a triangle (see Figure 7.2). Balance theory is concerned with the elements and their interrelations from the speaker's viewpoint. In our first example (Figure 7.2a), the speaker favors reduced taxes, perceives Liz Brown as favoring reduced taxes, and, therefore, intends to vote for Brown. This system is balanced. By definition, a balanced state is one in which all three sentiment relations are positive or in which one is positive and

the other two are negative. For example, this system would also be balanced if the speaker still favored reduced taxes (+) and, therefore, decided not to vote for Liz Brown (–) because she was opposed to reducing taxes (–) (Figure 7.2b).

Imbalance and Change. According to balance theory, an imbalanced state is one in which two of the relationships between elements are positive and one is negative or in which all three are negative. This is easiest to illustrate with friendships. Consider Haley and Ellen, who are starting their junior year in high school. They have been friends since fifth grade and spend all their free time together. This past summer, Haley grew close to Aaliyah, another girl at their high school, while working together at a local day camp. Ellen thinks Aaliyah is a gossip and does not like her. Figure 7.2c illustrates the situation from Haley's viewpoint. Haley feels positively toward Ellen and Aaliyah, but Ellen is not positive toward Aaliyah. Thus, there is an imbalance.

In general, an imbalanced situation like this is unpleasant. Balance theory assumes that people will try to restore balance among their attitudes. There are three basic ways to do this.

First, Haley may change her attitudes so the sign of one of the relations is reversed (Tyler & Sears, 1977). For instance, she may decide that she really does not like Aaliyah (Figure 7.2d). Alternatively, Haley may decide that she and Ellen have grown apart and she does not like her as much as she used to, or she may persuade Ellen to give Aaliyah a chance and to get to know her better so she can see how wrong her initial impressions are. Each of these involves changing one relationship so the system of beliefs contains either zero or two negative relationships.

Second, Haley can restore balance by changing a positive or negative relation to

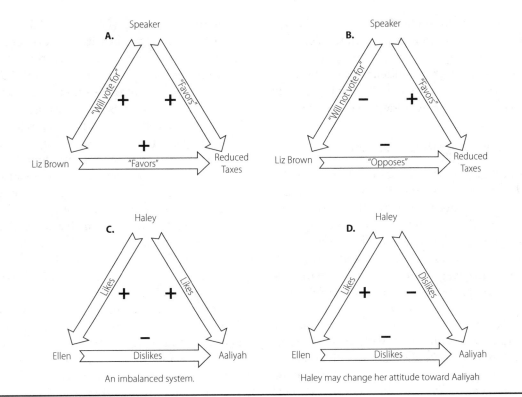

FIGURE 7.2 Balanced Cognitive Systems and Resolution of Imbalanced Systems

When the relationships among all three cognitive elements are positive (A) or when one relationship is positive and the other two are negative (B), the cognitive system is balanced. When two relationships are positive and one negative, the cognitive system is imbalanced. In (C), Ellen's negative attitude toward Aaliyah creates an unpleasant psychological state for Haley. Haley can resolve the imbalance by deciding she does not want to be friends with Aaliyah (D), deciding she does not like Ellen anymore, or persuading Ellen to like Aaliyah.

a null relation (Steiner & Rogers, 1963). Haley may decide that Ellen doesn't know anything about Aaliyah and her attitude toward her is irrelevant.

Third, Haley can restore balance by differentiating the attributes of the other person or object (Stroebe, Thompson, Insko, & Reisman, 1970). For instance, Haley may distinguish between types of friends—work friends, who you share few personal details with, and close friends, who you can trust with anything. Ellen might be correct in her belief that Aaliyah is a gossip. However, Haley believes she can be friends with both if she is careful what she shares with Aaliyah

so as to protect herself (and if she tells Ellen that this is her intention).

Which technique will a person use to remove the imbalance? Balance is usually restored by whatever means are easiest (Rosenberg & Abelson, 1960). If one relationship is weaker than the other two, the easiest mode of restoring balance is to change the weaker relationship (Feather, 1967). Because Haley and Ellen have been friends for over five years, it would be very difficult for Haley to change her sentiments toward Ellen; it would be easier for her to change her attitude toward Aaliyah. However, Haley really likes both girls and would prefer to maintain both friendships. Therefore, she may attempt to change Ellen's attitude, perhaps by differentiating the object (Aaliyah). If this influence attempt fails, theory suggests that Haley will probably change her own attitude toward Aaliyah.

Theory of Cognitive Dissonance

Another major consistency theory is the **theory of cognitive dissonance**. Whereas balance theory deals with the relationships among three cognitions, dissonance theory deals with consistency between two or more elements (behaviors and attitudes). For example, given Alysia's attitude toward intentional, environmentally sound consumption, we would never expect her to buy an SUV. If she did, then her behavior would be inconsistent with her attitudes, and this would likely cause her dissonance.

There are two situations in which dissonance commonly occurs: (1) after a decision, or (2) when one acts in a way that is inconsistent with one's beliefs.

Postdecisional Dissonance. Taylor will begin his sophomore year of college next week. He needs to work part time so he can pay for school. After two weeks of searching for work, he receives two offers. One is a part-time job doing library research for a faculty member he admires, and it pays $7 per hour with flexible working hours. The other is a job in a restaurant as a busser that pays $10 per hour but has set working hours—5 p.m. to 11 p.m., Thursdays, Fridays, and Saturdays. He has no experience bussing tables.

Taylor has a hard time choosing between these jobs. Both are located near campus, and he thinks he would like either one. Whereas the research job offers flexible hours, the busser's job pays more and offers him the opportunity to meet interesting people. In the end, Taylor chooses the bussing job, but he is experiencing dissonance.

Dissonance theory (Festinger, 1957) assumes there are three possible relationships between any two cognitions. Cognitions are consistent or consonant if one naturally or logically follows from the other. They are dissonant when one is inconsistent with the other. The logic involved is psycho logic (Rosenberg & Abelson, 1960)—that is, logic as it appears to the individual, not logic in a formal sense. Two cognitive elements also may be irrelevant; one may have nothing to do with the other. In Taylor's case, the decision to take the position clearing tables is consonant with (1) the job's convenient location, (2) the higher pay, and (3) the opportunities to meet people, but it is dissonant with the fact that (1) he is unsure of his ability to bus tables and (2) he has to work weekend nights and will miss out on hanging out with his friends (see Figure 7.3).

Having made the choice, Taylor is experiencing **cognitive dissonance**, a state of psychological tension induced by dissonant relationships between cognitive elements. Some decisions produce a large amount of cognitive dissonance, others very little. The magnitude of dissonance experienced depends in part on the proportion of elements that are dissonant with a person's decision. In Taylor's case, there are three consonant and only two dissonant cognitions, so he will only experience moderate dissonance. The magnitude is also influenced by the importance of the elements. He will experience less dissonance if it is not very important to hang out with his friends on the weekends but more dissonance if an active social life on weekends is important to him.

Dissonance is an uncomfortable state. To reduce dissonance, the theory predicts, Taylor will change his attitudes by changing either the cognitive elements themselves or the importance of the elements.

It is hard to change cognitions. He chose the restaurant job, and he made a commitment to work weekend nights and to take a

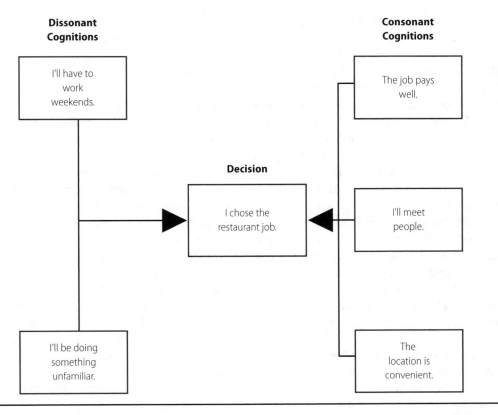

Dissonant Cognitions

I'll have to work weekends.

I'll be doing something unfamiliar.

Consonant Cognitions

The job pays well.

I'll meet people.

The location is convenient.

Decision

I chose the restaurant job.

FIGURE 7.3 Postdecisional Dissonance

Whenever we make a decision, there are some cognitions—attitudes, beliefs, knowledge—that are consonant with that decision and other cognitions that are dissonant with it. Dissonant cognitions create an unpleasant psychological state that we are motivated to reduce or eliminate. In this example, Taylor has chosen a job and is experiencing dissonance. Although three cognitions are consistent with his decision, two other dissonant cognitions are creating psychological tension.

job he had no experience in. Alternatively, Taylor can rationalize his choice by changing the relative importance of his cognitions. He can emphasize the importance of one or more of the consonant cognitions and deemphasize one or more of the dissonant cognitions. Although he has to do a job that is unfamiliar to him, he can emphasize the fact that it pays well. Although he would prefer to be able to go out on weekends, he can decide that this is less important because the restaurant job will still allow him to meet interesting people.

Decisions often result in dissonance. Regardless of the job he decided to take,

Taylor would have to work to reduce dissonance. If he had decided, instead, to do research for his professor, he would still experience dissonance because he chose to forgo the more lucrative position even though he needs money to stay in school. He would still try to rationalize his choice to reduce dissonance. It would probably work. If you asked him soon after he started his job if he would make the same decision again, he would likely say he would (Wee, 2013).

Elias Dinas (2013) argues that postdecisional dissonance (Brehm, 1956) and the cognitive efforts individuals use to reduce that dissonance partially explains the

effects of voting on subsequent party identification. Although some may argue that
party identification comes first, influencing
who one votes for, Dinas argues that consistency theories provide a compelling argument for how voting can lead to party
identification. Voting demands constituents choose from a number of alternatives. When we have a number of objects
to choose from, we are more likely to engage in rationalization for our final choice.
We might rationalize a vote for a political
candidate by seeing that candidate as more
attractive somehow and aligning oneself
with the party the candidate represents.
Once aligned, the constituent is more likely
to vote for candidates in that party, and
each vote choice further fortifies the voter's
identification with the political party.

Counterattitudinal Behavior. Dissonance
can also occur when we behave in ways that
are inconsistent with our attitudes. Such
situations may involve forced compliance—
that is, pressures on a person to comply
with a request to engage in counterattitudinal behavior (Joule and Azdia, 2003).

Imagine you have volunteered to serve
in a psychology experiment. You arrive at
the lab and are told you are participating
in a study of performance. You are given a
pegboard and told to turn each peg exactly
one-quarter turn. After you have turned the
last peg, you are told to start over, to turn
each peg another one-quarter turn. Later
you are told to remove each peg from the
pegboard and then to put each peg back.
After an hour of such activity, the experimenter indicates you are finished. The
experimenter says, "We are comparing
the performance of participants who are
briefed in advance with that of others who
are not briefed. You did not receive a brief-
ing. The next participant is supposed to be
briefed, but my assistant who usually does
this couldn't come to work today." He then
asks you to help out by telling a waiting participant that the tasks you have just completed were fun and exciting. For your help,
he offers you either $1 or $20.

In effect, you are being asked to lie—to
say the boring and monotonous tasks you
just performed were enjoyable. If you actually tell the next participant the tasks are
fun, you may experience cognitive dissonance afterward. Your behavior is inconsistent with your attitude about the task (that
it is boring). Moreover, lying to the next
participant is dissonant with your beliefs
about yourself (that you are moral and honest). To reduce dissonance, you can change
one of the cognitions. Which one will you
change? You cannot change your awareness
that you told the next participant the task
is fun. The only cognition open to change
is your attitude toward the task, which can
change in the direction of greater liking for
the task.

The theory of cognitive dissonance predicts (1) that you will change your attitudes
toward the tasks (like them better), and (2)
that the amount of change will depend on
the incentive you were paid to tell the lie.
Specifically, the theory predicts that greater
attitude change will occur when the incentive to tell the lie is low ($1) rather than high
($20), because you will experience greater
dissonance under low incentive than you
would under high incentive and will, therefore, be more motivated to change your
attitude.

These predictions were tested in a classic experiment by Festinger and Carlsmith
(1959). Participants in the experiment
completed the boring peg task and, when
asked by the experimenter to brief the next
participant, most agreed. The participants
told the next person who arrived at the laboratory that the experimental tasks were
interesting and they had fun doing them.
A secretary then asked each participant to
fill out a postexperimental questionnaire

on which they would rate the experiment and the tasks. These ratings provided the measures of the dependent variable. As expected, control participants who did not brief anyone and were not offered money rated the tasks as very unenjoyable and did not want to participate in the experiment again.

What about the participants who were paid money to tell a lie? For those receiving $20, the situation was not very dissonant. The money provided ample justification for engaging in counterattitudinal behavior (lying). You could think to yourself that you were being paid to act, not to tell the truth. In the $1 condition, however, the participants experienced greater dissonance because they did not have the justification for lying that the large amount of money provided. These participants could not deny they lied, so they reduced dissonance by changing their attitude—that is, by increasing their liking for the task and the experiment. The results of this study confirmed the predictions from dissonance theory. Participants in the high-incentive ($20) condition experienced little dissonance and rated the task and experiment negatively on the postexperimental questionnaire, whereas those in the low-incentive ($1) condition experienced more dissonance and rated the task and experiment positively.

Dissonance occurs only in some situations (Wicklund & Brehm, 1976). To experience dissonance, a person must be committed to a belief or course of action (Brehm & Cohen, 1962). Moreover, the person must believe that he or she chose to act voluntarily and is, thus, responsible for the outcome of the decision (Linder, Cooper, & Jones, 1967). This is shown in the case of Taylor, who chose the job bussing tables. If the owner of the restaurant were Taylor's father who demanded he work for him, Taylor would have had little or no postdecisional dissonance because

Psychologists find that hand washing helps ease the postdecisional dissonance people feel after making a choice between two alternatives (Lee & Schwarz, 2010). They believe that physical cleansing helps people feel psychologically cleansed, like they have wiped the slate clean. © snokid/iStock

he could blame his father for the choice he made. Likewise, if the experimenter had forced the participants to lie—rather than asking whether they would be willing to help—the level of dissonance would have been lower.

Researchers have found that some individuals—referred to as maximizers—are more prone to postdecisional dissonance than others. Maximizers are individuals who always strive to make the best possible decision. Conversely satisficers are people who will be content with an option as long as it is good enough (B. Schwartz, 2004). Standing in front of the cereal aisle, a satisficer would simply be focused on choosing a box of cereal they like. A maximizer would be focused on choosing the best of all the cereal options. When it comes to making choices, maximizers engage in more predecision fact finding, perceive more time pressure, experience more postdecisional dissonance and dissatisfaction, and are more likely to change their initial choices if given the opportunity to do so than are satisficers (Chowdhury, Ratneshwar, & Mohanty, 2009; Misuraca & Teuscher, 2013).

BOX 7.2 Selling with Cognitive Dissonance

Cognitive dissonance is a ubiquitous part of our daily lives. We encounter it almost wherever we go and in almost whatever we do. One social interaction in which we are very likely to encounter cognitive dissonance is when we encounter a salesperson—particularly one who uses high-pressure sales techniques, such as in automobile sales. Many sales techniques have harnessed the power of cognitive dissonance and use it to increase the chances of convincing the customer to buy. How does this occur?

First, salespeople often make use of a technique called the "foot-in-the-door" (Freedman & Fraser, 1966). In this case, the salesperson attempts to get the customer to agree to some kind of small request and, having established a pattern of compliance, will ask the customer to do bigger things, including purchasing the product. Salespeople might request an appointment at your home, ask you to fill out paperwork, or get you to take a test drive. This is one of the reasons so many businesses will offer free estimates to potential clients. Once the small request is fulfilled, an inconsistency is produced if you do not go ahead and buy the product (Burger, 1986, 1999). Your refusal to buy causes some dissonance because it is inconsistent with your previous compliant behavior. Of course, this is not always enough to get you to buy, but it can reduce sales resistance.

A second technique, often used by unscrupulous salespeople, is called "low-balling" (Burger & Petty, 1981; Weyant, 1996). In this technique, the salesperson will offer the buyer a very good price on a product. The buyer agrees, and the salesperson sets about to do all the paperwork. Before it is completed, though, the salesperson "discovers" that he or she has made an error and that the price is going to be higher than initially promised. Under these circumstances, the buyer has a tendency to accept the higher price; after all, he or she has already agreed to buy—why should a few more dollars make that much of a difference? Interestingly, though, social psychologists have found that buyers will often pay more than their original upper limit when confronted with the low-balling technique (Cialdini, 1993; Cialdini, Cacioppo, Basset, & Miller, 1978). If you walk into a car dealership knowing that you can buy a certain car for $20,000 elsewhere and are low-balled with an offer of $19,500, you may end up paying $20,500 for the car in the end!

In a third technique that involves consistency, salespeople usually work very hard to get us to like them (Gordon, 1996). In fact, they are often trained in many specific techniques to get buyers to feel like they are friends with the salesperson. It is no surprise that we are more likely to buy things from people we like than from people we do not like, but why does this occur? One reason is that refusing a request from someone we like is inconsistent with our liking them. When a friend asks us to purchase candy for a fundraiser, turning him or her down can be difficult because such behavior is incompatible with the friendship. Salespeople can use this underlying tendency to increase compliance as well (Jones, 1964; Liden & Mitchell, 1988).

THE RELATIONSHIP BETWEEN ATTITUDES AND BEHAVIOR

Do Attitudes Predict Behavior?

We have seen how our behavior can affect our attitudes and how people sometimes change their attitudes when their behavior appears to contradict those attitudes. However, many people think of attitudes as the source of behavior. We often assume that when we know a person's attitude toward an object or another person (a colleague, a political issue, a sports team), we can predict how that person will behave toward the object. If you know Haley likes Aaliyah, you would expect her to accept an invitation to Aaliyah's barbecue. If you know that Justin supports same-sex marriage, you would expect him to vote for a candidate who made that part of their political platform. If you know that I am a Mets fan, you would expect me not only to cheer for the Mets but also to root for any team playing against the Yankees. We like to predict others' behaviors so we can decide how to behave toward that person in order to achieve our own goals. But can we truly predict someone's behavior if we only know his or her attitudes?

In 1930, the social scientist Richard LaPiere traveled around the United States by car with a Chinese couple. At that time, there was considerable prejudice against the Chinese, particularly in the West. The three travelers stopped at more than 60 hotels, auto camps, and tourist homes as well as more than 180 restaurants. They kept careful notes about how they were treated. In all their travels and stops, they were only denied service once. Later, LaPiere sent a questionnaire to each place, asking whether they would accept Chinese guests. He received responses from 128 of the establishments; 92 percent of them indicated that they would *not* serve Chinese guests (LaPiere, 1934). Evidently there can be a great discrepancy between what people do and what they say.

Many studies on the topic have found only a modest correlation between attitude and behavior (Glasman & Albarracín, 2006). Several reasons have been suggested for this tenuous relationship. In this section, we consider four of these: (1) the accessibility and activation of the attitude, (2) the characteristics of the attitude, (3) the correspondence between attitude and behavior, and (4) situational constraints on behavior.

Accessibility and Activation of the Attitude

Each of us has thousands of attitudes. Most of the time, a particular attitude is not within our conscious awareness. Moreover, much of our behavior is mindless or spontaneous (Fazio, 1990). We act without thinking—that is, without considering our attitudes. For an attitude to influence behavior, it must be activated; it must be brought from memory into conscious awareness (Zanna & Fazio, 1982). The most accessible attitudes are most easily activated.

Attitudes become activated when something in the environment triggers them, like encountering the attitude object (Fazio & Towles-Schwen, 1999). For example, earlier sections of this chapter may have activated your attitudes toward many objects, such as the Yankees, snakes, same-sex marriage, and voting. These triggers are particularly effective if the attitude was originally formed through direct experience with the object (Fazio, Powell, & Herr, 1983). Thus, one way to activate attitudes is to arrange situations in which persons are exposed to the relevant objects. Soft lighting, a cozy fire, and glasses of wine are all associated with seduction; we often set up these cues in the hope of activating someone's positive attitudes toward romance and intimacy.

Attitudes differ in the ease with which they can be activated because they differ in accessibility. Some attitudes, such as stereotypes or a fear of snakes, are highly accessible and are activated automatically by the perception of the stereotyped object or the snake (Devine, 1989). These are often called implicit attitudes (Greenwald, Poehlman, Uhlmann, & Banaji, 2009). Other attitudes are situated deeper in our memory, making them less accessible and, therefore, activated more slowly (Fazio, Sanbonmatsu, Powell, & Kardes, 1986). It takes more than a brief encounter to activate these attitudes. You

might be able to provide an almost immediate reaction if someone asked you about
your favorite (or least favorite) restaurant in
town, but it would take you longer to access
an attitude toward a restaurant you were
less familiar with. The more accessible an
attitude is, the greater its influence on categorizing and judging objects (Smith, Fazio,
& Cejka, 1996). Applying this to restaurants
again, you are more likely to compare new
restaurants you visit to your favorite place
in town than to places you are less familiar
with because your attitude about the former
is more accessible than the latter.

Evidence also suggests that the more accessible an attitude, the more it is likely to
guide future behavior. This was shown, for
example, in a study of the impact of accessibility on voting in the 1984 presidential
election (Fazio & Williams, 1986). In June
and July 1984, 245 people were questioned
about their attitudes toward two presidential candidates (Ronald Reagan and Walter
Mondale). The latency of the answer—how
quickly the person replied to the question
about each candidate—was used as a measure of accessibility. After the election, each
person was asked whom he or she voted for.
The more accessible the attitude—that is,
the more quickly the person replied to the
original question about the candidate—the
more likely the person was to vote for that
same candidate in November.

Characteristics of the Attitude

The relationship between attitude and behavior is also affected by the nature of the
attitude itself. Four characteristics of attitudes may influence the attitude-behavior
relationship: (1) the degree of consistency
between the affective (evaluative) and the
cognitive components, (2) the extent to
which the attitude is grounded in personal
experience, (3) the strength of the attitude,
and (4) the attitude's stability.

Affective-Cognitive Consistency. The
beginning of the chapter introduced three
components of attitudes: cognition, evaluation (affect), and behavioral predisposition. When we consider the relation between attitude and behavior, we are looking
at the relationship between the first two
components and the third. Not surprisingly, research has shown that the degree of
consistency between the affective and cognitive components influences the attitude-
behavior relationship. That is, the greater
the consistency between cognition and
evaluation, the greater the strength of the
attitude-behavior relation.

Recall that the cognitive component is a
belief about the attitude object (for example, "My human sexuality course is boring.
The teacher drones on, and the text is too
difficult to read.") and the affective component is the emotion associated with the
object (for example, "I strongly dislike the
course."). In this case, there is a high degree
of affective-cognitive consistency. Now suppose another person also thinks the class is
boring but actually likes the course—perhaps because she is taking it with friends
or finds the subject matter is interesting.
Whose behavior could you confidently predict? The first person is much more likely to
skip class or to not do the reading than the
second person.

Social psychologists find that affective-cognitive consistency can predict intentions to help the poor (Tagler & Cozzarelli, 2013). Individuals' affective evaluations of the poor—if they described their
feelings toward the poor as positive or negative—were most likely to influence intentions to help the poor if individuals' cognitions about the poor were consistent with
those affective evaluations. For example,
if respondents who viewed the poor positively also believed that poverty was caused
by structural forces (see the discussion of
attributions for poverty in Chapter 6), their

affective evaluation and cognitions were consistent. If respondents thought that laziness or lack of effort contributes to poverty yet still viewed the poor positively, this suggested attitude inconsistency.

Affective-cognitive consistency not only predicts behavior but also increases the resistance of attitudes to change. When individuals have high affective-cognitive consistency, they tend to discredit information that is discrepant with their attitude or to minimize its importance. This makes attitudes more resistant to change.

Direct Experience. Suppose you have a positive attitude toward an activity based on having done it once, and your roommate has a positive attitude based on hearing you rave about it. Which of you is more likely to accept an invitation to engage in that activity?

One study (Regan & Fazio, 1977) provides an answer to this question. The behavior of interest was the proportion of time spent playing with several kinds of puzzles. Participants in the direct-experience condition played with sample puzzles; those in the indirect experience condition were given only descriptions of the puzzles. Researchers then asked participants to respond to some attitude measures and later gave participants an opportunity to play with the puzzles. Not surprisingly, they discovered that the average correlation between attitude and behavior was much higher for participants who had direct experience than for those who did not.

Attitudes based on direct experience are more predictive of subsequent behavior for a number of reasons (Fazio & Zanna, 1981). First, the best predictor of future behavior is past behavior; the more frequently you have played tennis in the past, the more likely you are to play it in the future (Fredricks & Dossett, 1983). Second, direct experience makes more information available

about the attitude object itself (Kelman, 1974). When we engage in planned and deliberate behavior, we draw on available information to choose the course of action. If we are using information we have about an attitude object to determine our behavior, there is likely to be a strong link between attitude and behavior (Fazio & Towles-Schwen, 1999). Third, attitudes based on direct experience with the object may be held with greater certainty—leading us to the third factor in the likelihood that attitudes influence behavior, attitude strength.

Strength. Suppose you ask two friends which candidate they like in the upcoming presidential election. One replies, "I'm voting for X!" The other hedges a bit, saying, "Well, maybe I'll vote for Y." Which person's behavior do you think you could predict? In general, the greater the strength of an attitude, the more likely it is to influence behavior. Studies of the link between attitudes toward candidates and subsequent voting behavior find that many of the errors in predictions occur among those who report indifference to the election—that is, people who hold weak or uncertain attitudes (Schuman & Johnson, 1976).

The relevance of an attitude—the extent to which the issue or object directly affects the person—also influences the strength of the attitude. Framing an issue in relevant terms (say, tuition increases on your college campus) brings to mind important consequences for you, such as the need for greater income or having to take out additional student loans. Framing it in irrelevant terms (say, tuition increases on campuses in Russia) may elicit no thought of personal consequences (Lieberman & Chaiken, 1996). When a political issue is relevant to an individual, there will be a much stronger relationship between attitudes and voting on the issue (Crano, 1997). This is, in part, because personal relevance increases attitude strength. Individuals who have a gay family member or friend are more likely not only to hold a more favorable attitude toward gays and lesbians but also to be more certain about that attitude (Herek & Capitanio, 1996).

As noted earlier in the chapter, certainty about an attitude is also influenced by whether affect or cognition was involved in the creation of the attitude. Attitudes formed based on affect (for example, fear of snakes) are more certain than attitudes based on cognition (for example, a preference for the Prius because it is the best hybrid car) (Edwards, 1990).

Attitude Stability. Most studies attempting to predict behavior from attitudes measure people's attitudes first and their behavior weeks or months later. A modest or small correlation may mean a weak attitude-behavior relationship—or it could mean people's attitudes have changed in the interim period. If the attitude changes after it is measured, the person's behavior may be consistent with his or her present attitude, although it appears inconsistent with our measure of the attitude.

In general, we would expect that the longer the time between the measurement of attitude and that of behavior, the more likely the attitude will change and the smaller the attitude-behavior relationship will be. In a study designed to test this possibility (Schwartz, 1978), an appeal was mailed to almost 300 students to volunteer as tutors for blind children. Earlier, students had filled out a questionnaire measuring general attitudes toward helping others, including questions about tutoring blind children. Some students had filled out the questionnaire six months earlier; some, three months earlier; some, both three and six months earlier; and still others had not seen the questionnaire. The correlation between attitude toward tutoring and actually volunteering was greater over the three-month period than over the six-month period. Thus, to avoid problems of temporal instability, the amount of time between the measurement of attitudes and that of behavior should be brief.

However, some attitudes evidence a remarkable degree of stability. Marwell, Aiken, and Demerath (1987) studied the political attitudes of 220 White young people who spent the summer of 1964 organizing Blacks in the South to vote. They measured the same attitudes of two-thirds of these activists two decades later, in 1984. The extreme radical attitudes these people held in 1965 had softened in the intervening 20 years, but in general these people remained liberal and committed to the needs of disadvantaged groups. This stability of their attitudes likely stemmed from the direct experience the activists had with the issues from their time in the South.

Attitude-Behavior Correspondence

Attitudes are more likely to predict behavior when the two are at the same level of specificity (Schuman & Johnson, 1976). For example, suppose you have invited a casual acquaintance to dinner, and you want to plan the menu. You know she likes an Italian restaurant in town, so you infer she likes Italian food. But can you predict with confidence that she will eat spinach noodles with clam sauce? Probably not. A favorable attitude toward a type of cuisine does not mean the person will eat every dish of that type.

Many studies have attempted to predict from general attitudes to specific behaviors (Ajzen, 1991; Green, 1972). For instance, some studies of families have tried to predict men's specific contributions to housework and childrearing (how often he vacuums or changes diapers, for example) from their gender role attitudes. Perhaps not

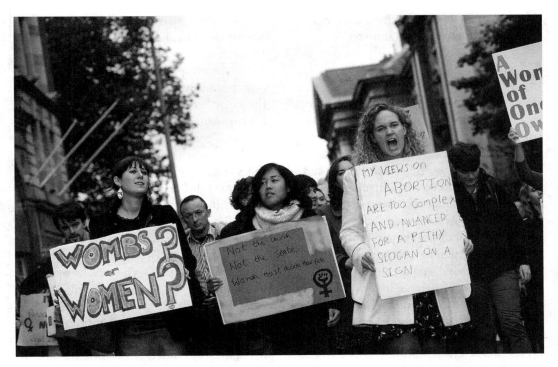

Although most Americans have attitudes about abortion, only a minority act on their beliefs like these demonstrators. People with strong attitudes, whether pro or con, are more likely to engage in such behavior. © wwwPhotographyServicesie/iStock

surprisingly, there is little congruence. Although many men express egalitarian gender role attitudes, this is generally not reflected in their specific gender role behavior (Araji, 1977). A general attitude is a summary of many feelings either about an object under a variety of conditions or about a whole class of objects. Logically, it should not predict behavior in any particular single situation. However, it might predict a composite measure of several relevant behaviors (Weigel & Newman, 1976). For example, although a man with egalitarian attitudes may do little more vacuuming than a man with more traditional gender role attitudes, he may be engaged in other egalitarian behaviors or have a less-gendered division of labor on the whole in his household than the more traditional man.

What about predicting a specific behavior, such as whether your Italian food–

loving guest will eat spinach noodles and clam sauce? Just as general attitudes best predict a composite index of behavior, we need a specific measure of attitude to predict a specific behavior. We can think of an attitude and a behavior as having four elements: an action (eating), an object or target (spinach noodles and clam sauce), a context (in your home), and a time (tomorrow night). The greater the degree of **correspondence**—that is, the number of elements that are the same in the attitude and the behavior—the better we can predict behavior from attitudes (Ajzen & Fishbein, 1977). If you know that your casual acquaintance likes to eat (correspondent action) spinach noodles (correspondent object) for dinner (correspondent time) at the Italian restaurant (noncorrespondent context), you can better predict her behavior than if all you know is that she likes to eat (correspondent action) at the Italian restaurant (noncorrespondent context).

Situational Constraints

If you believe tuition increases at your college are necessary to maintain the quality of your education—to retain the best faculty, provide ready access to books, journals, and computers, and so on—and you attend a meeting of Students for Educational Quality, your behavior reflects your attitude.

Suppose, however, that you oppose tuition increases but find yourself in a conversation with a date who expresses support for the increases. Would you voice your opposition—that is, behave in a manner consistent with your attitudes—or not? Your reaction would probably depend partly on the strength and certainty of your attitude (Pratkanis & Greenwald, 1989). If you are strongly opposed to tuition increases, you may speak your mind. But if you are moderately opposed, you may decide to avoid an argument and behave in a way that is inconsistent with your attitude. In LaPiere's study discussed earlier, for instance, hotel and restaurant employees confronted by a White man and a Chinese couple may have felt compelled to serve them rather than run the risk of creating a scene by refusing to do so.

Situational constraint refers to an influence on behavior due to the likelihood that other persons will learn about the behavior and respond positively or negatively to it. Situational constraints often determine whether our behavior is consistent with our attitudes. In fact, how we behave is frequently a result of the interaction between our attitudes and the constraints present in the situation (Warner & DeFleur, 1969; Klein, Snyder, & Livingston, 2004). The greater the agreement among others about how we should behave, the greater the situational constraint on persons whose atti-

tudes are inconsistent with the situational norms (Schutte, Kendrick, & Sadalla, 1985). In other words, you would be more likely to share your opposition in conversation with one friend who supported the increases than you would if you were in a group of four in which the other three were in support and you were the only opposed.

The greater the situational constraint, the weaker the relationship is between attitudes and behavior. Consequently, the less visible our behavior is to others, the more likely our behavior and attitudes will be consistent (Acock & Scott, 1980). With respect to attitudes about race and gender, many scholars who study prejudice have noted a shift in how people express prejudicial attitudes. As the social environment has become less accepting of overt expressions of racism and sexism, people may have responded to the situational constraints by hiding their attitudes and finding different, more subtle ways of expressing prejudice (Gawronski & Strack, 2004). This has shifted how we measure attitudes related to racism, sexism, and other socially sensitive attitudes (see Box 7.1) and how we think about sexism (and racism) in society (see Box 7.3).

Reference Groups

Several studies have assessed the impact of reference groups on the attitude-behavior relationship. Such research involves measuring participants' attitudes and behaviors toward some object and then asking them to indicate the positions of various social groups regarding that object.

One survey assessed adults' attitudes toward drinking alcoholic beverages and the degree to which their friends approved of drinking (Rabow, Neuman, & Hernandez, 1987). When attitudes and social support were congruent—that is, when the respondents' and their friends' views about drinking were the same—there was a much stronger relation between attitudes and behavior than when attitudes and social support were not congruent. We are much more likely to act in ways that are consistent with our attitudes when people who we perceive as members of our in-group hold similar attitudes (Terry & Hogg, 1996; White, Hogg, & Terry, 2002).

THE REASONED ACTION MODEL

In the preceding sections, we identified several influences on the relationship between a single attitude and behavior. However, at times, an object or situation may elicit multiple attitudes. In these cases, predicting behavior is more difficult. When several attitudes are invoked, the individual often engages in deliberative processing of information (Fazio, 1990). He or she considers the attributes of the object or situation, the relevant attitudes, and the costs and benefits of potential behaviors. The **theory of reasoned action**, developed by Fishbein and Ajzen (1975; Ajzen & Fishbein, 1980), considers the influence of these factors in the link between attitudes and behavior. This model is based on assumptions of a dual-process model: While some behavior based on attitudes is relatively automatic—jumping at a snake, for instance—other behavior based on attitudes—voting for a political candidate—is quite deliberate (Ajzen & Sexton, 1999).

According to the reasoned action model, behavior is determined by behavioral intention. This intention stems from a consideration of (1) an attitude about performing the specific behavior and (2) **subjective norms** (an individual's perception of others' beliefs about whether a behavior is appropriate as well as their motivation to comply with those expectations). It is important to note that the attitudes here are not general at-

titudes about an object ("The Toyota Prius is the best hybrid car") but rather attitudes about performing a particular behavior ("I want to buy a Prius instead of a Corolla"). This attitude is influenced by a person's beliefs about the likely consequences of the behavior and a person's evaluation—positive or negative—of each of those outcomes. Individuals systematically weigh what they know to be outcomes of engaging in the behavior they are considering ("If I buy a Prius, I will have a larger car payment, but I will also get better gas mileage") and the subjective norms ("My friends think buying a Prius is a good thing to do") in deciding whether to engage in attitude-consistent behavior.

Of course, we must also have the resources or the ability needed to carry out the intention. Consequently, it has been suggested that an additional variable should be added to the model, **perceived behavioral control** (Ajzen, 1985). A study of intentions to engage in safer sex among 403 undergraduates found that attitude and subjective norms explained substantial variation in the intention to use condoms in the next three months. However, even more variance was explained when one's comfort level with using condoms was added to the analysis (Wulfert & Wan, 1995). The revised model is referred to as the **theory of planned behavior**.

Not all of our behavior is planned (Liska, 1984). In addition to the automatic behavior discussed earlier, habit can also play a role in what we do. For example, whether one has donated blood in the past is a much better predictor of whether he or she will donate blood in the next four months than a statement about their intention to do so (Bagozzi, 1981). One of the reasons that behavior influences subsequent behavior is because engaging in that behavior becomes part of our identity (Granberg & Holmberg, 1990). If you regularly give blood, you may adopt "blood donor" as an important identity, and this will influence future behavior. In fact, social psychologists have found support that such a process occurs among regular donors (Piliavin & Callero, 1991). Similarly, research suggests that the best predictor of pro-environmental behavior is not pro-environmental attitudes but rather a pro-environmental identity (Stets & Biga, 2003).

SUMMARY

The Nature of Attitudes. (1) Every attitude has three components: cognition, evaluation, and a behavioral predisposition toward some object. (2) We learn attitudes through reinforcement, through repeated associations of stimuli and responses, and by observing others. (3) Attitudes are useful; they may serve heuristic and knowledge functions, and they define and maintain self.

Attitude Organization. An attitude is usually embedded in a larger cognitive structure and is based on one or more fundamental or primitive beliefs. Attitudes derived from primitive beliefs form a vertical structure. When multiple underlying beliefs support an attitude, these beliefs have a horizontal structure that helps the attitude persist.

Cognitive Consistency. Consistency theories assume that when cognitive elements are inconsistent, individuals will be motivated to change their attitudes or behavior to restore harmony. Balance theory assesses the relationships among three cognitive elements and suggests ways to resolve imbalance. Dissonance theory identifies two situations in which inconsistency often occurs: after a choice between alternatives or when people engage in behavior that is inconsistent with their attitudes. The theory also cites two ways to reduce dissonance: by

BOX 7.3 Test Yourself: Ambivalent Sexism Inventory

Although women have made tremendous strides in both the private and public spheres—particularly since the advent of the women's movement in the 1970s (Bolzendahl & Myers, 2004)—men still dominate high status positions in government and business around the world. While there was a time when women were seen as second class citizens, undeserving of the rights and responsibilities of men, these overtly prejudicial attitudes are much less common than they once were. How can we explain men's dominance in an era when attitudes about women have shifted?

Social psychologists argue that, while attitudes have changed, sexism is alive and well. **Sexism**—prejudice or discrimination based on a person's sex—has simply changed shape, shifting from overt and hostile forms of sexism to subtle, less recognizable forms (Fiske, 1998; Glick & Fiske, 2001; Nelson, 2002).

The survey opposite measures two forms of sexism—hostile and benevolent. How do you score? Can you tell the difference between them?

Both hostile and benevolent sexism help justify men's higher status in society. However, rather than assert that men are in these positions because women are somehow less-deserving or should be held in contempt, benevolent sexism suggests that women are simply different. They should be cherished, provided for, and protected, and it is men's responsibility to do that. Benevolent sexism is particularly insidious because it does not seem like prejudice to male perpetrators, because it is not contemptuous, and because women may find it alluring,

0 DISAGREE STRONGLY	1 DISAGREE SOMEWHAT	2 DISAGREE SLIGHTLY	3 AGREE SLIGHTLY	4 AGREE SOMEWHAT	5 AGREE STRONGLY

1. _____ No matter how accomplished he is, a man is not truly complete as a person unless he has the love of a good woman.

2. _____ Many women are actually seeking special favors, such as hiring practices that favor them over men, under the guise of asking for "equality."

3. _____ In a disaster, women ought to be rescued before men.

4. _____ Most women interpret innocent remarks or acts as being sexist.

5. _____ Women are too easily offended.

6. _____ Many women have a quality of purity that few men possess.

7. _____ Feminists want women to have more power than men.

8. _____ Most women fail to appreciate fully all that men do for them.

9. _____ Women seem to gain power by getting control over men.

10. _____ Women should be cherished and protected by men.

11. _____ Every man ought to have a woman whom he adores.

12. _____ A good woman should be set on a pedestal by her man.

13. _____ Women exaggerate problems they have at work.

14. _____ Women, compared to men, tend to have a superior moral sensibility.

15. _____ Men should be willing to sacrifice their own well-being in order to provide financially for those who are dependent on them.

16. _____ Once a woman gets a man to commit to her, she usually tries to put him on a tight leash.

17. _____ Women, as compared to men, tend to have a more refined sense of culture and good taste.

18. _____ Men are incomplete without women.

19. _____ Many women get a kick out of leading men on.

20. _____ When women lose to men in a fair competition, they typically complain about being discriminated against.

To determine your Hostile Sexism score, average items 2, 4, 5, 7, 8, 9, 13, 16, 19, 20.
To determine your Benevolent Sexism score, average items 1, 3, 6, 10, 11, 12, 14, 15, 17, 18

disarming, and difficult to resist. In fact, although women are significantly more likely than men to reject hostile sexism, they are much more accepting of benevolent sexism—with rates in the United States quite similar to men (Glick, et al. 2000).

Source: Adapted from Glick & Fiske, 2001.

changing one of the elements or by changing the importance of the cognitions involved.

The Relationship Between Attitudes and Behavior. The attitude-behavior relationship is influenced by six variables: accessibility and activation of the attitude, characteristics of the attitude, attitude-behavior correspondence, situational constraints, reference groups, and reasoning. (1) For an attitude to influence behavior, it must be activated, and the person must use it as a guide for behavior. (2) The relationship is stronger if affective-cognitive consistency is high and if the attitude is based on direct experience, is strong (relevant), and is stable. (3) The relationship is stronger when the measures of attitude and behavior correspond in action, object, context, and time. (4) Situational constraints may facilitate or prevent the expression of attitudes in behavior. (5) Attitudes are more likely to influence behavior if reference groups hold similar attitudes. (6) The theory of reasoned action argues that behavior is determined by behavioral intention, and this intention is determined by a person's attitudes toward a particular line of action and perceptions of social norms. Reasoning is not involved in automatic behaviors or those determined by habit.

List of Key Terms and Concepts

attitude (p. 244)
balance theory (p. 252)
cognitions (p. 244)
cognitive dissonance (p. 254)
correspondence (p. 263)
perceived behavioral control (p. 265)
prejudice (p. 248)
primitive belief (p. 250)
sexism (p. 266)
situational constraint (p. 264)
subjective norms (p. 265)

theory of cognitive dissonance (p. 254)
theory of planned behavior (p. 265)
theory of reasoned action (p. 265)

Critical Thinking Skill:
Analyzing Attitudes

This chapter opened your eyes to the components of attitudes and made you think about where they come from, how they relate to one another, and how your attitudes may—or may not—influence your behavior. What are some of the ways this knowledge might change the way you think about or respond to your own attitudes and those of others?

It is important to recognize the central role our beliefs play in shaping our attitudes. For example, you are likely to have a more positive attitude toward environmentally conscious living if you believe humans are causing climate change and that climate change has a negative impact on our world, our lives, or those of future generations. It is also important to consider where those beliefs come from and why we hold them.

Other critical thinking exercises in this book encourage you to gather evidence and investigate claims. These are certainly important. However, critical thinking also requires you to consider why you hold the beliefs you do in the first place.

For example, why would someone think humans are causing climate change? Not everyone does. And why might someone believe climate change is having a negative impact on the world? Some argue that certain crops in certain places are benefiting from higher temperatures.

To evaluate assumptions we might have, we need to think critically about where they come from and why we hold them. Why might someone believe the claims above?

Think back to Chapter 6 and the discussion of the differences between what social science students thought caused poverty and what business students believed. What accounts for these differences?

Consider the example of Justin from this chapter and his beliefs about same-sex marriage, equality, and acceptance of the Constitution. Why might he hold these beliefs?

What is it about Justin or these students' cultures—the time period they live in, their communities, the media messages they are exposed to, their roles and experiences, and so forth—that might cause them to hold these beliefs? For example, you might not think climate change has a negative effect on our world because you live in an area that has been relatively unaffected by it; someone who lives on the Gulf Coast of the United States may think quite differently. You might believe the poor are lazy because your classes do not require you to systematically consider structural forces. You might be against same-sex marriage because you see marriage as a religious institution rather than a civil one.

What are some of your attitudes? What are the beliefs that influence them? Where might those beliefs originate from?

Once you realize why you or others hold certain attitudes and beliefs, you can consider potential biases and alternative ways of thinking. Would you feel differently about climate change if you lived in Darfur or in Alaska? Would you think differently about poverty if you had been poor or your favorite shows were *Maury Povich* and *Cops*? Are your beliefs about same-sex marriage different from your grandparents'? Would you feel the same way you do now if you had lived two generations ago? Questions like these help us understand our own views and the views of others, thereby increasing both cultural competence and critical thinking.

CHAPTER 8

SYMBOLIC COMMUNICATION
AND LANGUAGE

INTRODUCTION

Imagine that you wake up tomorrow morning and you cannot speak. How would you manage to get through the day? How would it affect your interactions with roommates, partners, professors, employers? Now, imagine that you wake up the next day and you can speak again! But you can't move your arms or hands. How would that influence your ability to interact with those same people? Communication is a basic ingredient of every social situation. Without communication, interaction breaks down; indeed, it would be simply impossible to participate in a class, purchase something, or arrange a birthday party or any other social occasion.

Communication is the process whereby people transmit information about their ideas, feelings, and intentions to one another. We communicate through spoken and written words, through voice qualities and physical closeness, through gestures and posture. Often, communication is deliberate: We smile, clasp our beloved in our arms, and whisper, "I love you." Other times, we communicate meanings that are unintentional. A Freudian slip, for instance, may tell our listeners more than we want them to know.

Because people do not share each other's experiences directly, they must convey their ideas and feelings to each other in ways that others will notice and understand. We often do this by means of symbols. **Symbols** are arbitrary forms that are used to refer to ideas, feelings, intentions, or any other object.

Symbols represent our experiences in ways that others can perceive with their sensory organs—through sounds, gestures, pictures, even fragrances. But if we are to interpret symbols as others intend them to be understood, their meanings must be socially shared. To communicate successfully, we must master the ways for expressing ideas and feelings that are accepted in our community.

Symbols are arbitrary stand-ins for what they represent. A green light could as reasonably stand for "stop" as for "go," the sound *luv* as reasonably for negative as for positive feelings. The arbitrariness of symbols becomes painfully obvious when we travel in foreign countries. We are then likely to discover that the words and even the gestures we take for granted fail to communicate accurately. A North American who makes a circle with thumb and index finger to express satisfaction to a waiter may be in for a rude surprise if he or she is eating at a restaurant in Ghana, where the waiter may interpret this gesture as a sexual invitation. In Venezuela, it may be interpreted as a sexual insult! The traveler may then have serious difficulties straightening out these misunderstandings because he and the waiter lack a shared language of verbal symbols to discuss them.

Language and nonverbal forms of communication are amazingly complex. They must be understood and used with flexibility and creativity. Most of us fail on occasion to communicate our ideas and feelings with accuracy or to understand others' communications as well as we might wish. Yet, considering the problems a communicator must solve, most people do surprisingly well. This chapter begins with an examination of language, moves on to nonverbal communication, then analyzes the impacts of communication and social relationships on each other. Finally, this chapter considers the delicate coordination involved in our most common social activity—conversation. This chapter addresses the following questions:

1. What is the nature of language, and how is it used to grasp meanings and intentions?

2. What are the major types of nonverbal communication, and how do they combine with language to convey emotions and ideas?

3. How do social relationships shape communication, and how does it in turn express or modify those relationships?

4. What rules and skills do people employ to maintain a smooth flow of conversation and to avoid disruptive blunders?

LANGUAGE AND VERBAL COMMUNICATION

Although people have created numerous symbol systems (such as mathematics, music, painting), language is the main vehicle of human communication. All people possess a spoken language. There are thousands of different languages in the world (Katzner, 1995). This section addresses several crucial topics regarding the role of language in communication. These include the nature of language, three perspectives on how people attain understanding through language

Signing by the interpreter parallels the oral message by the speaker. Although sign language lacks the phonetic component, it possesses the morphologic, semantic, and syntactic components of language. © AP Photo/Charles Dharapak

use, and the relation between language and thought (see Box 8.1).

Linguistic Communication

Little is known about the origins of language, but humans have possessed complex spoken languages since earliest times (Kiparsky, 1976; Lieberman, 1975). **Spoken language** is a socially acquired system of sound patterns with meanings agreed on by the members of a group. We will examine the basic components of spoken language and some of the advantages of language use.

Basic Components. Spoken languages include sounds, words, meanings, and grammatical rules. Consider the following statement of one roommate to another: "Wherewereyoulastnight?" What the listener hears is a string of sounds much like this, rather than the sentence "Where were you last night?" To understand a string of sounds and to produce an appropriate response, people must recognize the following components: (1) the distinct sounds of which the language is composed (the phonetic component); (2) the combination of sounds into words (the morphologic component); (3) the common meaning of the words (the semantic component); and (4) the conventions for putting words together built into the language (the syntactic component, or grammar). We are rarely conscious of manipulating all these components during conversation, though we do so regularly and with impressive speed.

Unspoken languages, such as Morse code, computer programming languages, and sign languages, lack a phonetic component, although they do possess the remaining components of spoken language. People who use sign languages, for example, use upper body movements to signal words (morphology) with shared meanings (semantics), and they combine these words

BOX 8.1   Research Update: The Linguistic Relativity Hypothesis

Does the language we speak influence the way we think about and experience the world? The most famous theory on this question—the Sapir-Whorf linguistic relativity hypothesis—holds that language "is not merely a reproducing instrument for voicing ideas, but is itself a shaper of ideas, the program and guide for the individual's mental activity" (Whorf, 1956). Two forms of this hypothesis—strong and weak—have been proposed.

According to the strong form of the linguistic relativity hypothesis, language determines our perceptions of reality, so we cannot perceive or comprehend distinctions that don't exist in our own language. Orwell's description of Newspeak, the language developed by the totalitarian rulers in his novel *Nineteen Eighty-Four*, portrays in frightening terms how language restricts thought:

> Don't you see that the whole aim of Newspeak is to narrow the range of thought? In the end we shall make thought crime literally impossible because there will be no words in which to express it. . . . Every year fewer and fewer words, and the range of consciousness always a little smaller. . . . The revolution will be complete when the language is perfect. (George Orwell, *Nineteen Eighty-Four,* 1949; 46–47)

Orwell's description suggests that language determines thought through the words it makes available to people. We cannot talk about objects or ideas for which we lack words. The ways we think about the world are determined by the way our language slices up reality.

The strong form of the linguistic relativity hypothesis has not fared well in research. Consider some of the facts. Some languages have only two basic words (*dark* and *white*) to cover the whole spectrum of colors. Yet people from these and all other known language groups can discriminate between and communicate about whatever large numbers of colors they are shown (Heider & Olivier, 1972). Most likely, any concept can be expressed in any language, though not with the same degree of ease and efficiency. Before either TV or the word *television* existed, for example, someone undoubtedly referred to the concept of "a device that can transmit pictures and sounds over a distance." When new concepts are encountered, people invent words (*laser*) or borrow them from other languages (*sabotage* from French, *goulash* from Hungarian).

Thus, the strong linguistic relativity hypothesis that language determines thought has found little support. But there is considerable evidence for a weak form of this hypothesis. The weak

---

into sentences according to rules of order (syntax). For a communication system to be considered a language, morphology, semantics, and syntax are all essential. Linguists study these components, seeking to uncover the rules that give structure to language. Social psychologists are more interested in how language fits into social interaction and influences it and in how language expresses and modifies social relationships (Giles, Hewstone, & St. Clair, 1981).

Advantages of Language Use. Words— the symbols around which languages are constructed—provide abundant resources

with which to represent ideas and feelings. The average adult native speaker of English knows the meanings of some 35,000 words, and actively uses close to 5,000. Because it is a symbol system, language enhances our capacity for social action in several ways.

First, language frees us from the constraints of the here and now. Using words to symbolize objects, events, or relationships, we can communicate about things that happened last week or last year, and we can discuss things that may happen in the future. The ability to do the latter allows us to coordinate our behavior with the activities of others. In thinking about losing your voice form of the linguistic relativity hypothesis says that each language facilitates particular forms of thinking because it makes some events and objects more easily codable or symbolizable. In fact, the availability of linguistic symbols for objects or events has been shown to have two clear effects: (1) it improves the efficiency of communication about these objects and events, and (2) it enhances success in remembering them.

Counting is difficult for people whose language does not include numbers. The Piraha, a group living in the Amazon, have only two words for numbers, words that mean *one* and *two*. When an experimenter lined up several batteries and asked a member of the tribe to match it, the member did well when the line contained two or three, but had a difficult time if there were more than three batteries in the experimenter's line (Gordon, 2004).

Language influences what we pay attention to. Native speakers of Ndonga (spoken in parts of Africa) and of English were compared on three color cognition tasks. Ndonga has no terms for orange, pink, and purple. Participants were presented with colors that exploited this fact. Speakers of both performed well at sorting colors based on similarity. However, they differed in performance on a task that required them to search for specific colors; native speakers of En-

glish were better (Pilling & Davies, 2004). This same influence of language was demonstrated in experiments using speakers of English. Participants who were primed with (shown) abstract terms focused on general features in a categorization task, whereas those primed using concrete terms focused on specific aspects in performing the task (Stapel & Semin, 2007).

The availability of linguistic symbols also affects memory for objects and persons. This was shown in a study that involved subjects who spoke English or Chinese (Hoffman, Lau, & Johnson, 1986). This study used English- and Chinese-language descriptions of two people whose traits could be easily labeled in English but not in Chinese and of two other people whose traits could be easily labeled in Chinese but not in English. Three groups of participants read the descriptions: English monolinguals, Chinese-English bilinguals who read in Chinese, and Chinese-English bilinguals who read in English. The participants' memory of the descriptions was assessed. The results showed that memory was much better when the information about the target conformed to labels in the participant's language of processing. These results lend support to the weak form of the linguistic relativity hypothesis.

for the day, it may have occurred to you that it would very difficult to make appointments, schedule a meeting, or plan a trip.

Second, language allows us to communicate with others about experiences we do not share directly. You cannot know directly the joy and hope your friend feels at bearing a child, nor her grief and despair at her mother's death. Yet she can convey a good sense of her emotions and concerns to you through words, even in writing, because these shared symbols elicit the same meanings for you both.

Third, language enables us to transmit, preserve, and create culture. Through the

spoken and the written word, vast quantities of information pass from person to person and from generation to generation. Language also enhances our ability to go beyond what is already known and to add to the store of cultural ideas and objects. Working with linguistic symbols, people generate theories, design and build new products, and invent social institutions.

We turn now to three models of communication: the encoder-decoder model, the intentionalist model, and the perspective-taking model. We will consider how each model views the communication process and discusses communication accuracy.

The Encoder-Decoder Model

Language is often thought of as a medium of communication that one person uses to transmit information to another. The **encoder-decoder model** views communication as a process in which an idea or feeling is encoded into symbols by a source, transmitted to a receiver, and decoded into the original idea or feeling (Krauss & Fussell, 1996). This process is portrayed in Figure 8.1.

Communication Process. According to this model, the basic unit of communication is the message, which has its origin in the desire of the speaker to communicate. A message is constructed when the speaker encodes the information he or she wishes to communicate into a combination of verbal and nonverbal symbols. The message is sent via a channel, whether by face-to-face interaction, telephone, electronic communication, or in writing. The listener must decode the message in order to arrive at the information he or she believes the speaker wanted to communicate.

Communication Accuracy. The goal of communication is to accurately transfer the message content from speaker to listener.

The speaker hopes to create in the listener the mental image or feeling that the speaker intends to convey. The listener is also motivated to achieve accuracy, in order to coordinate his or her behavior with that of the speaker. **Communication accuracy** refers to the extent to which the message inferred by the listener matches the message intended by the speaker. According to this model, the primary influence on accuracy is *codability*, which is the extent of interpersonal agreement about what something is called. Codability is partly a function of language. Early research focused on the codability of colors (Lantz & Stefflre, 1964). In this research, one person (the encoder) was shown a color and asked to describe that color in words. This verbal message was then sent to a second person (the decoder), who tried to use the verbal description to identify the color intended by the encoder. Some colors are much more easily coded in the English language (fire-engine red) than others (the reddish color of a sunset). By extension, some ideas and feelings are easily expressed in English, whereas others are much more difficult to put into words. In general, messages that are easily coded will be more accurately transmitted.

Codability involves agreement about what something is to be called. It also de-

FIGURE 8.1 The Encoder-Decoder Model

According to the encoder-decoder model, communication originates in the speaker's desire to convey an idea or feeling. He or she encodes the message into a set of symbols and transmits it to the hearer. The hearer decodes the message. The more codable the idea or feeling in the language, the more accurate the communication.

pends on the extent to which speaker and listener define symbols (such as words or gestures) in the same way. This in turn depends on the language to which each was socialized. Thus, a common cause of miscommunication is differences in language between speaker and listener. This is obvious when we try to converse with someone from a different country. It is less obvious, but perhaps just as important, when we converse with someone of a different race, class, or gender (Maynard & Whalen, 1995).

At times, the processes of encoding and decoding are very deliberate or mindful (Giles & Coupland, 1991). If we are preparing a speech, we may consciously consider alternative ways to phrase a message and alternative gestures to use when communicating. Listening to a speaker, we may pay careful attention to the words used, the speed and volume of the spoken message, the gestures, and the posture of the speaker in order to decide which message is the correct one. We are often mindful of the encoding and decoding process in novel situations or in communicating about novel topics.

Communication is not always a process of consciously translating ideas and feelings into symbols and then transmitting these symbols deliberately in hopes that the listener will interpret them correctly. Much communication occurs without any self-conscious planning. In familiar or routine situations, we often rely on a conversational script—a sequentially organized series of utterances that occur with little or no conscious thought. Thus, when you enter a restaurant, you can interact with the server without much mental effort, because you both follow a conversational script that specifies what each of you should say and in what sequence. Communication accuracy is typically high in situations governed by conversational scripts. When you order food in a fast-food outlet, you usually get exactly what you want with minimum effort.

If conversation is scripted, listeners will probably not pay careful attention to the idiosyncratic features of a message. They will tend to remember the generic content of a message but not its unusual characteristics. In a field experiment testing this prediction, students were approached by a stranger who asked for a piece of paper. Prior to the request, one-half of the students were asked to pay attention to the request; the other half were not forewarned. Later, the forewarned students were more likely to remember the specific words used in the request than the unprepared students (Kitayama & Burnstein, 1988).

The Intentionalist Model

The encoder-decoder model emphasizes messages consisting of symbols whose meaning is widely understood. It directs our attention to the literal meaning of verbal messages. Often, however, messages are not interpreted literally. For example, in many theaters, the feature film is preceded by the message "Please, silence during the show." But are members of the audience expected to be silent? No. They can laugh if the film is a comedy, boo at the villain, and applaud when the bad guy or gal gets what he or she deserves. Most of us understand this message in terms of its intention: We should not whisper or talk to those seated near us. For this type of communication, we need a different model.

According to the **intentionalist model**, communication involves the exchange of communicative intentions, and messages are merely the means to this end (Krauss & Fussell, 1996). The speaker selects the message he or she believes is most likely to accomplish his or her intent. "Please, silence during the show" is intended to keep us from disturbing other members of the audience, and that is how we understand it.

Communication Process. The origin of communication is the speaker's intent to achieve some goal or to have some effect on the listener. But there is not a fixed, one-to-one relation between words and intended effects, so the speaker can use a variety of messages or utterances to achieve his or her intended effect. For example, imagine you are studying in your living room, and you want your roommate to bring you something to drink. Table 8.1 lists some of the utterances you might use to make the request. Which one would you choose?

According to the intentionalist model, decoding the literal meaning of a message is only part of the process of communication. The hearer must also infer the speaker's underlying intention in order to respond appropriately. To the question "How is that lemonade we bought?" a satisfactory response to the literal message is "Good." If the communication is to be successful, however, your roommate needs to infer your intention—that he should bring you a glass of lemonade. Both selecting a message to convey your intention and inferring another's intention from their utterance are carried out according to social conventions.

TABLE 8.1 "Get Me a Drink of Lemonade."

1.	Get me a glass of lemonade.
2.	Can you get me some lemonade?
3.	Would you get me some lemonade?
4.	Would you get me something to drink?
5.	Would you mind if I asked you to get me some lemonade?
6.	I'm thirsty.
7.	Did you buy some lemonade at the store?
8.	How is that lemonade we bought?

Communication Accuracy. According to this model, accuracy in communication is accuracy in understanding the intentions of the speaker. To achieve accuracy requires more sophisticated processing than merely interpreting the literal meaning of the message. When inferring the speaker's intention, the listener needs to take into account the context, especially (1) the status or role relationship between speaker and listener, and (2) the social context in which the communication occurs. If you and your roommate are lovers, you might choose a less polite form of the request, such as option 2 in Table 8.1, and you would expect a less polite response than if the two of you are simply sharing the residence. If your parents are visiting at the time, your request to them is likely to take a different form, such as option 3.

According to **speech act theory**, utterances both state something and do something (Searle, 1979). In Table 8.1, utterances 1 to 6 state the speaker's desire for a drink (or specifically for lemonade), whereas utterances 7 and 8 do not. But all eight of the utterances perform an action; each has the force of a request. The significance of an utterance is not its literal meaning, but what it contributes to the work of the interaction in which it occurs (Geis, 1995). The use of language to perform actions is rule-governed; these rules influence both the creation and the interpretation of speech acts. To achieve accurate communication, both speaker and listener must be aware of these rules. Miscommunication is caused not only by the lack of shared meaning of symbols, but also by a lack of shared understanding of the rules governing the use of speech to perform actions.

To determine whether the message has achieved the intended effect, the speaker relies on the feedback provided by the listener's reaction. If the reaction indicates that the listener interpreted the message accurately, the speaker may elaborate, change the topic, or end the interaction. However, if the reaction suggests that the listener inferred a meaning different from the intended one, the speaker will often attempt to send the same message, perhaps using different words and gestures. For example, when James asked Jasmine, a coworker, to go out with him, Jasmine replied that she liked him as a friend and that she was busy Saturday night. Her intended message was that she was not interested in developing a romantic relationship with James. Several days later, James tried to give Jasmine six red roses. Inferring that James had not received her intended message, she refused the roses and told him directly that she was not interested in seeing him.

The Cooperative Principle. Mutual understanding is a cooperative enterprise. Because language does not convey thoughts and feelings in an unambiguous manner, people must work together to attain a shared understanding of each other's utterances (Goffman, 1983). A speaker must cooperate with a listener by formulating the content of speech acts in a manner that reflects the listener's way of thinking about objects, events, and relationships.

In turn, the listener must cooperate by actively trying to understand. He or she must go beyond the literal meanings of words to infer what the speaker is really saying. A listener must make a creative effort to cope with a speaker's tendency to formulate speech acts indirectly. Without such an effort, a listener would not understand speech acts that leave out words ("Paper come?"), abbreviate familiar terms ("See ya in calc"), and include vague references ("He told him he would come later").

According to Grice (1975), listeners assume that most talk is based on the **cooperative principle**. That is, listeners ordinarily assume that the speaker is behaving cooperatively by trying to be informative (giving as much information as is necessary and no more), truthful, relevant to the aims of the ongoing conversation, and clear (avoiding ambiguity and wordiness).

The cooperative principle is more than a code of conversational etiquette. It is crucial to the accurate transmission of meaning. Often, a listener can reach a correct understanding of otherwise ambiguous talk only by assuming that the speaker is trying to satisfy this principle. Consider, for example, how the maxim of relevance enables the conversationalists to understand each other in the following exchange:

JUAN: I'm exhausted.
MARIA: Fred will be back next Monday.

On the surface, Maria's statement seems unrelated to Juan's declaration. In some contexts, we might infer that she has changed the subject, indirectly sending the message that she does not care about his physical state. In fact, however, Maria is stating that she and Juan won't have to work as hard after their colleague Fred returns to the office next week. But why does she expect that Juan will understand this? Because she expects him to assume that she is adhering to the relevance maxim—that her comment relates to what he said.

The cooperative principle is also crucial for speech forms like sarcasm or understatement to succeed. In sarcasm or understatement, speakers want listeners to recognize that their words mean something quite different from their literal interpretation. One way we signal listeners that we intend our words to imply something different is by obviously violating one or two component maxims of the cooperative principle while holding to the rest. Consider Carrie's sarcastic reply when asked what she thought of the lecturer: "He was so exciting that he came close to keeping most of us awake the first half hour." By flouting the maxim of clarity (responding in an unclear, wordy way) while still being informative, truthful, and relevant, Carrie implies that the lecturer was in fact a bore.

The Perspective-Taking Model

A third model is based on symbolic interaction theory (see Chap. 1). It views the process of communication as both creating and reflecting a shared context between speaker and listener. This approach maintains that symbols do not have a meaning that is invariant across situations (see Box 8.1). According to the **perspective-taking model**, communication involves the exchange of messages using symbols whose meaning grows out of the interaction itself.

Communication Process. Communication involves the use of verbal and nonverbal symbols whose meaning depends on the shared context created by the participants. The development of this shared context requires reciprocal role taking, in which each participant places himself or herself in the role of the other in an attempt to view the situation from the other's perspective. The context created by the ongoing interaction changes from minute to minute; each actor must be attentive to these changes in order to communicate successfully as both speaker and listener.

Communication Accuracy. In the perspective-taking model, communication is much more than transmitting and receiving words with fixed, shared meanings. Conversationalists must select and discover the meanings of words through their context. In ordinary social interaction, the meanings of whole sentences and conversations may be ambiguous. Speakers and listeners must jointly work out these meanings as they go along.

Successful communication depends on **intersubjectivity**; each participant needs information about the other's status, view of the situation, and plans or intentions. Strangers rely on social conventions and rules about interpersonal communication. They categorize other participants and use stereotypes as a basis for making inferences about the plans and intentions of the other person(s) who are present in the setting. Notice that this practice perpetuates stereotypes via the self-fulfilling prophecy (see Chap. 6). Persons who know each other can draw on their past experience with each other as a basis for effective communication.

Interpersonal Context. According to this model, both the production and the interpretation of communication is heavily influenced by the interpersonal context in which it occurs (Giles & Coupland, 1991). This context influences communication through norms, cognitive representations of prior similar situations, and emotional arousal.

Every social situation includes norms regarding communicative behavior. These norms specify what topics are appropriate and inappropriate for discussion, what language is to be used, and how persons of varying status should be addressed. Depending on these norms, we use one or another of various speech repertoires, ways of communicating the same literal message that vary in words, tone, and so on (Giles & Coupland, 1991). Imagine a man who wishes another person to close a door. To his son in his home, he might say, "Close the door." To his son at work, he might say, "Please close the door, Tom." To an employee, he could say, "Would you close the door?" These different ways of making a request reflect differences in speech rules, which depend on the relationship between speaker and listener, and on the setting.

Each new situation evokes representations of prior similar situations and the language one has used or heard in them (Chapman et al., 1992). These conversational histories provide us with the contents of our speech repertoires. Each of us has a set of things we say when we meet a stranger our own age at a party; these are opening lines that in the past have been effective in facilitating conversation with strangers at parties. If, instead, you met the same stranger on a plane, you might use different speech acts.

The processing of messages by listeners is also influenced by these contextual factors. Listeners interpret messages in light of the rules operating in situations, their past experience, and the emotions elicited in them. When speaker and listener have the same understanding of the normative demands, communication should be quite accurate. Similarly, if a situation evokes the same representations and emotions in both, it is likely that the listener will accurately interpret the speaker's message. Communication across group and cultural boundaries is often difficult precisely because speaker and listener differ in their assumptions and experiences, even though they may speak the same language.

The accuracy of indirect or covert communication depends heavily on shared knowledge. In a series of experiments, participants were asked to compose messages—either in writing or on videotape—taking a position in which they did not believe. They were also instructed to try to covertly inform the reader or viewer that they did not hold that position. The majority of the participants used the device of including false information about themselves in the message. Friends of the participants who read or viewed the message detected the deception, whereas strangers did not (Fleming, Darley, Hilton, & Kojetin, 1991).

Members of a group share a **linguistic intergroup bias** (Maass & Arcuri, 1992).

That is, there are subtle and systematic differences in the language we use to describe events as a function of our group membership and the group to which the actor or target belongs. We describe other members of our own group behaving properly and members of out-groups behaving improperly at very abstract levels (say, "Jim [in-group · member] is helpful"; "George [out-group member] is aggressive"). This encourages positive stereotypes of us and negative stereotypes of them. When in-group members behave badly or out-group members behave well, we describe the events concretely ("Jim pushed that guy out of his way"; "George held the door for a woman carrying a baby"). This technique encourages an attribution to the individual rather than to the group. Research with Danish youth found evidence that the influence of this bias increased significantly from age 8 to age 19 (Werkman, Wigboldus, & Semin, 1999).

Sociolinguistic Competence. To attain mutual understanding, language performance must be appropriate to the social and cultural context. Otherwise, even grammatically acceptable sentences will not make sense. "My mother eats raw termites" is grammatically correct and meaningful; it reflects linguistic competence. But as a serious assertion by a North American, this utterance would draw amazed looks. It expresses an idea that is incongruous with American culture, and listeners would have difficulty interpreting it. In a termite-eating culture, however, the same utterance would be quite sensible. This example shows that successful communication requires **sociolinguistic competence**—knowledge of the implicit rules for generating socially appropriate sentences. Such sentences make sense to listeners, because they fit with the listeners' social knowledge (Hymes, 1974).

Speech that clashes with what is known about the social relationship to which it refers suggests that a speaker is not socio-linguistically competent (Grimshaw, 1990). Speakers are expected to use language that is appropriate to the status of the individuals they are discussing and to their relationship of intimacy. For example, competent speakers would not state seriously, "The janitor ordered the president to turn off the lights in the Oval Office." They know that low-status persons do not "order" those of much higher status; at most, they "hint" or "suggest." Referring to a relationship of true intimacy, sociolinguistically competent speakers would not say, "The lover bullied her beloved." Rather, they would select such socially appropriate verbs as "coaxed" or "persuaded." In short, competent speakers recognize that social and cultural constraints make some statements interpretable and others uninterpretable in a given situation.

Thus, successful communication is a complex undertaking. A speaker must produce a message that has not only an appropriate literal meaning, but also an intention or goal appropriate to the relationship and setting. The message must reflect the present degree of intersubjectivity between speaker and hearer, consistent with the interactional context. The message must also signify the statuses of the participants (Geis, 1995). Given these requirements, it is remarkable that each of us communicates successfully many times each day.

NONVERBAL COMMUNICATION

In the introduction, we asked you to think about what it would be like to communicate without using words. Imagine that you are looking out of a window of your third-floor dorm room or apartment. You notice a man on the sidewalk below, dressed immacu-

lately in a three-piece suit, pacing back and forth. He looks up and sees you and immediately begins to gesture. He points to you, then to some other window, and then to his watch. His movements are quick and sharp. His face is tense. What is he trying to communicate to you?

Even without the use of words, most of us can make some inferences about the man's message and emotional state. We do so by interpreting his nonverbal communication. This section examines three questions concerning nonverbal communication: (1) What are the major types of nonverbal communication? (2) What is communicated by the human face? (3) What is gained and what problems arise when nonverbal and verbal communication are combined in ordinary interaction?

Types of Nonverbal Communication

By one estimate, the human face can make some 250,000 different expressions (Bird-whistell, 1970). In addition to facial expressions, nonverbal communication uses many other bodily and gestural cues. Four major types of nonverbal cues (summarized in Table 8.2) are described next.

Paralanguage. Speaking involves a great deal more than the production of words. Vocal behavior includes loudness, pitch, speed, emphasis, inflection, breathiness, stretching or clipping of words, pauses, and so on. All the vocal aspects of speech other than words are called **paralanguage**. This includes such highly communicative vocalizations as moaning, sighing, laughing, and even crying. Shrillness of voice and rapid delivery communicate tension and excitement in most situations (Scherer, 1979). Various uses and interpretations of paralinguistic and other nonverbal cues will be examined later in this chapter. For now, see how many distinct meanings you can give to

TABLE 8.2 Types of Nonverbal Communication

TYPE OF CUE	DEFINITION	EXAMPLES	CHANNEL
Paralanguage	Vocal but nonverbal behavior involved in speaking	Loudness, speed, pauses in speech	Auditory
Body language (kinesics)	Silent motions of the body	Gestures, facial expressions, eye gaze	Visual
Interpersonal spacing (proxemics)	Positioning of body at varying distances and angles from others	Intimate closeness, facing head-on, looking away, turning one's back	Primarily visual; also touch, smell, and auditory
Choice of personal effects	Selecting and displaying objects that others will associate with you	Clothing, makeup, room decorations	Primarily visual; also auditory and smell

the sentence "George is on the phone again" by varying the paralinguistic cues you use.

Body Language. The silent movement of body parts—scowls, smiles, nods, gazing, gestures, leg movements, postural shifts, caressing, slapping, and so on—all constitute **body language**. Because body language entails movement, it is known as *kinesics* (from the Greek *kinein* meaning "to move"). Whereas paralinguistic cues are auditory, we perceive kinesic cues visually. The body movements of the man in our example were probably particularly useful to you in interpreting his feelings and intentions. Researchers investigated the use of head tilts to the side and shoulder shrugs during debates (Debras & Cienki, 2012). Head tilts served to point to other persons or objects, to call attention to them, whereas shrugs were markers of disengagement.

The handshake is a common nonverbal behavior. There are a variety of beliefs about the meaning of a handshake, depending on whether it is firm or limp, dry or damp. Research on how we interpret handshakes involved 4 trained coders (2 men, 2 women); each shook hands twice with 112 men and women and rated the participants on four measures of personality. The man or woman with a firm handshake was rated by the coders as extroverted and emotionally expressive and given low ratings on shyness. Women who shook hands firmly were also rated as open to new experience (Chaplin, Phillips, Brown, Clanton, & Stein, 2000). Thus, a handshake can make a strong first impression and influence future interactions.

Interpersonal Spacing. We also communicate nonverbally by using **interpersonal spacing** cues—positioning ourselves at varying distances and angles from others (for example, standing close or far away, facing head-on or to one side, adopting various postures, and creating barriers with books or other objects). Because proximity is a major means of communication between people, this type of cue is also called *proxemics*. When there is very close positioning, proxemics can convey information through smell and touch as well.

What types of communication by wait staff influence your emotional reactions in a restaurant? Researchers surveyed several hundred diners in family restaurants in Seoul, Korea; diners completed a 31-item questionnaire while waiting for dessert. The survey assessed diners' reactions to the server's verbal, paralinguistic, kinesic and proxemic behaviors. The results indicated that eye contact, smiles, bodily positioning, and touch determined whether the customer reported a positive or negative experience; the server's language and paralanguage were not related to diner's impressions (Jung & Yoon, 2011).

Choice of Personal Effects. Though we usually think of communication as expressed through our bodies, people also communicate nonverbally through the personal effects they select—their choices of clothing, hairstyle, makeup, eyewear (contact lenses), and the like. A uniform, for example, may communicate social status, political opinion, lifestyle, and occupation, revealing a great deal about how its wearer is likely to behave (Joseph & Alex, 1972). You may have made assumptions about the status and lifestyle of the man in our sketch based on the fact that he wore a three-piece suit. The deliberate use of bodily hair and tattoos to influence the impressions of others is discussed in Chapter 4.

Clothing can convey a great deal of information about the wearer. Interviews with 38 young people found that clothing choices conveyed information about group membership (Piacentini & Mailer, 2004). The wearing of gold jewelry signaled membership in one group, whereas dressing in "joggies" and "trackies" indicated membership in a very different group. Wearing expensive, branded clothing conveyed one's social class status to other students and staff. Clothing was also chosen to fit and communicate the role that the person was performing.

In spaces that a person controls, such as a bedroom, dormitory room, or office, objects that are displayed will be associated with the person. Persons who enter the space will make inferences about the occupant based on what objects are displayed,

their relative position or prominence, and so on. A survey of eighth- and ninth-graders focused on the contents of their bedrooms found gender differences in the objects and decorations; boys' rooms contained sports equipment and things they had built, whereas girls' rooms contained stuffed animals and photographs of people/family members (Jones et al., 2007). Girls' rooms were much more likely to contain makeup tables and have matching bedspread, curtains, and rugs. Similar differences have been found in the living spaces of college

The meaning of a gesture can vary greatly from one culture to another. A good example is the "thumbs up." In the United States, the gesture is often associated with the late film critic Roger Ebert. When he and his TV co-host, Gene Siskel, both reviewed a film positively, they gave it "two thumbs up," meaning it was an excellent film. It is widely used to signal "good work" or "awesome," and it has that meaning in Russia and several other countries. However, in several Middle Eastern countries it is a vile insult. In Iran it means "F—you!" © Featureflash/Shutterstock.com students and recent graduates (Gosling et al., 2005). Furniture in residences reflects and displays the patterns of social interaction preferred by residents. Furniture creates and constrains possibilities for interaction, and is often purchased and arranged for that purpose. A study of the tables purchased by Australians found that purchasers of a rectangular table used it to display the family hierarchy, with adults sitting at the short ends; a round table was purchased and used by two people who preferred an equalitarian style of interaction (Bjorkvall & Karlsson, 2011).

For the most part, nonverbal cues, like language, are learned rather than innate. As a result, the meanings of particular nonverbal cues may vary from culture to culture. One example is the meaning of "thumbs up." Other features of nonverbal communication may have universal meanings, however. These universals are based on our biological nature.

Computer Mediated Communication

The preceding discussion implicitly assumes that communication is face-to-face. In the past century, new forms of communication aided by technology have become widely used. The first was the telephone, which allowed communication at a distance; it involves spoken language and paralanguage, but body language, proxemics, and the impact of personal effects are lost. There is less shared context for the communication, unless the actors know each other. More recently the cell phone has freed communicators from connection to "landlines" and allows communication from almost anywhere at any time, This is an advantage in increasing the spontaneity and sense of connection, but a disadvantage to the extent that it happens at inappropriate times such as a meeting, a performance, during a class, or during a religious service.

The development and adoption of computer-mediated communication (CMC) has been especially rapid. E-mail and texting (SMS, or short message service) are almost universal in certain segments of U.S. society. In CMC, communication is entirely by written language, removing the paralingual cues, kinesics, and proxemics—that is, aural and visual feedback (Kiesler, Siegel & McGuire, 1984). We noted earlier that these are very important in providing context, which aids in interpreting the words, and is often the mode by which emotion is communicated. This obviously makes many messages harder to code, potentially restricting the topics of communication, and increases risk of inaccuracy. The widespread use of emoticons is an effort to compensate for the difficulty of conveying emotion, as is the use of textual devices such as CAPITAL LETTERs to indicate shouting. CMC also involves the limited *cyberself* (discussed in Chap. 4), rather than the embodied person.

E-mail and text are also asynchronous, meaning that there is no immediate feedback from others. As we note later in the chapter, *back-channel feedback* (eye contact, smiles, nods) makes an important contribution to accuracy of communication, and to the smooth flow of interaction (a relationship). The absence of immediate feedback makes the time lag between the sending of a message and receiving an answer potentially meaningful to the sender: "Why did she wait one hour/one day/one week to respond to my invitation?" The lack of a synchronous connection is taken advantage of when a communicator uses e-mail or text to send "bad news." College students acknowledge using text messages instead of face-to-face contacts to break up with a partner (Harrison & Gilmore, 2012). Perhaps not surprisingly, in class discussions of texting this is a common complaint! Students also report sending messages at times some would consider inappropriate, such as while on a date, interacting with friends or family, on an airplane in flight, or even while having sex. In other words, CMC users regularly violate the temporal and spatial boundaries that separate intimate life, social activities, work, and religion (Kiesler, Siegel, & McGuire, 1984). These breaches suggest that CMC encourages disinhibition and lack of attention to ongoing social activity.

What's in a Face?

The face is an important communication channel. Typically, we pay attention to the face of persons with whom we interact. Moreover, the face is capable of many nonverbal behaviors; one dictionary lists 98 behaviors, of which 25 involve the face (Rashotte, 2002). They include baring the teeth, closing one's eyes, frowning, grinning, licking the lips, nodding, tilting the head, raising one's eyebrows, and smiling. The physical features of the face combined with these movements convey a variety of messages, including information about social identities, personality, and emotions (see Chap. 5).

The physical features of the face, including skin color, often provide cues to racial or ethnic identity. The features, in combination with grooming, makeup, and jewelry, virtually always indicate gender. Thus, inferences about two important social identities are made the moment we see someone's face, and these inferences shape our interaction with that person.

Physiognomy, the art of "reading" faces, is based on the belief that personality traits can be inferred from facial features. In research designed to test this, participants were given photographs and descriptions of a target person. The photographs were selected based on ratings by other participants on the confidence, charisma, and dominance of the person in the photo; one-half of the photos were of people rated high

Successful communication is a complex process. These two kids are combining languages, interpersonal spacing, and body language to accomplish the sharing of a secret. © Tetiana Kolinko/123rf

on these, and the other half were of people rated low on them. Participants were asked to rate the target on 13 personality scales. When the verbal description was ambiguous, the characteristics of the photo significantly influenced ratings (Hassin & Trope, 2000). This research suggests that people do make inferences about personality based on facial features. The idea that there are basic facial expressions implies that we interpret facial expressions without reference to context. In fact, research has demonstrated that identical facial expressions are interpreted differently, depending upon context. In a specific context, we expect certain facial expressions, and we compare the expression(s) displayed to what we expect in interpreting it (Aviezer et al., 2008).

Later in this chapter, we discuss research on facial maturity and how it influences interaction.

Combining Nonverbal and Verbal Communication

When we speak on the telephone or shout to a friend in another room, we are limited to communicating through verbal and paralinguistic channels. When we wave to arriving or departing passengers at the airport, we use only the kinesic channel. Ordinarily, however, communication is multichanneled. Information is conveyed simultaneously through verbal, paralinguistic, kinesic, and proxemic cues.

What is gained and what problems are caused when different communication channels are combined? If they appear to convey consistent information, they reinforce each other, and communication becomes more accurate. But if different channels convey information that is inconsistent, the message may produce confusion or even arouse a suspicion of deception. In this section, we examine some outcomes of apparent consistency and inconsistency among channels.

Reinforcement and Increased Accuracy. The multiple cues we receive often seem redundant, each carrying the same message. A smile accompanies a compliment delivered in a warm tone of voice; a scowl accompanies a vehemently shouted threat. But multiple cues are seldom entirely redundant, and they are better viewed as complementary (Poyatos, 1983). The smile and warm tone convey that the compliment is sincere; the scowl and vehement shout imply that the threat will be carried out. Thus, multiple cues convey added information, reduce ambiguity, and increase the accuracy of communication (Krauss, Morrel-Samuels, & Colasante, 1991).

Taken alone, each channel lacks the capacity to carry the entire weight of the messages exchanged in the course of a conversation. By themselves, the verbal aspects of language are insufficient for accurate communication. Paralinguistic and kinesic cues supplement verbal cues by supporting and emphasizing them. The importance of paralinguistic cues is illustrated in a study of students from a Nigerian secondary school and teachers' college (Grayshon, 1980). Although these students took courses in English and knew the verbal language well, they did not know the paralinguistic cues of British native speakers. The students listened to two British recordings with identical verbal content. In one recording, paralinguistic cues indicated that the speaker was giving the listener a brush-off. In the other recording, paralinguistic cues indicated that the speaker was apologizing. Of 251 students, 97 percent failed to perceive any difference in the meanings the speaker was conveying. Failure to distinguish a brush-off from an apology could be disastrous in everyday communication. Accurate understanding requires paralinguistic as well as verbal knowledge.

Our accuracy in interpreting events is greatly enhanced if we have multiple communication cues rather than verbal information alone. The value of a full set of cues was demonstrated in a study of U.S. undergraduates' interpretations of various scenes (Archer & Akert, 1977). Participants observed scenes of social interaction that were either displayed in a video broadcast or described verbally in a transcript of the video broadcast. Thus, students received either full, multichannel communication or verbal cues alone. Afterward, students were asked to answer questions about what was going on in each scene—questions that required going beyond the obvious facts. Observers who received the full set of verbal and nonverbal cues were substantially more accurate in interpreting social interactions. For instance, of those receiving multichannel cues, 56 percent correctly identified which of three women engaged in a conversation had no children; this compared with only 17 percent of those limited to verbal cues. These findings convincingly demonstrate the gain in accuracy from multichannel communication.

Resolving Inconsistency. At times, the messages conveyed by different channels appear inconsistent with one another. This makes communication and interaction problematic. What would you do, for example, if your instructor welcomed you during office hours with warm words, a frowning face, and an annoyed tone of voice? You might well react with uncertainty and caution, puzzled by the apparent inconsistency between the verbal and nonverbal cues you were receiving. You would certainly try to figure out the instructor's true feelings and desires, and you might also try to guess why the instructor was sending such confusing cues.

The strategies people use to resolve apparently inconsistent cues depend on their inferences about the reasons for the apparent inconsistency (Zuckerman et al., 1981). Inconsistency could be due to the communicator's ambivalent feelings (Mongrain & Vettes 2003), to poor communication skills, or to an intention to deceive. A large body of research has compared the relative weight we give to messages in different channels when we do not suspect deception.

In one set of studies, people judged the emotion expressed by actors who posed contradictory verbal, paralinguistic, and facial signals (Mehrabian, 1972). These studies showed that facial cues were most important in determining which feelings are interpreted as true. Paralinguistic cues were second, and verbal cues were a distant third. Later research exposing receivers to more complete combinations of visual and auditory cues replicated the finding that people rely more on facial than on paralinguistic cues when the two conflict. This preference for facial cues increases with age from childhood to adulthood, indicating that it is a learned strategy (DePaulo, Rosenthal, Eisenstat, Rogers, & Finkelstein, 1978).

People also use social context to help them judge which channel is more credible (Bugenthal, 1974). They consider whether the facial expression, tone of voice, or verbal content is appropriate to the particular social situation. If people recognize a situation as highly stressful, for example, they rely more on the cues that seem consistent with a stressful context (such as a strained tone of voice) and less on cues that seem to contradict it (such as a happy face or a verbal assertion of calmness). If the emotional expression is ambiguous, situational cues determine the emotion that observers attribute to the person (Carroll & Russell, 1996). For example, a person in a frightening situation displaying an expression of moderate anger was judged to be afraid. In short, people tend to resolve apparent inconsistencies between channels in favor of the channels whose message seems most appropriate to the social context.

SOCIAL STRUCTURE AND COMMUNICATIONS

So far, this chapter has examined the nature of verbal, nonverbal, and computer-mediated communication. How do social relationships shape communication? And how does communication express, maintain, or modify social relationships? These questions pinpoint social psychology's concern with the reciprocal impacts of social structure and communication on each other. This section examines four aspects of these impacts. First, it discusses gender differences in communication. Second, it considers the links between styles of speech and position in the social stratification system. Third, it analyzes the ways in which communication creates and expresses the two central dimensions of relationships—status and intimacy. Finally, it examines the social norms that regulate interaction distances and some of the outcomes when these norms are violated.

Gender and Communication

A fundamental question about how social structure influences communication is whether there are systematic differences between men and women in communication style. Many empirical studies have been conducted since 1970. Typically, each study focuses on one or two aspects of interaction and compares men and women on it. The most widely studied aspect has been interruptions. Research by Zimmerman and West (1975) reported that in casual conversation of mixed-gender dyads, men interrupted women much more frequently than the reverse. Other research suggested that women's speech involves more frequent use of tag questions ("It's really hot, isn't it?"), hedges ("In my opinion, . . ."), and disclaimers ("I may be wrong but . . ."). These three are often linked and have been said to indicate that women's speech is more tentative than men's. Some studies report that women are more likely to use intensifiers ("It's really hot, isn't it?"). In the nonverbal realm, women smile more often than men and are less likely to look at the other person as they interact. These and other findings of gender differences are the basis for the assertion that there are vast differences in style of interaction between men and women. In addition to academic researchers who take this position, it has been popularized in books such as *You Just Don't Understand: Women and Men in Conversation* (Tannen, 1991) and *Men Are from Mars, Women Are from Venus* (Gray, 1992) (see Box 8.2). The early academic interpretation of these differences was that they reflect the fact that men have greater power than women. Thus, interruptions, declarative statements instead of tentative ones, and speech without intensifiers all reflect the possession of power—that is, the stratification system of the society.

Research on gender differences in communication has gotten more sophisticated in recent years. Instead of descriptive research comparing men and women on a small number of behaviors, researchers now study these processes in specific social contexts. Thus, researchers study how gender and contextual variables such as type of relationship, group task, or authority structure interact to influence communication. For example, studies in the 1970s and 1980s found that when men attempted to change the topic of conversation, they succeeded 96 percent of the time; in contrast, attempts by women succeeded only 36 percent of the time (Fishman, 1983). This was interpreted as reflecting the difference in status of men and women. But if we take a broader look, we see that (1) there are several types of topic shifts in interaction, and (2) any group of three or more people tends to develop an internal status structure that is influenced by the setting, task, and characteristics of the specific people present. A recent study of six-person task-oriented groups found that topic shifts are more sensitive to the internal status structure of the group than to gender (Okamoto & Smith-Lovin, 2001). Moreover, topic shifts often occurred following a lapse in the discussion or an obvious conclusion to the current topic, suggesting that they are not displays of power.

Research on other aspects of communication has reached similar conclusions. A study of nonverbal behavior recruited participants in a company's headquarters; 42 employees each participated in two interactions with another, randomly chosen employee. As a result, the dyads varied in the corporate status of participants. There were 10 all-male, 9 all-female, and 25 mixed-gender dyads. During each interaction, the pair was given two tasks. Interaction was video- and audiotaped, and the tapes were coded by trained observers. The data were analyzed by gender and by corporate status. Some nonverbal behavior varied by gender and some varied by status. The differences

BOX 8.2 Gender Differences in Communication

Two of the best-selling books of the 1990s, *You Just Don't Understand* (Tannen, 1991) and *Men Are from Mars, Women Are from Venus* (Gray, 1992), proclaim that there are important differences in the way men and women communicate. According to Tannen, men and women have different goals in conversation. Men intend to exert control, maintain their independence, and enhance their status; women want to establish and maintain relationships. Men engage in conversational dominance, women in conversational maintenance. (Does this sound like the gender stereotypes discussed in Box 6.2?)

Lakoff (1979) called attention to the greater use by women of tag questions—statements that are between an assertion ("male" speech style) and a question. For example, "Richard is here, isn't he?" Lakoff and others argue that tag questions express a lack of confidence in the speaker—a desire to avoid commitment to a statement and potential conflict. Empirical results with regard to gender differences in the use of tag questions are conflicting: In some studies, women use them more; in other studies, men use them more; and in some studies, there are no differences. Also, if we look at the functions of tag questions in conversation, we see that there are several: They may express uncertainty, but they also may express solidarity ("You were really sad about losing her, weren't you?") or politeness ("Sit down, won't you?"). A closer look suggests that it is too simplistic to interpret the use of tag questions as an indication of lack of confidence, regardless of the gender of the person using them (Aries, 1996).

Another oft-discussed difference is in the use of back-channel feedback—small vocal comments a listener makes while a speaker is talking. Women use less intrusive responses than men to indicate attention or agreement during conver-sation. Women prefer head nods and "M-hmn" rather than the more assertive "Yeah" or "Right." Women also make more such responses than men. Again, research shows that gender interacts with other variables. Back-channel responses occur more often in cooperative than in competitive interactions, carry different meaning depending on whether they are inserted in the middle (showing active attention) or at the end of a long utterance (indicating an end to the topic). Back-channel comments are not consistently associated with power or dominance.

There are also gender differences in nonverbal behavior. Men tend to signal dominance through freer staring, pointing, and walking slightly ahead of the women they are with. Women are more likely to avert or lower their eyes and move out of a man's way when they are passing him (LaFrance & Mayo, 1978; Leffler, Gillespie, & Conaty, 1982). However, when men are in subordinate positions to women, they avert their eyes or move out of her way. Thus, the gender difference is really a difference in the numbers of men and women who occupy superordinate positions. An observational study of 799 instances of intentional touch found that in public situations—at shopping malls, outdoors on a college campus—men are more likely to touch women. In greeting or leave-taking situations—at bus stations and airports—there was no asymmetry by gender (Major, Schmidlin, & Williams, 1990).

Thus, a comprehensive review of the literature on gender differences in communication leads to the conclusion that speech patterns, conversational style, and nonverbal behavior vary not only by gender but by characteristics of the context, such as the goals of the interaction and the roles of the participants. Anyone is capable of displaying "masculine" or "feminine" styles of communication when it is appropriate.

associated with status did not correspond to the differences associated with gender. Although women smiled more, there were no differences in smiling by status. There were no stable differences across gender or status, suggesting that the differences observed reflected local or corporate practices and participants' motives (Hall & Friedman, 1999).

In short, men and women do not form two different, homogeneous groups with respect to communication style (Cameron, 1998). Generalizations about gender and communication require taking into account the context and particular local (group, organizational) communication practices (Eckert & McConnell-Ginet, 1999).

Social Stratification and Speech Style

The way we speak both reflects and re-creates our social relationships (Giles & Coupland, 1991). Every sociolinguistic community recognizes variation in the way its members talk. One style is usually the preferred or standard style. In addition to this preferred style, there are often other, nonpreferred styles.

Standard and Nonstandard Speech. Consider an example of each style. As you enter a theater, a young man approaches you. He asks, "Would you please fill out this short survey for me?" Depending on your mood, you might comply with his request. But what if he asked, "Wud ja ansa sum questions?" Many people would be less likely to comply with this request.

The first request employs standard American English. **Standard speech** is defined as characterized by diverse vocabulary, proper pronunciation, correct grammar, and abstract content. It takes into account the listener's perspective. Note the inclusion of "please" in the first request, which indicates that the speaker recognizes

that he is asking for a favor. **Nonstandard speech** is defined as characterized by limited vocabulary, improper pronunciation, incorrect grammar, and directness. It is egocentric; the absence of "please" and "for me" in the second request makes it sound like an order, even though it is phrased as a question.

In the United States, as in many other countries, speech style is associated with social status (Giles & Coupland, 1991). The use of standard speech is associated with high socioeconomic status and with power. People in positions of economic and political power are usually very articulate and grammatically correct in their public statements. In contrast, the use of nonstandard speech is associated with low socioeconomic status and low power.

These variations in speech are often used in mass media to index social class (Stamou, 2011). An analysis of a very popular Greek TV series describes the standard speech used by Constantine, a 40-something professor. He uses a formal speech style, peppered with obsolete language forms and ancient Greek proverbs. He lives with Helen, a 40-something barmaid, who uses everyday and colloquial speech, and throws in expressions from youth language ("pissed off"). Their consistent use of these styles contrasts with two other characters, both lawyers, who switch from one style to the other depending on the occasion. Given the class gulf between them, it is not surprising that Constantine and Helen don't cohabit happily ever after. You can probably think of a TV series or film that uses speech style to mark social class.

Speech style is also influenced by the interpersonal context. In informal conversations with others of equal status, such as at some parties or in bars, we often use nonstandard speech, regardless of our socioeconomic status. In more formal settings, especially public ones, we usually shift to standard speech. Thus, our choice of standard or nonstandard speech gives listeners information about how we perceive the situation.

Studies in a variety of cultures have found systematic differences in how people evaluate speakers using standard and nonstandard speech. In one study, students in Kentucky listened to tape recordings of young men and women describing themselves. Four of the recordings, two by men and two by women, were of speakers with "standard" American accents. Four others, identical in content, were of speakers with Kentucky accents. On the average, students gave the standard speakers high ratings on status and the nonstandard speakers low ratings on status (Luhman, 1990).

Is mumbling macho? Women's speech has somewhat greater phonetic distinctiveness than men's; women speak with more dispersed vowels (better enunciation) and more precise articulation of consonants. Radio DJs report altering their speech to fit the audience, so they might use more masculine styles when broadcasting heavy metal and country music, and less masculine styles when playing popular and classical music. Eight on-air DJs were recorded on XM satellite radio; one-minute samples were created for each, and rated by male and female undergraduates on ten Likert scales. Recordings were also analyzed using acoustic computer software. Those DJs whose speech was acoustically less distinctive (that is, they mumbled more) were rated as significantly more masculine by the listeners. As predicted they were the DJs on the heavy metal and country music channels (Heffernan, 2010).

African-American Vernacular English. Nonstandard speech involves limited vocabulary, is rooted in the present, and does not allow for elaboration and qualification of ideas. As a result, some analysts advocate

so-called *deficit theories*, which claim that people who use nonstandard speech are less capable of abstract and complex thought. These theories also claim that nonstandard speech styles are typical of lower-class, Black, and other culturally disadvantaged groups in the United States, Great Britain, and other societies. Combining these two claims, deficit theorists argue that the children from disadvantaged groups perform poorly in school because their restricted language makes them cognitively inferior. Their poor academic performance in turn leads to unemployment and poverty in later life.

The strongest criticism of deficit theories has come from Labov (1972). Based on interviews in natural environments, he demonstrated that "Black English," which has been described as nonstandard speech, is every bit as rich and subtle as standard English. Black English differs from standard English mainly in surface details like pronunciation ("ax" = *ask*) and grammatical forms ("He be busy" = *He's always busy*). Nonstandard speech may appear impoverished because nonstandard speakers feel less relaxed in the social contexts where they are typically observed (such as schools or interviews), and so they limit their speech. Anxiety may be the reason the one young man asked "Wud ja ansa sum questions?" Social researchers or other "outsiders" who observe nonstandard speakers may also inhibit their language (Grimshaw, 1973). When interviewed by a member of their own race, for instance, Black job applicants used longer sentences and richer vocabularies and employed words more creatively (Ledvinka, 1971). Overall, speech differences between groups have not been shown to reflect differences in cognitive ability (Thorlundsson, 1987), and deficit theories have not received much empirical support.

In 1996, the Oakland, California, school board adopted a resolution stating that Black

English, which the resolution called **ebonics** (ebony phonics), is a distinctive language. The board decided to provide some instruction in ebonics to facilitate the education of students and encourage "their mastery of English language skills." The board's action set off a national debate. Numerous scholars and organizations now recognize the legitimacy and cultural value of this language spoken by many African Americans, referred to as *African-American Vernacular English* (AAVE) (Rodriguez, Cargile, & Rich, 2004). Some teachers use AAVE in an effort to enhance the comprehension and learning of African-American students (Bohn, 2003). For example, one seventh-grade teacher in a predominantly minority school encourages students to journal and write poetry in AAVE, which facilitates self-expression, and requires students to produce an "errorless draft" of a paper adhering to all the conventions of Standard English (SE) (Hill, 2009). A field researcher in one high school in Washington, D.C., observed that for many African-American students, AAVE was the preferred speech style; they associated SE with White, majority culture, and its history of oppressing Blacks (Fordham, 1999). For these students, SE is the nonstandard vernacular, and they "dissed" (disrespected) those Blacks who used it. These students "leased" SE—that is, used it when they had to while in school, from 9:00 a.m. to 3:00 p.m., but not outside the school building. Two researchers collected essays from 52 African-American tenth-graders (Godley & Escher, 2012). Twenty-three (45 percent) argued that only AAVE should be spoken in the classroom, because they were more proficient and comfortable speaking it. Eighteen said both AAVE and SE should be spoken; they said AAVE facilitates group work and brainstorming, and that SE should be used for "practicing" communication in future contexts. Ten students argued that only SE should be spoken, to prepare them for future academic and professional endeavors.

We noted earlier that evaluation of speakers is influenced by their speech style. Do people evaluate speakers of AAVE differently? In a carefully designed experiment, majority and minority students evaluated recordings of speakers using strong AAVE (11 features), moderate AAVE (6 features), or U.S. Standard English (USE). Listeners rated the strong AAVE speakers as less attractive and lower-status than the speakers of moderate AAVE. They rated speakers of moderate AAVE as lower in attractiveness and status than speakers of USE (Rodriguez, Cargile, & Rich, 2004). Other research has attempted to identify the specific features that cause listeners to distinguish AAVE from USE; the results are inconclusive (Thomas & Reaser, 2004).

Communicating Status and Intimacy

The two central dimensions of social relationships are status and intimacy. Status is concerned with the exercise of power and control. Intimacy is concerned with the expression of affiliation and affection that creates social solidarity (Kemper, 1973). Verbal and nonverbal communication express and maintain particular levels of intimacy and relative status in relationships. Moreover, through communication we may challenge existing levels of intimacy and relative status and negotiate new ones (Scotton, 1983).

Communication can signal our view of a relationship only if we recognize which communication behaviors are appropriate for an expected level of intimacy or status, and which are inappropriate. The following examples suggest that we easily recognize when communication behaviors are inappropriate. What if you

- repeatedly addressed your mother as Mrs. X?

- used vulgar slang during a job interview?
- draped your arm on your professor's shoulder as he or she explained how to improve your test answers?
- looked away each time your beloved gazed into your eyes?

Each of these communication behaviors would probably make you uncomfortable, and they would doubtlessly cause others to think you inept, disturbed, or hostile. Each behavior expresses levels of intimacy or relative status easily recognized as inappropriate to the relationship. In the following section, we survey systematically how specific communication behaviors express, maintain, and change status and intimacy in relationships.

Status. Forms of address clearly communicate relative status in relationships. Inferiors use formal address (title and last name) for their superiors (for example, "When is the exam, Professor Levine?"), whereas superiors address inferiors with familiar forms (first name or nickname; for example, "On Friday, Daphne"). Status equals use the same form of address with one another. Both use either formal (Ms./Mr./Mrs.) or familiar forms (Carol/Bill), depending on the degree of intimacy between them (Brown, 1965). When status differences are ambiguous, individuals may even avoid addressing each other directly. They shy away from choosing an address form because it might grant too much or too little status.

A shift in forms of address signals a change in social relationships, or at least an attempted change. During the French Revolution, in order to promote equality and fraternity, the revolutionaries demanded that everyone use only the familiar (*tu*) and not the formal (*vous*) form of the second-person pronoun, regardless of past status differences. Presidential candidates

try to reduce their differences with voters by inviting the use of familiar names (John, Barack). In cases where there is a clear status difference between people, the right to initiate the use of the more familiar or equal forms of address belongs to the superior (for example, "Why don't you drop that 'Doctor' stuff?"). This principle also applies to other communication behaviors. It is the higher-status person who usually initiates changes toward more familiar behaviors such as greater eye contact, physical proximity, touch, or self-disclosure.

We each have a speech repertoire, different pronunciations, dialects, and a varied vocabulary from which to choose when speaking. Our choices of language to use with other people express a view of our relative status and may influence our relationships. People usually make language choices smoothly, easily expressing status differences appropriate to the situation (Gumperz, 1976; Stiles, Orth, Scherwitz, Hennrikus, & Vallbona, 1984). Teachers in a Norwegian town, for instance, were observed to lecture to their students in the standard language (Blom & Gumperz, 1972). When they wished to encourage student discussion, however, they switched to the local dialect, thereby reducing status differences. Note how your teachers also switch to more informal language when trying to promote student participation.

An experiment involving groups composed of a manager and two workers studied the effect of authority and gender composition of the group on verbal and nonverbal communication (Johnson, 1994). The researcher created a simulated retail store; the manager gave instructions to the subordinates and monitored their work for 30 minutes. The interaction was coded as it occurred. Authority affected verbal behavior; subordinates talked less, were less directive, and gave less feedback compared to superiors, regardless of gender. Gender

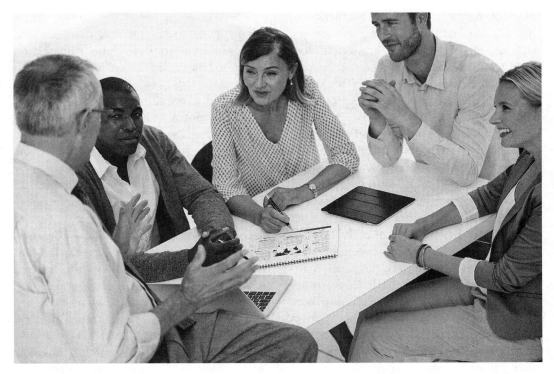

Kinesic and proxemic cues are all we need to decipher the status relations displayed in this photo. His position, half sitting in a relaxed posture with active hand gestures, tells us which one is the boss; their seated postures, direct eye contact, and uniform smiles identify the employees. © pixdeluxe/iStock

affected the nonverbal behaviors of smiling and laughing; women in all-female groups smiled more than men in all-male groups.

Paralinguistic cues also communicate and reinforce status in relationships. An experimental study of influence in three-person groups systematically varied the paralanguage of one member (Ridgeway, 1987). This member, a confederate, was most influential when she spoke rapidly, in a confident tone, and gave quick responses. She was less influential when she behaved dominantly (that is, spoke loudly, gave orders) or submissively (that is, spoke softly, in a pleading tone). A subsequent study found that a person who spoke in a task-oriented style (that is, rapid speech, upright posture, eye contact) or a social style (that is, moderate volume, relaxed posture) was more influential (Carli, LaFleur, & Loeber, 1995). Persons who spoke using dominant or submissive paralanguage were less influential. Thus, engaging in the paralinguistic behaviors appropriate to the statuses of group members—in these experiments equals—enhances one's influence; engaging in behaviors inappropriate to one's status (say, like a superior toward equals) reduces one's influence.

Body language also serves to express status. When status is unequal, people of higher status tend to adopt relatively relaxed postures with their arms and legs in asymmetrical positions. Those of lower status stand or sit in more tense and symmetrical positions. The amount of time we spend looking at our partner, and the timing, also indicate status. Higher-status persons look more when speaking than when listening, whereas lower-status persons look more when listening than when speaking. Overall, inferiors look more at their partners, but they are also first to break the gaze between partners. Finally, superiors are much more likely to intrude physically on inferiors by touching or pointing at them (Dovidio & Ellyson, 1982; LaFrance & Mayo, 1978; Leffler, Gillespie, & Conaty, 1982).

An important phenomenon that both expresses and produces status differences is silencing. In many interactions, being silent is not a passive state reflecting the absence of a desire to communicate. The silence of one or more of the actors may reflect an active state produced by the ongoing interaction. A common form of silencing involves not replying to a comment or question addressed to you, which may silence the other person. Bodily movement may contribute to silencing, as when you turn away from someone and pick up the TV remote, or leave the room. Silencing can be an especially complex process when it occurs in a group setting, as illustrated by a detailed analysis of the silencing of one student during a classroom discussion (Leander, 2002). In response to a teacher's question about equal rights for women, one woman, Chelle, sitting in the back of the room, says quietly, "No, we don't have equal rights." A young man in front of her gestures with his thumb over his shoulder and says, "We got somebody back here who says they don't have equal rights." The young man, by gesturing rather than looking at Chelle, and by invoking we-they (in-group vs. out-group identities), is attempting to silence her. Both students are sitting near friends, and the friends become engaged in the conversation, so that interacting groups are now attempting to control the discourse. This contest by the groups is facilitated by seating arrangements, and participants turn their bodies and direct their gaze in ways that signal alignment. Other techniques employed included speaking over a member of the other group, and ridicule of an example given by one of the women. Thus, silencing involves language, gaze, gesture, bodily orientation, and symbolic invocation of group ties within the setting.

Intimacy. Communication also expresses another central dimension of relationships—intimacy. The exchange of title and last names is common for strangers. One way we signal intimacy or solidarity is by addressing each other with first names. In other languages, speakers express intimacy by their choice of familiar versus formal second-person pronouns. As noted earlier, the French can choose between the familiar *tu* or the formal *vous*; the Spanish have *tu* or *usted*; the Germans *du* or *sie*; and so on.

Our choice of language is another way to express intimacy. For example, the residents of a Norwegian town were found to use the formal version of their language with strangers and the local dialect with friends. They spoke the formal language when transacting official business in government offices, then switched to dialect for a personal chat with the clerk after completing their business (Blom & Gumperz, 1972). The use of slang gives strong expression to in-group intimacy and solidarity. Through slang, group members assert their own shared social identity and express their alienation from and rejection of the out-group of slang illiterates.

Choice of language, or *code switching*, is a strategy that is employed in a variety of situations. Deliberate choice of a language may play a central role in the construction of ethnicity (De Fina, 2007). Members of *Il Circolo*, an Italian-American community with 48 members (men), gathered monthly for dinner and cards. All spoke both English and Italian, and some also spoke a dialect. Public communication, verbal and written, and club business during dinner was conducted in English. Informal conversation, including talk during card games, was typically in Italian; if the men knew the dialect, that language might be used. The dialect and Italian were spoken to emphasize the men's common ethnic background.

Code switching may also reflect the desire to maintain or revitalize an ethnic community. Young adults of Mayan descent living in Guatemala were less likely to use Spanish, compared to older (Mayan) adults. The youth spoke in the Mayan dialect more often to demonstrate their resistance to Spanish culture and to revitalize the Mayan language (Barrett, 2008). Note the similarity to the use of AAVE by Black high school students to resist White U.S. culture discussed earlier.

Code switching is a common occurrence in language classes where native speakers of one language are learning a second language. Observation in high school English-as-a-second-language classes for immigrants from China (Liang, 2006), and Spanish classrooms where 10- to 12-year-old native speakers of Spanish were learning Catalan (Unamuno, 2008), found that students switched back to native language when it facilitated completion of class assignments. Thus, the goals of interaction influence language choice.

You can even observe code switching in CMC. Swiss of German descent who visited Internet chat rooms often used dialect instead of German in their messages. Frequency of dialect use reflected not only the preference of individual message senders, but also the relative use of dialect in the thread—that is, context (Siebenhaar, 2006). This is especially remarkable because a written version of the dialect was rarely used prior to the Internet.

The intimacy of a relationship is clearly reflected in and reinforced by the content of conversation. As a relationship becomes more intimate, we disclose more personal information about ourselves. Intimacy is also conveyed by conversational style. In one study (Hornstein, 1985), telephone conversations were recorded and later analyzed; the conversations were between strangers, acquaintances, and friends. Compared to strangers, friends used more implicit openings ("Hi," or "Hi, it's me"), raised more topics, and were more responsive to the other conversationalist (for example, asked more questions). Friends also used more complex closings (for example, making concrete arrangements for the next contact). Conversations of acquaintances were more like those of strangers.

The **theory of speech accommodation** (Beebe & Giles, 1984; Giles, 1980) illustrates an important way in which people use verbal and paralinguistic behavior to express intimacy or liking. According to this theory, people express or reject intimacy by adjusting their speech behavior during interaction to converge with or diverge from their partner's. To express liking or evoke approval, they make their own speech behavior more similar to their partner's. To reject intimacy or communicate disapproval, they accentuate the differences between their own speech and their partner's.

A detailed analysis of 18 interviews illustrates speech accommodation based on both ethnicity and familiarity (Scanlon & Wassink, 2010). A 65-year old, middle-class, African-American woman interviewed 14 African-American and 4 White adults who grew up in the same multiethnic neighborhood. She had known some of the interviewees growing up in that neighborhood but not others. Her speech patterns were recorded and analyzed acoustically for use of features common to AAVE. She was more likely to use tokens common to AAVE in interviews with African Americans; she rarely used them in interviews with whites—that is, she used SE patterns with them. Also, she was more likely to match speech patterns with persons she had known growing up than with strangers.

Adjustments of paralinguistic behavior demonstrate speech accommodation during conversations (Taylor & Royer, 1980; Thakerar, Giles, & Cheshire, 1982). Individuals who wish to express liking tend to shift their own pronunciation, speech rate, vocal intensity, pause lengths, and utterance lengths during conversation to match those of their partner. Individuals who wish to communicate disapproval modify these vocal behaviors in ways that make them diverge more from their partner's. Researchers recruited 100 romantically involved couples. Following an initial 3-minute conversation, couples were separated and randomly assigned to one of five conditions; one member was instructed to engage in very low, low, high, or very high intimacy in a subsequent 3-minute interaction, or were given no instruction. The second interaction was videotaped, and the frequency of 11 behaviors reflecting intimacy was coded for each participant. As expected, the partner adjusted his or her behavior by reciprocating the behaviors exhibited by the confederate. Reciprocity was especially evident on verbal expressions of intimacy and nonverbal indicators of involvement, for example, facial pleasantness (Guerreo, Jones, & Burgoon, 2000).

Among bilinguals, speech accommodation may also determine the choice of language (Bourhis, Giles, Leyens, & Tajfel, 1979). To increase intimacy, bilinguals choose the language they believe their partner would prefer to speak. To reject intimacy, they choose their partner's less preferred language.

If greater intimacy leads to accommodation, can accommodation lead to greater intimacy? Research suggests that extreme accommodation, in the form of mimicry, leads to behaviors associated with greater intimacy. Using the methodology of the field experiment, 60 groups of customers in a restaurant were randomly assigned to one of two conditions. In one condition,

a waitress literally repeated the orders of her customers; in the other, she merely acknowledged the orders by saying "Okay" or "Coming up." Customers whose orders were mimicked were more generous, giving significantly larger tips than those in the other condition (van Baaren, Holland, Steenaert, & van Knippenberg, 2003). In a related experiment conducted in a laboratory, the experimenter mimicked the posture (bodily orientation, positions of arms and legs) of one-half of the participants during a 6-minute interaction; those whom she mimicked were more likely to help her later when she dropped some pens (van Baaren, Holland, Kawakami, & van Knippenberg, 2004).

Accommodation is evident even in very subtle paralinguistic cues. Using audiotapes of interviews by talk-show host Larry King of 25 guests (stars, athletes, politicians), analyses indicated voice convergence between partners (Gregory & Webster, 1996). Lower-status persons accommodated their voices to higher-status persons. Moreover, student ratings of the status of Larry King and of his guests were correlated with the voice characteristics that showed convergence.

The ways we express intimacy through body language and interpersonal spacing are well-recognized. For instance, research supports the folklore that lovers gaze more into each other's eyes (Rubin, 1970). In fact, we tend to interpret a high level of eye contact from others as a sign of intimacy. We communicate liking by assuming moderately relaxed postures, moving closer and leaning toward others, orienting ourselves face-to-face, and touching them (Mehrabian, 1972). Increasing emotional intimacy is often accompanied by increasing body engagement, from an arm around the shoulders to a full embrace (Gurevitch, 1990). There is an important qualification to these generalizations, however. Mutual gaze, close distance, and touch reflect intimacy and promote it only when the interaction has a positive cast. If the interaction is generally negative—if the setting is competitive, the verbal content unpleasant, or the past relationship antagonistic—these same nonverbal behaviors intensify negative feelings (Schiffenbauer & Schiavo, 1976).

The Case of "Dude." Let's apply the themes in this section to a concrete case. Language is continually evolving; some words and phrases fall into disuse (remember "valley girl"?) while new ones appear, like "dude." Think about the last time you used "dude" in conversation; to whom were you talking, and what was the context? Research using diaries, surveys of students, and analysis of conversations yields a snapshot of its use (Kiesling, 2004). "Dude" is used primarily by young men in conversation with other young men, suggesting that it is a marker of youth and masculinity. Further, men rarely use the term in conversation with parents and professors; its use indexes a relationship between persons of equal status. In terms of intimacy, it occurs in conversations involving friends, but not close friends; this suggests to the researcher that "dude" is used to indicate a "cool solidarity," an effortless interaction with other men. Like many terms that are adopted widely by youth, "dude" has many uses, as a greeting ("What's up, dude?"), an exclamation ("Dude!"), to one-up someone ("That's lame, dude"), and to express agreement. Thus, like all use of speech, the use of this term is governed by sociolinguistic norms, and reflects group membership and the status and intimacy of the relationship between the conversationalists.

NORMATIVE DISTANCES FOR INTERACTION

American and Northern European tourists in Cairo are often surprised to see men touching and staring intently into each other's eyes as they converse in public. Surprise may turn to discomfort if the tourist engages an Arab man in conversation. Bathed in the warmth of his breath, the tourist may feel sexually threatened. In our own communities, in contrast, we are rarely made uncomfortable by the overly close approach of another. People apparently know the norms for interaction distances in their own cultures and they conform to them. What are these norms, and what happens when they are violated?

Normative Distances

Edward Hall (1966) has described four spatial zones that are normatively prescribed for interaction among middle-class Americans. Each zone is considered appropriate for particular types of activities and relationships. Public distance (12 to 25 feet) is prescribed for interaction in formal encounters, lectures, trials, and other public events. At this distance, communication is often one way, sensory stimulation is very weak, people speak loudly, and they choose language carefully. Social distance (4 to 12 feet) is prescribed for many casual social and business transactions. Here, sensory stimulation is low. People speak at normal volume, do not touch one another, and use frequent eye contact to maintain smooth communication. Personal distance (1.5 to 4 feet) is prescribed for interaction among friends and relatives. Here, people speak softly, touch one another, and receive substantial sensory stimulation by sight, sound, and smell. Intimate distance (0 to 18 inches) is prescribed for giving comfort, making love, and aggressing physically. This distance provides intense stimulation from touch, smell, breath, and body heat. It signals unmistakable involvement.

Many studies support the idea that people know and conform to the normatively prescribed distances for particular kinds of encounters (LaFrance & Mayo, 1978).

When we compare different cultural and social groups, both similarities and differences in distance norms emerge. All cultures prescribe closer distances for friends than for strangers, for example. The specific distances for preferred interactions vary widely, however. With regard to personal distance, research using participants from several cultural groupings found that Anglo-Saxons (people from the United States, the United Kingdom, and Canada) preferred the largest zone or distance, followed by Asians and Caucasians (Western Europe), with Mediterraneans and Latinos preferring the smallest zone (Beaulieu, 2004). Women tend to interact with one another at closer distances than men do in Western cultures (Sussman & Rosenfeld, 1982), whereas two men interact at close distances in some Muslim countries (Hewitt & Alqahtani, 2003). Social class may also influence interpersonal spacing. In Canadian school yards, lower-class primary-school children were observed to interact at closer distances than middle-class children, regardless of race (Scherer, 1974). Observational research on Boy Scout and Girl Scout troop meetings suggests that maintaining the appropriate physical and emotional distance from peers is associated with peer acceptance (Stiles & Raney, 2004).

Differences in distance norms may cause discomfort in cross-cultural interaction. People from different countries or social classes may have difficulty in interpreting the amount of intimacy implied by each other's interpersonal spacing and in finding mutually comfortable interaction distances. Cross-cultural training in nonverbal communication can reduce such discomfort. For instance, Englishmen were liked more by Arabs with whom they interacted when the Englishmen had been trained to behave nonverbally like Arabs—to stand closer, smile more, look more, and touch more (Collett, 1971).

Two aspects of interpersonal spacing that clearly influence and reflect status are physical distance and the amount of space each person occupies. Equal-status individuals jointly determine comfortable interaction distances and tend to occupy approximately equal amounts of space with their bodies and with the possessions that surround them. When status is unequal, superiors tend to control interaction distances, keeping greater physical distance than equals would choose. Superiors also claim more direct space with their bodies and possessions than inferiors (Gifford, 1982; Hayduk, 1978; Leffler et al., 1982).

Violations of Personal Space. What happens when people violate distance norms by coming too close? In particular, what do we do when strangers intrude on our personal space?

The earliest systematic examination of this question included two parallel studies (Felipe & Sommer, 1966). In one, strangers approached lone male patients in mental hospitals to a point only 6 inches away. In the other, strangers sat down 12 inches away from lone female students in a university library. The mental patients and the female students who were approached left the scene much more quickly than the other patients and students who were not approached. After only 2 minutes, 30 percent of the patients who were intruded on had fled, compared with none of the others. Among the students, 70 percent of those whose space was violated had fled by the end of 30 minutes, compared with only 13 percent of the others. The results of this study are shown in Figure 8.2.

Research in a university library in Pakistan replicated the study of invasions involving students. A female invader, dressed like a student, selected a person sitting alone (51 men, 50 women) and sat down within three feet (Khan & Kamal, 2010). She remained seated for 10 minutes, or until the other person left the table ("flight"). Observers recorded other reactions: stare/glance, browse books, lean away, use cell phone, initiate conversation, or no reaction. Ninety-four percent of the men and women reacted (in a control condition, only six percent of students sitting alone performed any of the behaviors in a 10-minute period). The most common reactions were stare/glance and use cell phone. Men who fled on

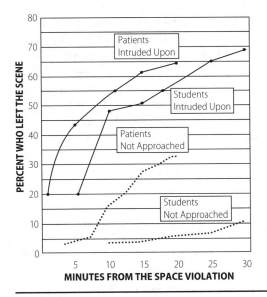

FIGURE 8.2 Reactions to Violations of Personal Space

How do people react when strangers violate norms of interpersonal distance and intrude on their personal space? A common reaction is illustrated here. Strangers sat down 12 inches away from lone female students in a library or approached lone male patients in a mental hospital to within 6 inches. Those who were approached left the scene much more quickly than control subjects who were not approached. Violations of personal space often produce flight. Source: *Social Problems* by N. J. Felipe and R. Sommer. Copyright 1966 by University of California Press—Journals. Reproduced with permission of University of California Press—Journals in the format Textbook and extranet posting via Copyright Clearance Center.

average left within 2 minutes, whereas for women (the same gender as the invader) it was 9 minutes.

The reaction to violations depends in part on the setting in which they occur. Whereas violations of space norms at library tables may lead to flight, violations in library aisles lead to the person spending more time in the aisle (Ruback, 1987). Similarly, intrusion into the space of someone using a public telephone is associated with the caller spending more time on the phone (Ruback, Pape, & Doriot, 1989). It is possible that when you are looking for a book or talking on the phone, a violation of distance norms is distracting, so it takes you longer to complete your task.

Staring is a powerful way to violate another's privacy without direct physical intrusion. Staring by strangers elicits avoidance responses, indicating that it is experienced as an intense negative stimulus. When stared at by strangers, for instance, pedestrians cross the street more rapidly, and drivers speed away from intersections more quickly (Ellsworth, Carlsmith, & Henson, 1972; Greenbaum & Rosenfeld, 1978).

As the energy crisis worsens, more people are considering alternatives to the car as a means of transportation. Yet many people are unwilling to use mass transit, even when it is more convenient and equally fast. Why? Possibly because on crowded buses, streetcars, and commuter trains, passengers experience violations of personal space. Interviews with auto users identified influences associated with the decision to drive versus use transit; one theme was negative affect due to violations of personal space on transit vehicles (Mann & Abraham, 2006). Research involving 139 passenger train commuters found that both self-reports of stress and increases in salivary cortisol, a hormonal indicator of stress, were related to local seating density within the rail coach. People experienced adverse reactions when they had to sit close to others (Evans & Wener, 2007).

In the contemporary world, crowded public transportation facilities like airplanes and airports are also very noisy. Travelers are likely to encounter violations of their aural space, by the noise of crowds, jet engines, crying infants, noisy teens, loud cell phone conversations, and so one. Perhaps this accounts for the marketing success of noise-cancelling headphones (Hagood, 2011). They allow the user to at least create a quiet space, if not an uncrowded one.

Despite the crowded circumstances, the people on this subway train are maintaining some privacy. Strangers feel uncomfortable when they must intrude on each other's personal space. To overcome this discomfort, they studiously ignore each other, avoiding touch, eye contact, and verbal exchanges. © Nick White/Image Source/ Corbis

CONVERSATIONAL ANALYSIS

Although conversation is a common daily activity, we all have trouble communicating at times. The list of what can go wrong is long and painful: inability to get started, irritating interruptions, awkward silences, failure to give others a chance to talk, failure to notice that listeners are bored or have lost interest, changing topics inappropriately, assuming incorrectly that others understand, and so on. This section examines the ways people avoid these embarrassing and annoying blunders. To maintain smooth-flowing conversation requires knowledge of certain rules and communication skills that are often taken for granted. We will discuss some of the rules and skills that are crucial for initiating conversations, regulating turn taking, and coordinating conversation through verbal and nonverbal feedback.

Initiating Conversations

Conversations must be initiated with an attention-getting device—a summons to interaction. Greetings, questions, or the ringing of a telephone can serve as the summons. But conversations do not get under way until potential partners signal that they are attending and willing to converse. Eye contact is the crucial nonverbal signal of availability for face-to-face interaction. Goffman (1963a) suggests that eye contact places a person under an obligation to interact: When a waitress permits eye contact, she places herself under the power of the eye-catcher.

The most common verbal lead into conversation is a **summons-answer sequence** (Schegloff, 1968). Response to a summons ("Jack, you home?" "Yeah") indicates availability. More important, this response initiates the mutual obligation to speak and to listen that produces conversational turn

Flirting is a complex behavior that conveys interest in being approached by another person. These young people are using posture, smiles, and direct gaze to attract each other's attention. © Lise Gagne/iStock

taking. The summoner is expected to provide the first topic—a conversational rule that little children exasperatingly overlook. Our reactions when people violate the summons-answer sequence demonstrate its widespread acceptance as an obligatory rule. When people ignore a summons, we conclude either that they are intentionally insulting us, socially incompetent, or psychologically absent (sleeping, drunk, or crazy).

Telephone conversations exhibit a common sequential organization. Consider the following conversation between a caller and a recipient:

0. (ring)
1. Recipient: Hello?
2. Caller: This is John.
3. R: Hi.
4. C: How are you?
5. R: Fine. How are you?
6. C: Good. Listen, I'm calling about . . .

The conversation begins with a summons-answer sequence (lines 0, 1). This is followed by an identification-recognition sequence (lines 2, 3); in this example, the recipient knows that the caller, John, recognizes his voice, so he does not state his name. Next, there is a trading of "How are you?" sequences (lines 4 through 6). Finally, at line 6, John states the reason for the call. This organization is found in many types of telephone calls. However, in an emergency, when seconds count, the organization is quite different (Whalen & Zimmerman, 1987). Consider the following example:

0. (ring)
1. R: Mid-City Emergency.
2. C: Um, yeah. There's a fire in my garage.
3. R: What's your address?

Notice that the opening sequence is shortened; both the greeting and the

"How are you?" sequences are omitted. In emergency calls, the reason for the call is stated sooner. Note also that the recognition element of the identification-recognition sequence is moved forward, to line 1. Both of these changes facilitate communication in an anonymous, urgent situation. However, if the dispatcher answers a call and the caller says, "This is John," that signals an ordinary call. Thus, the organization of conversation clearly reflects situational contingencies.

Regulating Turn Taking

A pervasive rule of conversation is to avoid bumping into someone verbally. To regulate turn taking, people use many verbal and nonverbal cues, singly and together, with varying degrees of success (Duncan & Fiske, 1977; Kendon, Harris, & Key, 1975; Sacks, Schegloff, & Jefferson, 1978).

Signaling Turns. Speakers indicate their willingness to yield the floor by looking directly at a listener with a sustained gaze toward the end of an utterance. People also signal readiness to give over the speaking role by pausing and by stretching the final syllable of their speech in a drawl, terminating hand gestures, dropping voice volume, and tacking relatively meaningless expressions (such as "You know") onto the end of their utterances. Listeners indicate their desire to talk by inhaling audibly as if preparing to speak. They also tense and move their hands, shift their head away from the speaker, and emit especially loud vocal signs of interest (such as "Yeah," "M-hmn").

Speakers retain their turn by avoiding eye contact with listeners, tensing their hands and gesticulating, and increasing voice volume to overpower others when simultaneous speech occurs. People who persist in these behaviors are soon viewed by others as egocentric and domineering. They have

violated an implicit social rule: "It's all right to hold a conversation, but you should let go of it now and then" (Richard Armour).

Verbal content and grammatical form of speech also provide important cues for turn taking. People usually exchange turns at the end of a meaningful speech act, after an idea has been completed. The first priority for the next turn goes to any person explicitly addressed by the current speaker with a question, complaint, or other invitation to talk. People expect turn changes to occur after almost every question, but not necessarily after other pauses in conversation (Hanni, 1980). It is difficult to exchange turns without using questions. When speakers in one study were permitted to use all methods except questions for signaling their desire to gain or relinquish the floor, the length of each speaking turn virtually doubled (Kent, Davis, & Shapiro, 1978).

Turn Allocation. Much of our conversation takes place in settings where turn taking is more organized than in spontaneous conversations. In class discussions, meetings, interviews, and therapy sessions, for example, responsibility for allocating turns tends to be controlled by one person, and turns are often allocated in advance. Prior allocation of turns reduces strains that arise from people either competing for speaking time or avoiding their responsibilities to speak. Allocation of turns also increases the efficiency of talk. It can arrange a distribution of turns that best fits the task or situation—a precisely equal distribution (as in a formal debate) or just one speaker (as in a football huddle).

Much of the early work on the structure of conversation was based on English-language talk. Recently, researchers have examined talk within a broader range of languages and communities/cultures. These comparative studies are leading to the identification of a generic series of problems in conversation, and an understanding of how the solution varies, reflecting local/cultural context (Sidnell, 2007).

Feedback and Coordination

We engage in conversation to attain interpersonal goals—to inform, persuade, impress, control, and so on. To do this effectively, we must assess how what we say is affecting our partner's interest and understanding as we go along. Both verbal and nonverbal feedback help conversationalists in making this assessment. Through feedback, conversationalists coordinate what they are saying to each other from moment to moment. The responses called **back-channel feedback** are especially important for regulating speech as it is happening. These are the small vocal and visual comments that a listener makes while a speaker is talking, without taking over the speaking turn. They include such responses as "Yeah," "M-hmn," short clarifying questions (such as "What?" "Huh?"), brief repetitions of the speaker's words or completions of his or her utterances, head nods, and brief smiles. When conversations are proceeding smoothly, the fine rhythmic body movements of listeners (such as swaying, rocking, blinking) are precisely synchronized with the speech sounds of speakers who address them (Condon & Ogston, 1967). These automatic listener movements are another source of feedback that indicates to speakers whether they are being properly tracked and understood (Kendon, 1970).

Both the presence (or absence) and the timing of back-channel feedback influence speakers. In smooth conversation, listeners time their signs of interest, agreement, or understanding to occur at the end of long utterances, or when the speaker turns his or her head toward them. When speakers are denied feedback, the quality of their speech deteriorates. They become less coherent and communicate less accurately. Their speech becomes more wordy, less organized, and more poorly fitted to the situation (Bavelas, Coates, & Johnson, 2000). Lack of feedback causes such deterioration because it prevents speakers from learning several things about their partners. They cannot discern whether their partners (1) have relevant prior knowledge they need not repeat; (2) understand already so they can wrap up the point or abbreviate; (3) have misinformation they should correct; (4) feel confused so they should backtrack and clarify; or (5) feel bored so they should stop talking or change topics.

Alerted to the possible loss of listener attention and involvement by the absence of feedback, speakers employ attention-getting devices to evoke feedback. One such attention-getting device is the phrase "You know." Speakers frequently insert "You know" into long speaking turns immediately prior to or following pauses if their partner seems to be ignoring their invitation to provide feedback or to accept a speaking turn (Fishman, 1980).

Another device a speaker can use to regain the attention of another participant is to ask him or her a question. Such displays of uncertainty (for example, "What was the name of that guy on the *Idol* show?") restructure the interaction by getting listeners more involved (Goodwin, 1987). If the speaker shifts his or her gaze to a specific person as he or she asks the question, it will draw that person into the conversation.

The fact that feedback influences the quality of speech has another interesting consequence. Listeners who frequently provide their conversational partners with feedback also understand their partner's communication more fully and accurately. Through their feedback, active listeners help shape the conversation to fit their own needs. The information needed varies on several dimensions, one of which is precision; recall that the cooperative principle assumes the actors provide relevant precision. In responding to an invitation, it may be sufficient, if exaggerated, to say, "I don't have any money," but in bankruptcy court, counsel or the judge will want greater precision. When we fail to provide relevant precision, we will be challenged by an alert listener (Drew, 2003). This reinforces a central theme of this chapter: Accurate communication is a shared social accomplishment.

Feedback is important not only in conversations, but also in formal lectures. Lecturers usually monitor members of the audience for feedback. If listeners are looking at the speaker attentively and nodding their heads in agreement, the lecturer infers that his or her message is understood. On the other hand, quizzical or out-of-focus expressions suggest failure to understand. Similarly, members of the audience use feedback from the lecturer to regulate their own behavior; a penetrating look from the speaker may be sufficient to end a whispered conversation between listeners.

An important form of feedback in many lectures is applause. Speakers may want applause for a variety of reasons, not just ego gratification. Sometimes, lecturers subtly signal the audience when to applaud; audiences watch for such signals in order to maintain their involvement. For instance, an analysis of 42 hours of recorded political speeches suggests that there is a narrow range of message content that stimulates applause (Heritage & Greatbatch, 1986). Attacks on political opponents, foreign persons, and collectivities; statements of support for one's own positions, record, or party; and commendations of individuals or groups generate applause. When these messages are framed within particular rhetorical devices, applause is from two to eight times more likely. For example:

SPEAKER: Governments will argue [pause]

that resources are not available [short pause] to help disabled people. [long pause]

The fact is that too much is spent on the munitions of war, [long pause]

and too little is spent [applause begins]

on the munitions of peace.

In this example, the speaker uses the rhetorical device of contrast or antithesis. Using this device, the speaker's point is made twice. Audiences can anticipate the completion point of the statement by mentally matching the second half with the first. This rhetorical device is an "invitation to applaud," and in the example, the audience begins to applaud even before the speaker completes the second half.

SUMMARY

Communication is the process whereby people transmit information about their ideas and feelings to one another.

Language and Verbal Communication. Language is the main vehicle of human communication. (1) All spoken languages consist of sounds that are combined into words with arbitrary meanings and put together according to grammatical rules. (2) According to the encoder-decoder model, communication involves the encoding and sending of a message by a speaker, and the decoding of the message by a listener. Accuracy depends on the codability of the idea or feeling being communicated. (3) In contrast, the intentionalist model argues that communication involves the speaker's desire to affect the listener, or the transmission of an intention. The context of the communication influences how messages are sent and interpreted. (4) The perspective-taking model argues that communication requires intersubjectivity—the shared context created by speaker and listener. Thus, communication is a complex undertaking; to attain mutual understanding, conversationalists must express their message in ways listeners can interpret, take account of others' current knowledge, and actively work to decipher meanings.

Nonverbal Communication. A great deal of information is communicated nonverbally during interaction. (1) Four major types of nonverbal communication are paralanguage, body language, interpersonal spacing, and choice of personal effects. (2) CMC involves only written language, eliminating paralinguistic and visual cues that contribute to accuracy and regulation of interaction. It also encourages disinhibition. (3) The face is an important channel of communication; it provides information that observers use to infer social identities and personal characteristics. (4) Information is usually conveyed simultaneously through nonverbal and verbal channels. Multiple cues may add information to each other, reduce ambiguity, and increase accuracy. But if cues appear inconsistent, people must determine which cues reveal the speaker's true intentions.

Social Structure and Communication. The ways we communicate with others reflect and influence our relationships with them. (1) Gender is related to communication style; its impact depends on the interpersonal, group, or organizational context. (2) In every society, speech that adheres to rules governing vocabulary, pronunciation, and grammar is preferred or standard. Its use is associated with high status or power and is evaluated favorably by listeners. Nonstandard speech is often used by lower-status persons and evaluated negatively. (3) We express, maintain, or challenge the levels of relative status and intimacy in our relationships through our verbal and nonverbal behavior. Status and intimacy influence and are influenced by forms of address, choice of dialect or language, interruptions, matching of speech styles, gestures, eye contact, posture, and interaction distances. (4) The appropriate interaction distances for particular types of activities and relationships are normatively prescribed. These distances vary from one culture to another. When strangers violate distance norms, people flee the scene or use other devices to protect their privacy.

Conversational Analysis. Smooth conversation depends on conversational rules and communication skills that are often taken for granted. (1) Conversations are initiated by a summons to interaction. They get under way only if potential partners signal availability, usually through eye contact or verbal response. (2) Conversationalists avoid verbal collisions by taking turns. They signal either a willingness to yield the floor or a desire to talk through verbal and nonverbal cues. In some situations, turns are allocated in advance. (3) Effective conversationalists assess their partner's understanding and interest as they go along through vocal and visual feedback. If feedback is absent or poorly timed, the quality of communication deteriorates. An effective speech also involves coordination between speaker and audience; the timing of applause is a joint accomplishment.

List of Key Terms and Concepts

back-channel feedback (p. 305)
body language (p. 283)
communication (p. 272)
communication accuracy (p. 275)

Critical Thinking Skill:
Understanding the Importance
of Clear Communication

Our lives consist of our relationships with other people—parents or caregivers, siblings, lovers, friends, supervisors, coworkers. The quality of our lives rests on the quality of these relationships. And what does the quality of a relationship depend on? Communication. As we discuss in Chapter 11, an essential aspect of developing a relationship is self-disclosure. Self-disclosure involves telling the other person personal information about yourself—that is, communicating (also see Chap. 4).

For many people, good, satisfying relationships are those in which we get some of our needs met, whatever the needs may be—help, emotional support, information, money, or sexual pleasure. In order for that to happen, the other person has to know what our needs are and how to satisfy them. We often wish the person would know without our having to tell them; we wish they could read our minds. Or we think, "If you were really a good mother/friend/lover,

you would know what I want." Some reflection, or critical thinking, will reveal these beliefs to be false.

In order for another person to meet our needs, we must communicate clearly and honestly. This can be harder than it sounds. Our communication usually follows well-rehearsed scripts, as in ordering food in a restaurant, talking individually with an instructor, or flirting at a party. We rely on social conventions, but these may not communicate clearly who we are and what we want. Look at the "Get me a drink" example earlier in this chapter. "Did you buy some lemonade at the store?" is a pretty indirect request if your goal is to have her bring you some lemonade. "Yes" or "No" is a sufficient response, leaving you mildly frustrated. Clear, direct communication—"Please bring me a glass of lemonade"—is much more likely to get you a glass of lemonade.

Communication involves not only words but also paralanguage—the way one speaks: warmly, coldly, with hostility; loudly or softly; fast or slow. As we noted, these cues may communicate the speaker's emotional state. Perhaps you have been in conversations where the words didn't match the person's mood; or you tried to hide your anger. When your coworker asks if you are mad that he or she is late for your meeting or for work, you may say "No!" but your tone and the loudness of your voice may give you away. Your effort to avoid clear, honest communication may not work.

Communication also involves nonverbal behavior and body language. A tense body, arms folded across the chest, and avoidance of eye contact probably indicate anger or withdrawal from the conversation. On the other hand, relaxed posture, a smile, and a nodding head indicate engagement and desire to communicate.

Clear communication requires effort and critical thinking. First, you need to understand yourself. What do you want to say?

Once you identify your intention, think about how best to communicate it. Be aware that social scripts and conventions may not provide the means for clear, honest communication. Use direct language. Choose the context: time and place. Consider the other person's communication style. Be direct, and try to match your words to your paralinguistic and nonverbal cues.

Now it's time to apply this skill. Think about a circumstance in your life that could be improved by clear communication—at home, at school, at work, in a relationship.

What is the circumstance or problem? What is your goal? What do you want to achieve? Now think about ways that you could communicate clearly to the other(s) involved. What language would clearly convey what you want? What would be a good time and place to talk about it? Next is the hard part: Do it. Recognize that clear communication takes practice; it may not work the first time. In fact, things may get worse before they get better. But you may also be surprised to learn that the other(s) want to do things differently as much as you do!

CHAPTER 9

SOCIAL INFLUENCE AND PERSUASION

INTRODUCTION

Consider some examples of social influence:

- In front of her condominium, Julie is met by Erika, a neighbor. Erika has heard that a waste management company plans to open a new landfill only a mile from their complex. Trying to mobilize opposition, Erika argues that the landfill would pose dangers to health and lower property values. She asks Julie to attend a meeting and sign a petition against the landfill. Somewhat alarmed by developments, Julie finds Erika's view persuasive, and she agrees to sign.

- One evening, the owner of a 24-hour convenience store is confronted by a man wearing a ski mask and brandishing a pistol. The man threatens, "Hand over your money or I'll blow you away!" Facing a choice between two undesirable alternatives—losing his money or his life—the victim opens the cash register and hands over the money.

- During a military action in Afghanistan, a U.S. commander orders a platoon of men to attack a series of caves where terrorists are thought to be hiding. The danger involved is great. Night has fallen, the entire area is covered with antipersonnel mines, and the enemy has been firing on the troops from the hills. Despite these obstacles, the troops move out as ordered.

These stories illustrate various forms of **social influence**. By definition, social influence occurs when one person (the **source**) engages in some behavior (such as persuading, threatening, promising, or issuing orders) that causes another person (the **target**) to behave differently from how he or she would otherwise behave. In the preceding illustrations, the sources were Erika (persuading Julie), the thief (threatening his victim), and the infantry commander (or-

dering his troops to enter a dangerous situation).

Social influence leads to a variety of outcomes. In some cases, the influencing source may produce **attitude change**—a change in the target's beliefs and attitudes about some issue, person, or situation. Attitude change is a fairly common result of social influence. In other cases, however, the source may not really care about changing the target's attitudes but only about securing compliance. **Compliance** occurs when the target's behavior conforms to the source's requests or demands. Some social influence attempts, of course, produce both attitude change and compliance.

Moreover, we must recognize that many social influence attempts prove ineffective, producing little or no change in the target. Orders issued by direct authority frequently obtain compliance, but at other times, their targets may respond with defiance or open revolt. Because influence attempts vary in their degree of success, one concern of this chapter is to discern the conditions under which influence attempts are most effective.

Forms of Social Influence

Influence attempts can be either open or covertly manipulative (Tedeschi, Schlenker, & Lindskold, 1972). In open influence, the attempt is readily apparent to the target. The target understands that someone is trying to change his or her attitudes or behavior. In manipulative influence, the attempt is hidden from the target. Manipulative influence strategies like ingratiation and tactical self-presentation were covered in Chapter 4. This chapter focuses on open influence.

There are many forms of open influence. Among the more important forms are (1) the use of persuasive communication to change the target's attitudes or beliefs, (2) the use of threats or promises to gain compliance, and (3) the use of orders based on legitimate authority to gain compliance.

Consider first the resources involved in persuasion. When attempting to persuade, the source uses information to change the target's attitudes and beliefs about some issue, person, or situation. Certain types of information are more useful than others in bringing about persuasion. For instance, Erika's persuasion attempt is more likely to succeed if she can introduce facts that Julie did not already know about the landfill and its effects; likewise, success is more likely if the source can advance compelling and valid arguments the target had not previously considered. Having the right type of information is important in effective persuasion.

Influence attempted by means of threats or promises is based on punishments and rewards rather than on information. If a threat is to produce compliance, the target must believe that the source can impose punishment. The convenience store owner was more likely to hand over the money in the register because the brandished pistol substantiated the robber's threat. The same is true for influence based on promises, except that it involves the control of rewards rather than punishments. If the target believes that the source has no real control over the punishments or rewards involved, the threat or promise is unlikely to succeed.

Influence through the use of orders from an authority or officeholder is based on the target's accepting the authority's legitimacy. Influence of this type is especially common within formal groups or organizations. When attempting influence by invoking legitimate authority, the source makes demands on the target that are vested in his or her role within the group. Such an attempt will succeed only if the target believes the source actually holds a position of authority and has the right to issue orders of the kind involved in the influence attempt. The chain of command in the military helps explain why troops would willingly walk toward danger.

Because influence attempts can vary greatly in their degree of success and because we all use social influence in our relationships with others, it is important to understand the conditions under which influence attempts are effective. Specifically, in this chapter we will address the following questions:

1. What factors determine whether a communication will succeed in persuading a target to change his or her beliefs or attitudes? In what ways, for instance, do characteristics of the source and target and properties of the message itself determine whether the persuasion attempt will be effective?

2. Under what conditions do threats and promises prove successful in gaining compliance from the target?

3. When a person in authority issues an order, under what conditions are targets likely to obey it?

4. How can persons resist persuasion attempts and maintain their original attitudes?

ATTITUDE CHANGE VIA PERSUASION

Day in and day out, others bombard us with messages with the intent to persuade. As an example, consider what happens to Maria Castillo on a typical day. Early in the morning, Maria's clock radio comes on. Before Maria can get out of bed, a cheerful announcer is trying to sell her a new breakfast sandwich. Her Facebook and Twitter feeds are filled with messages from friends

FIGURE 9.1 The Communication-Persuasion Paradigm

urging others to get out and vote for a particular candidate in the upcoming election. As she sits on the bus, she reads the advertisements overhead. The cashier at the coffee shop asks her if she would like to donate her change to help a local charity. Once at her desk, Maria checks e-mail and finds a message from her favorite clothing store offering free shipping on any purchases today. Minutes later, a coworker drops by to ask Maria whether she would like to buy wrapping paper for his daughter's school fundraiser. At lunch, a friend mentions her plans to attend a concert the following weekend and urges Maria to come along. In midafternoon, she listens to an argument from a coworker who wants to change some paperwork procedures in the office. When she arrives home in the evening, Maria opens her mail. One letter is a carefully worded appeal from a charitable organization asking her to volunteer her time. Other letters are junk mail fliers asking for money or offering discounts at local restaurants and stores. Later that night, when Maria is watching television, advertisers bombard her endlessly with ads for their products—insurance, light beers, cosmetics, and imported sports cars.

All these messages Maria received have something in common: They seek to persuade. **Persuasion** may be defined as changing the beliefs, attitudes, or behaviors of a target through the use of information or argument. Persuasion is widespread in social interaction and assumes many different forms (McGuire, 1985).

This section considers various facets of message-based persuasion, including the communication-persuasion paradigm and the characteristics of sources, messages, and targets that affect the persuasiveness of a message.

Communication-Persuasion Paradigm

Consider the question, "Who says what to whom with what effect?" This question is one way of organizing modern research on persuasion. In this question, the "who" refers to the source of a persuasive message, the "whom" refers to the target, and the "what" refers to the content of the message. The phrase "with what effect" refers to the various responses of the target to the message. These elements (source, message, target, response) are fundamental components of the **communication-persuasion paradigm.** Figure 9.1 displays this paradigm and shows how these components are interrelated. First, the properties of the source can affect how the target audience will construe the message. For instance, characteristics such as the expertise and trustworthiness of the source can affect whether a target changes attitudes. Second, the properties of the message itself can have a significant impact on its persuasiveness. For instance, whether a message carries a fear appeal or presents only one-sided arguments can affect whether a persuasion attempt is successful. Third, the characteristics of the target are also important. For instance, what a target already believes about an issue as well as the extent of the target person's involvement in the issue and commitment to a position can affect whether a message will be rejected or will lead to attitude change.

The Source

Suppose we ask 25 persons selected at random to read a persuasive communication (such as a newspaper editorial) that advocates a position on a nutrition-related topic. We tell this group that the message came from a Nobel Prize–winning biologist. At the same time, we ask 25 other persons to read the same message, but we tell this group that it came from a cook at a local fast-food establishment. Subsequently, we ask both groups to indicate their attitude toward the position advocated in the message. Which group of persons will be more persuaded by the communication? Most likely, the persons who read the message ascribed to the prize-winning biologist will be more persuaded than those who read the message ascribed to the fast-food cook.

Why should the source's identity make any difference? The identity of the source provides the target with information above and beyond the content of the message itself. Because some sources are more credible than others, the target may pay attention to the source's identity when deciding whether to believe the message. **Communicator credibility** denotes the extent to which the target perceives the communicator as a believable source of information. Note that the communicator's credibility is "in the eye of the beholder"—a given source may be credible for some audiences but not for others. Many consider Fox News a credible source; others do not.

A variety of factors influence the extent to which a source is credible. Two of these, the source's expertise and the source's trustworthiness, are of special importance.

Expertise. Generally, a message from a source having a high level of expertise relevant to the issue will bring about greater attitude change than a similar message from a source with a lower level of expertise (Chebat, Filiatrault, & Perrien, 1990; Hass, 1981; Maddux & Rogers, 1980). This may occur because targets may be more accepting and less critical of messages from high-expertise sources.

The impact of source expertise is illustrated by a study in which participants were exposed to health information online (Hu & Sundar, 2010). The information came from either a doctor (Chris Park, MD, a high-credibility source) or layperson (Chris Park, low-credibility source). One message discouraged the use of sunscreen so as to prevent Vitamin D deficiency and the other advocated consuming raw milk instead of pasteurized milk. Participants believed that both messages were more credible when they came from a doctor than from a layperson.

Even if a persuasion attempt from a low-credibility source fails at first, there is sometimes a sleeper effect in which the target can later be persuaded. However, this only occurs if the target noted the important arguments in the message and has forgotten that she or he originally considered the source to be noncredible (Kumkale & Albarracín, 2004; Pratkanis, Greenwald, Leippe, & Baumgardner, 1988).

The source's expertise interacts with the target's involvement and knowledge in determining attitude change. When the target has little involvement—meaning that the issue is of little personal importance—or prior knowledge on a given issue, messages from highly expert sources produce more attitude change than those from less expert sources. But the more personally relevant the issue is to the target or the more knowledgeable the target is about the issue, the less likely it is that communicator expertise will make much difference in persuasion (Rhine & Severance, 1970). When involvement and knowledge are high, the target is more likely to engage in detailed processing and elaboration, so the content of the message itself becomes the overriding determinant of attitude change (Petty & Cacioppo, 1979a, 1979b, 1990; Stiff, 1986).

Trustworthiness. Although expertise is an important factor in communicator credibility, it is not the only one. Under some conditions, a source can be highly expert but still not very credible. As an example, suppose your car is running poorly, so you take it into a garage for a tune-up. A mechanic you have never met before inspects your car. He identifies several problems, one of which involves major repair work on the engine. The mechanic offers to complete this work for $870 and claims that your car will soon fall apart without it. The mechanic may be an expert, but can you accept his word

that the expensive repair is necessary? How much does he stand to gain if you believe his message?

As this example shows, the target pays attention not only to a communicator's expertise but also to his or her motives. If the message appears highly self-serving and beneficial to the source, the recipient may distrust the source and discount the message (Hass, 1981). In contrast, communicators who argue against their own vested interests seem especially candid and trustworthy. For example, suppose an employee of a local business told you that you should not purchase a product made by her company but rather should buy one made by a Japanese competitor. Her remarks would probably be unexpected, but they would have more impact than if she had argued for purchasing her own American-made model. Even if you normally prefer to buy products made in the United States, you might think twice in this case. A source who

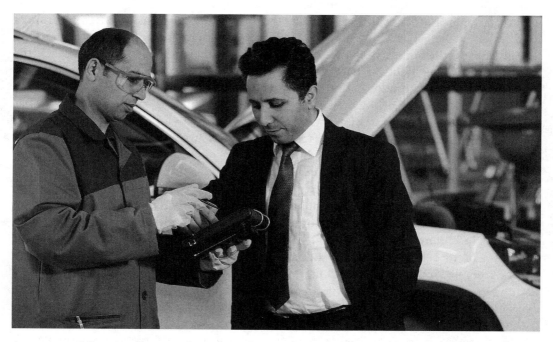

As an automobile owner listens to the message from the garage mechanic, he assesses not only the quality of the argument but also the credibility of the communicator. The mechanic may have expertise, but can he be trusted? © savas keskiner/iStock

violates our initial expectations by arguing against her vested interest will, therefore, be especially persuasive (Eagly, Wood, & Chaiken, 1978; Walster [Hatfield], Aronson, & Abrahams, 1966).

Trustworthiness also depends on the source's identity, because this carries information about the source's goals and values. A source perceived as having goals similar to the audience will be more persuasive than one perceived as having dissimilar goals (Berscheid, 1966; Cantor, Alfonso, & Zillmann, 1976). A study exploring consumer reactions to religious symbols in advertising (for example, an ichthys or cross) found that the symbols had mixed effects (Taylor, Halstead, & Haynes, 2010). In general, such symbols enhanced consumer evaluations and purchase intentions, but the positive effect was largest for evangelical Christians. This was, in part, because the symbols signaled attitude similarity and trustworthiness to Christian consumers. However, the reverse was true among less religious young adults. This group reported that they were less likely to purchase goods or services from a business that used a religious symbol in advertising than businesses that did not. Also related to similarity, endorsements from men increase men's intent to purchase goods, while endorsements from women increase women's intent to do so (Caballero, Lumpkin, & Madden, 1989).

Attractiveness and Likability. The physical attractiveness of the source—determined at a glance, without great cognitive effort—can also affect the persuasiveness of a message. Advertisers regularly select attractive individuals as spokespersons for their products in television and magazine advertisements. Because it is rewarding to look at attractive spokespersons, these advertising messages receive more attention than they otherwise would. Higher source attractiveness leads us to give greater attention to the message, and higher levels of attention facilitate greater persuasion (Chaiken, 1986). Moreover, because physical attractiveness leads to liking, we like attractive persons more and, thus, are sometimes more positively disposed to accept products or positions they advocate (Burger et al., 2001; Eagly & Chaiken, 1975; Horai, Naccari, & Fatoullah, 1974). Whatever the source of likability (similarity, attractiveness, or simple contact), likability tends to increase persuasive influence because we want to maintain and enhance relationships with those we like (Cialdini, 2001; Roskos-Ewoldsen, Bichsel, & Hoffman, 2002).

A source's attractiveness can have greater effect when combined with other factors, like message strength. Strong arguments tend to be detailed, compelling, and substantiated by fact (Wood, Kallgren, & Preisler, 1985). Conversely, weak arguments are of lower quality. In one study investigating the impact of persuasive advertisements for sun-tanning oil, the participants received a message that—depending on treatment—contained either strong or weak arguments and came from either an attractive or an unattractive female spokesperson (DeBono & Telesca, 1990). Results showed that, in general, the attractive source was more persuasive than the unattractive one. But the attractive source was especially persuasive when the message arguments were strong rather than weak. When the arguments were weak, attractiveness made very little difference in persuasion.

Effect of Multiple Sources. Factors other than the source's expertise and trustworthiness can affect whether a message is persuasive. **Social impact theory** (Jackson, 1987; Latané, 1981; Sedikides & Jackson, 1990), a general framework applicable to both persuasion and obedience, states that the impact of an influence attempt is a direct function of strength (that is, social status or power), immediacy (that is, physical or psychological distance), and number of influencing sources. A target will be more influenced when the sources are strong (rather than weak), when the sources are physically close (rather than remote), and when the sources are numerous (rather than few).

Although not all the predictions from social impact theory have been fully tested (Jackson, 1986; Mullen, 1985), two social scientists devised an interesting test of two of the factors (immediacy and number of sources) using Facebook (Egebark & Ekström, 2011). With users' permission, the researchers posted identical status updates in real Facebook accounts and then varied the numbers of "likes" that the updates had and who the likes were from. For each of these status updates, friends of the users either saw that (1) one unknown user had liked the status update, (2) three unknown users had liked the status update, or (3) one of their peers—a mutual friend, with a number of friends in common with the user—had liked the status update. Consistent with social impact theory's predictions, friends of the users were more than twice as likely to like (or comment on) a status update that had first been liked by at least three people (number of sources) or liked by a mutual friend (immediacy) than they were to like a status update that had only one like from a stranger. These results are consistent with previous studies that suggest a message presented by several different sources is more persuasive than the same message presented by a single source (Harkins & Petty, 1981b, 1987; Wolf & Bugaj, 1990; Wolf & Latané, 1983). This is especially true when the arguments presented in the message are strong rather than weak. Strong messages coming from multiple sources receive greater scrutiny and foster more issue-relevant thinking by the target, which leads to

attitude change; however, weak messages from multiple sources may receive added scrutiny but will produce no extra attitude change (Harkins & Petty, 1981a).

Certain qualifications apply to this multiple-source effect. First, for multiple sources to have more impact than a single source, the target must perceive the multiple sources to be independent of one another. If the target believes that the sources colluded in sending their messages, the added impact of multiple sources will vanish and the communication will have no more effect than if it came from a single source (Harkins & Petty, 1983).

Second, there is an upper limit to the multiple-source effect (Tanford & Penrod, 1984). Adding more and more sources will increase persuasion, but only up to a point. For instance, a message from three independent sources will be more persuasive than the same message from a single source, but a message coming from, say, 13 sources may not be appreciably more persuasive than the same message coming from 11 sources.

The Message

Persuasive communications differ dramatically in their content. Some messages contain arguments that are highly factual and rational, whereas others contain emotional appeals that motivate action by arousing fear or greed. Messages differ in their detail and complexity (simple versus complex arguments), their strength of presentation (strong versus weak arguments), and their balance of presentation (one-sided versus two-sided arguments). These properties affect how a person will scrutinize, interpret, and elaborate a message.

Message Discrepancy. Suppose a woman told you that Elizabeth II, the Queen of England, is five feet four inches tall. Would you believe her? What if she said five feet ten inches tall—would you believe that? How about six feet three inches? Or seven feet six inches? You may not know how tall the queen actually is, but you probably have a rough idea. Although you might believe five feet ten inches, you would probably doubt six feet three inches and certainly doubt seven feet six inches. The message asserting that the queen is seven feet six inches tall is highly discrepant from your beliefs.

By definition, a **discrepant message** is one advocating a position that is different from what the target believes. Discrepancy is a matter of degree; some messages are highly discrepant, others less so. To cause a change in beliefs and attitudes, a message must be at least somewhat discrepant from the target's current position; otherwise, it would just reaffirm what the target already believes. Up to a certain point, greater levels of message discrepancy will lead to greater change in attitudes (Jaccard, 1981). A message that is moderately discrepant will be more effective in changing a target's beliefs and attitudes than a message that is only slightly discrepant. Of course, it is possible for a message to be so discrepant that the target will simply dismiss it. To say that the Queen of England is seven feet six inches tall is just not believable.

There is an important interaction between message discrepancy and source expertise. Sources with high credibility produce more attitude change at higher levels of discrepancy than do sources with low credibility. Thus, a target is more likely to accept a highly discrepant message from a high-credibility source than from a low-credibility source. This is particularly true if the argument is strong rather than weak (Clark, Wegener, Habashi, & Evans, 2012). Highly discrepant messages from a low-credibility source are ineffective because the target will quickly derogate the source. Figure 9.2 summarizes the combined impact of message discrepancy, communicator credibility, and argument strength on attitude change.

Many empirical studies report findings consistent with the relationships shown in Figure 9.2 (Aronson, Turner, & Carlsmith, 1963; Fink, Kaplowitz, & Bauer, 1983; Rhine & Severance, 1970). In one experiment, for instance, participants were given a written message on the number of hours of sleep that people need each night to function effectively (Bochner & Insko, 1966). In some cases, the message was attributed to a Nobel Prize–winning physiologist (high credibility), whereas in other cases it was attributed to a YMCA director (medium credibility). The arguments contained in the message were identical for all participants, with one important exception. In some cases the message proposed that people need eight hours of sleep per night; in others, the message proposed seven hours; in others, six hours; and so on down to zero hours of sleep per night. Most participants began the experiment believing that people need approximately eight hours of sleep each night. Therefore, these messages differed in level of discrepancy. The results suggested that the more discrepant the position advocated by the high-credibility source (the Nobel Prize winner), the greater the amount of attitude change. Only when this source argued for the most extreme position (zero hours of sleep) did the participants refuse to believe the message. The same pattern appeared for the medium-credibility source (the YMCA director), except that his effectiveness peaked out at moderate levels of discrepancy (three hours of sleep per night). For very extreme positions (two hours of sleep or less), the medium-credibility source was less effective. Thus, this study demonstrates that sources with higher credibility produce greater amounts of attitude change at higher levels of discrepancy.

FIGURE 9.2 Attitude Change as a Function of Source Expertise, Message Discrepancy, and Argument Strength

These figures illustrate attitude change toward junk food taxation after reading an argument (strong or weak) from a source high or low in expertise (a leading scholar in health and food sciences or a high school junior). Participants who had a favorable view toward taxing junk food before reading the argument were most influenced by the strength of the argument of someone who was low on expertise. The reverse was true for those with relatively high message discrepancy. For those participants, argument quality had the largest effect when the source was an expert. Adapted from Clark et al., 2012, Figure 1.

Fear Arousal. Most messages intended to persuade incorporate either rational appeals or emotional appeals. Rational appeals are factual in nature; they present specific, verifiable evidence to support claims. Rational appeals frequently address a need already felt by the audience and provide the missing solution; that is, these messages are drive reducing. Emotional appeals, in contrast, try to arouse basic drives and to stimulate a need where none was present. These messages are drive creating.

Perhaps the most common emotional appeals are those involving fear. Fear-arousing messages are especially useful when the source is trying to motivate the target to take some specific action. A political candidate, for example, may warn that if voters elect her opponent to office, the nation will

become embroiled in international conflict. Likewise, in an antismoking advertisement on TV, a victim dying of throat cancer and emphysema warns young persons that if they start smoking cigarettes, they may end up as diseased victims themselves. In each of these cases, the source is using a fear-arousing communication. Messages of this type direct the target's attention to some negative or undesired outcome that is likely to occur unless the target takes certain actions advocated by the source (Higbee, 1969; Ruiter, Kok, Verplanken, & van Eersel, 2003).

Some studies have shown that communications arousing high levels of fear produce more change in attitude than do communications arousing low levels of fear (Dembroski, Lasater, & Ramires, 1978; Leventhal, 1970). If a message arouses fear and the targets believe that attending to the message will show them how to cope with this fear, then they may analyze the message carefully and change their attitudes (Petty, 1995). Fear-arousing communications have been effective in persuading people to do many things, including reducing their cigarette smoking, driving more safely, improving their dental hygiene practices, changing their attitudes toward Communist China, and so on (Insko, Arkoff, & Insko, 1965; Leventhal, 1970; Leventhal & Singer, 1966).

Some studies suggest, however, that fear-arousing messages can fail if they are too strong and create too much fear. If people feel very threatened, they may become defensive and deny the reality or the importance of the threat rather than think rationally about the issue (Johnson, 1991; Lieberman & Chaiken, 1992). In this sense, a message arousing moderate fear may prove more effective than one arousing extremely high fear.

The impact of fear-arousing communications is shown clearly by a study in which college students received messages advocating inoculations against tetanus (Dabbs & Leventhal, 1966). These messages described tetanus as easy to catch and as producing serious, even fatal consequences. The message also indicated that inoculation against tetanus, which could be obtained easily, provided effective protection against the disease. Depending on experimental treatment, the participants received either high-fear, low-fear, or control communications. In the high-fear condition, the messages described tetanus in extremely vivid terms, thereby creating a high level of fear and apprehension. In the low-fear condition, the messages described tetanus in less detailed terms, thereby creating no more than low to moderate fear. In the control condition, the message provided little detail about the disease, thereby arousing no fear.

To determine the message's effectiveness, the students were asked whether they thought it was important to get a tetanus inoculation and whether they actually intended to get one. The responses showed that students exposed to the high-fear message had stronger intentions to get shots than those exposed to the other messages. Moreover, records kept at the university health service indicated that students receiving the high-fear message were more likely to actually be inoculated during the following month than were students receiving the other messages.

This study demonstrates that fear-arousing messages can change attitudes. In general, however, fear-arousing messages are effective only when certain conditions are met. First, the message must assert that if the target does not change behavior, he or she will suffer serious negative consequences. Second, the message must show convincingly that these negative consequences are highly probable. Third, the message must recommend a specific course of action that, if adopted, will enable the target to avoid the negative consequences. A message that predicts negative consequences but fails to assure the target that he or she can avoid them by taking specific action will produce little attitude change. Instead, it will leave the target feeling that the negative consequences are inevitable regardless of what he or she may do (Job, 1988; Maddux & Rogers, 1983; Patterson & Neufeld, 1987).

Recent research on cultural orientations and the persuasiveness of fear appeals finds that such appeals are most effective when the messages reflect receivers' internalized cultural beliefs (Lee & Park, 2012). Anti-smoking public service announcements (PSAs) that emphasized the health risks of smoking to the participants themselves ("When you smoke, you suffer.") were more effective among participants with an individualistic orientation, as is common in the United States. PSAs with identical imagery and facts but that framed smoking as a threat to participants' family members ("When you smoke, they suffer.") were more effective among those with a collectivist cultural orientation.

One-Sided versus Two-Sided Messages. When a source uses rational rather than emotional appeals, other message characteristics also come into play. One such characteristic is the number of viewpoints, or sides, represented in the message. A one-sided message emphasizes only those facts that explicitly support the position advocated by the source ("Sun tanning causes skin cancer" or "Sun tanning causes wrinkles"). A two-sided message, in contrast, presents not only the position advocated by the source but also opposing viewpoints ("Sun tanning helps to maintain vitamin D levels but causes skin cancer" or "Sun tanning gives you an attractive glow, but causes wrinkles").

Which is more effective—a one-sided message or a two-sided message? The answer depends heavily on the nature of the target audience. One-sided messages have the advantage of being uncomplicated and easy to grasp. They are more effective when the audience already agrees with the source; they also tend to be effective when the audience does not know much about the issue, for they keep the audience blind to opposing viewpoints. Two-sided messages are more complex, so they attract more attention and are processed more thoroughly than one-sided messages (Eisend, 2007; Petty & Cacioppo, 1986a). They also have the advantage of making the source appear less biased and more trustworthy. Such messages tend to be more effective when the audience initially opposes the source's viewpoint or knows a lot about the alternative positions (Karlins & Abelson, 1970; Sawyer, 1973). In the case of the sun-tanning messages above,

the most effective of the four messages (two one-sided, two two-sided) in decreasing individuals' intentions to suntan was the two-sided appearance-focused appeal: "Sun tanning gives you an attractive glow, but causes wrinkles" (Cornelis, Cauberghe, & De Pelsmacker, 2013). Because most people who sun tan do so for appearance-focused benefits rather than health-focused (to increase vitamin D levels), the statement tapping into such a motivation is more effective than one less consistent with individuals' experiences or motives.

The Target

So far, we have discussed how the characteristics of the source and the content of the message affect persuasion. Yet it is also true that the characteristics of the target play a role in persuasion. One important target characteristic that affects persuasion is the target's level of intelligence. Another is the degree to which the target is involved with the issue, a topic discussed briefly earlier in the chapter. Moreover, any persuasion attempt may also be affected by personality factors, such as how much the target person likes thinking things through or if they are an anxious person. Finally, how focused or distracted the target is during the persuasion attempt also plays a role in susceptibility.

Intelligence. Individuals who are more intelligent tend to be more resistant to influence for a number of reasons. Intelligent targets generally know more about any given issue than less intelligent targets (Rhodes & Wood, 1992). Even if they know little or nothing about the issue, bright people are better able to critically evaluate both the source's specific appeal and the message itself (Wood, Kallgren, & Preisler, 1985). This is not only a matter of innate intelligence (IQ), but also knowledge acquired through experience and education. In a study of susceptibility to phishing, the group most susceptible to such scams was 18- to 25-year-olds. Despite their comfort with technology, people in this age group had lower levels of education and less experience with e-mail than those who were older (Sheng, et al., 2010).

Involvement with the Issue. One important attribute of targets is the extent of their involvement with a particular issue (Johnson & Eagly, 1989; Petty & Cacioppo, 1990). Suppose, for example, that someone advocates a fundamental change at your college, such as increasing the degree requirements, specifically proposing a comprehensive exam in students' major areas in order to graduate. The proposed change would take effect at the beginning of the next year. Many students would be very involved with this issue because the change would affect the difficulty of completing their degrees. Now, suppose the source advocated instead that the change take place ten years in the future rather than next year. Current students would probably have little interest in this proposal because they will finish college long before any changes take effect.

Your involvement with the issue fundamentally affects the way you process a message. When highly involved, a target will want to scrutinize the message closely and think carefully about its content. In such cases, strong arguments will likely produce substantial attitude change, whereas weak arguments will produce little or no attitude change. In contrast, the target who is uninvolved will have less motivation to think carefully about the message. If any change in attitude occurs, it will result more from peripheral factors, such as source expertise or trustworthiness, than from the arguments themselves (Chaiken, 1980; Leippe & Elkin, 1987; Petty, Cacioppo, & Heesacker, 1981).

In one study, a message similar to the one just described was presented to a group of college students (Petty, Cacioppo, & Goldman, 1981). The message proposed that college seniors be required to take a comprehensive exam before graduation. Three independent variables were manipulated in this study. The first variable was personal involvement with the issue. Half the participants were told that the new policy would take effect next year at their college (high involvement), whereas the other half were told that the policy would take effect ten years in the future (low involvement). The second variable was the strength of the message's argument. Half the participants received eight strong and cogent arguments in favor of the proposal; the other participants received eight weak and specious arguments. The third variable was the expertise of the source. Half of the participants were told that the source of the message was a professor of education at Princeton University (high-expertise source); the other half were told that the source was a student at a local high school (low-expertise source).

In the high-involvement condition, the target's attitude toward comprehensive exams was determined primarily by the strength of the arguments. Strong arguments produced significantly more attitude change than weak ones. The expertise of the source had no significant impact on attitude change. In the low-involvement condition, attitudes were determined primarily by the source's expertise; the high-expertise source produced more attitude change than the low-expertise source. The strength of the arguments had little effect on this group.

Thus, the target's involvement with the issue moderated which factor was the primary determinant of attitude change. For participants with high involvement, the strength of the argument was more important than source expertise because participants cared about the issue. For those

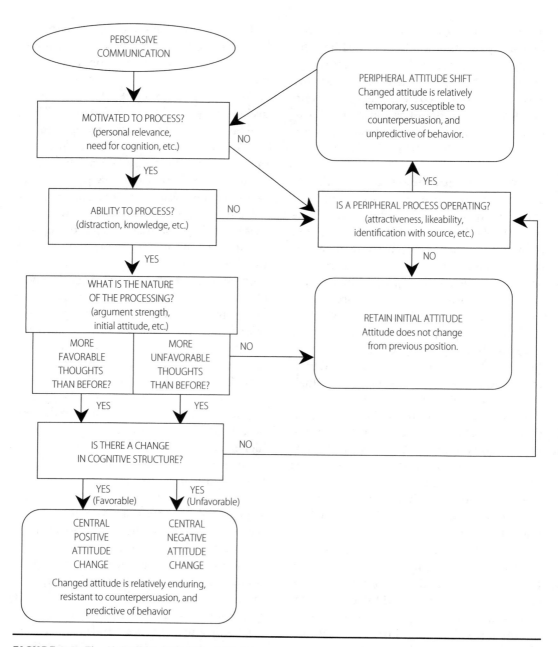

FIGURE 9.3 The Elaboration Likelihood Model

A popular dual-process theory of persuasion is the Elaboration Likelihood Model. Depending on an individual's motivation and ability to process a persuasion attempt, one of two routes is activated. Persuasion in the peripheral process relies on heuristics (attractiveness, likeability, shared identity) and tends to lead to weaker attitude change. The central persuasion process requires more thought and attention (higher levels of elaboration of the argument) and results in more enduring attitude change. Adapted from Petty & Wegener, 1999, Figure 3.1.

with low involvement, source expertise was more important because the participants had little motivation to scrutinize the arguments. Similar findings have been reported more recently (Byrne, et al., 2012; Chaiken & Maheswaran, 1994).

Personality. Beyond involvement with the issue, how much an individual enjoys puzzling through problems and thinking about issues plays an important role in persuasion attempts. Those who do enjoy these thinking tasks are said to have a high need for cognition (Cacioppo, Petty, Feinstein, & Jarvis, 1996) and are motivated to examine arguments more carefully and thoroughly than those who have a low need for cognition (Shestowsky, Wegener, & Fabrigar, 1998). Thus, they are more likely to engage the content of argument and more likely to ignore the peripheral cues, making them resistant to persuasion (Haugvedt & Petty, 1992). When facing an audience of people with a high need for cognition (for example, college professors), one would be wise to pay careful attention to constructing a solid set of arguments that will stand up to the scrutiny of full engagement.

In addition to the need for cognition, other personality traits affect individuals' susceptibility to persuasion. One popular model of personality in psychology that considers a range of personality traits is the **five-factor model** (Costa & McCrae, 1992; Digman, 1990) or Big Five. The model takes a wide variety of personality traits and organizes them into five factors, or categories. These factors and examples of associated traits are agreeableness (warmth, friendliness), conscientiousness (efficiency, dependability), extraversion (outgoingness, assertiveness), openness (curiosity, insight), and neuroticism (confidence, sensitivity). Research finds that individuals who are high on neuroticism—for example, those

who feel socially anxious or depressed—are more susceptible to persuasion (Hovland, Janis, & Kelley, 1953), as are people who are high on openness (Gerber et al., 2013). There is less consensus on the effects of extraversion, agreeableness, or conscientiousness and their relationship to susceptibility to social influence.

Distraction. Even people with a high need for cognition who are strongly involved in an issue will sometimes have trouble paying attention to arguments. This can occur because the audience is distracted by any number of things—perhaps they aren't feeling well, maybe there is street noise that makes it hard to hear, perhaps the speaker has an annoying habit that bothers the listener, and so on. Anything that prevents the target from giving full attention to the argument will impair the target's ability or motivation to evaluate an argument or appeal effectively and, therefore, influence the persuasion attempt (Albarracín, 2002). Given the discussion so far, it will be no surprise to learn that when we are distracted, we are more likely to use peripheral cues when forming our opinions. The distracting element in the environment prevents us from fully engaging and appreciating the details of the argument, and therefore, we fall back on peripheral indicators such as the attractiveness of the speaker (Petty & Brock, 1981; Petty, Wells, & Brock, 1976).

COMPLIANCE WITH THREATS AND PROMISES

As important as attitude change is, it is not the only outcome of social influence. Another important outcome is compliance—that is, behavioral conformity by the target to the source's requests or demands. With compliance, the fundamental concern is

BOX 9.1 Media Campaigns

One Monday in March 2013, the Human Rights Campaign (HRC) encouraged people—using e-mail, Facebook feeds, and a website announcement—to change their profile pictures to a pink-on-red equal sign to demonstrate support of same-sex marriage. Although there was no way to measure exactly how many users adopted the new picture (or one of the many variants of it), the next day, 2.7 million (120%) more users changed their profile than did so one week prior (Bakshy, 2013). For anyone using Facebook at the time, the profile photos were a strong statement of the widespread support, particularly among those between their early twenties and late thirties, for marriage equality. The immediate spread across Facebook demonstrated the speed and reach of social media, but what did it tell us about social media's role in persuasion?

A **media campaign** is a systematic attempt by a source to use the **mass media**—channels of communication that enable a source to reach a large audience (the Internet, television, newspapers, magazines, and radio)—to change the attitudes and beliefs of a select target audience. Media campaigns are common in the industrialized world. Advertisers use them to sell new products or services, and political parties use them to sway voters' sentiments. Also, public officials use them to change citizens' behavior through public service announcements that attempt to stop drunk driving, encourage people to try to quit smoking, get people to vote on election day, and so on (Cummings, Sciandra, Davis, & Rimer, 1989; Farhar-Pilgrim & Shoemaker, 1981; Solomon, 1982). To what extent are communications transmitted by the mass media effective in changing the beliefs and attitudes of large numbers of people? Furthermore, when Facebook users changed

their profile photos to a pink equal sign, did it reflect a change in their opinions about same-sex marriage or simply serve as a statement of a pre-existing attitude? The latter is much more likely. Although social media and technology make it increasingly easy to participate in a media campaign by changing a profile photo or clicking a button to send a message to an elected official or to send $10 to a relief fund, it is as ineffective as other mass media are at persuading users to change their view or behaviors.

Each year, advertisers spend hundreds of billions of dollars on media campaigns. Nevertheless, most media campaigns do not produce large amounts of attitude change. In general, messages sent via the mass media have only a small impact on their target audience's attitudes (Barber & Grichting, 1990; Bauer, 1964; Finkel, 1993). There are several reasons media campaigns are usually able to produce only small amounts of attitude change. First, there is the phenomenon of selective exposure. Many messages do not reach the audience they are intended to influence because audience members attend mostly to those sources with which they agree. Instead of reaching persons who disagree with the message—and whose opinions might, thus, be changeable—many media communications are received by persons who already agree with the message and whose opinions will, therefore, be reinforced, not changed. The HRC's initial message went only to people affiliated with the HRC in some way (supporters and those who subscribe to the organization's Facebook and Twitter feeds) and then was shared on users' timelines—spaces most likely viewed by others with similar attitudes because of humans' propensity to befriend similar others. The media exposes people to more messages that support their preexisting attitudes than those that contradict them (Klitzner, Gruenewald, & Bamberger, 1991; Sears & Freedman, 1967). Some have argued, however, that selective exposure is being reduced with the advance of modern communication technology. People are now exposed to a greater variety of viewpoints through both Internet and television news programming and advertising (Garrett, Carnahan, & Lynch, 2011; Mutz & Martin, 2001). However, there is still a tendency for the messages to reinforce previously held attitudes (Ansolabehere & Iyengar, 1994), and the plethora of partisan sources makes it easier to avoid attitude-discrepant information (Garrett, 2009).

Second, even if the intended targets receive messages from the media, they may reject them or derogate the source. Recipients of media communications are certainly not passive, and the impact of a message depends heavily on the uses and gratifications that the audience can obtain from the information (Dervin, 1981; Swanson, 1979). For example, in selling consumer products, media persuasion is more effective when the target's involvement with the decision is low and when he or she perceives relatively small differences between alternative products. In contrast, the impact of the media will be slight when target involvement with the decision is high and the differences between products appear clear-cut (Chaffee, 1981; Ray, 1973).

Third, even when a target finds a media message compelling, he or she may be subject to counter-pressures that inhibit attitude change (Atkin, 1981). Some of these pressures come from social groups such as family, friends, and co-workers; these groups may exert influence that nullifies a media campaign's impact. Moreover, targets are exposed to conflicting persuasive communications and cross-pressures transmitted via the media. For example, beer advertisements would probably be enormously successful if only one manufacturer advertised its product. But because many brands advertise, media messages offset one another.

Other Effects of Media Campaigns

Although media campaigns do not usually cause a massive change in attitudes, they do exert other impacts on audiences. First, they are effective in strengthening preexisting attitudes. In other words, they reinforce and buttress preferences already held by the target audience (Ansolabehere & Iyengar, 1994).

In addition to strengthening preexisting attitudes, mass media are successful in creating attitudes toward objects that previously were unknown or unimportant to the audience. Advertisers use media campaigns to cultivate positive attitudes toward newly introduced products (smartphones, beverages, new toys for children). Political parties also use media campaigns to create positive attitudes toward new, little-known candidates running for office. Today, former Presidents Jimmy Carter and Bill Clinton are well known to the American public. But when both began running for the presidency, the situation was very different. Both had been the governors of southern states, but both were almost entirely unknown outside the South. Carter had even appeared on the game show What's My Line?, and none of the celebrity panel was able to guess who he was. To win the Democratic nomination for president, both candidates launched massive media campaigns to make themselves recognizable to Americans. At the same time the candidates were introducing themselves, they also worked hard to establish a positive public image of themselves.

producing a particular behavior from the target, irrespective of whether the target's beliefs and attitudes change. Of course, in some cases, compliance can be obtained indirectly by changing attitudes—if someone can change what we believe, he or she might also change how we behave. But persuasion is not necessary to change behavior. French and Raven (1959; Raven, 1992) proposed that there are six kinds of social power that can be used to induce compliance—some of which require actual persuasion and some of which do not (see Box 9.2). In this section, we examine two in more detail: threats and promises.

Consider a homeowner, Richard Sorenson, who lives in an area of Michigan where it snows heavily. One cold day in January, a snowstorm dumps 12 inches of snow on his driveway and sidewalk. Although Richard has been the person in his household who has always shoveled the snow, he believes his teenage son is now old enough to take on the task and has been considering the best way to shift the responsibility. He could approach his son and say, "I'll give you $20 if you shovel the snow out of the driveway." This would be an attempt to gain compliance in the form of a promise: Richard promises to pay $20 in return for a specified performance. Or he could use a threat: "Shovel the snow or else I won't let you use the car for a week." Here, compliance is demanded or Richard will levy a penalty.

Influence based on promises and threats differs from persuasion attempts in a fundamental way. When using persuasion, the source tries to change the way a target views the situation. Sorenson, for example, might have attempted to persuade his son that shoveling snow is enormous fun or that clearing out the driveway would make him a good son. These appeals, if successful, would change how the teen looks at the situation, but they would not actually change the situation itself. This contrasts with the use of promises or threats, in which the source does restructure the situation. By promising to pay money for a clear driveway or threatening punishment if it is not done, Sorenson has added a new reinforcement contingency to the situation—money in return for snow removal or the inconvenience of walking if it is not removed. In both cases, he hopes the looming reinforcement will induce his son to comply, but which approach will be most effective?

Effectiveness of Threats and Promises

A **threat** is a communication from one person (the source) to another (the target) that takes the general form, "If you don't do X [which I want], then I will do Y [which you don't want]" (Boulding, 1981; Tedeschi, Bonoma, & Schlenker, 1972). For example, an employer might say to her employee, "If you don't complete this project before the deadline, I'll withhold your bonus." If the employee needs her bonus to pay medical bills and has no other job prospects, she will take the threat seriously and do her best to comply with the demand.

When a source issues a threat, the sanction threatened can be virtually anything—a physical beating, the loss of a job, a monetary fine, the loss of love. The important point is that for a threat to be effective, the target must want to avoid the sanction. If the employee threatened by her boss happens to have a new job lined up elsewhere, she will not care whether her boss intends to cut her bonus, and the threat will have little impact.

In the context of compliance, a **promise** is similar to a threat, except that it involves contingent rewards, not punishments. A person using a promise says, "If you do X [which I want], then I will do Y [which you want]." Notice that a promise involves a reward controlled by the source. Richard Sorenson promises a payment of $20 if his

BOX 9.2 Social Power and Compliance

Suppose a high school student did not do well on her last set of exams and her father wants to try to influence her to study harder for her winter finals. The father can choose from a number of different tactics to try to produce compliance. These tactics can be organized by the type of power the father might use to influence the daughter. According to a model forwarded by French and Raven (1959; Raven, 1992), there are six major social bases of power that can be used in such a situation.

1. Promise of Reward. One way of inducing compliance is to promise to provide a reward if the target performs the desired behavior. The father might tell his daughter, "If you spend two hours a day studying for the next two weeks, I will buy you a new cell phone." Oftentimes, explicit agreements about behavior and rewards are made, but other times they are more subtle, such as when we work hard to gain approval from our parents even though we have never explicitly agreed on such an arrangement.

2. Coercion Through Threat. In contrast to the reward strategy, the father might use the threat of a negative outcome to induce compliance. "If you don't do better on your exams next time, you will not go on the spring break trip you are planning." As with rewards, the threats do not necessarily have to be explicit in order to be effective.

3. Referent Power. **Referent power** uses our desire to be accepted by members of valued social groups. When we seek acceptance, we may be more likely to comply with the demands of the group or we may try to become more similar to the group by imitating the behavior of its members (see Chapter 13). To use referent power, the father could identify people whom his daughter admires and then point out how studious those people are: "Your older sister spends at least two hours a day studying."

4. Legitimate Power. The social positions people occupy often supply them with power over other individuals, and this hierarchical arrangement is often accepted by both the higher-power and lower-power persons involved (see Chapter 14). Bosses have the power to tell employees what to do, parents have the power to tell children what to do, and police officers have the power to tell motorists what to do. When authority is accepted as a right associated with a social role, it is called **legitimate power**. The father in our example could invoke legitimate power by saying, "I'm the parent, and one of my jobs as a parent is to make sure you study. So get to work!" If the daughter accepts the traditional authority arrangement, she will head off to study, even if she does not really want to.

5. Information. Sometimes, we can actually change people's attitudes about the behavior we want them to exhibit, and the behavior change will then follow in order to produce consistency with the attitude. One way of doing this is to provide information about the effects of the behavior. "The grades you have now are not going to be high enough for you to get into college. The average grades of entering students at State College last year were in the B range. You currently only have a C average."

6. Expertise. Information can play a less direct role in compliance as well. There are many times in life when we do not need to know all information about the behavior as long as we think the person telling us what to do is an expert. We assume that because the person is an expert, she knows what she is talking about and, thus, we will comply with her request. When a doctor prescribes drugs, we usually take them even if we don't know exactly how they work because we can rely on the expertise of the doctor. In the case of the father and the high school student, he might refer to an expert on studying who claims that an additional two hours of studying per day will raise a student's GPA by a full letter grade.

teenage son clears the driveway and sidewalk. People frequently use promises in exchanges, both monetary and nonmonetary.

By issuing a promise, the source creates a set of options for the target. Suppose, for example, that the source makes the promise, "I'll give you $20 if you clear the snow from the driveway." In response, the target can (1) comply with the source's request and clear the driveway, (2) refuse to comply and let the matter drop, or (3) make a counteroffer, such as "How about $30? It's a long driveway, and the snow is very deep." In similar fashion, a threat creates a choice for the target. Once a threat is issued, the target can (1) comply with the threat, (2) refuse to comply, or (3) issue a counter-threat (Boulding, 1981).

The range of possible responses to threats and promises raises a fundamental question: Under what conditions will threats and promises be successful in gaining compliance, and under what conditions will they fail? Certain characteristics of threats and promises, such as their magnitude and credibility, affect the probability that the target will comply.

Magnitude of Threats and Promises.

In promises, the greater the magnitude of the reward offered by a source, the greater the probability of compliance by the target (Lindskold & Tedeschi, 1971). For example, a factory supervisor might obtain compliance from a worker by offering a large incentive: "If you are willing to work the late shift next month, I'll approve your request for four extra days of vacation in September." The worker's reaction might be less accommodating, however, if his supervisor offered only a trivial incentive: "If you work the late shift next month, I'll let you take your coffee break five minutes early today."

A similar principle holds for threats. Compliance with threats varies directly with the magnitude of the punishment in-

A robber holds a store clerk at gunpoint. Targets are more likely to comply when threats are both large and credible. © Pixtal / SuperStock

volved. Other factors being equal, targets will dismiss threats that entail trivial consequences, but they will more likely comply with threats that entail large and serious consequences (Miranne & Gray, 1987). Consistent with this, researchers find that the more severe the possible punishments for cheating, the more likely students are to adhere to an honor code (McCabe, Treviño, & Butterfield, 1999, 2001).

Credibility of Threats and Promises. Suppose you own a little puppy that often runs wild. Your not-so-nice neighbor hates dogs. One day, he issues a threat: "If you don't keep your dog off my property, I will call animal control." This threat is troublesome, because your dog romps on his property frequently. But would your neighbor really do what he says, or is he merely bluffing? You will comply and tether your dog if the threat is real, but you do not want to comply if it is merely a bluff. Unfortunately, there is no surefire, risk-free way to find out whether the threat is credible. The only true way to test your neighbor's credibility is to call his bluff—that is, to refuse to comply. Then, if your neighbor was merely bluffing, that fact will quickly become evident. Of course, if he was not bluffing, you will suffer the consequences. Retrieving your puppy from animal control may cost some money and entail some anxious moments.

Bluffing or not, any threatener wants the target to believe the threat is credible and to comply with his demand. He does not want the target to call his bluff. After all, a successful threat is one that obtains compliance without actually having to be carried out. If the target refuses to comply, the threatener must either admit he is bluffing or incur the costs of carrying out the threat.

To judge the credibility of a threat, targets gauge the cost to the source of carrying out the threat. Threats that cost a lot to carry out are less credible than those costing less. Calling animal control would require very little of your neighbor's time. Targets also estimate the credibility of a threat from the social identity of the source. A threat involving physical violence, for example, will be more credible if it comes from a karate expert wearing a black belt than if it comes from the proverbial 97-pound weakling. Finally, previous behavior affects the credibility of the threat. If your neighbor has called animal control to pick up other neighbors' dogs, you are more likely to take his threat seriously. While threats are seen as most credible when they are consistently followed through with, credibility can be established with only occasional enforcement because even that increases the perception that this is one of the times when the source will follow through.

The SEV Model. A threat's **subjective expected value (SEV)** is a measure of the pressure that the target feels from the threat. The level of SEV depends on several factors. SEV increases as the threat's credibility increases and as the magnitude of punishment threatened increases (Stafford, Gray, Menke, & Ward, 1986; Tedeschi, Bonoma, & Schlenker, 1972). When both credibility and punishment magnitude

are high, the SEV of the threat will be high; consequently, the target will feel a lot of pressure to comply. When both credibility and punishment magnitude are low, SEV is low; consequently, the target will feel little or no pressure to comply. When one is high and the other is low (as, for example, when magnitude is high but credibility is low), the threat will have a moderate to low SEV.

The SEV model of threat effectiveness predicts that a target's compliance with a threat depends on not only the SEV of the threat but also the cost to the target of complying with the threat (Tedeschi, Schlenker, & Lindskold, 1972). That is, when deciding whether to comply with the threat, a target will estimate both the SEV of the threat and the cost of complying. These factors will have opposite effects on compliance. The probability of compliance will increase directly as a function of SEV but will decrease as a function of the cost to the target of complying.

Although the above description links the SEV model with threats, it also applies to promises. Of course, the relevant variables in this case are the magnitude of the reward and the credibility of the promise. The results of one study showed that targets were more influenced when the reward promised was large rather than small and when the source had credibility in following through on the promises (Lindskold, Cullen, Gahagan, & Tedeschi, 1970). Consistent with the SEV view, these conclusions hold true only when the reward promised for compliance is greater than the reward(s) that might be gained from refusing to comply.

OBEDIENCE TO AUTHORITY

As important as persuasion and compliance are, they are not the only forms of social influence used in everyday life. We have all witnessed situations in which—without the

The lines of authority become salient as a military commander gives orders to his recruits. © panda3800/ shutterstock

use of threat, promises, or persuasion—one person issues an order and another person complies. For example, a baseball umpire tosses an unruly manager out of the game and orders him to leave the field; the manager, after showing his resentment by throwing his cap to the ground and kicking first base, grudgingly complies. The umpire does not attempt to persuade the manager to leave voluntarily; he simply issues an order directing the manager to leave. Compliance in this case is based on the fact that both the umpire and the manager are participating in a larger social system (two ball clubs playing a game) in which behavior is regulated by rules and roles. The capacity of the source (the umpire) to influence the target (the manager) stems from the rights conferred by their roles within the game. Under the rules of the game, the umpire has the right to throw the manager out of the game for disruptive behavior.

When persons occupy roles within a group, organization, or larger social system, they accept certain rights and obligations vis-à-vis other members in that social unit. Typically, these rights and obligations give one person authority over another with respect to certain acts and performances. **Authority** refers to the capacity of one member to issue orders to others—that is, to direct or regulate the behavior of other members by invoking rights that are vested in his or her role. When the umpire tosses the manager out of the game, the basis of his power is legitimate authority.

Orders by police officers, decisions by judges, directives by parents, and exhortations by clergymen—all these entail authority and the invocation of norms. A source can exercise authority only when, by virtue of the role that he or she occupies in a social group, others accept his or her right to prescribe behavior regarding the issue at hand

(Kelman & Hamilton, 1989; Raven & Kruglanski, 1970). In exercising authority, the source invokes a norm and, thereby, obliges the target(s) to comply. The greater the number of persons the source can directly or indirectly influence in this manner and the wider the range of behaviors over which the source has jurisdiction, the greater his or her authority within the group (Michener & Burt, 1974; Zelditch, 1972).

In this section, we will discuss influence based on legitimate authority. First, we will consider some interesting experimental studies of destructive obedience. These studies illustrate the extremes to which authorities can push behavior. Second, we will consider some factors that determine whether a target will comply or refuse to comply with an authority's directives.

Experimental Study of Obedience

Obedience to authority frequently produces beneficial results because it facilitates coordination among persons in groups or collective settings. Civil order hinges on obedience to orders from police officers and judicial officials, and effective performance in work settings often depends on following bosses' or employers' directives. Yet if obedience to authority is unquestioning, it can sometimes produce disquieting or undesirable outcomes.

At the 2012 Sundance film festival, a number of viewers walked out of the showing of *Compliance*, a docudrama recounting the disturbing events that transpired at a Kentucky restaurant in 2004. The audience was shocked and uncomfortable to learn how far someone might go as they yielded to requests from an authority figure.

It was a busy Friday night when a man posing as "Officer Scott" called the local McDonald's and asked an assistant manager, Donna Summers, for help with a police investigation. Scott told Summers that one of her employees had been accused of theft. He gave a vague description of an employee, who Summers recognized as a young woman working the front counter. Scott claimed that there were no officers available to come conduct the investigation and so he would need her assistance. He assured Summers that her general manager was aware of the situation and that he had given permission for her to help the officer. Scott asked Summers to take the employee to the office. He then began to give her instructions on how to proceed: first asking Summers to search the employee's possessions, then to strip search her. When things picked up in the restaurant and Summers was needed up front, Scott asked her to bring in someone else who she could trust to continue with the procedure. Summers asked her fiancé, Walter Nix, to come to the restaurant and help. For the next two hours, Scott demanded that Nix have the employee engage in acts of humiliation, including a body cavity search and performing a sex act. When Nix became uncomfortable with the situation and told his fiancée that he needed to leave, a still-rushed Summers asked the restaurant's maintenance man to help out. When the maintenance man realized what was happening in the restaurant's office, he refused to play any part in it. His reaction sparked something in Summers. She became suspicious and called the store's general manager to see whether he had, in fact, talked with Scott. He had not. The call had been a hoax. Summers and Nix were not the only unknowing accomplices who had complied with disturbing commands from an unknown caller. Similar events—most likely from the same perpetrator—occurred throughout the United States.

Research in social psychology also documents the disconcerting outcomes of obedience to authority. In one study, hospital nurses received orders from doctors to administer a drug to a patient. The order came by telephone, and the nurses involved did not previously know the doctors giving the order. The drug was one not often used in the hospital; hence, it was not very familiar to the nurses. The dosage prescribed was heavy and substantially exceeded the maximum listed on the package. The results showed that nearly all the nurses in this study were nevertheless ready to follow orders and administer the drug at the prescribed dosage (Hofling et al., 1966).

Of course, the conditions in this study—like conditions in the Kentucky McDonald's—were very favorable for obedience; under different conditions, obedience rates will not be so high. Subsequent research has indicated, for instance, that when nurses are more familiar with the medicine involved and are able to consult freely with their colleagues, the rates of obedience are considerably lower (Rank & Jacobson, 1977).

In some cases, obedience to authority can produce very negative consequences, especially if the orders involve actions that are morally questionable or reprehensible. History provides many examples, such as the My Lai Massacre during the Vietnam War, at which soldiers obeyed Lieutenant Calley's orders to kill innocent villagers, or the activity of the Third Reich of Nazi Germany during the 1930s and 1940s that produced the Holocaust. In complying with the dictates of Hitler's authoritarian government, some German citizens committed acts that most people consider morally unconscionable—beatings, confiscation of property, torture, and murder of millions of people. This may seem like madness, but Hannah Arendt (1965) has argued that most participants in the Holocaust were not psychotics or sadists who enjoyed committing mass murder but ordinary individuals exposed to powerful social pressures.

To explore the limits of obedience to legitimate authority, Stanley Milgram carried out a program of experimental research in a laboratory setting (Milgram, 1965, 1974, 1976; Miller, Collins, & Brief, 1995). Milgram created a hierarchy in which one person (the experimenter, who assumed the role of authority) directed another person (the participant) to engage in actions that ostensibly hurt a third person (a confederate, who played the role of victim). The primary goal of this research was to understand the conditions under which participants would follow morally questionable orders to hurt the confederate.

At the outset, Milgram (1963) recruited 40 adult men to serve as participants. These men, contacted through newspaper advertisements, were adults (aged 20 to 50) with diverse occupations (labor, blue collar, white collar, and professional). When a participant arrived for the experiment, he found that another person (a gentle, 47-year-old male accountant) had also responded to the newspaper advertisement. This person, though ostensibly another participant, was actually a confederate of the experimenter. The experimenter told the participants that the purpose of the research was to study the effects of punishment (that is, electric shock) on learning. One of the participants was to occupy the role of learner, whereas the other was to occupy the role of teacher. Participants drew a slip of paper to determine their roles; unknown to the participant, the drawing was rigged so the confederate was always selected as the learner. The confederate was then taken into the adjacent room and strapped into an "electric chair," and electrodes were attached to his wrist. He mentioned that he had some heart trouble and expressed concern that the shock might prove dangerous. The experimenter, who was dressed in a lab coat, replied that the shock would be painful but would not cause permanent damage.

The participant and the confederate then participated in a paired-associates learning task. The participant, in the role of teacher, read pairs of words over an intercom system to the confederate in the adjacent room, and the confederate was supposed to memorize these. After reciting the entire list of paired words, the participant then tested the amount the confederate learned. Going through the list again, he read aloud the first word of each pair and four alternatives for the second word of the pair, much like a multiple-choice exam. The confederate's task was to select the correct alternative response for each item.

Consistent with the cover story that they were investigating the effects of punishment on learning, the experimenter ordered the participant to shock the learner whenever he made an incorrect response. This shock was to be administered by means of an electric generator that had 30 voltage levels, ranging from 15 to 450 volts. The participant was directed to set the first shock at the lowest level (15 volts) and then, with each successive error, increase to the next higher voltage. That is, the participant was to increase the voltages from 15 to 30 to 45, and so on up to the 450-volt maximum. On the shock generator, the lowest voltage level (15 volts) was labeled *slight shock*; a higher level (135 volts) read *strong shock*; higher still (375 volts) read *danger: severe shock*; the highest level (450 volts) was ominously marked *XXX*. In actuality, this equipment was a dummy generator, and the confederate never received any actual shocks, but its appearance was quite convincing to participants.

Soon after the session began, it became apparent that the confederate was a slow learner. Although he got a few answers right, his responses were incorrect on most trials. The participants reacted by administering ever-higher levels of shock, as they had been ordered to do. When the shock level reached 75 volts, the confederate (who was still in the adjacent room) grunted loudly. At 120 volts, he shouted that the shocks were becoming painful. At 150 volts, he demanded to be released from the experiment ("Get me out of here! I won't be in the experiment anymore! I refuse to go on!"). At 270 volts, his response to the shock was an agonized scream. (Actually, the shouts and screams that participants heard from the adjacent room came from tape recordings so the learner's response was uniform for all participants.)

Whenever a participant expressed concern or dismay about the procedure, the experimenter urged him to persist ("The experiment must continue" and "You have no other choice—you must go on."). At the 300-volt level, the confederate shouted in desperation that he wanted to be released from the electric chair and would not provide any further answers to the test. In reaction, the experimenter directed the participant to treat any refusal to answer as an incorrect response. At the 315-volt level, the learner gave out a violent scream. At the 330-volt level, he fell completely silent, and from that point on nothing more was heard from him. Stoically, the experimenter directed the participant to continue toward the 450-volt maximum, even though the learner did not respond.

The basic question this study addressed was, "What percentage of the participants would continue to administer shocks up to the 450-volt maximum?" The results showed that of the 40 participants, 26 (65%) continued to the end of the shock series (450 volts). Although they could have refused to proceed, not a single participant stopped before administering 300 volts. Despite the tortured reactions of the confederate, most participants followed the experimenter's orders.

Understandably, this situation was very stressful for the participants, and many felt some concern for the learner's welfare. As the shock level rose, the participants grew increasingly worried and agitated. Some began to sweat or laugh nervously, and many pleaded with the experimenter to check the learner's condition or to end the study immediately. A few participants became so distressed that they refused to follow the experimenter's orders. The overall level of compliance in this study, however, was quite high, reflecting the enormous impact of directives from a legitimate authority.

It is important to note that Milgram's experiment could not be conducted today because scientists are now bound by rules designed to protect individuals who participate in research. Being put in a situation in which you are required to shock someone—even with the ability to leave and even later discovering during debriefing that it was all a ruse—is disturbing and can lead to post-traumatic stress. Institutional Review Boards at universities, hospitals, and other organizations now evaluate detailed plans for any research that involves human subjects, weighing the risks and potential benefits, and must approve the plans before research can begin.

Factors Affecting Obedience to Authority

As Milgram's results show, persons in authority usually obtain compliance with their orders, especially when these are accepted as legitimate or backed by potential force. Nevertheless, orders from an authority can set off a complex process that can lead to various responses (Blass, 1991). Compliance does not always occur, and subordinate members sometimes defy orders from an authority. Although most participants in Milgram's research obeyed orders, some refused to comply. Other studies have reported similar effects: Obedience is the most common response to authority, but defiance occurs in some cases (Martin & Sell, 1986; Michener & Burt,

1975). This raises a basic question: Under what conditions will people comply with authority, and under what conditions will they refuse? What factors affect the probability that group members will comply with authority?

Certain factors affecting compliance are straightforward. For instance, other things being equal, a direct display of authority symbols—like a uniform or badge—will increase compliance (Bushman, 1988). In one study (Sedikides & Jackson, 1990), visitors at the bird exhibit of the Bronx Zoo were approached by a person who told them not to touch the handrail of the exhibit. They were significantly more likely to obey this directive when it came from a person dressed in a zookeeper uniform than when it came from a person dressed in casual clothes. The use of authoritative symbols may also have played a part in the Milgram studies, in which the experimenter wore a gray lab coat.

Another factor that matters is whether the person in authority can back up his or her demands with punishment in the event of noncompliance. Although this was not an explicit factor in Milgram's studies, other research has manipulated the magnitude of the potential punishment the authority wielded, and the results support the view that greater punishment magnitude leads to higher levels of compliance (Michener & Burt, 1975).

Milgram (1974) extended his basic experiment to study some other factors that affect compliance with orders. For instance, one variation manipulated the degree of surveillance by the experimenter over the participant (Milgram, 1965, 1974). In one condition, the experimenter sat a few feet away from the participant during the experiment, maintaining direct surveillance; in another condition, after giving basic instructions, the experimenter departed from the laboratory and issued orders by telephone from a remote location. The results show that the number of obedient participants was almost three times greater in the face-to-face condition than in the order-by-telephone condition. In other words, obedience was greater when participants were under direct surveillance than under remote surveillance. During the telephone conversations, some participants specifically assured the experimenter they were raising the shock level when, in actuality, they were using only the lowest shock and nothing more. This tactic enabled them to ease their conscience while at the same time avoiding a direct confrontation with authority.

In another variation, Milgram (1974) manipulated the participant's physical proximity to the victim. The findings showed that bringing the victim closer to the participant—and, therefore, increasing the participant's awareness of the learner's suffering—substantially reduced the participant's willingness to administer shock. In the extreme case, when the victim was seated right next to the participant, obedience decreased substantially. Tilker (1970) reported similar results and also showed that expressly making participants totally responsible for their own actions rendered them less likely to administer shocks to the learner.

Obedience to authority is also affected by the participant's position in a larger chain of command. Kilham and Mann (1974) used a Milgram-like situation in which one participant (the executant) actually pushed the buttons to administer shock, while another participant (the transmitter) simply conveyed the orders from the experimenter. The results showed that obedience rates were approximately twice as high among transmitters as among executants. In other words, persons positioned closer to the authority but farther from the unhappy task of throwing the switch were more obedient.

RESISTING INFLUENCE AND PERSUASION

It is important to note that we are not simply hapless victims of the persuasion and compliance efforts of other people. Social psychologists have identified a number of factors that enhance our ability to resist attitude change. In this section, we discuss three major contributors to persuasion resistance: inoculation, forewarning, and reactance.

Inoculation

Interested in how persons develop resistance to persuasion, McGuire (1964) proposed that a target can be inoculated against persuasion. He specified various **attitude inoculation** treatments that would enable target persons to defend their beliefs against persuasion attempts. One such treatment, called a *refutational defense*, is analogous to medical inoculation, in which a patient receives a small dose of a pathogen so that he or she can develop antibodies. The refutational defense consists of giving the target (1) information that is discrepant with their beliefs and (2) arguments that counter the discrepant information and that support their original beliefs. By exposing a target to weak attacks and allowing the target to refute them, this inoculation builds up the target's resistance and prepares the target to resist stronger attacks on their attitudes in the future.

Some research (McGuire & Papageorgis, 1961) has demonstrated the effectiveness of a refutational defense against persuasion attempts. College students received messages attacking three commonly held beliefs or "cultural truisms." Two days before the attack, the students had received an inoculation treatment to foster their resistance to persuasion. For one truism, they received a refutational defense. For a second truism, they received a different immunization treatment called a *supportive defense*—information containing elaborate arguments in favor of the truism. For the third truism, they received no defense. Following exposure to attacks on their attitudes, students rated the extent of their agreement with each of the truisms. The results show that the refutational defense provided the highest level of resistance to persuasion. The supportive defense provided less resistance, and when no defense was present, there was still less resistance to persuasion. Later research extended the reach of refutational defenses beyond cultural truisms to other types of attitudes (politics, health).

Forewarning

A second aid to resisting influence is simply warning people that they are about to be exposed to a persuasion attempt. It is not necessary to provide information to refute the arguments for this effect to occur—if we are warned that our attitudes will be coming under attack, we begin to develop our own counterarguments (Freedman & Sears, 1965). However, combining forewarning with refutational defenses is particularly effective. As an example, exposing middle school students to public service announcements that included both warning of an impending threat to their existing beliefs ("No matter how much you want to stay a nonsmoker, the truth is that the pressure to smoke in junior high will be higher than at any other time in your life.") and demonstrated refutations to counterarguments (*Smoking is cool.* "It is definitely not cool for friends to expect you to do something stupid. Real friends respect your decision

to live a healthy life because they will want what's best for you.") effectively protected antismoking attitudes and curbed dangerous behaviors, particularly among the most vulnerable (Pfau, Van Bockern, & Kang, 1992).

The more advance notice people have that the persuasion attempt is coming, the more time they have to develop counterarguments. If motivated to develop such arguments, they may be more resistant to the persuasion attempt than will those with less time (Chen, Reardon, Rea, & Moore, 1992; Petty & Cacioppo, 1979a). This brings up an important qualification for the positive effect of forewarning. The targets of the persuasion attempt must care about and be psychologically involved in the issue. If they do care about the issue, then the warning motivates them to defend their position. If, however, they do not care about the issue, the forewarning may have little effect and, in some instances, can even produce greater attitude change (Apsler & Sears, 1968).

Reactance

Sometimes, persuasion attempts can go too far. When trying to convince people to change their attitudes, we may become too heavy-handed and actually produce a reaction in the direction opposite to that we intended. This phenomenon is called **reactance**—or the boomerang effect—and it occurs when the target of the persuasion attempt begins to feel that their independence and freedom are being threatened (Brehm, 1966). Feeling the need to reassert control, the targets will behave in a way counter to the persuasion attempt in order to demonstrate their independence. Reactance effects have been demonstrated in studies of antidrinking, ant-smoking, and antigraffiti persuasion attempts; physician's advice; and warning labels on television programming and alcoholic beverages (for example, Bensley & Wu, 1991; Bushman & Stack, 1996; Pennebaker & Sanders, 1976; Ringold, 2002).

SUMMARY

Social influence occurs when behavior by one person (the source) causes another person (the target) to change an opinion or to perform an action he or she would not otherwise perform. Important forms of open influence include persuasion, use of threats and promises, and exercise of legitimate authority.

Attitude Change via Persuasion. Persuasion is a widely used form of social influence intended to produce attitude change. (1) The communication-persuasion paradigm points to many factors—properties of the source, the message, and the target—that affect whether a message will change beliefs and attitudes. (2) Certain attributes of the source affect a message's impact. Sources who are credible (that is, highly expert and trustworthy) are more persuasive than sources who are not. Attractive sources are more persuasive than unattractive ones, especially if message arguments are strong. A message coming from multiple, independent sources will have more impact than the same message from a single source. (3) Message characteristics also determine a message's effectiveness. Highly discrepant messages are more persuasive when they come from a source having high credibility. Fear-arousing messages are most effective when they specify a course of action that can avert impending negative consequences. One-sided messages have more impact than two-sided messages when the target already agrees with the speaker's viewpoint or is not well informed. (4) Attributes of the target also determine a message's effectiveness. Targets who are highly involved with

an issue, who like thinking issues through in detail, and who are not distracted tend to scrutinize messages closely and are more influenced by the strength of the arguments than by peripheral factors.

Compliance with Threats and Promises. Threats and promises are influence techniques used to achieve compliance (not attitude change) from the target. In using threats and promises, the source alters the environment of the target by directly manipulating reward contingencies. The effectiveness of a threat depends on both the magnitude of the punishment involved and the probability that it will be carried out. Greater compliance results from high magnitude and high probability. Similar effects hold true for promises, although these involve rewards rather than punishments.

Obedience to Authority. *Authority* refers to the capacity of one group member to issue orders or make requests of other members by invoking rights vested in his or her role. (1) Research on obedience to authority shows that participants will comply with orders to administer extreme levels of electric shock to an innocent victim. (2) Obedience to authority is more likely to occur when the authority is dressed in uniform, when the authority can back up orders with punishments, when participants are under direct surveillance by the person issuing orders, when participants are distant from rather than close to the victim, and when participants are transmitters rather than executants of a command.

Resisting Influence and Persuasion. Resistance to persuasion attempts can be increased through inoculation processes, in which targets are exposed to some of the source's arguments before the persuasion attempt occurs and provided with counterarguments. Persuasion can also be reduced by warning the target that a persuasion attempt is going to occur. Finally, if a persuasion attempt is too heavy-handed, targets may feel their freedom is threatened and attempt to reestablish their independence by defying the persuasion attempt.

List of Key Terms and Concepts

attitude change (p. 312)
attitude inoculation (p. 337)
authority (p. 332)
communication-persuasion paradigm (p. 314)
communicator credibility (p. 315)
compliance (p. 312)
discrepant message (p. 315)
five-factor model (p. 312)
legitimate power (p. 329)
mass media (p. 316)
media campaign (p. 316)
persuasion (p. 314)
promise (p. 328)
reactance (p. 338)
referent power (p. 329)
social impact theory (p. 317)
social influence (p. 312)
source (p. 312)
subjective expected value (SEV) (p. 331)
target (p. 312)
threat (p. 328)

Critical Thinking Skill: Evaluating Persuasive Messages

As this chapter illustrated, we are inundated with persuasive statements throughout our daily lives. Some of these are messages worth being persuaded by; others are not. Critical thinking can help you discern between the two.

Think about your dentist's regular encouragement to brush and floss regularly. This message is consistent with toothpaste, mouthwash, and toothbrush ads encouraging you to practice good dental hygiene (and use their product in doing so). There is nothing inherently wrong about any of these messages. Certainly no one would argue that we should neglect our teeth and gums.

However, you may be exposed to similar persuasive messages from friends who regularly encourage you to go out drinking to have a good time. This message is consistent with the commercials and other advertisements that show glamorous-looking people having a good time while drinking alcohol. Like the dental hygiene messages, the messages of advertisers and an individual who you know might be consistent with one another, offering multiple sources of information in support of their claims. However, there are important differences in the two sets of messages. Based on what you learned in this chapter, what are some of the ways these persuasive attempts differ? Think of these before you continue.

You might have thought about the reliability and trustworthiness of the source. Your dentist has little to gain by having you take better care of your teeth. In fact, you would spend more time in the dentist's office—and pay more for your dentist's services—if you did not heed her advice and neglected your teeth.

You might have also thought about the purpose of the message. Your friends might genuinely care about you and whether you have a good time, but they also want to have others to hang out with when they go out, and if they drink regularly, they want others to drink regularly too in order to make them feel more normal. It might be self-serving to encourage you to join them. Advertisers, whether selling vodka or mouthwash, have their bottom line in mind, so they are sources to be skeptical of. Consider whether a message is biased or self-serving.

You might have also considered the source's evidence and credentials. Your dentist knows quite a bit about dental hygiene. Messages from advertisers for oral hygiene products often include supporting evidence: "Kills 99% of germs in clinical tests," "4 out of 5 dentists recommend." What evidence do your friends or the alcohol advertisers have that people have a better time out at the bars than elsewhere? Is there an assumption that people are having a good time? Do your friends or the alcohol advertisers make any effort to prove this claim or substantiate it? Thinking critically, you should evaluate a message's argument. Is it compelling? Are the ideas presented in a logical, reasoned way that follow from one another and lead to a particular conclusion?

Understanding what differentiates a valid persuasive message from an invalid one not only helps us be more critical consumers of information but can also help us become more effective in persuading others.

ALTRUISM AND
PROSOCIAL BEHAVIOR

Jennifer Beyer, age 22, was driving along Old River Road in Appleton, Wisconsin, on a cold day in February. She was on the way to visit a friend, but when a soaking wet child flagged her down, she pulled over immediately. Shivering and frightened, Jeff Laszewski hurriedly explained that he and his friend, nine-year-old Colin Deeg, had been playing on the frozen Fox River when the ice gave way. Jeff had managed to climb back onto the ice and make it to shore, but Colin was still in the water and couldn't get out.

Starting down the river bank, Jennifer saw Colin splashing in the frigid water. At the point where many others would have stopped due to the great personal risk, she went onto the frozen river to rescue him. Inching her way onto the ice, she tried to use her scarf to pull Colin out, but the ice cracked and she plunged into the water. At this point, Colin was still conscious but fading fast. In the meantime, Jeff reached another adult, Cyndy Graf, who quickly dialed 911 for help and then ran to the river.

Jennifer grabbed Colin to keep him from going under and tried to get him out of the water. This proved impossible, however. Colin soon passed out and the weight of his wet clothes made him too heavy to push onto land. Jennifer's limbs were numb with cold by the time police arrived and fire teams reached the river with rescue equipment, but she had kept Colin's head above water and prevented him from drowning. Officers rushed the pair to nearby St. Elizabeth's hospital, where doctors used a bypass machine to warm Colin's blood, which had dropped in temperature to 78 degrees. Jennifer was treated for hypothermia. A week later, Colin was doing fine.

Jennifer Beyer's story is extraordinary for its valor and heroism, but everyday life is filled with smaller tales of people helping others in need. Individuals help others in many ways. They may give someone a ride, help change a flat tire, donate blood, make contributions to charity, return lost items to their owners, assist victims of accidents, and so on. Of course, the mere fact that someone needs help does not mean others will rush to give aid. Humans are capable of vastly different responses to persons in need. Although Jennifer Beyer went onto the ice to rescue Colin Deeg, many others would not have taken that risk. Some will not even stop to help a stranded motorist or make contributions to charitable causes. Thus, a challenge for social psychologists is to explain variations in helping behavior. When will people help others, when will they refuse to, and why? Drawing on research and theory, this chapter addresses the following questions:

1. What motivates us to help one another?

2. How do characteristics of the person in need of help influence giving by others?

3. What impact do cultural factors such as norms and roles have on helping behavior?

4. How do characteristics of the situation affect helping behavior?

5. In emergency situations, what factors determine whether bystanders will intervene and offer help?

6. When help is given, which factors determine the recipient's reactions?

When discussing the positive end of social behaviors, social psychologists use three interrelated terms. **Prosocial behavior** is a broad category of actions considered beneficial to others and as having positive social consequences. These include donating to charity, intervention in emergencies, cooperation, sharing, volunteering, sacrifice, and the like. This contrasts with antisocial behavior that is aggressive, violent, or destructive. **Helping** is prosocial behavior that has the consequence of providing some benefit to or improving the well-being of another person (Dovidio, Piliavin, Schroeder, & Penner, 2006). Intent is unimportant. There is no requirement that the helper intends to benefit another person with his or her action. Furthermore, the helper can also benefit from helping; under this definition, helping behavior may involve either selfish or egoistic motives. Another type of prosocial behavior is altruism. Although there is some disagreement on what behaviors count as altruistic (Kalmijn & De Graaf, 2012), here we define **altruism** as helping that is intended to provide aid to someone else without expectation of any reward (other than the good feeling that may result) and that comes at a cost to the helper. Note that, for altruism, intentions do matter. Under this definition, the helper must intend to benefit the other (Piliavin & Charng, 1990; Schroeder, Penner, Dovidio, & Piliavin, 1995; Simmons, 1991). In fact, this must be the primary goal of the altruistic action (Batson, 2011).

MOTIVATION TO HELP

What motivates one person to help another? There are at least three major views on the issue, each rooted in different conceptions of human nature. The first view depicts humans as egoistic or selfish beings, concerned primarily with their own gratification. Helping originates from some ulterior, self-serving motive. Potential helpers weigh the costs and benefits of helping to decide whether they will do so. The second view depicts humans as rather more generous and unselfish beings, capable of real concern for the welfare of others. For instance, a bystander may rush to rescue an accident victim to relieve the victim's pain and anguish. Our human ability to empathize with others motivates us to alleviate their distress. The third view, from evolutionary psychology, sees prosocial behavior as an evolved trait that helps ensure individuals will pass along their genes to the next generation. In this section, we look at these three views in more detail.

Egoism

One view of human nature regards us all as fundamentally selfish beings, concerned primarily with our own gratification. This seemingly simple seed is used throughout the social sciences to explain a huge variety of social behavior, including prosocial acts. Although this view acknowledges that helping behavior occurs with considerable frequency, it treats helping as always originating from some ulterior, self-serving consideration (Gelfand & Hartmann, 1982). For instance, a student might help a peer with a difficult assignment to get admiration and approval from the other, to avoid feelings of guilt or shame, to obligate the other to her, or to bolster her own self-esteem. Helping behavior motivated by self-gratification is called **egoism**.

Even in the most other-oriented, charitable behavior, there is little doubt that considerations of reward and cost influence decisions to give or withhold help. Every helping act imposes some costs on the helper (danger, loss of time, financial costs, expenditure of effort). In general, the greater these costs, the less likely persons are to help (Kerber, 1984; Shotland & Stebbins, 1983). Would you be more likely to help someone study for an exam you are also studying for than for an exam you took last semester? If you are also studying for the exam, ensuring someone else understands the material takes little additional time and might actually help you understand the material better (in addition to the potential benefits of helping another student outlined above). Helping someone study for an exam for a class that you are not enrolled in, however, comes at a cost; it takes away valuable time that you could spend studying another subject and offers you fewer direct benefits.

There may also be some costs to potential helpers for *not* helping (public disapproval by others, embarrassment and loss of face, and condemnation by the victim). The evaluation of these costs is important in determining helping behavior, and many theorists believe individuals will generally not give help unless they think the rewards (even if not immediate) will outweigh the costs (Lynch & Cohen, 1978; Piliavin, Dovidio, Gaertner, & Clark, 1981).

The rewards that motivate potential helpers are many and varied. They may include such things as thanks from the victim, admiration and approval from others, financial rewards and prizes, and recognition for competence. People will help more if they anticipate rewards such as status enhancement (Bienenstock & Bianchi, 2004; Kerber, 1984). Even small rewards—like the small chocolate that the local Goodwill offers with every donation—tend to increase individuals' helping behavior. Getting something in return helps people make a self-interested justification for the behavior (Holmes, Miller, & Lerner, 2002; Perlow & Weeks, 2002).

The form of help that someone offers may depend on the specific rewards he or she seeks, and these may, in turn, depend on his or her own needs. For example, a study invited students to volunteer for a range of prosocial activities with similar rewards. When given a choice, students volunteered for activities related to their personal values and preferences. For example, those who enjoyed novelty volunteered more frequently to help with a project on unusual states of consciousness, ESP, and hypnosis, and those who liked close social relationships volunteered more frequently to help troubled high school students (Gergen, Gergen, & Meter, 1972).

Altruism and Empathetic Concern

People often react to the distress of others on an emotional level and offer help in response. The term **empathy** refers to the vicarious experience of an emotion that is congruent with—or possibly identical to—the emotion that another person is experiencing (Barnett, 1987; Eisenberg & Miller, 1987). For example, when a mother sees her child in pain, she may experience a very similar emotion to the child. There is considerable evidence that feelings of empathy for a person in need will lead to helping behavior (Batson et al., 1981; Dovidio, Allen, & Schroeder, 1990; Eisenberg & Miller, 1987; Fultz et al., 1986).

The Empathy-Altruism Model. The *empathy-altruism model* proposes that adults can experience two distinct states of emotional arousal while witnessing another's suffering: distress and empathy. Distress involves unpleasant emotions such as shock, alarm, worry, and upset at seeing another person suffer. Empathy, however, entails such emotions as compassion, concern, warmth, and tenderness toward the other (Batson, 1987, 1991; Batson & Coke, 1981; Batson & Oleson, 1991). These states of emotional arousal give rise to different motivations, but both can lead to helping behavior. If the bystander experiences distress at seeing another suffering, he or she may be motivated to reduce this distress (egoism). This contrasts with the situation in which a bystander experiences empathy when wit-

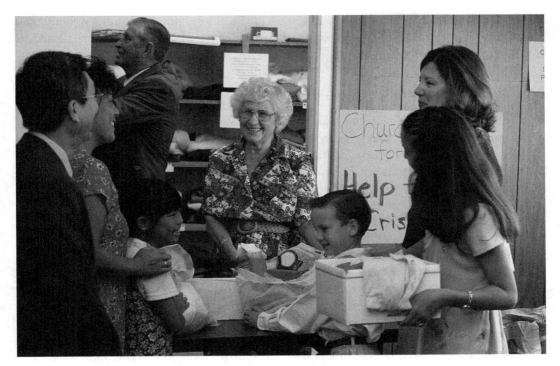

Who will volunteer at this church charity drive? Who will donate goods? Personal characteristics sometimes drive the decision to help, but cost-benefit calculations, cultural norms, situational factors, and even genetics also play important roles. © Ocean/Corbis

nessing the suffering of another. Feelings of this type may cause the bystander to help the victim, but this help is motivated fundamentally by a desire to reduce the other's distress (altruism). The empathy-altruism model has received support from many experiments. Typically, the participants in these studies witness a person in distress and must decide whether to offer help. The independent variables in these studies are the level of empathy and the ease of escape from the situation. When empathy is high, the frequency of helping behavior is also high, irrespective of whether it was easy to avoid the situation. However, when distress is high, the frequency of helping behavior drops off substantially when escape is easy; participants leave the situation rather than absorbing the costs of helping (Batson et al., 1983). Distress can be alleviated by leaving the situation; empathy cannot.

Altruistically motivated helping, fueled by empathy, appears to lead to more sustained giving than helping that is motivated by egoism (Piferi, Jobe, & Jones, 2006). In a study on the motivations for helping after the September 11 terrorist attacks, researchers found that individuals who gave money, blood, goods, or other forms of assistance because of other-focused motives (giving to reduce another's discomfort) were almost four times more likely to still be giving support one year later than those whose original motivation was to reduce personal distress (egoistic motives). This effect likely stems from differences in emotional arousal. The events of September 11 emotionally affected people throughout the United States. Those who gave to reduce their own distress reduced their emotional arousal with their initial gift, discharging that emotional distress. However, those who gave to reduce others' distress did not stop empathizing with victims who continued to struggle long after the attacks.

Evolutionary Perspectives

A third view on prosocial behavior takes an evolutionary perspective. The basic notion driving this theory is that any genetically determined physical attribute or trait that helps an individual survive will be passed on to the next generation. Eventually, individuals with the attribute will become more numerous than those without. The evolutionary perspective often points to others in the animal kingdom to demonstrate its propositions. For example, helping behaviors and even altruistic, self-sacrificing behaviors are common in nature. Ground squirrels, for instance, frequently sound alarm calls when a predator approaches. These calls warn other squirrels of the threat, but they also draw the attention of the predator to the individual sounding the alarm, thereby increasing the chances of that individual being killed (Sherman, 1980). Other animals sacrifice themselves to predators to protect the larger group (Wilson, 1971). At first, these patterns of self-sacrificing behavior seem to run counter to evolutionary theory. Altruism among animals often means that those who are the most helpful will be the least likely to survive. This means they will be less likely to have offspring and may not have any at all. How, then, could the altruistic tendency persist generations later? The same question can be posed, of course, with respect to humans.

Evolutionary psychology and a related theoretical perspective called *sociobiology* (Archer, 1991; Buss, 1999; Ketelaar & Ellis, 2000; Wilson, 1975, 1978) have constructed a response to the problem of altruism and have assembled evidence that supports the view that altruism has roots in evolution (Buss & Kenrick, 1998; Krebs & Miller,

1985). To understand how helping can make sense in an evolutionary context, it is important to appreciate that the "fittest" animal is the one that passes on its genes to subsequent generations. This can happen either by the animal itself producing offspring or by the animal's close relatives, such as brothers, sisters, and cousins (who share many of its genes), producing offspring. So although it is true that altruistic behavior will not have survival value for an individual, altruistic acts can increase the survival of one's genes if directed toward others who share the same genes (Hamilton, 1964; Meyer, 2000). Consider a mother bird who sacrifices herself to save the lives of her eight babies. Each of the babies carries half of the genes of the mother; thus, between them, they have four times as many of the mother's genes as she does herself.

Furthermore, some sociobiologists have argued that altruistic behavior is perpetuated because of reciprocation. If all the animals in a group engage in helping behavior, they will all be better off in the long run (Hardy & van Vugt, 2006). If, for example, the animals all take turns playing the role of sentry and warning the group of approaching predators, many more members of that group will survive and reproduce than if none of them had warned the group.

Evolutionary approaches to altruism have produced a considerable body of interesting research and theoretical propositions. For example, animals should be most altruistic toward those that most closely resemble them genetically—that is, they should help immediate family members more than distant cousins, and distant cousins more than outsiders or strangers (Burnstein, Crandall, & Kitayama, 1994; Rushton, Russell, & Wells, 1984). Second, parents will tend to behave altruistically toward healthy offspring, who are likely to survive and pass on their genes, but less altruistically toward sick or unhealthy offspring, who are likely to die before reproducing (Dovidio et al., 1991). Third, helping behavior should only favor those who can still reproduce. Thus, helping behavior should be targeted more toward young women than to older women who are past the age of menopause (Kruger, 2001).

Generally speaking, these evolutionary propositions have found support in studies. However, there are also exceptions and alternative explanations (Buss & Kenrick, 1998; Caporeal, 2001; Dovidio et al., 1991). For example, Sime (1983) examined peo-

ple in a fire emergency and found that they were much more likely to endanger themselves by searching for family members than by searching for friends. Rather than attributing this behavior to genetic kin selection, however, we may just as likely assume that people would sacrifice more to save someone they love than someone who is simply an acquaintance because losing the former would cause them more distress.

Although interesting, the sociobiological perspective is controversial, especially as applied to humans. For example, critics

---

BOX 10.1 Research Update: Gossip as Prosocial Behavior

Gossip is a complex social behavior; although it is very common, it is also widely criticized. An evolutionary perspective would argue that gossip exists because it serves a purpose. According to psychologist Robin Dunbar, that purpose is a prosocial one. Dunbar (1996) hypothesized that gossip became more and more prominent as a linguistic practice as humans began to live in larger and larger groups. Without being able to directly observe others' behavior, group members would use gossip to track one another's reputation as trustworthy group members.

A team of social psychologists tested Dunbar's assumption about the prosociality of gossip in a series of experiments. Feinberg, Willer, Stellar, & Keltner (2012) put participants in situations in which they watched another participant (the transgressor) act selfishly. The researchers then gave the participants the opportunity to gossip about the transgressor to the participant who would interact with the transgressor next in the experiment. More than half the students chose to gossip, and 96% of those gossip messages moved beyond serving a selfish, personal end. Examples of prosocial gossip messages were: "[He] didn't send anything back last round. I'd advise not sending anything" or "Try to keep all the money you can, because [she] will not give you much in return."

Using a battery of self-reports and heart rate monitors, the researchers explored why gossip—and, particularly, prosocial gossip—was so common. They found that people with a more prosocial orientation, whose personality reflected more other-directed concerns, tend to gossip more than those with an egoistic orientation and that participants would gossip even if there was no potential of harm toward the transgressor and when it was costly to gossip. What made gossip so attractive?

Results suggest that witnessing the unfair acts of transgressors evoked negative arousal, especially among more prosocial individuals. The more negative affect participants felt, the more compelled they were to engage in prosocial gossip. Furthermore, engaging in prosocial gossip actually reduced their levels of negative affect. This was especially true for more prosocial individuals.

Gossip also had an important effect on behavior. Participants behaved more cooperatively when they knew that observers could potentially gossip about them.

Source: Adapted from Feinberg, Willer, Stellar, & Keltner, 2012.

have questioned whether altruism is genetically transmitted (Buck & Ginsburg, 1991; Kitcher, 1985). By this model, animals and humans would help only close relatives and rarely or never help those who are genetically unrelated. Yet we know humans often help others who are unrelated—even total strangers. Some critics argue that to explain altruism among unrelated persons, it is necessary to rely on cultural constructs, such as religious values, that define unrelated others as appropriate recipients of help. At best, then, evolution is an incomplete explanation for altruism.

CHARACTERISTICS OF THE NEEDY THAT FOSTER HELPING

When in need, some people have a much better chance of receiving help than others do. Our willingness to help needy persons depends on various factors. Important among these are whether we know and like them, whether they are similar to or different from us, and whether we consider them truly deserving of help.

Acquaintanceship and Liking

We are especially inclined to help people whom we know and to whom we feel close. Studies of reactions following natural disasters, for example, indicate that whereas people generally become very helpful toward others, they tend to give aid first to needy family members, then to friends and neighbors, and last to strangers (Dynes & Quarantelli, 1980; Form & Nosow, 1958). Research suggests this tendency stems, in part, from an increased ability to empathize with those we know well (Maner & Gailliot, 2007). We are better able to take their perspective and vicariously experience their emotional distress, thereby motivating altruistic helping. Relationships

increase helping because they involve relatively stronger normative obligations, more intense emotion and empathy, and greater costs if we fail to help. Even a brief acquaintanceship is sufficient to make us more likely to help someone (Pearce, 1980). A simple introduction or comment, and sometimes less, is enough to transform a complete stranger into a "familiar stranger" (Milgram, 1977) and increase the likelihood of helping.

We are also more likely to help someone we like than to help someone we do not like. This effect occurs whether our positive feelings about the other are based on his or her physical appearance, personal characteristics, or friendly behavior (Kelley & Byrne, 1976; Mallozzi, McDermott, & Kayson, 1990). Moreover, we are more likely to help someone who likes us than to help someone who does not (Baron, 1971).

Similarity

In general, we are more likely to help others who are similar to ourselves than to help others who are dissimilar (Dovidio, 1984). That is, we are more likely to help those who resemble us in race, attitudes, political ideologies, and even mode of dress. For instance, with respect to race, several studies have reported that in situations where refusing to help may be easily justified, Whites are more likely to help other Whites than to help Blacks (Benson, Karabenick, & Lerner, 1973; Dovidio & Gaertner, 1981). Similarity of opinions and political ideologies also increases helping (Hornstein, 1978). In a series of field studies, New York pedestrians came across "lost" wallets or letters that had been planted by researchers in conspicuous places. These objects contained information indicating the original owner's views on the Arab-Israeli conflict, on worthy or unpopular organizations, or on trivial opinion items. The owner's views on these top-

BOX 10.2 Research Update: Group Boundaries and Helping Behavior

We tend to help others who are like us. A regular cyclist is more likely to stop to help a cyclist with a flat tire than to help a stranded motorist. Additionally, race, gender, and other strongly held group identities play an important role in our willingness to help others, but what impact might other, less salient identities have? For example, can similarity based on being a fan of a particular sport team or even a particular sport, like baseball, encourage helping behavior?

A group of researchers set out to explore the influence of these sports-related group memberships by using a choreographed accident in which a confederate fell down and feigned a painful injury in the presence of a subject. Prior to the accident, the subjects had taken a survey questionnaire about their favorite soccer team, thereby priming their identity as fans of their favorite team. Then, the subjects were directed to walk to a different location for the second part of the soccer study in which they were supposed to watch a video about soccer teams. Along the way, they passed the confederate, who fell and pretended to be hurt. The outcome of interest was whether the subjects stopped to help and, if so, how much help was offered.

The manipulation in the experiment was simple: The confederate wore a shirt identified with the subjects' favorite team, a shirt identified with the main rival of the subjects' favorite team, or a neutral shirt that did not identify with any team at all. The results were surprisingly stark. Confederates wearing the favorite team's shirt received help from the subjects over 90% of the time, whereas those wearing a plain shirt or the rival team's shirt received help less than one-third of the time.

In the second experiment, these same researchers attempted to examine a more diffuse identity: that of soccer fans in general rather than those of a particular team. This experiment followed a similar procedure as the first, except that instead of priming the subjects' identity about their favorite team, the researchers primed the subjects to think about their identity as soccer fans in general. They did this by telling the subjects that there are a few troublemakers among soccer fans who got into drunken brawls and, thereby, gave soccer fans a bad name. However, there are also many positive aspects about being soccer fans, and the purpose of the research was to examine these positive aspects. After hearing this information, the subjects filled out a survey about being soccer fans. The remainder of the experiment proceeded as before. Again, the primed identity had a strong effect on helping, but the pattern was different. If the confederate was wearing either soccer shirt, help was received about 75% of the time. If the confederate wore the generic shirt, help was received less than 25% of the time.

Source: Adapted from Levine, Prosser, Evans, and Reicher, 2005.

ics either resembled or differed from the views known to characterize the neighborhoods in which the objects were dropped. Persons finding the wallets or letters took steps to return them to the owner much more frequently when the owner's views were similar to their own. As Box 10.2 illustrates, even a characteristic as seemingly trivial as liking the same sport can influence the chances of helping (and hurting).

Much of the effect of similarity is a product of perceived group membership. Although groups and group processes will be discussed in more detail in Chapters 13 and 14, people tend to help in-group members (people who share a particular characteristic) more than out-group members (people who are different from them on a particular characteristic). This is, in part, because individuals are better able to ascribe emotions to in-group members. A study of helping after Hurricane Katrina illustrates this effect (Cuddy, Rock, & Norton, 2007). Researchers had White, Black, and Latino participants read a fictionalized account of a mother who had lost her child during Hurricane Katrina. Names cued readers into the victims' race (Tanesha/Amanda and Tyrell/Joshua). After reading the news story, participants were asked to describe the emotions the mothers were experiencing and whether they planned to volunteer or had already volunteered time toward Hurricane Katrina relief efforts.

Of primary interest to the researchers was the role of emotion in helping. They distinguished between two types of emotions—primary and secondary—to determine their relative effects. Primary emotions are emotions that are a direct result of an external cue. They are closely related to the situation at hand. For example, the moment an intimate relationship ends—the breakup—causes a rush of emotion that can be directly attributed to the breakup. You might experience sadness, hurt, and frustration. Secondary emotions are the more enduring effects of these immediate emotions. The rush of sadness may give way to insecurity, anxiety, or depression.

Results showed that participants inferred similar primary emotions—sadness, distress, pain, fear, and so on—for in-group and out-group members. In other words, whether a Black or White participant read the story of Tanesha or Amanda, they believed the mothers would feel similar levels of sadness. However, when participants were asked to rate secondary emotions—grief, sorrow, mourning, guilt, and so on—differences emerged. Specifically, participants inferred lower levels of secondary emotions to out-group members, thinking they would experience less grief than someone in their in-group. Importantly, empathizing with someone in need based on

these secondary emotions has more of an influence on helping than simply empathizing on primary emotions.

Deservingness

After Hurricane Katrina, some Americans felt that the residents of New Orleans who stayed in the city during the storm did not deserve help. After all, it seemed like they decided to ignore officials' orders to evacuate. Whether we see someone as deserving help has important implications for our desire to act on their behalf.

Suppose you received a call asking you to help elderly people who had just suffered a sharp reduction in income after losing their jobs. Would it matter whether they lost their jobs because they were caught stealing and lying or because their work program was being phased out? A study of Wisconsin residents who received such a call showed that respondents were more likely to help if the elderly people had become dependent because their program was cut than because they had been caught stealing (Schwartz & Fleishman, 1978).

What matters in this situation is the potential helpers' causal attribution regarding the origin of need (such attributions were covered in Chapter 6). Potential helpers respond more favorably when a person's need is caused by circumstances beyond his or her control. Such people are true "innocent victims" who deserve help. In contrast, needs caused by a person's own actions, misdeeds, or failings elicit little desire to help (Bryan & Davenport, 1968; Frey & Gaertner, 1986). For instance, one study found that students were less sympathetic and less likely to help a person who developed AIDS through promiscuous sexual contact than through a blood transfusion (Weiner, Perry, & Magnusson, 1988). In the United States, we tend to commit the fundamental attribution error (the tendency to overemphasize personality in making attributions) and assume that those in need are somewhat to blame for their situation and to downplay or ignore the importance of circumstances outside of their control that may have led to the need or made it difficult to overcome it. Needs thought to stem from illegitimate sources—including individual choices—undermine helping by inhibiting empathic concerns, blocking our sense of normative obligation, and increasing the possibility of condemnation rather than social approval for helping.

Even in emergencies, potential helpers are influenced by whether they consider a victim deserving. Consider responses to an emergency staged by experimenters on the New York City subway (Piliavin, Ro-

ABC's program *What Would You Do* puts unsuspecting people in situations in which they can either intervene to help or choose to ignore someone in need. In one episode, *What Would You Do* had an actor—dressed like a homeless man—fall to the ground on a busy sidewalk. Although people stopped more quickly when the person who fell was a well-dressed woman, a number of onlookers did call 911 for the man. However, when the same man fell to the ground with a beer can in his hand, only one woman, named Linda Hamilton, stopped. She tried to get other people's attention, to no avail. Hamilton, who is sometimes homeless herself, then threw the beer can away, hoping it would elicit more help. After she realized that passersby would not stop on their own, she explicitly asked a woman to call 911. Immediately after this second woman stopped, others also came to the man's aid. © *ABC News*

din, & Piliavin, 1969). Shortly after the subway train left the station, a young man (a confederate) collapsed to the floor and lay staring at the ceiling during the seven-and-a-half minute trip to the next station. In one experimental condition, the man carried a cane and appeared crippled. In another condition, he carried a liquor bottle and reeked of whiskey. Bystanders helped the seemingly crippled man immediately but waited several minutes, on average, before helping the man who appeared drunk.

NORMATIVE FACTORS IN HELPING

Would you intervene in a heated argument between a man and a woman you believe are married? In one experiment (Shotland & Straw, 1976), participants unexpectedly witnessed a realistic fight between a man and a woman in an elevator. The man attacked the woman, shaking her violently, while she struggled and resisted. In one treatment, the man and woman were depicted as strangers; the woman screamed, "Get away from me! I don't know you!" In the other treatment, she screamed, "Get away from me! I don't know why I ever married you!" This simple variation greatly affected the participants' propensity to help. Whereas 65% of the subjects intervened in the stranger fight, fewer than 20% intervened in the married fight.

This difference may have been due, in part, to the participants' perceptions of a greater likelihood of injury to the woman in the stranger fight than in the married fight. They assumed that an attack by a stranger might progress further than an attack by a husband. However, this reticence may have also been due to normative expectations. The participants who witnessed the married fight said they hesitated to take action because they were not sure their help was wanted. Almost all the participants who did not intervene said they felt the fight was "none of my business." Clearly, "wife" and "husband" are social roles, and some widely understood norms regulate the relations between wives and husbands (and outsiders). One of these is that, except in the case of physical abuse, outsiders should basically mind their own business and let married couples resolve disputes as they will. When the woman in the elevator identified herself as the man's wife, this norm suddenly became relevant and changed the meaning of intervention. To intervene in the fight would be an intrusion on the marital relationship and might invite reprisals from the husband, the wife, or both. In fact, participants who thought the attacker was the woman's husband believed he was more likely to attack them if they intervened than did participants who believed the attacker was a stranger. This fear of eliciting an attack on oneself when intervening makes men—who see themselves as more able to protect themselves in such an attack—more likely to intervene when they see a woman being abused than other women are (Laner, Benin, & Ventrone, 2001).

Norms of Responsibility and Reciprocity

Cultural norms mandate helping as appropriate under some conditions, and they define it as inappropriate under others. When mandated as appropriate, helping becomes an approved behavior, supported by social sanctions. Broad social norms indicate when helping is appropriate.

Social Responsibility Norm. The **social responsibility norm** is a general norm stating that individuals should help others who are dependent on them. People often mention their sense of what they "ought to do"—their internalized standards—when asked why they offer to help (Berkowitz,

1972). For example, Simmons (1991) reports the words of a bone marrow donor prior to giving: "This is a life and death situation and you must do anything you can to help that person, whether it is family, friends, or [someone] unknown" (p. 14). The word "must" in this statement suggests that a norm is operative.

Applicable in many situations, the social responsibility norm is readily activated. Some research suggests that simply informing individuals that another person—even a stranger—is dependent on them is enough to elicit help (Berkowitz, Klanderman, & Harris, 1964). Recognize, however, that there are stronger and weaker versions of the social responsibility norm. Whereas the norm that we must help dependent kin or needy friends is widely held, the belief that we must help needy strangers or unknown persons is not so universally accepted. Although the awareness of a stranger's dependency will sometimes elicit help, it does not always do so. Speeding passersby, for example, frequently disregard stranded motorists they notice on the roadside. Bystanders watch, apparently fascinated but immobile, during rapes and other assaults. Thousands of people reject charity appeals every day.

Some theorists have suggested that the social responsibility norm effectively motivates helping only when people are expressly reminded of it. In a test of this hypothesis (Darley & Batson, 1973), theological students were asked to write and record a talk. Some students prepared remarks on the parable of the Good Samaritan, others wrote about job opportunities. On the way to record their talk, the students passed a man slumped in a doorway. Although the students who wrote about the Good Samaritan were presumably thinking about the virtues of altruism as they passed the man, they helped the stranger only slightly more than the students who had prepared a talk on the unrelated topic.

These findings suggest that the social responsibility norm is a fairly weak source of motivation to help and is easily negated by the costs of helping.

The Norm of Reciprocity. Another cultural standard, the **norm of reciprocity**, states that people should (1) help those who have helped them and (2) not help those who have denied them help for no legitimate reason (Schroeder et al., 1995; Trivers, 1983). Imagine your roommate's car has broken down and he asks you for a ride to the grocery store to pick up a few things. You are much more likely to help him if he did a favor for you the last time you needed one. However, if he turned down a previous request to help you—say, when you needed a ride to campus from the bus station after returning from winter break—you are much less likely to agree. This reciprocity norm applies to anyone who has previously received some benefit from another. The norm is found in different cultures around the world (Gergen, Ellsworth, Maslach, & Siepel, 1975). Small kindnesses that create the conditions for reciprocity are a common feature of family, friendship, and work relationships.

People not only report that the reciprocity norm influences their behavior; behavioral studies have actually demonstrated reciprocity in action (Bar-Tal, 1976; Wilke & Lanzetta, 1982). Reciprocity is especially likely when the person expects to see the helper again (Carnevale, Pruitt, & Carrington, 1982). People try to match the amount of help they give to the quantity they received earlier. By matching benefits, people maintain equity in their relationships and avoid becoming overly indebted to others. Understanding the norm of reciprocity, those in need are less likely to ask for help when they believe they will not be able to repay the aid in some form (Fisher, Nadler, & Whitcher-Alagna, 1982; Nadler,

Mayseless, Peri, & Chemerinski, 1985). That said, people do not reciprocate every benefit they receive. Whether we feel obligated to reciprocate depends in part on the intentions we attribute to the person who helped us. We feel more obligated to reciprocate if we perceive that the original help was given voluntarily rather than coerced and that it was chosen consciously rather than accidentally (Gergen et al., 1975; Greenberg & Frisch, 1972).

Personal Norms

Although broad norms like social responsibility and reciprocity undoubtedly affect helping behavior, they are, by themselves, inadequate bases from which to predict the occurrence of helping behavior with precision. There are several reasons for this. First, given the wide variety of contingencies that people encounter, these norms are simply too general to dictate our behavior with any precision in all cases. Second, not everyone in society accepts these norms to the same degree; some individuals internalize them to a greater extent than others do. Third, the social norms that apply to any given situation occasionally conflict with one another; the social responsibility norm may obligate us to help an abused wife, for example, but the widely accepted norm against meddling in others' marriages tells us not to intervene.

In response to these criticisms, a different type of normative theory has been developed by social psychologists (Schwartz & Howard, 1981, 1984). This theory explains not only the conditions under which norms are likely to motivate helping but also individual differences in helping in particular situations. Instead of dealing with broad social norms, this theory focuses on **personal norms**—feelings of moral obligation to perform specific actions that stem from an individual's internalized system of values.

For example, a survey on medical transplants might ask, "If a stranger needed a bone marrow transplant, and you were a suitable donor, would you feel a moral obligation to donate bone marrow?" This survey would then be followed by an apparently unrelated encounter with a representative of an organization who would ask these individuals for help. In various studies, individuals' personal norms have predicted differences in their willingness to donate bone marrow or blood, to tutor blind children, to work for increased welfare payments for the needy (Schwartz & Howard, 1982), and to participate in community recycling programs (Hopper & Nielsen, 1991).

These personal norms may stem from role identities (Piliavin, Grube, & Callero, 2002). We are driven to act in ways consistent with our identities to experience ourselves as authentic and to uphold those identities (see Chapter 4). For example, a religious person might help because it is "the Christian thing to do" or because they believe in the golden rule: "Do unto others as you would like done to you." Similarly, someone who has adopted an identity as a "blood donor" is more likely to give blood than someone who has not (Piliavin & Callero, 1991). Helping is most likely to occur when conditions simultaneously foster the activation of personal norms and suppress any defenses that might neutralize personal norms.

Gender Norms

Although there are not significant gender differences in how much people help, there are significant differences in the ways men and women help. These differences are related to gender role norms and expectations (Piliavin & Unger, 1985). For example, research findings suggest that men are more likely than women to intervene and offer assistance in emergency situations that entail danger (Eagly & Crowley,

1986). In a study of people who had been publicly recognized as heroes by the state of California (that is, persons who had intervened to protect someone during a dangerous criminal act, such as a mugging or bank robbery), all of the heroes but one was a man (Huston, Ruggiero, Conner, & Geis, 1981). Acting heroically by confronting risk and danger is often considered part of the traditional male role. Women, however, are more likely to help in situations requiring nurturance, caretaking, and emotional support. Women are more likely to help children they witness being abused than men are (Laner, Benin, & Ventrone, 2001) and women care for children and aging parents more on a day-to-day basis than men do, fulfilling an important help-giving function (Brody, 2004). Women are also more likely than men to provide their friends with personal favors, emotional support, and informational counseling (Eisenberg & Fabes, 1991; Otten, Penner, & Waugh, 1988).

SITUATIONAL INFLUENCES

Prosocial behavior is influenced by not only normative factors but also situational influences on potential helpers. For example, we are more likely to help when we feel we have time to. In the earlier study of theological students who were on their way to give a speech on the parable of the Good Samaritan (Darley & Batson, 1973), being in a hurry had a much stronger effect on whether the students stopped to help than the topic of the speech did. Students who were in a hurry offered much less help than those who were not, in part because they felt a sense of social responsibility toward those who were waiting on them (Batson et al., 1978). In this section we consider a handful of other such factors: experiences with models of helping, mood, and the potential costs of helping (or not).

Modeling

An important factor that affects helping and aggression is the presence of behavioral models—someone else who is helping. The presence of a behavioral model tends to increase helping for several reasons. First, a model demonstrates what kinds of actions are possible or effective in the situation. Others who previously did not know how to help can emulate the model. As an example, even if a young college student wants to help a stranded motorist on the highway, he or she might not know anything about cars and, therefore, be unsure of how they might help the motorist. However, if the student had previously been in a car with someone else who, in a similar instance, made note of the mile marker and pulled out their cell phone and called highway patrol to notify the police of the stranded motorist and their location, the student would have a model of a possible behavior and would be more likely to respond similarly if a comparable situation occurred.

Second, a helping model conveys the message that to offer help is appropriate in the particular situation. A model may, for example, increase the salience of the social responsibility norm. Once aware of this norm, others may decide to help. A popular series of insurance commercials demonstrated this nicely, showing the sense of responsibility spreading through the city. It begins with a mother watching as a man stops to pick up her child's toy. She makes note of this and, later, in a restaurant, pushes a coffee cup—teetering on the edge of a table and at risk of falling—back toward the center of the table. A passerby witnesses this act of kindness and later stops to help a man up from a wet sidewalk. The commercial continues through a long series of models and observers who eventually become models for another observer.

Finally, a model provides information about the costs and risks involved in help-ing—a consideration that is especially important in situations involving danger. By offering help under conditions of danger or potential damage to self, models demonstrate to others that the risks incurred are tolerable or justified.

Mood

As discussed in Chapter 5, a mood is a transitory feeling, such as being happy and elated or being frustrated and depressed. Both good and bad moods can help or hinder a person's likelihood of helping another.

Good Moods and Helping. When individuals are in a good mood, they are more likely to help others than when they are in a neutral mood (Salovey, Mayer, & Rosenhan, 1991). Good moods promote both spontaneous helping and compliance with requests for help. There are several reasons that being in a good mood increases our propensity to help others (Carlson, Charlin, & Miller, 1988). First, people who are in a good mood are less preoccupied with themselves and less concerned with their own problems. This allows them to focus more attention on the needs and problems of others, which, through empathy, often leads to helping. Second, people in a good mood often feel relatively fortunate compared to others who are deprived. They recognize that their good fortune is out of balance with others' needs, and to restore balance, they use their resources to help others (Rosenhan, Salovey, & Hargis, 1981). Third, people in a good mood tend to see the world in a positive light and want to retain the warm glow of happiness. Thus, if they can maintain or even increase their own positive feelings through prosocial behavior, they will do so.

That said, good moods may also inhibit helping in particular situations. Those in a good mood may avoid forms of helping that involve unpleasant or embarrassing activities that threaten to interrupt or end their good mood (Cunningham, Steinberg, & Grev, 1980).

Bad Moods and Helping. The effects of a bad mood—feeling sad or depressed—can have rather complex effects on helping. Under some conditions, a bad mood inhibits helping. Under other conditions, however, it promotes helping (Carlson & Miller, 1987; Rosenhan, Salovey, & Hargis, 1981).

Bad moods can suppress helping for several reasons. First, a bad mood has an impact on the salience of others' needs. In contrast to those in a good mood, people in a bad mood are concerned about their own problems and less likely to notice others' needs than are people in a neutral or good mood. When others' needs do not grab the attention of a potential helper, help is less likely to be given (Aderman & Berkowitz, 1983; Rogers, Miller, Mayer, & Duval, 1982). Second, people in a bad mood often see themselves as less fortunate than others. Feeling relatively impoverished, they may resist using their own resources to help others, lest they become even more disadvantaged (Rosenhan et al., 1981).

Conversely, bad moods can sometimes increase helping. One explanation for this is the *negative-state relief hypothesis* (Cialdini, Kendrick, & Baumann, 1982; Cialdini et al., 1987). This hypothesis assumes that (1) individuals experiencing unpleasant feelings will be motivated to reduce them, and (2) people have learned since childhood that helping others will improve their own mood, often through the receipt of thanks or praise. The hypothesis predicts that people in bad moods will help others to boost their own spirits. Although this is an egoistic rather than altruistic motive for helping because individuals are offering help primarily to relieve sadness in themselves rather than to relieve suffering in others,

the effect is the same. However, two important implications of this hypothesis are that (1) a negative mood will only motivate helping if people believe that doing so will improve their mood (Manucia, Baumann, & Cialdini, 1984), and (2) they will only help if there is not an accessible alternative way to relieve the bad mood (Schaller & Cialdini, 1988).

Costs

When making a decision to help, people usually make a calculation about the potential costs and benefits of their action. Cost calculations for helping involve both the costs to the helper and the needs of the victim. Helpers may be willing to endure higher costs to themselves if the costs to the victim of not receiving help are extremely high (Dovidio et al., 1991; Piliavin et al., 1981). Jennifer Byer realized that Colin would likely die if she did nothing. This potential cost was so great that she was willing to take the risk of falling into the frozen river herself to prevent it.

Bystanders often take into account several kinds of costs to themselves in emergency situations. First, bystanders consider the cost of giving direct help. This includes the costs to them if they offer help—lost time, exposure to danger, expenditure of effort, exposure to disgusting experiences, and the like. Second, bystanders consider the cost of not giving help. Costs borne by the bystanders if the victim receives no help include the burden of unpleasant emotional arousal while witnessing another's suffering and the costs associated with one's personal failure to act in the face of another's need (self-blame, possible blame from others, embarrassment, and the like).

Various studies have documented that cost influences prosocial behavior. First, research finds that the greater the cost to self of giving direct help, the less likely one

Would you intervene here? High potential costs inhibit bystander intervention in this fight. Most bystanders would feel little responsibility for either man and would wish to avoid entanglement in the fight that is still in progress. © Cathy Yeulet/123rf

is to help (Darley & Batson, 1973; Shotland & Straw, 1976). This was demonstrated, for instance, in a study conducted in the New York City subway (Allen, 1972). Aboard a subway car, a bewildered-looking man asked the participant (a passenger) whether the train was going uptown or downtown. The man in the neighboring seat—a muscular type reading a bodybuilding magazine—responded quickly but gave an obviously wrong answer. Both the bewildered man and the bodybuilder were confederates. The participant could help by correcting this misinformation, but only at the risk of challenging the bodybuilder. Whether the participants helped depended on how threatening the bodybuilder appeared to be. Threat was manipulated by varying his reaction to an incident a minute before. When the bodybuilder had previously threatened physical harm to a person who had stumbled over his outstretched feet, only 16% of the participants helped. When the bodybuilder had only insulted and embarrassed the stumbler, 28% helped. When the bodybuilder had given no reaction to the stumbler, 52% helped. Thus, the greater the anticipated cost of antagonizing the misin-

forming bodybuilder, the less likely people were to help the bewildered man.

BYSTANDER INTERVENTION IN EMERGENCY SITUATIONS

Some of the earliest and most interesting social psychological research on helping was inspired by the tragic murder of a young woman named Catherine (Kitty) Genovese. Shortly before 3:20 a.m. on March 13, 1964, Kitty was attacked near her home. Milton Hatch awoke at the first scream. Staring from his apartment window, he saw a woman kneeling on the sidewalk directly across the street and a small man standing over her. "Help me! Help me! Oh, God, he's stabbed me!" she cried. Leaning out his window, Hatch shouted, "Let that girl alone!" As other windows opened and lights went on, the assailant fled in his car. No one called the police. With many eyes now following her, Kitty dragged herself along the street—but not quickly enough. More than ten minutes passed before the neighbors saw her assailant reappear, hunting for her. When he stabbed her a second time, she screamed, "I'm dying! I'm dying!" Still, no one called the police. The third, fatal attack occurred in the vestibule of a building a few doors from Kitty's own entrance. Finally, at 3:55—35 minutes after Kitty's first scream—Harold Klein, who lived at the top of the stairs where Kitty was murdered, called the police. The first patrol car arrived within two minutes, but by then it was too late (Seedman & Hellman, 1975). It was subsequently discovered that a total of 38 people had witnessed the stalking and stabbing.

The tragic story quickly became front page news in New York and across the country, setting off a flurry of social psychological research. The fundamental questions raised by Kitty's murder were, "Under what conditions will bystanders and witnesses intervene in an emergency and give help?" and, "Why do people help in some emergency situations but not in others?" In this section, we will consider this issue in detail and look at various factors that influence whether a bystander will help a victim.

The Decision to Intervene

The term **bystander intervention** denotes a (quick) response by a person witnessing an emergency to help another who is endangered by events. Whether and how to intervene in an emergency is a complex decision because providing assistance often places the helper in considerable danger. These decisions require integration of a great deal of information about self and the environment. Given that there is not time to accurately assess the situation, it is not particularly difficult for the decision-making process to break down and prevent emergency intervention. Latané and Darley (1970) produced a model of this decision-making process made up of five steps. If any of these steps fail, the decision-making process ends and the bystander does not provide assistance.

1. The bystander must notice the situation. Some studies have manipulated how preoccupied potential helpers were, and unsurprisingly, those who were more caught up in their own thoughts were less likely to notice the emergency situation and, therefore, less likely to respond (Darley & Batson, 1973).

2. Once the bystander has noticed the situation, he or she must interpret it as an emergency. Most emergency situations are quite ambiguous, and failure to interpret them as emergencies will produce inaction among bystanders.

3. The bystander must decide that they have some personal responsibility in the situation. One famous study created a situation at a beach where the researchers staged the theft of a radio while its owner was swimming. Most people—about 80%—did nothing to try to stop the thief or to intervene in any manner. However, when the owner of the radio asked the person next to her to keep an eye on the radio while she was swimming, almost all of them confronted the person stealing the radio (Moriarty, 1975). Once they had taken on the responsibility for the radio, they were much more likely to act to help the victim. If bystanders interpret the situation to be "none of their business," they will not respond.

4. The bystander must believe that they know how to help. Sometimes, the assistance required is something very simple, like dialing 911 for assistance. Other times, the situation is more complex. When witnessing an epileptic seizure, most people have no idea how to respond, and so they do nothing. People with medical training are much more likely to attempt to provide assistance at accident sites than are those without medical knowhow (Cramer, McMaster, Bartell, & Dragna, 1988).

5. The bystander must make the decision to act. Even if all of the first four conditions are fulfilled, people often will hesitate to act because they are afraid of negative consequences to themselves. Typically, people engage in some kind of risk calculation before they act in emergency situations (Fritzsche, Finkelstein, & Penner, 2000). For example, we are often hesitant to break up a fight between other individuals because we are afraid of getting hurt accidentally—or even that the two combatants will turn on us.

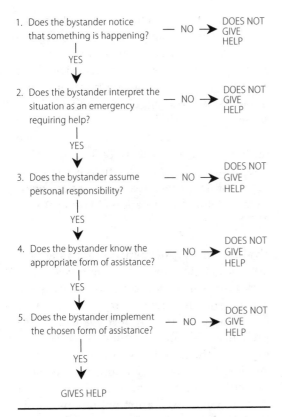

1. Does the bystander notice that something is happening? — NO → DOES NOT GIVE HELP

YES ↓

2. Does the bystander interpret the situation as an emergency requiring help? — NO → DOES NOT GIVE HELP

YES ↓

3. Does the bystander assume personal responsibility? — NO → DOES NOT GIVE HELP

YES ↓

4. Does the bystander know the appropriate form of assistance? — NO → DOES NOT GIVE HELP

YES ↓

5. Does the bystander implement the chosen form of assistance? — NO → DOES NOT GIVE HELP

YES ↓

GIVES HELP

FIGURE 10.1 Decisions Leading to Intervention in an Emergency

The Bystander Effect

In emergency situations, potential helpers are influenced by their relationship to other bystanders (Dovidio, 1984; Latané & Darley, 1970). This influence is apparent at each step in the decision-making process. To investigate the nature of bystander influence, researchers conducted a variety of laboratory studies that simulated emergencies of one kind or another. For instance, in an early experiment (Latané & Rodin, 1969), participants heard a loud crash from the room next door, followed by a woman screaming, "Oh my God, my foot! I . . . can't move it. Oh my ankle. I . . . can't get this thing off me." In another experiment (Darley & Latané, 1968), participants engaged

in a discussion over an intercom suddenly heard someone in the group begin to choke, gasp, and call for help, apparently gripped by an epileptic seizure.

In each experiment, the number of people who were supposedly present when the emergency occurred varied. Participants either believed they were alone with the victim or that one or more bystanders were present. Time and again, the same finding emerged: As the number of bystanders increased, the likelihood that any one of them would help decreased (Latané & Nida, 1981). Bystanders helped most often and most quickly when they were alone with the victim. In other words, simply knowing that other potential helpers were also present inhibited intervention in an emergency. Furthermore, as the number of bystanders increases, the likelihood that any one bystander will help a victim decreases. Social psychologists termed this the **bystander effect**.

Theorists have identified several distinct processes that contribute to the bystander effect. These include social influence regarding the interpretation of the situation, evaluation apprehension, and diffusion of responsibility (Latané, Nida, & Wilson, 1981; Piliavin et al., 1981). Each of these processes affects specific steps in the decision-making process.

Interpreting the Situation. One important element of emergencies is the ambiguity of the situation. In retrospect, the Kitty Genovese situation does not seem that ambiguous at all, but in the heat of the moment, people are often not certain how to respond to unusual situations. Was she really stabbed? Is this a domestic argument that is being dramatized to embarrass one party? Is she acting as bait so the two of them can mug someone else? These and other questions delay reactions and stall a decision to act. During that pause, people look to the

FIGURE 10.2 The Bystander Effect

Students who were discussing, via intercom, their adjustment to college life heard one participant begin to choke, then gasp and call for help, as if he were undergoing a serious nervous seizure. Students intervened to help the victim most quickly and most often when they believed they were the lone bystander to witness the emergency. More than 90% of lone bystanders helped within the first 90 seconds after the seizure. Among those who believed other bystanders were present, however, fewer than 50% intervened in the first two minutes and fewer than 70% did so even after four minutes. The bystander effect refers to the fact that the greater the number of bystanders in an emergency, the less likely any one bystander will help.

Source: Adapted from Darley and Latane, "Bystander Intervention in Emergencies: Diffusion of Responsibility," *Journal of Personality and Social Psychology*, 8, 377–383. Copyright 1968 by the American Psychological Association.

reactions of others for cues about what is going on and how to react. If others appear calm, the bystander may decide that nothing special is happening or that whatever is happening requires no help. Likewise, the failure of others to act may signal to the bystander that there is no appropriate way to help. In this way, they inhibit each other from helping.

Bystanders often try to appear calm, avoiding overt signs of worry until they see whether others are alarmed. Through such cautiousness, onlookers unintentionally encourage one another to define the situation as not problematic. The larger the number of apparently unruffled bystanders, the stronger their inhibiting influence

is on one another. This effect is illustrated in Figure 10.2, using data from an experiment in which a false epileptic seizure was portrayed. However, consistent with this explanation, increasing the number of bystanders does not inhibit individual helping under certain conditions, such as (1) when observation reveals that others are indeed alarmed (Darley, Teger, & Lewis, 1973), and (2) when the need for help is so unambiguous that others' reactions are unnecessary to define the situation (Clark & Word, 1972).

Evaluation Apprehension. Bystanders are not only interested in others' reactions; they also realize that other bystanders are an audience for their own reactions. As a result, bystanders may feel evaluation apprehension—concern about what others expect of them and how others will evaluate their behavior. Evaluation apprehension can either inhibit or promote helping. On the one hand, evaluation apprehension inhibits helping when bystanders fear that others will view their intervention as foolish, inappropriate, or wrong. When they see that other witnesses to an emergency are not reacting (as in the Kitty Genovese case), they may infer that the others do not see a need to intervene or might even oppose intervention. In the decision-making sequence, evaluation apprehension mainly affects step 4 (choosing a way to react) and step 5 (deciding whether to implement a chosen course of action). On the other hand, evaluation apprehension promotes helping if there are no cues to suggest that other witnesses oppose intervention or if there is a sense of mutual awareness that some intervention is necessary (Schwartz & Gottlieb, 1976).

Diffusion of Responsibility. When one and only one bystander witnesses an emergency, the responsibility to intervene is focused wholly on that individual. But when there are multiple bystanders, the responsibility to intervene is shared, as is the blame if the victim is not helped. Therefore, a witness is less likely to intervene when others are present. The process wherein a bystander does not take action because others share the responsibility for intervening is called **diffusion of responsibility**. In the decision sequence, diffusion of responsibility operates primarily as step 3 (bystander decides whether he or she has the responsibility to act).

Diffusion of responsibility occurs only when a bystander believes that the other witnesses are capable of helping. We diffuse responsibility less to witnesses who are too far away to take effective action or who are too young to cope with the emergency (Bickman, 1971; Ross, 1971). Similarly, the tendency to diffuse responsibility is particularly strong if a bystander feels less competent than others who are present. Bystanders helped less, for example, when one of the other witnesses to a seizure was a premed student with experience working in an emergency ward (Pantin & Carver, 1982; Schwartz & Clausen, 1970).

SEEKING AND RECEIVING HELP

Although the bulk of this chapter focused on giving help rather than receiving it, recipients' reactions to receiving help—and people's willingness to seek help in the first place—are important topics that also deserve attention. It seems obvious that the generally expected response to helping is gratitude and appreciation. But that is not always the case. In fact, help can elicit resentment, hostility, and anxiety.

Help and Obligation. When help is sought and received, resources (such as labor and materials) are transferred from one person to another. If the norm of reciprocity is salient in the situation, the person receiving help may feel obligated or indebted to the helper (Greenberg & Westcott, 1983). In consequence, needy persons (in nonemergency situations) sometimes experience a dilemma. On the one hand, they can ask for help and possibly endure some embarrassment or social obligation; on the other hand, they can suffer through the difficulties of trying to solve their problems on their own (Gross & McMullen, 1983). In cases in which the recipient has the opportunity and ability to reciprocate, there may be no problem. But in cases in which this is more difficult, it may create a lingering sense of indebtedness in the needy toward the helper (Nadler, 1991; Wills, 1992), and they may develop resentment and negative sentiments toward the benefactor (Clark, Gotay, & Mills, 1974; Gross & Latané, 1974).

Threats to Self-Esteem. In studying people's reactions to receiving help, theorists have proposed that an important determinant of whether help is appreciated or resented is the extent to which the help undermines the recipient's self-esteem (Nadler, 1991; Nadler & Fisher, 1986; Shell & Eisenberg, 1992). Although helping provides relief, it can also impair a recipient's self-esteem and sense of self-reliance. The avowed purpose of welfare, for instance, has been to aid impoverished individuals and to help families escape hunger while they establish themselves as self-supporting. Yet welfare and other forms of assistance are sometimes given reluctantly or in ways that do not promote these outcomes. Intentionally or otherwise, helpers may communicate the message that those who need and accept help are inferior in status and ability because they fail to display self-reliance and achievement (DePaulo & Fisher, 1980; Rosen, 1984). Taking help can cause embarrassment for recipients because it challenges the norm of self-reliance: an expectation that individuals should take care of themselves and their dependents. Similarly, students might be reticent to ask for help for fear that their professor or peers will consider them incompetent or unintelligent.

Similarity of Help Provider. Surveys regarding help seeking for personal and psychological problems indicate that we are most likely to ask people who are similar to us for assistance. Wills (1992) finds that persons looking for help of this type are several times more likely to seek it from friends, acquaintances, or family members than from professionals or strangers.

However, the helper's similarity to the recipient is a complex factor in help giving and help seeking. Help that implies an important inadequacy is often more threatening to our self-esteem when we receive it from those who are similar to us in attitudes or background than from those who are dissimilar (Nadler, 1987; Nadler & Fisher, 1984). Similarity can aggravate recipients' self-evaluations, because similar helpers are relevant targets for self-comparison (say, "If we are both alike, why do I need help while you can give it?"). People who accept aid from helpers similar to themselves on a task central to their self-concept report lower self-esteem, less self-confidence, and more personal threat than when they accept aid from dissimilar helpers (DePaulo, Nadler & Fisher, 1983; Nadler, Fisher, & Ben-Itzhak, 1983).

**OTHER FORMS OF
PROSOCIAL BEHAVIOR**

Although much of this chapter focused on helping specific others, there are more organizationally based forms of prosocial behavior that are also of interest to social psychologists. This final section highlights

two specific types: philanthropy and volunteering.

Philanthropy. Charitable giving, or philanthropy, includes both small-scale donations (dropping your change in the plastic container at the grocery store counter) or large monetary donations (making a large gift to endow an annual scholarship at your local university). Such giving is particularly prevalent in churches and religious organizations, in which there is a tithing norm that encourages members to donate 10% of their income to charity or the church. In part because of the large amount of religious charitable giving, the United States is considered a "giving culture" (Wright, 2001). However, researchers suggest that this culture is sustained, in part, because people in the United Stated tend to feel that they have something to gain by giving, whether tax credits and deductions, enhanced social status, or something else.

People are more likely to give when certain factors are present. In addition to some discussed earlier (for example, an awareness of need and perceptions of deservingness), research suggests that individuals' are more motivated to donate money when they are directly asked to contribute. In other words, we are more likely to give when we are approached and made aware of the opportunity to give (Bryant, Jeon-Slaughter, Kang, & Tax, 2003). We are also more likely to give when the organization who needs contributions reflects values that are similar to our own and when we feel that our gift can make an important difference (Parsons, 2003). Giving not only helps charitable organizations but has also been shown to result in an enhanced mood—"a warm glow"—after giving (Meier, 2006).

Volunteering. Volunteering—freely giving time for the benefit of another person, group, or organization—also benefits organizations (Wilson, 2000). It has four distinct attributes that set it apart from other forms of prosocial behavior: *longevity* (it is usually institutionalized, ongoing, and quite often repeated), *planfulness* (it is thought out before being done), *nonobligatory* (it is not motivated by a concern for a specific individual with whom one has a relationship), and is done in *an organizational context* (most volunteering is not an individual acting alone) (Penner, 2002).

Certain qualities of individuals make them much more likely to volunteer. For example, greater social integration—being embedded in social networks—increases both the chances that someone will be asked to volunteer and their likelihood of agreeing to do so (Penner, Dovidio, Piliavin, & Schroeder, 2005). Being socially integrated might also give individuals greater awareness of problems that need attention. Research also suggests that those who are married, religious, and/or well educated are more likely to volunteer, as are women and those of higher social classes (Wilson, 2000; Wilson & Janoski, 1995; Wilson & Musick, 1997). Although findings are mixed, it appears that volunteering is beneficial to one's health, particularly mental health and well-being (Greenfield & Marks, 2004).

SUMMARY

Prosocial behavior is any behavior that helps another. Helping is a specific type of prosocial behavior that benefits others. Altruism, another kind of prosocial behavior, is voluntary behavior intended to benefit another with no expectation of external reward. This intent is an important component of altruism.

Motivation to Help. Actors often engage in some kind of calculation of costs and benefits before engaging in prosocial behavior and will often help others for some type of reward. However, helping without intention of benefit (altruism) typically stems from humans' ability to experience empathy. Prosocial behavior may also be passed from parent to child through evolutionary processes that enhance the persistence of an individual's genes in future generations. Even self-sacrifice can be beneficial in perpetuating one's genes if targeted at those who share genetic material. If the net costs are too high, however, they will not act.

Helpers and Targets. Many characteristics of individuals affect the chance of receiving help from another. Acquaintanceship and liking of another person can increase the chances of helping behavior when that person is in need. Similarity between actors and targets can substantially increase the chances of helping behavior. Potential helpers also consider whether the target deserves help. Innocent individuals are more likely to receive help.

The Contexts of Prosocial Behavior. External factors, both norms and situational influences, can have powerful effects on prosocial behavior. We are more likely to help those who are dependent on us (the norm of social responsibility) and those who have helped us in the past (the norm of reciprocity). Personal norms that facilitate helping and determine how we help are often related to salient role and social identities, including gender. The presence of a model who demonstrates prosocial behavior facilitates helping. However, moods have mixed effects. In deciding when to help, we weigh the benefits and costs both to the persons in need and to ourselves. Individuals can learn about the costs and benefits through a social learning process.

Bystander Intervention in Emergency Situations. Prior to actually giving help in emergencies, bystanders go through a decision sequence. A bystander must realize that something is happening, interpret the situation as an emergency, decide that he or she has the responsibility to act, know or recognize an appropriate form of assistance, and decide to implement the chosen behavior. Ambiguous social situations cause participants to look for cues that might lead toward helping. Depending on others for these cues can produce a failure to provide help while everyone waits for cues from others that action is required, known as the *bystander effect*. The more observers there are to an emergency, the less likely any one person is to act because of a diffusion of responsibility.

Seeking and Receiving Help. Help is not always sought after or easily accepted by the targets because they are sometimes reticent to bear the obligations the help entails and because the assistance may threaten their self-esteem. The more similar a target is to a helper, the more embarrassing it may be to accept assistance.

Other Forms of Prosocial Behavior. Volunteering and philanthropy are prosocial behaviors that tend to benefit organizations rather than individuals.

List of Key Terms and Concepts

altruism (p. 345)
bystander effect (p. 361)
bystander intervention (p. 360)
diffusion of responsibility (p. 363)
egoism (p. 345)
empathy (p. 346)
helping (p. 345)
norm of reciprocity (p. 355)
personal norms (p. 355)
prosocial behavior (p. 344)
social responsibility norm (p. 354)

Critical Thinking Skill: Creative Thinking

Throughout this book, you have been exposed to research that may or may not relate to your personal experience. Although it might be interesting to you, you might ask what you can or cannot do with that information in your own life.

Take, for example, research suggesting that heterosexual married couples who engage in prosocial behaviors, like small acts of kindness and displays of respect and affection, and who are willing to forgive each other's faults or mistakes experienced more marital satisfaction and were less likely to imagine divorcing their partner (Dew & Wilcox, 2013). You likely know people who are married, so you could share this information with them in hopes of improving their relationship or helping to explain why they are so happily married. But could it have further-reaching influence? What might you take from it if you are not married?

To engage in critical creative thinking, we search for alternative applications of what we have learned.

The most obvious application would be to nonmarried couples. Whether cohabiting or simply dating, whether heterosexual or same-sex, these same behaviors from the Dew and Wilcox (2013) study likely strengthen relationships and lessen the chances of either person imagining ending the relationship. Can you think of examples of this?

But what about other types of relationships? Can you use these findings and the basis for them to enhance your platonic friendships or to create a better relationship with your mother or your daughter? What types of kindnesses, displays of respect, and forgiveness would be applicable in those relationships? What about your relationships with your neighbors or coworkers? Could you share the findings with your employer to help her think of ways she might increase employee satisfaction and reduce turnover?

Scientists often use this type of creative thinking to consider what questions to explore next. A sociologist reading this research might consider recruiting a sample of same-sex couples and asking similar questions to determine whether the relationship between prosocial behaviors and relationship satisfaction and commitment was as strong or perhaps stronger in those couples (Carrington, 1999). However, even if you are not planning to conduct your own research, you can benefit from this creative thinking as well. Considering alternative applications not only helps you understand the specific material but also encourages you to engage with the world in a deliberate and involved way.

AGGRESSION

INTRODUCTION

- On April 16, 2007, a single gunman, a senior at Virginia Tech, entered a residence hall on campus and gunned down two students. About two hours later, he entered the engineering building and chained the doors shut. He proceeded to enter a classroom and ended up killing 32 people before he finally killed himself. One professor, Livi Librescu, held the classroom door against the gunman's attempts to enter while his students escaped out the window. He was killed by bullets shot through the door he was holding shut.

- In November 2011, a 15-year-old-girl was sexually assaulted at a party by four young men. One of the boys took pictures of the assault that he passed on to his friends and their fellow schoolmates. The photos soon made their way onto social media websites, including Facebook. The girl in the photo, Rehtaeh Parsons, was taunted by her peers. She was bombarded with texts and messages. Some called her a slut, others asked to have sex with her, some claimed she only cried rape because she regretted that her actions became public. In April of 2013, unable to handle the bullying anymore, Rehtaeh committed suicide.

- Under investigation for murdering his wife, Josh Powell was allowed a supervised visit with his two young sons, Charlie, 7, and Braden, 5. As soon as the social worker pulled up to the rental house with his children, the boys ran toward the front door, anxious to see their father. Powell let the boys in, locked the social worker out, and proceeded to attack the boys with a hatchet. As the social worker called to report him for locking her out, Powell set the house on fire, killing both his sons and himself in a murder-suicide.

These disturbing incidents are stark demonstrations of persons' ability to inflict pain and death on others. How can we account for such incidents and for the many forms of aggression that commonly occur in the United States and throughout the world? These phenomena are the focus of this chapter.

What Is Aggression?

Defining aggression seems simple: Aggression is any behavior that hurts another, whether physically or emotionally. But further thought makes us recognize it is not the outcome so much as the intention that we must consider. We would not consider a surgeon an aggressor if a heart transplant patient died on the operating table despite heroic efforts to save the patient's life. Following Krebs (1982), we will define **aggression** as any behavior intended to harm another person (the target). Importantly, this harm must be something the target wants to avoid. According to this definition, a bungled assassination is an act of aggression, whereas heart surgery—approved by the patient and intended to improve his or

American culture tends to associate physical violence with aggression and ignores psychological and emotional abuse as additional types of aggression. If social service agencies and others can broaden individuals' conception of abuse, they can encourage more victims to seek help. © miriam-doerr

her health—is clearly not aggression, even if the patient dies.

Aggression should not be equated with physical violence. Aggressive actions vary widely. The intended harm may be physical, psychological, or social—ranging from homicide or battery, to emotional abuse and cyber-bullying, to active neglect or harming a target's reputation.

Drawing on research and theory, this chapter addresses the following questions:

1. What motivates people to act aggressively?

2. How do characteristics of the target influence aggression?

3. How do characteristics of the situation influence aggression?

4. How can we reduce the frequency of aggressive behavior in society?

5. What influences the incidence of interpersonal aggression—abuse, bullying, assault, sexual assault, and murder—in our society?

AGGRESSION AND THE MOTIVATION TO HARM

As the examples in the introduction show, human beings have a remarkable capacity to harm others—even those they love or are expected to protect. Why do people turn against others? What motivates human aggression? There are at least four possible answers: (1) people are instinctively aggressive; (2) people become aggressive in response to events that are frustrating; (3) people aggress against others as a result of aversive emotion; and (4) people learn to use aggression as a means of obtaining what they want. This section considers each of these in turn.

Aggression as Instinct

A deep history of psychological thought, going back at least to Sigmund Freud (1930, 1950), has considered aggression to be a basic human instinct—that is, an innate behavior that seems to emerge even without socialization or training. To Freud, the innate urge to destroy is as natural as our need to breathe. This instinct constantly generates hostile impulses that demand release. We often release these hostile impulses by aggressing against others, but we can also turn violently against ourselves (suicide) or suffer internal distress (physical or mental illness).

If our aggressive impulses are innate, that means they must be passed to us through our genetic code and are a result of long evolutionary processes. As discussed in earlier chapters, evolutionary theories rely on the Darwinian principle of survival of the fittest. According to Lorenz (1966, 1974), the aggressive instinct has evolved because it contributed to an animal's survival. For instance, in many species, the strongest and most aggressive animals occupy the top positions in the group's social hierarchy. To fight for position in this hierarchy is adaptive in a Darwinian sense, for it gives the animal control over food, shelter, and other resources needed to survive as well as access to mating partners.

Proponents of instinct theories are pessimistic about the possibility of controlling human aggression. At best, they believe, aggression can be channeled into approved competitive activities such as athletics, academics, or business. In these types of activities, there are social rules to govern the expression of aggression intended to prevent competition from degenerating into destructiveness. Quite often, however, socially approved competition stimulates aggression: Football and hockey players start throwing punches, soccer fans riot violently, and businesspeople destroy competitors or cheat the public through ruthless practices.

Although the propensity for aggression can be passed through human generations and aggression is common in social life, most social psychologists have not seen instinct theories of aggression as particularly useful. One reason is that generalizing findings about animal behavior to human behavior is hazardous. Moreover, cross-cultural studies suggest that human aggression lacks two characteristics that are typical of instinctive behavior in animals—universality and periodicity. The need to eat and breathe, for example, are universal to all members of a species. They are also periodic, for they rise after deprivation and fall when satisfied. Aggression, in contrast, is not universal in humans. It pervades some individuals and societies but is virtually absent in others. Moreover, human aggression is not periodic. The occurrence of human aggression is largely governed by specific social circumstances. Aggressive behavior does not increase when people have not aggressed for a long time or decrease after they have recently aggressed. Thus, our biological makeup provides only the capacity for aggression, not an inevitable urge to aggress.

Frustration-Aggression Hypothesis

The second possible explanation for aggressive behavior is that aggression is an internal state that is elicited by certain events. The most famous view of aggression as an elicited drive is the **frustration-aggression hypothesis** (Dollard et al., 1939). This hypothesis asserts that (1) every frustration leads to some form of aggression and (2) every aggressive act is due to some prior frustration. In contrast to instinct theories, this hypothesis states that aggression is instigated by external, environmental events.

In one early demonstration (Barker, Dembo, & Lewin, 1941), researchers showed children a room full of attractive toys. They allowed some children to play with the toys immediately while others were made to wait 20 minutes. The children who waited behaved much more destructively during play, smashing the toys on the floor and against the walls. Here, aggression is a direct response to **frustration**—that is, to the blocking of a goal-directed activity. By blocking the children's access to the tempting toys, the researchers frustrated them. This, in turn, elicited an aggressive drive that the children expressed by destroying the researchers' toys. More recent research suggests that the link between frustration and aggression may be an important cause for the positive link between video games and violence. More competitive games tend to increase aggressive behavior, supporting the role of frustration—from losing in a competitive situation—on increasing aggression (Adachi & Willoughby, 2011).

Several decades of research have led to modifications of the original hypothesis (Berkowitz, 1978). First, studies have shown that frustration does not always produce aggressive responses (Zillman, 1979)—frustrated individuals often restrain themselves due to fear of punishment. Take, for example, being laid off. Losing one's job is a frustrating experience. Researchers predicted that small increases in layoffs would lead to violence in communities. Large increases, however, would lead to reduced violence because those still working would be afraid of being laid off for causing trouble (Catalano, Novaco, & McConnell, 1997). Data from San Francisco supported these predictions. Frustration can also lead responses other than aggression, such as despair, depression, or withdrawal. Second, research indicates that aggression can occur without prior frustration (Berkowitz, 1989). The ruthless businessperson or scientist may attempt to sabotage competitors due to the desire for wealth and fame, even though the competitors have not blocked his or her goal-directed activity.

Aggressive acts often stem from frustration. Both the mother who yells at her children and a player who yells at an umpire do so because they are frustrated, one with her children fighting and the other with the umpire's call. *Left:* © Ocean/Corbis; *right:* © Gabe Palmer/Corbis

The frustration-aggression hypothesis implies that the nature of the frustration influences the intensity of the resulting aggression. Two factors that intensify aggression are the strength and the arbitrariness of frustration.

Strength of Frustration. The more we desire a goal and the closer we are to achieving it, the more frustrated and aroused we become if blocked. If someone cuts ahead of us just as we reach the front of a very long line, our frustration will be especially strong and result in a more aggressive response than if we were further back. Researchers demonstrated this in a field experiment (Harris, 1974). They had confederates cut ahead of people in lines at theaters, restaurants, and grocery checkout counters. The confederate cut in front of either the second or the twelfth person in line. Observers recorded the reactions of the person. As predicted, people at the front of the line responded more aggressively. They directed more than twice as many abusive remarks toward the confederate than people at the back of the line.

Cases of "road rage" also exemplify the frustration-aggression hypothesis and the relationship between the intensity of frustration and intensity of aggression. Road rage most commonly occurs when one motorist engages in a behavior that causes frustration in another driver, blocking the driver's attempt to reach a goal, such as arriving on time for an appointment or securing an available parking spot. This frustration may lead to many types of aggression. Social psychologists distinguish between driver aggression (honking, tailing, making obscene gestures) and driver violence (chasing the other car or its driver, throwing objects, or shooting at him or her). Mild frustration tends to cause the former, whereas stronger frustration causes the latter. Research finds that men and women are equally likely to report engaging in driver aggression in response to frustrating events, but only men reported driver violence (Hennessy & Wiesenthal, 2001).

Arbitrariness of Frustration. People are also apt to feel more hostile when they believe the frustration is arbitrary, unprovoked, or illegitimate than when they attribute it to a reasonable, accidental, or legitimate cause.

In a study demonstrating this principle, researchers asked students to make appeals for a charity over the telephone (Kulick & Brown, 1979). The students were frustrated by refusals from all the potential donors (in reality, confederates). In the legitimate frustration condition, potential donors offered good reasons for refusing (such as "I just lost my job"). In the illegitimate frustration con-

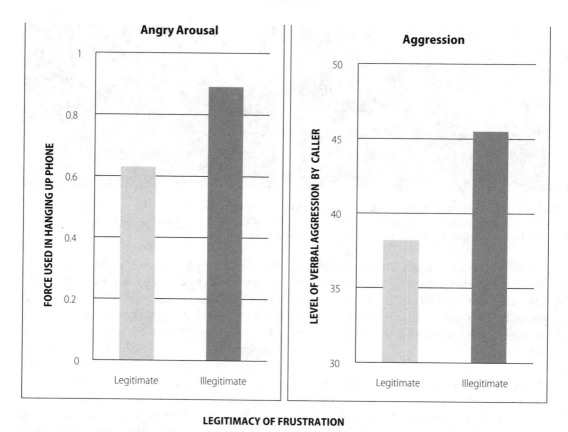

FIGURE 11.1 Effect of Legitimacy of Frustration on Aggressive Responses

Source: Adapted from "Frustration, Attribution of Blame, and Aggression" by Kulick and Brown, *Journal of Experimental Social Psychology,* 15: 183–194. Copyright 1979, with permission from Elsevier.

dition, they offered weak, arbitrary reasons (such as "charities are a rip-off"). As shown in Figure 11.1, individuals exposed to illegitimate frustration were more emotionally aroused than those exposed to legitimate frustration. They also directed more verbal aggression against the potential donors.

Aversive Emotional Arousal

In the eight decades since the original statement of the frustration-aggression hypothesis, research has identified several other causes of aggression. In one study, community residents and university students were asked what events upset or angered them (Averill, 1982). Some replied that legitimate

actions by others and unavoidable accidents could trigger aggressive reactions. Physical pain, such as stubbing one's toe, and verbal and physical attacks can arouse us and elicit an aggressive response. Insults—especially those involving traits that we value, perhaps intelligence, honesty, ethnicity, or attractiveness—can also provoke aggression. Repeated insults and bullying by classmates contributed to Columbine and other more recent school shootings by students.

Accidents, attacks, and insults tend to increase aggression because they all arouse **aversive affect**—negative emotion that people seek to reduce or eliminate (Berkowitz, 1989). When persons act aggressively in response to this negative affect, the aggression is often instrumental. That is, it is intended to reduce or eliminate the cause of the affect. Often, this affect is anger, but it can be pain or other types of discomfort. For example, one of the reasons violence is higher in the summer months is because the higher temperatures produce discomfort and people look for a way to discharge this aversive affect (Anderson, Anderson, & Deuser, 1996). Turning on the air conditioner, yelling at your little sister, kicking the dog, or shooting someone who insults you are instrumental actions to deal with the discomfort.

Aggression resulting from aversive affect is called **affective aggression**. Affective aggression is more common among persons who believe that acting aggressively will make them feel better. If someone believes that acting aggressively will not decrease the discomfort or negative affect, he or she will engage in other instrumental actions.

Social Learning and Aggression

Social learning theories provide a fourth explanation for aggressive behavior. Two processes by which aggression can be learned are imitation and reinforcement.

Imitation. Many people learn their aggressive behaviors by observing others commit aggressive acts and then enacting these same behaviors themselves. In one experiment, children observed an adult playing with a five-foot-tall, inflated rubber Bobo doll (Bandura, Ross, & Ross, 1961). In one experimental condition, the adult engaged in aggressive behavior toward the doll, including punching and kicking it and sitting on it. These actions, accompanied by the shouting of aggressive words and phrases, continued for nine minutes. Later, each child was intentionally frustrated and then left alone in a room with various toys, including a smaller Bobo doll. The children who had observed the aggressive model were much

more aggressive toward the doll than those who had observed a nonaggressive model. They engaged in aggressive behavior such as kicking the doll and made comments similar to those they had observed.

Many children learn aggressive behavior from their parents. Indeed, 90% of parents in the United States report using physical punishment to discipline their children (see Chapter 3). Children who are spanked or slapped for transgressions are learning that if someone's behavior breaks rules or makes you angry, it is okay to punish them physically. A longitudinal study of 717 boys found that boys who experienced harsh parenting practices at ages 10 to 12 were more likely to be involved in violent dating relationships at age 16 (Lavoie et al., 2002). Much of the other aggressive behavior within the family—child abuse, intimate partner abuse, or sibling abuse—can also be explained with social learning theory. People who abuse their intimate partners or children often grew up in families in which they either witnessed or were the targets of abuse (Gelles & Cornell, 1990). Growing up in a family in which some members abuse others teaches the child that not only is it acceptable to engage in physical aggression but that occupants of certain roles—such as husbands, girlfriends, or children—are also appropriate targets for aggression.

Reinforcement. Social learning theory holds that aggressive responses are acquired and maintained—like any other social behavior—through experiences of reinforcement and reward (Bandura, 1973). Individuals learn early on that aggression can be associated with desired outcomes, thereby reinforcing the behavior. Muggers may attack a person to take his or her money. One child knocks down another to obtain the toy he or she desires. Students bully other students to gain esteem or deference from their peers. Even if we do not consciously consider the rewards we might gain, we can learn that aggression leads to individual gain, thus reinforcing the behavior.

CHARACTERISTICS OF TARGETS THAT INFLUENCE AGGRESSION

The preceding section introduced four potential sources of the motivation to aggress. Once aroused, such motives incline us toward aggressive behavior. Whether aggression occurs, however, also depends on the characteristics of the **target**—the person toward whom the aggressive behavior is directed. In this section, we discuss four target characteristics related to aggression: race and gender, attributions for the aggressor's attack, and retaliatory capacity.

Gender and Race

Aggression does not occur at random. If it did, we would observe aggressive behaviors by all kinds of people directed at targets of both genders, all ethnic groups, and all ages. In fact, aggression is patterned. First, aggressive behavior usually involves two people of the same race or ethnicity. This is true of aggression within the family, as most families are racially and ethnically homogeneous. But it is also true of violent crimes such as assault, sexual assault, and murder. Table 11.1 reports FBI murder statistics that demonstrate this within-race tendency.

The relationship between aggression and gender depends on the type of aggressive behavior. In cases of abuse within the family, both genders are targets. Boys and girls are equally likely to be abused by a parent. Wives abuse their husbands as often as husbands abuse their wives (Gelles & Strauss, 1988). However, the types of abuse are different. Women are more likely to slap, kick, bite, or to try to hit their partner with an object. Men are more likely to beat up their partner and to push, grab, or shove. In cases of violence involving current or former intimate partners, women are the victims of 74% of the murders and 85% of the assaults and sexual assaults (Greenfeld et al., 1998). These patterns are found among Blacks, Latinos, and Whites (Rennison, 2001), but the rates appear to be lower among Asian and Pacific Islanders (Johnson & Ferraro, 2000).

Although men and women are equally likely to engage in *aggressive* behavior, men engage in significantly more *violent* behavior. Of reported cases of rape or sexual assault, 95% involve a male offender and female victim. As Table 11.1 reports, men were responsible for almost 90% of murders, of both men and women, committed in 2009. Most murders and **aggravated assaults**—an attack by one person on another with the intent of causing bodily injury—involve two men.

These patterns indicate that the display of aggression is channeled by social beliefs and norms. Observing violence within one's family teaches children that violence within the family is acceptable. Similarly, beliefs and norms in U.S. society encourage men to direct physical and sexual aggression toward women and other men. For example, masculine gender norms encourage men to be dominant over women (Connell, 2005). These gender norms also associate masculinity with status and toughness, motivating men to use aggression to gain the respect of others (Thompson & Pleck, 1986). Men in our society frequently compete with each other for various rewards, such as influence over one another, status in a group, the companionship of a woman, or other symbols of success. These competitions often lead to insults that provoke anger or direct physical challenges. There are norms in some groups, cultures, or subcultures that require men to defend themselves in such situations. For example, observers have often described the American South as having

TABLE 11.1 Race and Sex of Murder Victim by Race and Sex of Offender, 2009

	TOTAL	RACE OF OFFENDER				SEX OF OFFENDER	
		WHITE	BLACK	OTHER	UNKNOWN	MALE	FEMALE
Race of Victim							
White	3518	84.2%	12.9%	1.1%	1.7%	87.7%	8.7%
Black	2867	7.3%	90.8%	0.5%	1.4%	88.5%	10.0%
Other	181	27.6%	14.4%	57.5%	0.6%	89.5%	9.9%
Unknown	65	41.5%	33.8%	1.5%	23.1	67.7%	9.2%
Sex of Victim							
Male	4638	44.3%	52.2%	1.9%	1.6%	87.9%	10.4%
Female	1928	60.6%	34.3%	3.7%	1.4%	89.2%	9.4%

Note: This table is based on incidents in which some information about the offender is known by law enforcement. Therefore, when the offender's age, sex, and race are all reported as unknown, these data are excluded from the table. For summaries related to sex, percentages for those of an unknown sex are omitted.

Source: FBI Homicide Data.

a norm that requires men to defend themselves against insults—a "culture of honor" (see Box 11.1).

Attribution of Intention

Direct attacks, both verbal and physical, typically produce an aggressive reaction (Geen, 1968; White & Gruber, 1982). Nevertheless, we withhold retaliation when we perceive that an attack was not intentional. We are unlikely to respond aggressively, for example, if we see that a man who has smashed his grocery cart into our car in the parking lot was trying to save a child from an oncoming car. However, we must first realize the man's intention. Aggression following harm is both more probable and stronger when we attribute the attack to the actor's intentions rather than to accidental or legitimate external pressures (Dyck & Rule, 1978). In the former case, the target of our aggressive response deserves that response more than when the harm is accidental.

The general aggression model (Anderson & Bushman, 2002), based on a dual-process model, proposes that after an initial immediate appraisal (or attribution) of an attack or hostile situation, a reappraisal of the situation only occurs if there are sufficient resources (for example, time or cognitive capacity) and the initial appraisal is somehow unsatisfactory.

These appraisals of the situation as well as related attributions for harm have important implications for our responses to aggression. In one study of 70 abused women, those living with their violent partner sometimes blamed themselves for the abuse. They attributed it to their incompetence, unattractiveness, or talking back to the partner. Other women blamed situational factors such as their partner's stress. The women most likely to leave their abusive partners were those who blamed him—rather than themselves or the situation—for the abuse (Andrews & Brewin, 1990).

An important influence on attributions is whether an attacker apologizes. An apology often states or implies that the harm another did to us was unintentional. In one study, an experimenter made mistakes that caused the participant to fail at the tasks. When the experimenter apologized, the participants

BOX 11.1 Research Update: The Culture of Honor

Students were milling around the cafeteria of Spring High School—just outside of Houston, Texas—before school on a September morning. Some were eating breakfast, others catching up on their homework, many simply talking with friends before the first bell rang. Just outside the cafeteria, Joshua Broussard "bumped" into Luis Alfaro as he moved through the crowded hallway. The two exchanged words. Moments later, Alfaro pulled out a knife and attacked Broussard. As students scattered, Broussard collapsed in the school hallway and died.

The attack at Spring High School is not unusual. A large number of the homicides that occur in any given year are triggered by arguments, and many of these disputes are over trivial matters, including offensive comments or name calling. However, what is most interesting about the incident is its similarity to a series of social psychological experiments conducted 20 years earlier on the "culture of honor" (Cohen, Nisbett, Bowdle, & Schwarz, 1996).

In those experiments, both "Northerner" and "Southerner"* students from the University of Michigan were invited to the laboratory for what they believed was an experiment on response times and human judgment. Upon arrival, they were asked to fill out initial paperwork and take it to a table at the end of a long, narrow hallway. Unbeknownst to the participants, the experimental treatment actually occurred during the walk to this table. As some of the participants made their way down the hallway, a confederate bumped the unsuspecting student and called him an "asshole." Observers situated in the hallway, ostensibly working on their homework, gauged the participants' reactions. Participants then participated in a series of judgment tasks to gauge their reactions to the incident.

Comparisons of the reactions of Southerners and Northerners supported the idea of a "culture of honor" in the South. Social scientists argue that individuals from places with a "culture of honor" are more likely to perceive a benign incident as an interpersonal threat. Furthermore, once offended or insulted, those who accept a "culture of honor" will feel the need to restore honor by retaliating against the insult. Sure enough, Southerners who were bumped by the confederate were more likely to see the insult as a cause for anger rather than amusement and to see violence as an appropriate reaction to an "affront." Whereas Northerners were able to brush off the insult and remain unaffected, Southerners who were insulted were primed for aggression and would act out if given the right stimulus. Later studies found that Southerners were also more prepared to aggress on a physiological level, with higher cortisol and testosterone levels than Northerners who had also been insulted.

A tremendous amount of research on the culture of honor conducted since these early studies supports these findings. Social psychologists recently considered this concept in relation to school violence and found that high school students in culture-of-honor states—including Texas—were more likely to bring a weapon to school and were at higher risk of school shootings than were students in other states (Brown, Osterman, & Barnes, 2009). Although many attributed the tragedy at Spring High to gang violence, the culture of honor may have also played an important role in the events of that September morning.

---

*Students were classified as "Southern" if they lived in one of the following states for at least six years: Delaware, Maryland, West Virginia, Virginia, North Carolina, South Carolina, Georgia, Florida, Kentucky, Tennessee, Alabama, Mississippi, Arkansas, Louisiana, or Texas. All other students, except those who lived in Washington, DC, were considered "Northern." On average, those classified as "Southern" had lived 87% of their lives in the South, whereas those classified as "Northern" had spent only 4% of their lives in the South.

refrained from acting aggressively toward her. Apologies may also lessen resulting aggression because they sometimes provide mitigating information—accounts of external causes of the offending action—that facilitate a reappraisal (Barlett & Anderson, 2011). However, it is important to note that as the severity of the harm increases, the effectiveness of apologies decreases (Ohbuchi, Kameda, & Agarie, 1989).

Retaliatory Capacity

One of the consequences that we might consider in calculating the costs (and benefits) of aggression is the likelihood of retaliation by the target.

Research suggests that the threat of retaliation reduces aggressive behavior. In one experiment, participants were told to deliver electric shocks to another person and that they could select the intensity of the shock. In one condition, participants were told that after they had delivered the shocks, the experiment would be over. In another condition, participants were told that after they had delivered shocks, they would change places with the other person. In other words, they would be in a position in which the other person would be delivering shocks (and could retaliate). Participants in the latter condition delivered significantly less intense shocks than in the former condition (Prentice-Dunn & Rogers, 1980). These findings help explain why anonymous cyber-bullying is described as more severe than nonanonymous forms of bullying. Bullies may be inclined to engage in more aggressive acts when they use fake aliases or post on anonymous websites like ask.fm because the risk of retaliation is significantly smaller.

Sometimes, there are instances of **displaced aggression**—defined as aggression toward a target that exceeds what is justified by provocation by that target. This often oc-

curs because the aggression is instigated by a different source and then displaced onto a less powerful or more available target who had no responsibility for the initial response (Umberson, Williams & Anderson, 2002). Displaced aggression is a common explanation for aggression directed toward partners, children, or pets—"She is taking her bad day out on us."—but does it actually occur? A meta-analysis of social psychological research on the subject provides substantial evidence that displaced aggression is quite real (Marcus-Newhall, Pedersen, Carlson & Miller, 2000). Some argue that displaced aggression may partially account for higher incidences of domestic violence in poor and working-class households (Umberson, Anderson, Glick & Shapiro, 1998). Frustration with a lack of control over events outside the home, whether related to work or in other interactions, ends up directed toward family members (see the discussion of spillover from work to home in Chapter 15). Similar processes can also help explain why children who are bullied are more likely to be bullies themselves (Salmivalli & Nieminen, 2002).

Research on displaced aggression also finds that the more negative the insult, attack, or frustration and the more similar the instigator and the target, the greater the likelihood that displaced aggression will occur.

SITUATIONAL IMPACTS ON AGGRESSION

There are a number of specific characteristics of situations that make aggression more likely. Five covered in this chapter are potential rewards, presence of models, norms, stress, and aggressive cues.

Potential Rewards

Three types of rewards that promote aggression are direct material benefits, social approval, and attention.

The material benefits that armed robbers and Mafiosi obtain by using violence support their aggression. If the material benefits are reduced—say, by vigorous law enforcement—this type of aggressive violence will decline.

Although aggression is generally condemned, social approval is a second common reward for aggressive acts. Virtually every society has norms that approve aggression against particular targets in particular circumstances. We honor soldiers for shooting the enemy in war. We praise children for defending their siblings in a fight. Most of us, on occasion, urge friends to respond aggressively to insults or exploitation.

Attention is the third type of reward for aggressive acts. The teenager who taunts or bullies a classmate basks in the spotlight of attention from peers, even as he is reproached by school authorities. Research conducted in elementary school classrooms shows that even though aggressive children are generally disliked by their peers, the aggressive behavior at school is positively reinforced with laughter and interest from classmates (Powers & Bierman, 2013). Although few today would suggest that we should ignore bullying, research does show that a strategy that coupled rewards for cooperation and ignored aggressive behavior was effective in reducing aggression among preschool children (Brown & Elliott, 1965).

Modeling

A second situational factor that increases aggression is the presence of behavioral models. Just as aggressive behavior is learned by observing and then imitating a model (Bandura, Ross, & Ross, 1961), a model's aggressive behavior in a specific situation may encourage others to behave in similar ways. This "peer contagion" (Dishion & Dodge, 2005) has been found not only among elementary students and teenagers but also among adults.

Just as the last chapter discussed the importance of models in demonstrating types of helping acts that are possible, aggressive models demonstrate the possible negative behaviors. Consider the riots that occurred in London and other parts of the United Kingdom in 2011. What began as a peaceful protest of police brutality devolved quickly into a violent clash between protestors and police that included looting, arson, and total chaos. A panel argued that social media and the 24-hour news coverage actually made the riot worse. The incident was dubbed the "BlackBerry Riots" because of the importance of mobile devices and social media in organizing riot activities, spreading inflammatory and inaccurate accounts, and circulating photos of the destruction and chaos.

Media coverage exaggerated the extent of rioting in some areas, which made rioting a self-fulfilling prophecy as it encouraged others to join in. Social media and news outlet images and film also provided aggressive models. Aggressive models provide three types of information that influence observers. First, models demonstrate specific aggressive acts that are possible in a situation. Second, models provide information about the appropriateness of aggression—about whether it is normatively appropriate in a setting. The behavior of the initial participants in the UK riots signaled that violence was appropriate. The live television coverage of the riot news stations provided unwittingly—and the social media more intentionally—transmitted this message to tens of thousands of others who could join in and add to the chaotic scenes. Finally, models provide information about the consequences of acting aggressively. Observers see whether the model succeeds in attaining goals and whether the behavior is punished or rewarded. Not surprisingly, observers are more likely to imitate aggressive behaviors that yield rewards and avoid punishment. The modeling of aggression also helps account for why prior riots in one city are associated with subsequent riots in the same city (Olzak, Shanahan, & McEneaney, 1996) and why riots seem to spread from one city to another with mass media coverage (Myers, 1997).

These models matter little when observers are not motivated to do harm. But people who feel provoked and who are suppressing any urge to aggress often lose their inhibitions after observing an aggressive model. They are the most likely to imitate aggression. In other words, the news coverage of school shootings like Columbine is unlikely to cause an observer who is not motivated to do harm to consider bringing a gun to school or to hurt a classmate. However, such coverage might provoke someone who has an underlying urge to harm their peers by showing them that lashing out violently at school is not only possible but also perhaps both common and rewarded through mass media attention (Coleman, 2004).

Norms

Just as there is a positive norm of reciprocity (see Chapter 10), there is also a *negative norm of reciprocity*. This norm—"an eye for an eye, a tooth for a tooth"—justifies retaliation for attacks. Research on the culture of honor (see Box 11.1) suggests that the belief that one should respond to an attack on one's family property or self with aggression—and even killing—varies across cultural group. There is also evidence that men are more likely to endorse this honor ideology than women are (Barnes, Brown & Osterman, 2012). Such norms influence behavior. Among ex-offenders, endorsing "an eye for an eye" and similar statements was correlated with reports of more frequent violent behavior during the past year (Markowitz & Felson, 1998).

The negative reciprocity norm requires that the retaliation be proportionate to the provocation. Numerous experiments indicate that people match the level of retaliation to the level of the attack (Taylor, 1967). In the heat of anger, however, we are likely to overestimate the strength of another's provocation and to underestimate the intensity of our own response. When angry, we are also more likely to misinterpret responses that have no aggressive intent as intentional provocation. Thus, even when people strive to match retaliation to provocation, aggression may escalate.

A study of 444 assaults against police officers revealed that escalation of retaliation due to mutual misunderstanding was the most common factor leading to violence (Toch, 1969). Typically, the police officer began with a routine request for information. The person confronted interpreted the officer's request as threatening, arbitrary, and unfair and, thus, refused to comply. The officer interpreted this noncompliance as an attack on his or her own authority and reacted by declaring the suspect under arrest. Angered further by the officer's seemingly illegitimate assertion of power, the suspect retaliated with verbal insults and obscenities. From there the incident escalated quickly. The officer angrily grabbed the suspect, who retaliated by attacking physically. This sequence illustrates how a confrontation can spiral into violent aggression even when the angry participants feel they are merely matching their opponents' level of attack.

Experiments also support this norm of negative reciprocity. Two participants engaged in a competitive reaction time task in a laboratory; after each trial, the faster person could direct a noxious blast of noise at the slower person (Bushman, Baumeister, & Strack, 1999). The experiment was rigged so the participant received the noise on one-half of the trials (randomly selected) and could deliver noise on the other half. Over time, the participant increasingly matched the noise level delivered to him or her—clear evidence of reciprocity.

Stress

Stress also increases the likelihood of aggressive behavior. Social stressors, such as chronic unemployment and the experience of discrimination, are related to aggression because of their effects on frustration and anger. A study on the impact of economic distress on violence in married and cohabiting couples found that objective indicators such as reported household income were negatively related to abuse; as household income increased, the frequency of physical violence decreased. However, regardless of actual income, when either partner wished that the other worked more hours (or earned more money), this discrepancy between desire and reality was positively related to physical violence (Fox, Benson, DeMaris, & Van Wyk, 2002).

There are several other sources of stress within couples that may lead to intimate violence. Some potential stressors include: a short relationship duration (that is, the couple doesn't know each other well), a mismatch in gender role definitions (one has traditional views, the other more modern views), substance abuse, and large numbers of children. These are related to intimate violence in part through their relationship to more frequent disagreements as well as a more heated disagreement style that causes disagreements to escalate (DeMaris, Benson, Fox, Hill & Van Wyk, 2003). This process of escalation occurs, in part, because the longer an argument or fight continues, the more likely each person is to introduce past grievances rather than focusing solely on the issue at hand.

Stress can also stem from living conditions. Research finds that intimate violence occurs more frequently in economically disadvantaged neighborhoods (Benson & Fox, 2004), even among those who are better off financially than their neighbors (Fox & Benson, 2006). These same processes suggest, though, that neighborhood characteristics can also reduce intimate violence. Research linking survey data, census data, and homicide data for the city of Chicago found that, even in disadvantaged neighborhoods, if residents share a sense of collective efficacy (for example, "people in this neighborhood can be trusted") and a sense that neighbors could be counted on, rates of intimate violence were lower (Browning & Cagney, 2003). Such sentiments could be interpreted as indicators of lower levels of stress stemming from the neighborhood environment.

Other situational stressors can also produce high levels of aggression. Several studies have shown that temperature is related to the occurrence of a number of violent crimes, including assault, sexual assault, murder, and riots (Anderson, 1987, Baron & Ransberger, 1978). This is, in part, because temperatures increase discomfort and feelings of hostility (Anderson, 2001). Recent research finds that climate controls like air conditioning have the potential to curb heat-related violence, but access to such technologies is not uniform and their reach is limited (Rotton & Cohn, 2004). Interestingly, taking into account the time of day—because more crime occurs at night, but temperatures tend to be lower then—rates of violence peak at a temperature between 80 and 90 degrees (Cohn & Rotton, 2005). Temperatures beyond that lead to reduced violence, perhaps because people want to escape the heat and break off interaction with others (Cohn & Rotton, 1997).

Heat also influences aggression indirectly by increasing the prevalence of aggressive thoughts that may subsequently lead to aggressive behavior. Researchers found that exposure to words related to hot temperatures (sunburn, boils, roasted, hot, sweats), regardless of the actual temperature in the laboratory, resulted in more aggressive thoughts and hostile perceptions than exposure to either cold (frostbite, freezes, cold, shivers) or neutral words unrelated to temperature (DeWall & Bushman, 2009).

Aggressive Cues

Situations that produce aggression often start out in ways that are ambiguous to those involved in them. Should that insult be interpreted as a good-natured joke or a challenge to a man's masculinity? Is a jovial conversation between your boyfriend and another woman perfectly innocent, friendly banter, or an unwelcome attempt at flirting? Observers and participants involved in such incidents need help from the environment to figure out what is happening and how they should respond.

Aggressive cues in the environment can increase the likelihood of an aggressive response (Berkowitz, 1989). These cues may intensify the aggressive motivation or lower inhibitions even if they are not directly involved in the immediate situation. For example, people who have been aroused or frustrated respond more aggressively when in the presence of a gun than in the presence of neutral objects, even when the object has nothing to do with the aggression (Carlson, Marcus-Newhall, & Miller, 1990). The so-called **weapons effect** occurs when people are already aroused. The effect involves cognitive priming; the sight of a weapon makes more accessible or primes aggression-related concepts or scripts for behavior (Anderson, Benjamin, & Bartholow, 1998).

Aggressive cues also affect aggression by a process of ruminative thought (Marcus-Newhall et al., 2000). **Rumination** is a self-focused attention toward one's distress and the possible causes and consequences of the distress rather than ways to overcome it. When someone is thinking about an earlier provocation, they may respond aggressively to a mildly annoying event (a trigger). If your roommate is thinking of an incident in which her professor embarrassed her in class earlier in the day as she stirs the spaghetti sauce on the stove, she might snap at you for asking when she will be finished cooking. If she is instead thinking of the weekend ahead, she will be more likely to simply tell you that dinner will be done in a few minutes.

To test the effect of ruminating on aggression, social psychologists had a group of undergraduates participate in a three-part experiment (Bushman et al., 2005). In the first part of the experiment, the provocation phase, the participants were asked to solve difficult anagrams (for example, to unscramble NVTNIMEREON to spell ENVIRONMENT) while loud and distracting music played in the background. After a few minutes, the experimenter collected the anagram sheets, turned off the music, and left to score the sheet. The experimenter returned later and informed the participants that their score was well below average and they really should repeat the task but added—in an exasperated tone—that repeating the first part would be a waste of time and they should just proceed to part two. For part two, a random group of participants were assigned to the rumination phase and asked to respond to a number of self-focused phrases ("what kind of person you are," "why people treat you the way they do"). Others responded to externally focused or mood-enhancing phrases. In the final part of the experiment, the trigger phase, all the participants played a trivia game. When the research assistant read the trivia questions too quickly, mispronounced some of the names (pronouncing Leonardo da Vinci as Leon Divinsky), and occasionally mixed up the possible responses, participants who had been in the rumination condition reacted significantly more aggressively—recommending the research assistant not be hired for a permanent position and experiencing more negative emotions—than did those who had been assigned to the other groups in part two or who had not experienced an annoying trigger in the final part of the experiment (see Figure 11.2).

REDUCING AGGRESSIVE BEHAVIOR

Aggressive behavior is often costly to individuals and the groups and society to which they belong. Given the problems associated with aggressive behavior, reducing aggression has been an important topic of research. Four strategies that hold some promise are reducing frustration, punishing aggressive behavior, providing nonaggressive models, and providing opportunities for catharsis.

Reducing Frustration

Given that frustration is so central to aggression, we might be able to reduce aggressive behavior by reducing the frequency or strength of frustration. A major source of frustration in American society, for example, is inadequate resources. Studies comparing crime rates across different cities (e.g., Land, McCall, & Cohen, 1990) and nations (Gartner, 1990) find that economic deprivation is the best predictor for crime. Many cases of robbery, assault, and murder are motivated simply by a desire for money or property. Frustration and, therefore, aggression could be reduced if everyone had access to life's necessities.

Many of the frustrations we experience arise from conflicts with other people.

FIGURE 11.2 The Interaction Between Rumination and a Mild Annoyance on Aggression

When participants were prompted to ruminate about an aggressive provocation, a subsequent minor trigger caused a significantly more aggressive reaction than for those who were provoked but not asked to ruminate or for those who ruminated but were not exposed to the minor trigger.

Source: Figure 1, Bushman et al. (2005). "Chewing on It Can Chew You Up: Effects of Rumination on Triggered Displaced Aggression." Journal of Personality and Social Psychology, 88, 969–983.

Thus, another way to reduce aggressive behavior is to provide people with alternative means of resolving interpersonal conflicts. Recent innovations in dispute resolution involve the increasing use of professionally trained mediators and the training of selected community members in conflict-resolution techniques. These innovations have also been implemented in schools. Conflict-resolution programs using peers as mediators have been introduced partly in response to the rise in mass shootings and bullying in schools.

Punishment

Punishment is often used to control aggression because of a widely held belief that punishment is an effective deterrent. Threats can indeed be effective in eliminating aggression, but only under certain narrowly defined conditions (Baron, 1977). For threats to inhibit aggression, the anticipated punishment must be great and the probability that it will occur very high. Even so, threatened punishment is largely ineffective when potential aggressors are extremely angry.

Actual (not just anticipated or threatened) punishment can also control aggression, but again, strict conditions must be met (Baron, 1977): (1) The punishment must follow the aggressive act promptly, (2) it must be seen as the logical outcome of that act, and (3) it must not violate legitimate social norms. Unless these conditions are met, people perceive punishment as unjustified, and this increases the likelihood that they will respond with anger or aggression.

Although research demonstrates the importance of these conditions for deterrence, the criminal justice system often fails to meet these conditions. The probability than any single criminal act will be punished is low, simply because most criminals are not caught. Even when criminals are caught, punishment rarely follows the crime promptly. Moreover, few criminals see the punishment as a logical or legitimate outcome of their act. Finally, criminals often have much to gain through their aggression. A longitudinal study of adult offenders found that perception of risk of sanctions was not related to criminal activity. The most significant predictor of crime was the perception of opportunities to gain economically by breaking the law (Piliavin et al., 1986). As a result, the criminal justice system is not very effective in deterring criminal aggression.

Nonaggressive Models

Just as aggressive models may increase aggression, nonaggressive models may reduce it. Mahatma Gandhi, who led the movement to free India of British colonialism, used pacifist tactics that have since been imitated by protesters around the world. Laboratory research has also demonstrated the restraining influence of nonaggressive models. In one study (Baron & Kepner, 1970), participants observed an aggressive model deliver many more shocks to a confederate than required by the task. Other participants observed a nonaggressive model who gave the minimum number of shocks required. A control group observed no model. The results showed that the participants who observed the nonaggressive model displayed less subsequent aggression than did the participants in either the control group or the participants who saw the aggressive model. Other research shows that nonaggressive models not only reduce aggression but can also offset the influence of aggressive models (Baron, 1971).

Catharsis

Infuriated by a day of catering to the whims of her boss, Christina turned on her teenage son as he drove her home. "Why must you drive like a maniac?" she snapped in a fit of displaced aggression. Miguel was stunned. He was driving a sedate 35 miles per hour and had done nothing to provoke his mother's aggression. Did Christina feel better after venting her anger on Miguel?

Many people believe that letting off steam is better than "bottling up" hostility. A very old psychological concept captures this idea (Aristotle, *Poetics*, Book 6). **Catharsis** is the notion that one can reduce aggressive arousal by performing aggressive acts. The catharsis hypothesis states that we can purge ourselves of hostile emotions by experiencing these emotions while acting aggressively. A broader view suggests that by observing aggression as an involved spectator to drama, television, or sports, we also release aggressive emotions.

Numerous studies support the usefulness of catharsis and show that it does indeed reduce aggression (Geen & Quanty, 1977). But again, conditions are everything. For catharsis to occur, the aggressive act must be directed at the source of the frustration and not someone else. Misdirected or displaced aggression, such as kicking the dog or yelling at Miguel, often does not result in catharsis. We also must feel that the aggression we display will be viewed as acceptable by others, and we cannot feel guilty about it afterward.

In fact, with few exceptions, research has shown that performing aggressive acts will increase future aggression, not reduce it. This is true whether the initial aggression is a verbal attack, a physical attack, or even aggressive play (Bushman, Baumeister, & Stack, 1999; Geen, Stonner, & Shope, 1975). For example, research finds higher rates of both psychological and physical dating violence used by collegiate athletes in contact sports (wrestling, basketball) versus those in noncontact sports (track and field, swimming) (Burns, 2009).

Initial aggression promotes further aggression because initial aggressive acts produce disinhibition—the reduction of ordinary internal controls against socially disapproved behavior. Disinhibition is reflected in the reports of murderers and soldiers who commented that killing was difficult the first time but became easier thereafter. Second, initial aggressive acts serve to arouse our anger even further. Third, they give us experience in harming others, and thus, it becomes a more accessible part of our behavioral repertoires. Finally, if we do experience catharsis following aggression, this reinforces aggression, and behaviors we find rewarding are repeated more frequently.

AGGRESSION IN SOCIETY

Over the last two decades, there has been increasing recognition that aggressive behavior is at the heart of several major social problems. This awareness is due, in part, to the widespread publicity given to certain incidents like school shootings and other mass murders. But, fortunately, mass murders are rare. Much more common are other types of interpersonal violence, in which one person directs physical aggression toward another with the intent to injure or kill the target. This final section of the chapter on aggression discusses three specific aspects of interpersonal violence. First, it looks at the causes and consequences of sexual assault. Next, it examines the impact of pornography on sexual assault. Finally, it discusses whether television programming and video games contribute to violence.

Sexual Assault

Sexual assault is sexual touching or intercourse without consent, accomplished by coercion, manipulation, or either the threat or use of force. The greater the force used or the resulting injury, the more severe the assault. One study of sexual coercion surveyed from 165 men and 131 women who were new members of fraternities and sororities. Men were as likely as women to report being coerced into unwanted sexual contact, but only women reported being physically forced to do so (Larimer, Lydum, Anderson, & Turner, 1999). Most cases involve offenders and victims from the same racial or ethnic group.

In some cases, the offender is motivated by sexual desire. In other cases, however, the offender's intent is to dominate, humiliate, or injure the victim. Sexual assault is one form of sexual aggression; sexual aggression is really a continuum, ranging from the use of bribes through verbal pressure, the intentional use of alcohol or drugs, physical force, and kidnapping to sexual murder (Jewkes, Sen, & Garcia-Moreno, 2002).

What Causes Sexual Aggression? There are several answers to this question. One is a specific set of cultural beliefs and practices creates conditions that encourage rape. In a rape-prone society, the sexual assault of women by men is allowed or overlooked (Sanday, 1981, 2003). Rape-prone societies share several characteristics. First, there are high levels of interpersonal violence. Second, there is an ideology of male dominance that subordinates women, suggesting that women are the property of men and should be subject to men's control. Third, men and women are regularly separated (during religious rituals, for example) in rape-prone societies. The United States is a rape-prone society. Rates of violent crime are high. Until recently, men dominated women politically, economically, and sexually. There is also a continuing separation of men and women in certain spheres (athletic programs, workplaces).

Rape-proneness has also been applied to college campuses. Researchers find that when fraternities or men's dorms are allowed to have parties, whereas sororities and women's dorms are not, men are more likely to be able to structure the party and control the movement and behavior of their guests (Armstrong, Hamilton, & Sweeney, 2006). Men also regulate and distribute the alcohol, an important factor in sexual assault on college campuses (Logan, Walker, Cole, & Keukefeld, 2002). With men as hosts, women are also expected to be nice and to defer to men in interaction, ultimately supporting male dominance in the situation and contributing to the rape-prone environment of campus parties (Armstrong, Hamilton, & Sweeney, 2006).

Perpetrators of Sexual Assault. Of course, individuals rather than societies or cultures commit rape. A second approach to determining the causes of sexual assault is to identify men's characteristics that may be related to their aggressive behavior. Research suggests that some men are sexually aggressive—that is, they rely on aggressive behaviors in their relationships with women (Malamuth, Heavey, & Linz, 1993). These men tend to score highly on measures of the desire to dominate women and of hostility toward women. They also have a variety of attitudes that facilitate aggression toward women, including rape myths, such as the belief that women secretly desire to be raped and enjoy it, that victims cause rape, and that other men are prone to rape (see Box 11.2) (Koss & Leonard, 1984; Malamuth, 1984). These men also tend to be sexually aroused by portrayals of rape. In laboratory studies, men who endorse rape myths are more likely to aggress against a woman who has mildly insulted or rejected them (Check & Malamuth, 1983). In addition to these specific gender attitudes, findings from research suggest that pornography use and alcohol abuse are also significant predictors of the perpetration of sexual violence (Carr & VanDeusen, 2004).

Men's tendency to be sexually aggressive is stable over time. Researchers collected data on 423 young men, including

BOX 11.2 Test Yourself: Rape Myths

Among the causes of sexual aggression are cultural beliefs that encourage rape. These beliefs are rape myths—prejudicial, stereotyped, and false beliefs about rape, rape victims, and persons who commit rape (Burt, 1980). Examples of these myths are "She asked for it," "He didn't mean to," and "It wasn't really rape." These beliefs create a climate that encourages sexual assault and is suspicious of and hostile toward victims.

An attitude scale that is widely used to assess these beliefs is the Rape Myth Acceptance Scale, developed by Burt (1980). Below are some of the items from an updated version of the scale intended for college students (McMahon & Farmer, 2011). Read each statement and circle the appropriate response: Strongly Agree (SA), Agree (A), Don't know (?), Disagree (D), or Strongly Disagree (SD).

1. If a girl goes to a room alone with a guy at a party, it is her own fault if she is raped.

    SA   A   ?   D   SD

2. If a girl doesn't physically fight back, you can't really say it was rape.

    SA   A   ?   D   SD

3. When girls go to parties wearing slutty clothes, they are asking for trouble.

    SA   A   ?   D   SD

4. If a girl initiates kissing or hooking up, she should not be surprised if a guy assumes she wants to have sex.

    SA   A   ?   D   SD

5. If a girl is raped while she is drunk, she is at least somewhat responsible for letting things get out of hand.

    SA   A   ?   D   SD

6. Rape happens when a guy's sex drive goes out of control.

    SA   A   ?   D   SD

7. A lot of times, girls who say they were raped agreed to have sex and then regret it.

    SA   A   ?   D   SD

8. Rape accusations are often used as a way of getting back at guys.

    SA   A   ?   D   SD

9. If a girl doesn't say "no," she can't claim rape.

    SA   A   ?   D   SD

10. If a guy is drunk, he might rape someone unintentionally.

    SA   A   ?   D   SD

Scores for each question range from 1 (strongly agree) to 5 (strongly disagree). Scores should be totaled for a cumulative score. Higher scores indicate greater rejection of rape myths. A man with a lower score likely believes that if he engages in sexual activity with a woman who comes home with him on the first date after they have both been drinking, it is not rape, even if she offers some resistance. This is one of the dangers of rape myths. They provide scripts that legitimize sexual activity to which the woman may not have overtly consented. Another type of rape myth—that claims of rape are not true—creates an environment in which such claims are not believed, and therefore, sexual assault is not punished.

There have been many studies on the correlates of endorsing rape myths. One review summarizes the findings of 72 studies (Anderson, Cooper, & Okamura, 1997). Men, older persons, and persons from lower socioeconomic backgrounds are more likely to hold such attitudes. Acceptance of rape was associated with traditional beliefs about gender roles, an adversarial view of male-female relationships, and conservative political beliefs. These results are consistent with the theory that rape myth acceptance is the result of socialization to gender types and conservative beliefs.

measures of hostility toward women and attitudes supportive of violence. Ten years later, they reinterviewed a number of the men and their female partners (Malamuth, Linz, Heavey, Barnes, & Acker, 1995). The characteristics measured ten years earlier predicted which men were later sexually aggressive toward their partners, as reported both by men and their partners. This research suggests that men who commit sexual assault have learned a script for heterosexual interactions that includes the use of verbal abuse or physical force to exercise influence over or obtain sexual gratification from a woman (Huesmann, 1986). Once learned, it is used to regulate behavior in various situations. Research suggests that this script is learned in childhood (Jacobson & Gottman, 1998), likely when the child observes aggression frequently, is reinforced for aggressive behavior, and is the object of aggression.

Victims of Sexual Assault. Victims of sexual assault are primarily women between the ages of 15 and 24. Some women—a minority of all victims—are assaulted by men they do not know. These assaults by strangers often occur outdoors, in parks, deserted parking lots, or in the victim's residence. The offenders in these cases are often opportunistic, attacking any woman who is available or appears to be vulnerable.

Much more often, however, women are assaulted by someone they know. This may be a man they are dating (date rape) or a neighbor or coworker (acquaintance rape). The victims in most cases of date rape are young, single women—often high school or college students. A recent study found that 78% of unwanted sexual contact on a college campus took place while "hooking up" (Flack et al., 2007). In part because of their involvement in rape-prone fraternities on campus and in the hook-up culture, White college students are at a higher risk of sexual assault than are other racial groups on campuses (Armstrong, Hamilton, & Sweeney, 2006).

Several factors contribute to the occurrence of sexual assault. One is alcohol, which is a factor in more than half of all sexual assaults (whether involving alcohol consumption by the perpetrator, victim, or both) (Abbey, 2002). Alcohol lowers internal inhibitions that might otherwise prevent aggression. It also influences judgment. Both surveys and experiments provide evidence that people are more likely to engage in risky behavior—including entering a risky situation—when they have been drinking. In fact, some men use alcohol or drugs intentionally to make a woman more likely to take risks voluntarily (Abbey et al., 2001). One study randomly assigned male participants to one of two conditions. In one, the men consumed alcohol. In the other, the participants drank a nonalcoholic beverage. The participants were then presented with an acquaintance rape scenario. Intoxicated participants found the male character's use of force to obtain sex more acceptable and were more willing to act in a similar manner than the sober participants (Abbey, 2011). The effects of alcohol were strongest for men who already held hostile attitudes toward women.

Another factor in sexual assault is misinterpreted verbal or nonverbal messages. A woman may engage in some behavior that a man incorrectly interprets as a sexual invitation (Bondurant & Donat, 1999). Misinterpretations not only increase the prevalence of sexual assault but also influence attributions about the causes of assault. When responsibility for a sexual assault is placed on the victim rather than the perpetrator, it is referred to as **victim-blame**. Those engaged in victim-blame argue that a woman's flirting or provocative dress can somehow lead a man to believe that a woman is consenting to sexual contact or intercourse. Men tend to perceive more sexual intent in women's behavior than other women do (Farris, Treat, Viken, & McFall, 2008).

Cultural beliefs are a third factor that contributes to sexual assault. According to one survey of 14- to 17-year-olds, teenagers of both genders believe that a man is justified in forcing a woman to have intercourse if she gets him sexually excited, leads him on, or has dated him for a long time (Goodchilds & Zellman, 1984). Other influential cultural beliefs include that men cannot stop once they have started to become sexually aroused, that husbands cannot rape their wives, and that women enjoy rape (Edwards et al., 2011; Ryan, 2011).

Misperceptions and cultural beliefs also influence women's interpretation of forced, nonconsensual sexual activity. Many women who experience sexual assault do not perceive the experience as rape (Kahn, Mathie, & Torgler, 1994). This may be because their experience—being assaulted by someone they know during a date after some sexual foreplay—does not match their script for rape: a violent attack by a stranger (Ryan, 1988). In one study, researchers asked women to write a description "of events before, during, and after a rape" and to describe their past experiences with assault. There were some women who reported that they had been forced to have sex but who also replied "no" to the question, "Have you ever been raped?" These women were more likely to describe rape as an attack by a stranger than were women who reported that they had been raped. Similarly, women's script for a loving relationship is one of equality and romance, which encourages individuals to overlook their partner's bad behavior, with an emphasis on male rather than female sexual drive (Lloyd & Emery, 2000). An experience of aggression does not fit this script and so may be ignored. This is a good example of

the power of scripts to shape experience (see Chapter 6).

Pornography and Violence

One possible source for scripts that encourage sexual aggression is growing up in an abusive family. Another is viewing or reading pornography (Ryan, 2011).

On August 1, 2013, Ariel Castro was sentenced to life plus 1,000 years for the kidnapping, rape, and assault of three women whom he held captive in his home in Cleveland, Ohio. At the sentencing hearing, Castro blamed his behaviors on an addiction to pornography and joined a growing number of perpetrators—including Ted Bundy, a serial murderer who confessed to killing at least 24 young women—who have used pornography addiction as a defense for their heinous actions. Such claims generate great interest in the connection between pornography and violence, a link that social psychologists have conducted considerable research to explore.

Nonaggressive Pornography. Various studies have shown that the effect of pornography on behavior depends on what the pornography portrays. Pornography that explicitly depicts adults engaging in consenting sexual activity is termed **nonaggressive pornography** or erotica. Reading or viewing nonaggressive pornography creates sexual arousal (Byrne & Kelley, 1984), usually through the mechanism of cognitive and imaginative processing.

Nonaggressive pornography by itself does not produce aggression toward women (Donnerstein & Linz, 1998). However, when the viewer's inhibitions are lowered—as they may be if he is intoxicated—or if a man is already at risk for sexual aggression, it may do so (Vega & Malamuth, 2007). Research finds that when men are angered or frustrated and then view nonaggressive pornographic images, they show more aggressive behavior toward women (Donnerstein & Barrett, 1978). The mechanism is thought to be transfer of arousal: The sexual arousal that results from viewing pornography is added to the arousal induced by the anger, resulting in sexual aggression.

Hollywood films, while not considered pornography, increasingly include apparently consensual sexual activity that is degrading or humiliating to women. For example, a study of James Bond films found that both the sexual activity and harm to women shown in the films has been increasing steadily over time (Neuendorf et al., 2010). An experiment explored the effect of viewing scenes that objectified women. Men and women who participated in the experiment saw either selections from *9½ Weeks* and *Showgirls* or scenes from animated cartoons. Participants subsequently read and evaluated a magazine story about a date rape or a stranger rape. Men who saw the sexualized film clips were more likely to say that the victim of the data rape enjoyed it and "got what she wanted" (Milburn, Mather, & Conrad, 2000). These results have important implications given the rise of depictions of sexual violence toward women in advertising and print media (Cortese, 2004).

Aggressive Pornography. Exposure to **aggressive pornography**—explicit depictions of sexual activity in which force is threatened or used to coerce a woman to engage in sex—also influences behavior, especially aggression toward women (Malamuth, 1984; Malamuth, Addison, & Koss, 2000). Unlike erotica, aggressive pornography has lasting effects on both attitudes and behavior. In a study of its effects on attitudes (Donnerstein, 1984), men viewed one of three films featuring either aggression, nonaggressive sexual activity, or aggressive sexual activity. Following the film, the participants completed several attitude scales, including one that measured acceptance of rape myths. Men who saw the films depicting aggression or aggressive sexual activity scored higher on the rape myth acceptance scale (see Box 11.2) than did men who saw the film depicting nonaggressive sexual activity. These men also indicated greater willingness to use force to obtain sex. The fact that both films depicting aggression, even nonsexual aggression, affected attitudes more than the nonaggressive film suggests that it is aggression rather than explicit portrayals of sex that influences attitudes toward sexual aggression. Experimental research like this is important for demonstrating the effects of viewing pornography to counter the argument that the relationship between pornography and aggression only goes the other direction: that men who consume pornography already have aggressive tendencies toward women and are, therefore, attracted to aggressive pornography (Malamuth, Addison, & Koss, 2000). Although that certainly may be the case, exposure to pornography also influences sexual aggression.

In another experimental study (Donnerstein & Berkowitz, 1981), male participants were either angered or treated neutrally by a male or female confederate. The participants then viewed one of four films: a neutral film, a nonaggressive pornographic film, or one of two aggressive pornographic films. In the latter films, a young woman is shoved around, tied up, stripped, and raped. In one version, she finds the experience disgusting, whereas in the other she is smiling at the end. Following the film, the men were given an opportunity to aggress against a male or female confederate by delivering electric shocks. The films did not affect aggression toward the male confederate. However, participants who saw the aggressive films delivered more intense electric shocks to the female confederate.

The fact that aggressive pornography produces aggressive behavior reflects three influences: sexual arousal, aggressive cues, and reduced inhibitions. Some men experience high levels of arousal in response to such portrayals. Moreover, such pornography portrays women as targets of aggression. In the experiment conducted by Donnerstein and Berkowitz, the film created an association in the viewer's mind between the victim in the film and the woman who angered him, suggesting aggression toward the latter. Note that aggressive films led to increased violence toward the female confederate and not the male confederate, a finding consistent with this interpretation. These films may also reduce inhibitions to aggression by suggesting that aggression directed toward women has positive outcomes.

One important question is whether we can generalize from the results of laboratory research to natural settings. Does the viewing of aggressive pornography in nonlaboratory settings contribute to violence against women? One study found a correlation between the availability of pornography and rates of violent crime (Baron & Straus, 1984). Results suggested that the circulation index of eight "sex magazines" (including *Playboy* and *Hustler*) in a state was the strongest predictor of rape in that state. Another study examined the influence of intentional exposure to X-rated material on sexually aggressive behavior among 10- to 15-year-olds (Ybarra et al., 2011). After accounting for other potential influences related to both exposure and sexual aggression (for example, substance abuse and being a victim of sexual aggression), researchers found that boys and girls who were exposed to violent X-rated material were six times as likely to report perpetrating a sexually aggressive behavior as were those who had either not viewed X-rated material or who had only been exposed to nonviolent X-rated material.

Media Violence and Aggression

If one thing has changed about American lifestyles over the past century, it is the amount of time spent consuming entertainment and news through visual media, both online and on television. These media are replete with violence, sex, and aggressive behaviors of all kinds. Given the ubiquity of media and the widespread belief that violence—sexual, physical, and psychological—is increasing around the world, both researchers and the public are interested in the effects media exposure has on behavior.

Violent Television and Aggression. Evelyn Wagler was carrying a two-gallon can of gasoline back to her stalled car. She was cornered by six young men who forced her to douse herself with the fuel. Then, one of the men tossed a lighted match. She burned to death. Two nights earlier, a similar murder had been depicted on national television.

Violence pervades television. Both heroes and villains perform aggression on television. Not just humans, but also cartoon characters torment each other in astonishingly creative ways. During prime-time television, three to five violent incidents occur per hour of programming, and 20 to 25 violent incidents occur per hour during Saturday morning children's shows (American Psychological Association, 1993). In all, 60% of television programs and 70% of the programming intended for children contains violence (Wilson et al., 2002). By age 18, the average American child is likely to have seen about 200,000 violent acts on television, including 40,000 homicides (Plagens, Miller, Foote, & Yoffe, 1991). Only one-quarter of these violent acts results in any punishment for the perpetrators (National Television Violence Study, 1996). Although research suggests that watching violent television is correlated with aggressive behavior (Anderson et al., 2003; Coyne et al., 2011), correlation is not the same as causation.

Does exposure to television violence encourage viewers to behave aggressively? Experimental research—where one group is exposed to violent media in a controlled setting while another group is not and then both groups' behavior and attitudes are measured—suggests that there is a causal connection (Comstock, 1984; Friedrich-Cofer & Huston, 1986; Murray & Kippax, 1979). This research also points to five processes that explain why exposure to media violence might increase aggressive behavior (Huesmann & Moise, 1996).

- *Imitation.* Viewers learn specific techniques of aggression from media models. Social learning evidently played a role in the violent attack on Evelyn Wagler.

- *Cognitive priming.* Portrayals of violence activate aggressive thoughts and pro-aggression attitudes. The activation of an attitude increases the likelihood that it will be expressed in behavior.

- *Legitimization/justification.* Exposure to violence that leads to goal attainment and has positive outcomes (for example, punishes wrongdoers) legitimizes aggression and makes it more acceptable (Bushmann & Huesmann, 2001).

- *Desensitization.* After observing violence repeatedly, viewers become less sensitive to aggression. This makes them less reluctant to hurt others and less inclined to ease others' suffering.

- *Arousal.* Viewing violence on television produces excitement and physiological arousal, which may amplify aggressive responses in situations that would otherwise elicit milder anger.

Moreover, these results have been found in experiments with boys and girls of all ages, races, social classes, and levels of intelligence as well as in many countries (Huesmann & Moise, 1996). A meta-analysis of all the research available at the time reports that virtually every study—whether cross-sectional (n=86), longitudinal (n=46), or experimental (n=152)—finds a significant relationship between exposure to media violence and aggression (Anderson & Bushman, 2002). This is true of television, movies, and Internet media (Ybarra, Diener-West, Markow, Leaf, Hamburger, & Boxer, 2008).

Violence on the Internet takes a number of forms, including violent videos, like some posted on the sites YouTube or Vine, or violent images and scenarios depicted in photos and ads showing physical and sexual aggression. Other violence on the Internet takes the form of psychological violence. "Hate pages" are devoted to harassing and degrading specific groups, and cyber-bullying runs rampant on Facebook, ask.fm, and other social media sites. Users—particularly adolescents who are highly susceptible to peer pressure—frequently imitate this displayed aggression, both on- and offline (Ybarra et al., 2008).

However, the relationship between violent media and aggression is not one directional. A growing body of evidence suggests that the link between aggression and media usage is actually circular (Friedrich-Cofer & Huston, 1986). Because aggressive children are relatively unpopular with their peers, they spend more time watching television as well as online and playing video games. This exposes them to more violence, teaches them aggressive scripts and behaviors, and reassures them that their behavior is appropriate. When they then try to enact these scripts in interactions with others, they become even more unpopular and are driven back to television—and the vicious cycle continues (Huesmann, 1986; Singer & Singer, 1983).

Despite all this evidence on the connection between media violence and violent behavior, scientists have been unable to convince film and television producers to decrease the amount of violence shown in television and movies. In fact, over time, film ratings have relaxed to allow more violent content in PG-13 films than was allowed in previous years (Leone & Barowski, 2011). To approach the issue from another side, researchers have turned their attention toward developing interventions to limit the negative effect of media violence (Rosenkoetter, Rosenkoetter, & Acock, 2009).

Social psychologists have used experimental methods—both in the field and the laboratory—to test strategies that parents, teachers, and others might use to counteract the deleterious effects of violent media (Rosenkoetter, Rosenkoetter, & Acock, 2009). Previous work suggests that aggression is lower among individuals who are high in empathy (Dean & Malamuth, 1997). Drawing on this, researchers tried to induce empathy among viewers. When adults ask children to empathize with the victim, children are less accepting of aggression and find the aggression in cartoons less humorous (Nathanson & Cantor, 2000). Adults can also reduce children's imitation of aggression by making negative comments about the violence. A neutral comment, however, is no less effective than no comment at all (Cantor & Wilson, 2003).

Interventions are most effective when they are long term. A year-long program for elementary students that emphasized the ways that television distorts the reality of aggression not only resulted in less positive attitudes about violence on television but also reduced identification with violent heroes and led children to watch less violent programming. Participating in the program also lowered aggressive behav-iors among boys, who watch more violent programming than girls do (Rosenkoetter, Rosenkoetter, Ozretich, and Acock, 2004; Dodge, Coie, & Lynam, 2006).

Violent Video Games and Aggression. One late summer afternoon, an eight-year-old boy shot Marie Smothers, his elderly caregiver, in the back of the head as she sat in her living room watching television. Media reports claimed the shooting was intentional and blamed the violent video game *Grand Theft Auto*—which the boy had been playing just moments before he killed Smothers—for his violent actions. Although it is difficult to determine the causes of acts of aggression, research suggests that there is a relationship between both short- and long-term exposure to violence in video games and aggression (Anderson et al., 2010). Both men and women who report playing violent video games are more likely to report engaging in various aggressive behaviors (Bushman, Baumeister, & Stack, 1999).

Although video game playing was once restricted to arcades and television consoles, today people also play video games on computers, handheld devices, iPods, and cell phones. Technological advances have improved the sound effects and graphics, making video games more engrossing than they were in the past (Ivory & Kalyanaraman, 2007). In 2008, 97% of teenagers between 12 and 17 reported playing video games, with 31% playing every day (Lenhart et al., 2008). Many of these video games portray interpersonal violence. A content analysis of 33 popular video games found that 80% of them involved aggression or violence as part of the strategy. About half encourage violence directed at people, and 21% included violence directed at women (Dietz, 1998).

Playing video games involves a number of the psychological processes discussed earlier. Playing violent video games leads

Technological advances have greatly expanded young people's access to media, including violent media, and have limited adults' knowledge of what young people are exposed to and the opportunity to discuss the images together. © CREATISTA/ shutterstock

to both physiological (heart rate, body temperature) and emotional arousal (anger, hostility) (Anderson et al. 2010). Players, like the young boy discussed at the beginning of the section, might imitate what they see. More lasting, though, is acquiring the behavior patterns or scripts that include violence as a means of achieving higher scores (observational learning) and having these rewarded (reinforcement) (Funk, Flores, Buchman, & Germann, 1999). Ongoing exposure to violence also desensitizes players to violence, making it seem more normal and natural (Krahé, 2013), and primes them to later react more aggressively to minor annoyances (Anderson & Dill, 2000). This occurs, in part, through disinhibition.

Features of games either dampen or amplify the effect of violence on aggression. For example, both more visible blood in games and controllers in the shape of a realistic gun tend to heighten arousal and hostility (Barlett, Harris, & Baldassaro, 2007; Barlett, Harris & Bruey, 2008). Similarity to and identification with aggressive video game characters also increase the effects of video games on aggression (Williams, 2010). Finally, research finds that playing a video game that sexualized and objectified women—with provocative dress— increased men's rape acceptance and led them to judge rape victims more negatively than did playing an identical game with fully clothed women as characters (Stermer & Burkley, 2012).

SUMMARY

Aggression is behavior intended to harm another person that the target person wants to avoid.

Aggression and the Motivation to Harm. There are four main theories regarding the motivation for aggression. (1) People are instinctively aggressive. (2) People become aggressive in response to events that are frustrating. (3) People aggress against others as a result of aversive emotion. (4) People are motivated by rewards and learn to use aggression as a means of obtaining what they want.

Characteristics of Targets That Affect Aggression. Once aggressive motivation has been aroused, target characteristics influence whether aggressive behavior occurs. Aggressive behavior is more likely if the target is of the same race or ethnicity. The target's gender also influences the response. When we are attacked, our response is influenced by the attributions we make about the attacker's intentions. We are less likely to engage in aggression toward a target who we believe is capable of retaliation. We may, however, engage in displaced aggression against another.

Situational Impacts on Aggression. Situational conditions are important influences on aggressive behavior. Rewards that encourage aggression include material benefits, social approval, and attention. Aggressive models provide information about available options, normative appropriateness, and consequences (or lack thereof) of aggressive acts. The negative reciprocity norm encourages aggressive behavior in certain situations. Aggressive behavior is more likely when stressors, such as high temperature, are present. Aggressive behavior is also more likely in the presence of aggressive cues, especially weapons.

Reducing Aggressive Behavior. Frustration levels could be reduced by guaranteeing everyone the basic necessities, therefore limiting aggression motivated by rewards. Punishment is effective in controlling aggression only when it promptly follows the aggressive act, is seen as the logical outcome of that act, and does not violate social norms. Nonaggressive models reduce the likelihood of aggression and can offset the effect of aggressive models. Although catharsis may follow aggressive acts, such acts may still promote later aggression.

Aggression in Society. Interpersonal violence is a serious problem in American society. Rates of sexual assault and acceptance of the behavior are influenced by societal characteristics, such as male domination of women, and by scripts that encourage male aggression toward women. Nonaggressive pornography and aggressive pornography both influence attitudes and behavior, although the latter to a much higher degree.

Experimental research shows that observing violence in film, on television and the Internet, and in video games increases aggressive attitudes and behavior in everyday settings.

List of Key Terms and Concepts

affective aggression (p. 375)
aggravated assault (p. 376)
aggression (p. 370)
aggressive pornography (p. 391)
aversive affect (p. 374)
catharsis (p. 386)
displaced aggression (p. 379)
frustration (p. 372)
frustration-aggression hypothesis (p. 372)
nonaggressive pornography (p. 372)
rumination (p. 383)
sexual assault (p. 386)
target (p. 376)
victim-blame (p. 389)
weapons effect (p. 383)

Critical Thinking Skill: Applying Scientific Research to Policy Decisions

Gun violence in the United States has many people concerned. However, both politicians and citizens are divided on how best to curb this violence. Some argue that only police and the military should have guns, others argue that automatic weapons should be restricted or guns should be harder to purchase, while still others assert that access to guns is not the problem and that other measures should be taken. How should the average citizen or a policymaker decide their stance on this critical issue? The best way to make a good decision is to use the best available scientific evidence and think clearly about it. The evidence might come from correlational methods, like field studies and surveys, or from experiments.

The current discourse around gun violence centers on access. To determine whether the widespread availability of guns increases gun violence using a correlational method, a scientist might compare rates of lethal gun violence (deaths related to gunshot wounds) in countries where gun ownership is legal to the rates in countries where citizens are not allowed to buy guns through legal channels. The researchers would then see whether there is a correlation between accessibility and lethal gun violence. Suppose the correlation is positive and significant—that is, the more accessible guns are to citizens (legal to own, easy to purchase, and so forth), the larger the number of people who die from gun-related violence each year. This evidence provides support for policies that limit access to guns. However, because it is a correlational study, it cannot tell us whether access actually influences violence.

Another way to get at the question would be with an experiment. In a field experiment, scientists might choose two cities with similar rates of gun violence that are similar on other characteristics (racial diversity, economic inequality, education and income levels, and so forth). They would then have politicians institute a law that limited access to firearms in one of the cities. By tracking gun violence in the two cities, they could gauge whether restricting access lessened violence. However, there are a number of confounding factors that make such an experiment problematic and the findings difficult to interpret.

Alternatively, scientists could run a laboratory experiment in which they put subjects in a situation—something like a video game—in which they either had easy access to a gun or a gun was difficult or costly to acquire. The researchers could then expose subjects to frustrating situations in which they had the opportunity to use the gun or deal with their aggression in another way and then compare the likelihood that subjects would choose responses other than gun violence. Although laboratory experiments allow scientists significant control over conditions, the problem here is that it is a video game. Furthermore, in such a research setting, participants are acutely aware that their behavior is being tracked. Perhaps the findings would not generalize to a natural environment.

What are the benefits and limitations of the above studies? What are other studies you might conduct?

We can be most confident of a conclusion if there is converging evidence from multiple studies, both correlational and experimental. Considering these hypothetical studies together would give us more confidence in our ultimate decision because each study addresses some of the limitations of the others.

How can these studies inform a policy decision? At this point, a good policy decision would involve a cost-benefit analysis. Reducing citizens' access to guns might make those citizens more vulnerable to the violent attacks of others. Gun manufacturers and retailers would lose money if their only clients were police and military. These are costs. What are other costs? However, fewer gun deaths—whether accidental or intentional—would be a benefit. Are there other benefits?

In general, when making policy decisions when scientific evidence is available, we should evaluate the quality of that evidence and then weigh the costs and benefits of implementing policies based on the evidence.

CHAPTER 12

INTERPERSONAL ATTRACTION AND RELATIONSHIPS

INTRODUCTION

Dan was looking forward to the new semester. Now that he was a junior, he would be taking more interesting classes. He walked into the lecture hall and found a seat halfway down the aisle. As he looked toward the front, he noticed a very pretty young woman removing her coat; as he watched, she sat down in the front row.

Dan noticed her at every class; she always sat in the same seat. One morning, he passed up his usual spot and sat down next to her.

"Hi," he said. "You must like this class. You never miss it."

"I do, but it sure is a lot of work."

As they talked, they discovered they were from the same city and both were economics majors. When the professor announced the first exam, Dan asked Mia if she wanted to study for it with him. They worked together for several hours the night before the exam, along with Mia's roommate. Dan and Mia did very well on the exam.

The next week, he took her to a film at a campus theater. The week after, she asked him to a party at her dormitory. That night, as they were walking back to her room, Mia told Dan that her roommate's parents had just separated and that her roommate was severely depressed. Dan replied that he knew how she felt because his older brother had just left his wife. Because it was late, they agreed to meet the next morning for breakfast. They spent all day Sunday talking about love, marriage, parents, and their hopes for the future. By the end of the semester, Mia and Dan were seeing each other two or three times a week.

At its outset, the relationship between Dan and Mia was based on **interpersonal attraction**—a positive attitude held by one person toward another person. Over time, however, the development of their relationship involved increasing interdependence and increasing intimacy.

The development and outcome of personal relationships involves several stages. This chapter discusses each of these stages. Specifically, it considers the following questions:

1. Who is available? What determines with whom we come into contact?

2. Who is desirable? Of those available, what determines with whom we attempt to establish relationships?

3. What are the determinants of attraction or liking?

4. How do friendship and love develop between two people?

5. What is love?

6. What determines whether love thrives or dies?

WHO IS AVAILABLE ?

Hundreds or thousands of persons may go to school or live or work where you do. Most of them remain strangers—persons with whom you have no contact. Those persons with whom we come into contact, no matter how fleeting, constitute the field of **availables**—the pool of potential friends and lovers (Kerckhoff, 1974). What determines who is available? Is it mere chance that George rather than Bill is your roommate, or that Dan met Mia rather than Heather? The answer, of course, is no.

Two basic influences determine who is available. First, institutional structures influence our personal encounters. The admissions office of your school, the faculty committees that decide degree requirements, and the scheduling office all influence whether Dan and Mia enroll in the same class. Second, individuals' personal characteristics influence their choice of activities. Dan chose to take the economics class where he met Mia because of an interest in that field and a desire to go to graduate school in business. Thus, institutional and personal characteristics together determine who is available.

Given a set of persons who are available, how do we make contact with one or two of these persons? Three influences progressively narrow our choices: routine activities, proximity, and familiarity.

Routine Activities

Much of our life consists of a routine of activities that we repeat daily or weekly. We attend the same classes and sit in the same seats, eat in the same places at the same tables, shop in the same stores, ride the same bus, and work with the same people. These activities provide opportunities to interact with some availables but not with others. More important, the activity provides a focus for our initial interactions. We rarely establish a relationship by saying "Let's be friends" at a first meeting. To do so is risky, because the other person may decide to exploit us. Or that person may reject such an opening, which may damage our self-esteem. Instead, we begin by talking about something shared—a class, an ethnic background, a school, or the weather.

Most relationships begin in the context of routine activities. A study of college students found that relationships began with a meeting in a class, a dorm, or at work (36 percent); with an introduction by a third person (38 percent); or at parties (18 percent) or bars (14 percent). A study of 3,342 adults aged 18 to 59 asked how respondents met their sexual partners (Laumann, Gagnon, Michael, & Michaels, 1994). One-third reported that they were introduced by a friend, and another third said they were in-

troduced by family members or coworkers. Thus, social networks play an important role in the development of relationships. Studies of the friendship patterns of city dwellers have found that friends are selected from relatives, coworkers, and neighbors (Fischer, 1984). Thus, routine activities and social networks are important influences on the development of relationships.

How has the Internet affected where couples meet? A study of 2,462 heterosexual couple and 462 same-sex couples documents the changes (Rosenfeld & Thomas, 2012). Figure 12.1 displays the results. Since 1995, the percentage of couples meeting through family and friends has declined steadily, while the percentage meeting online has increased. The Internet has especially changed how same-sex couples meet.

Proximity

Although routine activities bring us into the same classroom, dining hall, or workplace, we are not equally likely to meet every person who is present. Rather, we are more likely to develop a relationship with someone who is in close physical proximity to us.

In classroom settings, seating patterns are an important influence on the development of friendships. One study (Byrne, 1961a) varied the seating arrangements for three classes of about 25 students each. In one class, they remained in the same seats for the entire semester (14 weeks). In the second class, they were assigned new seats halfway through the semester. In the third class, they were assigned new seats every 3½ weeks. The relationships among students were assessed at the beginning and at the end of the semester. Few relationships developed among the students in the class where seats were changed every 3½ weeks. In the other two classes, students in neighboring seats became acquainted in greater numbers than students in nonneighboring

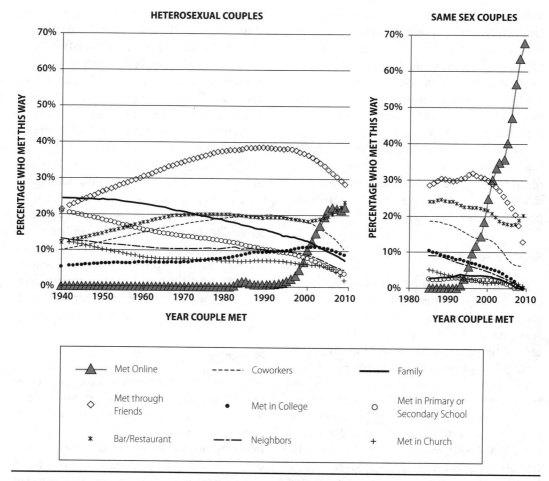

FIGURE 12.1 The Impact of the Internet on Where People Meet

A unique data set allows us a glimpse at how the Internet has affected where people meet. A survey of 2,462 heterosexual couples and 462 same-sex couples asked where they met and the year they met. The results are displayed above. Among heterosexual couples, meeting through friends has become less important since 1995; in 2010, about 20 percent met on the Internet. Among same-sex couples, there have been dramatic declines in the importance of all the traditional sources, with almost 70 percent of those meeting in 2010 reporting they met on the Internet.

Source: M. J. Rosenfeld & R. J. Thomas (2012). "Searching for a mate: The rise of the Internet as a social intermediary." *American Sociological Review,* 77: 523–547.

seats. Moreover, the relationships were closer in the class where seat assignments were not changed.

Similar positive associations between physical proximity and friendship have been found in a variety of natural settings, including dormitories (Priest & Sawyer, 1967), married student housing complexes (Festinger, Schachter, & Back, 1950), and business offices (Schutte & Light, 1978).

We are more likely to develop friendships with persons in close proximity because such relationships provide interpersonal rewards at the lowest cost. Interaction is easier with those who are close by. It costs less time and energy to interact with the

When we think about where people meet available partners, we often picture the singles bar. However, studies of heterosexual relationships have found that relatively few people met their partners at a bar. Much more common were meetings in classes, dorms, or workplaces. © Kzenon/Shutterstock

person sitting next to you than with someone on the other side of the room.

Familiarity

As time passes, people who take the same classes, live in the same apartment building, or do their laundry in the same place become familiar with each other. Having seen a person several times, sooner or later we will smile or nod. Repeated exposure to the same novel stimulus is sufficient to produce a positive attitude toward it; this is called the **mere exposure effect** (Zajonc, 1968). In other words, familiarity breeds liking, not contempt. This effect is highly general and has been demonstrated for a wide variety of stimuli—such as music, visual art, and comic strips—under many different conditions (Harrison, 1977).

Does mere exposure produce attraction? The answer appears to be yes. In one experiment, female undergraduates were asked to participate in an experiment on their sense of taste. They entered a series of booths in pairs and rated the taste of various liquids. The schedule was set up so that two participants shared the same booth either once, twice, five times, ten times, or not at all. At the end of the experiment, each woman rated how much she liked each of the other participants. As predicted, the more frequently a woman had been in the same booth with another participant, the higher the rating (Saegert, Swap, & Zajonc, 1973). Interestingly, the increase in liking as a function of frequency of exposure is greater for stimuli that are presented subliminally, of which the person is not consciously aware (Bornstein, 1992).

WHO IS DESIRABLE?

We come into contact with many potential partners, but contact by itself does not ensure the development of a relationship. Whether a relationship of some type actually develops between two persons depends on whether each is attracted to the other. Initial attraction is influenced by social norms, physical attractiveness, and processes of interpersonal exchange. If the attraction is mutual, the interaction that occurs is governed by scripts.

Social Norms

Each culture specifies the types of relationships that people may have. For each type, norms specify what kinds of people are allowed to have such a relationship. These norms tell us which persons are appropriate as friends, lovers, and mentors. In U.S. society, there is a **norm of homogamy**—a norm requiring that friends, lovers, and spouses be similar in age, race, religion, and socioeconomic status (Kerckhoff, 1974). Research shows that homogamy is characteristic of all types of social relationships from acquaintance to intimate (McPherson, Smith-Lovin, & Cook, 2001). Interviews with 832 students attending the same (all-White) high school obtained data on their romantic/sexual relationships (Bearman, Moody, & Stovel, 2004). The students' relationships were homophilous on IQ, family socioeconomic status (SES), getting drunk, sexual activity, and college plans.

A survey of 3,342 adults assessed the extent to which partners in relationships were similar on the following dimensions (Laumann et al., 1994): 75 to 83 percent were homophilous (similar) by age, 82 to 87 percent by education, 88 to 93 percent by race/ ethnicity, and 53 to 72 percent by religion. Differences on one or more of these dimensions make a person less appropriate

as an intimate partner and more appropriate for some other kind of relationship. Thus, a person who is much older but of the same social class and ethnicity may be appropriate as a mentor—someone who can provide advice about how to manage your career. Potential dates are single persons (of the opposite sex) who are of similar age, class, ethnicity, and religion. Same-sex couples are less likely to be homogeneous on race/ethnicity, age, and education, perhaps due to the limited availability of partners (Schwartz & Graf, 2007).

Norms that define appropriateness influence the development of relationships in several ways. First, each of us uses norms to monitor our own behavior. We hesitate to establish a relationship with someone who is defined by norms as an inappropriate partner. Thus, a low-status person is unlikely to approach a high-status person as a potential friend. For example, the law clerk who just joined a firm would not discuss his hobbies with the senior partner (unless she asked). Second, if one person attempts to initiate a relationship with someone who is defined by norms as inappropriate, the other person will probably refuse to reciprocate. If the clerk did launch into an extended description of the joys of restoring antique model trains, the senior partner would probably end the interaction. Third, even if both persons are willing to interact, third parties often enforce the norms that prohibit the relationship (Kerckhoff, 1974). Another member of the firm might later chide the clerk for presuming that the senior partner cared about his personal interests.

At the beginning of the twenty-first century, interracial relationships continue to be rare in the United States. A study of adolescent friendships found that "best friends" are typically of the same race/ethnicity, particularly among Whites (92 percent) and Blacks (85 percent), compared to Hispanics

According to the matching hypothesis, people seek partners whose level of social desirability is about equal to their own. We frequently encounter couples who are matched—that is, who are similar in age, race, ethnicity, social class, and physical attractiveness. © Cathy Yeulet/123rf

(51 percent) and Asians (48 percent) (Kao & Joyner, 2004). In 2010, only 9.5 percent of married couples were interracial; of these, 38 percent were White-Hispanic, 8 percent were Black-White, and the rest were White-other (U.S. Bureau of the Census, 2010). The norm of homogamy remains especially strong on this dimension (Blackwell & Lichter, 2004). Research on interracial romantic relationships found that non-White males reported more disapproval from their White female partners' family and friends than any other race/gender combination (Miller, Olson, & Fazio, 2004).

Physical Attractiveness

In addition to social norms that define who is appropriate, individuals also have personal preferences regarding desirability. Someone may be normatively appropriate but still not appeal to you. Physical attractiveness can have a significant impact on desirability.

Impact of Physical Attractiveness. A great deal of evidence shows that given a choice of more than one potential partner, individuals will prefer the one who is more physically attractive (Hendrick & Hendrick, 1992). A study of 752 first-year college students, for example, demonstrates that most individuals prefer more attractive persons as dates (Walster [Hatfield], Aronson, Abrahams, & Rottman, 1966). As part of the study, students were invited to attend a dance. Before the dance, each student's physical attractiveness was secretly rated by four people, and each student completed a questionnaire. Although the students were told they would be paired by the computer, in fact, men and women were paired randomly. At the dance, during the intermission, students filled out a questionnaire that measured their impressions of their dates.

This study tested the **matching hypothesis**—the idea that each of us looks for someone who is of approximately the same level of social desirability. The researchers predicted that the students whose dates matched their own level of attractiveness would like their dates most. Those whose dates were very different in attractiveness were expected to rate their dates as less desirable. Contrary to the hypothesis, in this situation, students preferred a more attractive date, regardless of their own attractiveness.

How can we explain the significance of attractiveness? One factor is simply esthetic; generally, we prefer what is beautiful. Although beauty is, to a degree, "in the eye of the beholder," cultural standards influence our esthetic judgments. A study of female facial beauty found substantial agreement among male college students about which features are attractive (Cunningham, 1986). These men rated such features as large eyes, small nose, and small chin as more attractive than small eyes, large nose, and large chin. What male features do women find attractive? Female college students rated men with large eyes, prominent cheekbones, and a large chin as more attractive (Cunningham, Barbee, & Pike, 1990). Research has also found a high level of agreement among men that certain female body shapes are more appealing than others (Wiggins, Wiggins, & Conger, 1968) and agreement among women about which male body shapes are attractive (Beck, Ward-Hull, & McLear, 1976).

A second factor is that we anticipate more rewards when we associate with attractive persons. A man accompanied by an extremely attractive woman receives more attention and prestige from other persons than if he is seen with an unattractive woman, and vice versa (Sigall & Landy, 1973).

The Attractiveness Stereotype. A third factor is the **attractiveness stereotype**— the belief that "what is beautiful is good" (Dion, Berscheid, & Walster [Hatfield], 1972). We assume that an attractive per-

son possesses other desirable qualities. Research consistently finds that we infer that physically attractive people possess more favorable personality traits and are more likely to experience successful outcomes in their personal and social lives (Berscheid & Reis, 1998; Lorenzo et al., 2010).

There are limits to the influence of this stereotype. A meta-analysis of more than 70 studies found that attractiveness has a moderate influence on judgments of social competence—how sensitive, kind, and interesting a person is (Eagly, Ashmore, Makhijani, & Longo, 1991). It has less influence on judgments of adjustment and intelligence, and no influence on judgments of integrity or concern for others. Also, the influence of attractiveness on judgments of intellectual competence is reduced when other information about the person's competence is available (Jackson, Hunter, & Hodge, 1995).

When we believe another person possesses certain qualities, those beliefs influence our behavior toward that person. Our actions may then lead him or her to behave in ways that are consistent with our beliefs (see Chap. 6). In one experiment, men were shown photographs of either an attractive or an unattractive woman. They were then asked to interact with that woman via intercom for 10 minutes. The woman was actually a student volunteer. Each conversation was tape-recorded and rated by judges. Women who were perceived as attractive by the men were rated as behaving in a more friendly, likable, and sociable way than women who were perceived as unattractive. This happened in part because the men gave the target person opportunities to act in ways that would confirm their expectations based on the attractiveness stereotype (Snyder et al., 1977). This is a good example of the self-fulfilling prophecy.

Judgments of attractiveness seem to be based on several dimensions. College students were asked to sort photographs of 95 female fashion models. Analyses suggested that both men and women distinguished three dimensions in their judgments—sexy, cute (youthful), and trendy (up to date in clothing and grooming) (Ashmore, Solomon, & Longo, 1996).

Each of us knows that physically attractive people may receive preferential treatment. As a result, we spend tremendous amounts of time and money trying to increase our own attractiveness to others. Men and women purchase clothing, jewelry, perfumes, colognes, and hair color products in an effort to enhance their physical attractiveness. Our choice of products reflects current standards of what looks good.

Increasingly, people are using cosmetic surgery to enhance their appearance. Plastic surgeons can lift your eyelids; pin your ears; fill your wrinkles; reshape your nose, jaw, or chin; enlarge your breasts, pectorals, or penis; and suck the fat from your abdomen, thighs, or ankles. In 2012, over 10 million cosmetic procedures were performed by board certified persons in the United States, 1.7 million of them involving surgery (American Society for Aesthetic Plastic Surgery, 2013). The vast majority are elective—that is, intended to enhance appearance, reflecting the impact of the attractiveness stereotype. Ninety percent of the procedures are performed on women, reflecting the greater importance of attractiveness to them. Critics point out that the procedures don't always work; they may result in misshapen features, serious scarring, or even death. This is another example of the downside of self-presentational concerns (see Box 4.5).

Not everyone prefers attractive persons. Many of us were taught—and some of us believe—that "beauty is only skin deep," and "you can't judge a book by its cover." What kinds of people are influenced by another's attractiveness, and what kinds of people "read the book" before making a judgment?

Research suggests that people who hold traditional attitudes toward men and women are those whose judgments are much more likely to be influenced by beauty (Touhey, 1979).

Evolutionary Perspective on Attractiveness. According to the evolutionary perspective, men and women have an evolved disposition to mate with healthy individuals so that they will produce healthy offspring, who will in turn successfully mate and pass on their genetic code. According to this view, facial and bodily physical attractiveness are markers for physical and hormonal health (Thornhill & Grammar, 1999). Thus, we prefer young, attractive partners because they have high reproductive potential.

Research based on this perspective argues that women and men face different adaptive problems in short-term (casual) mating compared to long-term mating and reproduction. These differences lead to different strategies or behaviors designed to solve these problems. In short-term mating, a woman may choose a partner who offers her immediate resources such as food or money (drinks, dinner?). In long-term mating, she will prefer a partner who appears willing and able to provide resources for the indefinite future (marriage?). A man may choose a sexually available woman for a short-term liaison and avoid such women when looking for a long-term mate. A study of mating strategies found that physical attractiveness and possession of resources were judged important in selecting a long-term mate, whereas sexual availability and giving gifts were judged more important in selecting a partner for a "one-night stand" (Schmitt & Buss, 1996). Moreover, both men and women are more selective when choosing a partner for a long-term relationship (Stewart, Stinnett, & Rosenfeld, 2000). It is not surprising, according to this perspective, that singles ads emphasize attractiveness and resources. It is also worth noting that mate-selection criteria do not vary much by age in the range from age 20 to age 60 (Buunk, Dijkstra, Fetchenhauer, & Kenrick, 2002).

Attractiveness Isn't Everything. Physical attractiveness may have a major influence on our judgments of others because it is readily observable. When we meet someone for the first time, one characteristic we can assess quickly is his or her attractiveness. If other relevant information is available, it might reduce or eliminate the impact of attractiveness on our judgments. In fact, an analysis of 70 studies found that when perceivers have other personal information about the target person, the effect of the attractiveness stereotype is smaller (Eagly et al., 1991).

Exchange Processes

How do we move from the stage of awareness of another person to the stage of contact? Recall that in our introduction, Dan noticed Mia at every lecture. Because she was young and not wearing a wedding ring, Dan hoped that she was available. She was certainly desirable—she was very pretty and seemed like a friendly person. What factors did Dan consider when deciding whether to initiate contact? One important factor in this decision is the availability and desirability of alternative relationships (Backman, 1990). Thus, before Dan chose to initiate contact with Mia, he probably considered whether there was anyone else who might be a better choice.

Choosing Friends. We can view each actual or potential relationship—whether involving a friend, coworker, roommate, or romance—as promising rewards but entailing costs. Rewards are the pleasures or gratifications we derive from a relationship.

These might include companionship, a gain in knowledge, enhanced self-esteem, satisfaction of emotional needs, or sexual gratification. Costs are the negative aspects of a relationship, such as time spent, physical or mental effort, embarrassment, anxiety, and money.

Exchange theory proposes that this is, in fact, the way people view their interactions (Blau, 1964; Homans, 1974). People evaluate interactions and relationships in terms of the rewards and costs that each is likely to entail. They calculate likely outcomes by subtracting the anticipated costs from the anticipated rewards. If the expected outcome is positive, people are inclined to initiate or maintain the relationship. If the expected outcome is negative, they are unlikely to initiate a new relationship or to stay in an ongoing relationship. Dan anticipated that a relationship with Mia would be rewarding; she would be fun to do things with, and others would be impressed that he was with such an attractive woman. At the same time, he anticipated that Mia would expect him to be committed to her and that he would have to spend time and money on her. He would also have less time to play pickup basketball.

What standards can we use to evaluate the outcomes of a relationship? Two standards have been proposed (Kelley & Thibaut, 1978; Thibaut & Kelley, 1959). One is the **comparison level** (CL), the level of outcomes expected based on the average of a person's experience in past relevant relationships. Each relationship is evaluated as to whether it is above or below that person's CL—that is, better or worse than the average of past relevant relationships. Relationships that fall above a person's CL are satisfying, whereas those that fall below it are unsatisfying.

If this were the only standard, we would always initiate relationships that appeared to promise outcomes better than those we already experienced and avoid relationships that appeared to promise poorer outcomes. Sometimes, however, we use a second standard. The **comparison level for alternatives** (CLalt) is the lowest level of outcomes a person will accept in light of the available alternatives. A person's CLalt varies depending on the outcomes that he or she believes can be obtained from the best of the available alternative relationships. The use of CLalt explains why we may sometimes turn down opportunities that appear promising or why we may remain in a relationship even though we feel that the other person is getting all the benefits.

Whether a person initiates a new relationship or not will depend on both the CL and the CLalt. An individual usually avoids relationships whose anticipated outcomes fall below the CL. If a potential relationship appears likely to yield outcomes above a person's CL, initiation will depend on whether the outcomes are expected to exceed the CLalt. Dan believed that a relationship with Mia would be very satisfying. He was seeing another woman, and that relationship was not gratifying. Thus, the potential relationship with Mia was above both CL and CLalt, leading Dan to initiate contact.

Whereas CL is an absolute, relatively unchanging standard, several factors influence a person's CLalt. These factors include the extent to which routine activities provide opportunities to meet people, the size of the pool of eligible persons, and one's skills in initiating relationships.

Making Contact. Once we decide to initiate interaction, the next step is to make contact. Sometimes we use technology, such as the telephone or e-mail. Often, we arrange to get physically close to the person. At parties and in bars, people often circulate, which brings them into physical proximity with many of the other guests.

Once in proximity, a stranger attracted to another person wants to communicate interest without making a commitment to interaction. In initial encounters, the problem can be resolved by using ambiguous cues. In opposite-sex encounters, the gender that has "more to lose" (the woman) will try to control the interaction; to do so, she will initially use nonverbal cues that the man may not consciously perceive (Grammar, Kruck, Juette, & Fink, 2000). Researchers observed 45 male-female pairs of strangers (aged 18 to 23) left alone in a waiting room. Questionnaires completed later were used to assess each participant's interest in the other person. Women interested in the man were more likely to display several cues, including short glances, coy smiles, and primping (adjusting clothing without a visible reason). Men interested in the woman were more likely to speak to her in the first 3 minutes (a direct cue); if she responded with head nods, his rate of speech increased. This pattern is probably repeated many times every day in airplanes, on trains and buses, and in classes and waiting rooms (see Box 12.1).

Scripts. The development of relationships is influenced by an event schema or script. A script specifies (1) the definition of the situation (a hook-up, date, or job interview), (2) the identities of the social actors involved, and (3) the range and sequence of permissible behaviors (see Chap. 6). Recall our discussion of symbolic interaction theory in Chapter 1.

The initiation of a relationship requires an opening line. Often, it is about some feature of the situation. At the beginning of this chapter, Dan initiated the conversation by commenting that Mia never missed the class. Two people waiting to participate in a psychology experiment may begin talking by speculating about the purpose of the experiment. The weather is a widely used

BOX 12.1 Research Update: Flirting

A distinctive class of communicative behaviors is flirting, or courtship signaling (Birdwhistell, 1970). The term refers to a class of nonverbal behaviors exhibited by a man/woman that serves to attract the attention and elicit the approach of another man/woman (after Moore, 1985). A catalog of movements used by adult women to attract men has been developed by Moore (1985), and a catalog of movements used by men to attract women has been developed by Renninger, Wade, and Grammar (2004); both are based on naturalistic observation. Traditional flirting includes gestures such as hair tossing, licking lips, or smiling, primping, touching hair or clothing, eye movements such as arching an eyebrow or direct glance, bodily movements that mirror another person's movement, or the wearing of revealing or seductive clothing (Whitty, 2004).

Renninger and colleagues observed men in bars; each man was observed for 30 minutes, and each occurrence of 14 nonverbal behaviors that might attract a woman's attention was recorded. The average interobserver reliability was 0.84. The outcome, making contact, was defined as 1 minute or more of continual conversation with a female. The results showed that men who engaged in short, direct glances at the woman, who used more space with their bodily position and movements, used fewer closed-body movements (for example, arms folded), and engaged in more nonreciprocated touching of other men were more likely to make contact.

While often it is the man who physically approaches and initiates verbal interaction, research indicates that women take the initiative, using nonverbal signals, in encouraging the man to initiate contact. Men (and women) are reluctant to approach another person without invitation because of the possibility of rejection. Evolutionary analyses of mating point out that since women make the greater investment in offspring, they are the choosers. Thus, women selectively encourage some men to approach but not others.

Women are said to be looking for a high-status male. The male behaviors identified by Renninger and colleagues as successful in producing contact, such as nonreciprocated touching and use of greater space, are thought to be behaviors that indicate high status.

Moore (1985) began her research by observing 200 White women, judged to be aged 18 to 35, and recording their nonverbal behavior. A woman not accompanied by a man was selected

topic for openings. Following a first contact or meeting, we may check out the other person online, at Facebook, LinkedIn, or similar sites.

Once initiated, scripts specify the permissible next steps. American society—or at least the subculture of college students—is characterized by a specific script for "first dates" (Rose & Frieze, 1993). When asked to describe "actions that a woman (man) would typically take" on a first date, both men and women identified a core action sequence: dress, be nervous, pick up date, leave (meeting place), confirm plans, get to know, evaluate, talk, laugh, joke, eat, attempt to make out/accept or reject, take date home, kiss, go home. In general, both men and women ascribed a proactive/aggressive role to the man and a reactive role to the woman. Recent research asked undergraduates to describe a "typical date"; in general, the descriptions were very similar to those reported 15 years earlier, indicating the persistence of the traditional, gendered script (Bartoli & Clark, 2006). Research has examined differences between Black and White undergraduates in the emphasis they place on certain aspects of dating (Jackson at random and observed for at least 30 minutes in settings where there were at least 20 men and women present. Observers recorded every behavior of the focal subject and its consequences. Flirting, or a nonverbal solicitation behavior, was defined as a behavior that resulted in a man's attention within 15 seconds. Subsequent research (Moore & Butler, 1989) describes behaviors that attract male attention and those that maintain his attention after interaction begins. Male attention is likely to follow a room-encompassing glance, a smile while looking at him, patting or smoothing the hair, the "lip lick," or a head toss. Once verbal interaction begins, male attention is maintained by frequent head nods while he talks, leaning close to him, and touching or brushing part of the body against him.

Moore and Renninger, and others, provide contextual evidence for the assertion that these behaviors are courtship signals. If these behaviors are intended to attract male/female attention, we should observe them in contexts where such solicitations are likely, such as bars, but not in settings where no members of the other gender are present. Moore studied 10 women in each of four social settings: singles bar, university snack bar, university library, and women's center meeting. Again, focal sampling was employed; a woman was observed only if at least 25 people were present and she was not accompanied by a man. The display of courtship signals was clearly context-specific. Women were much more likely to engage in these behaviors in the singles bar, and least likely to engage in them at women's center meetings.

Once a couple begins to interact, flirting is reciprocal (Back et al., 2011). Three-minute interactions were videotaped in a speed-dating setting. Raters viewed the tapes and rated how much each person was flirting every 30 seconds. Flirting by one person was highly correlated with being flirted at by the other.

Most research on flirting has been done in romantic settings where the motivation is to meet someone. However, these behaviors occur in other settings, and may reflect other motivations (Henningsen et al., 2008). One study assessed motives for flirting in samples of undergraduates (average age 20) and full-time workers (average age 33.5). Students viewed flirting as motivated by sexual interest or the desire to advance a relationship. Workers were more likely to view flirting as intended to achieve an instrumental goal, for example, get a coworker to do a favor or make a sale.

et al., 2011). African Americans place more importance on giving and receiving gifts, and meeting members of the date's family. Whites place greater emphasis on hanging out with the date's friends.

Actual first dates, of course, are characterized by departures from the script. A study of college students focused on whether the roles of men and women are changing (Lottes, 1993). Both men and women were asked about the extent to which they had experienced the woman's initiating a date, initiating sexual intimacy, and paying for a date. Increasing propor-

tions of women are engaging in these traditionally male activities.

Since 2000, the "hook-up" has become increasingly common on college campuses, and some observers suggest it has replaced dating. Research suggests that hook-ups are very similar to dates. Men still initiate contact and direct activities, couples still talk and evaluate possible relationships/activities, leave the meeting place, and eventually go home (Eaton & Rose, 2011). The difference is that dates are perceived as the first stage in the development of a longer-term relationship, whereas the hook-up is not.

In the traditional dating script, males paid for the activity, but young men and women report that the female is increasingly paying, at least some of the time. © gchutka/iStock

How do we learn these scripts, and the departures from them? One source is the mass media. Both men and women learn about relationships and how to handle them from popular magazines. A study of magazines oriented toward women (*Cosmopolitan*, *Glamour*, and *Self*) and men (*Playboy*, *Penthouse*, and *GQ*) found that they portrayed relationships in similar terms (Duran & Prusank, 1997). The dominant focus in both types of magazines was sexual relationships. In women's magazines (January 1990 to December 1991), the themes were (1) women are less skilled at and more anxious about sex and (2) sex is enjoyed most in caring relationships. In men's magazines during the same period, the themes were (1) men are under attack in sexual relationships and (2) men have natural virility and strong sexual appetites. Also, the articles in women's magazines portrayed men as incompetent about relationships.

THE DETERMINANTS OF LIKING

Once two people make contact and begin to interact, several factors will determine the extent to which each person will like the other. Three of these factors are considered in this section: similarity, shared activities, and reciprocal liking.

Similarity

How important is similarity? Do "birds of a feather flock together"? Or do "opposites attract"? These two aphorisms about the determinants of liking are inconsistent and provide opposing predictions. A good deal of research has been devoted to finding out which one is more accurate. The evidence indicates that birds of a feather do flock together—that is, we are attracted to people who are similar to ourselves (Markey & Markey, 2007). Probably the most important kind of similarity is **attitudinal similarity**—the sharing of beliefs, opinions, likes, and dislikes.

Attitudinal Similarity. A widely employed technique for studying attitudinal similarity is the attraction-to-a-stranger paradigm, initially developed by Byrne (1961b). Potential participants fill out an attitude questionnaire that measures their beliefs about various topics, such as life on a college campus. Later, participants receive information about a stranger as part of a seemingly unrelated study. The information they receive describes the stranger's personality or social background and may include a photograph. They also are given a copy of the same questionnaire they completed earlier, ostensibly filled out by the stranger. In fact, the stranger's questionnaire is completed by the experimenter, who systematically varies the degree to which the stranger's supposed responses match the participant's responses. After seeing the stranger's questionnaire, the participants are asked how much they like or dislike the stranger and how much they would enjoy working with that person.

In most cases, the participant's attraction to the stranger is positively associated with the percentage of attitude statements by the stranger that agree with the participant's own attitudes (Byrne & Nelson, 1965; Gonzales, Davis, Loney, Lukens, & Junghans, 1983). We rarely agree with our friends about everything; what matters is that we agree on a high proportion of issues. This relationship between similarity of attitudes and liking is very general; it has been replicated in studies using both men and women as participants and strangers under a variety of conditions (Berscheid & Walster [Hatfield], 1978).

In the attraction-to-a-stranger paradigm, the participant forms an impression of a stranger without any interaction. This allows researchers to determine the precise relationship between similarity and liking. But what do you think the relationship would be if two people were allowed to interact? Would similarity have as strong an effect?

A study attempting to answer this question arranged dates for 44 couples (Byrne, Ervin, & Lamberth, 1970). Researchers distributed a 50-item questionnaire measuring attitudes and personality to a large sample of undergraduates. From these questionnaires, they selected 24 male-female couples whose answers were very similar (66 to 74 percent identical) and 20 couples whose answers were not similar (24 to 40 percent identical). Each couple was introduced, told they had been matched by a computer, and asked to spend the next 30 minutes together at the student union; they were even offered free sodas. The experimenter rated each participant's attractive-

ness before he or she left on the date. When they returned, the couple rated each other's sexual attractiveness, desirability as a date, and desirability as a marriage partner, and indicated how much they liked each other. The experimenter also recorded the physical distance between the two as they stood in front of his desk.

The results of this experiment showed that both attitudinal similarity and physical attractiveness influenced liking. Partners who were attractive and who held highly similar attitudes were rated as more likable. Moreover, similar partners were rated as more intelligent and more desirable as a date and marriage partner. The couples high in similarity stood closer together after their date than the couples low in similarity—another indication that similarity creates liking.

At the end of the semester, 74 of the 88 participants in this study were contacted and asked whether they (1) could remember their date's name, (2) had talked to their date since their first meeting, (3) had dated their partner, or (4) wanted to date their partner. Participants in the high attractiveness/high similarity condition were more likely to remember their partner's name, to report having talked to their partner, and to report wanting to date their partner than those in the low attractiveness/low similarity condition.

The story of Dan and Mia at the beginning of this chapter illustrates the importance of similarity in the early stages of a relationship. After their initial meeting, they discovered they had several things in common. They were from the same city. They had chosen the same major and held similar beliefs about their field and about how useful a bachelor's degree would be in that field. Each also found the other attractive; like the participants in the high attraction/high similarity condition, Dan and Mia continued to talk after their first meeting.

Why Is Similarity Important? Why does attitudinal similarity produce liking? One reason is the desire for consistency between our attitudes and perceptions. The other reason focuses on our preference for rewarding experiences.

Most people desire cognitive consistency—consistency between attitudes and perceptions of whom and what we like and dislike. If you have positive attitudes toward certain objects and discover that another person has favorable attitudes toward the same objects, your cognitions will be consistent if you like that person (Newcomb, 1971). When Dan discovered that Mia had a positive attitude toward his major, his desire for consistency produced a positive attitude toward Mia (see Balance Theory, Chap. 7). Our desire for consistency attracts us to persons who hold the same attitudes toward important objects.

Another reason we like persons with attitudes similar to our own is because our interaction with them provides three kinds of reinforcement. First, interacting with persons who share similar attitudes usually leads to positive outcomes (Lott & Lott, 1974). At the beginning of this chapter, Dan anticipated that he and Mia would get along well because they shared similar likes and dislikes.

Second, similarity validates our own view of the world. We all want to evaluate and verify our attitudes and beliefs against some standard. Sometimes, physical reality provides objective criteria for our beliefs. But often there is no physical standard, and so we must compare our attitudes with those of others (Festinger, 1954). Persons who hold similar attitudes provide us with support for our own opinions, which allows us to deal with the world more confidently (Byrne, 1971). Such support is particularly important in areas, such as political attitudes, where we realize that others hold attitudes dissimilar to our own (Rosenbaum, 1986).

Research indicates that similarity in mood is also an important influence on attraction. In the attraction-to-a-stranger paradigm, nondepressed participants prefer nondepressed strangers (Rosenblatt & Greenberg, 1988). In an experiment, male and female students interacted with a depressed or nondepressed person of the same sex. People in homogeneous pairs (both depressed or both nondepressed) were more satisfied with the interaction than people in mixed pairs (Locke & Horowitz, 1990). In another study, researchers measured the depression levels of people and of their best friends. Depressed people had best friends who were also depressed (Rosenblatt & Greenberg, 1991).

Third, we like others who share similar attitudes because we expect that they will like us. In one experiment, college students were given information about a stranger's attitudes and the stranger's evaluation of them (Condon & Crano, 1988). The participants' perceptions of the stranger's similarity to and evaluation of them were also assessed. The students were attracted to strangers whom they perceived as evaluating them positively, and that accounted for the influence of similar attitudes.

Shared Activities

As people interact, they share activities. Recall that after Mia and Dan met, they began to sit together in class and to discuss course work. When the professor announced the first exam, Dan invited Mia to study for it with him. Mia's roommate was also in the class; the three of them reviewed the material together the night before the exam. Mia and Dan both got As on the exam, and each felt that studying together helped. The next week, they went to a movie together. Several days later, she invited Dan to a party.

Shared activities provide opportunities for each person to experience reinforcement. Some of these reinforcements come from the other person; Mia finds Dan's interest in her very reinforcing. Often, the other person is associated with a positive experience, which leads us to like the other person (Byrne & Clore, 1970). Getting an A on the examination was a very positive experience for both Dan and Mia. The association of the other person with that experience led to increased liking for the other.

Thus, as a relationship develops, the sharing of activities contributes to increased liking. This was shown in a study in which pairs of friends of the same sex both filled out attitude questionnaires and listed their preferences for various activities (Werner & Parmelee, 1979). The duration of the friendships averaged 5 years. The results of the study showed similarity between friends in both activity preferences and attitudes. A study of romantic relationships found that sharing of tasks or activities was a strong predictor of liking (Stafford & Canary, 1991). Thus, participation in mutually satisfying activities is a strong influence on the development and maintenance of relationships. The results of a series of five studies indicate that participation in novel and arousing activities rather than mundane and trivial pursuits is associated with relationship quality (Aron, Norman, Aron, McKenna, & Heyman, 2000). As Dan and Mia got to know each other, their shared experiences—studying, seeing movies, going to parties—became the basis for their relationship, supplementing the effect of similar attitudes.

If shared activities are important, what happens when a couple does not do things together? This is not an idle question; many students and working adults are separated from their partner by distance, and may see each other (share activities) only occasionally. What about secret relationships, where contact is limited by the need to prevent others from learning about it? Some

research suggests that secrecy will be associated with greater attraction (Wegner, Lane, & Dimitri, 1994). But if shared activities are important, absence will prevent the development of shared reinforcements and may increase costs, such as a sense of burden (a sense that the relationship is difficult to coordinate, requires a great deal of work, energy). A series of studies found that participants in secret relationships reported greater burden, less satisfaction, and lower relationship quality than persons in open ones (Foster & Campbell, 2005). People in secret relationships also reported significantly less love for their partner. These results strengthen the conclusion that shared activities make an important difference.

Reciprocal Liking

One of the most consistent research findings is the strong positive relationship between our liking someone and the perception that the other person will like us in return (Backman, 1990). In most relationships, we expect reciprocity of attraction; the greater the liking of one person for the other, the greater the other person's liking will be in return. But will the degree of reciprocity increase over time as partners have greater opportunities to interact? To answer this question, one study obtained liking ratings from 48 persons (32 men and 16 women) who had been acquainted for 1, 2, 4, 6, or 8 weeks (Kenney & La Voie, 1982). The results showed a positive correlation between each person's liking rating and the other's, and the reciprocity of attraction increased somewhat with the duration of the acquaintance. Some participants in this study were roommates rather than friends; they would be expected to like each other due to the proximity effect. When roommate pairs were eliminated from the results, the correlation between liking ratings increased substantially.

BOX 12.2 Online Relationships: Are They Different?

Most of the literature reviewed so far in this chapter is based on or assumes face-to-face interaction. Internet technologies, especially instant messaging and chat rooms, which allow synchronous interaction, create the possibility of developing or sustaining intimate relationships without meeting face-to-face. How do the processes involved differ?

We discussed self-presentation online in Chapter 4. In face-to-face interaction, potential partners have access to a broad array of nonverbal cues in addition to verbal messages in forming an impression. Online, potential partners only have access to messages crafted by the person. Participants realize that self-presentation in the making contact stage is critical, because potential partners will use it to decide whether to explore possible relationships. So, in crafting a self-presentation, the person wants to emphasize positive characteristics; at the same time, if there is a possibility or hope of meeting, the presentation must be credible, if not authentic (Ellison, Heino, & Gibbs, 2006). Also, as in offline relationships, accurate self-disclosure is related to the development of intimacy, increasing motivation to be honest.

Research indicates that some online daters engage in misrepresentation. In an online survey of 6,581 Canadian users of such services, more than 25 percent reported misrepresenting themselves online; the most common areas were age (14 percent), marital status (10 percent), and appearance (10 percent) (Brym & Lenton, 2001). Ellison and colleagues (2006) interviewed 34 participants in Connect.com; half were male, most were in their 30s or 40s. They found that because participants wanted to create a positive impression, some described online a future, potential self, rather than the (current) self; they did not perceive this as misrepresentation. Another source of misrepresentation is limited self-awareness; as we saw earlier, we do not necessarily see ourselves as others see us.

Another study focused on accuracy of profiles posted on online dating sites. Researchers recruited subscribers to these sites; the sample was 50 percent male, and many participants were in their 20s. Participants were given a printed copy of their profile and asked to rate the accuracy of 15 informational items and of their photo. Upon completion of the ratings, the height and weight of the participant were measured, and age listed

THE GROWTH OF RELATIONSHIPS

We have traced the development of relationships from the stage of zero contact through awareness (who is available) and surface contact (who is desirable) to mutuality (liking). At the beginning of this chapter, Dan and Mia met, discovered that they had similar attitudes and interests, and shared pleasant experiences, such as doing well on an examination, going to a movie, and later, going to a party.

Many of our relationships remain at the "minor" level of mutuality. We have numerous acquaintances, neighbors, and coworkers whom we like and interact with regularly but to whom we do not feel especially close. A few of our relationships grow closer; they proceed through "moderate" to "major" mutuality. Three aspects of this continued growth of relationships are examined in this section: self-disclosure, trust, and interdependence. As the degree of mutuality increases between friends, roommates, and coworkers, self-disclosure, trust, and interdependence also will increase.

Self-Disclosure

Recall that when Dan and Mia returned from the party, Mia told Dan that her roommate's parents had just separated and that on the profile was compared with age on the driver's license. Differences were very common, and usually small. Men were more likely to lie about their height, women to lie about their weight; the more the person deviated from the average, the bigger the lie. Overall, the participants rated their profile photos as least accurate, and their reported relationship status as most accurate (Toma, Hancock, & Ellison, 2008).

Recognizing that others are motivated to present a positive image and may misrepresent themselves, participants in online dating carefully attend to subtle cues in others' messages. They scrutinize the writing for spelling or grammatical mistakes, the style of the writing, and descriptors of the person. The inclusion/exclusion of sexual language is noted. Other aspects, such as user name, service provider, and time of day the message was sent, may influence inferences by the recipient.

Gibbs, Ellison, and Heino (2006) conducted an online survey of members of Match.com; 56 percent of the respondents were female, 93 percent were White, and many were in their 40s. Participants adapt their behavior/responses to the verbal and linguistic cues in messages they receive. The survey contained a three-item measure of relational goals: the importance of long-term dating, of meeting a special person, and of finding a life/marital partner. Those who rated these goals as more important reported that they were more honest and intentional in their online self-disclosures.

We noted earlier that the inclusion or exclusion of sexual language is considered significant by recipients of messages. Talk about sex can be sexually arousing, providing one motive for its inclusion. Expressions by another of sexual desire for you may give your self-esteem a boost. Also, if one's relational goal is a relationship that involves sexual intimacy, that needs to be communicated to potential partners. On the other hand, others may be turned off by direct, explicit statements of sexual interest. A study of 30-minute conversations from English and Spanish chat rooms examined the conversational negotiation of sexuality. Participants often embedded sexual content in a "play" frame, characterized by the use of emoticons and acronyms conveying laughter and joking, using verbal reproductions of humorous or childish pronunciations of sexual terms, and the taking on of alternative roles via humorous, or subtly sexual screen names. These techniques balance the inclusion of sexual content and adherence to constraints on public sex talk (del-Teso-Craviotto, 2006).

her roommate was very depressed. Mia said that she didn't know how to help her roommate—that she felt unable to deal with the situation. At this point, Mia was engaging in self-disclosure—the act of revealing personal information about oneself to another person. Self-disclosure usually increases over time in a relationship. Initially, people reveal things about themselves that are not especially intimate and that they believe the other will readily accept. Over time, they disclose increasingly intimate details about their beliefs or behavior, including information they are less certain the other will accept (Backman, 1990).

Self-disclosure increases as a relationship grows. In one study, same-sex pairs of previously unacquainted college students were brought into a laboratory setting and asked to get acquainted (Davis, 1976). They were given a list of 72 topics. Each topic had been rated earlier by other students on a scale of intimacy from 1 to 11. The participants were asked to select topics from this list and to take turns talking about each topic for at least 1 minute while their partner remained silent. The interaction continued until each partner had spoken on 12 of the 72 topics. The results showed that the intimacy of the topic selected increased steadily from the first to the twelfth topic chosen. The average intimacy of topics discussed by each couple increased from 3.9 to 5.4 over the 12 disclosures. Research also indicates that greater self-disclosure during a 10-minute conversation was associated with an increase in positive affect—happiness, excitement—and attraction to the partner (Vittengl & Holt, 2000).

When Mia told Dan about the situation with her roommate, Dan replied that he knew how she felt, because his older brother had just separated from his wife. This exchange reflects reciprocity in self-disclosure; as one person reveals an intimate detail, the other person usually discloses information at about the same level of intimacy (Altman & Taylor, 1973). In the Davis (1976) study, each participant selected a topic at the same level of intimacy as the preceding one or at the next level of intimacy. However, reciprocity decreases as a relationship develops. In another study, a researcher recruited students to be participants and asked each to bring an acquaintance, a friend, or a best friend to the laboratory (Won-Doornink, 1985). Each dyad was given a list of topics that varied in degree of intimacy. Each was instructed to take at least four turns choosing and discussing a topic. Each conversation was tape-recorded and later analyzed for evidence of reciprocity. The association between the stage of the relationship and the reciprocity of intimate disclosures was curvilinear—that is, there was greater reciprocity of intimate disclosures between friends than between acquaintances but less reciprocity between best friends than among friends (see Figure 12.2).

Not all people divulge increasingly personal information as you get to know them. You have probably known people who were very open—who readily disclosed information about themselves—and others who said little about themselves. In this regard, we often think of men as less likely to discuss their feelings than women. However,

research has shown that self-disclosure depends not only on gender but also on the nature of the relationship. In casual relationships (with men or women), men are less likely to disclose personal information than women (Reis, Senchak, & Solomon, 1985). In dating couples, the amount of disclosure is related more to gender role orientation than to gender. Men and women with traditional gender role orientations disclose less to their partners than those with egalitarian gender role orientations (Rubin, Hill, Peplau, & Dunkel-Scheker, 1980). Traditional gender roles are more segregated, with each person responsible for certain tasks, whereas egalitarian orientations emphasize sharing. An emphasis on joint activity leads to greater self-disclosure. In intimate heterosexual relationships, men and women do not differ in the degree of self-disclosure (Hatfield, 1982; Mitchell et al., 2008).

A study of self-disclosure by young adults inquired about the extent to which each had disclosed in a variety of domains, including sexual activities, shameful events, personal health, and feelings and traumas. Generally, there were no differences between men and women. African-American and young men were significantly less likely to disclose, but analyses suggested this was related to low income rather than to ethnicity and gender (Consedine, Sabag-Cohen, & Krivoshekova, 2007).

The work discussed so far is concerned with the intimacy of self-disclosure. But self-disclosure is a complex phenomenon and has several characteristics including content (information about self or about the relationship), amount, and emotional tone (Bradford, Feeney, & Campbell, 2002). Using diaries, researchers gathered data on 1,908 conversations lasting more than 10 minutes from both members of the couple. The results indicated that disclosures could be scored on these dimensions and that there were differences in intimacy and

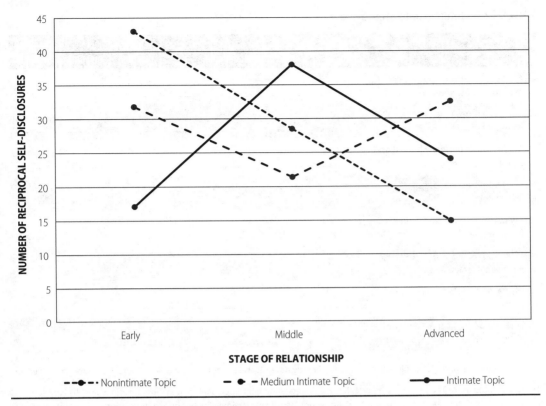

FIGURE 12.2 The Relationship Between Reciprocity and Intimacy

Reciprocity—picking a topic of conversation that is as intimate as the last topic introduced by your partner—is the process by which relationships become more intimate. The extent of reciprocity depends on the intimacy of the topic and the stage of the relationship. Students talked with an acquaintance (early stage), friend (middle stage), or best friend (advanced stage). With topics that were not intimate (such as the weather), reciprocity declined steadily as the stage increased. With intimate topics, in contrast, reciprocity was greatest at the middle stage, less at the advanced stage, and least at the early stage of a relationship.

Source: Adapted from Won-Doornink, 1985, Figure 4.

amount of disclosure related to the partner's attachment style.

Trust

Why did Dan confide in Mia that his brother had just left his wife? Perhaps he was offering reciprocity in self-disclosure. Because Mia had confided in Dan, she expected him to reciprocate. But had he been suspicious of Mia's motives, he might not have. This suggests the importance of trust in the development of a relationship.

When we **trust** someone, we believe that person is both honest and benevolent (Larzelere & Huston, 1980). We believe that the person tells us the truth—or at least does not lie to us—and that his or her intentions toward us are positive. One measure of interpersonal trust is the interpersonal trust scale reproduced in Table 12.1. The questions focus on whether the other person is selfish, honest, sincere, fair, or considerate. We are more likely to disclose personal information to someone we trust. How much do you trust your partner? Answer the

TABLE 12.1 Interpersonal Trust Scale

	STRONGLY AGREE	AGREE	SLIGHTLY AGREE	?	SLIGHTLY DISAGREE	DISAGREE	STRONGLY DISAGREE
1. My partner is primarily interested in his or her own welfare.	___	___	___	___	___	___	___
2. There are times when my partner cannot be trusted.	___	___	___	___	___	___	___
3. My partner is perfectly honest and truthful with me.	___	___	___	___	___	___	___
4. I feel I can trust my partner completely.	___	___	___	___	___	___	___
5. My partner is truly sincere in his or her promises.	___	___	___	___	___	___	___
6. I feel my partner does not show me enough consideration.	___	___	___	___	___	___	___
7. My partner treats me fairly and justly.	___	___	___	___	___	___	___
8. I feel my partner can be counted on to help me.	___	___	___	___	___	___	___

Note: For items 1, 2, and 6, Strongly Agree 1, Agree 2, Slightly Agree 3, and so on. For items 3, 4, 5, 7, and 8, the scoring is reversed.

Source: Adapted from "The Dyadic Trust Scale: Toward Understanding Interpersonal Trust in Close Relationships," by Larzelere and Huston, *Journal of Marriage and the Family,* 42(3). Copyright 1980 by the National Council on Family Relations, 3989 Central Ave. NE, Suite 550, Minneapolis, MN 55421. Reprinted by permission.

questions on the scale and determine your score. Higher scores indicate greater trust.

To study the relationship between trust and self-disclosure, researchers recruited men and women from university classes, from a list of people who had recently obtained marriage licenses, and by calling persons randomly selected from the telephone directory. Each person was asked to complete a questionnaire concerning his or her spouse or current or most recent date. The survey included the scale in Table 12.1. Researchers averaged the trust scores for seven types of relationships, as shown in Figure 12.3. Note that as the relationship becomes more exclusive, trust scores increase significantly. Is there a relationship between trust and self-disclosure?

Each person was also asked how much he or she had disclosed to the partner in each of six areas—religion, family, emotions, relationships with others, school or work, and marriage. Trust scores were positively correlated with self-disclosure—that is, the more the person trusted the partner, the greater the degree of self-disclosure.

Other research on interpersonal trust suggests that in addition to honesty and benevolence, reliability is an important aspect of trust. We are more likely to trust someone who we feel is reliable—on whom we can count (Johnson-George & Swap, 1982)—and predictable (Rempel, Holmes, & Zanna, 1985).

Many couples today are involved in long-distance relationships; they are com-

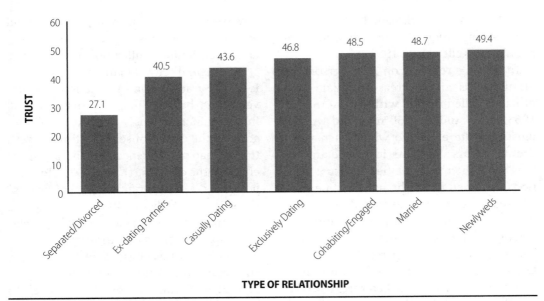

FIGURE 12.3 Average Interpersonal Trust Scores for Seven Types of Heterosexual Relationships

Trust involves two components: the belief that a person is honest and that his or her intentions are benevolent. More than 300 persons completed the interpersonal trust scale (see Table 12.1) for their current or most recent heterosexual partner. Results showed a strong relationship between the degree of intimacy in a relationship and the degree of trust.

Source: Adapted from "The Dyadic Trust Scale: Toward Understanding Interpersonal Trust in Close Relationships," by Larzelere and Huston, *Journal of Marriage and the Family,* 42(3). Copyright 1980 by the National Council on Family Relations, 3989 Central Ave. NE, Suite 550, Minneapolis, MN, 55421. Reprinted by permission.

mitted to each other but do not live in the same city or state or even country. A longitudinal study of student couples who were exclusively dating compared couples in same-city and long-distance relationships (Cameron & Ross, 2007). Researchers reasoned that relational security, a sense of trust and faith in the partner, would be especially important in the survival of long-distance relationships. High relational security among both men and women predicted stability of all relationships one year later. Long-distance relationships were significantly more likely to break up; long-distance relationships in which the man reported lower relational security and higher negative affect (low self-esteem, optimism) at Time 1 were more likely to break up.

Interdependence

Earlier in this chapter, we noted that people evaluate potential and actual relationships in terms of the outcomes (rewards minus costs) they expect to receive. Dan initiated contact with Mia because he anticipated that he would experience positive outcomes. Mia encouraged the development of a relationship because she, also, expected the rewards to exceed the costs. As their relationship developed, each discovered that the relationship was rewarding. Consequently, they increased the time and energy devoted to their relationship and decreased their involvement in alternative relationships. As their relationship became increasingly mutual, Mia and Dan became increasingly dependent on each other for various rewards (Backman, 1990). The result is strong, frequent, and diverse interdependence (Kelley et al., 1983).

Increasing reliance on one person for gratifications and decreasing reliance on others is called **dyadic withdrawal** (Slater, 1963). One study of 750 men and women illustrates the extent to which such withdrawal occurs. Students identified the intensity of their current heterosexual relationships, then listed the names of persons whose opinions they considered important. They also indicated how important each person's opinions were and how much they had disclosed to that person (Johnson & Leslie, 1982). As predicted, the more intimate his or her current heterosexual relationship, the smaller the number of friends listed by the respondent; there was no difference in the number of relatives listed. Furthermore, as the degree of involvement increased, the proportion of mutual friends of the couple also increased (Milardo, 1982). Other studies have found that as heterosexual relationships become more intimate, each partner spends less time interacting with friends, whereas interaction with relatives may increase (Surra, 1990).

Interdependence evolves out of the process of negotiation (Backman, 1990). Each person offers various potential rewards to the partner; the partner accepts some and rejects others. As the relationship develops, the exchanges stabilize. Shared activities are an important potential source of rewards. Each person has activity preferences. As the relationship develops, the couple must blend their separate preferences into joint activities. A study of dating couples found that men liked sex, games, and sports better than women, whereas women preferred companionship, entertainment, and cultural activities (Surra & Longstreth, 1990). Some couples achieved a blend by taking turns, alternately engaging in activities preferred by each. Others cooperated, engaging in activities they both liked, such as preparing food and running errands. Some couples experienced continuing conflict over what to do.

A potential reward in many relationships is sexual gratification. As relationships develop and become more mutual, physical intimacy increases as well. The couple negotiates the extent of sexual intimacy, with the woman's preferences having a greater effect on the outcome (Lear, 1997). How important is sexual gratification in dating relationships? A study of 149 couples assessed the importance of various rewards in relationships of increasing intimacy (preferred date, going steady, engaged, living together, and married). Among intimate couples, sexual gratification was much more likely to be cited as a major basis for the relationship (Centers, 1975). Other surveys indicate that the more emotionally intimate a couple is, the more likely they are to engage in sexual intimacy (Christopher & Roosa, 1991).

LOVE AND LOVING

It is fair to say that what we feel for our friends, roommates, coworkers, and some of the people we date is attraction. But is that all we feel? Occasionally, at least, we experience something more intense than a positive attitude toward others. Sometimes we feel, and even say, "I love you."

How does loving differ from liking? Much of the research in social psychology on attraction or liking is summarized earlier in this chapter. By contrast, there has been less research on love. Three views of love are considered in this section: the distinction between liking and loving, passionate love, and romantic love.

Liking versus Loving

One of the first empirical studies of love distinguished between liking and loving

(Rubin, 1970). Love is more than intense liking; it is the attachment to and caring about another person (Rubin, 1974). Attachment involves a powerful desire to be with and be cared about by another person. Caring involves making the satisfaction of another person's needs as significant as the satisfaction of your own.

Based on this distinction, Rubin developed scales to measure both liking and love. The liking scale evaluates one's dating partner, lover, or spouse on various dimensions, including adjustment, maturity, responsibility, and likability. The love scale measures attachment to and caring for one's partner, and intimacy (self-disclosure). These scales were completed by each member of 182 dating couples, both for her or his partner and best friend of the same sex (Rubin, 1970). The results showed a high degree of internal consistency within each scale and a low correlation between scales. Thus, the two scales do measure different things.

If the distinction between liking and loving is valid, how do you think you would rate a dating partner and your best friend on these scales? Rubin predicted high scores on both liking and love scales for the dating partner, lover, or spouse, and a high liking score but lower love score for the (platonic) friend. The average scores of the 182 couples confirmed these predictions. Research work by Davis (1985) also distinguishes between friendship and love. Friendship involves several qualities, including trust, understanding, and mutual assistance. Love involves all of these plus caring (giving the utmost to and being an advocate for the other) and passion (obsessive thought, sexual desire).

Passionate Love

Love certainly involves attachment and caring. But is that all? What about the agony of jealousy and the ecstasy of being loved by another person? An alternative view of love emphasizes emotions such as these. It focuses on **passionate love**—a state of intense physiological arousal and intense longing for union with another (Hatfield & Walster, 1978).

Cognitive and emotional factors interact to produce passionate love. Each of us learns about love from parents (Trotter, 2010), friends, and entertainment media (Ward, 2003). We learn with whom it is appropriate to fall in love, how it feels, and how we should behave when we are in love. We experience an emotion only when we are physiologically aroused. Thus, we experience passionate love when we experience intense arousal and the circumstances fit the cultural definitions we have learned.

Passionate love has three components: cognitive, emotional, and behavioral (Hatfield & Sprecher, 1986). The cognitive components include a preoccupation with the loved one, an idealization of the person or the relationship, and a desire to know the other and be known by him or her. Emotional components include physiological arousal, sexual attraction, and desire for union. Behavioral elements include serving the other and maintaining physical closeness to him or her. A scale designed to measure passionate love is reproduced in Box 12.3. Notice that each item deals with one of these components.

Research in the United States using the passionate love scale finds that the items are closely related—that is, all of them measure a single factor (Hendrick & Hendrick, 1989). A study of 60 men and 60 women found that scores on the scale are related to the stage of the relationship. Passionate love increases substantially from the early stage of dating to the stage of an exclusive relationship. It does not increase further as the relationship moves from exclusively dating to living together or becoming engaged

(Hatfield & Sprecher, 1986). A study of 197 couples at various stages of courtship, including recently married, found that passionate love did decline as the length of the relationship increased (Sprecher & Regan, 1998).

Passionate love is associated with other intense emotions. When our love is reciprocated and we experience closeness or psychological union with the other person, we experience fulfillment, joy, and ecstasy. Conversely, positive emotional experiences—excitement, sexual excitement—can enhance passionate love. The study of 197 couples found that passionate love and sexual desire were positively related (Sprecher & Regan, 1998). Interestingly, sexual desire and sexual activity are not related (Regan, 2000). Unrequited love, on the other hand, is often associated with jealousy, anxiety, or despair. Loss of a love can be emotionally devastating.

There are four widely used scales that measure love. A meta-analysis pooled the data from 81 studies, involving more than 19,000 participants, and analyzed the structure of the four scales (Graham, 2011). Three higher-order factors or dimensions underlying the items were identified: love, romantic obsession, and friendship. As relationship length increased, love scores increased and obsession scores decreased. These results are consistent with the research showing that passionate love generally decreases over time. Love scores were also positively related to relationship satisfaction.

An important question is whether passionate love is universal or only found in some (Western?) cultures. Analyses of answers to the 15-item scale using data from nine cultural groups (1,809 participants) identified a common-factor structure; the six dimensions included commitment/affection, security/insecurity, and self-/other-centered (Landis & O'Shea, 2000). More detailed analyses of the responses separating men and women identified variation in the relative importance of the factors across culture by gender groups.

The Romantic Love Ideal

The studies and theories of love discussed so far assume that love consists of a particular set of feelings and behaviors. Furthermore, most of us assume that we will experience this emotion at least once in our lives. But these are very culture-bound assumptions. There are societies in which the state or experience we call "love" is unheard of. In fact, U.S. society is almost alone in accepting love as the major basis for marriage.

In U.S. society, we are socialized to accept a set of beliefs about love—beliefs that guide much of our behavior. The following five beliefs are known collectively as the **romantic love ideal**:

1. True love can strike without prior interaction ("love at first sight").
2. For each of us, there is only one other person who will inspire true love.
3. True love can overcome any obstacle ("Love conquers all").
4. Our beloved is (nearly) perfect.
5. We should follow our feelings—that is, we should base our choice of partners on love rather than on other, more rational considerations (Lantz, Keyes, & Schultz, 1975).

Researchers have developed a scale to measure the extent to which individuals hold these beliefs (Sprecher & Metts, 1989). When the scale was completed by a sample of 730 undergraduates, the results indicated that the first four beliefs are held by many young people. Interestingly, male students are more likely to hold these beliefs than female students.

Research suggests that the fourth belief, idealization of the partner, is an important

BOX 12.3 Test Yourself: Passionate Love

Think of the person you love most passionately right now. If you are not in love right now, think of the last person you loved passionately. If you have never been in love, think of the person you came closest to caring for in that way. Keep that person in mind as you complete this questionnaire. Try to record how you felt at the time when your feelings were the most intense.

Use the following scale to answer each item:

    1   2   3   4   5   6   7   8   9
Not at all true   Moderately true   Definitely true

1. I would feel deep despair if _____ left me.

2. Sometimes I feel I can't control my thoughts; they are obsessively on _____.

3. I feel happy when I am doing something to make _____ happy.

4. I would rather be with _____ than anyone else.

5. I'd get jealous if I thought _____ were falling in love with someone else.

6. I yearn to know all about _____.

7. I want _____ physically, emotionally, and mentally.

8. I have an endless appetite for affection from _____.

9. For me, _____ is the perfect romantic partner.

10. I sense my body responding when _____ touches me.

11. _____ always seems to be on my mind.

12. I want _____ to know me—my thoughts, my fears, and my hopes.

13. I eagerly look for signs indicating _____'s desire for me.

14. I possess a powerful attraction for _____.

15. I get extremely depressed when things don't go right in my relationship with _____.

Source: Adapted from "Scale for Determining Passionate Love" by Hatfield and Sprecher, *Journal of Adolescence,* 9, 383–410. © Copyright 1986, with permission from Elsevier.

influence on relationship satisfaction. Two studies of Dutch adults found that many of them believed that their relationship was better than the relationships of others, and that this belief was associated with reported happiness (Buunk & van der Eijnden, 1997). The perceived superiority of one's own relationship reflects strong commitment to that relationship, and is probably a resource in times of relational stress. In another study, researchers asked the members of dating (98) and married (60) couples to rate themselves, their partners, and their ideal partners on 21 interpersonal characteristics (Murray, Holmes, & Griffin, 1996a). Analyses indicated that the participant's ratings of the partner were more similar to the ratings of the self and the ideal partner than to the partner's self-ratings. Furthermore, people who idealized their partners and whose partners idealized them were happier. A longitudinal study found that over a 1-year period, partners came to share the individual's idealized image of him or her (Murray, Holmes, & Griffin, 1996b).

The romantic love ideal has not always been popular in the United States. A group of researchers conducted an analysis of best-selling magazines published during four historical periods (Lantz et al., 1975; Lantz, Schultz, & O'Hara, 1977). They counted the number of times the magazines mentioned one or more of the five beliefs that make up the romantic love ideal. The number of times the ideal was discussed increased steadily over time. These findings suggest that American acceptance of the romantic love ideal occurred gradually from 1741 to 1865. The romantic love ideal first really came into its own about the time of the Civil War.

Love as a Story

When we think of love, our thoughts often turn to the great love stories: Romeo and Juliet, Cinderella and the prince (Julia Roberts and Richard Gere), King Edward VIII and Wallis Simpson, and *Pygmalion/My Fair Lady*. According to Sternberg (1998), these stories are much more than entertainment. They shape our beliefs about love and relationships, and our beliefs in turn influence our behavior.

> Zach and Tammy have been married 28 years. Their friends have been predicting divorce since the day they were married. They fight almost constantly. Tammy threatens to leave Zach; he tells her that nothing would make him happier. They lived happily ever after.
>
> Valerie and Leonard had a perfect marriage. They told each other and all of their friends that they did. Their children say they never fought. Leonard met someone at his office and left Valerie. They are divorced (adapted from Sternberg, 1998).

Wait a minute! Aren't those endings reversed? Zach and Tammy should be divorced, and Valerie and Leonard should be living happily ever after, right? If love is merely the interaction between two people—how they communicate and behave—you're right; the stories have the wrong endings. But there is more to love than interaction; what matters is how each partner interprets the interaction. To make sense out of what happens in our relationships, we rely on our love stories.

A **love story** is a story (script) about what love should be like; it has characters, plot, and theme. There are two central characters in every love story, and they play roles that complement each other. The plot details the kinds of events that occur in the relationship. The theme is central; it provides the meaning of the events that make up the plot, and it gives direction to the behavior of the principals. The love story guiding Zach and Tammy's relationship is the "War" story. Each views love as war—that is, a good relationship involves constant fighting. The two central characters are warriors, fighting for what they believe, to maintain their independence. The plot consists of arguments, fights, threats to leave—in short, battles. The theme is that love is war; one may win or lose particular battles, but the war continues. Zach and Tammy's relationship endures because they share this view, and it fits their temperaments. Can you imagine how long a wimp would last in a relationship with either of them?

According to this view, falling in love occurs when you meet someone with whom you can create a relationship that fits your love story. Furthermore, we are satisfied with relationships in which we and our partner match the characters in our story (Beall & Sternberg, 1995). Valerie and Leonard's marriage looked great on the surface, but it didn't fit Leonard's love story. He left when he met his "true love"—that is, a woman who could play the complementary role in his primary love story.

Where do our love stories come from? Many of them have their origins in the culture—in folk tales, literature, theater, films, and television programs. The cultural context interacts with our own personal experience and characteristics to create the stories that each of us has (Sternberg, 1996). As we experience relationships, our stories evolve, taking account of unexpected events. Each person has more than one story; the stories often form a hierarchy. One of Leonard's stories was "House and Home"; home was the center of the relationship, and he (in his role of Caretaker) showered attention on the house and kids—not on Valerie. But when he met Sharon with her aloof air, ambiguous past, and dark glasses, he was hooked; she elicited the "Love Is a Mystery" story that was more salient to Leonard. He could not explain why he left Valerie and the kids; like most of us, he was not consciously aware of his love stories. It should be obvious from these examples that love stories derive their power from the fact that they are self-fulfilling. We create in our relationships events according to the plot and then interpret those events according to the theme. Our love relationships are literally social constructions. Because our love stories are self-confirming, they can be very difficult to change.

Sternberg and his colleagues have identified five categories of love stories found in U.S. culture, and several specific stories within each category. They have also developed a series of statements that reflect the themes in each story. People who agree with the statements "I think fights actually make a relationship more vital" and "I actually like to fight with my partner" are likely to hold the "War" story. Sternberg and Hojjat studied samples of 43 and 55 couples (Sternberg, 1998). They found that couples generally held similar stories. The more discrepant the stories of the partners, the less happy the couple was. Some stories were associated with high satisfaction—for example, the "Garden" story, in which love is a garden that needs ongoing cultivation. Two stories associated with low satisfaction were the "Business" story (especially the version in which the roles are Employer and Employee), and the "Horror" story, in which the roles are Terrorizer and Victim.

Love stories, or implicit theories of relationships (Franiuk, Cohen, & Pomerantz, 2002), are stable over time. Persons who believe there is a one-and-only love, or "soul mate," for them believe that finding the right person is the key to a satisfying relationship; people who believe that a successful relationship requires continuing work, Sternberg's "garden," believe that hard work is the key. So men and women in the first group emphasize the partner's characteristics in assessing their satisfaction with the relationship; if they decide their partner is not Ms. or Mr. Right, they may leave in search of the true love. Gardeners view the relationship as a work in progress and place less emphasis on the partner in assessing their satisfaction; if unhappy, they work harder and apply more water and fertilizer.

Sternberg states that love stories reflect the culture. Does that mean that the stories or themes he has identified are unique to U.S. culture? Researchers recruited 61 dating and 81 married couples in the United States (mostly White), and 46 dating and 94 married couples in China. A measure developed by Sternberg to measure preferences for themes was completed by the U.S. participants; a careful translation into Chinese was completed by the Chinese participants. Analyses revealed several components, including devotion/caring and pragmatism, that were common to both cultures. The themes of love as war and love as a fairy tale were unique to the United States. Love as the tending of a garden and the incomprehensibility of a lover were unique to China. Devotion/caring was the strongest predictor of relationship satisfaction (Jackson, Chen, Guo & Gao, 2006).

BREAKING UP

Progress? Chaos?

You may have noticed that much of the work we have reviewed assumes or implies that intimate relationships develop or progress in a linear way. We meet, disclose, trust, disclose more, trust more, become sexually intimate, become interdependent, fall in love, and (we hope) live happily ever after. This linear model underlies much of the work on relationships and relationship stability/instability. There is, however, an alternative model that may be (more) appropriate: chaos theory (Weigel & Murray, 2000). Chaos theory suggests that relationships do not develop in a steady linear progression. Instead, relationships may shift suddenly or spontaneously; they may go up (get better) or down (get worse). A small event (say, a missed phone call) may have a major impact; a traumatic event (say, a diagnosis of cancer) may have little or no effect. As a result, it may be impossible to predict the future of an individual relationship. We are just beginning to explore the implications of this model of intimacy.

Whether linear or not, few relationships last forever. Roommates who once did everything together lose touch after they finish school. Two women who were once best friends gradually stop talking. Couples fall out of love and break up. What causes the dissolution of relationships? Research suggests two answers: unequal outcomes and unequal commitment.

Unequal Outcomes and Instability

Earlier in this chapter, we discussed the importance of outcomes in establishing and maintaining relationships. Our decision to initiate a relationship is based on what we expect to get out of it. In ongoing relationships, we can assess our actual outcomes; we can evaluate the rewards we are obtaining relative to the costs of maintaining the relationship. A survey of college students examined the impact of several factors on satisfaction with a relationship; one factor was the value of overall outcomes compared with a person's CL (Michaels, Edwards, & Acock, 1984). In an analysis of the reports of men and women involved in exclusive relationships, the outcomes being experienced were most closely related to satisfaction with the relationship. Several other studies report the same results (Surra, 1990).

The CLalt is also an important standard used in evaluating outcomes. Are the outcomes from this relationship better than those obtainable from the best available alternative? One dimension on which people may evaluate relationships is physical appearance. A relationship with a physically attractive person may be rewarding. Two people who are equally attractive physically will experience similar outcomes on this dimension. What about two people who differ in attractiveness? The less attractive person will benefit from associating with the more attractive one, whereas the more attractive person will experience less positive outcomes. Because attractiveness is a valued and highly visible asset, the more physically attractive person is likely to find alternative relationships available and to expect some of them to yield more positive outcomes.

This reasoning was tested in a study of 123 dating couples. Photographs of each person in the study were rated by five men and five women for physical attractiveness, and a relative attractiveness score was calculated for each member of each couple. Both men and women who were more attractive than their partners reported having more friends of the opposite sex—that is, alternatives—than men and women who were not more attractive than their partners. Follow-up data collected 9 months later indicated that dating couples who were rated as similar in attractiveness were more likely to be still dating each other (White, 1980). These results are consistent with the hypothesis that persons experiencing outcomes below CLalt are more likely to terminate the relationship.

But not everyone compares their current outcomes with those available in alternative relationships. Individuals in White's study who were committed—that is, cohabiting, engaged, or married—did not vary in the number of alternatives they reported. Also, their relative attractiveness was not related to whether they were still in the relationship 9 months later. Persons who are committed to each other may be more concerned with equity than with alternatives.

Weight is one aspect of physical attractiveness. A study of 1,405 adolescent and young adult couples investigated matching and trading (providing more of one input to compensate for less of another) in relationships involving obese persons (BMI greater than 30) (Carmalt et al., 2008). Obese men and women were less likely to have a physically attractive partner. The disadvantage was greater for women than men, and for Black women than for White women. Greater education, a more attractive personality, and better grooming (self-presentation) offset the disadvantage of obesity for some persons, resulting in a more attractive partner than would be expected.

Equity theory (Walster [Hatfield], Berscheid, & Walster, 1973) postulates that each of us compares the rewards we receive from a relationship to our costs or contributions. In general, we expect to get more out of the relationship if we put more into it. Thus, we compare our outcomes (rewards minus costs) to the outcomes our partner is receiving. The theory predicts that **equitable relationships**—in which the outcomes are equivalent—will be stable, whereas inequitable ones will be unstable.

This prediction was tested in a study involving 537 college students who were dating someone at the time (Walster [Hatfield], Walster, & Traupmann, 1978). Each student read a list of things that someone might contribute to a relationship, including good looks, intelligence, loving, understanding, and helping the other make decisions. Each student also read a list of potential consequences of a relationship, including various personal, emotional, and day-to-day rewards and frustrations. Each student was then asked to evaluate the contributions he or she made to the relationship, the contributions the partner made, the things he or she received, and the things the partner received. Each evaluation was made using an 8-point scale that ranged from extremely positive (+4) to extremely negative (−4). The researchers calculated the person's overall outcomes by dividing the rating of consequences by the rating of contributions. They calculated the perceived outcomes of the partner by dividing the rating of the consequences the partner received by the rating of the contributions the partner was making. By comparing the person's outcomes with the perceived partner's outcomes, the researchers determined whether the relationship was perceived as equitable.

Students were interviewed 14 weeks later to assess the stability of their relationships. Stability was determined by whether they were still dating their partner and by how long they had been going together (or how long they had gone together). The results clearly demonstrated that inequitable relationships were unstable. The less equitable the relationship was at the start, the less likely the couple was to be still dating 14 weeks later. Furthermore, students who perceived that their outcomes did not equal their partner's outcomes reported that their relationships were of shorter duration.

Differential Commitment and Dissolution

Are outcomes (rewards minus costs) the only thing we consider when deciding whether to continue a relationship? What about emotional attachment or involvement? We often continue a relationship because we have developed an emotional commitment to the person and feel a sense of loyalty to and responsibility for that person's welfare. The importance of commitment is illustrated by the results of a survey of 234 college students (Simpson, 1987). Each student was involved in a dating relationship and answered questions about 10 aspects of the relationship. Three months later, each respondent was recontacted to determine whether he or she was still dating the partner. The characteristics that were most closely related to stability included length and exclusivity of the relationship and having engaged in sexual intimacy; all three are aspects of commitment. A review of research on premarital relationships concludes that commitment—the person's intent to remain in the relationship—is consistently related to stability (Cate, Levin, & Richmond, 2002).

A meta-analysis of the longitudinal studies of the stability of nonmarital romantic relationships included data from more than 37,000 participants in 137 studies (Le et al., 2010). Researchers assessed the relationships between 16 often measured variables and stability; the average time between Time 1 and the last follow-up across studies was 145 weeks. The three major predictors of lasting relationships were greater commitment, greater love for the partner, and more positive illusions about the partner.

A study of 101 heterosexual dating couples tested the hypothesis that unequal involvement is related to greater instability. Each partner completed a questionnaire at baseline, and follow-up surveys at 6, 18, 30, and 42 months. At time 5 (42 months), 41 of the couples were still together; 28 of the 41 were married. Perceptions of unequal emotional involvement were common; in 75 percent of the couples, at least one member reported that he or she, or the partner, was less involved. Less involved partners perceived themselves as more powerful— this reflects the "principle of least interest." Equal involvement was related to greater satisfaction (Sprecher, Schmeeckle, & Felmlee, 2006).

The importance of equal degrees of involvement is illustrated in another study. Couples were recruited from four colleges and universities in the Boston area (Hill, Rubin, & Peplau, 1976). Each member of 231 couples filled out an initial questionnaire and completed three follow-up questionnaires 6 months, 1 year, and 2 years later. At the time the initial data were collected, couples had been dating an average of 8 months; most were dating exclusively, and 10 percent were engaged. Two years later, researchers were able to determine the status of 221 of the couples. Some were still together, whereas others had broken up.

What distinguished the couples who were together 2 years later from those who had broken up? Couples who were more involved initially—who were dating exclusively, who rated themselves as very close, who said they were in love, and who estimated a high probability that they would get married—were more likely to be together 2 years later. Of the couples who reported equal involvement initially, only 23 percent broke up in the following 2 years. But of the couples who reported unequal involvement initially, 54 percent were no longer seeing each other 2 years later.

Not surprisingly, the break up of a couple was usually initiated by the person who

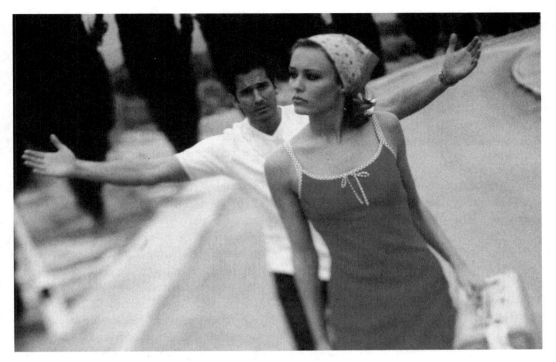

Breaking up is very painful. It can be especially hard on the person who is more committed to the relationship. The person left behind may experience a variety of powerful, negative emotions. © Thomas Schweizer/Corbis

was less involved. Of those whose relationships ended, 85 percent reported that one person wanted to break up more than the other. There was also a distinct pattern in the timing of breakups; they were much more likely to occur in May through June, September, and December through January. This suggests that factors outside the relationship—such as graduation, moving, and arriving at school—led one person to initiate the breakup. Such changes, or life course transitions (see Chap. 3), are likely to increase the costs, such as the difficulty of meeting, or of continuing a relationship. Interestingly, other research shows that college students are also more likely to break up in the two weeks around Valentine's Day (Morse & Neuberg, 2004). This cultural event emphasizes what intimate relationships should be like; perhaps the hype leads participants in declining relationships

to decide to quit, and perhaps to look for alternatives.

We suggested earlier that breaking up is costly. Who experiences greater costs? One study surveyed both rejectors and rejectees (Perilloux & Buss, 2008). Women were more likely to report loss of male protection and post breakup stalking by the ex. Women also reported more negative emotions than men. Both men and women who were rejected experienced greater loss of self-esteem and depression than rejectors. In another study of students, greater distress was reported by rejectees, persons whose breakup was recent, and those who had not entered a new relationship (Field et al., 2011).

The dissolution of a relationship is often painful. But breaking up is not necessarily undesirable. It can be thought of as part of a filtering process through which people who are not suited to each other terminate their relationships. Furthermore, coping with and learning from the breakup may lead to personal growth and more successful relationships in the future (Tashiro, Frazier, & Berman, 2006).

Responses to Dissatisfaction

Not all relationships that involve unequal outcomes or differential commitment break up. What makes the difference? The answer is, in part, the person's reaction to these situations. The level of outcomes a person experiences and his or her commitment to the relationship are influences on satisfaction with that relationship (Bui, Peplau, & Hill, 1996; Rusbult et al., 1986). A study of 60 students and 36 married couples found that an important influence on satisfaction is the perception that your partner supports your attempts to achieve goals that are important to you (Brunstein, Dangelmayer, & Schultheiss, 1996). As long as the person is satisfied, whatever the level of rewards or commitment, he or she will want to continue the relationship. People who are satisfied are more likely to engage in **accommodation**—to respond to potentially destructive acts by the partner in a constructive way (Rusbult, Verette, Whitney, Slovik, & Lipkus, 1991). A study of Black and White married couples over 14 years found that reports of frequent conflict and of using insults, name-calling, and shouting in response to conflict (in other words, not engaging in accommodation) predicted subsequent divorce (Orbuch, Veroff, Hassan, & Horrocks, 2002).

An individual in an unsatisfactory relationship has four basic alternatives (Goodwin, 1991; Rusbult, Zembrodt, & Gunn, 1982): exit (termination), voice (discuss with your partner), loyalty (grin and bear it), and neglect (stay in the relationship but not contribute much). Which of these alternatives the person selects depends on the anticipated costs of breaking up, the availability of alternative relationships, and the level of reward obtained from the relationship in the past.

To assess the costs of breaking up, the individual weighs the costs of an unsatisfactory relationship against the costs of ending that relationship. There are three types of barriers or costs to leaving a relationship: material, symbolic, and affectual (Levinger, 1976). Material costs are especially significant for partners who have pooled their financial resources. Breaking up will require agreeing on who gets what, and it may produce a lower standard of living for each person. Symbolic costs include the reactions of others. A survey of 254 persons, 123 of whom were in relationships, measured the perception of friends' and family members' support for the relationship and commitment to it (Cox, Wexler, Rusbult, & Gaines, 1997). Persons who perceived more support were more committed, in both dating and married couples. Will close friends and family members support or criticize the termination of the relationship? A longitudinal study of dating couples found that lower levels of support by friends for the relationship were associated with later termination of it (Felmlee, Sprecher, & Bassin, 1990). Affectual costs involve changes in one's relationships with others. Breaking up may cause the loss of friends and reduce or eliminate contact with relatives—that is, it may result in loneliness (see Box 12.4). A study of married persons asked each to name "the most important factors keeping you together"; the most frequently mentioned barriers were children (31 percent of respondents), religion (13 percent), and financial need (6 percent) (Previti & Amato, 2003).

A second factor in this assessment is the availability of alternatives. The absence of an attractive alternative may lead the indi-

BOX 12.4 Are You Lonely Tonight?

Did you feel lonely when you first entered school here? If you did, you weren't alone. People entering a college or university are likely to feel lonely for the first several weeks or months (Cutrona, 1982). In fact, most people have experienced loneliness sometime during their lives.

Loneliness is an unpleasant, subjective experience that results from the lack of social relationships satisfying in either quantity or quality (Perlman, 1988). Loneliness is different from being alone or social isolation. Social isolation is an objective situation, whereas loneliness is a subjective, internal experience. You can feel lonely in the midst of a family reunion, and you can be alone in your room and yet feel connected to others.

Loneliness is different from shyness. Shyness is a personality trait that reflects characteristics of the person rather than the state of one's social ties. Shyness is defined as "discomfort and inhibition in the presence of others" (Jones, Briggs, & Smith, 1986). A study of several measures of shyness found that the common element in these measures is distress in and avoidance of interpersonal situations. When shy people interact with others, they are afraid they are being evaluated by the other person and are more likely to think they are making a negative impression on the other person (Asendorpf, 1987).

There are two types of loneliness (Weiss, 1973), which differ in their cause. One is social loneliness, which results from a lack of social relationships or ties to others. Several studies have found that people with few or no friends and few or no family ties are more likely to feel lonely (Stokes, 1985). Thus, events that disrupt ties to social networks can cause loneliness (Marangoni & Ickes, 1989).

The other type is emotional loneliness, which results from the lack of emotionally intimate re-lationships. One study of adolescents found a strong association between self-disclosure and loneliness; greater self-disclosure to others was associated with reduced loneliness (Davis & Franzoi, 1986). Thus, shyness can cause loneliness by inhibiting self-disclosure. There is evidence that loneliness in men is the result of having few or no relationships with others, whereas in women it is the result of having no intimate relationships (Stokes & Levin, 1986). Clearly, loneliness is tied to the state of one's interpersonal relationships.

Because loneliness is related to the number and quality of interpersonal relationships, we can predict that people in some circumstances are more likely to experience it. First, people undergoing a major social transition are generally at greater risk of loneliness. The transition from school to work may be accompanied by feelings of loneliness, especially when this transition involves a geographic move. Second, living arrangements are related to feeling lonely. A study of 554 adult men and women found that living alone was the most important determinant of these feelings (de Jong-Gierveld, 1987). Third, one's relationship status is important. Earlier in this chapter, we described the increasing self-disclosure and interdependence that accompanies the development of romantic relationships; people who report that interdependence developed more rapidly and more broadly and who feel a strong sense of "we-ness" in their relationship are less likely to report loneliness (Flora & Segrin, 2000). Conversely, people who have recently gone through the termination of an intimate relationship—through breaking up, divorce, or death of a partner—may be especially vulnerable to loneliness.

vidual to maintain an unrewarding relationship, whereas the appearance of an attractive alternative may trigger the dissatisfied person to dissolve the relationship.

We noted at the beginning of this chapter that two factors influence who is available: personal characteristics and institutional structure. With regard to the first, people who are in relationships perceive opposite-sex persons of the same age as less physically attractive than do people who are not in relationships (Simpson, Gangestad, & Lerum, 1990). This devaluation of potential partners contributes to relationship maintenance. However, a longitudinal study found that the perceived quality of alternative partners increased among persons whose relationships subsequently ended (Johnson & Rusbult, 1989). With regard to institutional structures, the sex ratio in a community determines the number of eligible partners. Research combining survey data with census data for the area where the respondent lived found that the risk of divorce is greatest in areas where husbands or wives encounter numerous alternatives (South, Trent, & Shen, 2001).

A third factor is the level of rewards experienced before the relationship became dissatisfying. If the relationship was particularly rewarding in the past, the individual is less likely to decide to terminate it.

How important are each of these three factors? That is, which factors are most important in determining whether a dissatisfied person responds by discussing the situation with his or her partner, waiting for things to improve, neglecting the partner, or terminating the relationship? In one study, participants were given short stories describing relationships in which these three factors varied. They were asked what they would do in each situation (Rusbult et al., 1982). The results showed that the lower the prior satisfaction—that is, the less satisfied and the less positive their feelings and caring for their partners—the more likely they were to neglect or terminate the relationship. The less the investment—that is, the degree of disclosure and how much a person stands to lose—the more likely participants were to engage in neglect or termination. Finally, the presence of attractive alternatives increased the probability of terminating the relationship. A later study of ongoing relationships yielded the same results (Rusbult, 1983).

A study of the stability of the relationships of 167 couples over a 15-year period also found that satisfaction, level of investments, and quality of alternatives predicted commitment. Relationships in which commitment was high were more likely to endure (Bui et al., 1996).

SUMMARY

Interpersonal attraction is a positive attitude held by one person toward another person. It is the basis for the development, maintenance, and dissolution of close personal relationships.

Who Is Available? Institutional structures and personal characteristics influence who is available to us as potential friends, roommates, coworkers, and lovers. Three factors influence whom we select from this pool. (1) Our daily routines make some persons more accessible. (2) Proximity makes it more rewarding and less costly to interact with some people rather than others. (3) Familiarity produces a positive attitude toward those with whom we repeatedly come into contact.

Who Is Desirable? Among the available candidates, we choose based on several criteria. (1) Social norms tell us what kinds of people are appropriate as friends, lovers, and mentors. Homogamy—similarity in age, race, religion, and SES—is characteristic of intimate relationships in the United States. (2) We prefer a more physically attractive person, both for esthetic reasons and because we expect rewards from associating with that person. Attractiveness is more influential when we have no other information about a person. (3) We choose based on our expectations about the rewards and costs of potential relationships. We choose to develop those relationships whose outcomes we expect will exceed both comparison level (CL) and comparison level for alternatives (CLalt). We implement our choices by making contact; the development of the relationship is guided by a script.

The Determinants of Liking. Many relationships—between friends, roommates, coworkers, or lovers—involve liking. The extent to which we like someone is determined by three factors.

(1) The major influence is the degree to which two people have similar attitudes. The greater the proportion of similar attitudes, the more they like each other. Similarity produces liking because we prefer cognitive consistency and because we expect interaction with similar others to be reinforcing. (2) Shared activities become an important influence on our liking for another person as we spend time with them. (3) We like those who like us; as we experience positive feedback from another, it increases our liking for them.

The Growth of Relationships. As relationships grow, they change on three dimensions. (1) There may be a gradual increase in the disclosure of intimate information about the self. Self-disclosure is usually reciprocal, with each person revealing something about themselves in response to revelations by the other. (2) Trust in the other person—a belief in his or her honesty, be-

nevolence, and reliability—also increases as relationships develop. Trust may be especially important in long-distance relationships. (3) Interdependence for various gratifications also increases, often accompanied by a decline in reliance on and number of relationships with others.

Love and Loving. (1) Whereas liking refers to a positive attitude toward an object, love involves attachment to and caring for another person. Love also may involve passion—a state of intense physiological arousal and intense absorption in the other. (2) The experience of passionate love involves cognitive, emotional, and behavioral elements. Love increases as the length of the relationship increases, but passion may decline. (3) The concept of love does not exist in all societies; the romantic love ideal emerged gradually in the United States and came into its own about the time of the Civil War. (4) Love stories—scripts—shape our beliefs about love and relationships, and our beliefs influence how we behave in and interpret our relationships.

Breaking Up. There are three major influences on whether a relationship dissolves. (1) Breaking up may result if one person feels that outcomes (rewards minus costs) are inadequate. A person may evaluate present outcomes against what could be obtained from an alternative relationship. Alternatively, a person may look at the outcomes the partner is experiencing and assess whether the relationship is equitable. (2) The degree of commitment to a relationship is an important influence on whether it continues. Someone who feels a low level of emotional attachment to and concern for his or her partner is more likely to break up with that person. (3) Responses to dissatisfaction with a relationship include exit, voice, loyalty, or neglect. Which response occurs depends on the anticipated economic and emotional costs, the availability of attractive alternatives, and the level of prior satisfaction in the relationship.

List of Key Terms and Concepts

accommodation (p. 432)

attitudinal similarity (p. 412)

attractiveness stereotype (p. 416)

availables (p. 400)

comparison level (p. 408)

comparison level for alternatives (p. 409)

dyadic withdrawal (p. 422)

equitable relationships (p. 429)

interpersonal attraction (p. 400)

loneliness (p. 433)

love story (p. 426)

matching hypothesis (p. 405)

mere exposure effect (p. 403)

norm of homogamy (p. 404)

passionate love (p. 423)

romantic love ideal (p. 424)

trust (p. 419)

Critical Thinking Skill: (Relationship) Decision Making and Problem Solving

In making good decisions, it helps to (1) identify your goal(s) in the situation; (2) list at least two possible actions or solutions to the problem; (3) evaluate the quality of each solution (Does it help you meet your goal? Does it have any negative aspects?); and (4) decide on the best one. Consider the following scenario.

Britney, a student at your school, has been seeing Craig for a month. He seems to really like her, and she certainly is attracted to him. At a party on campus, she sees Shelly flirting with Craig and starts to worry that Shelly is trying to steal him. Back at her own apartment, Britney tries to decide what to do to keep Craig. They have not had intercourse yet, but have done just about everything else. She thinks maybe the thing to do is send him a nude photo of herself to arouse his interest and make herself seem hot.

What should Britney do? Apply the techniques listed above to consider what her best decision is. (1) What is her goal? (2) What are at least two possible solutions? (3) Evaluate each solution in terms of whether it helps her meet her goal and whether it has any negative aspects. Do this before you read on.

Britney's goal is to maintain and develop a relationship with Craig. One solution is to send him the nude photo. Another is to do nothing; doing "nothing" is doing something: waiting to see if there is a problem before doing something else. Did you think of other potential solutions? A third is to text him a positive, enthusiastic message without a photo. A fourth solution would be to make sure she sees him before class the next day and be friendly. It would be best if Britney takes out a piece of paper and systematically evaluates these options.

Here are some evaluations of each solution.

1. Send Craig the nude photo. It might help her achieve her goal of keeping him, but it might backfire if Craig forms a negative impression of her. A definite negative is that Britney cannot assume that Craig will keep the photo private. He might decide to forward it to his buddies, causing her great embarrassment.

2. Do nothing. This may not contribute positively to Britney's achieving her goal, but it also carries no risk. She can assess whether Craig behaves differently the next time she sees him.

3. and 4. Send a positive text or see him in person the next day. These are sim-

ilar solutions; both involve making contact, an important part of attraction, as discussed earlier in the chapter. Positive contact is also important, as discussed by exchange theory. They differ in whether the contact is electronic or in person. Either one (or both) help Britney achieve her goal, and neither seems to have any negative aspects.

Overall, then, the key to making good decisions is to "Think first!" Be clear about your goal. Think of multiple solutions; don't stop after the first or most obvious one (especially if the obvious one involves lashing out angrily). Then carefully evaluate each possible solution. Choose the one that seems likely to help you achieve your goal and has few or no negative consequences.

UNDERSTANDING GROUPS

INTRODUCTION

Groups are everywhere. We all participate in them, spending a significant portion of our days engaging in group activities. Take Brandon Harris, for example. Brandon is the star cornerback on his university's football team. He is close to his parents and his two younger sisters and enjoys spending time with his extended family when he is home during school breaks. He regularly attends the local Islamic Society Mosque and is working closely with a group of students in his Business 102 class on a semester-long project. Although he thought about moving into the fraternity house, he has really enjoyed living in Reilly for the last few years. He thinks that dorm life keeps him grounded. He gets along well with his three roommates and found serving as treasurer of the dorm's council a valuable experience. During the off-season, Brandon also holds down a work-study job, shelving books in the library. He is friendly with the other work-study students and looks forward to the evenings he spends in the stacks. He and his girlfriend have been together since their first year of college, when they met in a sociology class. It has been a busy quarter for Brandon, and he is genuinely looking forward to spring break. He plans to kick it off with a long-awaited beach vacation with a group of his closest high school friends, a group he affectionately refers to as the Zoo Crew.

Brandon is clearly busy, but even if our own social lives are less active than his, groups are a pervasive part of our everyday experiences as well. We are members of families, work groups, sports teams, street gangs, classes and seminars, therapy and rehabilitation groups, classical quartets and rock groups, small military units, neighborhood clubs, church groups, and so on. Groups are important because they provide social support, a cultural framework to guide performance, and rewards and resources of all kinds. Without groups, most individuals would be isolated, unloved, disoriented, relatively unproductive, and very possibly hungry.

To better understand groups and the significant influence they have on our lives, this chapter provides the tools—both concepts and theories—used to classify and study groups. The next chapter (Chapter 14) delves more deeply into the within-group processes of interest to social psychologists.

What Is a Group?

We all have a notion of a "group," but our commonsense notion is too broad for use in social psychology. In this chapter and the next, the term **group** specifically refers to a social unit that consists of two or more persons with all of the following attributes:

1. **Membership.** To be a member of a group, we must identify ourselves as belonging to the group and must also be recognized by other members as belonging to the group (Lickel et al., 2000).
2. **Interaction among members.** Group members also must interact—communicating with one another and influencing one another, whether in person, online, or through other mediums.
3. **Goals shared by members.** Group members may have goals that are the same, unique, or complementary. Either way, group members should be interdependent with respect to goal attainment. In other words, progress by one member toward his or her objectives makes it more likely that another member will also reach his or her objectives.
4. **Shared norms.** Group members hold a set of expectations (that is,

norms or rules) that place limits on members' behavior and guide action.

As this definition suggests, groups are not simply collections of individuals; rather, they are organized systems in which the relations among individuals are structured and patterned. For our purposes here, not all social units of two or more persons are groups. For example, persons in a theater crowd escaping in panic from a fire would not constitute a group. Although there may be some communication among the individuals in the crowd, there are no explicit normative expectations or a sense of shared membership among those present. Likewise, a commercial transaction between a customer and a cashier ringing up a basket of groceries would not qualify as a group interaction. In such a situation, there is no common goal or explicit basis for group membership.

Social psychologists typically divide groups into two categories: primary and secondary (Cooley, 1909). **Primary groups** tend to be smaller groups with strong emotional ties and bonds that endure over time. They are more informal and intimate than other groups that individuals belong to. Brandon's family and close friends—the Zoo Crew—are examples of primary groups. Conversely, **secondary groups** are more formal and impersonal. They tend to be organized around instrumental goals—like the group working on the Business 102 class project with Brandon or the other work-study students shelving books at the library—and have few emotional ties. Occasionally, secondary groups begin to take on some of the qualities of primary groups. For instance, over time the football team began to feel like family to Brandon, as team members' shared goals extended beyond the instrumental goals of winning a game or having an undefeated season toward something more intimate and diffuse, like encouraging

one another and offering emotional support both on and off the field.

This chapter introduces a social psychological view of groups, specifically focused on the forces that unify a group and define the behavior of its members. In doing so, it addresses the following questions:

1. What factors hold members together as a unit? That is, what produces cohesion—or the lack of it—in groups?

2. How does a group define its structure and goals?

3. What are group norms and in what ways do they regulate members' behavior? How do groups influence their members to conform?

4. What are the causes of intergroup conflict, and how can it be lessened or resolved?

5. How does conflict affect the intragroup processes outlined above?

GROUP COHESION

Groups vary in their connectedness. Take the Jaguars—a recreational softball club—as an example of a tight-knit, secondary group. The Jaguars have a long record of championships in the city league. The Jaguar players take pride in their performance and are very committed to their team. At practice and during games, this team is a model of enthusiasm and coordination. On the rare occasion when they have a losing streak, all of the team members voluntarily hold extra practice sessions to sharpen their skills and teamwork. The players like one another, and they enjoy playing together and celebrating their victories. Although they do not always agree on strategy, the Jaguars resolve their differences quickly. Several of the players consider teammates their best friends, and they often spend time together off the field. The Jaguars team rarely loses any of its players—not even its second-stringers.

The players of another team in the league—the Penguins—provide a very different story. The Penguins have finished in last place for the last three seasons. Occasionally, the Penguins have to forfeit a game because they cannot even field a team of nine players. The team is not a high priority for the players—they are often busy with other activities, and they often miss practice. The players seldom run into one another outside of team activities. The Penguins' planning session last spring dissolved into chaos when the players could not agree on how to pay for some new equipment. The friction was so bad that there is doubt about whether the team will even participate in the league next year.

The Jaguars and the Penguins differ in a number of respects. For one thing, the Jaguars win a lot more than the Penguins. But the teams also differ notably in their members' willingness to participate in the group. The Jaguar players care about their membership on the team and want to interact with one another, whereas the Penguin players seem to care much less. The Jaguars have a stronger grip on members' loyalty than the Penguins do, and the team has bonded together more firmly—the Jaguars have a higher level of group cohesion than the Penguins do.

Group cohesion refers to the extent to which members of a group desire to remain in a group and resist leaving it (Balkwell, 1994; Cartwright, 1968). A highly cohesive group generally maintains a firm hold over its members' time, energy, loyalty, and commitment. Cohesive groups are marked by strong ties among members, a positive emotional feeling about membership, and a tendency for members to perceive events in similar terms (Bollen & Hoyle, 1990; Braaten, 1991; Evans & Jarvis, 1980). Because members of a cohesive group desire to belong, the interactions among them will typically have a positive, upbeat character and reflect a "we" feeling.

The Nature of Group Cohesion

People may have very different motives for joining and staying in groups. Some may belong to a group because they like the tasks they perform in the group, because they enjoy interacting with the other members, because the group reflects their own values, or because the group helps them get something they want (such as prestige, money, future opportunities, protection, or social contacts). These varied motives lead to different levels and types of cohesion among the members (Cota et al., 1995; Hogg & Haines, 1996; Mullen & Copper, 1994; Tziner, 1982).

One of the fundamental types of group cohesion is *social cohesion* (Dion, 2000). A group has social cohesion if its members stay in the group primarily because they like one another as persons and desire to interact with one another (Aiken, 1992; Lott & Lott, 1965). All other things being equal, social cohesion will be greater when group members are similar. Similarity increases liking; therefore, groups whose members have similar education, ethnicity, and status, and hold similar attitudes will have greater social cohesion.

The other major type of group cohesion is *task cohesion*. When a group has high task cohesion, its members remain together primarily because they are heavily involved with the group's task(s). Task cohesion will be greater if members find the group's task(s) intrinsically valuable, interesting, and challenging. It will also be

BOX 13.1 Research Update: The Ties That Bind: Attachments to a Sorority

Why are people strongly attached to some groups? Social psychologists have identified a number of different factors that strengthen cohesion among group members. Recent work on the problem has produced a new proposition: Emotional cohesion develops from the network structure in a group. That is, patterns of who knows whom, and who interacts with whom, produce emotional commitments to the group and the ensuing effects of cohesion (conformity to group norms, productivity of the group, and so on).

To be emotionally attached to the group, individuals must feel they are full members of the group—that they belong to the group—and they must feel good about being members of the group—belonging to it makes them happy. Being emotionally attached implies that having to detach from the group produces negative emotional costs. If someone separates from a group in which he or she does not feel very connected, it would not produce much negative emotion because the individual does not feel connected in the first place. Likewise, if someone is a member of a group and is not happy about it (perhaps it is a group that is constantly arguing), he or she will not suffer much from separating.

Sociologists Pamela Paxton and James Moody believed that differences in an individu-

al's involvement and position in the network of individuals inside the group would produce differences in the sense of belonging and the individual's emotional satisfaction with the group.

To test these ideas, Paxton and Moody studied the relationships among the members of a sorority at a college in the southern United States. Each member of the sorority was asked who in the sorority was her best friend, who she went out with socially on a regular basis, and in whom she would confide. As expected, some members were named more often than others, and those people were considered more central to the sorority network.

The researchers found, not surprisingly, that sorority sisters who were more central to the network felt more belonging to the group and were happier with their membership. But the researchers also located several subgroups or cliques within the larger sorority. They found that people who were more central to those subgroups were lower on their emotional attachment to the group. In terms of group cohesion, then, relationships with others can increase cohesion, but if cohesion among a subgroup becomes strong enough, it can damage the commitment of its members to the larger group.

Source: Adapted from Paxton and Moody, 2003.

---

greater if the group's objectives (and the related tasks) are clearly defined (Raven & Rietsema, 1957). Groups that succeed at achieving their goals (like the Jaguars) often have higher task cohesion than do groups that fail repeatedly (like the Penguins).

Sources and Consequences of Cohesion

Social psychological research suggests that positive emotions attributed to the group are an important source of cohesion (Lawler, Thye, & Yoon, 2000, 2008). For exam-

ple, when the Jaguar players feel good after winning a game, they make attributions about the source of their happiness (see Chapter 6). Given that the team had to work together to win and the positive emotions came from winning, the players attribute their positive affect to the team and its joint action. Focusing on the group as an entity increases the group orientation of the members. The players are more likely to think of the team as an important unit and to invest further in the group (Lawler, Thye & Yoon, 2000).

Implicit in the above is cohesion's relationship to interdependence. That is, the more that group members must rely on one another to achieve the goals that generate positive emotion, the more likely they are to attribute any positive emotion they experience to the group (Lawler 2001, Lawler, Thye, & Yoon, 2008). If the Jaguars won because of the actions of a star player and not a group effort, the positive emotions associated with winning would be much less likely to strengthen group ties because the win would be attributed to the one player rather than any joint action on the part of the team.

Cohesion begets increased cohesion. Given the opportunity, members of highly cohesive groups communicate more with one another than do members of less cohesive groups (Moran, 1966), and the interaction is of higher quality. Interaction among members in highly cohesive groups is usually friendlier, more cooperative, and entails more attempts to reach agreements and to improve coordination (Shaw & Shaw, 1962).

Families are primary groups, with strong and intimate ties. Engaging in activities that require teamwork and generate positive emotions, like this family is, increases cohesion among group members. The positive affect the activity generates is attributed to the group, enhancing a sense of "we-ness." Members of highly cohesive groups invest more time and energy into group activities than those in less cohesive groups. © Hero Images/Corbis

Members of high-cohesion groups also have more influence on one another than do members of low-cohesion groups (Lott & Lott, 1965). This is not only because members of high-cohesion groups try to influence one another more but also because they are more likely to be successful at doing so. Conformity is higher in cohesive groups than less cohesive ones (Sakurai, 1975; Wyer, 1966).

Members of groups with high cohesion are more likely to invest both time and energy into their groups (Lawler, Thye, & Yoon, 2000) because they want them to perform well. This helps explain why cohesion tends to increase the productivity and performance of groups. However, cohesion does not always contribute to success (Evans & Dion, 1991; Gully, Devine, & Whitney, 1995; Mullen & Copper, 1994). The effects of cohesion ultimately depend on the type of cohesion holding the group together. Task cohesion (that is, members' commitment to the group's task) has a significant effect on group productivity, but other forms of cohesion (such as social cohesion and group pride) have little or no effect on productivity (Mullen & Copper, 1994). This may be because members of socially cohesive groups prefer to spend their time socializing rather than producing.

GROUP GOALS

Groups can also be characterized by their goals and by the structure they adopt in pursuit of their goals. A **group goal** is an outcome group members view as desirable and important to attain. These goals can differ in terms of specificity, ranging from general statements about what the group does and why it exists to more specific targets and tasks that the group members attempt to achieve along the way to its larger goals. Primary groups tend to have more general or diffuse goals (like supporting or caring for one another). Conversely, secondary groups are likely to have specific goals (like winning football games or completing a course project).

Group Goals and Individual Goals

Although individual and group goals may be related, they are not always the same, and these differences can be very important for the functioning of the group.

Most groups function best when there is compatibility between group goals and the individual goals of its members. The term **goal isomorphism** refers to a state in which group goals and individual goals are compatible in the sense that actions leading to group goals also lead to the attainment of individual goals. High isomorphism benefits the group and vice versa because members are motivated to pursue group goals and to contribute resources and effort to the group (Sniezek & May, 1990). The common admonition among coaches—"There's no I in team"—is an effort to remind players that individuals' goals can sometimes interfere with group goals. A basketball player who refuses to pass might be trying to increase his own stats and notoriety, but this can be detrimental to the team's performance, causing them to lose points or keeping them from learning to work effectively as a unit.

Groups use a number of strategies to heighten isomorphism. First, many groups recruit selectively—that is, only admit persons who strongly support the group's main goal(s) as members. Second, groups use socialization and training. For example, a basketball coach might bench a star player who consistently hogs the ball in an effort to socialize him into being more of a team player or run drills in practice that incorporate a number of passes. Finally, increasing members' awareness that they belong to the group and making their identity as

members more salient can enhance individuals' support for group goals (Mackie & Goethals, 1987). Strategies toward this end include increasing the proximity of members to one another, the experiences they share in common, and the amount of social contact and communication among them (Turner, 1981). Using a common designation to label group members (Penguins, Tri-Delts, Crips) also makes salient a united identity (Dion, 1979).

GROUP NORMS

A **norm** is a rule or standard that specifies how group members are expected to behave under given circumstances (Hechter & Opp, 2001). Most groups develop a variety of norms that regulate their members' activities. For example, a Freecycle group may have norms specifying how many requests a community member can make for free items before they must offer an item of their own on the website. Norms of this type will obviously have an impact on the ratio of requests to offers and influence members' perceptions of the group's goals. A group of college admissions officers may have norms that regulate how the officers make judgments; the nature of these norms will indirectly affect which applicants will be admitted and which will not. A family may have norms regulating who washes the dishes or mows the lawn.

Functions of Norms

Norms serve a number of important functions for groups (Feldman, 1984). First, they foster coordination among members while in pursuit of group goals. Because norms usually reflect a group's fundamental value system, they prescribe behaviors that help the group in the attainment of important goals. When members conform to group

Group norms can extend to any aspect of behavior, including dress and appearance. Bikers have a different dress code from corporate executives, but conformity is high in each group. *Left:* © hroe/iStock; *right:* © Squaredpixels/iStock

norms, they know what to expect of one another, facilitating coordination among them. If a family has established a norm of gathering together for Sunday dinner, this limits the needs to make explicit plans for the dinner or for family members to wonder whether they will be free for other activities on an upcoming Sunday.

Second, norms provide a cognitive frame of reference through which group members interpret and judge their environment. That is, norms provide a basis for distinguishing good from bad, important from unimportant, tenable from untenable. They are especially useful in novel or ambiguous situations, where they serve as pointers on how to behave. Because norms are anchored in the group's values and culture, norms bring predictability and coherence to group activities.

Third, norms define and enhance the common identity of group members. This is especially true when group norms require members to behave differently from persons outside the group. Thus, norms that prescribe distinctive dress (for example, clothing or hairstyles) or distinctive speech patterns (for example, dialects or vocabulary) will differentiate group members from nonmembers. These norms demarcate group boundaries and reinforce the group's distinctive identity.

Conformity and Influence

Norms do not mean much unless the group can somehow oblige its members to live up to its norms. When an individual adheres to group norms and standards, it is called **conformity**. Much of the behavior we witness in daily life involves conformity to one group norm or another. Group members often change their behavior expressly so it will conform to group norms.

The Asch Conformity Paradigm. In groups, influence flows in many directions—members influence other members and are influenced in turn. Of special importance, however, is the influence the group's majority exercises over individual members' behavior. Social psychologists use the term **majority influence** to refer to the processes by which a group's majority pressures an individual member to conform or to adopt a specific position on some issue.

The impact of majority influence on individual group members was illustrated in a series of classic experiments by Asch (1951, 1955, 1957). Using a laboratory setting, Asch created a situation in which an individual was confronted by a majority that agreed unanimously on a factual matter (spatial judgments) but was obviously in error. These studies showed that, within limits, groups can pressure their members to change their judgments and conform with the majority's position even when that position is obviously incorrect.

In the basic Asch experiment, a group of eight persons participated in an investigation of "visual discrimination." In fact, all but one of the participants in each group were confederates working for the experimenter. The remaining individual was a naive participant. In front of the experimental room, large cards displayed a standard line and three comparison lines, as shown in Figure 13.1. The participant's objective was to decide which of the three comparison lines was closest in length to the standard line.

The task seemed simple and straightforward: one of the comparison lines was the same length as the standard line, whereas the other two were very different. The group repeated this task 18 times, using

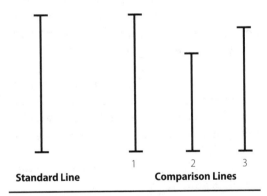

Standard Line   **Comparison Lines**

FIGURE 13.1 Judgmental Task Used in Asch Conformity Studies

In the Asch paradigm, naive participants are shown one standard line and three comparison lines. The task is to judge which of the three comparison lines is closest in length to the standard line. By itself, this task appears easy. However, participants are surrounded by other persons (supposedly also naive participants but actually experimental confederates) who publicly announce erroneous judgments regarding the match between lines. Such a situation imposes pressure on the participant to conform to their erroneous judgments.

Source: Adapted from Asch, 1952.

a different set of lines each time. On each trial, the standard line matched one of the three comparison lines. During each trial of the experiment, the confederates announced their judgments publicly, one after another. The group was seated so that the confederates responded prior to the real participant, who also announced his or her opinion publicly. Although this task seemed easy, it turned out to be a difficult experience for the naive participant. On 6 of the 18 trials, the confederates gave a correct response, but on the other 12 trials, the confederates responded incorrectly. The confederates' erroneous responses put the naive participants in a trying position. On the one hand, they knew the correct response based on their own perception of the lines. On the other hand, they heard all the other persons (whom they believed to be sincere) unanimously announcing a different and incorrect judgment on 12 trials.

The results showed that majority opinion, even when obviously incorrect, strongly influenced the judgments the naive participants announced. In the 12 critical trials, nearly one-third of the responses by participants were incorrect (Asch, 1957). Only one-quarter of the participants showed no conformity and remained independent throughout; the remainder conformed, at least to some degree. One-third of the participants conformed on 50% or more of the critical trials. This is striking compared to the control condition. With no confederates present and participants recording their judgments privately on paper, the error rate was less than 1%.

Interviews conducted after the experiment revealed that most of the participants were quite aware of the discrepancy between the majority's judgments and their own. They felt puzzled and under pressure, and they tried to figure out what might be happening. Some wondered whether they had misunderstood the experimental instructions; others began to look for other explanations or to question their eyesight. Even those participants who did not conform to the majority felt some apprehension but eventually decided that the problem rested more with the majority than with themselves. The interviews indicated that participants' conformity in this study was of a particular type: public compliance without private acceptance: Although many participants conformed publicly, they privately did not believe or accept the majority's judgment. In effect, they viewed public compliance as the best choice in a difficult situation.

Why Conform? The occurrence of majority influence and conformity in groups can be explained generally by the fact that individual members are dependent on the majority cognitively, socially, and for utilitarian reasons as well. For one thing, members seek information about social reality, and they depend on the majority to validate their understanding of and opinions about the group and the world. For another, individual members want to obtain various rewards and benefits—not the least of which is the acceptance of their continuing membership in the group—and they depend heavily on the majority for these outcomes. The dependence of group members on the majority thus leads to the majority's exercise of influence in groups because it can withhold these outcomes from the minority.

Normative Influence. Many analyses distinguish between normative influence and informational influence (Cialdini & Trost, 1998; Deutsch & Gerard, 1955; Kaplan, 1987; Turner, 1991). **Normative influence** occurs when a member conforms to expectations held by others (that is, to norms) in order to receive the social rewards or avoid the punishments that are contingent on meeting these expectations (Janes & Olson,

2000). Being liked and accepted by other members is one important reward in normative influence. To exercise influence of this type, a group will need to maintain at least some degree of surveillance over its members' behavior. The impact of normative influence is heightened, for instance, when members respond publicly rather than anonymously (Insko et al., 1983; Insko et al., 1985).

Conformity to social norms may also be a utility-seeking activity, less in terms of directly avoiding punishments or currying favor but rather as a means to stabilize relationships and enhance the predictability of behavior in the group. Conforming to norms and enforcing them produces more easily understandable relationships among people, making exchanges in these relationships easier (Horne, 2004). If, for example, Bob wishes to sell an item on eBay, he must follow the prescribed norms about describing his product accurately, adequately packaging his product for shipping, and charging reasonable shipping and handling costs. He is motivated to conform to the standards of the eBay community, not just because he will be sanctioned (by negative testimonials and perhaps even losing his account) if he does not but also because following the norms enhances the trading system for everyone involved. It makes buying and selling behavior predictable, comfortable, and easy to manage.

Informational Influence. Informational influence occurs when a group member accepts information from others as valid evidence about reality. This type of influence is likely when members need to reduce uncertainty—as in situations that involve ambiguity or that entail an absence of objective standards to guide judgment (Baron, Vandello, & Brunsman, 1996). More concretely, informational influence often occurs in situations in which members are trying to solve a complex problem unfamiliar to them (Kaplan & Miller, 1987). Think back to your first time in the high school cafeteria. You might not have known what to expect, but there probably were not explicit instructions anywhere. You looked to what others were doing to determine how you should proceed. Members considered more expert or knowledgeable are especially likely to exercise informational influence during such tasks. This type of influence also occurs frequently in crisis situations when members must act immediately but lack knowledge about the appropriate action.

With respect to the Asch line judgment task, it seems that normative influence was operating prominently in the situation. Of those participants who conformed in the Asch experiment, many did so to avoid being embarrassed, ridiculed, or laughed at by the majority. They were seeking acceptance by the majority (or at least to avoid outright public rejection). In one variation, Asch retested his participants on the same stimuli with the majority group no longer present, and they gave correct answers; their experience of judging lines in the presence of the majority did not permanently alter their understanding of the lines' lengths, suggesting that informational influence was not an influential factor.

Although informational influence was relatively unimportant in the Asch situation, we should not underestimate its importance in other situations. A famous study by Sherif (1935, 1936)—conducted years before Asch did his line judgment research—dramatically illustrates the impact of informational influence under conditions of uncertainty. Sherif's study used a physical phenomenon known as the autokinetic effect (meaning "moves by itself"). The autokinetic effect occurs when a person stares at a stationary pinpoint of light located at a distance in a completely dark room. For most people, this light will appear to move

in an erratic fashion, even though the light is not actually moving at all. Sherif used the autokinetic effect as a basis for studying informational influence in groups. First, he placed participants in a laboratory setting by themselves and asked them to estimate how far the light moved. In making these judgments, the participants were literally in the dark—they had no external frame of reference. From their individual estimates, the researcher was able to determine a stable range for each participant. Participants differed quite a bit in this respect. Whereas some thought the light was moving only one or two inches, others believed it was moving as much as eight or ten inches.

Shortly thereafter, Sherif put the same participants together in groups of three and placed them back in the autokinetic situation. Although the estimates the participants had made when alone were different, the estimates they made in groups converged on a common standard. This change in members' judgments provides evidence for the operation of informational influence. Lacking an external frame of reference and being uncertain about their own judgment, group members began to use one another's estimates as a basis for defining reality. Each group established its own arbitrary standard, and members used this as a frame of reference. This process of norm formation can be quite subtle; in fact, other research (Hood & Sherif, 1962) has shown that participants involved in an autokinetic experiment are often unaware that other members are influencing their judgments.

Another interesting finding from Sherif's original study emerged when, a week or two after their initial exposure, the participants were again placed alone in the autokinetic situation. The results showed that the participants used the acquired group norm as the framework for their new, individual judgments. Although not all studies have found evidence of such enduring norm internalization, at least one study retested individual participants in the autokinetic task a year after their initial exposure to the group norm and found evidence that the group norm still influenced participants' judgments despite the passage of time (Rohrer, Baron, Hoffman, & Swander, 1954).

Increasing Conformity

An individual's tendency to conform will be greater under some conditions than under others. Social psychologists have identified a number of factors that affect conformity in groups.

Size of the Majority. If the majority is unanimous—that is, if all the members of the majority are united in their position—then the size of the majority will have an impact on the behavior of the participant. As the size of the unanimous majority increases, the amount of participants' conformity increases (Asch, 1955; Rosenberg, 1961). For example, a participant confronted by one other person in an Asch-type situation will conform very little; he or she will answer independently and correctly on nearly all trials. However, when confronted by two persons, the participant will experience more pressure and will agree with the majority's erroneous answer more of the time. Confronted by three persons, the participant will conform at a still higher rate. In his early studies, Asch (1951) found that conformity to unanimous false judgments increased with majority size up to three members and then remained essentially constant beyond that point. Although some research (Bond & Smith, 1996; Gerard, Wilhelmy, & Conolley, 1968) has questioned the exact point at which the effect of majority size begins to level off, there does seem to be some point at which additional persons do not further increase conformity.

Unanimity. What happens when the group's majority is not unanimous? Basically, lack of unanimity among majority members has a liberating effect on participants' behavior. A participant will be less likely to conform if another member breaks away from the majority (Gorfein, 1964; Morris & Miller, 1975). One explanation for this is that the member who abandons the majority provides validation and social support for the participant. For example, if one or several members in an experiment like Asch's abandon the majority and announce correct judgments, their behavior will reaffirm the participant's own perception of reality and reduce his or her tendency to conform to the majority.

Beyond this, however, any breach in the majority—whether it provides social support or not—will reduce the pressure on the participant to conform (Allen & Levine, 1971; Levine, Saxe, & Ranelli, 1975). In one study (Allen & Levine, 1969), individuals participated in groups of five persons, four of whom were confederates. The participants made judgments on a variety of items. These included visual tasks similar to those used by Asch as well as informational items (for example, "In thousands of miles, how far is it from San Francisco to New York?") and opinion items for which there were no correct answers ("Agree or disagree: 'Most young people get too much education'"). Depending on the experimental condition, participants were confronted with either a unanimous majority of four persons (control condition), a majority of three persons and a fourth person who broke from the majority and gave the correct answer (social support condition), or a majority of three persons and a fourth person who broke from the majority but gave an answer even more erroneous than that of the majority (extreme erroneous dissent condition).

The control condition, which involved a unanimous majority, produced the highest level of conformity. The social support condition, in which the dissenter joined the participant, produced significantly less conformity than the control condition. Even the extreme erroneous dissent condition, in which the dissenter gave an answer that was more extreme and incorrect than the majority's, produced significantly less conformity. Thus, any breach in the majority reduced conformity because it called into question the correctness of the majority's position and reduced the participant's tendency to conform.

Attraction to the Group. Members who are highly attracted to a group will conform more to group norms than will members who are less attracted to it (Kiesler & Kiesler, 1969; Mehrabian & Ksionzky, 1970). One explanation for this is that when individuals are attracted to a group, they also wish to be accepted personally by its members. Because acceptance and friendship are strengthened when members hold similar attitudes and standards, individuals who are highly attracted to a group conform more to the views held by the other members (Feather & Armstrong, 1967; McLeod, Price, & Harburg, 1966). However, attraction to a group will increase conformity only if that conformity leads to acceptance by others in the group (Walker & Heyns, 1962).

Commitment to Future Interaction. Members are more likely to conform to group norms when they anticipate that their relationship with the group will be permanent or enduring, as opposed to short term (Lewis, Langan, & Hollander, 1972). This is true regardless of whether members are attracted to a group (Forsyth, 1999). For example, even if you dislike your coworkers and your job, you are likely to continue to conform to group norms (coming in to work on time, being friendly, helping customers) when you know you will be continuing to work there for the foreseeable future.

Competence. Another factor affecting conformity is an individual member's level of expertise relative to that of other members. If members who are skilled at the group's task differ from the majority's view, they will resist pressure to the degree that they believe themselves to be more competent than the other group members (Ettinger et al., 1971). Interestingly, the extent to which a person believes that he or she is competent may be more important than the actual level of competence (Stang, 1972). Persons who, in fact, are not competent will still resist conformity pressure and perhaps try to persuade other members to change their positions if they believe they have more skill than the other members.

Priming. Two researchers combined the work of Sherif and Asch to do a study on the effects of priming in conformity. Louise Pendry and Rachael Carrick (2001) asked their subjects to count the number of beeps they heard—a task not as ambiguous as the Sherif autokinetic effect but still subject to considerable error by many subjects. Each time, the subjects actually heard 100 beeps, but the confederates (as in the Asch experiments) were instructed to lie and report between 120 and 125 beeps. Not surprisingly, the subjects often conformed and reported much higher than 100 beeps.

However, what was most interesting was that the experimenters were able to manipulate conformity through a process of **priming**—brief exposure to a stimulus meant to influence the response to a second stimulus. The researchers exposed their subjects to either a "punk" stimulus (representing anarchy and nonconformity), an "accountant" stimulus (representing the neat and orderly conformist), or no stimulus (the control condition) by showing

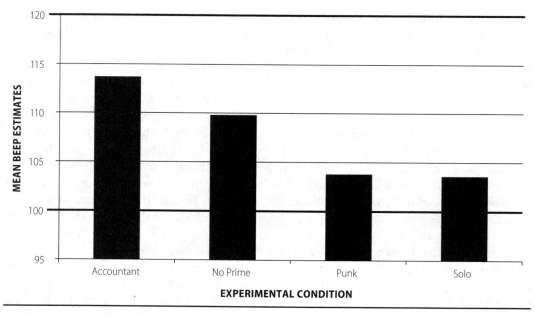

FIGURE 13.2 Effects of Priming on Conformity

In an experiment that combined Asch (conformity paradigm) and Sherif (ambiguous situation), researchers found that priming influenced conformity. Participants primed to think about accountants conformed significantly more than any other group. Furthermore, participants who were primed with punk before the experiment did not differ from those who completed the task alone (without any type of influence).

Source: Adapted from Pendry & Carrick, 2001.

them a photo and asking them to read text that described the person in the text as either a punk rocker or an accountant. The results showed that the accountant-primed subjects conformed to the confederates' estimates of the number of beeps the most of the three groups. The group that received no prime conformed, but less so than the accountant-primed group. The punk-primed group essentially did not conform at all. Their estimates were not significantly different from subjects who performed the beep-counting task in isolation (and thus had no conformity pressure).

INTERGROUP CONFLICT

Processes between groups heavily influence processes within groups. Groups seldom

exist in isolation as they do in the laboratory. Sports teams and gangs have rivals. Families and friendship groups have contemporaries. The United States is one of many countries in the world. One intergroup process with profound implications on groups is intergroup conflict.

The term **intergroup conflict** is often used in two distinct ways. First, we use it when referring to conflict between organized groups—each group consisting of members who interact with one another, who have well-defined role relationships, and who have interdependent goals. Second, we also use intergroup conflict to refer to what might be better described as conflict between persons belonging to different social categories. Although not necessarily members of organized groups, these people perceive themselves as members of the same social category and are involved emotionally in this common definition of themselves. For instance, conflict between members of ethnic or racial categories (such as neighborhood conflicts between Blacks and Hispanics in Miami) is usually considered intergroup conflict, even though the individuals involved may not belong to organized groups.

Effects of Intergroup Conflict on Within-Group Processes

Intergroup conflict produces changes in the internal structure of the groups participating in the conflict that can promote escalation and make conflict resolution more difficult (Coser, 1967). Three main changes that can occur are increased group cohesion, increased militancy of group leaders, and an alteration of norms in the group.

Group Cohesion. Research finds that when a group engages in conflict against another group or is threatened by another group, it will become more cohesive (Dion, 1979; Ryen & Kahn, 1975; Worchel & Norvell, 1980). During conflict, a group's boundaries will become more firmly etched, and its members will generally show higher levels of loyalty, commitment, and cooperativeness to the group (Sherif, 1966; Sherif & Sherif, 1982).

Why does intergroup conflict lead to higher cohesion? First, as the conflict escalates, a group's cause becomes more significant to its members, and thus they increase their commitment to it. Second, intergroup conflict frequently entails threats; if an outgroup issues a threat, that action quickly identifies the out-group as an enemy. Having a common enemy heightens perceived similarity among in-group members and increases cohesion (Holmes & Grant, 1979; Samuels, 1970).

What are the consequences of heightened in-group cohesion during intergroup conflict? As noted previously, if a group is cohesive, its members will desire to remain in it and resist leaving it. A highly cohesive group will, in general, maintain a firm hold over its members' time, energy, loyalty, and commitment. Because conformity and cooperation tend to be greater in high-cohesion groups than in low-cohesion groups (Sakurai, 1975), cohesive groups are capable of taking well-coordinated action in pursuit of their goals. In the context of intergroup conflict, high-cohesion groups are often more vigorous and contentious than low-cohesion groups.

Of course, there are some limits to this effect. If a group is embroiled in a conflict in which it cannot possibly prevail, members may give up all hope. When this occurs, cohesion can decline, and some members may leave the group. But under conditions in which success is still possible, in-group cohesion will usually increase when conflict develops with another group.

Leadership Militancy. Group leaders act differently under conditions of intergroup conflict than under conditions of peace. Under conflict, leaders have to direct the charge against the adversary. They plan the group's strategic moves, obtain resources needed for the conflict, coordinate members' actions, and serve as spokespersons in negotiations with the adversary. How well these activities are performed will have an important impact on a group's success or failure in intergroup conflict.

It is not uncommon for groups embroiled in heavy conflict to change leaders. If the campaign against an opposing group is not progressing well, rivals for leadership may emerge within the in-group. Frequently, these rivals will be angrier, more radical, and more militant than the existing leaders. This challenge from rivals will place the existing leaders under pressure. To defend against this threat, they may react by adopting a harder line and taking stronger action against the out-group. Under conditions of threat, group members are more likely to be influenced by their leaders and, therefore, are more accepting of this increased militancy. Although existing leaders do not always react to threat in this way, they are especially prone to do so when their own position within the group is insecure or precarious (Rabbie & Bekkers, 1978).

Norms and Conformity. Intergroup conflict not only increases group cohesion and leadership militancy; it also changes group norms and goals. Once serious intergroup hostilities have begun, group members will grow concerned with winning (or surviving) the conflict. Some behaviors and activities the group considered valuable prior to the conflict may now seem useless or even detrimental to success in the conflict; if this happens, the group will reorder goal priorities and favor those behaviors that can help it win the conflict.

As part of this, the group may reassess the importance of various tasks and make corresponding changes in members' role definitions and task assignments. This can result in a redistribution of status and rewards among members that—if judged by preconflict standards—would not appear fair. The reallocation of tasks may impose an unequal sharing of costs and hardships, and it may not reflect members' seniority or past contributions. Changes such as these can increase tensions among members within the group (Leventhal, 1979). But if the conflict is intense, concerns about group effectiveness and survival will overshadow concerns about equity and fairness.

Under severe conflict, the members will increase their demands on one another for conformity to group norms and standards. Enhanced coordination and task performance will help the group achieve success in the conflict. There will also be pressure to adopt the group's negative attitudes and stereotypes regarding the adversary—a form of "right thinking." The importance of loyalty to the in-group will increase, and members will increasingly expect one another to display a distrusting, competitive orientation toward the out-group. Those who do not will be trusted less by the group and may even be ostracized or ejected from the group.

These conformity pressures may well impinge on the rights and liberties of individual members. Yet the group will care less about these rights than it did before the conflict, and there will be less tolerance of dissent (Korten, 1962). If internal dissent does occur, the majority will likely react by suppressing it or by forcing the dissidents out of the group, especially if they suspect them of sympathizing with the adversary or engaging in behavior that jeopardizes the group's chance of victory.

All three of these processes—increased cohesion, leadership militancy, and norms and conformity—were evident in the United States immediately following 9/11. The perceived threat from outside not only brought most of the country together, however briefly, but also allowed George W. Bush to get support to increase surveillance of citizens, significantly enhance airport security regulations, and devote more military personnel and monies to the War on Terror. Furthermore, those who refused to conform to these norms were often considered anti-American.

SOURCES OF INTERGROUP CONFLICT

In the case of 9/11, intergroup conflict stemmed from a single aversive event, a series of terrorist attacks on U.S. soil. There are several other origins of intergroup conflict. Overt conflict can develop because groups have an underlying opposition of interests. When this opposition prevents them from achieving their goals simultaneously, it can lead to antagonism and friction and, eventually, to open conflict. Conflict can also develop because members of one group view themselves as different in important ways from members of another group and act in a discriminatory way toward the other group. Or conflict may occur because one group suddenly threatens or deprives another group and, thereby, provokes an aggressive reaction. These factors are not mutually exclusive; in fact, they often work together to cause conflict between groups (Taylor & Moghaddam, 1987).

Realistic Group Conflict

Years ago, Muzafer Sherif and his colleagues conducted an important study of intergroup conflict at Robbers Cave State Park in Oklahoma (Sherif, 1966; Sherif et al., 1961; Sherif & Sherif, 1982). The participants in this experiment were well-adjusted, academically successful, White, middle-class American boys, aged 11 and 12. These boys attended a two-week experimental summer camp and participated in camp activities, unaware that their behavior was under systematic observation. The research objective was to investigate how an underlying opposition of interest might lead to overt intergroup conflict. Therefore, the boys were divided into two groups, named the Eagles and the Rattlers.

The experiment progressed in several stages. The first stage, which lasted about a week, was designed to produce cohesion within each of the groups. The boys arrived at the camp on two separate buses and settled into cabins located a considerable distance apart. By design, contact within each group was high, but contact between the two groups was minimal.

The boys within each group engaged in various activities, many of which required cooperative effort for achievement. They camped out, cooked, worked on improving swimming holes, transported canoes over rough terrain to the water, and played various games. As they worked together, the boys in each group pooled their efforts, organized duties, and divided tasks of work and play. Eventually, the boys identified more and more with their own groups, and each unit developed a high degree of group cohesion and solidarity.

Next, the experimenters began the second stage, in which conflict was induced between the groups. Specifically, the camp staff arranged a tournament of games, including baseball, touch football, tug-of-war, and a treasure hunt. In this tournament, prizes were awarded only to the victorious group. Thus, one group could attain its goal only at the expense of the other.

The tournament started in the spirit of good sportsmanship, but as it progressed, the positive feelings faded. The good sportsmanship cheer that customarily follows a game, "two-four-six-eight, who do we appreciate," turned into "two-four-six-eight, who do we appreci-HATE." Intergroup hostility intensified, and members of each group began to refer to their rivals as "sneaks" and "cheats." After suffering a stinging defeat in one game, the Eagles burned a banner left behind by the Rattlers. When the Rattlers discovered this "desecration," they confronted the Eagles, and a fistfight nearly broke out. The next morning, the Rattlers seized the Eagles' flag. Name calling, threats, physical scuffling, and cabin raids by the opposing groups became increasingly frequent. When asked by the experimenters to rate each other's characters, a large proportion of the boys in each group gave negative ratings to all the boys in the other group. When the tournament was finally over, the two groups refused to have anything to do with each other.

This study is a classic illustration of **realistic group conflict theory**, a well-established theory that provides one explanation for the development of intergroup conflict. The basic propositions of realistic group conflict theory are (1) when groups are pursuing objectives in which a gain by one group necessarily results in a loss by the other, they have what is called an opposition of interest; (2) this opposition of interest causes members of each group to experience frustration and to develop antagonistic attitudes toward the other group; (3) as members of one group develop negative attitudes and unfavorable perceptions about members of the other group, they become more strongly identified with and attached to their own group; (4) as solidarity and cohesion within each group increase, the likelihood of overt conflict between groups increases, and even a very slight provocation can trigger direct action by one group against another.

The pattern of conflict in the relationship between the Eagles and the Rattlers is consistent with this theory. Intergroup conflict stemming from an underlying opposition of interest is also apparent in the everyday struggle for economic survival, such as the competition between ethnic groups for access to jobs, housing, and schooling (Bobo, 1983, 1999, 2000; Olzak, 1992).

Social Identity

Another factor in intergroup conflict is how strongly members identify with their own group. Even when an underlying opposition of interest is not present, strong group identification can, by itself, produce biased behavior toward out-groups.

People have a fundamental tendency to like their own group (the in-group) and to dislike competing or opposing groups (the out-groups) (Sumner, 1906). This is because of **ethnocentrism**—the tendency to regard one's own group as the center of everything and as superior to out-groups. Ethnocen-

trism involves a pervasive and rigid distinction between the in-group and one or more out-groups. It entails stereotyped positive imagery and favorable attitudes regarding the in-group combined with stereotyped negative imagery and hostile attitudes regarding the out-groups. For example, seeing the in-group as superior and the out-group as inferior, viewing the in-group as strong and the out-group as weak, and construing the in-group as honest and peaceful and the out-group as treacherous and hostile (LeVine & Campbell, 1972; Wilder, 1981).

Ethnocentric attitudes not only cause in-group members to devalue and demean out-group members; they also lead to **discrimination**—overt acts that treat members of certain out-groups in an unfair or disadvantageous manner. The simple process of social categorization—placing people into arbitrarily defined groups that have no important meaning—is sufficient to produce intergroup discrimination (Tajfel, 1982b; Tajfel & Billig, 1974).

This effect has been demonstrated consistently using an experimental paradigm called the **minimal group paradigm**. This research finds that even arbitrary or trivial distinctions between groups trigger in-group and out-group processes. In one instance, participants were openly assigned to categories at random based on a coin toss. The results still show the same pattern as well-entrenched groups: Participants discriminate in favor of their own in-group and against the out-group. This bias is reflected both in attitudinal and evaluation measures and in the allocation of money and other rewards (Brewer, 1979; Brewer & Brown, 1998; Oakes & Turner, 1980; Tajfel, 1981).

Social identity theory of intergroup behavior, developed by Tajfel and others (Tajfel, 1981, 1982a; Tajfel & Turner, 1986), offers an account for this discrimination even when there is no utilitarian value in those beliefs or behaviors. This theory starts

Research in the minimal group paradigm consistently shows that even arbitrary group distinctions can trigger in-group and out-group processes like ethnocentrism and biased evaluations of group performance. Contact with members from the out-group can break down stereotypes and lessen intergroup conflict. Comic courtesy of xkcd.com.

by assuming that individuals want to hold a positive self-concept. According to this view, the self-concept has two components, a personal identity and a social identity, and improving the evaluation of either of these can improve one's self-concept. The social identity component depends primarily on the groups or social categories to which one belongs, and the evaluation of one's own group is determined in part by a comparison with other groups. Thus, positive social identity depends on whether the comparisons made between one's in-group and some relevant out-groups are favorable.

The desire to maintain a positive self-concept, then, creates pressures to evaluate one's own group positively. Thus, in the minimal group situation, when an individual is assigned to a group, he or she ends up thinking of that group (the in-group) as better than the other (the out-group) and as a result will have higher personal self-esteem (Aberson, Healy, & Romero, 2000; Rubin & Hewstone, 1998). He or she will also engage in actions to support this idea, such as allocating money to members of the in-group.

Aversive Events

A single aversive event, like the 9/11 terrorist attack mentioned earlier, can pro-voke open hostilities between groups (Berkowitz, 1972; Konecni, 1979). An **aversive event** is a behavioral episode caused by or attributed to an out-group that entails undesirable outcomes for members of an in-group. The unexpected loss of the basketball game is an aversive event for fans of the home team, and it can trigger conflict extending far beyond the hardwood court. Although aversive events can assume many forms, they always involve outcomes that people would prefer to avoid, and they include such things as being physically or verbally attacked, being slighted or humiliated, or being subjected to a loss of income or property.

The idea that aversive events trigger overt intergroup conflict is based on the general frustration-aggression hypothesis (see Chapter 11). This hypothesis holds that frustration leads to annoyance or anger, which can quickly turn into aggression if situational conditions are conducive (Berkowitz, 1989; Gustafson, 1989). The hypothesis is true for groups as well as individuals. If provoked by an aversive event seen to be caused by an out-group, an in-group will mobilize and attack the out-group. This response is most likely to happen when an underlying opposition of interest exists between groups, when easily identifiable characteristics (such as language, religion, or members' skin color) serve as a basis for differentiation between groups, and when members of one group already hold antagonistic attitudes and negative stereotypes regarding the other.

PERSISTENCE OF INTERGROUP CONFLICT

Intergroup conflict persists, in large part, because of biased perceptions of the out-group. In intergroup conflict, it is not uncommon for members of an in-group to harbor unrealistic impressions regarding out-group members. When in-group members hold mistaken perceptions of the out-group, disputes become increasingly difficult to resolve. Mistaken impressions arise from certain biases inherent in group perception, including the illusion that the out-group is homogeneous, an excessive reliance on stereotypes, errors in causal attribution, and incorrect evaluation of in-group performance relative to that of the out-group.

Out-Group Homogeneity

There is a tendency for in-group members to overestimate the degree of similarity or homogeneity among out-group members (Linville, Fischer, & Salovey, 1989; Quattrone, 1986). Although in-group members perceive and appreciate the diversity within the in-group, individuals usually perceive less variability among members of the out-group (Mullen & Hu, 1989; Rothbart, Dawes, & Park, 1984). In other words, they tend to perceive the out-group members as "all alike." This is referred to as the **illusion of out-group homogeneity**.

This perceptual bias is quite general and widespread. It has been observed in men's and women's perceptions of each other (Park & Rothbart, 1982), of students attending rival universities (Quattrone & Jones, 1980), of young and elderly persons (Brewer & Lui, 1984), and of people in different occupations (Brauer, 2001). Quattrone (1986) suggests that limited contact with out-group members and richer contact with in-group members contributes to this bias. Fewer experiences with an out-group make it less likely that the perceivers will have a chance to see or appreciate the extent to which out-group members differ from one another in important ways.

Group Stereotypes and Images

In-group members often make use of stereotypes (see Chapter 6) of the out-group. Although stereotypes do have certain virtues (for instance, they make it possible to process information more quickly), reliance on them can foster mistaken impressions of the out-group and its members. For one thing, stereotypes often exaggerate or accentuate the differences between an in-group and an out-group; they make the groups seem to differ from one another to a greater extent than they really do (Eiser, 1984). Moreover, many stereotypes are depreciatory, and they often ascribe negatively valued traits or characteristics to out-group members.

Individuals are also likely to overestimate similarities between themselves and their in-groups relative to themselves and their out-groups. Thus, the stereotypes created of out-groups tend to attribute characteristics to its members that are opposed to the individual's view of self and in-group: They are stingy, we are generous. This, in turn, helps create unrealistic contrasts between in-groups and out-groups, exaggerating differences and promoting intergroup conflict (Riketta, 2005). One such difference is to perceive the in-group and its behavior as relatively peaceful and cooperative and to perceive the adversary as aggressive and competitive (Bronfenbrenner, 1961).

Another important characteristic of stereotypes is that they tend to have low schematic complexity—that is, they are oversimplified and unrealistic (Linville & Jones, 1980). This lower schematic complexity puts in-group members at risk of neglecting or misinterpreting new information about the activities of the out-group, especially if it is inconsistent with the stereotype. For instance, if a peaceful overture by the out-group is difficult to understand in light of the in-group's stereotype of the out-group, the in-group members may incorrectly reinterpret the action as a veiled threat and react with hostility.

Ultimate Attribution Error

Several studies have revealed a perceptual bias that Pettigrew (1979) has called the **ultimate attribution error**. When a member of our own in-group behaves in a positive or desirable manner, we are likely to attribute that behavior to the member's internal, stable characteristics (such as positive personality dispositions). If that same person behaves in a negative or undesirable manner, we will tend to discount it and attribute it to external, unstable factors (she was operating under unusual stress or having a bad day). However, when perceiving a member of an out-group, we display the opposite bias. Positive behaviors by outgroup members are attributed to unstable, external factors (situational pressures or luck). Negative behaviors are attributed to stable, internal factors (undesirable personal traits or dispositions). In other words, you are more likely to blame the out-group for negative outcomes but are less likely to give it credit for positive outcomes (Cooper & Fazio, 1986; Hewstone, 1990; Taylor & Jaggi, 1974). These attribution biases tend to maintain each side's negative view re-

garding the character and motives of the other side.

Biased Evaluation of Group Performance

Another common bias is for in-group members to rate the performance of their own group more favorably than that of the out-group, even when there is no objective basis for this difference (Hinkle & Schopler, 1986). One illustration of this bias appeared in the Robbers Cave study discussed earlier. When antagonism between the Eagles and the Rattlers was at its peak, the investigators arranged for the boys to participate in a bean-collecting contest. They scattered beans on the ground, and the boys collected as many as possible in one minute. Each boy stored his beans in a sack with a narrow opening, so he could not check the number of beans in it. Later, the experimenters projected a picture of the beans gathered by each boy on a screen in a large room. Boys from both groups tried to estimate the number of beans in each boy's collection. The projection time was very short and precluded counting. In reality, the experimenters projected the same number of beans (35) each time, although in different arrangements. The boys' estimates revealed a strong in-group bias; they overestimated the number of beans collected by members of their own group and underestimated the number collected by the out-group. This bias increases as the distinction between ingroup and out-group becomes more salient (Brewer, 1979).

Bias in the evaluation of group performance can produce a variety of consequences. It can serve as a positive motivational device that strengthens the in-group's effort, boosts group morale, and helps members avoid complacency (Worchel, Lind, & Kaufman, 1975). However, overvaluation of an in-group's relative performance can lead to faulty decision making or groupthink

(Janis, 1982; see Chapter 14). Overestimation of a group's capacity relative to that of an adversary may cause the in-group to become overconfident and, hence, too willing to continue a fight that realistically should be abandoned or settled.

RESOLVING INTERGROUP CONFLICT

One cannot resolve intergroup conflict merely by "reversing" the processes that initially caused it. It is often impossible to eliminate the underlying opposition of interest, to diminish the ethnocentric identification with the in-group, or to forestall aversive events. Nevertheless, investigators and practitioners have developed various techniques to reduce or resolve intergroup conflict. In this section, we discuss four of them.

Superordinate Goals

One of the most effective techniques for resolving intergroup conflict is to develop what are called superordinate goals. A **superordinate goal** is an objective held in common by all groups in a conflict that cannot be achieved by any one group without the supportive efforts of the other group. Research confirms that, once introduced, superordinate goals usually reduce in-group bias and intergroup conflict (Bettencourt, Brewer, Croak, & Miller, 1992; Gaertner et al., 1999; Sherif et al., 1961).

When the conflict between the Eagles and the Rattlers was at its peak in the Robbers Cave experiment, the researchers introduced several goals that involved important shared needs. First, the researchers arranged for the system that supplied water to both groups to break down. To find the source of the problem and restore water to the camp, the two groups of boys had to work together. Next, the food delivery truck

became stuck along the roadway. If the boys were to eat, they had to work together to free the heavy vehicle and push it up a steep grade. By inducing some cooperation between the groups, the superordinate goal structure also reduced hostility (Sherif et al., 1961).

The impact of superordinate goals on conflict reduction is not usually immediate but rather gradual and cumulative. The results are stronger when several goals are introduced one after another rather than a single goal. Because superordinate goals are cumulative in effect, they have greater impact when they are massed (Blake, Shepard, & Mouton, 1964; Sherif et al., 1961).

Why does this work? First, superordinate goals serve as a basis for restructuring the relationship between groups. Superordinate goals create cooperative interdependence between the in-group and the out-group. By changing a hostile win-lose situation into one of collaborative problem solving, with the possibility of a win-win outcome, a superordinate goal reduces friction between groups. The activities of out-group members will become valued by in-group members because members of one group are contributing to outcomes desired by the other.

Second, the introduction of a superordinate goal often increases interaction between in-group and out-group members. Increased contact by itself is generally not sufficient to reduce intergroup bias or hostility, but if some of the interaction with the out-group members is personalized rather than just task-oriented or if it provides information that reduces stereotyping, the superordinate goal will reduce bias and hostility (Bettencourt et al., 1992; Brewer & Miller, 1984; Worchel, 1986).

Third, the introduction of a superordinate goal can generate a new, superordinate social identity shared by all members. The superordinate goal reduces the sharp distinction between the in-group ("us") and the out-group ("them"), and a new common identity applying to all members of both groups is created. One theory of recategorization, termed the common in-group identity model, proposes that when persons belonging to separate social groups come to view themselves as members of a single social unit or category, their attitudes toward one another will become more positive (Dovidio, Gaertner, Isen, & Lowrance, 1995; Gaertner et al., 1993; Gaertner, Mann, Murrell, & Dovidio, 1989). Former out-group members will increase in attractiveness, and the favoritism that in-group members originally afforded their own group will now be extended to the whole collective.

Intergroup Contact

An increase in contact and communication between members of opposing groups can also reduce intergroup conflict. According to the **intergroup contact hypothesis**, increased contact should lessen stereotypes and reduce bias and, consequently, lessen antagonism between groups (Allport, 1954; Pettigrew & Tropp, 2006). For example, research finds that more contact with the homeless—whether having a homeless relative, interacting with them at a shelter, reading an article about the problem of homelessness, or even living in a neighborhood with a large homeless population—increases sympathy toward the group and fosters a willingness to sacrifice to help a homeless person (Lee, Farrell, & Link, 2004).

Although intergroup contact often reduces prejudice and conflict between groups in some cases, it does not always do so (Brewer & Kramer, 1985; Herek & Capitanio, 1996; Hewstone & Brown, 1986; Pettigrew, 1997; Riordan, 1978). School desegregation, for instance, increased contact between Black and White children, but it did not always produce positive changes in intergroup relations (Cook, 1984; Gerard, 1983). In some instances, increasing the level of intergroup contact can actually increase conflict (Brewer, 1986). Given these mixed findings, social psychologists have focused their attention on identifying the conditions under which intergroup contact leads to reduced bias and conflict as well as the conditions under which it does not.

Sustained Close Contact. Findings suggest that contact between members of different groups is more effective in reducing conflict if the contact is sustained and personal rather than brief and superficial (Amir, 1976; Brown & Turner, 1981; Levin, van Laar, & Sidanius, 2003). Low levels of intimacy will have little effect on intergroup prejudice and stereotyping (Segal, 1965).

There are several reasons why sustained close contact tends to reduce prejudice and stereotyping. First, cognitive dissonance may produce attitude change. If individuals with negative attitudes find themselves subject to situational pressures that increase interaction, and if they consequently engage in positive actions toward members of an out-group, their behavior will be inconsistent with their attitudes, which may create a state of cognitive dissonance (see Chapter 7). The theory of cognitive dissonance predicts that these persons will end up changing their attitudes—becoming more positive toward the out-group—as a means of justifying to themselves their new behavior.

Second, during close contact, members of different groups may engage in self-disclosure. Higher levels of self-disclosure generally promote interpersonal liking, provided that the attributes one person reveals are viewed positively—or at least not negatively—by the other (Collins & Miller, 1994).

BOX 13.2 Using *Remember the Titans* to Understand Intergroup Conflict Reduction

Many of the social psychological processes discussed in this book are illustrated in popular television shows and movies. Intergroup processes are no exception.

Remember the Titans follows the football team at Alexandria, Virginia's T. C. Williams High School during the 1971 season, its first as an integrated school and team. Herman Boone, played by Denzel Washington, is tasked with winning football games. However, he realizes that intergroup dynamics may stand in the way of that goal, and he employs specific strategies to reduce the conflict evident between the Black and White players.

The "coming together" of the Titans over the course of the film clearly illustrates three important sociological theories of intergroup conflict reduction—intergroup contact, superordinate goals, and shared identities.

Coach Boone began by trying to make Black and White students interact by having them sit together on the bus to camp, room together while there, and dine together at meals. When this contact failed at first to lessen the animosity between groups or forge an integrated community, Boone specifically instructs the players to spend time getting to know players of another race—things about their families, about their likes and dislikes. The stereotypes and generalizations prevalent between the groups become clear in the scenes that follow. At one point, a White player begrudgingly sits down to learn more about a Black player and asks, "What does your daddy do?" Before the player can answer, the White player says, "You do have a daddy,

right?" Only through ongoing, meaningful conversations are these stereotypes broken down.

Some of these conversations lead to close friendships. Scenes from the movie convey the importance of these friendships between group members, specifically because they offer numerous opportunities for anxiety reduction, empathy, and knowledge. Most notable is the friendship between the White team captain, Gerry Bertier, and a Black standout, Julius Campbell. When these two players move beyond superficial conversation to honestly assessing one another's strengths and weaknesses both on and off the field, their friendship begins. This relationship moves to a new level during a scene in the locker room at camp. One of the Black players makes a joke about Gerry Bertier's mama. Clearly upset, Gerry poises for a physically violent counterattack, but Julius comes and puts his hand on Bertier's shoulder and, smiling, shoots an insult back at the antagonist. This begins a round of "mama jokes" and exposes Bertier to this side of locker room banter that is apparently common among his Black teammates. The scene ends a few mama jokes later when another White player makes a joke that elicits raucous laughter and Bertier exclaims with good cheer, "Now that's a mama joke!"

Throughout the film, the shared goal of becoming an excellent football team and winning games provides a powerful superordinate goal for the players. Here, Boone himself plays a critical role as a no-nonsense authority figure. Superordinate goals are most effective when initiated by an authority figure or an individual or cause

Third, sustained close contact between members of different groups can serve to break down stereotypes. Of course, contact with a single representative or "token" member of an out-group is usually not sufficient on its own to change group stereotypes because that person can too easily be viewed as an exception who is not representative of the entire out-group (Weber & Crocker, 1983). But close contact with multiple members of an out-group sustained over time may provide enough contrary information to compel a change in old stereotypes.

outside of the groups themselves (Johnson and Lewicki, 1969)—institutional support for the intergroup contact. Coach Boone makes it clear that he is such an authority figure—without vested interest in either racial group. He does not automatically side with the Black students because he is a Black man himself and does not stand for any behavior that gets in the way of winning. Early on, Boone informs his staff that he is there as a football coach, nothing else, and he came to win, and he tells his players that when they put on that Titan uniform, they better come out to win. Therefore, winning and overcoming any barriers that might exist to accomplishing that become the team's superordinate goal.

A pivotal moment in the establishment of this goal occurs during football camp. Boone rouses the team at three in the morning to take a run through the woods surrounding Gettysburg College. Despite a reminder from his assistant coach that this is a high school football team and not the Marines, Boone pushes the players harder. As the sun comes up, the team ends up at the field where the Gettysburg Battle was fought, and Boone turns to them and says,

> Fifty-thousand died fighting the same fight we're still fighting today. . . . Take a lesson from the dead. If we don't come together right now on this hallowed ground, we too will be destroyed. . . . Respect each other [and] learn to play this game like men.

Boone takes winning one game at a time and, with each achievement, gains more legitimacy with players and coaches alike, slowly breaking down the barriers between the racial groups and enhancing the positive effect of the superordinate goals.

Finally, integrating the in- and out-group (in this case, the Black and the White players) into a single group results in a reduction of bias. At a number of times in the film, Coach Boone reminds the team that they are in this together and they are all Titans. The viewer watches as the use of "they," "them," and "those people" lessens and there is an increase in the use of "we," "us," and "the Titans." However, the emergent shared identity is best illustrated with the team chants and choreographed dances emphasizing unity:

> Everywhere we go, people want to know . . .
> Who we are, who we are . . .
> So we tell them, so we tell them . . .
> We are the Titans, the mighty-mighty Titans.

Scenes of segregated stands of football spectators and conflict in the school as a whole remind the viewer that the players' shared identity as football players gives them a special perspective the other students lack. With time, however, the community and school come around. Students celebrate together, spectators sit together integrated by race, and town businesses proclaim that this is "Titan Country." Although the film occasionally departs from the specific historical reality of the Titans, as a narrative, it captures the spirit of social psychological research on conflict reduction in integrated schools; athletic teams really do serve an important role in school integration.

Source: Adapted from Collett, Kelly, & Sobolewski, 2010.

Equal-Status Contact. Intergroup contact is also more likely to reduce conflict when in-group and out-group members occupy positions of equal status than when they occupy positions of unequal status (Riordan, 1978; Robinson & Preston, 1976). One early demonstration of equal-status contact comes from a classic study conducted in the military during World War II (Mannheimer & Williams, 1949). At that time, the U.S. Army was still largely segregated by race; only a few companies were integrated. This study showed that White soldiers changed their attitudes toward Black soldiers after the two racial groups fought in combat as equals, side by side. When asked how they felt about their company including Black as well as White platoons, only 7% of the White soldiers from integrated units reacted negatively. In contrast, 62% of the soldiers in completely segregated White companies reacted negatively to the prospect of having Black platoons in their unit. Equal-status contact has been effective in reducing prejudice in other situations as well, including among Black and White children at interracial summer camps (Clore, Bray, Itkin, & Murphy, 1978) and in interracial housing situations (Hamilton & Bishop, 1976).

To better understand why equal-status contact is important, consider what happens when contact is not based on equal status (Cohen, 1984). When status is unequal, members of a higher-status group may refuse to accept influence or to learn from a lower-status group. They can justify this to themselves on the grounds that the lower-status group has less skill or experience. With one side unwilling to accept influence, expectations of lesser competence will appear to be supported, and stereotypes will be all the more difficult to overcome. To have any impact, the lower-status group will need to demonstrate repeatedly to the higher-status group that it is as good as the other in relevant respects. For all these reasons, intergroup contact is more effective in reducing prejudice and conflict if members of the different groups enter a situation on an equal footing.

Institutionally Supported Contact. Finally, intergroup contact is more likely to reduce stereotyping and create favorable attitudes if it is backed by social norms that promote equality among groups (Adlerfer, 1982; Cohen, 1980; Williams, 1977). If the norms support openness, friendliness, and mutual respect, the contact has a greater chance of changing attitudes and reducing prejudice than if they do not.

Institutionally supported intergroup contact—that is, contacts sanctioned by an outside authority or by established customs—are more likely to produce positive changes than unsupported contacts. Without institutional support, members of an in-group may be reluctant to interact with outsiders because they feel doing so is deviant or simply inappropriate. With the presence of institutional support, however, contact between groups is more likely to be seen as appropriate, expected, and worthwhile. For instance, with respect to desegregation in elementary schools, there is evidence that students were more highly motivated and learned more in classes conducted by teachers (that is, authority figures) who supported rather than opposed desegregation (Epstein, 1985).

In sum, intergroup contact tends to reduce conflict when it is anchored by institutional or authoritative support, when it is based on equal rather than unequal status, and when it is personal rather than superficial in character.

SUMMARY

What Is a Group? A group is a social unit that consists of two or more persons and has certain defining attributes, including recognized membership, interaction among members, shared goals and objectives, and norms that guide members' behavior. Primary and secondary groups differ on types of goals and level of intimacy. A cohesive group is one that can strongly attract and hold its members. Interdependence coupled with positive emotion enhances cohesion. Two important types of cohesion are social cohesion and task cohesion, and the level of a group's cohesion affects the interaction among members. Members in highly cohesive groups communicate more than those in less cohesive groups; they also exert more influence over one another, and their interaction is friendlier and more cooperative. A group goal is a desirable outcome that members strive collectively to bring about. Group goals differ from individual goals—outcomes desired by members for themselves.

Conformity to Group Norms. A norm is a rule or standard that specifies how group members are expected to behave under given circumstances. Group norms coordinate activity among members, provide a frame of reference that enables members to interpret their environment, and define the common identity of group members. Conformity means adherence by an individual to group norms and expectations. The Asch conformity paradigm uses a simple visual discrimination task to investigate conditions that produce individuals' conformity to the majority's judgment. Groups can use both normative influence and informational influence to exert pressure on individual members. Sherif's autokinetic effect studies illustrate the impact of informational influence on group members. Many factors affect the level of conformity in Asch-type situations. Conformity increases with group size up to three, and it is greater when the majority is unanimous than when it is not. Group members are also more likely to conform when they are highly attracted to a group and when conformity will lead to liking and acceptance by other members. Commitment to future interaction affects conformity. Finally, task competence affects conformity; members who oppose the majority's view will resist conformity pressures to the extent that they believe themselves to be more competent than other members.

Intergroup Conflict. Conflict between groups influences processes within groups. Conflict increases the level of cohesion of the in-group as members increase their commitment and unite to face a common adversary. However, it may also produce rivalry for leadership among in-group members, and this rivalry can produce more militant leadership. Conflict often changes the normative structure of the in-group and both increases the pressure on in-group members to conform and lessens the majority's tolerance of dissenters.

Development of Intergroup Conflict. Intergroup conflict has several origins. (1) Groups often have opposing interests that prevent them from achieving their goals simultaneously, leading to friction, hostility, and overt conflict. (2) A high level of in-group identification, accompanied by ethnocentric attitudes, may create discrimination between groups, which escalates conflict. (3) One group, by threatening or depriving another, may create an aversive event that turns submerged antagonism into overt conflict.

Persistence of Intergroup Conflict. Although some conflicts between groups dissipate quickly, others last for a long time. Several mechanisms support the persistence of intergroup conflict. Perception of the out-group by in-group members is often biased. This bias, caused by insufficient information regarding the out-group and excessive reliance on stereotypes, produces an incorrect understanding of the characteristics and intentions of out-group members and an overestimation of in-group capabilities.

Resolution of Intergroup Conflict. Several techniques can be used to reduce intergroup conflict. One is to introduce superordinate goals into the conflict. Because goals of this type can be achieved only through the joint efforts of opposing sides, they promote cooperative behavior and serve as a basis for restructuring the relationship between groups. Another technique is to increase intergroup contact. This approach is more effective in reducing bias and conflict when contact is sustained, close, based on equal status, and supported institutionally.

List of Key Terms and Concepts

aversive event (p. 457)
conformity (p. 446)
discrimination (p. 456)
ethnocentrism (p. 456)
goal isomorphism (p. 445)
group (p. 440)
group cohesion (p. 442)
group goal (p. 444)
illusion of out-group homogeneity (p. 458)
informational influence (p. 448)
intergroup conflict (p. 452)
intergroup contact hypothesis (p. 461)
majority influence (p. 446)
minimal group paradigm (p. 456)
norm (p. 445)
normative influence (p. 448)
primary group (p. 441)
priming (p. 451)
realistic group conflict theory (p. 455)
secondary group (p. 441)
social identity theory of intergroup
  behavior (p. 456)
superordinate goal (p. 460)
ultimate attribution error (p. 459)

Critical Thinking Skill:
Promoting Higher Order Cognitive Skills

As you read this chapter, are you stopping to ask yourself questions? What kinds of questions are you asking or would you ask someone else if you were testing each other's understandings of the material? When you study the material, how are you engaging with it?

By this point in the semester, critical engagement—that is beneficial for both understanding and retention—should be coming naturally to you. However, this exercise is a good opportunity to step back and evaluate the types of questions you are asking yourself and the depth of the connections you are making (Bloom, 1956).

At the most basic level, questions test what you remember. Are the questions that you are asking things like, "What are the four attributes of a group?" or "What is the definition of a norm?" These questions simply ask you to recall data or information. Anyone could memorize these things without truly understanding them. It is slightly more cognitively demanding to also require evidence of understanding the information we retain. For example, "What is intergroup conflict? Describe how it affects group processes." Or "In your own words, summarize how the Titans were able to overcome intergroup conflict and to become a cohesive unit."

Higher-order questions require application, analysis, synthesis, or evaluation.

Application questions ask you to transfer the concepts you are learning to new situations. An example might be, "What is a group that you belong to? Demonstrate how it fits the four attributes of a group." The benefit of this question is that to answer it, you must have the knowledge of the four attributes of a group (a lower-order skill), but you are also using a higher-order process by applying the concepts to a novel situation that is personally relevant.

Questions that engage skills of analysis encourage you to divide material or information into its component parts and then demonstrate how to put it back together. If you asked yourself to "Use the tenets of

Realistic Group Conflict Theory to explain a specific instance of enduring intergroup conflict in contemporary society," you must know the theory, including its individual propositions, and be able to engage each of those propositions in tandem to support your single example.

A question that requires synthesis pulls together seemingly separate or distinct knowledge to create a more complete picture or enhance an outcome: "The chapter discusses conformity as related to group norms, but how is conformity linked to other topics related to groups, including cohesion, goals, and intergroup conflict? How might making these connections enhance our understanding of conformity and groups?"

Finally, an evaluation question asks you to make judgments about the value of ideas, to develop opinions based on specific criteria. An example of such a question might be, "Imagine that your dorm's resident adviser approaches you for help. He heard you were taking a social psychology class and hopes you might have a solution for how to restore harmony between two roommates who can't seem to get along. If you were to give him a solution that is grounded in theory from this chapter, providing evidence of its effectiveness, what would it be?" This question should also prompt you to use creativity to solve a problem, another higher-order skill.

In sum, asking ourselves questions as we read is an invaluable way to stay alert and to learn material. However, we must also evaluate the types of questions we are asking. Although knowledge is important, higher-order questions require more critical thinking and reap more benefits for engagement, retention, and understanding.

What types of questions are you asking yourself? If they are currently higher-order questions, that is wonderful—keep it up! If not, how could you take what you learned here to shift your approach to studying?

GROUP
PROCESSES

INTRODUCTION

The trial has ended, and now it is time to deliberate. You think the defendant is probably guilty, but you want to hear how the others feel. Delivering a guilty verdict is not a trivial matter. You look around at the other jurors who are sitting at the table in the deliberation room.

- Alex is a senior at Yale, where he is apparently at the top of his class. He is heading to medical school after graduation.
- Sophia looks tired. She has talked about her three children and how difficult it has been to keep up with things around the house because of the long days in court. She misses staying home with her toddler while the twins are at school.
- LaToya is anxious to get back to work. She is concerned about how her oncology patients and their families are doing without her on the nursing rotation.
- Charlotte has been quiet during the meals the jury has shared, but you cannot help but notice how beautiful she is. You heard her tell Sophia that she just got a modeling contract in New York.
- Martin is vice president of a local grocery store chain. Judging by the wisps of gray in his sandy-brown hair, he is in his late forties. With his confident demeanor, it is no surprise he has been so successful in business.

The judge has instructed you six to choose a foreperson, someone who will keep the jury on task and communicate with the court if necessary. The six of you look around at one another. Who will you choose? How will that choice affect the behavior of the jury and the group's ultimate decision?

Social psychologists have studied small groups like this jury for over 50 years. Their findings show that what happens next in that jury deliberation room is not based on chance but rather is the result of highly structured—and, therefore, predictable—group processes. Attributes of the group members (gender, race, age, occupation, attractiveness) and of the group itself (a collective task, a designated foreperson) influence both individuals' behavior in the group and the group's effectiveness at achieving its goals.

This chapter introduces the variety of intergroup processes of interest to social psychologists today. In doing so it addresses the following questions:

1. How do group leaders emerge? What types of leaders are there? Why might people take on roles in groups?

2. Who is afforded more status in groups, and why? How are groups influenced by the diversity of the individuals involved in them?

3. How do groups make decisions? What can social psychology tell us about why they sometimes make the wrong decision? How are individuals' opinions influenced by the group?

4. Why do some people have more power in relationships, whereas other people are dependent? How do trust and commitment emerge between people? How does interaction affect emotional attachment to others?

5. What principles do people use to determine what is fair? How do they respond when they perceive outcomes or processes to be unfair?

THE SYSTEMATIC STUDY OF GROUPS

Although social psychologists have long been interested in groups and their influence on individuals (Allport, 1924; Cooley, 1902; Simmel, 1902), the systematic study of group processes did not begin until the mid-twentieth century, when Robert Bales (1950) started to record detailed accounts of interaction in small groups. His interest in group processes began while he was a research associate at Yale, working in alcohol studies. As part of that position, he observed therapeutic treatment groups for alcohol addicts. Watching these groups and the individuals who participated in them, Bales began to consider how individuals' behavior in groups stemmed not only from their personal characteristics but also from characteristics of the group. He formulated a method—Interaction Process Analysis (IPA)—to systematically document group members' behavior so he could better understand group-level patterns. With this method, Bales did not focus on the specific content of communication between group members; rather, he was interested in capturing the types of contributions group members made (a joke, a suggestion, a criticism), which group member made it, and to whom it was directed. Figure 14.1 shows his coding scheme.

Group processes researchers often study groups of students—or other community members (Milgram, 1974, Zimbardo, 1973)—in the laboratory to control as much of the situation as possible. Bales was no exception. The participants in much of his research were Harvard undergraduates whom he invited to a laboratory in the Harvard Social Relations department. Bales would have the groups work on a **collective task**—a task that cannot be achieved without the participation of all group members. In one such task, Bales had the groups discuss a case, not unlike the criminal cases that juries deliberate, and then reach a unanimous

agreement on a recommended punishment. Although a discussion is not generally seen as a collective task, making a unanimous decision is. As the group worked together, Bales and his research assistants would observe, meticulously categorize, and record every group-oriented behavior that group members made.

The small groups that Bales studied were **homogeneous**—that is, they were similar on a number of factors. They were all white, undergraduate men (Harvard was a men's college until 1977). They were typically sophomores, in their second year of study at the university.

Bales and his research team screened subjects to ensure that the students interacting in groups would not know one another. He wanted to be absolutely sure that the group dynamics he was studying were not influenced by anything beyond what he and his research team could manipulate and observe in the laboratory. Bales discovered that when members of these homogeneous groups of strangers started to discuss their problem, specific patterns emerged. For one, the initial equality among members disappeared, and distinctions quickly materialized between them.

Bales noted that some members participated more than others and exercised more influence regarding the group's decision. The most talkative member in the problem-solving groups typically initiated 40 to 45 percent of all communicative acts. The second-most active person initiated approximately 20 to 30 percent of all communication. This pattern is apparent in Table 14.1, which summarizes the percentage of acts initiated by each member for groups ranging from three to eight members. As the size of the group increased, the most talkative person still initiated a large percentage of the communicative acts, whereas the less talkative individuals were crowded out almost completely (Bales, 1970).

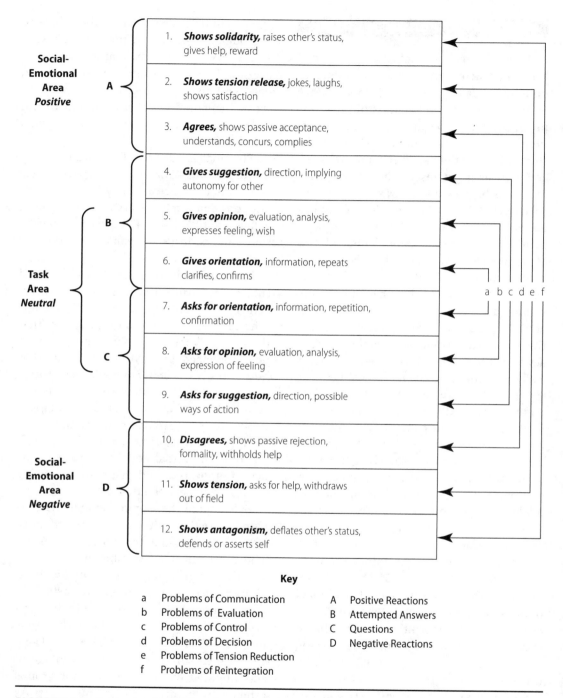

FIGURE 14.1 Categorization Scheme for Interaction Process Observations

Source: Adapted from Bales, *Interaction Process Analysis: A Method for the Study of Small Groups.* 1950.

TABLE 14.1 Percentage of Total Acts Initiated by Each Group Member as a Function of Group Size

MEMBER NUMBER	GROUP SIZE					
	3	4	5	6	7	8
1	44	32	47	43	43	40
2	33	29	22	19	15	17
3	23	23	15	14	12	13
4		16	10	11	10	10
5			6	8	9	9
6				5	6	6
7					5	4
8						3

Note: Data are based on a total of 134,421 acts observed in 167 groups consisting of 3 to 8 members.

Source: Adapted from Bales, 1970, pp. 467–474.

These patterns remain tremendously stable once developed (Fisek, 1974). The group member who initiates the most communication during the beginning minutes of interaction is very likely to continue doing so throughout the interaction. Furthermore, these patterns tend to hold for the life of the group. If the same group meets for several sessions, the member who ranked highest in participation during the first session is likely to rank highest during subsequent sessions.

Of course, Bales was more interested in the quality of communications than the quantity. He wanted to know the specific types of contributions group members made and how these affected individuals' perceptions of their fellow group members. Observers scored the types of contributions (using the coding scheme illustrated in Figure 14.1), and then, at the end of the discussion period, group members filled out questionnaires and rated one another. Items included things like, "Who had the best ideas in the group?" "Who did the most to guide the group discussion?" and "Which group member was the most likable?"

Typically, there was high agreement among group members in their answers regarding ideas and guidance. In short, the person initiating the most communicative acts—generally the person who talked the most—was perceived as the group's task leader (guiding discussion, having the best ideas). But this task leader was not usually the best-liked member. In fact, he was sometimes the least-liked member. In most groups, the second-highest initiator was the best-liked member. Why does this occur?

In general, the highest initiator is someone who drives the group toward the attainment of its goals. Most of the acts this person initiates are task oriented (see the clustering of contributions on the left side of Figure 14.1). For this reason, social psychologists call the high initiator the group's **task specialist**. However, in an effort to get things done, the task specialist also tends to engage in negative behaviors. This type of leader might be pushy or even openly antagonistic, and even if it helps influence group opinion, this aggressive behavior can create tension.

Importantly, the negative behavior of the task-specialist opens the door for some other member, the **social-emotional specialist**, to ease the tension and soothe hurt feelings in the group. The acts this person initiates are likely to be acts that release tension and encourage solidarity (see the positive social-emotional categories in Figure 14.1). The social-emotional specialist is the group member who exercises tact or tells a joke at just the right moment. This person helps to ease tensions and maintain good spirits within the group. Not surprisingly, the social-emotional specialist is often the best-liked member of the group.

Thus, in task groups, there are two basic functions—getting things done and keeping relations pleasant—that are typically performed by different members. When group members divide up functions in this manner, we say that **role differentiation** has occurred in the group. Although role differentiation is common, it is not inevitable. In 20 to 30 percent of case studies in the laboratory, a single member performs both the task-oriented and the social-emotional functions (Lewis, 1972). For groups in natural, nonlaboratory settings, the incidence of combined roles may be higher (Rees & Segal, 1984).

Both informal and formal groups tend to engage in role differentiation for efficiency. Usually, it is not productive for all members of a group to try to perform the same tasks. Instead, the group engages in a division of labor in which members are assigned different tasks, or roles.

A **role** is a cluster of rules or expectations indicating the set of duties to be performed by a member occupying a given position within a group; it describes the function that a group member serves for the group. Because group members hold role expectations regarding one another's performance, they feel justified in making demands on one another. For instance, the members of a sales group expect the salespeople to contact potential customers, to identify customers' needs, and to offer customers the products that meet these needs. If, for some reason, one of the salespeople suddenly stopped contacting customers, other members of the sales group would view it as a violation of role expectations and would doubtless take action to correct the situation.

STATUS AND EXPECTATIONS

In their research on group participation, Bales and his graduate student researchers discovered a strange phenomenon. In some groups, role and status differences—measured by members' rate of participation, their influence over group decisions, and the types of acts they contributed—emerged rather slowly. In others, it happened almost instantaneously. In trying to locate an explanation, the researchers realized that there was an important difference between these groups: some began the group task with more knowledge about one another than others.

Remember that Bales intended for these groups to be strangers. He was careful to ensure that the young men participating in a group had no prior interaction with one another. However, he had been less cautious once the men were in the laboratory. In some cases, there was time for the participants to chat before the experiment began. Think about the small talk you might make with other students in a waiting room. You might ask them where they are from, what year they are, and what they are majoring in. At Harvard, where almost all students live on campus for the entire four years of school, students would also ask one another what hall they lived in. These halls, not unlike fraternities, had reputations. The researchers realized that even though this information was completely unrelated to the task at hand, group members drew on it when determining who to turn to as a leader (Willer & Walker, 2007).

Think back to the jury at the beginning of the chapter. Given the little that you know about the jury members—the tidbits that you have picked up throughout the trial and based on what you can observe—who do you think is most likely to be chosen as foreperson?

Status Characteristics

What happens in newly formed groups whose members are not identical in social attributes? What about groups, like the jury, that are composed of members who differ in gender, race, age, education, attractiveness, and occupation? We encounter such groups every day—PTAs, student committees, neighborhood associations, church groups, and so on. Social psychologists find that many of the within-group differences in participation and influence that emerge in heterogeneous groups are based on their members' characteristics.

A **status characteristic** is any social attribute of a person around which evaluations and beliefs about that person come to be organized. When a characteristic is imbued with status value, certain states of that status characteristic are afforded more esteem in a culture than are other states (Ridgeway & Walker, 1995). For example, in the United States, gender is a status characteristic, with men thought to be more competent than women; race is a status characteristic, with Whites perceived of as more capable than Blacks; education is a status characteristic, with graduate students believed to be more skilled than people who only completed high school and a student at Yale as more intelligent than a student from Southern Connecticut State University.

These cultural beliefs about status characteristics are carried into small-group settings, where they influence interactions. In problem-solving groups like the ones Bales studied, individuals of higher status are expected to make more contributions, and their contributions are perceived as more valuable. These expectations lead to the formation of a **power and prestige order** in groups, with those of lower status often deferring to those of higher status and those of higher status taking the lead in decision making (Berger & Webster, 2006).

Types of Status Characteristics. There are two types of status characteristics that guide performance expectations: diffuse and specific.

Diffuse status characteristics influence ideas about general competence. For example, in most cultures around the world, people assume that men are more competent than women across a range of tasks (analytic ability, conversation, driving). Men, therefore, benefit from greater esteem and are thought of as worthy of more respect than women not only in those domains but also overall (Ridgeway, 2011). In fact, because of the *burden-of-proof process*, diffuse status characteristics are assumed to be relevant and operative across a range of situations unless those attributes are explicitly demonstrated to be unrelated to task performance (Berger, Cohen, & Zelditch, 1972). In other words, group members will assume that men will perform better at being a foreperson unless they are aware of evidence that gender is not at all related to the task or that women have actually been found to perform better on it.

Specific status characteristics (mathematical ability, athleticism) also influence performance expectations. However, these characteristics must be relevant to the task to influence expectations and can only be applied to a more circumscribed set of tasks. These attributes more directly and precisely indicate someone's level of ability on the task to be performed by the group. For example, if the trial was about a nurse who had accidentally administered the wrong drug to a patient, the group might

With gender a diffuse status characteristic, men are often afforded more influence in task groups regardless of the task at hand. However, if the group task is feminized—as some types of design might be—then women may be able to exert more influence in group decision making.
© monkeybusinessimages/iStock

decide that LaToya possessed a specific status characteristic (her experience as a nurse) that would make her more qualified to be foreperson—or to have informal influence over deliberations—than if the case was about tax evasion.

Status Generalization

Studies show that persons with high standing on status characteristics are accorded more respect and esteem than are other members, and they are chosen more frequently as leaders. Their contributions to group problem solving are evaluated more positively, they are given more opportunities to participate in discussions, and they exert more influence over group decisions (Balkwell, 1991; Berger, Cohen, & Zelditch, 1972; Webster & Foschi, 1988). The tendency for members' status characteristics to affect group structure and interaction is called status generalization.

When **status generalization** occurs, a member's status outside a group affects his or her status inside that group. That is, the members who hold higher status in society at large will tend to hold higher status in the group (Cohen & Zhou, 1991).

For example, you—like many Americans—might begin jury deliberations believing that Martin, as a professional with experience, would be a more competent leader than Sophia, who is a stay-at-home mom. Because of the influence of status characteristics on the power and prestige order, you and the other jury members will likely decide that Martin should be foreperson. Although the foreperson is not a formal leadership role, you will find that you and the rest of the group increasingly defer to him. As a foreperson, he will likely talk more than other jurors (Ellison & Munro, 2010). The other members of the jury are more likely to ask what he thinks, cede the floor to him when he wants it, and defer to him. They are also inclined to select the verdict that he suggests in deliberations. This is not just conjecture from students in laboratory experiments; these trends have been supported using research on mock jury deliberations, with juries composed of people from a typical jury pool (Strodtbeck, Simon, & Hawkins, 1965). Social psychologists found that men on these mock juries initiated more interaction than did women. Furthermore, those with occupations of higher status—both men and women—participated more than those of lower status. A questionnaire completed by mock jurors at the end of the sessions provided information on their perceptions of one another, including who was "most helpful in reaching the verdict." This measure reflected the amount of influence each member—as perceived by the other members—had over the group decision. The findings are very similar to those on the rates of participation in groups. On average, male jurors were perceived as more helpful than female jurors, and jurors of high occupational status were perceived as more helpful than those of lower occupational status.

Overall, this jury study revealed the typical impact of status generalization: Persons with higher standing in terms of gender and occupation became the group members with the higher status inside the group.

Although the findings in this study seem clear-cut, the interpretation in terms of status generalization is open to criticism. A critic might argue that a person's status inside a group is not a function of his or her status outside the group but is, instead, caused by the same qualities or personal traits that determine that person's status outside the group. One might hypothesize, for instance, that people of high intelligence translate their intelligence into both high occupational status and better contributions to the group. If this were the case, a person's standing inside a group would not be caused by his or her external occupational status; rather, both internal and external status would be caused by a third factor—intelligence.

To check the possibility of unseen, confounding factors, several studies have manipulated status characteristics experimentally. One of these studies (Moore, 1968) investigated pairs of female participants. Both women were shown a series of figures made up of smaller black-and-white rectangles. They were told that the test measured contrast sensitivity and their task was to judge which of the two colors—black or white—covered the greater area in each of the figures. This task was difficult because the black and white areas were in fact approximately equal, making the task ambiguous.

The participants, who were seated so they could not see or talk with each other, signaled their initial judgments to one another using a console with lights (these experiments are now conducted over computer networks). The participants knew they would each make a final judgment after seeing each other's initial judgments. They were told that they should weigh their own answers against their partner's answers to make accurate final judgments.

What the participants did not know was that the lights on the consoles were, in fact, controlled by the experimenter. The experimenters were manipulating how often a participant learned that her partner's initial judgment was different from her own and then measuring how often the participant changed her judgment if that was the case.

All the participants in this experiment were students at a junior college in the Bay

BOX 14.1 Research Update: Motherhood as a Status Characteristic

A number of studies suggest that mothers with similar occupations, education, and training make, on average, less money than women without children. However, these studies rely on data that lacks measures of productivity. Perhaps mothers are paid less because they are taking more time off from work or are more distracted in their jobs than are non-mothers. To better understand the underlying mechanism for the pay gap between mothers and nonmothers, researchers would have to find a way to control for all the extraneous factors. A laboratory experiment allowed Shelley Correll and her colleagues to do just that.

Correll has always been interested in how cultural schemas influence performance expectations. Her earlier research (Correll, 2001, 2004) explored the link between stereotypes about women being less skilled at math than men and girls' self-assessments about mathematical ability and their plans to pursue math and science careers. In the case of mothers, Correll argued that cultural understandings of the motherhood role (warm, nurturing, devoted to her children) are in tension with the cultural understandings of the "ideal worker" role (rational, devoted to work). These schemas might lead evaluators, perhaps unconsciously, to expect mothers to be less competent and less committed to their jobs (Blair-Loy, 2003; Ridgeway & Correll, 2004).

To test her ideas, Correll paid undergraduate participants to rate a pair of equally qualified, same-gender (either male or female), same-race (either Black or White) job applicants who differed on parental status. The job applicant files were created by Correll and her research team so they could be as similar as possible—with both candidates having similar education and experience along with equivalent skills, goals, and productivity levels—but the students believed the files they were reading were real. They thought that they were evaluating the candidates for a communications company that was interested in gathering input from college students who were heavy consumers of new communication technology. The only differences between the files were the names—this is how Correll cued race and gender—and parental status (the résumés of parents included a line about PTA involvement, and the mention of a family in an attached memo included children).

After reading each application, participants were asked to report their initial impressions of the applicants, to provide pros and cons for the applicant, and then to complete an evaluation sheet that assessed applicants' competence

Area. As a manipulation of status, one-half of the participants were told that their partner was a high school student (a lower-status partner), whereas the other half were told that their partner was from Stanford University (a higher-status partner). The results show that the women who believed their partner to be of higher status changed their answers on the judgmental task significantly more often than those who thought themselves to have higher status than their partner. In other words, they were likely to be influenced by those of higher status and

more likely to resist influence from those of lower status. The random assignment of participants to experimental treatments eliminated the possibility that participants differed systematically in intelligence or ability on the judgment task.

In the years since this experiment, research finds that many other status distinctions affect whether research participants are likely to change their initial responses or to stay with their original judgments. These include but are not limited to physical attractiveness, race and ethnicity, mili-

	MOTHERS	NONMOTHERS	FATHERS	NONFATHERS
Competence	*5.19*	*5.75*	*5.51*	*5.44*
Commitment	*67.0*	*79.2*	*78.5*	*74.2*
Salary Recommended ($)	*137,000*	*148,000*	*150,000*	*144,000*
Proportion Recommended for Management	*.691*	*.862*	*.936*	*.851*
Likelihood of Promotion	*2.74*	*3.42*	*3.30*	*3.11*
Proportion Recommended for Hire	*.468*	*.840*	*.734*	*.617*

and commitment and made recommendations on hiring, salary, additional training, and other job-related outcomes.

A selection of the results are summarized in the table above.

The italicized numbers are those that differ significantly (more than expected by chance) from their counterparts (mothers from nonmothers, fathers from nonfathers). Even though their job-relevant file characteristics were identical, mothers were significantly disadvantaged on all measures. They were seen as less competent and less committed. The students recommended lower starting salaries and were less likely to recommend mothers for management, see them as promotable, or recommend them for hire. Interestingly, men experienced the reverse effect. Whereas mothers suffered a "motherhood penalty," fathers were given a "fatherhood bonus" in which they were advantaged compared to their nonfather counterparts on all dimensions except perceptions of competence. In a follow-up audit study, Correll and her team sent the fake résumés to similar positions that were listed in the newspaper. Results support the experimental findings. Mothers received significantly fewer callbacks than did their childless peers.

The connection between perceptions of competence and motherhood suggests that motherhood does, indeed, act as a salient status characteristic in the workplace, and status processes and performance expectations play an important role in women's ongoing disadvantage across occupational spheres.

Source: Correll, Benard, & Paik, 2007.

tary rank, sexual orientation, age, and occupation (Webster & Foschi, 1988). Research on status effects has also extended beyond influence to examine other outcomes. For example, the research discussed in Box 14.1 explores how status affects hiring and salary decisions.

Overcoming Status Generalization

Because group members often treat diffuse status characteristics as relevant to performance expectations even when they are not, status generalization can work to an individual's disadvantage (Forsyth, 1999). In a mixed setting with both men and women, for example, the women may find that they are not permitted to influence the group's decision significantly even though they are as qualified as—and may be more qualified than—men with respect to the problem under discussion. Because of the burden-of-proof process discussed earlier, without a clear demonstration that gender is irrelevant to performance, verbal protests regarding gender equality may be to no avail (Pugh

& Wahrman, 1983). Status generalization is also not something that only influences people's beliefs about others; we also have performance expectations for ourselves. These can influence our aspirations—leading fewer girls and young women to aspire to math careers, for example (Correll, 2001, 2004)—and our performance (Lovaglia, Lucas, & Thye, 1998; see also the discussion of stereotype threat in Chapter 6). Because irrelevant diffuse status characteristics can so easily place someone at a disadvantage, researchers have asked whether status generalization can be overcome or eliminated in face-to-face interaction.

Early research tried to overcome status generalization by raising the expectations of lower-status persons regarding their own performance on group tasks so they could, in turn, force a change in other people's expectations regarding their performance. Unfortunately, this approach does not work very well. Social psychologists discovered that to overcome status generalization, one must change everyone's performance expectations—not only those held by low-status group members but also those held by high-status group members. One effective way to overcome status generalization, then, is to supply all group members with information that contradicts performance expectations inferred from a diffuse status characteristic (Berger, Rosenholtz, & Zelditch, 1980; Cohen & Roper, 1972; Riordan & Ruggiero, 1980).

However, it can be quite difficult to overcome status generalization because expectations and evaluations of status groups tend to reflect prevailing cultural stereotypes (Berger, Rosenholtz, & Zelditch, 1980; Ellard & Bates, 1990; Meeker, 1981). Although we may not think of ourselves as holding such views, as previous chapters suggest, these beliefs and their effect on our behavior in group settings are likely automatic (Fiske Lin, & Neuberg, 1999).

Further complicating things, interactions in groups not only are based on cultural beliefs but also often serve to reinforce them. If Martin had been selected as the jury's foreperson and he had influenced the group's ultimate decision, you and the other jury members would likely leave the courthouse seeing him—and those who possess similar status characteristics—as a good leader. He would provide confirmation of your status beliefs. In this way status beliefs and their influence on the power and prestige order function as a type of self-fulfilling prophecy that thereby perpetuates inequalities based on status long after the specific encounter (Ridgeway and Smith-Lovin, 1999).

Status Construction and Status Value

We acquire many of these cultural beliefs through socialization, but how is it that any particular attribute becomes imbued with status? According to Cecilia Ridgeway (2006, 2011), our beliefs about status are formed in interaction. We acquire them in daily encounters. When we come upon a new type of nominal attribute, one that we have not learned status meanings for, we will look for clues about how that attribute's categories are organized in a status hierarchy. For example, if you know nothing about the fraternities on campus, you may look at fraternities' resources (attractiveness of pledges, wealth, popularity) to decide which fraternities are higher or lower status. In effect, you are constructing your own status hierarchy, and these status beliefs will influence your performance expectations for the various groups. When you treat those groups based on those expectations and draw on these status beliefs in interaction, you create a status system.

We are also formulating and maintaining status meanings when we interact with others who are different on salient attributes that we are already aware of as status characteristics (race, gender, sexual identity) because we attend to evidence about status. We note that men have better-paying jobs and are afforded more authority, influence, and respect. We come to understand men as having higher status. When we carry these beliefs into interactions, we also carry them out of interaction. This process continuously constructs and reconstructs the status system.

Like attributes, objects can also acquire status value. Objects that are associated with high-status actors become more valuable than those linked to low-status actors (Thye, 2000). Within hours of the release of the first official family portrait of Prince William, Kate Middleton, and their son George, the $79 dress she wore for the photo shoot sold out. The next month, the company that made the dress doubled their sales figures. Although the publicity of the photo shoot played a role in the business's success, status value likely did as well. Once the dress—and brand—became associated with someone as high status as the Duchess, it became more valuable. Buyers believed that the particular dress the Duchess had worn was more valuable than other $79 dresses.

GROUP DECISION MAKING

Social psychologists have also studied group decision making without a specific focus on status and individual influence. All other things aside, group decision making should be fairly easy and involves several basic steps (Janis & Mann, 1977). To make a decision effectively, group members need to (1) define a set of possible options, (2) gather all the relevant information about these options, (3) share this information among themselves, (4) carefully assess all the potential consequences of each option under consideration, and then (5) calculate the overall value of each option. Once this is done, (6) the group selects the most attractive option as the group's choice.

In practice, however, group decision making is not always so easy or straightforward, for the decision-making process can go awry in various ways. Information regarding certain options may prove hard to obtain, leading to incomplete or inadequate consideration of these options. Even if the individual members do have all the relevant information, they may fail to share it fully with one another (Stasser, 1992; Stasser & Titus, 1987). If members hold different values, they may disagree regarding which options are most attractive. This disagreement can spawn arguments and block consensus within the group. As the previous sections suggest, some group members may have more influence over the group, and conformity pressures within the group may impel members to abbreviate or short-circuit the deliberation processes. If this happens, group discussion may lead to ill-considered or unrealistic decisions.

Groupthink

Aberrations in decision making can plague any group, even those at the highest levels of business and government. The infamous Bay of Pigs invasion, for example, was planned by a small group of top government officials immediately after President John Kennedy took office in 1961. The group included what some considered to be the nation's "best and brightest": McGeorge Bundy, Dean Rusk, Robert McNamara, Douglas Dillon, Robert Kennedy, Arthur Schlesinger, Jr., and President Kennedy himself along with representatives of the Pentagon and the Central Intelligence Agency (CIA). This group decided to invade Cuba in April 1961, using a small band of 1,400 Cuban exiles as troops. The invasion was to be staged at the Bay of Pigs and assisted covertly by the U.S. Navy, Air Force, and CIA. As it turned out, the invasion was poorly conceived. The materials and reserve ammunition on which the exiles were depending never arrived because Castro's air force sank the supply ships. The exiles were promptly surrounded by 20,000 well-equipped Cuban soldiers, and within three days, virtually all the exiles had been captured or killed. The United States suffered a humiliating defeat in the eyes of the world, and Castro's communist government became more strongly entrenched on the Caribbean island.

How could it happen? How could a group of such capable and experienced men make a decision that turned out so poorly? In a post hoc analysis, Janis (1982) suggests that a specific group process, *groupthink*, may have led to the ill-fated decision. Although Janis's interpretation of events has been called into question, particularly since the release of recordings made during the Bay of Pigs briefings, the model he developed has largely endured (Esser, 1998).

Groupthink refers to a faulty mode of thinking by group members in which pressures for unanimity within the group overwhelm their desire to realistically evaluate alternative courses of action. In other words, the group members neglect to appraise alternatives critically and to weigh the pros and cons carefully because they fear disrupting the perception of consensus. Once groupthink sets in, the typical result is a poor decision.

Symptoms of Groupthink. By studying what happened during various important foreign policy decisions, Janis (1982) was able to ascertain certain symptoms that indicate when groupthink is operating. These include:

1. **Illusions of invulnerability.** Group members may think they are invulnerable and cannot fail, and therefore, they display excessive optimism and take excessive risks.
2. **Illusions of morality.** Members may display an unquestioned belief in the group's inherent superior morality, and this may incline them to ignore the ethical consequences of their decisions.
3. **Collective rationalization.** Members may discount warnings that, if heeded, would cause them to reconsider their assumptions.
4. **Stereotyping of the adversary.** Especially in the political sphere, the group may develop a stereotyped view of enemy leaders as too evil to warrant genuine attempts to negotiate or as too weak to mount effective counteractions.
5. **Self-censorship.** Members may engage in self-censorship of any deviation from the apparent group consensus, with each member inclined to minimize the importance of his or her own doubts.
6. **Pressure on dissenters.** The majority may exert direct pressure on any member who dissents or argues against any of the group's stereotypes, illusions, or commitments.
7. **Mindguarding.** There may emerge in the group some self-appointed "mind guards"—members who protect against information that might shatter the complacency about the effectiveness and morality of the group's decisions.
8. **Apparent unanimity.** Despite their personal doubts, group members may share an illusion that unanimity regarding the decision exists within the group.

Janis suggests that some of these symptoms were present during the decision-making process for the Bay of Pigs invasion. For example, there was an assumed air of consensus that caused members of the decision-making group to ignore some glaring defects in their plan. Although several of Kennedy's senior advisers had strong doubts about the planning, the group's atmosphere inhibited them from voicing criticism. Several members emerged as "mind guards" within the group; they suppressed opposing views by arguing that the decision to invade had already been made and that everyone should help the president instead of distracting him with dissension. Open inquiry and clearheaded exploration were discouraged. Even the contingency planning was unrealistic. For instance, if the exiles failed in their primary military objective at the Bay of Pigs, they were supposed to join the anti-Castro guerrillas known to be operating in the Escambray Mountains. Apparently, no one was troubled by the fact that 80 miles of impassable swamp and jungle stood between the guerrillas in the mountains and the exiles.

Groupthink might not be such a concern—except for the recognition that it can occur and recur in many groups. Janis notes that the Bay of Pigs invasion is not the only fiasco in which groupthink played an important role. He suggests groupthink was also involved in other high-level government decisions, including the decision to invade North Korea during the Korean War, the failure to defend Pearl Harbor on the eve of World War II, the decision to escalate the Vietnam War, and the decision to engage in the Watergate cover-up. More recent work argues that groupthink played a role in the *Challenger* disaster (Esser, 1995; Moorhead, Ference, & Neck, 1991) and the decision to invade Iraq in 2003 (Badie, 2010; Rinehart & Dunwoody, 2005).

Causes of Groupthink. Various factors cause groupthink, including homogeneity of members, insulation of the group from its environment, lack of clear-cut rules to guide decision-making behavior within the group, and high levels of group stress (Hensley & Griffin, 1986; Manz & Sims, 1982; Moorhead & Montanari, 1986). Another contributing factor is promotional leadership—that is, a leader who actively promotes his or her own favored solution to the problem facing the group, to the neglect of other possible solutions (Leana, 1985; McCauley, 1989). According to Janis, each of these factors contributes to groupthink, and their simultaneous occurrence makes groupthink very probable.

Janis also argued that groupthink is more likely to occur in high-cohesion groups than in low-cohesion groups, but there is only limited support for this hypothesis (Aldag & Fuller, 1993; Michener & Wasserman, 1995; Park, 1990). The inconsistency in findings on the relationship between cohesion and groupthink may arise in part because the levels of cohesion that can be induced in laboratory studies are low compared to what can emerge in real-life situations.

Avoiding Groupthink. If groupthink produces poor decisions and outcomes, how can one guard against it? There are several ways to prevent groupthink from occurring (Janis, 1982).

1. A group's leader should encourage dissent and call on each member to express any objections and doubts.
2. A leader should be impartial and not announce a preference for any particular option or plan. By describing a problem rather than recommending a solution, a leader can foster an atmosphere of open inquiry and impartial exploration.

3. A group should divide itself into several independent subgroups, each working on the same problem and carrying out its deliberation independently. This will prevent the premature development of consensus in the main group.

4. After a tentative consensus has been reached, a group should hold a "second-chance" meeting, at which each member can express any remaining doubts before a firm decision is taken.

5. A group can appoint a "devil's advocate" who is responsible for challenging the positions of other group members even if he or she really agrees with them (Hirt & Markmann, 1995).

These methods are effective because they increase the probability that a group will obtain all the information relevant to a decision and then evaluate that information with care. The net result of these steps will be a better, more realistic decision.

Risky Shift, Cautious Shift, and Group Polarization

Even when group decision making is not dysfunctional and follows a fairly rational course, it can still produce surprising consequences. For instance, there is some evidence that discussion in groups causes individuals to favor courses of action that are either riskier or more cautious than what they would choose if they made the decision alone (Stoner, 1968; Vinokur, 1971).

In one experiment (Stoner, 1968), individuals responded to 12 different choice dilemmas entailing various degrees of risk. After responding to these choice dilemmas alone, the participants assembled in groups of six and discussed each item until they reached a unanimous decision. The participants were then separated and asked again to review each item and indicate an individual decision. The basic finding was that the group decisions following discussion were, on the average, riskier than the decisions made by individual members prior to the discussion. Moreover, the responses made individually after participating in the group were also riskier on average than the responses prior to discussion. This tendency to advocate more risk following a group discussion is termed a **risky shift**. This phenomenon has been observed in many studies (Cartwright, 1971; Dion, Baron, & Miller, 1970).

Other studies using similar tasks, however, have revealed something directly opposite to the risky shift. On certain issues, when members are more likely to be cautious or risk avoidant, group discussion actually causes members to become even more cautious than they were initially (Fraser, Gouge, & Billig, 1971; Stoner, 1968; Turner, Wetherell, & Hogg, 1989). This move away from risk following a group discussion is termed a **cautious shift**. So although group discussion leads to more extreme decisions, these are not necessarily riskier decisions.

Both risk shift and cautious shift are forms of an underlying phenomenon called **group polarization** (Levine & Moreland, 1998). Polarization occurs when group members shift their opinions toward a position that is similar to—but more extreme—than their opinions before group discussion. Thus, if members favored a moderately risky position prior to a group discussion, polarization would occur if they shifted toward greater risk following the discussion. Likewise, if they initially favored a moderately cautious position, polarization would occur if they shifted in the direction of even greater caution after the group discussion (Myers & Lamm, 1976).

The tendency for group discussion to create polarization is quite general. That is, discussion produces polarization not only on decisions involving risk but also on judgments and attitudes in general. For example, polarization has been observed with respect to political attitudes (Paicheler & Bouchet, 1973), jury verdicts (Isozaki, 1984; Myers & Kaplan, 1976), satisfaction with new consumer products (Johnson & Andrews, 1971), judgments of physical dimensions (Vidmar, 1974), ethical decisions (Horne & Long, 1972), perceptions of other persons (Myers, 1975), and interpersonal bargaining and negotiating (Lamm & Sauer, 1974).

SOCIAL EXCHANGE

Around the same time that Bales was studying decision making and the types of interactions that occur in groups, George Homans (1958, 1961) was trying to develop a general theory of human behavior based on what we might observe in group interaction. As part of this general theory, Homans argued that interaction between people should be conceptualized as an exchange—a phenomenon he called "social exchange."

Conventional ideas about exchange tend to focus on tangible goods. For example, two college students might make a trade—Ryan lends Jason his car for the weekend and, in return, Jason gives Ryan his tickets to an upcoming concert. However, much of what we exchange in social life is intangible. You smile at a passerby and they smile back. You tell your friend that you like her new dress and she either expresses gratitude or deflects the compliment. Martin shares his opinion on the case and some of his fellow jurors nod as others express disagreement. In this framework, all interaction occurs through a **relation**—a connection between two people—with people contributing benefits and potentially deriving them from the interaction. Because people are self-inter-

A popular application of exchange theory is to think of the "benefits" people bring to dating and marriage relationships. In one version of this, men offer status and financial resources in exchange for women's youth and beauty. Analyses of personal ads support gendered trends in benefits sought and offered. Heterosexual women tend to offer attractiveness in ads while seeking success in potential dates, and heterosexual men do the reverse, offering success while seeking attractiveness (Davis, 1990). © leaf/iStock

ested, Homans argued, the relative payoffs of relations shape interaction. For example, Ryan is less likely to lend Jason his car if Jason offers nothing—tangible or intangible—in return. The relative payoffs determine both Ryan and Jason's behavior.

The social exchange perspective (Cook, 1987; Homans, 1974; Kelley & Thibaut, 1978) focuses on (1) *actors* who exchange (2) *resources* using (3) an exchange *process* while situated in (4) an exchange *structure* (Molm, 2006) and assumes that individuals have freedom of choice and often face social situations in which they must choose among alternative actions. Ryan can decide whether or not he wants to lend Jason his car.

Any action provides some rewards and entails some costs. Even if Jason gives Ryan nothing tangible in return, there could be benefits. Jason could be indebted to Ryan. Ryan could feel good about himself for helping out a friend, or he might impress a girl he is interested in with his act of kindness. The costs can vary too. If Ryan will be unable to run his regular weekend errands or meet friends because he is without a car, these might be significant costs. If his car would sit idle all weekend if he chose not to lend it to someone, the cost of lending it out is small. People tend to choose actions that produce good profits and avoid actions that produce poor profits.

In this way, social exchange draws on operant psychology and reinforcement theories. These theories suggest that people will be more likely to perform a specific behavior if it is followed directly by the occurrence of something pleasurable or by the removal of something aversive; likewise, people will more likely refrain from performing a particular behavior if it is followed by the occurrence of something aversive or by the removal of something pleasant.

This view of human behavior might seem overly rational and calculated, but social exchange theory suggests that these choices to engage in or refrain from a line of action are often given little thought because they are the result of conditioning—learning as the result of positive or negative responses to behavior (Mazur, 1998; Skinner, 1953). Humans have the ability to learn the natural consequences of actions and to behave in ways that minimize costs and maximize rewards, either consciously or unconsciously (Emerson, 1972).

Social psychologists who study social exchange study mutually dependent and recurring exchange relationships. In other words, social psychology is less interested in a one-shot exchange, between people who will never see one another again (a gas station attendant and a motorist passing through town), than they are in the ongoing exchange relationship among friends like Ryan and Jason, who both derive benefits from their relationship with one another.

Power and Dependence

In the same way that Robert Bales formalized the study of groups, Richard Emerson formalized the study of social exchange by taking Homan's ideas and testing and refining them in laboratory experiments.

One of Emerson's (1972) main contributions was his emphasis on the networks that exchange relationships are nested in (Thibaut & Kelley, 1959). Rarely are two people completely cut off from everyone else; there are always alternative exchange partners. Imagine that Ryan's other roommate, Max, also wants to borrow his car for the weekend. Ryan would find out what both Max and Jason had to offer before deciding to whom he would lend the car.

Emerson argued that individuals' positions in these networks, more than their personalities, influence their exchange behavior. He found that this is true even when people are ignorant about the exchange structure and their relative position (Emerson, 1981). It might be hard to believe that a position rather than your personality can influence your behavior—especially a position that you are unaware of—but social psychological research suggests that it can. People who are in powerful positions will demand more benefits and get more from exchange than will actors who are in weaker positions. But where does power

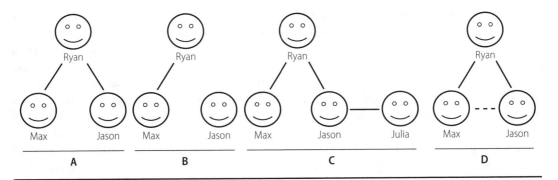

FIGURE 14.2 Achieving Balance in an Exchange Relation

The relationship between Jason and Ryan is unbalanced in (A) because Ryan has Max as an alternative source of benefits. To achieve a more balanced relation, Jason might decrease his interest in Ryan's car (B), find an alternative source of a car (C), or form a coalition with Max (D).

come from? Social exchange argues that *power*—one's ability to direct or influence the behavior of others—is not an attribute of an actor but of a position. In exchange networks, power depends, in part, on the availability (and attractiveness) of alternative exchange partners (Molm, Peterson, & Takahashi 2001; Skvoretz & Willer, 1993).

If both Max and Jason want to borrow Ryan's car, Ryan is in a powerful position. This power comes from Max's and Jason's dependence on him for a desired benefit (see Figure 14.2a). Remember, Jason was originally willing to trade the car for concert tickets. However, if he learned that someone else wanted the car, Jason would feel like he needed to increase the incentive for Ryan to choose to lend it to him. He might offer to do Ryan's laundry in addition to giving him the concert tickets.

According to Emerson (1962), there are four ways that Jason could decrease Ryan's power over him, leading to a more balanced system:

First, he could decide that he was not all that interested in borrowing Ryan's car for the weekend, perhaps convincing himself that he needed to stay on campus and study. Because Ryan's power stems from Jason's dependence, Ryan would no longer have power in the relationship if Jason were no longer motivated to exchange with him (see Figure 14.2b).

Second, Jason could find an alternative source for the benefit that Ryan has to offer. What if Jason's chemistry partner, Julia, also had a car on campus, and he could ask her instead? This would alter the structure that Ryan and Jason's exchange relationship is embedded in (see Figure 14.2c). This change in structure would decrease Ryan's power over Jason because it introduces an alternative for Jason, thereby decreasing his dependence on Ryan for the valued resource (a car).

Third, he could work to increase Ryan's interest in what he had to offer. If Ryan was as excited to go to the concert as Jason was to borrow the car, the exchange relation would be balanced. Of course, if Ryan was absolutely desperate to go to the concert and offered Jason the car as an incentive to give him the tickets, the power in the relation could be reversed, and Jason could be the one with the upper hand. In such a scenario, Ryan is more dependent on Jason for a desired outcome than Jason is on Ryan.

Finally, Jason could form a coalition with Max. They—either with or without Ryan's knowledge—could agree to share the car regardless of who Ryan gave it to. By forming a coalition, Max and Jason are decreasing Ryan's ability to play them against one another (see Figure 14.2D). They have become one collective actor and thereby increase their power relative to Ryan by decreasing their dependence on him.

Commitment and Trust

More recent work in exchange focuses less on power and dependence and more on the affective outcomes of exchange—how people feel about the people they exchange with—and how these feelings influence behavior. Two of these outcomes are trust and commitment. These are considered *emergent outcomes* because they develop over time in ongoing exchange relations.

Commitment can be measured in two ways in social exchange. The first is a behavioral measure. Using this metric, an individual is committed to an exchange partner if they repeatedly exchange with them even if there are alternative exchange partners available (Cook & Emerson, 1978). Take, for example, two colleagues who meet for lunch every Thursday. There are many other people in the office who go out to lunch and who the two women enjoy spending time with, but these two women continue to meet at the same time and same place every Thursday. This recurrent behavior is interpreted as a sign of commitment to the exchange relation.

Another way to measure commitment is as an emotional attachment, a sense of liking of the exchange partner or partners (Lawler & Yoon, 1996). This sense of solidarity is important. People who have an emotional commitment to exchange relations are more likely to stay in relationships

and to invest in them. For example, a study of teachers found that those who felt emotionally connected to the other teachers at their schools were more likely to invest their own time and money in professional development, from acting as a mentor to getting more training in instruction techniques (Price & Collett, 2012). These teachers were also more committed to staying at their current school than were those who did not have the same emotional connection to the school.

Trust is another emergent outcome of exchange. Social exchange requires that we trust an exchange partner to honor the terms of exchange. However, exchange also fosters trust because the more times an exchange partner fulfills his or her obligations to us, the more we believe they are trustworthy. Returning to Ryan and Jason, Ryan and Jason must trust one another to follow through on their end of the agreement—either handing over the tickets or the car keys—for a successful exchange to occur. However, such exchanges also build trust. The more times that Ryan and Jason have honored previous agreements, the easier it is for them to trust one another in a subsequent exchange.

Trust usually evolves in relationships. Early transactions require little trust. As the relationship continues and partners demonstrate their trustworthiness, exchanges often require more and more trust (Molm, 2006). When you first meet a new person, you might share superficial things with them. However, as they increasingly demonstrate that they are accepting and honest, you will come to share more personal experiences with them. It is unlikely that Ryan would lend Jason his car for an entire weekend if they had just met; it is much more likely that Ryan and Jason have roomed together for a while. Jason has demonstrated that he is conscientious with the things he borrows from Ryan—his toothpaste, a pen, his flash drive, and then a leather jacket—and that he makes good on what he promises in return. This exchange history influences the trust Ryan has in Jason.

Forms of Exchange

There are a number of processes through which exchange occurs. Social psychologists find that, even with all else being equal, the form that an exchange takes has important effects on commitment, trust, and other affective and cognitive outcomes (Molm, Collett, & Schaefer, 2007). The four forms social psychologists study most often are negotiated, reciprocal, generalized, and productive. These are illustrated in Figure 14.3.

Negotiated Exchange. In negotiated exchange, actors engage in a joint decision process, like bargaining, to establish and agree on the terms of exchange (Molm, 1997). If you and your professor decide that she will give you five extra-credit points if you participate in a social psychology experiment, that is a negotiated exchange. Each person's obligation is clear.

Reciprocal Exchange. When we engage in an exchange with someone without direct negotiation—and in which the giving of benefits is performed separately—this is considered reciprocal exchange. For example, you and a friend might have established a reciprocal trend in paying for the first round at happy hour. You paid for the first round two weeks ago, your friend picked up the tab last week, and now you are ready to take the check again. You might assume that they will pay next week, but you cannot be sure. You are giving someone something without knowing when or even if they will reciprocate.

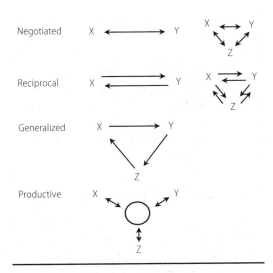

FIGURE 14.3 Forms of Exchange

The above figures illustrate the four main exchange types—negotiated, reciprocal, generalized, and productive—in two- and three-person exchange networks.

Generalized Exchange. Most people understand generalized exchange as the obligation to "pay it forward." In a generalized exchange relation, givers and receivers are not matched in pairs. With reciprocal exchange, the benefits and costs flow back and forth between two actors. With generalized exchange, the benefits (and costs) flow to an exchange partner and then to someone else and then to someone else (or perhaps back to you). If the person in front of you holds the door for you, and then you hold it for someone else, who holds it for yet another person, you are engaged in generalized exchange. Those who have been given a benefit give a benefit to someone else.

Productive Exchange. The last form of exchange of interest to social psychologists is productive exchange. In productive exchange, there is a jointly produced good that exchange partners create and receive benefits from. An example might be a group project that a small group of students does for a class. Each group member ostensibly makes some individual contribution to the project, and they will benefit from the grade they receive for the group's work. Cooperation is key here, as individuals must coordinate efforts and combine resources to generate a collective good (Lawler, 2001); it is not something any single person could create on his or her own.

Contemporary Exchange Theories

Two prominent theories explore the effects of form of exchange on affective and cognitive outcomes, including commitment, trust, and perceptions of fairness.

The **affect theory of social exchange** focuses on interdependence (Lawler, 2001). This theory proposes that the greater the perceptions of shared responsibility for the outcome—that is, the more the group had to work together to achieve it—the more likely that the exchange process will produce positive outcomes (solidarity, positive emotion, commitment behaviors). Not surprisingly given its focus on shared responsibility, tests of this theory find that productive exchanges produce the most positive outcomes of the four types of exchange. However, the affect theory also predicts that negotiated exchange, with the joint decision process and shared responsibility inherent in bargaining, will foster more solidarity and positive emotion than reciprocal exchange. Results of studies testing this proposition are mixed (Lawler, Thye, & Yoon, 2008).

Rather than focus on interdependence, **reciprocity theory** is concerned with conflict, risk, and the expressive value of exchange. Reciprocity theory argues that the level of conflict inherent in an exchange process inhibits the development of trust and decreases the solidarity and positive affect between exchange partners. The back and forth nature of bargaining, like that in

negotiated exchange, seems competitive. Therefore, generalized and reciprocal exchange strategies—forms that lessen the perception that exchange is competitive—will produce more trust and positive emotion than will negotiated exchange. When someone fails to live up to his or her end of a bargain in a negotiated exchange, this can easily be interpreted as an attempt to gain something at the expense of the other. In a relationship built on reciprocal exchange, however, failure to follow through is an act of omission rather than one of commission. This makes it less likely that the action (or lack thereof) will be seen as a transgression. Consider two of the examples above. If Ryan refuses to lend Jason his car after Jason has already given him the concert tickets and fulfilled his end of an explicit agreement, this has a different tenor than if you buy the first round at happy hour one week and your friend does not offer to do the same the next week.

Reciprocity theory also proposes that reciprocal and generalized exchanges entail more risk—because there is no guarantee of receiving something in return—and this increased risk encourages the development of trust. The structure of giving in reciprocal and generalized exchange also enhances affective outcomes because an act of giving (or reciprocity) for which there is no explicit agreement has expressive value beyond the instrumental benefits of the act (Molm, Collett, & Schaefer, 2007). Negotiated agreements lack this symbolic value.

EQUITY AND JUSTICE

On October 1, 2013, the U.S. government shut down. Although there were many issues plaguing Congress, the primary point of contention was whether the government should fund the Affordable Care Act—"Obamacare." One issue of concern was that if the government provided income-based subsidies for health care, this would benefit some Americans and not others. Why should the same benefits be more expensive for some than for others?

Distributive Justice Principles

Distributive justice is the perceived fairness of a distribution of rewards. There are many principles that people use to judge distributive justice (Deutsch, 1985; Elliott & Meeker, 1986; Saito, 1988). The three that are most common are equity, equality, and relative need.

When group members follow the *equity principle*, they distribute rewards in proportion to members' contributions. For example, if three students started a business together, under the equity principle, the partner who invested the most resources in it (either initially or over time) would expect to take a larger share of the business's profits.

When group members use the *equality principle*, they distribute rewards equally among members, regardless of members' contributions. Using this principle, the three friends would divide the profits evenly, regardless of initial contribution or the hours each put into the business as it continued.

Finally, when they follow the *relative needs principle*, group members distribute rewards according to members' personal needs, regardless of contributions (Lamm & Schwinger, 1980). The most profits would go to the partner who had the most debts, the largest family, or some other measure of need. Because this is the least common principle in most Westernized cultures, instances of this principle—like an income-based subsidy—are often met with skepticism or outright disdain.

When allocating rewards among members, a group may rely exclusively on one of these justice principles or may apply several of them simultaneously. These justice principles usually lead to different distributions of rewards, but they can be combined. For example, the students above could divide the monthly profits they make from running their business equally but plan to divide any profits they make from the sale of the company based on an equity principle. In this case, each student's proportion of profits from the sale of the company would be equal to the proportion of the start-up funds they had initially provided.

Not surprisingly, the principles' relative importance varies from group to group and from situation to situation. For instance, the equality principle often prevails in situations in which members are concerned with solidarity and wish to avoid conflict (Leventhal, Michaels, & Sanford, 1972). It also prevails in cultural settings that are relationship oriented rather than economically oriented (Mannix, Neale, & Northcraft, 1995). There is some evidence that women favor the equality principle over the equity principle more than men do (Leventhal & Lane, 1970; Watts, Messe, & Vallacher, 1982) and that friends are more likely to follow the equality norm than are strangers (Austin, 1980). Research findings also suggest that members of small (3-person) groups are more likely to favor equality than members of large (12-person) groups (Allison, McQueen, & Schaerfl, 1992).

The needs principle is frequently salient in close or intimate relationships involving friends, lovers, and relatives. However, this principle has also been invoked in other contexts. Karl Marx, for example, advocated the adoption of the needs principle in communist societies, in which individuals would contribute according to their abilities and receive according to their needs.

The equity principle is often used in work situations, where many persons want their share of rewards to reflect the importance

BOX 14.2   Research Applications: Exchange in Families

Recent research has applied both reciprocity theory and the affect theory of social exchange to couples with young children. Initial results show support for the theory of reciprocity (Molm, 2010; Molm, Collett, & Schaefer, 2007). It appears that couples who engage in reciprocal exchange are happier and more satisfied with their relationship than are those who explicitly negotiate the division of labor in their households. Carla and Ben are an example of such a couple.

Carla and Ben have been together for twelve years and have three children. Ben uses finances to illustrate how reciprocity works between them. Although they have separate bank accounts, they work in tandem to support the household:

> When we were both working, we would always just pay the bills together. There would be some days, though, that she would just go and pay a bill, and I didn't even know about it, and the bill would come in and be already paid. Well, I would do the same thing.

He emphasizes that they do not engage in explicit bargaining in their relationship. Although they sometimes openly discuss what needs to be done, they usually just step up and do what they need to do without discussing it directly. This includes the laundry—whoever notices it needs to be done takes charge of it.

Carla and Ben were one of many couples in the interviews who used meals to exemplify reciprocal exchange patterns in their relationships. In their household, Carla does the cooking and Ben cleans up the dishes and kitchen. Although they will sometimes switch roles, Larissa and Robert are similar. Larissa explains, "Like, if I cook, he'll clean. And if he cooks, I clean." The couples state that these divisions of labor just happened and believe they are a sign that the couple just clicked and are meant to be together.

Other couples engage in explicit negotiation. This is particularly common among newer couples or those who have yet to really put down roots. Couples who primarily use a strategy of negotiation seem less sure of their relationship and less happy. One such couple is Olivia and Mason. They started with a reciprocal system but recently moved to a more negotiated strategy. It is not going well. Parents of two young children, both Olivia and Mason work outside the home. She is a teacher and he is a counselor. At the beginning of their relationship, they tried to just fill in the gaps and to establish a sense of turn-taking or reciprocity in household tasks. Olivia soon realized, though, that she was doing the majority of the household labor. She tried talking to Mason about it. She asked for help and made suggestions, but nothing seems to work. She finally decided to keep her frustration to herself, which caused major strife in the relationship because she was constantly angry and Mason had no idea what needed to be done.

Realizing that the quality of their marriage was suffering, Olivia reached out to her married friends. She said they told her, "It's a husband thing . . . you have to just talk about and talk about and talk about [it] until you get it right."

of their contribution. For example, in an industrial work group in the United States, a worker normally would expect to receive better outcomes (salary, benefits) than others if his or her job required higher skill, more hours per week, and so on. Likewise, a woman would probably feel some inequity if she contributes more to the family than her partner but receives little help or love in return. As these examples suggest, equity judgments are made when one group member compares his or her own outcomes and inputs against those of another member (Brockner & Wiesenfeld, 1996; Greenberg

She ended up doing just that. Olivia and Mason sat down and decided that they needed to draft a plan and explicitly agree on who should do what, when, and how. Unfortunately, it seemed to make matters worse. When Mason failed to pitch in as much as he'd agreed to in the plan, Olivia was even angrier than she was initially because it wasn't only that she was still doing more; he also wasn't upholding his end of the bargain.

As predicted by reciprocity theory, conflict was more salient in the negotiated exchange setting than the reciprocal one, and Olivia viewed Mason's actions, or lack thereof, as intentional. At the time of the last interview, in an even more explicit negotiation process, they sat down and put the expectations for chores on paper. Olivia likens the document to "closing procedures" in a workplace—everything that needs to be done before one can leave having completed one's work—but they are both unsure whether this new method will work any better than previous attempts.

Although the researchers found reciprocal exchanges to be beneficial for relationships, reciprocity alone was not enough. The couples with the best outcomes also perceive supporting a family as a highly interdependent task, regardless of their family structure (for example, breadwinner-homemaker or dual-career). Couples who see themselves as a team and believe they share responsibility for important outcomes in their relationship are much more satisfied with and committed to their relationships.

For example, Aldo continues to do housework at Sabrina's house even after they separated because he feels he should "play a very strong role in [his] children's upbringing." The two of them view parenthood as something they will do together, regardless of whether they're in a relationship. Aldo describes this approach to an interviewer:

> Yeah, if I go out there, and I see the trash and stuff in the yard, and [we] will get out there and clean it up, yeah. Mop the floor or whatever needs to be done... Regardless of, of what beef you have with people, you know, it's, it's not only me doing that for her, it's for me doing those... Doing that for those children, too. You know what I'm saying? So I'm like, she needs me to clean her bathroom, I'm going to clean [it]. If I think it needs to be done, I'm going to do it.

Aldo and Sabrina's experience demonstrates the importance of interdependence in satisfaction with a relationship. Even as their romantic connection dissipates, the reciprocity in their relationship is evident, and they are able to stay close friends and generate positive emotions from working together as parents.

The findings from these interviews demonstrate the mutuality of the affect theory of social exchange and reciprocity theory. They also suggest that perceptions of interdependence, likely fostered by reciprocity or a sense of shared responsibility in making their families work, may be more important than the objective level of interdependence inherent in negotiation.

Source: Collett & Avelis, 2011.

& Cohen, 1982; Homans, 1974; Walster [Hatfield], Walster, & Berscheid, 1978).

To make this more concrete, consider the case of two women employed by the same company. One of the women (Anita) receives a high outcome—a salary of $100,000 a year, four weeks of paid vacation, reserved parking in the company's lot, and a fancy corner office with thick rugs and a nice view. The other woman (Candace) is about the same age but receives a lesser outcome—a salary of $40,000 per year, no paid vacation, no reserved parking, and a cramped, noisy office with no windows.

Will Anita and Candace feel that this distribution of rewards is equitable? If their inputs to the company are identical, the arrangement will almost certainly be experienced as distressing, especially by Candace. For example, if both work a 40-hour week, have only high school educations, and have approximately equal experience, there is little basis for paying Anita more than Candace. Candace will probably feel angry because the reward distribution is inequitable, and Anita may feel uncomfortable or guilty.

But suppose instead that Anita's inputs are much greater than Candace's. Say that she works a 60-hour week, holds an advanced degree such as an M.B.A., and has 12 more years of relevant experience than Candace. Additionally, suppose that Anita's job involves a high level of stress because it entails the risk of serious failure and financial loss for the company. In this event, Anita not only has greater "investments" (that is, education and experience) but also is bearing greater immediate "costs" (60 hours of work a week plus high stress). Under these conditions, both Anita and Candace may feel that their outcomes, although not equal, are nevertheless equitable.

Responses to Inequity

Inequity produces distress (anger, guilt) and reduces productivity and commitment to the group. There are two distinct types of inequity: underreward and overreward. **Underreward** occurs when a person's outcomes are too low relative to his or her inputs; **overreward occurs** when a person's outcomes are too high relative to his or her inputs. Both make it likely that there will be direct attempts to change the conditions that produce the inequity.

Responses to Underreward. Persons who are underrewarded typically become dis-

satisfied or angry (Austin & Walster [Hatfield], 1974; Cropanzano, 1993; Scher, 1997; Sweeney, 1990). The greater the degree of underreward, the greater the dissatisfaction and desire to reestablish equity. Equity can be restored by increasing the outcomes to the underrewarded, decreasing the inputs from the underrewarded, decreasing the outcomes to the overrewarded, or increasing the inputs from the overrewarded. For example, a person who feels their salary is too low compared to their peers might aggressively seek a pay raise (increasing outcomes). Alternatively, they might reduce their effort (decreasing inputs). The latter would reduce group productivity (Andrews, 1967; Lawler & O'Gara, 1967). Feelings of underreward have been connected to other negative outcomes, including increasing the likelihood that workers will steal from their employers or engage in other forms of work-related sabotage (Greenberg & Scott, 1996).

Not everyone responds to underreward behaviorally. Some engage in cognitive efforts to reduce distress. They might search for an external source to blame for the inequity—maybe there is a pay scale that caps what a new employee can make. When injustice can be attributed to an external source rather than an individual, people are less likely to address inequity behaviorally.

Responses to Overreward. What happens when a person receives more than his or her fair share in a relationship? Will he or she be content just to enjoy the benefits? Although overreward is apparently less troubling to individuals than is underreward (Greenberg, 1996), it can still create feelings of inequity, often in the form of guilt rather than anger (Perry, 1993; Sweeney, 1990). To reduce this distress, a person who feels guilty may attempt to rectify the inequity (Austin & Walster [Hatfield], 1974).

Research findings show that in some situations, overrewarded persons sacrifice some of their rewards to increase those of others. However, the extent of the redistribution often will not be complete, and equity may be only partially restored (Leventhal, Weiss, & Long, 1969). There is some evidence that overrewarded members prefer to restore equity by increasing their inputs. For example, in a work situation, overrewarded members can strive to produce more or better products as a means of reducing inequity (Goodman & Friedman, 1971; Patrick & Jackson, 1991); this enables them to restore equity without sacrificing any of the outcomes they receive.

This process was investigated in a classic study in which students were hired to work as proofreaders (Adams & Jacobsen, 1964). In one condition, participants were told that they were not really qualified for the job—due to inadequate experience and poor test scores—but that they would nevertheless be paid the same rate as professional proofreaders (30 cents per page). In a second condition, participants were told that due to their lack of qualifications, they would be paid a reduced rate (20 cents per page). In a third condition, participants were told that they had adequate experience and ability for the job and that they would be paid the full rate (30 cents per page). Thus, the participants in the first condition viewed themselves as overrewarded, whereas those in the second and third conditions saw their pay as equitable. Measures of the quality of the students' work showed that the overrewarded students caught significantly more errors than the equitably paid students. In fact, the overrewarded students were so vigilant that they often challenged the accuracy of material that was correct. These results indicate that the overrewarded students increased their inputs, thereby restoring equity. Similar findings appear in related studies (Adams & Rosenbaum, 1962; Goodman & Friedman, 1969).

Procedural Justice

Social psychologists increasingly find that the fairness of distributions, or outcomes, is only one measure of fairness. People also gauge the fairness of the procedures or processes that determine distributions, what many call **procedural justice**. There are two different components of procedural justice—instrumental and relational.

In instrumental terms, the justness of a process is related to the amount of control an individual feels they have in shaping the process and determining the outcome (Thibaut & Walker, 1975, 1978). The more control an individual has, the more just they believe the procedure is. If a teenager is allowed to give input on the punishment she receives for breaking curfew, she will see this as more just than if her parents decide this without consulting her. For example, if they ask her what she thinks is fair, she will see the process as more just.

Procedural justice is important because the fairer an individual believes a process is, the fairer he or she will perceive the outcome to be (Tyler, Boeckmann, Smith, & Huo, 1997). In other words, the teenager will see the exact same punishment—perhaps a week without her cell phone or being grounded from the homecoming dance—as more fair if she is somehow involved in the process than if her parents simply announce the punishment.

In early research, these instrumental concerns dominated the research on procedural justice. However, over time the conception of procedural justice expanded and began to consider whether processes make an individual feel included and valued beyond just giving them control. Social psychologists who attend to relational factors in processes would argue that including the teenager in discussions about punishment gives her *voice*—the opportunity to give her opinion (Greenberg & Folger, 1983). Having a say is important, even if it does not influence the outcome. People will perceive a process as fairer if they have such an opportunity, even if it comes after a decision has already been made (Lind, Kanfer, & Earley, 1990). If the teenager's parents let her express her disappointment rather than simply sending her to her room, she will feel that the process was fairer. People are also more likely to rate a procedure as fair if it promotes relationships among group members, makes people feel included within the group, indicates standing in the group, and demonstrates neutrality (Lind & Tyler, 1988; Tyler & Lind, 1992).

Allocation procedures are more likely to be seen as fair if they meet a number of criteria (Leventhal, Karuza, & Fry, 1980): suppression of bias, consistency, representation of all parties' interests, accuracy of information, ethicality, and correctability. For example, a teenage daughter is more likely to see the process of choosing a punishment as fair if her parents ensure that they have all the information about why she broke curfew (accuracy of information), they use the same process they would use for a sibling (suppression of bias) and one that is similar to those they have used previously (consistency), and they use a process that is seen as ethical (ethicality) and flexible enough that there is the possibility for change if there is a problem with the process or new information comes to light (correctability).

Procedural and distributive justice are related to a number of other concepts in social psychology. For example, recent work in social exchange finds that people tend to perceive identical outcomes as more fair when they come from reciprocal exchange than when they are a result of negotiated exchange (Molm, Peterson, & Takahashi, 2003). They also see exchange partners in reciprocal exchanges as more fair as well (Molm, Collett, & Schaefer, 2006). These effects are likely because conflict increases attention to inequities (Deutsch, 2000), and conflict is lower in reciprocal exchange than it is in negotiated exchanges (Molm, 2010). Social psychologists have also explored the link between attributions (Chapter 6) and reactions to injustice. An individual is less likely to respond to perceived injustice if they attribute the injustice to an external source than if they attribute it to an individual (Utne & Kidd, 1980). This is one of the reasons people react more negatively if it is a fair procedure—versus an unfair one—that leads to an unfavorable outcome. If the process is flawed, one can expect the outcome to be flawed. If the process is fair, it is much more difficult to make sense of an outcome that is perceived of as unfair.

SUMMARY

The Systematic Study of Groups. Robert Bales was the first to study groups in a systematic fashion, using his Interaction Process Analysis to document what type of contributions group members made and to whom they directed those communications. His research showed that status and influence differences emerge, even in initially homogeneous groups, and then persist for the life of the group. Over time, group members take on particular roles in groups. Two roles that influence group dynamics are the task specialist and social-emotional specialist.

Status Characteristics and Expectations. Most groups are not homogenous. The diversity in groups affects within-group processes, with those who are higher in status being afforded more influence in groups. Status characteristics are attributes that are connected to group members' expectations and evaluations of people and performances through a status generalization process. Diffuse status characteristics are attributes that are thought to influence performance on a wide range of tasks, whereas specific status characteristics only influence performance expectations if they are explicitly connected to the group task.

Group Decision Making. There are a series of steps that groups go through during a group decision-making process. Sometimes these processes go awry. One problem plaguing group decision making is groupthink, a fault mode of thinking that often leads to ill-conceived outcomes. Social psychologists have located a number of symptoms and causes of groupthink as well as recommended ways to avoid falling victim to groupthink. Group decision making and discussion also leads to group polarization, causing group members to make either more cautious or more risky decisions than they would alone.

Social Exchange. Social psychologists see interaction as a process of exchange, whereby individuals trade benefits and rewards with one another in interaction. The central premise of social exchange is that actors exchange resources using an exchange process while situated in an exchange network. These resources can be tangible or intangible. Social exchange theorists study attributes of relations and positions rather than individuals. Although early research in social exchange focused on network structure, power, and dependence, more recent research examines exchange form, trust, and commitment.

Equity and Justice. There are three distribution principles that shape justice evaluations—equity, equality, and need. When individuals feel they have been underrewarded or overrewarded, they experience distress and engage in behavioral or cognitive efforts to restore a perception of equity (in which an individual gets what he or she deserves). Perceptions of fairness of procedures are also important in justice evaluations. Procedures that afford participants control over the process and outcome and make individuals feel like a valued part of the group are seen as most fair.

List of Key Terms and Concepts

affect theory of social exchange (p. 490)
cautious shift (p. 484)
collective task (p. 471)
diffuse status characteristics (p. 475)
distributive justice (p. 491)
group polarization (p. 484)
groupthink (p. 482)
homogeneous (p. 471)
overreward (p. 494)
power and prestige order (p. 475)
procedural justice (p. 495)
reciprocity theory (p. 490)
relation (p. 485)
risky shift (p. 484)
role (p. 474)
role differentiation (p. 474)
social-emotional specialist (p. 473)
specific status characteristics (p. 475)
status characteristic (p. 475)
status generalization (p. 476)
task specialist (p. 473)
underreward (p. 494)

Critical Thinking Skill:
Understanding Theory as a Bridge

Much of the research on group processes relies on laboratory experiments. As we have seen throughout this text, it is nearly impossible to create conditions in the laboratory that approximate the world outside the laboratory (experimentalists tend to avoid the phrase "the real world" because the laboratory is very real). However, reproducing that outside world is not the goal of experiments (Zelditch, 1969); instead, experimental social psychologists are interested in testing theories—theories that are based on and apply to the life outside the laboratory.

Social psychologists consider a process they see in social life—for example, why you trust your current boyfriend more than your last boyfriend—and generate a theory about why that might be the case. Is it that his personality is different—he's inherently more trustworthy—or is there a social process at play? Thinking back on a previous relationship, perhaps you were together almost all the time, giving little opportunity to a partner to build trust in your absence. In your current relationship, you have your own life and your own interests and friends, and this gives you and your partner the opportunity to act in a trustworthy manner. You think that this difference might be one of the reasons you have greater trust now than previously. How could you test that?

If you were to create an experiment, you would have to think abstractly. What is it about being apart that facilitates trust in couples? What facilitates trust in other situations and relationships?

You might generate a theory—a statement of the relationship of facts about the social world—about the genesis of trust in relationships. Based on your experiences, you might decide that trust emerges from

(1) situations of risk and uncertainty (for example, when a couple is not together) and (2) when the group members do not take advantage of the others' trust (for example, if a partner remains faithful).

In fact, Linda Molm had a similar theory. Instead of bringing couples into the laboratory, however, she brought students in and had some exchange points using processes with very low levels of risk and others with very high levels of risk (Molm, Schaefer, & Collett, 2009). Unbeknownst to the students, they were exchanging with computerized actors. Some were programmed to behave in a trustworthy manner, others in an untrustworthy manner. Molm found support for her theory. The highest levels of trust were among those students who exchanged points in a high-risk situation with partners who engaged in a trustworthy manner. She argued this supported her "theory of reciprocity."

Collett and Avelis (2011) were able to use Molm's theory as the bridge between the laboratory and the couples they studied (see Box 14.2). They were not using the results of the experiment—that exchanging points over computers led to different levels of trust. They were using the theory—that acting in a trustworthy manner in a situation of risk increases trust and enhances relationships. This is how theory can work as the bridge. It connects the outside world to the laboratory and the laboratory back to the outside world.

Although there are many examples of this from the text, one of the most famous is Latané and Darley's theory of bystander intervention. Their research was inspired by something they saw outside the laboratory—the way people reacted to the attack on Kitty Genovese. They came up with a theory about the diffusion of responsibility to explain why Kitty's neighbors failed to help her. They tested this theory in a series of laboratory experiments. None of the situations involved attacks or neighbors; they involved students and emergencies that might occur in a laboratory on campus. For those who apply the theory today, it is unimportant that Latané and Darley's research findings were related to billowing smoke or students' seizures. Using theory as the bridge, what the researchers learned can be used to explain countless situations in which individuals failed to act in an emergency—or when they did.

Can you think of how you might use the theories in this chapter to understand life outside the laboratory?

CHAPTER 15

SOCIAL STRUCTURE AND PERSONALITY

INTRODUCTION

Fred is 38, married, the father of two children, and sells pacemakers to hospitals. He travels 2 or 3 days a week and works at home the rest of the time in his $300,000 house in the suburbs. He earns almost $150,000 a year. Because his income is based entirely on commission, Fred worries about his sales falling off; but on the whole, he is satisfied with his life. His values are conservative, and he voted for Mitt Romney in 2012.

Jose is also 38 and has a wife and two children. He runs a service station and works 6 days a week from early morning until 6:00 or 7:00 p.m. Jose and his family live in a small, three-bedroom house. Last year, he made about $60,000. He worries a lot about money and has been very tense the past year. He has liberal values and usually votes for Democratic candidates.

Marie is 39. She is nurse manager in a hospital pediatric unit. Last year, her salary was $83,500. Although she enjoys her young patients, she hates all the paperwork and the personnel problems. Some of her values are conservative, whereas others are liberal; she considers herself an Independent.

Fred, Jose, and Marie are three very different people. Each has a different occupation, which produces differences in income and lifestyle. They differ in their *values*—in what they believe is important—and in the amount of stress they feel.

Where do these differences come from? Often, they are the result of one's location in society. Every person occupies a social **position**—a designated location in a social system (Biddle, 1986). The ordered and persisting relationships among these positions in a social system make up the **social structure** (House, 1981).

This chapter considers the impact of social structure on the individual. There are three ways in which social structure influences a person's life. First, every person occupies one or more positions in the social structure. Each position carries a set of expectations about the behavior of the occupant of that position, called a **role** (Rommetveit, 1955). Role expectations are anticipations of how a person will behave based on the knowledge of his or her position. Through socialization and personal experience, each of us knows the role expectations associated with our positions (Heiss, 1990). For example, Fred enacts several roles, including salesman, husband, and father. The expectations associated with these roles are a major influence on his behavior.

A second way that social structure influences the individual is through **social networks**—the sets of relationships associated with the various positions a person occupies. Each of us is woven into several networks, including those involving coworkers, family, and friends. Ties between the person and a family member or friend reflect a **primary relationship**—one that is personal, emotionally involving, and of long duration. Such relationships have a substantial effect on one's behavior and self-image (Cooley, 1902).

A third way in which social structure influences the individual is through **status**—the social ranking of a person's position. In every society, some positions are accorded greater prestige than others. Differences in ranking indicate a person's relative standing—his or her status—in the social structure. Each of us occupies several positions of differing status. In the United States, occupational status is especially influential. It is the major determinant of income, which has a substantial effect on one's lifestyle. One of the obvious differences between Fred and Jose, for instance, is their annual income.

Each person's location in social structure is the most important determinant of many of his or her life experiences. This chapter focuses on the relationships between social location and several characteristics that determine the nature and quality of one's life, including education and occupation, values, health, and strength of connection to the society. Specifically, it considers four questions:

1. How does location in society affect educational and occupational achievement?

2. How does social location influence people's values?

3. How does social location influence a person's physical and mental health?

4. How does social location influence a person's sense of belonging in society, or the lack thereof?

STATUS ATTAINMENT

The individual's relative standing or status in the social structure is perhaps the single most important influence on his or her life. Status determines access to resources—to money and to influence over others. In the United States, occupation is the main determinant of status. This section considers the nature of occupational status, the determinants of the status that particular individuals attain or achieve, and the impact of social networks on the attainment of status.

Occupational Status

Occupational status is a key component of social standing and a major determinant of income and lifestyle. Fred is a sales representative for a company that makes pacemakers and other electronic medical equipment. These items are in great demand, and few companies make them. Fred sells a single pacemaker for $7,200 and keeps 25 percent of the money as his commission.

He needs to be on the road only 2 or 3 days per week to earn $150,000 a year. He has a beautiful suburban home and two cars. Jose, by contrast, owns a service station. He works from morning until night pumping gas and repairing cars. His station is in a good location, but his overhead is high; he earned only $60,000 last year, and he worries that this year, that figure will be lower. Jose and his family live in a smaller, older house and have a 6-year-old car.

The benefits that Fred and Jose receive from their occupational statuses are clearly different. First, Fred earns twice as much money as Jose. This determines the quality of housing, clothing, and medical care his family receives. Fred also has much greater control over his own time. Within limits, he can choose which days he works and how much he works; this, in turn, affects the time he can spend with family and friends. Jose doesn't have much free time. Finally, Fred receives a great deal of respect from the people with whom he works. He controls a scarce resource, so doctors and hospital personnel generally treat him well. Jose, however, deals with people who are usually preoccupied or angry because their cars are not running properly. As a result, Jose's job is much more stressful.

In addition to these tangible benefits, occupational status is associated with prestige. Several surveys in the United States have found that there is widespread agreement about the prestige ranking of specific occupations. In these studies, respondents typically are given a list of occupations and asked to rate each occupation in terms of its "general standing" or "social standing." The average rating is often used as a measure of relative prestige. The prestige scores for the United States shown in Table 15.1 were taken from an occupational prestige scale of 0–100 (Nakao & Treas, 1994). Surprisingly, there is considerable agreement across diverse societies in the average ranking of

TABLE 15.1 Occupational Prestige in the United States

OCCUPATION	NAKAO-TREAS PRESTIGE SCORE
Physician	86
Lawyer	75
College or university professor	74
Registered nurse	66
Electrical engineer	64
Elementary school teacher	64
Police officer	60
Social worker	52
Dental hygienist	52
Office manager	51
Electrician	51
Housewife	51
Office secretary	46
Data-entry keyer	41
Farmer	40
Auto mechanic	40
Beautician	36
Assembly-line worker	35
Housekeeper (private home)	34
Precision assembler	31
Truck driver	30
Cashier	29
Waitress/waiter	28
Garbage collector	28
Hotel chambermaid	20
Househusband	14

Source: Hauser and Warren, 1997.

occupations. Even adults in China give rankings similar to those displayed in Table 15.1 (Lin & Xie, 1988). This agreement may reflect the fact that modern societies develop a similar division of labor in order to function effectively (van Leeuwen & Maas, 2010).

The social structure of the United States can be viewed as consisting of several groups or social classes. A **social class** con-sists of persons who share a common sta-tus in the society. There are various views regarding the nature of social classes in the United States. One view of social class em-phasizes occupational prestige in conjunc-tion with income and education in defining class boundaries. This approach ordinarily classifies people into upper upper, lower upper, upper middle, lower middle, work-ing, and lower classes (Coleman & Neugar-ten, 1971). A very different approach em-phasizes a relational view of class, especially the control, or lack of control, an individ-ual has over his or her work and coworkers as the main determinant of class standing (Wright, Costello, Hachen, & Sprague, 1982).

Intergenerational Mobility

When a person moves from an occupation lower in prestige and income to one higher in prestige and income, he or she is expe-riencing **upward mobility**. To what extent is upward mobility possible in the United States? On the one hand, we have the Hora-tio Alger rags-to-riches imagery in our cul-ture: Anyone who is determined and works hard can achieve economic success. This imagery is fueled by stories about the aston-ishing success of Oprah Winfrey as a media mogul, Bill Gates's success as founder and head of Microsoft, Martha Stewart's suc-cess as a businesswoman, and so on. Many Americans believe that they can become rich in their lifetime (DiPrete, 2007). On the other hand, some argue that America is a caste society—that our eventual occupa-tional and economic achievements are fixed at birth by our parents' social class, our ethnicity, and our gender. To be sure, ev-ery city has families that have been wealthy for generations and families that have been poor for as long. This suggests that the United States is characterized by castes—groups whose members are prevented by rigid class boundaries from changing their social status.

These two views of upward mobility in American society are concerned with intergenerational mobility—the extent of change in social status from one generation to the next. To measure intergenerational mobility, we compare the social status of persons with that of their parents. If the rags-to-riches image is accurate, we should find that a large number of adults attain a social status significantly higher than their parents'. If the caste society image is correct, we should find little or no upward mobility.

What are the influences on upward (intergenerational) mobility in American society? In this section, we consider the impact of three factors: socioeconomic background, gender, and occupational segregation.

Socioeconomic Background. Occupational attainment in U.S. society rests heavily on educational achievement. To be a doctor, dental assistant, computer programmer, lawyer, or business executive, one needs the required education. To become a registered nurse, Marie (whom we met in the introduction) had to complete nursing school. Fred, our medical equipment salesman, earned a bachelor's degree in business.

Beyond education, what other factors influence occupational attainment? To answer this question effectively, we need to trace the occupational careers of individuals over their life course. Such longitudinal data are available from a research project begun in the 1950s (Sewell & Hauser, 1980). In 1957, all high school seniors in Wisconsin were surveyed about their post–high school plans. From this population, a random sample of 10,317 was selected for continuing study. In 1964, researchers obtained information from students' parents about

post–high school education, military service, marital status, and current occupation. Later, they obtained information about the students' earnings and about the colleges or universities they attended. In 1975, 97 percent of the original sample were located, and most were interviewed by telephone. The interview focused on post–high school education, work history, and family characteristics. The data from this study enabled researchers to trace the impact of the characteristics of high school seniors on subsequent education, occupation, earnings, and work experience.

Figure 15.1 presents a diagram of the relationships found among the variables studied. The arrows indicate causal influences. Variables are arranged from left to right to reflect the order in which they affect the person through time. These results indicate that children from more affluent homes have greater ability and higher aspirations, and receive more education. Children with higher ability get better grades, which reward them for their academic work and reinforce their aspirations. Children who do well are also encouraged by significant others, such as teachers and relatives, which also contributes to their high aspirations. These children are likely to choose courses that will prepare them for college. They are likely to spend more time on academic pursuits and less time on dating and social activities (Jessor, Costa, Jessor, & Donovan, 1983). As a result, they are likely to continue their education beyond high school and perhaps beyond college. Finally, high ability, encouragement of significant others, and high educational attainment lead to greater occupational status and earnings.

Note that socioeconomic background and grades have an indirect effect on occupational status and a direct effect on educational attainment. This does not mean that parental socioeconomic status and an individual's grades are unrelated to occupa-

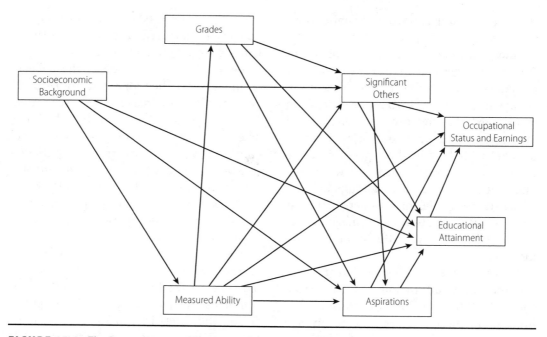

FIGURE 15.1 The Determinants of Occupational Status Attainment

This figure summarizes the influences that determine educational and occupational status over the life course. Socio-economic background (parents' education, occupation, and income) influences ability, aspirations, and educational attainment. Ability influences grades, which, in turn, affect encouragement from significant others and aspirations for educational attainment. Occupational status is affected by education and also by ability, aspirations, and significant others.

Source: Adapted from William H. Sewell and Robert M. Hauser, "The Wisconsin Longitudinal Study of Social and Psychological Factors in Aspirations and Achievements," *Research in Sociology of and Education and Socialization,* Vol. 1, 1980, pp. 59–99.

tional status. Rather, it indicates that status and grades influence occupational attainment through other variables—like aspirations—that have a direct impact on occupational attainment (Sewell & Hauser, 1975). A meta-analysis of the interrelationship of intelligence and parental socioeconomic status (SES) on individuals' attainment included studies that measured all of the relevant variables and used a longitudinal design (Strenze, 2007). It used data from 85 data sets, involving 135 samples. An index of parental SES (education, occupation, and income), intelligence/ability measured while the individual was still in school, and academic performance/grades predicted later educational and occupational attainment and income.

In the research summarized in Figure 15.1, the family characteristics studied are mothers' and fathers' socioeconomic standing—education, occupation, and income. How is it that variables such as your father's education and your mother's income influence your educational attainment? Parents often use their resources to create a home environment that facilitates doing well in school (Teachman, 1987). Thus, they provide such aids as a quiet place to study, encyclopedias, and a laptop or tablet computer. Moreover, they may provide cultural enrichment activities, such as attending concerts and sports events (DiMaggio & Mohr, 1985). A study of the daily activities of children aged 3 to 11 found that children of highly educated parents spent more time reading and studying and less time watching TV (Bianchi & Robinson, 1997). In high school, students whose parents have bachelor's degrees are more likely to study, and spend more hours studying (Allard, 2008).

One review of the research on the intergenerational transmission of poverty concludes that children raised in poor families will complete fewer years of school, are less likely to attend college, and are more likely to be poor as adults (Corcoran, 1995). On the other hand, many Black families, though not wealthy, do give their children the motivation and the skills to succeed in school (McAdoo, 1997).

Family structure also plays a role in the attainment process. A study of a national sample of 30- to 59-year-old men and women compared those raised in original two-parent families with those raised in other family structures. Those raised in original families earned more as adults (Powell & Parcell, 1997). Among Blacks, the presence of two parents, both employed outside the home, is essential to mobility (McAdoo, 1997).

The experiences of Fred and Jose clearly reflect the importance of these processes. Fred's parents were upper middle class; they sent him to preschool at age 4 and encouraged him to learn to read. Jose's parents were working class; they encouraged him to get out and play and not to waste time reading. Fred did well in school; his grades were always high. Jose struggled with his schoolwork, especially math. By eighth grade, Fred had an excellent record, and his teachers gave him lots of encouragement; Jose's teachers, on the other hand, didn't pay much attention to him. Fred worked hard in high school, got good grades, and, with the support of his teachers and family, went to a university. After finishing high school, Jose went into the army, where he learned vehicle mechanics. When Fred finished college, he got a job in a

medical equipment firm. Ten years after he graduated from high school, Fred was selling $200,000 worth of equipment per year and earning 20 percent commissions. After he finished his military service, Jose went to work in a gas station. Ten years after Jose graduated from high school, he was earning $28,000 per year working in a gas station.

Thus, there is some upward mobility in U.S. society, and one's socioeconomic background does not fix one's occupational attainment and earnings. Through greater education, many persons achieve an occupational status and income larger than would be expected based solely on their background. Thus, America is not a caste society. At the same time, one's socioeconomic background is not irrelevant to one's educational and occupational attainment. Not everyone can be a doctor, lawyer, or engineer. Opportunities for upward mobility are not unlimited.

Education. The research summarized in the preceding section clearly indicates the importance of education in determining one's occupational attainment and adult status. Thus, differences in the amount of education completed will result in differences in status. In U.S. society, there are large disparities in educational attainment by ethnicity. The percentage of all persons who have completed high school (and more) and college (and more) in 2010 are displayed in Table 15.2. Looking at the data, Asian Americans are the most educated (one-half complete college), followed by Whites (30 percent), Blacks (18, 21 percent), and Hispanics (13, 15 percent). Not surprisingly, these differences translate into differences in occupations, which in turn create differences in income (see below) and lifestyle.

Gender. Is the process of status attainment different for men and women? According to the data obtained on Wisconsin high

TABLE 15.2 Educational Attainment by Ethnicity and Gender, 2010

	WHITE		BLACK		ASIAN & PAIS		HISPANIC	
	MALE %	FEMALE %	MALE %	FEMALE %	MALE %	FEMALE %	MALE %	FEMALE %
High school graduate or more	86.9	88.2	83.6	84.6	91.2	87.0	61.4	64.4
College graduate or more	30.8	29.9	17.2	21.4	55.6	49.5	12.9	14.9

Source: U.S. Census Bureau, Statistical Abstract of the United States: 2012, Table 230.

school students, the determinants of occupational status as depicted in Figure 15.2 are the same for both men and women, although the size of some relationships varies. Using a prestige scale of 0–100, the first jobs held by women were, on the average, 6 points higher than the first jobs held by men. Women's first jobs were concentrated within a narrow range of prestige, whereas there was much greater variation in the prestige scores of first jobs held by men (Sewell, Hauser, & Wolf, 1980). Table 15.1 reveals how this occurred. The first jobs that women held included registered nurse, schoolteacher, social worker, dental assistant, and secretary. The prestige scores of these jobs range from 66 to 46. In contrast, men's first jobs ranged from physician (86) to garbage collector (28).

When the researchers looked at 1975 occupations, they found that men had gained an average of 9 points in status in the 18-year period since their graduation from high school. Women, on the other hand, had actually lost status; the average prestige of current occupations for women was 2 points lower than the average prestige of their first jobs. Men experience upward mobility because they work continuously. Moreover, they are in occupations with possibilities of promotion and advancement. Women's work careers are often interrupted by marriage and by raising children; when they return to work, they often take up the same job. Thus, women are less able to build

up enough continuous experience to gain promotions. Moving also interferes with women's advancement, especially when the purpose of the move is to further the man's career (Shihadeh, 1991). Advancement is also more limited in occupations held largely by women. The top positions in schools, social work, airlines, and sales are more often held by men than by women. So the occupational status achieved by men and women differs over the course of their careers.

These differences are evident in the lives of Fred, Jose, and Marie, who were introduced earlier in this chapter. After college, Fred began in sales (prestige score 49), and his income increased substantially every year. If he wanted, he could move up in the company to regional sales manager, national sales manager, and perhaps vice president of sales. Jose has moved from gas station attendant (prestige score 21) to owner of a service station (prestige score 44). Like Fred, Marie went to college and earned a bachelor's degree. Her first job involved working on a surgical unit in a large hospital (prestige score 66). As nurse manager in pediatrics, she works days now, gets weekends off, and earns more, but her occupation is unchanged. She could move up to director of nursing, but she is unlikely to strive for this, because the added responsibility isn't balanced by added pay.

Occupational Segregation. In the preceding section, we saw that the influence of

Segregation of occupations by gender is widespread in the United States; for example, most construction workers are men, whereas most nurses and unit clerks in hospitals are women. This segregation has serious consequences for a woman's earnings and occupational prestige. *Left:* © kozmoat98/iStock; *right:* © Helen King/Corbis

factors such as socioeconomic background and ability on occupational attainment is similar for men and women. At the same time, working men and women are not proportionately distributed across occupational categories. Look back at Table 15.1. As you look at each occupation in the list, which gender comes to mind? Chances are that when you think of engineers, carpenters, or auto mechanics, you picture men performing those jobs. In 2012, of those employed in these occupations, 84 percent, 98 percent, and 98 percent, respectively, were men (U.S. Bureau of Labor Statistics, 2013a). Similarly, when you think of registered nurse or dental hygienist, you picture women in these roles; in 2012, of those employed in these occupations, 91 percent and 99 percent, respectively, were women. Many occupations consist overwhelmingly of either men or women; there is substantial occupational level segregation by gender (Reskin & Padavic, 1994). As occupation is the basis of prestige and a major determinant of income, this segregation has serious consequences.

There are several processes that perpetuate occupational segregation. Our awareness of the gender composition of occupations through our daily experience and via media portrayals influences our aspirations. Further, cultural beliefs about gender differences in skills and abilities, for example, that girls are less skilled than boys at math, influence educational decisions and career choices (Correll, 2004) in ways that maintain occupational segregation (men become engineers) (see Box 15.1).

Direct experience with occupational segregation begins in adolescence. Data from a sample of 3,101 tenth- and eleventh-grade students in suburban high schools provide concrete evidence (Greenberger & Steinberg, 1983). Adolescents' first jobs are segregated by sex, with girls earning a lower hourly wage. These differences reflect differential opportunity; employers hire primarily girls or primarily boys for a particular job (for example, laborer, fast-food sales), and they pay boys more. Performing different roles results in differences in the skills developed by gender.

Adults often experience gender segregation in the workplace. In a survey of 290 organizations with a total of more than 50,000 employees, the results indicated that men and women rarely perform similar work in a single organization; when they do, they usually have different job titles (Bielby & Baron, 1986). There is little evidence that employers' practices in this regard are a rational response to differences between men and women. Jobs held by men in one organization are held by women in other organizations. What happens when a person of the other gender enters a segregated occupation? That person may experience stereotyping and harassment by coworkers or supervisors, and may leave the job. On the other hand, the person may experience unusual rewards and rapid advancement. Elementary school teachers are primarily women (81.4 percent in 2012); research comparing the outcomes of men and women elementary teachers found that men were more likely than women to be promoted to administrative positions (Cognard-Black, 2004). Either way, the dominance of one gender in the occupation is maintained.

Differences in work performed or in job titles often result in large differences in pay. In the first quarter of 2013, the median weekly earnings (in current dollars) of White women employed full-time was $723, whereas the median for White men was $888 (U.S. Bureau of Labor Statistics, 2013b). Thus, the median annual earnings of a White woman was $37,596, whereas the median for a White man was $46,167—a difference of $8,580. Thus, women's earnings are, on average, 81 percent of men's earnings. An analysis of local labor markets found that the more segregated a labor market was, the larger the gap between men's and women's wages (Cohen, 2003).

There are also differences in earnings by race and ethnicity. In 2013, the median weekly earnings of Black women was $597, whereas the earnings of Hispanic women was $531. Thus, Black women earned $126 per week less than White women, and the White/Hispanic difference was $192. The median earnings of Black men was $666, and of Hispanic men $593. The White/Black difference was $222 per week and the White/Hispanic gap was $295. (U.S. Bureau

of Labor Statistics, 2013b). Asian men and women enjoy the highest average weekly earnings in the U.S., $1,058 and $831 respectively. Part of these gaps is due to differences in occupations by race and gender, reflecting differences in (access to) education and training. However, a substantial proportion is due to discrimination, not to differences in measures of workers' skills.

Social Networks. We have seen that socioeconomic background, ability, educational attainment, and earlier jobs influence occupational attainment over the life course. In part, this is because differences in experiences create differences in an individual's aspirations and abilities to cope with the occupational world. Varied experiences also move people into different social networks. This exposes them to varied social contacts, which have an important effect on their upward mobility. This section considers some of the ways in which position in social networks affects the person.

Networks provide channels for the flow of information, including information about job opportunities. What types of networks are likely to provide information on finding new jobs? You might think it is networks characterized by strong ties, such as families or peer groups. Surprisingly, employment opportunities are often found through networks characterized by weak ties—relationships involving infrequent interaction and little closeness or emotional depth (Marsden & Campbell, 1984). Those to whom our ties are weak are involved in different groups and activities than we are. Consequently, they will be exposed to information that is different from the information we and our friends already have. For this reason, new information is more likely to come via a weak tie than via a strong one. In one study, of those who found jobs through contacts, only 17 percent were obtained through strong ties (Granovetter, 1973).

BOX 15.1 Can Girls Do Math? Cultural Beliefs and Occupational Segregation

The power of cultural beliefs was convincingly demonstrated by the controversy in early 2005 over remarks made by the president of Harvard University, Lawrence Summers. Speaking at a meeting of the National Bureau of Economic Research on January 14, Summers suggested three reasons why women are underrepresented "in high-end scientific professions. One is what I would call . . . the high-powered job hypothesis. The second is what I would call different avail-ability of aptitude at the high end, and the third is what I would call different socialization and patterns of discrimination in a search" (Summers, 2005). In an elaboration of the second point, he suggested that, among those with the very high-est abilities in science and math, the ratio of men to women was probably 5:1. Summers is restat-ing a widely held cultural belief in the United States, that girls/women are inferior at math and, by extension, will not succeed in occupations that require high mathematical ability. A profes-sor of biology at MIT, Dr. Nancy Hopkins, walked out on Summers, and later discussed his remarks with a reporter.

One reason why many reacted to his remarks with indignation is that these beliefs become a self-fulfilling prophecy (see Chap 6). Many teach-ers and guidance counselors (and many parents) believe girls are inferior at math and so they cau-tion girls not to take advanced math or science courses. This, of course, restricts the number of girls who take the courses needed to later pur-sue degrees in these fields. This belief is held by many boys and girls, and influences the way they interact with one another. Furthermore, a girl who believes she is less skilled will not work as hard or be as persistent as a girl who believes she can do it, making it less likely that she will succeed (see Chap. 3, self-efficacy). If we really want to encourage members of a group to enter an occupational field in larger numbers, we need to stop constraining them by voicing and acting upon such beliefs. It is especially upsetting when someone of Summers's status, president of one of the oldest universities in the United States, voices them.

More important, Summers is wrong. There have been hundreds of studies of differences in mathematical and related skills and abilities, at all age levels. These studies have been the focus of large-scale meta-analyses; one of them used data from more than 100 studies, testing 3 mil-lion persons (Hyde, Fenema, & Lamon, 1990; Hyde, Lindberg, Linn, Ellis, & Williams, 2008). Overall, the average effect size was $d = 0.05$— that is, it was basically zero. When the analysis was done by age, the results indicated that there is no gender difference in math performance in elementary or middle school, but a significant difference emerges in high school. These results flatly reject the hypothesis that there are innate differences in ability, and are entirely consistent with the hypothesis that girls and boys are being socialized to believe there is a difference, and that that cultural belief increasingly affects math performance as females progress through the school system. It is not differential ability, but dif-ferential socialization that results in few women in top positions in science.

Another explanation for the underrepresen-tation of women at top levels of science is that it reflects their lifestyle choices—to have children and spend time with family—not discrimination. This explanation was put forward in a paper in the prestigious Proceedings of the National Academy of Science (Ceci & Williams, 2011). It was widely covered by major media outlets. The problem is that there is no data supporting the hypothesis (Barnett & Rivers, 2011). The authoritative scien-tific report is "Beyond Bias and Barriers" (Commit-tee, 2007). It cites more than 500 sources of data showing that women face widespread discrimi-nation in science and engineering. This discrimi-nation is evident in the results of an experiment (Moss-Racusin, et al., 2012). Science faculty at major universities rated the application materials of a student, who was randomly assigned either a male or female name. Faculty rated the male more competent and more hireable, selected a higher starting salary, and offered more mento-ring to him.

A study of the hiring process in a mid-sized high-tech organization gathered information on all 35,229 applicants over a 10-year period (1985–1994). The results indicated that there were only small differences in hiring by gender, and they were accounted for entirely by age and education. For ethnic minorities, on the other hand, some of the differences were accounted for by referral method; members of minority groups lacked access to the informal networks that were associated with success in getting hired (Petersen, Saporta, & Seidel, 2000).

We noted earlier that women are less likely than men to experience upward occupational mobility during their careers. Might this occur because men and women differ in their access to networks that carry job information? Our ties to networks grow out of the activities we share with others. The organizations we belong to are a major setting for such activities (Feld, 1981). The larger the organization, the larger the potential number of weak rather than strong ties. If men belong to larger organizations than women, they would have more weak ties and, hence, better access to information useful in finding jobs.

To examine this possibility, 1,799 adults were asked the name and size of each organization to which they belonged (Miller-McPherson & Smith-Lovin, 1982). On average, men belonged to organizations such as business and professional groups and labor unions, whereas women were more likely to belong to smaller charitable, church, neighborhood, and community groups. Moreover, job-related contacts are more likely to develop in business, professional, and union groups. Findings showed that men had an average of 170 job-related potential contacts, whereas women had an average of fewer than 35. The difference was as large comparing men and women who worked as comparing men who worked

and women in traditional roles. Apparently, men are in networks that allow greater access to information about and opportunities for advancement. Contemporary researchers refer to access to organizational networks as *bridging social capital* to highlight its value as an influence on one's resources (Coffe & Geys, 2008).

It is common to advise people seeking jobs to network, to seek information and assistance from people they know, in person, online, or through networking sites. Thus, men are likely to network with men and women with women, so women are often networking with people who have lower-paid jobs in gender-segregated firms. This, of course, perpetuates gender segregation in employment and the earnings gap between men and women (Munsch, 2013).

Social networks also contribute to mobility within one's workplace. A longitudinal study of employees in one high-tech firm found that having a large network of informal ties was associated with promotions and salary increases (Podolny & Baron, 1997).

INDIVIDUAL VALUES

Last year, Fred, Jose, and Marie were each approached by a labor union organizer. Fred, the sales representative, was approached by a member of Retail Clerks International. The organizer explained that under a union contract, Fred would spend fewer days on the road and would receive a travel allowance from his employer. Jose was approached by a representative of the Teamsters. The organizer sympathized with the problems of independent service station owners and urged Jose to let the Teamsters represent his interests in dealing with his supplier. Marie was approached by the president of United Health Care Workers; she was promised higher wages and greater respect from physicians if she would join.

Fred flatly rejected the invitation, believing that a union contract would limit his freedom and perhaps reduce his income. Jose's reaction was mixed. On the one hand, he felt he was at the mercy of "Big Oil." On the other hand, he was also a self-employed businessman; like Fred, he didn't want to join a labor organization that might limit his ability to determine his prices and the pace at which he worked. Marie reacted very favorably to her invitation and began to attend union meetings "to see what they are like." She felt that a union might lead to higher pay and might force the hospital to give her more freedom in determining the pace at which she worked.

In making their decisions, Fred, Jose, and Marie used their personal **values**, which are enduring beliefs that certain patterns of behavior or end states are preferable to others (Rokeach, 1973). All three were concerned with protecting or enhancing their freedom and income. These values provided criteria for making decisions. Thus, each person weighed the potential effect of joining a union on freedom and income. Fred felt that the effect on both would be negative. Jose was sure that union membership would limit his freedom but uncertain about its effect on his income. Marie perceived a potential gain in both freedom and income, so she decided to explore union membership.

An important theory of values has been developed by Schwartz (1992, 1994). He identifies 10 motivationally distinct values; these are portrayed in Figure 15.2. One study assessed the values of 999 adults, 52 percent of them women. There were no differences by gender in either the structure of values or the mean ratings of the importance of each value. The rated importance of specific values was related to age; older persons gave higher ratings to tradition and benevolence, and lower ratings to

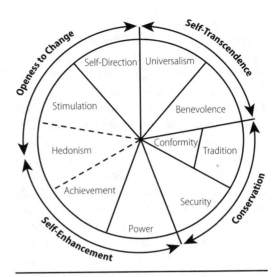

FIGURE 15.2 The Structure of Individual Values

A theory of values developed by Schwartz (1992) identifies 10 motivationally distinct types of values. Each value is defined in terms of its central goal. The theory also specifies a structure of relationships among the values. Values that lead to actions that conflict with each other are located opposite each other; complementary values are located close to each other. Thus, actions that provide hedonistic rewards often conflict with social norms and traditions; actions that conform to social norms enhance security. Finally, the values can be thought of as lying along two dimensions, from self-enhancement to self-transcendence, and from conservation to openness to change.

Source: Value priorities and gender. (1998). By Prince-Gibson and Schwartz, *Social Psychological Quarterly,* 61, 49–67.

achievement and hedonism. Education was also related to importance; as education increased, persons gave lower ratings to tradition, conformity, and power, and higher ratings to stimulation, self-direction, and universalism (Prince-Gibson & Schwartz, 1998).

Because values are general, they can provide integration or coherence across the many roles an individual plays (Hitlin, 2003). Although general, they influence many specific attitudes, choices, and behaviors as well. For example, values are related to our attitudes toward public policy. Thus, the importance one places on personal property and on social equality is related to one's attitudes toward paying higher taxes to help the poor (Tetlock, 1986). Those who place greater value on property will oppose higher taxes, whereas those who place greater importance on equality will favor increasing taxes to help the poor. Those who feel these values are equally important should find it hard to decide.

Values are related to choices. A study of university students assessed their values and asked them to respond to 10 hypothetical scenarios. Each scenario required a choice between two options, each representing a different value. The respondents' choices were consistent with their values (Feather, 1995).

Values are related to preference for convenience foods. A sample of adults responsible for food purchasing and preparation in Thessaloniki, Greece, were interviewed (Botanaki & Mattas, 2010). Their values were measured based on the Schwartz model, as were their attitudes toward convenience in the domains of meal planning, shopping, preparation, and consumption. Pro-convenience food attitudes were positively associated with values of stimulation and achievement—that is, seeking new experiences and acting independently. Valuing conservation and self-transcendence were associated with negative attitudes toward convenience foods.

How do value systems arise? They are influenced by our location in the social structure. This section examines two aspects of social position that affect individual values: occupational role and education.

Occupational Role

We spend up to half of our waking hours at work, so it is not surprising that our work influences our values. But occupational experiences vary tremendously. To determine their effect on values, we must identify the basic differences among occupations. Three important characteristics have been suggested (Kohn, 1969). The first is closeness of supervision—the extent to which the worker is under the direct surveillance and control of a supervisor. As a traveling salesman, Fred is rarely under close supervision, whereas Marie's work is supervised by the director of nursing and various physicians. The second occupational characteristic is routinization of work—the extent to which tasks are repetitive and predictable. Much of Jose's work is routine—pumping gas, tuning engines, relining brakes. But his work is not highly predictable. From one day to the next, he never knows what kind of auto breakdown he will encounter or what unusual request some customer may make. The third characteristic is substantive complexity of the work—how complicated the work tasks are. Work with people is usually more complex than work with data or work with objects. Marie's occupation as a nurse is especially complex because she must constantly cope with the problems posed by doctors, patients, and families.

All three of these characteristics were measured in several studies of employed

Workers on an assembly line often experience alienation. Assembly-line jobs are monotonous, do not allow workers to exercise initiative, and give them no influence over working conditions.
© gerenme/iStock

men to determine the impact of occupational role on values and personality (Kohn & Schooler, 1983). The results of these studies show a relationship between particular occupational characteristics and particular values: Men whose jobs were less closely supervised, less routine, and more complex placed especially high value on responsibility, good sense, and curiosity. Men whose work was closely supervised, routine, and not complex were more likely to value conformity. Thus, the occupational conditions that encourage self-direction—less supervised, nonroutine, complex tasks—are associated with valuing individual qualities that facilitate adjustment and success in a self-directed environment: responsibility, curiosity, and good sense. Occupational conditions that encourage adherence to a prescribed routine—close supervision and routine and simple tasks, such as bolting bumpers on new cars—are associated with qualities that facilitate success in that environment, such as neatness and obedience. This pattern has emerged in studies of employed men and women (Miller, Schooler, Kohn, & Miller, 1979) and in studies conducted in several countries including the United States, Japan, and Poland (Slomczynski, Miller, & Kohn, 1981).

Early studies of the relationships between workers' values and their occupational conditions revealed that workers exposed to particular conditions hold particular values. However, these studies were unable to determine with certainty whether adjustment to occupational conditions actually caused people to value particular qualities. Perhaps men who value curiosity and desire responsibility select occupations that allow them to exercise these traits (Kohn & Schooler, 1973). In attempting to identify the causal order, researchers compared the men's values and occupational conditions in 1974 with their values and occupational conditions 10 years earlier (Kohn & Schooler,

1982). What they found indicated causal effects in both directions between values and occupational conditions. Men who had valued self-direction highly in 1964 were more likely to be in work roles that were more complex, less routine, and less closely supervised 10 years later. Thus, values influenced job selection. At the same time, men who were in occupations that allowed or required self-direction in 1964 placed greater value on responsibility, curiosity, and good sense in 1974. Thus, their earlier job conditions influenced their later values.

Do these effects persist into later life? Men and women interviewed in 1974 were interviewed again in 1994 (Schooler, Mulatu, & Oates, 2004). The results replicated those in the original 10-year longitudinal study. Persons high in self-direction in 1974 were more likely to work in jobs that encourage self-direction in 1994, and scored higher on measures of self-direction and intellectual flexibility. Jobs providing greater independence and self-direction—physician, lawyer, professor, accountant, CEO—are higher in social status, providing their occupants with greater advantages.

A recent review of research on cross-national psychological differences concludes that opportunities for self-direction in one's work are consistently associated with differences in values in a number of countries (Schooler, 1996).

Education

Are differences in education also related to differences in an individual's values? The research by Kohn and his colleagues described in the preceding section demonstrated that men in jobs that are nonroutine, substantively complex, and not closely supervised value self-direction, whereas men in jobs with the opposite characteristics value conformity. Education is associated with the value one places on these characteristics;

the higher one's education, the greater the value placed on self-direction.

Substantively complex occupations involve working independently with people, objects, or data. Such work requires intellectual flexibility, the ability to evaluate information or situations, and the ability to solve problems. These abilities should be related to educational attainment, so education should be related to intellectual flexibility. Analyses of data from a sample of 3,101 men indicate that as education increases, so does intellectual flexibility (Kohn & Schooler, 1973). Thus, education influences both the value placed on self-direction and the abilities needed for success in substantively complex occupations.

SOCIAL INFLUENCES ON HEALTH

Most of us attribute diseases to biological rather than social factors. But the transmission of disease obviously depends on people's interactions, and our physical susceptibility to disease is influenced by our lifestyles. This is true, for instance, with a disease such as AIDS. Similarly, our mental health is influenced by our relationships with relatives, friends, lovers, professors, supervisors, and so on. Thus, social position affects both physical and mental health. This section examines the impact of occupation, gender, marital role, and social class on physical health. It also considers the relationship between these factors and mental health.

Physical Health

Occupational Roles. What do the physician addicted to oxycotin, the executive with an ulcer, the coal miner with black lung disease (chronic obstructive pulmonary disease), and the factory worker with chronic back pain all have in common? The answer: health problems that may be due largely to their occupational roles.

Occupational roles affect physical health in two ways. First, some occupations directly expose workers to health hazards. Miners who are exposed to coal dust, workers exposed to chemical fumes, and workers who process grain often suffer damage to lung tissue. Waitstaff, bartenders, and kitchen workers exposed to cigarette smoke may develop lung cancer. Workers exposed to various toxic chemicals may die of bladder cancer. Occupational conditions caused 4,609 deaths in 2011 (U.S. Bureau of Labor Statistics, 2012a), and 3 million injuries and illnesses (U.S. Bureau of Labor Statistics, 2012b). The highest death and injury rates are in transportation, followed by manufacturing and construction.

Second, many occupational roles expose individuals to stresses that affect physical health indirectly. Each of the roles we play carries a set of obligations or duties. Meeting these demands requires time, energy, and resources. When these demands exceed the person's perceived ability to meet them, the result is stress (Lazarus, 1991).

There are several types or sources of stressors with different consequences (Thoits, 2010). A common source is *stressful life events.* Upcoming exams, a major project deadline, an acute illness, and a move within the same city are all events that cause some stress; their effects are generally short-lived, and end following the event. Negative life events are associated with reduced physical and mental health. In one study, researchers asked adults to report the amount of stress in their lives and their health problems 20 times over a 6-month period. Those who reported higher levels of stress also reported more health problems, including sore throats, headaches, and flu. Increased stress was associated with more ailments on the same day and on subsequent days (DeLongis, Folkman, & Lazarus,

1988). The connection between stress and physical health is the body's immune system. A study of college students found that as their reports of stress increased, the concentration of antibodies in their saliva decreased (Jemmott & Magloire, 1988). The lower the level of antibodies, the more susceptible one is to illness.

Another perspective on stress considers *daily hassles* of life and their effect on health. The Daily Inventory of Stressful Events (Almeida, Wethington, & Kessler, 2002) assesses whether the person has experienced each of a broad range of stressors, including arguments about various personal and family issues, work or school overload or difficulties, or issues involving one's residence (money, needing repairs). Interviews with a national sample ($N = 1031$) found that respondents reported at least one hassle on 40 percent of the days and multiple hassles on 11 percent of them. Respondents who reported more frequent interpersonal stressors and concerns regarding the self (the way you feel about yourself, the way others feel about you) were more likely to report daily physical symptoms.

A second source is *chronic stressors* or strains. Insufficient income to support the family, caring for a chronically ill (for example, with AIDS) or disabled person, and living in a dangerous neighborhood (Boardman, 2004) are all examples. Chronic conflict leading to a breakup and chronic unemployment are also examples. These conditions are continuous over time, and so is the stress associated with them. Chronic stress may lead to physical illness. Excellent evidence of this link comes from a longitudinal study of two samples of adults (140 and 190 persons, respectively) employed at a large company (Maddi, Bartone, & Puccetti, 1987). Each person's level of stress was assessed by a carefully designed measure of stressful life events. Then, 1 or 2 years later, each person completed a questionnaire regarding illness that included both mild (for example, influenza) and serious (for example, heart attack) conditions. There were strong associations between the level of stress experienced initially and reported illness 1 or 2 years later. Research indicates that the impact of cumulative or chronic stress on health is greater than the impact of life events, and that females, members of minority groups, and poor and working-class persons experience significantly more chronic stress (Thoits, 2010).

A third type are *traumas*, extreme threats to the person's psychological or physical well-being. Examples include physical or sexual assault, military combat experiences, and natural disasters. An earthquake and its aftershocks may last only one day. But the devastation and disruption experienced by survivors may affect them for months. Data from numerous countries document the association of earthquakes with increased cardiovascular risks, such as pulmonary embolism (Dimsdale, 2008).

Many people spend energy, time, and money jogging, playing tennis, or working out. Does it do any good? There is evidence that people who are physically fit are less likely to experience stress-related illness. One study of students obtained self-reports of time spent per week in each of 14 fitness activities. The researchers also assessed fitness directly, measuring blood pressure, aerobic capacity, and endurance. Higher levels of self-reported fitness were associated with higher levels of health. Greater fitness as measured directly was associated with fewer visits to the student health center (Brown, 1991b). However, whereas stress is related to health, it is not related to self-reported fitness (Roth, Wiebe, Fillingian, & Shay, 1989). Fitness does not reduce the amount of stress one experiences, but it does reduce illness. A review of literature, including randomized clinical trials of physical-activity interventions, concludes

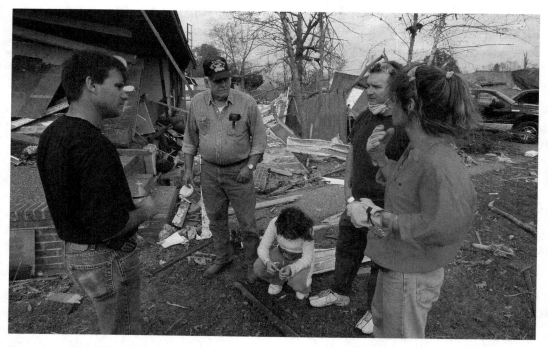

Traumatic events, like hurricanes, earthquakes, tornadoes, or major floods, may cause high levels of stress in survivors lasting for years. Rebuilding one's residence, one's financial base, and re-establishing daily routines may take several years, or more. © Leif Skoogfors/FEMA

that persons who engage in regular physical activity are less likely to experience several diseases and have a better quality of life (Penedo & Dahn, 2005).

The most widely studied relationship between job characteristics and physical health is the impact of occupational stress on coronary heart disease. As one's workload increases—including perceived demands and number of hours worked—so does the incidence of coronary heart disease (Dimsdale, 2008). Heart attacks are associated with a high level of serum cholesterol in the blood. Several studies report that the level of serum cholesterol rises among persons under high work-related stress (Chandola, Brunner, & Marmot, 2006). This suggests another tangible link between role demands and physical health. Furthermore, some studies suggest that the job-stressed individual may hyperrespond to stressors outside the work environment.

An important aspect of jobs that are associated with an increased risk of heart attack is the lack of control over work pace and task demands (Dimsdale, 2008). Occupations associated with the highest risk include cooks, waitstaff, assembly-line operators, and gas station attendants. These jobs are characterized by high demand—heavy workload and rapid pace—over which the worker has little or no control. Cashiers and waiters are four to five times more likely to have a heart attack than foresters or civil engineers. One study assessed the contribution of lack of control on the job to coronary heart disease, controlling for other factors, including individual risk factors and the availability of social support (Marmot, Bosma, Hemingway, Brunner, & Stansfeld, 1997). Longitudinal data were obtained from 7,372 employed men and women at three points in time. A reported lack of control at Time 1 was associated with increased incidence of self-reported chest pain and angina, and doctor-diagnosed angina or heart attack, at Times 2 and 3.

Gender Roles. Who is more likely to experience coronary heart disease, cirrhosis of the liver, or lung cancer—men or women? You probably picked men, and if you did, you are right. Men are twice as likely as women to die from these conditions. More generally, research consistently finds that women live longer than men but suffer from more illnesses in many countries around the world (Read & Gorman, 2010). Although there is evidence that genetic and hormonal factors play a role, traditional role expectations for men and women and occupational role segregation are also significant factors.

Some gender differences in health are associated with reproductive roles (Macintyre, Hunt, & Sweeting, 1996). Health problems related to reproduction, such as premenstrual syndrome and pregnancy-related conditions, are most likely among women of childbearing age. Men exposed to various chemicals, heat, or radiation, usually on the job, may experience reduced sperm production, abnormal sperm types, or impaired sperm transfer (National Institute of Occupational Safety and Health, 2002). Hormonal changes at menopause affect the physical health of some women, causing osteoporosis and an increased likelihood of broken bones. Older men are very likely to experience enlarged prostate glands, and may die of prostate cancer.

The top three causes of death are the same for men and women in the United States: heart disease, cancer, and respiratory diseases. However, age-adjusted death rates indicate that males are at greater risk for all three (1.6 to 1.3) (National Center for Health Statistics, 2012). One analysis suggests that the greater likelihood of male death from these illnesses is related to smoking (Case & Paxson, 2004). There is

also variation by ethnicity. Blacks have the highest age-adjusted death rates of heart disease, cerebrovascular disease, and cancer, while Hispanics have the lowest rates of these three, with Whites intermediate. Research on Black/White differences in mortality suggests that differences in social class—education, income, and job complexity—are responsible (Warner & Hayward, 2006). These differences have persisted for 50 years (Syme, 2008), indicating that we need new approaches to reducing these disparities.

Role overload, in which the demands of one's role(s) exceed the amount of time, energy, and other resources one has, is associated with coronary heart disease. Professionals such as physicians, lawyers, accountants, and so on are especially vulnerable to overload; until recently, the persons holding these positions have been primarily men. Other studies have shown that heart attacks are correlated with certain personality traits known as *coronary-prone behavior patterns* (Jenkins, Rosenman, & Zyzanski, 1974). People who exhibit these behavior patterns are work-oriented, aggressive, competitive, and impatient. They often initiate two or more tasks simultaneously (Kurmeyer & Biggers, 1988). Men are much more likely to be characterized by this behavior pattern than women.

We documented above the differences in income of men and women in the contemporary United States (and it is found in many other countries as well). Women's lower earnings limit their access to health-related resources compared to men (Read & Gorman, 2010).

Men are more prone than women to have cirrhosis of the liver because they are more likely than women (1.7 to 1) to be heavy drinkers (Schoenborn, 2004). Until recently, men were much more likely to smoke cigarettes and, therefore, more likely than women to contract lung cancer and emphysema. Men are 2.5 times more likely to die in auto accidents (National Center for Health Statistics, 2012), both because of higher rates of driving under the influence of alcohol (4 of 5 arrests for DWI are of men) and because of poor driving habits (Waldron, 1976).

Clearly, certain behaviors increase the risk of illness or death. The transmission of these health risk behaviors, such as not eating an adequate diet, smoking, and drinking, was the focus of a study of 330 teenagers and their parents. The results showed that the father's lifestyle affected only boys and the mother's lifestyle affected only girls (Wickrama, Conger, Wallace, & Elder, 1999). Thus, health risk behaviors are learned as part of gender role socialization.

These generalizations highlight overall differences between men and women, but we need to recognize that gender roles vary by culture and subculture—and that gender roles are changing (Watkins & Whaley, 2000); for example, increasing numbers of women are smoking, and so the gender gap in deaths due to lung cancer will gradually get smaller.

Marital Roles. Marriage is associated with physical health. Married men and women are less likely to report conditions such as back pain and headaches, and limitations on activity (Schoenborn, 2004). They experience fewer acute and chronic health conditions (Ross, Mirowsky, & Goldsteen, 1990). On a variety of indicators, widowed persons are more likely than the divorced or separated to experience health problems. These patterns are found in Whites, Blacks, and Hispanics.

Why is it that being married protects people against illness and accidents? The most likely explanation is that married persons are less likely to engage in behaviors that expose them to illness and accidents. They probably eat and sleep better than

unmarried persons. They are less likely to smoke and drink (Schoenborn, 2004). They may take fewer risks, reducing the likelihood they will be involved in accidents. Finally, they may be more likely to seek medical care when ill (Verbrugge, 1979).

This explanation suggests that the health advantage of married people is the result of living with another person. To test this interpretation, data were analyzed from a national sample of women. Measures of illness included the number of days spent in bed and the number of doctor visits in the past year. Women who lived with another adult reported no more illness than married women, regardless of whether they were single, separated, divorced, or widowed (Anson, 1989). When another adult is present, she or he can provide emotional support, help identify illness early, and provide care that encourages rapid recovery.

Is merely being married sufficient to reduce risk? Perhaps. But being happily married is even more beneficial. According to one study, married men and women who were satisfied with their marital roles reported better physical health than those who were dissatisfied (Wickrama, Conger, Lorenz, & Matthews, 1995). On the other hand, marital conflict has been shown to have direct negative influences on cardiovascular, immune, and other physiological mechanisms. Marital stress also has indirect consequences for health by increasing depression and by negatively affecting health behaviors (Kiecolt-Glaser & Newton, 2001).

In contemporary U.S. society, one-half of marriages end in divorce, and most divorced persons remarry. How do these transitions—which are often stressful—affect health? A longitudinal study of the relationship between marital status and mortality in a sample of 12,484 people shows that the longer one is married, the greater one's life expectancy. Women especially

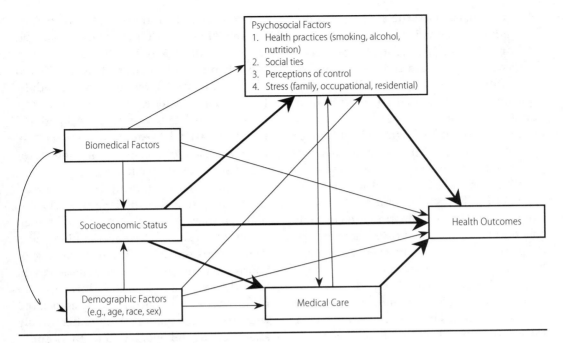

FIGURE 15.3 A Model of the Influences on Health

There are several influences on a person's physical and mental health. Biomedical, socioeconomic (such as occupation), and demographic (including age, race, gender, and marital status) factors all influence health, both directly and indirectly. All influence such immediate psychosocial factors as health practices and stress. Socioeconomic status is the major influence on the amount and quality of medical care available to the person: The availability of medical care, in conjunction with the other factors, influences how physically and mentally healthy one is.

Source: From "Socioeconomic Differentials in Health: A Review and Redirection" (1990) by David R. Williams, *Social Psychology Quarterly,* 53(2), 82. Used with permission from the American Sociological Association.

benefit from not being single. On the other hand, any transition—to (re)marriage, divorce, or widowhood—increases the risk of death (Brockmann & Klein, 2002).

What about cohabiting couples? Do they enjoy the same health advantage as married persons? Research suggests they do not. Comparisons of the health of men and women living in same-sex and different sex relationships found that cohabiters had higher odds of poorer health than married couples (Denney, Gorman, & Barrera, 2013). Among different-gender couples, women experienced a greater disadvantage compared to their married counterparts. There was little difference between same-sex cohabiting men and women.

Social Class. We noted earlier that status has a major impact on lifestyle. One aspect of this impact is the effect of social class on physical health.

A model of the influences on health is presented in Figure 15.3 (Williams, 1990). In this model, socioeconomic status is one of three influences on health. Whether education, occupation, or income is used as the indicator of status, lower-socioeconomic-status groups in the United States experience higher death rates. A study of 18,733 deaths in 1986 found that social class was strongly correlated with mortality (Rogers, 1995). The highest mortality was found among persons who were single and poor. Rates of infant mortality are also negatively related to social class; the rate of mortality among Black infants is twice as high as the rate for White infants. Controlling for class, differences by race are reduced. However, racial differences do persist. Blacks have higher death rates, tend to become ill at younger ages (for example, Black women are more likely to be diagnosed with breast cancer before age 40) and some diseases progress faster in Blacks than whites (for example, chronic kidney disease) (Williams, 2012). Racism and minority person's experiences of discrimination are certainly a factor in these elevated risks; these experiences are stressful, and may occur on a daily basis, causing chronic stress.

Several factors have been identified as causes of the negative relationship between class and health. First, persons with higher status are more likely to be employed full-time, to have subjectively rewarding jobs, and to have higher income. Second, higher-status persons are more likely to have a sense of control on the job and of control over their lives and health. Finally, higher-status persons are less likely to engage in health risk behaviors—smoking and heavy drinking—and more likely to eat properly, exercise, and use health-care services. In other words, social class is associated with several of the factors discussed earlier. Analyses of data from two national probability samples found that full-time employment, sense of control on the job, and lifestyle were all related to self-reported health (Ross & Wu, 1995). A study of mortality differences between men and women found that differences in death rates by class (income, occupation) were as large for women as for men (Koskinen & Martelin, 1994). The exception was among married women, whose death rates varied little by class—that is, being married compensates for the health risks experienced by working-class single women.

Class differences in physical health vary across the life course (House et al., 1994).

Differences in health associated with class are small in early adulthood (25 to 44), then increase with age (45 to 54) until late in life, when they become small again (75 and older). The large differences in later adulthood reflect greater exposure of lower-class persons to risk factors such as occupational health hazards, lack of control on the job, excessive alcohol consumption, and number of stressful life events.

In sum, the relationship between social status and physical health is complex. Occupational roles may expose men and women directly to health risks, causing illness and death, or to the stressful effects of lack of control on the job. Gender differences in reproductive roles lead to differences in health risks. Role overload is associated with some occupations and differentially affects men and women due to occupational segregation. Being married or living with another adult reduces one's health risk compared to being single. Social class is also associated with differences in mortality, due to its association with occupation and lifestyle. The bottom line is that improving the physical health of people in the United States requires interventions that improve the socioeconomic circumstances and occupational conditions within which people live (Syme, 2008).

Mental Health

At the beginning of this chapter, we introduced Jose, who owns a service station, works long hours, and earns about $60,000 per year. He has two children, a large mortgage on his home, and he has trouble making ends meet. He comes home from work every day exhausted. He worries about the economy and whether there will be another energy crisis, leading to inadequate supplies of gasoline, or an oil glut, leading to gasoline price wars. Either one would ruin his business, because more than one-half of his income is from gasoline sales. The ups and downs of gas prices in 2012 were very stressful.

Like many Americans, Jose finds that his life situation is very demanding. His customers expect him to do high-quality repair work at low prices, his wife expects him to support the family and spend time with her, and his children want more toys and electronics than he can afford. At times, the demands made on him by others exceed his ability to cope with them, causing psychological stress. People who are under stress often become tense and anxious, are troubled by poor appetite, or experience insomnia. A widely used questionnaire designed to measure stress-related symptoms is reproduced in Box 15.2. Many of the items on this scale measure behavior, thoughts, and feelings associated with depression.

Stress is a major influence on mental health. Short-term stressors, such as final exam week or an approaching deadline, may produce a temporary increase in stress-related symptoms or depression. As soon as the exams are over or the deadline passes, mood may return to normal. Long-term stressors, such as the continuing economic worries that Jose experiences, may produce impaired psychological functioning. Neuroses, schizophrenia, and affective disorders such as depression are among the mental illnesses associated with severe stress. The experience of stress and impaired psychological functioning varies by occupation, by gender, by marital and work roles, by membership in social networks, and by social class. Some events have an impact on large numbers of people simultaneously. Box 15.3 provides an example of such a stressful event.

Occupational Roles. Work-related stress not only affects physical health but also can affect mental health. We noted earlier that occupations that involve heavy workloads and in which workers have little or no control over their work pace are stressful. Physicians are under high levels of stress; they are expected to heal their patients, to be available to others whenever needed, to be compassionate, and to be cost-effective. These expectations are internalized by most physicians, and they may be exacerbated by personal traits such as perfectionism. The high rates of suicide, depression, substance abuse, and marital problems among physicians appear to result from these stresses (Miller & Megowen, 2000).

Beyond the stresses associated with specific occupations, one's economic circumstances are an important source of stress (Voydanoff, 1990). Economic hardship—insufficient income to meet basic needs—is stressful. Interviews with more than 2,000 adults showed that not having enough money to provide food, clothing, and medical care for self or family was the major variable associated with depression scores (Pearlin & Johnson, 1977).

Economic uncertainty—concern over one's prospects of finding or keeping a job—is also stressful. A study of 7,095 workers found that the level of unemployment in an industry as a whole is associated with the level of distress experienced by employed workers in that industry (Reynolds, 1997). The relationship was stronger for workers in complex, rewarding jobs. Unemployment is especially debilitating (Vinokur, Price, & Caplan, 1996). It is associated with anxiety, depression, and admission to mental hospitals (Voydanoff, 1990), and with an increased risk of death (Voss, Nylén, Floderus, Diderichsen, & Terry, 2004). In addition to economic rewards, one's work is a highly salient role identity for many people. The meaning the individual attaches to work influences its importance to psychological well-being (Simon, 1997). The impact of unemployment is greater on men than on women, probably because the work role identity is more salient for men.

BOX 15.2 Test Yourself: How Do You Respond to Stress?

Stress is a discrepancy between the demands on a person and his or her ability to successfully respond to those demands. Individuals under stress experience a variety of physical and psychological symptoms. A widely used measure of these symptoms is reproduced here. Read the instructions and complete the scale.

Here is a list of ways you might have felt or behaved in the past week. Read each of the following statements and then circle the appropriate number to the right of the statement to indicate how often you have felt this way during the past week.

These questions measure depression, a common response to stress. This is the CES-D (Center for Epidemiological Studies Depression) scale.

You can determine your score by adding up the numbers you circled (0, 1, 2, or 3) for all of the items except items 4, 8, 12, and 16. Notice that these four items refer to positive feelings, whereas the other items refer to negative ones. To score items 4, 8, 12, and 16, give yourself 0 if you circled 3, 1 if you circled 2, 2 if you circled 1, and 3 if you circled 0. Total scores on the scale may range from 0 to 60. If your score is more than 16 points, you could be diagnosed as depressed.

DURING THE PAST WEEK	RARELY OR NONE OF THE TIME (LESS THAN 1 DAY)	SOME OR A LITTLE OF THE TIME (1–2 DAYS)	OCCASIONALLY OR MODERATE AMOUNT OF THE TIME (3–4 DAYS)	MOST OR ALL OF THE TIME (5–7 DAYS)
1. I was bothered by things that usually don't bother me.	0	1	2	3
2. I did not feel like eating; my appetite was poor.	0	1	2	3
3. I felt I could not shake off the blues even with help from my family and friends.	0	1	2	3
4. I felt that I was just as good as other people.	0	1	2	3
5. I had trouble keeping my mind on what I was doing.	0	1	2	3
6. I felt depressed.	0	1	2	3
7. I felt that everything I did was an effort.	0	1	2	3
8. I felt hopeful about the future.	0	1	2	3
9. I thought my life had been a failure.	0	1	2	3
10. I felt fearful.	0	1	2	3
11. My sleep was restless.	0	1	2	3
12. I was happy.	0	1	2	3
13. I talked less than usual.	0	1	2	3
14. I felt lonely.	0	1	2	3
15. People were unfriendly.	0	1	2	3
16. I enjoyed life.	0	1	2	3
17. I had crying spells.	0	1	2	3
18. I felt sad.	0	1	2	3
19. I felt that people disliked me.	0	1	2	3
20. I could not "get going."	0	1	2	3

In some instances, the stress associated with unemployment leads to violence. Each year, there are incidents in which a fired employee returns to the workplace with guns or rifles, often seeking the person(s) believed responsible for his or her being fired. These incidents can lead to injuries and deaths, and to suicide by the former employee.

A daily hassle experienced frequently by many residents of the United Sates is eth-nic/racial discrimination. *Microaggressions*, acts of disregarding the person of color based on biased beliefs, are experienced often, and require management of anger and emotional upset. Inability to successfully resolve these issues causes race-related stress (Franklin, Boyd-Franklin, & Kelly, 2006). It is not surprising, therefore, that a study of 6,082 African Americans, Caribbean Blacks, and Whites found that Afri-can-Americans and Caribbean Blacks have substantially higher rates of chronic major depressive disorder, and are more likely to report that it is severe and disabling (Williams et al., 2007).

Gender Roles. Adult women in the United States have somewhat poorer mental health than men. On measures of distress, women attain significantly higher scores than men. For example, Macintyre, Hunt, and Sweeting (1996) found that women report greater malaise (sleep problems, difficulty concentrating, worry, and fatigue) than men at all ages. Are women under greater stress? Or are they more likely to report symptoms of distress than men? One study assessed the frequency of experiencing emotions such as anger, sadness, and happiness and the levels of distress in men and women (Mirowsky & Ross, 1995). The results indicated that women expressed emotions more freely than men, but this did not fully account for the differences in stress scores. Overall, women experienced stress about 30 percent more often than men.

In an attempt to identify sources of chronic stress in women's lives, researchers asked female students, professionals, and mothers to write items representing stressful situations for women. A factor analysis yielded five factors, including fear of being unattractive, of victimization, and of failing to be nurturing (Watkins & Whaley, 2000). These sources of stress may be unique to women.

There also may be a gender difference in how people respond to stress. Whereas men experiencing high stress report higher rates of substance use and abuse, women experiencing high stress report higher rates of impaired psychological functioning. In a survey of 3,131 adults, stress was measured by the number of life events experienced by the person, or by someone close to him or her, in the prior 6 months. Respondents were also asked questions about participation in various behaviors and psychological functioning. Men experiencing stress were more likely to report alcohol or drug use or dependence, whereas women experiencing stress reported increased anxiety and emotional disorders (Armeli, Carney, Tennen, Affleck, & O'Neil, 2000).

Marital Roles. Just as married men and women are physically healthier than people who are not married, they are characterized by greater psychological well-being and less depression than single, separated, divorced, or widowed persons (Ross et al., 1990). Again, it appears that it is the presence of another adult in the residence—rather than being married per se—that is associated with being healthy.

Of course, it might be that people who have higher levels of well-being are more likely to marry or cohabit, whereas persons with lower levels remain single. A longitudinal study of 18- to 24-year-old men and women, some of whom married whereas others remained single, found that marriage did improve well-being (Horowitz, White,

BOX 15.3 The Impact of Large-scale Traumas on Psychological Functioning

On July 20, 2012, about 12:30 AM, a young man dressed in tactical clothing entered a crowded movie theater in Aurora, Colorado. He activated two canisters which released gas and smoke, and then started firing in turn a shotgun, a semi-automatic weapon, and a handgun. The shooting lasted two minutes, and resulted in 12 deaths and 70 injuries.

The research summarized in this chapter indicates that relatively common, "everyday" stressors such as moving, starting a new job, changes in relationships, and conflict with family or coworkers affect individuals' physical and mental health, in some cases seriously. Occasionally, a large group or a population experiences extreme situations—events that Dohrenwend (2000) terms *fateful*. **Fateful events** share several characteristics: They are beyond the individual's control, unpredictable, often life-threatening, and often large in magnitude, and they disrupt people's usual activities. Such events have consequences far beyond those of everyday stressors. The Aurora theater shooting affected several hundred people directly and hundreds of others indirectly. There are the immediate stresses of death and injury, and impacts on family, friends, and coworkers. Because the event and its consequences were uncontrollable, thousands of people in the community experienced fear, anger, and rage that could not be channelled into effective action.

A wide variety of responses are seen in adults following such traumatic events. In addition to the emotions just listed, they include disbelief, irritability, anxiety, depression, sleep disturbances, and increases in alcohol and other substance use. For most individuals, these acute traumatic stress symptoms resolve over time. For some, however, the intensity and duration of the symptoms justify the diagnosis of posttraumatic stress disorder (PTSD) (Norwood, Ursano, & Fullerton, 2002).

The most researched such event in the United States was the terrorist attacks on September 11, 2001, on the World Trade Center and the Pentagon. More than 2,800 people were killed, affecting hundreds of workplaces and thousands of families. There was the immediate stress of the deaths and destruction, the continuing stress for persons in New York and Washington due to the disruption of their lives, and the continuing stress for most Americans due to the uncertainty about further attacks.

Excellent data on the impact of the terrorist attacks comes from the longitudinal National Tragedy Survey conducted by the National Opinion Research Center (NORC) at the University of Chicago (Rasinski, Berktold, Smith, & Albertson, 2002). Two weeks after the attacks, a probability sample of 1,013 Americans and a probability sample of 406 residents of New York City were interviewed. Four to 6 months later, in January to March 2002, re-interviews were completed with 805 Americans (79 percent of the original sample) and 296 residents of New York City (73 percent).

To begin, consider national pride. One goal of the terrorist attacks was to demoralize the American population. However, measures of pride taken 2 weeks after September 11 either remained the same or increased compared to previous NORC surveys. For example, 97 percent of those surveyed said they would rather be a citizen of America than of any other country. On the other hand, confidence in major institutions, including the executive branch, Congress, and banks and financial institutions, fell by 7 to 13 percent; the exception was confidence in the U.S. military, which remained at pre-attack levels (81 percent).

The interview included questions assessing the experience of stress. In the first survey, respondents were asked which of 15 symptoms they had experienced following the attacks. Nine symptoms were reported by 20 percent or more of the national sample; the five most common were crying (60.3 percent), trouble sleeping (51.2

percent), feeling nervous or tense (49.9 percent), feeling dazed and numb (45.7 percent), and feeling more tired than usual (37.5 percent). In the sample of New York City residents, 12 symptoms were reported by 20 percent or more; the five most common were crying (74.1 percent), feeling nervous or tense (62.5 percent), trouble sleeping (59.4 percent), feeling more tired than usual (47.6 percent), and not feeling like eating (46.4 percent). Not surprisingly, New York City residents were somewhat more likely to report specific symptoms. Clearly, the impact of the attacks was substantial, measured by the numbers who experienced symptoms of stress.

At the re-interview 4 to 6 months later, reports of symptoms experienced in the past 2 weeks were generally lower than in the initial survey. In the national sample, the numbers reporting crying declined 40 percent, those reporting trouble sleeping declined 20 percent, feeling tense and nervous 22 percent, and feeling dazed and numb 33 percent. Comparable declines were observed in the reports of New York City residents. These longitudinal results indicate a trend toward recovery—that is, reduced incidence of stress. Declines were greatest among those who reported that they knew someone who had been hurt or killed in the attacks. African Americans, on the average, reported fewer symptoms in September, but showed little decline in the follow-up interviews. Slower recovery was also observed in persons with less than a high school education and with family incomes less than $40,000 per year. The follow-up interview included a standard measure of PTSD. Among the New York City residents, 15 percent scored in the range indicative of the disorder. In the national sample, the percentage scoring in this range was 8 percent. The highest PTSD scores were observed among those with poor general health, less education, and less income.

These results suggest that those of vulnerable social status have more or longer-lasting adverse reactions to fateful events. Research on a broad variety of disasters, including natural disasters such as earthquakes (Seplaki, Goldman, Weinstein, & Lin, 2003) and hurricanes, finds that persons of low SES in that society (whether the country is rich or poor), people who are socially isolated, and people who are directly affected by the disaster report higher levels of depressive symptoms. Several hypotheses have been offered to account for the increased vulnerability of low-SES persons. First, such persons may be more likely to have suffered as a result of the event due to poor housing or inadequate public services. Second, economic assets and education can enhance recovery because the individual has access to resources. Third, persons who are of low SES may also be socially isolated, lacking the social support that family and friends can provide. According to one observer, "disasters most often exacerbate social inequality" (de Waal, 2006).

In response to the rise in reports of symptoms and of widespread PTSD after traumatic events, debriefing has become standard clinical practice. Debriefing involves group sessions in which those affected by a fateful event are encouraged to process their emotional reactions. Following many recent traumatic events, such as 9/11 and the Northern Illinois University shooting (February, 2008), large numbers of persons have participated in debriefings. Do they help persons cope with traumatic events? An expert panel assembled by the National Institute of Mental Health (2002), having reviewed the empirical evidence, concludes that early interventions such as debriefing do not reduce the risk of later or continuing disorder. Research, such as the surveys following the 9/11 attacks, shows that most people are resilient; relying on their own resources, social support networks, and community services, they will recover (van Emmerik, Kamphuis, Hulsbosch, & Emmelkamp, 2002). Psychological services should be available for those whose personal resources are not sufficient or who do not recover on their own.

& Howell-White, 1996). Another study with data from a national sample compared persons who were stably married with those who experienced separation or divorce. Persons who experienced a loss reported increased symptoms on the CES-D (see Box 15.2); the effect was greater on persons who believed marriage should be a lifelong commitment (Simon & Marcussen, 1999).

The greater well-being of married persons reflects the beneficial effects of social support. A spouse can provide social support—care, advice, and aid in times of stress—and emotional support. Do husbands and wives share equally in receiving these benefits? Apparently not. Married men are characterized by better mental health than married women (Kurdek, 1991).

A study of a representative sample of more than 13,000 adults assessed the relationship between roles and mental health in four ethnic groups (Jackson, 1997). Occupying the spousal role was associated with greater well-being among Blacks, Mexican Americans, Puerto Ricans, and non-Hispanic Whites. Occupying other family roles, especially sibling, was related to better mental health in all groups except Puerto Ricans.

Some researchers focus on the interrelations of work and family roles. Of particular interest is work-family conflict—the extent to which the demands associated with one role are incompatible with the other. One common circumstance is **spillover**, in which the stress experienced at work or in the family is carried into the other domain (Bolger, DeLongis, Kessler, & Wethington, 1989). A study of air traffic controllers and their wives documented the impact of work stress on marital interaction (Repetti, 1989). As the controllers' daily workload increased (larger number of planes handled, poorer visibility), wives reported that the men were more withdrawn at home. A longitudinal study of 166 married couples obtained completed diaries from both part-

ners for either 28 or 42 consecutive days. Each person reported on stressors at work (too much to do, arguments with coworkers) and at home (too much to do, arguments with spouse, arguments with child). For both husbands and wives, increased stress at work was associated with increased stress at home (Bolger et al., 1989).

Stress associated with marital roles can influence work role performance. The research by Bolger and colleagues (1989) also found that for husbands, increased stress at home was associated with increased stress at work. Forthofer, Markman, Cox, Stanley, and Kessler (1996) analyzed data from a study of 8,098 persons aged 15 to 54; they focused on 1,431 employed married men and 1,138 employed married women. The results indicated that problems within the marriage were related to the number of days the person was "unable to function" in the preceding month among both men and women.

If marital strains can lead to reduced performance at work, can positive experiences at home enhance work experience? Two studies suggest that the answer is yes. Barnett (1994) studied 300 full-time employed women in dual-earner couples. Positive experiences in the roles of partner or parent buffered the effects of negative job experiences on distress. A longitudinal study found that increases/decreases in marital satisfaction are related to increases/decreases in work satisfaction among employed men and women, but not the reverse (Rogers & May, 2003).

Work/family conflict can affect the quality of the marital relationship by influencing the couple's interaction. Research demonstrated that and the resulting distress effects on two dimensions of marital interaction: hostility and warmth. As distress increases, both the person and the spouse report greater hostility and less warmth (Matthews, Conger, & Wickrama, 1996). Work/family conflict also is related to alcohol consumption. A study of employed adults aged 35 to 65 found that higher levels of marital disagreement (regarding spending money or household tasks) and stress at work (too much to do, conflicting demands) were each related to reports of problem drinking. Positive spillover from family (talking at home, expressions of love) to work was associated with less frequent reports of problem drinking; interestingly, both positive and negative spillover from work to family were associated with greater problem drinking (Grzywacz & Marks, 2000).

Another type of spillover involves the worker using behavior patterns acquired or reinforced at work in interactions with family members. This possibility was explored in a study that linked occupational conditions to the use of violence by a man against his female partner. The results showed that men in violent (for example, law enforcement) and dangerous (for example, construction) occupations were more likely to engage in violence directed at the partner (Melzer, 2002). This may reflect a spillover of the stress associated with these occupations, or the violence-supportive attitudes learned on the job.

How do people cope with work/family conflict? They use one or more of several strategies. In one study, wives reported the use of planning and cognitive restructuring—changing their definition of the situation—for example, deciding the house does not need to be cleaned every week. Husbands reported restructuring and withdrawing from interaction (Padden & Buehler, 1995). In a study of 221 managers, both men and women reported the use of prioritizing, reducing their personal standards (restructuring), asking others for help, and ending involvement in one or more roles (for example, in community organizations) (Kirchmeyer, 1993).

Thus, the relationships among occupational, gender, and marital roles and psychological well-being are complex (Ross et al., 1990). The demands of work roles may lead to distress; this is especially likely when work demands are high and not under the person's control. Economic hardship and unemployment cause distress. Men typically have somewhat better mental health than women, in part because men react to stress by drug and alcohol use, whereas women respond psychologically. Married men report greater well-being than married women, apparently because wives are more likely to experience family-related strains (Mennino, Rubin, & Brayfield, 2005). Stresses experienced at work can spill over and affect marital relationships; conversely, strain at home can produce losses at work. In any case, the social roles one occupies are major influences on mental health.

Social Networks. Up to this point, we have reviewed evidence showing that our relationships with others—that is, our membership in social networks—can be major sources of stress. At the same time, social networks can serve as an important resource in coping with stress (Wellman & Worley, 1990).

Two examples of social networks are depicted in Figure 15.4. Both networks center on a single individual, Aurora.. The network on the left depicts the pattern of relationships among Aurora and her friends that has evolved out of their shared experience. For example, the ties between Aurora, Ian, and Casey developed because they took graduate courses together. Bailey, Becca, and Sean are friends she met in high school. Aurora described this network when asked to name the people to whom she is closest, excluding relatives. When asked to include relatives, Aurora described the network on the right of Figure 15.4. The most striking difference is the greater number of direct ties among the persons in the network on the right. This network is dense—most of

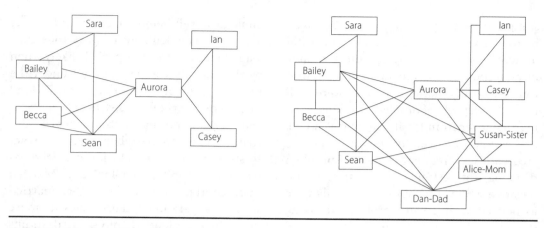

FIGURE 15.4 Social Networks

These two networks are focused on Aurora. When asked to name her best friends, excluding relatives, she described the network on the left. Bailey, Becca, and Sean are her best friends from "home," where she grew up. She met two of them through work. Ian and Casey are her best friends where she lives now; she met them both through her graduate work. Aurora and her friends from home all know each other, but her home friends are not connected to her school friends. The network on the right includes Aurora's relatives, including Alice (her mom), Dan (her dad), and Susan (her sister). This network is a dense one, because each person has close ties to several of the others.

the persons in it know each other independently of their ties to Aurora (Milardo, 1988).

First, a network of close friends and kin eases the impact of stressful events by providing various types of support (Cooke, Rossmann, McCubbin, & Patterson, 1988; House, 1981). One type is emotional support—letting us know that they care for and are concerned about us. Emotional support is an important buffer for negative psychological states like depression (Harlow & Cantor, 1995). A second type is esteem support—providing us with positive feedback about our abilities and worth as a person. A poor grade, for example, is less stressful if our friends let us know they think we are good students. Informational support from others prepares us to avoid problems or to handle them when they arise. Advice from friends on how to handle job interviews, for example, improves our ability to cope with this situation. Finally, network members provide each other with instrumental support—money, labor, and time. Research

shows that people who report poor well-being tend to seek out others who can provide the type of support they need (Harlow & Cantor, 1995).

The presence or absence of support is a major determinant of the impact of a stressful life event. A study of 882 women seeking an abortion obtained longitudinal data from 615 of them. Before the abortion, each woman rated the degree to which she received positive (expressed concern, offered help) and negative (argued, criticized) support from her partner, mother, and friends. Perceptions of positive support from each source were associated with greater well-being following the abortion (Major, Zubek, Cooper, Cozarelli, & Richards, 1997).

Research has documented the impact of supportive relationships on the individual's ability to cope with stress. A longitudinal study of a representative sample of 900 adults focused on the relationship between social network membership and physical health (Seeman, Seeman, & Sayles, 1985). Persons who reported in the initial interview that they had instrumental support available (that is, persons who, when ill, had others who would call, express concern, and offer help) were in better physical health 1 year later. Another longitudinal study assessed the impact of family support on mental health (Aldwin & Revenson, 1987). The sample consisted of 245 men and 248 women from randomly selected families in an urban area. The availability of support from one's family at the time of the initial survey was associated with better psychological adjustment one year later. Other research indicates that individuals with family support are more likely to cope with stressful events by using active strategies rather than avoidance or withdrawal strategies (Holahan & Moos, 1990). A longitudinal study of the relation between coping strategies and mental health found that people who used active strategies at the time of the initial survey reported fewer psychological symptoms on the second survey (Aldwin & Revenson, 1987). Finally, using active behavioral coping strategies is associated with shorter duration of several types of stressful events (Harnish, Aseltine, & Gore, 2000).

A second way in which social networks reduce stress is by teaching us strategies for coping with stressful events or crises when they occur. When members of a group are all subjected to similar stressors, the group may develop coping strategies. A study of interns and residents in a hospital found that they were subjected to long hours of demanding work in often poor facilities (Mizrahi, 1984). These physicians coped with stress by minimizing the time spent with each patient, by limiting interaction with patients to "relevant topics," and by treating patients as nonpersons—for example, by focusing exclusively on their illness. These strategies were passed on from experienced group members to new ones.

Several types of relationships can provide support, including primary kin (parents, siblings, and adult children), secondary kin, and friends and neighbors. The kind of support provided depends on the type of relationship. Persons to whom we have strong ties provide emotional support and companionship. Primary kin provide us with financial aid and services, whereas friends and neighbors give us services and emotional support (Wellman & Worley, 1990). Research indicates that, among Blacks, kin primarily provide services such as transportation and child care, whereas among Whites, kin are more likely to provide financial support; however, the data suggest that this difference may have more to do with social class than with race (Sarkisian & Gerstel, 2004). Also, Black women are more likely to engage in reciprocal exchanges of services, and White women to engage in reciprocal exchanges of emotional support. Research on provision of support among low-income families suggests that these exchanges of services provide an important resource for coping with daily demands (Henley, Danziger, & Offer, 2005).

There is evidence that neighborhood disadvantage is associated with poorer mental health among residents. These neighborhoods are characterized by poor

Family members help us to cope with stressful events, such as the death of a relative or a close friend. They are an important source of emotional support and may help by temporarily taking over some of our role obligations. © Rubberball/iStock

access to health services, transportation, quality housing, jobs, and desirable partners. There may also be significant rates of crime and violence. These conditions may create chronic stress in residents, leading to depressive symptoms and fearful anxiety (Hill, Ross, & Angel, 2005). These, in turn, create distress, which negatively affects health. Supportive social networks, close relationships with nearby kin and neighbors, mediate the relationship between neighborhoods and symptoms by providing emotional support and services, reducing depressive symptoms (Haines, Beggs, & Hurlbert, 2011).

Recognizing the significance of supportive relationships, an innovative approach—social network mapping—is being used to assess the support available to organ transplant recipients (Lewis, Winsett, Cetingok, Martin, & Hathaway, 2000). The map both increases the person's awareness of the resources available and enables health professionals and social workers to work with the person more effectively.

Social Class. The lower a person's socioeconomic status, the greater the amount of stress reported (Mirowsky & Ross, 1986). According to data from interviews with a representative sample of U.S. adults, 8.3 percent of the poor, 5.3 percent of the near-poor, and 2 percent of the nonpoor are characterized by serious psychological distress (National Center for Health Statistics, 2004). Education, occupation, and income are the principal measures of socioeconomic status. An analysis of data from surveys of eight quite diverse samples (Kessler, 1982) shows that each contributes separately to stress. The relative importance of these three components as sources of stress is different for men and women. For men, income appears most important; for women (employed or not), education appears to be

the most important component. Occupational attainment is the least important determinant of stress for both genders.

How does education affect stress? Research shows that people who are well-educated have lower levels of distress, primarily because of paid work and financial resources (Ross & van Willigen, 1997). The evidence suggests that the relationship between social class and health also reflects lifestyle differences; persons higher in socioeconomic status are more likely to have a healthy diet, exercise regularly, and get adequate sleep, and less likely to smoke (Mulatu & Schooler, 2002).

In the United States, a large percentage of the lower class are Black. As a result, one might expect Blacks to have poorer mental health than Whites. However, the results of research comparing the psychological functioning of Blacks and Whites are inconsistent; whereas some studies find higher average symptom scores among Blacks, others do not (Vega & Rumbaut, 1991).

Further analyses have sought to identify the causes of the negative relationship between social status and stress. Are lower-class persons exposed to greater stress, or are they simply less able to cope effectively with stressful events? The answer is, both (Kessler & Cleary, 1980). On the one hand, lower-class persons are more likely to experience *economic hardship*—not having enough money to provide adequate food, clothing, and medical care (Pearlin & Radabaugh, 1976). They also experience higher rates of a variety of physical illnesses (Syme & Berkman, 1976).

Both economic hardship and illness increase the stress that an individual experiences. Furthermore, persons who are low in income, education, and occupational attainment lack the resources that would enable them to cope with these stresses effectively. Low income reduces their ability to cope with illness. Moreover, low-status persons are less likely to have a sense of control over their environment, and they have less access to political power or influence. For this reason, they are less likely to attempt to change stressful conditions or events.

Resilience to economic adversity—that is, no increase in distress scores in response to hardship—is provided by several resources. A longitudinal study of 558 rural youths and their families began when the youths were in seventh grade. Resilience among the parents was associated with marital support, effective problem-solving skills, and a sense of mastery. Resilience among the youths was promoted by nurturance (support) by parents and support by older siblings (providing warmth, not drinking alcohol) and friends (Conger & Conger, 2002).

If stress increases as socioeconomic status decreases, we would expect persons lower in status to have poorer mental health. Research over the past 60 years has consistently confirmed this expectation; there is a strong correlation between social class and serious mental disorders (Eaton, 1980). This correlation has been found in studies conducted in numerous countries (Dohrenwend & Dohrenwend, 1974). In general, persons in the lowest socioeconomic class have the highest rates of mental illness (Hudson, 2005).

The differences by social class in rates of mental disorders are due in part to differences in stress. Persons in low-status occupations are more likely to experience lack of control over work. They may also experience economic uncertainty due to risk of layoff or seasonal variations in employment opportunities. This stress is likely to spill over into family interaction patterns, causing familial relations to become an added source of stress rather than a buffer. Research indicates that the shift from adequate to inadequate employment, involuntary part-time work, or low-wage jobs is as-

sociated with increased depression, and the shift to unemployment is related to even higher depression scores (Dooley, Prause, & Ham-Rowbottom, 2000). Unemployment is especially stressful, and rates of unemployment are highest among the least educated (U.S. Bureau of the Labor Statistics, 2012). Finally, the members of the social networks of the least educated have fewer economic and emotional resources.

ALIENATION

Jim dragged himself out of bed and headed for the shower. As the water poured over him, he thought, "Thursday . . . another 10-hour shift . . . if the line doesn't shut down, I'll bolt 500 bumpers . . . sick of car frames . . . I'd rather do almost anything else . . . if only I'd finished high school . . . damn the money! . . . Let 'em take the job and shove it . . . but what else pays a guy who quit school $24.36 an hour?"

Jim is experiencing **alienation**—the sense that one is uninvolved in the social world or lacks control over it, a sense of separation or disconnect from one's social surroundings (Nair & Vohra, 2012). Several types of alienation have been identified (Seeman, 1975). Two will be discussed here: self-estrangement and powerlessness. An analysis of scales measuring alienation verified that these two dimensions are central ones (Lacourse, Villeneuve, & Claes, 2003).

Self-Estrangement

Jim's hatred for his job reflects **self-estrangement**—the awareness that he is engaging in activities that are not rewarding in themselves. Work is an important part of one's waking hours. When work is meaningless, the individual perceives the self as devoting time and energy to something unrewarding—that is, something "alien."

Whereas social background and individual characteristics have some influence, alienation from work is primarily determined by the occupational and organizational conditions of work (Mortimer & Lorence, 1995).

What makes a job intrinsically rewarding? Perhaps the most important feature is autonomy. Work that requires the individual to use judgment, exercise initiative, and surmount obstacles contributes to self-respect and a sense of mastery. A second feature is variety in the tasks that the person performs. Jim has no autonomy; his job does not allow him to exercise judgment or initiative. It also has no variety; it is monotonous and boring.

Four features of industrial technology produce self-estrangement. First, self-estrangement will be higher if the worker has no connection with the finished product itself. Second, it will be higher if the worker has no control over company policies. Third, it will be higher if the worker has little influence over the conditions of employment—over which days, which hours, or how long he or she works. Finally, it will be higher if the worker has no control over the work process—for example, the speed with which he or she must perform tasks (Blauner, 1964). Notice that alienation, like stress, is caused by lack of control over the conditions of work. Research indicates that persons from high SES backgrounds are more likely to experience alienation under these conditions (Nair & Vohra, 2012), probably because such environments are inconsistent with their values and skills (see earlier discussion of Occupational Roles).

These features are especially characteristic of assembly-line work, in which each person performs the same highly specialized task many times per day. Thus, workers on assembly lines should be more likely to experience self-estrangement than other workers. A study testing this hypothesis (Blauner, 1964) compared assembly-line workers in textile and automobile plants with skilled printers and chemical industry technicians. As expected, assembly-line workers were more alienated than skilled workers who had jobs that were more varied and involved the exercise of judgment and initiative.

Work in bureaucratic organizations—like large insurance companies or government agencies—may also produce self-estrangement. In many bureaucratic organizations, workers have little or no control over the work process and do not participate in organizational decision making. Thus, workers at the lowest levels of such organizations should experience self-estrangement or dissatisfaction with their work. Conversely, workers who are involved in decision making should be less alienated. A survey of 8,000 employees in 100 companies located in the United States or Japan found that workers involved in participatory decision-making structures had higher commitment to their work (Lincoln & Kalleberg, 1985). Such workers were willing to work harder and were proud to be employed by and wanted to remain with the company.

More generally, the extent to which workers are alienated depends on the system of production in which they work. Hodson (1996) identifies five systems: craft, where each worker produces a product; direct supervision; assembly line; bureaucratic; and participatory. A review of studies of all five types of workplaces reveals a U-shaped relationship between workers' attitudes and the system of production (see Figure 15.5). Both craft and participatory systems are associated with high job satisfaction and pride in one's work; direct supervision is the most alienating system. Results such as these have led many large firms, such as General Motors, to introduce participatory systems.

As noted earlier, individual characteristics do influence reactions to work (Mor-

FIGURE 15.5 Systems of Production and Alienation from Work

The way in which work is organized, or the system of production, is a major influence on people's attitudes toward their work. Historically, five different systems of production have been used: craft, where each worker has considerable autonomy; direct supervision, where another person monitors one's work; assembly line, where the work activity is determined by the organization and speed of the line; bureaucratic, where many aspects of work are governed by impersonal rules; and participatory organization, where teams of managers and workers make decisions.

A review of the research literature suggests that the pride workers have in their work and their job satisfaction vary depending on the system in which they work. The graph displays these variations, indicating that although participative systems are less alienating than the assembly lines and bureaucratic forms they replaced, they are not as satisfying as the craft system of production.

Source: Hodson, "Dignity in the Workplace under Participative Management," *American Sociological Review*, 61(5), 730 (1996). Used with permission of the American Sociological Association.

timer & Lorence, 1995). Surveys indicate that job satisfaction and involvement are most stable among workers aged 30 to 45. Women are as committed to work as men, though they place greater emphasis on the quality of interpersonal relations in the workplace. Among those holding comparable jobs, Blacks are as committed as Whites to their jobs and employers.

According to the theory developed more than a century ago by Karl Marx (Bottomore, 1964), whether a person will experience self-estrangement is determined by his or her relation to the means of production. The most alienated employees are hypothesized to be those who have no autonomy, who do not have the freedom to solve nonroutine problems, and who have no subordinates. Marx referred to such workers as the *proletariat*. In contemporary society, assembly-line workers, sales-clerks, file clerks, and laborers are all in occupations that have these characteristics. A survey of 1,499 working adults found that 46 percent were in jobs of this type (Wright et al., 1982). Several studies have found that men whose jobs are characterized by lack of autonomy and complexity typically have high scores on measures of self-estrangement (Kohn, 1976) and low scores on measures of job involvement (Lorence & Mortimer, 1985).

There is some evidence that the characteristics of the work environment influence psychological well-being. One researcher assessed the common environment of office workers by averaging the ratings of all of those employed in each of 37 branch offices; each worker's own ratings were used as a measure of his or her immediate environment (Repetti, 1987). Workers who rated their branches more positively (on interpersonal climate and support and respect from coworkers) reported lower levels of anxiety and depression. Aggregate ratings by the workers of the environment in the branch were also related to anxiety and depression scores.

Powerlessness

Consider the facts that vandalism is widespread in certain sections of large cities, that many adults do not vote in presidential elections, and that some people on welfare

The graffiti gracing walls and buildings in American cities are responses to alienation. Spray-painted messages, sometimes including the painter's initials, reflect the lack of control over their lives that many youth feel. © stevegeer/iStock

make no effort to find a job. These facts all have something in common. They reflect, at least in part, people's sense of **powerlessness**—the sense of having little or no control over events.

Powerlessness is a generalized orientation toward the social world. People who feel powerless believe they have no influence on political affairs and world events; this is different from feeling a lack of control over events in day-to-day life. A typical measure of powerlessness includes items like "This world is run by a few people in power and there is not much the little guy can do about it." Agreement with such statements indicates powerlessness. Most people's scores on measures of powerlessness are quite stable over a period of many years (Neal & Groat, 1974). There is some evidence that a sense of powerlessness develops during childhood (Seeman, 1975).

Research with a sample of high school students identified powerlessness as a significant factor in alienation in adolescence (Lacourse et al., 2003). Interestingly, a sense of powerlessness is not associated with social class—that is, income, occupation, or education.

Statements that measure powerlessness, such as "People like me have no say" and "Politicians don't care what I think," were included in several surveys between 1952 and 1980. Analysis of patterns of agreement with these items shows that powerlessness or political alienation declined from 1952 to 1960, rose steadily from 1960 to 1976, and then declined (Rahn & Mason, 1987). The increase in the 1960s and 1970s was associated with increased concern about such political and social issues as civil rights for Blacks, the war in Vietnam, and the Watergate political scandal. Thus, fluctuations in powerlessness reflect, at least in part, events in the larger society.

Although the sense of powerlessness is found in all classes, upper and lower classes may have different means of expressing it. Middle-class and upper-class persons may be more likely to stay home on election day or to feel apathetic about political affairs or organizations that influence public policy. Lower-class persons may be more likely to have a hostile attitude toward city officials and to vandalize city buses, subway trains, and businesses in their neighborhoods. Thus, how an individual expresses frustration over his or her lack of influence on the world may depend on his or her social position.

SUMMARY

This chapter considers the impact of social structure on four areas of a person's life: achievement, values, physical and mental health, and sense of belonging in society. Social structure influences the individual through the expectations associated with one's roles, the social networks to which one belongs, and the status associated with one's positions.

Status Attainment. An individual's status determines his or her access to resources—money, lifestyle, and influence over others. Three generalizations can be made about status in the United States. (1) An individual's status is closely tied to his or her occupation. (2) Occupational attainment is influenced directly by the individual's educational level and ability and indirectly by socioeconomic background. Among women, occupational status and earnings are limited by gender segregation. (3) Information about job opportunities is often obtained via social networks, especially those characterized by weak ties.

Individual Values. Two aspects of the individual's position in society influence his or her values (1) Particular values are reliably associated with certain occupational role characteristics. Men and women whose jobs are closely supervised, routine, and not complex value conformity, whereas those whose jobs are less closely supervised, less routine, and more complex value self-direction. (2) Higher education is associated with placing greater value on self-direction and with greater intellectual flexibility.

Social Influences on Health. Physical health is influenced by occupation, gender, marital roles, and social class. (1) Occupational roles determine the health hazards to which individuals are exposed and whether they experience role overload. (2) The traditional role expectations for men and women make men more vulnerable than women to illnesses such as coronary heart disease. (3) Marriage protects both men and women from illness and premature death. (4) Members of lower-status groups and Blacks experience higher rates of illness, disability, and death.

Mental health is also influenced by social factors. (1) Economic hardship, uncertainty, and unemployment are associated with poor mental health. (2) Women have somewhat poorer mental health than men. (3) Marriage is associated with reduced stress for both men and women. Working adults may experience spillover of stress from work into family relationships. (4) Social networks are an important resource in coping with stress; they provide the person with emotional, esteem, and informational support, as well as instrumental aid. (5) Lower-class persons report greater stress and experience a higher incidence of mental illness.

Alienation. Two types of alienation are self-estrangement and powerlessness. (1)

Self-estrangement is associated with work roles that do not allow workers a sense of autonomy, such as assembly-line jobs. (2) Powerlessness is a generalized sense that one has little or no control over the world.

List of Key Terms and Concepts

alienation (p. 533)
fateful events (p. 536)
position (p. 502)
powerlessness (p. 536)
primary relationship (p. 502)
role (p. 502)
role overload (p. 519)
self-estrangement (p. 533)
social class (p. 504)
social networks (p. 502)
social structure (p. 502)
spillover (p. 528)
status (p. 502)
upward mobility (p. 504)
values (p. 513)

Critical Thinking Skill:
Thinking as Hypothesis Testing

In everyday life, we function like intuitive scientists. Events occur and we want to explain and perhaps control them. To do that, we use the same skills as a scientist testing a hypothesis: (1) we accumulate observations; (2) we formulate hypotheses or explanations; (3) we use the information to see if it confirms or disconfirms the hypothesis.

A common experience for many people today is stress—feeling tense, anxious, overworked. Stress may result in depressed mood, feeling overwhelmed and unhappy with life. When we experience stress, we usually want to reduce it or escape from it. To do that successfully, we need to determine the source of the stress. The research summarized in this chapter identifies sev-

eral sources of stress in contemporary life. Your stress may reflect economic hardship, being overworked at school or work (which can spill over at home), problems in an intimate relationship (marital strain), or lack of a supportive social network. Obviously, to cope with stress effectively requires identifying the source(s) of it. Often, we look around and focus on the most obvious or most recent person or event. If you have a partner, that person is perhaps the most obvious, especially if you have been fighting. But your fights may be a result of economic hardship, your overload at work, or stresses at school, not problems with the relationship. In fact, breaking up with your partner will probably add to your stress rather than reduce it.

A better strategy is to think like a scientist. Accumulate some observations. In what situation(s) do you feel more stress—at work, at home? When do you feel most stressed—during the week, on the weekend, when you pay the bills? Does the stress fluctuate from week to week? If so, is that associated with the deadlines at work, or arguments with a superior, or your partner, or visits with family? If you observe systematically, you will hopefully identify some patterns that suggest a hypothesis. Suppose you observe that the stress is greatest when you pay bills, when there is an unexpected expense, when your partner asks for extra money. That suggests economic hardship, not your partner, as the source. Collect some data over the next several weeks. Note each time you feel stress and the events that occurred recently. This process will take some time. You might want to keep some notes.

If your observations verify the hypothesis, you can turn to the question of how to cope with the problem. If you think it is economic hardship, there are two general strategies you can use: increase your income, or decrease your expenses. There are several ways to implement each strategy. You could increase income by taking a second or third job. Note, however, that this will add to your stress unless you cut back on school, work, or time spent with your partner or friends or family. You could borrow money, or take out a loan. Or you could reduce your expenses. Sometimes it is relatively easy. Three Starbucks per day cost $15; three coffees from McDonald's cost $3.

Maybe you can rent videos from your cable company instead of going to the theater. If you are in a relationship, you will want to communicate with your partner about your observations and choices of strategy. If you adopt a strategy and the hypothesis is correct, your stress should gradually decline. If the stress doesn't decline, like a scientist, you need to start over again and develop a new hypothesis.

CHAPTER 16

DEVIANT BEHAVIOR AND SOCIAL REACTION

INTRODUCTION

Megan and Hanna wandered through the boutique, stopping briefly to look at blouses and then going to the lingerie section. Each looked at several bra and panty sets. Hanna kept returning to a burgundy set priced at $69.50. Finally, she picked it up, glanced quickly around her, and dropped it into her shoulder bag.

The only other shopper in the vicinity, a well-dressed man in his 40s, saw Hanna take the clothing. He looked around the store, spotted a clerk, and walked toward her. Megan stammered to Hanna, "I, uh, I don't think we should do this."

"Oh, it's okay. Nothing will happen," Hanna replied, before walking quickly out of the store. Moments later, Megan followed her. As Hanna entered the mall, the clerk stepped up to her, took her by the elbow, and said, "Come with me, please."

Shoplifting episodes like this one occur many times every day in the United States. Shoplifting is one of several types of **deviant behavior**—behavior that violates the norms that apply in a given situation. In addition to crime, deviance includes cheating, substance use or abuse, fraud, corruption, delinquent behavior, harassment, and behavior considered symptomatic of mental illness.

There are two major reasons why social psychologists study deviant behavior, one theoretical and one practical. First, social norms and conformity are the basic means by which the orderly social interaction necessary to maintain society is achieved. By studying nonconformity, we learn about the processes that produce social order. For example, we might conclude that Hanna took the lingerie because there were no store employees nearby, suggesting the importance of surveillance in maintaining order. Second, social psychologists study deviant behavior to better understand its causes.

Deviant behaviors such as alcoholism, drug addiction, and crime are perceived as serious threats to society. Once we understand its causes, we may be able to develop better programs that reduce or eliminate deviance or that help people change their deviant behavior.

This chapter addresses four fundamental questions:

1. What are the causes of deviant behavior?

2. How important for deviant behavior is the reaction of observers? That is, does someone have to react to behavior in particular ways for it to be considered deviant?

3. Why do some people engage in deviance repeatedly? Why do they adopt a lifestyle that involves regular participation in deviant activities?

4. What determines how authorities and agents of social control deal with incidents of deviance? Is their reaction influenced by the deviant person's gender, social status, or other characteristics of the situation?

THE VIOLATION OF NORMS

When we read or hear that someone is accused of murder, or embezzling money from her employer, or engaging in illegal accounting practices, we often ask, "Why?" In Hanna's case, we would ask, "Why did she take that lingerie?" In this section, we consider first the nature of norms and then look at several theories about the causes of deviant behavior. These include anomie theory, control theory, differential association theory, and routine activities theory.

Norms

Most people would regard Hanna's behavior in the department store as deviant because it violated social norms. Specifically, she violated laws that define taking merchandise from stores without paying for it as a criminal act. Thus, deviance is a social construction; whether a behavior is deviant or not depends on the norms or expectations for behavior in the situation in which it occurs.

In any situation, our behavior is governed by norms derived from several sources (Suttles, 1968). First, there are purely "local" and group norms. Thus, roommates and families develop norms about what personal topics can and cannot be discussed at meals. Second, there are subcultural norms that apply to large numbers of persons who share some characteristic. For example, there are racial or ethnic group norms governing the behavior of Blacks or persons of Polish descent that do not apply to other Americans. A subculture that is particularly relevant to the discussion of deviance is the subculture of violence, which will be discussed later. Third, there are societal norms, such as those requiring certain types of dress or those limiting sexual activity to certain relationships and situations. Thus, the norms that govern our daily behavior have a variety of origins, including family and friends; socioeconomic, religious, or ethnic subcultures; and the society in general.

The repercussions of deviant behavior depend on which type of norm an individual violates. Violations of local norms may be of concern only to a certain group. Failing to do the dishes when it is your turn may result in your roommate being angry, although your friends may not care about that deviance. Subcultural norms are often held in common by most of those with whom we interact, whether they are friends, family members, or coworkers. Violations of these norms may affect most of one's day-to-day interactions. Violations of societal norms may subject a person to action by formal agencies of control, such as the police or the courts. Earlier in this book, we discussed the violation of local norms (see Chap. 4) and group norms (see Chap. 13). In this chapter, we focus on the violation of societal norms and on reactions to norm violations.

Anomie Theory

The **anomie theory** of deviance (Merton, 1957) suggests that deviance arises when people striving to achieve culturally valued goals, such as wealth, find that they do not have any legitimate way to attain these goals. These people then break the rules, often in an attempt to attain these goals illegitimately.

Anomie. Every society provides its members with goals to aspire to. If the members of a society value religion, they are likely to socialize their youths and adults to aspire to salvation. If the members value power, they will teach people to seek positions in which they can dominate others. U.S. culture extols wealth as the appropriate goal for most members of society, and the means to happiness. In every society, there are also norms that define acceptable ways of striving for goals, called **legitimate means**. In the United States, legitimate means for attaining wealth include education, working hard at a job to earn money, starting a business, and making wise investments.

A person socialized into U.S. society will most likely desire material wealth and will strive to succeed in a desirable occupation—to become a sales rep, teacher, nurse, business executive, doctor, or the like. The legitimate means of attaining these goals are to obtain a formal education and to climb the ladder of occupational prestige (see Chap. 15). The person who has access to these means—who can afford to go to college and has the accepted skin color, ethnic background, and gender—can attain these socially desirable goals.

What about those who do not have access to the legitimate means? As Americans, these people will desire material wealth like everyone else, but they will be blocked in their strivings. Because of the way society is structured, certain members are denied access to legitimate means. Government decisions regarding budgeting, building schools, or closing schools determine the availability of education to individuals. Similarly, certain members of society are denied access to jobs. Not only individual characteristics, such as lack of education, but also social factors, such as the profitability of making autos in Detroit, determine who is unemployed.

A person who strives to attain a legitimate goal but is denied access to legitimate means will experience anomie—a state that reduces commitment to norms or the pursuit of goals. There are four ways a person may respond to anomie; each is a distinct type of deviance. First, an individual may reject the goals, and give up trying to achieve success, but continue to conform to social norms. This adaptation is termed *ritualism*. The poorly paid stock clerk who never misses a day of work in 45 years is a ritualist. He is deviant because he has given up the struggle for success. Second, the individual might reject both the goals and the means, withdrawing from active participation in society by *retreatism*. This may take the form of drinking, drug use, withdrawal into mental illness, or other kinds of escape. Third, one might remain committed to the goals but turn to disapproved or illegal ways of achieving success. This adaptation is termed *innovation*. Earning a living as a burglar, commercial sex worker, or loan

Most Americans are socialized to strive for economic success. But some people do not have access to legitimate employment, so they seek wealth by alternative, sometimes illegal means, such as commercial sex work. © Karen Kasmauski/Corbis

shark is an innovative means of attaining wealth. Finally, one might attempt to overthrow the existing system and create different goals and means through *rebellion*.

Shoplifting is a form of innovation. Like other types of economic crime, it represents a rejection of the normatively prescribed means (paying for what you want) while continuing to strive for the goal (possessing merchandise). According to anomie theory, Hanna, the shoplifter, has been socialized to desire wealth but does not have access to a well-paying job due to her poor education. As a result, she steals what she wants because she does not have the money to pay for it.

Another influence on an individual's adaptation is access to deviant roles. Using a means of goal achievement—whether legitimate or illegitimate—requires access to two structures (Cloward, 1959). The first is a **learning structure**—an environment in which an individual can learn the information and skills required. A shoplifter needs to learn how to conceal objects quickly, how to spot electronic anti-theft devices, and so forth. The second is an **opportunity structure**—an environment in which an individual has opportunities to play a role, which usually requires the assistance of those in complementary roles. Anomie theory assumes that anyone can be an innovator—through shoplifting, prostitution, or professional theft. But not everyone has access to the special knowledge and skills needed to succeed as a commercial sex worker (Heyl, 1977) or a black-market banker (Weigand, 1994). Just as access to legitimate means to achieve goals is limited, so is access to illegitimate means. Only those who have both the learning and opportunity structures necessary to become a shoplifter, commercial sex worker, or embezzler can use these alternative routes to success (Coleman, 1987).

The opportunities for deviance available to a person depend on age, sex, kinship, ethnicity, and social class (Cloward, 1959). These characteristics, with the possible exception of class, are beyond the individual's control. Thus, commercial sex work in our society primarily involves young, physically attractive persons. People who do not have access to the learning or opportunity structures necessary for deviance cannot succeed either through legitimate or through illegitimate means. Such failure often produces retreatism. Drug addicts, alcoholics, and mentally ill persons may be losers in both the conventional and criminal worlds.

Anomie and Social Class. Anomie theory emphasizes access to education and employment. Those who have access to both should not engage in deviant behavior. Those who do not have access to one or both should experience anomie and are likely to engage in deviance. A survey of 1,614 youths aged 15 to 18 measured commitment to success goals ("making a lot of money") and perceived access to college education (Farnworth & Leiber, 1989). Respondents who said they wanted to make a lot of money but did not expect to complete college were much more likely to report delinquent behavior.

One measure of access to legitimate means is the unemployment rate. According to the theory, as unemployment increases, rates of deviance also should increase. One study analyzed the relationship between unemployment rates and crime rates in the United States for each year of the 1948–1985 period (Devine, Sheley, & Smith, 1988). There was a strong relationship; as unemployment increases, so does crime. The relationship is stronger for economic crime (burglary) than for violent crime (murder). An analysis of increases and decreases in the homicide rate from 1970 to 2000 in major U.S. cities found that increases and decreases in relative deprivation (percentage of families living in poverty, median family income) was related to number of murders (McCall, Parker, & MacDonald, 2008). Evidence of a direct connection between unemployment and economic crime comes from a longitudinal study in which ex-addicts, ex-offenders, and "dropout" youths reported their legal and illegal income for up to 3 years; as the unemployment rate in the city increased, youths reported greater income from illegal activities (Uggen & Thompson, 2003).

Two studies suggest that it is relative rather than absolute socioeconomic standing that determines whether one experiences anomie. A study of arrest rates for burglary and robbery from 1957 to 1990 found that as income inequality among Blacks increased, so did Black arrest rates (LaFree & Drass, 1996). Similarly, an analysis of the number of Latinos murdered in 1980 found that the degree of income inequality among Latinos was an important factor (Martinez, 1996). Thus, it is one's economic standing relative to similar others, in this case in one's ethnic group, that matters, not one's standing in the society as a whole.

The relationship between socioeconomic disadvantage and crime is not limited to minority groups. A study of 124 central cities with substantial Black populations found that, in cities where the economic circumstances (such as rates of home ownership) of Blacks and Whites were similar, murder rates were similar as well (Boardman, Finch, Ellison, Williams, & Jackson, 2001). Another study used a composite score of disadvantages, including the percentage of households below poverty and male unemployment rates. Neighborhood disadvantage was associated with increased exposure to social stressors (illness, criminal victimization) and psychological distress (feeling sad, anxious, hopeless); all three were associated with drug use, especially among those with the lowest incomes. These results are consistent with anomie theory.

Anomie theory directs our attention to the importance of social class. Because lower-class members are more frequently excluded from quality education and jobs, the theory predicts that they will commit more crimes. Data collected by police departments and the FBI generally confirm this prediction, showing that a disproportionate number of those arrested for crimes are poor, minority men. This has led some to conclude that crime and social class are inversely related—that the highest crime rates are found in the lower social strata (Cloward, 1959).

However, there is a class bias built into the official statistics on crime. Not all illegitimate economic activities are included in these statistics. Whereas data on burglary, robbery, and larceny are compiled by police departments, data on income tax evasion, price fixing, and insider trading are not. Police and FBI statistics are much more likely to include "street" crimes than the kinds of economic crimes committed by the wealthy, corporate executives, and stockbrokers. The latter are called *white-collar crime—*

activities that violate norms of trust, usually for personal gain (Shapiro, 1990). To embezzle or misappropriate funds or engage in insider trading of stocks, one needs access to a position of trust. Such positions usually are filled by middle-class and upper-class persons. These crimes are facilitated by the social organization of trust; the acts of trustees are invisible, hidden in a network of often electronic connections between organizations. Widespread crimes of this type in the investment and banking industries caused the economic crisis of 2008–2010. Thus, although specific crimes may vary by class, illegitimate economic activity may be common to all classes.

General Strain Theory. One limitation of anomie theory is that it does not specify the mechanism by which the lack of access to legitimate means produces delinquent or criminal behavior. One attempt to do so is Agnew's general strain theory (Agnew, 1992; Agnew & White, 1992). Agnew proposes that emotion connects the experience of strain with deviant behavior; strain elicits negative affective states—frustration, anger, or fear—that create the motivation to act. These actions may be deviant or criminal. Such actions include crimes that provide access to the goal (robbery, burglary, selling drugs), aggression against people perceived as responsible for the strain (abuse, assault), or drug and alcohol use to escape the emotions. The role of emotion can explain incidents such as an angry former employee returning to the workplace and killing supervisor(s) and former coworkers.

A longitudinal study of high school youths provides data to test the theory. Youths in the ninth, tenth, and eleventh grades in three primarily White suburban communities were interviewed three times over a 2-year period. The research measured life stress and family conflict, anger and anxiety, aggressive delinquency (damaging property, carrying a weapon, fighting) and nonaggressive delinquency (stealing, joyriding, running away), and marijuana use. The results indicated that life stressors and family conflict were related to delinquency and marijuana use. As predicted by the theory, family conflict was related to anger, and anger was related to engaging in aggressive delinquency. However, anger was not related to nonaggressive delinquency or marijuana use, and anxiety was not related to any of the three types of behaviors (Aseltine, Gore, & Gordon, 2000). Thus, the results provide only modest support for the key predictions.

A longitudinal study of youths living in Dade County, Florida, yielded a sample with substantial numbers of African Americans and Hispanics, as well as Whites, allowing a test of the theory among these minorities. To the extent that there are differences by racial/ethnic group in criminal behavior, general strain theory suggests that these are caused by differences between groups in strain. The research included three measures of strain: recent life events (in the preceding 12 months), chronic stressors (for example, unemployment, relationship, child care, residence), and lifetime major events (for example, abandonment, school failure, divorce, physical or sexual assault) (see Chap. 15). It also included measures of social support. Using data from 898 young men, analyses indicated that strain as measured by recent life events was related to criminal activity, and that greater involvement of African Americans in crime was associated with greater exposure to major lifetime events (Eitle & Turner, 2003).

A survey of a random sample of residents of Raleigh, North Carolina, tested strain theory with an adult population. Respondents were asked to report the likelihood they would commit violence, a property violation (for example, theft), a minor offense, or illegal drug use. A measure of strain, including frequency of unpleasant experiences and how well one has achieved his or her goals, predicted likelihood of offending. However, the relationship was not mediated by negative emotions (feeling upset, angry, depressed) (Tittle, Broidy, & Gertz, 2008).

Control Theory

If you were asked why you don't shoplift clothing from stores, you might reply, "Because my parents (or lover, or friends) would kill me if they found out." According to **control theory**, social ties influence our tendency to engage in deviant behavior. We often conform to social norms because we are sensitive to the wishes and expectations of others. This sensitivity creates a bond between the individual and other persons. The stronger the bond is, the less likely the individual is to engage in deviant behavior.

There are four components of the social bond (Hirschi, 1969). The first is attachment—ties of affection and respect for others. Attachment to parents is especially important, because they are the primary socializing agents of a child. A strong attachment to them leads the child to internalize social norms. The second component is commitment to long-term educational and occupational goals. Someone who aspires to go to law school is unlikely to commit a crime, because a criminal record would be an obstacle to a career in law. The third component is involvement. People who are involved in sports, Scouts, church groups, and other conventional activities simply have less time to engage in deviance. The fourth component is belief—a respect for the law and for persons in positions of authority.

We can apply control theory to the shoplifting incident described in the introduction. Hanna does not feel attached to law-abiding adults; therefore, she was not concerned about their reactions to her

These Boy Scouts are attending a Memorial Day parade. Participation in such group activities increases attachment to and involvement in conventional society, reducing the likelihood of delinquency. © Jonathan Alcorn/Reuters/Corbis

behavior. Nor did she seem deterred by commitment when she said, "Nothing will happen." Hanna's deviant act reflects the absence of a bond with conventional society.

The relationship between delinquency and the four components of the social bond has been the focus of numerous studies. Several studies have found a relationship between a lack of attachment and delinquency; young people from homes characterized by a lack of parental supervision, communication, and support report more delinquent behavior (Hoffman, 2002; Hundleby & Mercer, 1987; Messner & Krohn, 1990). Attachment to school, measured by grades, is also associated with delinquency. Boys and girls who do well in school are less likely to be delinquent. Regarding commitment to long-term goals, research indicates that youths who are committed to educational and career goals are less likely to engage in property crimes such as robbery and theft (Johnson, 1979; Shover, Novland, James, & Thornton, 1979). Findings relevant to the third component, involvement, are mixed. Whereas involvement in studying and homework is negatively associated with reported delinquency, participation

in athletics, hobbies, and work is unrelated to reported delinquency. Involvement in religion, as reflected in frequent church attendance and rating religion as important in one's life, is associated with reduced delinquency (Sloane & Potrin, 1986). Finally, evidence suggests that conventional beliefs reduce the frequency of delinquent behavior (Gardner & Shoemaker, 1989).

Control theory asserts that attachment to parents leads to reduced delinquency. Implicitly, the theory assumes that parents do not encourage delinquent behavior. Although this assumption may be correct in most instances, there are exceptions. Studies suggest that some parents encourage delinquent and criminal behaviors. Some parents explicitly teach their children how to shoplift, commit burglaries, and steal cars and trucks (Butterfield, 2002). A longitudinal study of criminal convictions in a Dutch sample found that same-sex parent's convictions significantly predicted son's/daughter's convictions (van De Rakt, Nieuwbeerta, & Apel, 2009). However, same-sex sibling's convictions were the strongest predictor. These data provide a stringent test, since the outcome measure is convictions. These are cases in which crime really does "run in the family." In these instances, parental (and sibling) attachment leads to increased delinquency and crime. The influence of sex suggests the importance of learning and imitation.

Does a lack of attachment to parents in childhood relate to adult deviant behavior? Yes. Research consistently shows that children who are physically and sexually abused are more likely to be involved as adults in violent and property crime, prostitution, and alcohol and substance abuse (Macmillan, 2001). The strength of adult social bonds is also related to adult criminal behavior. One study assessed month-to-month variations in circumstances that could strengthen or weaken the bond, and related this variation to the occurrence of criminal behavior (Horney, Osgood, & Marshall, 1995). The circumstances were starting/stopping school, starting/stopping work, and starting/stopping living with a girlfriend or wife. Interviews were conducted with 658 men in prison who had committed felonies. Increases in criminal behavior were closely related to changes that reduced the men's bonds to others—stopping school or work, and stopping living with a girlfriend or wife.

A well-established finding in the study of delinquency and crime is the "age-crime curve"—rates of offending rise sharply in adolescence, peak in young adulthood, and decline steadily thereafter (Stolzenberg & D'Alessio, 2008; see Figure 16.1). Most offenses are committed by men, but the curve is the same for women's offenses. Typical adolescent offenses include vandalism, auto theft, and burglary. Persons aged 18 to 28 are more likely to be involved in drug violations and homicide. Middle-aged persons are more frequently involved in gambling offenses. These variations suggest life-course changes in attachments and opportunities lead to different types of offenses, and to desistance as one ages.

One longitudinal study indicates that the strength of the social bond influences whether adults engage in deviant behavior (Sampson & Laub, 1990). The researchers studied 500 boys aged 10 to 17 who were in a correctional school and 500 boys of the same age from public school. Each boy was followed until he was 32. Generally, strong ties to social institutions were associated with reduced rates of crime, alcohol abuse, gambling, and divorce. In adolescents, the important attachments were to family and school. In young adults, the influential ties were to school, work, or marriage. In later adulthood, the important ties were to work, marriage, and parenthood.

What about women? Would work, marriage, and parenthood be associated with

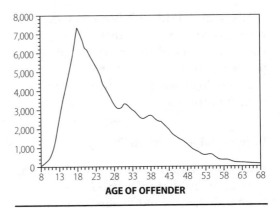

FIGURE 16.1 The Relationship Between Age and Crime

Involvement in delinquency and crime varies across the life course, responding to changes in economic conditions, changes in social roles, and opportunities. While rates of offenses vary by gender and race, the shape of the curve is the same across these groups.

Source: Stolzenberg & D'Alessio, "Co-offending and the Age-Crime Curve," *Journal of Research in Crime and Delinquency*, 45, 65–86, 2008.

desistance from crime among women who were serious delinquents in adolescence? A study comparing women and men who were in institutions during adolescence found that neither job stability nor marriage was associated with adult desistance. In narratives of their lives, women were more likely than men to describe their children and religious transformation as the forces for change in their lives (Giordano, Cernkovich, & Rudolph, 2002). Moreover, it was not the fact of having children or a good job that was important; it was a transformation in the woman's identity or her thinking about those aspects of her life. These results are consistent with symbolic interaction theory and its emphasis on meaning constructed by the person in interaction with others.

Ethnographic research on women who smuggle drugs from Mexico to the United States illustrates how strong adult attachment to male family members, lovers, or spouses may lead to a woman's involvement in crime. Some of these women were coerced by these others into smuggling, whereas others perceived involvement as a means of increasing their income and independence from men (Campbell, 2008).

Differential Association Theory

Vince and Arturo were roommates in the Phi Kappa Sly house. They were both taking Human Sexuality, and the first exam was in three days. Arturo asked Vince if he wanted to study with him. Vince replied, "I'm just going to review the old exams in the file the night before." Arturo replied, "But that's cheating!" Vince said, "I got to get an A. I saw Butch and George using the file last night." Arturo said, "Well, I want to learn the material, so count me out." Arturo studied for several hours and got an A-; Vince looked at old exams for one hour and got a C.

Vince's behavior reflects a conflict between two sets of norms. His college has rules defining cheating as academic misconduct. Academic work such as writing papers and preparing for tests should be done by the student, not by relying on paper or exam files or materials on the Internet. Arturo's behavior reflects this set of norms. Fraternity members, on the other hand, believe academic work is not important, and help their brothers minimize effort by maintaining an exam file. Butch's and George's behavior represents this set of norms. Vince is not insensitive to the expectations of others. In fact, he is highly sensitive to the expectations of his "brothers."

This view of deviance is the basis of **differential association theory**, developed by Sutherland. He argued that although the law provides a uniform standard for deviance, one group may define a behavior as deviant, whereas another group defines it as desirable. Some groups believe cheating is wrong

because (1) it violates academic regulations, (2) it claims credit for work that is not your own, and (3) it is unfair to other students who do their own work. Other groups believe it is acceptable because (1) it saves time, (2) the professor will never know, and (3) everybody (like Butch and George) is doing it. The latter are referred to as *neutralizing beliefs* (Rettinger & Kramer, 2009; Sykes and Matza, 1957); they neutralize the influence of definitions/beliefs unfavorable to the behavior.

Attitudes about behaviors are learned through associations with others, usually in primary group settings. People learn motives, drives, and techniques of engaging in specific behaviors. What they learn depends on with whom they interact—that is, on their differential associations. Whether someone engages in a specific behavior depends on how frequently he or she is exposed to attitudes and beliefs that are favorable toward that behavior.

The principle of differential association states that a "person becomes delinquent because of an excess of definitions favorable to violation of the law over definitions unfavorable to violation of the law" (Sutherland, Cressey, & Luckenbill, 1992). Studies designed to test this principle typically ask individuals questions about their attitudes toward a specific behavior and about their participation in that behavior. One study revealed that the number of definitions favorable to delinquency accurately predicted which young men reported delinquent behavior (Matsueda, 1982). The larger the number of definitions a youth endorsed, the larger the number of delinquent acts he reported having committed in the preceding year. A subsequent study found that associating with delinquent peers was also related to delinquent behavior (Heimer & Matsueda, 1994).

Research on cheating by students found that direct knowledge of cheating by other students is the most powerful predictor of cheating (O'Rourke et al., 2010). Thus, seeing Butch and George use the exam file was probably a major influence on Vince's behavior.

Certain groups within the United States hold a set of beliefs that justify the use of physical aggression in certain situations. This set of beliefs is referred to as the *subculture of violence*. Within this subculture, violence is considered appropriate when used as a means of self-defense and protection of one's home, or to defend one's reputation. A review of state laws governing spouse abuse, corporal punishment, and capital punishment found that Southern states have laws that are more accepting of violence (Cohen, 1996). Several studies report a relationship between these beliefs and behavior. Felson, Liska, South, and McNulty (1994) studied young men in 87 high schools. The young men were asked whether aggressive responses were appropriate in three situations involving insults or threats. Those young men who endorsed the use of violence were much more likely to report involvement in eight types of interpersonal violence, including striking a parent or teacher, fighting, and using weapons in disputes. Endorsing the use of violence was also associated with delinquency within the school, including cheating, tardiness, and truancy.

The theory of differential association does not specify the process by which people learn criminal or deviant behavior. For this reason, Burgess and Akers (1966) developed a modified theory of differential association. This modified version emphasizes the influence of positive and negative reinforcement on the acquisition of behavior. Much of this reinforcement comes from friends and associates.

A survey of 3,056 high school students was conducted to test the theory (Akers, Krohn, Lanza-Kaduce, & Radosevich, 1979). In particular, it assessed the relationship between differential association, reinforcement, and adolescents' drinking behavior and marijuana use. Differential association was measured by three questions: "How many of your (1) best friends, (2) friends you spend the most time with, and (3) friends you have known longest smoke marijuana and/or drink?" The survey also assessed students' definitions of drug and alcohol laws. Both social reinforcement (whether the adolescent expected praise or punishment for use from parents and peers) and nonsocial reinforcement (whether the effects of substance use were positive or negative) were measured. The findings of this survey showed that differential association was closely related to the use of alcohol or drugs. The larger the number of friends who drank or smoked marijuana, the more likely the student was to drink alcohol or smoke marijuana. Reinforcement was also related to behavior; those who used a substance reported that it had positive effects. The students' definitions were also related to those with whom they associated; if their friends drank or used marijuana, they were more likely to have positive attitudes toward the behavior and negative attitudes toward laws defining that behavior as criminal. Finally, students' attitudes were consistent with their behavior. Those who opposed marijuana use and supported the marijuana laws were much less likely to use that substance.

A similar study (Akers, LaGreca, Cochran, & Sellers, 1989) focused on drinking among older persons. Interviews were conducted with 1,410 people aged 60 and over. The measures used were the same or similar to those used with adolescents. The results were essentially the same. The drinking behavior of persons 60 and older was related to the drinking behavior of spouse, family, or friends; reinforcements; and an individual's attitudes toward drinking.

Survey data collected at one point in time often cannot be used to test hypotheses about cause-effect relationships. However, survey data collected from the same people at two or more times can be. Stein, Newcomb, and Bentler (1987) analyzed data from 654 young people who were surveyed three times at 4-year intervals that began when they were in junior high school. The measures included peer drug use, adult drug use, and community approval of drug use. The results showed that adolescents who believed that both peers and adults were using drugs were more likely to become drug users.

Persons who are members of a group should be most heavily influenced by it. A study analyzing longitudinal data collected over a 6-year period, from adolescence into young adulthood (Pollard et al., 2013), differentiated three positions: member (more than 50 percent of friends are members of same group), liaison (has friends in more than one group), and isolate (only one tie to the group/network). Members of a group with one or more binge drinkers at Time 1, in high school, were much more likely to become long-term heavy bingers. This may reflect the point noted above, that observing deviance is the best predictor of engaging in the behavior.

Thus, differential association emphasizes interacting with groups and learning pro-conformity or neutralizing beliefs with regard to the behavior. Learning emphasizes modeling and imitation in learning the behavior (see Chap. 3) and reinforcement, a positive or negative experience including feedback from others. A meta-analysis considered the results of 133 studies testing the relationship between these and crime or deviant behavior. The results indicate that measures of interaction and beliefs are consistently stronger in cross-sectional but not longitudinal studies (Pratt, Cullen, Sellers, et al., 2013).

In addition to being modeled by peers or family, deviant behaviors can sometimes be provoked by media coverage, as detailed in Box 16.1.

Recall from Chapter 15 that an important characteristic of social networks is density—the extent to which each member of the network or group knows the other members. Networks that are dense should have more influence on their members' behavior; if all of your friends drink alcohol, it will be hard for you to "just say no." A study of a nationally representative sample of seventh to twelfth graders found that peers' delinquency has a stronger association with an adolescent's delinquency when the friendship network is dense (Haynie, 2001).

Because each person usually associates with several groups, the consistency or inconsistency in definitions across groups is also an important influence on behavior (Krohn, 1986). *Network multiplexity* refers to the degree to which individuals who interact in one context also interact in other contexts. When you interact with the same people at church, at school, on the athletic field, and at parties, multiplexity is high. When you interact with different people in each of these settings, multiplexity is low. When multiplexity is high, the definitions of an activity will be consistent across groups; when it is low, definitions may be inconsistent across groups. Thus, differential associations should have the greatest impact on attitudes and beliefs when multiplexity is high. A survey of 1,435 high school students measured the extent to which individuals interacted with parents and with the same peers in each of several activities (Krohn, Massey, & Zielinski, 1988). Students who participated jointly with parents and peers in various activities were less likely to smoke cigarettes.

Routine Activities Perspective

So far, we have considered characteristics of the person (motivation, beliefs) and of his associations with others (parents, friends). These have been shown to be related to delinquency, assault, murder, burglary, economic crimes, suicide, and alcohol and drug use. The **routine activities perspective** focuses on a third class of influences—how these behaviors emerge from the routines of everyday life (Felson, 1994).

Each instance of deviant behavior requires the convergence of the elements necessary for the behavior to occur. Crimes such as burglary, larceny, or robbery require the convergence of an offender and a likely target (residence, store, or person) and the absence of some guardian who could intervene. In the illustration at the beginning of the chapter, the shoplifting incident involves such a convergence: Hanna, the lingerie, and the absence of a clerk or security guard. Illegal consumption requires two offenders (seller and user), a substance, and a setting with no guardian; "crack houses" provide the latter in many large cities. Without such convergence, deviance will not occur. We can understand another aspect of deviance if we analyze everyday activity from the perspective of how it facilitates or prevents such convergences. This perspective calls our attention to the contributions of situations to behavior.

One class of situations that facilitates deviance is unstructured socializing with peers in the absence of an authority figure (Osgood, Wilson, O'Malley, Bachman, & Johnston, 1996). The presence of peers makes it likely that definitions will be shared, including definitions favorable to particular forms of deviance. The absence of an authority figure or guardian reduces the likelihood of punishment for deviance. Lack of structure makes time available for deviance. What situations have these characteristics? They include cruising in a car with friends, going to parties, and "hanging out" with friends. Data from a longitudinal study of a national sample of 1,200 persons

aged 18 to 26 allowed researchers to relate involvement in these situations to deviance. Frequency of participation in them was related to alcohol and marijuana use, dangerous driving, and criminal behavior. Changes across five waves of data collection in an individual's participation in these activities were related to changes in his or her involvement in deviance.

Researchers have consistently noted that men are much more likely to commit criminal acts than women. This is not only true of street crime but also of economic crimes involving violation of trust, such as insider trading. The routine activities perspective explains this as due to gender role socialization, which teaches women different norms and definitions; to lack of access to tutelage in various forms of deviance; and to restrictions on activities that keep women out of certain settings (Steffensmeier & Allan, 1996). Thus, few women commit either burglary or insider trading because of their lack of access in everyday life to the apprenticeships where one learns these behaviors. Similarly, we are not surprised that the corporate executives of Enron, WorldCom, and other companies who committed fraud in the period 1995–2003 were men; the "glass ceiling" prevents most women from occupying such roles.

Research on youths aged 9 to 19 living in 12 high-poverty neighborhoods demonstrates that some elements simultaneously increase and decrease the likelihood of criminal activity. Carrying a gun in such a neighborhood makes it available for use in a crime, but also available to defend oneself in case of attack. Similarly, employment creates a conventional attachment and provides income by a legitimate means, but also creates the risk of injury or death during a robbery (Spano, Freilich, & Bolland, 2008).

The anomie, control, differential association, and routine activities perspectives are

BOX 16.1 The Power of Suggestion

Rape, robbery, murder, and other types of deviant behavior receive a substantial amount of coverage in newspapers and on radio and television. One function of publicizing deviance is to remind us of norms—to tell us what we should not do (Erikson, 1964). But is this the only consequence? Could the publicity given to particular deviant activities increase the frequency with which they occur? In some cases, the answer appears to be yes.

A study of the relationship between the publicity given to suicides and suicide rates suggests that the two are positively correlated (Phillips, 1974). This study identified every time a suicide was publicized in three major U.S. daily newspapers during the years 1947–1968. Next, the researchers calculated the number of expected suicides for the following month by averaging the suicide rates for that same month from the year before and the year after. For example, the researchers noted that the suicide of a Ku Klux Klan leader on November 1, 1965, was widely publicized. They then obtained the expected number of suicides (1,652) by averaging the total number of suicides for November 1964 (1,639) and November 1966 (1,665). In fact, there were 1,710 suicides in November 1965; the difference between the observed and the expected rates (58) could be due to suggestion via the mass media.

The results of this study showed that suicides increased in the month following reports of a suicide in major daily papers. Moreover, the more publicity a story was given—as measured by the number of days the story was on the front page—the larger the rise in suicides. If a story was published locally—in Chicago but not in New York, for example—the rise in suicides occurred only in the area where it was publicized.

Why should such publicity lead other persons to kill themselves? There must be some factor that predisposes a small number of persons to take their own lives following a publicized suicide. That predisposing factor may be anomie. According to this theory, suicide is a form of retreatism—of withdrawal from the struggle for success. Persons who don't have access to legitimate means are looking for some way to adapt to their situation. Publicity given to a suicide may suggest a solution to their problem.

These results were replicated by a study in Australia, which measured the amount of publicity in newspapers and on radio and TV given suicides during a one-year period (Pirkis, Burgess, Francis, et al., 2006). Media reports were more likely to be associated with increases in suicides if they were broadcast on television, the suicide was successful, and other suicides were reported on the same day.

When we think of suicide, we think of shooting oneself, taking an overdose of a drug, or jumping off a building. We distinguish suicide from accidents, in which we presume the person did not intend to harm himself or herself. But the

not incompatible. Anomie theory suggests that culturally valued goals and the opportunities available to achieve these goals are major influences on behavior. Opportunities to learn and occupy particular roles are influenced by age, social class, gender, race, and ethnic background—that is, by the structuring of everyday life based on these variables. According to control theory, we are also influenced by our attachments to others and our commitment to attaining success. Our position in the social structure and our attachments to parents and peers determine our differential associations—the kinds of groups to which we belong. Within these groups, we learn definitions favorable to particular behaviors, and we learn that we face sanctions when we choose behaviors that group members define as deviant.

critical difference is the person's intent, not the event itself. Some apparent accidents may be suicides. For example, when a car hits a bridge abutment well away from the pavement on a clear day with no evidence of mechanical malfunction, this may be suicide.

If some auto accidents are, in fact, suicides, we should observe an increase in motor vehicle accidents following newspaper stories about a suicide. In fact, data from newspapers and motor vehicle deaths in San Francisco and Los Angeles verify this hypothesis (Phillips, 1979). Statistics show a marked increase in the number of deaths due to automobile accidents 2 and 3 days after a suicide is publicized, especially accidents involving a single vehicle. In the Detroit metropolitan area, an analysis of motor vehicle fatalities for the years 1973–1976 revealed an average increase in fatalities of 35 to 40 percent the third day after a suicide story appeared in the daily papers (Bollen & Phillips, 1981). Again, the more publicity, the greater the increase. Finally, if the person whose suicide is publicized was young, deaths of young drivers increase, whereas if the person killing himself was older, the increase in fatalities involves more older drivers.

Does an increase in suicide follow any publicized suicide, or are some suicides more likely to be imitated than others? Stack (1987) studied instances in which celebrities killed themselves. The effect of publicized suicide is gender- and race-specific. Suicide by a male celebrity was followed by an increase in the number of men who killed themselves but not in the number of women who took their lives, and vice versa. Similarly, an increase in suicides by Whites followed a publicized case involving a White celebrity, whereas rates among Blacks were unaffected. The fact that the effects of publicized suicide are age-, gender-, and race-specific is consistent with the concept of imitation.

A detailed study of the impact of one suicide identified several consequences. The suicide of a well-known male TV reporter in Quebec was the subject of 65 news articles in the following week. It was followed by an increase in suicides among men aged 20 to 49 in Quebec in the four months following his death. There was a cluster of six suicides in the community where he died, all by hanging, which was the means of his death. There was also a significant, almost 100 percent increase in calls to the Suicide Prevention Centre (Tousignant, Mishara, Caillaud, Fortin, & St-Laurent, 2005).

A very different explanation of suicide is that it reflects a lack of social integration. The imitation explanation would be strengthened if we find clustering of suicides after controlling for the effects of variables such as marital and residential stability. Such an analysis was performed of suicide rates for U.S. counties from 1989 to 1991. Interestingly, the variance in suicide rates in the western third of the United States was explained by integration; in the non-West, clustering remained, strengthening the argument that suicide involves imitation (Baller & Richardson, 2002).

REACTIONS TO NORM VIOLATIONS

When we think of murder, robbery, or sexual assault, we think of cases we have read about or heard of on radio or television. We frequently refer to police and FBI statistics as measures of the number of crimes that have occurred in our city or county. Our knowledge of alcohol or drug abuse depends on knowing or hearing about persons who engage in these behaviors. All of these instances of deviance share another important characteristic as well: In every case, the behavior was discovered by someone who called it to the attention of others.

Does it matter that these instances involve both an action (by a person) and a reaction (by a victim or an observer)? Isn't an act equally deviant regardless of whether others find out about it? Let's go back to Hanna's theft of the lingerie. Suppose Hanna had left the store without being stopped by the clerk. In that case, she and Megan would have known she had taken the lingerie, but she would not have faced sanctions from others. She would not have experienced the embarrassment of being confronted and accused of a crime. Moreover, she would have had some beautiful lingerie. But the fact is that she was stopped by the clerk. She will be questioned, the police will be called, and she may be arrested. Thus, the consequences of committing a deviant act are quite different when certain reactions follow.

Whether a rule violation becomes "known about" depends in part on the actor's social and economic resources (Jackson-Jacobs, 2004). Consider two crack users, both 21-year-old men. DuShawn lives in a deteriorating neighborhood; he works at a car wash, and his earnings support his habit. When he isn't working, he hangs out with other users. Sometimes, he commits burglary to get more money. He shoots up in a "crack house," the only place where he can get some privacy and escape surveillance. He is at risk of assault by fellow users, who know he is a user; they want his money or his drugs. Doug is a junior at a university. He lives in an apartment near campus, where he can use heroin with little risk. His part-time job supplies the money. His schedule of classes and work make it relatively easy for him to restrict his use to leisure times in his apartment, with carefully selected friends. Joseph's legitimate and sufficient income, control over his life, and access to private space make it unlikely he will be arrested.

This reasoning is the basis of **labeling theory**—the view that reactions to a norm violation are a critical element in deviance. Only after an act is discovered and labeled "deviant" is the act recognized as such. If the same act is not discovered and labeled, it is not deviant (Becker, 1963).

If deviance depends on the reactions of others to an act rather than on the act itself, the key social psychological question becomes, "Why do particular audiences choose to label an act as deviant, whereas other audiences may not?" Labeling theory is an attempt to understand how and why acts are labeled deviant. In the case of the stolen lingerie, labeling analysts would not be concerned with Hanna's behavior. Rather, they would be interested in the responses to Hanna's act by Megan, the male customer, and the clerk. Only if an observer challenges Hanna's behavior or alerts a store employee does the act of taking the lingerie become deviant.

Reactions to Rule Breaking

Labeling theorists refer to behavior that violates norms as **rule breaking**, to emphasize that the act by itself is not deviant. Most rule violations are "secret," in the sense that no one other than the actor (and on occasion, the actor's accomplices) is aware of them. Many cases of theft and tax evasion, many violations of drug laws, and some burglaries are never detected. These activities can be carried out by a single person. Other acts, such as robberies, assaults, and various sexual activities, involve other people who will know about them, but who may not label the act as deviant. Instances of assault, domestic violence, rape, and sexual abuse of children are not reported because the victim is unwilling or unable to do so.

How will members of an audience respond to a rule violation? It depends on the circumstances, but studies suggest that people very often ignore it. When wives of men hospitalized for psychiatric treatment were asked how they reacted to their husband's bizarre behavior, for example, they often replied that they had not considered their husbands ill or in need of help (Yarrow,

Schwartz, Murphy, & Deasy, 1955). People react to isolated episodes of unusual behavior in one of four ways. A common response is denial, in which the person simply does not recognize that a rule violation occurred. In one study, denial was typically the first response of women to their husbands' excessive drinking (Jackson, 1954). A second response is normalization, in which the observer recognizes that the act occurred but defines it as normal or common. Thus, wives often reacted to excessive drinking as normal, assuming that many men drink a lot. Third, the person may recognize the act as a rule violation but excuse it, attributing its occurrence to situational or transient factors; this reaction is attenuation. Thus, some wives of men who were later hospitalized believed that the episodes of bizarre behavior were caused by unusually high levels of stress or by physical illness. Finally, people may respond to the rule violation by balancing it, recognizing it as a violation but de-emphasizing its significance in light of the actor's good qualities.

The man who witnessed Hanna's behavior looked around, spotted the clerk, and reported the act. In doing so, he labeled the actor. Labeling involves a (re)definition of the actor's social status; the man placed Hanna into the category of "shoplifter" or "thief." The clerk, in turn, probably defined Hanna as "another shoplifter." Although labeling is triggered by a behavior, it results in a redefinition or typing of the actor. As we shall see, this has a major impact on people's perceptions of and behavior toward the actor.

Determinants of the Reaction

What determines how an observer reacts to rule breaking? Reactions depend on three aspects of the rule violation, including the nature of the actor, the audience, and the situation.

Actor Characteristics. Reactions to a type of deviance, such as mental illness, depend on the specific behavior. Given a vignette describing a person who meets the diagnostic criteria for mental illness, adults are more unwilling to interact with (for example, have as a neighbor or coworker) someone who is dependent on drugs (72 percent) or alcohol (56 percent) than someone who has schizophrenia (48 percent) or depression (37 percent). People who view these behaviors as caused by stress are less likely to reject interaction with the person. The belief most closely associated with rejection is the belief that such persons are dangerous (Martin, Pescosolido, & Tuch, 2000). The extent to which people have the same reaction depends on the degree of *normative consensus* about the act (Schmidtke, 2007). We noted that there are often both definitions favorable and unfavorable to a behavior; the greater the agreement that the act is undesirable/deviant/criminal, the more likely observers will label the actor.

Reaction to a rule violation often depends on who performs the act. First, people are more tolerant of rule breaking by family members than by strangers. The research cited earlier reveals extraordinary tolerance of spouses for bizarre, disruptive, and even physically abusive behavior. Many of us probably know of a family attempting to care for a member whose behavior creates problems for them. Second, people are more tolerant of rule violations by persons who make positive contributions in other ways. In small groups, tolerance is greater for persons who contribute to the achievement of group goals (Hollander & Julian, 1970). We seem to tolerate deviance when we are dependent on the person committing the act—perhaps because if we punish the actor, it will be costly for us. Third, a study of employee theft from restaurants found that coworkers were less likely to label the act as theft if they perceived the actor as more similar to themselves (Schmidtke, 2007). Fourth, we are less tolerant if the person has a history of rule breaking (Whitt & Meile, 1985).

Does gender affect reactions to deviant behavior? It depends on the behavior. An ingenious field experiment suggests that it does not affect responses to shoplifting. With the cooperation of stores, shoplifting events were staged near customers who could see the event. The experiment was conducted in a small grocery store, a large supermarket, and a large discount department store. The gender of the shoplifter, the appearance of the shoplifter, and the gender of the observer were varied. Neither the shoplifter's nor the customer's gender had an effect on the frequency with which the customer reported the apparent theft (Steffensmeier & Terry, 1973). Gender does affect reactions to persons who are mentally ill. People are more willing to interact with a woman who is described as having schizophrenia, depression, or drug or alcohol dependence than with a man described the same way. This is partly explained by the fact that women are perceived as less dangerous than men (Schnittker, 2000). We are less likely to label women than men for violations of criminal law (Haskell & Yablonsky, 1983), women are less likely to be kept in jail between arraignment and trial, and they receive more lenient sentences than men. One explanation for this differential treatment is that women are subject to greater informal control by family members and friends, and so are treated more leniently in the courts. A study of the influences on pretrial release and sentence severity found that both men and women with families received more lenient treatment; the effect was stronger for women (Daly, 1987).

On the other hand, research suggests that psychiatrists are more likely to label women as having a personality disorder than men (Dixon, Gordon, & Khomusi, 1995). Case histories were prepared that included symptoms of clinical disorders (as defined in the then-current *Diagnostic and Statistical Manual of Mental Disorders*, "*DSM-III*"; American Psychiatric Association, 1981) and personality disorders (*DSM-III*, Axis II). Personality disorders are generally less serious and more ambiguously defined than clinical disorders. The case histories were identical except for gender: male, female, or unspecified. The psychiatrists' diagnoses of clinical disorders were not influenced by gender, but they were more likely to diagnose women as having personality disorders than men with the same symptoms.

Audience Characteristics. The reaction to a violation of rules also depends on who witnesses it. Because groups vary in their norms, audiences vary in their expectations. People enjoying a city park on a warm day will react quite differently to a nude man walking through the park than will a group of people in a nudist park. Recognizing this variation in reaction, people who contemplate breaking the rules—by smoking marijuana, drinking in public, or jaywalking, for example—often make sure no one is around who will punish them.

People who violate rules often belong to groups. What influences whether other group members will ignore or punish a violation? One variable is the cohesiveness of the group. A laboratory experiment found that members of a cohesive group are more likely to reward a member who punished a deviant person than members of groups low in cohesion (Horne, 2001). As a result, members were more likely to punish violators. The effect was found in all-male groups and all-female groups.

Social identity theory (see Chap. 4) suggests that the group membership of the deviant person and the audience both influence reactions. We are motivated to maintain a positive in-group identity, and one means we employ is to maximize the differences we perceive between our group and other groups. Thus, we negatively judge members of our in-group who deviate, especially if the deviation is negative. We judge favorably an out-group member who deviates from his or her group's norms. A laboratory experiment tested these predictions; the results supported them (Abrams, Marques, Brown, & Henson, 2000).

An important influence on whether a witness will label a rule violation is the level of concern in the community about the behavior. Citizens who are concerned about drug use as a social problem are probably more alert for signs of drug sales and use, and are more likely to label someone as a drug user. A major determinant of the level of concern is the amount of activity by politicians, service providers, and the mass media calling attention to the problem (Beckett, 1994). Political rhetoric, intense media attention, and public concern over a perceived threat may combine to create a *moral panic* (Fox, 2013), leading to demands that rule-breakers be labeled and punished/treated.

Officials who routinely deal with suspects react very differently to suspected offenders than do most citizens. One study focused on officials working in a court-affiliated unit who evaluated suspected murderers following arrest. These officials had a stereotyped image of the type of person who commits murder (Swigert & Farrell, 1977). When lower-class male members of ethnic minorities committed murder, these officials believed that it was in response to a threat to their masculinity. For example, if an Italian-American truck driver was arrested for murder, they were likely to assume that he had killed the other man in response to verbal insults. This labeling based on a stereotype had important consequences. Suspects who fit this stereotype were less likely to be defended by a private attorney, more

likely to be denied bail, more likely to plead guilty, and more likely to be convicted on more severe charges.

Consider the example of a student with a drinking problem seeking help at a university counseling center. The treatment will depend on how counselors view student "troubles." One study found that the staff of a university clinic believed that students' problems could be classified into one of the following categories: problems in studying, choosing a career, achieving sexual intimacy, or handling personal finances; conflict with family or friends; and stress arising from sociopolitical activities. When a student came to the clinic because of excessive drinking, the therapist first decided which of these categories applied to this person's troubles; that is, which type of problem was causing this student to drink excessively. How the problem was defined in turn determined what the therapist did to try to help the student (Kahne & Schwartz, 1978).

Situational Characteristics. Whether a behavior is construed as normal or labeled as deviant also depends on the definition of the situation in which the behavior occurs. Marijuana and alcohol use, for example, are much more acceptable at a party than at work (Orcutt, 1975). Various sexual activities expected between spouses in the privacy of their home would elicit condemnation if performed in a public park in many parts of the United States.

Consider so-called gang violence. In some major cities, incidents in which teenage gangs assault each other are common. News media, police, and other outsiders often refer to such incidents as "gang wars." These events often occur in the neighborhoods where the gang members live. How do their parents, relatives, and friends react to such incidents? According to a study of one Chicano community, it depends on the situation (Horowitz, 1987). Young men are expected to protect their families, women, and masculinity. When violence results from a challenge to honor, the community generally tolerates it. On the other hand, if the violence disrupts a community affair, such as a dance or a wedding, it is not tolerated.

We often rely on the behavior of others to help us define situations. Our reaction to a rule violation may be influenced by the reactions of other members of the audience. The influence of the reactions of others is demonstrated in a field experiment of intrusions into waiting lines (Milgram, Liberty, Toledo, & Wackenhut, 1986). Members of the research team intruded into 129 waiting lines with an average length of six persons. One or two confederates approached the line and stepped between the third and fourth person. In some cases, other confederates served as buffers; they occupied the fourth and fifth positions and did not react to the intrusion. When the buffers were present, others in the line were much less likely to react verbally or nonverbally to the intrusion.

A good deal of research suggests that interpersonal violence—especially assaults and murders—often involves two young men and is triggered by a verbal insult (Katz, 1988). An aggressive response by a male to an insult often reflects masculine overcompensation; reaction to a threat to one's masculinity with an exaggerated demonstration of masculinity (Willer, Conlon, Rogalin, & Wojnowicz, 2013). But whether a remark is an insult is a matter of social definition. Not surprisingly, fights are more likely to erupt following a remark when there is a male audience and when the men have been drinking (Felson, 1994). A remark is less likely to lead to a fight if the audience includes women.

Consequences of Labeling

Assume that an audience defines an act as deviant. What are the consequences for the

actor and the audience? We will consider four possible outcomes.

Institutionalization of Deviance. In some cases, individuals who label a behavior as deviant may decide that it is in their own interest for the person to continue the behavior. They may, in fact, reward that person for the deviant behavior. If you learn that a good friend is selling drugs, you may decide to use this man as a source and purchase drugs from him. Over time, your expectations will change; you will come to expect him to sell drugs. If your drug-selling friend then decides to stop dealing, you may treat him as a rule breaker. Illegal activities by stockbrokers are likely to be ignored or encouraged by other employees and supervisors when all of them benefit economically from the activity (Zey, 1993). The process by which members of a group come to expect and support deviance by another member over time is called **institutionalization of deviance** (Dentler & Erikson, 1959).

Consider the following sworn statement by a former Enron employee, Timothy N. Belden:

> I was Director of Enron's California energy trading desk . . . [We] marketed and supplied electricity to Californian wholesale customers. . . . Beginning in approximately 1998, and ending in approximately 2001, I and other individuals in Enron agreed to devise and implement a series of fraudulent schemes through these markets. We designed the schemes to obtain increased revenue for Enron. . . .
>
> We exported and then imported amounts of electricity generated within California in order to receive higher, out-of-state prices from the [ISO] when it purchased "out of market." We scheduled energy that we did not have, or did not intend to supply. (*United States of America v. Timothy Belden*, U.S. Dis-

trict Court, Northern District of California, Doc. CR 02-0313 MJJ, October 17, 2002)

Note the repeated use of "we"; Belden and other Enron employees supported (and expected the support of) one another as they engaged in these deviant activities. It is possible that support for their criminal activities extended to the highest levels of the corporation.

Sadly, history repeats itself. The Federal Energy Regulatory Commission had charged JP Morgan Ventures Energy with the same manipulation of the electricity markets in the western United States in 2010 and 2011. Notice that JP Morgan acknowledged the violations and the assessment of a civil penalty of $285 million was issued July 30, 2013 (Docket Nos. IN11-8-000, IN13-5-000: ORDER APPROVING STIPULATION AND CONSENT AGREEMENT, http://www.ferc.gov/EventCalendar/Files/20130730080931-IN11-8-000.pdf). These activities clearly reflect differential association among corporate employees, and a corporate culture that prioritizes making money over obeying the rules.

Backtracking. Even when an audience reacts favorably to a rule violation, the actor may decide to discontinue the behavior. This second consequence of labeling is called *backtracking*. It may occur after the actor learns that others label his or her act as deviant. Though some audiences react favorably, the actor may wish to avoid the reaction of those who would not react favorably—and the resulting punishment. Many teenagers try substances like marijuana once or twice. Although their friends may encourage its continued use, some youths backtrack because they want to avoid their parents' or others' negative reactions.

Effective Social Control. An audience that reacts negatively to rule breaking and

threatens or attempts to punish the actor may force the actor to give up further involvement in the deviant activity. This third consequence of labeling is known as *effective social control*. This reaction is common among friends or family members, who often threaten to end their association with an actor who continues to engage in deviance. Similarly, they may threaten to break off their relationship if the person does not seek professional help. In these instances, the satisfaction of the actor's needs is contingent on changing his or her behavior. Members of the audience also may insist that the actor renounce aspects of his or her life that they see as contributing to future deviance (Sagarin, 1975). If excessive drinking is due to job-related stressors, for example, family members may demand that the person find a different type of employment. Displays of remorse may also lead to reduced punishment for an offense (Robinson, Smith-Lovin, & Tsoudis, 1994).

Unanticipated Deviance. Still another possibility is that the individual may engage in further or unanticipated deviance. Note the use of the term "unanticipated." Negative reactions by members of an audience are intended to terminate rule-breaking activity. However, such reactions may, in fact, produce further deviance. This occurs when the audience's response sets in motion a process that leads the actor to greater involvement in deviance. This process and its outcomes are the focus of the next section.

LABELING AND SECONDARY DEVIANCE

Labeling a person as deviant may set in motion a process that has important effects on the individual. The process of societal reaction produces changes in the behavior of others toward the labeled individual and may lead to corresponding changes in his or her self-image. A frequent consequence of the process is involvement in secondary deviance and participation in a deviant subculture. In this section, we consider this process in detail.

Societal Reaction

Earlier in this chapter, we mentioned that labeling is a process of redefining a person. By categorizing a person as a particular kind of deviant, we place that person in a stigmatized social status (see Chap. 4). The deviant person (sex addict, "bipolar," thief) is defined as undesirable—not acceptable in conventional society—and frequently treated as inferior. There are two important consequences of stigma: status loss and social discrimination (Link & Phelan, 2001). The loss of status causes a gradual change in self-conception; the person comes to perceive the self as a type of deviant. Discriminatory behavior by others not only affects one's self-concept but constrains one's behavior and opportunities.

Being caught in a deviant act has important consequences. This youth may experience disrupted schooling and separation from family and friends as a result of being arrested. © filo/ iStock

Changes in the Behavior of Others. When we learn that someone is an alcoholic, a convicted "sex offender," or mentally ill, our perceptions and behavior toward that person change. For example, if we learn that someone has a drinking problem, we may respond to his or her request for a drink with "Do you think you should?" or "Why don't you wait until the food is served?" to convey our objection. We may avoid jokes about drinking in the person's presence, and we may stop inviting him or her to parties or gatherings where alcohol will be served.

A more severe behavioral reaction involves withdrawal from the stigmatized person (Kitsuse, 1964). For instance, the labeled shoplifter, alcoholic, or out(ed) gay teacher may be fired from his or her job. Behavioral withdrawal may occur because of hostility toward the deviant person, or it may reflect a sincere desire to help the person. For example, the employer who fires an alcoholic may do so because he dislikes alcoholics or because he believes that relief from work obligations will reduce the stress that may be causing the drinking problem.

Paradoxically, our reaction to deviance may produce additional rule breaking by the labeled person. We expect people who are psychologically disturbed to be irritable or unpredictable, so we avoid them to avoid an unpleasant interaction. The other person may sense that he or she is being avoided and respond with anger or distrust. This anger may cause coworkers to gossip behind his or her back; he or she may respond with suspicion and become paranoid. When members of an audience behave toward a person according to a label and cause the person to respond in ways that confirm the label, they have produced a **self-fulfilling prophecy** (Merton, 1957). Lemert (1962) documents a case in which such a sequence led to a man's hospitalization for paranoia.

Self-Perception of the Deviant. Another consequence of stigmatized social status is that it changes the deviant person's self-image. A person labeled deviant often incorporates the label into his or her identity. This redefinition of oneself is due partly to feedback from others who treat the person as deviant. Moreover, the new self-image may be reinforced by the individual's own behavior. Repeated participation in shoplifting, for example, may lead Hanna to define herself as a thief.

Redefinition is facilitated by the social programs and agencies that deal with specific types of deviant persons. Such agencies pressure persons to acknowledge that they are deviant. Admitting that one purchased a term paper on the Internet will often lead student personnel workers and deans to go easy on a cheater, especially if it is a first offense. Failure to acknowledge the action may lead to suspension or dismissal from the college. Admitting that one is mentally ill is often a prerequisite for psychiatric treatment (Goffman, 1959a). Mental health professionals believe that a patient cannot be helped until the individual recognizes his or her problem. Employees of an agency that provided jobs for unemployed persons viewed their clients' employment problems as partly the result of individual failure (Miller, 1991). To receive agency services, clients had to agree with this view and change their behavior accordingly.

Thus, the deviant person experiences numerous pressures to accept a stigmatized identity. Acceptance of a stigmatized identity has important effects on self-perception. Everyone has beliefs about what people think of specific types of deviant persons. Accepting a label such as "thief," "drunk," or "bipolar" leads a person to expect that others will stigmatize and reject him or her, which in turn produces self-rejection. Self-rejection makes subsequent deviance more likely (Kaplan, Martin, & Johnson,

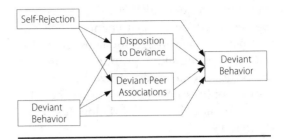

FIGURE 16.2 The Relationship of Self-Rejection to Deviant Behavior

A person who engages in deviant behavior anticipates that others will reject him or her, which, in turn, can lead to self-rejection. A longitudinal study collected data from junior high school students three times, each 1 year apart. At Time 1, reported participation in deviance was positively related to self-rejection (feeling one is no good, a failure, rejected by parents and teachers). Self-rejection at Time 1 was associated with more favorable dispositions (attitudes) toward deviance but a decreased likelihood of associating with other deviants 1 year later (at Time 2). Favorable dispositions and deviant associations at Time 2, as well as deviance at Time 1, were related to increased deviance—theft, gang violence, drug use, and truancy—at Time 3.

Source: Kaplan, Johnson, & Bailey, "Deviant Peers and Deviant Behavior: Further Elaboration of a Model," *Social Psychology Quarterly,* 50(3), 281, 1987. Used with permission from the American Sociological Association.

1986). In a study of junior high school students, data were collected three times at 1-year intervals. Self-rejection (that is, feeling that one is no good, a failure, rejected by parents and teachers) was related to more favorable dispositions (definitions) toward deviance and to an increased likelihood of associating with deviant persons 1 year later. A high disposition and associations with deviant peers were related to increased deviance—theft, gang violence, drug use, and truancy—1 year later (Kaplan, Johnson, & Bailey, 1987). Figure 16.2 summarizes these relationships. Delinquent behavior, in turn, is associated with reduced self-esteem (McCarthy & Hoge, 1984).

In short, labeling may set in motion a cycle in which changes in the labeled person's behavior produce changes in other people's behavior, which in turn changes the deviant person's self-image and subsequent behavior. Self-fulfilling prophecies can also be positive. One study assessed the expectations of 98 sixth-grade math teachers for their students (N 1,539) (Madon, Jussim, & Eccles, 1997). Teachers' expectations (positive or negative) predicted performance much better for students who were low achievers. Also, teachers' overestimates—that is, positive expectations—predicted actual achievement better than their underestimates. Perhaps positive expectations inspire underachievers.

Although more attention has been given to situations in which others label the person, some persons become committed to deviance without such labeling. For example, some persons voluntarily seek psychiatric treatment; some of these cases reflect self-labeling (Thoits, 1985). People know that others view certain behaviors as symptoms of mental illness. If they observe themselves engaging in those behaviors, they may label themselves as mentally ill. A study of persons who had experienced a psychiatric disorder in the prior 12 months, measured by self-reports of symptoms, found that persons with more education, and who are not living in poverty, were more likely to voluntarily seek treatment (Thoits, 2005). This probably reflects in part greater information about mental illness and access to mental health services.

Secondary Deviance

A frequent outcome of the societal reaction process is **secondary deviance**, in which a person engages increasingly in deviant behavior as an adjustment to others' reactions (Lemert, 1951). Usually, the individual becomes openly and actively involved in the deviant role, adopting the clothes, speech, and mannerisms associated with it. For ex-

ample, initially, a person with a drinking problem may drink only at night and on weekends to prevent his or her drinking from interfering with work. Once the person adopts the role of "heavy drinker" or "alcoholic," however, he or she may drink continuously. An attractive 19-year-old latina woman answered an ad for models; at first, she modeled lingerie in provocative poses, somewhat tentatively and anxiously. At the urging of the photographer, and for more money, she did some nude shots, and as she got increasingly comfortable displaying her body, finally engaged in some explicit stills. Her parents found some of the photos and were horrified; they kicked her out. Within 6 months, she moved to San Fernando Valley and signed on with Vivid Entertainment. She makes $1,500 per film and hangs with other actors and film producers in the community.

As an individual becomes openly and regularly involved in deviance, he or she may increasingly associate with others who routinely engage in the same or related activity. The individual may join a **deviant subculture**—a group of people whose norms encourage participation in the deviance and who regard positively those who engage in it. Subcultures provide not only acceptance but also the opportunity to enact deviant roles. Through a deviant subculture, the would-be drug dealer or commercial sex worker can gain access to customers more readily.

Subcultural groups are an attractive alternative for deviant persons for two reasons. First, these people are often forced out of nondeviant relationships and groups through others' reactions. As family and friends progressively break off relationships with them, they are compelled to seek acceptance elsewhere. Second, membership in subcultural groups may result from the deviant person's desire to associate with persons who are similar and who can provide them with feelings of social acceptance and self-worth (Cohen, 1966). Deviant persons are no different from others in their need for positive reflected appraisals.

Deviant subcultures help persons cope with the stigma associated with deviant status. We have already noted that deviant persons are often treated with disrespect and sanctioned by others for their activity. Such treatment threatens self-esteem and produces fear of additional sanctions. Subcultures help the deviant person cope with these feelings. They provide a vocabulary of motives—beliefs that explain and justify the individual's participation in the behavior.

The norms and belief systems of subcultures support a positive self-conception. In the early 1970s, a commercial sex workers' rights group, COYOTE (Cast Off Your Old, Tired Ethics), emerged in San Francisco. Although it has not obtained the legalization of prostitution, it did enhance the self-images of its members (Weitzer, 1991). In 2012 it had branches in San Francisco and Los Angeles, and continued to advocate for sex workers' rights. Many people think that nudists are exhibitionists who take off their clothes to get sexual kicks. Nudists, on the other hand, consider themselves morally respectable and hold several beliefs designed to enhance that claim: (1) nudity and sexuality are unrelated, (2) there is nothing shameful about the human body, (3) nudity promotes a feeling of freedom and natural pleasure, and (4) nude exposure to the sun promotes physical, mental, and spiritual well-being. There are also specific norms—"no staring," "no sex talk," and "no body contact"—designed to sustain these general beliefs (Weinberg, 1976). The belief systems of deviant subcultures provide the social support the person needs to maintain a positive self-image.

A study of the networks of persons having their first contact with the mental health system clearly documents these dynamics (Perry, 2011). Respondents reported experiences of people being anxious around them, unwilling to make friends, and cutting off relationships with them. Respondents diagnosed with schizophrenia and bipolar disorder, and who had high levels of symptoms, were more likely to report these reactions. At the same time, some respondents reported having supportive networks of people who knew about their illness and helped them to cope with it. People with more perceptible cognitive, emotional and behavioral symptoms were more likely to report having a supportive core group, perhaps because the visible symptoms elicited concern in others.

Joining a deviant subculture often stabilizes participation in one form of deviance. It also may lead to involvement in additional forms of deviant behavior. For instance, many commercial sex workers become drug users through participation in a subculture.

FORMAL SOCIAL CONTROLS

So far, this chapter has been concerned with **informal social control**—the reactions of family, friends, and acquaintances to rule violations by individuals. Informal controls are probably the major influence on an individual's behavior. In modern societies, however, there are often elaborate systems set up specifically to process rule breakers. Collectively, these are called **formal social controls**—agencies given responsibility for dealing with violations of rules or laws. Typically, the rules enforced are written, and, in some cases, punishments also may be specified. The most prominent system of formal social control in our society is the criminal justice system, which includes police, courts, jails, and prisons. A second system of formal social control is the juvenile

Deviant subcultures create opportunities for people to enact roles not acceptable elsewhere in society. This nudist camp provides a place where people can undress without attracting attention or being arrested. © Regis Duvignau/Reuters/Corbis

justice system, which includes juvenile officers, social workers, probation officers, courts, and treatment or detention facilities. A third system of formal social control deals with mental illness. It includes mental health professionals, commitment procedures, and institutions for the mentally ill and mentally impaired.

Formal Labeling and the Creation of Deviance

Most of us think of these agencies as reactive—as simply processing individuals who have already committed crimes or who are mentally retarded or in need of psychiatric treatment. But these agencies do much more than take care of persons already known to be deviant. It can be argued that the function of formal social control agencies is to select members of society and identify or certify them as deviant (Erikson, 1964).

In the 1990s, crime control became big business in U.S. society. Federal and state governments provided funds to hire thousands of additional police officers, sheriff's deputies, and federal agents. Many states built new prisons. Additional officers and new prisons require large investments in new equipment. It has been suggested that there is a crime control industry, with many people lobbying for its preservation and growth (Chambliss, 1994). More officers and prisons lead to more arrests and further increases in prison populations. Is this expansion due to real increases in crime? No. Crime has not increased substantially in the past 25 years. In fact, rates of violent crime were stable from 1973 to 1993; since 1993, they have fallen by more than 52 percent. Rates of property crime have been declining steadily since 1975 (U.S. Department of Justice, 2011). What has increased is political rhetoric on and mass media attention to the level of crime, leading the public to perceive an increase. Politicians have used this perception as a basis for fear campaigns to enlist support for the expansion of formal control systems.

Functions of Labeling. Of what value is labeling people as "criminals," "delinquents," or "mentally ill"? There are three functions of labeling persons as deviant: (1) to provide concrete examples of undesirable behavior, (2) to provide scapegoats for the release of tensions, and (3) to unify the group or society.

First, the public identification of deviance provides concrete examples of how we should not behave (Cohen, 1966). When someone is actually apprehended and sanctioned for deviance, the norms of society are made starkly clear. For instance, the arrest of someone for shoplifting dramatizes the possible consequences of taking things that do not belong to us. Scandals involving sexual misconduct by high-profile politicians heighten awareness of politicians engaging in sexual harassment, sexting, and sexual activity with commercial sex workers.

According to the **deterrence hypothesis**, the arrest and punishment of some individuals for violations of the law deters other persons from committing the same violations. To what extent does general deterrence really affect people's behavior? Most analysts agree that the objective possibility of arrest and punishment does not deter people from breaking the law. Rather, conformity is based on people's perceptions of the likelihood and severity of punishment. Thus, youths who perceive a higher probability that they will be caught and that the punishment will be severe are less likely to engage in delinquent behavior (Jensen, Erickson, & Gibbs, 1978). Perceptions of risk are affected by personal experience; youths who have committed specific acts of delinquency but have not been punished perceive lower risk of sanction for those

acts (Carmichael, Langton, Pendell, Reitzel, & Piqure, 2005). Similarly, a study of theft of company property by employees found that those who perceived greater certainty and severity of organizational sanctions for theft were less likely to have stolen property (Hollinger & Clark, 1983).

For the punishment of some offenders to deter others, others must be aware of it. Again, research with youths found that those who had observed their peers getting away with delinquent acts perceived less risk of punishment, whereas those who observed peers receiving punishment following delinquent acts perceived greater risk (Matsueda, Kreager, & Huizinga, 2006). What about publicity? Does publicizing punishment influence perceived risk? In recent years, executions of murderers have been widely publicized. Does this publicity deter murder? Specifically, does coverage of executions on the evening news on network television lead to a reduction in homicide rates? A study of news coverage and homicide rates from 1976 through 1987 found no relationship (Bailey, 1990).

Perceived certainty of sanctions generally has a much greater effect on persons who have low levels of moral commitment (Silberman, 1976; Wright, Caspi, Moffit, & Paternoster, 2004). People whose morals define a behavior as wrong are not as affected by the threat of punishment. For example, personal moral beliefs are a more important influence on whether adults use marijuana than the fear of legal sanctions (Meier & Johnson, 1977). Adults who believe that the use of marijuana is wrong do not use it, regardless of their perception of the likelihood that they will be sanctioned for its use.

We have seen that personal experience or peers' experience of punishment is associated with greater perceived risk. This suggests that more vigorous or aggressive arrest practices (a "crackdown")

Some crime and delinquency prevention programs involve having persons convicted of breaking the law talk to youths about the nature and consequences of deviance. By publicizing the penalties for deviance, such programs attempt to deter others from breaking the law. © AP Photo/ Matt Rourke

should increase perceived risk, which in turn should reduce crime. A study of arrest practices in one precinct in New York City found that increases in the number of arrests per officer and total arrests for violent crimes produced decreases in cases of robbery and burglary. But the effect was not linear; beyond a threshold, further increases in arrests produced a larger number of robberies and burglaries. Also, arrest vigor did not produce decreases in assault, suggesting that deterrence effects of crackdowns occur for economic crimes and crimes in public, but not noneconomic crimes that occur in private (Kane, 2006).

A second function of the public identification of deviant persons is to provide a scapegoat for the release of tension. Many people face threats to the stability and security of their daily lives. Some fear the possibility that they will be victimized by aggressive behavior or the criminal activity of others. The existence of such threats arouses tension. Persons identified publicly as deviant persons provide a focus for these fears and insecurities. Thus, the publicly identified deviant person becomes the concrete threat we can deal with decisively.

This scapegoating process is illustrated among the Puritans, who came to New England in the 1600s to establish a community based on a specific Christian theology. As time passed, groups within the community periodically challenged the ministers' claims that they were the sole interpreters of the theology. Furthermore, the community faced the threat of Native American attacks and the problems of daily survival in a harsh environment. In 1692, a group of young women began to behave in such bizarre ways as screaming, convulsing, crawling on all fours, and barking like dogs. The community focused attention on these women. The physicians defined them as "witches," representatives of Satan, and the entire community banded together in search of others who were under the "Devil's influence." The community imprisoned many persons suspected of sorcery and sent 22 persons to their deaths. Thus, the witch hunt provided a scapegoat—an outlet for people's fears and anxieties (Erikson, 1966).

A third function of the public identification of deviant persons is to increase the cohesion and solidarity of society. Nothing unites the members of a group like a common enemy (Cohen, 1966). Deviant persons, in this context, are "internal enemies"—persons whose behavior threatens the morale and efficiency of a group. Should the solidarity of the group be threatened, it can be restored by identifying one member as deviant and imposing appropriate sanctions. Suppose you are given the case study of a boy with a history of delinquency who is to be sentenced for a minor crime. You are asked to discuss the case with three other persons and decide what should be done. One member of the group argues for extreme discipline, whereas you and the other two favor leniency. Suddenly, an expert in criminal justice, who has been sitting quietly in the corner, announces that your group should not be allowed to reach a decision. How might you deal with this threat to the group's existence? The reasoning just outlined suggests that the person who took the extreme position will be identified as the cause of the group's poor performance and that the other members will try to exclude him or her from future group meetings. A laboratory study used exactly this setup, contrasting the reaction of threatened groups to the person taking the extreme position with the reaction of nonthreatened groups. In the former condition, the person taking the extreme position was more likely to be stigmatized and rejected (Lauderdale, 1976).

Thus, controlled amounts of deviant behavior serve important functions. If deviance is useful, we might expect control agencies to "create" deviance when the functions it serves are needed. In fact, the number of persons who are publicly identified as deviant seems to reflect the levels of stress and integration in society (Scott, 1976). When integration declines, there is an increased probability of deviance. Eventually, the level and severity of deviance may reach a point where citizens will demand a "crackdown." Social control agencies will step up their activity, increasing the number of publicly identified deviant persons. This, in turn, will increase solidarity and lower stress, leading to an increase in the amount of informal control and a reduction in deviance.

The Process of Labeling. Labeling is not a simple, one-step procedure for formal agencies. The processing of rule breakers usually involves a sequence of decisions. At each step, someone has to decide whether to terminate the process or to pass the rule breaker on to the next step. Figure 16.3 shows the sequence of steps involved in processing criminal defendants.

Each of the control agents—police officers, prosecutors, and judges—has to make many decisions every day. Like anyone else, they develop cognitive schemas and rules that simplify their decision making. A very common police-citizen encounter occurs when an officer stops a motorist who has been drinking. What determines whether a driver who has been drinking is labeled a "drunken driver"? Officers on the street rely on a variety of subjective data, such as visible intoxication or the odor of alcohol (Myrstol, 2012), since the Breathalyzer or blood or urine test are usually available only at the police station. Research suggests that police officers develop a series of informal guidelines that they use in deciding whether to arrest the motorist. In one study of 195 police encounters with persons who had been drinking, arrests were more likely if the encounter occurred downtown and if the citizen was disrespectful (Lundman, 1974).

Prosecutors also develop informal rules that govern their decisions. For example, in one large Midwestern city, taking an object worth less than $100 is a misdemeanor, and conviction normally results in a fine. The theft of a more valuable object is a felony and results in a prison sentence. Because felony theft cases require much more time and effort, the prosecutor charged most persons arrested for shoplifting with misdemeanors, even if they had taken jewelry worth hundreds of dollars.

In many jurisdictions, probation officers are asked to prepare a presentencing report and to recommend a sentence for the convicted person. Research indicates that these officers have a set of typologies or schemas into which they sort persons (Lurigis & Carroll, 1985). Semistructured interviews with probation officers in one community identified 10 schemas, including *burglar, addict, gang member, welfare fraud,* and *conman.* Each schema was associated with beliefs about the motive for the crime and the appropriate treatment and prognosis. When officers were asked to evaluate sample cases, those fitting a schema were evaluated more

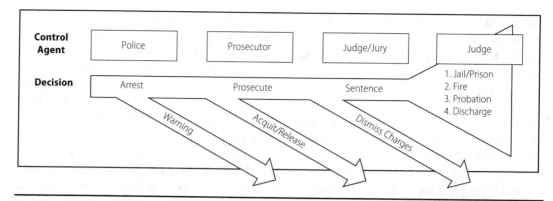

FIGURE 16.3 Formal Social Control: Processing Criminal Defendants

Formal social control often involves several control agents, each of whom makes one or more decisions. The first step in the criminal justice system is an encounter with a law enforcement officer. If you are arrested, the case is passed to a prosecutor, who decides whether to prosecute. If your case goes to court, the judge or jury decides whether you are guilty. Finally, the judge renders a sentence. These decision makers are influenced by their own personal attitudes, cognitive schemas, role expectations, and the attitudes of others regarding their decisions. Much research is devoted to the social psychological aspects of decision making in the criminal justice system.

quickly and confidently. More experienced officers were more likely to use similar schemas (Drass & Spencer, 1987).

Each step in this process involves interaction between professionals and the alleged rule breaker—and often members of his or her family. The professional's goal is to have the rule breaker and other laypersons accept the label. Research on the labeling of children with developmental disabilities suggests that family members are more likely to accept a diagnosis if the professional elicits family members' schemas and frames the diagnosis/label in those terms (Gill & Maynard, 1995).

Biases in Social Control. Not all persons who violate the rules are labeled. Most social control agencies process only some of those who engage in rule-breaking behavior. In the study of police encounters with drunken persons, only 31 percent were arrested (Lundman, 1974). In some cases, control agents may be influenced by the demeanor of the rule breaker, by the agent's schema, or by where the violation occurs.

This leads one to ask whether systematic biases exist in the social control system.

It has been suggested that control agents are more likely to label those people who have the least power to resist their certification as deviant (Quinney, 1970). This hypothesis predicts that lower-class persons and members of racial and ethnic minorities are more likely to be certified as deviant than upper-class, middle-class, and White persons. This hypothesis offers a radically different explanation for the correlation between crime and social class. Earlier in this chapter, we suggested that crime rates are higher for lower-class persons because they do not have access to nondeviant means of economic success. Here we are suggesting that crime rates are higher among lower-class persons because they are more likely to be arrested, prosecuted, and found guilty, even though the underlying rate of deviant activity may not vary as a function of social class.

Does social class or race influence how an individual is treated by control agents? One way to answer this question is by

Whether a police officer gives a citizen a traffic ticket or not depends partly on the demeanor of the citizen. Officers are more likely to ticket or arrest hostile, argumentative persons than polite and submissive ones. © Kali Nine LLC/iStock

studying police-citizen encounters through the ride-along method, in which trained observers ride in squad cars and systematically record data about police-citizen encounters. In the largest study of this kind, observers rode with some officers on all shifts every day for 7 weeks. Data were collected in Boston, Washington, and Chicago, and included 5,713 encounters. There was no evidence that Blacks were more likely to be arrested than Whites. Rather, arrests were more likely when a third party demanded an arrest, when the evidence was strong, and when the crime was serious (Black, 1980). A study of how police officers managed violent encounters between citizens found that arrest was more likely if the incident involved White persons; two men instead of one woman and one man, or two women; or if one person acted abusively toward the officer (Smith, 1987). On the other hand, research that included ride-alongs in

Washington, D.C., suggests that at least in that city, Blacks are subjected to more intense police surveillance than other racial/ethnic groups (Chambliss, 1994).

Police officers frequently have to make a quick decision about whether someone is dangerous or a "criminal." As noted above, they rely on schemas they learn in training and on the job. Research indicates that they rely on nonverbal cues such as speech disruptions, inappropriate smiles, and avoidance of eye contact as indicators of nervousness or deception. An analysis of videotaped police-citizen encounters included interactions with 40 African-American, 40 Caucasian and 40 Hispanic persons who were innocent, and 40 from each group in which there was evidence that the suspect had committed a crime. While guilty White men and women did display more frequent speech disruptions, innocent African-American persons were more likely to display these nonverbal behaviors than guilty ones (Johnson, 2007).

What about decisions by prosecutors? Do they entail discrimination based on race or class? Prosecutors are generally motivated to maximize the ratio of convictions to trials. This may be one criterion that citizens use in evaluating the performance of a district attorney. Prosecutors develop beliefs about which cases are "strong"—that is, likely to result in conviction. A study of a random sample of 980 defendants charged with felonies found that prosecutors are more likely to prosecute cases involving serious crimes where the evidence is strong and the defendant has a serious prior police record. Race was not generally influential (Myers & Hagan, 1979).

Does the social class of an arrested person influence how he or she is treated by the courts? Several studies of the handling of juvenile cases report little evidence of class or race bias. A study of cases in Denver and Memphis found that the seriousness of the offense and the youth's prior record were the major determinants of the sentence given (Cohen & Kluegel, 1978). Two longitudinal studies, of 9,945 boys in Philadelphia (Thornberry & Christenson, 1984) and of cases in Florida (Henretta, Frazier, & Bishop, 1986), found that the most important influence on the disposition of a charge was the disposition imposed for a prior offense or offenses.

A common practice in adult criminal cases is plea bargaining, in which a prosecutor and a defendant's lawyer negotiate a plea to avoid the time and expense of a trial. A single action frequently violates several laws. For instance, if a driver who has been drinking runs a red light and hits a pedestrian who later dies, that incident involves at last three crimes: drunken driving, failure to obey a signal, and vehicular manslaughter. These offenses vary in seriousness and thus in their associated sentences.

The prosecutor may offer not to indict the driver for manslaughter if a plea of guilty is entered to a drunken driving charge. The attorney may accept the offer, provided the prosecutor also recommends a suspended sentence.

Are the members of certain groups more likely to be tried or to get bigger reductions in sentences? An analysis of charge reduction or plea bargaining in a sample of 1,435 criminal defendants found that women and Whites received slightly more favorable reductions than men and Blacks (Bernstein, Kick, Leung, & Schulz, 1977). Another study of 1,213 men charged with felonies found that the characteristics of an offense—especially the seriousness of the crime and the strength of the evidence—were most important in determining the disposition. The outcomes of the cases were not related to age, ethnicity, or employment status (Bernstein, Kelly, & Doyle, 1977). A study of 296 women who killed another person found that whereas they were all initially charged with murder, in two-thirds of the cases, the charge was reduced to manslaughter or a lesser offense (Mann, 1996). Women in Southern cities and women who killed men were less likely to have the charge(s) reduced and received more severe sentences if convicted.

Among the persons convicted, do we find a class or racial bias in the length of the sentences given? One study focused on the sentences received by 10,488 persons in three Southern states: North Carolina, South Carolina, and Florida (Chiricos & Waldo, 1975). The researchers examined sentences for 17 different offenses and found no relationship between socioeconomic status or race and sentence length. Again, the individual's prior record was the principal variable related to sentence length. A study of a random sample of 16,798 felons convicted during the years 1976–1982 in Georgia looked at racial differences in sentencing (Myers & Talarico, 1986). In general, the seriousness of a crime was the principal influence on the sentence length. Another study of the influence of race on sentencing analyzed federal court proceedings for the years 1993–1996. The sentences given male defendants varied by race/ethnicity. For offenses of the same seriousness, there were small to moderate effects, with Whites receiving shorter sentences and Hispanics receiving longer ones; Blacks received intermediate sentences (Steffensmeier & Demuth, 2000).

Earlier, we discussed white-collar crime, which is often committed by middle-class and upper-class persons. Are white-collar offenders more likely to receive lenient sentences? A study of persons charged with embezzlement and tax, lending, credit, postal, and wire fraud found that within this group, high-status persons were no less likely to be imprisoned or to receive shorter sentences (Benson & Walker, 1988). The significant influences were the total amount of dollars involved and how widespread the offenses were. Blacks did receive longer sentences than Whites. It is sometimes argued that judges are lenient on high-status offenders because they suffer serious informal sanctions, such as the loss of a job. A study of the likelihood of job loss and the influence of job loss on sentence severity found no relationship (Benson, 1989). However, class position did influence job loss; high-status offenders and those whose frauds were larger in scale were less likely to lose their jobs.

Persons sentenced to prison may become eligible for parole. What influences decisions at this stage? A study in Alabama analyzed the influence of race. Alabama uses a two-stage process: a screening to determine who should be considered for parole, and a parole decision—whether to release the prisoner. Considering 762 cases, the results showed that race did not have a significant effect at either stage. At the preliminary stage, significant influences were seriousness of offense, time served, discipline while in prison, and parole officer's recommendation. The only significant influence on the decision was recommendations by prison personnel (Morgan & Smith, 2008).

Long-Term Effects of Formal Labeling

How long does the official label of "deviant" stick to a person? Can it be shaken? In contrast to the trial or hearing in which a person is formally certified as deviant, there is no formal ceremony terminating one's deviant status (Erikson, 1964). People are simply released from prison or mental hospital, or the final day of probation passes—with no fanfare. Does the individual regain his former status upon release, or does deviant status in our society tend to be for life?

Some argue that ex-convicts, ex-patients, and others who have been labeled as deviant face continuing pressures from family, friends, employers, and coworkers that prevent them from readjusting to normal life. Such pressures constitute a reminder of their former deviant status.

One domain in which persons who have been officially labeled might face discrimination is employment. In the United States, a good job is essential to health and welfare as an adult. Labeling theory asserts that contact with authorities will reduce one's occupational attainment, independently of the rule-breaking or deviant behavior. Longitudinal data allowed a study of the effect of contact with authorities (suspended from school, stopped by police, charged, convicted, sentenced, jailed) at ages 15 to 23 on status (employed, status, income) during ages 29 to 37 (Davies & Tanner, 2003). For males, suspension or being stopped had little effect; the more serious forms of contact, especially being jailed, had significant negative effects on average hours worked, status of job, and income. For women, suspension had negative effects; also, being sentenced and jailed had substantial impact, with incarceration resulting in a reduction in annual income of more than 50 percent! Another study of data from more than 3,600 men compared those who had been incarcerated with men who had not (Western, 2002); overall, incarceration reduced subsequent earnings by 19 percent, and also resulted in slower wage growth in later years. The impact on Black and Hispanic men was about twice as large as the impact on White men.

Discrimination in employment following formal labeling may occur because others perceive these persons as "delinquents," "ex-cons," or "crazies," and expect them to behave in ways consistent with the label. A study of the impact of a criminal record on decisions by employers used the audit method, which involves sending matched pairs of people (testers) to apply for real job openings. The pairs differ on some characteristic, and the researcher observes whether employers respond differently to the two people. Two young White men and two young Black men, matched on age, physical appearance, and style, applied for the same jobs 1 day apart. One man of each race had a criminal record—a felony drug conviction that resulted in 18 months in prison. Each tester posed as the convicted felon in alternate weeks. The dependent variable was whether the employer called back the young man for an interview. Having a record had a significant effect. For the White pair, the man without the record was called 34 percent of the time, whereas the man with the record was called 17 percent of the time. Among the Black testers, the percentages were 14 percent and 5 percent (Pager, 2003). Thus, the combination of being Black and having a criminal record makes it unlikely one will be called for an interview. This contributes to the high rates of unemployment in some minority communities.

Questionnaires and interviews with men hoping to transition from AIDS disability back to work focused on issues of identity. The men countered the stigma of living with AIDS by developing a romanticized anticipatory identity as worker/gay man/recovered. As they sought re-employment, they experienced discrimination and shame, and had to adjust to medical and other constraints, producing an actualized identity at odds with the anticipatory one. The transition back into the worker role was thus very stressful for some (Ghaziani, 2004).

Another approach to studying the long-term effects is to compare persons who have and have not been labeled. A study of psychiatrically disturbed persons compared the income and employment status of those who had been treated (labeled) with the income and status of those who had not been treated. Treatment was negatively associated with both income and employment (Link, 1982). The impact seemed to depend partly on whether occupational competence was developed before or after the onset of the illness. Men who had no history of competent work performance had more difficulty obtaining employment following hospitalization. Men who had a history of occupational competence usually kept their jobs, even during periods when their work performance was seriously affected.

Some persons turn a career history of deviance into an occupational asset by becoming a "professional ex-" (Brown, 1991a). Individuals with histories of alcohol or drug abuse or other problem behaviors sometimes become counselors, working with others who are involved in these behaviors. Professionalizing rather than giving up the deviant identity is another way of going straight.

A study of the long-term impact of being labeled as mentally ill suggests that it is not the label by itself that has impact but the label combined with changes in self-perception (Link, 1987). The study compared samples of residents and clinic patients from the same area of New York City. Three samples involved people who had been labeled: first-treatment contact patients, repeat-treatment contact patients, and formerly treated community residents. The other two groups were untreated "cases" (people with symptoms) and a sample of residents. All participants completed a scale that measured the belief that mental patients are stigmatized and discriminated against. High scores on the measure were associated with reduced income and unemployment in the labeled groups but not in the unlabeled ones. Later research shows that when people enter treatment, those who expect discrimination use strategies such as keeping their condition secret or withdrawing from interaction (Link, Cullen, Struening, Shrout, & Dohrenwend, 1989). This tends to cut them off from social support and interfere with their work performance.

A longitudinal study of recovery from mental illness obtained data from members of self-help groups ($N = 590$) and outpatients ($N = 90$) two times, 18 months apart. The results indicate that recovery is a complex process. As reported satisfaction with job status, income, place of residence, and time spent with family and friends increase, symptoms decrease. Decreases in symptoms over the 18-month period were associated with increases in self-esteem. In turn, we would expect increases in self-esteem to be associated with reduced symptoms and recovery (Markowitz, 2001). Thus, an important part of recovery is the quality of social, economic, and occupational roles available to the person.

The long-term effects of formal labeling on the reactions of others may be limited, because persons who have been labeled in the past engage in various tactics to prevent others from learning about their stigma. These tactics include selective concealment of past labeling, preventive disclosure to close friends, and various deception strategies (Miall, 1986). On the other hand, longitudinal research suggests that persons who have been publicly labeled and treated continue to anticipate rejection from others even though they no longer engage in the symptomatic behavior (Link, Struening, Rahav, Phelan, & Nuttbrock, 1997). A longitudinal study of 88 persons released following an average of 8 years of hospitalization measured experiences with rejection following release. Those who reported a larger number of such experiences subsequently attained low scores on mastery. Former patients' self-views appear to fluctuate, perhaps in response to alternating experiences of acceptance and stigma (Wright, Gronfein, & Owens, 2000). Thus, stigma may have lasting effects on a person's psychological well-being.

SUMMARY

Deviant behavior is any act that violates the social norms that apply in a given situation.

The Violation of Norms. (1) Norms are local, subcultural, or societal in scope. The repercussions of deviant behavior depend on which type of norm an individual violates. (2) Anomie theory asserts that deviance occurs when persons do not have legitimate means available for attaining cultural success goals. Possible responses to anomie include ritualism, retreatism, innovation, and rebellion. General strain theory suggests that emotions link structural position and behavior. (3) Control theory states that deviance occurs when an individual is not responsive to the expectations of others. This responsiveness, or social bond, includes attachment to others, commitment to long-term goals, involvement in conventional activities, and a respect for law and authority. Research indicates that social integration is associated with reduced rates of deviance in adolescence and adulthood. (4) Differential association theory emphasizes the importance of learning through interaction with others. Individuals often learn the motives and actions that constitute deviant behavior just as they learn socially approved behavior. (5) The routine activities perspective calls attention to situations that facilitate the convergence of offenders and targets, in the absence of a guardian.

Reactions to Norm Violations. Deviant behavior involves not only acts that violate social norms but also the societal reactions to these acts. (1) There are numerous possible responses to rule breaking. Very often, we ignore it. At other times, we deny that the act occurred, define the act as normal, excuse the perpetrator, or recognize the act but de-emphasize its significance. Only after an act is discovered and labeled "deviant" is it recognized as such. (2) Our reaction to rule breaking depends on the characteristics of the actor, the audience, and the situation. People often have a stereotyped image of deviant persons; these stereotypes influence how audiences react to rule violations. (3) The consequences of rule breaking depend on the reactions of the audience and the response of the rule breaker. If members of the audience reward the person, the deviance may become institutionalized. Alternatively, the person may decide to avoid further deviance, in spite of others' encouragement. If the person is punished, he or she may either give up the behavior or respond with additional rule violations.

Labeling and Secondary Deviance. The process of labeling has two important consequences. (1) It leads members of an audience to change their perceptions of and

behavior toward the actor. If they withdraw from the stigmatized person, they may create a self-fulfilling prophecy and elicit the behavior they expected from the actor. (2) Labeling often causes the actor to change his or her self-image and to come to define the self as deviant. This, in turn, may lead to secondary deviance—an open and active involvement in a lifestyle based on deviance. Such lifestyles are often embedded in deviant subcultures.

Formal Social Controls. Every society gives certain agents the authority to respond to deviant behavior. (1) In U.S. society, the major formal social control agents are the criminal justice, juvenile justice, and mental health systems. These agencies select persons and identify them as deviant through a sequence of decisions. In the criminal justice system, the sequence includes the decisions to arrest, prosecute, and sentence the person. Various factors influence each step in decision making, including the strength of the evidence, the seriousness of the rule violation, and the individual's prior record, and sometimes gender and race. (2) Contrary to popular belief, people do not systematically stigmatize former deviant persons. Most families do not continue to stigmatize relatives following their release from mental hospitals, and most employers do not stigmatize ex-patients who have established competent work records. On the other hand, employers may stigmatize minority men with prison records, and stigma may have long-term effects on the ex-deviant person's psychological well-being.

List of Key Terms and Concepts

Critical Thinking Skill:
Applying Stigmatizing Labels Critically

A major contribution of the labeling perspective on deviance is calling our attention to the fact that many of the words we use to describe people who engage in deviance are stigmatizing. Labels like "slut," "jd" (juvenile delinquent), "retard," "child molester," and "murderer" carry a strong negative evaluation. If we use such labels in conversation, it changes the attitudes of others toward the person; eventually the label gets back to the person and may have a negative impact on his self-image and mental health. So it is really important that we use these labels only when they are accurate. Therefore, the issues are (1) to what does the label refer exactly, and (2) does the person actually have that characteristic?

One concern is that the meaning of some labels is ambiguous to begin with. The term *slut* is used to refer to someone who is sexually promiscuous; but what does that mean? In practice it probably means different things to different people. So whether a woman is a slut is subjective; it depends on the standards of the person doing the labeling. They may have very different standards than you do.

We also reviewed research in this chapter that indicates that often a person is labeled a slut, gay or lesbian, or an alcoholic based on indirect evidence. The person applying the label may not have observed relevant behavior—sex with multiple partners, or excessive drinking. Labeling is often based on dress—showing a lot of skin, wearing colorful clothing—hanging out with a certain group, working in a certain occupation, or being a type of athlete ("all ___ are lesbians").

Labels are communicated through social interaction. If a friend tells you that Jade is lesbian and you repeat the label to others, you are uncritically accepting another person's judgment—a judgment you might not agree with if you knew "the facts." This, of course, is gossip, which can ruin another person's reputation, possibly wrongly. People have been forced to change schools and jobs, lost relationships, and even committed suicide because of gossip.

A critical thinker should not accept without question the accuracy of such labels. At a minimum, we should inquire how the person applying the label knows it is accurate. If the answer is "So-and-so said so" or "Everybody knows!" we should be skeptical.

CHAPTER 17

COLLECTIVE BEHAVIOR AND
SOCIAL MOVEMENTS

INTRODUCTION

- On March 12, 2011, at least 85,000 protestors gathered on the Capital Square in Madison, Wisconsin, alternately marching, yelling, chanting slogans, singing, and listening to speeches. They were protesting the passage (at 12:30 a.m. in a hastily called session) by the Republican-controlled legislature of Act 10, which severely curtailed public employees' union protections.

- On October 29, 2012, the San Francisco Giants baseball team won the World Series in a rare 4-game sweep of the Detroit Tigers in Detroit. Fans in San Francisco converged on the Civic Center, and small groups fanned out and set fires, broke windows, and vandalized cars and at least one city bus.

- On July 28, 2013, a large crowd moved through Huntington Beach, California, fighting, looting, and trashing property. Thousands of people had attended the U.S. Open of Surfing earlier in the day. A large fight broke out after the event ended; when police tried to break it up, the crowd surged into the downtown area.

- On August 14, 2013, hundreds of protestors marched through the streets of Alexandria, Egypt, armed with wooden clubs. The protestors, backers of ousted Egyptian president Mohamed Morsi, set fires, beat restaurant patrons, and stormed a police station.

Events such as these occur daily and sometimes receive international media coverage. In part because they occur frequently and often result in injuries, deaths, and property damage, they have been of interest to social scientists since the turn of the twentieth century.

Collective behavior refers to two or more persons engaged in behavior judged common or concerted on one or more dimensions (McPhail, 1991). This is an intentionally broad definition, because a wide range of events have been studied by social scientists as examples of collective behavior, including the four just described.

Collective behavior has three dimensions: spatial, temporal, and scale. With regard to space, collective behavior may occur at a single point (such as a street corner or building), at a larger site (such as a football stadium), or across an entire city or state. Temporal duration can vary from a few minutes (such as a violent attack by a gang) to several hours (such as a victory celebration) to several days (such as the widespread rioting in Stockholm, Sweden, in May of 2013). Collective behavior also varies in terms of the scale of the activity. We usually only learn about large-scale events, because newspapers and television news programs tend to report only the largest rallies, demonstrations, riots, victory celebrations, or political campaigns (Oliver & Myers, 1999; Myers & Caniglia, 2004). This focus on large-scale events colors the public's perception of the nature of collective behavior.

Research on "collective behavior" usually focuses on short-term, unorganized events—crowd behavior—but another segment of the field examines longer-term, relatively organized activities called "social movements."

In this chapter, we will examine both by discussing the following questions:

1. What social processes are involved in collective behavior?

2. What causes collective behavior? That is, what conditions facilitate it, and what conditions precipitate particular collective activities?

3. What factors influence the behavior of people when they gather in a crowd?

4. How do social movements develop? What are the processes by which social movements define issues and attract members?

5. How do social movement organizations mobilize supporters, especially into high-risk activism?

COLLECTIVE BEHAVIOR

Several years ago, the University of Wisconsin Badgers, playing a football game at home, beat the University of Michigan Wolverines, 13 to 10. When the game ended, fans in the stadium rushed onto the field to celebrate the win. An estimated 12,000 persons attempted to move forward onto the field from two sections of the stadium, seemingly in unison. But their progress was blocked by a 3-foot-high iron railing in front of the stands and by a 6-foot-high chain-link fence just beyond it. As the people in the back pressed forward, those in front were crushed against the barrier, and many fell and were trampled. The force ripped the railing out of its concrete moorings and flattened the fence. At least 68 people were injured, and 16 were hospitalized for at least one night. Miraculously, no one was killed. The incident received nationwide publicity.

Can social psychology help us understand incidents like these? Since the very beginnings of the discipline, social psychologists have been concerned with crowd behavior. As we will see, however, the earliest, or classic, perspectives on the crowd were largely uninformed by actual empirical study and, in fact, most of these theoretical notions have been thoroughly debunked

(McPhail, 1991). But these ideas about crowds and "mob psychology" live on in the popular press and the mind of the public. Therefore, we discuss them not only to provide an understanding of the historical development of thinking about collective behavior, but also to show that some of these popular ideas are, in fact, myths.

Crowds

A **crowd** is a temporary gathering of persons in close physical proximity, engaging in joint activity that is unconventional (Snow & Oliver, 1995). Participants may engage in one common activity (such as listening to a speech or spontaneously singing a song) or in concerted action (such as vandalizing cars or rescuing victims from a collapsed building) or in a large variety of activities (such as observing others in the crowd, milling, discussing actions with friends, looting, and running away from police). Crowd incidents often seem to be marked by high levels of emotion (Turner & Killian, 1972). For instance, in the surge at the Wisconsin football game, most persons in the stadium were Wisconsin fans and were elated at the unexpected victory over a powerful rival.

The classic perspective on crowds has its roots in the writings of Gustave Le Bon (1895) and focuses much of its attention on emotion in the crowd. According to Le Bon and other early writers, emotion in a crowd produces unity among its members and gives direction to the crowd's behavior (Locher, 2002; McPhail, 1991; Miller, 2000). Le Bon referred to this as "the mental unity of the crowd." This unanimity is then supposed to lead participants to think, feel, and act in ways that are different than if each member were alone. Thus, the elation shared by the Wisconsin fans led them to want to celebrate on the field, whereas they might not have tried to enter the field if it weren't for the influence of others. If these persons all had different feelings, the surge would not have occurred.

Deindividuation. One influence on behavior in crowds is that the members may feel more anonymous in the large group than they usually do. This **deindividuation** can result in a temporary reduction in self-awareness and sense of personal responsibility (Festinger, Pepitone, & Newcomb, 1952). This can make it easier for the person to act on impulse and to engage in behavior that violates social norms—such as shoving hard against others, breaking windows, or overturning cars. Social psychologists have long thought that this effect arises from a reduced sense of self-awareness (Diener, 1980), increased arousal, and the diffusion of responsibility (Zimbardo, 1969) (see Chap. 10). More recently, however, some social psychologists have recognized the possibility that behavior in deindividuated situations may actually be the result of conforming to norms that are specific to the situation (Postmes & Spears, 1998). This view is more consistent with sociological understandings of crowds such as the emergent norm theory discussed later. Furthermore, although the effects of deindividuation have been amply demonstrated in laboratory settings, it is considerably more controversial whether individuals in crowds experience marked degrees of deindividuation in the first place. In fact, most people in crowds attend as part of a group of friends or family members and are thus not particularly anonymous (McPhail, 1991). At the protest in Madison, most persons came with family, friends, or coworkers rather than as individuals.

Contagion. People in general have a tendency to imitate the behavior of others. When many people are crowded into a relatively small area, imitation can spread a behavior very quickly. When one person provides a novel model for behavior, it can quickly be assessed and performed by others in the crowd. The outbreak of violence in the Super Bowl XXXII celebration that followed the Denver Broncos win occurred when a group of people began kicking in the windows of an Athlete's Foot store. This behavior spread; others began to break windows in neighboring stores.

Le Bon's understanding of crowd behavior was deeply influenced by his understanding and observation of French politics (Miller, 2000). The tremendous interpersonal violence that accompanied the French Revolution and its long aftermath provided a frightening model of crowd behavior. Le

The behavior that occurs in groups and crowds often seems very different from behavior in our daily routines. Coordination of activity in a crowd can produce an innocuous, even fun, outcome, such as this water balloon attack. Or it can result in something much more serious, such as a destructive riot. Collective behavior scholars try to understand the dynamics that produce both kinds of action. © Matthias Balk/dpa/Corbis

Bon tried to understand how people could participate in such extraordinary fits of violence and revert to their normal routines only hours later. He concluded that a disease-like **contagion** was spreading through the crowd and infecting everyone present. Thus, an unconscious contagious effect transformed individuals in crowds into a unanimous mass. He thought the hypnotized mass was highly suggestible and thus could easily be turned to destructive behavior.

Contemporary events that appear to reflect contagion involve a number of people in close proximity displaying the same behavior or symptoms of illness, with no apparent physical (chemical, biological) cause. A highly publicized case involved more than 20 high school students in Le Roy, New York, who in 2011 developed uncontrollable arm swings or tics within a 3-month period. An investigation revealed no plausible physical cause. These incidents are variously termed mass or collective hysteria, or *mass psychogenic illness.* It is believed that these events occur when someone who is under stress "converts" the emotional disturbance into a physical symptom. Others in the vicinity experiencing stress observe the behavior and adopt it. These events often occur in schools or workplaces. Most such incidents involve women. In one 3-day period in 2005, 29 students in a Michigan high school became ill, experiencing headache and light-headedness. The school was evacuated twice, so that emergency response teams could search for possible causes. After the second evacuation, federal and state specialists were brought in. A thorough assessment was carried out of the air, water, and infrastructure of the building over the next 3 days; all of the findings were normal. Investigators concluded this was probably a case of MPI (US DHHS, 2006). All of the evidence suggests that the students' "symptoms" were

reactions to unusual things happening to others in the vicinity; 22 of the 29 persons experiencing symptoms were female; and symptoms resolved within minutes or a few hours of leaving the building. Such incidents gain momentum from attention and prolonged media exposure. Camera crews from major networks descended on Le Roy, New York, and were constantly trying to interview those affected, their families, and friends and neighbors. Such attention can encourage the spread of the behavior.

Myths about Crowds. Although casual and unsystematic observation of crowds has a tendency to produce impressions similar to Le Bon's, social scientists have produced evidence that these notions of contagion and the accompanying view of mob psychology are simply wrong (McPhail, 1991; Miller, 2000). Over 40 years ago, sociologist Carl Couch (1968) summarized research on crowds and identified a number of stereotypes of crowds held by social scientists and the broader public. These stereotypes have been so difficult to shake that collective behavior scholars now refer to them as "myths"! Recently, David Schweingruber and Ronald Wohlstein (2005) summarized the seven dominant myths about crowds:

- **Irrationality.** Although people in crowds do things that to the outsider look irrational, research shows that people are no less rational in their decision-making processes when they are in crowd situations than they are at other times. Even in emergency evacuation situations where we might expect people to panic (for example, the evacuation of the World Trade Center during the September 11, 2001, attacks), people remain orderly and calm throughout (Tierney, 2002).
- **Emotionality.** People are engaged emotionally in crowd situations, but

crowds do not cause individuals to supplant rationality with emotion, nor is emotionality the exclusive domain of crowds by any means.

- **Suggestibility.** Despite how it may appear to an outsider, people in crowds are not particularly likely to obey the directives of others or to imitate mindlessly other behavior they see. If crowds are so easily suggestible, one might ask why they do not disperse immediately when asked to by the authorities!

- **Destructiveness.** Crowd situations sometimes end up producing some kind of destruction or violence. But even though these violent episodes may be emphasized by the media, and thus become associated with crowds (Myers & Caniglia, 2004), violent crowds are very much the exception rather than the rule (McPhail, 1994). Furthermore, even in crowds that do produce violence, only a small fraction of the crowd is engaged in any kind of destructive act. In San Francisco, of the thousands of fans gathered at the Civic Center, only an estimated 100 engaged in destructive acts. Therefore, it does not seem that being in a crowd causes all/most/many individuals to become violent.

- **Spontaneity.** Crowds are often thought to be spontaneous in producing action that is not thought through, not rational, and unpredictable. Once again, this myth seems to emerge from the outsider not being able to predict what the crowd will do rather than from those in the crowd engaging in unplanned action. Much crowd action, and in particular the protest crowds that are so often the focus of crowd psychology, require a great deal of planning. Furthermore, those in crowds rely on well-established scripts

and norms to guide their action much of the time (Tilly, 1995). Consider the emergence of the "wave" in a football stadium. Although the individual fan might not be able to predict when it will occur, the crowd at the game is responding to an action planned by the cheer squad and knows what to do as a result of prior experience seeing or being part of the wave. It is not a spontaneous act.

- **Anonymity.** As mentioned earlier, individuals are rarely anonymous in crowds. They assemble at the event with friends and family and usually stay with that group throughout the event.

- **Unanimity.** Although people in crowds are sometimes thought to all be doing the same thing at the same time, those who have actually systematically observed crowds have found that people are engaged in a huge variety of activities while in crowds (Turner & Killian, 1987), and rarely can one observe even near-unanimous activity—even at a rally where everyone is supposed to be paying attention to a speaker or praying together (Schweingruber & McPhail, 1999).

Some of these seven beliefs about crowds may seem very intuitively attractive to you, but as has often been shown to be the case throughout this textbook, systematic social psychology does not always verify our commonsense understandings. To better illustrate various aspects (perhaps unexpected) of crowd behavior, Box 17.1 discusses a crowd rush at a rock concert, and how people's behavior in the rush was quite different than the portrayals of the event in the popular press suggested.

Emergent Norms. *Emergent norm theory,* proposed by Turner and Killian (1972,

BOX 17.1 "Stampede" at The Who Concert

In December of 1979, the rock group The Who were preparing to play a concert at Cincinnati's Riverfront Coliseum. The concert promoters had arranged open seating for the concert, meaning that whoever got to a seat first claimed it for the concert. As a result, concertgoers began gathering at the Coliseum some 6 hours before the concert was scheduled to begin. By the time the doors opened, thousands of people were waiting to enter the concert. As the crowd surged forward to enter the Coliseum, the crowd became compacted and people near the front were caught in a massive crush. Some fell and were trampled by the crowd. In the end, 11 people were killed and many more injured.

The press and other observers reacted angrily to the incident, decrying the "mob psychology" that seemed to have produced incredibly callous behavior on the part of the concertgoers. The press called on traditional theories of crowd behavior to characterize what happened. They believed either that the crowd situation had transformed people into ruthless monsters who were willing to kill other people just to get a better seat at the concert or that the concert was a gathering of sociopaths who "stomped 11 persons to death [after] having numbed their brains on weed, chemicals, and Southern Comfort" (Ryoko, 1979).

Aware that the traditional theories of crowd behavior had serious shortcomings, sociologist Norris Johnson examined the crush at the concert to determine how accurate the press had been in characterizing the events, and if there was any empirical evidence for or against the traditional theories of crowds. Johnson found that systematic, detailed investigation revealed a quite different set of behaviors than what had been reported. First, the concertgoers' behavior could not be described as "unregulated competition" for seats. People in the crowd near the area where the injuries occurred reported that everyone in the area was desperately trying to help others. When the first group of approximately 25 people fell, others tried to form a protective ring around them. Unfortunately, the immense pressure from behind them forced them either to walk across the fallen group or to fall into it themselves. Others reported trying to help or to get help for other people, but everyone around was trapped by the crowd. People reported not being able to move their arms, and others were carried along by the crowd, unable to touch the ground for long periods.

Second, social norms were not suspended during the surge. For example, one norm in our society is that men, by virtue of being stronger, should help women. During the crush, men did not abandon this norm and just attend to their own interests. Instead, they offered much more help than they received, and offered the majority of their help to women.

In the end, it is clear that the structure of the situation had much more to do with the emergence of the crush than with transformative contagion or amoral, individualistic behavior.

For one thing, communication in the crowd was extremely limited. The only ones who knew that people were being hurt were those close to the injured. The vast majority of the people in the crowd had no idea what was happening and were just moving forward in what they perceived as a routine situation. A second structural problem was that the crowd had been allowed to build up to such a large number with no place to go until the doors were opened. When the doors were opened, too few were opened to accommodate the large number of people who were waiting. Those at the back of the crowd could see that the doors were open—a signal to move forward—but they had no idea that they were moving forward more rapidly than those in the front could move through the doors.

Source: Adapted from Norris R. Johnson, "Panic at The Who Concert Stampede: An Empirical Assessment," *Social Problems*, Vol. 34, No. 4: 362–373. © 1987, The Society for the Study of Social Problems Inc. Used by permission. All rights reserved. http://www.ucpress.edu/journals.

1987), was constructed to correct the mistakes of earlier crowd theorists. Emergent norm theory applies to collective behavior that occurs when people find themselves in an undefined or unanticipated situation. The situation may be novel, so there are few cultural norms to guide or direct action. For instance, in recent years, there have been several incidents in which a person with a gun walked into a school and opened fire. On December 14, 2012, Adam Lanza entered Sandy Hook Elementary School in Newtown, Connecticut, by shooting his way through a locked door. Confronted by three school personnel, he shot and killed two of them, then entered a first-grade classroom and shot and killed all but one of the students. Witnesses described chaotic scenes in several classrooms during the attack. Such incidents are completely unexpected, and there are no behavioral guidelines; people don't know what to do. In other cases, the social structure may be temporarily disrupted by a natural disaster—such as a tornado—or by an event such as a citywide strike by police officers. Another possibility is that there may be conflicting definitions of how people should behave. To act in these situations, those present must develop a shared definition of the situation and the associated behavioral norms.

In all these circumstances, people want to find out what is going on or what they should do. Because they need information, conventional barriers to communication may break down. Strangers talk to one another or to members of groups they usually avoid. Furthermore, the usual standards of judgment and morality may be suspended (although research has shown that this is usually quite rare). **Rumor**—communication through informal and often novel channels that cannot be validated—can exert a major influence on the emerging definition of the situation (Knopf, 1975). In August 2002, a riot broke out in Indianap-

olis after a police bullet fired in a drug raid ricocheted and hit a young bystander in the arm. Rumors quickly spread that the police had aimed at the boy, producing a quite different understanding of the situation. In some incidents, rumors are broadcast by radio and TV stations, making them appear to be true. In other incidents, milling—the movement of persons within a setting, and the consequent exchange of information between crowd members—is the primary method through which rumor is transmitted. Persons who are not physically present may learn about the emerging situation from radio or television reports or through telephone calls (McPhail, 1991).

Diverse interpretations and action tendencies are usually present in a crowd situation (Turner & Killian, 1972). Someone initiates an act—perhaps in the belief that others will support him or her. Once a person initiates an act, the support of those nearby determines whether that person will persist in attempts to influence others. If enough people reinforce that person's position or behavior, a shared understanding will emerge. The definition of the situation that results from interaction in an initially ambiguous situation is termed an **emergent norm**. The emergent norm is usually not completely novel; it involves a modification or transformation of preexisting norms (Killian, 1984).

Once a definition of the situation develops, people are able to act purposively. In a crowd, behaviors consistent with the norms are encouraged, whereas behaviors inconsistent with the norms are discouraged. Thus, there are normative limits on the behavior of crowd participants. Crowds celebrating a football championship usually do not engage in looting. Conversely, crowds of looters in the inner city do not congregate in bars for several hours, drinking alcoholic beverages and chanting for their victorious team.

A distinctive image of crowds emerges from this perspective. People in crowds are viewed as emotional. Crowd activity reflects the rapid spread of a behavior—often one that violates social norms, such as looting stores—through the crowd. The spread is facilitated by anonymity; people can engage in deviance without fear of sanction, because the others present don't know them. But people are still making rational decisions in line with their current understanding of the situation. Nevertheless, when large numbers of people engage in the same behavior, unintended and undesirable outcomes can occur, such as the injuries suffered in the surge at the Wisconsin-Michigan game.

While the emergent norm perspective has been helpful in understanding certain kinds of actions in a limited set of collective settings, it has been criticized because emerging norms via negotiation are not unique or even especially relevant to crowd situations. Norms emerge in many social situations, including but hardly limited to crowds. Furthermore, norms of behavior that individuals have prior to being in a crowd are used and acted on within the crowd settings.

Gatherings

The traditional view of crowds as emotional is at best incomplete and at times misleading. An alternative perspective has been developed that calls our attention to other aspects of crowd incidents and collective behavior (McPhail, 1991, 1994). This perspective uses such concepts as the gathering, the phases of a gathering, and companion clusters to analyze collective behavior (McPhail, 1997).

According to this view, the social setting for many forms of collective behavior is a **gathering**—that is, a temporary collection of two or more persons occupying a common space and time frame (McPhail, 1991).

Gatherings are the basis of collective behavior. People may gather for a variety of reasons. Some gatherings are for purposes of recreation or "hanging out," as in parks, theaters, swimming pools, or at the scene of a fire, accident, or arrest. Other gatherings are demonstrations that involve two or more people meeting in public to protest or celebrate some person, principle, or condition; these may be political or religious in nature, or involve an athletic event. Still other gatherings are ceremonies, intended to mark a change in status or a life-course transition; these may be semipublic or private events.

Behavior in Gatherings. The behaviors of persons in gatherings reflect their purposes. Many persons who attend share the stated purpose (say, to celebrate a victory). But others come with other purposes—to accompany a friend, to meet potential dates, or to pick someone's pocket. What occurs reflects two influences: (1) participants' purposes and (2) features of the situation. Consider again the surge at the Wisconsin-Michigan game. At the end of the game, some of those in the student section wanted to go onto the field to celebrate. Others wanted to leave the stadium. Others wanted to get something to eat or drink. Each of these required movement toward the lower level of the stands. A situational feature, unknown to most of them, was the iron railing; because it was only 3 feet high, it was not visible to those standing more than a few rows back. The interaction of the participants' purposes and the situational feature—the railing—caused the undesirable outcome: injuries to 68 people.

Gatherings have three phases: assembling, activities, and dispersal (McPhail, 1991). We will briefly examine each in turn.

Assembling. Any gathering is the result of people coming together in a common location at the same time (McPhail, 2006). This process may involve convergence, or it may reflect the ecology of the location at which the gathering occurs.

Convergence refers to the situation in which those present at a gathering share certain qualities. The spectators at a football game are there to see the game. They may have other, more idiosyncratic purposes as well, but they are fans, and this fact influences their behavior. Indeed, because the crowd has so many fans in it and because they have gathered because they are fans, their identity as fans may become more salient to them and contribute more to their behavior than it does in other circumstances. The surge at the Wisconsin-Michigan game occurred in part because many fans wanted to celebrate the unexpected victory. Convergence at a gathering is much more likely if the gathering has been publicized in advance. It is also more likely if the media broadcast news of it in advance or as it occurs.

More often, the composition of a gathering reflects the social ecology of the environment. Other factors being equal, the greater the density of an area, the larger the number of potential participants. Crowd events are much more likely to occur in central cities than in suburbs or rural areas. Organizers of demonstrations learned many years ago that they need to provide buses if sympathizers are not located near the site of the demonstration.

Research suggests that many individuals come to gatherings in small groups of two to five people (McPhail, 1991). These small groups are usually made up of acquaintances, friends, or family members. This group-within-a-group composition is important because the presence of others who know the person establishes some informal social control over his or her behavior. The classic perspective on crowds—which emphasized anonymity and the resulting lack

of control over participants' behavior—was incorrect on this point. Although it is true that many participants in gatherings do not know one another, each participant is often part of a small group. These groups form the fundamental social unit in collective behavior situations—they discuss what is happening, decide jointly how to interpret the activities of others, and act together.

Activities. The activities of participants in gatherings are not random. McPhail (1991, 2006) has identified the "elementary forms of collective action." Four common vocal activities are conversing, singing, praying, and cheering. Data collected at the Promisekeepers March on Washington, October 4, 1997, found that praying and singing were solicited by speakers from the podium, whereas conversing and cheering were more spontaneous. Physically, participants may congregate in **companion clusters**—of family, friends, or acquaintances. A second activity form is the queue or line, as participants wait for admission, access, or service. A third form is arcs or rings of participants around performers, speakers, or fights.

Certain activities are common in particular types of gatherings. For instance, religious, concert, and sport gatherings involve celebration rituals—individual or collective chanting, singing, or praying, combined with symbolic gestures, such as the "wave" or holding up cigarette lighters to request an encore. Most members of the culture are familiar with these rituals because of childhood socialization or exposure via mass media. Thus, even a first-time participant in a religious service can act in unison with others. Ceremonial gatherings often involve singing, dancing, and musical performances; these are sometimes quite complex and require considerable advance planning and coordination. Retirement and farewell ceremonies and funerals often involve tributes to the person and have a typical form.

Dispersal. Gatherings end or disperse in one of four ways: routine, coerced, emergency, or negotiated. By far the most common but least studied is the *routine* type, in which those present leave the setting in an orderly fashion. People often queue as they leave an airplane, football stadium, or concert hall. They typically leave in the company of the same people with whom they assembled. When there are large numbers of persons or vehicles, officials may facilitate dispersal by directing traffic. In more open settings, such as a concert in a park, people may leave in clusters.

Coerced dispersal refers to the situation in which social control agents, such as police officers or firefighters, direct people to leave before the intended purpose of the gathering is achieved. This occurs when the authorities suspect that those gathered are in some danger, are causing others to be in danger, or because the assembled group is being too disruptive of others' life routines. An example is police directing citizens to leave a stadium or concert because of a bomb threat. Another type of coerced dispersal occurred in downtown Denver during the Super Bowl victory celebration, when the police used tear gas to force the revelers to leave the area.

The most frequently studied is *emergency* dispersal. This refers to situations where people have to deal with a suddenly disrupted or dangerous environment. The evacuation of the World Trade Center on September 11, 2001, after the first plane hit the tower is one example of an emergency dispersal. Studies have shown that even in such extraordinary circumstances, most people do not panic (Perry & Pugh, 1978). In fact, critical thinking and problem solving may even be enhanced in these dangerous situations. The speed and efficiency of emergency dispersal can be improved by rehearsal. Thus, fire (bomb) drills in schools, buildings, or ships, rehearsals of response to shooter scenarios on college campuses, or disaster preparedness training are all designed to reduce confusion, injuries, and death. Conversely, failure to hold an evacuation drill may have contributed to the 32 deaths that occurred during the sinking of the cruise ship *Costa Concordia* after it ran aground on January 13, 2012.

Negotiated dispersals are possible when event or protest organizers and law enforcement personnel collaborate before or during protest events. This allows for an advance agreement about the time, place, and manner of dispersal of crowds.

Underlying Causes of Collective Behavior

Having considered the internal dynamics of gatherings, we turn now to the causes of collective behavior. In some instances, collective behavior is simply a response to some event, such as a natural disaster, an athletic victory, or an assassination. Other types of collective behaviors—demonstrations, boycotts, lynchings, lootings, and epidemics—frequently are thought to involve not only a specific event but also more basic underlying conditions in the larger society. Three such conditions are strain, relative deprivation, and grievances.

Strain. Society may be viewed as normally in a state of equilibrium, maintaining a relative balance between the emphasis on achieving society's goals and the provision of the means to achieve them—education and jobs (Merton, 1957) (see Chap. 16). At times, however, social change may disrupt this equilibrium, so that one aspect of society is no longer in balance with other aspects. Advances in technology, for example, demand changes in occupational structure. Machines and robots have replaced many blue-collar workers in automobile plants. This change has contributed to plant closings and high unemployment in cities like Detroit that depend heavily on the auto industry. Such change produces strains in society that cause some individuals to experience stress (see Chap. 15). Although those who are affected may not recognize the source (for example, automation), they experience stress or frustration, which has been theorized to contribute to collective behavior.

Historically, economic issues have often been the key grievances articulated by protestors (Rudé, 1964). Food riots to protest the lack of sufficient food, attacks on factories and businesses to prevent mechanization, and sabotage to disable machinery and other property are often economically motivated. These activities were common in preindustrial England and France (Hobsbawm & Rudé, 1975; Tilly, 1995). More recently, bank failures in Japan and Korea produced economic crises in several Southeast Asian countries, where currencies declined sharply in value. The reduced purchasing power that resulted led to widespread rioting in Indonesia in February 1998 ("Indonesians die," 1998). Rioters frequently targeted businesses and homes of ethnic Chinese, whom they blamed for soaring prices. These protests may reflect the strain caused by widespread unemployment and inadequate incomes.

The evidence that economic issues drive strain and produce collective action is mixed. Whereas economic grievances seem to be related to people's attitudes and their support of radical policies (Plutzer, 1987), other researchers have had great difficulty connecting economic conditions to actual collective behavior or protest (Myers, 1997; Shorter & Tilly, 1974; Spilerman, 1970, 1976). Useem (1998) argues that these ambiguous findings can be clarified if we make a distinction between routine (election rallies, peaceful protest) and nonroutine (riots, rebellion, violence) collective action. Whereas routine collective action cannot be well explained by strain, there is more evidence that strain does produce nonroutine collective action (Myers, 1997; Myers & Li, 2001; Olzak & Shanahan, 1996).

Surveys of three distinctive groups, German students, Indian Muslims, and British Muslims, tested a theory of the antecedents of normative (demonstrations, picketing) and nonnormative (civil disobedience, riots) collective action. Perceptions of unfair group disadvantage are predicted to lead to group-based anger and aggressive, nonnormative, action. Perceptions of disadvantage combined with the belief in the group's efficacy to solve its problems are predicted to lead to normative action. The results supported the theory, suggesting a group's response to relative deprivation depends partly on its beliefs about the efficacy of normative protest (Tausch et. al., 2011). A meta-analysis finds that perceived efficacy is highly related to participation in protest (van Zomeren et al., 2008).

Relative Deprivation. In the eighteenth century, the revolt against the feudal socioeconomic structure occurred first in France. Yet France had already lost many feudal characteristics by the time the French Revolution began in 1789. The French peasant was free to travel, to buy and sell goods, and to contract services. In Germany, however, the feudal social structure was still intact. Thus, based on objective conditions, we would have expected a revolution to occur in Germany before it did in France. Why didn't it? One analyst (de Tocqueville, 1856/1955) argued that the decline of medieval institutions in France caused peasants to become obsessed with the ownership of land. The improvement in their objective situation created subjective expectations for further improvement. Peasant participation in the French Revolution was motivated by the desire to fulfill subjective expectations—to obtain land—rather than by a desire to eliminate oppressive conditions.

This basic notion about the causes of revolutions was expanded into a more systematic view. According to the **J-curve theory** (Davies, 1962, 1971), the "state of mind" of citizens determines whether there is political stability or revolution. Based on external conditions, individuals develop expectations regarding the satisfaction of their needs. Under certain conditions, persons expect continuing improvement in the satisfaction of their needs. If these expectations are met, people are content, and political stability results. But if the gap between expectations and reality becomes too great, people can become frustrated and engage in protest and rebellious activity.

Some have posited that revolutions occur when the level of actual satisfaction declines following a period of rising expectations and their relative satisfaction (Davies, 1971). These relationships are summarized in Figure 17.1. Note the J shape of the actual need satisfaction curve; as satisfaction declines, an intolerable gap between expected need satisfaction and actual need satisfaction emerges.

Such a gap between one's desired level of need satisfaction and one's actual need satisfaction is called **relative deprivation**. Relative deprivation arises when people make a comparison between their own circumstances and some comparison situation. The comparison might be made by an individual comparing oneself or one's group to people from a different group or to an expected standard. For example, an African-American person might experience relative deprivation by comparing his or her own salary to the salaries of Whites, by comparing the overall level of Black salaries to White salaries, or by comparing to what that individual thinks is a fair salary level. Thus, even if things are improving, relative deprivation can still occur.

Although it has been hypothesized that increasing relative deprivation in a group

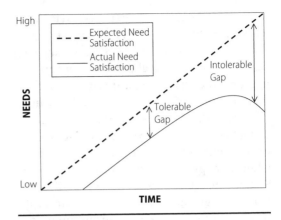

FIGURE 17.1 The J-Curve Model

One theory of the causes of revolt is the J-curve theory. According to this model, rebellion occurs when there is an intolerable gap between people's expectations of need satisfaction and the actual level of satisfaction they experience. In response to improved economic and social conditions, people expect continuing improvement in the satisfaction of their needs. As long as they experience satisfaction, there is political stability, even if there is a gap between expected and actual satisfaction. If the level of actual satisfaction declines, the gap gets bigger; at some point it becomes intolerable, and collective action occurs.

Source: Adapted from Davies, "Toward a Theory of Revolution," *American Sociological Review,* 27, 5–19, 1962.

should increase the chances that collective behavior will break out, a large number of studies have failed to find such a relationship (Gurney & Tierney, 1982). Other studies have tried to measure and analyze the relationship between the individual's level of frustration or deprivation and his or her participation in protest. These studies found no differences in frustration or relative deprivation between participants and nonparticipants (McPhail, 1994).

On the other hand, there have been successes for relative deprivation theory as well. Corning and Myers (2002), for example, measured relative deprivation among women by focusing on group comparisons and found that women with higher relative deprivation scores were more likely to have engaged in collective behavior and were more likely to expect to participate in the future. This and other research suggest that it is the feeling about one's group being deprived that is most important, rather than feelings about one's own individual condition (Begley & Alker, 1982; Guimond & Dubé-Simard, 1983). In one laboratory experiment, the researchers manipulated whether deprivation (the loss of a promised $10 payment) was seen as due to individual failure or group membership. Participants who perceived it as due to group membership were more supportive of collective action (Foster & Matheson, 1995).

Grievances and Competition. In any society, certain resources are highly valued but scarce. These resources include income or property, skills of certain types, and power and influence over others. Because of their scarcity, such resources are unequally distributed. Some groups have more access to a given resource than others. When one group has a grievance—discontent with the existing distribution of resources—collective behavior may occur to change that distribution (Oberschall, 1973). Attempts to change the existing arrangement frequently elicit responses by other groups that are designed to preserve the status quo. The result may be a series of actions by challengers and power holders.

There are three types of collective actions (Tilly, Tilly, & Tilly, 1975). *Competitive* action involves conflict between communal groups, usually on a local scale. One example is conflict and violence directed toward members of certain ethnic groups. Such incidents are more likely when members of the two groups are competing for low-wage jobs or where there are sharp increases in immigration (Olzak, 1989, 1992). The high rates of lynching of Blacks in the South in the 1890s is another example. From 1865 to 1880, Blacks enjoyed

large gains in political influence. By 1890, however, Whites were attempting to regain political control. Between 1890 and 1900, several state legislatures discussed laws that would have taken the vote away from Blacks. During these years, the number of Blacks lynched in Alabama, Georgia, Louisiana, Mississippi, and South Carolina reached a peak (Wasserman, 1977). The lynching of Blacks also increased during economic downturns—for example, when the price of cotton was declining (Beck & Tolnay, 1990).

A second type of collective action, called *reactive*, involves a conflict between a local group and the agents of a national political system. Tax rebellions, draft resistance movements, and protests of governmental policy are reactive. Such behavior is a response to attempts by the state to enforce its rules (regarding military service, for example) or to extend its control (such as imposing a new tax). Thus, such events represent resistance to the centralization of authority.

A third type of collective action, called *proactive*, involves demands for material resources, rights, or power. Unlike reactive behavior, it is an attempt to influence rather than resist authority. Strikes by workers, demonstrations for equal rights or against abortion, and various nonviolent protest activities are all proactive. Most proactive situations involve broad coalitions rather than one or two locally based groups.

The three underlying conditions discussed in this section differ in their emphasis. The strain model emphasizes the individual's emotional state in explaining collective behavior. The relative deprivation view emphasizes the person's subjective assessment of need satisfaction. The grievance model suggests that collective behavior results from rational attempts to redistribute resources in society (Zurcher & Snow, 1990).

Precipitating Incidents

Conditions of strain, relative deprivation, and grievances may be present in a society over extended periods of time. By contrast, incidents of collective behavior are often sporadic. Frequently, there are warning signals that a group is frustrated or dissatisfied. Members of the dissatisfied group or third parties may attempt to convince those in power to make changes (Oberschall, 1973). If these changes are not made, members may increasingly perceive legitimate channels as ineffective, leading to marches, protests, or other activities. Eventually, an incident may occur that adversely affects members of the group and highlights the problem, triggering collective behavior by group members; such an incident is referred to as a *precipitating event*. Such incidents appear to increase sharply the dissatisfaction of those who may have had low levels of grievance prior to the event (Opp, 1988).

An incident is more likely to trigger collective behavior if it occurs in an area accessible to many members of the affected group; this facilitates the assembling process. It is also more likely to lead to collective action if it occurs in a location that has special significance to group members (Oberschall, 1973). An event that occurs in such a place may produce a stronger reaction than would the same incident in a less meaningful location.

In April 1992, a California jury acquitted four police officers charged with beating a Black motorist, Rodney King. Word of the acquittal was broadcast throughout Southern California. Within minutes, a crowd of young men gathered at the intersection of Florence and Normandie in mostly Black South Central Los Angeles. At first, some of the men shouted at and harassed passing motorists. As their numbers grew, others began stopping cars and beating the occu-

pants. Many of those present merely observed these activities. Violence and looting spread rapidly. The ensuing disorder lasted 3 days, resulting in 53 deaths and the destruction of 10,000 businesses.

The acquittal of the officers symbolized for many Blacks their inferior position. The relations between Black citizens and White police officers in Los Angeles and other cities have been characterized by hostility for many years. The videotaped beating of Rodney King was a graphic example of the mistreatment many Blacks had suffered. The verdict suggested that White police officers could abuse Black citizens without fear of punishment. This increased the frustration felt by large numbers of Blacks. Some of them acted, and others quickly joined in.

Empirical Studies of Riots

Because they are unpredictable, hostile crowd events such as the one in Los Angeles are difficult to study empirically. Nevertheless, extensive and sophisticated research has been conducted on past racial disturbances, such as occurred in many U.S. cities between 1965 and 1971. These studies have made careful attempts to examine many of the theories presented earlier in this chapter.

In the first 9 months of 1967, there were more than 160 serious racial disturbances. In response, President Lyndon Johnson appointed a commission to study the causes of these incidents. In its report (National Advisory Commission on Civil Disorders, 1968), the commission concluded that the racial disturbances were caused by the underlying social and economic conditions affecting Blacks in our society. The report pointed to the high rates of unemployment, poverty, and the poor health and sanitation conditions in Black ghettos; the exploitation of Blacks by retail merchants; and the experience of racial discrimination, all of which produced a sense of deprivation and frustration among Blacks.

The Commission studied 24 disorders in 23 cities in depth. It concluded that

> disorder was generated out of an increasingly disturbed social atmosphere, in which typically a series of tension-heightening incidents over a period of weeks or months became linked in the minds of many in the Negro community with a reservoir of underlying grievances. At some point in the mounting tension, a further incident—in itself often routine or trivial—became the breaking point, and the tension spilled over into violence. Violence usually occurred almost immediately following the occurrence of the final precipitating incident, and then escalated rapidly. Disorder generally began with rock and bottle throwing and window breaking. Once store windows were broken, looting usually followed. (National Advisory Commission on Civil Disorders, 1968, p. 6)

The precipitating event frequently involved contacts between police officers and Blacks. In Tampa, Florida, a disturbance in 1967 began after a policeman shot a fleeing robbery suspect. A rumor quickly spread that the Black suspect was surrendering when the officer shot him. In other cities, disorder was triggered by incidents involving police attempts to disperse a crowd in a shopping district or to arrest predominantly Black patrons of a tavern selling alcoholic beverages after the legal closing time (Bergesen, 1982). To many Blacks, police officers symbolize White society and are therefore a readily available target for grievances and frustration. When a police officer arrests or injures a Black under ambiguous circumstances, it provides a concrete focus for discontent and a poignant reminder of grievances.

Severity of Disturbances. In some cities, racial disorders involved a few dozen people, and there was little property damage. In other cities, they involved thousands of people, and millions of dollars worth of property was destroyed. What determined how severe a disorder was?

The commission's report suggested that the deprivations experienced by Blacks fueled the disorders. Numerous researchers have studied this hypothesis. One question is whether absolute or relative deprivation is more influential. Are grievances greater only when unemployment, poor housing, and poor health are widespread, or are grievances greater when the conditions experienced by Blacks are poorer than the conditions experienced by Whites?

Measures of both absolute and relative deprivation were included in a series of studies of riots that occurred from 1961 to 1968 (Spilerman, 1970, 1976). The absolute level of deprivation was measured by the unemployment rate, the average income, and the average education of non-Whites in each city where a disturbance occurred. Relative deprivation was measured by the differences between White and non-White unemployment rates, average income, average education, and average occupational status. Spilerman examined both the frequency and the severity of rioting. The results were sobering for deprivation theorists. Spilerman found that although both severity and frequency of disturbances were associated with the size of the non-White population of a city and its location in the Southern region of the United States, neither absolute nor relative deprivation was associated with the severity of disorders. This finding was challenged by subsequent work, and other analysts have located small effects of relative deprivation and strain-related variables (Carter, 1983, 1990; Myers, 1997; Olzak & Shanahan, 1996). Nevertheless, these explanations do not appear to be very important in predicting where and when rioting will occur.

These results suggest that Black protests were not due to local community conditions but to general features of the society, such as increased Black consciousness, heightened racial awareness, and greater identification with other Blacks because of the civil rights movement. Television may have contributed to the disorders of the late 1960s by providing role models: Blacks in one city witnessed and later copied the actions of those in other cities (Myers, 2000). Blacks who were engaged in vandalism, looting, and other collective behavior served as a model for Blacks experiencing grievances and deprivation.

Temperature and Collective Violence. It is often suggested that high temperatures contribute to large-scale racial disturbances. The report of the National Advisory Commission on Civil Disorders (1968) noted that 60 percent of the 164 racial disorders that occurred in U.S. cities in 1967 took place in July, during hot weather. Of the 24 serious disturbances studied in detail, in most instances the temperature during the day on which violence first erupted was very high.

One study of the relationship between temperature and collective violence focused on 102 incidents that occurred between 1967 and 1971 (Baron & Ransberger, 1978). The results showed a strong relationship between temperature and the occurrence of violence. The incidents of collective violence were much more likely to have begun on days when the temperature was high (71–90 degrees). This relationship is depicted in Figure 17.2.

As Figure 17.2 indicates, there were few riots on days when the temperature was higher than 90 degrees. Does this indicate that it is too hot on such days, or that there are very few days when the temperature

is that high? To answer this question, the researchers estimated the probability of a disturbance, controlling for the number of days in each temperature range. The results show a direct relationship (Carlsmith & Anderson, 1979). In other words, the higher the temperature, the more likely a disturbance is to occur. One interpretation of this relationship is that in high-density neighborhoods with little air conditioning, the number of people on the streets increases with the temperature. Large street crowds facilitate the transmission of rumors and increase the likelihood of supportive responses to acts initiated by an individual or a small group.

If high temperature is associated with the occurrence of collective violence, an obvious question is whether high temperature is related to other types of violent behaviors (Anderson, 2001). One readily available measure of behavior is the rate of violent crime—of murder, sexual assault, and assault. One study analyzed the relationship between rates of violent crime and average temperature in data from 260 cities for the year 1980 (Anderson, 1987). As expected, the higher the average temperature, the higher the rates of violent crime in a city. Another study analyzed data from Dayton, Ohio, for a 2-year period (Rotton & Frey, 1985). The researchers looked at daily variations in the number of reports to police of assaults and family disturbances. The number of each was positively associated with the temperature. These results suggest that people are more irritable in hot weather and, thus, more likely to engage in aggressive or violent behavior (Berkowitz, 1993).

Some analysts have wondered if the relationship between violence and heat is merely an artifact of other processes related to heat, and not a product of increased aggressiveness. As in the case of riots, people may be outside, interacting in

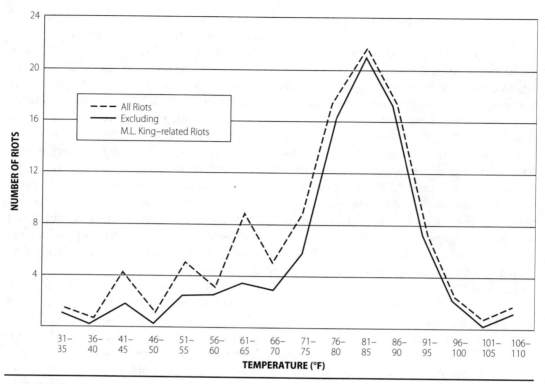

FIGURE 17.2 Ambient Temperature and Collective Violence

There is a strong relationship between mean temperature and the occurrence of collective disturbances. An analysis of 102 incidents between 1967 and 1971 generated this graph. As the temperature increased, the frequency of riots also increased. As the temperature increases, so does the number of people who are outside. Large numbers of people on the streets facilitate the development of a crowd.

Source: Baron and Ransberger, "Ambient Temperatures and the Occurrence of Collective Violence," *Journal of Personality and Social Psychology,* 36: 351–360, 1978. Copyright 1978 by the American Psychological Association.

different kinds of circumstances, and providing themselves with more opportunities for violent behavior in the summer rather than in the winter. If violence is more likely to occur in places where people sell illegal drugs, for example, could it be that people are more willing to go and buy drugs in the summer, or more likely to spend more time in the area than they would in the winter?

Although we do not know for certain how much these kinds of artifacts contribute to the heat-violence relationship, some field studies and laboratory studies confirm an increase in irritability and aggression, even when gathering processes are held constant (Anderson, Anderson, Dorr, DeNeve, & Flanagan, 2000). For example, Reifman, Larrick, and Fein (1991) found that baseball pitchers are more likely to hit batters with a pitch on hot days. This result suggests that aggression is partially a direct product of heat irritability.

Selection of Targets. Looting during a civil disturbance does not occur randomly. During racial disorders, such as the one in Los Angeles in 1992, property damage is primarily to retail stores. Residences, public buildings such as schools, and medical facilities such as clinics and hospitals are usually

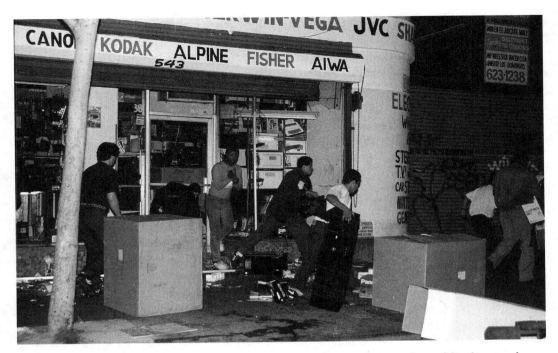

Civil disorders, which occur periodically in American cities, often involve members of disadvantaged groups. Looting and vandalism are common, with businesses whose owners are disliked as the likely targets. © Lee Celano/Reuters/Corbis

unaffected. Moreover, the looting and vandalism of businesses is often selective. Some stores are cleaned out, whereas others in the same block are untouched.

According to one survey (Berk & Aldrich, 1972), the reason for this discrepancy is that businesses with higher average prices of merchandise (that is, more attractive merchandise) were more likely to be attacked. A second factor was familiarity with the interior of the store. The larger the percentage of Black customers, the more likely the store was to be looted. Retaliation was also a factor; stores whose owners refused to cash checks and give credit to Blacks were more likely to be attacked. White ownership by itself was the least important factor.

Thus, the selection of targets during a riot reflects the desire of participants to obtain expensive consumer goods and to retaliate against anti-Black owners. This may reflect the operation of social control

within the crowd. Emergent norms may define some buildings and types of stores as appropriate targets and others as inappropriate targets. These norms are probably enforced by members of the crowd itself (Oberschall, 1973).

Even in deadly collective violence, assailants retain a clear sense of rationality as they choose whom they are going to kill. In a careful study of ethnic riots in which people were attacked and killed, Horowitz (2001) documents the great pains rioters often go to as they try to avoid what he calls "false positives." In other words, rioters work very hard to make sure that they do not kill people who do not belong to the group they wish to attack.

Social Control and Collective Behavior. Social control agents such as police officers strongly influence the course of a collective incident once it begins. In some cases, the mere appearance of authorities at the scene of an incident sets off collective action.

The importance of control agents is especially clear in protest situations. Protesters usually enter a situation with (1) beliefs about the efficacy of violence and (2) norms regarding the use of violence (Kritzer, 1977). If the participants' norms do not oppose violence, and if they believe violence may be effective, they are predisposed to choose violent tactics. Similarly, control agents enter a situation with (1) beliefs about what tactics the protesters are likely to use and (2) informal norms regarding violence. If the police anticipate violence, they prepare by bringing specially trained personnel and special equipment. Based on these beliefs and expectations, either the control agents or the protesters may initiate violence. Violence by one group is likely to produce a violent response from the other. Data from 126 protest events support this view (Kritzer, 1977).

In some instances, the response of authorities determines the severity and the duration of disorders (Spiegel, 1969). In any disturbance, there are two critical points at which either undercontrol or overcontrol can cause a protest to escalate. The first is the authorities' response to the initial phase. Undercontrol by police in reaction to the initial disorder may be interpreted by protesters as an "invitation to act." It suggests that illegal behavior will not be punished. Overcontrol at this point—such as an unnecessary show of force or large numbers of arrests—may arouse moral indignation, which may attract new participants and increase violence. In Madison in 2011, there were many law enforcement personnel in the area but they maintained a low profile; officers assembled and remained in areas away from the center of the protest.

The second critical point in a disturbance is the response to widespread disorder and looting during the second day. As the disorder progresses, participants gradually become physically exhausted. Undercontrol by authorities may facilitate the collapse of the protest. Overcontrol may result in incidents that fuel hostility, draw in new participants, and increase the intensity of the disturbance.

Three strategies for protest policing have been identified (Earl, 2011). The first is *escalated force*, in which police are present in large numbers and confront protestors. The second is *negotiated management*, which involves requiring permits; this provides police with an opportunity to negotiate crowd control in advance, and monitor it. Some scholars suggest negotiation replaced the use of force in the 1970s in the United States as a result of experiences during the riots in the 1960s. During this period, however, police also developed specialized units like SWAT teams to be used in crowd control. The anti–World Trade Organization protests in Seattle in 1999, involving more than 40,000 protestors, led to the development of a third strategy, *strategic incapacitation* (Noakes & Gillham, 2007), involving the creation of large no-protest zones, the use of nonlethal weapons, and strategic arrests. Obviously, which strategy police use may determine the course of a protest.

The response of authorities to one incident also may affect the severity of subsequent disorders in the same city (Spilerman, 1976). One study investigating incidents of collective violence in France, Germany, and Italy between 1830 and 1930 (Tilly et al., 1975) found that episodes involving violence were often preceded by nonviolent collective action. Moreover, a substantial amount of the violence consisted of the forcible reaction of authorities (often military or police forces employed by the government) to the nonviolent protests of citizens. Thus, violence was not necessarily associated with attempts to influence authority. It was equally associated with reactions to such attempts by the agents of authority. A study of supporters of the Irish Republican Army found that they supported the use of violence only when they viewed peaceful protest as ineffective and knew others who had experienced repressive acts by authorities (White, 1989). A survey of the death rate associated with political violence in 49 countries in the period from 1968 to 1977 found that the death rate was higher in countries with moderate scores on an index of regime repressiveness (Muller, 1985).

SOCIAL MOVEMENTS

The difference between collective behavior and social movements is in part one of degree. Both involve gatherings of people who engage in unconventional behavior—behavior that is inconsistent with some norms of society or is unconventional for the social space and time in which it occurs (Snow & Oliver, 1995). Both are caused by social conditions that generate strain, frustration, or grievances. The differences lie in their degree of organization. Crowd incidents are often unorganized; they occur spontaneously, with no widely recognized leaders and no specific goals.

A **social movement** is a collective activity that expresses a high level of concern about some issue (Zurcher & Snow, 1990). Its participants are people who feel strongly enough about an issue to act. Persons involved in a movement take a variety of actions—sign petitions, donate time or money, talk to family or friends, participate in rallies and marches, engage in civil disobedience, or campaign for candidates. These activities are drawn from the repertoire of ordinary political activities in society, but are often outside the conventional two-party structure. Within the movement, an organization may emerge—a group of persons with defined roles who engage in sustained activity to promote or resist social change (Turner & Killian, 1972).

In this part of the chapter, we first discuss the development of a social movement. Then we consider the movement organization and some influences on how it operates.

Preconditions

By themselves, strain or grievances cannot create a social movement. For a movement to appear, people must perceive their discontent as the result of controllable forces external to themselves (Ferree & Miller, 1985; McAdam, 1999). If they attribute their discontent to such internal forces as their own failings or bad luck, they are not predisposed to attempt to change their environment. Moreover, people must believe they have a right to the satisfaction of their unmet expectations (Oberschall, 1973). These attributions are often the result of interaction with others in similar circumstances. The moral principles used to legitimize their demand may be taken from the culture or from a specific ideology or philosophy (Snow, Rochford, Worden, & Benford, 1986). Thus, at the core of any social movement are beliefs rooted in the larger society.

A current social movement taking place in the United States involves abortion. In the late 1960s, an organized social movement developed that pressed for change in the laws restricting the availability of abortion. This movement culminated in the Supreme Court decision *Roe* v. *Wade* on January 22, 1973. This decision held that the state cannot interfere in an abortion decision by a woman and her physician during the first 3 months of pregnancy. The increasingly widespread availability of abortion created strain for others in our society. Many people view a fetus as a person and thus define abortion as murder. Drawing primarily on conservative Christian theology, these people gradually organized a movement in the mid-1970s to obtain legislation that would sharply restrict a woman's right to abortion.

In addition to perceiving unmet needs, people in a social movement must believe that the satisfaction of their needs cannot be achieved through established channels. This perception may be based on a lack of access to such channels (Graham & Hogan, 1990), or it may result from the failure of attempts to bring about change through those channels. At first, the anti-abortion movement emphasized lobbying and attempts to influence elections. As these activities did not produce the legislative or judicial action they sought, the movement increasingly adopted more aggressive tactics, including attempts to physically prevent women from entering abortion clinics. In the 1990s and 2000s, some individuals engaged in violent acts, including bombing clinics where abortions were performed and killing physicians who performed the procedure.

Another precondition may be a solution—action that people believe will ameliorate their discontent or redress their grievance (Wilmoth & Ball, 1995). A case study of the movement to control world population growth suggests that the development of birth control in the 1960s—especially oral contraceptives and surgical sterilization procedures—provided a feasible solution to the problem of overpopulation. As a result, population control efforts were more organized and successful in the 1970s than they had been in the 1950s.

Ideology and Framing

As affected individuals interact, an ideology or generalized belief emerges. **Ideology** is a conception of reality that emphasizes certain values and justifies a movement (Turner & Killian, 1972; Zurcher & Snow, 1990). Ideologies are often developed by

movement participants as the movement grows.

The anti-abortion, or pro-life, ideology rests on several assumptions. First, each conception is an act of God. Thus, abortion violates God's will. Second, the fetus is an individual who has a constitutional right to life. Third, every human life is unique and should be valued by every other human being. Pro-life forces view the status of abortion as temporary—a departure from the past when it was morally unacceptable. Persons and programs (such as sex education) are evaluated in terms of whether they support or undermine these beliefs. Any person or group who favors continued legal abortion is defined as immoral. In recent elections in many communities, a candidate's position on abortion has been a major political issue. Pro-life activists believe that by opposing people and programs that encourage abortion, they will cause a sharp decline in its availability and redefine it as illegitimate.

Such an ideology fulfills a variety of functions (Turner & Killian, 1972). First, it provides a way of identifying people and events and a set of beliefs regarding appropriate behavior toward them. Ideology is usually oversimplified because it emphasizes one or a few values at the expense of others. A second function of ideology is that it gives a movement a temporal perspective. It provides a history (what caused the present undesirable situation), an assessment of the present (what is wrong), and a conception of the future (what goals can be attained by the movement) (Martin, Scully, & Levitt, 1990; Snow et al., 1986). Third, it defines group interests and gives preference to them. Finally, it creates villains. It identifies certain persons or aspects of society as responsible for the discontent. This latter function is essential because it provides the rationale for the activity designed to produce change (Oberschall, 1973).

A common element of the ideology of contemporary groups seeking to produce change is the rhetoric of "the public good" (Williams, 1995). Like other elements of ideology, this rhetoric is drawn from the larger culture and provides a resource that movements use in making their claims.

Once social movement groups have identified and committed to ideological positions, they must articulate and present their ideas to others in the broader social environment so that they can win support, recruit participants, and gather the resources they need to accomplish their goals. In essence, they must sell their ideas and causes to others. The processes of articulating their idea for the consumption of others is called social movement **framing** (Snow et al., 1986; Snow & Benford, 1992).

When activists frame their issues, they attempt to link them in some way with the values and ideologies potential recruits already hold. For example, in the United States, people commonly accept the notion that "all men are created equal" and that individuals, by their mere existence, have certain rights. These two general values, equality and basic rights, can be tapped into by activists to align others to their cause. For example, in a battle over gay rights in Cincinnati, those supporting the gay and lesbian cause argued that gay men and lesbian women were being denied basic rights and that all activists wanted was a guarantee of the same rights (to be free from employment discrimination, for example) that everyone should enjoy (Dugan, 2004). The opposition, however, argued that the gay and lesbian cause would provide special privileges to a select group, thereby violating equality notions: The rights of gay and lesbian people were equally protected by general principles that applied to everyone in Cincinnati—why should there be special treatment of this particular group? In this particular case, the frame chosen by the opposition resonated more with the population of Cincinnati—the framing attempts made by the gay and lesbian population were unsuccessful and were defeated.

These results and the many other studies of movement framing demonstrate the importance of social construction in protest. It is not enough for social problems to exist that are not being addressed by traditional government and institutional approaches. These problems have to diagnosed, the population has to be convinced that the problems are worthy of correction because they are unjust, and activists must also develop a corrective action plan that will be accepted (Gamson, 1992). Without these critical processes, social movements will fail to even get off the ground.

Recruitment

The development and continuing existence of any movement depends on recruitment—the process of attracting supporters. Some people are attracted to a movement because they share some distinctive attributes (Zurcher & Snow, 1990). In many instances, these are persons who experience the discontent or grievances at the base of the movement.

A study comparing people who participated in the movement to prevent the reopening of Pennsylvania's Three Mile Island nuclear power plant with a group of nonparticipants found that the activists had opposed commercial and military uses of nuclear energy before the accident, and the accident had served to increase their discontent substantially (Walsh & Warland, 1983). There are limitations, however, to this grassroots view of recruitment (Turner & Killian, 1972). Many studies have found that the supporters of a movement are not the most deprived or frustrated. Also, the goals of a movement may not be aimed at removing the sources of the discontent.

The content of the ideology reflects several influences—not just a desire to eliminate a particular source of frustration. Once the movement has developed, people may be attracted by the ideology who do not share the discontent.

Recruitment depends heavily on three catalysts: ideology, identity, and existing social networks (Zurcher & Snow, 1990). The content and framing of the ideology is what attracts supporters. The ideology spreads, at least in part, through existing social networks. Supporters communicate the ideology to their friends, families, and coworkers as they interact with them.

Research on recruitment into religious movements documents the importance of friendship and kinship ties (Stark & Bainbridge, 1980). Adherents to the Mormon religion, for example, are called to proselytize. They establish friendship ties with nonmembers, then gradually introduce their beliefs to their new friends. Likewise, the members of a doomsday cult who believed the Earth would soon be destroyed often were relatives of other members. Those with kinship ties were less likely to leave the cult.

A study of conversion to Catholic Pentecostalism compared 150 converts with a control group of non-Pentecostal Catholics (Heirich, 1977). The major difference between the two groups was in their social networks. Converts had been introduced to the "born again" movement by someone they trusted—a parent, priest, or teacher. Converts also reported positive or neutral reactions to their participation from family and friends.

Sometimes, entire groups are recruited all at once (Oberschall, 1973). The civil rights movement in the South in the 1950s is one example. Because of their religious views, Black ministers were predisposed to support a movement whose ideology emphasized freedom and equality. These ministers recruited their entire congregations and communicated the ideology to other ministers. As a result, the movement spread rapidly. More recently, the pro-life movement has grown by recruiting entire congregations of Catholics and Mormons. Such en bloc recruitment is much more efficient than recruiting individuals (Jenkins, 1983). Pro-life protests in many cities are the result of recruiting members of one or two congregations to assemble at the protest site. Pro-choice protests often are the result of recruiting members of feminist and women's health advocacy groups.

An alternative mechanism for recruitment is the mass media. On Wednesday, August 28, 2013, over 100,000 people gathered on the National Mall in Washington, D.C., to commemorate the fiftieth anniversary of Dr. Martin Luther King's "I Have a Dream" speech. Most had come from outside the Washington area, from New York, Maine, and California. The organizers had publicized the event for weeks, and it was listed on many websites and announced in many venues.

Thus, the media play an important role in social movements. Media reports convey a movement's ideology and attract members by providing role models or by providing information about the time and place of activities. It is no accident that movement groups devote considerable effort to getting reporters and camera crews to cover their activities. Media attention—time on television and radio, space in newspapers and magazines—is a scarce resource. To get it, movement groups may have to engage in novel or dramatic acts (Holgartner & Bosk, 1988). Such actions may lead to confrontation and violence.

No matter what ideology drives a movement group and what kinds of social networks guide recruitment, successful mobilization is also dependent on a successful notion of collective identity. **Collective**

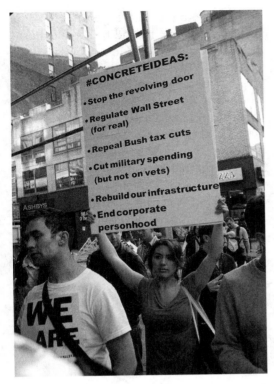

This demonstration was part of the Occupy Wall Street movement. Organizers of such events hope for coverage by the mass media, because reports of movement activities may attract additional supporters. © Owen Franken/Corbis

identity is a shared understanding that a group of people has of who they are as a group—who is a member of the group, who is not, and what the boundary is that separates them (Taylor, 1989; Taylor & Whittier, 1992). Constructing the identity boundary for an activist group is a critical activity and often requires a great deal of work. If the group defines its boundaries too widely, it will not be able to present itself as an alternative to the status quo, and its members will not feel they are contributing to change. If the collective identity is too narrow and its boundaries are too rigidly drawn, the group risks alienating potential members, thwarting its chances of having a political impact, and being viewed

as a fringe group with little relevance to the social and political realities of the day (McVeigh, Myers, & Sikkink, 2004).

Mobilization

Having attracted supporters, a movement must induce some of them to become committed members (Zurcher & Snow, 1990). Commitment involves the creation of links between the interests of an individual and those of the movement so that the individual will be willing to contribute actively to the achievement of movement goals. **Mobilization** is the process through which individuals surrender personal resources and commit them to the pursuit of group or organizational goals (Oberschall, 1978). Resources can be many things: money or other material goods, time and energy, leadership or other skills, or moral or political authority. From the individual's viewpoint, mobilization often involves a rational decision. The person weighs the costs and benefits of various actions. If the potential rewards outweigh the potential risks, a particular course of action is taken. Mobilization also involves group processes, such as collective rituals and democratic decision making, which increase the individual's commitment to movement actions (Hirsch, 1990).

Among committed members, some may become leaders. Taking a leadership role in a movement organization may be risky but potentially very rewarding (Oberschall, 1973). If the movement is successful, leaders may attain prestige, visibility, a permanent, well-paid position with the organization, and opportunities to interact with powerful, high-status members of society. Leaders of movements are often persons with substantial education (such as lawyers, writers, professors, and students) and at least moderate status in society (Weed, 1990). They are frequently persons whose skills cannot be confiscated by authorities, who can expect social support, and who will be dealt with leniently if arrested. Thus, their risk-reward ratio is favorable for involvement.

For a movement to succeed, others also must be induced to follow and work actively in the organization (Zurcher & Snow, 1990). One basis of commitment is moral—anchoring an individual's worldview in the movement's ideology. Members who are attracted by the ideology tend to see their own interests as furthered by the achievement of movement goals. Many women become involved in pro-abortion organizations because preserving freedom of choice for all women will benefit them. At the same time, movement adherents clarify, extend, and even reinterpret the ideology as they attempt to persuade others to commit resources to the movement (Snow et al., 1986). A second basis of commitment is a sense of belonging, which is facilitated by collective rituals in which members participate. One advantage of recruiting preexisting groups, such as church congregations, is that this sense of belonging is already developed. A third basis of commitment is instrumental. If the organization has enough resources at its disposal, it can provide utilitarian rewards for committed members. These rewards may be distributed equally among members or selectively to members who make a particular contribution (Oliver, 1980).

Depending on its overall strategy, a movement organization can use moral, affective, or instrumental rewards as bases for building commitment. These are sufficient for most organizations to induce members to contribute time, materials, and other resources. Other organizations demand that members commit themselves to exclusive participation. They require that members renounce other roles and commitments and undergo **conversion**—the process through which a movement's ideology becomes the individual's fundamental perspective. This degree of commitment is required by some religious movements and by so-called utopian communities. Conversion involves persuasion and "consciousness raising"; it is an attempt to change the individual's worldview. Conversion is usually accomplished during a period of intensive interaction with other movement members. It is thus a very labor-intensive mobilization strategy (Ferree & Miller, 1985). An organization seeking volunteers for high-risk activities, such as those involving the risk of arrest, must use powerful inducements. A study of volunteers for a project to register voters in rural Mississippi in 1964 found that several characteristics distinguished participants from volunteers who decided not to go (McAdam, 1986). Participants had intense ideological commitment, previous experience with activism, and ties to other activists (see Figure 17.3) or all of the above.

Conservative Movements in the United States

Since the 1980s, political conservatives have become a major force in the United States, partly through the rise and success of a number of social movements. These include movements against same-sex marriage, sex education, abortion, and immigration, and for unrestricted gun ownership. The ideology of some of these movements includes strongly held conspiratorial beliefs, distrust of and the desire to curtail democratic processes, and advocacy of criminal action or violence. Scholars in the first half of the twentieth century attributed such movements to factors such as status anxiety (the view that one's political or economic power is waning), ignorance, or psychological disorder, at least among their leaders (Blee & Creasap, 2010). However, there is evidence that these movements attract ordinary, middle-class people, many of whom are wealthy and powerful.

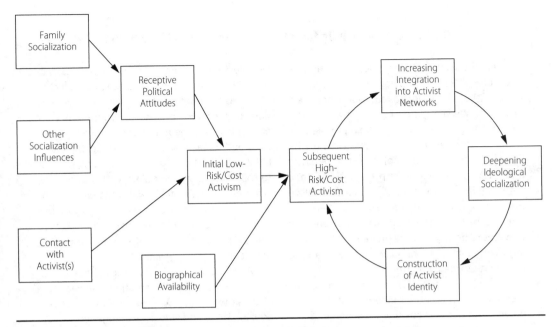

FIGURE 17.3 Influences on Recruitment to High-Risk Activism

Many social movement activities are low-risk—involving little or no cost to participants. Such activities include donating money, distributing leaflets, and attending rallies. Sometimes, however, movement leaders decide to engage in activities that are high-risk—involving the risk of injury or death. Political activism in the rural South in 1964 is an example of a high-risk activity. A study of the characteristics associated with the willingness to participate in this activity compared those who went with those who initially volunteered but decided not to go. Analyses suggested that a sequence of experiences, beginning with particular socialization experiences and including contact with other activists and prior activism, were associated with being available for and participating in the high-risk activity. Once involved, participation facilitated greater involvement.

Source: McAdam, "Recruitment to High-Risk Activism: The Case of Freedom Summer," *American Journal of Sociology,* 92, 64–90, 1986. Copyright © 1986, The University of Chicago Press.

Many movements in the second half of the twentieth century were "progressive," focused on securing rights for disadvantaged and stigmatized groups. As such, their goals were often to enact new legislation that would guarantee rights and create social programs to increase the status and improve the living standards of such groups. Movements to improve the status of women, Blacks, immigrants, the poor, and similar groups were the focus of much of the research on social movements by scholars from 1970 to 2000. These groups were engaging in *proactive* actions. Rightist movements do not support changes or policies; they oppose them. In fact, they have often arisen in opposition to these progressive movements, and attempt to counter or even push back advances made by them. Thus, they may focus on lobbying to repeal legislation rather than protest marches, and lawsuits to overturn legislation or court decisions. These groups are engaging in *reactive* actions. Thus, the tactics used by the two types of movements differ a great deal. How else do they differ?

We noted above that religious and civil rights movements recruited members through existing social networks. They recruited by mobilizing members to recruit family and friends. They also recruited

BOX 17.2 Research Update: Emotions and Social Movements

We began this chapter by reviewing early theories of collective behavior, which attributed many of these behaviors to emotional processes in crowds. We summarized research and theory that challenged these views, leading to the conclusion that some of the early ideas were myths. From 1970 to 2000, views of collective behavior and social movements were primarily concerned with cognitive processes and resource mobilization issues, usually ignoring emotion. Recently, scholars have rediscovered the important role that emotions play in these phenomena, discussing them in much more nuanced ways than the early writers treated them.

Psychologists of all types have been heavily focused on how emotions emerge. But there is a different set of questions that uses emotions not as a dependent, or outcome, variable, but rather looks at the effects of emotions on the individual, on other people, and on the social environment. These approaches treat emotions as independent variables—the sources as opposed to the outcomes. Researchers recognize, of course, that the experience and expression of emotions are part of complicated cycles in which felt emotions are expressed and cause changes in the social context. These changes introduce feedback in the system that can result in new emotions being experienced and introduced to the environment or in changes in the original emotions. These issues are of great interest in the study of social movements.

Some researchers who examine political and social activism have come to see emotions as a key element that drives individuals to participate. Oftentimes, activists face very difficult challenges as they pursue their goals, and the emotions they experience can play a very important part in keeping them involved or causing them to abandon their activism. In Doug McAdam's (1986) study of college students who traveled to the South to register Black voters during the civil rights movement, it was apparent that the volunteers had transformative emotional experiences—ranging from fear that had to be overcome, to anger that strengthened their resolve, to love for their fellow activists.

More recently, Erika Summers-Effler (2005) has been studying the emotional experiences of those who live and work in Catholic worker houses. These individuals are engaged in very challenging and highly involved activism in service to the poor in inner cities. They essentially give their lives to the Catholic worker movement, abandoning their possessions and former lives to live in the inner-city environment. The Catholic worker house hosts "guests," who essentially are anyone who wishes to live at the house and typically are those who would otherwise be homeless. In addition to hosting the guests in the house, the Catholic workers also provide meals for people in the neighborhood, maintain a clothing pantry for those in need in the neighborhood, and provide after-school tutoring. The challenges are many and the support systems are sparse, resulting in difficult daily challenges that can stretch the workers to their limits.

through organizational networks such as churches and labor groups. Conservative movements, by contrast, recruited through cultural events, including music concerts and amusement parks, and using publishing houses to publish books and sponsor tours by authors. Another strategy was the identification and vilification of enemies: working women, abortion providers, immigrants, and especially sexual minorities. These campaigns attracted like-minded people to participation in the movements. Their anti-gay efforts were particularly successful in the 1990s.

Conservative movements also use particular strategies to mobilize their support-

Given these kinds of extreme challenges, Catholic workers need intangible support in order to continue with their work—they need emotional outlets and emotional rituals that give them the fortitude to continue on and maintain their commitments. Summers-Effler documents a number of critical emotional processes that provide this kind of support. For one, she emphasizes the importance of laughter in the community. Humor, she found, allowed individuals to face difficult situations and maintain a sense of cohesion within the group. Joint laughter allowed individuals to escape any shame they might have felt or any sense of failure by recognizing the absurd in the situation without giving in to it. This story illustrates that process:

> Lynn said that the ice cream was in the basement because the refrigerator was broken. I asked, half seriously, if they were waiting for God to get them a new refrigerator. Everyone thought this was really funny; most were doubled over in laughter. The laughter was irresistible, contagious.
>
> I found myself laughing as well . . . Finally, Lynn stopped laughing long enough to say that she was debating whether to call the repair man or not, and that she had had a few discussions with St. Francis about it . . . she was immediately consumed with laughter again. (pp. 143–144)

A second key process related to emotion was its relationship to rituals in the community. The Catholic worker environment was full of both emotion and ritual—rituals both formal and informal. What Summers-Effler found was that emotion and ritual combined to produce positive outcomes for the workers; in particular, greater solidarity. What seemed to occur was that negative emotion was processed by the ritual and the result was a strengthening of bonds among the group. One example was the weekly community gathering:

> Once a week the extended community, mostly white middle class supporters but also some guests and people from the neighborhood, participate in a community dinner at the Catholic worker house . . . during this weekly ritual, which often involves the formal ritual of liturgy, the extended group reaffirms the Catholic workers as sacred symbols of the community. Because the Catholic workers are the center of attention and praise, these weekly dinners are an emotional boost to the Catholic workers from their extended community.

Thus, we can see some ways that emotions produce important social outcomes, and therefore their role as inputs into social situations should be considered as carefully as are questions about how emotions emerge from social situations.

Source: Excerpted from Summers-Effler, 2005.

ers. They have heavily utilized alternative media, such as blogs, bulletin boards, and chat rooms, to disseminate their views. Use of the Internet makes their efforts much less visible, and it allows people to support and participate in the movement relatively anonymously. Music and media events, rather than rallies and protest marches, allow members to meet and create involvement.

Thus, the "new" conservative and right-wing social movements use different strategies to recruit and mobilize supporters, and use different tactics to achieve their goals. The study of these groups has revitalized the study of social movements.

SUMMARY

This chapter discusses both collective behavior and social movements.

Collective Behavior. (1) The classic perspective on collective behavior focuses on the crowd. Early crowd theorists focused on ideas about crowd behavior that included unanimity of feeling, deindividuation, and contagion. Later analysts debunked some of these ideas and focused instead on how people in undefined situations, such as disasters, develop new norms and social organization. (2) An alternative perspective considers the gathering. Gatherings have a purpose; participants' behaviors reflect that purpose in interaction with features of the setting. (3) Three conditions have been studied as underlying causes of collective behavior: strain, relative deprivation, and grievances. (4) Collective behavior is often triggered by an event that adversely affects those already experiencing strain, deprivation, or grievances. (5) Empirical studies of riots suggest that the severity of a disturbance is influenced mainly by the number of potential participants and less so by differences in underlying social conditions. Once it begins, the course of a collective incident and the likelihood of future disorders are influenced by the behavior of police and other social control agents.

Social Movements. A social movement is collective activity that expresses a high level of concern about some issue. The development of a social movement rests on several factors. First, people must experience strain or deprivation, believe they have a right to satisfy their unmet needs, and believe that satisfaction cannot be achieved through established channels. Second, as participants interact, an ideology must emerge that justifies collective activity. Third, to sustain the movement, additional people must be recruited by spreading the ideology, often through existing social networks. Development of a movement organization depends on mobilization—getting individuals to commit personal resources to the group. Conservative movements differ from progressive ones in the content of their ideology, and in the tactics they use to recruit and mobilize supporters.

List of Key Terms and Concepts

collective behavior (p. 580)
collective identity (p. 602)
companion clusters (p. 588)
contagion (p. 583)
conversion (p. 604)
crowd (p. 581)
deindividuation (p. 582)
emergent norm (p. 586)
framing (p. 601)
gathering (p. 587)
ideology (p. 600)
J-curve theory (p. 591)
mobilization (p. 603)
relative deprivation (p. 591)
rumor (p. 586)
social movement (p. 599)

Critical Thinking Skill: Understanding the Difference Between Anecdotal and Scientific Evidence

Large-scale riots occurred in London and several other British cities August 6 to 11, 2011. Thousands of people engaged in looting, arson, and mass destruction of property—homes, businesses, automobiles, and buses. The precipitating event was the shooting of Mark Duggan in Tottenham by police following a traffic stop. Duggan, a 29-year-old local resident, died. More than 3,100 people were arrested during the days of rioting.

Max Hastings posted the following commentary on a British blog on August 10, 2011:

If you live a normal life of absolute futility, which we can assume most of this week's rioters do, excitement of any kind is welcome. The people who wrecked swathes of property, burned vehicles and terrorised communities have no moral compass to make them susceptible to guilt or shame.

Most have no jobs to go to or exams they might pass. They know no family role models, for most live in homes in which the father is unemployed, or from which he has decamped.

They are illiterate and innumerate, beyond maybe some dexterity with computer games and BlackBerries. They are essentially wild beasts.

This is an example of anecdotal evidence, a claim of evidence based on personal interpretation.

This chapter has reviewed the social scientific evidence about riots, collected over several decades. You can see in the synopsis of the British riots several features of riots identified by researchers and scholars.

This body of research led to the identification of several myths about collective behavior that we summarized early in this chapter. How many of the myths are reflected in the comments by Mr. Hastings? Irrationality? Emotionality? Destructiveness? Spontaneity? Unanimity? We are exposed to such anecdotal interpretations of events daily, and more frequently given the proliferation of social media and blogs. We need to be very careful not to take them too seriously. Such commentaries usually reflect one very narrow point of view, picking out one or two elements of a complex series of events, and emphasizing them. The reality, as reflected in the scientific evidence, is much more complex.

A

Access display A signal (verbal or nonverbal) from one person indicating to another that further social interaction is permissible.

Accommodation A constructive response to a potentially destructive act by a partner in a romantic relationship.

Accounts Explanations people offer after they have performed acts that threaten their social identities. Accounts take two forms—excuses that minimize one's responsibility and justifications that redefine acts in a more socially acceptable manner.

Action units A configuration of facial muscles or a discernible movement originating from them.

Actor-observer difference The bias in attribution whereby actors tend to see their own behavior as due to characteristics of the external situation, whereas observers tend to attribute actors' behavior to the actors' internal, personal characteristics.

Affect A subjective positive or negative evaluation of an object, which can vary in direction, intensity, and activity.

Affective aggression Aggression resulting from aversive affect (negative emotion that people seek to reduce or eliminate). More common among persons who believe that acting aggressively will make them feel better.

Affect theory of social exchange A theory that focuses on the genesis of emotion during social exchange and the cognitive and behavioral effects of that emotion.

Aggravated assault An attack by one person on another with the intent of causing bodily injury.

Aggression Behavior that is intended to harm another person and that the other wants to avoid.

Aggressive pornography Explicit depiction—in film, video, photograph, or story—of sexual activity in which force is threatened or used to coerce a person to engage in sex. *See also* Nonaggressive pornography.

Alienation The sense that one is uninvolved in the social world or lacks control over it.

Aligning actions Actions people use to define their apparently questionable conduct as actually in line with cultural norms, thereby repairing social identities, restoring meaning to situations, and reestablishing smooth interaction.

Altercasting Tactics we use to impose roles and identities on others that produce outcomes to our advantage.

Altruism Actions performed voluntarily with the intention of helping someone else that entail no expectation of receiving a reward or benefit in return (except possibly an internal feeling of having done a good deed for someone).

Anomie theory The theory that deviant behavior arises when people striving to achieve culturally valued goals find they do not have access to the legitimate means of attaining these goals.

Arbitrator In situations of conflict, a neutral third party who has the power to decide how a conflict will be resolved. *See also* Mediator.

Archival research A research method that involves the acquisition and analysis (or reanalysis) of existing information collected by others.

Attachment A warm, close relationship with an adult who provides an infant with a sense of security and stimulation.

Attitude A predisposition to respond to a particular object in a generally favorable or unfavorable way.

Attitude change A change in a person's attitudes about some issue, person, or situation.

Attitude inoculation A process that helps a target person to resist persuasion attempts by exposing him or her to a weak version of the arguments.

Attitudinal similarity The sharing by two people of beliefs, opinions, likes, and dislikes.

Attractiveness stereotype The belief that "what is beautiful is good"; the assumption that an attractive person possesses other desirable qualities.

Attribution The process by which people make inferences about the causes of behavior or attitudes.

Authority The capacity of one group member to issue orders to others—that is, to direct or regulate the behavior of other members by invoking rights that are vested in his or her role.

Availables Those persons with whom we come into contact and who constitute the pool of potential friends and lovers.

Aversive affect Negative emotion that people seek to reduce or eliminate.

Aversive event In intergroup relations, a situation or event caused by or attributed to an outside group that produces negative or undesirable outcomes for members of the target group.

B

Back-channel feedback The small vocal and visual comments a listener makes while a speaker is talking, without taking over the speaking turn. This includes responses such as "Yeah," "Huh?" "M-hmn," head nods, brief smiles, and completions of the speaker's words. Back-channel feedback is crucial to coordinate conversation smoothly.

Back regions A setting used to manage appearances. In back regions, people allow themselves to violate appearances while they prepare, rehearse, and rehash performances. Contrasts with front regions, where people carry out interaction performances and exert efforts to maintain appropriate appearances.

Balance theory A theory concerning the determinants of consistency in three-element cognitive systems.

Belief perseverance A tendency to continue to view an initial assumption as correct despite evidence to the contradictory.

Birth cohort A group of people who were born during the same period of one or several years and who are, therefore, all exposed to particular historical events at approximately the same age.

Body language (kinesics) Communication through the silent motion of body parts—scowls, smiles, nods, gazes, gestures, leg movements, postural shifts, caresses, slaps, and so on. Because body language entails movement, it is also known as *kinesics*.

Borderwork Interaction across gender boundaries that is based on and strengthens such boundaries.

Brainstorming In groups, a procedure intended to generate a large number of high-quality, novel ideas in a brief period. Brainstorming is based on the principles that members should freely express any idea that comes to mind,

withhold criticism and defer judgment until later, try to generate as many ideas as possible, and build on ideas suggested by others.

Bystander effect The tendency for bystanders in an emergency to help less often and less quickly as the number of bystanders present increases.

Bystander intervention In an emergency situation, a quick response by a person witnessing the emergency to help another who is endangered by events.

C

Career A sequence of roles—each role with its own set of activities—that a person enacts during his or her lifetime. People's most important careers are in the domains of family and friends, education, and work.

Categorization The tendency to perceive stimuli as members of groups or classes rather than as isolated entities; the act of encoding stimuli as members of classes.

Catharsis The reduction of aggressive arousal by means of performing aggressive acts. The catharsis hypothesis states that we can purge ourselves of hostile emotions by intensely experiencing these emotions while performing aggression.

Cautious shift In group decision making, the tendency for decisions made in groups after discussion to be more cautious (less risky) than decisions made by individual members prior to discussion. *See also* Risky shift.

Cognitions An element of cognitive structure. Cognitions include attitudes, beliefs, and perceptions of behavior.

Cognitive dissonance A state of psychological tension induced by dissonant relationships between cognitive elements.

Cognitive labeling theory A theory that proposes that emotional experience is the result of a three-step sequence: (1) an event in the environment produces a physiological reaction, (2) we notice the physiological reaction and search for an appropriate explanation, and (3) by examining situational cues we find an emotional label for the reaction.

Cognitive processes The mental activities of an individual, including perception, memory, reasoning, problem solving, and decision making.

Cognitive structure Any form of organization among a person's concepts and beliefs.

Cognitive theory A theoretical perspective based on the premise that an individual's mental activities (perception, memory, and reasoning) are important determinants of behavior.

Collective behavior Emergent and extrainstitutional behavior that is often spontaneous and subject to norms created by the participants.

Collective identity A shared understanding that a group of people has of who they are as a group.

Collective task A task that requires group members to take into account the views of other group members to achieve a successful outcome.

Collectivist cultures Cultures that emphasize group over individual. The focus is on the interconnectedness of individuals, particularly the interdependent nature of their social relationships and identities. *See also* Individualist cultures.

Communication The process through which people transmit information about their ideas and feelings to one another.

Communication accuracy The extent to which the message inferred by a listener from a communication matches the message intended by the speaker.

Communication-persuasion paradigm A research paradigm that conceptualizes persuasion attempts in terms of source, message, target, channel, and impact—that is, who says what to whom by what medium with what effect.

Communicator credibility In persuasion, the extent to which the communicator is perceived by the target audience as a believable source of information.

Companion clusters Groups of family, friends, or acquaintances who remain together throughout a gathering.

Comparison level (CL) A standard used to evaluate the outcomes of a relationship, based on the average of the person's experience in past relevant relationships.

Comparison level for alternatives (CLalt) A standard specifying the lowest level of outcomes a person will accept in light of available alternatives; the level of profit available to an individual in his or her best alternative relationship.

Complexity-extremity effect The bias where less complex schemas lead to more extreme judgments and evaluations.

Compliance In social influence, adherence by the target to the source's requests or demands.

Compliance may occur either with or without concomitant change in attitudes.

Conditioning A process of learning in which, if a person performs a particular response and if this response is then reinforced, the response is strengthened.

Confirmation bias The tendency to focus on information relevant to a belief and ignoring or downplaying information that is inconsistent with that belief.

Conformity Adherence by an individual to group norms so that behavior lies within the range of tolerable behavior.

Conjunctive tasks A type of unitary group task in which the group's performance depends entirely on that of its weakest or slowest member. *See also* Additive tasks, Disjunctive tasks.

Contagion The rapid spread through a group of visible and often unusual symptoms or behavior.

Content analysis A research method that involves a systematic scrutiny of documents or messages to identify specific characteristics and then making inferences based on their occurrence.

Contingencies (of self-esteem) Characteristics of self or categories of outcomes on which a person stakes his or her self-esteem.

Contingency model of leadership effectiveness A middle-range theory of leadership effectiveness that maintains that group performance is a function of the interaction between a leader's style (task-oriented or relationship-oriented) and various situational factors such as the leader's personal relations with members, the degree of task structure, and the leader's position power.

Control theory The theory that an individual's tendency to engage in deviant behavior is influenced by his or her ties to other persons. There are four components of such ties: attachment, commitment, involvement, and belief.

Conversion The process through which the ideology of a social movement becomes the individual's fundamental perspective.

Cooling-out A response to repeated or glaring failures that gently persuades an offender to accept a less desirable though still reasonable alternative identity.

Cooperative principle The assumption conversationalists ordinarily make that a speaker is behaving cooperatively by trying to be (1) informative, (2) truthful, (3) relevant to the aims of the ongoing conversation, and (4) clear.

Correspondence The degree to which the action, context, target, and time in a measure of attitude is the same as those in a measure of behavior.

Crowd A substantial number of persons who engage in behavior recognized as unusual by participants and observers.

Cultural routines Recurrent and predictable activities that are basic to day-to-day social life.

D

Definition of the situation In symbolic interaction theory, a person's interpretation or construal of a situation and the objects in it. An agreement among persons about who they are, what actions are appropriate in the setting, and what their behaviors mean.

Deindividuation A temporary reduction of self-awareness and sense of personal responsibility; it may be brought on by such situational conditions as anonymity, a crowd, darkness, and consciousness-altering drugs.

Dependent variable In an experiment, the variable that is measured to determine whether it is affected by the manipulation of one or more other variables (independent variables).

Deterrence hypothesis The view that the arrest and punishment of some individuals for violation of laws deters other persons from committing the same violations.

Deviant behavior Behavior that violates the norms that apply in a given situation.

Deviant subculture A group of people whose norms encourage participation in a specific form of deviance and who regard positively those who engage in it.

Differential association theory The theory that deviant behavior occurs when people learn definitions favorable to the behavior through their associations with other persons.

Diffuse status characteristics Social attribute of a person that influences evaluations and beliefs about that person's general competence. *See also* Specific status characteristics.

Diffusion of responsibility The process wherein a bystander does not take action (e.g., in an emergency situation) because there are other bystanders who share the responsibility for intervening.

Disclaimer A verbal assertion intended to ward off any negative implications of impending actions by defining these actions as irrelevant to one's established social identity. By using disclaimers, a person suggests that although the impending acts may ordinarily imply a negative identity, his or hers is an extraordinary case.

Discrepant message In persuasion, a message advocating a position that is different from what the target believes.

Discrimination Overt acts, occurring without apparent justification, that treat members of certain out-groups in an unfair or disadvantageous manner.

Disjunctive tasks A type of unitary group task in which the group's performance depends entirely on that of its strongest or fastest member. *See also* Additive tasks, Conjunctive tasks.

Displaced aggression Aggression toward a target that exceeds what is justified by provocation by that target. Often occurs because aggression instigated by a different source is displaced onto a less powerful or more available target who had no responsibility for the negative response.

Display rules Cultural norms that dictate how we must modify our facial expressions to make them fit particular situations.

Dispositional attribution A decision by an observer to attribute a behavior to the internal state(s) of the person who performed it rather than to factors in that person's environment. *See also* Situational attribution.

Distributive justice principles A criterion in terms of which group members can judge the fairness and appropriateness of the distribution of rewards. Three of the most important are the equality principle, the equity principle, and the relative needs principle.

Dyadic withdrawal The process of increasing reliance on one person for gratification and decreasing reliance on others.

E

Ebonics A variety of American English spoken by many Blacks, with distinctive pronunciation of some words; African-American Vernacular English (AAVE).

Egoism Helping behavior motivated by a helper's own sense of self-gratification.

Embarrassment The feeling that people experience when interaction is disrupted because the identity they have claimed in an encounter is discredited.

Emergent norm The definition of the situation that results from interaction in an initially ambiguous situation.

Emotional deviance When individuals project an emotion that is inappropriate or too high or low in intensity for a particular situation.

Emotional intelligence One's ability to read, understand, and respond to others' emotional cues and behavior.

Emotional labor Emotion work that is done as an occupational requirement or expectation.

Emotions Short-lived reactions to a stimulus, a type of affect. The four components of an emotion are (1) a situational stimulus, (2) physiological changes, (3) expressive gesturing of some kind, and (4) a label to identify a cluster of the first three.

Emotion work Efforts to change the intensity or quality of feelings to bring them into line with the requirements of the occasion.

Empathy An emotional response to others as if we ourselves were in that person's situation; feeling pleasure at another's pleasure or pain at another's pain.

Encoder-decoder model A theory that views communication as a linear process in which the message is encoded by a transmitter, transmitted, and decoded by a receiver.

Endorsement An attitude held by a group member indicating the extent to which he or she supports the group's leader.

Equitable relationships A relationship in which the outcomes received by each person are equivalent.

Equity When people receive rewards in proportion to the contributions they make toward the attainment of group goals.

Ethnocentrism In intergroup relations, the tendency to regard one's own group as the center of everything and to evaluate other groups in reference to it; the tendency to regard one's in-group as superior to all out-groups.

Evolutionary psychology A theoretical perspective positing that predispositions toward some social behaviors are passed genetically from generation to generation and shaped by the process of natural selection.

Experiment A research method used to investigate cause-and-effect relations between one variable (the independent variable) and another (the dependent variable). In an experiment, the investigator manipulates the independent variable, randomly assigns participants to various levels of that variable, and measures the dependent variable.

External validity The extent to which it is possible to generalize the results of one study to other populations, settings, or times.

Extraneous variable A variable that is not explicitly included in a research hypothesis but has a causal impact on the dependent variable.

Extrinsically motivated behavior A behavior that results from the motivation to obtain a reward (food, praise) or avoid a punishment (spanking, criticism) controlled by someone else.

F

Fateful events Events that are beyond an individual's control, unpredictable, often life-threatening, often large in magnitude, and that disrupt people's usual activities.

Feeling rules Norms that dictate which emotions are appropriate for particular roles in a social context.

Field study An investigation that involves the collection of data about ongoing activity in everyday settings.

Five-factor model A psychological model that takes a wide variety of personality traits and organizes them into five factors, or categories. These factors and examples of associated traits are agreeableness (warmth, friendliness), conscientiousness (efficiency, dependability), extraversion (outgoingness, assertiveness), openness (curiosity, insight), and neuroticism (confidence, sensitivity). Also called the "Big Five."

Focus-of-attention bias The tendency to overestimate the causal impact of whomever or whatever we focus our attention on.

Formal social controls Agencies that are given responsibility for dealing with violations of rules or laws.

Frame A set of widely understood rules or conventions pertaining to a transient but repetitive social situation that indicate which roles should be enacted and which behaviors are proper.

Framing The attempts social movement activists make to articulate and present their ideas to broader audiences in hopes of winning support.

Front regions A setting used to manage appearances. In front regions, people carry out interaction performances and exert efforts to maintain appropriate appearances. Contrasts with back regions, where they allow themselves to violate appearances while they prepare, rehearse, and rehash performances.

Frustration The blocking of goal-directed activity. According to the frustration-aggression hypothesis, frustration leads to aggression.

Frustration-aggression hypothesis The hypothesis that every frustration leads to some form of aggression and every aggressive act is due to some prior frustration.

Fundamental attribution error The tendency to underestimate the importance of situational influences and to overestimate personal, dispositional factors as causes of behavior.

G

Game stage Mead's second stage of social experience, in which children enter organized activities and learn to imagine the viewpoints of several others at the same time.

Gathering A temporary collection of two or more people occupying a common space and time frame.

Gender role The behavioral expectations associated with gender.

Generalized other A conception of the attitudes and expectations held in common by the members of the organized groups with whom one interacts.

Goal isomorphism In groups, a state in which group goals and individual goals held by a member are similar in the sense that actions leading to the attainment of group goals also lead simultaneously to the attainment of individual goals.

Group A social unit that consists of two or more persons and has the following characteristics: shared goal(s), interaction (communication and influence) among members, normative expectations (norms and roles), and identification of members with the unit.

Group cohesion A property of a group, specifically the degree to which members of a group desire to remain in that group and resist leaving it. A highly cohesive group will maintain a firm hold over its members' time, energy, loyalty, and commitment.

Group goal A desirable outcome that group members strive collectively to accomplish or bring about.

Group goal effect An empirical generalization regarding group productivity—namely, that if a group establishes explicit, demanding objectives with respect to the group's performance, and if the group's members are highly committed to those objectives, then the group will perform at a higher level than if it does not do these things.

Group polarization In group decision making, the tendency for group members to shift their opinions toward a position that is similar to but more extreme than the positions they held prior to group discussion; both the risky shift and the cautious shift are instances of group polarization.

Group productivity The level of a group's output (per unit of time) gauged relative to something else, such as the level of resources used by the group or the group's targeted objectives.

Group self-esteem An individual's evaluation of self as a member of a racial or ethnic group.

Groupthink A mode of thinking within a cohesive group whereby pressures for unanimity overwhelm the members' motivation to realistically appraise alternative courses of action.

H

Halo effect The tendency of our general or overall liking for a person to influence our assessment of more specific traits of that person. The halo effect can produce inaccuracy in our ratings of others' traits and performances.

Helping Any behavior that has the consequences of providing some benefit to or improving the well-being of another person.

Heuristics Mental shortcuts that allow individuals to quickly select and apply schemas to new or ambiguous situations.

Homogenous Similar in important qualities.

Hypothesis A conjectural statement of the relation between two or more variables. Some hypotheses are explicitly causal in nature, whereas others are noncausal.

I

Identity The categories people use to specify who they are—that is, to locate themselves relative to other people.

Identity control theory Proposes that an actor uses the social meaning of his or her identity as a reference point for assessing what is occurring in the situation.

Identity degradation A response to repeated or glaring failures that destroys the offender's current identity and transforms him or her into a "lower" social type.

Identity theory A sociological theory that emphasizes the importance of self-meanings (role, group, social, and person identities) in guiding behavior.

Ideology In the study of social movements, a conception of reality that emphasizes certain values and justifies the movement.

Illusion of out-group homogeneity The tendency among in-group members to overestimate the extent to which out-group members are homogeneous or all alike.

Imitation A process of learning in which the learner watches another person's response and observes whether that person receives reinforcement.

Implicit personality theory A set of unstated assumptions about which personality traits are correlated with one another.

Impression formation The process of organizing diverse information into a unified impression of a person.

Independent variable In an experiment, the variable that is manipulated by the investigator to study the effects on one or more other (dependent) variables.

Individualist cultures Cultures that emphasize the individual and value individual achievement. *See also* Collectivist cultures.

Informal social control The reactions of family, friends, and acquaintances to rule violations by individuals.

Informational influence In groups, a form of influence that occurs when a group member accepts information from others as valid evidence about reality. Influence of this type is particularly likely to occur in situations of uncertainty or where there are no external or "objective" standards of reference.

Informed consent Voluntary consent by an individual to participate in a research project based on information received about what his or her participation will entail.

Ingratiation The deliberate use of deception to increase a target person's liking for us in hopes of gaining tangible benefits that the target person controls. Techniques such as flattery, expressing agreement with the target person's attitudes, and exaggerating one's own admirable qualities may be used.

Institutionalization of deviance The process by which members of a group come to expect and support deviance by another member over time.

Instrumental conditioning The process through which an individual learns a behavior in response to a stimulus to obtain a reward or avoid a punishment.

Intentionalist model A theory that views communication as the exchange of communicative intentions and views messages transmitted as merely the means to this end.

Intergroup conflict A state of affairs in which groups having opposing interests take antagonistic actions toward one another to control some outcome important to them.

Intergroup contact hypothesis An hypothesis holding that in intergroup relations, increased interpersonal contact between groups will reduce stereotypes and prejudice and, consequently, reduce antagonism between groups.

Internalization The process through which initially external behavioral standards become internal and subsequently guide an individual's behavior.

Internal validity The extent to which research findings are free from contamination by extraneous variables.

Interpersonal attraction A positive attitude held by one person toward another person.

Interpersonal spacing (proxemics) Nonverbal communication involving the ways in which people position themselves at varying distances and angles from others. Because *interpersonal spacing* refers to the proximity of people, it is also known as *proxemics*.

Intersubjectivity The information that each participant in an interaction needs about the other participant(s) in order for communication to be successful.

Interview survey A method of research in which a person (i.e., an interviewer) asks a series of questions and systematically records the answers from the respondents. *See also* Questionnaire survey.

Intrinsically motivated behavior A behavior that results from the motivation to achieve an internal state that an individual finds rewarding.

J

J-curve theory The theory that revolutions occur when there is an intolerable gap between people's expectations of need satisfaction and the actual level of satisfaction they experience.

L

Labeling theory The view that reactions of, and characterizations by, others are an essential element in deviance.

Leadership In groups, the process whereby one member influences and coordinates the behavior of other members in pursuit of group goals. The enactment of several functions necessary for successful group performance, including planning, organizing, and controlling the activities of group members.

Learning structure An environment in which an individual can learn the information and skills required to enact a role.

Legitimate means Those ways of striving to achieve goals that are defined as acceptable by social norms.

Legitimate power Authority that is accepted as a normal part of a social role.

Life course An individual's progression through a series of socially defined, age-linked social roles.

Life event An episode marking a transition point in the life course that provokes coping and readjustment.

Likert scale A technique for measuring attitudes that asks a respondent to indicate the extent to which he or she agrees with each of a series of statements about an object.

Linguistic intergroup bias Subtle and systematic differences in the language we use to describe events as a function of our group membership and the group to which the actor or target belongs.

Loneliness An unpleasant, subjective experience that results from the lack of social relationships satisfying in either quantity or quality.

Looking-glass self The term coined by Cooley that describes the self-schema we create based on how we think we appear to others.

Love story A script about what love should be like; it has characters, plot, and theme.

M

Majority influence The process by which a group's majority pressures an individual to adopt a specific position on some issue.

Mass media Those channels of communication (TV, radio, newspapers, and the Internet) that enable a source to reach and influence a large audience.

Matching hypothesis The hypothesis that each person looks for someone to date who is of approximately the same level of social desirability.

Media campaign A systematic attempt by an influencing source to use the mass media to change attitudes and beliefs of a target audience.

Mediator A third party who helps groups in conflict to identify issues and agree on some resolution to the conflict. Mediators usually serve as advisers rather than as decision makers. *See also* Arbitrator.

Mere exposure effect Repeated exposure to the same stimulus that produces a positive attitude toward it.

Meta-analysis A statistical technique that allows the researcher to combine the results from all previous studies of a question.

Methodology A set of systematic procedures used to conduct empirical research. Usually these procedures pertain to how data will be collected and analyzed.

Middle-range theories Narrow, focused, theoretical frameworks that explain the conditions that produce some specific social behavior. *See also* Theoretical perspective.

Minimal group paradigm Placing people into arbitrarily defined groups that have no important meaning is sufficient to trigger in-group and out-group processes and produce intergroup discrimination.

Minority influence An attempt by an active minority within a group to persuade majority members to accept their viewpoint and adopt a new position.

Mobilization The process through which individuals surrender personal resources and commit them to the pursuit of group or organizational goals.

Mood A general psychological condition that characterizes an individual's experience and emotional orientation for hours or even days. Considerably less specific than an emotion.

Moral development The process through which children become capable of making moral judgments.

N

Nonaggressive pornography Explicit depictions—in film, video, photograph, or story—of adults engaging in consenting sexual activity. *See also* Aggressive pornography.

Nonstandard speech A style of speech characterized by limited vocabulary, improper pronunciation, and incorrect grammar. The use of this style is associated with low status and low power. *See also* Standard speech.

Norm In groups, a standard or rule that specifies how members are expected to behave under given circumstances; expectations concerning which behaviors are acceptable and which are unacceptable for specific persons in specific situations.

Normative influence In groups, a form of influence that occurs when a member conforms to group norms in order to receive the rewards or avoid the punishments that are contingent on adherence to these norms.

Normative life stage A discrete period in the life course during which individuals are expected to perform the set of activities associated with a distinct age-related role.

Normative transition Socially expected changes made by all or most members of a defined population.

Norm of homogamy A social norm requiring that friends, lovers, and spouses be characterized by similarity in age, race, religion, and socioeconomic status.

Norm of reciprocity A social norm stating that people should (1) help those who have previously helped them and (2) not help those who have denied them help for no legitimate reason.

O

Observational learning The acquisition of behavior based on the observation of another person's behavior and of its consequences for that person. Also known as *modeling*.

Opportunity structure An environment in which an individual has opportunities to enact a role, which usually requires the assistance of those in complementary roles.

Overreward A situation in which an individual's outcomes are too high relative to his or her inputs. *See also* Underreward.

P

Panel study A method of research in which a given sample of respondents is surveyed at one point in time and then resurveyed at a later point (or several later points). Also known as a *longitudinal survey*.

Paralanguage All the vocal aspects of speech other than words, including loudness, pitch, speed of speaking, pauses, sighs, laughter, and so on.

Passionate love A state of intense longing for union with another and intense physiological arousal.

Perceived behavioral control The tendency of our behavior to be influenced not only by intentions but also by whether we are able to carry out those intentions.

Personal norms Feelings of moral obligation to perform specific actions that stem from an individual's internalized system of values.

Perspective-taking model A theory that views communication as the exchange of messages using symbols whose meaning is created by the interaction itself.

Persuasion An effort by a source to change the beliefs or attitudes of a target person through the use of information or argument.

Play stage Mead's first stage of social experience, in which young children imitate the activities of people around them.

Population A set of all people whose attitudes, behavior, or characteristics are of interest to the researcher.

Position A designated location in a social system.

Power and prestige order A structure of influence that emerges in task groups, with those of lower status often deferring to those of higher status and those of higher status taking the lead in decision making.

Powerlessness The sense of having little or no control over events.

Prejudice A strong like or dislike for members of a specific group.

Primacy effect The tendency, when forming an impression, to be most influenced by the earliest information received. The primacy effect accounts for the fact that first impressions are especially powerful.

Primary group A group with strong emotional ties and bonds that endure over time. This type of group tends to be more informal and intimate than other groups that individuals belong to. *See also* Secondary group.

Primary relationship An interpersonal relationship that is personal, emotionally involving, and of long duration.

Priming An implicit cognition effect, whereby exposure to one stimulus influences a response to another stimulus.

Primitive belief A belief based on our own personal experience or from a credible authority.

Principle of cognitive consistency In cognitive theory, a principle maintaining that if a person holds several ideas that are incongruous or inconsistent with one another, he or she will experience discomfort or conflict and will subsequently change one or more of the ideas to render them consistent.

Principle of covariation A principle that attributes behavior to the potential cause that is present when the behavior occurs and absent when the behavior fails to occur.

Procedural justice Perceptions of fairness of processes or procedures used to determine distributions.

Production blocking In brainstorming groups, a phenomenon that inhibits the production of novel ideas. Production blocking occurs when participants in a brainstorming group are unable to express their ideas due to bottlenecks caused by turn taking among members.

Promise An influence technique that is a communication taking the general form, "If you do X (which I want), then I will do Y (which you want)." *See also* Threat.

Prosocial behaviors A broad category of actions considered by society as being beneficial to others and as having positive social consequences. A wide variety of specific behaviors qualify as prosocial, including donation to charity, intervention in emergencies, cooperation, sharing, volunteering, sacrifice, and the like.

Prototype In person perception, an abstraction that represents the "typical" or quintessential instance of a class or group.

Punishment A painful or discomforting stimulus that reduces the frequency with which the target behavior occurs.

Q

Questionnaire survey A method of research in which a series of questions appear on a printed questionnaire and the respondents read and answer them online at their own pace. Usually no interviewer is present. *See also* Interview survey.

R

Random assignment In an experiment, the assignment of participants to experimental conditions on the basis of chance.

Reactance Resistance to persuasion attempts that occurs when the persuasion attempt threatens the independence or freedom of the target.

Realistic group conflict theory A theory of intergroup conflict that explains the development and the resolution of conflict in terms of the goals of each group. Its central hypothesis is that groups will engage in conflictive behavior when their goals involve opposition of interest.

Recency effect The tendency, when forming an impression, to be most influenced by the latest information received.

Reciprocity theory An exchange theory that focuses on conflict, risk, and the expressive value of exchange.

Referent power Social influence that occurs because individuals seek to be liked and accepted by valued social groups.

Reflexive self The ability to act toward oneself, taking the role of both the subject and the object in a situation; a uniquely human trait.

Reinforcement Any favorable outcome or consequence that results from a behavioral response by a person. Reinforcement strengthens the response—that is, it increases the probability it will be repeated.

Reinforcement theory A theoretical perspective based on the premise that social behavior is governed by external events, especially rewards and punishments.

Relation A connection between two people, with people contributing benefits and potentially deriving them from interactions with each other.

Relative deprivation A gap between the expected level and the actual level of satisfaction of the individual's needs in which the level expected by the individual exceeds the level of need satisfaction experienced.

Reliability The degree to which a measuring instrument produces the same results each time it is employed under a set of specified conditions.

Response rate In a survey, the percentage of people contacted who complete the survey.

Risk-benefit analysis A technique that weighs the potential risks to research participants against the anticipated benefits to participants and the importance of the knowledge that may result from the research.

Risky shift In group decision making, the tendency for decisions made in groups after discussion to be riskier than decisions made by individual members prior to discussion. *See also* Cautious shift.

Role A set of functions to be performed by a person on behalf of a group of which he or she is a member; a cluster of rules indicating the set of duties to be performed by a member occupying a given position within a group; the set of expectations governing the behavior of an occupant of a specific position within a social structure.

Role differentiation The emergence of distinct roles within a group; the division of labor within a group.

Role identities Individuals' concept of self in specific social roles.

Role overload The condition in which the demands placed on a person by his or her roles exceed the amount of time, energy, and other resources available to meet those demands.

Role taking In symbolic interaction theory, the process of imaginatively occupying the position of another person and viewing the situation and the self from that person's perspective; the process of imagining the other's attitudes and anticipating that person's responses.

Role theory A theoretical perspective based on the premise that a substantial portion of observable, day-to-day social behavior is simply persons carrying out role expectations.

Romantic love ideal Five beliefs regarding love, including the belief (1) in love at first sight, (2) that there is one and only one true love for each person, (3) that love conquers all, (4) that our beloved is (nearly) perfect, and (5) that one should follow his or her heart.

Routine activities perspective A theory that considers how deviant behavior, such as crime and substance abuse, emerges from the routines of everyday life.

Rule breaking Behavior that violates social norms.

Rumination Self-focused attention toward one's distress and the possible causes and consequences of the distress rather than ways to overcome it.

Rumor Communication via informal and often novel channels that cannot be validated.

S

Salience The relative importance of a specific role identity to the individual's self-schema. The salience hierarchy refers to the ordering of an individual's role identities according to their importance.

Schema A specific cognitive structure that organizes the processing of complex information about other persons, groups, and situations. Our schemas guide what we perceive in the environment, how we organize information in memory, and what inferences and judgments we make about people and things.

Secondary deviance Deviant behavior employed by a person as a means of defense or adjustment to the problems created by others' reactions to rule breaking by him or her.

Secondary group A group that is formal and impersonal, often organized around instrumental goals. *See also* Primary group.

Self The individual viewed as both the active source and the passive object of reflexive behavior.

Self-awareness A state in which we take the self as the object of our attention and focus on our own appearance, actions, and thoughts.

Self-disclosure The process of revealing personal information (aspects of our feelings and behaviors) to another person. Self-disclosure is sometimes used as an impression-management tactic.

Self-discrepancy The state in which a component of the individual's actual self is the opposite of a component of the ideal self or the ought self.

Self-esteem The evaluative component of the self-concept. The positive and negative evaluations people have of themselves.

Self-estrangement The awareness that one is engaging in activities that are not rewarding in themselves.

Self-fulfilling prophecy When persons behave toward another person according to a label (impression) and cause the person to respond in ways that confirm the label.

Self-presentation All conscious and unconscious attempts by people to control the images of self they project in social interaction.

Self-reinforcement An individual's use of internalized standards to judge his or her own behavior and reward the self.

Self-schema The organized structure of information that people have about themselves; the primary influence on the processing of information about the self.

Self-serving bias In attribution, the tendency for people to take personal credit for acts that yield positive outcomes and to deflect blame for bad outcomes by attributing them to external causes.

Sentiment The social aspect of emotion. Components of human responses that separate them from analogous responses animals would have.

Sexism Prejudice or discrimination on the basis of sex.

Sexual assault Sexual touching or intercourse without consent, accomplished by coercion, manipulation, or either the threat or use of force. The greater the force used or the resulting injury, the more severe the assault.

Shaping The learning process in which an agent initially reinforces any behavior that remotely resembles the desired response and subsequently requires increasing correspondence between the learner's behavior and the desired response before providing reinforcement.

Significant others People whose views and attitudes are very important and worthy of consideration. The reflected views of a significant other have great influence on the individual's self-concept and self-regulation.

Simple random sample A sample of individuals selected from a population in such a way that everyone is equally likely to be selected. *See also* Stratified sample.

Situated identity A conception held by a person in a situation that indicates who he or she is in relation to the other people involved in that situation.

Situated self The subset of self-concepts that constitutes the self people recognize in a particular situation. Selected from the person's various identities, qualities, and self-evaluations, the situated self depends on the demands of the situation.

Situational attribution A decision by an observer to attribute a behavior to environmental forces facing the person who performed it rather than to that person's internal state. *See also* Dispositional attribution.

Situational constraint An influence on behavior due to the likelihood that other persons will learn about that behavior and respond positively or negatively to it.

Social class Persons who share a common status in society. One's class standing may be based on occupational prestige and income.

Social-emotional specialist In groups, a person who strives to keep emotional relationships pleasant among members; a person who initiates acts that ease the tension and soothe hurt feelings.

Social emotions Emotions that cannot be understood or defined without reference to the social world; emotions that (1) involve an awareness of oneself in the social context, (2) emerge out of interaction with at least one other actor, and (3) are often experienced in reference to some kind of societal standard.

Social exchange theory A theoretical perspective, based on the principle of reinforcement, that assumes that people will likely choose actions that maximize rewards and minimize costs.

Social facilitation A phenomenon in which the mere presence of other individuals causes persons to perform better.

Social identity A definition of the self in terms of the defining characteristics of a social group.

Social identity theory of intergroup behavior A theory of intergroup relations based on the premise that people spontaneously categorize the social world into various groups (specifically, in-groups and out-groups) and experience high self-esteem to the extent that the in-groups to which they belong have more status than the out-groups.

Social impact theory A theoretical framework, applicable to both persuasion and obedience, stating that the impact of an influence attempt is a function of strength, immediacy, and number of sources that are present.

Social influence An interaction process in which one person's behavior causes another person to change an opinion or to perform an action that he or she would not otherwise do.

Socialization The process through which individuals learn skills, knowledge, values, motives, and roles appropriate to their positions in a group or society.

Social learning theory A theoretical perspective maintaining that one person (the learner) can acquire new responses without enacting them simply by observing the behavior of another person (the model). This learning process, called *imitation*, is distinguished by the fact that the learner neither performs a response nor receives any reinforcement.

Social loafing The tendency by group members to slack off and reduce their effort on additive tasks, which causes the group's output to fall short of its potential.

Social movement Collective activity that expresses a high level of concern about some issue; the activity may include participation in discussions, petition drives, demonstrations, or election campaigns.

Social networks The sets of interpersonal relationships associated with the social positions a person occupies.

Social perception The process through which we construct an understanding of the social world out of the data we obtain through our senses; more narrowly defined, the processes through which we use available information to form impressions of people.

Social psychology The field that systematically studies the nature and causes of human social behavior.

Social responsibility norm A widely accepted social norm stating that individuals should help people who are dependent on them.

Social structure The ordered and persisting relationships among the positions in a social system.

Sociolinguistic competence Knowledge of the implicit rules for generating socially appropriate sentences that make sense because they fit the listeners' social knowledge.

Source In social influence, the person who intentionally engages in some behavior (persuasion, threat, promise) to cause another person to behave in a manner different from how he or she otherwise would. *See also* Target.

Specific status characteristics Attributes that influence performance expectations for tasks that are relevant to that attribute (e.g., mathematical ability on a math test). *See also* Diffuse status characteristics.

Speech act theory The theory that verbal utterances both state something and do something.

Spillover Stress experienced at work or in the family is carried over into the other domain.

Spoken language A socially acquired system of sound patterns with meanings agreed on by the members of a group.

Standard speech A speech style characterized by diverse vocabulary, proper pronunciation, correct grammar, and abstract content. The use of this style is associated with high status and power. *See also* Nonstandard speech.

Status The social ranking of a person's position.

Status characteristic Any property of a person around which evaluations and beliefs about that person come to be organized; properties such as race, occupation, age, sex, ethnicity, education, and so on.

Status generalization A process through which differences in members' status characteristics lead to different performance expectations and, hence, affect patterns of interaction in groups; the tendency for a member's status inside a group to reflect his or her status outside that group.

Stereotypes Fixed sets of characteristics that are attributed to all the members of a group; simplistic and rigid perceptions of members of one group that are widely shared by others.

Stereotype threat The suspicion a member of a group holds that he or she will be judged based on a common stereotype of the group.

Stigma Personal characteristics that others view as insurmountable handicaps preventing competent or morally trustworthy behavior.

Stratified sample In survey research, a sampling design whereby researchers subdivide the population into groups according to characteristics known or thought to be important, select a random sample of groups, and then draw a sample of units within each selected group. *See also* Simple random sample.

Stress The condition in which the demands made on the person exceed the individual's ability to cope with them.

Subjective expected value (SEV) With respect to threats, the product of a threat's credibility times its magnitude; with respect to promises, the product of a promise's credibility times its magnitude.

Subjective norms An individual's perception of others' beliefs about whether a behavior is appropriate and their motivation to comply with those expectations.

Subtractive rule When making attributions about the influence of personal dispositions on a behavior, the observer subtracts the perceived impact of situational forces from the personal disposition implied by the behavior itself.

Subtyping A process through which perceivers create subcategories of stereotyped groups who serve as exceptions to the rule without threatening the overarching stereotype. Cognitive strategies like these help people explain away contradictory information and preserve their stereotypes.

Summons-answer sequence The most common verbal method for initiating a conversation, in which one person summons the other as with a question or greeting, and the other indicates his or her availability for conversation by responding. This sequence establishes the mutual obligation to speak and to listen that produces conversational turn taking.

Superordinate goal In intergroup conflict, an objective held in common by all conflicting groups that cannot be achieved by any one group without the supportive efforts of the others.

Supplication An impression management tactic that involves convincing a target person that you are needy and deserving.

Symbolic interaction theory A theoretical perspective based on the premise that human nature and social order are products of communication among people. Also know as *symbolic interactionism.*

Symbols Forms used to represent ideas, feelings, thoughts, intentions, or any other object. Symbols represent our experiences in a way that others can perceive with their sensory organs—through sounds, gestures, pictures, and so on.

T

Tactical impression management The selective use of self-presentation tactics by a person who wishes to manipulate the impressions that others form of him or her.

Target In social influence, the person who is affected by a social influence attempt from the source. In aggression, the person toward whom an aggressive act is directed. *See also* Source.

Task specialist In groups, a member who pushes the group toward the attainment of its goals; a person who contributes many ideas and suggestions to the group.

Theoretical perspectives Theories that make broad assumptions about human nature and offer general explanations of a wide range of diverse behaviors. *See also* Middle-range theories.

Theory A set of interrelated propositions that organizes and explains a set of observed facts; a network of hypotheses that may be used as a basis for prediction.

Theory of cognitive dissonance A theory concerning the sources and effects of inconsistency in cognitive systems with two or more elements.

Theory of planned behavior A revised model of the theory of reasoned action that argues that the link between intention and behavior will be strongest when an individual perceives individual control over the behavior.

Theory of reasoned action The theory that behavior is determined by behavioral intention, which in turn is determined by both attitude and subjective norm.

Theory of speech accommodation The theory that people express or reject intimacy with others by adjusting their speech behavior (accent, vocabulary, or language) during interaction. They make their own speech behavior more similar to their partner's to express liking, and more dissimilar to reject intimacy.

Threat An influence technique that is a communication taking the general form, "If you don't do X (which I want), then I will do Y (which you don't want)." *See also* Promise.

Trait centrality A personality trait has a high level of trait centrality when information about a person's standing on that trait has a large impact on the overall impression that others form of that person. The warm-cold trait, for instance, is highly central.

Transactional leadership Leadership in groups based on an exchange between the leader and other group members. The leader performs actions that move the group toward the attainment of its goals; in return, the leader receives support, endorsement, and rewards.

Transformational leadership Leadership that strengthens group performance by changing the way members view their group, its opportunities, and its mission; leadership that conveys an extraordinary sense of mission to group members and arouses new ways of thinking within the group.

Trust The belief that a person is both honest and benevolent.

U

Ultimate attribution error A perceptual bias occurring in intergroup relations. Negative behaviors by out-group members are attributed to stable, internal factors such as undesirable personal traits or dispositions, but positive behaviors by out-group members are attributed to unstable, external factors such as situational pressures or luck. As a result, in-group observers will blame the out-group for negative outcomes but will not give it credit for positive outcomes.

Underreward When a person's outcomes are too low relative to his or her inputs. *See also* Overreward.

Upward mobility Movement of a person from an occupation lower in prestige and income to one higher in prestige and income.

V

Values Enduring beliefs that certain patterns of behavior or end states are preferable to others.

Victim-blame When responsibility for a sexual assault is placed on the victim rather than the perpetrator.

W

Weapons effect A cognitive priming effect, when the sight of a weapon makes more accessible or primes aggression-related concepts or scripts for behavior.

Abbey, A. (2002). Alcohol-related sexual assault: A common problem among college students. *Journal of Studies on Alcohol and Drugs, 14*, 118–128.

Abbey, A., Jacques-Tiura, A. J., & LeBreton, J. M. (2011). Risk factors for sexual aggression in young men: An expansion of the confluence model.*Aggressive Behavior, 37*(5), 450–464.

Abbey, A., McAuslan, P., Zawacki, T., Clinton, A. M., & Buck, P. O. (2001). Attitudinal, experiential, and situational predictors of sexual assault perpetration. *Journal of Interpersonal Violence, 16*(8), 784–807.

Abele, A. E. (2003). The dynamics of masculine-agentic and feminine-communal traits: Findings from a prospective study. *Journal of Personality and Social Psychology, 85*, 768–776.

Abelson, R. P. (1981). The psychological status of the script concept. *American Psychologist, 36*, 715–729.

Aberson, C. L., Healy, M., & Romero, V. (2000). Ingroup bias and self-esteem: A meta-analysis. *Personality and Social Psychology Review, 4*, 157–173.

Abrams, D., Marques, J., Brown, N., & Henson, M. (2000). Pro-norm and anti-norm deviance within and between groups. *Journal of Personality and Social Psychology, 78*, 906–912.

Acock, A., & Scott, W. (1980). A model for predicting behavior: The effect of attitude and social class on high and low visibility political participation. *Social Psychology Quarterly, 43*, 59–72.

Adachi, P. J., & Willoughby, T. (2011). The effect of video game competition and violence on aggressive behavior: Which characteristic has the greatest influence? *Psychology of Violence, 1*(4), 259.

Adams, J. S. (1963). Toward an understanding of inequity. *Journal of Abnormal and Social Psychology, 67*, 422–436.

Adams, J. S., & Jacobsen, P. R. (1964). Effects of wage inequities on work quality. *Journal of Abnormal and Social Psychology, 69*, 19–25.

Adams, J. S., & Rosenbaum, W. B. (1962). The relationship of worker productivity to cognitive dissonance about wage inequities. *Journal of Applied Psychology, 46*, 161–164.

Adelman, R., & Verbrugge, L. (2000). Death makes news: The social impact of disease on newspaper coverage. *Journal of Health and Social Behavior, 41*, 347–367.

Aderman, D., & Berkowitz, L. (1983). Self-concern and the unwillingness to be helpful. *Social Psychology Quarterly, 46*(4), 293–301.

Adler, P. A., & Adler, P. (1995). Dynamics of inclusion and exclusion in preadolescent cliques. *Social Psychology Quarterly, 58*, 145–162.

Adlerfer, C. P. (1982). Problems in changing White males' behavior and beliefs concerning race relations. In P. Goodman (Ed.), *Change in organizations* (pp. 122–165). San Francisco: Jossey-Bass.

Agnew, R. (1992). Foundation for a general strain theory of crime and delinquency. *Criminology, 30*, 47–87.

Agnew, R., & White, H. R. (1992). An empirical test of general strain theory. *Criminology, 30*, 475–499.

Aiken, L. R. (1992). Some measures of interpersonal attraction and group cohesiveness. *Educational and Psychological Measurement, 52*(1), 63–67.

Ainsworth, M. (1979). Infant-mother attachment. *American Psychologist, 34*, 932–937.

Ajzen, I. (1982). On behaving in accordance with one's attitudes. In M. Zanna, E. Higgins, & C. Herman (Eds.), *Consistency in social behavior: The Ontario symposium* (Vol. 2) (pp. 131–146). Hillsdale, NJ: Erlbaum.

Ajzen, I. (1985). From intentions to action: A theory of planned behavior. In J. Kuhl & J. Beckman (Eds.), *Action control: From cognition to behavior.* (pp. 11–39). Heidelberg: Springer Verlag.

Ajzen, I. (1991). The theory of planned behavior. *Organizational behavior and human decision processes, 50*(2), 179–211.

Ajzen, I., & Fishbein, M. (1977). Attitude-behavior relations: A theoretical analysis and review of research. *Psychological Bulletin, 84*, 888–918.

Ajzen, I., & Fishbein, M. (1980). *Understanding attitudes and predicting social behavior.* Englewood Cliffs, NJ: Prentice Hall.

Ajzen, I., & Holmes, W. H. (1976). Uniqueness of behavioral effects in causal attribution. *Journal of Personality, 44*, 98–108.

Ajzen, I., & Sexton, J. (1999). Depth of processing, belief congruence, and attitude-behavior correspondence. In S. Chjaiken and Y. Trope (Eds.), *Dual-process theories in social psychology* (pp. 117–138). New York: Guilford.

Akers, R. L., Krohn, M., Lanza-Kaduce, L., & Radosevich, M. (1979). Social learning and deviant behavior: A specific test of a general theory. *American Sociological Review, 44*, 636–655.

Akers, R. L., LaGreca, H. J., Cochran, J., & Sellers, C. (1989). Social learning theory and alcohol behavior among the elderly. *Sociological Quarterly, 30*, 625–638.

Albarracín, D. (2002). Cognition in persuasion: An analysis of information processing in response to persuasive communications. *Advances in Experimental Social Psychology, 34*, 61–130.

Aldag, R. J., & Fuller, S. F. (1993). Beyond fiasco: A reappraisal of the groupthink phenomenon and a new model of group decision processes. *Psychological Bulletin, 113*, 533–552.

Aldwin, C., & Revenson, T. (1987). Does coping help? A reexamination of the relationship between coping and mental health. *Journal of Personality and Social Psychology, 53*, 337–348.

Alexander, C. N., & Rudd, J. (1984). Predicting behaviors from situated identities. *Social Psychology Quarterly, 47*, 172–177.

Alexander, C. N., & Wiley, M. G. (1981). Situated activity and identity formation. In M. Rosenberg & R. Turner (Eds.), *Social psychology: Sociological perspectives*. (pp. 269–289). New York: Basic Books.

Allan, E. A., & Steffensmeier, D. J. (1989). Youth underemployment and property crime: Differential effects of job availability and job quality on juvenile and young adult arrest rates. *American Sociological Review, 54*, 107–123.

Allard, M. D. (2008). How high school students use time: A visual essay. *Monthly Labor Review, 131*(11), 51–57.

Allen, H. (1972). Bystander intervention and helping on the subway. In L. Bickman & T. Henchy (Eds.), *Beyond the laboratory: Field research in social psychology*. (pp. 22–33). New York: McGraw-Hill.

Allen, V. L., & Levine, J. M. (1969). Consensus and conformity. *Journal of Experimental Social Psychology, 5*, 389–399.

Allen, V. L., & Levine, J. M. (1971). Social support and conformity: The role of independent assessment of reality. *Journal of Experimental Social Psychology, 7*, 48–58.

Allen, V. L., & Van de Vliert, E. (1982). A role theoretical perspective on transitional processes. In V. L. Allen & E. Van de Vliert (Eds.), *Role transitions: Explorations and explanations* (pp. 3–18). New York: Plenum.

Allison, S. T., Mackie, D. M., Muller, M. M., & Worth, L. T. (1993). Sequential correspondence biases and perceptions of change: The Castro studies revisited. *Personality and Social Psychology Bulletin, 19*, 151–157.

Allison, S. T., McQueen, L. R., & Schaerfl, L. M. (1992). Social decision making processes and the equal partitioning of shared resources. *Journal of Experimental Social Psychology, 28*, 23–42.

Allport, F. H. (1920). The influence of the group upon association and thought. *Journal of Experimental Psychology, 3*, 159–182.

Allport, F. H. (1924). *Social psychology*. Cambridge, MA: Houghton Mifflin.

Allport, G. W. (1935). Attitudes. In C. Murchison (Ed.), *Handbook of social psychology*. (pp. 798–844). Worcester, MA: Clark University Press.

Allport, G. W. (1954). *The nature of prejudice*. Reading, MA: Addison-Wesley.

Allport, G. W. (1961). *Pattern and growth in personality*. New York: Holt, Rinehart and Winston.

Allport, G. W., & Postman, L. J. (1947). *The psychology of rumor*. New York: Holt, Rinehart & Winston.

Almeida, D., Wethington, E., & Kessler, R. (2002). The daily inventory of stressful events: An interview-based approach for measuring daily stressors. *Assessment, 9*, 41–55.

Altman, I., & Taylor, D. A. (1973). *Social penetration: The development of interpersonal relationships*. New York: Holt, Rinehart and Winston.

Alwin, D. F. (1986). Religion and parental child-rearing orientations: Evidence of Catholic-Protestant convergence. *American Journal of Sociology, 92*, 412–440.

Alwin, D. F. (1990). Cohort replacement and changes in parental socialization values. *Journal of Marriage and the Family, 52*, 347–360.

Al-Zahrani, S. S. A., & Kaplowitz, S. A. (1993). Attributional biases in individualistic and collectivistic cultures: A comparison of Americans with Saudis. *Social Psychology Quarterly, 56*, 223–233.

Amato, P. R. (2001). The consequences of divorce for adults and children. In R. Milardo (Ed.), *Understanding families into the new millennium: A decade in review* (pp. 488–506). Minneapolis, MN: National Council on Family Relations.

Amato, P. R., & Cheadle, J. (2005). The long-reach of divorce: Divorce and child well-being across three generations. *Journal of Marriage and Family, 67*, 191–206.

Amato, P. R., & Fowler, F. (2002). Parenting practices, child adjustment, and family diversity. *Journal of Marriage and Family, 64*, 703–716.

American Association of University Women. (1992). *The AAUW report: How schools shortchange girls*. Washington, DC: Author.

American Psychiatric Association. (1981). *Diagnostic and statistical manual of mental disorders* (3rd ed.). Washington, DC: Author.

American Psychological Association. (1993). *Summary report of the APA Commission on Violence and Youth*. Washington, DC: Author.

American Society for Aesthetic Plastic Surgery. (2013). Cosmetic procedures increase in 2012. www.surgery.org/media/news-releases/cosmetic-procedures-increase-in-2012.

Amir, Y. (1969). Contact hypothesis in ethnic relations. *Psychological Bulletin, 71*, 319–342.

Amir, Y. (1976). The role of intergroup contact in change of prejudice and ethnic relations. In P. A. Katz (Ed.), *Towards the elimination of racism* (pp. 245–308). New York: Pergamon.

Anderson, B. A., & Silver, B. D. (1987). The validity of survey responses: Insights from interviews of married couples in a survey of Soviet emigrants. *Social Forces, 66*, 537–554.

Anderson, C. A. (1987). Temperature and aggression: Effects on quarterly, yearly, and city rates of violent and nonviolent crime. *Journal of Personality and Social Psychology, 52*, 1161–1173.

Anderson, C. A. (2001). Heat and violence. *Current Directions in Psychological Science, 10*, 33–38.

Anderson, C. A., Anderson, K. B., & Deuser, W. E. (1996). Examining an affective aggression framework: Weapon and temperature effects on aggressive thoughts, affect, and attitudes. *Personality and Social Psychology Bulletin, 22*, 366–376.

Anderson, C. A., Anderson, K. B., Dorr, N., DeNeve, K. M., & Flanagan, M. (2000). Temperature and aggression. In M. Zanna (Ed.), *Advances in experimental social psychology* (Vol. 32, pp. 63–133). New York: Academic Press.

Anderson, C. A., Benjamin, A. J., & Bartholow, B. D. (1998). Does the gun pull the trigger? Automatic priming effects of weapon pictures and weapon names. *Psychological Science, 9,* 308–314.

Anderson, C. A., Berkowitz, L., Donnerstein, E., Huesmann, L. R., Johnson, J., Linz, D., et al. (2003). The influence of media violence on youth. *Psychological Science in the Public Interest, 4,* 81–110.

Anderson, C. A., & Bushman, B. J. (2002). Human aggression. *Annual Review of Psychology, 53*(1), 27–51.

Anderson, C. A., & Dill, K. E. (2000). Video games and aggressive thoughts, feelings, and behavior in the laboratory and in life. *Journal of Personality and Social Psychology, 78*(4), 772–790.

Anderson, C. A., & Sedikides, C. (1991). Thinking about people: Contribution of a typological alternative to associationistic and dimensional models of person perception. *Journal of Personality and Social Psychology, 60,* 203–217.

Anderson, C. A., Shibuya, A., Ihori, N., Swing, E. L., Bushman, B. J., Sakamoto, A., Rothstein, H. R., & Saleem, M. (2010). Violent video game effects on aggression, empathy, and prosocial behavior in eastern and western countries: a meta-analytic review. *Psychological Bulletin, 136*(2), 151.

Anderson, K. (2010). *Benign bigotry: The psychology of subtle prejudice.* Cambridge, UK: Cambridge University Press.

Anderson, K. B., Cooper, H., & Okamura, L. (1997). Individual differences and attitudes toward rape: A meta-analytic review. *Personality and Social Psychology Bulletin, 23*(3), 295–315.

Anderson, W. P. (2006). A procedure for coding self-regard from narrative self-descriptions. *Psychological Reports, 99,* 879–893.

Andrews, B., & Brewin, C. R. (1990). Attributions of blame for marital violence: A study of antecedents and consequences. *Journal of Marriage and the Family, 52*(3), 757–767.

Andrews, I. R. (1967). Wage inequity and job performance: An experimental study. *Journal of Applied Psychology, 51,* 39–45.

Ansolabehere, S., & Iyengar, S. (1994). Of horseshoes and horse races: Experimental studies of the impact of poll results on electoral behavior. *Political Communication, 11,* 412–430.

Anson, O. (1989). Marital status and women's health revisited: The importance of a proximate adult. *Journal of Marriage and the Family, 51,* 185–194.

Antaki, C., Barnes, R., & Leudar, I. (2005). Diagnostic formulations in psychotherapy. *Discourse Studies, 7,* 627–647.

Appleton, W. (1981). *Fathers and daughters.* New York: Doubleday.

Apsler, R., & Sears, D. O. (1968). Warning, personal involvement, and attitude change. *Journal of Personality and Social Psychology, 9,* 162–166.

Aquino, K. F., & Reed, A. (2002). The self-importance of moral identity. *Journal of Personality and Social Psychology, 83,* 1423–1440.

Araji, S. K. (1977). Husbands' and wives' attitude-behavior congruence on family roles. *Journal of Marriage and the Family,* 309–320.

Arbuthnot, J., & Wayner, M. (1982). Minority influence: Effects of size, conversion, and sex. *Journal of Psychology, 111,* 285–295.

Archer, D., & Akert, R. (1977). Words and everything else: Verbal and nonverbal cues in social interpretation. *Journal of Personality and Social Psychology, 35,* 443–449.

Archer, J. (1991). Human sociobiology: Basic concepts and limitations. *Journal of Social Issues, 47*(3), 11–26.

Archer, R. L. (1980). Self-disclosure. In D. M. Wegner & R. R. Vallacher (Eds.), *The self in social psychology.* (pp. 409–427). New York: Oxford University Press.

Arditti, J. A. (1999). Rethinking relationships between divorced mothers and their children: Capitalizing on family strengths. *Family Relations, 48,* 109–119.

Arendt, H. (1965). *Eichmann in Jerusalem: A report on the banality of evil.* New York: Viking.

Aries, E. (1996). *Men and women in interaction.* New York: Oxford University Press.

Armeli, S., Carney, M. A., Tennen, H., Affleck, G., & O'Neil, T. P. (2000). Stress and alcohol use: A daily process examination of the stressor-vulnerability model. *Journal of Personality and Social Psychology, 78,* 979–994.

Armstrong, E. A., Hamilton, L., & Sweeney, B. (2006). Sexual assault on campus: A multilevel, integrative approach to party rape. *Social Problems, 53*(4), 483–499.

Aron, A., Norman, C., Aron, E., McKenna, C., & Heyman, R. (2000). Couples' shared participation in novel and arousing activities and experienced relationship quality. *Journal of Personality and Social Psychology, 78,* 273–284.

Aronfreed, J., & Reber, A. (1965). Internalized behavior suppression and the timing of social punishment. *Journal of Personality and Social Psychology, 1,* 3–16.

Aronson, E., Ellsworth, P. C., Carlsmith, J. M., & Gonzales, J. H. (1990). *Methods of research in social psychology* (2nd ed.). New York: McGraw-Hill.

Aronson, E., Turner, J. A., & Carlsmith, J. M. (1963). Communicator credibility and communication discrepancy as determinants of opinion change. *Journal of Abnormal and Social Psychology, 67,* 31–36.

Aronson, E., Wilson, T., & Brewer, M. (1998). Experimentation in social psychology. In D. Gilbert, S. Fiske, & G. Lindzey (Eds.), *The handbook of social psychology* (4th ed., Vol. 1, pp. 99–142). Boston: McGraw-Hill.

Arriaga, X., Reed, J., Goodfriend, W., & Agnew, C. (2006). Relationship perceptions and persistence: Do fluctuations in perceived partner commitment undermine dating relationships? *Journal of Personality and Social Psychology, 91,* 1045–1065.

Asch, S. E. (1946). Forming impressions of personality. *Journal of Abnormal and Social Psychology, 41,* 258–290.

Asch, S. E. (1951). Effects of group pressure upon the modification and distortion of judgments. In H. Guetzkow (Ed.), *Groups, leadership, and men.* (pp. 177–190). Pittsburgh, PA: Carnegie Press.

Asch, S. E. (1952). *Social psychology.* Englewood Cliffs, NJ: Prentice Hall.

Asch, S. E. (1955). Opinions and social pressure. *Scientific American, 193,* 31–35.

Asch, S. E. (1957). An experimental investigation of group influence. In *Symposium on preventive and social psychiatry.* (pp. 15–17). Washington, DC: Walter Reed Army Institute of Research.

Aseltine, R., Gore, S., & Gordon, J. (2000). Life stress, anger and anxiety, and delinquency: An empirical test of general strain theory. *Journal of Health and Social Behavior, 41,* 256–275.

Asendorpf, J. B. (1987). Videotape reconstruction of emotions and cognitions related to shyness. *Journal of Personality and Social Psychology, 53,* 542–549.

Ashforth, B., & Lee, R. (1990). Defensive behavior in organizations: A preliminary model. *Human Relations, 43,* 621–648.

Ashmore, R. D. (1981). Sex stereotypes and implicit personality theory. In D. L. Hamilton (Ed.), *Cognitive processes in stereotyping and intergroup behavior* (pp. 37–81). Hillsdale, NJ: Erlbaum.

Ashmore, R. D., Solomon, M. R., & Longo, L. C. (1996). Thinking about fashion models' looks: A multidimensional approach to the structure of perceived physical attractiveness. *Personality and Social Psychology Bulletin, 22,* 1083–1104.

Astone, N., & McLanahan, S. S. (1991). Family structure, parental practices, and high school completion. *American Sociological Review, 56,* 309–320.

Atkin, C. K. (1981). Mass media information campaign effectiveness. In R. E. Rice & W. J. Paisley (Eds.), *Public communication campaigns.* (pp. 265–279). Beverly Hills, CA: Sage.

Attridge, M., Berscheid, E., & Simpson, J. A. (1995). Predicting relationship stability from both partners vs. one. *Journal of Personality and Social Psychology, 69,* 254–268.

Attrill, A., & Jalil, R. (2011). Revealing only the superficial me: Exploring categorical self-disclosure online. *Computers in Human Behavior, 27,* 1634–1642.

Aubrey, J. S., & Harrison, K. (2004). The gender-role content of children's favorite television programs and its links to their gender-related perception. *Media Psychology, 6,* 111–146.

Austin, W. (1980). Friendship and fairness: Effects of type of relationship and task performance on choice distribution rules. *Personality and Social Psychology Bulletin, 6,* 402–408.

Austin, W., & Walster [Hatfield], E. (1974). Participants' reactions to "equity with the world." *Journal of Experimental Social Psychology, 10,* 528–548.

Averill, J. R. (1980). A constructivist view of emotion. *Emotion: Theory, research, and experience, 1,* 305–339.

Aviezer, H., Hassin, R., Ryan, J., Grady, C., Susskind, J., Anderson, A., Muscovitch. M., & Bentin, S. (2008). Angry, disgusted, or afraid? Studies on the malleability of emotion perception. *Psychological Science, 19,* 724–732.

Babcock, M. K., & Sabini, J. (1990). On differentiating embarrassment from shame. *European Journal of Social Psychology, 20*(2), 151–169.

Back, M. D., Penke, L., Schmukle, S. C., Sachse, K., Borkenau, P., & Asendorpf, J. B. (2011). Why mate choices are not as reciprocal as we assume: The role of personality, flirting, and physical attractiveness. *European Journal of Personality, 25,* 120–132.

Backman, C. (1990). Attraction in interpersonal relationships. In M. Rosenberg & R. Turner (Eds.), *Social psychology: Sociological perspectives.* (pp. 235–268). New Brunswick, NJ: Transaction.

Backman, C., & Secord, P. (1962). Liking, selective interaction, and misperception in congruent interpersonal relations. *Sociometry, 25,* 321–325.

Badie, D. (2010). Groupthink, Iraq, and the war on terror: Explaining US policy shift toward Iraq. *Foreign Policy Analysis, 6*(4), 277–296.

Bagozzi, R. P. (1981). Attitudes, intentions, and behavior: A test of some key hypotheses. *Journal of Personality and Social Psychology, 41,* 607–627.

Bailey, J. M., Kim, P., Hills, A., & Linsenmeier, J. (1997). Butch, femme, or straight acting? Partner preferences of gay men and lesbians. *Journal of Personality and Social Psychology, 73,* 960–973.

Bailey, W. C. (1990). Murder, capital punishment, and television: Execution publicity and homicide rates. *American Sociological Review, 55,* 628–633.

Baker, K., & Raney, A. (2007). Equally super? Gender-role stereotyping of superheroes in children's animated programs. *Mass Communications and Society, 10,* 25–41.

Bakshy, E., (2013, March 29). Showing support for marriage equality on Facebook. *Facebook Data Science* (Notes). www.facebook.com/notes/facebook-data-science/showing-support-for-marriage-equality-on-facebook/10151430548593859.

Bales, R. F. (1950). *Interaction process analysis: A method for the study of small groups.* Cambridge, MA: Addison-Wesley.

Bales, R. F. (1953). The equilibrium problem in small groups. In T. Parsons, R. F. Bales, & E. A. Shils (Eds.), *Working papers in the theory of action.* (pp. 115–134). New York: Free Press.

Bales, R. F. (1965). Task roles and social roles in problem solving groups. In I. D. Steiner & M. Fishbein (Eds.), *Current studies in social psychology* (pp. 321–333). New York: Holt, Rinehart and Winston.

Bales, R. F. (1970). *Personality and interpersonal behavior.* New York: Holt, Rinehart and Winston.

Balk, S. J., Fisher, D. E., & Geller, A. C. (2013). Teens and indoor tanning: A cancer prevention opportunity for pediatricians. *Pediatrics, 131*, 772–785.

Balkwell, J. W. (1991). From expectations to behavior: An improved postulate for expectation states theory. *American Sociological Review, 56*, 355–369.

Balkwell, J. W. (1994). Status. In M. Foschi & E. J. Lawler (Eds.), *Group processes: Sociological analyses* (pp. 119–148). Chicago: Nelson-Hall.

Ball, D. W. (1976). Failure in sports. *American Sociological Review, 41*, 726–739.

Baller, R., & Richardson, K. (2002). Social integration, imitation and the geographic patterning of suicide. *American Sociological Review, 67*, 873–888.

Baltes, P., & Willis, S. (1982). Plasticity and enhancement of intellectual functioning in old age: Penn State's adult development and enrichment project. In F. Craik & S. Trehub (Eds.), *Aging and cognitive processes.* (pp. 353–389). New York: Plenum.

Banaji, M., & Prentice, D. (1994). The self in social contexts. *Annual Review of Psychology, 45*, 297–332.

Bandura, A. (1965). Influence of models' reinforcement contingencies on the acquisition of imitative responses. *Journal of Personality and Social Psychology, 1*, 589–595.

Bandura, A. (1969). Social-learning theory of identificatory processes. In D. Goslin (Ed.), *Handbook of socialization theory and research.* (pp. 213–262). Chicago: Rand McNally.

Bandura, A. (1973). *Aggression: A social learning analysis.* Englewood Cliffs, NJ: Prentice Hall.

Bandura, A. (1977). *Social learning theory.* Englewood Cliffs, NJ: Prentice Hall.

Bandura, A. (1982a). The psychology of chance encounters and life paths. *American Psychologist, 37*, 747–755.

Bandura, A. (1982b). Self-efficacy mechanism in human agency. *American Psychologist, 37*, 122–147.

Bandura, A. (1982c). Self-appraisal and self-regulation. In J. Suls (Ed.), *Psychological perspectives on the self* (Vol. 1). Hillsdale, NJ: Erlbaum.

Bandura, A., Ross, D., & Ross, S. (1961). Transmission of aggression through imitation of aggressive models. *Journal of Abnormal and Social Psychology, 63*, 575–582.

Barber, J. J., & Grichting, W. L. (1990). Australia's media campaign against drug abuse. *International Journal of the Addictions, 25*, 693–708.

Barker, R. G., Dembo, T., & Lewin, K. (1941). Frustration and aggression: An experiment with young children. *University of Iowa Studies in Child Welfare, 18*, 1–34.

Barlett, C. P., & Anderson, C. A. (2011). Reappraising the situation and its impact on aggressive behavior. *Personality and Social Psychology Bulletin, 37*(12), 1564–1573.

Barlett, C. P., Harris, R. J., & Baldassaro, R. (2007). Longer you play, the more hostile you feel: Examination of first person shooter video games and aggression during video game play. *Aggressive Behavior, 33*(6), 486–497.

Barlett, C. P., Harris, R. J., & Bruey, C. (2008). The effect of the amount of blood in a violent video game on aggression, hostility, and arousal. *Journal of Experimental Social Psychology, 44*(3), 539–546.

Barnes, C. D., Brown, R. P., & Osterman, L. L. (2012). Don't tread on me: Masculine honor ideology in the us and militant responses to terrorism. *Personality and Social Psychology Bulletin, 38*(8), 1018–1029.

Barnes, G., Farrell, M., & Cairns, A. (1986). Parental socialization factors and adolescent drinking behavior. *Journal of Marriage and the Family, 48*, 27–36.

Barnett, M. A. (1987). Empathy and related responses in children. In N. Eisenberg & J. Strayer (Eds.), *Empathy and its development* (pp. 146–162). New York: Cambridge University Press.

Barnett, R. C. (1994). Home-to-work spillover revisited: A study of full-time employed women in dual-earner couples. *Journal of Marriage and the Family, 56*, 647–656.

Barnett, R., & Rivers, C. (2011). Flawed study dismissing job bias thrills media. www.womensenews.org/story/women-in-science/110218.

Baron, L., & Straus, M. A. (1984). Sexual stratification, pornography, and rape in the United States. In N. M. Malamuth and E. I. Donnerstein (Eds.), *Pornography and sexual aggression* (pp. 185–209). Orlando, FL: Academic Press.

Baron, R., & Ransberger, V. (1978). Ambient temperature and the occurrence of collective violence: The "long, hot summer" revisited. *Journal of Personality and Social Psychology, 36*, 351–360.

Baron, R. A. (1971). Reducing the influence of an aggressive model: The restraining effects of discrepant modeling cues. *Journal of Personality and Social Psychology, 20*, 240–245.

Baron, R. A. (1977). *Human aggression.* New York: Plenum.

Baron, R. A., & Kepner, C. R. (1970). Model's behavior and attraction toward the model as determinants of adult aggressive behavior. *Journal of Personality and Social Psychology, 14*, 335–344.

Baron, R. S., & Roper, G. (1976). A reaffirmation of a social comparison view of choice shifts, averaging, and extremity effects in autokinetic situations. *Journal of Personality and Social Psychology, 33*, 521–530.

Baron, R. S., Vandello, U. A., & Brunsman, B. (1996). The forgotten variable in conformity research: Impact of task importance on social influence. *Journal of Personality and Social Psychology, 71*, 915–927.

Barrett, L. F., & Kensinger, E. A. (2010). Context is routinely encoded during emotion perception. *Psychological Science, 21*(4), 595–599.

Barrett, R. (2008). Linguistic differentiation and Mayan language revitalization in Guatemala. *Journal of Sociolinguistics, 12*, 275–305.

Bar-Tal, D. (1976). *Prosocial behavior: Theory and research.* New York: Halsted.

Barlett, C. P., & Anderson, C. A. (2011). Reappraising the situation and its impact on aggressive behavior.

Personality and Social Psychology Bulletin, 37(12), 1564–1573.

Barnes, C. D., Brown, R. P., & Osterman, L. L. (2012). Don't tread on me: Masculine honor ideology in the US and militant responses to terrorism. *Personality and Social Psychology Bulletin, 38*(8), 1018–1029.

Barrett, K. C. (1995). A functionalist approach to shame and guilt. In J. P. Tangney & K. W. Fischer (Eds), *Self-conscious emotions: The psychology of shame, guilt, embarrassment, and pride* (pp. 25–63). New York: Guilford Press.

Barrett, L. F., & Kensinger, E. A. (2010). Context is routinely encoded during emotion perception. *Psychological Science, 21*(4), 595–599.

Bartlett, M. S., Littlewort, G., Frank, M., Lainscsek, C., Fasel, I., & Movellan, J. (2006, April). Fully automatic facial action recognition in spontaneous behavior. In *Automatic Face and Gesture Recognition, 2006. FGR 2006.* 7th International Conference on Automatic Face and Gesture Recognition (pp. 223–230). IEEE.

Bartley, S., Blanton, P., & Gilliard, J. (2005). Husband and wives in dual-earner marriages: Decision-making, gender role attitudes, division of household labor, and equity. *Marriage and Family Review, 37,* 69–93.

Bartoli, A. M., & Clark, M. D. (2006). The dating game: Similarities and differences in dating scripts among college students. *Sexuality and Culture, 10,* 54–80.

Basic HHS Policy for Protection of Human Research Subjects. (2005). 45 C.F.R. Pt. 46.101–46.124.

Basil, D. Z., Ridgway, N. M., & Basil, M. D. (2008). Guilt and giving: A process model of empathy and efficacy. *Psychology & Marketing, 25*(1), 1–23.

Bass, B. M. (1990). *Bass & Stogdill's handbook of leadership: Theory, research, and managerial applications* (3rd ed.). New York: Free Press.

Bates, E., O'Connell, B., & Shore, C. (1987). Language and communication in infancy. In J. Osofsky (Ed.), *Handbook of infant competence* (2nd ed., pp. 149–203). New York: Wiley.

Batson, C. D. (1987). Prosocial motivation: Is it ever truly altruistic? In L. Berkowitz (Ed.), *Advances in experimental social psychology* (Vol. 20, pp. 65–122). New York: Academic Press.

Batson, C. D. (1991). The altruism question: Toward a social psychological answer. Hillsdale, NJ: Erlbaum.

Batson, C. D. (2011). *Altruism in humans.* New York: Oxford University Press.

Batson, C. D., Cochran, P. J., Biederman, M. F., Blosser, J. L., Ryan, M. J., & Vogt, B. (1978). Failure to help when in a hurry: Callousness or conflict? *Personality and Social Psychology Bulletin, 4*(1), 97–101.

Batson, C. D., & Coke, J. S. (1981). Empathy: A source of altruistic motivation for helping? In J. P. Rushton & R. M. Sorrentino (Eds.), *Altruism and helping behavior.* (pp. 167–187). Hillsdale, NJ: Erlbaum.

Batson, C. D., Duncan, B., Ackerman, P., Buckley, T., & Birch, K. (1981). Is empathic emotion a source of altruistic motivation? *Journal of Personality and Social Psychology, 40,* 290–302.

Batson, C. D., & Oleson, K. C. (1991). Current status of the empathy-altruism hypothesis. In M. S. Clark (Ed.), *Review of personality and social psychology: Vol. 12. Prosocial behavior* (pp. 62–85). Newbury Park, CA: Sage.

Batson, C. D., O'Quin, K., Fultz, J., Vanderplas, M., & Isen, A. M. (1983). Influence of self-reported distress and empathy on egoistic versus altruistic motivation to help. *Journal of Personality and Social Psychology, 45,* 706–718.

Baudson, T. G., & Preckel, F. (2013). Teachers' implicit personality theories about the gifted: An experimental approach. *School Psychology Quarterly, 28*(1), 37–46.

Bauer, R. (1964). The obstinate audience: The influence process from the point of view of social communication. *American Psychologist, 19,* 319–328.

Baumeister, R. F. (1982). A self-presentational view of social phenomena. *Psychological Bulletin, 91,* 3–26.

Baumeister, R. F. (1998). The self. In D. Gilbert, S. Fiske, & G. Lindzey (Eds.), *The handbook of social psychology* (4th ed., Vol. 1, pp. 680–740). Boston: McGraw-Hill.

Baumeister, R. F., Stillwell, A. M., & Heatherton, T. F. (1994). Guilt: An interpersonal approach. *Psychological Bulletin, 115*(2), 243–267.

Baumrind, D. (1980). New directions in socialization research. *American Psychologist, 35,* 639–652.

Bavelas, J., Coates, L., & Johnson, T. (2000). Listeners as co-narrators. *Journal of Personality and Social Psychology, 79,* 941–952.

Beall, A., & Sternberg, R. (1995). The social construction of love. *Journal of Social and Personal Relationships, 12,* 417–438.

Bearman, P., Moody, J., & Stovel, K. (2004). Chains of affection: The structure of adolescent romantic and sexual networks. *American Journal of Sociology, 110,* 44–91.

Beaulieu, C. (2004). Intercultural study of personal space: A case study. *Journal of Applied Social Psychology, 34,* 794–805.

Beck, E., & Tolnay, S. E. (1990). The killing fields of the deep South: The market for cotton and the lynching of Blacks, 1882–1930. *American Sociological Review, 55,* 526–539.

Beck, S. B., Ward-Hull, C. I., & McLear, P. M. (1976). Variables related to women's somatic preferences of the male and female body. *Journal of Personality and Social Psychology, 34,* 1200–1210.

Becker, H. S. (1963). *Outsiders: Studies in the sociology of deviance.* New York: Free Press.

Beckett, K. (1994). Setting the public agenda: "Street crime" and drug use in American politics. *Social Problems, 41,* 425–447.

Beebe, L. M., & Giles, H. (1984). Speech accommodation theories: A discussion in terms of second language learning. *International Journal of the Sociology of Language, 46,* 5–32.

Begley, T., & Alker, H. (1982). Anti-busing protest: Attitudes and actions. *Social Psychology Quarterly, 45,* 187–197.

Bell, R. (1979). Parent, child, and reciprocal influences. *American Psychologist, 34*, 821–826.

Bellavia, G., & Murray, S. (2003). Did I do that? Self-esteem related differences in reactions to romantic partners' moods. *Personal Relationships, 10*, 77–95.

Bellugi, U. & Brown, R. (1964). The acquisition of language. In D. Rioch & E. Weinstein (Eds.), *Proceedings of the association for research in nervous and mental disease, Vol. 42: Disorders of communication.* (pp. 1–192). Baltimore, MD: Williams and Wilkins.

Belsky, J. (2006). Early child care and early child development: Major findings of the NICHD study of Early Child Care. *European Journal of Developmental Psychology, 3*, 95–110.

Bem, D. J. (1970). *Beliefs, attitudes, and human affairs.* Belmont, CA: Brooks/Cole.

Bem, S. (1974). The measurement of psychological androgyny. *Journal of Consulting and Clinical Psychology, 42*, 155–162.

Bender, A. (2012). Secrets and magic pills: Constructing masculinity and sexual "normalcy" following spinal cord injury. In Carpenter, L., & DeLamater, J. (Eds.), *Sex for life: from virginity to Viagra, how sexuality changes throughout our lives* (pp. 198–214). New York: New York University Press.

Bennett, M. (1990). Children's understanding of the mitigating function of disclaimers. *Journal of Social Psychology, 130*, 29–37.

Bennett, M., & Dewberry, C. (1989). Embarrassment at others' failures: A test of the Semin and Manstead model. *Journal of Social Psychology, 129*, 557–559.

Benokraitis, N. V. (1997). *Subtle sexism: Current practice and prospects for change.* Thousand Oaks, CA: Sage.

Benokraitis, N., & Feagin, J. (1986). *Modern sexism.* Englewood Cliffs, NJ: Prentice Hall.

Bensley, L. S., & Wu, R. (1991). The role of psychological reactance in drinking following alcohol prevention messages. *Journal of Applied Social Psychology, 21*, 1111–1124.

Benson, M. L. (1989). The influence of class position on the formal and informal sanctioning of white-collar offenders. *Sociological Quarterly, 30*, 465–479.

Benson, M. L., & Fox, G. L. (2004). When violence hits home: How economics and neighborhood play a role, Research in Brief. *NCJ, 205004.*

Benson, M. L., & Walker, E. (1988). Sentencing the white-collar offender. *American Sociological Review, 53*, 294–302.

Benson, P. L., Karabenick, S. A., & Lerner, R. M. (1973). Pretty pleases: The effect of physical attraction, race, and sex on receiving help. *Journal of Experimental Social Psychology, 12*, 409–415.

Ben-Ze'ev, A. (2001). *The subtlety of emotions.* Cambridge, MA: MIT Press.

Bergen, D., & Williams, J. (1991). Sex stereotypes in the United States revisited: 1972–1988. *Sex Roles, 24*, 413–423.

Berger, J., Cohen, B. P., & Zelditch, M. (1972). Status characteristics and social interaction. *American Sociological Review, 37*, 241–255.

Berger, J., Rosenholtz, S. J., & Zelditch, M. (1980). Status organizing processes. In A. Inkeles, N. J. Smelser, & R. H. Turner (Eds.), *Annual Review of Sociology* (Vol. 6, pp. 479–508). Palo Alto, CA: Annual Reviews.

Berger, J., & Webster Jr, M. (2006). Expectations, status, and behavior. In P. J. Burke (Ed.), *Contemporary social psychological theories* (pp. 268–300). Stanford, CA: Stanford Social Sciences.

Berger, L., Brooks-Gunn, J., Paxson, C., & Waldfogel, J. (2008). First-year maternal employment and child outcomes: Differences across racial and ethnic groups. *Children and Youth Services Review, 30*, 365–387.

Berger, P. L., & Luckmann, T. (1966), The social construction of reality: A treatise in the sociology of knowledge. Garden City, NY: Anchor Books.

Bergesen, A. (1982). Race riots of 1967: An analysis of police violence in Detroit and Newark. *Journal of Black Studies, 12*, 261–274.

Berk, R. A., & Aldrich, H. (1972). Patterns of vandalism during civil disorders as an indicator of selection of targets. *American Sociological Review, 37*, 533–547.

Berkowitz, D., & Marsiglio, W. (2007). Gay men: Negotiating procreative, father, and family identities. *Journal of Marriage and the Family, 69*, 36–381.

Berkowitz, L. (1972). Frustrations, comparisons, and other sources of emotion arousal as contributors to social unrest. *Journal of Social Issues, 28*(1), 77–91.

Berkowitz, L. (1978). Whatever happened to the frustration-aggression hypothesis? *American Behavioral Scientist, 21*, 691–708.

Berkowitz, L. (1989). Frustration-aggression hypothesis: Examination and reformulation. *Psychological Bulletin, 106*, 59–73.

Berkowitz, L. (1993). Aggression: Its cause, consequences, and control. New York: McGraw Hill.

Berkowitz, L., Klanderman, S. B., & Harris, R. (1964). Effects of experimenter awareness and sex of subject and experimenter on reactions to dependency relationships. *Sociometry, 27*, 327–337.

Berkowitz, M. W., Mueller, C. W., Schnell, S. V., & Pudberg, M. T. (1986). Moral reasoning and judgments of aggression. *Journal of Personality and Social Psychology, 51*, 885–891.

Berlin, L. J., Ispa, J. M., Fine, M. A., et al. (2009). Correlates and consequences of spanking and verbal punishment for low-income White, African American, and Mexican American Toddlers. *Child Development, 80*, 1403–1420.

Bernstein, I., Kelly, W., & Doyle, P. (1977). Societal reaction to deviants: The case of criminal defendants. *American Sociological Review, 42*, 743–755.

Bernstein, I., Kick, E., Leung, J., & Schulz, B. (1977). Charge reduction: An intermediary stage in the process of labelling criminal defendants. *Social Forces, 56*, 362–384.

Bernstein, W. M., Stephan, W. G., & Davis, M. H. (1979). Explaining attributions for achievement: A path analytic approach. *Journal of Personality and Social Psychology, 37*, 1810–1821.

Bernuth, K. (2006, October 22). Amnesia victim, Al, struggles to bring past into present. *Denver Post.* www.denverpost.com/news/ci_4530616.

Berry, D. S., & Landry, J. R. (1997). Facial maturity and daily social interaction. *Journal of Personality and Social Psychology, 72*, 570–580.

Berscheid, E. (1966). Opinion change and communicator-communicatee similarity and dissimilarity. *Journal of Personality and Social Psychology, 4*, 670–680.

Berscheid, E., & Reis, H. (1998). Attraction and close relationships. In D. Gilbert, S. Fiske, & G. Lindzey (Eds.), *The handbook of social psychology* (4th ed., Vol. 2, pp. 193–281). Boston: McGraw-Hill.

Berscheid, E., & Walster [Hatfield], E. (1978). *Interpersonal attraction* (2nd ed.). Reading, MA: Addison-Wesley.

Bertenthal, B. I., & Fischer, K. (1978). Development of self-recognition in the infant. *Developmental Psychology, 14*, 44–50.

Bessenoff, G. (2006). Can the media affect us? Social comparison, self-discrepancy, and the thin ideal. *Psychology of Women Quarterly, 30*, 239–251.

Bettencourt, B. A., Brewer, M. B., Croak, M. R., & Miller, N. (1992). Cooperation and the reduction of intergroup bias: The role of reward structure and social orientation. *Journal of Experimental Social Psychology, 28*, 301–319.

Bianchi, S. M., & Robinson, J. (1997). What did you do today? Children's use of time, family composition, and the acquisition of social capital. *Journal of Marriage and the Family, 59*, 332–344.

Biblarz, T., & Stacy, J. (2010). Does the gender of parents matter? *Journal of Marriage and Family, 72*, 3–22.

Bickman, L. (1971). The effect of social status on the honesty of others. *Journal of Social Psychology, 85*(1), 87–92.

Biddle, B. J. (1979). *Role theory: Expectations, identities, and behaviors.* New York: Academic Press.

Biddle, B. J. (1986). Recent developments in role theory. In A. Inkeles, J. Coleman, & N. Smelser (Eds.), *Annual Review of Sociology* (Vol. 12, pp. 67–92). Palo Alto, CA: Annual Reviews.

Bielby, W., & Baron, J. (1986). Men and women at work: Sex segregation and statistical discrimination. *American Journal of Sociology, 91*, 759–799.

Bienenstock, E., & Bianchi, A. (2004). Activating performance expectations and status differences through gift exchange: Experimental results. *Social Psychology Quarterly, 67*, 310–318.

Birdwhistell, R. L. (1970). *Kinesics in context: Essays on body motion communications.* Philadelphia: University of Pennsylvania Press.

Bjorkvall, A., & Karlsson, A. (2011). The materiality of discourses and the semiotics of materials: A social perspective on the meaning potentials of written texts and furniture. *Semiotica, 187*, 141–165.

Black, D. (1980). *The manners and customs of the police.* New York: Academic Press.

Blackwell, D., & Lichter, D. (2004). Homogamy among dating, cohabiting, and married couples. *Sociological Quarterly, 45*, 719–737.

Blair-Loy, M. (2003). *Competing devotions: Career and family among women executives.* Cambridge, MA: Harvard University Press.

Blake, R. R., Shepard, H. A., & Mouton, J. S. (1964). *Managing intergroup conflict in industry.* Houston, TX: Gulf.

Blanck, P. D., & Rosenthal, R. (1982). Developing strategies for decoding "leaky" messages. In R. S. Feldman (Ed.), *Development of nonverbal behavior in children.* (pp. 203–229). New York: Springer Verlag.

Blascovich, J., Ginsburg, G. P., & Veach, T. L. (1975). A pluralistic explanation of choice shifts on the risk dimension. *Journal of Personality and Social Psychology, 31*, 422–429.

Blascovich, J., Mendes, W. B., Hunter, S., Lickel, B., & Kowai-Bell, N. (2001). Perceiver threat in social interactions with stigmatized others. *Journal of Personality and Social Psychology, 80*, 253–267.

Blass, T. (1991). Understanding behavior in the Milgram obedience experiment: The role of personality, situations, and their interactions. *Journal of Personality and Social Psychology, 60*, 398–413.

Blau, P. (1964). *Exchange and power in social life.* New York: Wiley.

Blauner, R. (1964). *Alienation and freedom.* Chicago: University of Chicago Press.

Blee, K. M., & Creasap, K. A. (2010). Conservative and right-wing movements. *Annual Review of Sociology, 36*, 269–286.

Blom, J. P., & Gumperz, J. J. (1972). Social meaning and linguistic structure: Code-switching in Norway. In J. J. Gumperz & D. Hymes (Eds.), *Directions in sociolinguistics.* (pp. 407–434). New York: Holt, Rinehart and Winston.

Bloom, B. S. (1956). Taxonomy of educational objectives: The classification of educational goals. Handbook 1: Cognitive domain. New York: David McKay.

Blumberg, S. J., & Luke, J. V. (2012). Wireless substitution: Early release of estimates from the National Health Interview Survey, January–June 2012. Washington, DC: National Center for Health Statistics. www.cdc.goc/nchs/nhis.htm.

Blumenthal, M., Kahn, R. L., Andrews, F. M., & Head, K. B. (1972). *Justifying violence: Attitudes of American men.* Ann Arbor, MI: Institute for Social Research.

Blumer, H. (1962). Society and symbolic interactionism. In A. M. Rose (Ed.), *Human behavior and social processes.* (pp. 179–192). Boston: Houghton Mifflin.

Blumer, H (1969). *Symbolic interactionism: Perspective and method.* Englewood Cliffs, NJ: Prentice-Hall.

Blumstein, P. W. (1974). The honoring of accounts. *American Sociological Review, 39*, 551–566.

Boardman, J., Finch, B. K., Ellison, C., Williams, D., & Jackson, J. (2001). Neighborhood disadvantage, stress, and drug use among adults. *Journal of Health and Social Behavior, 42*, 151–165.

Boardman, J. S. (2004). Stress and physical health: The role of neighborhoods as mediating or moderating mechanisms. *Social Science and Medicine, 58*, 2473–2483.

Bobo, L. (1983). Whites' opposition to busing: Symbolic racism or realistic group conflict. *Journal of Personality and Social Psychology, 45*, 1196–1210.

Bobo, L. (1999). Prejudice as group position: Micro-foundations of a sociological approach to racism and race relations. *Journal of Social Issues, 55*, 445–472.

Bobo, L. (2000). Race and beliefs about affirmative action: Assessing the effects of interests, group threat, ideology and racism. In D. O. Sears, J. Sidanius, & L. Bobo (Eds.), *Racialized politics: The debate about racism in America.* (pp. 137–164). Chicago: University of Chicago Press.

Bochner, S., & Insko, C. A. (1966). Communicator discrepancy, source credibility, and opinion change. *Journal of Personality and Social Psychology, 4*, 614–621.

Bodenhausen, G. V., & Lichtenstein, M. (1987). Social stereotypes and information processing strategies: The impact of task complexity. *Journal of Personality and Social Psychology, 52*, 871–880.

Bodenhausen, G., & Wyer, R. (1985). Effects of stereotypes on decision making and information-processing strategies. *Journal of Personality and Social Psychology, 48*, 267–282.

Body rebuilding. (1997, January 26). *Wisconsin State Journal*, p. 1G.

Bogle, K. A. (2007). The shift from dating to hooking up in college: What scholars have missed. *Sociology Compass, 1*(2), 775–788.

Bohn, A. (2003). Familiar voices: Using Ebonics communication techniques in the primary classroom. *Urban Education, 38*, 688–707.

Bohra, K. A., & Pandey, J. (1984). Ingratiation toward strangers, friends, and bosses. *Journal of Social Psychology, 122*, 217–222.

Bolger, N., DeLongis, A., Kessler, R. C., & Wethington, E. (1989). The contagion of stress across multiple roles. *Journal of Marriage and the Family, 51*, 175–183.

Bollen, K. A. (1989). *Structural equations with latent variables.* New York: Wiley.

Bollen, K. A., & Hoyle, R. H. (1990). Perceived cohesion: A conceptual and empirical examination. *Social Forces, 69*, 479–504.

Bollen, K. A., & Phillips, D. P. (1981). Suicidal motor vehicle fatalities in Detroit: A replication. *American Journal of Sociology, 87*, 404–412.

Bolzendahl, C. I., & Myers, D. J. (2004). Feminist attitudes and support for gender equality: Opinion change in women and men, 1974–1998. *Social Forces, 83*(2), 759–789.

Bond, R., & Smith, P. B. (1996). Culture and conformity: A meta-analysis of studies using Asch's line judgment task. *Psychological Bulletin, 119*, 111–137.

Bondurant, B., & Donat, P. L. (1999). Perceptions of women's sexual interest and acquaintance rape: The role of sexual overperception and affective attitudes. *Psychology of Women Quarterly, 23*(4), 691–705.

Bord, R. J. (1976). The impact of imputed deviant identities in structuring evaluations and reactions. *Sociometry, 39*, 108–116.

Bornstein, R. (1992). Subliminal mere exposure effects. In R. Bornstein & T. Pittman (Eds.), *Perception without awareness: Cognitive, clinical, and social perspectives* (pp. 101–210). New York: Guilford Press.

Bornstein, R. F., & Pittman, T. S. (1992, March). *Perception without awareness: Cognitive, clinical, and social perspectives.* Paper presented at "Perception Without Awareness: Cognitive, Clinical and Social Perspectives" Conference, Gettysburg College. Gettysburg, PA: Guilford Press.

Bosker, B. (2013, January 1). Affectiva's emotion recognition tech: when machines know what you're feeling. *Huffington Post.* www.huffingtonpost.com/2012/12/24/affectiva-emotion-recognition-technology_n_2360136.html.

Botanaki, A., & Mattas, K. (2010). Revealing the values behind convenience food consumption. *Appetite, 55*, 629–638.

Bottomore, T. B. (Ed.). (1964). *Karl Marx' early writings.* New York: McGraw-Hill.

Bouchard, T. J., Barsaloux, J., & Drauden, G. (1974). Brainstorming procedure, group size, and sex as determinants of the problem-solving effectiveness of groups and individuals. *Journal of Applied Psychology, 59*, 135–138.

Bouchard, T. J., & Hare, M. (1970). Size, performance, and potential in brainstorming groups. *Journal of Applied Psychology, 54*, 51–55.

Boulding, K. E. (1981). *Ecodynamics: A new theory of societal evolution.* Beverly Hills, CA: Sage.

Bourhis, R. Y., Giles, H., Leyens, J. P., & Tajfel, H. (1979). Psycholinguistic distinctiveness: Language divergence in Belgium. In H. Giles & R. N. St. Clair (Eds.), *Language and social psychology.* (pp. 158–185). Oxford, UK: Blackwell.

Bowlby, J. (1965). Maternal care and mental health (1953). In J. Bowlby (Ed.), *Child care and the growth of love.* London: Penguin.

Braaten, L. J. (1991). Group cohesion: A new multidimensional model. *Group, 15*, 39–55.

Brackett, M. A., & Mayer, J. D. (2003). Convergent, discriminant, and incremental validity of competing measures of emotional intelligence. *Personality and Social Psychology Bulletin, 29*(9), 1147–1158.

Bradford, S., Feeney, J., & Campbell, L. (2002). Links between attachment orientations and dispositional and diary-based measures of disclosure in dating couples: A study of actor and partner effects. *Personal Relationships, 9*, 491–506.

Bradley, G. W. (1978). Self-serving biases in the attribution process: A reexamination of the fact or fiction question. *Journal of Personality and Social Psychology, 36*, 56–71.

Braesicke, K., Parkinson, J. A., Reekie, Y., Man, M. S.,

Hopewell, L., Pears, A., Crofts, H., Schnell, C. R., & Roberts, A. C. (2005). Autonomic arousal in an appetitive context in primates: A behavioural and neural analysis. *European Journal of Neuroscience, 21*(6), 1733–1740.

Brand, R. J., Bonatsos, A., D'Orazio, R., & DeShong, H. (2012). What is beautiful is good, even online: Correlations between photo attractiveness and text attractiveness in men's online dating profiles. *Computers in Human Behavior, 28*(1), 166–170.

Brauer, M. (2001). Intergroup perception in the social context: The effects of social status and group membership on perceived out-group homogeneity and ethnocentrism. *Journal of Experimental Social Psychology, 37*, 15–31.

Bray, R. M., Kerr, N. L., & Atkin, R. S. (1978). Effects of group size, problem difficulty, and sex on group performance and member reactions. *Journal of Personality and Social Psychology, 36*, 1224–1240.

Brehm, J. W. (1956). Postdecision changes in the desirability of alternatives. *Journal of Abnormal and Social Psychology, 52*, 384–389.

Brehm, J. W., & Cohen, A. (1962). *Explorations in cognitive dissonance.* New York: Wiley.

Brehm, P. (1966). *A theory of psychological reactance.* New York: Academic Press.

Brewer, M. B. (1979). In-group bias in the minimal intergroup situation: A cognitive-motivational analysis. *Psychological Bulletin, 86*, 307–324.

Brewer, M. B. (1986). The role of ethnocentrism in intergroup conflict. In S. Worchel & W. G. Austin (Eds.), *Psychology of intergroup relations* (2nd ed., pp. 88–102). Chicago: Nelson-Hall.

Brewer, M. B., & Brown, R. J. (1998). Intergroup relations. In D. T. Gilbert, S. T. Fiske, & G. Lindzey (Eds.), *The handbook of social psychology* (4th ed., pp. 554–594). New York: McGraw-Hill.

Brewer, M. B., & Campbell, D. T. (1976). *Ethnocentrism and intergroup attitudes: East African evidence.* New York: Halsted.

Brewer, M. B., & Kramer, R. M. (1985). The psychology of intergroup attitudes and behavior. *Annual Review of Psychology, 36*, 219–243.

Brewer, M. B., & Lui, L. (1984). Categorization of the elderly by the elderly: Effects of perceiver's category membership. *Personality and Social Psychology Bulletin, 10*, 585–595.

Brewer, M. B., & Miller, N. (1984). Beyond the contact hypothesis: Theoretical perspectives on desegregation. In N. Miller & M. B. Brewer (Eds.), *Groups in contact: The psychology of desegregation* (pp. 281–302). Orlando, FL: Academic Press.

Brewer, M. B., & Pierce, K. P. (2005). Social identity complexity and out-group tolerance. *Personality and Social Psychology Bulletin, 31*, 428–437.

Brickner, M. A., Harkins, S. G., & Ostrom, T. M. (1986). Effects of personal involvement: Thought provoking implications for social loafing. *Journal of Personality and Social Psychology, 51*, 763–769.

Briggs, J. L. (1970). *Never in anger: Portrait of an Eskimo family* (Vol. 12). Cambridge, MA: Harvard University Press.

Brim, O. G., & Ryff, C. (1980). On the properties of life events. In P. Baltes & O. G. Brim (Eds.), *Life-span development and behavior* (Vol. 3, pp. 368–388). New York: Academic Press.

Brockmann, H., & Klein, T. (2002). Love and death in Germany: The marital biography and its impact on health (Working Paper 2002–15). Rostock, Germany: Max Planck Institute.

Brockner, J., & Wiesenfeld, B. M. (1996). An integrative framework for explaining reactions to a decision: The interactive effects of outcomes and procedures. *Psychological Bulletin, 120*, 189–208.

Brody, E. M. (2004). *Women in the middle: Their parent care years.* New York: Springer.

Bronfenbrenner, U. (1961). The mirror image in Soviet-American relations: A social psychologist's report. *Journal of Social Issues, 17*(3), 45–56.

Broverman, I., Vogel, S., Broverman, D., Clarkson, F., & Rosenkrantz, P. (1972). Sex-role stereotypes: A current appraisal. *Journal of Social Issues, 28*(2), 59–78.

Brown, G. L, Manglesdorf, S. C., & Neff, C. (2012). Father involvement, paternal sensitivity and father-child attachment security in the first 3 years. *Journal of Family Psychology, 26*, 421–430.

Brown, J. D. (1991a). The professional ex-: An alternative for exiting the deviant career. *Sociological Quarterly, 32*, 219–230.

Brown, J. D. (1991b). Staying fit and staying well: Physical fitness as a moderator of life stress. *Journal of Personality and Social Psychology, 60*, 555–561.

Brown, J. D., Collins, R. L., & Schmidt, G. W. (1988). Self-esteem and direct vs. indirect forms of self-enhancement. *Journal of Personality and Social Psychology, 55*, 445–453.

Brown, P., & Elliott, R. (1965). Control of aggression in a nursery school class. *Journal of Experimental Child Psychology, 2*, 103–107.

Brown, R. (1965). *Social psychology.* Glencoe, IL: Free Press.

Brown, R., & Fraser, C. (1963). The acquisition of syntax. In C. Cofer & B. Musgrave (Eds.), *Verbal behavior and learning.* (pp. 43–79). New York: McGraw-Hill.

Brown, R. J., & Turner, J. C. (1981). Interpersonal and intergroup behavior. In J. Turner & H. Giles (Eds.), *Intergroup behavior* (pp. 33–65). Chicago: University of Chicago Press.

Brown, R. P., Osterman, L. L., & Barnes, C. D. (2009). School violence and the culture of honor. *Psychological Science, 20*(11), 1400–1405.

Brown, S., Sessions, J., & Taylor, K. (2004). What will I be when I grow up? An analysis of childhood expectations and career outcomes (Working Paper 05/2). University of Leicester, Department of Economics.

Brown, T., & Warner, D. (2008). Divergent pathways? Racial/ethnic differences on older women's labor force withdrawal. *Journal of Gerontology: Social Sciences, 63B*, S122–S134.

Browning, C. R., & Cagney, K. A. (2003). Moving beyond poverty: Neighborhood structure, social processes, and health. *Journal of Health and Social Behavior*, *44*(4), 552–571.

Brunstein, J. C., Dangelmayer, G., & Schultheiss, O. C. (1996). Personal goals and social support in close relationships: Effects on relationship mood and marital satisfaction. *Journal of Personality and Social Psychology*, *71*, 1006–1019.

Bryan, J. H., & Davenport, M. (1968). *Donations to the needy: Correlates of financial contributions to the destitute* (Research Bulletin No. 68–1). Princeton, NJ: Educational Testing Service.

Bryant, W. K, Jeon-Slaughter, H., Kang, H., & Tax, A. (2003). Participation in philanthropic activities: Donating money and time. *Journal of Consumer Policy*, *26*, 43–73.

Brym, R., & Lenton, R. (2001). *Love online: A report on digital dating in Canada*. www.bestsoftworks.com/docs/loveonline.pdf.

Bryson, B. (1996). "Anything but heavy metal": Symbolic exclusion and musical dislikes. *American Sociological Review*, *61*(5), 884–899.

Buck, R., & Ginsburg, B. (1991). Emotional communication and altruism: The communicative gene hypothesis. *Altruism: Review of Personality and Social Psychology*, *12*, 149–175.

Bugenthal, D. E. (1974). Interpretations of naturally occurring discrepancies between words and intonation: Modes of inconsistency resolution. *Journal of Personality and Social Psychology*, *30*, 125–133.

Buhrmester, M., Kwang, T., & Gosling, S. D. (2011). Amazon's Mechanical Turk: A new source of inexpensive, yet high-quality data? *Perspectives on Psychological Science*, *6*, 3–5.

Bui, K.-V. T., Peplau, L. A., & Hill, C. T. (1996). Testing the Rusbult model of relationship commitment and stability in a 15-year study of heterosexual couples. *Personality and Social Psychology Bulletin*, *22*, 1244–1257.

Burawoy, M. (2003). Revisits: An outline of a theory of reflexive ethnography. *American Sociological Review*, *68*, 645–679.

Burger, J. M. (1986). Increasing compliance by improving the deal: The That's-Not-All technique. *Journal of Personality and Social Psychology*, *51*, 277–283.

Burger, J. M. (1999). The foot-in-the-door compliance procedure: A multiple-process analysis and review. *Personality and Social Psychology Review*, *3*, 303–325.

Burger, J. M., & Petty, R. E. (1981). The low-ball compliance technique: Task or person commitment? *Journal of Personality and Social Psychology*, *40*, 492–500.

Burger, J. M., Soroka, S., Gonzago, K., Murphy, E., & Somervell, E. (2001). The effect of fleeting attraction on compliance to requests. *Personality and Social Psychology Bulletin*, *27*, 1578–1586.

Burgess, R. L., & Akers, K. L. (1966). A differential association-reinforcement theory of criminal behavior. *Social Problems*, *14*, 128–147.

Burke, P. (2004). Identities and social structure: The 2003 Cooley-Mead Award Address. *Social Psychology Quarterly*, *67*, 5–15.

Burke, P. J. (1991). Identity processes and social stress. *American Sociological Review*, *56*, 836–849.

Burke, P. J., & Reitzes, D. (1981). The link between identity and role performance. *Social Psychology Quarterly*, *44*, 83–92.

Burke, P. J., & Stets, J. E. (2009). *Identity theory*. Oxford University Press.

Burns, D. (2009). The experience and expression of anger and aggression in dating relationships for male college athletes in contact and non-contact sports. Doctoral dissertation, Oklahoma State University.

Burnstein, E. (1982). Persuasion as argument processing. In H. Brandstatter, J. H. Davis, & G. Stocher-Kreichgauer (Eds.), *Contemporary problems in group decision-making* (pp. 103–124). New York: Academic Press.

Burnstein, E., Crandall, C., & Kitayama, S. (1994). An evolved heuristic for altruism: Evidence for a human propensity to calculate inclusive fitness. *Journal of Personality and Social Psychology*, *67*, 773–789.

Burnstein, E., & Vinokur, A. (1973). Testing two classes of theories about group-induced shifts in individual choice. *Journal of Experimental Social Psychology*, *9*, 123–137.

Burt, M. R. (1980). Cultural myths and supports for rape. *Journal of Personality and Social Psychology*, *38*(2), 217–230.

Burton, L. M., Bonilla-Silva, E., Ray, V, et al. (2010). Critical race theories, colorism, and the decade's research on families of color. *Journal of Marriage and Family*, *72*, 440–459.

Bushman, B. J. (1988). The effects of apparel on compliance: A field experiment with a female authority figure. *Personality and Social Psychology Bulletin*, *14*, 459–467.

Bushman, B., Baumeister, R., & Stack, A. (1999). Catharsis, aggression, and persuasive influence: Self-fulfilling or self-defeating prophecies. *Journal of Personality and Social Psychology*, *76*, 367–376.

Bushman, B. J., Bonacci, A. M., Pedersen, W. C., Vasquez, E. A., & Miller, N. (2005). Chewing on it can chew you up: effects of rumination on triggered displaced aggression. *Journal of Personality and Social Psychology*, *88*(6), 969.

Bushman, B. J., & Huesmann, L. R. (2001). Effects of televised violence on aggression. In D. G. Singer, & J. L. Singer (Eds.), *Handbook of children and the media* (pp. 223–254). Thousand Oaks, CA: Sage.

Bushman, B. J., & Stack, A. D. (1996). Forbidden fruit versus tainted fruit: Effects of warning labels on attraction to television violence. *Journal of Experimental Psychology: Applied*, *2*, 207–226.

Buss, D. M. (1994). *The evolution of desire: Strategies of human mating*. New York: Basic Books.

Buss, D. M. (1999). *Evolutionary psychology*. Boston: Allyn and Bacon.

Buss, D. M., & Kenrick, D. T. (1998). Evolutionary social psychology. In D. T. Gilbert, S. T. Fiske, & G. Lindzey (Eds.), *The handbook of social psychology* (4th ed., pp. 982–1026). Boston: McGraw-Hill.

Butterfield, F. (2002, August 21). Father steals best: Crime in an American family. *New York Times.*

Buunk, B., Dijkstra, P., Fetchenhauer, D., & Kenrick, D. (2002). Age and gender differences in mate selection criteria for various involvement levels. *Personal Relationships, 9,* 271–278.

Buunk, B. P., & van der Eijnden, R. (1997). Perceived prevalence, perceived superiority, and relationship satisfaction: Most relationships are good but ours is the best. *Personality and Social Psychology Bulletin, 23,* 219–228.

Byrne, D. (1961a). The influence of propinquity and opportunities for interaction on classroom relationships. *Human Relations, 14,* 63–69.

Byrne, D. (1961b). Interpersonal attraction and attitude similarity. *Journal of Abnormal and Social Psychology, 62,* 713–715.

Byrne, D. (1971). *The attraction paradigm.* New York: Academic Press.

Byrne, D., & Clore, G. L. (1970). A reinforcement model of evaluative responses. *Personality: An International Journal, 1,* 103–128.

Byrne, D., Ervin, C., & Lamberth, J. (1970). Continuity between the experimental study of attraction and real-life computer dating. *Journal of Personality and Social Psychology, 16,* 157–165.

Byrne, D., & Kelley, K. (1984). Introduction: Pornography and sex research. In N. M. Malamuth & E. Donnerstein (Eds.), *Pornography and sexual aggression.* (pp. 1–15). Orlando, FL: Academic Press.

Byrne, D., & Nelson, D. (1965). Attraction as a linear function of proportion of positive reinforcements. *Journal of Personality and Social Psychology, 1,* 659–663.

Byrne, S., Guillory, J. E., Mathios, A. D., Avery, R. J., & Hart, P. S. (2012). The unintended consequences of disclosure: effect of manipulating sponsor identification on the perceived credibility and effectiveness of smoking cessation advertisements. *Journal of Health Communication, 17,* 1119–1137.

CNN. (2012, March 20). 911 calls paint picture of chaos after Florida teen is shot. http://news.blogs.cnn.com/2012/03/20/911-calls-paint-picture-of-chaos-after-florida-teen-is-shot/.

Caballero, M., Lumpkin, J., & Madden, C. (1989). Using physical attractiveness as an advertising tool: An empirical test of attraction phenomenon. *Journal of Advertising, 29,* 16–22.

Cacioppo, J. T., Petty, R. E., Feinstein, J. A., & Jarvis, W. B. G. (1996). Dispositional differences in cognitive motivation: The life and times of individuals varying in need for cognition. *Psychological Bulletin, 119,* 197–253.

Cadinu, M. R., & Rothbart, M. (1996). Self-anchoring and differentiation processes in minimal group settings. *Journal of Personality and Social Psychology, 70,* 661–677.

Cahill, S. (1987). Children and civility: Ceremonial deviance and the acquisition of ritual competence. *Social Psychology Quarterly, 50,* 312–321.

Cahill, S. E. (1999). Emotional capital and professional socialization: The case of mortuary science students (and me). *Social Psychology Quarterly, 62,* 101–116.

Callaway, M. R., & Esser, J. K. (1984). Groupthink: Effects of cohesiveness and problem-solving procedures on group decision making. *Social Behavior and Personality, 12,* 157–164.

Callero, P. (1985). Role-identity salience. *Social Psychology Quarterly, 48,* 203–214.

Cameron, D. (1998). Gender, language, and discourse: A review essay. *Signs: Journal of Women in Culture and Society, 23,* 945–973.

Cameron, J., & Ross, M. (2007). In times of uncertainty: Predicting the survival of long-distance relationships. *Journal of Social Psychology, 147,* 581–606.

Campbell, D. T. (1967). Stereotypes in the perception of group differences. *American Psychologist, 22,* 817–829.

Campbell, H. (2008). Female drug smugglers on the U.S.-Mexico border: Gender, crime, and empowerment. *Anthropological Quarterly, 81,* 233–267.

Campbell, J. D. (1990). Self-esteem and clarity of self-concept. *Journal of Personality and Social Psychology, 59,* 538–549.

Campbell, W. K., Hoyle, R. H., & Bradfield, E. K. (2011). Compensating, resisting, and breaking: A meta-analytic examination of reactions to self-esteem threat. *Personality and Social Psychology Review, 15*(1), 51–74.

Campbell, W. K., & Sedikides, C. (1999). Self-threat magnifies the self-serving bias: A meta-analysis integration. *Review of General Psychology, 3,* 23–43.

Cano, I., Hopkins, N., & Islam, M. R. (1991). Memory for stereotype-related material: A replication study with real-life social groups. *European Journal of Social Psychology, 21,* 349–357.

Cantor, J., Alfonso, H., & Zillmann, D. (1976). The persuasive effectiveness of the peer appeal and a communicator's first hand experience. *Communication Research, 3,* 293–310.

Cantor, J., & Wilson, B. J. (2003). Media and violence: Intervention strategies for reducing aggression. *Media Psychology, 5,* 363–403.

Caplan, F. (1973). *The first twelve months of life.* New York: Grosset and Dunlap.

Caporeal, L. R. (2001). Evolutionary psychology: Toward a unifying theory and a hybrid science. *Annual Review of Psychology, 52,* 607–628.

Carli, L. L., LaFleur, S. J., & Loeber, C. C. (1995). Nonverbal behavior, gender, and influence. *Journal of Personality and Social Psychology, 68,* 1030–1041.

Carlsmith, J. M., & Anderson, C. (1979). Ambient temperature and the occurrence of collective violence. *Journal of Personality and Social Psychology, 37,* 337–344.

Carlson, M., Charlin, V., & Miller, N. (1988). Positive mood and helping behavior: A test of six hypotheses.

Journal of Personality and Social Psychology, 55(2), 211–229.

Carlson, M., Marcus-Newhall, A., & Miller, N. (1990). Effects of situational aggression cues: A quantitative review. *Journal of Personality and Social Psychology, 58*, 622–633.

Carlson, M., & Miller, N. (1987). Explanation of the relation between negative mood and helping. *Psychological Bulletin, 102*(1), 91.

Carmalt, J. H., Cawley, J., Joyner, K., & Sobal, J. (2008). Body weight and matching with a physically attractive romantic partner. *Journal of Marriage and the Family, 70*, 1287–1296.

Carmichael, S., Langton, L., Pendell, G., Reitzel, J., & Piqure, A. (2005). Do the experiential and deterrent effect operate differently across gender? *Journal of Criminal Justice, 33*, 267–276.

Carnevale, P. J., & Henry, R. A. (1989). Determinants of mediator behavior: A test of the strategic choice model. *Journal of Applied Social Psychology, 19*, 481–498.

Carnevale, P. J., & Pegnetter, R. (1985). The selection of mediation tactics in public sector disputes: A contingency analysis. *Journal of Social Issues, 41*(2), 65–81.

Carnevale, P. J., Pruitt, D. G., & Carrington, P. I. (1982). Effects of future dependence, liking, and repeated requests for help on helping behavior. *Social Psychology Quarterly, 45*(1), 9–14.

Carr, J. L., & VanDeusen, K. M. (2004). Risk factors for male sexual aggression on college campuses. *Journal of Family Violence, 19*(5), 279–289.

Carrington, C. (1999). *No place like home: Relationships and family life among lesbians and gay men.* Chicago: University of Chicago Press.

Carroll, J. M., & Russell, J. A. (1996). Do facial expressions signal specific emotions? Judging emotion from face in context. *Journal of Personality and Social Psychology, 70*, 205–218.

Carter, G. L. (1983). Explaining the severity of the 1960's Black rioting. Unpublished dissertation, Columbia University, Department of Sociology.

Carter, G. L. (1990). Black attitudes and the 1960s Black riots: An aggregate-level analysis of the Kerner Commission's "15 cities" data. *Sociological Quarterly, 31*, 269–286.

Cartwright, D. (1968). The nature of group cohesiveness. In D. Cartwright & A. Zander (Eds.), *Group dynamics* (3rd ed., pp. 91–109). New York: Harper & Row.

Cartwright, D. (1971). Risk taking by individuals and groups: An assessment of research employing choice dilemmas. *Journal of Personality and Social Psychology, 20*, 361–378.

Case, A., & Paxson, C. (2004). Sex differences in morbidity and mortality (Working Paper w10653). Cambridge, MA: National Bureau of Economic Research.

Caspi, A. (1989) Turning points and pathways to change. Symposium: *Surmounting childhood disadvantage.* Society for Research in Child Development. Kansas City, MO.

Caspi, A., & Herbener, E. S. (1990). Continuity and change: Assortative marriage and the consistency of personality in adulthood. *Journal of Personality and Social Psychology, 58*, 250–258.

Catalano, R., Novaco, R., & McConnell, W. (1997). A model of the net effect of job loss on violence. *Journal of Personality and Social Psychology, 72*(6), 1440–1447.

Cate, R., Levin, L., & Richmond, L. (2002). Premarital relationship stability: A review of recent research. *Journal of Social and Personal Relationships, 19*, 261–284.

Catrambone, R., & Markus, H. (1987). The role of self-schemas in going beyond the information given. *Social Cognition, 5*, 349–368.

Ceci, S. J., & Williams, W. M. (2011). Understanding current causes of women's underrepresentation in science. *PNAS 2011, 108*, 3157–3162.

Center on Addiction and Substance Abuse. (2003). *Teen tipplers: America's underage drinking epidemic.* New York: Columbia University.

Centers, R. (1975). Attitude similarity-dissimilarity as a correlate of heterosexual attraction and love. *Journal of Marriage and the Family, 37*, 305–312.

Chaffee, S. (1981). Mass media in political campaigns: An expanding role. In R. E. Rice & W. J. Paisley (Eds.), *Public communication campaigns.* (pp. 181–198). Beverly Hills, CA: Sage.

Chaiken, S. (1980). Heuristic versus systematic information processing and the use of source versus message cues in persuasion. *Journal of Personality and Social Psychology, 39*, 752–766.

Chaiken, S. (1986). Physical appearance and social influence. In C. P. Herman, M. P. Zanna, & E. T. Higgins (Eds.), *Physical appearance, stigma, and social behavior: The Ontario Symposium* (Vol. 3, pp. 143–177). Hillsdale, NJ: Erlbaum.

Chaiken, S., & Maheswaran, D. (1994). Heuristic processing can bias systematic processing: Effects of source credibility, argument ambiguity, and task importance on attitude judgment. *Journal of Personality and Social Psychology, 66*, 460–473.

Chaiken, S., & Yates, S. (1985). Affective-cognitive consistency and thought-induced polarization. *Journal of Personality and Social Psychology, 49*, 1470–1481.

Chambliss, W. J. (1994). Policing the ghetto underclass: The politics of law and law enforcement. *Social Problems, 41*, 177–193.

Chandola, T., Brunner, E., & Marmot, M. (2006). Chronic stress at work and the metabolic syndrome: Prospective study. *British Medical Journal, 332*, 521–525.

Chao, R. (1994). Beyond parental control and authoritarian parenting style: Understanding Chinese parenting through the cultural notion of training. *Child Development, 65*, 1111–1119.

Chaplin, W., Phillips, J., Brown, J., Clanton, N., & Stein, J. (2000). Handshaking, gender, personality, and first impressions. *Journal of Personality and Social Psychology, 79*, 110–117.

Chapman, R. S., Streim, N. W., Crais, E. R., Salmon, D., Strand, E. A., & Negri, N. A. (1992). Child talk: Assumptions of a developmental process model for early language learning. In R. S. Chapman (Ed.), *Processes in language acquisition and disorder*. (pp. 3–19). Chicago: Mosby/Year Book.

Charon, J. M. (1995). *Symbolic interactionism: An introduction, interpretation, and integration* (5th ed.). Englewood Cliffs, NJ: Prentice Hall.

Chebat, J.-C., Filiatrault, P., & Perrien, J. (1990). Limits of credibility: The case of political persuasion. *Journal of Social Psychology, 130*, 157–167.

Check, J. V., & Malamuth, N. M. (1983). Sex role stereotyping and reactions to depictions of stranger versus acquaintance rape. *Journal of Personality and Social Psychology, 45*(2), 344–356.

Chen, H. C., Reardon, R., Rea, C., & Moore, D. J. (1992). Forewarning of content and involvement: Consequences for persuasion and resistance to persuasion. *Journal of Experimental Social Psychology, 22*, 23–33.

Chen, Y. R., & Church, A. H. (1993). Reward allocation preferences in groups and organizations. *International Journal of Conflict Management, 4*(1), 25–59.

Cheng, P. W., & Novick, L. R. (1990). A probabilistic contrast model of causal induction. *Journal of Personality and Social Psychology, 58*, 545–567.

Cherlin, A. J. (2010). Demographic trends in the United States: A review of research in the 2000s. *Journal of Marriage and Family, 72*, 403–419.

Cherlin, A. J., Chase-Lansdale, P. L., & McRae, C. (1998). Effects of divorce on mental health throughout the life course. *American Sociological Review, 63*, 239–249.

Chiricos, T., & Waldo, G. (1975). Socioeconomic status and criminal sentencing: An empirical assessment of a conflict proposition. *American Sociological Review, 40*, 753–772.

Chowdhury, T. G., Ratneshwar, S., & Mohanty, P. (2009). The time-harried shopper: Exploring the differences between maximizers and satisficers. *Marketing Letters, 20*(2), 155–167.

Christopher, F. S., & Roosa, M. (1991). Factors affecting sexual decisions in the premarital relationships of adolescents and young adults. In K. McKinney & S. Sprecher (Eds.), *Sexuality in close relationships* (pp. 111–133). Hillsdale, NJ: Erlbaum.

Cialdini, R. B. (1993). *Influence: Science and practice* (3rd ed.). New York: HarperCollins.

Cialdini, R. B. (2001). *Influence: Science and practice* (4th ed.). Boston: Allyn and Bacon.

Cialdini, R. B., Borden, R., Thorne, A., Walker, M., & Freeman, S. (1976). Basking in reflected glory: Three (football) field studies. *Journal of Personality and Social Psychology, 34*, 366–375.

Cialdini, R. B., Cacioppo, J. T., Basset, R., & Miller, J. A. (1978). Low-ball procedure for producing compliance: Commitment, then cost. *Journal of Personality and Social Psychology, 36*, 463–476.

Cialdini, R. B., Kenrick, D. T., & Baumann, D. J. (1982). Effects of mood on prosocial behavior in children and adults. *The development of prosocial behavior*, 339–359.

Cialdini, R. B., Schaller, M., Houlihan, D., Arps, K., Fultz, J., & Beaman, A. L. (1987). Empathy-based helping: Is it selflessly or selfishly motivated. *Journal of Personality and Social Psychology, 52*(4), 749–758.

Cialdini, R. B., & Trost, M. R. (1998). Social influence: Social norms, conformity, and compliance. In D. T. Gilbert, S. T. Fiske, & G. Lindzey (Eds.), *Handbook of social psychology*. (pp. 151–192). Boston: McGraw-Hill.

Clark, E. V. (1976). From gesture to word: On the natural history of deixis in language acquisition. In J. S. Bruner & A. Gartner (Eds.), *Human growth and development*. (pp. 85–120). Oxford, UK: Clarendon.

Clark, J. K., Wegener, D. T., Habashi, M. M., & Evans, A. T. (2012). Source expertise and persuasion the effects of perceived opposition or support on message scrutiny. *Personality and Social Psychology Bulletin, 38*, 90–100.

Clark, M. S., Gotay, C. C., & Mills, J. (1974). Acceptance of help as a function of the potential helper and opportunity to repay. *Journal of Applied Social Psychology, 4*, 224–229.

Clark, R. D., & Word, L. E. (1972). Why don't bystanders help? Because of ambiguity? *Journal of Personality and Social Psychology, 24*, 392–400.

Clore, G. L., Bray, R. M., Itkin, S. M., & Murphy, P. (1978). Interracial attitudes and behavior at a summer camp. *Journal of Personality and Social Psychology, 36*, 107–116.

Cloward, R. (1959). Illegitimate means, anomie, and deviant behavior. *American Sociological Review, 24*, 164–176.

CNPAAEMI (Council of National Psychological Associations for the Advancement of Ethnic Minority Interests). (2000). *Guidelines for research in ethnic minority communities*. Washington, DC: American Psychological Association.

Coffe, H., & Geys, B. (2008). Measuring the bridging nature of voluntary associations: The importance of association size. *Sociology, 42*(2), 357–369.

Cognard-Black, A. (2004). Will they stay, or will they go? Sex-atypical work among token men who teach. *Sociological Quarterly, 45*, 113–139.

Cohen, A. (1966). *Deviance and control*. Englewood Cliffs, NJ: Prentice Hall.

Cohen, B. P., & Zhou, X. (1991). Status processes in enduring work groups. *American Sociological Review, 56*, 179–188.

Cohen, C. E. (1981). Person categories and social perception: Testing some boundaries of the processing effects of prior knowledge. *Journal of Personality and Social Psychology, 40*, 441–452.

Cohen, D. (1996). Law, social policy, and violence: The impact of regional cultures. *Journal of Personality and Social Psychology, 70*, 961–978.

Cohen, E. G. (1980). Design and redesign of the desegregated school: Problems of status, power, and conflict. In W. G. Stephan & J. Feagin (Eds.), *School desegregation*. (pp. 251–280). New York: Academic Press.

Cohen, E. G. (1984). The desegregated school: Problems in status power and interethnic climate. In N. Miller

& M. Brewer (Eds.), *Groups in contact: The psychology of desegregation* (pp. 77–96). Orlando, FL: Academic Press.

Cohen, D., Nisbett, R. E., Bowdle, B. F., & Schwarz, N. (1996). Insult, aggression, and the southern culture of honor: An "experimental ethnography." *Journal of Personality and Social Psychology, 70*(5), 945–960.

Cohen, E. G., & Roper, S. (1972). Modification of interracial interaction disability: An application of status characteristic theory. *American Sociological Review, 37,* 643–657.

Cohen, G., Steele, C. M., & Ross, L. D. (1999). The mentor's dilemma: Providing critical feedback across the racial divide. *Personality and Social Psychology Bulletin, 25,* 1302–1318.

Cohen, L., & Kluegel, J. (1978). Determinants of juvenile court dispositions: Ascriptive and achieved factors in two metropolitan courts. *American Sociological Review, 43,* 162–176.

Cohen, M. J., & Wade, T. J. (2012). Individual differences in first and fourth year college women's short term mating strategy preferences and perceptions. *Psychology, 3*(11), 966–973.

Cohen, P. (2003). Occupational segregation and the devaluation of women's work across U.S. labor markets. *Social Forces, 81,* 881–908.

Cohn, E. G., & Rotton, J. (1997). Assault as a function of time and temperature: A moderator-variable time-series analysis. *Journal of Personality and Social Psychology, 72*(6), 1322–1334.

Cohn, E. G., & Rotton, J. (2005). The curve is still out there: A reply to Bushman, Wang, and Anderson's (2005) Is the curve relating temperature to aggression linear or curvilinear? *Journal of Personality and Social Psychology, 89*(1), 67–70.

Cohn, R. M. (1978). The effect of employment status change on self-attitudes. *Social Psychology, 41,* 81–93.

Cole, T. (2001). Lying to the one you love: The use of deception in romantic relationships. *Journal of Social and Personal Relationships, 18,* 107–129.

Coleman, J. W. (1987). Toward an integrated theory of white-collar crime. *American Journal of Sociology, 93,* 406–439.

Coleman, L. (2004). *The copycat effect: How the media and popular culture trigger the mayhem in tomorrow's headlines.* New York: Paraview.

Coleman, R. P., & Neugarten, B. (1971). *Social status in the city.* San Francisco: Jossey-Bass.

Collett, J. L., & Avelis, J. (2011). Building a life together: Reciprocal and negotiated exchange in fragile families. *Advances in Group Processes, 28,* 227–254.

Collett, J. L., Kelly, S., & Sobolewski, C. (2010). Using *Remember the Titans* to teach theories of conflict reduction. *Teaching Sociology, 38,* 258–266.

Collett, J. L., & Lizardo, O. (2010). Occupational status and the experience of anger. *Social Forces, 88*(5), 2079–2104.

Collett, P. (1971). On training Englishmen in the nonverbal behavior of Arabs: An experiment in intercultural communication. *International Journal of Psychology, 6,* 209–215.

Colley, A., Mulhern, G., Maltby, J., & Wood, A. M. (2009). The short form BSRI: Instrumentality, expressiveness and gender associations among a United Kingdom sample. *Personality and individual differences, 46*(3), 384–387.

Collins, N. L., & Miller, L. C. (1994). Self-disclosure and liking: A meta-analytic review. *Psychological Bulletin, 116,* 457–475.

Committee on Maximizing the Potential of Women. (2007). *Beyond bias and barriers: Fulfilling the potential of women in academic science and engineering.* Washington, DC: National Academy Press.

Comstock, G. (1984). Media influences on aggression. In A. Goldstein (Ed.), *Prevention and control of aggression: Principles, practices, and research.* (pp. 241–272). New York: Pergamon.

Comstock, G. S., Chaffee, S., Katzman, N., McCombs, M., & Roberts, D. (1978). *Television and human behavior.* New York: Columbia University Press.

Condon, J. W., & Crano, W. D. (1988). Inferred evaluation and the relation between attitude similarity and interpersonal attraction. *Journal of Personality and Social Psychology, 54,* 789–797.

Condon, W. S., & Ogston, W. D. (1967). A segmentation of behavior. *Journal of Psychiatric Research, 5,* 221–235.

Conger, J. A., Kanungo, R. N., & Menon, S. T. (2000). Charismatic leadership and follower outcome effects. *Journal of Organizational Behavior, 21,* 747–767.

Conger, R., & Conger, K. (2002). Resilience in Midwestern families: Selected findings from the first decade of a prospective, longitudinal study. *Journal of Marriage and the Family, 64,* 361–373.

Connell, R. W. (2005). *Masculinities.* Berkeley: University of California Press.

Consedine, N., Sabag-Cohen, S., & Krivoshekova, Y. (2007). Ethnic, gender, and socioeconomic differences in young adults' self-disclosure: Who discloses what to whom? *Cultural Diversity and Ethnic Minority Psychology, 13,* 254–263.

Cook, K. (Ed.). (1987). *Social exchange theory.* Newbury Park, CA: Sage.

Cook, K. S., & Emerson, R. M. (1978). Power, equity and commitment in exchange networks. *American Sociological Review,* 721–739.

Cook, S. W. (1984). The 1954 social science statement and school desegregation: A reply to Gerard. *American Psychologist, 39,* 819–832.

Cook, S. W. (1985). Experimenting on social issues: The case of school desegregation. *American Psychologist, 40,* 452–460.

Cooke, B., Rossmann, M., McCubbin, H., & Patterson, J. (1988). Examining the definition and measurement of social support: A resource for individuals and families. *Family Relations, 37,* 211–216.

Cooley, C. H. (1902). *Human nature and the social order.* New York: Charles Scribner's Sons.

Cooley, C. H. (1908). A study of the early use of self-words by a child. *Psychological Review, 15*, 339–357.

Cooley, C. H. (1909). *Social organization: A study of the larger mind.* New York: Scribner.

Cooper, J., & Fazio, R. H. (1986). The formation and persistence of attitudes that support intergroup conflict. In S. Worchel & W. G. Austin (Eds.), *Psychology of intergroup relations* (2nd ed., pp. 183–195). Chicago: Nelson-Hall.

Cooper, W. H. (1981). Ubiquitous halo. *Psychological Bulletin, 90*, 218–244.

Coopersmith, S. (1967). *The antecedents of self-esteem.* San Francisco: Freeman.

Corcoran, M. (1995). From rags to riches: Poverty and mobility in the United States. *Annual Review of Sociology, 21*, 237–267.

Cornelis, E., Cauberghe, V., & De Pelsmacker, P. (2013). Being healthy or looking good? The effectiveness of health versus appearance focused arguments in two-sided messages. *Journal of Health Psychology.*

Corning, A. F., & Myers, D. J. (2002). Individual orientation toward engagement in social action. *Political Psychology, 23*, 703–729.

Correll, S. (2004). Constraints into preferences: Gender, status and emerging career aspirations. *American Sociological Review, 69*, 93–113.

Correll, S. J. (2001). Gender and the career choice process: the role of biased self-assessments. *American Journal of Sociology, 106*(6), 1691–1730.

Correll, S. J., Benard, S., & Paik, I. (2007). Getting a job: Is there a motherhood penalty? *American Journal of Sociology, 112*(5), 1297–1339.

Corsaro, W. A., & Eder, D. (1995). Development and socialization of children and adolescents. In K. S. Cook, G. A. Fine, & J. S. House (Eds.), *Sociological perspectives on social psychology* (pp. 421–451). Boston: Allyn and Bacon.

Corsaro, W., & Fingerson, L. (2006). Development and socialization in childhood. In J. DeLamater (Ed.), *Handbook of social psychology.* (pp. 125–165). New York: Kluwer/ Plenum.

Corsaro, W., & Molinari, L. (2000). Priming events and Italian children's transition from preschool to elementary school: Representations and actions. *Social Psychology Quarterly, 63*, 16–33.

Corsaro, W. A., & Rizzo, T. A. (1988). *Discussione* and friendship: Socialization processes in the peer culture of Italian nursery school children. *American Sociological Review, 53*, 879–894.

Cortese, A. J. (2004). *Provocateur: Images of women and minorities in advertising.* Lanham, MD: Rowman & Littlefield.

Coser, L. A. (1967). *Continuities in the study of social conflict.* New York: Free Press.

Costa, M., Dinsbach, W., & Manstead, A. (2001). Social presence, embarrassment, and nonverbal behavior. *Journal of Nonverbal Behavior, 25*, 225–240.

Costa, P. T. Jr., & McCrae, R. R. (1992). *Revised NEO Personality Inventory (NEO-PI-R) and NEO Five-Factor Inventory (NEO-FFI) manual.* Odessa, FL: Psychological Assessment Resources.

Cota, A. A., & Dion, K. L. (1986). Salience of gender and sex composition of ad hoc groups: An experimental test of distinctiveness theory. *Journal of Personality and Social Psychology, 50*, 770–776.

Cota, A. A., Evans, C. R., Dion, K. L., Kilik, L., & Longman, R. S. (1995). The structure of group cohesion. *Personality and Social Psychology Bulletin, 21*, 572–580.

Cotter, D., Hermsen, J., & Vanneman, R. (2004). *Gender inequality at work.* New York: Russell Sage Foundation.

Couch, C. J. (1968). Collective behavior: An examination of some stereotypes. *Social Problems, 15*, 310–322.

Courtright, J. A. (1978). A laboratory investigation of group-think. *Communications Monographs, 45*, 229–246.

Cowan, P. A. (1991). Individual and family life transitions: A proposal for a new definition. In D. A. Cowan & M. Hetherington (Eds.), *Family transitions.* (pp. 3–30). Hillsdale, NJ: Erlbaum.

Cox, C. L., Wexler, M. O., Rusbult, C. E., & Gaines, S. O. (1997). Prescriptive support and commitment processes in close relationships. *Social Psychology Quarterly, 60*, 79–90.

Coyne, S. M., Nelson, D. A., Graham-Kevan, N., Tew, E., Meng, K. N., & Olsen, J. A. (2011). Media depictions of physical and relational aggression: connections with aggression in young adults' romantic relationships. *Aggressive Behavior, 37*(1), 56–62.

Cozby, P. C. (1972). Self-disclosure, reciprocity, and liking. *Sociometry, 35*, 151–160.

Cramer, R., McMaster, M., Bartell, P., & Dragna, M. (1988). Subject competence and minimization of the bystander effect. *Journal of Applied Social Psychology, 18*, 1132–1148.

Crandall, C. S., Tsang, J., Goldman, S., & Pennington, J. (1999). Newsworthy moral dilemmas: Justice, caring, and gender. *Sex Roles, 40*, 187–210.

Crano, W. D. (1977). Primacy versus recency in retention of information and opinion change. *Journal of Social Psychology, 101*(1), 87–96.

Crano, W. (1997). Vested interests, symbolic politics, and attitude-behavior consistency. *Journal of Personality and Social Psychology, 72*, 485–491.

Crisp, R. J., & Turner, R. N. (2011). Cognitive adaptation to the experience of social and cultural diversity. *Psychological Bulletin, 137*(2), 242–266.

Crocker, J., & Major, B. (1989). Social stigma and self-esteem: The self-protective properties of stigma. *Psychological Review, 96*, 608–630.

Crocker, J., Thompson, L. L., McGraw, K. M., & Ingerman, C. (1987). Downward comparison, prejudice, and evaluations of others: Effects of self-esteem and threat. *Journal of Personality and Social Psychology, 52*, 907–916.

Crocker, J., Voelkl, K., Testa, M., & Major, B. (1991). Social stigma: The affective consequences of attributional ambiguity. *Journal of Personality and Social Psychology, 60*, 218–228.

Crocker, J., & Wolfe, C. (2001). Contingencies of self-worth. *Psychological Review, 108*, 593–623.

Cropanzano, R. (1993). *Justice in the workplace: Approaching fairness in human resource management.* Hillsdale, NJ: Erlbaum.

Crosnoe, R., & Cavanagh, S. E. (2010). Families with children and adolescents: A review, critique, and future agenda. *Journal of Marriage and Family, 72,* 594–611.

Cuddy, A. J., Fiske, S. T., & Glick, P. (2007). The BIAS map: Behaviors from intergroup affect and stereotypes. *Journal of Personality and Social Psychology, 92*(4), 631–648.

Cuddy, A. J., Rock, M. S., & Norton, M. I. (2007). Aid in the aftermath of Hurricane Katrina: Inferences of secondary emotions and intergroup helping. *Group Processes & Intergroup Relations, 10*(1), 107–118.

Cummings, K. M., Sciandra, R., Davis, S., & Rimer, B. (1989). Response to anti-smoking campaign aimed at mothers with young children. *Health Education Research, 4,* 429–437.

Cunningham, M. R. (1986). Measuring the physical in physical attractiveness: Quasi-experiments on the sociobiology of female facial beauty. *Journal of Personality and Social Psychology, 50,* 925–935.

Cunningham, M. R., Barbee, A. P., & Pike, C. L. (1990). What do women want? Facial metric assessment of multiple motives in the perception of male physical attractiveness. *Journal of Personality and Social Psychology, 59,* 61–72.

Cunningham, M. R., Steinberg, J., & Grev, R. (1980). Wanting to and having to help: Separate motivations for positive mood and guilt-induced helping. *Journal of Personality and Social Psychology, 38*(2), 181.

Cushman, F., Young, L., & Hauser, M. (2006). The role of conscious reasoning and intuition in moral judgment: testing three principles of harm. *Psychological Science, 17*(2), 1082–1089.

Cutrona, C. E. (1982). Transition to college: Loneliness and the process of social adjustment. In L. A. Peplau & D. Perlman (Eds.), *Loneliness: A resource book of current theory research and therapy.* (pp. 291–309). New York: Wiley.

Dabbs, J. M., & Leventhal, H. (1966). Effects of varying the recommendations in a fear-arousing communication. *Journal of Personality and Social Psychology, 4,* 525–531.

Daher, D. M., & Banikiotes, P. G. (1976). Interpersonal attraction and rewarding aspects of disclosure content and level. *Journal of Personality and Social Psychology, 33,* 492–496.

Dahmen, N., & Cozma, R. (2009). *Media takes: On again.* Sacramento, CA: International Longevity Center-USA and Aging Services of California.

Daly, K. (1987). Discrimination in the criminal courts: Family, gender, and the problem of equal treatment. *Social Forces, 66,* 152–175.

Darley, J. M., & Batson, C. D. (1973). From Jerusalem to Jericho: A study of situational and dispositional vari-ables in helping behavior. *Journal of Personality and Social Psychology, 27,* 100–108.

Darley, J. M., & Fazio, R. H. (1980). Expectancy confirmation processes arising in the social interaction sequence. *American Psychologist, 35,* 867–881.

Darley, J. M., & Latané, B. (1968). Bystander intervention in emergencies: Diffusion of responsibility. *Journal of Personality and Social Psychology, 8,* 377–383.

Darley, J. M., Teger, A. I., & Lewis, L. D. (1973). Do groups always inhibit individuals' response to potential emergencies? *Journal of Personality and Social Psychology, 26,* 395–399.

Darwin, C. (1998). *The expression of the emotions in man and animals.* Oxford, UK: Oxford University Press.

Davidson, A. R., & Jaccard, J. (1979). Variables that moderate the attitude-behavior relation: Results of a longitudinal survey. *Journal of Personality and Social Psychology, 37,* 1364–1376.

Davidson, A. R., Yantis, S., Norwood, M., & Montano, D. (1985). Amount of information about the attitude object and attitude-behavior consistency. *Journal of Personality and Social Psychology, 49,* 1184–1198.

Davies, J. C. (1962). Toward a theory of revolution. *American Sociological Review, 27,* 5–19.

Davies, J. C. (Ed.). (1971). *When men revolt—and why.* New York: Free Press.

Davies, S., & Tanner, J. (2003). The long arm of the law: Effects of labeling on employment. *Sociological Quarterly, 44,* 385–404.

Davis, D., & Perkowitz, W. T. (1979). Consequences of responsiveness in dyadic interaction: Effects of probability of response and proportion of content-related responses on interpersonal attraction. *Journal of Personality and Social Psychology, 37,* 534–550.

Davis, F. (1961). Deviance disavowal: The management of strained interaction by the visibly handicapped. *Social Problems, 9,* 120–132.

Davis, J. A., Smith, T. W., & Marsden, P. V. (2000). *General social surveys, 1972–2000.* Ann Arbor, MI: Inter-University Consortium for Political and Social Research. www.icpsr.umich.edu:8080/ICPSR-STUDY/03197.xml.

Davis, J. D. (1976). Self-disclosure in an acquaintance exercise: Responsibility for level of intimacy. *Journal of Personality and Social Psychology, 33,* 787–792.

Davis, K. (1947). Final note on a case of extreme isolation. *American Journal of Sociology, 52,* 432–437.

Davis, K. E. (1985, February). Near and dear: Friendship and love. *Psychology Today, 22,* 22–30.

Davis, L. R., & Harris, O. (1998). Race and ethnicity in US sports media. *MediaSport,* 154–169.

Davis, M. H., & Franzoi, S. L. (1986). Adolescent loneliness, self-disclosure, and private self-consciousness: A longitudinal investigation. *Journal of Personality and Social Psychology, 51,* 595–608.

Davis, S. (1990). Men as success objects and women as sex objects: A study of personal advertisements. *Sex Roles, 23*(1–2), 43–50.

Dawes, R. M. (1998). Behavioral decision making and

judgement. In D. Gilbert, S. Fiske, & G. Lindzey (Eds.), *The handbook of social psychology* (4th ed., Vol. 1, pp. 497–548). New York: McGraw-Hill.

Dawkins, R. (1982). *The extended phenotype.* San Francisco: Freeman.

Dean, K. E., & Malamuth, N. M. (1997). Characteristics of men who aggress sexually and of men who imagine aggressing: Risk and moderating variables. *Journal of Personality and Social Psychology, 72*(2), 449–455.

Debras, C., & Cienki, A. (2012). Some uses of head tilts and shoulder shrugs during human interaction, and their relation to stancetaking. *International Conference on Privacy, Security, Risk and Trust* (PASSAT), *136*, 932–937.

De Fina, A. (2007). Code-switching and the construction of ethnic identity in a community of practice. *Language in Society, 36*, 371–392.

de Jong-Gierveld, J. (1987). Developing and testing a model of loneliness. *Journal of Personality and Social Psychology, 53*, 119–128.

de Tocqueville, A. (1955). *The old regime and the French Revolution* (S. Gilbert, Trans.). Garden City, NY: Doubleday. (Original work published 1856).

De Waal, A. (2006). An imperfect storm: Narratives of calamity in a liberal-technocratic age. *Items and Issues, 5*, 1–8. (Social Science Research Council).

De Wolff, M. S., & Van Ijzendoorn, M. H. (1997). Sensitivity and attachment: A meta-analysis on parental antecedents of infant attachment. *Child Development, 68*, 571–591.

Deater-Deckard, K., & Dodge, K. (1997). Externalizing behavior problems and discipline revisited: Nonlinear effects and variation by culture, context, and gender. *Psychological Inquiry, 8*, 161–175.

Deaux, K., & Lewis, L. (1983). Components of gender stereotypes. *Psychological Documents, 13*, 25 (No. 2583).

Deaux, K., & Martin, D. (2003). Interpersonal networks and social categories: Specifying levels of context in identity processes. *Social Psychology Quarterly, 66*, 101–117.

DeBono, K. G., & Telesca, C. (1990). The influence of source physical attractiveness on advertising effectiveness: A functional perspective. *Journal of Applied Social Psychology, 20*, 1383–1395.

Deci, E. (1975). *Intrinsic motivation.* New York: Plenum.

DeDreu, C., & DeVries, N. (Eds.). (2001). *Group consensus and minority influence.* Oxford, UK: Blackwell.

Degelman, D., & Price, N. (2002). Tattoos and ratings of personal characteristics. *Psychological Reports, 90*, 507–514.

DeLamater, J., & Moorman, S. (2007). Sexual behavior in later life. *Journal of Aging and Health, 19*, 921–945.

DeLongis, A., Folkman, J., & Lazarus, R. S. (1988). The impact of daily stress on health and mood: Psychological and social resources as mediators. *Journal of Personality and Social Psychology, 54*, 486–495.

Del-Teso-Craviotto, M. (2006). Language and sexuality in Spanish and English dating chats. *Journal of Sociolinguistics, 10*, 460–480.

DeMaris, A., Benson, M. L., Fox, G. L., Hill, T., & Van Wyk, J. (2003). Distal and proximal factors in domestic violence: A test of an integrated model. *Journal of Marriage and Family, 65*(3), 652–667.

Dembroski, T. M., Lasater, T. M., & Ramires, A. (1978). Communicator similarity, fear-arousing communications, and compliance with health care recommendations. *Journal of Applied Social Psychology, 8*, 254–269.

Demo, D. H. (1992). The self-concept over time: Research issues and directions. *Annual Review of Sociology, 18*, 303–326.

Demo, D. H., & Acock, A. C. (1988). The impact of divorce on children. *Journal of Marriage and the Family, 50*, 619–648.

Demo, D., & Cox, M. (2001). Families with young children: A review of research in the 1990s. In R. Milardo (Ed.), *Understanding families into the new millennium: A decade in review* (pp. 95–114). Minneapolis, MN: National Council on Family Relations.

Demo, D. H., & Hughes, M. (1990). Socialization and racial identity among Black Americans. *Social Psychology Quarterly, 53*, 364–374.

Denney, J. T., Gorman, B. K., & Barrera, C. B. (2013). Families, resources and adult health: Where do sexual minorities fit? *Journal of Health and Social Behavior, 54*, 46–63.

Dentler, R., & Erikson, K. (1959). The functions of deviance in groups. *Social Problems, 7*, 98–107.

Denton, K., & Krebs, D. (1990). From the scene to the crime: The effect of alcohol and social context on moral judgment. *Journal of Personality and Social Psychology, 59*, 242–248.

Denzin, N. (1977). *Childhood socialization: Studies in the development of language, social behavior, and identity.* San Francisco: Jossey-Bass.

DePaulo, B. M. (1992). Nonverbal behavior and self-presentation. *Psychological Bulletin, 111*, 203–243.

DePaulo, B. M., & Fisher, J. D. (1980). The costs of asking for help. *Basic and Applied Social Psychology, 1*, 23–35.

DePaulo, B. M., Lassiter, G. D., & Stone, J. T. (1982). Attentional determinants of success at determining deception and truth. *Personality and Social Psychology Bulletin, 8*, 273–279.

DePaulo, B. M., Nadler, A., & Fisher, J. D. (1983). *New directions in helping: Help seeking* (Vol. 2). New York: Academic Press.

DePaulo, B. M., & Rosenthal, R. (1979). Ambivalence, discrepancy, and deception in nonverbal communication. In R. Rosenthal (Ed.), *Skill in nonverbal communication.* (pp. 204–248). Cambridge, MA: Oelgeschlager, Gunn and Hain.

DePaulo, B. M., Rosenthal, R., Eisenstat, R. A., Rogers, P. L., & Finkelstein, S. (1978). Decoding discrepant nonverbal cues. *Journal of Personality and Social Psychology, 36*, 313–323.

DePaulo, B. M., Stone, J. I., & Lassiter, G. D. (1985). Deceiving and detecting deceit. In B. R. Schlenker (Ed.),

The self and social life (pp. 323–370). New York: Mc-Graw-Hill.

DePaulo, B. M., Zuckerman, M., & Rosenthal, R. (1980). Detecting deception: Modality effects. In L. Wheeler (Ed.), *Review of personality and social psychology* (Vol. 1, pp. 125–162). Beverly Hills, CA: Sage.

Der-Karabetian, A., & Smith, A. (1977). Sex-role stereotyping in the United States: Is it changing? *Sex Roles, 3,* 193–198.

Derlega, V. J., & Grzelak, J. (1979). Appropriate self-disclosure. In G. J. Chelune et al. (Eds.), *Self-disclosure: Origins, patterns, and implications of openness in interpersonal relationships* (pp. 151–176). San Francisco: Jossey-Bass.

Derlega, V. J., Metts, S., Petronio, S., & Margulis, S. T. (1993). *Self-disclosure.* Newbury Park, CA: Sage.

Dervin, B. (1981). Mass communicating: Changing conceptions of the audience. In R. E. Rice & W. J. Paisley (Eds.), *Public communication campaigns.* (pp. 71–87). Beverly Hills, CA: Sage.

Deutsch, M. (1985). *Distributive justice: A social psychological perspective.* New Haven, CT: Yale University Press.

Deutsch, M. (2000). Justice and conflict. In M. Deutsch and & P. T. Coleman (Eds.), *The handbook of conflict resolution: Theory and practice* (pp. 41–64). San Francisco: Jossey-Boss.

Deutsch, M., & Gerard, H. B. (1955). A study of normative and informational social influences upon individual judgment. *Journal of Abnormal and Social Psychology, 51,* 629–636.

Devine, J. A., Sheley, J. F., & Smith, M. D. (1988). Macroeconomic and social-control policy influences on crime-rate changes, 1948–1985. *American Sociological Review, 53,* 407–420.

Devine, P. C. (1989). Stereotypes and prejudice: Their automatic and controlled components. *Journal of Personality and Social Psychology, 56,* 5–18.

Dew, J., & Wilcox, B. W. (2013). Generosity and the maintenance of marital quality. *Journal of Marriage and Family, 75*(5), 1218–1228.

DeWall, N. C., & Bushman, B. J. (2009). Hot under the collar in a lukewarm environment: Words associated with hot temperature increase aggressive thoughts and hostile perceptions. *Journal of Experimental Social Psychology, 45*(4), 1045–1047.

Diehl, M., & Stroebe, W. (1987). Productivity loss in brainstorming groups: Toward the solution of a riddle. *Journal of Personality and Social Psychology, 53,* 497–509.

Diehl, M., & Stroebe, W. (1991). Productivity loss in idea-generating groups: Tracking down the blocking effect. *Journal of Personality and Social Psychology, 61,* 392–403.

Diekman, A. B., Eagly, A. H., Mladinic, A., & Ferreira, M. C. (2005). Dynamic stereotypes about women and men in Latin America and the United States. *Journal of Cross-Cultural Psychology, 36,* 209–226.

Diener, E. (1980). Deindividuation: The absence of

self-awareness and self-regulation in group members. In P. B. Paulus (Ed.), *Psychology of group influence.* (pp. 209–242). Hillsdale, NJ: Erlbaum.

Dietz, T. L. (1998). An examination of violence and gender role portrayals in video games: Implications for gender socialization and aggressive behavior. *Sex Roles, 38*(5–6), 425–442.

Digman, J. M. (1990). Personality structure: Emergence of the five-factor model. *Annual Review of Psychology, 41,* 417–440.

DiMaggio, P., & Mohr, J. (1985). Cultural capital, educational attainment, and marital selection. *American Journal of Sociology, 90,* 1231–1257.

Dimsdale, J. (2008). Psychological stress and cardiovascular disease. *Journal of the American College of Cardiology, 51,* 1237–1246.

Dinas, E. (2013). Does choice bring loyalty? Electoral participation and the development of party identification. *American Journal of Political Science, 58,* 449–465.

Dion, K. L. (1979). Intergroup conflict and intragroup cohesiveness. In W. G. Austin & S. Worchel (Eds.), *The social psychology of intergroup relations* (pp. 211–224). Monterey, CA: Brooks/Cole.

Dion, K. L. (2000). Group cohesion: From "field of forces" to multidimensional construct. *Group Dynamics: Theory, Research, and Practice, 4,* 7–26.

Dion, K., Baron, R., & Miller, N. (1970). Why do groups make riskier decisions than individuals? In L. Berkowitz (Ed.), *Advances in experimental social psychology* (Vol. 5, pp. 305–377). New York: Academic Press.

Dion, K., Berscheid, E., & Walster [Hatfield], E. (1972). What is beautiful is good. *Journal of Personality and Social Psychology, 24,* 285–290.

Dion, K. L., & Schuller, R. A. (1991). The Ms. stereotype: Its generality and its relation to managerial and marital status stereotypes. *Canadian Journal of Behavioural Science, 23,* 25–40.

DiPrete, T. (2007). Is this a great country? Upward mobility and the chance for riches in contemporary America. *Research in Social Stratification and Mobility, 25,* 89–95.

Dishion, T. J., & Dodge, K. A. (2005). Peer contagion in interventions for children and adolescents: Moving towards an understanding of the ecology and dynamics of change. *Journal of Abnormal Child Psychology, 33,* 395–400.

Dixon, J., Gordon, C., & Khomusi, T. (1995). Sexual symmetry in psychiatric diagnosis. *Social Problems, 42,* 429–448.

Dodge, K. A., Coie, J. D., & Lynam, D. (2006). Aggression and antisocial behavior in youth. In N. Eisenberg, W. Damon, R. L. Lerner (Eds), *Handbook of child psychology: Vol. 3. Social, emotional, and personality development* (pp. 719–788), New York: Wiley.

Dodson, L., & Dickert, J. (2004). Girls' family labor in low-income households: A decade of qualitative research. *Journal of Marriage and Family, 66,* 318–332.

Dohrenwend, B. P. (1961). The social psychological nature of stress: A framework for causal inquiry. *Journal of Abnormal and Social Psychology, 62,* 294–302.

Dohrenwend, B. P. (2000). The role of adversity and stress in psychopathology: Some evidence and its implications for theory and research. *Journal of Health and Social Behavior, 41,* 1–19.

Dohrenwend, B. P., & Dohrenwend, B. S. (1974). Social and cultural influences on psychopathology. *Annual Review of Psychology, 25,* 417–452.

Dollard, J., Doob, J., Miller, N., Mowrer, O., & Sears, R. (1939). *Frustration and aggression.* New Haven, CT: Yale University Press.

Donald, M. (1991). *Origins of the modern mind: Three stages in the evolution of culture and cognition.* Cambridge, MA: Harvard University Press.

Donnerstein, E. (1984). Pornography: Its effect on violence against women. In N. M. Malamuth & E. Donnerstein (Eds.), *Pornography and sexual aggression.* (pp. 53–81). Orlando, FL: Academic Press.

Donnerstein, E., & Barrett, G. (1978). The effects of erotic stimuli on male aggression toward females. *Journal of Personality and Social Psychology, 36,* 180–188.

Donnerstein, E., & Berkowitz, L. (1981). Victim reactions in aggressive erotic films as a factor in violence toward women. *Journal of Personality and Social Psychology, 41,* 710–724.

Donnerstein, E, and Linz, D. (1998). Mass media, violence and the male viewer. In M. E. Oden and J. Clay-Warner (Eds): *Confronting rape and sexual assault* (pp 181–198). Wilmington, DE: SR Books/Scholarly Resources.

Donohue, W. A., Allen, M., & Burrell, N. (1988). Mediator communication competence. *Communication Monographs, 55,* 104–119.

Dooley, D., Prause, J., & Ham-Rowbottom, K. (2000). Underemployment and depression: Longitudinal relationships. *Journal of Health and Social Behavior, 41,* 421–436.

Dovidio, J. F. (1984). Helping behavior and altruism: An empirical and conceptual overview. In L. Berkowitz (Ed.), *Advances in experimental social psychology* (Vol. 17, pp. 362–427). New York: Academic Press.

Dovidio, J. F., Allen, J. L., & Schroeder, D. A. (1990). Specificity of empathy-induced helping: Evidence for altruistic motivation. *Journal of Personality and Social Psychology, 59,* 249–260.

Dovidio, J., Brigham, J. C., Johnson, B., & Gaertner, S. (1996). Stereotyping, prejudice, and discrimination: Another look. In N. Macrea, M. Hewstone, & C. Stangor (Eds.), *Foundations of stereotypes and stereotyping.* (pp. 276–319). New York: Guilford Press.

Dovidio, J. F., & Ellyson, S. L. (1982). Decoding visual dominance: Attributions of power based on relative percentages of looking while speaking and looking while listening. *Social Psychology Quarterly, 45,* 106–113.

Dovidio, J. F., & Gaertner, S. L. (1981). The effects of race, status, and ability on helping behavior. *Social Psychology Quarterly, 44,* 192–203.

Dovidio, J. F., & Gaertner, S. L. (1996). Affirmative action, unintentional racial biases, and intergroup relations. *Journal of Social Issues, 52*(4), 51–75.

Dovidio, J. F., Gaertner, S. L., Isen, A. M., & Lowrance, R. (1995). Group representations and intergroup bias: Positive affect, similarity, and group size. *Personality and Social Psychology Bulletin, 21,* 856–865.

Dovidio, J. F., Piliavin, J. A., Gaertner, S. L., Schroeder, D. A., & Clark, R. D. (1991). The arousal/cost-reward model and the process of intervention: A review of the evidence. In M. S. Clark (Ed.), *Review of personality and social psychology: Vol. 12. Prosocial behavior* (pp. 86–118). Newbury Park, CA: Sage.

Dovidio, J. F., Piliavin, J. A., Schroeder, D. A., & Penner, L. (2006). *The social psychology of prosocial behavior.* Hillsdale, NJ: Erlbaum.

Draghi-Lorenz, R., Reddy, V., & Costall, A. (2001). Rethinking the development of "nonbasic" emotions: A critical review of existing theories. *Developmental Review, 21*(3), 263–304.

Drass, K. A., & Spencer, J. W. (1987). Accounting for presentencing recommendations: Typologies and probation officers' theory of office. *Social Problems, 34,* 277–293.

Dreben, E. K., Fiske, S. T., & Hastie, R. (1979). The independence of evaluative and item information: Impression and recall order effects in behavior-based impression formation. *Journal of Personality and Social Psychology, 37,* 1758–1768.

Dreger, A. (2008). The controversy surrounding the man who would be queen: A case history of the politics of sciencce, identity, and sex in the Internet age. *Archives of Sexual Behavior, 37,* 366–421.

Drew, P. (2003). Precision and exaggeration in interaction. *American Sociological Review, 68,* 917–938.

Drews, D., Allison, C., & Probst, J. (2000). Behavioral and self-concept differences in tattooed and nontattooed college students. *Psychological Reports, 86,* 475–481.

Duesterhoeft, D. (1987). An unholy alliance? A case study comparison of religious and feminist anti-pornography activists. Unpublished masters' thesis, University of Wisconsin.

Dugan, K. (2005). *The struggle over gay, lesbian, and bi-sexual rights: Facing off in Cincinnati.* New York: Routledge.

Dugan, K. B. (2004). Strategy and "Spin": Opposing movement frames in an anti-gay voter initiative. *Sociological Focus, 37,* 213–235.

Dukes, R. L., & Stein, J. A. (2011). Ink and holes: Correlates and predictive associations of body modification among adolescents. *Youth and Society, 43,* 1547–1569.

Dunbar, R. (1996). *Grooming, gossip, and the evolution of language.* Harvard University Press.

Duncan, S., & Fiske, D. W. (1977). *Face-to-face interaction: Research methods and theory.* Hillsdale, NJ: Erlbaum.

Duneier, M. (2001). *Sidewalk.* New York: Farrar, Straus, and Giroux.

Duran, R. L., & Prusank, D. T. (1997). Relational themes in men's and women's popular nonfiction magazine articles. *Journal of Social and Personal Relationships, 14*, 165–189.

Dutton, D., & Aron, A. (1974). Some evidence for heightened sexual attraction under conditions of high anxiety. *Journal of Personality and Social Psychology, 30*, 510–517.

Dutton, D., & Lake, R. (1973). Threat of own prejudice and reverse discrimination in interracial situations. *Journal of Personality and Social Psychology, 28*, 94–100.

Dyck, R. J., & Rule, B. G. (1978). Effect on retaliation of causal attribution concerning attack. *Journal of Personality and Social Psychology, 36*, 521–529.

Dynes, R. R., & Quarantelli, E. L. (1980). Helping behavior in large-scale disasters. In D. H. Smith & J. Macaulay (Eds.), *Participation in social and political activities* (pp. 339–354). San Francisco: Jossey-Bass.

Eagly, A. H., Ashmore, R. D., Makhijani, M. G., & Longo, L. C. (1991). What is beautiful is good, but . . . : A meta-analytic review of research on the physical attractiveness stereotype. *Psychological Bulletin, 110*, 109–128.

Eagly, A. H., & Chaiken, S. (1975). An attribution analysis of the effects of communicator characteristics on opinion change: The case of communicator attractiveness. *Journal of Personality and Social Psychology, 32*, 136–144.

Eagly, A. H., & Crowley, M. (1986). Gender and helping behavior: A meta-analytic review of the social psychological literature. *Psychological Bulletin, 100*, 283–308.

Eagly, A., & Steffen, V. J. (1984). Gender stereotypes stem from distribution of women and men into social roles. *Journal of Personality and Social Psychology, 46*, 735–754.

Eagly, A. H., Wood, W., & Chaiken, S. (1978). Causal inferences about communicators and their effect on attitude change. *Journal of Personality and Social Psychology, 36*, 424–435.

Earl, J. (2011). Political repression: Iron fists, velvet gloves, and diffuse control. *Annual Review of Sociology, 37*, 261–284.

East, P. L. (1998). Racial and ethnic differences in girls' sexual, marital, and birth expectations. *Journal of Marriage and the Family, 60*, 150–162.

Eaton, A. A., & Rose, S. (2011). Has dating become more egalitarian? A 35 year review using *Sex Roles*. *Sex Roles, 64*, 843–862.

Eaton, W. (1980). *The sociology of mental disorders.* New York: Praeger.

Ebbesen, E. B., & Bowers, R. J. (1974). Proportion of risky to conservative arguments in a group discussion and choice shift. *Journal of Personality and Social Psychology, 29*, 316–327.

Ebert, J. (2005). A broken heart harms your health. *Nature online.* www.nature.com/news/2005/050207/full/ 050207-11.html.

Eckert, P., & McConnell-Ginet, S. (1999). New generalizations and explanations in language and gender research. *Language in Society, 28*, 185–201.

Eckes, T. (1995). Features of situations: A two-mode clustering study of situation prototypes. *Personality and Social Psychology Bulletin, 21*, 366–374.

Edelmann, R. J. (1985). Social embarrassment: An analysis of the process. *Journal of Social and Personal Relationships, 2*, 195–213.

Edelmann, R. J. (1987). *The psychology of embarrassment.* Chichester, UK: Wiley.

Edelmann, R. J., Evans, G., Pegg, I., & Tremain, M. (1983). Responses to physical stigma. *Perceptual and Motor Skills, 57*, 294.

Edelmann, R. J., & Iwaki, S. (1987). Self-reported expression and consequences of embarrassment in the United Kingdom and Japan. *Psychologia, 30*, 205–216.

Eder, D. (with Evans, C. C., & Parker, S.). (1995). *School talk: Gender and adolescent culture.* New Brunswick, NJ: Rutgers University Press.

Editorial. (2004). True lies. *Nature, 428*, 679.

Edwards, C. P., Knoche, L., & Kumru, A. (2001). Play patterns and gender. In J. Worell (Ed.), *Encyclopedia of gender* (pp. 809–816). San Diego, CA: Academic Press.

Edwards, K. (1990). The interplay of affect and cognition in attitude formation and change. *Journal of Personality and Social Psychology, 59*, 202–216.

Edwards, K. M., Turchik, J. A., Dardis, C. M., Reynolds, N., & Gidycz, C. A. (2011). Rape myths: History, individual and institutional-level presence, and implications for change. *Sex Roles, 65*(11–12), 761–773.

Eisenberg, N., Cumberland, A., Guthrie, I., Murphy, B., & Shepard, S. (2005). Age changes in prosocial responding and moral reasoning in adolescence and early adulthood. *Journal of Research on Adolescence, 15*, 235–260.

Eisenberg, N., & Fabes, R. A. (1991). Prosocial behavior and empathy: A multimethod developmental perspective. In M. S. Clark (ed.), *Review of personality and social psychology, Vol. 12. Prosocial behavior* (pp. 34–61). Newbury Park, CA: Sage.

Egebark, J., & Ekström, M. (2011). Like what you like or like what others like? Conformity and peer effects on Facebook. Stockholm: Research Institute of Industrial Economics IFN Working Paper, 866.

Eibl-Eibesfeldt, I. (1979). Human ethology: Methods and limits. *Behavioral and Brain Sciences, 2*(1), 50–57.

Eisenberg, N., & Miller, P. A. (1987). The relation of empathy to prosocial and related behaviors. *Psychological Bulletin, 101*, 91–119.

Eisend, M. (2007). Understanding two-sided persuasion: An empirical assessment of theoretical approaches. *Psychology & Marketing, 24*, 615–640.

Eiser, J. R. (Ed.). (1984). *Attitudinal judgment.* New York: Springer Verlag.

Eitle, D., & Turner, R. J. (2003). Stress exposure, race, and young adult male crime. *Sociological Quarterly, 44*, 243–269.

Ekman, P. (1972). Universal and cultural differences in facial expression of emotion. In J. R. Cole (Ed.), *Nebraska Symposium on Motivation, 1971* (Vol. 19, pp. 207–283). Lincoln: Nebraska University Press.

Ekman, P. (1992). An argument for basic emotions. *Cognition and Emotion, 6*(3–4), 169–200.

Ekman, P., & Friesen, W. V. (1969). Nonverbal leakage and clues to deception. *Psychiatry, 32,* 88–106.

Ekman, P., & Friesen, W. V. (1971). Constants across cultures in the face and emotion. *Journal of Personality and Social Psychology, 17,* 124–129.

Ekman, P., & Friesen, W. V. (1974). Detecting deception from the body or face. *Journal of Personality and Social Psychology, 29,* 288–298.

Ekman, P., & Friesen, W. V. (1975). *Unmasking the face: A guide to recognizing emotions from facial cues.* Englewood Cliffs, NJ: Prentice-Hall.

Ekman, P. and Friesen, W. V. (1978). *Facial action coding system: A technique for the measurement of facial movement.* Palo Alto, CA: Consulting Psychologists Press.

Ekman, P., & Friesen, W. V. (1986). A new pan-cultural facial expression of emotion. *Motivation and emotion, 10*(2), 159–168.

Ekman P., & Friesen, M. (1987). Single judgment emotion task. *Journal of Personality and Social Psychology, 53,* 712–717.

Ekman, P., Friesen, W. V., & O'Sullivan, M. (1988). Smiles when lying. *Journal of Personality and Social Psychology, 54,* 414–420.

Ekman, P., Friesen, W. V., & Scherer, K. R. (1976). Body movements and voice pitch in deceptive interaction. *Semiotica, 16,* 23–27.

Ekman, P., & O'Sullivan, M. (1991). Who can catch a liar? *American Psychologist, 46,* 913–920.

Ekman, P., O'Sullivan, M., & Frank, M. (1999). A few can catch a liar. *Psychological Science, 10,* 263–266.

Ekman, P., Sorenson, E. R., & Friesen, W. V. (1969). Pan-cultural elements in facial displays of emotion. *Science, 164*(3875), 86–88.

Elder, G. H. (1975). Age differentiation and the life course. In A. Inkeles, J. Coleman, & N. Smelser (Eds.), *Annual Review of Sociology* (Vol. 1, pp. 165–190). Palo Alto, CA: Annual Reviews.

Elder, G. H., & O'Rand, A. M. (1995). Adult lives in a changing society. In K. S. Cook, G. A. Fine, & J. S. House (Eds.), *Sociological perspectives on social psychology* (pp. 452–475). Needham Heights, MA: Allyn and Bacon.

Elkin, F., & Handel, G. (1989). *The child and society: The process of socialization* (5th ed.). New York: Random House.

Ellard, J. H., & Bates, D. D. (1990). Evidence for the role of the justice motive in status generalization processes. *Social Justice Research, 4*(2), 115–134.

Elliott, G. C., & Meeker, B. F. (1986). Achieving fairness in the face of competing concerns: The different effects of individual and group characteristics. *Journal of Personality and Social Psychology, 50,* 754–760.

Ellis, L., & Ratnasingam, M. (2006). Gender, sexual orientation and occupational interests: Evidence of androgen influences. *Mankind Quarterly, 53,* 36–80.

Ellison, L., & Munro, V. E. (2010). Getting to (not) guilty: Examining jurors' deliberative processes in, and beyond, the context of a mock rape trial. *Legal Studies, 30*(1), 74–97.

Ellison, N., Heino, R., & Gibbs, J. (2006). Managing impressions online: Self-presentational processes in the online dating environment. *Journal of Computer-Mediated Communication, 11,* 415–441.

Ellison, N. B., Hancock, J. T., & Toma, C. L. (2011). Profile as promise: A framework for conceptualizing veracity in online dating self-presentations. *New Media & Society, 14,* 45–62.

Ellsworth, P. C., Carlsmith, J. M., & Henson, A. (1972). The stare as a stimulus to flight in human subjects. *Journal of Personality and Social Psychology, 21,* 302–311.

Emerson, R. M. (1962). Power-dependence relations. *American Sociological Review, 31*–41.

Emerson, R. M. (1972). Exchange theory, part II: exchange relations and networks. *Sociological Theories in Progress, 2,* 58–87.

Emerson, R. M. (1981). Social exchange theory. In M. Rosenberg and R. Turner, *Social psychology: Sociological perspectives* (pp. 30–65). New York: Basic Books.

Emmons, R. A., & Diener, E. (1986). Situation selection as a moderator of response consistency and stability. *Journal of Personality and Social Psychology, 51,* 1013–1019.

Emmons, R. A., Diener, E., & Larsen, R. J. (1986). Choice and avoidance of everyday situations and affect congruence: Two models of reciprocal interactionism. *Journal of Personality and Social Psychology, 51,* 815–826.

Epstein, J. L. (1985). After the bus arrives: Resegregation in desegregated schools. *Journal of Social Issues, 41*(3), 23–44.

Erikson, E. H. (1968). *Identity: Youth and crisis.* New York: Norton.

Erikson, K. (1964). Notes on the sociology of deviance. In H. Becker (Ed.), *The other side: Perspectives on deviance.* (pp. 307–314). New York: Free Press.

Erikson, K. (1966). *The wayward Puritans.* New York: Wiley.

Erol, R. Y., & Orth, U. (2011). Self-esteem development from age 14 to 30 years: A longitudinal study. *Journal of Personality and Social Psychology, 101,* 607–619.

Esser, J. K. (1995). *Groupthink from Pearl Harbor to the Challenger: Failure of Decision-making groups.* Beaumont, TX: Lamar University-Beaumont.

Esser, J. K. (1998). Alive and well after 25 years: A review of groupthink research. *Organizational Behavior and Human Decision Processes, 73*(2), 116–141.

Ettinger, R. F., Marino, C. J., Endler, N. S., Geller, S. H., & Natziuk, T. (1971). Effects of agreement and correctness on relative competence and conformity. *Journal of Personality and Social Psychology, 19,* 204–212.

Evans, C. R., & Dion, K. L. (1991). Group cohesion and performance: A meta-analysis. *Small Group Research, 22*, 175–186.

Evans, G., & Wener, R. (2007). Crowding and personal space invasion on the train: Please don't make me sit in the middle. *Journal of Environmental Psychology, 27*, 90–94.

Evans, N. J., & Jarvis, P. A. (1980). Group cohesion: A review and reevaluation. *Small Group Behavior, 11*, 359–370.

Fader, J. J. (2011). Conditions of a successful status graduation ceremony: Formerly incarcerated urban youth and their tenuous grip on success. *Punishment and Society, 13*, 29–46.

Falci, C. D. (2011). Self-esteem and mastery trajectories in high school by social class and gender. *Social Science Research, 40*, 586–601.

Farhar-Pilgrim, B., & Shoemaker, F. F. (1981). Campaigns to affect energy behavior. In R. E. Rice & W. J. Paisley (Eds.), *Public communication campaigns.* (pp. 161–180). Beverly Hills, CA: Sage.

Farina, A., Gliha, D., Boudreau, L. A., Allen, J. G., & Sherman, M. (1971). Mental illness and the impact of believing others know it. *Journal of Abnormal Psychology, 77*, 1–5.

Farnworth, M., & Leiber, M. J. (1989). Strain theory revisited: Economic goals, educational means, and delinquency. *American Sociological Review, 54*, 263–274.

Farris, C., Treat, T. A., Viken, R. J., & McFall, R. M. (2008). Sexual coercion and the misperception of sexual intent. *Clinical Psychology Review, 28*(1), 48–66.

Fazio, R. H. (1990). Multiple processes by which attitudes guide behavior: The MODE model as an integrative framework. In L. Berkowitz (Ed.), *Advances in experimental social psychology* (Vol. 23, pp. 75–109). New York: Academic Press.

Fazio, R. H. (1995). Attitudes as object-evaluation associations: Determinants, consequences, and correlates of attitude accessibility. In R. E. Petty and J. A. Krosnick (Eds.), *Attitude strength: Antecedents and consequences* (pp. 247–282). Hillsdale, NJ: Erlbaum.

Fazio, R. H., Powell, M., & Herr, P. (1983). Toward a process model of the attitude-behavior relation: Accessing one's attitude upon mere observation of the attitude object. *Journal of Personality and Social Psychology, 44*, 723–735.

Fazio, R. H., Sanbonmatsu, D. M., Powell, M. C., & Kardes, F. R. (1986). On the automatic activation of attitudes. *Journal of Personality and Social Psychology, 50*, 229–238.

Fazio, R. H., & Towles-Schwen, T. (1999). The MODE model of attitude-behavior processes. In S. Chaiken and Y. Trope (Eds.), *Dual-process theories in social psychology*, 97–116. New York: Guilford.

Fazio, R. H., & Williams, C. J. (1986). Attitude accessibility as a moderator of the attitude-perception and attitude-behavior relations: An investigation of the 1984 presidential election. *Journal of Personality and Social Psychology, 51*, 505–514.

Fazio, R. H., & Zanna, M. (1981). Direct experience and attitude-behavior consistency. In L. Berkowitz (Ed.), *Advances in experimental social psychology* (Vol. 14, pp. 161–202). New York: Academic Press.

Feather, N. T. (1967). A structural balance approach to the analysis of communication effects. In L. Berkowitz (Ed.), *Advances in experimental social psychology* (Vol. 3, pp. 99–165). New York: Academic Press.

Feather, N. T. (1995). Values, valences, and choice: The influence of values on the perceived attractiveness and choice of alternatives. *Journal of Personality and Social Psychology, 68*, 1135–1151.

Feather, N. T., & Armstrong, D. J. (1967). Effects of variations in source attitude, receiver attitude, and communication stand on reactions to source and contents of communications. *Journal of Personality, 35*, 435–455.

Feeney, J. A. (1999). Adult romantic attachment and couple relationships. In J. Cassidy & P. R. Shaver (Eds.), *Handbook of attachment: Theory, research, and clinical applications* (pp. 355–377). New York: Guilford.

Feeney, J. A., & Noller, P. (1990). Attachment style as a predictor of adult romantic relationships. *Journal of Personality and Social Psychology, 58*, 281–291.

Feijten, P., & van Ham, M. (n.d.). Residential mobility and migration of the divorced and separated. *Demographic Research, 17*, Article 21, 623–653. www.demographic-research.org.

Feinberg, M., Willer, R., Stellar, J., & Keltner, D. (2012). The virtues of gossip: Reputational information sharing as prosocial behavior. *Journal of Personality and Social Psychology, 102*(5), 1015–1030.

Feijten P., & van Ham, M. (2010). The impact of splitting up and divorce on housing careers in the UK. *Housing Studies, 25*, 483–507.

Fejfar, M. C., & Hoyle, R. H. (2000). Effect of private self-awareness on negative affect and self-referent attribution. *Personality and Social Psychology Review, 4*, 132–142.

Feld, S. (1981). The focused organization of social ties. *American Journal of Sociology, 86*, 1015–1035.

Felipe, N. J., & Sommer, R. (1966). Invasions of personal space. *Social Problems, 14*, 206–214.

Feldman, D. C. (1984). The development and enforcement of group norms. *Academy of Management Review, 9*, 47–53.

Felfe, C., & Hsin, A. (2012). Maternal work conditions and child development. *Economics of Education Review, 31*, 1037–1057.

Felmlee, D., Sprecher, S., & Bassin, E. (1990). The dissolution of intimate relationships: A hazard model. *Social Psychology Quarterly, 53*, 13–30.

Felson, M. (1994). *Crime and everyday life: Insights and implications for society.* Thousand Oaks, CA: Pine Forge Press.

Felson, R. B. (1981). Ambiguity and bias in the self-concept. *Social Psychology Quarterly, 44*, 64–69.

Felson, R. B. (1985). Reflected appraisal and the development of self. *Social Psychology Quarterly, 48*, 71–78.

Felson, R. B. (1989). Parents and the reflected appraisal process: A longitudinal analysis. *Journal of Personality and Social Psychology, 56*, 965–971.

Felson, R. B., Liska, A. E., South, S. J., & McNulty, T. L. (1994). The subculture of violence and delinquency: Individual vs. school context effects. *Social Forces, 73*, 155–173.

Felson, R. B., & Reed, M. (1986). The effects of parents on the self-appraisals of children. *Social Psychology Quarterly, 49*, 302–308.

Felson, R. B., & Zielinski, M. A. (1989). Children's self-esteem and parental support. *Journal of Marriage and the Family, 51*, 727–735.

Fernández-Dols, J. M., & Ruiz-Belda, M. A. (1995). Are smiles a sign of happiness? Gold medal winners at the Olympic Games. *Journal of Personality and Social Psychology, 69*(6), 1113–1119.

Ferree, M. M., & Miller, F. D. (1985). Mobilization and meaning: Toward an integration of social psychological and resource perspectives on social movements. *Sociological Inquiry, 55*, 38–55.

Festinger, L. (1954). A theory of social comparison processes. *Human Relations, 7*, 117–140.

Festinger, L. (1957). *A theory of cognitive dissonance.* Stanford, CA: Stanford University Press.

Festinger, L., & Carlsmith, J. (1959). Cognitive consequences of forced compliance. *Journal of Abnormal and Social Psychology, 58*, 203–210.

Festinger, L., Pepitone, A., & Newcomb, T. (1952). Some consequences of de-individuation in a group. *Journal of Abnormal and Social Psychology, 47*, 382–389.

Festinger, L., Schachter, S., & Back, K. W. (1950). *Social pressures in informal groups.* New York: Harper & Row.

Fiedler, F. E. (1978a). Recent developments in research on the contingency model. In L. Berkowitz (Ed.), *Group processes.* (pp. 209–225). New York: Academic Press.

Fiedler, F. E. (1978b). The contingency model and the dynamics of the leadership process. In L. Berkowitz (Ed.), *Advances in experimental social psychology* (Vol. 11, pp. 59–112). New York: Academic Press.

Fiedler, F. E. (1981). Leadership effectiveness. *American Behavioral Scientist, 24*, 619–632.

Field, T., Diego, M., Pelaez, M., Deeds, O., & Delgado, J, (2011). Breakup distress in university students: A review. *College Student Journal, 45*, 461–480.

File, T. (2013). Computer and internet use in the United States. *Current Population Survey Reports*, P20–568. Washington, DC: U.S. Census Bureau.

Fine, G. A. (1995). Building blocks and the quadrant of action. In K. Cook, G. A. Fine, and J. S. House (Eds.), *Sociological perspectives on social psychology* (pp. 1–7). Boston: Allyn and Bacon.

Fine, G. A. (2000). Games and truths: Learning to construct social problems in high school debate. *Sociological Quarterly, 41*, 103–123.

Fink, E. L., Kaplowitz, S. A., & Bauer, C. L. (1983). Positional discrepancy, psychological discrepancy, and attitude change: Experimental tests of some mathematical models. *Communication Monographs, 50*, 413–430.

Finkel, S. E. (1993). Reexamining the "minimal effects" model in recent presidential elections. *Journal of Politics, 55*, 1–21.

Fischer, C. S. (1984). *The urban experience* (2nd ed.). San Diego, CA: Harcourt Brace Jovanovich.

Fisek, M. H. (1974). A model for the evolution of status structures in task-oriented discussion groups. In J. Berger, T. L. Conner, & M. H. Fisek (Eds.), *Expectation states theory.* (pp. 55–83). Cambridge, MA: Winthrop.

Fishbein, M., & Ajzen, I. (1975). *Belief, attitude, intention, and behavior.* Reading, MA: Addison-Wesley.

Fisher, J., Nadler, D., & Whitcher-Alagna, S. (1982). Recipient reactions to aid. *Psychological Bulletin, 91*, 33–54.

Fishman, P. (1983). Interaction: The work women do. In B. Thorne, C. Kramerae, & N. Henley (Eds.), *Language, gender, and society* (pp. 89–101). Rowley, MA: Newbury House.

Fishman, P. M. (1980). Conversational insecurity. In H. Giles & W. P. Robinson (Eds.), *Language: Social psychological perspectives.* (pp. 127–132). New York: Pergamon.

Fisicaro, S. A. (1988). A reexamination of the relation between halo error and accuracy. *Journal of Applied Psychology, 73*, 239–244.

Fiske, S. T. (1998). Stereotyping, prejudice, and discrimination. In D. T. Gilbert, S. T. Fiske, & G. Lindzey (Eds.), *Handbook of social psychology* (4th ed., pp. 357–411). New York: McGraw-Hill.

Fiske, S. T., Cuddy, A. J., & Glick, P. (2007). Universal dimensions of social cognition: Warmth and competence. *Trends in Cognitive Sciences, 11*(2), 77–83.

Fiske, S. T., Cuddy, A. J., Glick, P., & Xu, J. (2002). A model of (often mixed) stereotype content: Competence and warmth respectively follow from perceived status and competition. *Journal of Personality and Social Psychology, 82*(6), 878–902.

Fiske, S. T., Lin, M., & Neuberg, S. L. (1999). The continuum model: Ten years later. In S. Chaiken and Y. Trope, *Dual-process theories in social psychology* (pp. 231–254). New York: Guilford.

Fiske, S. T., & Linville, P. (1980). What does the schema concept buy us? *Personality and Social Psychology Bulletin, 6*, 543–557.

Fiske, S. T., & Neuberg, S. L. (1990). A continuum model of impression formation, from category-based to individuating processes: Influence of information and motivation on attention and interpretation. In M. P. Zanna (Ed.), *Advances in experimental social psychology* (Vol. 23, pp. 1–74). San Diego, CA: Academic Press.

Fiske, S. T., & Taylor, S. E. (1991). *Social cognition* (2nd ed.). New York: McGraw-Hill.

Fitzpatrick, M. J., & McPherson, B. J. (2010). Coloring within the lines: Gender stereotypes within contemporary coloring books. *Sex Roles, 62*, 127–137.

Flack, W. F., Daubman, K. A., Caron, M. L., Asadorian, J. A., D'Aureli, N. R., Gigliotti, S. N., Hall, A. T. et al. (2007). Risk Factors and consequences of unwanted sex among university students hooking up, alcohol, and stress response. *Journal of Interpersonal Violence*, 22(2), 139–157.

Flavell, J., Shipstead, S., & Croft, K. (1978). *What young children think you see when their eyes are closed*. Unpublished report, Stanford University.

Fleming, J. H., Darley, J. M., Hilton, J. L., & Kojetin, B. A. (1991). Multiple audience problem: A strategic communication perspective on social perception. *Journal of Personality and Social Psychology*, 58, 593–609.

Flora, J., & Segrin, C. (2000). Relationship development in dating couples: Implications for relational satisfaction and loneliness. *Journal of Social and Personal Relationships*, 17, 811–825.

Flowers, M. L. (1977). A laboratory test of some implications of Janis's groupthink hypothesis. *Journal of Personality and Social Psychology*, 35, 888–896.

Fodor, E. M., & Smith, T. (1982). The power motive as an influence on group decision making. *Journal of Personality and Social Psychology*, 42, 178–185.

Forbes, G. (2001). College students with tattoos and piercings: Motives, family experiences, personality factors, and perception by others. *Psychological Reports*, 89, 774–786.

Forbes, G. B., Adams-Curtis, L. E., White, K. B., & Hamm, N. R. (2002). Perceptions of married women and married men with hyphenated surnames. *Sex Roles*, 46(5–6), 167–175.

Fordham, S. (1999). Dissin' "the standard": Ebonics as guerrilla warfare at Capital High. *Anthropology and Education Quarterly*, 30, 272–293.

Forgas, J. P. (2011). Can negative affect eliminate the power of first impressions? Affective influences on primacy and recency effects in impression formation. *Journal of Experimental Social Psychology*, 47(2), 425–429.

Form, W. H., & Nosow, S. (1958). *Community in disaster*. New York: Harper.

Formoso, D., Gonzales, N., Barrera, M., & Dumka, L. (2007). Interparental relations, maternal employment, and fathering in Mexican American families. *Journal of Marriage and the Family*, 69, 26–39.

Forsyth, D. R. (1999). *Group dynamics* (3rd ed.). Belmont, CA: Wadsworth.

Forsyth, D. R., Berger, R. E., & Mitchell, T. (1981). The effects of self-serving vs. other-serving claims of responsibility on attraction and attribution in groups. *Social Psychology Quarterly*, 44, 59–64.

Forthofer, M. S., Markman, H. J., Cox, M., Stanley, S., & Kessler, R. C. (1996). Associations between marital distress and work loss in a national sample. *Journal of Marriage and the Family*, 58, 597–605.

Foster, C., & Campbell, W. K. (2005). The adversity of secret relationships. *Personal Relationships*, 12, 125–143.

Foster, M. D., & Matheson, K. (1995). Double relative

deprivation: Combining the personal and political. *Personality and Social Psychology Bulletin*, 21, 1167–1177.

Fox, G. L., & Benson, M. L. (2006). Household and neighborhood contexts of intimate partner violence. *Public Health Reports*, 121(4), 419–427.

Fox, G. L., Benson, M. L., DeMaris, A. A., & Wyk, J. (2002). Economic distress and intimate violence: Testing family stress and resources theories. *Journal of Marriage and Family*, 64(3), 793–807.

Fox, K. (2013). Incurable sex offenders, lousy judges, and the media: Moral panic sustenance in the age of new media. *American Journal of Criminal Justice*, 38, 160–181.

Francis, L. (1997). Ideology and interpersonal emotion management: Redefining identity in two support groups. *Social Psychology Quarterly*, 60, 153–171.

Franiuk, R., Cohen, D., & Pomerantz, E. (2002). Implicit theories of relationships: Implications for relationship satisfaction and longevity. *Personal Relationships*, 9, 345–367.

Frank, F., & Anderson, L. R. (1971). Effects of task and group size upon group productivity and member satisfaction. *Sociometry*, 34, 135–149.

Franklin, A., Boyd-Franklin, N., & Kelly, S. (2006). Racism and invisibility: Race-related stress, emotional abuse, and psychological trauma for people of color. *Journal of Emotional Abuse*, 6, 9–30.

Franks, D., & Marolla, J. (1976). Efficacious action and social approval as interacting dimensions of self-esteem. *Sociometry*, 39, 324–341.

Fraser, C., Gouge, C., & Billig, M. (1971). Risky shifts, cautious shifts, and group polarization. *European Journal of Social Psychology*, 1, 7–30.

Fredricks, A., & Dossett, D. (1983). Attitude-behavior relations: A comparison of the Fishbein-Ajzen and the Bentler-Speckart models. *Journal of Personality and Social Psychology*, 45, 501–512.

Freedman, J., & Fraser, S. (1966). Compliance without pressure: The foot-in-the-door technique. *Journal of Personality and Social Psychology*, 4, 195–202.

Freedman, J. L., & Sears, D. O. (1965). Warning, distraction, and resistance to influence. *Journal of Personality and Social Psychology*, 1, 262–266.

French, J. R. P., & Raven, B. (1959). Bases of social power. In D. Cartwright (Ed.), *Studies in social power*. (pp. 150–167). Ann Arbor: University of Michigan.

Freud, S. (1930). *Civilization and its discontents*. London: Hogarth Press.

Freud, S. (1950). Why war? In J. Strachey (Ed.), *Collected papers* (Vol. 5, pp. 195–216). London: Hogarth Press.

Freud, S. (1962). *Three essays on the theory of sexuality* (Trans. James Strachey). New York: Basic Books.

Frey, D. (1978). Reactions to success and failure in public and private conditions. *Journal of Experimental Social Psychology*, 14, 172–179.

Frey, D. L., & Gaertner, S. L. (1986). Helping and the avoidance of inappropriate interracial behavior: A strategy that perpetuates a nonprejudiced self-image. *Journal of Personality and Social Psychology, 50,* 1083–1090.

Frey, K. S., & Ruble, D. N. (1985). What children say when the teacher is not around: Conflicting goals in social comparison and performance assessment in the classroom. *Journal of Personality and Social Psychology, 48,* 550–562.

Friedrich-Cofer, L., & Huston, A. C. (1986). Television violence and aggression: The debate continues. *Psychological Bulletin, 100,* 364–371.

Fries, A., & Pollak, S. (2004). Emotion understanding in postinstitutionalized Eastern European children. *Development and Psychopathology, 16,* 355–369.

Frieze, I., & Weiner, B. (1971). Cue utilization and attributional judgments for success and failure. *Journal of Personality, 39,* 591–605.

Frijda, N. H., & Mesquita, B. (1994). The social roles and functions of emotions. In S. Kitayama & H. R. Markus (Eds), *Emotion and culture: Empirical studies of mutual influence* (pp. 51–87). Washington, DC: American Psychological Association.

Fritzsche, B. A., Finkelstein, M. A., & Penner, L. A. (2000). To help or not to help: Capturing individuals' decision policies. *Social Behavior and Personality, 28,* 561–578.

Fultz, J., Batson, C. D., Fortenbach, V. A., McCarthy, P. M., & Varney, L. L. (1986). Social evaluation and the empathy-altruism hypothesis. *Journal of Personality and Social Psychology, 50,* 761–769.

Furnham, A. (1986). The robustness of the recency effect: Studies using legal evidence. *Journal of General Psychology, 113*(4), 351–357.

Furstenberg, F., & Kiernan, K. (2001). Delayed parental divorce: How much do children suffer? *Journal of Marriage and the Family, 63,* 446–457.

Gaertner, S. L., Dovidio, J. F., Anastasio, P. A., Bachman, B. A., & Rust, M. C. (1993). The common ingroup identity model: Recategorization and the reduction of intergroup bias. In W. Stroebe & H. Hewstone (Eds.), *European review of social psychology* (Vol. 4, pp. 1–26). Chichester, UK: Wiley.

Gaertner, S. L., Dovidio, J. F., Rust, M. C., Nier, J. A., Banker, B., Ward, C. M., et al. (1999). Reducing intergroup bias: Elements of intergroup cooperation. *Journal of Personality and Social Psychology, 76,* 388–402.

Gaertner, S. L., Mann, J., Murrell, A., & Dovidio, J. F. (1989). Reducing intergroup bias: The benefits of recategorization. *Journal of Personality and Social Psychology, 57,* 239–249.

Galton, M. (1987). An ORACLE chronicle: A decade of classroom research. *Teaching and Teacher Education, 3,* 299–313.

Gamson, W. A. (1992). Social psychology of collective action. In A. D. Morris & C. M. Mueller (Eds.), *Frontiers of social movement theory.* (pp. 53–76). New Haven, CT: Yale University Press.

Gardner, L., & Shoemaker, D. J. (1989). Social bonding and delinquency: A comparative analysis. *Sociological Quarterly, 30,* 481–500.

Garfinkel, H. (1956). Conditions of successful degradation ceremonies. *American Sociological Review, 61,* 420–424.

Garfinkel, I., & McLanahan, S. S. (1986). *Single mothers and their children: A new American dilemma.* Washington, DC: Urban Institute.

Garrett, P., & Baquedano-Lopez, P. (2002). Language socialization: Reproduction and continuity, transformation and change. *Annual Review of Anthropology, 31,* 339–361.

Garrett, R. K. (2009). Echo chambers online?: Politically motivated selective exposure among Internet news users. *Journal of Computer-Mediated Communication, 14,* 265–285.

Garrett, R. K., Carnahan, D., & Lynch, E. K. (2011). A turn toward avoidance? Selective exposure to online political information, 2004–2008. *Political Behavior, 1,* 1–22.

Garrido, C. O., R. B. Adams, A. J. Nelson, U. Hess, & R. E. Kleck. (2013). Age-related facial markers as mechanisms driving attributions of sadness to neutral elderly faces. Presentation at the Association for Psychological Science Annual Convention. Washington, DC. May 24, 2013.

Gartner, R. (1990). The victims of homicide: A temporal and cross-national comparison. *American Sociological Review, 55,* 92–106.

Gates, G. S. (1924). The effect of an audience upon performance. *Journal of Abnormal and Social Psychology, 18,* 334–342.

Gawronski, B., & Strack, F. (2004). On the propositional nature of cognitive consistency: Dissonance changes explicit, but not implicit attitudes. *Journal of Experimental Social Psychology, 40,* 535–542.

Gecas, V. (1990). Contexts of socialization. In M. Rosenberg & R. Turner (Eds.), *Social psychology: Sociological perspectives.* (pp. 165–199). New Brunswick, NJ: Transaction.

Gecas, V., & Burke, P. J. (1995). Self and identity. In K. S. Cook, G. A. Fine, & J. S. House (Eds.), *Sociological perspectives on social psychology* (pp. 41–67). Needham Heights, MA: Allyn and Bacon.

Gecas, V., & Schwalbe, M. (1983). Beyond the looking-glass self: Social structure and efficacy-based self-esteem. *Social Psychology Quarterly, 46,* 77–88.

Geen, R. G. (1968). Effects of frustration, attack, and prior training in aggressiveness upon aggressive behavior. *Journal of Personality and Social Psychology, 9*(4), 316–321.

Geen, R. G., & Quanty, M. G. (1977). The catharsis of aggression: An analysis of a hypothesis. In L. Berkowitz (Ed.), *Advances in experimental social psychology* (Vol. 10, pp. 1–37). New York: Academic Press.

Geen, R. G., Stonner, L., & Shope, G. L. (1975). The facilitation of aggression by aggression: A study in response inhibition and disinhibition. *Journal of Personality and Social Psychology, 31,* 721–726.

Geis, M. L. (1995). *Speech acts and conversational interaction.* New York: Cambridge University Press.

Gelfand, D. M., & Hartmann, D. P. (1982). Response consequences and attributions: Two contributors to prosocial behavior. In N. Eisenberg (Ed.), *The development of prosocial behavior.* (pp. 165–196). New York: Academic Press.

Geller, V. (1977). The role of visual access in impression management and impression formation. Unpublished doctoral dissertation, Columbia University, New York.

Gelles, R. J., & Cornell, C. P. (1997). *Intimate violence in families.* Newbury Park, CA: Sage.

Gelles, R. J., & Strauss, M. A. (1988). *Intimate violence.* New York: Simon and Schuster.

Gerard, H. B. (1983). School desegregation: The social science role. *American Psychologist, 38,* 869–877.

Gerard, H. B., Wilhelmy, R. A., & Conolley, E. S. (1968). Conformity and group size. *Journal of Personality and Social Psychology, 8,* 79–82.

Gerber, A. S., Huber, G. A., Doherty, D., Dowling, C. M., & Panagopoulos, C. (2013). Big five personality traits and responses to persuasive appeals: Results from voter turnout experiments. *Political Behavior, 35*(4), 687–728.

Gergen, K. J., Ellsworth, P., Maslach, C., & Siepel, M. (1975). Obligation, donor resources, and reactions to aid in three cultures. *Journal of Personality and Social Psychology, 31,* 390–400.

Gergen, K. J., Gergen, M. M., & Meter, K. (1972). Individual orientations to prosocial behavior. *Journal of Social Issues, 28(3),* 105–130.

Gesell, A., & Ilg, F. (1943). *Infant and child in the culture of today.* New York: Harper & Row.

Ghaziani, A. (2004). Anticipatory and actualized identities: A cultural analysis of the transition from AIDS disability to work. *Sociological Quarterly, 45,* 273–301.

Gibbons, F. X., Smith, T. W., Ingram, R. E., Pearce, K., Brehm, S. S., & Schroeder, D. J. (1985). Self-awareness and self-confrontation: Effects of self-focused attention on members of a clinical population. *Journal of Personality and Social Psychology, 48,* 662–675.

Gibbs, J., Ellison, N., & Heino, R. (2006). Self-presentation in online personals: The role of anticipated future interaction, self-disclosure, and perceived success in Internet dating. *Communication Research, 33,* 152–177.

Gifford, R. (1982). Projected interpersonal distance and orientation choices: Personality, sex, and social situation. *Social Psychology Quarterly, 45,* 145–152.

Gilbert, D. T., & Malone, P. S. (1995). The correspondence bias. *Psychological Bulletin, 117,* 21–38.

Gilbert, T. F. (1978). *Human competence.* New York: McGraw-Hill.

Giles, H. (1980). Accommodation theory: Some new directions. In S. deSilva (Ed.), *Aspects of linguistic behavior.* (pp. 105–136). York, UK: York University Press.

Giles, H., & Coupland, N. (1991). *Language: Contexts and consequences.* Pacific Grove, CA: Brooks/Cole.

Giles, H., Hewstone, M., & St. Clair, R. (1981). Speech as an independent and dependent variable of social situations: An introduction and new theoretical framework. In H. Giles & R. St. Clair (Eds.), *The social psychological significance of speech.* Hillsdale, NJ: Erlbaum.

Gill, V. T., & Maynard, D. W. (1995). On "labeling" in actual interactions: Delivering and receiving diagnoses of developmental disabilities. *Social Problems, 42,* 11–37.

Gilligan, C. (1982). *In a different voice.* Cambridge, MA: Harvard University Press.

Ginorio, A., Gutierrez, L., Cauce, A. M., & Acosta, M. (1995). Psychological issues for Latinas. In H. Landrine (Ed.), *Bringing cultural diversity to feminist psychology: Theory, research, and practice* (pp. 241–263). Washington, DC: American Psychological Association.

Giordano, P., Cernkovich, S., & Rudolph, J. (2002). Gender, crime, and desistance: Toward a theory of cognitive transformation. *American Journal of Sociology, 107,* 990–1064.

Glasman, L. R., & Albarracín, D. (2006). Forming attitudes that predict future behavior: a meta-analysis of the attitude-behavior relation. *Psychological Bulletin, 132*(5), 778–822.

Glass, J., Bengston, V. L., & Dunham, C. (1986). Attitude similarity in three-generation families: Status inheritance or reciprocal influence? *American Sociological Review, 51,* 685–698.

Glenn, N., & Marquardt, E. (2001). *Hooking up, hanging out, and hoping for Mr. Right.* New York: Institute for American Values. www.americanvalues.org/search/item.php?id=18.

Glick, P., & Fiske, S. T. (2001). An ambivalent alliance: Hostile and benevolent sexism as complementary justifications for gender inequality. *American Psychologist, 56*(2), 109–118.

Glick, P., Fiske, S. T., Mladinic, A., Saiz, J. L., Abrams, D., Masser, B., & López, W. L. (2000). Beyond prejudice as simple antipathy: hostile and benevolent sexism across cultures. *Journal of Personality and Social Psychology, 79*(5), 763–775.

Godley, A., & Escher, A. (2012). Bidialectical African American adolescents' beliefs about spoken language expectations in English classrooms. *Journal of Adolescent and Adult Literacy, 55,* 704–713.

Goethals, G. R., & Zanna, M. P. (1979). The role of social comparison in choice shift. *Journal of Personality and Social Psychology, 37,* 1469–1476.

Goffman, E. (1952). Cooling the mark out: Some adaptations to failure. *Psychiatry, 15,* 451–463.

Goffman, E. (1956). Embarrassment and social organization. *American Journal of Sociology, 62*(3), 264–271.

Goffman, E. (1959a). The moral career of the mental patient. *Psychiatry, 22,* 125–169.

Goffman, E. (1959b). *The presentation of self in everyday life.* Garden City, NY: Anchor/Doubleday.

Goffman, E. (1963a). *Behavior in public places.* New York: Free Press.

Goffman, E. (1963b). *Stigma: Notes on the management of spoiled identity*. Englewood Cliffs, NJ: Spectrum/Prentice Hall.

Goffman, E. (1967). *Interaction ritual*. Chicago: Aldine.

Goffman, E. (1974). *Frame analysis*. New York: Harper and Row.

Goffman, E. (1983). Felicity's condition. *American Journal of Sociology, 89*, 1–53.

Goldberg, W., Prause, J., Lucas-Thompson, R., & Himsel, A. (2008). Maternal employment and children's achievement in context: A meta-analysis of four decades of research. *Psychological Bulletin, 134*, 77–108.

Goldstein, B., & Oldham, J. (1979). *Children and work: A study of socialization*. New Brunswick, NJ: Transaction.

Goleman, D. (1996) *Emotional intelligence*. London: Bloomsbury.

Goleman, D. (2006). *Emotional intelligence*. New York: Random House.

Gonos, G. (1977). "Situation" vs. "frame": The "interactionist" and the "structuralist" analysis of everyday life. *American Sociological Review, 42*, 854–867.

Gonzales, M. H., Davis, J. M., Loney, G. L., Lukens, C. K., & Junghans, C. M. (1983). Interactional approach to interpersonal attraction. *Journal of Personality and Social Psychology, 44*, 1192–1197.

Goodchilds, J. D., & Zellman, G. L. (1984). Sexual signaling and sexual aggression in adolescent relationships. In N. M. Malamuth & E. I. Donnerstein (Eds.), *Pornography and sexual aggression* (pp. 234–243). Orlando, FL: Academic Press.

Gooden, A. M., & Gooden, M. A. (2001). Gender representation in notable children's picture books: 1995–1999. *Sex Roles, 45*, 89–101.

Goodman, P. S., & Friedman, A. (1969). An examination of quantity and quality of performance under conditions of overpayment in piece rate. *Organizational Behavior and Human Performance, 4*, 365–374.

Goodman, P. S., & Friedman, A. (1971). An examination of Adams' theory of inequity. *Administrative Science Quarterly, 16*, 271–288.

Goodwin, C. (1987). Forgetfulness as an interactive resource. *Social Psychology Quarterly, 50*, 115–131.

Goodwin, R. (1991). A re-examination of Rusbult's responses to dissatisfaction typology. *Journal of Social and Personal Relationships, 8*, 569–574.

Goodwin, S. A., Gubin, A., Fiske, S. T., & Yzerbyt, V. Y. (2000). Power can bias impression processes: Stereotyping subordinates by default and by design. *Group Processes and Intergroup Relations, 3*, 227–256.

Gordon, C. (1968). Self-conceptions: Configurations of content. In C. Gordon & K. J. Gergen (Eds.), *The self in social interaction I: Classic and contemporary perspectives* (pp. 115–136). New York: Wiley.

Gordon, P. (2004). Numerical cognition without words: Evidence from Amazonia. *Science, 306*, 496–499.

Gordon, R. A. (1996). Impact of ingratiation on judgments and evaluations: A meta-analytic investigation. *Journal of Personality and Social Psychology, 71*(1), 54–70.

Gordon, S. (1990). Social structural effects on emotion. In T. D. Kemper (Ed.) *Research agendas in the sociology of emotion* (pp.145–79). Albany: State University of New York Press.

Gorfein, D. S. (1964). The effects of a nonunanimous majority on attitude change. *Journal of Social Psychology, 63*, 333–338.

Gosling, S. D., Craik, K. H., Martin, N. R., & Pryor. M. R. (2005). Material attributes of personal living spaces. *Home Cultures, 2*, 51–88.

Gove, W., Hughes, M., & Geerken, M. R. (1980). Playing dumb: A form of impression management with undesirable effects. *Social Psychology Quarterly, 43*, 89–102.

Gowen, C. R. (1986). Managing work group performance by individual goals and group goals for an interdependent group task. *Journal of Organizational Behavior Management, 7*(3–4), 5–27.

Graham, J. M. (2011). Measuring love in romantic relationships: A meta-analysis. *Journal of Social and Personal Relationships, 28*, 748–771.

Graham, L., & Hogan, R. (1990). Social class and tactics: Neighborhood opposition to group homes. *Sociological Quarterly, 31*, 513–529.

Gramling, R., & Forsyth, C. J. (1987). Exploiting stigma. *Sociological Forum, 2*, 401–415.

Grammar, K., Kruck, K., Juette, A., & Fink, B. (2000). Non-verbal control as courtship signals: The role of control and choice in selecting partners. *Evolution and Human Behavior, 21*, 371–390.

Granberg, D., & Holmberg, S. (1990). The intention-behavior relationship among U.S. and Swedish voters. *Social Psychology Quarterly, 53*, 44–54.

Granovetter, M. S. (1973). The strength of weak ties. *American Journal of Sociology, 78*, 1360–1380.

Grant, P. R., & Holmes, J. G. (1981). The integration of implicit personality schemas and stereotype images. *Social Psychology Quarterly, 44*, 107–115.

Gray, J. (1992). *Men are from Mars, women are from Venus: A practical guide for improving communication and getting what you want in your relationships*. New York: HarperCollins.

Gray-Little, B., & Hafdahl, A. (2000). Factors influencing racial comparisons of self-esteem: A quantitative review. *Psychological Bulletin, 126*, 26–54.

Grayshon, M. C. (1980). Social grammar, social psychology, and linguistics. In H. Giles, W. P. Robinson, & P. M. Smith (Eds.), *Language: Social psychological perspectives.* (pp. 155–169). New York: Pergamon.

Green, A. (2002, July 13). Teen-agers are misunderstood. *Wisconsin State Journal*, p. D1.

Green, J. A. (1972). Attitudinal and situational determinants of intended behavior toward Blacks. *Journal of Personality and Social Psychology, 22*, 13–17.

Greenbaum, P., & Rosenfeld, H. (1978). Patterns of avoidance in response to interpersonal staring and proximity: Effects of bystanders on drivers at a traffic intersection. *Journal of Personality and Social Psychology, 36*, 575–587.

Greenberg, J. (1996). *The quest for justice on the job: Essays and experiments.* Thousand Oaks, CA: Sage.

Greenberg, J., & Cohen, R. L. (1982). *Equity and justice in social behavior.* New York: Academic Press.

Greenberg, J., & Folger, R. (1983). Procedural justice, participation, and the fair process effect in groups and organizations. In P. B. Paulus (Ed.), *Basic group processes* (pp. 235–256). New York: Springer-Verlag.

Greenberg, J., & Scott, K. S. (1996). Why do workers bite the hands that feed them? Employee theft as a social exchange process. In B. M. Staw & L. L. Cummings (Eds.), *Research in organizational behavior* (Vol. 18, pp. 111–156). Greenwich, CT: JAI Press.

Greenberg, M., & Frisch, D. (1972). Effect of intentionality on willingness to reciprocate a favor. *Journal of Experimental Social Psychology, 8,* 99–111.

Greenberg, M. S., & Westcott, D. R. (1983). Indebtedness as a mediator of reactions to aid. In J. D. Fisher, A. Nadler, & B. M. DePaulo (Eds.), *New directions in helping: Vol. 1. Recipient reactions to aid* (pp. 85–112). San Diego, CA: Academic Press.

Greenberger, E., & Steinberg, L. (1983). Sex differences in early labor force participation. *Social Forces, 62,* 467–486.

Greenfeld, L., Rand, M., Craven, D., Klaus, P., Perkins, C., Ringel, C., et al. (1998). *Violence by intimates.* Washington, DC: U.S. Department of Justice, Bureau of Justice Statistics.

Greenfield, E. A., & Marks, N. F. (2004). Formal volunteering as a protective factor for older adults' psychological well-being. *Journal of Gerontology, 59B,* 258–264.

Greenwald, A., & Farnham, S. (2000). Using the implicit association test to measure self-esteem and self-concept. *Journal of Personality and Social Psychology, 79,* 1022–1038.

Greenwald, A. G., Nosek, B. A., & Banaji, M. R. (2003). Understanding and using the implicit association test: I. An improved scoring algorithm. *Journal of Personality and Social Psychology, 85*(2), 197–216.

Greenwald, A. G., Poehlman, T. A., Uhlmann, E. L., & Banaji, M. R. (2009). Understanding and using the Implicit Association Test: III. Meta-analysis of predictive validity. *Journal of Personality and Social Psychology, 97*(1), 17–41.

Gregory, S. W., & Webster, S. (1996). A nonverbal signal in voices of interview partners effectively predicts communication accommodation and social status perceptions. *Journal of Personality and Social Psychology, 70,* 1231–1240.

Grice, P. H. (1975). Logic and conversation. In P. Cole & J. L. Morgan (Eds.), *Syntax and semantics, Vol. 3: Speech acts.* (pp. 41–58). New York: Academic Press.

Griffin, D., Gonzalez, R., & Varey, C. (2001). The heuristics and biases approach to judgment under uncertainty. In A. Tesser & N. Schwartz (Eds.), *Blackwell handbook of social psychology: Intraindividual processes.* (pp. 207–235). Oxford, UK: Blackwell.

Grimshaw, A. D. (1973). On language in society. Part 1. *Contemporary Sociology, 2,* 575–585.

Grimshaw, A. D. (1990). Talk and social control. In M. Rosenberg & R. H. Turner (Eds.), *Social psychology: Sociological perspectives.* (pp. 200–232). New Brunswick, NJ: Transaction.

Gross, A. E., & Latané, J. G. (1974). Receiving help, reciprocation, and interpersonal attraction. *Journal of Applied Social Psychology, 4,* 210–223.

Gross, A. E., & McMullen, P. A. (1983). Models of the help seeking process. In B. M. DePaulo, A. Nadler, & J. D. Fisher (Eds.), *New directions in helping: Vol. 2. Help seeking* (pp. 47–73). New York: Academic Press.

Gross, E., & Stone, G. P. (1970). Embarrassment and the analysis of role requirements. In G. P. Stone & H. A. Farberman (Eds.), *Social psychology through symbolic interaction.* (pp. 1–15). Waltham, MA: Ginn-Blaisdell.

Grzywacz, J., & Marks, N. (2000). Family, work, work-family spillover, and problem drinking during midlife. *Journal of Marriage and the Family, 62,* 336–348.

Guadagno, R. E., & Cialdini, R. B. (2007). Gender differences in impression management in organizations: A qualitative review. *Sex Roles, 56,* 483–494.

Gueguen, N. (2012). Tattoos, piercings, and sexual activity. *Social Behavior and Personality, 40,* 1543–1548.

Guerreo, L., Jones, S., & Burgoon, J. (2000). Responses to nonverbal intimacy change in romantic dyads: Effects of behavioral valence and degree of behavioral change on nonverbal and verbal reactions. *Communication Monographs, 67*(4), 325–346.

Guimond, S., Begin, G., & Palmer, D. L. (1989). Education and causal attributions: The development of "person-blame" and "system-blame" ideology. *Social Psychology Quarterly, 52*(2), 126–140.

Guimond, S., & Dubé-Simard, L. (1983). Relative deprivation theory and the Quebec nationalist movement: The cognition-emotion distinction and the personal-group deprivation issue. *Journal of Personality and Social Psychology, 44,* 526–535.

Guimond, S., & Palmer, D. L. (1990). Type of academic training and causal attributions for social problems. *European Journal of Social Psychology, 20*(1), 61–75.

Gully, S. M., Devine, D. J., & Whitney, D. J. (1995). A meta-analysis of cohesion and performance: Effects of level of analysis and task interdependence. *Small Group Research, 26,* 497–520.

Gumperz, J. J. (1976). The sociolinguistic significance of conversational code-switching. In J. Cook-Gumperz & J. J. Gumperz (Eds.), *Papers on language and context.* (pp. 1–34). Berkeley, CA: University of California, Language Behavior Research Laboratory.

Gurevitch, Z. D. (1990). The embrace: On the element of non-distance in human relations. *Sociological Quarterly, 31,* 187–201.

Gurney, J. F., & Tierney, K. J. (1982). Relative deprivation and social movements: A critical look at twenty years of theory and research. *Sociological Quarterly, 23,* 33–47.

Guryan, J., Hurst, E., & Kearney, M. (2008). Parental education and parental time with children (Working

Paper 13993). Cambridge, MA: National Bureau of Economic Research.

Gustafson, R. (1989). Frustration and successful vs. unsuccessful aggression: A test of Berkowitz's completion hypothesis. *Aggressive Behavior*, *15*(1), 5–12.

Haan, N. (1978). Two moralities in action contexts. Relationships to thought, ego regulation, and development. *Journal of Personality and Social Psychology*, *36*, 286–305.

Haan, N. (1986). Systematic variability in the quality of moral action, as defined in two paradigms. *Journal of Personality and Social Psychology*, *50*, 1271–1284.

Hackman, J. R., & Morris, C. G. (1975). Group tasks, group interaction process, and group performance effectiveness: A review and proposed integration. In L. Berkowitz (Ed.), *Advances in experimental social psychology* (Vol. 8, pp. 45–99). New York: Academic Press.

Hagood, M. (2011). Quiet comfort: Noise, otherness and the mobile production of personal space. *American Quarterly*, *63*, 573–589.

Hahlweg, K., Heinrichs, N., Bertram, H., et al. (2008). Corporal punishment: Prevalence and impact on psychological development of preschool children. *Kindheit und Entwicklung*, *17*, 45–56.

Haidt, J., & Keltner, D. (1999). Culture and facial expression: Open-ended methods find more expressions and a gradient of recognition. *Cognition and Emotion*, *13*(3), 225–266.

Haines, V. A., Beggs, J. J., & Hurlbert, J. S. (2011). Neighborhood disadvantage, network social capital, and depressive symptoms. *Journal of Health and Social Behavior*, *52*, 58–73.

Halberstam, D. (1979). *The powers that be.* New York: Knopf.

Hall, E. T. (1966). *The hidden dimension.* Garden City, NY: Doubleday.

Hall, J., & Friedman, G. (1999). Status, gender, and nonverbal behavior: A study of structured interactions between employees of a company. *Personality and Social Psychology Bulletin*, *25*, 1082–1091.

Halpern, D. F. (1998). Teaching critical thinking for transfer across domains: Dispositions, skills, structure training, and metacognitive monitoring. *American Psychologist*, *53*(4), 449–455.

Halpern, D. F. (2002). Teaching for critical thinking: A four-part model to enhance thinking skills. In W. J. McKeachie, S. F. Davis, C. L. Brewes, and W. Buskist (Eds.), *The teaching of psychology: Essays in honor of Wilbert J. McKeachie and Charles L. Brewer* (pp. 91–106). Mahwah, NJ: Erlbaum.

Hamilton, D. L. (1979). A cognitive-attributional analysis of stereotyping. In L. Berkowitz (Ed.), *Advances in experimental social psychology* (Vol. 12, pp. 53–85). New York: Academic Press.

Hamilton, D. L. (1981). Stereotyping and intergroup behavior: Some thoughts on the cognitive approach. In D. L. Hamilton (Ed.), *Cognitive processes in stereotyping and intergroup behavior* (pp. 333–353). Hillsdale, NJ: Erlbaum.

Hamilton, D. L., & Bishop, G. D. (1976). Attitudinal and behavioral effects of initial integration of White suburban neighborhoods. *Journal of Social Issues*, *32*(2), 47–67.

Hamilton, M. C., Anderson, D., Broaddus, M., & Young, K. (2006). Gender stereotyping and under-representation of female characters in 200 popular children's books: A twenty-first century update. *Sex Roles*, *55*, 757–765.

Hamilton, W. (1964). The genetical evolution of social behavior, I & II. *Journal of Theoretical Biology*, *7*, 1–52.

Hamilton, W. D. (1964). The genetical evolution of social behaviour. I. *Journal of Theoretical Biology*, *7*(1), 1–16.

Hanni, R. (1980). What is planned during speech pauses? In H. Giles, W. P. Robinson, & P. M. Smith (Eds.), *Language: Social psychological perspectives.* (pp. 321–326). New York: Pergamon.

Harasty, A. (1997). The interpersonal nature of social stereotypes: Discussion patterns about in-groups and out-groups. *Personality and Social Psychology Bulletin*, *23*, 270–284.

Hardy, C., & Latané, B. (1986). Social loafing on a cheering task. *Social Science*, *71*, 165–172.

Hardy, C., & Van Vugt, M. (2006). Nice guys finish first: The competitive altruism hypothesis. *Personality and Social Psychology Bulletin*, *32*, 1402–1413.

Harkins, S. G., & Petty, R. E. (1981a). The effects of source magnification of cognitive effect on attitudes: An information processing view. *Journal of Personality and Social Psychology*, *40*, 401–413.

Harkins, S. G., & Petty, R. E. (1981b). The multiple source effect in persuasion: The effects of distraction. *Personality and Social Psychology Bulletin*, *4*, 627–635.

Harkins, S. G., & Petty, R. E. (1982). Effects of task difficulty and task uniqueness on social loafing. *Journal of Personality and Social Psychology*, *43*, 1214–1229.

Harkins, S. G., & Petty, R. E. (1983). Social context effects in persuasion: The effects of multiple sources and multiple targets. In P. B. Paulus (Ed.), *Basic group processes.* (pp. 149–175). New York: Springer Verlag.

Harkins, S. G., & Petty, R. E. (1987). Information utility and the multiple source effect. *Journal of Personality and Social Psychology*, *52*, 260–268.

Harkins, S. G., & Szymanski, K. (1987). Social loafing and social facilitation. In C. Hendrick (Ed.), *Group processes and intergroup relations* (pp. 167–188). Newbury Park, CA: Sage.

Harlow, R. E., & Cantor, N. (1995). To whom do people turn when things go poorly? Task orientation and functional social contacts. *Journal of Personality and Social Psychology*, *69*, 329–340.

Harnish, J., Aseltine, R., & Gore, S. (2000). Resolution of stressful experiences as an indicator of coping effectiveness in young adults: An event history analysis. *Journal of Health and Social Behavior*, *41*, 121–136.

Harris, M. B. (1974). Mediators between frustration and aggression in a field experiment. *Journal of Experimental Social Psychology*, *10*, 561–571.

Harris, P., & Sachau, D. (2005). Is cleanliness next to godliness? The role of housekeeping in impression formation. *Environment and Behavior, 37,* 81–101.

Harrison, A. (1977). Mere exposure. In L. Berkowitz (Ed.), *Advances in experimental social psychology* (Vol. 10, pp. 39–83). New York: Academic Press.

Harrison, M. A., & Gilmore, A. L. (2012). U txt WHEN? College students' social contexts of text messaging. *Social Science Journal, 49,* 513–518.

Harvey, E. (1999). Short-term and long-term effects of parental employment on children of the National Longitudinal Study of Youth. *Developmental Psychology, 35,* 445–459.

Harvey, J. H., Weber, A. L., & Orbuch, T. L. (1990). *Interpersonal accounts.* Oxford, UK: Blackwell.

Haskell, M. R., & Yablonsky, L. (1983). *Criminology: Crime and Criminality* (3rd ed.). Boston: Houghton Mifflin.

Haslam, S. A., & McCarty, C. (2004). Experimental design and causality in social psychology research. In Sansone, C., Morf, C. C., & Panter, A. T. (Eds.), *The Sage handbook of methods in social psychology* (pp. 237–264). Thousand Oaks, CA: Sage.

Hass, R. G. (1981). Effects of source characteristics on cognitive responses in persuasion. In R. E. Petty, T. M. Ostrom, & T. C. Brock (Eds.), *Cognitive responses in persuasion* (pp. 141–172). Hillsdale, NJ: Erlbaum.

Hassin, R., & Trope, Y. (2000). Facing faces: Studies on the cognitive aspects of physiognomy. *Journal of Personality and Social Psychology, 78,* 837–852.

Hastorf, A. H., Wildfogel, J., & Cassman, T. (1979). Acknowledgment of a handicap as a tactic in social interaction. *Journal of Personality and Social Psychology, 31,* 1790–1797.

Hater, J. J., & Bass, B. M. (1988). Supervisors' evaluations and subordinates' perceptions of transformational and transactional leadership. *Journal of Applied Psychology, 73,* 695–702.

Hatfield, E. (1982). What do women and men want from love and sex? In E. R. Allgeier & N. B. McCormick (Eds.), *Changing boundaries: Gender roles and sexual behavior.* (pp. 106–134). Palo Alto, CA: Mayfield.

Hatfield, E., & Sprecher, S. (1986). Measuring passionate love in intimate relationships. *Journal of Adolescence, 9,* 383–410.

Hatfield, E., & Walster, G. W. (1978). *A new look at love.* Lanham, MA: University Press of America.

Haugtvedt, C. P., & Petty, R. E. (1992). Personality and persuasion: Need for cognition moderates the persistence and resistance of attitude changes. *Journal of Personality and Social Psychology, 63*(2), 308–319.

Hauser, R. M., & Warren, J. R. (1997). Socioeconomic indexes for occupations: A review, update, and critique. *Sociological Methodology 1997* (pp. 177–298). Cambridge, MA: Basil Blackwell.

Haveman, R., Wolfe, B., & Spaulding, J. (1991). Childhood events and circumstances influencing high school completion. *Demography, 28,* 133–157.

Hawkes, D., Senn, C., & Thom, C. (2004). Factors that influence attitudes toward women with tattoos. *Sex Roles, 50,* 593–604.

Hawkins, A. (2004). Reflections on body hair. *Off Our Backs, 34,* 40–41.

Hayduk, L. A. (1978). Personal space: An evaluation and orienting review. *Psychological Bulletin, 85,* 117–134.

Haynie, D. (2001). Delinquent peers revisited: Does network structure matter? *American Journal of Sociology, 106,* 1013–1057.

Hazan, C., & Shaver, P. (1987). Romantic love conceptualized as an attachment process. *Journal of Personality and Social Psychology, 52,* 511–524.

Heard, H. (2007). Fathers, mothers, and family structure: Family trajectories, parent gender, and adolescent schooling. *Journal of Marriage and the Family, 69,* 435–450.

Hebl, M., & Dovidio, J. (2005). Promoting the "social" in the examination of social stigmas. *Personality and Social Psychology Review, 9,* 156–182.

Hechter, M., & Opp, K. (2001). *Social norms.* New York: Russell Sage Foundation.

Heffernan, K. (2010). Mumbling is macho: Phonetic distinctiveness in the speech of American radio DJs. *American Speech, 85,* 67–90.

Hegtvedt, K. A. (2006). Justice frameworks. In P. J. Burke (Ed.), *Contemporary social psychological theories* (pp. 46–69). Stanford, CA: Stanford Social Services.

Heider, E. R., & Olivier, D. (1972). The structure of the color space in naming and memory of two languages. *Cognitive Psychology, 3,* 337–354.

Heider, F. (1944). Social perception and phenomenal causality. *Psychological Review, 51,* 258–374.

Heider, F. (1958). *The psychology of interpersonal relations.* New York: Wiley.

Heimer, K., & Matsueda, R. (1994). Role-taking, role commitment, and delinquency: A theory of differential social control. *American Sociological Review, 59,* 365–390.

Heirich, M. (1977). Change of heart: A test of some widely held theories about religious conversion. *American Journal of Sociology, 83,* 653–680.

Heise, D. R., & Calhan, C. (1995). Emotion norms in interpersonal events. *Social Psychology Quarterly, 58,* 223–240.

Heiss, D. (1979). *Understanding events: Affect and the construction of social action.* New York: Cambridge University Press.

Heiss, J. (1981). Social roles. In M. Rosenberg & R. H. Turner (Eds.), *Social psychology: Sociological perspectives.* (pp. 94–132). New York: Basic Books.

Heiss, J. (1990). Social roles. In M. Rosenberg & R. Turner (Eds.), *Social psychology: Sociological perspectives.* (pp. 94–129). New Brunswick, NH: Transaction.

Hendrick, C., & Hendrick, S. (1989). Research on love: Does it measure up? *Journal of Personality and Social Psychology, 56,* 784–794.

Hendrick, S., & Hendrick, C. (1992). *Liking, loving, and relating* (2nd ed.). Pacific Grove, CA: Brooks/ Cole.

Henley, J., Danziger, S., & Offer, S. (2005). The contribution of social support to the material well-being of low-income families. *Journal of Marriage and Family, 67*, 122–140.

Hennessy, D. A., & Wiesenthal, D. L. (2001). Gender, driver aggression, and driver violence: An applied evaluation. *Sex Roles, 44*(11–12), 661–676.

Henningsen, D. D., Braz, M., & Davies, E. (2008). Why do we flirt? Flirting motivations and sex differences in working and social contexts. *Journal of Business Communication, 45*, 483–502.

Henretta, J. C., Frazier, C., & Bishop, D. (1986). The effect of prior case outcome on juvenile justice decision-making. *Social Forces, 65*, 554–562.

Henrich, J., Heine, S. J., & Norenzayan, A. (2010). The weirdest people in the world. *Behavioral and Brain Sciences, 33*(2–3), 61–83.

Hensley, T. R., & Griffin, G. W. (1986). Victims of groupthink: The Kent State University board of trustees and the 1977 gymnasium controversy. *Journal of Conflict Resolution, 30*, 497–531.

Hepburn, C., & Locksley, A. (1983). Subjective awareness of stereotyping: Do we know when our judgments are prejudiced? *Social Psychology Quarterly, 45*, 311–318.

Herek, G. M., & Capitanio, J. P. (1996). "Some of my best friends": Intergroup contact, concealable stigma, and heterosexuals' attitudes toward gay men and lesbians. *Personality and Social Psychology Bulletin, 22*, 412–424.

Heritage, J., & Greatbatch, D. (1986). Generating applause: A study of rhetoric and response at party political conferences. *American Journal of Sociology, 92*, 110–157.

Hess, T. M., Auman, C., Colcombe, S. J., & Rahhal, T. A. (2003). The impact of stereotype threat on age differences in memory performance. *Journals of Gerontology Series B: Psychological Sciences and Social Sciences, 58*(1), P3-P11.

Hess, T. M., & Slaughter, S. J. (1990). Schematic knowledge influences on memory for scene information in young and older adults. *Developmental Psychology, 26*, 855–865.

Hess, U. (2013). Smiling and angry wrinkles: The impact of aging on the clarity of emotional facial expressions. Presentation at the Association for Psychological Science Annual Convention. Washington, DC. May 24, 2013.

Hetherington, E. M. (1999). Should we stay together for the sake of the children? In E. M. Hetherington (Ed.), *Coping with divorce, single parenting, and remarriage: A risk and resiliency perspective* (pp. 93–116). Mahwah, NJ: Erlbaum.

Hewitt, J., & Alqahtain, M. (2003). Differences between Saudi and U.S. students in reaction to same- and mixed-sex intimacy shown by others. *Journal of Social Psychology, 134*, 233–242.

Hewitt, J. P. (1997). *Self and society* (7th ed.). Boston: Allyn and Bacon.

Hewitt, J. P. (2000). *Self and society: A symbolic interactionist social psychology* (8th ed.). Boston: Allyn and Bacon.

Hewitt, J. P., & Stokes, R. (1975). Disclaimers. *American Sociological Review, 40*, 1–11.

Hewstone, M. (1990). The "ultimate attribution error"? A review of the literature on intergroup causal attribution. *European Journal of Social Psychology, 20*, 311–335.

Hewstone, M., & Brown, R. (1986). Contact is not enough: An intergroup perspective on the contact hypothesis. In M. Hewstone & R. Brown (Eds.), *Contact and conflict in intergroup encounters* (pp. 1–44). Oxford, UK: Blackwell.

Hewstone, M., & Jaspars, J. (1987). Covariation and causal attribution: A logical model of the intuitive analysis of variance. *Journal of Personality and Social Psychology, 53*, 663–672.

Heyl, B. S. (1977). The Madam as teacher: The training of house prostitutes. *Social Problems, 24*, 545–555.

Higbee, K. L. (1969). Fifteen years of fear arousal: Research on threat appeals, 1953–1968. *Psychological Bulletin, 72*, 426–444.

Higgins, C., & Judge, T. (2004). The effect of applicant influence tactics on recruiter perceptions of fit and hiring recommendations: A field study. *Journal of Applied Psychology, 89*, 622–632.

Higgins, E. T. (1989). Self-discrepancy theory: What patterns of self-beliefs cause people to suffer? In L. Berkowitz (Ed.), *Advances in experimental social psychology* (Vol. 22, pp. 93–136). New York: Academic Press.

Higgins, E. T., & Bargh, J. A. (1987). Social cognition and social perception. *Annual Review of Psychology, 38*, 369–425.

Higgins, E. T., & Bryant, S. L. (1982). Consensus information and the fundamental attribution error: The role of development and in-group versus out-group knowledge. *Journal of Personality and Social Psychology, 47*, 422–435.

Higgins, E. T., Klein, R., & Strauman, T. (1985). Self-concept discrepancy theory: A psychological model for distinguishing among different aspects of depression and anxiety. *Social Cognition, 3*, 51–76.

Higuchi, M., & Fukada, H. (2002). A comparison of four causal factors of embarrassment in public and private situations. *Journal of Psychology, 136*, 399–406.

Hill, C., Rubin, Z., & Peplau, L. (1976). Breakups before marriage: The end of 103 affairs. *Journal of Social Issues, 32*(1), 147–168.

Hill, K. D. (2009). Code-switching pedagogies and African American student voices: Acceptance and resistance. *Journal of Adolescent and Adult Literacy, 53*, 120–131.

Hill, T. D., Ross, C. E., & Angel, R. J. (2005). Neighborhood disorder, psychophysiological distress, and health. *Journal of Health and Social Behavior, 46*, 170–186.

Hiltrop, J. M. (1985). Mediator behavior and the settlement of collective bargaining disputes in Britain. *Journal of Social Issues, 41*(2), 83–99.

Hines, M., Golombok, S., Rust, J., Johnson, K., Golding, J., et al. (2002). Testosterone during pregnancy and gender role behavior of preschool children: A longitudinal, population study. *Child Development, 73*, 1678–1687.

Hinkle, S., & Schopler, J. (1986). Bias in the evaluation of in-group and out-group performance. In S. Worchel & W. G. Austin (Eds.), *Psychology of intergroup relations* (2nd ed., pp. 196–212). Chicago: Nelson-Hall.

Hirsch, E. L. (1990). Sacrifice for the cause: Group processes, recruitment, and commitment in a student social movement. *American Sociological Review, 55*, 243–254.

Hirschi, T. (1969). *Causes of delinquency.* Berkeley: University of California Press.

Hirt, E. R., & Markmann, K. D. (1995). Multiple explanation: A consider-an-alternative strategy for debiasing judgments. *Journal of Personality and Social Psychology, 69*, 1069–1086.

Hitlin, S. (2003). Values as the core of personal identity: Drawing links between two theories of self. *Social Psychology Quarterly, 66*, 118–137.

Ho, D., Fu, W., & Ng, S. (2004). Guilt, shame and embarrassment: Revelations of face and self. *Culture and Psychology, 10*, 64–84.

Hobsbawm, E., & Rudé, G. (1975). *Captain Swing: A social history of the great English agricultural uprising of 1830.* New York: Norton.

Hochschild, A. R. (1983). *The managed heart: Commercialization of human feeling.* Berkeley: University of California Press.

Hodson, R. (1996). Dignity in the workplace under participative management. *American Sociological Review, 61*, 719–738.

Hoelter, J. W. (1983). The effects of role evaluation and commitment on identity salience. *Social Psychology Quarterly, 46*, 140–147.

Hoelter, J. W. (1984). Relative effects of significant others on self-evaluation. *Social Psychology Quarterly, 47*, 255–262.

Hoelter, J. W. (1986). The relationship between specific and global evaluations of self: A comparison of several models. *Social Psychology Quarterly, 49*, 129–141.

Hofferth, S. (2003). Race/ethnic differences in father involvement in two-parent families: Culture, context, or economy? *Journal of Family Issues, 24*, 185–216.

Hofferth, S., & Sandberg, J. (2001). How American children spend their time. *Journal of Marriage and the Family, 63*, 295–308.

Hoffman, C., Lau, I., & Johnson, D. (1986). The linguistic relativity of person cognition: An English-Chinese comparison. *Journal of Personality and Social Psychology, 51*, 1097–1105.

Hoffmann, J. (2002). The community context of family structure and adolescent drug use. *Journal of Marriage and the Family, 64*, 314–330.

Hoffman, M. L. (2001). *Empathy and moral development: Implications for caring and justice.* Cambridge, UK: Cambridge University Press.

Hofling, C. K., Brotz, E., Dalrymple, S., Graves, N., & Pierce, C. M. (1966). An experimental study of nurse-physician relationships. *Journal of Nervous and Mental Disease, 143*, 171–180.

Hogg, M. A. (2006). Social identity theory. In P. J. Burke (Ed.), *Contemporary social psychological theories* (pp. 111–136). Palo Alto, CA: Stanford University Press.

Hogg, M. A. (2013). Intergroup relations. In DeLamater, J. D, and Ward, A. (Eds.), *Handbook of Social Psychology* (2nd ed., pp. 533–561). New York: Springer.

Hogg, M. A., & Haines, S. C. (1996). Intergroup relations and group solidarity: Effects of group identification and social beliefs on depersonalized attraction. *Journal of Personality and Social Psychology, 70*, 25–39.

Hogg, M. A., Terry, D. J., & Jaines, S. C. (1996). Intergroup relations and group solidarity: Effects of group identification and social beliefs on depersonalized attraction. *Journal of Personality and Social Psychology, 70*, 25–39.

Holgartner, S., & Bosk, C. L. (1988). The rise and fall of social problems: A public arenas model. *American Journal of Sociology, 94*, 53–78.

Hollander, E. P. (1985). Leadership and power. In G. Lindzey & E. Aronson (Eds.), *Handbook of social psychology* (3rd ed., Vol. 2, pp. 485–537). New York: Random House.

Hollander, E. P., Fallon, B. J., & Edwards, M. T. (1977). Some aspects of influence and acceptability for appointed and elected group leaders. *Journal of Psychology, 95*, 289–296.

Hollander, E. P., & Julian, J. W. (1970). Studies in leader legitimacy, influence, and innovation. In L. Berkowitz (Ed.), *Advances in experimental social psychology* (Vol. 5, pp. 33–69). New York: Academic Press.

Hollinger, R. C., & Clark, J. P. (1983). Deterrence in the workplace: Perceived certainty, perceived severity, and employee theft. *Social Forces, 62*, 398–418.

Holmes, D. S. (1971). Compensation for ego threat: Two experiments. *Journal of Personality and Social Psychology, 18*, 234–237.

Holmes, J. G., & Grant, P. (1979). Ethnocentric reactions to social threats. In L. H. Strickland (Ed.), *Social psychology: East-West perspectives.* Oxford, UK: Pergamon.

Holmes, J. G., Miller, D. T., & Lerner, M. J. (2002). Committing altruism under the cloak of self-interest: The exchange fiction. *Journal of Experimental Social Psychology, 38*(2), 144–151.

Holohan, C. J., & Moos, R. (1990). Life stressors, resistance factors, and improved psychological functioning: An extension of the stress resistance paradigm. *Journal of Personality and Social Psychology, 58*, 909–917.

Holst, V. F., & Pezdek, K. (1992). Scripts for typical crimes and their effects on memory for eyewitness testimony. *Applied Cognitive Psychology, 6*(7), 573–587.

Holt, C. L., & Ellis, J. B. (1998). Assessing the current validity of the Bem Sex-Role Inventory. *Sex Roles, 39*(11–12), 929–941.

Homans, G. C. (1958). Social behavior as exchange. *American Journal of Sociology*, 597–606.

Homans, G. C. (1961). *Social behavior: Its elementary forms.* Oxford, UK: Harcourt-Brace.

Homans, G. C. (1974). *Social behavior: Its elementary forms* (2nd ed.). New York: Harcourt Brace Jovanovich.

Homer, P. M., & Kahle, L. R. (1988). A structural-equation test of the value-attitude-behavior hierarchy. *Journal of Personality and Social Psychology, 54,* 638–646.

Hood, W. R., & Sherif, M. (1962). Verbal report and judgment of an unstructured stimulus. *Journal of Psychology, 54,* 121–130.

Hopper, J. R., & Nielsen, J. M. (1991). Recycling as altruistic behavior: Normative and behavioral strategies to expand participation in a community recycling program. *Environment and Behavior, 23,* 195–220.

Horai, J., Naccari, N., & Fatoullah, E. (1974). The effects of expertise and physical attractiveness upon opinion agreement and liking. *Sociometry, 37,* 601–606.

Horne, C. (2001). The enforcement of norms: Group cohesion and meta-norms. *Social Psychology Quarterly, 64,* 253–266.

Horne, C. (2004). Collective benefits, exchange interests, and norm enforcement. *Social Forces, 82,* 1037–1062.

Horne, W. C., & Long, G. (1972). Effect of group discussion on universalistic-particularistic orientation. *Journal of Experimental Social Psychology, 8,* 236–246.

Horney, J., Osgood, D. W., & Marshall, I. H. (1995). Criminal careers in the short-term: Intra-individual variability in crime and its relation to local life circumstances. *American Sociological Review, 60,* 655–673.

Hornstein, G. (1985). Intimacy in conversational style as a function of the degree of closeness between members of a dyad. *Journal of Personality and Social Psychology, 49,* 671–681.

Hornstein, H. A. (1978). Promotive tension and prosocial behavior: A Lewinian analysis. In L. Wispe (Ed.), *Altruism, sympathy, and helping.* (pp. 177–207). New York: Academic Press.

Horowitz, D. L. (2001). *The deadly ethnic riot.* Berkeley: University of California Press.

Horowitz, H. V., White, H. R., & Howell-White, S. (1996). Becoming married and mental health: A longitudinal study of a cohort of young adults. *Journal of Marriage and the Family, 58,* 895–907.

Horowitz, R. (1987). Community tolerance of gang violence. *Social Problems, 34,* 437–450.

Hostetler, A., Sweet, S., & Moen, P. (2007). Gendered career paths: A life-course perspective in returning to school. *Sex Roles, 56,* 85–103.

House, J. S. (1977). The three faces of social psychology. *Sociometry, 40,* 161–177.

House, J. S. (1981). *Work stress and social support.* Reading, MA: Addison-Wesley.

House, J. S., Lepkowski, J. M., Kinney, A. M., Mero, R. P., Kessler, R. C., & Herzog, A. R. (1994). The social stratification of aging and health. *Journal of Health and Social Behavior, 35,* 213–234.

Hovland, C. I., Janis, I. L., & Kelley, H. H. (1953). *Communication and persuasion: Psychological studies of opinion change.* New Haven, CT: Yale University Press.

Howard, J. (2000). Social psychology of identities. *Annual Review of Sociology, 26,* 367–393.

Hu, Y., & Sundar, S. S. (2010). Effects of online health sources on credibility and behavioral intentions. *Communication Research, 37,* 105–132.

Hudson, C. G. (2005). Socioeconomic status and mental illness: Tests of the social causation and selection hypotheses. *American Journal of Orthopsychiatry, 75,* 3–18.

Hue, C., & Erickson, J. R. (1991). Normative studies of sequence strength and scene structure of 30 scripts. *American Journal of Psychology, 104,* 229–240.

Huesmann, L. R. (1986). Psychological processes promoting the relation between exposure to media violence and aggressive behavior by the viewer. *Journal of Social Issues, 42*(3), 125–139.

Huesmann, L. R., & Moise, J. (1996). Media violence: A demonstrated public health threat to children. *Harvard Mental Health Letter, 12*(12), 5–7.

Hughes, D., & Surra, C. (2000). The reported influence of research participation on premarital relationships. *Journal of Marriage and the Family, 62,* 822–832.

Hughes, M., & Demo, D. H. (1989). Self-perceptions of Black Americans: Self-esteem and personal efficacy. *American Journal of Sociology, 95,* 132–159.

Hull, C. L. (1943). *Principles of behavior.* New York: Appleton-Century-Crofts.

Hultsch, D., & Plemons, J. (1979). Life events and life span development. In P. Baltes & O. G. Brim (Eds.), *Life-span development and behavior* (Vol. 2, pp. 1–36). New York: Academic Press.

Hundleby, J. D., & Mercer, G. W. (1987). Family and friends as social environments and their relationship to young adolescents' use of alcohol, tobacco, and marijuana. *Journal of Marriage and the Family, 49,* 151–164.

Hunter, C. H. (1984). Aligning actions: Types and social distribution. *Symbolic Interaction, 7,* 155–174.

Hunter, J. A., Stringer, M., & Watson, R. P. (1991). Intergroup violence and intergroup attributions. *British Journal of Social Psychology, 30,* 261–266.

Huston, T. L., Ruggiero, M., Conner, R., & Geis, G. (1981). Bystander intervention into crime: A study based on naturally-occurring episodes. *Social Psychology Quarterly, 14,* 23.

Hyde, J., Fenema, E., & Lamon, S. (1990). Gender differences in mathematics performance: A meta-analysis. *Psychological Bulletin, 107,* 139–155.

Hyde, J., Lindberg, S., Linn, M., Ellis, A., & Williams, C. (2008). Gender similarities characterize math performance. *Science, 321,* 494–495.

Hyde, J. S. (1984). How large are gender differences in aggression? A developmental meta-analysis. *Developmental Psychology, 20,* 722–736.

Hyde, J. S. (2005). The gender similarities hypothesis. *American Psychologist, 60*(6), 581–592.

Hyde, J. S., & Else-Quest, N. (2012). *Half the human experience* (8th ed.). Belmont, CA: Wadsworth/Cengage.

Hymes, D. (1974). *Foundations in sociolinguistics.* London: Tavistock.

Iervolino, A., Hines, M., Golombok, S., Rust, J., & Plomin, R. (2005). Genetic and environmental influences on sex-typed behavior during the preschool years. *Child Development, 76*, 826–840.

Indonesians die as riots over price rises widen. (1998, February 15). *New York Times*, p. A10.

Ingham, A. G., Levinger, G., Graves, J., & Peckham, V. (1974). The Ringelmann effect: Studies of group size and group performance. *Journal of Experimental Social Psychology, 10*, 371–384.

Insko, C. A., Arkoff, A., & Insko, V. M. (1965). Effects of high and low fear-arousing communications upon opinions toward smoking. *Journal of Experimental Social Psychology, 40*, 256–266.

Insko, C. A., Drenan, S., Solomon, M. R., Smith, R., & Wade, T. J. (1983). Conformity as a function of the consistency of positive self-evaluation with being liked and being right. *Journal of Experimental Social Psychology, 19*, 341–358.

Insko, C. A., Smith, R. H., Alicke, M. S., Wade, J., & Taylor, S. (1985). Conformity and group size: The concern with being right and the concern with being liked. *Personality and Social Psychology Bulletin, 11*, 41–50.

Isenberg, D. J. (1986). Group polarization: A critical review and meta-analysis. *Journal of Personality and Social Psychology, 50*, 1141–1151.

Ishii, K., Reyes, J. A., & Kitayama, S. (2003). Spontaneous attention to word content versus emotional tone differences among three cultures. *Psychological Science, 14*(1), 39–46.

Isozaki, M. (1984). The effect of discussion on polarization of judgments. *Japanese Psychological Research, 26*, 187–193.

Ivory, J. D., & Kalyanaraman, S. (2007). The effects of technological advancement and violent content in video games on players' feelings of presence, involvement, physiological arousal, and aggression. *Journal of Communication, 57*(3), 532–555.

Jaccard, J. (1981). Toward theories of persuasion and belief change. *Journal of Personality and Social Psychology, 40*, 260–269.

Jackson, J. (1954). The adjustment of the family to the crisis of alcoholism. *Quarterly Journal of Studies on Alcohol, 15*, 564–586.

Jackson, J. M. (1986). In defense of social impact theory: Comment on Mullen. *Journal of Personality and Social Psychology, 50*, 511–513.

Jackson, J. M. (1987). Social impact theory: A social forces model of influence. In B. Mullen & G. R. Goethals (Eds.), *Theories of group behavior* (pp. 111–124). New York: Springer Verlag.

Jackson, L. A., Hunter, J. E., & Hodge, C. N. (1995). Physical attractiveness and intellectual competence: A meta-analytic review. *Social Psychology Quarterly, 58*, 108–122.

Jackson, P. B. (1997). Role occupancy and minority mental health. *Journal of Health and Social Behavior, 38*, 237–255.

Jackson, P. B., Kleiner, S., Geist, C., & Cebulko, K. (2011). Conventions of courtship: Gender and race differences in the significance of dating rituals. *Journal of Family Issues, 32*, 629–652.

Jackson, T., Chen, H., Guo, C., & Gao, X. (2006). Stories we love by: Conceptions of love among couples from the People's Republic of China and the United States. *Journal of Cross-Cultural Psychology, 37*, 446–464.

Jackson-Jacobs, C. (2004). Hard drugs in a soft context: Managing trouble and crack use on a college campus. *Sociological Quarterly, 45*, 835–856.

Jacobson, N. S., & Gottman, J. M. (1998). *When men batter women: New insights into ending abusive relationships*. New York: Simon and Schuster.

Jacques, J. M., & Chason, K. (1977). Self-esteem and low status groups: A changing scene? *Sociological Quarterly, 18*, 399–412.

Jaffee, S., & Hyde, J. S. (2000). Gender differences in moral orientation: A meta-analysis. *Psychological Bulletin, 126*, 703–726.

James, W. (1890). *Principles of psychology*. New York: Holt, Rinehart and Winston.

Janes, L., & Olson, J. M. (2000). Jeer pressure: The behavioral effects of observing ridicule of others. *Personality and Social Psychology Bulletin, 26*, 474–485.

Janis, I. L. (1982). *Groupthink* (2nd ed.). Boston: Houghton Mifflin.

Janis, I. L., & Mann, L. (1977). *Decision making: A psychological analysis of conflict, choice, and commitment*. New York: Free Press.

Jankowski, S., Videka-Sherman, L., & Laquidara-Dickinson, K. (1996). Social support networks of confidants to people with AIDS. *Social Work, 41*, 206–213.

Jekielek, S. M. (1998). Parental conflict, marital disruption, and children's emotional well-being. *Social Forces, 76*, 905–935.

Jellison, J. M., & Riskind, J. (1970). A social comparison of abilities interpretation of risk-taking behavior. *Journal of Personality and Social Psychology, 15*, 375–390.

Jemmott, J. B., & Magloire, K. (1988). Academic stress, social support, and secretory immunoglobulin. *Journal of Personality and Social Psychology, 55*, 803–810.

Jenkins, C., Rosenman, R., & Zyzanski, S. (1974). Prediction of clinical coronary heart disease by a test for coronary prone behavior pattern. *New England Journal of Medicine, 290*, 1271–1275.

Jenkins, J. C. (1983). Resource mobilization theory and the study of social movements. In R. H. Turner & J. F. Short (Eds.), *Annual Review of Sociology* (Vol. 9, pp. 527–553). Palo Alto, CA: Annual Reviews.

Jensen, G., Erickson, M., & Gibbs, J. (1978). Perceived risk of punishment and self-reported delinquency. *Social Forces, 57*, 57–78.

Jessor, R., Costa, F., Jessor, L., & Donovan, J. (1983). Time of first intercourse: A prospective study. *Journal of Personality and Social Psychology, 44*, 608–626.

Jewkes, R., Sen, P., & Garcia-Moreno, C. (2002). Sexual violence. In E. G. Krug, L. L. Dahlberg, J. A. Mercy, A. B. Zwi, & R. Lozano (Eds), *World report on violence and health* (pp. 149–181). Geneva: World Health Organization.

Job, R. F. S. (1988). Effective and ineffective use of fear in health promotion campaigns. *American Journal of Public Health, 78,* 163–167.

Johnson, B. T. (1991). Insight about attitudes: Metaanalytic perspectives. *Personality and Social Psychology Bulletin, 17,* 289–299.

Johnson, B. T., & Eagly, A. H. (1989). Effects of involvement on persuasion: A meta-analysis. *Psychological Bulletin, 106,* 290–314.

Johnson, C. (1994). Gender, legitimate authority, and leader-subordinate conversations. *American Sociological Review, 59,* 122–135.

Johnson, D. J., & Rusbult, C. E. (1989). Resisting temptation: Devaluation of alternative partners as a means of maintaining commitment in close relationships. *Journal of Personality and Social Psychology, 57,* 967–980.

Johnson, D. L., & Andrews, I. R. (1971). The risky-shift hypothesis tested with consumer products as stimuli. *Journal of Personality and Social Psychology, 20,* 382–385.

Johnson, J. T., & Boyd, K. R. (1995). Dispositional traits versus the content of experience: Actor/ observer differences in judgments of the "authentic self." *Personality and Social Psychology Bulletin, 21,* 375–383.

Johnson, K. J., Lund, D. A., & Dimond, M. F. (1986). Stress, self-esteem, and coping during bereavement among the elderly. *Social Psychology Quarterly, 49,* 273–279.

Johnson, M., & Leslie, L. (1982). Couple involvement and network structure: A test of the dyadic withdrawal hypothesis. *Social Psychology Quarterly, 45,* 34–43.

Johnson, M. P., & Ferraro, K. J. (2000). Research on domestic violence in the 1990s: Making distinctions. *Journal of Marriage and Family, 62*(4), 948–963.

Johnson, R. E. (1979). *Juvenile delinquency and its origins.* New York: Cambridge University Press.

Johnson, R. R. (2007). Race and police reliance on suspicious non-verbal cues. *Policing: An International Journal of Police Strategies & Management, 30,* 277–299.

Johnson-George, C., & Swap, W. (1982). Measurement of specific interpersonal trust: Construction and validation of a scale to assess trust in a specific other. *Journal of Personality and Social Psychology, 43,* 1306–1317.

Jones, E. E. (1964). *Ingratiation: A social psychology perspective.* New York: Appleton-Century-Crofts.

Jones, E. E. (1979). The rocky road from acts to dispositions. *American Psychologist, 34,* 107–117.

Jones, E. E., & Davis, K. E. (1965). From acts to dispositions. In L. Berkowitz (Ed.), *Advances in experimental social psychology* (Vol. 2, pp. 219–266). New York: Academic Press.

Jones, E. E., Davis, K. E., & Gergen, K. J. (1961). Role playing variations and their informational value for person perception. *Journal of Abnormal and Social Psychology, 63,* 302–310.

Jones, E. E., Farina, A., Hastorf, A. H., Markus, H., Miller, D. T., & Scott, R. A. (1984). *Social stigma.* New York: Freeman.

Jones, E. E., Gergen, K. J., Gumpert, P., & Thibaut, J. (1965). Some conditions affecting the use of ingratiation to influence performance evaluation. *Journal of Personality and Social Psychology, 1,* 613–626.

Jones, E. E., & Goethals, G. R. (1971). *Order effects in impression formation: Attribution context and the nature of the entity.* Morristown, NJ: General Learning Press.

Jones, E. E., & Harris, V. A. (1967). The attribution of attitudes. *Journal of Experimental Social Psychology, 3,* 1–24.

Jones, E. E., & McGillis, D. (1976). Correspondent inferences and the attribution cube: A comparative reappraisal. In J. H. Harvey, W. J. Ickes, & R. F. Kidd (Eds.), *New directions in attribution research* (Vol. 1, pp. 389–420). Hillsdale, NJ: Erlbaum.

Jones, E. E., & Nisbett, R. (1972). The actor and observer: Divergent perceptions of the causes of behavior. In E. E. Jones, D. E. Kanouse, H. H. Kelley, R. E. Nisbett, S. Valins, & B. W. Weiner (Eds.), *Attribution: Perceiving the causes of behavior.* (pp. 79–94). Morristown, NJ: General Learning Press.

Jones, E. E., & Pittman, T. S. (1982). Toward a general theory of strategic self-presentation. In J. Suls (Ed.), *Psychological perspectives on the self* (Vol. 1, pp. 231–262). Hillsdale, NJ: Erlbaum.

Jones, E. E., Rock, L., Shaver, K. G., Goethals, G. R., & Ward, L. M. (1968). Pattern of performance and ability attribution: An unexpected primacy effect. *Journal of Personality and Social Psychology, 10,* 317–340.

Jones, E. E., & Wortman, C. (1973). *Ingratiation: An attributional approach.* Morristown, NJ: General Learning Press.

Jones, R. M., Taylor, D. E., Dick, A. J., Singh, A, & Cook, J. L. (2007). Bedroom design and decoration: Gender differences in preference and activity. *Adolescence, 42,* 539–553.

Jones, V. C. (1948). *The Hatfields and the McCoys.* Chapel Hill, NC: University of North Carolina Press.

Jones, W. H., Briggs, S. R., & Smith, T. G. (1986). Shyness: Conceptualization and measurement. *Journal of Personality and Social Psychology, 51,* 629–639.

Jong, P. (1999). Communicative and remedial effects of social blushing. *Journal of Nonverbal Behavior, 23,* 197–217.

Jöreskög, K. G., & Sörbom, D. (1979). *Advances in factor analysis and structural equation models.* Cambridge, MA: Abt Books.

Joseph, N., & Alex, N. (1972). The uniform: A sociological perspective. *American Journal of Sociology, 77,* 719–730.

Joule, R., & Azdia, T. (2003). Cognitive dissonance, double forced compliance, and commitment. *European Journal of Social Psychology, 33,* 565–571.

Jourard, S. M. (1971). *Self-disclosure.* New York: Wiley.

Judd, C. M., Drake, R. A., Downing, J. W., & Krosnick, J.

A. (1991). Some dynamic properties of attitude structures: Context-induced response facilitation and polarization. *Journal of Personality and Social Psychology*, 60, 193–202.

Judge, T. A., & Bono, J. E. (2000). Five-factor model of personality and transformational leadership. *Journal of Applied Psychology*, 85, 751–765.

Jung, H. S., & Yoon, H. H. (2011). The effects of nonverbal communication of employees in the family restaurant upon customers' emotional responses and customer satisfaction. *International Journal of Hospitality Management*, 30, 542–550.

Jussim, L., Coleman, L., & Nassau, S. (1987). The influence of self-esteem on perceptions of performance and feedback. *Social Psychology Quarterly*, 50, 95–99.

Kacmar, K. M., Carlson, D., & Bratton, V. (2004). Situational and dispositional factors as antecedents of ingratiatory behaviors in organizational settings. *Journal of Vocational Behavior*, 65, 309–331.

Kahn, A. S., Mathie, V. A., & Torgler, C. (1994). Rape scripts and rape acknowledgment. *Psychology of Women Quarterly*, 18(1), 53–66.

Kahne, M., & Schwartz, C. (1978). Negotiating trouble: The social construction and management of trouble in a psychiatric context. *Social Problems*, 25, 461–475.

Kahneman, D., & Tversky, A. (1973). On the psychology of prediction. *Psychological Review*, 80, 237–251.

Kalmijn, M., & De Graaf, P. M. (2012). Life course changes of children and well-being of parents. *Journal of Marriage and Family*, 74(2), 269–280.

Kalven, H., & Zeisel, H. (1966). *The American jury*. Boston: Little, Brown.

Kane, R. (2006). On the limits of social control: Structural deterrence and the policing of "suppressible" crime. *Justice Quarterly*, 23, 186–213.

Kao, G., & Joyner, K. (2004). Do race and ethnicity matter among friends? Activities among interracial, interethnic, and intraethnic adolescent friends. *Sociological Quarterly*, 45, 557–573.

Kaplan, H. B., Johnson, R., & Bailey, C. A. (1987). Deviant peers and deviant behavior: Further elaboration of a model. *Social Psychology Quarterly*, 50, 277–284.

Kaplan, H. B., Martin, S. S., & Johnson, R. J. (1986). Self-rejection and the explanation of deviance: Specification of the structure among latent constructs. *American Journal of Sociology*, 92, 384–411.

Kaplan, M. F. (1977). Discussion polarization effects in a modified jury discussion paradigm: Informational influences. *Sociometry*, 40, 262–271.

Kaplan, M. F. (1987). The influencing process in group decision-making. In C. Hendrick (Ed.), *Group processes*. (pp. 189–212). Newbury Park, CA: Sage.

Kaplan, M. F., & Miller, C. E. (1987). Group decision making and normative versus informational influence: Effects of type of issue and assigned decision rule. *Journal of Personality and Social Psychology*, 53, 306–313.

Karau, S. J., & Williams, K. D. (1993). Social loafing: A meta-analytic review and theoretical integration. *Journal of Personality and Social Psychology*, 65, 681–706.

Karau, S. J., & Williams, K. D. (1995). Social loafing: Research findings, implications, and future directions. *Current Directions in Psychological Science*, 4(5), 134–140.

Karau, S. J., & Williams, K. D. (2001). Understanding individual motivation in groups: The collective effort model. In M. E. Turner (Ed.), *Groups at work: Advances in theory and research* (pp. 113–141). Mahwah, NJ: Erlbaum.

Karlins, M., & Abelson, H. I. (1970). *How opinions and attitudes are changed* (2nd ed.). New York: Springer Verlag.

Karlins, M., Coffman, T. L., & Walters, G. (1969). On the fading of social stereotypes: Studies on three generations of college students. *Journal of Personality and Social Psychology*, 13, 1–16.

Karraker, A., & DeLamater, J. (2013). Past year sexual inactivity among older married persons and their partners. *Journal of Marriage and Family*, 75, 142–163.

Katz, D. (1960). The functional approach to the study of attitudes. *Public Opinion Quarterly*, 24, 163–204.

Katz, D., & Braly, K. (1933). Racial stereotypes of one hundred college students. *Journal of Abnormal and Social Psychology*, 28, 280–290.

Katz, I. (1970). Experimental study in Negro-White relationships. In L. Berkowitz (Ed.), *Advances in experimental social psychology* (Vol. 5, pp. 71–117). New York: Academic Press.

Katz, I. (1981). *Stigma: A social psychological analysis*. Hillsdale, NJ: Erlbaum.

Katz, I., Wackenhut, J., & Glass, D. C. (1986). An ambivalence-amplification theory of behavior toward the stigmatized. In S. Worchel & W. G. Austin (Eds.), *Psychology of intergroup relations* (2nd ed., pp. 103–117). Chicago: Nelson-Hall.

Katz, J. (1988). *Seductions of crime: Moral and sensual attractions in doing evil*. New York: Basic Books.

Katzner, K. (1995). *The languages of the world* (3rd ed.). London: Routledge.

Kauffman, D. R., & Steiner, I. D. (1968). Some variables affecting the use of conformity as an ingratiation technique. *Journal of Experimental Social Psychology*, 4, 400–414.

Kaufman, J., & Johnson, K. (2004). Stigmatized individuals and the process of identity. *Sociological Quarterly*, 45, 807–833.

Kelley, H. H. (1950). The warm-cold variable in first impressions. *Journal of Personality*, 18, 431–439.

Kelley, H. H. (1967). Attribution theory in social psychology. In D. Levine (Ed.), *Nebraska symposium in motivation, 1967*. (pp. 192–238). Lincoln: University of Nebraska Press.

Kelley, H. H. (1972). Causal schemata and the attribution process. In E. Jones, D. Kanouse, H. Kelley, R. Nisbett, S. Valms, & B. Weiner (Eds.), *Attribution: Perceiving the causes of behavior*. (pp. 151–176). Morristown, NJ: General Learning Press.

Kelley, H. H. (1973). The process of causal attribution. *American Psychologist, 28*, 107–128.

Kelley, H. H., Berscheid, E., Christensen, A., Harvey, H. H., Huston, T., Levinger, G., et al. (1983). *Close relationships*. New York: Freeman.

Kelley, H. H., & Michela, J. L. (1980). Attribution theory and research. *Annual Review of Psychology, 31*, 457–501.

Kelley, H. H., & Thibaut, J. W. (1978). *Interpersonal relations: A theory of interdependence*. New York: Wiley.

Kelley, K., & Byrne, D. (1976). Attraction and altruism: With a little help from my friends. *Journal of Research in Personality, 10*, 59–68.

Kelman, H. C. (1974). Attitudes are alive and well and gainfully employed in the sphere of action. *American Psychologist, 29*, 310–324.

Kelman, H. C., & Hamilton, V. L. (1989). *Crimes of obedience: Toward a social psychology of authority and responsibility*. New Haven, CT: Yale University Press.

Keltner, D. (1996). Evidence for the distinctness of embarrassment, shame, and guilt: A study of recalled antecedents and facial expressions of emotion. *Cognition and Emotion, 10*(2), 155–172.

Kemper, T. D. (1973). The fundamental dimensions of social relationship: A theoretical statement. *Acta Sociologica, 6*, 41–57.

Kemper, T. D. (1978). *A social interactional theory of emotions*. New York: Wiley.

Kendall, D. E. (2011). *Framing class: Media representations of wealth and poverty in America*. Rowman and Littlefield.

Kendon, A. (1970). Movement coordination in social interaction: Some examples described. *Acta Psychologica, 32*, 100–125.

Kendon, A., Harris, R. M., & Key, M. R. (1975). *Organization of behavior in face-to-face interaction*. The Hague: Mouton.

Kendzierski, D., & Whitaker, D. J. (1997). The role of self-schema in linking intention with behavior. *Personality and Social Psychology Bulletin, 23*, 139–147.

Kenney, D., & La Voie, L. (1982). Reciprocity of interpersonal attraction: A confirmed hypothesis. *Social Psychology Quarterly, 45*, 54–58.

Kenrick, D. T. (1995). Evolutionary theory versus the confederacy of dunces. *Psychological Inquiry, 6*, 56–62.

Kenrick, D. T., McCreath, H. E., Govern, J., King, R., & Bordin, J. (1990). Person-environment intersections: Everyday settings and common trait dimensions. *Journal of Personality and Social Psychology, 58*, 685–698.

Kent, G., Davis, J., & Shapiro, D. (1978). Resources required in the construction and reconstruction of conversations. *Journal of Personality and Social Psychology, 36*, 13–22.

Kerber, K. W. (1984). The perception of nonemergency helping situations: Costs, rewards, and the altruistic personality. *Journal of Personality, 52*, 177–187.

Kerckhoff, A. C. (1974). The social context of interpersonal attraction. In T. Huston (Ed.), *Foundations of interpersonal attraction* (pp. 61–78). New York: Academic Press.

Kerr, N., & Bruun, S. (1981). Ringelmann revisited: Alternative explanations for the social loafing effect. *Personality and Social Psychology Bulletin, 7*, 224–231.

Kerr, N. L., & Bruun, S. (1983). The dispensability of member effort and group motivation losses: Free rider effects. *Personality and Social Psychology Bulletin, 44*, 78–94.

Kessler, R. C. (1982). A disaggregation of the relationship between socioeconomic status and psychological distress. *American Sociological Review, 47*, 752–764.

Kessler, R. C., & Cleary, P. (1980). Social class and psychological distress. *American Sociological Review, 45*, 463–478.

Ketelaar, T., & Ellis, B. J. (2000). Are evolutionary explanations unfalsifiable? Evolutionary psychology and the Lakatosian philosophy of science. *Psychological Inquiry, 11*, 1–21.

Khan, A. Y., & Kamal, A. (2010). Exploring reactions to invasion of personal space in university students. *Journal of Behavioral Sciences, 20*, 80–97.

Khanna, N. (2004). The role of reflected appraisals in racial identity: The case of multiracial Asians. *Social Psychology Quarterly, 67*, 115–131.

Kiecolt-Glaser, J. K., & Newton, T. L. (2001). Marriage and health: His and hers. *Psychological Bulletin, 127*, 472–503.

Kiesler, C. A., & Corbin, L. H. (1965). Commitment, attraction, and conformity. *Journal of Personality and Social Psychology, 2*, 890–895.

Kiesler, C. A., & Kiesler, S. B. (1969). *Conformity*. Reading, MA: Addison-Wesley.

Kiesler, C. A., Zanna, M., & DeSalvo, J. (1966). Deviation and conformity: Opinion change as a function of commitment, attraction, and the presence of a deviate. *Journal of Personality and Social Psychology, 3*, 458–467.

Kiesling, S. (2004). Dude. *American Speech, 79*, 281–305.

Kiesler, S. Siegel, J., & McGuire, T. W. (1984). Social psychological aspects of computer-mediated communication. *American Psychologist, 39*, 1123–1134.

Kilham, W., & Mann, L. (1974). Level of destructive obedience as a function of transmitter and executant roles in the Milgram obedience paradigm. *Journal of Personality and Social Psychology, 29*, 696–702.

Killian, L. (1984). Organization, rationality, and spontaneity in the civil rights movement. *American Sociological Review, 49*, 770–783.

Kim, J., Collins, K., Zylbergold, B. A., et al. (2007). From sex to sexuality: Exposing the heterosexual script on primetime network television. *Journal of Sex Research, 44*, 145–157.

Kiparsky, P. (1976). Historical linguistics and the origin of language. *Annals of the New York Academy of Sciences, 280*, 97–103.

Kirchmeyer, C. (1993). Nonwork-to-work spillover: A more balanced view of the experiences and coping of professional men and women. *Sex Roles, 28*, 531–552.

Kitayama, S., & Burnstein, E. (1988). Automaticity in conversations: A reexamination of the mindlessness hypothesis. *Journal of Personality and Social Psychology, 54,* 219–224.

Kitcher, P. (1985). *Vaulting ambition: Sociobiology and the quest for human nature.* Cambridge, MA: MIT Press.

Kitsuse, J. (1964). Societal reaction to deviant behavior: Problems of theory and method. In H. Becker (Ed.), *The other side: Perspectives on deviance.* (pp. 87–100). New York: Free Press.

Klapper, J. T. (1960). *The effects of mass communication.* New York: Free Press.

Kleck, R. E., & Strenta, A. (1980). Perceptions of the impact of negatively valued physical characteristics on social interaction. *Journal of Personality and Social Psychology, 39,* 861–873.

Klein, O., Snyder, M., & Livingston, R. W. (2004). Prejudice on the stage: Self-monitoring and the public expression of group attitudes. *British Journal of Social Psychology, 43,* 299–314.

Kling, K. C., Hyde, J., Showers, C., & Buswell, B. (1999). Gender differences in self-esteem: A meta-analysis. *Psychological Bulletin, 125,* 470–500.

Klitzner, M., Gruenewald, P. J., & Bamberger, E. (1991). Cigarette advertising and adolescent experimentation with smoking. *British Journal of Addiction, 86,* 287–298.

Knapp, M. L., Stafford, L., & Daly, J. A. (1986). Regrettable messages: Things people wish they hadn't said. *Journal of Communication, 36,* 40–58.

Knopf, T. A. (1975). *Rumors, race, and riots.* New Brunswick, NJ: Transaction.

Knutson, M. C. (2002). Tattooing, piercing, and branding: A guide for clinicians. *Medscape.* www.medscape.com/viewarticle/444871.

Kogan, N., & Wallach, M. (1964). *Risk taking: A study in cognition and personality.* New York: Holt, Rinehart and Winston.

Kohl, W. L., Steers, R., & Terborg, J. (1995). The effects of transformational leadership on teacher attitudes and student performance in Singapore. *Journal of Organizational Behavior, 73,* 695–703.

Kohlberg, L. (1969). Stage and sequence: The cognitive-developmental approach to socialization. In D. Goslin (Ed.), *Handbook of socialization theory and research.* (pp. 347–380). Chicago: Rand McNally.

Kohn, M. (1969). *Class and conformity: A study in values.* Homewood, IL: Dorsey Press.

Kohn, M. (1976). Occupational structure and alienation. *American Journal of Sociology, 82,* 111–130.

Kohn, M. L. (1989). Social structure and personality: A quintessentially sociological approach to social psychology. *Social Forces, 68*(1), 26–33.

Kohn, M., Naoi, A., Schoenbach, C., Schooler, C., & Slomczynski, K. M. (1990). Position in the class structure and psychological functioning in the United States, Japan, and Poland. *American Journal of Sociology, 95,* 964–1008.

Kohn, M., & Schooler, C. (1973). Occupational experience and psychological functioning: An assessment of reciprocal effects. *American Sociological Review, 38,* 97–118.

Kohn, M., & Schooler, C. (1982). Job conditions and personality: A longitudinal assessment of their reciprocal effects. *American Journal of Sociology, 87,* 1257–1286.

Kohn, M., & Schooler, C. (with Miller, J., Miller, K., Schoenbach, S., & Schoenberg, R.). (1983). *Work and personality: An inquiry into the impact of social stratification.* Norwood, NJ: Ablex.

Konecni, V. J. (1979). The role of aversive events in the development of intergroup conflict. In W. G. Austin & S. Worchel (Eds.), *The social psychology of intergroup relations.* (pp. 85–102). Monterey, CA: Brooks/Cole.

Korten, D. C. (1962). Situational determinants of leadership structure. *Journal of Conflict Resolution, 6,* 222–235.

Koskinen, S., & Martelin, T. (1994). Why are socioeconomic mortality differences smaller among women than among men? *Social Science and Medicine, 38,* 1385–1396.

Koss, M. P., & Leonard, K. E. (1984). Sexually aggressive men: Empirical findings and theoretical implications. In N. M. Malamuth & E. I. Donnerstein (Eds.), *Pornography and sexual aggression* (pp. 213–232). Orlando, FL: Academic Press.

Kothandapani, V. (1971). Validation of feeling, belief, and intention to act as three components of attitude and their contribution to prediction of contraceptive behavior. *Journal of Personality and Social Psychology, 19,* 321–333.

Kozielecki, J. (1984). Rodzaje samoprezentacji [Types of self-presentation]. *Psychologia Wychowawcza, 27,* 129–137.

Krahé, B. (2013). Violent video games and aggression. In K. E. Dill (Ed.), *The Oxford handbook of media psychology* (pp. 352–372). New York: Oxford University Press.

Kraus, S. (Ed.). (1962). *The great debates.* Bloomington: Indiana University Press.

Krauss, R. M., & Fussell, S. K. (1996). Social psychological models of interpersonal communication. In E. T. Higgins & A. Kruglanski (Eds.), *Social psychology: Handbook of basic principles* (pp. 655–701). New York: Guilford Press.

Krauss, R. M., Morrel-Samuels, P., & Colasante, C. (1991). Do conversational hand gestures communicate? *Journal of Personality and Social Psychology, 61,* 743–754.

Kraut, R. E. (1980). Humans as lie-detectors: Some second thoughts. *Journal of Communication, 30,* 209–216.

Kraut, R. E., & Poe, D. (1980). Behavior roots of person perception: The deception judgments of customs inspectors and laymen. *Journal of Personality and Social Psychology, 39,* 784–798.

Kravitz, D. A., & Martin, B. (1986). Ringelmann rediscovered: The original article. *Journal of Personality and Social Psychology, 50,* 936–941.

Krebs, D. L. (1982). Psychological approaches to altruism: An evaluation. *Ethics, 92*, 147–158.

Krebs, D. L., & Miller, D. T. (1985). Altruism and aggression. In G. Lindzey & E. Aronson (Eds.), *The handbook of social psychology* (3rd ed., pp. 1–71). New York: Random House.

Kreider, R. M., & Ellis, R. (2011). Living arrangements of children, 2009. *Current Population Reports*, P70–126. Washuington, DC: U.S. Census Bureau.

Kressel, K., & Pruitt, D. G. (1985). Themes in the mediation of social conflict. *Journal of Social Issues, 41*(2), 179–198.

Kriesberg, L. (1973). *The sociology of social conflicts*. Englewood Cliffs, NJ: Prentice Hall.

Kritzer, H. (1977). Political protest and political violence: A nonrecursive causal model. *Social Forces, 55*, 630–640.

Krohn, M. D. (1986). The web of conformity: A network approach to the explanation of delinquent behavior. *Social Problems, 33*, 581–593.

Krohn, M. D., Massey, J. L., & Zielinski, M. (1988). Role overlap, network multiplexity, and adolescent deviant behavior. *Social Psychology Quarterly, 51*, 346–356.

Kruger, D. J. (2001). Inclusive fitness and judgments of helping behaviors: Adaptations for kin directed altruism. *Social Behavior and Personality, 29*, 323–330.

Krull, D. S., & Dill, J. C. (1996). On thinking first and responding fast: Flexibility in social inference processes. *Personality and Social Psychology Bulletin, 22*, 949–959.

Kuhn, D., Langer, J., Kohlberg, L., & Haan, N. (1977). The development of formal operations in logical and moral judgement. *Genetic Psychology Monographs, 95*, 97–188.

Kuhn, M. H., & McPartland, T. (1954). An empirical investigation of self-attitudes. *American Sociological Review, 19*, 68–76.

Kulick, J. A., & Brown, R. (1979). Frustration, attribution of blame, and aggression. *Journal of Experimental Social Psychology, 15*, 183–194.

Kumkale, G. T., & Albarracín, D. (2004). The sleeper effect in persuasion: A meta-analytic review. *Psychological Bulletin, 130*, 143–172.

Kurdek, L. A. (1991). The relation between reported well-being and divorce history, availability of proximate adult, and gender. *Journal of Marriage and the Family, 53*, 71–78.

Kurmeyer, S. L., & Biggers, K. (1988). Environmental demand and demand engendering behavior: An observational analysis of the Type A pattern. *Journal of Personality and Social Psychology, 54*, 997–1005.

Kurtines, M. M. (1986). Moral behavior as rule governed behavior: Person and situation effects on moral decision-making. *Journal of Personality and Social Psychology, 50*, 784–791.

Kuyper, L., Wit, J., Adam, P., & Woertman, L. (2012). Doing more good than harm? The defects of participation in sex research on young people in the Netherlands. *Archives of Sexual Behavior, 41*, 497–506.

Kwang, T., & Swann, W. B. Jr. (2010). Do people embrace praise even when they feel unworthy? A review of critical tests of self-enhancement versus self-verification. *Personality and Social Psychology Review, 14*, 263–280.

Kyjonkova, H., & Lacinova, L. (2010). Private speech and activity type in preschool children. *Ceskoslovenska Psychologie, 54*, 342–356.

Kyratzis, A. (2004). Talk and interaction among children and the co-construction of peer groups and peer culture. *Annual Review of Anthropology, 33*, 625–649.

Labov, W. (1972). *Sociolinguistic patterns*. Philadelphia: University of Pennsylvania Press.

Lachman, S. J., & Bass, A. R. (1985). A direct study of halo effect. *Journal of Psychology, 119*, 535–540.

Lacourse, E., Villeneuve, M., & Claes, M. (2003). Theoretical structure of adolescent alienation: A multigroup confirmatory factor analysis. *Adolescence, 38*, 639–650.

LaFrance, M., & Mayo, C. (1978). *Moving bodies: Nonverbal communication in social relationships*. Monterey, CA: Brooks/Cole.

LaFree, G., & Drass, K. A. (1996). The effect of changes in intraracial income inequality and educational attainment on changes in arrest rates for African Americans and Whites, 1957–1990. *American Sociological Review, 61*, 614–634.

Lakoff, R. T. (1979). Women's language. In O. Buturff & E. L. Epstein (Eds.), *Women's language and style.* (pp. 139–158). Akron, OH: University of Akron.

Lamb, M. E. (1979). Paternal influence and the father's role: A personal perspective. *American Psychologist, 34*, 938–993.

Lamm, H. (1988). A review of our research on group polarization: Eleven experiments on the effects of group discussion on risk acceptance, probability estimation, and negotiation positions. *Psychological Reports, 62*, 807–813.

Lamm, H., & Sauer, C. (1974). Discussion-induced shift toward higher demands in negotiation. *European Journal of Social Psychology, 4*, 85–88.

Lamm, H., & Schwinger, T. (1980). Norms concerning distributive justice: Are needs taken into consideration in allocation decisions? *Social Psychology Quarterly, 43*, 425–429.

Lamm, H., & Trommsdorff, G. (1973). Group versus individual performance on tasks requiring ideational proficiency (brainstorming): A review. *European Journal of Social Psychology, 3*, 361–388.

Land, K. C., McCall, P. L., & Cohen, L. E. (1990). Structural correlates of homicide rates: Are there invariances across time and social space? *American Journal of Sociology, 95*, 922–963.

Landis, D., & O'Shea, W. (2000). Cross-cultural aspects of passionate love: An individual differences analysis. *Journal of Cross-Cultural Psychology, 31*, 752–777.

Landrine, H., Klonoff, E., & Brown-Collins, A. (1995). Cultural diversity and methodology in feminist psychology: Critique, proposal, empirical example. In

H. Landrine (Ed.), *Bringing cultural diversity to feminist psychology: Theory, research, and practice* (pp. 55–75). Washington, DC: American Psychological Association.

Laner, M. R., Benin, M. H., & Ventrone, N. A. (2001). Bystander attitudes toward victims of violence: Who's worth helping? *Deviant Behavior, 22*(1), 23–42.

Lange, C. G., & James, W. (1922). *The emotions* (Vol. 1). Baltimore, MD: Williams and Wilkins.

Lansford, J. E., Skinner, A. T., Sorbring, E., et al. (2012). Boys' and girls' relational and physical aggression in nine countries. *Aggressive Behavior, 38,* 298–308.

Lantieri, L., & Patti, J. (1996). *Waging peace in our schools.* Boston, MA: Beacon.

Lantz, D., & Stefflre, V. (1964). Language and cognition revisited. *Journal of Abnormal and Social Psychology, 69,* 472–481.

Lantz, H., Keyes, J., & Schultz, M. (1975). The American family in the preindustrial period: From base lines in history to change. *American Sociological Review, 40,* 21–36.

Lantz, H., Schultz, M., & O'Hara, M. (1977). The changing American family from the preindustrial to the industrial period: A final report. *American Sociological Review, 42,* 406–421.

LaPiere, R. (1934). Attitudes versus actions. *Social Forces, 13,* 230–237.

Larimer, M. E., Lydum, A. R., Anderson, B. K., & Turner, A. P. (1999). Male and female recipients of unwanted sexual contact in a college student sample: Prevalence rates, alcohol use, and depression symptoms. *Sex Roles, 40*(3–4), 295–308.

Larson, E. B., & Yao, X. (2005). Clinical empathy as emotional labor in the patient-physician relationship. *JAMA: The Journal of the American Medical Association, 293*(9), 1100–1106.

Larson, L. L., & Rowland, K. (1973). Leadership style, stress, and behavior in task performance. *Organizational Behavior and Human Performance, 9,* 407–421.

Larzelere, T., & Huston, T. (1980). The dyadic trust scale: Toward understanding interpersonal trust in close relationships. *Journal of Marriage and the Family, 42,* 595–604.

Latané, B. (1981). The psychology of social impact. *American Psychologist, 36,* 343–356.

Latané, B., & Darley, J. M. (1968). Group inhibition of bystander intervention in emergencies. *Journal of Personality and Social Psychology, 10*(3), 215–221.

Latané, B., & Darley, J. M. (1970). *The unresponsive bystander: Why doesn't he help?* New York: Appleton-Century-Crofts.

Latané, B., & Nida, S. (1981). Ten years of research on group size and helping. *Psychological Bulletin, 89*(2), 308–324.

Latané, B., Nida, S. A., & Wilson, D. W. (1981). The effects of group size on helping behavior. In J. P. Rushton & R. M. Sorrentino (Eds.), *Altruism and helping behavior: Social, personality, and developmental perspectives.* (pp. 287–313). Hillsdale, NJ: Erlbaum.

Latané, B., & Rodin, J. (1969). A lady in distress: Inhibiting effects of friends and strangers on bystander intervention. *Journal of Experimental Social Psychology, 5*(2), 189–202.

Latané, B., Williams, K., & Harkins, S. (1979). Many hands make light the work: The causes and consequences of social loafing. *Journal of Personality and Social Psychology, 37,* 822–832.

Lau, R. R. (1989). Individual and contextual influences on group identification. *Social Psychology Quarterly, 52,* 220–231.

Lau, R. R., & Russell, D. (1980). Attributions in the sports pages. *Journal of Personality and Social Psychology, 39,* 29–38.

Lauderdale, P. (1976). Deviance and moral boundaries. *American Sociological Review, 41,* 660–676.

Laughlin, P. R. (1980). Social combination processes of cooperative, problem-solving groups as verbal intellective tasks. In M. Fishbein (Ed.), *Progress in social psychology* (Vol. 1, pp. 127–155). Hillsdale, NJ: Erlbaum.

Laumann, E. O., Gagnon, J. H., Michael, R. T., & Michaels, S. (1994). *The social organization of sexuality.* Chicago: University of Chicago Press.

Lavoie, F., Hebert, M., Tremblay, R., Vitaro, F.,Vezina, L., & McDuff, P. (2002). History of family dysfunction and perpetration of dating violence by adolescent boys: A longitudinal study. *Journal of Adolescent Health, 30,* 375–383.

Lawler, E. J. (2001). An affect theory of social exchange. *American Journal of Sociology, 107,* 321–352.

Lawler, E. J., & O'Gara, P. W. (1967). Effects of inequity produced by underpayment on work output, work quality, and attitudes toward work. *Journal of Applied Psychology, 51,* 403–410.

Lawler, E. J., Thye, S. R., & Yoon, J. (2000). Emotion and group cohesion in productive exchange. *American Journal of Sociology, 106,* 616–657.

Lawler, E. J., Thye, S. R., & Yoon, J. (2008). Social exchange and micro social order. *American Sociological Review, 73,* 519–542.

Lawler, E. J., & Yoon, J. (1996). Commitment in exchange relations: Test of a theory of relational cohesion. *American Sociological Review, 61*(1), 89–108.

Lawton, C. A., Blakemore, J. E. O., & Vartanian, L. R. (2003). The new meaning of Ms.: Single, but too old for Miss. *Psychology of Women Quarterly, 27*(3), 215–220.

Lazarsfeld, P. F., Berelson, B., & Gaudet, H. (1948). *The people's choice: How the voter makes up his mind in a presidential campaign.* New York: Columbia University Press.

Lazarus, R. S. (1991). *Emotion and adaptation.* New York: Oxford University Press.

Le, B., Dove, N. L., Agnew, C. R., Korn, M. S, & Mutso, A. A. (2010). Predicting nonmarital romantic relationship dissolution: A meta-analytic synthesis. *Personal Relationships, 17,* 377–390.

Le Bon, G. (1895). *Psychologie des foules* [Crowd psychology]. London: Unwin (1903).

Leana, C. R. (1985). A partial test of Janis' groupthink model: Effects of group cohesiveness and leader behavior on defective decision making. *Journal of Management, 11*, 5–17.

Leander, K. (2002). Silencing in classroom interaction: Producing and relating social spaces. *Discourse Processes, 34*, 193–235.

Leaper, C., Anderson, K., & Sanders, P. (1998). Moderators of gender effects on parents' talk to their children: A meta-analysis. *Developmental Psychology, 34*, 3–27.

Leaper, C., & Smith, T. E. (2004). A meta-analytic review of gender variations in children's language use: talkativeness, affiliative speech, and assertive speech. *Developmental Psychology, 40*(6), 993–1027.

Lear, D. (1997). *Sex and sexuality: Risk and relationships in the age of AIDS.* Thousand Oaks, CA: Sage.

Leary, A., & Tobin, T. (2005, March 18). In schools, violence starting at earlier ages. *St. Petersburg Times.*

Leary, M., Tchividjian, L., & Kraxberger, B. (1994). Self-presentation can be hazardous to your health: Impression management and health risk. *Health Psychology, 13*, 461–470.

Leary, M. R. (1995). *Self-presentation: Impression management and interpersonal behavior.* Madison, WI: Brown & Benchmark.

Leary, M. R., & Kowalski, R. M. (1990). Impression management: A literature review and two-component model. *Psychological Bulletin, 107*, 34–47.

Ledvinka, J. (1971). Race of interviewer and the language elaboration of Black interviewees. *Journal of Social Issues, 27*, 185–197.

Lee, B. A., Farrell, C. R., & Link, B. G. (2004). Revisiting the contact hypothesis: The case of public exposure to homelessness. *American Sociological Review, 69*, 40–63.

Lee, H. (2006). Privacy, publicity, and accountability of self-presentation in an on-line discussion group. *Sociological Inquiry, 76*, 1–22.

Lee, H. S., & Park, J. S. (2012). Cultural orientation and the persuasive effects of fear appeals: The case of anti-smoking public service announcements. *Journal of Medical Marketing: Device, Diagnostic and Pharmaceutical Marketing, 12*, 73–80.

Lee, J. (2009). Escaping embarrassment: face-work in the rap cipher. *Social Psychology Quarterly, 72*(4), 306–324.

Lee, S. W., & Schwarz, N. (2010). Washing away postdecisional dissonance. *Science, 328*(5979), 709.

Leffler, A., Gillespie, D. L., & Conaty, J. C. (1982). The effects of status differentiation on nonverbal behavior. *Social Psychology Quarterly, 45*, 153–161.

Leippe, M. R., & Elkin, R. A. (1987). When motives clash: Issue involvement and response involvement as determinants of persuasion. *Journal of Personality and Social Psychology, 52*, 269–278.

Lemert, E. (1951). *Social pathology.* New York: McGraw-Hill.

Lemert, E. (1962). Paranoia and the dynamics of exclusion. *Sociometry, 25*, 2–20.

Lenhart, A., Kahne, J., Middaugh, E., Macgill, A. R., Evans, C., & Vitak, J. (2008). Teens, video games, and civics: teens' gaming experiences are diverse and include significant social interaction and civic engagement. *Pew Internet and American Life Project.*

Lenhart, A., Rainie, L., & Lewis, O. (2001, June 20). Teenage life online: The rise of the instant-message generation and the Internet's impact on friendships and family relationships. Pew Internet and American Life Project. www.pewinternet.org/~/media//Files/Reports/2001/PIP_Teens_Report.pdf.

Lennington, S. (1981). Child abuse: The limits of sociobiology. *Ethology and Sociobiology, 2*, 17–29.

Lennon, M. C., Link, B. G., Marbach, J. J., & Dohrenwend, B. P. (1989). The stigma of chronic facial pain and its impact on social relationships. *Social Problems, 36*, 117–134.

Leone, R., & Barowski, L. (2011). MPAA ratings creep: a longitudinal analysis of the PG-13 rating category in US movies. *Journal of Children and Media, 5*(01), 53–68.

Lepper, M., Greene, D., & Nisbett, R. (1973). Undermining children's intrinsic interest with extrinsic reward: A test of the "overjustification" hypothesis. *Journal of Personality and Social Psychology, 28*, 129–137.

Leventhal, G. S. (1979). Effects of external conflict on resource allocation and fairness within groups and organizations. In W. G. Austin & S. Worchel (Eds.), *The social psychology of intergroup relations.* (pp. 237–251). Monterey, CA: Brooks/Cole.

Leventhal, G. S., & Lane, D. W. (1970). Sex, age, and equity behavior. *Journal of Personality and Social Psychology, 15*, 312–316.

Leventhal, G. S., Karuza J. Jr., & Fry, W. R. (1980). Beyond fairness: A theory of allocation preferences. In G. Mikula (Ed.), *Justice and social interaction* (pp. 167–218). New York: Springer-Verlag.

Leventhal, G. S., Michaels, J. W., & Sanford, C. (1972). Inequity and interpersonal conflict: Reward allocation and secrecy about reward as methods of preventing conflict. *Journal of Personality and Social Psychology, 23*, 88–102.

Leventhal, G. S., Weiss, T., & Long, G. (1969). Equity, reciprocity, and reallocating the rewards in the dyad. *Journal of Personality and Social Psychology, 13*, 300–305.

Leventhal, H. (1970). Findings and theory in the study of fear communications. In L. Berkowitz (Ed.), *Advances in experimental social psychology* (Vol. 5, pp. 119–186). New York: Academic Press.

Leventhal, H. (1984). A perceptual-motor theory of emotion. *Advances in Experimental Social Psychology, 17*, 117–182.

Leventhal, H., & Singer, R. P. (1966). Affect arousal and positioning of recommendations in persuasive communications. *Journal of Personality and Social Psychology, 4*, 137–146.

Lever, J., Grov, C., Royce, T., & Gillespie, M. A. (2008). Searching for love in all the "write" places: Exploring

Internet personals use by sexual orientation, gender, and age. *International Journal of Sexual Health, 20,* 233–246.

Levin, J., & Arluke, A. (1982). Embarrassment and helping behavior. *Psychological Reports, 51,* 999–1002.

Levin, S., van Laar, C., & Sidanius, J. (2003). The effects of ingroup and outgroup friendships on ethnic attitudes in college: A longitudinal study. *Group Processes and Intergroup Relations, 6,* 76–92.

Levine, J. M., & Moreland, R. L. (1998). Small groups. In D. Gilbert, S. Fiske, & G. Lindzey (Eds.), *The handbook of social psychology* (4th ed., pp. 415–469). Boston: McGraw-Hill.

Levine, J. M., Saxe, L., & Ranelli, C. J. (1975). Extreme dissent, conformity reduction, and the bases of social influence. *Social Behavior and Personality, 3,* 117–126.

Levine, M., Prosser, A., Evans, D., & Reicher, S. (2005). Identity and emergency intervention: How social group membership and inclusiveness of group boundaries shape helping behavior. *Personality and Social Psychology Bulletin, 31,* 443–453.

LeVine, R. A., & Campbell, D. T. (1972). *Ethnocentrism: Theories of conflict, ethnic attitudes, and group behavior.* New York: Wiley.

Levinger, G. (1976). A social psychological perspective on marital dissolution. *Journal of Social Issues, 32*(1), 21–47.

Levinson, R., Powell, B., & Steelman, L. C. (1986). Social location, significant others, and body image among adolescents. *Social Psychology Quarterly, 49,* 330–337.

Levitin, T. E. (1975). Deviants are active participants in the labeling process: The visibly handicapped. *Social Problems, 22,* 548–557.

Lewin, D., Feuille, P., & Kochan, T. (1977). *Public sector labor relations: Analysis and readings.* Glen Springs, NJ: Thomas Horton.

Lewis, G. H. (1972). Role differentiation. *American Sociological Review, 37,* 424–434.

Lewis, K., Winsett, R., Cetingok, M., Martin, J., & Hathaway, D. (2000). Social network mapping with transplant recipients. *Progress in Transplantation, 10,* 262–266.

Lewis, M., & Brooks-Gunn, J. (1979). Toward a theory of social cognition: The development of self. In I. Uzgiris (Ed.), *Social interaction and communication during infancy. New directions for child development* (Vol. 4, pp. 1–20). San Francisco: Jossey-Bass.

Lewis, S. A., Langan, C. J., & Hollander, E. P. (1972). Expectation of future interaction and the choice of less desirable alternatives in conformity. *Sociometry, 35,* 440–447.

Lex, B. W. (1986). Measurement of alcohol consumption in fieldwork settings. *Medical Anthropology Quarterly, 17,* 95–98.

Liang, X. (2006). Identity and language functions: High school Chinese immigrant students' code-switching dilemmas in ESL classes. *Journal of Language, Identity, and Education, 5,* 143–167.

Lichter, D., & Qian, Z. (2004). *Marriage and family in a multiracial society.* New York: Russell Sage Foundation.

Lickel, B., Hamilton, D. L., Wieczorkowski, G., Lewis, A., Sherman, S. J., & Uhles, A. N. (2000). Varieties of groups and the perception of group entiativity. *Journal of Personality and Social Psychology, 78,* 223–246.

Liden, R. C., & Mitchell, T. R. (1988). Ingratiatory behaviors in organizational settings. *Academy of Management Review, 13,* 572–614.

Lieberman, A., & Chaiken, S. (1992). Defensive processing of personally relevant health messages. *Personality and Social Psychology Bulletin, 18,* 669–679.

Lieberman, A., & Chaiken, S. (1996). The direct effect of personal relevance on attitudes. *Personality and Social Psychology Bulletin, 22,* 269–279.

Lieberman, P. (1975). *On the origins of human language: An introduction to the evolution of human speech.* New York: MacMillan.

Lieberman, S. (1965). The effect of changes of roles on the attitudes of role occupants. In H. Proshansky & B. Seidenberg (Eds.), *Basic studies in social psychology* (pp. 485–494). New York: Holt, Rinehart and Winston.

Likert, R. (1932). A technique for the measurement of attitudes. *Archives of Psychology* (Whole no. 142).

Lin, N. (1974–1975). The McIntire march: A study of recruitment and commitment. *Public Opinion Quarterly, 38,* 562–573.

Lin, N., & Xie, W. (1988). Occupational prestige in urban China. *American Journal of Sociology, 93,* 793–832.

Lincoln, J., & Kalleberg, A. (1985). Work organization and workforce commitment: A study of plants and employees in the United States and Japan. *American Sociological Review, 50,* 738–760.

Lind, E. A., Kanfer, R., & Earley, P. C. (1990). Voice, control, and procedural justice: Instrumental and noninstrumental concerns in fairness judgments. *Journal of Personality and Social Psychology, 59*(5), 952.

Lind, E. A., & Tyler, T. (1988). *The social psychology of procedural justice.* New York: Plenum Press.

Lindberg, L. D., & Singh, S. (2008). Sexual behavior of single adult American women. *Perspectives on Sexual and Reproductive Health, 40,* 27–33.

Linder, D. E., Cooper, J., & Jones, E. (1967). Decision freedom as a determinant of the role of incentive magnitude in attitude change. *Journal of Personality and Social Psychology, 6,* 245–254.

Lindskold, S., Cullen, P., Gahagen, J., & Tedeschi, J. T. (1970). Developmental aspects of reaction to positive inducements. *Developmental Psychology, 3,* 277–284.

Lindskold, S., & Tedeschi, J. T. (1971). Reward power and attraction in interpersonal conflict. *Psychonomic Science, 22,* 211–213.

Link, B. G. (1982). Mental patient status, work, and income: An examination of the effects of a psychiatric label. *American Sociological Review, 47,* 202–215.

Link, B. G. (1987). Understanding labelling effects in the area of mental disorders: An assessment of the effects of expectations of rejection. *American Sociological Review, 52*, 96–112.

Link, B. G., Cullen, F. T., Struening, E., Shrout, P. E., & Dohrenwend, B. (1989). A modified labeling theory approach to mental disorders: An empirical assessment. *American Sociological Review, 54*, 400–423.

Link, B. G., & Phelan, J. C. (2001). Conceptualizing stigma. *Annual Review of Sociology, 27*, 363–385.

Link, B. G., Struening, E. L., Rahav, M., Phelan, J. C., & Nuttbrock, L. (1997). On stigma and its consequences: Evidence from a longitudinal study of men with dual diagnosis of mental illness and substance abuse. *Journal of Health and Social Behavior, 38*, 177–190.

Linville, P. W. (1982). The complexity-extremity effect and age-based stereotyping. *Journal of Personality and Social Psychology, 42*, 193–211.

Linville, P. W., Fischer, G. W., & Salovey, P. (1989). Perceived distributions of the characteristics of in-group and out-group members: Empirical evidence and a computer simulation. *Journal of Personality and Social Psychology, 57*, 165–188.

Linville, P. W., & Jones, E. E. (1980). Polarized appraisals of out-group members. *Journal of Personality and Social Psychology, 38*, 689–703.

Lipe, M. G. (1991). Counterfactual reasoning as a framework for attribution theories. *Psychological Bulletin, 109*, 456–471.

Liska, A. (1984). A critical examination of the causal structure of the Fishbein-Ajzen attitude-behavior model. *Social Psychology Quarterly, 47*, 61–74.

Littlepage, G. E. (1991). Effects of group size and task characteristics on group performance: A test of Steiner's model. *Personality and Social Psychology Bulletin, 17*, 449–456.

Littlepage, G., & Pineault, T. (1978). Verbal, facial, and paralinguistic cues to the detection of truth and lying. *Personality and Social Psychology Bulletin, 4*, 461–464.

Lizardo, O., & J. L. Collett (2013). Embarrassment and social organization: A multiple identities model. *Social Forces, 92*(1), 353–375.

Lloyd, S. A., & Emery, B. C. (2000). The context and dynamics of intimate aggression against women. *Journal of Social and Personal Relationships, 17*(4–5), 503–521.

Locher, D. A. (2002). *Collective behavior.* Upper Saddle River, NJ: Prentice Hall.

Locke, K. D., & Horowitz, L. M. (1990). Satisfaction in interpersonal interactions as a function of similarity in level of dysphoria. *Journal of Personality and Social Psychology, 58*, 823–831.

Logan, T. K., Walker, R., Cole, J., & Leukefeld, C. (2002). Victimization and substance abuse among women: contributing factors, interventions, and implications. *Review of General Psychology, 6*(4), 325.

Lohr, J. M., & Staats, A. (1973). Attitude conditioning in Sino-Tibetan languages. *Journal of Personality and Social Psychology, 26*, 196–200.

Lois, J. (2003). *Heroic efforts: The emotional culture of*

search and rescue volunteers. New York: New York University Press.

Longmore, M. A., Manning, W. D., & Giordano, P. C. (2006). Identity exploration and adolescents' high risk sexual behaviors: A longitudinal analysis (Working Paper No. 06–16). Center for Family and Demographic Research, Bowling Green State University.

Lonsdale, A. J. (2009). The social psychology of music and musical taste. Doctoral dissertation, Heriot Watt University, UK. www.ros.hw.ac.uk/handle/10399/2275.

Lonsdale, A. J., & North, A. C. (2012). Musical taste and the representativeness heuristic. *Psychology of Music, 40*(2), 131–142.

Lopes, P. N., Salovey, P., Côté, S., Beers, M., & Petty, R. E. (2005). Emotion regulation abilities and the quality of social interaction. *Emotion, 5*(1), 113–118.

Lord, C. G., Lepper, M. R., & Mackie, D. (1984). Attitude prototypes as determinants of attitude-behavior consistency. *Journal of Personality and Social Psychology, 46*, 1254–1266.

Lorence, J., & Mortimer, J. (1985). Job involvement through the life course: A panel study of three age groups. *American Sociological Review, 50*, 618–638.

Lorenz, K. (1966). *On aggression.* New York: Harcourt Brace Jovanovich.

Lorenz, K. (1974). *Civilized man's eight deadly sins.* New York: Harcourt Brace Jovanovich.

Lorenzo, G. L., Biesanz, J. C., & Human, L. J. (2010). What is beautiful is good and more accurately understood: Physical attractiveness and accuracy in first impressions of personality. *Psychological Science, 21*, 1777–1782.

Lott, A., & Lott, B. (1965). Group cohesiveness as interpersonal attraction: A review of relationships with antecedent and consequent variables. *Psychological Bulletin, 64*, 259–309.

Lott, A., & Lott, B. (1974). The role of reward in the formation of positive interpersonal attitudes. In T. Huston (Ed.), *Foundations of interpersonal attraction.* (pp. 171–192). New York: Academic Press.

Lottes, I. L. (1993). Nontraditional gender roles and the sexual experience of heterosexual college students. *Sex Roles, 29*, 645–669.

Lottes, I. L., & Kuriloff, P. J. (1994). The impact of college experience on political and social attitudes. *Sex Roles, 31*, 31–54.

Lovaglia, M. J., Lucas, J. W., & Thye, S. R. (1998). Status processes and mental ability test scores. *American Journal of Sociology, 104*, 195–228.

Lucas, J. W., & Lovaglia, M. J. (1998). Leadership status, gender, group size, and emotion in face-to-face groups. *Sociological Perspectives, 41*(3), 617–637.

Lucas-Thompson, R. G., Goldberg, W. A., & Prause, J. (2010). Maternal work early in the lives of children and its distal associations with achievement and behavior problems. *Psychological Bulletin, 136*, 915–942.

Luchins, A. S. (1957). Experimental attempts to minimize the impact of first impressions. In C. I. Hovland (Ed.),

The order of presentation in persuasion. (pp. 62–75). New Haven, CT: Yale University Press.

Luhman, R. (1990). Appalachian English stereotypes: Language attitudes in Kentucky. *Language in Society, 19*, 331–348.

Lundman, R. J. (1974). Routine police arrest practices: A commonweal perspective. *Social Problems, 22*, 127–141.

Lurigis, A. J., & Carroll, J. S. (1985). Probation officers' schemata of offenders: Content, development, and impact on treatment decisions. *Journal of Personality and Social Psychology, 48*, 1112–1126.

Lussier, P., Corrado, R., & Tzoumakis, S. (2012). Gender differences in physical aggression and associated developmental correlates in a sample of Canadian preschoolers. *Behavioral Sciences and Law, 30*, 643–671.

Lutfey, K., & Mortimer, J. (2003). Development and socialization through the adult life course. In J. DeLamater (Ed.), *Handbook of social psychology.* (pp. 183–202). New York: Kluwer-Plenum.

Lynch, J. C., & Cohen, J. L. (1978). The use of subjective expected utility theory as an aid to understanding variables that influence helping behavior. *Journal of Personality and Social Psychology, 36*, 1138–1151.

Maass, A., & Arcuri, L. (1992). The role of language in the persistence of stereotypes. In G. R. Semin & K. Fiedler (Eds.), *Language, interaction, and social cognition* (pp. 129–143). Newbury Park, CA: Sage.

MacEwen, K. E., & Barling, J. (1991). Effects of maternal employment experiences on children's behavior via mood, cognitive difficulties, and parenting behavior. *Journal of Marriage and the Family, 53*, 635–644.

Macintyre, S., Hunt, K., & Sweeting, H. (1996). Gender differences in health: Are things really as simple as they seem? *Social Science and Medicine, 42*, 617–624.

Mackie, D. M., & Goethals, G. R. (1987). Individual and group goals. In C. Hendrick (Ed.), *Group processes* (pp. 144–166). Newbury Park, CA: Sage.

Macmillan, R. (2001). Violence and the life course: The consequences of victimization for personal and social development. *Annual Review of Sociology, 27*, 1–22.

Maddi, S., Bartone, P., & Puccetti, M. (1987). Stressful events are indeed a factor in physical illness: Reply to Schroeder and Costa (1984). *Journal of Personality and Social Psychology, 52*, 833–843.

Maddux, J. E., & Rogers, R. W. (1980). Effects of source expertness, physical attractiveness, and supporting arguments on persuasion: A case of brains over beauty. *Journal of Personality and Social Psychology, 39*, 235–244.

Maddux, J. E., & Rogers, R. W. (1983). Protection motivation and self-efficacy: A revised theory of fear appeals and attitude change. *Journal of Experimental Social Psychology, 19*, 469–479.

Madon, S., Jussim, L., & Eccles, J. (1997). In search of the powerful self-fulfilling prophecy. *Journal of Personality and Social Psychology, 72*, 791–809.

Madsen, D. B. (1978). Issue importance and choice shifts: A persuasive arguments approach. *Journal of Personality and Social Psychology, 36*, 1118–1127.

Magnuson, M., & Dundes, L. (2008). Gender differences in "social portraits" reflected in MySpace profiles. *CyberPsychology and Behavior, 11*, 239–241.

Mahon, N. E. (1982). The relationship of self-disclosure, interpersonal dependency, and life changes to loneliness in young adults. *Nursing Research, 31*, 343–347.

Major, B., Schmidlin, A. M., & Williams, L. (1990). Gender patterns in social touch: The impact of setting and age. *Journal of Personality and Social Psychology, 58*, 634–643.

Major, B., Zubek, J. M., Cooper, M. L., Cozarelli, C., & Richards, C. (1997). Mixed messages: Implications of social conflict and social support within close relationships for adjustment to a stressful life event. *Journal of Personality and Social Psychology, 72*, 1349–1363.

Malamuth, N. M. (1984). Aggression against women: Cultural and individual causes. In N. M. Malamuth & E. Donnerstein (Eds.), *Pornography and sexual aggression.* (pp. 19–52). Orlando, FL: Academic Press.

Malamuth, N. M., Addison, T., & Koss, M. (2000). Pornography and sexual aggression: Are there reliable effects and can we understand them? *Annual Review of Sex Research, 11*(1), 26–91.

Malamuth, N. M., Heavey, C. L., & Linz, D. (1993). Predicting men's antisocial behavior against women: The interaction model of sexual aggression. In G. C. N. Hall (Ed.), *Sexual aggression: Issues in etiology, assessment, and treatment* (pp. 63–97). Washington, DC: Taylor and Francis.

Malamuth, N. M., Linz, D., Heavey, C. L., Barnes, G., & Acker, M. (1995). Using the confluence model of sexual aggression to predict men's conflict with women: A 10-year follow-up study. *Journal of Personality and Social Psychology, 69*(2), 353–369.

Mallozzi, J., McDermott, V., & Kayson, W. A. (1990). Effects of sex, type of dress, and location on altruistic behavior. *Psychological Reports, 67*, 1103–1106.

Malti, T., Gasser, L., & Gutzwiller-Helfenfinger, E. (2010). Children's interpretive understanding, moral judgments, and emotion attributions: Relations to social behavior. *British Journal of Developmental Psychology, 28*, 275–292.

Maner, J. K., & Gailliot, M. T. (2007). Altruism and egoism: Prosocial motivations for helping depend on relationship context. *European Journal of Social Psychology, 37*(2), 347–358.

Manis, M., Shedler, J., Jonides, J., & Nelson, T. E. (1993). Availability heuristic in judgments of set size and frequency of occurrence. *Journal of Personality and Social Personality, 65*, 448–457.

Mann, C. R. (1996). *When women kill.* Albany: State University of New York Press.

Mann, E., & Abraham, C. (2006). The role of affect in UK commuters' travel mode choices: An interpretative phenomenological analysis. *British Journal of Psychology, 97*, 155–176.

Mannheim, B. F. (1966). Reference groups, membership groups, and the self-image. *Sociometry, 29,* 265–279.

Mannheimer, D., & Williams, R. M. (1949). A note on Negro troops in combat. In S. A. Stouffer, E. A. Suchman, L. C. DeVinney, S. A. Star, & R. M. Williams (Eds.), *The American soldier* (Vol. 1, pp. 486–599). Princeton, NJ: Princeton University Press.

Manning, P. K., & Cullum-Swan, B. (1992). Semiotics and framing: Examples. *Semiotica, 92,* 239–257.

Mannix, E. A., Neale, M. A., & Northcraft, G. B. (1995). Equity, equality, or need? The effects of organizational culture on the allocation of benefits and burdens. *Organizational Behavior and Human Decision Processes, 63,* 276–286.

Manstead, A. S. R., Proffitt, C., & Smart, J. L. (1983). Predicting and understanding mother's infant-feeding intentions and behavior: Testing the theory of reasoned action. *Journal of Personality and Social Psychology, 44,* 657–671.

Manucia, G. K., Baumann, D. J., & Cialdini, R. B. (1984). Mood influences on helping: Direct effects or side effects. *Journal of Personality and Social Psychology, 46*(2), 357–364.

Manz, C. C., & Sims, H. P. (1982). The potential for "groupthink" in autonomous work groups. *Human Relations, 35,* 773–784.

Marangoni, C., & Ickes, W. (1989). Loneliness: A theoretical review with implications for measurement. *Journal of Social and Personal Relationships, 6,* 93–128.

Marchman, V. A. (1991). The acquisition of language in normally developing children: Some basic strategies and approaches. In I. Pavao-Martins, A. Castro-Caldas, H. Van Dongen, & A. Van Hout (Eds.), *Acquired aphasia in children.* (pp. 15–24). Dordrecht, The Netherlands: Kluwer.

Marcus, D. K., Wilson, J. R., & Miller, R. S. (1996). Are perceptions of emotion in the eye of the beholder? A social relations analysis of judgments of embarrassment. *Personality and Social Psychology Bulletin, 22*(12), 1220–1228.

Marcus-Newhall, A., Pedersen, W. C., Carlson, M., & Miller, N. (2000). Displaced aggression is alive and well: A meta-analytic review. *Journal of Personality and Social Psychology, 78*(4), 670–689.

Markey, P. M., & Markey, C. N. (2007). Romantic ideals, romantic obtainment, and relationship experiences: The complementarity of interpersonal traits among romantic partners. *Journal of Social and Personal Relationships, 24,* 517–533.

Markowitz, F. (2001). Modeling processes in recovery from mental illness: Relationships between symptoms, life satisfaction, and self-concept. *Journal of Health and Social Behavior, 42,* 64–79.

Markowitz, F., & Felson, R. (1998). Social-demographic differences in attitudes and violence. *Criminology, 36,* 401–422.

Markus, H. (1977). Self-schemas and processing information about the self. *Journal of Personality and Social Psychology, 35,* 63–78.

Markus, H., & Wurf, E. (1987). The dynamic self-concept: A social psychological perspective. *Annual Review of Psychology, 38,* 299–337.

Markus, H., & Zajonc, R. B. (1985). The cognitive perspective in social psychology. In G. Lindzey & E. Aronson (Eds.), *Handbook of social psychology* (3rd ed., Vol. 1, pp. 137–230). New York: Random House.

Markus, H. R., & Kitayama, S. (1991). Culture and the self: Implications for cognition, emotion, and motivation. *Psychological Review, 98,* 224–253.

Markus, H. R., Kitayama, S., & Hieman, R. J. (1996) Culture and "basic" psychological principles. In E. T. Higging & A. W. Kruglanski (Eds.), *Social psychology: Handbook of basic principles* (pp. 857–913). New York: Guilford Press.

Markus, H. R., Smith, J., & Moreland, R. L. (1985). Role of the self-concept in the perception of others. *Journal of Personality and Social Personality, 49,* 1494–1512.

Marmot, M. G., Bosma, H., Hemingway, H., Brunner, E., & Stansfeld, S. (1997). Contribution of job control and other risk factors to social variations in coronary heart disease. *The Lancet, 350,* 235–239.

Marsden, P., & Campbell, K. (1984). Measuring tie strength. *Social Forces, 63,* 482–501.

Marsh, H. W., Barnes, J., & Hocevar, D. (1985). Self-other agreement on multidimensional self-concept ratings: Factor analysis and multitraitmultimethod analysis. *Journal of Personality and Social Psychology, 49,* 1360–1377.

Martin, C. L. (1987). A ratio measure of sex stereotyping. *Journal of Personality and Social Psychology, 52,* 489–499.

Martin, K., Leary, M., & Rejeski, W. J. (2000). Self-presentational concerns in older adults: Implications for health and well-being. *Basic and Applied Social Psychology, 22,* 169–179.

Martin, J., Pescosolido, B., & Tuch, S. (2000). Of fear and loathing: The role of "disturbing behavior," labels, and causal attributions in shaping public attitudes toward people with mental illness. *Journal of Health and Social Behavior, 41,* 208–223.

Martin, J., Scully, M., & Levitt, B. (1990). Injustice and the legitimation of revolution: Damning the past, excusing the present, and neglecting the future. *Journal of Personality and Social Psychology, 58,* 281–290.

Martin, M. W., & Sell, J. (1986). Rejection of authority: The importance of type of distribution rule and extent of benefit. *Social Science Quarterly, 67,* 855–868.

Martinez, R. (1996). Latinos and lethal violence: The impact of poverty and inequality. *Social Problems, 43,* 131–145.

Mason, W., & Suri, S. (2012). Conducting behavioral research on Amazon's Mechanical Turk. *Behavioral Research, 44,* 1–23.

Marwell, G., Aiken, M. T., & Demerath, N. J. (1987). The persistence of political attitudes among 1960s civil rights activists. *Public Opinion Quarterly, 51,* 383–399.

Matsueda, R. (1982). Testing control theory and differential association: A causal modeling approach. *American Sociological Review, 47,* 489–504.

Matsueda, R., Kraeger, D., & Huizinga, D. (2006). Deterring delinquents: A rational choice model of theft and violence. *American Sociological Review, 71,* 93–122.

Matsueda, R. L. (1992). Reflected appraisals, parental labeling, and delinquency: Specifying a symbolic interactionist theory. *American Journal of Sociology, 97,* 1577–1611.

Matsumoto, D. (1987). The role of facial response in the experience of emotion: more methodological problems and a meta-analysis. *Journal of Personality and Social Psychology, 52*(4), 769–774.

Matsumoto, D. (1990). Cultural similarities and differences in display rules. *Motivation and Emotion, 14*(3), 195–214.

Matsumoto, D., & Ekman, P. (1989). American-Japanese cultural differences in intensity ratings of facial expressions of emotion. *Motivation and Emotion, 13*(2), 143–157.

Matthews, L. S., Conger, R. D., & Wickrama, K. A. S. (1996). Work-family conflict and marital quality: Mediating processes. *Social Psychology Quarterly, 59,* 62–79.

Maurer, T., Pleck, J., & Rane, T. (2001). Parental identity and reflected-appraisals: Measurement and gender dynamics. *Journal of Marriage and the Family, 63,* 309–321.

Mayer, J. D., Rapp, H. C., & Williams, L. (1993). Individual differences in behavioral prediction: The acquisition of personal-action schemata. *Personality and Social Psychology Bulletin, 19,* 443–451.

Maynard, D. W. (1983). Social order and plea bargaining in the court. *Sociological Quarterly, 24,* 215–233.

Maynard, D. W., & Whalen, M. R. (1995). Language, action, and social interaction. In K. S. Cook, G. A. Fine, & J. S. House (Eds.), *Sociological perspectives on social psychology* (pp. 149–175). Needham Heights, MA: Allyn and Bacon.

Mazur, J. E. (1998). *Learning and behavior* (4th ed.). Upper Saddle River, NJ: Prentice Hall.

McAdam, D. (1986). Recruitment to high-risk activism: The case of Freedom Summer. *American Journal of Sociology, 92,* 64–90.

McAdam, D. (1999). *Political process and the development of Black insurgency, 1930–1970* (2nd ed.). Chicago: University of Chicago Press.

McAdoo, H. P. (1997). Upward mobility across generations of African-American families. In H. P. McAdoo (Ed.), *Black families* (3rd ed., pp. 139–162). Thousand Oaks, CA: Sage.

McArthur, L. Z. (1972). The how and what of why: Some determinants and consequences of causal attribution. *Journal of Personality and Social Psychology, 22,* 171–193.

McArthur, L. Z., & Post, D. L. (1977). Figural emphasis and person perception. *Journal of Experimental Social Psychology, 13,* 520–535.

McCabe, D. L., Treviño, L. K., & Butterfield, K. D. (1999).

Academic integrity in honor code and non-honor code environments: A qualitative investigation. *Journal of Higher Education, 70*(2), 211–234.

McCabe, D. L., Treviño, L. K., & Butterfield, K. D. (2001). Cheating in academic institutions: A decade of research. *Ethics & Behavior, 11*(3), 219–232.

McCall, G. J., & Simmons, J. L. (1978). *Identities and interactions.* New York: Free Press.

McCall, P., Parker, K., & MacDonald, J. (2008). The dynamic relationship between homicide rates and social, economic, and political factors from 1970 to 2000. *Social Science Research, 37,* 721–735.

McCarthy, J. D., & Hoge, D. R. (1984). The dynamics of self-esteem and delinquency. *American Journal of Sociology, 90,* 396–410.

McCauley, C. (1989). The nature of social influence in groupthink: Compliance and internalization. *Journal of Personality and Social Psychology, 57,* 250–260.

McCauley, C., Stitt, C. L., & Segal, M. (1980). Stereotyping: From prejudice to prediction. *Psychological Bulletin, 87,* 195–208.

McConahay, J. B. (1983). Modern racism and modern discrimination: The effects of race, racial attitudes, and context on simulated hiring decisions. *Personality and Social Psychology Bulletin, 9,* 551–558.

McConahay, J. B. (1986). Modern racism, ambivalence, and the modern racism scale. In J. F. Dovidio & S. L. Gaertner (Eds.), *Prejudice, discrimination, and racism.* (pp. 91–125). Orlando, FL: Academic Press.

McConahay, J. B., Hardee, B. B., & Batts, V. (1981). Has racism declined in America? It depends on who is asking and what is asked. *Journal of Conflict Resolution, 25,* 563–579.

McFarland, C., & Ross, M. (1982). The impact of causal attributions on affective reactions to success and failure. *Journal of Personality and Social Psychology, 43,* 937–946.

McFarland, D. (2004). Resistance as a social drama: A study of change-oriented encounters. *American Journal of Sociology, 109,* 1249–1318.

McGarty, C., Yzerbyt, V. Y., & Spears, R. (Eds.). (2002). *Stereotypes as explanations: The formation of meaningful beliefs about social groups.* Cambridge University Press.

McGrath, J. E. (1984). *Groups: Interaction and performance.* Englewood Cliffs, NJ: Prentice Hall.

McGuire, W. J. (1964). Inducing resistance to persuasion: Some contemporary approaches. In L. Berkowitz (Ed.), *Advances in experimental social psychology* (Vol. 1, pp. 191–229). New York: Academic Press.

McGuire, W. J. (1985). Attitude and attitude change. In G. Lindzey & E. Aronson (Eds.), *The handbook of social psychology* (3rd ed., Vol. 2, pp. 233–346). New York: Random House.

McGuire, W. J., & McGuire, C. (1982). Significant others in self-space: Sex differences and developmental trends in the social self. In J. Suls (Ed.), *Psychological perspectives on the self* (Vol. 1, pp. 71–96). Hillsdale, NJ: Erlbaum.

McGuire, W. J., & McGuire, C. (1986). Differences in conceptualizing self versus conceptualizing other people as manifested in contrasting verb types used in natural speech. *Journal of Personality and Social Psychology, 51,* 1135–1143.

McGuire, W. J., & Papageorgis, D. (1961). The relative efficacy of various types of prior belief-defense in producing immunity against persuasion. *Journal of Abnormal and Social Psychology, 62,* 327–337.

McLanahan, S., & Booth, K. (1989). Mother-only families: Problems, prospects, and politics. *Journal of Marriage and the Family, 51,* 557–580.

McLanahan, S., & Sandefur, G. (1994). *Growing up with a single parent: What hurts, what helps?* Cambridge, MA: Harvard University Press.

McLeod, J. M., Price, K. O., & Harburg, E. (1966). Socialization, liking, and yielding of opinions in imbalanced situations. *Sociometry, 29,* 197–212.

McLoyd, V., Cauce, A. M., Takeuchi, D., & Wilson, L. (2001). Marital processes and parental socialization in families of color: A decade review of research. In R. Milardo (Ed.), *Understanding families into the new millennium: A decade in review.* (pp. 1070–1093). Minneapolis, MN: National Council on Family Relations.

McMahon, S., & Farmer, G. L. (2011). An updated measure for assessing subtle rape myths. *Social Work Research, 35*(2), 71–81.

McPhail, C. (1991). *The myth of the madding crowd.* Hawthorne, NY: Aldine de Gruyter.

McPhail, C. (1994). Presidential address—The dark side of purpose: Individual and collective violence in riots. *Sociological Quarterly, 35,* 1–32.

McPhail, C. (1997). Stereotypes of crowds and collective behavior: Looking backward, looking forward. *Studies in Symbolic Interactionism, 3,* 35–58.

McPhail, C. (2006). The crowd and collective behavior: Bringing symbolic interaction back in. *Symbolic Interaction, 29,* 433–464.

McPherson, M., Smith-Lovin, L., & Cook, J. (2001). Birds of a feather: Homophily in social networks. *Annual Review of Sociology, 27,* 415–444.

McVeigh, R., Myers, D. J., & Sikkink, D. (2004). Corn, Klansmen, and Coolidge: Structure and framing in social movements. *Social Forces, 83,* 653–690.

McWorter, G. A., & Crain, R. L. (1967). Subcommunity gladiatorial competition: Civil rights leadership as a competitive process. *Social Forces, 46,* 8–21.

Mead, G. H. (1934). *Mind, self, and society.* Chicago: University of Chicago Press.

Meeker, B. F. (1981). Expectation states and interpersonal behavior. In M. Rosenberg & R. H. Turner (Eds.), *Social psychology: Sociological perspectives* (pp. 290–319). New York: Basic Books.

Mehrabian, A. (1972). *Nonverbal communication.* New York: Aldine-Atherton.

Mehrabian, A., & Ksionzky, S. (1970). Models for affiliative and conformity behavior. *Psychological Bulletin, 74,* 110–126.

Meier, R. F., & Johnson, W. T. (1977). Deterrence as social control: The legal and extralegal production of conformity. *American Sociological Review, 42,* 292–304.

Meier, S. (2006). *The economics of non-selfish behaviour.* Northampton, MA: Edward Elgar.

Melzer, S. (2002). Gender, work, and intimate violence: Men's occupational violence spillover and compensatory violence. *Journal of Marriage and Family, 64,* 820–832.

Mendelsohn, H. (1973). Some reasons why information campaigns can succeed. *Public Opinion Quarterly, 37,* 50–61.

Mennino, S. F., Rubin, B., & Brayfield, A. (2005). Home-to-job and job-to-home spillover: The impact of company policies and workplace culture. *Sociological Quarterly, 46,* 107–135.

Merton, R. (1957). *Social theory and social structure.* Glencoe, IL: Free Press.

Mesquita, B., & Karasawa, M. (2002). Different emotional lives. *Cognition and Emotion, 16*(1), 127–141.

Messner, S. F., & Krohn, M. D. (1990). Class, compliance structure, and delinquency: Assessing integrated structural-Marxist theory. *American Journal of Sociology, 96,* 300–328.

Metts, S., & Cupach, W. R. (1989). Situational influence on the use of remedial strategies in embarrassing predicaments. *Communication Monographs, 56,* 151–162.

Meyer, P. (1999). The sociobiology of human cooperation: The interplay of ultimate and proximate causes. In J. M. G. van der Dennen, D. Smillie, & D. R. Wilson, (Eds.), *The Darwinian heritage and sociobiology* (pp. 49–65). Westport, CT: Praeger.

Meyer, P. (2000). The sociobiology of human cooperation: The interplay of ultimate and proximate causes. In J. M. G. van der Dennen, D. Smillie, & D. R. Wilson, (Eds.), *The Darwinian heritage and sociobiology.* (pp. 49–65). Westport, CT: Praeger.

Meyrowitz, J. (1985). *No sense of place: The impact of electronic media on social behavior.* New York: Oxford University Press.

Miall, C. E. (1986). The stigma of involuntary childlessness. *Social Problems, 33,* 268–282.

Michaels, J. W., Edwards, J. N., & Acock, A. C. (1984). Satisfaction in intimate relationships as a function of inequality, inequity, and outcomes. *Social Psychology Quarterly, 47,* 347–357.

Michener, H. A., & Burt, M. R. (1974). Legitimacy as a base of social influence. In J. T. Tedeschi (Ed.), *Perspectives on social power.* (pp. 310ff). Chicago: Aldine-Atherton.

Michener, H. A., & Burt, M. R. (1975). Components of "authority" as determinants of compliance. *Journal of Personality and Social Psychology, 31,* 605–614.

Michener, H. A., & Lawler, E. J. (1975). Endorsement of formal leaders: An integrative model. *Journal of Personality and Social Psychology, 31,* 216–223.

Michener, H. A., Plazewski, J. G., & Vaske, J. J. (1979). Ingratiation tactics channeled by target values and threat capability. *Journal of Personality, 47,* 36–56.

Michener, H. A., & Tausig, M. (1971). Usurpation and perceived support as determinants of the endorsement accorded formal leaders. *Journal of Personality and Social Psychology, 18*, 364–372.

Michener, H. A., & Wasserman, M. (1995). Group decision making. In K. S. Cook, G. A. Fine, & J. S. House (Eds.), *Sociological perspectives on social psychology* (pp. 336–361). Boston: Allyn and Bacon.

Milardo, R. (1988). Families and social networks: An overview of theory and methodology. In R. Milardo (Ed.), *Families and social networks.* (pp. 13–47). Newbury Park, CA: Sage.

Milardo, R. M. (1982). Friendship networks in developing relationships: Converging and diverging social environments. *Social Psychology Quarterly, 45*, 162–172.

Milburn, M. A. (1987). Ideological self-schemata and schematically induced attitude consistency. *Journal of Experimental Social Psychology, 23*, 383–398.

Milburn, M. A., Mather, R., & Conrad, S. D. (2000). The effects of viewing R-rated movie scenes that objectify women on perceptions of date rape. *Sex Roles, 43*(9–10), 645–664.

Miles, R. H. (1977). Role-set configuration as a predictor of role conflict and ambiguity in complex organizations. *Sociometry, 40*, 21–34.

Milgram, S. (1963). Behavioral study of obedience. *Journal of Abnormal and Social Psychology, 67*, 371–378.

Milgram, S. (1965). Some conditions of obedience and disobedience to authority. *Human Relations, 18*, 57–76.

Milgram, S. (1974). *Obedience to authority.* New York: Harper and Row.

Milgram, S. (1976). Obedience to criminal orders: The compulsion to do evil. In T. Blass (Ed.), *Contemporary social psychology: Representative readings* (pp. 175–184). Itasca, IL: Peacock.

Milgram, S. (1977). *The individual in a social world: Essays and experiments.* Reading, MA: Addison-Wesley Publishing Company.

Milgram, S., Liberty, H. J., Toledo, R., & Wackenhut, J. (1986). Response to intrusion into waiting lines. *Journal of Personality and Social Psychology, 51*, 683–689.

Miller, A. G. (1976). Constraint and target effects on the attribution of attitudes. *Journal of Experimental Social Psychology, 12*, 325–339.

Miller, A. G. (Ed.). (1982). *In the eye of the beholder: Contemporary issues in stereotyping.* New York: Praeger.

Miller, A. G., Collins, B. E., & Brief, D. E. (1995). Perspectives on obedience to authority: The legacy of the Milgram experiments. *Journal of Social Issues, 51*(3), 1–19.

Miller, C. E., & Komorita, S. S. (1995). Reward allocation in task-performing groups. *Journal of Personality and Social Psychology, 69*, 80–90.

Miller, D. L. (2000). *Introduction to collective behavior and collective action.* Prospect Heights, IL: Waveland Press.

Miller, G. (1991). Family as excuse and extenuating circumstance: Social organization and use of family rhetoric in a work incentive program. *Journal of Marriage and the Family, 53*, 609–621.

Miller, J., Schooler, C., Kohn, M., & Miller, K. (1979). Women and work: The psychological effects of occupational conditions. *American Journal of Sociology, 85*, 66–94.

Miller, K., Kohn, M., & Schooler, C. (1986). Educational self-direction and personality. *American Sociological Review, 51*, 372–390.

Miller, L. K., & Hamblin, R. L. (1963). Interdependence, differential rewarding, and productivity. *American Sociological Review, 43*, 193–204.

Miller, M., & Megowen, K. R. (2000). The painful truth: Physicians are not invincible. *Southern Medical Journal, 93*, 966–972.

Miller, R. S. (1987). Empathic embarrassment: Situational and personal determinants of reactions to the embarrassment of another. *Journal of Personality and Social Psychology, 53*, 1061–1069.

Miller, R. S. (1992). The nature and severity of self-reported embarrassing circumstances. *Personality and Social Psychology Bulletin, 18*, 190–198.

Miller, S., Olson, M., & Fazio, R. (2004). Perceived reactions to interracial romantic relationships: When race is used as a cue to status. *Group Processes and Inter-group Relations, 7*, 354–369.

Miller-McPherson, J., & Smith-Lovin, L. (1982). Women and weak ties: Differences by sex in the size of voluntary organizations. *American Journal of Sociology, 87*, 883–904.

Minnigerode, F., & Lee, J. A. (1978). Young adults' perceptions of sex roles across the lifespan. *Sex Roles, 4*, 563–569.

Miranne, A. C., & Gray, L. N. (1987). Deterrence: A laboratory experiment. *Deviant Behavior, 8*, 191–203.

Mirowsky, J., & Ross, C. (1986). Social patterns of distress. In A. Inkeles, J. Coleman, & N. Smelser (Eds.), *Annual Review of Sociology* (Vol. 12, pp. 23–45). Palo Alto, CA: Annual Reviews.

Mirowsky, J., & Ross, C. E. (1995). Sex differences in distress: Real or artifact? *American Sociological Review, 60*, 449–468.

Mischel, W., & Liebert, R. (1966). Effects of discrepancies between deserved and imposed reward criteria on their acquisition and transmission. *Journal of Personality and Social Psychology, 3*, 45–53.

Misuraca, R., & Teuscher, U. (2013). Time flies when you maximize: Maximizers and satisficers perceive time differently when making decisions. *Acta Psychologica, 143*(2), 176–180.

Mitchell, A., Castellani, A., Herrington, R., Joseph, J., Doss, B., & Snyder, D. (2008). Predictors of intimacy in couples' discussions of relationship injuries: An observational study. *Journal of Family Psychology, 22*, 21–29.

Miyamoto, S. F., & Dornbusch, S. (1956). A test of interactionist hypotheses of self-conception. *American Journal of Sociology, 61*, 399–403.

Mizrahi, T. (1984). Coping with patients: Subcultural

adjustments to the conditions of work among internists-in-training. *Social Problems, 32*, 156–166.

Modigliani, A. (1971). Embarrassment, face-work, and eye contact: Testing a theory of embarrassment. *Journal of Personality and Social Psychology, 17*, 15–24.

Moede, W. (1927). Die richtlinien der leistungs-psychologie [Guidelines for the psychology of achievement]. *Industrielle Psychotechnik, 4*, 193–209.

Molm, L. D. (1997). *Coercive power in social exchange.* Cambridge, UK: Cambridge University Press.

Molm, L. D. (2006). The social exchange framework. In P. J. Burke (Ed.), *Contemporary social psychological theories* (pp. 24–45). Palo Alto, CA: Stanford University Press.

Molm, L. D. (2010). The structure of reciprocity. *Social Psychology Quarterly, 73*(2), 119–131.

Molm, L. D., Collett, J. L., & Schaefer, D. R. (2006). Conflict and fairness in social exchange. *Social Forces, 84*, 2331–2352.

Molm, L. D., Collett, J. L., & Schaefer, D. R. (2007). Building solidarity through generalized exchange: A Theory of reciprocity. *American Journal of Sociology, 113*(1), 205–242.

Molm, L. D., Peterson, G., & Takahashi, N. (2001). The value of exchange. *Social Forces, 80*(1), 159–184.

Molm, L. D., Peterson, G., & Takahashi, N. (2003). In the eye of the beholder: Procedural justice in social exchange. *American Sociological Review, 68*, 128–152.

Molm, L. D., Schaefer, D. R., & Collett, J. L. (2009). Fragile and resilient trust: Risk and uncertainty in negotiated and reciprocal exchange. *Sociological Theory, 27*(1), 1–32.

Money, J., & Ehrhardt, A. (1972). *Man and woman, boy and girl.* Baltimore, MD: Johns Hopkins University Press.

Mongrain, M., & Vettese, L. (2003). Conflict over emotional expression: Implications for interpersonal communication. *Personality and Social Psychology Bulletin, 29*, 545–555.

Moore, J. C. (1968). Status and influence in small group interaction. *Sociometry, 31*, 47–63.

Moore, M. M. (1985). Nonverbal courtship patterns in women: Context and consequences. *Ethology and Sociobiology, 6*, 237–247.

Moore, M. M., & Butler, D. L. (1989). Predictive aspects of nonverbal courtship behavior in women. *Semiotica, 76*, 205–215.

Moore, R. (2004). Managing troubles in answering survey questions: Respondents' uses of projective reporting. *Social Psychology Quarterly, 67*, 50–69.

Moorhead, G., Ference, R., & Neck, C. P. (1991). Group decision fiascoes continue: Space shuttle *Challenger* and a revised groupthink framework. *Human Relations, 44*, 539–550.

Moorhead, G., & Montanari, J. R. (1986). An empirical investigation of the groupthink phenomenon. *Human Relations, 39*, 399–410.

Moran, G. (1966). Dyadic attraction and orientational consensus. *Journal of Personality and Social Psychology, 4*, 94–99.

Morgan, K., & Smith, B. (2008). The impact of race on parole decision-making. *Justice Quarterly, 25*, 411–435.

Morgan, W., Alwin, D., & Griffin, L. (1979). Social origins, parental values, and the transmission of inequality. *American Journal of Sociology, 85*, 156–166.

Moriarty, T. (1975). Crime, commitment, and the responsive bystander: Two field experiments. *Journal of Personality and Social Psychology, 31*, 370–376.

Morris, M. W., & Larrick, R. P. (1995). When one cause casts doubt on another: A normative analysis of discounting in causal attribution. *Psychological Review, 102*, 331–355.

Morris, W. N., & Miller, R. S. (1975). The effect of consensus-breaking and consensus-preempting partners on reduction of conformity. *Journal of Experimental Social Psychology, 11*, 215–223.

Morse, K., & Neuberg, S. (2004). How do holidays influence relationship processes and outcomes? Examining the instigating and catalytic effects of Valentine's Day. *Personal Relationships, 11*, 509–527.

Morse, S., & Gergen, K. (1970). Social comparison, self-consistency, and the concept of self. *Journal of Personality and Social Psychology, 16*, 148–156.

Mortimer, J. T., & Lorence, J. (1995). Social psychology of work. In K. S. Cook, G. A. Fine, & J. S. House (Eds.), *Sociological perspectives on social psychology* (pp. 497–523). Needham Heights, MA: Allyn and Bacon.

Mortimer, J. T., & Simmons, R. (1978). Adult socialization. In R. Turner, J. Coleman, & R. Fox (Eds.), *Annual Review of Sociology* (Vol. 4, pp. 421–454), Palo Alto, CA: Annual Reviews.

Moscovici, S. (1980). Toward a theory of conversion behavior. In L. Berkowitz (Ed.), *Advances in experimental social psychology* (Vol. 13, pp. 209–239). New York: Academic Press.

Moscovici, S. (1985a). Innovation and minority influence. In S. Moscovici, G. Mugny, & E. Van Avermaet (Eds.), *Perspectives on minority influence* (pp. 9–52). Cambridge, UK: Cambridge University Press.

Moscovici, S. (1985b). Social influence and conformity. In G. Lindzey & E. Aronson (Eds.), *Handbook of social psychology* (3rd ed., Vol. 2, pp. 347–412). New York: Random House.

Moscovici, S., & Lage, E. (1976). Studies in social influence III: Majority versus minority influence in a group. *European Journal of Social Psychology, 6*, 149–174.

Moscovici, S., Lage, E., & Naffrechoux, M. (1969). Influence of a consistent minority on the responses of a majority in a color perception task. *Sociometry, 32*, 365–379.

Moskowitz, G. B., Skurnik, I., & Galinsky, A. D. (1999). The history of dual-process notions, and the future of preconscious control. In S. Chaiken and Y. Trope, *Dual-process theories in social psychology* (pp. 12–36). New York: Guilford.

Moss-Racusin, C. A., Dovidio, J. F., Brescoll, V. L., Graham, M. J., & Handelsman, J. (2012). Science faculty's subtle gender biases favor male students. *Proceedings of the National Academy of Sciences, 109*(41), 16474–16479.

Muedeking, G. D. (1992). Authentic/inauthentic identities in the prison visiting room. *Symbolic Interaction, 15*, 227–236.

Mugny, G. (1982). *The power of minorities.* London: Academic Press.

Mugny, G. (1984). The influence of minorities: Ten years later. In H. Tajfel (Ed.), *The social dimension: European developments in social psychology* (Vol. 2, pp. 498–517). Cambridge, UK: Cambridge University Press.

Mulatu, M. S., & Schooler, C. (2002). Causal connections between socio-economic status and health: Reciprocal effects and mediating mechanisms. *Journal of Health and Social Behavior, 43*, 22–41.

Mullen, B. (1985). Strength and immediacy of sources: A meta-analytic evaluation of the forgotten elements of social impact theory. *Journal of Personality and Social Psychology, 48*, 1458–1466.

Mullen, B., & Copper, C. (1994). The relation between group cohesiveness and performance: An integration. *Psychological Bulletin, 115*, 210–227.

Mullen, B., & Hu, L. (1989). Perceptions of ingroup and outgroup variability: A meta-analytic integration. *Basic and Applied Social Psychology, 10*, 233–252.

Muller, C., Ride, S., Fouke, J., Whitney, T., Denton, D., Cantor, N., et al. (2005, February 18). Gender differences and performance in science. *Science, 307*, 1043.

Muller, E. (1985). Income inequality, regime repressiveness, and political violence. *American Sociological Review, 50*, 47–61.

Munsch, C. L. (2013). Women's jobs, men's jobs: How networking can lead women to lower paying jobs. Stanford University: The Clayman Institute for Gender Research. http://gender.stanford.edu/news/2013/womens-jobs-mens-jobs.

Murray, J. P., & Kippax, S. (1979). From the early window to the late night show: International trends in the study of television's impact on children and adults. In L. Berkowitz (Ed.), *Advances in experimental social psychology* (Vol. 12, pp. 253–320). New York: Academic Press.

Murray, S. L., Holmes, J. G., & Griffin, D. W. (1996a). The benefits of positive illusions: Idealization and the construction of satisfaction in close relationships. *Journal of Personality and Social Psychology, 70*, 79–98.

Murray, S. L., Holmes, J. G., & Griffin, D. W. (1996b). The self-fulfilling nature of positive illusions in romantic relationships: Love is not blind, but prescient. *Journal of Personality and Social Psychology, 71*, 1155–1180.

Musweiler, T., Strack, F., & Pfeiffer, T. (2000). Overcoming the inevitable anchoring effect: Considering the opposite compensates for selective accessibility. *Personality and Social Psychology Bulletin, 26*, 1142–1150.

Mustanski, B. (2001). Getting wired: Exploiting the Internet for the collection of valid sexuality data. *Journal of Sex Research, 38*, 292–301.

Mutz, D. C., & Martin, P. S. (2001). Facilitating communication across lines of political difference: The role of mass media. *American Political Science Review, 95*, 97–114.

Myers, D. G. (1975). Discussion-induced attitude polarization. *Human Relations, 28*, 699–714.

Myers, D. G., Bruggink, J. B., Kersting, R. C., & Schlosser, B. A. (1980). Does learning others' opinions change one's opinion? *Personality and Social Psychology Bulletin, 6*, 253–260.

Myers, D. G., & Kaplan, M. F. (1976). Group-induced polarization in simulated juries. *Personality and Social Psychology Bulletin, 2*, 63–66.

Myers, D. G., & Lamm, H. (1976). The group polarization phenomenon. *Psychological Bulletin, 83*, 602–627.

Myers, D. J. (1997). Racial rioting in the 1960s: An event history analysis of local conditions. *American Sociological Review, 62*, 94–112.

Myers, D. J. (2000). The diffusion of collective violence: Infectiousness, susceptibility, and mass media networks. *American Journal of Sociology, 106*, 173–208.

Myers, D. J., & Caniglia, B. S. (2004). All the rioting that's fit to print: Selection effects in national newspaper coverage of civil disorders, 1968–1969. *American Sociological Review, 69*, 519–543.

Myers, D. J., & Li, Y. E. (2001, August). *City conditions and riot susceptibility reconsidered.* Paper presented at the Annual Meeting of the American Sociological Association, Anaheim, CA.

Myers, M. A., & Hagan, J. (1979). Private and public trouble: Prosecutors and the allocation of court resources. *Social Problems, 26*, 439–451.

Myers, M. A., & Talarico, S. M. (1986). The social contexts of racial discrimination in sentencing. *Social Problems, 33*, 236–251.

Myrstol, B. A. (2012). The alcohol-related workload of patrol officers. *Policing: An International Journal of Police Strategies & Management, 35*, 55–75.

Nadler, A. (1987). Determinants of help seeking behaviour: The effects of helper's similarity, task centrality and recipient's self esteem. *European Journal of Social Psychology, 17*(1), 57–67.

Nadler, A. (1991). Help-seeking behavior: Psychological costs and instrumental benefits. In M. S. Clark (Ed.), *Review of personality and social psychology: Vol. 12. Prosocial behavior* (pp. 290–311). Newbury Park, CA: Sage.

Nadler, A., & Fisher, J. D. (1984). Effects of donor-recipient relationships on recipients' reactions to aid. In E. Staub, D. Bar-Tal, J. Karylowski, & J. Reykowski (Eds.), *Development and maintenance of prosocial behavior: International perspectives on positive morality.* (pp. 397–418). New York: Plenum.

Nadler, A., & Fisher, J. D. (1986). The role of threat to self-esteem and perceived control in recipient reaction to help: Theory development and empirical validation. In L. Berkowitz (Ed.), *Advances in experimental social psychology* (Vol. 19, pp. 81–122). San Diego, CA: Academic Press.

Nadler, A., Fisher, J. D., & Ben-Itzhak, S. (1983). With a little help from my friend: Effect of single or multiple act aid as a function of donor and task characteristics. *Journal of Personality and Social Psychology, 44,* 310–321.

Nadler, A., Mayseless, O., Peri, N., & Chemerinski, A. (1985). Effects of opportunity to reciprocate and self-esteem on help-seeking behavior. *Journal of Personality, 53,* 23–35.

Nagel, J. (1995). American Indian ethnic revival: Politics and the resurgence of identity. *American Sociological Review, 60,* 947–965.

Nail, P. R., Harton, H., & Decker, B. (2003). Political orientation and aversive versus modern racism: Tests of Dovidio and Gaertner's integrated model. *Journal of Personality and Social Psychology, 84,* 754–770.

Nair, N., & Vohra, N. (2012). The concept of alienation: Towards conceptual clarity. *International Journal of Organizational Analysis, 20,* 25–50.

Nakao, K., & Treas, J. (1994). Updating occupational prestige and socioeconomic scores: How the new measures measure up. In P. Marsden (Ed.), *Sociological methodology* (Vol. 24, pp. 1–72). Washington, DC: Basil Blackwell Publishers.

Nathanson, A. I., & Cantor, J. (2000). Reducing the aggression-promoting effect of violent cartoons by increasing children's fictional involvement with the victim. *Journal of Broadcasting and Electronic Media, 44,* 125–142.

National Advisory Commission on Civil Disorders. (1968). *Report of the National Advisory Commission on Civil Disorders.* New York: Bantam Books.

National Center for Health Statistics. (2004). *Health, United States, 2004.* (DHHS Publication No. 2004–1232, pp. 178–181). Hyattsville, MD: Author.

National Center for Health Statistics. (2004). Table 29. Age-adjusted death rates for selected causes of death, by sex, race, and Hispanic origin: United States, selected years 1950–2005. In *Health, United States, 2007* (DHHS Publication No. 2007–1232, pp. 178–181). Hyattsville, MD: Author.

National Center for Health Statistics. (2012). Deaths: Final data for 2010. *National Vital Statistics Reports, 61*(4). Washington, DC.

National Endowment for the Arts. (2008). Survey of public participation in the arts 2008 [MRDF]. Washington, DC: National Endowment for the Arts [producer]. Princeton, NJ: Cultural Policy and the Arts National Data Archive [distributor].

National Institute of Mental Health. (2002). Mental health and mass violence: Evidence-based early psychological intervention for victims/survivors of mass violence (NIH Publication No. 02–5138). Washington, DC: U.S. Government Printing Office.

National Institute of Occupational Safety and Health (NIOSH). (2002). The effects of workplace hazards on male reproductive health (NIOSH Publication No. 96–132). Washington, DC: Author.

National Institute of Occupational Safety and Health (NIOSH). (2004). Worker health chartbook, 2004, Figure 2–16 (NIOSH Publication No. 2004–146). www.cdc. gov/niosh/docs/204–146/detail.

National Public Radio. (2002, October 14). How pitchmen sell their wares at state fairs. *Morning Edition* [Program transcript]. Washington, DC: Public Broadcasting Service.

National Television Violence Study. (1996). *National Television Violence Study* (Vol. 1). Thousand Oaks, CA: Sage.

Navarro, M. (2005, April 24). When you contain multitudes. *New York Times,* pp. 1–2.

Neal, A. G., & Groat, H. (1974). Social class correlates of stability and change in levels of alienation: A longitudinal study. *Sociological Quarterly, 15,* 548–558.

Neal, J. W. (2010). Hanging out: Features of urban children's peer social networks. *Journal of Social and Personal Relationships, 27,* 982–1000.

Nelson, T. D. (2002). *The psychology of prejudice.* Boston: Allyn and Bacon.

Nemeth, C. J. (1986). Differential contributions of majority and minority influence. *Psychological Review, 93,* 23–32.

Nemeth, C. J., Swedlund, M., & Kanki, B. (1974). Patterning of the minority's responses and their influence on the majority. *European Journal of Social Psychology, 4,* 53–64.

Nemeth, C. J., Wachtler, J., & Endicott, J. (1977). Increasing the size of the minority: Some gains and some losses. *European Journal of Social Psychology, 7,* 15–27.

Neuendorf, K. A., Gore, T. D., Dalessandro, A., Janstova, P., & Snyder-Suhy, S. (2010). Shaken and stirred: A content analysis of women's portrayals in James Bond films. *Sex Roles, 62*(11–12), 747–761.

Neugarten, B. L., & Datan, N. (1973). Sociological perspectives on the life cycle. In P. Baltes & K. Schaie (Eds.), *Life-span developmental psychology: Personality and social processes.* (pp. 96–113). New York: Academic Press.

Newcomb, T. M. (1943). *Personality and social change.* New York: Dryden.

Newcomb, T. M. (1968). Interpersonal balance. In R. P. Abelson, W. J. McGuire, T. M. Newcomb, M. J. Rosenberg, & P. H. Tannenbaum (Eds.), *Theories of cognitive consistency: A sourcebook.* (pp. 28–51). Chicago: Rand McNally.

Newcomb, T. M. (1971). Dyadic balance as a source of clues about interpersonal attraction. In B. Murstein (Ed.), *Theories of attraction and love.* (pp. 31–45). New York: Springer Verlag.

Newspaper Advertising Bureau. (1980). Mass media in the family setting: Social patterns in media availability and use by parents. New York: Author.

NICHD Early Child Care Research Network. (1997a). Familial factors associated with the characteristics of nonmaternal care for infants. *Journal of Marriage and the Family, 59,* 389–408.

NICHD Early Child Care Research Network. (1997b).

The effects of infant child care on mother-infant attachment security: Results of the NICHD Study of Early Child Care. *Child Development, 68,* 860–879.

NICHD Early Child Care Research Network. (2002). Early child care and children's development prior to school entry: Results from the NICHD Study of Early Child Care. *American Educational Research Journal, 39,* 133–164.

Nickerson, R. S. (1998). Confirmation bias: A ubiquitous phenomenon in many guises. *Review of General Psychology, 2*(2), 175–220.

Nikolajeva, M. (2012). Guilt, empathy and the ethical potential of children's literature. *Barnboken-Journal of Children's Literature Research, 35,* 35.

Nisbett, R. E., Caputo, C., Legant, P., & Maracek, J. (1973). Behavior as seen by the actor and as seen by the observer. *Journal of Personality and Social Psychology, 27,* 154–164.

Noakes, J., & Gillham, P. F. (2007). Police and protestor innovation since Seattle. *Mobilization, 12,* 335–340.

Nomaguchi, K. M. (2006, December). Maternal employment, nonparental care, mother-child interactions, and child outcomes during preschool years. *Journal of Marriage and Family, 68*(5), 1341–1369.

Norenzayan, A., & Nisbett, R. E. (2000). Culture and causal cognition. *Current Directions in Psychological Science, 9,* 132–135.

Norstrom, T. (1995). The impact of alcohol, divorce, and unemployment on suicide. *Social Forces, 74,* 293–314.

Norton, M. I., Dunn, E. W., Carney, D. R., & Ariely, D. (2012). The persuasive "power" of stigma? *Organizational Behavior and Human Design Processes, 117,* 261–268.

Norwood, A., Ursano, R., & Fullerton, C. (2002). *Disaster psychiatry: Principles and practice.* American Psychiatric Association. www.psych.org/pract_of_psych/principles_and_practice3201.cfm.

Oakes, P. J., & Turner, J. C. (1980). Social categorization and intergroup behavior: Does minimal intergroup discrimination make social identity more positive? *European Journal of Social Psychology, 10,* 295–301.

Oberschall, A. (1973). *Social conflict and social movements.* Englewood Cliffs, NJ: Prentice Hall.

Oberschall, A. (1978). Theories of social conflict. In R. Turner, J. Coleman, & R. Fox (Eds.), *Annual Review of Sociology* (Vol. 4, pp. 291–315). Palo Alto, CA: Annual Reviews.

Ohbuchi, K. I., Kameda, M., & Agarie, N. (1989). Apology as aggression control: Its role in mediating appraisal of and response to harm. *Journal of Personality and Social Psychology, 56*(2), 219–227.

Okamoto, D. G., & Smith-Lovin, L. (2001). Changing the subject: Gender, status, and the dynamics of topic change. *American Sociological Review, 66,* 852–873.

O'Leary-Kelly, A. M., Martocchio, J. J., & Frink, D. D. (1994). A review of the influence of group goals on group performance. *Academy of Management Journal, 37,* 1285–1301.

Oliver, P. (1980). Rewards and punishments as selective incentives for collective action: Theoretical investigations. *American Journal of Sociology, 85,* 1356–1375.

Oliver, P. E., & Myers, D. J. (1999). How events enter the public sphere: Conflict, location, and sponsorship in local newspaper coverage of public events. *American Journal of Sociology, 105,* 38–87.

Olver, R. (1961). Developmental study of cognitive equivalence. Unpublished doctoral dissertation, Radcliffe College, Cambridge, MA.

Olzak, S. (1989). Labor unrest, immigration, and ethnic conflict in urban America, 1880–1914. *American Journal of Sociology, 94,* 1303–1333.

Olzak, S. (1992). *The dynamics of ethnic competition and conflict.* Palo Alto, CA: Stanford University Press.

Olzak, S., & Shanahan, S. (1996). Deprivation race riots: An extension of Spilerman's analysis. *Social Forces, 74,* 931–961.

Olzak, S., Shanahan, S., & McEneaney, E. H. (1996). Poverty, segregation, and race riots: 1960 to 1993. *American Sociological Review, 61*(4), 590–613.

Operario, D., & Fiske, S. T. (1999). Integrating social identity and social cognition: A framework for bridging diverse perspectives. In D. Abrams and M. A. Hogg, *Social identity and social cognition* (pp. 26–54). Malden, MA: Blackwell.

Opp, K.-D. (1988). Grievances and participation in social movements. *American Sociological Review, 53,* 853–864.

Oppenheimer, V. K. (1970). *The female labor force in the United States.* (Population Monograph Series No. 5). Berkeley, CA: Institute of International Studies.

Orbuch, T., Veroff, J., Hassan, H., & Horrocks, J. (2002). Who will divorce? A 14-year longitudinal study of Black couples and White couples. *Journal of Social and Personal Relationships, 19,* 549–568.

Orcutt, J. (1975). Deviance as a situated phenomenon: Variations in the social interpretation of marijuana and alcohol use. *Social Problems, 22,* 346–356.

O'Rourke, J., Barnes, J., Deaton, A., Fulks, K., Ryan, K., & Rettinger, D. (2010). Imitation is the sincerest form of cheating: The influence of direct knowledge and attitudes on academic dishonesty. *Ethics and Behavior, 20,* 47–64.

Orwell, G. (1949). *1984.* New York: Harcourt Brace Jovanovich.

Osborn, A. F. (1963). *Applied imagination* (3rd rev. ed.). New York: Scribner.

Osgood, C. E., Suci, G., & Tannenbaum, P. (1957). *The measurement of meaning.* Urbana: University of Illinois Press.

Osgood, D. W., Wilson, J. R., O'Malley, P. M., Bachman, J. G., & Johnston, L. D. (1996). Routine activities and deviant behavior. *American Sociological Review, 61,* 635–655.

Oskamp, S. (1991). *Attitudes and opinions.* Englewood Cliffs, NJ: Prentice Hall.

Otten, C. A., Penner, L. A., & Waugh, G. (1988). That's what friends are for: The determinants of psychological helping. *Journal of Social and Clinical Psychology*, *7*(1), 34–41.

Oyserman, D., Fryberg, S. A., & Yoder, N. (2007). Identity-based motivation and health. *Journal of Personality and Social Psychology*, *93*, 1011–1027.

Padden, S. L., & Buehler, C. (1995). Coping with the dual-income lifestyle. *Journal of Marriage and the Family*, *57*, 101–110.

Page, A. L., & Clelland, D. A. (1978). The Kanawha County textbook controversy: A study of the politics of lifestyle concern. *Social Forces*, *57*, 265–281.

Pager, D. (2003). The mark of a criminal record. *American Journal of Sociology*, *108*, 1249–1291.

Pager, D., Western, B., & Bonikowski, B. (2009). Discrimination in a low-wage labor market a field experiment. *American Sociological Review*, *74*(5), 777–799.

Paicheler, G., & Bouchet, J. (1973). Attitude polarization, familiarization, and group process. *European Journal of Social Psychology*, *3*, 83–90.

Pantin, H. M., & Carver, C. S. (1982). Induced competence and the bystander effect. *Journal of Applied Social Psychology*, *12*(2), 100–111.

Papastamou, S., & Mugny, G. (1985). Rigidity and minority influence: The influence of the social in social influence. In S. Moscovici, G. Mugny & E. Van Avermaet (Ed.), *Perspectives on minority influence* (pp. 113–136). Cambridge, UK: Cambridge University Press.

Park, W.-W. (1990). A review of research on groupthink. *Journal of Behavioral Decision Making*, *3*, 229–245.

Park, B., & Rothbart, M. (1982). Perception of out-group homogeneity and levels of social categorization: Memory for the subordinate attributes of in-group and out-group members. *Journal of Personality and Social Psychology*, *42*, 1051–1068.

Parke, R. (1969). Effectiveness of punishment as an interaction of intensity, timing, agent nurturance, and cognitive structuring. *Child Development*, *40*, 213–235.

Parke, R. (1970). The role of punishment in the socialization process. In R. Hoppe, G. Milton, & E. Simmel (Eds.), *Early experiences and the processes of socialization*. (pp. 81–108). New York: Academic Press.

Parke, R. D. (1996). *Fatherhood*. Cambridge, MA: Harvard University Press.

Parrott, W. G., & Smith, S. F. (1991). Embarrassment: Actual vs. typical cases, classical vs. prototypical representations. *Cognition and Emotion*, *5*, 467–488.

Parsons, L. M. (2003). Is accounting information from nonprofit organizations useful to donors? A review of charitable giving and value-relevance. *Journal of Accounting Literature*, *22*, 104–129.

Patrick, S. L., & Jackson, J. J. (1991). Further examination of the equity sensitivity construct. *Perceptual and Motor Skills*, *73*, 1091–1106.

Patterson, M. L., Mullens, S., & Romano, J. (1971). Compensatory reactions to spatial intrusion. *Sociometry*, *34*, 114–121.

Patterson, R. J., & Neufeld, R. W. J. (1987). Clear danger: Situational determinants of the appraisal of threat. *Psychological Bulletin*, *101*, 404–416.

Paul, E. L., & Hayes, K. A. (2002). The casualties of casual sex: A qualitative exploration of the phenomenology of college students' hookups. *Journal of Social and Personal Relationships*, *19*(5), 639–661.

Paulus, P. B. (1998). Developing consensus about groupthink after all these years. *Organizational Behavior and Human Decision Processes*, *73*, 362–374.

Paulus, P. B., Larey, T. S., & Dzindolet, M. T. (2001). Creativity in groups and teams. In M. Turner (Ed.), *Groups at work: Advances in theory and research* (pp. 319–338). Hillsdale, NJ: Erlbaum.

Pavlidis, J., Eberhardt, N., & Levine, J. (2002). Seeing through the face of deception. *Nature*, *415*, 35.

Paxton, P., & Moody, J. A. (2003). Structure and sentiment: Explaining emotional attachment to group. *Social Psychology Quarterly*, *66*, 34–47.

Pearce, P. L. (1980). Strangers, travelers, and Greyhound terminals: A study of small-scale helping behaviors. *Journal of Personality and Social Psychology*, *38*, 935–940.

Pearlin, L., & Johnson, J. (1977). Marital status, life-strains and depression. *American Sociological Review*, *42*, 704–715.

Pearlin, L., Nguyen, K., Schieman, S., & Milkie, M. (2007). The life-course origins of mastery among older people. *Journal of Health and Social Behavior*, *48*, 164–179.

Pearlin, L., & Radabaugh, C. (1976). Economic strains and the coping functions of alcohol. *American Journal of Sociology*, *82*, 652–663.

Peirce, K. (1993). Socialization of teenage girls through teen-magazine fiction: The making of a new woman or an old lady? *Sex Roles*, *29*, 59–68.

Pelham, B., Mirenberg, M., & Jones, J. (2002). Why Susie sells seashells by the seashore: Implicit egotism and major life decisions. *Journal of Personality and Social Psychology*, *82*, 469–487.

Pendry, L., & Carrick, R. (2001). Doing what the mob do: Priming effects on conformity. *European Journal of Social Psychology*, *31*, 83–92.

Penedo, F., & Dahn, J. (2005). Exercise and well-being: A review of mental and physical health benefits associated with physical activity. *Current Opinion in Psychiatry*, *18*, 189–193.

Pennebaker, J., & Sanders, D. (1976). American graffiti: Effects of authority and reactance arousal. *Personality and Social Psychology Bulletin*, *2*, 264–267.

Pennebaker, J. W. (1980). Perceptual and environmental determinants of coughing. *Basic and Applied Social Psychology*, *1*(1), 83–91.

Penner, L. A. (2002). Dispositional and organizational influences on sustained volunteerism: An interactionist perspective. *Journal of Social Issues*, *58*(3), 447–467.

Penner, L. A., Dovidio, J. F., Piliavin, J. A., & Schroeder, D. A. (2005). Prosocial behavior: Multilevel perspectives. *Annual Review of Psychology*, *56*, 365–392.

Perilloux, C., & Buss, D. (2008). Breaking up romantic relationships: Costs experienced and coping strategies deployed. *Evolutionary Psychology*, *6*, 164–181.

Perlman, D. (1988). Loneliness: A life-span family perspective. In R. Milardo (Ed.), *Families and social networks*. (pp. 190–220). Newbury Park, CA: Sage.

Perlow, L., & Weeks, J. (2002). Who's helping whom? Layers of culture and workplace behavior. *Journal of Organizational Behavior, 23*(4), 345–361.

Perry, B. (2011). The labeling paradox: Stigma, the sick role, and social networks in mental illness. *Journal of Health and Social Behavior, 52*, 460–477.

Perry, J. B., & Pugh, M. D. (1978). *Collective behavior: Response to social stress.* St. Paul, MN: West.

Perry, L. S. (1993). Effects of inequity on job satisfaction and self-evaluation in a national sample of African-American workers. *Journal of Social Psychology, 133*, 565–573.

Perry-Jenkins, M., Repetti, R., & Crouter, A. (2001). Work and family in the 1990s. In R. Milardo (Ed.), *Understanding families into the new millennium: A decade in review.* (pp. 981–998). Minneapolis, MN: National Council on Family Relations.

Pescosolido, A. T. (2001). Informal leaders and the development of group efficacy. *Small Group Research, 32*, 74–93.

Petersen, T., Saporta, I., & Seidel, M. L. (2000). Offering a job: Meritocracy and social networks. *American Journal of Sociology, 106*, 763–816.

Petrunik, M., & Shearing, C. D. (1983). Fragile façades: Stuttering and the strategic manipulation of awareness. *Social Problems, 31*, 125–138.

Pettigrew, T. F. (1979). The ultimate attribution error: Extending Allport's cognitive analysis of prejudice. *Personality and Social Psychology Bulletin, 5*, 461–476.

Pettigrew, T. F. (1997). Generalized intergroup contact effects on prejudice. *Personality and Social Psychology Bulletin, 23*, 173–185.

Pettigrew, T. F., & Tropp, L. R. (2006). A meta-analytic test of intergroup contact theory. *Journal of Personality and Social Psychology, 90*, 751–783.

Petty, R. E. (1995). Attitude change. In A. Tesser (Ed.), *Advanced social psychology* (pp. 195–255). New York: McGraw-Hill.

Petty, R. E., & Brock, T. C. (1981). Thought disruption and persuasion: Assessing the validity of attitude change experiments. In R. E. Petty, T. M. Ostrom, & T. C. Brock (Eds.), *Cognitive responses in persuasion.* (pp. 55–79). Hillsdale, NJ: Erlbaum.

Petty, R. E., & Cacioppo, J. T. (1979a). Effects of forewarning of persuasive intent and involvement on cognitive responses and persuasion. *Personality and Social Psychology Bulletin, 5*, 173–176.

Petty, R. E., & Cacioppo, J. T. (1979b). Issue involvement can increase or decrease persuasion by enhancing message-relevant cognitive responses. *Journal of Personality and Social Psychology, 37*, 1915–1926.

Petty, R. E., & Cacioppo, J. T. (1986a). *Communication and persuasion: Central and peripheral routes to attitude change.* New York: Springer Verlag.

Petty, R. E., & Cacioppo, J. T. (1986b). The elaboration likelihood model of persuasion. In L. Berkowitz (Ed.), *Advances in experimental social psychology* (Vol. 19, pp. 207–249). New York: Academic Press.

Petty, R. E., & Cacioppo, J. T. (1990). Involvement and persuasion: Tradition versus integration. *Psychological Bulletin, 107*, 367–374.

Petty, R. E., Cacioppo, J. T., & Goldman, R. (1981). Personal involvement as a determinant of argument-based persuasion. *Journal of Personality and Social Psychology, 41*, 847–855.

Petty, R. E., Cacioppo, J. T., & Heesacker, M. (1981). Effects of rhetorical questions on persuasion: A cognitive response analysis. *Journal of Personality and Social Psychology, 40*, 432–440.

Petty, R. E., & Wegener, D. T. (1999). The elaboration likelihood model: Current status and controversies. In S. Chaiken & Y. Trope (Eds.), *Dual process theories in social psychology* (pp. 41–72). New York: Guilford Press.

Petty, R. E., Wells, G. L., & Brock, T. C. (1976). Distraction can enhance or reduce yielding to propaganda: Thought disruption versus effort justification. *Journal of Personality and Social Psychology, 34*, 876–884.

Pfau, M., Van Bockern, S., & Kang, J. G. (1992). Use of inoculation to promote resistance to smoking initiation among adolescents. *Communications Monographs, 59*, 213–230.

Phillips, D. P. (1974). The influence of suggestion on suicide: Substantive and theoretical implications of the Werther effect. *American Sociological Review, 39*, 340–354.

Phillips, D. P. (1979). Suicide, motor vehicle fatalities, and the mass media: Evidence toward a theory of suggestion. *American Sociological Review, 84*, 1150–1174.

Piacentini, M., & Mailer, G. (2004). Symbolic consumption in teenagers' clothing choices. *Journal of Consumer Behavior, 3*, 251–262.

Piaget, J. (1954). *The construction of reality in the child.* New York: Basic Books.

Piaget, J. (1965). *The moral judgment of the child.* New York: Free Press.

Piferi, R. L., Jobe, R. L., & Jones, W. H. (2006). Giving to others during national tragedy: The effects of altruistic and egoistic motivations on long-term giving. *Journal of Social and Personal Relationships, 23*(1), 171–184.

Piliavin, I., Gartner, R., Thornton, C., & Matsueda, R. L. (1986). Crime, deterrence, and rational choice. *American Sociological Review, 51*(1), 101–119.

Piliavin, I. M., & Briar, S. (1964). Police encounters with juveniles. *American Journal of Sociology, 70*, 206–214.

Piliavin, I. M., Rodin, J., & Piliavin, J. A. (1969). Good samaritanism: An underground phenomenon. *Journal of Personality and Social Psychology, 13*(4), 289–299.

Piliavin, J. A., & Callero, P. L. (1991). *Giving blood: The development of an altruistic identity.* Baltimore, MD: Johns Hopkins University Press.

Piliavin, J. A., & Charng, H.-W. (1990). Altruism: A review of recent theory and research. *Annual Review of Sociology, 16*, 27–65.

Piliavin, J. A., Dovidio, J. F., Gaertner, S. L., & Clark, R. D. (1981). *Emergency intervention*. New York: Academic Press.

Piliavin, J. A., Grube, J. A., & P. L. Callero. (2002). Role as resource for action in public service. *Journal of Social Issues, 58*, 469–485.

Piliavin, J. A., & LePore, P. C. (1995). Biology and social psychology: Beyond nature versus nurture. In K. S. Cook, G. A. Fine, & J. S. House (Eds.), *Sociological perspectives on social psychology* (pp. 9–40). Boston: Allyn and Bacon.

Piliavin, J. A., & Unger, R. K. (1985). The helpful but helpless female: Myth or reality? In G. O' Leary, R. K. Unger, & B. S. Wallston (Eds.), *Women, gender and social psychology* (pp. 149–189). Hillsdale, HJ: Erlbaum.

Pilling, M., & Davies, I. (2004). Linguistic relativism and colour cognition. *British Journal of Psychology, 95*, 429–455.

Pinker, S. (1997). *How the mind works*. New York: Norton.

Pipher, M. (1994). *Reviving Ophelia: Saving the selves of adolescent girls*. New York: Ballantine Books.

Pirkis, J. E., Burgess, P. M., Francis, C., Blood, R. W., & Jolley, D. J. (2006). The relation between media reporting of suicide and actual suicide in Australia. *Social Science and Medicine, 62*, 2874–2886.

Plagens, P., Miller, M., Foote, D., & Yoffe, E. (1991, April). Violence in our culture. *Newsweek, 51*, 46–52.

Plant, E. A., & Peruche, B. M. (2005). The consequences of race for police officers' responses to criminal suspects. *Psychological Science, 16*(3), 180–183.

Plant, E. A., Peruche, B. M., & Butz, D. A. (2005). Eliminating automatic racial bias: Making race nondiagnostic for responses to criminal suspects. *Journal of Experimental Social Psychology, 41*(2), 141–156.

Pleck, J. H. (1976). The male sex role: Definitions, problems, and sources of change. *Journal of Social Issues, 32*(3), 155–164.

Plutzer, E. (1987). Determinants of leftist radical belief in the United States: A test of competing theories. *Social Forces, 65*, 1002–1017.

Plutzer, E. (1988). Work life, family life, and women's support of feminism. *American Sociological Review, 53*, 640–649.

Podolny, J. M., & Baron, J. N. (1997). Resources and relationships: Social networks and mobility in the workplace. *American Sociological Review, 62*, 673–693.

Pollard, M., Green, H. D., Kennedy, D., Go, M-H., & Tucker, J. S. (2013). Adolescent friendship networks and trajectories of binge drinking. Rand Corporation Working Papers, WR-998.

Porter, J. R., & Washington, R. E. (1993). Minority identity and self-esteem. *Annual Review of Sociology, 19*, 139–161.

Postmes, T., & Spears, R. (1998). Deindividuation and antinormative behavior: A meta-analysis. *Psychological Bulletin, 123*, 238–259.

Powell, M. A., & Parcell, T. L. (1997). Effects of family structure on the earnings attainment process: Differ-

ences by gender. *Journal of Marriage and the Family, 59*, 419–433.

Powers, C. J., & Bierman, K. L. (2013). The multifaceted impact of peer relations on aggressive–disruptive behavior in early elementary school. *Developmental Psychology, 49*(6), 1174–1186.

Powers, T. A., & Zuroff, D. C. (1988). Interpersonal consequences of overt self-criticism: A comparison with neutral and self-enhancing presentations of self. *Journal of Personality and Social Psychology, 54*, 1054–1062.

Poyatos, F. (1983). *New perspectives in nonverbal communication: Studies in cultural anthropology, social psychology, linguistics, literature, and semantics*. Oxford, UK: Pergamon.

Prager, I. G., & Cutler, B. L. (1990). Attributing traits to oneself and to others: The role of acquaintance level. *Personality and Social Psychology Bulletin, 16*, 309–319.

Pratkanis, A. R., & Greenwald, A. G. (1989). A sociocognitive model of attitude structure and function. In L. Berkowitz (Ed.), *Advances in experimental social psychology* (Vol. 22, pp. 245–285). New York: Academic Press.

Pratkanis, A. R., Greenwald, A. G., Leippe, M. R., & Baumgardner, M. H. (1988). In search of reliable persuasion effects: III. The sleeper effect is dead: Long live the sleeper effect. *Journal of Personality and Social Psychology, 54*(2), 203–218.

Pratt, T. C., Cullen, F. T., Sellers, C. S., Winfree, L. T. Jr., Madensen, T. D., Daigle, L. E., Fearn, N. E., & Gau, J. M. (2013). The empirical status of social learning theory: A meta-analysis. *Justice Quarterly, 27*, 765–802.

Prentice-Dunn, S., & Rogers, R. W. (1980). Effects of deindividuating situational cues and aggressive models on subjective deindividuation and aggression. *Journal of Personality and Social Psychology, 39*(1), 104–113.

Previti, D., & Amato, P. (2003). Why stay married? Rewards, barriers, and marital stability. *Journal of Marriage and Family, 65*, 561–573.

Price, H. E., & Collett, J. L. (2012). The role of exchange and emotion on commitment: A study of teachers. *Social Science Research, 41*(6), 1469–1479.

Priest, R. T., & Sawyer, J. (1967). Proximity and peership: Bases of balance in interpersonal attraction. *American Journal of Sociology, 72*, 633–649.

Prince-Gibson, E., & Schwartz, S. H. (1998). Value priorities and gender. *Social Psychology Quarterly, 61*, 49–67.

Pritchard, R. D., Jones, S. D., Roth, P. L., Stuebing, K. K., & Ekeberg, S. (1988). Effects of group feedback, goal setting, and incentives on organizational productivity. *Journal of Applied Psychology, 73*, 337–358.

Pritchard, R. D., & Watson, M. D. (1992). Understanding and measuring group productivity. In S. Worchel, W. Wood, & J. A. Simpson (Eds.), *Group process and productivity* (pp. 251–275). Newbury Park, CA: Sage.

Pruitt, D. G., & Insko, C. A. (1980). Extension of the Kelley attribution model: The role of comparison-object consensus, target-object consensus, distinctiveness, and consistency. *Journal of Personality and Social Psychology, 39*, 39–58.

Pugh, M. D., & Wahrman, R. (1983). Neutralizing sexism in mixed-sex groups: Do women have to be better than men? *American Journal of Sociology, 88*, 746–762.

Quattrone, G. A. (1986). On the perceptions of a group's variability. In S. Worchel & W. G. Austin (Eds.), *Psychology of intergroup relations* (2nd ed., pp. 25–48). Chicago: Nelson-Hall.

Quattrone, G. A., & Jones, E. E. (1980). The perception of variability within in-groups and out-groups: Implications for the law of small numbers. *Journal of Personality and Social Psychology, 38*, 141–152.

Quillian, L., & Campbell, M. (2003). Beyond black and white: The present and future of multiracial friendship segregation. *American Sociological Review, 68*, 540–566.

Quinn, D. M., & Chaudoir, S. R. (2009). Living with a concealable stigmatized identity: The impact of anticipated stigma, centrality, salience, and cultural stigma on psychological distress and health. *Journal of Personality and Social Psychology, 97*, 634–651.

Quinney, R. (1970). *The social reality of crime.* Boston: Little, Brown.

Rabbie, J. M., & Bekkers, F. (1978). Threatened leadership and intergroup competition. *European Journal of Social Psychology, 8*, 9–20.

Rabow, J., Neuman, C. A., & Hernandez, A. (1987). Cognitive consistency in attitudes, social support, and consumption of alcohol: Additive and interactive effects. *Social Psychology Quarterly, 50*, 56–63.

Rahn, J., & Mason, W. (1987). Political alienation, cohort size, and the Easterlin hypothesis. *American Sociological Review, 52*, 155–169.

Rahn, W. M. (1993). The role of partisan stereotypes in information processing about political candidates. *American Journal of Political Science, 37*(2), 472–496.

Ramirez, A., & Broneck, K. (2009). 'IM me': Instant messaging as relational maintenance and everyday communication. *Journal of Social and Personal Relationships, 26*, 291–314.

Rank, S. G., & Jacobson, C. K. (1977). Hospital nurses' compliance with medication overdose orders: A failure to replicate. *Journal of Health and Social Behavior, 18*, 188–193.

Rashotte, L. S. (2002). What does that smile mean? The meaning of nonverbal behaviors in social interaction. *Social Psychology Quarterly, 65*, 92–102.

Rasinski, K. A., Berktold, J., Smith, T. W., & Albertson, B. L. (2002). *America recovers: A follow-up to a national study of public responses to the September 11th terrorist attacks.* Chicago: National Opinion Research Center.

Ratzan, S. C. (1989). The real agenda setters: Pollsters in the 1988 presidential campaign. *American Behavioral Scientist, 32*, 451–463.

Raven, B. H. (1992). A power/interaction model of interpersonal influence: French and Raven thirty years later. *Journal of Social Behavior and Personality, 7*, 217–244.

Raven, B. H., & Kruglanski, A. W. (1970). Conflict and power. In P. Swingle (Ed.), *The structure of conflict.* (pp. 68–109). New York: Academic Press.

Raven, B. H., & Rietsema, J. (1957). The effects of varied clarity of group goal and group path upon the individual and his relation to the group. *Human Relations, 10*, 29–44.

Ray, M. (1973). Marketing communication and the hierarchy of effects. In P. Clarke (Ed.), *New models for communication research.* (pp. 146–175). Beverly Hills, CA: Sage.

Rea, L., & Parker, R. (1997). *Designing and conducting survey research: A comprehensive guide* (2nd ed.). San Francisco: Jossey-Bass.

Read, J. G., & Gorman, B. K. (2010). Gender and health inequality. In K. Cook & D. S. Masse (Eds.), *Annual Review of Sociology, 36*, 371–386.

Reed, A., & Aquino, K. F. (2003). Moral identity and the expanding circle of moral regard towards out-groups. *Journal of Personality and Social Psychology, 84*(6), 1270–1286.

Rees, C. R., & Segal, M. W. (1984). Role differentiation in groups: The relations between instrumental and expressive leadership. *Small Group Behavior, 15*, 109–123.

Regan, D. T., & Fazio, R. (1977). On the consistency between attitudes and behavior: Look to the method of attitude formation. *Journal of Experimental Social Psychology, 35*, 21–30.

Regan, P. (2000). The role of sexual desire and sexual activity in dating relationships. *Social Behavior and Personality, 28*, 51–59.

Reifenberg, R. J. (1986). The self-serving bias and the use of objective and subjective methods for measuring success and failure. *Journal of Social Psychology, 126*, 627–631.

Reifman, A. S., Larrick, R. P., & Fein, S. (1991). Temper and temperature on the diamond: The heat-aggression relationship in major-league baseball. *Personality and Social Psychology Bulletin, 17*, 580–585.

Reis, H. T., Senchak, M., & Solomon, B. (1985). Sex differences in the intimacy of social interaction: Further examination of potential explanations. *Journal of Personality and Social Psychology, 48*, 1204–1217.

Rempel, J. K., Holmes, J. G., & Zanna, M. P. (1985). Trust in a close relationship. *Journal of Personality and Social Psychology, 49*, 95–112.

Renfrow, D. (2004). A cartography of passing in everyday life. *Symbolic Interaction, 27*, 485–506.

Renninger, L., Wade, T., & Grammar, K. (2004). Getting that female glance: Patterns and consequences of male nonverbal behavior in courtship contexts. *Evolution and Human Behavior, 25*, 416–431.

Rennison, C. M. (2001). *Violent victimization and race, 1993–98.* U.S. Department of Justice, Office of Justice Programs, Bureau of Justice Statistics.

Rentfrow, P. J., & Gosling, S. D. (2007). The content and validity of music-genre stereotypes among college students. *Psychology of Music, 35*(2), 306–326.

Repetti, R. (1987). Individual and common components of the social environment at work and psychological well-being. *Journal of Personality and Social Psychology, 52,* 710–720.

Repetti, R. (1989). Effects of daily workload on subsequent behavior during marital interaction: The roles of social withdrawal and spouse support. *Journal of Personality and Social Psychology, 57,* 651–659.

Reskin, B., & Padavic, I. (1994). *Women and men at work.* Thousand Oaks, CA: Pine Forge Press.

Rettinger, D. A., & Kramer, Y. (2009). Situational and personal causes of student cheating. *Research in Higher Education, 50,* 293–313.

Reyers, A., & Matusitz, J. (2012). Emotional regulation at Walt Disney World: An impression management view. *Journal of Workplace Behavioral Health, 27*(3), 139–159.

Reynolds, J. R. (1997). The effects of industrial employment conditions on job-related distress. *Journal of Health and Social Behavior, 38,* 105–116.

Reynolds, P. D. (1984). Leaders never quit: Talking, silence, and influence in interpersonal groups. *Small Group Behavior, 15,* 404–413.

Rhine, R. J., & Severance, L. J. (1970). Ego-involvement, discrepancy, source credibility, and attitude change. *Journal of Personality and Social Psychology, 16,* 175–190.

Rhodes, N., & Wood, W. (1992). Self-esteem and intelligence affect influenceability: The mediating role of message reception. *Psychological Bulletin, 111,* 156.

Rice, R. W., Marwick, N. J., Chemers, M. M., & Bentley, J. C. (1982). Task performance and satisfaction: Least preferred coworker (LPC) as a moderator. *Personality and Social Psychology Bulletin, 8,* 534–541.

Richeson, J. A., & Ambady, N. (2003). Effects of situational power on automatic racial prejudice. *Journal of Experimental Social Psychology, 39,* 177–183.

Rideout, V., & Hamel, E. (2006). *The media family: Electronic media in the lives of infants, toddlers, preschoolers and their parents.* Menlo Park, CA: Kaiser Family Foundation.

Ridgeway, C. L. (1987). Nonverbal behavior, dominance, and the basis of status in task groups. *American Sociological Review, 52,* 683–694.

Ridgeway, C. L. (2006). Status construction theory. In P. J. Burke (Ed.), *Contemporary social psychological theories* (pp. 301–323). Palo Alto, CA: Stanford University Press.

Ridgeway, C. L. (2011). *Framed by gender: How gender inequality persists in the modern world.* New York: Oxford University Press.

Ridgeway, C. L., & Correll, S. J. (2004). Unpacking the gender system: A theoretical perspective on gender beliefs and social relations. *Gender and Society, 18*(4), 510–531.

Ridgeway, C. L., & Smith-Lovin, L. (1999). The gender system and interaction. *Annual Review of Sociology, 25,* 191–216.

Ridgeway, C. L., & Walker, H. A. (1995). Status structures. In K. S. Cook, G. A. Fine, & J. S. House (Eds.), *Sociological perspectives on social psychology* (pp. 281–310). Boston: Allyn and Bacon.

Riggio, R. E., & Friedman, H. S. (1983). Individual differences and cues to deception. *Journal of Personality and Social Psychology, 45,* 899–915.

Rigney, J. (1962). A developmental study of cognitive equivalence transformations and their use in the acquisition and processing of information. Unpublished honors thesis, Radcliffe College, Cambridge, MA.

Riketta, M. (2005). Cognitive differentiation between self, ingroup, and outgroup: The roles of identification and perceived intergroup conflict. *European Journal of Social Psychology, 35,* 97–106.

Riley, M. (1987). On the significance of age in sociology. *American Sociological Review, 52,* 1–14.

Rindfuss, R., Swicegood, C. G., & Rosenfeld, R. (1987). Disorder in the life course: How common and does it matter? *American Sociological Review, 52,* 785–801.

Rinehart, A. J., & Dunwoody, P. T. (2005, April). *Groupthink in the Bush administration's decision for Operation Iraqi Freedom.* Poster session presented at the annual Western Pennsylvania Undergraduate Psychology Conference, Chatham College, Pittsburgh, PA.

Ringelmann, M. (1913). Recherches sur les moteurs animés: Travail de l'homme [Research on animate sources of power: The work of man]. *Annales de l' Institut National Agronomique, 2e Série, 12,* 1–40.

Ringold, D. J. (2002). Boomerang effects in response to public health interventions: Some unintended consequences in the alcoholic beverage market. *Journal of Consumer Policy, 25,* 27–63.

Riordan, C. (1978). Equal-status interracial contact: A review and revision of the concept. *International Journal of Intercultural Relations, 2,* 161–185.

Riordan, C., & Ruggiero, J. A. (1980). Producing equal-status interracial interaction: A replication. *Social Psychology Quarterly, 43,* 131–136.

Riordan, C. A., Marlin, N. A., & Kellogg, R. T. (1983). The effectiveness of accounts following transgression. *Social Psychology Quarterly, 46,* 213–219.

Rivera, L. (2008). Managing "spoiled" national identity: War, tourism and memory in Croatia. *American Sociological Review, 73,* 613–634.

Robertson, J. F., & Simons, R. L. (1989). Family factors, self-esteem, and adolescent depression. *Journal of Marriage and the Family, 51,* 125–138.

Robinson, D. T., Smith-Lovin, L., & Tsoudis, O. (1994). Heinous crime or unfortunate accident: The effects of remorse on responses to mock criminal confessions. *Social Problems, 73,* 175–190.

Robinson, J. W., & Preston, J. D. (1976). Equal-status contact and the modification of racial prejudice: A reexamination of the contact hypothesis. *Social Forces, 54,* 911–924.

Rodriguez, J., Cargile, A., & Rich, M. (2004). Reactions to

African-American Vernacular English: Do more phonological features matter? *Western Journal of Black Studies, 28,* 407–414.

Rogers, M., Miller, N., Mayer, F. S., & Duval, S. (1982). Personal responsibility and salience of the request for help: Determinants of the relation between negative affect and helping behavior. *Journal of Personality and Social Psychology, 43*(5), 956–970.

Rogers, R. G. (1995). Marriage, sex, and mortality. *Journal of Marriage and the Family, 57,* 515–526.

Rogers, R. W. (1980). Expressions of aggression: Aggression-inhibiting effects of anonymity to authority and threatened retaliation. *Personality and Social Psychology Bulletin, 6,* 315–320.

Rogers, S., & May, D. (2003). Spillover between marital quality and job satisfaction: Long-term patterns and gender differences. *Journal of Marriage and Family, 65,* 482–495.

Rohrer, J. H., Baron, S. H., Hoffman, E. L., & Swander, D. V. (1954). The stability of autokinetic judgments. *Journal of Abnormal and Social Psychology, 49,* 595–597.

Rokeach, M. (1973). *The nature of human values.* New York: Free Press.

Rommetveit, R. (1955). *Social norms and roles.* Minneapolis: University of Minnesota Press.

Root, M. (1995). The psychology of Asian American women. In H. Landrine (Ed.), *Bringing cultural diversity to feminist psychology: Theory, research, and practice* (pp. 241–263). Washington, DC: American Psychological Association.

Rose, A., & Rudolph, K. (2006). A review of sex-differences in peer relationship processes: Potential trade-offs for the emotional and behavioral development of girls and boys. *Psychological Bulletin, 132,* 98–131.

Rose, H., & Rose, S. (2000). *Alas poor Darwin: Arguments against evolutionary psychology.* New York: Harmony Books.

Rose, S., & Frieze, I. H. (1993). Young singles' contemporary dating scripts. *Sex Roles, 28,* 499–509.

Rosen, L., Principe, C., & Langlois, J. (2013). Feedback seeking in early adolescence. *Journal of Early Adolescence, 33,* 363–377.

Rosen, S. (1984). Some paradoxical status implications of helping and being helped. In E. Staub, D. Bar-Tal, J. Karylowski, & J. Reykowski (Eds.), *Development and maintenance of prosocial behavior: International perspectives on positive morality.* (pp. 359–377). New York: Plenum.

Rosenbaum, M. E. (1986). The repulsion hypothesis: On the nondevelopment of relationships. *Journal of Personality and Social Psychology, 51,* 1156–1166.

Rosenberg, L. A. (1961). Group size, prior experience, and conformity. *Journal of Abnormal and Social Psychology, 63,* 436–437.

Rosenberg, M. (1965). *Society and the adolescent self-image.* Princeton, NJ: Princeton University Press.

Rosenberg, M. (1973). Which significant others? *American Behavioral Scientist, 16,* 829–860.

Rosenberg, M. (1990). The self-concept: Social product

and social force. In M. Rosenberg & R. H. Turner (Eds.), *Social psychology: Sociological perspectives.* (pp. 593–624). New Brunswick, NJ: Transaction.

Rosenberg, M., & Pearlin, L. (1978). Social class and self-esteem among children and adults. *American Journal of Sociology, 84,* 53–77.

Rosenberg, M., Schooler, C., & Schoenbach, C. (1989). Self-esteem and adolescent problems: Modeling reciprocal effects. *American Sociological Review, 54,* 1004–1018.

Rosenberg, M., Schooler, C., Schoenbach, C., & Rosenberg, F. (1995). Global self-esteem and specific self-esteem: Different concepts, different outcomes. *American Sociological Review, 60,* 141–156.

Rosenberg, M., & Simmons, R. (1972). *Black and White self-esteem: The urban school child.* Washington, DC: American Sociological Association.

Rosenberg, M. J., & Abelson, R. (1960). An analysis of cognitive balancing. In C. Hovland & M. Rosenberg (Eds.), *Attitude organization and change.* (pp. 112–163). New Haven, CT: Yale University Press.

Rosenberg, S. V., Nelson, C., & Vivekananthan, P. S. (1968). A multidimensional approach to the structure of personality impressions. *Journal of Personality and Social Psychology, 9,* 283–294.

Rosenberg, S. V., & Sedlak, A. (1972). Structural representations in implicit personality theory. In L. Berkowitz (Ed.), *Advances in experimental social psychology* (Vol. 6, pp. 235–297). New York: Academic Press.

Rosenblatt, A., & Greenberg, J. (1988). Depression and interpersonal attraction: The role of perceived similarity. *Journal of Personality and Social Psychology, 55,* 112–119.

Rosenblatt, A., & Greenberg, J. (1991). Examining the world of the depressed: Do depressed people prefer others who are depressed? *Journal of Personality and Social Psychology, 60,* 620–629.

Rosenfeld, M. J., & Thomas, R. J. (2012). Searching for a mate: The rise of the Internet as a social intermediary. *American Sociological Review, 77,* 523–547.

Rosenhan, D. L. (1973). On being sane in insane places. *Science, 179,* 250–258.

Rosenhan, D. L., Salovey, P., & Hargis, K. (1981). The joys of helping: Focus of attention mediates the impact of positive affect on altruism. *Journal of Personality and Social Psychology, 40*(5), 899–905.

Rosenkoetter, L. I., Rosenkoetter, S. E., & Acock, A. C. (2009). Television violence: An intervention to reduce its impact on children. *Journal of Applied Developmental Psychology, 30*(4), 381–397.

Rosenkoetter, L. I., Rosenkoetter, S. E., Ozretich, R. A., & Acock, A. C. (2004). Mitigating the harmful effects of violent television. *Journal of Applied Developmental Psychology, 25,* 25–47.

Rosenthal, R. (1966). *Experimenter effects in behavioral research.* New York: Appleton-Century-Crofts.

Rosenthal, R. (1980). Replicability and experimenter influence: Experimenter effects in behavioral research. *Parapsychology, 11,* 5–11.

Rosenthal, R., & Jacobson, L. (1968). *Pygmalion in the classroom: Teacher expectation and pupils' intellectual development*. New York: Rinehart and Winston.

Roskos-Ewoldsen, D. R., Bichsel, J., & Hoffman, K. (2002). The influence of accessibility of source likability on persuasion. *Journal of Experimental Social Psychology*, *38*, 137–143.

Ross, A. S. (1971). Effect of increased responsibility on bystander intervention: The presence of children. *Journal of Personality and Social Psychology*, *19*(3), 306.

Ross, C. E., Mirowsky, J., & Goldsteen, K. (1990). The impact of the family on health: The decade in review. *Journal of Marriage and the Family*, *52*, 1059–1078.

Ross, C. E., & Van Willigen, M. (1997). Education and the subjective quality of life. *Journal of Health and Social Behavior*, *38*, 275–297.

Ross, C. E., & Wu, C. (1995). The links between education and health. *American Sociological Review*, *60*, 719–745.

Ross, L. (1977). The intuitive psychologist and his shortcomings: Distortion in the attribution process. In L. Berkowitz (Ed.), *Advances in experimental social psychology* (Vol. 10, pp. 173–220). New York: Academic Press.

Ross, L., Lepper, M. R., & Hubbard, M. (1975). Perseverance in self-perception and social perception: biased attributional processes in the debriefing paradigm. *Journal of Personality and Social Psychology*, *32*(5), 880–892.

Ross, L. D. (2001). Getting down to fundamentals: Lay dispositionism and the attributions of psychologists. *Psychological Inquiry*, *12*, 37–40.

Ross, M., & Fletcher, G. (1985). Attribution and social perception. In G. Lindzey & E. Aronson (Eds.), *The handbook of social psychology* (3rd ed., pp. 73–122). Reading, MA: Addison-Wesley.

Ross, M., & Lumsden, H. (1982). Attributions of responsibility in sports settings: It's not how you play the game but whether you win or lose. In H. Hiebsch, H. Brandstatter & H. H. Kelley (Eds.), *Social psychology*. East Berlin: Deutscher Verlag der Wissenschaften.

Rotenberg, K. J., & Mann, L. (1986). The development of the norm of the reciprocity of self-disclosure and its function in children's attraction to peers. *Child Development*, *57*, 1349–1357.

Roth, D. L., Wiebe, D. J., Fillingian, R. B., & Shay, K. A. (1989). Life events, fitness, hardiness, and health: A simultaneous analysis of proposed stress-resistance effects. *Journal of Personality and Social Psychology*, *57*, 136–142.

Rothbart, M. (1996). Category-exemplar dynamics and stereotype change. *International Journal of Intercultural Relations*, *20*(3), 305–321.

Rothbart, M., Dawes, R., & Park, B. (1984). Stereotypes and sampling biases in intergroup perception. In J. R. Eiser (Ed.), *Attitudinal judgment* (pp. 109–134). New York: Springer Verlag.

Rothbart, M., Fulero, S., Jensen, C., Howard, J., & Birrell, B. (1978). From individual to group impressions: Availability heuristics in stereotype formation. *Journal of Experimental Social Psychology*, *14*, 237–255.

Rothbart, M., & John, O. P. (1985). Social categorization and behavioral episodes: A cognitive analysis of the effects of intergroup contact. *Journal of Social Issues*, *41*(3), 81–104.

Rotheram-Borus, M. J. (1990). Adolescents' reference group choices, self-esteem, and adjustment. *Journal of Personality and Social Psychology*, *59*, 1075–1081.

Rotton, J., & Cohn, E. G. (2004). Outdoor temperature, climate control, and criminal assault: The spatial and temporal ecology of violence. *Environment and Behavior*, *36*(2), 276–306.

Rotton, J., & Frey, J. (1985). Air pollution, weather, and violent crimes: Concomitant time-series analyses of archival data. *Journal of Personality and Social Psychology*, *49*, 1207–1220.

Ruback, R. (1987). Deserted (and nondeserted) aisles: Territorial intrusion can produce persistence, not flight. *Social Psychology Quarterly*, *50*, 270–276.

Ruback, R. B., Pape, K. D., & Doriot, P. (1989). Waiting for a phone: Intrusion on callers leads to territorial defense. *Social Psychology Quarterly*, *52*, 232–241.

Rubin, M., & Hewstone, M. (1998). Social identity theory's self-esteem hypothesis: A review and some suggestions for clarification. *Personality and Social Psychology Review*, *2*, 40–62.

Rubin, Z. (1970). Measurement of romantic love. *Journal of Personality and Social Psychology*, *16*, 265–273.

Rubin, Z. (1974). From liking to loving: Patterns of attraction in dating relationships. In T. Huston (Ed.), *Foundations of interpersonal attraction.* (pp. 383–402). New York: Academic Press.

Rubin, Z., Hill, C., Peplau, L., & Dunkel-Scheker, C. (1980). Self-disclosure in dating couples: Sex roles and the ethic of openness. *Journal of Marriage and the Family*, *42*, 305–317.

Rudé, G. (1964). *The crowd in history*. New York: Wiley.

Ruiter, R. A. C., Kok, G., Verplanken, B., & van Eersel, G. (2003). Strengthening the persuasive impact of fear appeals: The role of action framing. *Journal of Social Psychology*, *143*, 397–400.

Rusbult, C. E. (1983). A longitudinal test of the investment model: The development (and deterioration) of satisfaction and commitment in heterosexual involvements. *Journal of Personality and Social Psychology*, *45*, 101–117.

Rusbult, C. E., Johnson, D. J., & Morrow, G. D. (1986). Predicting satisfaction and commitment in adult romantic involvements: An assessment of the generalizability of the investment model. *Social Psychology Quarterly*, *49*, 81–89.

Rusbult, C. E., Verette, J., Whitney, G. A., Slovik, L. A., & Lipkus, I. (1991). Accommodation processes in close relationships: Theory and preliminary empirical evidence. *Journal of Personality and Social Psychology*, *60*, 53–78.

Rusbult, C. E., Zembrodt, I. M., & Gunn, L. K. (1982). Exit, voice, loyalty, and neglect: Responses to dissatisfaction in romantic involvement. *Journal of Personality and Social Psychology, 43,* 1230–1242.

Rushton, J. P., Russell, R. J., & Wells, P. A. (1984). Genetic similarity theory: Beyond kin selection. *Behaviour Genetics, 14,* 179–193.

Ryan, K. (1988). Rape and seduction scripts. *Psychology of Women Quarterly, 12,* 237–245.

Ryan, K. M. (2011). The relationship between rape myths and sexual scripts: The social construction of rape. *Sex Roles, 65*(11–12), 774–782.

Ryder, N. B. (1965). The cohort as a concept in the study of social change. *American Sociological Review, 30,* 843–861.

Ryen, A. H., & Kahn, A. (1975). The effects of intergroup orientation on group attitudes and proxemic behavior. *Journal of Personality and Social Psychology, 31,* 302–310.

Ryoko, M. (1979, December 4). The new barbarians: A glimpse of the future. *Cincinnati Post.*

Sabini, J., Siepmann, M., & Stein, J. (2001). The really fundamental attribution error in social psychological research. *Psychological Inquiry, 12,* 1–15.

Sacks, H., Schegloff, E., & Jefferson, G. (1978). A simplest systematics for the organization of turn-taking in conversations. In J. Schenkein (Ed.), *Studies in the organization of conversational interaction.* (pp. 696–735). New York: Academic Press.

Saegert, S. C., Swap, W., & Zajonc, R. B. (1973). Exposure, context, and interpersonal attraction. *Journal of Personality and Social Psychology, 25,* 234–242.

Sagarin, E. (1975). *Deviants and deviance.* New York: Praeger.

Sailes, G. A. (1998). The African American athlete: Social myths and stereotypes. In G. A. Sailes (Ed.), *African Americans in sport: Contemporary themes* (pp. 183–198). New Brunswick: NJ: Transaction.

Saito, Y. (1988). Situational characteristics as the determinants of adopting distributive justice principles: II. *Japanese Journal of Experimental Social Psychology, 27,* 131–138.

Sakurai, M. M. (1975). Small group cohesiveness and detrimental conformity. *Sociometry, 38,* 340–357.

Salmivalli, C., & Nieminen, E. (2002). Proactive and reactive aggression among school bullies, victims, and bully-victims. *Aggressive Behavior, 28*(1), 30–44.

Salovey, P., Mayer, J. D., & Rosenhan, D. L. (1991). Mood and helping: Mood as a motivator of helping and helping as a regulator of mood. In M. S. Clark (Ed.), *Review of personality and social psychology, Vol. 12. Prosocial behavior* (pp. 215–237). Newbury Park, CA: Sage.

Sammon, S., Reznikoff, M., & Geisinger, K. (1985). Psychosocial development and stressful life events among religious professionals. *Journal of Personality and Social Psychology, 48,* 676–687.

Sampson, R. J., & Laub, J. H. (1990). Crime and deviance over the life course: The salience of adult social bonds. *American Sociological Review, 55,* 609–627.

Samuels, F. (1970). The intra- and inter-competitive group. *Sociological Quarterly, 11,* 390–396.

Sanday, P. R. (1981). The socio-cultural context of rape: A cross-cultural study. *Journal of Social Issues, 37*(4), 5–27.

Sanday, P. R. (2003). Rape-free versus rape-prone: How culture makes a difference. In C. B. Travis (Ed.), *Evolution, gender, and rape,* 337–362. Cambridge, MA: MIT Press.

Sande, G. N., Goethals, G. R., & Radloff, C. E. (1988). Perceiving one's own traits and others': The multifaceted self. *Journal of Personality and Social Psychology, 54,* 13–20.

Sarbin, T., & Rosenberg, B. (1955). Contributions to role-taking theory IV: A method for obtaining a qualitative estimate of the self. *Journal of Social Psychology, 42,* 71–81.

Sarkisian, N., & Gerstel, N. (2004). Kin support among blacks and whites: Race and family organization. *American Sociological Review, 69,* 812–837.

Sawdon, A. M., Cooper, M., & Seabrook, R. (2007). The relationship between self-discrepancies, eating disorder and depressive symptoms in women. *European Eating Disorders Review, 15,* 207–212.

Sawyer, A. (1973). The effects of repetition of refutational and supportive advertising appeals. *Journal of Marketing Research, 10,* 23–33.

Sayer, L., Bianchi, S., & Robinson, J. (2004). Are parents investing less in children? Trends in mothers' and fathers' time with children. *American Journal of Sociology, 110,* 1–43.

Scanlon, M., & Wassink, A. B. (2010). African American English in Seattle: Accommodation and intraspeaker variation in the Pacific Northwest. *American Speech, 85,* 205–224.

Schachter, S. (1964). The interaction of cognitive and physiological determinants of emotional state. *Advances in Experimental Social Psychology, 1,* 49–80.

Schachter, S., & Singer, J. (1962). Cognitive, social, and physiological determinants of emotional state. *Psychological Review, 69*(5), 379–399.

Schaible, L. M., & Gecas, V. (2010). The impact of emotional labor and value dissonance on burnout among police officers. *Police Quarterly, 13*(3), 316–341.

Schaller, M., & Cialdini, R. B. (1988). The economics of empathic helping: Support for a mood management motive. *Journal of Experimental Social Psychology, 24*(2), 163–181.

Schank, R. C., & Abelson, R. P. (1977). *Scripts, plans, goals and understanding.* Hillsdale, NJ: Erlbaum.

Schau, H., & Gill, M. (2003). We are what we post? Self-presentation in personal web space. *Journal of Consumer Research, 30,* 385–404.

Scheff, T. (1966). *Being mentally ill.* Chicago: Aldine.

Scheff, T. J., & Retzinger, S. M. (2001). *Emotions and violence: Shame and rage in destructive conflicts.* Lincoln, NE: iUniverse.

Schegloff, E. (1968). Sequencing in conversational openings. *American Anthropologist, 70,* 1075–1095.

Scher, S. J. (1997). Measuring the consequences of injustice. *Personality and Social Psychology Bulletin, 23,* 482–497.

Scherer, K. R. (1979). Nonlinguistic vocal indicators of emotion and psychopathology. In C. E. Izard (Ed.), *Emotions in personality and psychopathology*. (pp. 493–529). New York: Plenum.

Scherer, S. E. (1974). Proxemic behavior of primary school children as a function of their socioeconomic class and subculture. *Journal of Personality and Social Psychology, 29*, 800–805.

Shestowsky, D., Wegener, D. T., & Fabrigar, L. R. (1998). Need for cognition and interpersonal influence: Individual differences in impact on dyadic decisions. *Journal of Personality and Social Psychology, 74*(5), 1317–1328.

Schiffenbauer, A., & Schiavo, R. S. (1976). Physical distance and attraction: An intensification effect. *Journal of Experimental Social Psychology, 12*, 274–282.

Schiffrin, D. (1977). Opening encounters. *American Sociological Review, 42*, 679–691.

Schifter, D. E., & Ajzen, I. (1985). Intention, perceived control, and weight loss: An application of the theory of planned behavior. *Journal of Personality and Social Psychology, 45*, 843–851.

Schlenker, B. R. (1975). Self-presentation. Managing the impression of consistency when reality interferes with self-enhancement. *Journal of Personality and Social Psychology, 32*, 1030–1037.

Schlenker, B. R. (2003). Self-presentation. In M. R. Leary & J. P. Tangney (Eds.), *Handbook of self and identity* (pp. 492–518). New York: Guilford.

Schlenker, B. R., & Weigold, M. F. (1992). Interpersonal processes involving impression regulation and management. *Annual Review of Psychology, 43*, 133–168.

Schlenker, B. R., Weigold, M. E., & Hallam, J. K. (1990). Self-serving attributions in social context: Effects of self-esteem and social pressure. *Journal of Personality and Social Psychology, 58*, 855–863.

Schmidtke, J. M. (2007). The relationship between social norm consensus, perceived similarity, and observer reactions to coworker theft. *Human Resource Management, 46*, 561–582.

Schmitt, D. P., Alcalay, L., Allik, J., Angleiter, A., Ault, L., Austers, I., et al. (2004). Patterns and universals of mate poaching across 53 nations: The effects of sex, culture, and personality on romantically attracting another person's partner. *Journal of Personality and Social Psychology, 86*(4), 560–584.

Schmitt, D. P., & Buss, D. M. (1996). Strategic self-promotion and competitor derogation: Sex and context effects in the perceived effectiveness of mate attraction tactics. *Journal of Personality and Social Psychology, 70*, 1185–1204.

Schmitt, D. P., & Buss, D. M. (2001). Human mate poaching: Tactics and temptations for infiltrating existing mateships. *Journal of Personality and Social Psychology, 80*(6), 894–917.

Schmitt, D. P., & Shackelford, T. K. (2003). Nifty ways to leave your lover: The tactics people use to entice and disguise the process of human mate poaching. *Personality and Social Psychology Bulletin, 29*(8), 1018–1035.

Schnabel, J. (2009). The black box. *Nature, 459*, 765–768.

Schnittker, J. (2000). Gender and reactions to psychological problems: An examination of social tolerance and perceived dangerousness. *Journal of Health and Social Behavior, 41*, 224–240.

Schnittker, J. (2002). The self-esteem of Chinese immigrants. *Social Psychology Quarterly, 65*, 56–76.

Schoenborn, C. (2004, December 15). Marital status and health: United States, 1999–2002. (Advance Data from Vital and Health Statistics No. 351). Hyattsville, MD: National Center for Health Statistics.

Schooler, C. (1996). Cultural and social-structural explanations of cross-national psychological differences. *Annual Review of Sociology, 22*, 323–349.

Schooler, C., Mulatu, M. S., & Oates, G. (2004). Occupational self-direction, intellectual functioning, and self-directed orientation in older workers: Findings and implications for individuals and societies. *American Journal of Sociology, 110*, 161–197.

Schrauger, J. S., & Schoeneman, T. (1979). Symbolic interactionist view of self-concept: Through the looking glass darkly. *Psychological Bulletin, 86*, 549–573.

Schroeder, D. A., Penner, L. A., Dovidio, J. F., & Piliavin, J. A. (1995). *The psychology of helping and altruism: Problems and puzzles*. New York: McGraw-Hill.

Schrum, W., & Creek, N. A. (1987). Social structure during the school years: Onset of the degrouping process. *American Sociological Review, 52*, 218–223.

Schulz, A., Williams, D., Israel, B., Becker, A., Parker, E., James, S., & Jackson, J. (2000). Unfair treatment, neighborhood effects, and mental health in the Detroit metropolitan area. *Journal of Health and Social Behavior, 41*, 314–332.

Schuman, H., & Johnson, M. (1976). Attitudes and behavior. In A. Inkeles, J. Coleman & N. Smelser (Eds.), *Annual Review of Sociology* (Vol. 2, pp. 161–207). Palo Alto, CA: Annual Reviews.

Schutte, J., & Light, J. (1978). The relative importance of proximity and status for friendship choices in social hierarchies. *Social Psychology, 41*, 260–264.

Schutte, N. S., Kendrick, D. T., & Sadalla, E. K. (1985). The search for predictable settings: Situational prototypes, constraint, and behavioral variation. *Journal of Personality and Social Psychology, 49*, 121–128.

Schwartz, B. (2004, December). The tyranny of choice. *Scientific American Mind*. www.scientificamerican.com/article/the-tyranny-of-choice.

Schwartz, C., & Graf, N. (2007). Assortative matching among same-sex and different-sex couples in the United States, 1990–2000 (Working paper No. 2007–21). Madison, WI: Center for Demography and Ecology.

Schwartz, S. H. (1978). Temporal instability as a moderator of the attitude-behavior relationship. *Journal of Personality and Social Psychology, 36*, 715–724.

Schwartz, S. H. (1992). Universals in the content and structure of values: Theoretical advances and empirical tests in 20 countries. In M. Zanna (Ed.), *Advances in experimental social psychology* (Vol. 25, pp. 1–65). Orlando, FL: Academic Press.

Schwartz, S. H. (1994). Are there universal aspects in the content and structure of values? *Journal of Social Issues, 50,* 19–45.

Schwartz, S. H., & Clausen, G. T. (1970). Responsibility, norms, and helping in an emergency. *Journal of Personality and Social Psychology, 16*(2), 299–310.

Schwartz, S. H., & Fleishman, J. (1978). Personal norms and the mediation of legitimacy effects on helping. *Social Psychology, 41,* 306–315.

Schwartz, S. H., & Gottlieb, A. (1976). Bystander reactions to a violent theft: Crime in Jerusalem. *Journal of Personality and Social Psychology, 34*(6), 1188–1199.

Schwartz, S. H., & Howard, J. A. (1980). Explanations of the moderating effect of responsibility denial on personal norm-behavior relationship. *Social Psychology Quarterly, 43,* 441–446.

Schwartz, S. H., & Howard, J. A. (1981). A normative decision-making model of altruism. In J. P. Rushton & R. M. Sorrentino (Eds.), *Altruism and helping behavior.* (pp. 189–211). Hillsdale, NJ: Erlbaum.

Schwartz, S. H., & Howard, J. A. (1982). Helping and cooperation: A self-based motivational model. In V. J. Derlega & J. Grzelak (Eds.), *Cooperation and helping behavior: Theories and research* (pp. 327–353). New York: Academic Press.

Schwartz, S. H., & Howard, J. A. (1984). Internalized values as motivators of altruism. In E. Staub, E. Bar-Tal, J. Karylowski, & J. Reykowski (Eds.), *Development and maintenance of prosocial behavior: International perspectives on positive morality.* (pp. 229–255). New York: Plenum.

Schwarz, N., Groves, R., & Schuman, H. (1998). Survey methods. In D. Gilbert, S. Fiske, & G. Lindzey (Eds.), *The handbook of social psychology* (4th ed., Vol. 1, pp. 143–179). Boston: McGraw-Hill.

Schweingruber, D., & McPhail, C. (1999). A method for systematically observing and recording collective action. *Sociological Methods and Research, 27*(4), 451–498.

Schweingruber, D., & Wohlstein, R. (2005). The madding crowd goes to school: Myths about crowds in introductory sociology textbooks. *Teaching Sociology, 33,* 136–153.

Scott, M., & Lyman, S. (1968). Accounts. *American Sociological Review, 33,* 46–62.

Scott, R. (1976). Deviance, sanctions, and social integration in small-scale societies. *Social Forces, 54,* 604–620.

Scotton, C. M. (1983). The negotiation of identities in conversation. *International Journal of the Sociology of Language, 44,* 115–136.

Searle, J. R. (1979). *Expression and meaning: Studies in the theory of speech acts.* Cambridge, UK: Cambridge University Press.

Sears, D., Fu, M., Henry, P. J., & Bui, K. (2003). The origins and persistence of ethnic identity among the "New Immigrant" groups. *Social Psychology Quarterly, 66,* 419–437.

Sears, D. O., & Freedman, J. L. (1967). Selective exposure to information: A critical review. *Public Opinion Quarterly, 31,* 194–213.

Sears, D. O., & Whitney, R. E. (1973). Political persuasion. In I. de S. Pool, W. Schramm, N. Maccoby, & E. Parker (Eds.), *Handbook of communication.* (pp. 153–289). Chicago: Rand McNally.

Sedikides, C., & Jackson, J. M. (1990). Social impact theory: A field test of source strength, source immediacy, and number of targets. *Basic and Applied Social Psychology, 11,* 273–281.

Seedman, A. A., & Hellman, P. (1975). *Chief!* New York: Avon.

Seeman, M. (1975). Alienation studies. In A. Inkeles, J. Coleman, & N. Smelser (Eds.), *Annual Review of Sociology* (Vol. 1, pp. 91–123). Palo Alto, CA: Annual Reviews.

Seeman, M., Seeman, M., & Sayles, M. (1985). Social networks and health status: A longitudinal analysis. *Social Psychology Quarterly, 48,* 237–248.

Segal, B. E. (1965). Contact, compliance, and distance among Jewish and non-Jewish undergraduates. *Social Problems, 13,* 66–74.

Select Committee on Intelligence, U.S. Senate. (2004). *Report on the U.S. intelligence community's prewar intelligence assessments on Iraq.* http://intelligence. senate.gov/ conclusions.pdf.

Semin, G. R., & Manstead, A. S. R. (1982). The social implications of embarrassment displays and restitution behaviour. *European Journal of Social Psychology, 12,* 367–377.

Semin, G. R., & Manstead, A. S. R. (1983). *The accountability of conduct: A social psychological analysis.* London: Academic Press.

Seplaki, C., Goldman, N., Weinstein, M., & Lin, Y.-H. (2003). Before and after the 1999 Chi-Chi earthquake: Traumatic events and depressive symptoms in an older population (Working Paper No. 2003–02). Princeton University: Office of Population Research.

Serbin, L., & O'Leary, K. (1975). How nursery schools teach girls to shut up. *Psychology Today, 9,* 56–58.

Serpe, R. T. (1987). Stability and change in self: A structural symbolic interactionist explanation. *Social Psychology Quarterly, 50,* 44–55.

Sewell, W. H., & Hauser, R. M. (1975). *Education, occupation, and earnings: Achievement in the early career.* New York: Academic Press.

Sewell, W. H., & Hauser, R. M. (1980). The Wisconsin longitudinal study of social and psychological factors in aspirations and achievements. *Research in Sociology of Education and Socialization, 1,* 59–99.

Sewell, W. H., Hauser, R. M., & Wolf, W. (1980). Sex, schooling, and occupational status. *American Journal of Sociology, 86,* 551–583.

Shapiro, S. P. (1990). Collaring the crime, not the criminal: Considering the concept of white-collar crime. *American Sociological Review, 55,* 346–365.

Sharkey, W., Kim, M., & Digs, R. (2001). Intentional embarrassment: A look at embarrassors' and targets' perspectives. *Personality and Individual Differences, 31,* 1261–1272.

Sharkey, W. F., & Stafford, L. (1990). Responses to embarrassment. *Human Communication Research, 17,* 315–342.

Shaver, P., Schwartz, J., Kirson, D., & O'Connor, C. (1987). Emotion knowledge: Further exploration of a prototype approach. *Journal of Personality and Social Psychology, 52*(6), 1061–1086.

Shaver, P. R., Wu, S., & Schwartz, J. C. (1992). *Cross-cultural similarities and differences in emotion and its representation.* Newbury Park, CA: Sage.

Shaw, B. A., Liang, J., & Krause, N. (2010). Age and race differences in trajectories of self-esteem. *Psychology and Aging, 25,* 84–94.

Shaw, M., & Costanzo, P. (1982). *Theories of social psychology* (2nd ed.). New York: McGraw-Hill.

Shaw, M. E., & Shaw, L. M. (1962). Some effects of sociometric grouping upon learning in a second grade classroom. *Journal of Social Psychology, 57,* 453–458.

Shell, R. M., & Eisenberg, N. (1992). A developmental model of recipients' reactions to aid. *Psychological Bulletin, 111,* 413–433.

Sheng, S., Holbrook, M., Kumaraguru, P., Cranor, L. F., & Downs, J. (2010, April). Who falls for phish? A demographic analysis of phishing susceptibility and effectiveness of interventions. In *Proceedings of the 28th international conference on human factors in computing systems* (pp. 373–382). ACM.

Sherif, M. (1935). A study of some social factors in perception. *Archives of Psychology, 27*(187), 1–60.

Sherif, M. (1936). *The psychology of social norms.* New York: Harper & Row.

Sherif, M. (1966). *In common predicament.* Boston: Houghton Mifflin.

Sherif, M., Harvey, O. J., White, B. J., Hood, W. R., & Sherif, C. W. (1961). *Intergroup cooperation and competition: The Robbers Cave experiment.* Norman, OK: University Book Exchange.

Sherif, M., & Sherif, C. (1964). *Exploration into conformity and deviation of adolescents.* New York: Harper & Row.

Sherif, M., & Sherif, C. W. (1982). Production of intergroup conflict and its resolution—Robbers Cave experiment. In J. W. Reich (Ed.), *Experimenting in society: Issues and examples in applied social psychology.* Glenview, IL: Scott, Foresman.

Sherman, J. W., Lee, A. Y., Bessenoff, G. R., & Frost, L. A. (1998). Stereotype efficiency reconsidered: Encoding flexibility under cognitive load. *Journal of Personality and Social Psychology, 75*(3), 589–606.

Sherman, P. (1980). The limits of ground squirrel nepotism. In G. Barlow & J. Silverberg (Eds.), *Sociobiology: Beyond nature/nurture?* (pp. 505–544). Boulder, CO: Westview.

Sherman, S. J., Judd, C. M., & Park, B. (1989). Social cognition. *Annual Review of Psychology, 40,* 281–326.

Sherwood, J. J. (1965). Self-identity and referent others. *Sociometry, 28,* 66–81.

Shibutani, T. (1961). *Society and personality.* Englewood Cliffs, NJ: Prentice Hall.

Shihadeh, E. S. (1991). The prevalence of husband-centered migration: Employment consequences for married mothers. *Journal of Marriage and the Family, 53,* 431–444.

Shorter, E., & Tilly, C. (1974). *Strikes in France: 1830–1968.* New York: Cambridge University Press.

Shotland, R. L., & Stebbins, C. A. (1983). Emergency and cost as determinants of helping behavior and the slow accumulation of social psychological knowledge. *Social Psychology Quarterly, 46,* 36–46.

Shotland, R. L., & Stebbins, C. A. (1983). Emergency and cost as determinants of helping behavior and the slow accumulation of social psychological knowledge. *Social Psychology Quarterly, 46,* 36–46.

Shotland, R. L., & Straw, M. K. (1976). Bystander response to an assault: When a man attacks a woman. *Journal of Personality and Social Psychology, 34,* 990–999.

Shott, S. (1979). Emotion and social life: A symbolic interactionist analysis. *American Journal of Sociology, 84*(6), 1317–1334.

Shover, N., Novland, S., James, J., & Thornton, W. (1979). Gender roles and delinquency. *Social Forces, 58,* 162–175.

Sidnell, J. (2007). Comparative studies in conversation analysis. *Annual Review of Anthropology, 36,* 229–244.

Siebenhaar, B. (2006). Code choice and code-switching in Swiss-German Internet relay chat rooms. *Journal of Sociolinguistics, 10,* 481–506.

Sigall, H., & Landy, D. (1973). Radiating beauty: The effects of having a physically attractive partner on person perception. *Journal of Personality and Social Psychology, 28,* 218–224.

Silberman, M. (1976). Toward a theory of criminal deterrence. *American Sociological Review, 41,* 442–461.

Sime, J. D. (1983). Affiliative behavior during escape to building exits. *Journal of Environmental Psychology, 3,* 21–41.

Simmel, G. (1902). The number of members as determining the sociological form of the group. I. *American Journal of Sociology, 8*(1), 1–46.

Simmons, R. G. (1991). Presidential address on altruism and sociology. *Sociological Quarterly, 32,* 1–22.

Simon, R. (1997). The meanings individuals attach to role-identities and their implications for mental health. *Journal of Health and Social Behavior, 38,* 256–274.

Simon, R., & Marcussen, K. (1999). Marital transitions, marital beliefs, and mental health. *Journal of Health and Social Behavior, 40,* 111–125.

Simon, W., & Gagnon, J. H. (2003). Sexual scripts: Origins, influences and changes. *Qualitative Sociology, 26*(4), 491–497.

Simons, R., Lin, K.-H., Gordon, L., Brody, G., Murry, V., & Conger, R. (2002). Community differences in the association between parenting practices and child conduct problems. *Journal of Marriage and Family, 64*, 331–345.

Simpson, J. A. (1987). The dissolution of romantic relationships: Factors involved in emotional stability and emotional distress. *Journal of Personality and Social Psychology, 53*, 683–692.

Simpson, J. A. (1990). Influence of attachment styles on romantic relationships. *Journal of Personality and Social Psychology, 59*, 971–980.

Simpson, J. A., Gangestad, S. W., & Lerum, M. (1990). Perception of physical attractiveness: Mechanisms involved in maintenance of romantic relationships. *Journal of Personality and Social Psychology, 59*, 1192–1201.

Sinclair, S., Dunn, E., & Lowery, B. S. (2005). The relationship between parental racial attitudes and children's implicit prejudice. *Journal of Experimental Social Psychology, 41*, 283–289.

Singer, J. L., & Singer, D. G. (1983). Psychologists look at television: Cognitive, developmental, personality, and social policy implications. *American Psychologist, 38*, 826–834.

Skinner, B. F. (1938). *The behavior of organisms: An experimental analysis.* Oxford, UK: Appleton-Century.

Skinner, B. F. (1953). *Science and human behavior.* New York: MacMillan.

Skinner, B. F. (1957). *Verbal behavior.* New York: Appleton-Century-Crofts.

Skinner, B. F. (1971). *Beyond freedom and dignity.* New York: Knopf.

Skowronski, J. J., & Carlston, D. E. (1989). Negativity and extremity biases in impression formation: A review of explanations. *Psychological Bulletin, 105*, 131–142.

Skvoretz, J., & Willer, D. (1993). Exclusion and power: a test of four theories of power in exchange networks. *American Sociological Review*, 801–818.

Slade, E. P., & Wissow, L. S. (2004). Spanking in early childhood and later behavior problems: A prospective study of infants and young toddlers. *Pediatrics, 113*, 1321–1330.

Slater, P. (1963). On social regression. *American Sociological Review, 28*, 339–364.

Slater, P. E. (1955). Role differentiation in small groups. *American Sociological Review, 20*, 300–310.

Sloane, D., & Potrin, R. H. (1986). Religion and delinquency: Cutting through the maze. *Social Forces, 65*, 87–105.

Slomczynski, K. M., Miller, J., & Kohn, M. (1981). Stratification, work, and values: A Polish-United States comparison. *American Sociological Review, 46*, 720–744.

Small, K. H., & Peterson, J. (1981). The divergent perceptions of actors and observers. *Journal of Social Psychology, 113*, 123–132.

Smardon, R. (2007). "I'd rather not take Prozac": Stigma and commodification in antidepressant consumer narratives. *Health: An Interdisciplinary Journal for the Social Study of Health, Illness, and Medicine, 12*, 67–86.

Smith III, A. C., & Kleinman, S. (1989). Managing emotions in medical school: Students' contacts with the living and the dead. *Social Psychology Quarterly*, 56–69.

Smith, D. A. (1987). Police response to interpersonal violence: Defining the parameters of legal control. *Social Forces, 65*, 767–782.

Smith, E. R., Fazio, R. H., & Cejka, M. A. (1996). Accessible attitudes influence categorization of multiply categorizable objects. *Journal of Personality and Social Psychology, 71*, 888–898.

Smith, E. R., & Henry, S. (1996). An in-group becomes part of the self: Response time evidence. *Personality and Social Psychology Bulletin, 22*, 635–642.

Smith, E. S., Powers, A. S., & Suarez, G. (2005). If Bill Clinton were a woman: The effectiveness of male and female politicians' account strategies following alleged transgressions. *Political Psychology, 26*, 115–134.

Smith, P. B., & Bond, M. H. (1994). *Social psychology across cultures: Analysis and perspectives.* Needham Heights, MA: Allyn and Bacon.

Smith-Lovin, L. (1990). Emotions as the confirmation and disconfirmation of identity: An affect control model. In T. D. Kemper (Ed.), *Research agendas in the sociology of emotion.* (pp. 238–270). Albany: State University of New York Press.

Smith-Lovin L. (1995). The sociology of affect and emotion. In K. Cook, G. A. Fine, & J. House (Eds.), *Sociological perspectives on social psychology* (pp. 118–148). Boston, MA: Allyn and Bacon.

Smith-Lovin, L., & Robinson, D. (2006). Control theories of identity, action and emotion: In search of testable differences between affect control theory and identity control theory. In K. A. McClelland & T. J. Fararo (Eds.), *Purpose, meaning, and action: Control systems theories in sociology.* (pp. 163–188). New York: Palgrave Macmillan.

Sniezek, J. A., & May, D. R. (1990). Conflict of interests and commitment in groups. *Journal of Applied Social Psychology, 20*, 1150–1165.

Snow, D. A., & Benford, R. D. (1992). Master frames and cycles of protest. In A. D. Morris & C. M. Mueller (Eds.), *Frontiers in social movement theory.* (pp. 133–155). New Haven, CT: Yale University Press.

Snow, D. A., & Oliver, P. E. (1995). Social movements and collective behavior: Social psychological dimensions and considerations. In K. S. Cook, G. A. Fine, & J. S. House (Eds.), *Sociological perspectives on social psychology* (pp. 571–599). Boston: Allyn and Bacon.

Snow, D. A., Rochford, E., Worden, S., & Benford, R. (1986). Frame alignment processes, micromobilization, and movement participation. *American Sociological Review, 51*, 464–481.

Snyder, C. R., Higgins, R. L., & Stucky, R. J. (1983). *Excuses: Masquerades in search of grace.* New York: Wiley.

Snyder, C. R., Lassegard, M. A., & Ford, C. E. (1986). Distancing after group success and failure: Basking in reflected glory and cutting off reflected failure. *Journal of Personality and Social Psychology, 51*, 382–388.

Snyder, M. (1981). On the self-perpetuating nature of social stereotypes. In D. L. Hamilton (Ed.), *Cognitive processes in stereotyping and intergroup behavior.* (pp. 183–212). Hillsdale, NJ: Erlbaum.

Snyder, M., & Swann, W. B. (1978). Hypothesis-testing processes in social interaction. *Journal of Personality and Social Psychology, 36,* 1202–1212.

Snyder, M., Tanke, E. D., & Berscheid, E. (1977). Social perception and interpersonal behavior: On the self-fulfilling nature of social stereotypes. *Journal of Personality and Social Psychology, 35,* 656–666.

Solano, C. H., Batten, P. G., & Parish, E. A. (1982). Loneliness and patterns of self-disclosure. *Journal of Personality and Social Psychology, 43,* 524–531.

Solomon, D. S. (1982). Mass media campaigns for health promotion. *Prevention in Human Services, 2,* 115–123.

Sommer, B. (2001). Menopause. In J. Worell (Ed.), *Encyclopedia of women and gender* (Vol. 2, pp. 729–738). San Diego, CA: Academic Press.

Sommers-Flanagan, R., Sommers-Flanagan, J., & Davis, B. (1993). What's happening on Music Television? A gender role content analysis. *Sex Roles, 28,* 745–753.

Sorrentino, R. M., & Field, N. (1986). Emergent leadership over time: The functional value of positive motivation. *Journal of Personality and Social Psychology, 50,* 1091–1099.

South, S., Trent, K., & Shen, Y. (2001). Changing partners: Toward a macrostructural-opportunity theory of marital dissolution. *Journal of Marriage and the Family, 63,* 743–754.

Spano, R., Freilich, J., & Bolland, J. (2008). Gang membership, gun carrying, and employment: Applying routine activities theory to explain violent victimization among inner city, minority youth living in extreme poverty. *Justice Quarterly, 25,* 381–410.

Spencer, J. W. (1987). Self-work in social interaction: Negotiating role-identities. *Social Psychology Quarterly, 50,* 131–142.

Spencer, S. J., Steele, C. M, & Quinn, D. M. (1999). Stereotype threat and women's math performance. *Journal of Experimental Social Psychology, 35,* 4–28.

Spiegel, J. P. (1969). Hostility, aggression, and violence. In A. Grimshaw (Ed.), *Patterns in American racial violence.* Chicago: Aldine.

Spilerman, S. (1970). The causes of racial disturbances: A comparison of alternative explanations. *American Sociological Review, 35,* 627–649.

Spilerman, S. (1976). Structural characteristics of cities and severity of racial disorders. *American Sociological Review, 41,* 771–793.

Spitz, R. (1945). Hospitalism. *Psychoanalytic Study of the Child, 1,* 53–72.

Spitz, R. (1946). Hospitalism: A follow-up report. *Psychoanalytic Study of the Child, 2,* 113–117.

Sprecher, S., & Metts, S. (1989). Development of the "Romantic Beliefs Scale" and examination of the effects of gender and gender role orientation. *Journal of Social and Personal Relationships, 6,* 387–411.

Sprecher, S., & Regan, P. (1998). Passionate and companionate love in courting and young married couples. *Sociological Inquiry, 68,* 163–185.

Sprecher, S., Schmeeckle, M., & Felmlee, D. (2006). The principle of least interest: Inequality in emotional involvement in romantic relationships. *Journal of Family Issues, 27,* 1–26.

Squier, W. (2002, April 15). My son goofs around, and I think it's great. *Newsweek,* p. 10.

St. C. Oates, G. (2004). The color of the undergraduate experience and the Black self-concept: Evidence from longitudinal data. *Social Psychology Quarterly, 67,* 16–32.

Staats, A. W., & Staats, C. (1958). Attitudes established by classical conditioning. *Journal of Abnormal and Social Psychology, 57,* 37–40.

Stack, S. (1987). Celebrities and suicide: A taxonomy and analysis, 1948–1983. *American Sociological Review, 52,* 401–412.

Stafford, L., & Canary, D. J., (1991). Maintenance strategies by romantic relationship type, gender, and relational characteristics. *Journal of Social and Personal Relationships, 8,* 217–242.

Stafford, M. C., Gray, L. N., Menke, B. A., & Ward, D. A. (1986). Modelling the deterrent effects of punishment. *Social Psychology Quarterly, 49,* 338–347.

Stamou, A. G. (2011). Speech style and the construction of social division: Evidence from Greek television. *Language and Communication, 31,* 329–344.

Stang, D. J. (1972). Conformity, ability, and self-esteem. *Representative Research in Social Psychology, 3,* 97–103.

Stapel, D., & Semin, G. (2007). The magic spell of language: Linguistic categories and their perceptual consequences. *Journal of Personality and Social Psychology, 93,* 23–33.

Stark, R., & Bainbridge, W. S. (1980). Networks of faith: Interpersonal bonds and recruitment in cults and sects. *American Journal of Sociology, 85,* 1376–1395.

Stasser, G. (1992). Pooling of unshared information during group discussion. In S. Worchel, W. Wood, & J. Simpson (Eds.), *Group process and productivity* (pp. 48–67). Newbury Park, CA: Sage.

Stasser, G., & Titus, W. (1987). Effects of information load and percentage of shared information on the dissemination of unshared information during group discussion. *Journal of Personality and Social Psychology, 53,* 81–93.

Steele, C. M. (1997). A threat in the air: How stereotypes shape the intellectual identities and performance of women and African-Americans. *American Psychologist, 52,* 613–629.

Steele, C. M. (1999, August). Thin ice: "Stereotype threat" and Black college students. *Atlantic Monthly, 284*(2), 44–47, 50–54.

Steele, C. M. (2010). *Whistling Vivaldi: And other clues to how stereotypes affect us.* New York: W. W. Norton.

Steele, C. M., & Aronson, J. (1995). Stereotype threat and the intellectual test performance of African-Americans. *Journal of Personality and Social Psychology, 69,* 797–811.

Steffensmeier, D., & Demuth, S. (2000). Ethnicity and sentencing outcomes in U.S. federal courts: Who is punished more harshly? *American Sociological Review, 65,* 705–729.

Steffensmeier, D. J., & Allan, E. (1996). Gender and crime: Toward a gendered theory of female offending. *Annual Review of Sociology, 22,* 459–487.

Steffensmeier, D. J., Allan, E. A., Haver, M. D., & Streifel, C. (1989). Age and the distribution of crime. *American Journal of Sociology, 94,* 803–831.

Steffensmeier, D. J., & Terry, R. M. (1973). Deviance and respectability: An observational study of reactions to shoplifting. *Social Forces, 51,* 417–426.

Steffy, L. (2005, January 12). CEOs are playing dumb in attempts to get off hook. *Houston Chronicle.* www. chron.com/disp/story.mpl/business/steffy/2988866. html.

Stein, J. A., Newcomb, M. D., & Bentler, P. M. (1987). An eight-year study of multiple influences on drug use and drug use consequences. *Journal of Personality and Social Psychology, 53,* 1094–1105.

Steiner, D. D., & Rain, J. S. (1989). Immediate and delayed primacy and recency effects in performance evaluation. *Journal of Applied Psychology, 74,* 136–142.

Steiner, I. D. (1972). *Group process and productivity.* New York: Academic Press.

Steiner, I. D., & Rogers, E. (1963). Alternative responses to dissonance. *Journal of Abnormal and Social Psychology, 66,* 128–136.

Stephan, W. G. (1987). The contact hypothesis in intergroup relations. In C. Hendrick (Ed.), *Group processes and intergroup relations* (pp. 13–40). Beverly Hills, CA: Sage.

Stephenson, W. (1953). *The study of behavior.* Chicago: University of Chicago Press.

Stermer, S. P., & Burkley, M. (2012). Xbox or seXbox? An examination of sexualized content in video games. *Social and Personality Psychology Compass, 6*(7), 525–535.

Sternberg, R. (1996). Love stories. *Personal Relationships, 3,* 59–79.

Sternberg, R. (1998). *Love is a story: A new theory of relationships.* New York: Oxford University Press.

Sternberg, R. J. (1985). Implicit theories of intelligence, creativity, and wisdom. *Journal of Personality and Social Psychology, 49,* 607–627.

Sternthal, B., Dholakia, R., & Leavitt, C. (1978). The persuasive effect of source credibility: A test of cognitive response analysis. *Journal of Consumer Research, 4,* 252–260.

Stets, J. E. (2003) Emotions and sentiments. In J. DeLamater (Ed.), *Handbook of social psychology* (pp. 309–335). New York: Kluwer Academic/Plenum.

Stets, J. E., & Biga, C. F. (2003). Bringing identity theory into environmental sociology. *Sociological Theory, 21*(4), 398–423.

Stets, J. E., & Burke, P. (2000). Identity theory and social identity theory. *Social Psychology Quarterly, 63,* 224–237.

Stevenson, M. B., Ver Hoeve, J. N., Roach, M. A., & Leavitt, L. A. (1986). The beginning of conversation: Early patterns of mother-infant vocal responsiveness. *Infant Behavior and Development, 9,* 423–440.

Stewart, A. (2000). *Uses of the past: Toward a psychology of generations.* Paper presented at the University of Michigan, Ann Arbor.

Stewart, A. (2002). *Gender, race, and generation in the psychology of women.* Paper presented at the Annual Meeting of the American Psychological Association, Chicago, IL.

Stewart, A. J., Henderson-King, D., Henderson-King, E., & Winter, D. G. (2000). *Work and family values: Life scripts in the Midwest in the 1950s.* Paper presented at Conference on Work and Families, San Francisco, CA.

Stewart, R. H. (1965). Effect of continuous responding on the order effect in personality impression formation. *Journal of Personality and Social Psychology, 1,* 161–165.

Stewart, S., Stinnett, H., & Rosenfeld, L. (2000). Sex differences in desired characteristics of short-term and long-term relationship partners. *Journal of Social and Personal Relationships, 17,* 843–853.

Sticca, F., & Perren, S. (2012). Is cyberbullying worse than traditional bullying? Examining the differential roles of medium, publicity, and anonymity for the perceived severity of bullying. *Journal of Youth and Adolescence, 42*(5), 739–750.

Stiff, J. B. (1986). Cognitive processing of persuasive message cues: A meta-analytic review of the effects of supporting information on attitudes. *Communication Monographs, 53,* 75–89.

Stiles, A., & Raney, T. (2004). Relationships among personal space boundaries, peer acceptance, and peer reputation in adolescence. *Journal of Child and Adolescent Psychiatric Nursing, 16,* 29–40.

Stiles, W., Orth, J., Scherwitz, L., Hennrikus, D., & Vallbona, C. (1984). Role behaviors in routine medical interviews with hypertensive patients: A repertoire of verbal exchanges. *Social Psychology Quarterly, 47,* 244–254.

Stokes, J. P. (1985). The relation of social network and individual difference variables to loneliness. *Journal of Personality and Social Psychology, 48,* 981–990.

Stokes, J., & Levin, I. (1986). Gender differences in predicting loneliness from social network characteristics. *Journal of Personality and Social Psychology, 51,* 1069–1074.

Stolzenberg, L., & D'Alessio, S. J. (2008). Co-offending and the age-crime curve. *Journal of Research in Crime and Delinquency, 45,* 65–86.

Stone, G. P. (1962). Appearances and the self. In A. Rose (Ed.), *Human behavior and social processes.* (pp. 86–118). Boston: Houghton Mifflin.

Stone, J., Lynch, C. I., Sjomeling, M., & Darley, J. M. (1999). Stereotype threat effects on Black and White athletic performance. *Journal of Personality and Social Psychology, 77*(6), 1213–1227.

Stoner, J. A. F. (1968). Risky and cautious shifts in group decisions: The influence of widely held values. *Journal of Experimental Social Psychology, 4,* 442–459.

Storms, M. D. (1973). Videotape and attribution process: Reversing actors' and observers' points of view. *Journal of Personality and Social Psychology, 27,* 165–175.

Strauman, T. J., Vookles, J., Berenstein, V., Chaiken, S., & Higgins, E. T. (1991). Self-discrepancies and vulnerability to body dissatisfaction and disordered eating. *Journal of Personality and Social Psychology, 61,* 946–956.

Straus, M., & Field, C. (2003). Psychological aggression by American parents: National data on prevalence, chronicity, and severity. *Journal of Marriage and Family, 65,* 795–808.

Straus, M., & Stewart, J. (1999). Corporal punishment by American parents: National data on prevalence, chronicity, severity, and duration, in relation to child and family characteristics. *Clinical Child and Family Psychology Review, 2,* 55–70.

Straus, M., Sugarman, D., & Giles-Sims, J. (1997). Spanking by parents and subsequent antisocial behavior of children. *Archives of Pediatric and Adolescent Medicine, 151,* 761–767.

Strenze, T. (2007). Intelligence and socioeconomic success: A meta-analytic review of longitudinal research. *Intelligence, 35,* 401–426.

Strodtbeck, F. L., Simon, R. J., & Hawkins, C. (1965). Social status in jury deliberations. In I. D. Steiner & M. Fishbein (Eds.), *Current studies in social psychology.* (pp. 333–342). New York: Holt, Rinehart and Winston.

Stroebe, W., Thompson, V., Insko, C., & Reisman, S. R. (1970). Balance and differentiation in the evaluation of linked attitude objects. *Journal of Personality and Social Psychology, 16,* 38–47.

Struch, N., & Schwartz, S. H. (1989). Intergroup aggression: Its predictors and distinctness from in-group bias. *Journal of Personality and Social Psychology, 56,* 364–373.

Stryker, S. (1980). *Symbolic interactionism: A social structural version.* Menlo Park, CA: Benjamin/Cummings.

Stryker, S. (1987). The vitalization of symbolic interactionism. *Social Psychology Quarterly, 50,* 83–94.

Stryker, S. (2001). Social psychology. In P. B. Baltes & N. J. Smelser (Eds.), *International encyclopedia of the social and behavioral sciences* (pp. 14409–14413). Oxford, UK: Pergamon.

Stryker, S., & Burke, P. J. (2000). The past, present, and future of an identity theory. *Social Psychology Quarterly,* 284–297.

Stryker, S., & Gottlieb, A. (1981). Attribution theory and symbolic interactionism: A comparison. In J. H. Hawes, W. Ickes, & R. F. Kidd (Eds.), *New directions in attribution theory* (Vol. 3, pp. 425–458). Hillsdale, NJ: Erlbaum.

Stryker, S., & Serpe, R. (1981). Commitment, identity salience and role behavior: Theory and research ex-

ample. In W. Ickes & E. Knowles (Eds.), *Personality, roles and social behavior.* (pp. 199–218). New York: Springer Verlag.

Stryker, S., & Serpe, R. (1982). Towards a theory of family influence in the socialization of children. In A. Kerckhoff (Ed.), *Research in sociology of education and socialization* (Vol. 4, pp. 47–71). Greenwich, CT: JAI Press.

Stryker, S., & Serpe, R. T. (1994). Identity salience and psychological centrality: Equivalent, overlapping, or complementary concepts? *Social Psychology Quarterly, 57*(1), 16–35.

Substance Abuse and Mental Health Services Administration. (2012). *The NSDUH Report: Monthly variation in substance use initiation among adolescents.* Rockville: MD: Center for Behavioral Health Statistics and Quality.

Sudman, S., & Bradburn, N. M. (1974). *Response effects in surveys.* Chicago: Aldine.

Sueda, K., & Wiseman, R. L. (1992). Embarrassment remediation in Japan and the United States. *International Journal of Intercultural Relations, 16*(2), 159–173.

Suls, J., Lemos, K., & Stewart, H. L. (2002). Self-esteem, construal, and comparisons with self, friends, and others. *Journal of Personality and Social Psychology, 82,* 252–261.

Suls, J. M., & Miller, R. (Eds.). (1977). *Social comparison processes: Theoretical and empirical perspectives.* New York: Wiley.

Summers, L. Archive of: Remarks at NBER Conference on Diversifying the Science & Engineering Workforce at the Wayback Machine (archived January 30, 2008). January 14, 2005. http://www.harvard.edu/president/speeches/summers_2005/nber.php

Summers-Effler, E. (2005). The emotional significance of solidarity for social movement communities: Sustaining Catholic worker community and service. In H. Flam & D. King (Eds.), *Emotion and social movements* (pp. 133–149). London and New York: Routledge.

Sumner, W. G. (1906). *Folkways.* New York: Ginn.

Sun, Y., & Li, Y. (2002). Children's well-being during parents' marital disruption process: A pooled time-series analysis. *Journal of Marriage and Family, 64,* 472–488.

Surra, C. (1990). Research and theory on mate selection and premarital relationships in the 1980s. *Journal of Marriage and the Family, 52,* 844–865.

Surra, C., & Longstreth, M. (1990). Similarity of outcomes, interdependence, and conflict in dating relationships. *Journal of Personality and Social Psychology, 59,* 501–516.

Suskind, R. (2004). *The price of loyalty: George W. Bush, the White House, and the education of Paul O'Neill.* New York: Simon and Schuster.

Sussman, N. M., & Rosenfeld, H. M. (1982). Influence of culture, language, and sex on conversational distance. *Journal of Personality and Social Psychology, 42,* 66–74.

Sutherland, E., Cressey, D., & Luckenbill, D. (1992). *Principles of criminology* (11th ed.). Dix Hills, NY: General Hall.

Suttles, G. (1968). *The social order of the slum.* Chicago: University of Chicago Press.

Swann, W. B. (1987). Identity negotiation: Where two roads meet. *Journal of Personality and Social Psychology, 53,* 1038–1051.

Swann, W. B., & Predmore, S. C. (1985). Intimates as agents of social support: Sources of consolation or despair? *Journal of Personality and Social Psychology, 49,* 1609–1617.

Swann, W. B., & Schroeder, D. G. (1995). The search for beauty and truth: A framework for understanding reactions to evaluations. *Personality and Social Psychology Bulletin, 21,* 1307–1318.

Swanson, D. L. (Ed.). (1979). The uses and gratifications approach to mass communications research. *Communication Research, 3,* 3–111.

Sweeney, P. D. (1990). Distributive justice and pay satisfaction: A field test of an equity theory prediction. *Journal of Business and Psychology, 4,* 329–341.

Sweet, J. A., & Bumpass, L. (1987). *American families and households.* New York: Russell Sage Foundation.

Swigert, V., & Farrell, R. (1977). Normal homicides and the law. *American Sociological Review, 42,* 16–32.

Swim, J. K., Aikin, K. J., Hall, W. S., & Hunter, B. A. (1995). Sexism and racism: Old fashioned and modern prejudices. *Journal of Personality and Social Psychology, 68,* 199–214.

Sykes, G. M., & Matza, D. (1957). Techniques of neutralization: A theory of delinquency. *American Sociological Review, 22,* 664–670.

Syme, L. (2008). Reducing racial and social-class inequalities in health: The need for a new approach. *Health affairs, 27,* 456–459.

Syme, S. L., & Berkman, L. (1976). Social class, susceptibility, and sickness. *American Journal of Epidemiology, 104,* 1–8.

Symons, D. (1992). On the use and misuse of Darwinism in the study of human behavior. In J. Barkow, L. Cosmides, & J. Tooby (Eds.), *The adapted mind: Evolutionary psychology and the generation of culture* (pp. 137–159). New York: Oxford University Press.

Tagler, M. J., & Cozzarelli, C. (2013). Feelings toward the poor and beliefs about the causes of poverty: The role of affective-cognitive consistency in help-giving. *Journal of Psychology, 147*(6), 517–539.

Tajfel, H. (1981). *Human groups and social categories: Studies in social psychology.* Cambridge, UK: Cambridge University Press.

Tajfel, H. (1982a). *Social identity and intergroup relations.* Cambridge, UK: Cambridge University Press.

Tajfel, H. (1982b). Social psychology of intergroup relations. *Annual Review of Psychology, 33,* 1–39.

Tajfel, H., & Billig, M. (1974). Familiarity and categorization in intergroup behavior. *Journal of Experimental Social Psychology, 10,* 159–170.

Tajfel, H., Billig, M. G., Bundy, R. P., & Flament, C. (1971).

Social categorization and intergroup behaviour. *European Journal of Social Psychology, 1,* 149–178.

Tajfel, H., & Turner, J. C. (1979). An integrative theory of intergroup conflict. In W. G. Austin & S. Worchel, *The social psychology of intergroup relations* (pp. 33–47). Monterey, CA: Brooks/Cole.

Tajfel, H., & Turner, J. (1986). The social identity theory of intergroup behavior. In S. Worchel & W. G. Austin (Eds.), *Psychology of intergroup relations* (2nd ed., pp. 7–24). Chicago: Nelson-Hall.

Tanford, S., & Penrod, S. (1984). Social influence model: A formal integration of research on majority and minority influence processes. *Psychological Bulletin, 95,* 189–225.

Tangney, J. P. (1995). Shame and guilt in interpersonal relations. In J. P. Tangney & K. W. Fisher (Eds.), *The psychology of guilt, shame, embarrassment and pride* (pp. 114–139). New York: Guilford.

Tangney, J. P., Miller, R. S., Flicker, L., & Barlow, D. H. (1996). Are shame, guilt, and embarrassment distinct emotions? *Journal of Personality and Social Psychology, 70*(6), 1256–1269.

Tannen, D. (1991). *You just don't understand: Women and men in conversation.* New York: Morrow.

Tashiro, T., Frazier, P., & Berman, M. (2006). Stress-related growth following divorce and relationship dissolution. In M. Fine & J. Harvey (Eds.), *Handbook of divorce and relationship dissolution* (pp. 361–384). Mahwah, NJ: Erlbaum.

Tausch, N., Becker, J. C., Spears, R., Christ, O., Saab, R., Singh, P., & Siddiqui, R. N. (2011). Explaining radical group behavior: Developing emotion and efficacy routes to normative and nonnormative collective action. *Journal of Personality and Social Psychology, 101,* 129–148.

Taylor, D. A., & Belgrave, F. Z. (1986). The effects of perceived intimacy and valence on self-disclosure reciprocity. *Personality and Social Psychology Bulletin, 12,* 247–255.

Taylor, D. M., & Jaggi, V. (1974). Ethnocentrism and causal attribution in a South Indian context. *Journal of CrossCultural Psychology, 5,* 162–171.

Taylor, D. M., & Moghaddam, F. M. (1987). *Theories of intergroup relations: International social psychological perspectives.* New York: Praeger.

Taylor, D. M., & Royer, L. (1980). Group processes affecting anticipated language choice in intergroup relations. In H. Giles, W. P. Robinson, & P. M. Smith (Eds.), *Language: Social psychological perspectives* (pp. 185–192). New York: Pergamon.

Taylor, D. W., Berry, P. C., & Block, C. (1958). Does group participation when using brainstorming facilitate creative thinking? *Administrative Science Quarterly, 3,* 23–47.

Taylor, S. E. (1981). A categorization approach to stereotyping. In D. L. Hamilton (Ed.), *Cognitive processes in stereotyping and intergroup behavior* (pp. 83–114). Hillsdale, NJ: Erlbaum.

Taylor, S. E., & Crocker, J. (1981). Schematic bases of

social information processing. In E. T. Higgins, C. P. Herman, & M. P. Zanna (Eds.), *Social cognition: The Ontario symposium* (Vol. 1, pp. 89–134). Hillsdale, NJ: Erlbaum.

Taylor, S. E., & Fiske, S. T. (1978). Salience, attention, and attribution: Top of the head phenomena. In L. Berkowitz (Ed.), *Advances in experimental social psychology* (Vol. 11, pp. 249–288). New York: Academic Press.

Taylor, S. E., Fiske, S. T., Etcoff, N. L., & Ruderman, A. J. (1978). The categorical and contextual bases of person memory and stereotyping. *Journal of Personality and Social Psychology, 36*, 778–793.

Taylor, S. P. (1967). Aggressive behavior and physiological arousal as a function of provocation and the tendency to inhibit aggression. *Journal of Personality, 35*, 297–310.

Taylor, V. (1989). Social movement continuity: The women's movement in abeyance. *American Sociological Review, 54*, 761–775.

Taylor, V., & Whittier, N. (1992). Collective identity in social movement communities: Lesbian feminist mobilization. In A. D. Morris & C. M. Mueller (Eds.), *Frontiers in social movement theory* (pp. 104–130). New Haven, CT: Yale University Press.

Taylor, V. A., Halstead, D., & Haynes, P. J. (2010). Consumer responses to Christian religious symbols in advertising. *Journal of Advertising, 39*, 79–92.

Teachman, J. (1987). Family background, educational resources, and educational attainment. *American Sociological Review, 52*, 548–557.

Tedeschi, J. T., Bonoma, T. V., & Schlenker, B. R. (1972). Influence, decision, and compliance. In J. T. Tedeschi (Ed.), *The social influence processes.* (pp. 418ff). Chicago: AldineAtherton.

Tedeschi, J. T., Schlenker, B. R., & Lindskold, S. (1972). The exercise of power and influence: The source of influence. In J. T. Tedeschi (Ed.), *The social influence processes.* (pp. 287–345). Chicago: Aldine-Atherton.

Terry, D. J., & Hogg, M. A. (1996). Group norms and the attitude-behavior relationship: A role for group identification. *Personality and Social Psychology Bulletin, 22*, 776–793.

Tesser, A., & Campbell, J. (1983). Self-definition and self-evaluation maintenance. In J. Suls & A. G. Greenwald (Eds.), *Psychological perspectives on the self* (Vol. 2, pp. 1–31). Hillsdale, NJ: Erlbaum.

Teti, D. M., & Lamb, M. E. (1989). Socioeconomic and marital outcomes of adolescent marriage, adolescent childbirth, and their co-occurrence. *Journal of Marriage and the Family, 51*, 203–212.

Teti, D., Lamb, M., & Elster, A. (1987). Long-range socioeconomic and marital consequences of adolescent marriage in three cohorts of adult males. *Journal of Marriage and the Family, 49*, 499–506.

Tetlock, P. E. (1986). A value pluralism model of ideological reasoning. *Journal of Personality and Social Psychology, 50*, 819–827.

Tetlock, P. E., & Manstead, A. S. R. (1985). Impression

management versus intrapsychic explanations in social psychology: A useful dichotomy? *Psychological Review, 92*, 59–77.

Thakerar, J. N., Giles, H., & Cheshire, J. (1982). Psychological and linguistic parameters of speech accommodation theory. In C. Fraser & K. R. Scherer (Eds.), *Advances in the social psychology of language.* (pp. 205–255). Cambridge, UK: Cambridge University Press.

Thibaut, J., & Kelley, H. (1959). *The social psychology of groups.* New York: Wiley.

Thibaut, J. W., & Walker, L. (1978). A theory of procedure. *California Law Review, 66*, 541–566.

Thibaut, J. W., & Walker, L. (1975). *Procedural justice: A psychological analysis.* New York: Wiley.

Thoennes, N. A., & Pearson, J. (1985). Predicting outcomes in divorce mediation: The influence of people and process. *Journal of Social Issues, 41*(2), 115–126.

Thoits, P. A. (1985). Self-labelling processes in mental illness: The role of emotional deviance. *American Journal of Sociology, 91*, 221–249.

Thoits, P. A. (1989). The sociology of emotions. *Annual Review of Sociology, 15*, 317–342.

Thoits, P. A. (1990). Emotional deviance: Research agendas. *Research Agendas in the Sociology of Emotions, 180*, 203.

Thoits, P. (2005). Differential labeling of mental illness by social status: A new look at an old problem. *Journal of Health and Social Behavior, 46*, 102–119.

Thoits, P. A. (2010). Stress and health: Major findings and policy implications. *Journal of Health and Social Behavior, 51*(S), 41–53.

Thoits, P. A. (2011). Resisting the stigma of mental illness. *Social Psychology Quarterly, 74*(1), 6–28.

Thomas, E., & Reaser, J. (2004). Delimiting perceptual cues used for the ethnic labeling of African American and European American voices. *Journal of Sociolinguistics, 8*, 54–87.

Thomas, L., De Bellis, M., Graham, R., & LaBar, K. (2007). Development of emotional facial recognition in late childhood and adolescence. *Developmental Science, 10*, 547–558.

Thomas, W. I., & Thomas, D. S. (1928). *The child in America: Behavior problems and programs.* New York: Alfred A. Knopf.

Thomas, W. I., & Znaniecki, F. (1918). *The Polish peasant in Europe and America* (Vol. 1). Boston: Badger.

Thompson, E. H., & Pleck, J. H. (1986). The structure of male role norms. *American Behavioral Scientist, 29*, 531–543.

Thompson, T. L., & Zerbinos, E. (1995). Gender roles in animated cartoons: Has the picture changed in 20 years? *Sex Roles, 32*, 651–673.

Thomsen, C. T., & Borgida, E. (1996). Throwing out the baby with the bathwater? Let's not overstate the overselling of the base rate fallacy. *Behavioral and Brain Sciences, 19*, 39–40.

Thorlundsson, T. (1987). Bernstein's sociolinguistics: An empirical test in Iceland. *Social Forces, 65*, 695–718.

Thornberry, T. D., & Christenson, R. L. (1984). Juvenile justice decision-making as a longitudinal process. *Social Forces, 63*, 433–444.

Thorndike, E. L. (1920). A constant error in psychological ratings. *Journal of Applied Psychology, 4*, 25–29.

Thorne, B. (1993). *Gender play: Girls and boys in school.* New Brunswick, NJ: Rutgers University Press.

Thornhill, R., & Grammar, K. (1999). The body and face of woman: One ornament that signals quality? *Evolution and Human Behavior, 20*, 105–120.

Thornton, A. (1984). Changing attitudes toward separation and divorce: Causes and consequences. *American Journal of Sociology, 90*, 856–872.

Thorton, A., Alwin, D. F., & Camburn, D. (1983). Causes and consequences of sex-role attitudes and attitude change. *American Sociological Review, 48*, 211–227.

Thornton, B., Lovley, A., Ryckman, R. M., & Gold, J. A. (2009). Playing dumb and knowing it all: Competitive orientation and impression management strategies. *Individual Differences Research, 7*, 265–271.

Thye, S. R. (2000). A status value theory of power in exchange relations. *American Sociological Review, 65*, 407–432.

Tierney, K. (2002). Strength of a city: A disaster research perspective on the World Trade Center attack. www.ssrc.org/sept11/essays/tierney.htm.

Tilker, H. A. (1970). Socially responsible behavior as a function of observer responsibility and victim feedback. *Journal of Personality and Social Psychology, 14*, 95–100.

Tilly, C. (1995). *Popular contention in Great Britain: 1758–1834.* Cambridge, MA: Harvard University Press.

Tilly, C., Tilly, L., & Tilly, R. (1975). *The rebellious century, 1830–1930.* Cambridge, MA: Harvard University Press.

Tittle, C., Broidy, L., & Gertz, M. (2008). Strain, crime, and contingencies. *Justice Quarterly, 25*, 283–312.

Toch, H. (1969). *Violent men: An inquiry into the psychology of violence.* Chicago: Aldine.

Toma, C., Hancock, J., & Ellison, N. (2008). Separating fact from fiction: An examination of deceptive self-presentation in online dating profiles. *Personality and Social Psychology Bulletin, 34*, 1023–1036.

Touhey, J. (1979). Sex-role stereotyping and individual differences in liking for the physically attractive. *Social Psychology Quarterly, 42*, 285–289.

Tousignant, M., Mishara, B., Caillaud, A., Fortin, V., & St-Laurent, D. (2005). The impact of media coverage of the suicide of a well-known Quebec reporter: The case of Gaetan Girouard. *Social Science and Medicine, 60*, 1919–1926.

Triandis, H. C. (1989). The self and social behavior in differing cultural contexts. *Psychological Review, 96*, 506–520.

Triandis, H. C. (1995). *Individualism and collectivism.* Boulder, CO: Westview Press.

Triandis, H. C., McCusker, C., & Hui, C. H. (1990). Multimethod probes of individualism and collectivism. *Journal of Personality and Social Psychology, 59*, 1006–1020.

Triplett, N. (1898). The dynamogenic factors in pacemaking and competition. *American Journal of Psychology, 9*, 507–533.

Trivers, R. L. (1971). The evolution of reciprocal altruism. *Quarterly Review of Biology, 46*, 35–57.

Trivers, R. L. (1983). The evolution of cooperation. In D. L. Bridgeman (Ed.), *The nature of prosocial behavior.* New York: Academic Press.

Trope, Y., & Cohen, O. (1989). Perceptual and inferential determinants of behavior-correspondent attributions. *Journal of Experimental Social Psychology, 25*(2), 142–158.

Trope, Y., Cohen, O., & Maoz, Y. (1988). The perceptual and inferential effects of situational inducements on dispositional attribution. *Journal of Personality and Social Psychology, 55*(2), 165–177.

Trotter, P. B. (2010). The influence of parental romantic relationships on college students' attitudes about romantic relationships. *College Student Journal, 44*, 71–83.

Trouilloud, D., & Amiel, C. (2011). Reflected appraisals of coaches, parents and teammates: A key component of athletes' self? *International Journal of Sport Psychology, 42*, 97–114.

Turner, J. C. (1981). The experimental social psychology of intergroup behavior. In J. C. Turner & H. Giles (Eds.), *Intergroup behavior* (pp. 66–101). Oxford, UK: Blackwell.

Turner, J. C. (1987). *Rediscovering the social group: A self-categorization theory.* Oxford, UK: Basil Blackwell.

Turner, J. C. (1991). *Social influence.* Pacific Grove, CA: Brooks/Cole.

Turner, J. C., Wetherell, M. S., & Hogg, M. A. (1989). Referent informational influence and group polarization. *British Journal of Social Psychology, 28*, 135–147.

Turner, J. S. (2011). Sex and the spectacle of music videos: An examination of the portrayal of race and sexuality in music videos. *Sex Roles, 64*, 173–191.

Turner, R. H. (1978). The role and the person. *American Journal of Sociology, 84*, 1–23.

Turner, R. H. (1990). Role change. In W. R. Scott & J. Blake (Eds.), *Annual Review of Sociology* (Vol. 16, pp. 87–110). Palo Alto, CA: Annual Reviews.

Turner, R. H., & Killian, L. M. (1972). *Collective behavior* (2nd ed.). Englewood Cliffs, NJ: Prentice Hall.

Turner, R. H., & Killian, L. M. (1987). *Collective behavior* (3rd ed.). Englewood Cliffs, NJ: Prentice Hall.

Tversky, A., & Kahneman, D. (1974). Judgment under uncertainty: Heuristics and biases. *Science, 185*, 1124–1131.

Twenge, J., & Crocker, J. (2002). Race and self-esteem: Meta-analyses comparing Whites, Blacks, Hispanics, Asians, and American Indians and comment on Gray-Little and Hafdahl (2000). *Psychological Bulletin, 128*, 371–408.

Tyler, T., & Lind, E. A. (1992). Relational model of authority in groups. In M. P. Zanna (Ed.), *Advances in experimental social psychology* (Vol. 25, pp. 115–191). San Diego, CA: Academic Press.

Tyler, T. R., Boeckmann, R. J., Smith, H. J., & Huo, Y. J. (1997). *Social justice in a diverse society.* Boulder, CO: Westview Press.

Tyler, T. R., & Sears, D. O. (1977). Coming to like obnoxious people when we must live with them. *Journal of Personality and Social Psychology, 35,* 200–211.

Tziner, A. (1982). Differential effects of group cohesiveness types: A clarifying overview. *Social Behavior and Personality, 10,* 227–239.

Uggen, C., & Thompson, M. (2003). The socioeconomic determinants of ill-gotten gains: Within-person changes in drug use and illegal earnings. *American Journal of Sociology, 109,* 146–185.

Umberson, D., Anderson, K., Glick, J., & Shapiro, A. (1998). Domestic violence, personal control, and gender. *Journal of Marriage and the Family, 60*(2), 442–452.

Umberson, D., Williams, K., & Anderson, K. (2002). Violent behavior: A measure of emotional upset? *Journal of Health and Social Behavior, 43*(2), 189–206.

U.S. Bureau of Labor Statistics. (2007). Table 11: Employed persons by detailed occupation, sex, race, and Hispanic or Latino ethnicity. In *Current Population Survey.* www.bls.gov/cps/cpsaat11.pdf.

U.S. Bureau of Labor Statistics. (2013a). Census of fatal occupational injuries summary, 2011. www.bls.gov/news.release/cfoi.nr0.htm.

U.S. Bureau of Labor Statistics. (2013b). Employed persons by detailed occupation, Table 11. www.bls.gov/cps/cpsaat11.pdf.

U.S. Bureau of Labor Statistics. (2013c). Usual weekly earnings of wage and salary workers. www.bls.gov/news.release/archives/wkyeng_04182013.htm.

U.S. Bureau of Labor Statistics. (2013d). Workplace injury and illness summary. www.bls.gov/news.release/osh.nr0.htm.

U.S. Bureau of the Census. (2000). *Statistical abstract of the United States: 2000* (120th ed.). Washington, DC: U.S. Government Printing Office.

U.S. Bureau of the Census. (2005). *Facts for features: Father's Day.* www.census.gov/Press-Release/www/releases/archives/facts_for_features_special_editions/004711.html.

U.S. Bureau of the Census. (2009). *Statistical abstract of the United States, 2007.* Washington, DC: U.S. Government Printing Office.

U.S. Bureau of the Census. (2010). *Households and families: 2010 Census brief.* Washington, DC: Bureau of the Census.

U.S. Bureau of the Census. (2012). Educational attainment by Race and Hispanic origin, 1970 to 2010. *Statistical Abstract of the United States: Tables 229, 230.*

U.S. Department of Health and Human Services. (2006). Health consultation: Saline High School, Saline, Washtenaw County, Michigan. Agency for Toxic Substances and Disease Registry, Public Health Service.

U.S. Department of Health and Human Services. (2010). *Code of Federal Regulations, Title 45, Part 46, "Protection of Human Subjects."* www.hhs.gov/ohrp/human subjects/guidance/ 45cfr46.htm.

U.S. Department of Justice. (2008). *Bureau of Justice Statistics Crime Trends.* www.ojp.usdoj.gov/bjs/glance. htm#Crime.

Unamuno, V. (2008). Multilingual switch in peer classroom interaction. *Linguistics and Education, 19,* 1–19.

Useem, B. (1998). Breakdown theories of collective action. *Annual Review of Sociology, 24,* 215–238.

Utne, M. K., & Kidd, R. F. (1980). Equity and attribution. In G. Mikula (Ed.), *Justice and social interaction: Experimental and theoretical contributions, from psychological research* (pp. 63–93). New York: Springer Verlag.

Valle, V. A., & Frieze, I. H. (1976). Stability of causal attributions as a mediator in changing expectations for success. *Journal of Personality and Social Psychology, 35,* 579–589.

van Aken, M., van Lieshout, C., & Haselager, G. (1996). Adolescents' competence and the mutuality of their self-descriptions and descriptions of them provided by others. *Journal of Youth and Adolescence, 25,* 285–306.

van Baaren, R., Holland, R., Kawakami, K., & Van Knippenberg, A. (2004). Mimicry and prosocial behavior. *Psychological Science, 15,* 71–74.

van Baaren, R., Holland, R., Steenaert, B., & Van Knippenberg, A. (2003). Mimicry for money: Behavioral consequences of imitation. *Journal of Experimental Social Psychology, 39,* 393–398.

Van Beek, Y., & Dubas, J. (2008). Age and gender differences in decoding basic and non-basic facial expressions in late childhood and early adolescence. *Journal of Nonverbal Behavior, 32,* 37–53.

Vandell, D. L., Belsky, J. Burchinal, M., et al. (2010). Do effects of early child care extend to age 15 years? Results from the NICHD Study of Early Child Care and Youth Development. *Child Development, 81,* 737–756.

van Dellen, M. R., Campbell, W. K., Hoyle, R. H., & Bradfield, E. K. (2011). Overcompensating, resisting, and breaking: A meta-analytic examination of theoretical models of reactions to self-esteem threat. *Personality and Social Psychology Review, 15,* 51–74.

Van De Rakt, M., Nieuwbeerta, P., & Apel, R. (2009). Association of criminal convictions between family members: Effects of siblings, fathers and mothers. *Criminal Behavior and Mental Health, 19,* 94–108.

Van Emmerik, A., Kamphuis, J., Hulsbosch, A., & Emmelkamp, P. (2002). Single session debriefing after psychological trauma: A meta-analysis. *The Lancet, 360,* 766–771.

van Leeuwen, M. H. D., & Maas, I. (2010). Historical studies of social mobility and stratification. In K. Cook & D. S. Masse (Eds.), *Annual Review of Sociology, 36,* 429–451.

Van Maanen, J. (1991). The smile factory: Work at Disneyland. In P. J. Frost, L. Moore, M. Louis, C. Lundberg, & J. Martin (Eds.). *Reframing organizational culture* (pp. 58–76). Newbury Park, CA: Sage.

Van Zomeren, M., Postmes, T., & Spears, R. (2008). Toward an integrative social identity model of collective action: A quantitative research synthesis of three socio-psychological perspectives. *Psychological Bulletin, 134,* 504–535.

Vega, V., & Malamuth, N. (2007). The role of pornography in the context of general and specific risk factors. *Aggressive Behavior, 33,* 104–117.

Vega, W. A., & Rumbaut, R. G. (1991). Ethnic minorities and mental health. *Annual Review of Sociology, 17,* 351–383.

Verbrugge, L. (1979). Marital status and health. *Journal of Marriage and the Family, 41,* 267–285.

Verplanck, W. S. (1955). The control of the content of conversation: Reinforcement of statements of opinion. *Journal of Abnormal and Social Psychology, 51,* 668–676.

Vidmar, N. (1974). Effects of group discussion on category width judgments. *Journal of Personality and Social Psychology, 29,* 187–195.

Vinokur, A. (1971). Cognitive and affective processes influencing risk taking in groups: An expected utility approach. *Journal of Personality and Social Psychology, 20*(3), 472.

Vinokur, A., & Burnstein, E. (1978). Novel argumentation and attitude change: The case of polarization following group discussion. *European Journal of Social Psychology, 8,* 335–348.

Vinokur, A. D., Price, R. H., & Caplan, R. D. (1996). Hard times and hurtful partners: How financial strain affects depression and relationship satisfaction of unemployed persons and their spouses. *Journal of Personality and Social Psychology, 71,* 166–179.

Vittengl, J., & Holt, C. S. (2000). Getting acquainted: The relationship of self-disclosure and social attraction to positive affect. *Journal of Social and Personal Relationships, 17,* 53–66.

Volling, B. L., & Belsky, J. (1991). Multiple determinants of father involvement during infancy in dual career and single-earner families. *Journal of Marriage and the Family, 53,* 461–474.

von Baeyer, C. L., Sherk, D. L., & Zanna, M. P. (1981). Impression management in the job interview: When the female applicant meets the male (chauvinist) interviewer. *Personality and Social Psychology Bulletin, 7,* 45–51.

von Hippel, W., Hawkins, C., & Schooler, J. (2001). Stereotype distinctiveness: How counterstereotypic behavior shapes the self-concept. (2001). *Journal of Personality and Social Psychology, 81,* 193–205.

Vonk, R. (2002). Self-serving interpretations of flattery: Why ingratiation works. *Journal of Personality and Social Psychology, 82,* 515–526.

Voss, M., Nylén, L., Floderus, B., Diderichsen, F., & Terry, P. (2004). Unemployment and early cause-specific mortality: A study based on the Swedish Twin Reg-

istry. *American Journal of Public Health, 94,* 2155–2161.

Voydanoff, P. (1990). Economic distress and family relations: A review of the eighties. *Journal of Marriage and the Family, 52,* 1099–1115.

Vygotsky, L. S. (1962). *Thought and language.* Cambridge, MA: MIT Press.

Waldman, D. A., Ramirez, G. G., House, R. J., & Puranam, P. (2001). Does leadership matter? CEO leadership attributes and profitability under conditions of perceived environmental uncertainty. *Academy of Management Journal, 44,* 134–143.

Waldron, I. (1976). Why do women live longer than men? *Social Science and Medicine, 10,* 349–362.

Walker, H. A., Thomas, G. M., & Zelditch, M. (1986). Legitimation, endorsement, and stability. *Social Forces, 64,* 620–643.

Walker, L. L., & Heyns, R. W. (1962). *An anatomy for conformity.* Englewood Cliffs, NJ: Prentice Hall.

Wallin, P. (1950). Cultural contradictions and sex roles: A repeat study. *American Sociological Review, 15,* 288–293.

Wallis, C. (2010). Performing gender: A content analysis of gender display in music videos. *Sex Roles, 64,* 160–172.

Walsh, E. J., & Taylor, M. (1982). Occupational correlates of multidimensional self-esteem: Comparisons among garbage collectors, bartenders, professors, and other workers. *Sociology and Social Research, 66,* 252–258.

Walsh, E. J., & Warland, R. H. (1983). Social movement involvement in the wake of a nuclear accident: Activists and free riders in the TMI area. *American Sociological Review, 48,* 764–780.

Walster [Hatfield], E., Aronson, E., & Abrahams, D. (1966). On increasing the persuasiveness of a low prestige communicator. *Journal of Experimental Social Psychology, 2,* 325–342.

Walster [Hatfield], E., Aronson, V., Abrahams, D., & Rottman, L. (1966). The importance of physical attractiveness in dating behavior. *Journal of Personality and Social Psychology, 4,* 508–516.

Walster [Hatfield], E., Berscheid, E., & Walster, G. W. (1973). New directions in equity research. *Journal of Personality and Social Psychology, 25,* 151–176.

Walster [Hatfield], E., Walster, G. W., & Berscheid, E. (1978). *Equity: Theory and research.* Boston: Allyn and Bacon.

Walster [Hatfield], E., Walster, G. W., & Traupmann, J. (1978). Equity and premarital sex. *Journal of Personality and Social Psychology, 36,* 82–92.

Walters, J., & Walters, L. (1980). Parent–child relationships: A review, 1970–1979. *Journal of Marriage and the Family, 42,* 807–822.

Walther, J. B. (2007). Selective self-presentation in computer-mediated communication: Hyperpersonal dimensions of technology, language, and cognition. *Computers in Human Behavior, 23,* 2538–2557.

Ward, L., Hansbrough, E., & Walker, E. (2005). Contributions of music video exposure to Black adolescents' gender and sexual schemas. *Journal of Adolescent Research, 20,* 143–166.

Ward, L. M. (2003). Understanding the role of entertainment media in the sexual socialization of American youth: A review of empirical research. *Developmental Review, 23,* 347–388.

Ward, L. M., & Friedman, K. (2006). Using TV as a guide: Associations between television viewing and adolescents' sexual attitudes and behavior. *Journal of Research on Adolescence, 16,* 133–156.

Warner, D. F., & Hayward, M. D. (2006). Early-life origins of the race gap in men's mortality. *Journal of Health and Social Behavior, 47,* 209–226.

Warner, L. C., & DeFleur, M. (1969). Attitude as an interactional concept: Social constraint and social distance as intervening variables between attitudes and action. *American Sociological Review, 34,* 153–169.

Wasserman, I. (1977). Southern violence and the political process. *American Sociological Review, 42,* 359–362.

Watkins, P. L., & Whaley, D. (2000). Gender role stressors and women's health. In R. Eisler & M. Hersen (Eds.), *Handbook of gender, culture, and health* (pp. 43–62). Mahwah, NJ: Erlbaum.

Watson, D. (1982). The actor and the observer: How are their perceptions of causality divergent? *Psychological Bulletin, 92,* 682–700.

Watts, B. L., Messe, L. A., & Vallacher, R. R. (1982). Toward understanding sex differences in pay allocation: Agency, communion, and reward distribution behavior. *Sex Roles, 8,* 1175–1187.

Webb, E. J., Campbell, D. J., Schwartz, R. D., & Sechrest, L. (1981). *Unobtrusive measures: Nonreactive research in the social sciences* (2nd ed.). Chicago: Rand McNally.

Weber, R., & Crocker, J. (1983). Cognitive processes in the revision of stereotypic beliefs. *Journal of Personality and Social Psychology, 45,* 961–977.

Webster, M., & Foschi, M. (1988). *Status generalization: New theory and research.* Stanford, CA: Stanford University Press.

Wee, S. (2013). Development and initial validation of the willingness to compromise scale. *Journal of Career Assessment, 21*(4), 487–501.

Weed, F. J. (1990). The victim-activist role in the anti-drunk driving movement. *Sociological Quarterly, 31,* 459–473.

Wegner, D. M., Lane, J. D., & Dimitri, S. (1994). The allure of secret relationships. *Journal of Personality and Social Psychology, 66,* 287–300.

Weigand, B. (1994). Black money in Belize: The ethnicity and social structure of black-market crime. *Social Forces, 73,* 135–154.

Weigel, D., & Murray, C. (2000). The paradox of stability and change in relationships: What does chaos theory offer for the study of romantic relationships? *Journal of Social and Personal Relationships, 17,* 425–449.

Weigel, R. H., & Newman, L. (1976). Increasing attitude-behavior correspondence by broadening the scope of the behavioral measure. *Journal of Personality and Social Psychology, 33,* 793–802.

Weinberg, M. (1976). The nudist management of respectability. In M. Weinberg (Ed.), *Sex research: Studies from the Kinsey Institute.* New York: Oxford University Press.

Weiner, B. (1985). An attributional theory of achievement motivation and emotion. *Psychological Review, 92,* 548–573.

Weiner, B. (1986). *An attributional theory of motivation and emotion.* New York: Springer Verlag.

Weiner, B., Amirkhan, J., Folkes, V. S., & Verette, J. A. (1987). An attributional analysis of excuse giving: Studies of a naive theory of emotion. *Journal of Personality and Social Psychology, 52,* 316–324.

Weiner, B., Frieze, I., Kukla, A., Reed, L., Rest, B., & Rosenbaum, R. M. (1971). *Perceiving the causes of success and failure.* Morristown, NJ: General Learning Press.

Weiner, B., Heckhausen, H., Meyer, W. U., & Cook, R. E. (1972). Causal ascriptions and achievement behavior: A conceptual analysis of effort and reanalysis of locus of control. *Journal of Personality and Social Psychology, 21,* 239–248.

Weiner, B., Perry, R. P., & Magnusson, J. (1988). An attributional analysis of reactions to stigmas. *Journal of Personality and Social Psychology, 55,* 738–748.

Weinstein, E. A., & Deutschberger, P. (1963). Some dimensions of altercasting. *Sociometry, 26,* 454–466.

Weiss, R. S. (1973). *Loneliness: The experience of emotional and social isolation.* Cambridge, MA: MIT Press.

Weitzer, R. (1991). Prostitutes' rights in the United States: The failure of a movement. *Sociological Quarterly, 32,* 23–41.

Weitzman, L. J., Eifler, D., Hokada, E., & Ross, K. (1972). Sex role socialization in picture books for pre-school children. *American Journal of Sociology, 77,* 1125–1150.

Weldon, E., & Weingart, L. R. (1993). Group goals and group performance. *British Journal of Social Psychology, 32,* 307–334.

Wellman, B., & Worley, S. (1990). Different strokes from different folks: Community ties and social support. *American Journal of Sociology, 96,* 558–588.

Wellman, H. M., Phillips, A. T., & Rodriguez, T. (2000). Young children's understanding of perception, desire, and emotion. *Child Development, 71*(4), 895–912.

Werkman, W., Wigboldus, D., & Semin, G. (1999). Children's communication of linguistic intergroup bias and its impact on cognitive inferences. *European Journal of Social Psychology, 29,* 95–104.

Werner, C., & Parmelee, P. (1979). Similarity of activity preferences among friends: Those who play together stay together. *Social Psychology Quarterly, 42,* 62–66.

Western, B. (2002). The impact of incarceration on wage mobility and inequality. *American Sociological Review, 67,* 526–546.

Weyant, J. (1996). Application of compliance techniques to direct-mail requests for charitable donations. *Psychology and Marketing, 13*, 157–170.

Whalen, M. R., & Zimmerman, D. H. (1987). Sequential and institutional contexts in calls for help. *Social Psychology Quarterly, 50*, 172–185.

White, C., Bushnell, N., & Regnemer, J. (1978). Moral development in Bahamian school children: A 3-year examination of Kohlberg's stages of moral development. *Developmental Psychology, 14*, 58–65.

White, G. (1980). Physical attractiveness and courtship progress. *Journal of Personality and Social Psychology, 39*, 660–668.

White, J. W., & Gruber, K. J. (1982). Instigative aggression as a function of past experience and target characteristics. *Journal of Personality and Social Psychology, 42*(6), 1069–1075.

White, K. M., Hogg, M. A., & Terry, D. J. (2002). Improving attitude-behavior correspondence through exposure to normative support from a salient ingroup. *Basic and Applied Social Psychology, 24*(2), 91–103.

White, R. W. (1989). From peaceful protest to guerilla war: Micromobilization of the Provisional Irish Republican Army. *American Journal of Sociology, 94*, 1277–1302.

Whitt, H. P., & Meile, R. L. (1985). Alignment, magnification, and snowballing: Processes in the definition of symptoms of mental illness. *Social Forces, 63*, 682–697.

Whitty, M. (2004). Cyber-flirting: An examination of men's and women's flirting behaviour both offline and on the Internet. *Behaviour Change, 21*, 115–126.

Whorf, B. L. (1956). Language, mind, and reality. In J. B. Carroll (Ed.), *Language, thought, and reality.* (pp. 245–270). Cambridge, MA: MIT Press.

Wicker, A. W. (1969). Attitudes versus actions: The relationship of verbal and overt behavioral responses to attitude objects. *Journal of Social Issues, 25*(4), 41–78.

Wicklund, R. A. (1975). Objective self-awareness. In L. Berkowitz (Ed.), *Advances in experimental social psychology* (Vol. 8, pp. 233–275). New York: Academic Press.

Wicklund, R. A., & Brehm, J. (1976). *Perspectives on cognitive dissonance.* Hillsdale, NJ: Erlbaum.

Wicklund, R. A., & Frey, D. (1980). Self-awareness theory: When the self makes a difference. In D. M. Wegner & R. R. Vallacher (Eds.), *The self in social psychology.* (pp. 54ff). New York: Oxford University Press.

Wickrama, K., Conger, R. D., Lorenz, F. O., & Matthews, L. (1995). Role identity, role satisfaction, and perceived physical health. *Social Psychology Quarterly, 58*, 270–283.

Wickrama, K. A. S., Conger, R., Wallace, L. E., & Elder, G. H. (1999). The inter-generational transmission of health-risk behaviors: Adolescent lifestyles and gender moderating effects. *Journal of Health and Social Behavior, 40*, 258–272.

Wickrama, K. A. S., Lorenz, F. O., Conger, R. D., & Elder, G. H. (1997). Marital quality and physical illness: A latent growth curve analysis. *Journal of Marriage and the Family, 59*, 143–155.

Wigboldus, D., Semin, G., & Spears, R. (2000). How do we communicate stereotypes? Linguistic biases and inferential consequences. *Journal of Personality and Social Psychology, 78*, 5–18.

Wiggins, J. S., Wiggins, N., & Conger, J. C. (1968). Correlates of heterosexual somatic preference. *Journal of Personality and Social Psychology, 10*, 82–90.

Wilcox, C., & Williams, L. (1990). Taking stock of schema theory. *Social Science Journal, 27*, 373–393.

Wilder, D. A. (1981). Perceiving persons as a group: Categorization and intergroup relations. In D. L. Hamilton (Ed.), *Cognitive processes in stereotyping and intergroup behavior* (pp. 213–257). Hillsdale, NJ: Erlbaum.

Wilder, D. A., & Thompson, J. E. (1980). Intergroup contact with independent manipulations on in-group and out-group interaction. *Journal of Personality and Social Psychology, 38*, 589–603.

Wilke, H., & Lanzetta, J. T. (1982). The obligation to help: Factors affecting response to help received. *European Journal of Social Psychology, 12*, 315–319.

Wilkins, A. C. (2008). "'Happier than non-Christians': Collective emotions and symbolic boundaries among Evangelical Christians." *Social Psychology Quarterly, 71*(3), pp. 281–301.

Wilkins, A. C. (2008). *Wannabes, goths, and Christians: The boundaries of sex, style, and status.* University of Chicago Press.

Willer, D., & Walker, H. A. (2007). *Building experiments: Testing social theory.* Stanford, CA: Stanford University Press.

Willer, R., Conlon, B., Rogalin, C. L., & Wojnowitz, M. T. (2013). Overdoing gender: A test of the masculine overcompensation thesis. *American Journal of Sociology, 118*, 980–1022.

Williams, D., Gonzalez, H., Neighbors, H., Nesse, R., Abelson, J., Swetman, J., & Jackson, J. (2007). Prevalence and distribution of major depressive disorder in African Americans, Caribbean Blacks, and Non-Hispanic Whites. *Archives of General Psychiatry, 64*, 305–315.

Williams, D. R. (1990). Socioeconomic differentials in health: A review and redirection. *Social Psychology Quarterly, 53*, 81–99.

Williams, D. R. (2012). Miles to go before we sleep: Racial inequities in health. *Journal of Health and Social Behavior, 53*, 279–295.

Williams, K. D. (2010). The effects of homophily, identification, and violent video games on players. *Mass Communication and Society, 14*(1), 3–24.

Williams, K. D., Harkins, S. G., & Latané, B. (1981). Identifiability as a deterrent to social loafing: Two cheering experiments. *Journal of Personality and Social Psychology, 40*, 303–311.

Williams, L. S. (2002). Trying on gender, gender regimes, and the process of becoming women. *Gender and Society, 16*, 29–52.

Williams, R. H. (1995). Constructing the public good: Social movements and cultural resources. *Social Problems, 42,* 124–144.

Williams, R. M. (1977). *Mutual accommodation: Ethnic conflict and cooperation.* Minneapolis: University of Minnesota Press.

Wills, T. A. (1992). The helping process in the context of personal relationships. In S. Spacapan & S. Oskamp (Eds.), *Helping and being helped: Naturalistic studies* (pp. 17–48). Newbury Park, CA: Sage.

Wilmoth, J. K., & Ball, P. (1995). Arguments and action in the life of a social problem: A case study of "over-population," 1946–1990. *Social Problems, 42,* 318–343.

Wilson, B. J., Smith, S. L., Potter, W. J., Kunkel, D., Linz, D., Colvin, C. M., & Donnerstein, E. (2002). Violence in children's television programming: Assessing the risks. *Journal of Communication, 52*(1), 5–35.

Wilson, E. O. (1971). *The insect societies.* Cambridge, MA: Belknap.

Wilson, E. O. (1975). *Sociobiology: The new synthesis.* Cambridge, MA: Harvard University Press.

Wilson, E. O. (1978). *On human nature.* Cambridge, MA: Harvard University Press.

Wilson, J. (2000). Volunteering. *Annual Review of Sociology, 26,* 215–240.

Wilson, J., & Janoski, T. (1995). The contribution of religion to volunteer work. *Sociology of Religion, 56*(2), 137–152.

Wilson, J., & Musick, M. (1997). Who cares? Toward an integrated theory of volunteer work. *American Sociological Review, 62*(5), 694–713.

Wilson, T. D., Houston, C. E., Etling, K. M., & Brekke, N. C. (1996). A new look at anchoring effects: Basic anchoring and its antecedents. *Journal of Experimental Psychology: General, 125,* 387–402.

Windle, M., & Dumenci, L. (1997). Parental and occupational stress as predictors of depressive symptoms among dual-income couples: A multilevel modeling approach. *Journal of Marriage and the Family, 59,* 625–634.

Winschild, P. D., & Wells, G. L. (1997). Behavioral consensus information affects people's inferences about population traits. *Personality and Social Psychology Bulletin, 23,* 148–156.

Winsler, A., Carlton, M. P., & Barry, M. J. (2000). Age-related changes in preschool children's systematic use of private speech in a natural setting. *Journal of Child Language, 27,* 665–687.

Wit, A., & Wilke, H. (1988). Subordinates' endorsement of an allocating leader in a commons dilemma: An equity theoretical approach. *Journal of Economic Psychology, 9,* 151–168.

Wit, A. P., Wilke, H. A. M., & Van Dijk, E. (1989). Attribution of leadership in a resource management situation. *European Journal of Social Psychology, 19,* 327–338.

Wittenbaum, G. M., Vaughan, S. I., & Stasser, G. (1998). Coordination in task-performing groups. In R. S. Tindale, L. Heath, J. D. Edwards, E. J. Posavac, F. B. Bryant, Y. Suarez-Balcazar, et al. (Eds.), *Social psy-*chological applications to social issues: Applications of theory and research on groups (pp. 177–204). New York: Plenum.

Wittenbrink, B., Judd, C. M., & Park, B. (2001). Evaluative versus conceptual judgments in automatic stereotyping and prejudice. *Journal of Experimental Social Psychology, 37*(3), 244–252.

Wolf, S., & Bugaj, A. M. (1990). The social impact of courtroom witnesses. *Social Behaviour, 5*(1), 1–13.

Wolf, S., & Latané, B. (1983). Majority and minority influences on restaurant preferences. *Journal of Personality and Social Psychology, 45,* 282–292.

Wood, W., Kallgren, C. A., & Preisler, R. M. (1985). Access to attitude-relevant information in memory as a determinant of persuasion: The role of message attributes. *Journal of Experimental Social Psychology, 21,* 73–85.

Wood, W., Lundgren, S., Ouellette, J. A., Busceme, S., & Blackstone, T. (1994). Minority influence: A meta-analytic review of social influence processes. *Psychological Bulletin, 115,* 323–345.

Won-Doornink, M. J. (1979). On getting to know you: The association between the stage of a relationship and the reciprocity of self-disclosure. *Journal of Experimental Social Psychology, 15,* 229–241.

Won-Doornink, M. J. (1985). Self-disclosure and reciprocity in conversation: A cross-national study. *Social Psychology Quarterly, 48,* 97–107.

Wong, J. (2002). What's in a name? An examination of social identities. *Journal for the Theory of Social Behavior, 32,* 451–463.

Worchel, S. (1986). The role of cooperation in reducing intergroup conflict. In S. Worchel & W. G. Austin (Eds.), *Psychology of intergroup relations* (2nd ed., pp. 288–304). Chicago: Nelson-Hall.

Worchel, S., Lind, E., & Kaufman, K. (1975). Evaluations of group products as a function of expectations of group longevity, outcome of competition, and publicity of evaluations. *Journal of Personality and Social Psychology, 31,* 1089–1097.

Worchel, S., & Norvell, N. (1980). Effect of perceived environmental conditions during cooperation on intergroup attraction. *Journal of Personality and Social Psychology, 38,* 764–772.

Wortman, C. B., & Linsenmeier, J. A. (1977). Interpersonal attraction and techniques of ingratiation in organizational settings. In B. M. Staw & G. R. Salancik (Eds.), *New directions in organizational behavior* (pp. 133–178). Chicago: St. Clair Press.

Wright, B., Caspi, A., Moffit, T., & Paternoster, R. (2004). Does the perceived risk of punishment deter criminally prone individuals? Rational choice, self-control, and crime. *Journal of Research in Crime and Delinquency, 41,* 180–213.

Wright, E. O., Costello, C., Hachen, D., & Sprague, J. (1982). The American class structure. *American Sociological Review, 47,* 709–726.

Wright, E., Gronfein, W., & Owens, T. (2000). Deinstitutionalization, social rejection, and the self-esteem of former mental patients. *Journal of Health and Social Behavior, 41,* 68–90.

Wright, K. (2000). *Generosity vs. altruism.* Center for Civil Society, London School of Economics, London.

Wright, K. (2001). Generosity vs. altruism: Philanthropy and charity in the United States and United Kingdom. *Voluntas: International Journal of Voluntary and Nonprofit Organizations, 12*(4), 399–416.

Wright, K. B. (2005). Researching Internet-based populations: Advantages and disadvantages of online survey research, online questionnaire authoring software packages, and web survey services. *Journal of Computer-Mediated Communication, 10*(3).

Wulfert, E., & Wan, C. K. (1995). Safer sex intentions and condom use viewed from a health belief, reasoned action, and social cognitive perspective. *Journal of Sex Research, 32,* 299–311.

Wyer, R. S. (1966). Effects of incentive to perform well, group attraction, and group acceptance on conformity in a judgmental task. *Journal of Personality and Social Psychology, 4,* 21–26.

Wyer, R. S., & Srull, T. K. (Eds.). (1984). *Handbook of social cognition* (Vols. 1–3). Hillsdale, NJ: Erlbaum.

Wylie, R. C. (1979). *The self-concept: Theory and research on selected topics* (rev. ed., Vol. 2). Lincoln: University of Nebraska Press.

Yarrow, M., Schwartz, C., Murphy, H., & Deasy, L. (1955). The psychological meaning of mental illness in the family. *Journal of Social Issues, 11,* 12–24.

Ybarra, M. L., Diener-West, M., Markow, D., Leaf, P. J., Hamburger, M., & Boxer, P. (2008). Linkages between Internet and other media violence with seriously violent behavior by youth. *Pediatrics, 122*(5), 929–937.

Ybarra, M. L., Mitchell, K. J., Hamburger, M., Diener-West, M., & Leaf, P. J. (2011). X-rated material and perpetration of sexually aggressive behavior among children and adolescents: Is there a link? *Aggressive Behavior, 37*(1), 1–18.

Yukl, G. (1981). *Leadership in organizations.* Englewood Cliffs, NJ: Prentice Hall.

Zaccaro, S. J. (1984). Social loafing: The role of task attractiveness. *Personality and Social Psychology Bulletin, 10,* 99–106.

Zajonc, R. (1998). Emotions. In D. T. Gilbert, S. T. Fiske, & G. Lindzey (Eds.), *The handbook of social psychology* (4th ed., Vol. 1, pp. 591–632). New York: McGraw-Hill.

Zajonc, R. B. (1965). Social facilitation. *Science, 149,* 269–274.

Zajonc, R. B. (1968). The attitudinal effects of mere exposure. *Journal of Personality and Social Psychology, 9* (Monograph Suppl. no. 2, Pt. 2), 1–27.

Zajonc, R. B., Heingartner, A., & Herman, E. M. (1969). Social enhancement and impairment of performance in the cockroach. *Journal of Personality and Social Psychology, 13,* 83–92.

Zajonc, R. B., & McIntosh, D. N. (1992). Emotions research: Some promising questions and some questionable promises. *Psychological Science, 3*(1), 70–74.

Zander, A. (1985). *The purposes of groups and organizations.* San Francisco, CA: Jossey-Bass.

Zanna, M., & Fazio, R. (1982). The attitude-behavior relation: Moving toward a third generation of research. In M. Zanna, E. Higgins, & C. Herman (Eds.), *Consistency in social behavior: The Ontario symposium* (Vol. 2, pp. 283–301). Hillsdale, NJ: Erlbaum.

Zanna, M. P., & Hamilton, D. L. (1977). Further evidence for meaning change in impression formation. *Journal of Experimental Social Psychology, 13,* 224–238.

Zartman, I. W., & Touval, S. (1985). International mediation: Conflict resolution and power politics. *Journal of Social Issues, 41*(2), 27–45.

Zebrowitz, L. A., Andreoletti, C., Collins, M. A., Lee, S. Y., & Blumenthal, J. (1998). Bright, bad, babyfaced boys: Appearance stereotypes do not always yield self-fulfilling prophecy effects. *Journal of Personality and Social Psychology, 75,* 1300–1320.

Zebrowitz, L., Voinescu, L., & Collins, M. A. (1996). "Wide-eyed" and "crooked-faced": Determinants of perceived and real honesty across the life span. *Personality and Social Psychology Bulletin, 22,* 1258–1269.

Zelditch, M. (1969). Can you really study an army in the laboratory? In A. Etzioni (Ed.), *A sociological reader on complex organizations* (pp. 528–539). New York: Rinehart and Winston.

Zelditch, M. (1972). Authority and performance expectations in bureaucratic organizations. In C. G. McClintock (Ed.), *Experimental social psychology.* (pp. 484–513). New York: Holt, Rinehart and Winston.

Zelditch, M., & Walker, H. A. (1984). Legitimacy and the stability of authority. In E. J. Lawler (Ed.), *Advances in group processes* (Vol. 1, pp. 1–26). Greenwich, CT: JAI Press.

Zey, M. (1993). *Banking on fraud: Junk bonds and buyouts.* New York: Aldine De Gruyter.

Zhao, S. (2005). The digital self: Through the looking glass of telecopresent others. *Symbolic Interaction, 28,* 387–405.

Zillmann, D. (1978). Attribution and misattribution of excitatory reactions. *New Directions in Attribution Research, 2,* 335–368.

Zillman, D. (1979). *Hostility and aggression.* Hillsdale, NJ: Erlbaum.

Zimbardo, P. (1969). The human choice: Individuation, reason, and order versus deindividuation, impulse, and chaos. In W. J. Arnold & D. Levine (Eds.), *Nebraska symposium on motivation* (Vol. 17, pp. 237–307). Lincoln: University of Nebraska Press.

Zimbardo, P. G. (1973). On the ethics of intervention in human psychological research: With special reference to the Stanford prison experiment. *Cognition, 2*(2), 243–256.

Zimmerman, D. H., & West, C. (1975). Sex roles, interruptions, and silences in conversations. In B. Thorne & N. Henley (Eds.), *Language and sex: Difference and dominance.* (pp. 105–129). Rowley, MA: Newbury House.

Zuckerman, E., Kim, T.-Y., Ukanwa, K., & von Rittman, J. (2003). Robust identities or nonentities? Typecasting in the feature-film labor market. *American Journal of Sociology, 108,* 1018–1074.

Zuckerman, M., DePaulo, B. M., & Rosenthal, R. (1981). Verbal and nonverbal communication of deception. In L. Berkowitz (Ed.), *Advances in experimental social psychology* (Vol. 14, pp. 59ff). New York: Academic Press.

Zuckerman, M., Koestner, R., & Alton, A. O. (1984). Learning to detect deception. *Journal of Personality and Social Psychology, 46,* 519–528.

Zurcher, L. A., & Snow, D. A. (1990). Collective behavior and social movements. In M. Rosenberg & R. H. Turner (Eds.), *Social psychology: Sociological perspectives.* (pp. 447–482). New Brunswick, NJ: Transaction.